THE INTERNATI(
FEDERA......

World of Tennis

1993

For the past 25 years *World of Tennis* has faithfully recorded the evolution of open tennis as it has developed from a fledgling sport into a multi-million dollar arm of the entertainment industry. This latest volume, illustrated as usual with photographs of all the star performers, continues the coverage with reports on all the principal events of another crowded year. 1992 will be remembered for the brilliance of Jennifer Capriati at the Games of the XXVth Olympiad in the torrid heat of Barcelona, where she became the youngest-ever champion; for the spectacular Wimbledon success of the charismatic American, Andre Agassi; for the staggering achievements of the Yugoslav-born teenager, Monica Seles, who for the second year running won three of the four Grand Slam crowns and caused a minor sensation at Wimbledon with her infamous grunt; for the heroic defence of his US Open title by the quiet Swede, Stefan Edberg; and for the rise to the top of the men's game by gentleman Jim Courier. All these moments are covered, along with reports on the re-emergence of the United States as Davis Cup champions and on the second success in the Federation Cup of Germany, led by Steffi Graf. As well as articles on each of the four Grand Slam Championships, the very cornerstones of the professional game, there are comprehensive reports on the men's and women's tours with the results in full of every main tournament and complete lists of every man and woman who took part, together with their nationalities and dates of birth. As always, the expanding worlds of international junior and veteran tennis are examined and, for the first time, the biographical section is headed by comprehensive details on the top ten men and women that include every result in Grand Slam, Davis Cup or Federation Cup play.

THE INTERNATIONAL TENNIS FEDERATION

World of Tennis

1993

Edited by John Barrett
Biographies by Christine Forrest

CollinsWillow
An Imprint of HarperCollins*Publishers*

Abbreviations used in this book

ARG	Argentina	**FRA**	France	**PAR**	Paraguay
AUS	Australia	**GBR**	Great Britain	**PER**	Peru
AUT	Austria	**GER**	Germany	**PHI**	Philippines
BAH	Bahamas	**GRE**	Greece	**POL**	Poland
BEL	Belgium	**HAI**	Haiti	**POR**	Portugal
BER	Bermuda	**HKG**	Hong Kong	**PRK**	Korea, DPR
BOL	Bolivia	**HUN**	Hungary	**PUR**	Puerto Rico
BRA	Brazil	**INA**	Indonesia	**ROM**	Rumania
BUL	Bulgaria	**IND**	India	**RSA**	South Africa
CAN	Canada	**IRL**	Ireland	**SEN**	Senegal
CHI	Chile	**IRN**	Iran	**SLO**	Slovenia
CHN	People's Republic of China	**ISR**	Israel	**SUI**	Switzerland
		ITA	Italy	**SWE**	Sweden
CIS	Commonwealth of Independent States	**JPN**	Japan	**TCH**	Czechoslovakia
		KEN	Kenya	**THA**	Thailand
CIV	Cite d'Ivoire	**KOR**	Korea	**TPE**	Chinese Taipei
COL	Colombia	**LUX**	Luxembourg	**TUR**	Turkey
CRO	Croatia	**MAR**	Morocco	**URU**	Uruguay
CUB	Cuba	**MAS**	Malaysia	**USA**	United States of America
DEN	Denmark	**MEX**	Mexico		
ECU	Ecuador	**NED**	Netherlands	**VEN**	Venezuela
EGY	Arab Republic of Egypt	**NGR**	Nigeria	**YUG**	Yugoslavia
		NOR	Norway	**ZIM**	Zimbabwe
ESP	Spain	**NZL**	New Zealand		
FIN	Finland	**PAK**	Pakistan		

Cover photograph: Jennifer Capriati wins gold medal at Barcelona Olympics – by T. Hindley

First published in 1993 by
Collins Willow
an imprint of HarperCollins*Publishers*
London

A CIP catalogue record for this book is available from the British Library

ISBN 0 00 218508 3

Typeset in Univers
Printed and bound in Great Britain by
Mackays of Chatham PLC, Chatham, Kent

CONTENTS

PREFACE

After 25 years of open tennis this is a perhaps an appropriate moment for reflection. Take your minds back to that momentous day in 1968 when the British Hard Court Championships in Bournemouth introduced honesty and a new era to the international game. In the chill of a British spring, Owen Davidson earned a place in history by beating John Clifton in the first match of the open era. His fellow Australian, Ken Rosewall, became the first open tournament winner with a four sets win over his old friend and rival of professional days, Rod Laver. From a women's field that contained only seven overseas challengers and none of the four newly signed 'professionals' of George McCall's National Tennis League (Billie Jean King, Rosie Casals, Ann Jones and Françoise Durr), Virginia Wade became the first woman to win an open title. Their prizes? Rosewall won a handsome £1,000 while Virginia's reward was £750!

To all of us involved with the transition these were heady days. But the future was uncertain, clouded by the political infighting between the governing body of the game, the International Lawn Tennis Federation (as the ITF was then known), and the two professional groups – Lamar Hunt's World Championship Tennis, and McCall's NTL. We had a mixture of categories under which players were grouped as each nation was allowed self-determination. Amateurs, contract professionals, teaching professionals and `players' were joined by registered players, and the two players' associations were still merely ideas in the minds of the deepest thinkers.

Little did we realise then how game would prosper. In that first year of open tennis total prize money for men and women at the 17 open events in eight countries fell considerably short of $1 million. In 1993, despite the worldwide recession, the men will play for some $56 million and the women for $33 million at 'official' tournament alone. In these last 25 years the astonishing rise in prize money has turned 123 men and 43 women into dollar millionaires from this source alone.

Alongside this spectacular growth in the professional game there has been an equally dramatic expansion in amateur tennis – particularly at the grass roots level in underdeveloped countries. Thanks to the $6 million that has already flowed into the ITF's Development Fund through the annual contribution from the Compaq Grand Slam Cup, some 100,000 youngsters per year are introduced to the joys of tennis and dozens of others are able to put their feet on the first rungs of the professional ladder as members of regional squads.

Perhaps the single most important achievement of the past quarter century, however, was to have tennis accepted as a full Olympic sport in 1988. The ramifications of this decision have led to an impressive worldwide growth for tennis as national governments have provided funds that were previously denied. For this we must thank the former President of the ITF, Philippe Chatrier, and his then General Secretary, the late David Gray. It was their vision and persuasiveness that turned the minds of doubting IOC committee members. As Mons. Chatrier ends his 20-year reign as the President of the French Federation, how appropriate it is that he takes on a major role with the IOC. All of us who have come to respect Philippe's genuine love for tennis and its finest traditions will wish him well as he starts to paint on a wider canvas.

In chronicling the changing face of international tennis over these turbulent 25 years of growth, the content and format of this publication have inevitably changed. This year's edition is no exception. In Christine Forrest's popular biographical section we offer for the first time a complete review of the top ten men and women which head two separate sections – another departure, this. Apart from full personal details and annual notes of their main achievements there are the results of every singles match they have ever played at the four Grand Slam Championships, as well as their complete Davis Cup or Federation Cup records. The usual information on a further 50 men and 50 women are included, plus details on the leading juniors. Thanks are due to Christine for this recast biographical information which I hope will provide a useful source of reference.

Thanks are also due to my talented colleagues among the writers and photographers whose expert contributions have once again brought to life the crowded events of another tennis year. As usual the bulk of the detailed material has been provided by Ian Barnes and his cheerful staff at the ITF but their efforts this year have been augmented by the dedicated work of an old friend and colleague from Slazenger days, Gerie Knights. How nice to have her back in the team! Leaving the ITF team is Marijke Volger who has been a tower of strength for the past three years. We all wish her well as she departs to a new role with the Dutch Tennis Federation.

Still an indispensable member of the team (and about to become even more closely integrated) is that remarkable American lady, Barbara Travers whose unfailing helpfulness in providing information on the men players is much appreciated. So is her cheerful disregard for conventional times of eating and sleeping. Her credo seems to be: 'If the work needs to be done, do it.'

Others who are equally dedicated include the two bands of cheerful workaholics representing the ATP Tour and the Women's Tennis Association, led respectively by Peter Alfano and Anna Leaird. Without the help of Greg Sharko at Ponte Vedra and Gene Beckwith in St. Petersburg it would be quite impossible to assemble the mass of statistical information we require each year. To them both my personal thanks. Then there are the teams on the road. Merely to see the loads of paper and electronic equipment these tireless packhorses tote around the globe on their punishing schedules is enough to question their sanity. However, George Rubenstein, Meg Donovan, Anna Legnani, Lauren Goldberg and Patricia Jolly at the ATP Tour and Renee Bloch Shallouf, Doug Clery, Tracey Robinson, Robin Reynolds and Ann Fahey at the WTA seem able retain their sanity more easily than some of my more demented colleagues. Long may they enjoy the punishment!

Finally, to our last and most fundamental innovation. For the first time this year all the material within these pages has been designed and set in house. When Tom Whiting of HarperCollins was assigned to this new role little did he realise what a gigantic task it would be. My admiration for his skill on the Macintosh is equalled only by my amazement at the speed with which he has mastered a difficult new subject. What is more, we have had no serious argument. The man deserves a medal!

Is it really twenty-five years since that day at a Stalybridge restaurant when my fellow tennis writers persuaded me that I should put together an annual on the first year of open tennis? Well, they say that time passes quickly when you are enjoying yourself. By that measurement I am the happiest man alive! I can only hope that after browsing through these pages, you are equally content.

JOHN BARRETT
London, March 1993

FOREWORD

If anything has marked the past few years in international tennis, it has been the explosion in interest, and enthusiasm, for the Davis Cup by NEC. This enthusiasm has been not only among the players but also the general public and is, almost certainly, the result of what are called 'big-time names' wanting to be involved. It is a tribute to the competition that so many of the stars of our game now ensure that their schedules make playing for their country a priority.

The last two finals – in Lyon where France won the trophy for the first time in 59 years by defeating the United States, and in Fort Worth, where the United States, with the so-called 'Dream Team' of Jim Courier, Andre Agassi, Pete Sampras and John McEnroe won for the 30th time – have also been remarkable for crowd involvement.

This has been generally good-natured and fun, but it also raises the question of whether it is fair to the players to have so many interruptions and delays. It is something on which a careful eye must be kept to ensure it does not go too far and spoil the enjoyment of other spectators, either in the stadium or watching on television.

The Davis Cup by NEC and the Federation Cup by NEC are our flagship events and their success is essential to our ability to carry on the vital work of development among our 176 member nations. This was one of the reasons for the decision during the year to play the Federation Cup by NEC in Frankfurt again in '93 and '94. The competition in 1992 was extremely well presented by the Deutscher Tennis Bund and we must build on that.

Tennis at the top level is now big business and one of the most widely watched sports – via television – in the world. The four Grand Slam championships and our international team competitions must provide not only first class entertainment but also the resources for us to invest in the future of the game. Tomorrow's champions are as important to us as today's winners of the major titles.

In 1992, of course, we had an extra opportunity to show the world just how international tennis has become via the Olympic Games in Barcelona. Players from some of the developing tennis nations such as Madagascar, Morocco and Indonesia were seen competing alongside some of the biggest names in the game which, in turn, encourages other less well-known tennis nations. The message that anyone with the right motivation and the opportunity to make the most of their talent can reach the pinnacle of the game was thus reinforced.

Promoting that message is one of the functions of this book which, in 1993, celebrates its 25th birthday. Over the last quarter of a century we have attempted to provide the tennis world with a definitive work of reference and, by emphasizing the achievements of the great champions of that time, to inspire young players to fulfil their ambitions.

Once again we have assembled facts and figures in an easy-to-follow fashion, provided comment on history-in-the-making from some of the game's leading writers and illustrated it all with the work of some of the sports world's leading photographers. We hope you will find their efforts enjoyable.

BRIAN TOBIN
President, International Tennis Federation

For the second year in a row Monica Seles won three of the four Grand Slam titles to maintain her position as the undisputed World Champion.   *(T. Hindley)*

THE YEAR IN REVIEW
Ronald Atkin

Rather like the world's trouble spots – the Middle East, the Balkans, the disintegrating former Soviet Union – professional tennis in 1992 was obsessed by the problem of power. Was technology ousting finesse? Had the men's game become too brutal, too fast, too prone to giants wielding super rackets and hitting the ball if not a thousand miles an hour, then uncomfortably close to 140 mph?

So concerned were the ATP Tour to address the chorus of criticism that they convened a forum in Miami during the Lipton Championships in March to address 'The Speed of the Game'. There was, as expected, lively discussion from players, officials, equipment manufacturers and media about possible measures to curb the problem. However, a few miles down the road a 5ft 8inch competitor called Michael Chang was busy proving it wasn't all that serious by winning the title on Key Biscayne's hard courts, defeating en route three of the hardest hitters in the sport: Marc Rosset, Pete Sampras and Jim Courier. It was, furthermore, Chang's second successive championship, having just captured the Grand Champion Cup crown on the (hard) courts of Indian Wells, California.

A coincidence? Wimbledon would provide the answer, with the bombardiers lined up to serve their cannonballs. Becker, Stich, Edberg, Sampras – surely one of these would prevail on the grass? Instead, Andre Agassi, clad becomingly in pure white, repelled the forces of power in brilliant style, fashioning his Championship on a glorious array of passing shots.

For those in search of symbols the Wimbledon men's final provided the perfect one: raw power, in the gangly shape of Goran Ivanisevic, versus Agassi's baseline skills. The Croatian left-hander produced another barrage of aces taking his total for the Championships to 205, but Agassi, long fair hair flowing beneath his white cap, became a slightly unlikely hero for those opposed to the brutalisation of tennis by winning in five sets. Thus, if only temporarily, was the matter of wide-bodied rackets, livelier balls and basketball-size players placed on the back burner to simmer gently until the next, inevitable outcry.

Agassi's Wimbledon performance may have made him the Official Eyeful of 1992 but an otherwise disappointing year ensured he would finish well adrift of the ITF's World Champion award. This went, for the first time in eight years, to another American, Jim Courier, while Monica Seles took the women's title for the second straight year. It was the first occasion the ITF had decided the men's winner by means of computer involvement but whether by resort to humans or machines, Courier rendered all argument invalid by winning two Grand Slams and ending the year as number one in the world rankings. Courier won the Australian Open and (for the second year) the French, sharing the victor's rostrum on both occasions with Seles, who enjoyed another phenomenal year.

While still short of her 19th birthday, the Yugoslav took the US Open to complete a 'three-Slam' year – Wimbledon once more eluding her – but was prevented, to her intense disappointment, from competing for Olympic gold at the Barcelona Games because she had not made herself available to compete during 1991 in the Federation Cup by NEC.

This rule also barred Martina Navratilova and Gabriela Sabatini and should have smoothed the route to gold of the 1988 Olympic champion, Steffi Graf. Instead, she succumbed in a three-set final to the 16-year-old American, Jennifer Capriati, whose delight (understandably) knew no bounds. Played out in stifling heat and over the best of five sets, the men's singles also produced an unexpected winner, and Switzerland's only gold of the Games, in Marc Rosset after the likes of Courier, Becker and Sampras had all perished in the third round. Rosset earned his medal the hard way against a local favourite, Jordi Arrese, overcoming fatigue and cramps to win over the full five sets in a little over five hours.

If the hopes of Spain, and in particular the talented Sanchez family, were dashed at the Olympics, it proved a year of solid achievement for Germany, once the nation had recovered from the shock of seeing its Davis Cup team, Boris Becker included, beaten by Brazil in the opening round of the 1992 competition. The women, with Steffi Graf firmly in charge, ensured maximum attendance figures by marching through the field at Frankfurt's Waldstadion to win the Federation Cup by NEC for Germany for the first time since 1987. With the competition due to be staged in Frankfurt for the next two years before switching in 1995 to a Davis Cup style format, another German victory is very much on the cards, particularly with the rise in the rankings of Anke Huber.

Graf rapidly followed the Frankfurt celebrations with an even bigger personal triumph, her fourth Wimbledon women's championship, in a distinctly one-sided and rain-ruined final against Seles. If her male compatriots, Becker and Stich, found themselves overshadowed at Wimbledon, there was success awaiting them in the late autumn. Becker, pronouncing himself newly motivated and playing with a verve and sharpness which had been absent for some time, provided more delight for the citizens of Frankfurt by winning the ATP Tour World Championships on his 25th birthday.

As if that was not enough to afford a rosy glow to German tennis, Michael Stich then proceeded to snaffle the $2 million first prize at the Compaq Grand Slam Cup in Munich. With Becker and Courier declining to take the place for which they had qualified, and with Ivan Lendl pulling out injured, Stich seized the moment to hammer out his most impressive sequence of victories since winning Wimbledon in 1991.

There was, again, talk in Munich of a women's Grand Slam Cup to honour those who had done well in the year's four premier tournaments. However, the ITF President, Brian Tobin, revealed that consideration was being given to staging a women's Grand Slam Cup at a separate event. This, at least, could overcome the thorny question of prize money parity often posed by representatives of the female players.

While such discussions continue, Monica Seles proceeded to clean up yet again on the women's circuit. In addition to the aforementioned three Grand Slams she won the season's-end Virginia Slims Championships in New York for the third year in succession, making short work of the only best-of-five-sets women's final on the year's programme by beating Martina Navratilova in straight sets.

Victory enabled Seles to equal her 1992 record of ten tournament wins and the first prize of $250 000 enabled her to break another record. With a bonus pool pay-out of $500 000, she ended the year with prize money of $2 622 352, more than any other tennis player, man or woman, has ever earned in a single year. The biggest cheers in Madison Square Garden were reserved, however, for Navratilova who had narrowly lost the opening set and led 3-1 in the second before losing 12 of the next 13 games and being left feeling, as she said, 'as if I had been run over by a Mack truck'. The nature of that defeat prompted the world's finest-ever woman tennis player to announce that 1993 would be her last full year of competition.

Navratilova also indulged in a spot of showbiz by joining the sport's elder statesman, the 40-year-old Jimmy Connors, in a so-called battle of the sexes match at Caesars Palace, Las Vegas. Connors won in gentlemanly fashion, kissed his opponent and then vowed to put in another hard year's work in 1993. Still battling along, too, is Ivan Lendl, who ended a 14-month barren spell by winning the Tokyo event in October. It was the 92nd success of his 15-year-career. But the other great name of the eighties, John McEnroe, opted to call it a day. His final year contained, as did all the others, much sublime tennis, an argument or two and – glory be – a Grand Slam title, albeit in doubles. In a Wimbledon final of record duration McEnroe combined with Stich to carry off the championship in a match that was carried over to the Monday following the end of The Championships and which attracted a full house (admitted free) to Court One.

McEnroe wept tears of joy, as he did four months later when a United States team inspired by his zest overcame the unexpectedly resilient challenge of Switzerland in the final of the Davis Cup by NEC. It was the 30th time the United States had captured the trophy which symbolises world tennis domination in team competition and the celebration among the Fort Worth crowd of 12,000 for once overwhelmed the cacophony provided by three Jumbo jet loads of Swiss supporters with their cowbells. Five days later came McEnroe's farewell to the game, defeat by Goran Ivanisevic at the Compaq Grand Slam Cup. It was a muted occasion, overshadowed by reports of difficulties with McEnroe's marriage to Tatum O'Neal.

The US success brought to a climax an eventful Davis Cup year in which the holders, France, went out to Switzerland in the second round and also said farewell to their captain, Yannick Noah, who had been such an inspiration in the final less than six months previously. The captaincy was something very much on McEnroe's mind, too. He made no secret of his ambitions in that direction and he was loudly supported by the other playing members of the American squad. It must have made embarrassing listening for the incumbent, Tom Gorman, who had come back with the trophy twice in three years. After some vacillation Gorman said he wanted to keep the job and in Munich Agassi spoke the truth when he said he thought McEnroe would find that 'the guys who wear suits and ties' at the US Tennis Association would stand between him and his ambitions. So it proved, with Gorman's re-selection duly announced just before the end of the year. McEnroe, it seems, is paying the price for stirring up emnities among the American tennis establishment over the years.

The 1993 Davis Cup entry has topped the hundred mark for the first time ever and the game continues to grow worldwide. Membership of the ITF grew last year to 176 nations (108 full and 68 associate) and tennis is flourishing in all corners of the world.

The social occasion of the year was the April marriage of Stefan Edberg to Annette Olsen, with the Swede offering his bride a belated present in the shape of a US Open championship hard won for the second straight year. Good news of the year was the victory won, on appeal, by the French Tennis Federation in its bid to extend the Roland Garros complex, a plan opposed by some local residents. This work will now go ahead, but without the guiding hand of Philippe Chatrier. After marrying Claudine Cros in a simple ceremony in a Brittany village in August, Chatrier announced in November that early in 1993 he would be stepping down after 20 years as President of the French Tennis Federation. Chatrier, 64, was also President of the ITF from 1977 to l991, and was elected to the International Olympic Committee in September1990.

Campaign of the year rapidly became the Aids Challenge set up at the US Open by Arthur Ashe, who made public earlier in the year his own HIV-positive status after hearing of newspaper plans to publish the story. The Arthur Ashe Foundation for the defeat of Aids aims to raise $5 million in 15 months and it produced an immediate and enthusiastic response within the tennis community. Finally, and sadly, Wimbledon lost two of it greatest names during 1992. Kitty Godfree, the oldest surviving Wimbledon champion, died at the age of 96 just prior to the start of the 1992 Championships. Having lost the 1923 final to Suzanne Lenglen, Kitty (then Miss McKane) defeated the formidable American, Helen Wills, to win the following year and repeated her success in 1926 with a win over Spain's Lili de Alvarez.

Then, on the very day that John McEnroe played his last tour match in Munich, came news of the death that morning of Dan Maskell at 84. Maskell, known as the 'Voice of Wimbledon', had announced his retirement from tennis commentating only ten months earlier. The presence of Maskell, and that wonderful voice, somehow summed up the essence of British summers. But there was much, much more to the man than that. 'Dan was a consummate professional, respected and loved the world over for his honest, informative and knowledgeable commentary,' said the Chairman of the All England Club, John Curry. 'He had great wisdom and a deep understanding of the game. He will be sorely missed.'

Despite retaining her Wimbledon title, Steffi Graf (above) could not challenge the authority of Monica Seles (left) who won all three of the other Grand Slam titles to end the year as the undisputed world No.1.
(T. Hindley)

PLAYERS OF THE YEAR

John Barrett

JIM COURIER

When, just two weeks after winning his first Australian Open title, Jim Courier reached the final in San Francisco, he became the tenth player to be ranked the No.1 player in the world since rankings began in 1973. It was an historic moment for the 21-year-old from Dade City and one he cherished. 'I'm very proud to have achieved the No.1 spot – but it's not something I worry about. If I just go out and play the best tennis I can, give it my best shot week in, week out, the ranking will take care of itself.' How right he was. Although Stefan Edberg did overtake him twice during the year, it was Courier who finished 1992 at the top. A second French Open title (where his victory speech in French was the PR coup of the year) plus wins in Tokyo, Hong Kong and Rome made sure of that. Jim is the first to admit that his highly individual, slugging, baseline style is not the prettiest sight in tennis. But he rightly asserts that there is a certain beauty in seeing an athlete give everything he has got in pursuit of excellence. No man works harder, no man competes more fiercely or more fairly, and no man deserves his success more completely than 'Gentleman Jim' Courier, *the* Player of the Year in 1992.

STEFAN EDBERG

Stefan Edberg may be a quiet, peaceful man but when he is challenged on a tennis court the 26-year-old Swede can fight like a tiger – as he proved at the 1992 US Open. Three times during the successful defence of his title Stefan was in a hopeless situation. In the fourth round against Richard Krajicek he had stood at 15–40 on his serve at 4–4 in the final set; one round later Ivan Lendl had led by a break in the fifth and was denied three points that would have given him a 5–3 lead; against Michael Chang in an epic semi-final that spanned a record breaking 5 hours and 26 minutes, Stefan had found himself 0–3 down in the fifth set and 15–40 on his serve. Somehow he escaped and broke for 2–3. But then, disaster! He immediately lost his own serve again to fall 2–4 behind. This was surely the end. But no! It is a measure of Stefan's nerve and character that from this desperate situation he reeled off 17 of the next 21 points for a heroic victory. After surviving such traumas it was no surprise that this elegant stroke-maker held off the challenge of Pete Sampras in the final. Long after he has stopped playing tennis Stefan will remember these performances, and the tournament wins in Hamburg (a first major success on clay, this) and New Haven that brought his career total to 36. But there was an even more important event in 1992 that he will remember for the rest of his life – his fairy-tale marriage in April to his long-time sweetheart, Annette Olsen. To her, Stefan will always be *the* Player of *every* Year.

ANDRE AGASSI

They said it was impossible. No longer, in an age of athletic giants wielding space-age rackets, was a baseliner capable of winning Wimbledon. But Andre Agassi proved them all wrong. With a display of piercing service returns and flashing passes, the like of which had never been seen on the famous old Centre Court, the 22-year-old Las Vegas showman – he of the flowing blond locks and the flailing forehand, of the gold earring and the golden double-handed backhand – brought down in succession Boris Becker, John McEnroe and Goran Ivanisevic to land the game's greatest prize. This first Grand Slam success after three failures at the last hurdle (two in Paris, one in New York), marked the

Stefan Edberg (above left) and Jim Courier (above right) shared the No.1 spot in the men's game, but perhaps the most memorable moments of 1992 were encapsulated in the performances of Andre Agassi (below left), winner at the Wimbledon Championships after eliminating some of the biggest servers in the game, and Jennifer Capriati (below right) who won an Olympic gold medal in the searing heat of Barcelona.

(M. Cole, T. Hindley)

fulfilment of a dream which Andre and his canny coach, Nick Bollettieri, had pursued for ten long years. More than that, this spectacular victory at last slayed the demon of self-doubt that had stalked Andre ever since he emerged on the scene as a precocious teenager with a reputation built on the shifting sands of promise rather than on the bedrock of fulfilment. On Sunday, 5th July 1992 Andre Agassi could at last call himself a true champion, and the world could salute him as an outstanding Player of the Year.

MARC ROSSET

For sheer courage – both physical and mental – the achievement of 21-year-old Marc Rosset in winning the Olympic title from a world class field in Barcelona's cauldron of a Centre Court has had few parallels. Ranked a modest 44 on the ATP computer and unseeded, this proud young giant from Geneva beat five seeds in succession on the slow red clay to win Switzerland's only gold medal of the Games. First South Africa's Wayne Ferreira(9) was felled in straight sets, then the overwhelming favourite, Jim Courier(1) of the United States who had won a second French Open only two months earlier, was similarly humbled – the upset of the year, this. Next it was the turn of local hero Emilio Sanchez(12) to feel the full force of Rosset's huge serve and rocket-like forehand as he went down in four sets. In the semi-finals Croatia's Goran Ivanisevic(4), exhausted by his four successive five-set wins (itself a record), could not garner a set. In the final, on another day of torrid heat, Rosset faced Barcelona-born Jordi Arrese(16) who had prepared all year for this moment. When Rosset won the first two sets an easy win seemed likely. But Arrese struck back to take the third set and then the fourth as Rosset, writhing with leg cramps, was treated by the trainer at the changeovers. Thoughts of quitting did pass through Marc's mind but the sight of his team-mates in the stands, urging him on, inspired him to one last great effort. In a noisy final set of unbearable tension, with the home crowd cheering every Arrese winner, Rosset held on to win it in the 14th game, appropriately with two huge forehands. It was wonderful to see how the Olympic spirit, for this brief moment, could transform a good player into a great one. Without question that performance stamped Marc Rosset as a Player of the Year.

MONICA SELES

Was there ever a more devastating striker of a tennis ball? For the second year in a row this remarkable Yugoslav-born teenager ruled the world of women's tennis with absolute authority. As in 1991, three of the four Grand Slam titles, as well as the season-ending Virginia Slims Championships, fell to her double-handed genius. Only at Wimbledon was her dominance interrupted. There the previous world champion, Steffi Graf, taking advantage of the furore surrounding the Seles grunt, interrupted her dominance of the major events for one brief moment. Elsewhere the 18-year-old left-hander lost only four matches in another all-conquering year which brought her ten more tournament wins that lifted her career total to 30. Only once, at the Lipton event, did she fail to reach the final and with her victory at Barcelona she became the youngest player ever to win 25 tour titles. No woman has ever played the way Monica does – with two-handed drives on both wings that are taken often as half-volleys. They speed to their target, deep and fast, with the unerring accuracy of a laser beam. Hard work on the practice court and growing physical strength have improved Monica's left-handed service considerably. No longer is it a weakness to be exploited. In fact it has become a weapon almost as potent as her drives. But her greatest asset is a mind that reacts to danger with the speed of a computer and makes her the finest match player of her generation. Yes, Monica Seles was certainly *the* Player of the Year in 1992.

STEFFI GRAF

With a welcome return to form after a disappointing start to the year that caused her to miss the Australian Open with ...what else...German measles, Germany's most famous woman athlete claimed a fourth Wimbledon title in 1992. With a devastating display of powerful serving and forehand hitting she completely destroyed the world champion,

Monica Seles, who could win only three games. That success alone was enough to make Steffi Graf a worthy player of the year, but in addition the 23-year-old right-hander won seven other titles and led Germany to victory in the Federation Cup. There were three major disappointments for Steffi in an otherwise excellent year. In Paris, despite playing almost flawless clay court tennis, she lost a magnificent final to Monica Seles after saving five match points; in the sweltering heat of Barcelona Steffi's Olympic crown was removed by the remarkable American teenager, Jennifer Capriati and Steffi had to be content with the silver medal; in her first match at the Virginia Slims Championships in New York Steffi lost disappointingly to Lori McNeil. Nevertheless it was clear that Seles and Graf were in a league of their own, well clear of their nearest challengers.

JENNIFER CAPRIATI

How many 16-year-olds in the world can boast of an Olympic Gold medal? Precious few in any sport. In tennis only the remarkable American prodigy Jennifer Capriati can make such a claim. In Barcelona's steam heat last summer Jennifer produced the best sustained performance of her young life to beat, in succession, Elna Reinach of South Africa, Argentina's Patricia Tarabini, Yayuk Basuki of Indonesia, German's No.7 seed Anke Huber, the local heroine Arantxa Sanchez-Vicario, seeded 2, and the holder and top seed, Steffi Graf of Germany. These six victories cost her only two sets. This was the high point of a year which had begun uncertainly. In the early tournaments Jennifer did not appear to be enjoying the game and there were rumours that she was debating whether to return to High School and the more normal life of an American teenager. Three outstanding successes convinced her that perhaps it was not so bad to be a professional tennis player after all. In March, at the Lipton tournament, Jennifer became one of only five players to beat world champion Monica Seles in 1992. After Wimbledon she went to Frankfurt for Federation Cup duty and proceeded to win every singles match as the United States reached the final. Then, inspired by her Olympic success, Jennifer went to San Diego and claimed her 5th tour title to take her career earnings past the $1 million mark. Yes, despite all her problems, Jennifer Capriati was certainly a Player of the Year in 1992.

ARANTXA SANCHEZ-VICARIO

For sheer consistency in singles and doubles, no-one could rival the smiling Spanish lass Arantxa Sanchez-Vicario in 1992. She appeared in no fewer than seven singles finals, including the US Open for the first time, and her two tournament victories, at the Lipton event in March and at the Canadian Open in August, included a rare win over the world champion Monica Seles at the latter. Her ten doubles victories with four different partners included the Australian Open and the Virginia Slims Championship titles with Helena Sukova. In addition Arantxa teamed up with Australia's Todd Woodbridge to win the mixed doubles at the French Open and reach the final in Australia. It was an exhausting schedule she had set herself but she seemed to thrive on all the hard work and by the end of the year she had banked $1.37 million to take her career earnings to almost $3.5 million. No wonder this most industrious Player of the Year smiled a lot!

THE ITF YEAR

THE ITF YEAR
DAVIS CUP
FEDERATION CUP

An heroic effort from Barcelona's Jordi Arrese contributed to a memorable Olympic final but the brave Spaniard had to be content with the silver medal in his home town.

(T. Hindley)

A win against the former world champion and title-holder, Steffi Graf, made Jennifer Capriati, at 16 years 4 months, the youngest-ever Olympic champion. (T. Hindley)

THE ITF YEAR

Ian Barnes

Olympic years have become something special in the International Tennis Federation calendar and 1992 was no exception. The Games of the 25th Olympiad, in Barcelona, provided the high spot of the year not only for the depth and drama of the competition but for the exposure tennis enjoyed as one of the Olympic movement's premier sports.

Two tennis players, Stefan Edberg of Sweden, the ITF's World Champion, and Goran Ivanisevic, of the newly independent Croatia, were chosen to carry their national flags in the spectacular Opening Ceremony parade. This was seen as a complement to a sport which had returned to the Games as a full medal sport only four years previously and a recognition that Edberg and Ivanisevic were the highest-profile sports personalities in their respective countries.

Edberg, unfortunately, had a short-lived exposure at the Games, losing in the first round of the singles to Andrei Chesnokov and with his partner, Anders Jarryd, going out at the same stage of the doubles to Jim Courier and Pete Sampras of the United States. Ivanisevic, in contrast, battled through four successive five-set matches before falling to eventual champion Marc Rosset, of Switzerland, in the semi-finals of the singles and also won a bronze medal in the doubles with Goran Prpic.

The Americans dominated the women's events with Jennifer Capriati, at 16, taking the singles gold medal – and incidentally preventing Steffi Graf from winning a third gold – and the unrelated Gigi Fernandez and Mary Joe Fernandez winning the doubles. Host nation Spain, inspired by the presence of King Carlos and Queen Sofia on several occasions during the 12 days of the tournament, collected a silver medal for Jordi Arrese in the men's singles and silver in the women's doubles in which Arantxa Sanchez-Vicario and Conchita Martinez were only narrowly defeated in a wonderfully entertaining final.

Being part of the Olympic movement has been one of the most significant factors in the recent growth of the ITF. Many countries find government funding for sports which are part of the Olympic family much easier to obtain and there is little doubt that it is in the interests of many of our member nations that our Olympic connection is maintained.

Some 176 nations are now either full or associate members of the ITF and any source of funds for development projects is important to many of them. The Grand Slam Development Fund – with the $2 million a year it now receives via the Grand Slam Committee from the Compaq Grand Slam Cup in Munich – continues to provide the bulk of the money invested in the future of the game but we have to encourage all our member nations to be as self-sufficient as possible.

The increase in membership came about in part from the political changes in Eastern Europe, particularly in the former Soviet Union and what was Yugoslavia. The Committee of Management granted provisional full membership to the Baltic States of Estonia, Latvia and Lithuania and to Croatia and Slovenia early in the year to enable athletes from those countries to compete in the Olympic Games and their decisions were endorsed by the Annual General Meeting which was held in the Dominican Republic in September. Full membership with five votes was also approved for the newly constituted All Russia Tennis Association and full membership with one vote each extended to Georgia and the Ukraine. Uzbekistan, another of the Republics within the former Soviet Union was provisionally admitted as an Associate Member. The Annual General Meeting also decided that Yugoslavia should remain a full member, but with reduced voting power.

These political changes also had a considerable impact on the Davis Cup by NEC. Yugoslavia, having been forced by circumstances in their country to play their World

Group first round tie against Australia in Cyprus, were defeated 5–0 and later, because of United Nations sanctions agreements, were barred from playing Cuba in the Qualifying Round for the World Group in 1993.

The Davis Cup Committee subsequently decided that Croatia should take the place of Yugoslavia in the Euro/African Zonal Group One in 1993 with Yugoslavia, which effectively comprised the regions of Serbia, Montenegro, Vojdovina and Kosovo, playing in the Zonal Group Three competition if the sanctions were lifted. Russia were selected to replace the Commonwealth of Independent States in the World Group of 1993 with Latvia, Estonia and Ukraine in Zonal Group Three.

Despite these problems, the 1992 Davis Cup by NEC was one of the most successful in terms of entry – a record 92 nations taking part – and excitement. Brazil, with the advantage of home ties, upset first Germany and then Italy before losing in the semi-finals to Switzerland, who had provided their own surprise by disposing of France, the Cup holders, in the second round. Switzerland's showing in the final against the United States in Fort Worth, Texas, where they carried the match into a third day before succumbing 3–1, exceeded the expectations of most neutral observers and will, no doubt, be seen to have been a tremendous shot in the arm for Swiss tennis.

The Federation Cup by NEC was also successfully staged at Frankfurt, Germany, with the home nation emerging as winners of the trophy for the second time by defeating the holders, Spain, in the final.

Decisions were also made during the year to return to Frankfurt in 1993 and 1994, after which the competition will be re-organized and run along Davis Cup lines with each match of four singles and a doubles being decided over two days.

Other competitions continued to flourish. Veteran and wheelchair events attracted ever-increasing numbers of competitors, and both the NEC World Youth Cup for players of 16 and under, in which France's boys and Belgium's girls triumphed, and the NTT World Junior Tennis competition for players of 14 and under – won by the Austrian boys and United States girls – enjoyed record entrie.

The Grand Slam championships also enjoyed a boom year. Attendances were higher than ever at the Ford Australian Open, Roland Garros and at the United States Open while at Wimbledon, which has been forced to reduce its capacity in recent years by Government legislation, a new roof on the Centre Court, supported by only four columns, enabled many more spectators an uninterrupted view of the action.

Monica Seles repeated her 1991 victories in Australia, France and the United States and was defeated only in the final, by Steffi Graf, at Wimbledon. She once again headed the Kraft Tour Point Standings to be named as the ITF World Champion for the year.

The men's World Champion was selected for the first time by a new computer program – the ITF World Champion Points Race – instead of the panel of former champions which had made the choice since the awards were introduced in 1978. Jim Courier, the winner of the Australian and French championships, a semi-finalist at the US Open and the man who clinched the winning point for the United States in the final of the Davis Cup by NEC, headed the table after the Compaq Grand Slam Cup in Munich, the final points-counting event of the year.

Unlike a roll-over ranking program, which reflects results over the most recent 52 weeks, the ITF World Champion Points Race program covers a calendar year. All competitive matches are taken into account, including the Grand Slams, Davis Cup by NEC, ATP Tour events, including the ATP World Finals in Frankfurt and the Compaq Grand Slam Cup. This was believed to be a more modern and accurate way to assess a player's performances during the year and brings the selection of the men's World Champion into line with the way the other champions are chosen.

For the ITF Development Department, 1992 was a year of expansion, thanks to the now regular injection of funds via the Grand Slam Committee from the Compaq Grand Slam Cup in Munich. Development officers were appointed in the Spanish and English speaking Carribean areas and the South Pacific and further big strides were made in Africa. With the newly formed Tennis South Africa back in the ITF fold, that Continent faces a much brighter future. A permanent training centre was set up in Johannesburg which, it was intended, would provide promising players from all over the Continent with opportunities to hone their skills and coaches with the chance to exchange views. The Compaq Grand Slam Cup itself, in its third year, became firmly established in the minds of the public and the players. Record crowds of more than 61,500 packed into the Munich Olympiahalle over the six days which culminated in victory, and the $2 million winner's cheque for local hero Michael Stich. Michael Chang, a semi-finalist in 1990, and runner-up to David Wheaton in 1991, was again the beaten finalist.

ITF WORLD CHAMPIONS

MEN

1978	Bjorn Borg	1986	Ivan Lendl
1979	Bjorn Borg	1987	Ivan Lend
1980	Bjorn Borg	1988	Mats Wilander
1981	John McEnroe	1989	Boris Becker
1982	Jimmy Connors	1990	Ivan Lendl
1983	John McEnroe	1991	Stefan Edberg
1984	John McEnroe	1992	Jim Courier
1985	Ivan Lend		

WOMEN

1978	Chris Evert	1986	Martina Navratilova
1979	Martina Navratilova	1987	Steffi Graf
1980	Chris Evert Lloyd	1988	Steffi Graf
1981	Chris Evert Lloyd	1989	Steffi Graf
1982	Martina Navratilova	1990	Steffi Graf
1983	Martina Navratilova	1991	Monica Seles
1984	Martina Navratilova	1992	Monica Seles
1985	Martina Navratilova		

ITF JUNIOR WORLD RANKING LEADERS

BOYS' SINGLES

1978 Ivan Lendl (TCH)
1979 Raul Viver (ECU)
1980 Thierry Tulasne (FRA)
1981 Pat Cash (AUS)
1982 Guy Forget (FRA)
1983 Stefan Edberg (SWE)
1984 Mark Kratzman (AUS)
1985 Claudio Pistolesi (ITA)
1986 Javier Sanchez (ESP)
1987 Jason Stoltenberg (AUS)
1988 Nicolas Pereira (VEN)
1989 Nicklas Kulti (SWE)
1990 Andrea Gaudenzi (ITA)
1991 Thomas Enqvist (SWE)
1992 Brian Dunn (USA)

GIRLS' SINGLES

1978 Hana Mandlikova (TCH)
1979 Mary-Lou Piatek (USA)
1980 Susan Mascarin (USA)
1981 Zina Garrison (USA)
1982 Gretchen Rush (USA)
1983 Pascale Paradis (FRA)
1984 Gabriela Sabatini (ARG)
1985 Laura Garrone (USA)
1986 Patricia Tarabini (ARG)
1987 Natalia Zvereva (URS)
1988 Cristina Tessi (ARG)
1989 Florencia Labat (ARG)
1990 Karina Habsudova (TCH)
1991 Zdenka Malkova (TCH)
1992 Rossana De Los Rios (PAR)

BOYS' DOUBLES

1982 Fernando Perez (MEX)
1983 Mark Kratzman (AUS)
1984 Augustin Moreno (MEX)
1985 Petr Korda (TCH)/ Cyril Suk (TCH)
1986 Tomas Carbonell (ESP)
1987 Jason Stoltenberg (AUS)
1988 David Rikl (TCH)/Tomas Zdrazila (TCH)
1989 Wayne Ferreira (RSA)
1990 Marten Renstroem (SWE)
1991 Karim Alami (MAR)
1992 Enrique Abaroa (MEX)

GIRLS' DOUBLES

1982 Beth Herr (USA)
1983 Larisa Savchenko (URS)
1984 Mercedes Paz (ARG)
1985 Mariana Perez Roldan (ARG)/Patricia Tarabini (ARG)
1986 Leila Meskhi (URS)
1987 Natalia Medvedeva (URS)
1988 JoAnne Faull (AUS)
1989 Andrea Strnadova (TCH)
1990 Karina Habsudova (TCH)
1991 Eva Martincova (TCH)
1992=Nancy Feber (BEL)
1992=Laurence Courtois (BEL)

Marc Rosset survived in the torrid heat and recovered his poise to claim the gold medal for Switzerland. It was their only medal of the Games. (T. Hindley)

THE OLYMPIC GAMES
John Barrett

It was appropriate that youth and courage were served in Barcelona as the world's leading men, and all but three of the top ranked women, interrupted their busy tournament schedules to strive for Olympic gold. Little did any of them realize just how exhausting it would be battling away for hour after hour on slow clay courts in the torrid heat of a Spanish summer.

At the end of a testing two weeks the American teenager, Jennifer Capriati, dethroned the reigning champion Steffi Graf 3–6 6–3 6–4 in a final of unbearable tension to become, at the age of 16, the youngest player to claim an Olympic crown. 'This was right up there with my win against Martina at Wimbledon...right now this means more to me than any of the Grand Slams,' said an emotional winner.

Then Marc Rosset of Switzerland, a giant at 6 ft 5 inches (1.96m) but rated no higher than 44th in the world, came back from the dead to beat the local hero, Jordi Arrese, seeded 16, in a fluctuating final that spanned 5 hours and 3 minutes of agonizing effort. The unseeded 21-year-old from Geneva had to summon every last ounce of energy to silence the noisy Spanish crowd with a 7–6 6–4 3–6 4–6 8–6 victory of truly heroic proportions. 'I was so exhausted in the fourth set I felt like quitting but I looked up at my team in the stands and knew that I must fight on to the end', admitted the delighted champion afterwards. His was the only medal won by Switzerland at the Games of the XXVth Olympiad.

With on-court temperatures soaring to 115 degrees fahrenheit and little breeze in the sheltered bowl of the centre court at the newly built Vall d'Hebron tennis centre, some of the leading men found the conditions too onerous to handle. Logically the finest clay court player was the world No.1 Jim Courier. The American was a strong favourite to add the Olympic title to his second French Open, won two months earlier. But after two straightforward victories against India's Ramesh Krishnan and Gilad Bloom of Israel, Courier faced a confident Rosset who had already disposed of the No.9 seed, Wayne Ferreira of South Africa. Courier could find no answer to Rosset's clever mixture of power and touch as he succumbed tamely 6–4 6–2 6–1 in a little over two hours. It was a tired and sad performance by a man whose early season performances had marked him as the game's toughest competitor.

Stefan Edberg's departure was equally unexpected. The former world No.1 had proudly carried the flag for Sweden during the spectacular but protracted opening ceremony. He was seeded No.2 and eager, he said, to improve upon the bronze medal he had won in Seoul. You would never have thought so when he lost the opening six games to Andrei Chesnokov of the Unified Team – as the former Soviet players were listed. Edberg was attempting to impose his usual serve-and-volley game against a shrewd opponent who knew exactly how to exploit the super-slow conditions. Chesnokov mixed short, low crosscourt passes with fierce drives and well flighted lobs to keep his opponent guessing. With his finger firmly upon the self-destruct button, Edberg went down 6–0 6–4 6–4 in 97 tortured minutes.

Nor was there any consolation for the quiet Swede in doubles. Unseeded because he had not played enough doubles to gain ranking points, Stefan was playing alongside his old friend Anders Jarryd, with whom he had won 12 titles, including the US and Australian Opens, as well as some crucial Davis Cup rubbers. Hard as they fought the Swedes were forced to swallow the bitter pill of defeat by the unseeded Americans Courier and Sampras who won 1–6 6–3 4–6 7–6 6–4.

Sadly, Chesnokov could not maintain his momentum and lost disappointingly to Renzo Furlan of Italy in the second round, but the other Andrei of the Unified Team, Andrei Cherkasov, kept the new flag flying. The 13th seed had looked most impressive in disposing of the tenacious Croatian, Goran Prpic, in four sets in the second round. I don't know if Pete Sampras, America's No.3 seed, had watched that match. If he did, he certainly did not learn from it. In building a two sets to one lead Sampras was having to work harder than he liked. The sheer physical effort had exacted a heavy price and the American was quite unable to match Cherkasov's relentless consistency and stamina in the closing stages as he went down 6–7 1–6 7–5 6–0 6–3. It was a spectacular success for Cherkasov who would carry his challenge through to the semi-finals where Arrese's speed and the support of the ecstatic home fans finally ended his hopes of silver or gold.

Germany's No.5 seed, Boris Becker, nearly became the most spectacular victim of all. His first round opponent was Christian Rudd of Norway, ranked a lowly 313 on the computer and lacking any experience of top level play. On the face of it this should have been a pleasant warm-up for the three-time Wimbledon champion. But when Becker went two sets to one down against an opponent whose response to the Olympic atmosphere had lifted his form to undreamed of heights, a sensational upset seemed a real possibility. Rudd led 2–0, 3–1, 4–2 and 6–5 in that fateful fourth set and was three points from victory in the 12th game on the German's serve. In the end it was only Becker's legendary strength and fitness, plus a cussed refusal to lose, that pulled him through 3–6 7–6 5–7 7–6 6–3.

In a match that had lasted nearly five hours, Becker had proved himself a formidable competitor but his relative weakness on slow clay was cruelly exposed two rounds later by the double-handed deception of the 19-year-old Frenchman, Fabrice Santoro. Teasing Becker with his early-taken flicks and well disguised lobs Santoro won their brief encounter 6–1 3–6 6–1 6–3. Becker was visibly shattered and said he was determined to make amends in the doubles.

Others who were quite unable to cope with the testing conditions against opponents in whom the Olympic flame burned brightly were Michael Chang (seeded 6), Guy Forget (seeded 7) and Michael Stich (seeded 8). All lost in the second round – Chang to Jaime Oncins of Brazil, Forget to the tall Swede, Magnus Larsson, and Stich to fellow German, Carl-Uwe Steeb – a fine performance this by the Stuttgart based left-hander.

The one highly ranked man who did excel was Wimbledon finalist Goran Ivanisevic. The No.4 seed had relished his role as the Croatian flag carrier and had set his heart on winning a medal for his country. The 20-year-old from Split would ultimately achieve his dream twice over by reaching the semi-finals in both singles and doubles (with Prpic). For a man whose best results have been achieved on fast surfaces and whose propensity to throw matches away half-heartedly has been the despair of his many supporters around the globe, this was a triumph of patience and determination. But the cost was immense. Four times in a row Ivanisevic had to go the full distance to dismiss, in turn, Bernado Motta of Portugal, Paul Haarhuis of Holland, the Swiss No.1 Jakob Hlasek(seeded 15) and Santoro. Hlasek, in fact, was two points from victory during their 16 game final set, and Santoro who had led 5–2 in the fifth, actually held two match points in the 10th game before being beaten 8–6. In the semi-final against Rosset, the determined Croat paid one last visit to the energy well but found it dry. He went down, defiant but exhausted, 6–3 7–5 6–2. Nevertheless, his bronze medal was the first earned by Croatia at the Games. In all Ivanisevic had spent more than 16 hours on court in singles and played 236 games. His four consecutive five set wins had given him an Open tennis record.

It was hardly surprising, therefore, that Ivanisevic had nothing left when the time came to play Ferreira and Piet Norval in the semi-finals of the doubles. In the previous round Goran had been within a point of disqualification against the Indians, Krishnan and Leander Paes, who had beaten the favourites Fitzgerald and Woodbridge in the second round. Prpic had held him together then but that task was beyond him against the agile South Africans. The Croatians went down 7–6 3–6 6–3 2–6 6–2 but even in defeat were proud that they had earned two more bronze medals for their new country.

Becker was as good as his word. He did, indeed, make himself a gold medallist at last.

Playing doubles with Stich for only the fourth time, he found an intensity that had seemed lacking in singles and nursed his partner through some awkward patches to clinch the final 7–6 4–6 7–6 6–3 against Ferreira and Norval. If Becker had not saved the set point he faced on his own serve in the 12th game of the opening set, the result might have been different. But his service winner saved the day and gave the Germans the breathing space they needed. Stich responded and in the end was playing as well as he had done two months earlier to win the Wimbledon title so memorably with John McEnroe.

The chief Spanish challenge, led by Sergi Bruguera and Emilio Sanchez, seeded respectively 11 and 12, faded disappointingly. Bruguera, having easily disposed of Britain's Andrew Castle, fell at the second hurdle to Mark Koevermans of Holland who won in four tame sets. Sanchez did at least fight through to the last eight, but there, inhibited both by the presence of the King and Queen and by the weight of national expectation from a noisy crowd, could win only one set as he became Rosset's third seeded victim.

It was left to Arrese to keep Spanish hopes alive. The boy from Barcelona, ranked at No. 30 in the world, had prepared for this moment ever since his selection at the start of the year, choosing to miss the entire Australian season and Wimbledon to concentrate on clay court tournaments in Europe. When countryman Carlos Costa did so well in the spring with wins in Estoril and Barceloina that lifted his ranking to No.10 by mid-May, the Spanish Federation approached Arrese to see if he would agree to swap places with Costa for the Olympics. To his credit, Costa refused to consider the move. 'Jordi is my friend and deserved to be selected', he said. 'I will not take his place.'

Arrese arrived home in Barcelona fresh from an appearance in the Hilversum final, his 14th tournament of the year. His progress to the Olympic final had been threatened only by his old rival Magnus Gustafsson of Sweden who had beaten him over five sets the

Beaten surprisingly early in the singles, Boris Becker and Michael Stich made amends for Germany by combining to take the gold medals in doubles.   *(T. Hindley)*

previous year – curiously enough also at Hilversum – which had been the Spaniard's 6th career tournament final. Playing in front of a patriotic crowd on the No.1 court in Barcelona, Arrese won 9–7 in the fifth set, his first ever five-set success. He then beat Furlan and Lavalle with ease before ending Cherkasov's hopes in a one-sided semi-final.

Rosset was also ready for his appointment with destiny. In their only previous meeting two years earlier the tall Swiss had prevailed 6–3 6–1 on an indoor carpet in Paris where his tremendous serving and heavy forehand had swept the lighter man away. Rosset realised that things would be rather different on slow clay.

In many ways it was an intriguing final, marked by some mighty blows from Rosset and some deadly passing from the Spaniard whose speed about the court and accuracy on the run were quite remarkable. When Rosset won the first set tie-break 7–2 and immediately broke Arrese in the first game of the second set (the only service break in the first twenty games), to earn a 2–0 lead after 128 minutes, it seemed the whole thing might be soon be over.

Two hours later it was two sets all. Halfway through the fourth set, as Rosset writhed with cramps and the trainer worked on his legs at the changeovers, it had seemed likely that the Swiss might be forced to retire. But as the afternoon turned to early evening the temperature began to drop and Rosset found a new lease of life. He was ahead in the early stages of the fifth set when a break for 3–1 was consolidated at 4–1. But then he faltered. With the packed stands echoing to the cheers for the local hero Rosset was broken in the 7th game as he delivered his 11th double fault.

To his credit Rosset never panicked amid the howling and screaming of the local populace. From 4–4 he held three times for the loss of only one point and in going ahead 6–5 he delivered three mighty serves to complete a love game – his 31st, 32nd and 33rd aces of the match. It was more than the brave Arrese could cope with. After resisting so stoutly for so long, at last he could resist no more. In the 14th game, leading 40–15, he missed with a backhand and failed to run down his opponent's next forehand volley. From deuce Rosset unleashed two mighty forehands from mid court and it was all over.

The absence of world No.1 Monica Seles, the No. 3 Gabriela Sabatini, and the No. 4 Martina Navratilova, robbed the women's event of full credibility. They were absent because all three had failed to make themselves available for the 1992 Federation Cup competition, a precondition for Olympic selection. Nevertheless, as the world's media focused upon the four top seeds – Graf, Sanchez-Vicario, Capriati and Mary Joe Fernandez – all of whom emerged to the semi-finals. It became clear that the absentees were the losers.

There were two notable casualties in the opening round. The 23-year-old Czech, Jana Novotna, seeded 9, lost 6–1 6–0 to her old rival Natalia Zvereva of the CIS (whose Olympic participants were all labelled EUN to signify Unified Team). Zvereva's command of the baseline and clever changes of pace recalled her progress to the French Open final in 1988. Poor Jana! All her attacking ploys came to nought on the ultra-slow clay courts against a clever opponent and the games slipped away before she had time to reorganize.

The 7–5 6–1 loss of Zina Garrison Jackson to the 20-year-old South African, Amanda Coetzer, was perhaps even more surprising because four years earlier Zina had been a bronze medallist in Korea where she had also won the gold with Pam Shriver in doubles. As with Novotna, the No.12 seed could not mount enough successful attacks without falling into error against an opponent whose excellent form belied her world ranking of 24.

It was commendable that the lowest ranked player, Sabine Appelmans of Belgium, came through to the quarter-finals without losing a set. She eliminated the Australian challenge single-handed by beating Rachael McQuillan and Nicole Provis and then accounted for Eugenia Maniakova from Moscow, who had removed the No.8 seed Katerina Maleeva, the middle sister of the famous Bulgarian family, in the second round. All three sisters were competing in Barcelona because the eldest, Manuela, the wife of Swiss coach Francois Fragnière, was representing Switzerland. Thus the Maleeva's created a new Olympic record. Admittedly the youngest, 17-year-old Magdelena, could make no headway against Graf in the third round, but nor could anyone else! At this stage the defending champion had lost a mere 11 games in four matches and looked invincible.

The athletic German was equally commanding in the semi-finals as she swept aside

Fernandez 6–4 6–2, her ninth successive straight sets win against the American. Fernandez, the Australian Open finalist for the second time last January, had not enjoyed a very good year. Nevertheless she had looked impressive in the previous round when beating the 6th seed, Maleeva Fragnière, 6–0 in the final set. But against Graf she was made to seem ponderous and deliberate. The champion was hitting the ball fast and true from the baseline and was serving with impressive power. This tenth consecutive singles win by Graf was the most by any man or woman in Olympic history and broke the record of South Africa's Charles Winslow who had won the gold medal with six wins in 1912 and added a bronze in 1912 with three more.

Capriati was almost as impressive on her way to the last four. She dismissed Elna Reinach of South Africa 6–1 6–0 and then had three workmanlike wins against an Argentine, an Indonesian and a German. Patricia Tarabini could win only five games from her but Yayuk Basuki earned 7 and Anke Huber (seeded 7) earned 9.

Jennifer's semi-final opponent was Sanchez-Vicario, upon whom the hopes of a medal for Spain rested because, in the previous round, the heroine of Spain's 1991 Federation Cup success had beaten her team-mate in that victory, Conchita Martinez (seeded 5), 6-4 6-4. With so much riding on it and the whole of Spain willing her to victory (including the King and Queen), Sanchez seemed inhibited.

This was not the free-hitting Sanchez who had beaten Capriati comprehensively the previous March at the Lipton tournament after the American had upset world No.1 Monica Seles. It was more like the anxious player who had been beaten 6–1 6–1 at Hilton Head in 1990 to become Capriati's first top-5 victim, soon after the precocious Floridian had entered the women's tour on the eve of her 14th birthday.

Some of the rallies were quite spectacular, fast and furious affairs, with both women showing great speed of foot and marvellous control of the ball at full stretch. But all too often they ended with a Spanish error. The combined 'ooohs' from 8,500 expectant Spanish throats was too much for the gallant Arantxa. Anxious glances towards her mother and father who sat with her brothers in the stands, demonstrated the strain she was under. Capriati's first set lead was wiped out by some industrious work from Sanchez but the American moved up a gear in the final set to inflict a 6–3 3–6 6–1 win against a disappointed loser.

The final started promisingly, developed intriguingly as Capriati endeavoured to end a run of four successive losses against the champion (the latest a 2–6 6–3 6–4 decision in Berlin) and then, in a final set of unbearable tension, became a minor classic.

Both players found the range in the very first game and at once were swapping drives of intimidating pace and accuracy. With the score at 2–2 there occurred one of those long and fluctuating games which did not seem particularly significant at the time but which, in retrospect, probably decided the issue. Graf, having conceded just one point in each of her service games, was made to struggle against a rampant youngster who clearly had decided that attack was her only hope, even on such a slow court. Four times Capriati held break point. Four times she was thwarted. Three of the lost opportunities came from her own forehand errors, two that flew long and one that finished in the net. In between Graf produced a beautiful service winner. Although Graf did survive after 13 deuces and went on the win that fierce 50 minute set 6–3, you knew that Capriati has started to believe in the possibility of a win. Graf knew it too.

The only break in the second set came in the eighth game with Capriati's relentless attack forcing Graf to overhit her forehand on the third set point. So, 5–3 to the young American. The way Capriati served out to love boded ill for the champion. Graf was immediately broken in the first game of the final set but broke right back after Capriati had led 30–0. This was a courageous game for Graf whose own penetration was the reason Capriati was forced into error.

Now the rallies reached breathtaking proportions with each in turn recovering miraculously to hit a winner from a seemingly impossible situation. Two-all, three-all, four-all. As the score mounted so did the tension. Something had to give. With both playing at the limits it was a matter of who would be the first to lose her nerve. To her credit, Capriati never wavered. She went on lambasting the ball fearlessly.

Suddenly Graf faltered. A third double fault made it 0–40. Two huge blows from the trusty forehand got her back to 30–40 and then Capriati's forehand just missed the line. Deuce. In the next rally Capriati forced Graf wide and the champion's crosscourt backhand flew wide. A fourth break point. Graf was playing too carefully now and Capriati unleashed another of those mighty forehands to break for 5–4. Here the American faced her sternest test. Would she finish the job cleanly and break the hoodoo of never having beaten the former world champion? Indeed she would! Bounding around the court with undisguised glee, Capriati held to 15 in a game that contained her 5th ace. Thus she completed her historic win in 2 hours and eight minutes.

It was the sort of positive climax that one always hopes for at the end of a really thrilling encounter and it transformed the attitude of one whose enthusiasm for tennis had waned so completely early in the year that she had even contemplated giving up the game. At the medal ceremony there were tears in the shining eyes of the new young gold medallist. She stood to attention on the high central podium with her right arm across her chest and her eyes raised towards the stars and stripes as it proudly climbed the tallest flagpole, obediently followed by the black, red, and gold of Germany and the red and yellow of Spain.

However, the German flag would soon enjoy it's moment of glory. Becker and Stich, the No. 6 seeds, made sure of that. Playing in only their fourth tournament together, the Davis Cup colleagues sunk their personal rivalries in the quest for gold. Playing with tremendous zest, they beat the young South Africans Wayne Ferreira and Piet Norval 7–6 4–6 7–6 6–3 in a battle that spanned 3 hours and 27 minutes. It was as if both former Wimbledon champions were trying to efface the memories of singles failures.

Most of the subtleties came from the South Africans but their relatively lightweight games were no match for German power. Becker was the general, always able to dig his team out of difficulties with his heavy blows. Stich, the reigning Wimbledon doubles champion with John McEnroe, was quite prepared to play a supporting role once again and in doing so provided some glorious touches of his own. Only once did he lose his serve and at the end he could look back proudly to the two key five set wins they had enjoyed, first against the local heroes Casal and Sanchez, seeded 3, and then against the 7th seeded Argentines, Frana and Miniussi. This was the first time a German doubles pair had won gold, though in 1896 in Athens Fritz Thraun, playing with John Boland of Ireland, had won the doubles.

The women's doubles became a Fernandez festival when the two Americans of that ilk, Mary Joe and Gigi, so often opponents on important doubles occasions but playing together for the first time, combined beautifully to thwart Spanish hopes of gold by beating Sanchez-Vicario and Martinez 7–5 2–6 6–2. Once again the pressure of national expectation helped to destroy the home team whose capture of the second set brought such prolonged applause that it was difficult at times for the umpire to retain control. Sanchez-Vicario, who earlier in the year had steadied her partner's nerves when they had won the French Open together and claimed five Federation Cup doubles matches without dropping a set, failed to cope with the pressure.

Although the arguments will rage on about the suitability of allowing fully fledged professionals in events like tennis and basketball to compete in the Olympic Games, there was no doubt about the opinions of the competitors themselves. You only had to see the emotion on the faces of the medal winners as their national anthems were being played to know that this moment would be etched on their memories for ever. In more and more sports the governing bodies have accepted that there is nothing immoral about the world's leading performers benefiting financially by their skills. If the Olympic Games is to retain its credibility it must surely embrace that honest principle and open its arms to excellence in all disciplines.

OLYMPIC GAMES, BARCELONA, 1992

MEN'S SINGLES – 1st round: J. Courier (1) d. R. Krishnan (WC) 6–2 4–6 6–1 6–4; G. Bloom (Q) d. M. Vajda (Q) 7–6 6–1 6–0; M. Rosset d. K. Alami (Q) 6–2 4–6 2–1 ret.; W. Ferreira (9) d. C. van Rensburg 7–5 6–2 2–6 6–4; E. Sanchez (12) d. T. Woodbridge 6–1 7–6 6–2; O. Camporese d. J. Rios (Q) 6–2 6–2

6–0; M. Larsson (WC) d. H. Skoff 6–2 6–3 6–3; G. Forget (7) d. C. Caratti 6–3 6–4 6–2; G. Ivanisevic (4) d. B. Mota (LL) 6–2 6–2 6–7 4–6 6–3; P. Haarhuis d. L. Mattar (LL) 4–6 6–3 6–2 6–2; A. Sznajder d. B. Wijaya (Q) 6–2 6–4 7–5; J. Hlasek (15) d. F. Maciel (Q) 6–3 6–4 4–6 6–2; J. Frana d. P. Arraya 6–2 6–0 6–7 6–7 6–2; F. Santoro d. C. Miniussi (LL) 6–1 7–6 6–4; Y. El Aynaoui (LL) d. C. Wilkinson (LL) 6–4 6–1 7–5; B. Becker (5) d. C. Ruud (LL) 3–6 7–6 5–7 7–6 6–3; M. Chang (WC) (6) d. A. Mancini 6–1 6–4 3–6 6–0; J. Oncins d. S. Muskatirovic (Q) 7–6 4–6 6–1; M. Koevermans (LL) d. L. Markovits (LL) 6–2 6–3 2–6 6–2; S. Bruguera (11) d. A. Castle (LL) 6–1 6–2 6–3; A. Cherkasov (13) d. R. Smith (Q) 6–1 6–0 3–6 6–1; G. Prpic d. K. Carlsen (Q) 6–4 4–6 6–3 7–5; J. Yzaga d. L. Paes (Q) 1–6 7–6 6–0 6–0; P. Sampras (3) d. W. Masur 6–1 7–6 6–4; M. Stich (8) d. R. Fromberg (Q) 6–3 3–6 6–1 3–6 6–3; C. Steeb (WC) d. A. Pavel (Q) 7–5 6–2 6–2; L. Lavalle d. J. Siemerink 6–4 6–4 6–2; H. Leconte (WC) d. T. Muster (10) 7–6 7–6 6–4; J. Arrese (16) d. E. Chang (Q) 6–4 6–2 6–2; M. Gustafsson d. O. Casey (LL) 7–6 6–1 6–4; R. Furlan (WC) d. S. Matsuoka 6–4 6–3 3–6 6–4; A. Chesnokov (WC) d. S. Edberg (2) 6–0 6–4 6–4. **2nd round:** Courier (1) d. Bloom (Q) 6–2 6–0 6–0; Rosset d. Ferreira (9) 6–4 6–0 6–2; E. Sanchez (12) d. Camporese 6–4 6–2 6–1; Larsson (WC) d. Forget 6–3 6–3 6–1; Ivanisevic (4) d. Haarhuis 6–7 6–2 1–6 6–3 6–2; Hlasek (15) d. Sznajder 4–6 6–4 6–3 7–5; Santoro d. Frana (LL) 4–6 6–2 6–1 6–1; Becker (5) d. El Aynaou (LL) 6–4 5–7 6–4 6–0; Oncins d. Chang (WC) (6) 6–2 3–6 6–3 6–3; Koevermans (LL) d. Bruguera (11) 1–6 6–3 6–3 6–2; Cherkasov (13) d. Prpic 6–4 6–7 6–4 6–3; Sampras (3) d. Yzaga 6–3 6–0 3–6 6–1; Steeb (WC) d. Stich (8) 6–4 6–2 4–6 6–3; Lavalle d. Leconte (WC) 6–4 3–6 4–6 6–3 10–8; Arrese (16) d. Gustafsson 6–2 4–6 6–1 3–6 9–7; Furlan (WC) d. Chesnokov (WC) 7–6 6–4 6–4. **3rd round:** Rosset d. Courier (1) 6–4 6–2 6–1; E. Sanchez (12) d. Larsson (WC) 6–4 7–6 6–7 6–4; Ivanisevic (4) d. Hlasek (15) 3–6 6–0 4–6 7–6 9–7; Santoro d. Becker (5) 6–1 3–6 6–1 6–3; Oncins d. Koevermans (LL) 7–6 6–0 7–6; Cherkasov (13) d. Sampras (3) 6–7 1–6 7–5 6–0 6–3; Lavalle d. Steeb (WC) 6–4 3–6 6–3 6–2; Arrese (16) d. Furlan (WC) 6–4 6–3 6–2. **Quarter-finals:** Rosset d. E. Sanchez (12) 6–4 7–6 3–6 7–6; Ivanisevic (4) d. Santoro 6–7 6–7 6–4 6–4 8–6; Cherkasov (13) d. Oncins 6–1 6–4 6–7 4–6 6–2; Arrese (16) d. Lavalle 6–1 7–6 6–1. **Semi-finals:** Rosset d. Ivanisevic (4) 6–3 7–5 6–2; Arrese (16) d. Cherkasov (13) 6–4 7–6 3–6 6–3. **Final:** Rosset d. Arrese (16) 7–6 6–3 3–6 4–6 8–6.

MEN'S DOUBLES – Semi-finals: Ferreira/P. Norval (4) d. Ivanisevic/Prpic 7–6 3–6 6–3 2–6 6–2; Becker/Stich (6) d. Frana/G. Miniussi (7) 7–6 6–2 6–7 2–6 6–4. **Final:** Becker/Stich (6) d. Ferreira/Norval (4) 7–6 4–6 7–6 6–3.

WOMEN'S SINGLES – 1st round: S. Graf (1) d. Novelo 6–1 6–1; B. Schultz d. L. Fang 7–5 6–7 6–4; Mag. Maleeva d. E. Zardo 6–2 6–4; K. Date (14) d. R. Simpson Alter 7–5 6–1; S. Appelmans (16) d. R. McQuillan 6–3 6–3; N. Provis d. K. Piccolini 6–1 6–0; E. Maniokova d. P. Ritter 6–1 7–6; K. Maleeva (8) d. L. Savchenko Neiland 7–6 6–2; M. J. Fernandez (4) d. L. Chen 6–2 6–3; P. Hy d. D. Randriantefy 6–2 6–1; S. Smith d. S. Gomer 2–6 6–3 6–1; N. Zvereva d. J. Novotna (9) 6–1 6–0; H. Sukova (11) d. N. Randriantefy 6–0 6–1; A. Gavaldon d. C. Lindqvist 6–4 6–3; R. Reggi Concato d. J. Byrne 6–4 7–6; M. Maleeva Fragnière (6) d. A. Vieira 6–2 6–3; P. Huber (7) d. N. Sawamatsu 6–0 4–6 6–2; B. Paulus d. M. Javer 6–7 6–4 6–3; N. Muns Jagerman d. I. Kim 6–4 6–4; J. Halard (15) d. K. Nowak 6–4 7–6; M. Pierce (13) d. L. Meskhi 7–6 7–5; Y. Basuki d. M. Paz 6–1 6–4; P. Tarabini d. M. de Swardt 6–4 6–2; J. Capriati (3) d. E. Reinach 6–1 6–0; C. Martinez (5) d. J. Wiesner 4–6 6–1 6–2; S. Cecchini d. P. Sepulveda 6–2 6–3; A. Blumberga d. C. Papadaki 4–6 6–1 6–2; A. Coetzer d. Z. Garrison Jackson (12) 7–5 6–1; N. Tauziat (10) d. R. Zrubakova 6–3 6–2; B. Rittner d. F. Labat 6–3 6–3; M. Endo d. E. Pampoulova Wagner 7–6 7–6; A. Sanchez-Vicario (2) d. I. Sprilea 6–1 6–3. **2nd round:** Graf (1) d. Schultz 6–2 6–4; Mag. Maleeva d. Date (14) 6–2 6–4; Appelmans (16) d. Provis 6–2 6–1; Maniokova d. K. Maleeva (8) 7–6 4–6 6–0; M. J. Fernandez (4) d. Hy 6–2 1–6 12–10; Zvereva d. Smith 6–1 6–2; Gavaldon d. Sukova (11) 4–6 6–4 5–3 ret.; Maleeva Fragnière (6) d. Reggi Concato 6–2 6–4; Huber (7) d. Paulus 6–4 6–1; Muns Jagerman d. Halard (15) 7–6 7–6; Basuki d. Pierce (13) 0–6 6–3 10–8; Capriati (3) d. Tarabini 6–4 6–1; Martinez (5) d. Cecchini 6–4 6–3; Coetzer d. Blumberga 6–2 6–4; Rittner d. Tauziat (10) 6–3 6–2; Sanchez-Vicario (2) d. Endo 6–0 6–1. **3rd round:** Graf (1) d. Mag. Maleeva 6–3 6–4; Appelmans (16) d. Maniokova 6–1 6–3; M. J. Fernandez (4) d. Zvereva 7–6 6–1; Maleeva Fragnière d. Gavaldon 6–0 6–3; Huber (7) d. Muns Jagerman 7–5 7–6; Capriati (3) d. Basuki 6–3 6–4; Martinez (5) d. Coetzer 6–4 6–3; Sanchez-Vicario (2) d. Rittner 4–6 6–3 6–1. **Quarter-finals:** Graf (1) d. Appelmans (16) 6–1 6–0; M. J. Fernandez (4) d. Maleeva Fragnière (6) 5–7 6–1 6–0; Capriati (3) d. Huber (7) 6–3 7–6; Sanchez-Vicario (2) d. Martinez (5) 6–4 6–4. **Semi-finals:** Graf (1) d. M. J. Fernandez (4) 6–4 6–2; Capriati (3) d. Sanchez-Vicario 6–3 3–6 6–1. **Final:** Capriati (3) d. Graf (1) 3–6 6–3 6–4.

WOMEN'S DOUBLES – Semi-finals: Martinez/Sanchez-Vicario (1) d. McQuillan/Provis (5) 6–1 6–2; G. Fernandez/M.J. Fernandez (2) d. Meskhi/Zvereva (4) 6–4 7–5. **Final:** G. Fernandez/M.J. Fernandez (2) d. Martinez/Sanchez-Vicario (1) 7–5 2–6 6–2.

With a 3-1 victory over the plucky Swiss
in Fort Worth, the United States (above,
Russ Adams) won the Davis Cup for the
30th time. Team: (L to R): Leach, Agassi,
Courier, J. McEnroe, Sampras, Gorman
(Capt.). Jakob Hlasek (left, T. Hindley)
was a powerful force in the Swiss team's
surprise progress to the final.

THE DAVIS CUP BY NEC

Ian Barnes

It was not really a surprise to see the Davis Cup by NEC back in American hands at the end of 1992. The squad Tom Gorman assembled to wipe out the memory of their defeat in the 1991 Final by France was just as much a 'Dream Team' as the basketball players who had been the golden heroes of the Olympic Games in Barcelona. Jim Courier, the Ford Australian and French Open champion, Andre Agassi, the Wimbledon title-holder, Pete Sampras, runner-up in the US Open and the incomparable John McEnroe, still a most formidable foe at the age of 34, knew what they had to do and then, in Agassi's favourite phrase, 'just did it'.

Having waltzed past Argentina, Czechoslovakia and the talented team from Sweden, they arrived for the final against Switzerland in Fort Worth bristling with confidence. Virtually the only dissenting voices belonged to Swiss captain Tim Sturdza, facing his first match in that role, and his players, Jakob Hlasek and Marc Rosset. Sturdza insisted: 'We reached the semi finals for the first time and the final for the first time. Now we are going to win the Cup for the first time'.

By the end of the first day, his words did not seem so outlandish. Agassi, it is true, had brushed aside Hlasek's challenge, 6–1, 6–2, 6–2 in just 88 minutes with the arrogance that comes from total self-belief.

But it was the nagging fear of failure which ate away and finally consumed Courier, who had come into the match against Rosset knowing that his Davis Cup record was far from impressive with four defeats in six previous singles outings. The result was a 1–1 scoreline at the end of the day and this heightened tension all round the arena. To say Courier was devastated by Olympic gold medallist Rosset's 6–3, 6–7, 3–6, 6–4, 6–4 victory would be an understatement. He was totally stunned. But such is the unique magic of Davis Cup that less than 48 hours later Courier was the American hero. A 6–3, 3–6, 6–3, 6–4 winner against Hlasek, Courier was hoisted in the air in triumph by his jubilant team-mates as the cheers of the flag waving American fans engulfed him.

After the Rosset set-back, Courier had been almost speechless. When he came down to earth after his Cup-clinching win over Hlasek he admitted: 'This is an amazing feeling. It is so special you could not buy it. Nothing has meant more to me than to bring the Cup back where it belongs.'

He went on to claim that, with their strength in depth, there was no reason to suppose the Americans could not now put a grip on the trophy 'for the next eight or nine years'. Only time will tell but the Americans have always had the strength in depth to be a force in the competition and, in Tom Gorman, they have one of the most experienced captains. He has now led various teams to three Cup wins in the first seven years of his captaincy and is the most successful captain, with 17 victories, in American tennis history.

For McEnroe, the final marked what he said would be the end of his singles career in a competition which he has always regarded as providing the highlights of his career. Certainly no American player, ancient of modern, has given more to his country's endeavours. He has played in a total of 30 ties, dating back to 1978, won 41 of 49 singles rubbers and 18 of 20 doubles matches with a variety of partners. More than anyone, he knows how Davis Cup fortunes can ebb and flow – a lesson that Germany learned at the beginning of the 1992 campaign which attracted a record 93 entries.

They were drawn to play in Brazil and found the experience too much for them, both mentally and physically. Boris Becker, so often the German hero, played one of the most gruelling matches of his life, saving six match points in the fourth set before overcoming

Luis Mattar 6-4, 5–7, 1–6, 7–6, 6–0 on a stifling, humid opening day, when Jaime Oncins defeated Carl-Uwe Steeb 6–3, 4–6, 6–2, 7–6 to level the score at 1–1.

Another exhausting match in the doubles, in which Casio Motta and Fernando Roese defeated Becker and Eric Jelen in three long sets, took so much out of Becker he was unable to start the reverse singles and Germany, to the surprise of all, except, perhaps, the Brazilians, found themselves facing a Qualifying Round match in late September as Oncins overcame substitute Markus Zoecke, 7–5 in the fifth.

The fall-out from the tie, and Brazil's subsequent second round defeat of Italy in Maceio, was considerable. Neither of the temporary venues, nor the conduct of the Brazilian crowds, was considered acceptable and led, after thorough investigation of all the circumstances, to a heavy fine on the Brazilian Federation and the drawing up of guidelines for the future staging of World Group ties. A rule allowing point penalties against players whose supporters were deemed to be behaving in a particularly partisan manner during play was also introduced to come into immediate effect.

Other first round matches in the World Group went more or less predictably with Sweden, the dominant team of the 1980s, coming back from 0–2 down to defeat Canada in Vancouver; Italy upsetting Spain 4–1; and France, the holders, beginning the defence of their title with a straightforward 5–0 defeat of Great Britain. The United States had a similar winning margin against Argentina in Hawaii.

The second round, in contrast, provided the unexpected defeat of France by Switzerland – after which Yannick Noah, who had played his 1991 heroes, Guy Forget and Henri Leconte, only in the doubles, resigned as captain – and the upset of Italy by Brazil.

Victory over France caused an outbreak of Cup fever in Switzerland that grew enormously before the semi final clash with Brazil, in Geneva, in September. Daily sell-out crowds of 17,000 willed Rosset and Hlasek to a clean-sweep victory and their country's first ever appearance in the final round of the competition.

The United States, meanwhile, with home advantage at every stage, cruised past Czechoslovakia and Sweden to claim their place in the final and give themselves the chance which Courier, Agassi, Sampras and McEnroe eventually took of a 30th Cup triumph.

The 1992 competition was also notable for the introduction of a Zonal Group Three competition, played in each area, at one venue in one week and the return of South Africa to the competition after an absence of 15 years. They made a winning return by losing only one of 31 sets in five ties they played in the Euro/African Zonal Group, which was played in Tunisia and were rewarded with promotion to Group Two for 1993.

Senegal, Algeria and Cameroon also earned promotion in the Euro/Africa Zone and were joined in the higher division by Iran and Kuwait in Asia/Oceania and Peurto Rico and Haiti in the American Zone.

The Commonwealth of Independent States (formerly USSR), Denmark, Austria, Israel, Korea, India, Cuba and Uruguay, earned the right to places in the Qualifying Round for 1993 alongside the 1992 World Group first round losers with five of them making the most of their opportunity. Denmark beat Argentina 3–2, Austria defeated Canada 3–1, Cuba were awarded a walk-over against Yugoslavia, who were unable to play because of United Nations sanctions, India made the most of home advantage to defeat Great Britain in Delhi and CIS had a comfortable 5–0 win over Korea in Moscow.

THE DAVIS CUP BY NEC, 1992

WORLD GROUP

FIRST ROUND – France d. Great Britain 5–0, Bayonne FRA: H. Leconte d. J. Bates 4–6 6–4 6–2 6–4; G. Forget d. M. Petchey 4–6 6–3 6–3 6–3; Forget/Leconte d. Bates/N. Broad 6–3 6–4 4–6 7–6(4); Forget d. Bates 6–2 6–4; Leconte d. Petchey 6–1 6–2. **Switzerland d. Netherlands 4–1, The Hague NED:** M. Rosset d. J. Siemerink 7–6(2) 6–2 7–6(4); J. Hlasek d. P. Haarhuis 4–6 6–4 6–3 7–6(2); Hlasek/Rosset d. Haarhuis/M. Koevermans 6–2 5–7 6–3 6–1; Hlasek d. J. Eltingh 6–2 6–4; Rosset lost Haarhuis 4–6 3–6. **Brazil d. Germany 3–1 (1 not played), Rio de Janeiro BRA:** L. Mattar lost B. Becker 4–6 7–5 6–1 6–7(2) 0–6; J. Oncins d. C–U. Steeb 6–3 4–6 6–2 7–6(5); C. Motta/F. Roese d. Becker/E. Jelen 7–5 6–3 6–3; Oncins d. M. Zoecke 1–6 6–4 7–6(3) 2–6 7–5; Mattar v Steeb not played. **Italy d. Spain 4–1, Bolzano ITA:** O. Camporese d. S. Bruguera 6–4 6–1 4–6 6–1; C. Caratti lost E. Sanchez 6–7(3) 6–4 6–3 5–7 5–7; Camporese/D. Nargiso d. S. Casal/E. Sanchez 7–6(4) 6–3 6–4; Camporese d. E. Sanchez 6–0 6–2 6–4; Caratti d. Bruguera 6–4 6–7(8) 6–1. **Australia d. Yugoslavia 5–0, Nicosia CYP** (Yugoslavia had choice of venue, but tie re-arranged in Cyprus because of civil unrest in Yugoslavia): R. Fromberg d. S. Zivojinovic 7–6(6) 0–0 ret.; W. Masur d. S. Muskatirovic 6–4 6–1 6–2; J. Fitzgerald/T. Woodbridge d. N. Djordjevic/A. Kitinov 7–5 6–3 7–6(2); Masur d. Djordjevic 6–3 6–0; Fromberg d. Muskatirovic 6–0 6–3. **Sweden d. Canada 3–2, Vancouver CAN:** M. Gustafsson lost G. Connell 6–7(5) 4–6 4–6; S. Edberg lost D. Nestor 6–4 3–6 6–1 3–6 4–6; Edberg/A. Jarryd d. Connell/G. Michibata 3–6 6–3 6–4 6–4; Edberg d. Connell 6–2 6–2 7–6(2); Gustafsson d. Nestor 6–4 2–6 3–6 7–5 6–4. **Czechoslovakia d. Belgium 5–0, Prague TCH:** K. Novacek d. B. Wuyts 6–7(7) 6–7(5) 6–3 6–4 6–4; P. Korda d. E. Masso 6–1 7–6(0) 6–3; Korda/C. Suk d. Masso/T. Van Houdt 6–3 6–3 6–3; Korda d. Wuyts 6–4 7–5; Novacek d. Masso 6–4 6–2. **USA d. Argentina 5–0, Mauna Lani HI USA:** P. Sampras d. M. Jaite 3–6 6–4 6–2 6–4; A. Agassi d. A. Mancini 6–4 6–4 6–4; R. Leach/J. McEnroe d. J. Frana/C. Miniussi 6–7(0) 6–2 6–2 6–1; Sampras d. Mancini 6–4 6–1; Agassi d. Jaite 7–5 6–3.

QUARTER-FINALS – Switzerland d. France 3–2, Nimes FRA: J. Hlasek d. A. Boetsch 3–6 7–6(3) 6–4 7–6(4); M. Rosset d. T. Champion 6–4 6–4 4–6 6–2; Hlasek/Rosset lost G. Forget/H. Leconte 6–4 6–4 2–6 6–7(5) 4–6; Hlasek d. Champion 6–3 4–6 7–6(6) 7–5; Rosset lost Boetsch 4–6 4–6. **Brazil d. Italy 3–1 (1 not played), Maceio BRA:** L. Mattar lost O. Camporese 3–6 7–5 4–6 7–6(9) 4–6; J. Oncins d. P. Cane 7–6(4) 4–6 5–7 7–5 6–3; C. Motta/F. Roese d. Camporese/D. Nargiso 6–4 6–2 5–7 3–6 6–3; Oncins d. S. Pescosolido 6–4 6–3 3–6 1–0 ret.; Mattar v Cane not played. **Sweden d. Australia 5–0, Lund SWE:** M. Gustafsson d. W. Masur 7–5 6–4 6–4; S. Edberg d. R. Fromberg 6–3 6–2 6–3; Edberg/A. Jarryd d. J. Fitzgerald/T. Woodbridge 6–3 6–3 6–1; Edberg d. Masur 6–4 7–6(4); C. Bergstrom d. Fromberg 6–4 7–5. **USA d. Czechoslovakia 3–2, Fort Myers FL USA:** P. Sampras d. K. Novacek 6–3 6–4 6–2; A. Agassi d. P. Korda 6–2 6–4 6–1; R. Leach/J. McEnroe lost Korda/C. Suk 3–6 4–6 4–6; Sampras lost Korda 4–6 3–6 6–2 3–6; Agassi d. Novacek 7–6(5) 6–0 6–0.

SEMI-FINALS – Switzerland d. Brazil 5–0, Geneva SUI: M. Rosset d. J. Oncins 6–3 7–5 7–5; J. Hlasek d. L. Mattar 6–2 6–3 6–7(5) 6–3; Hlasek/Rosset d. C. Motta/F. Roese 6–3 6–4 6–3; Hlasek d. Oncins 6–4 6–2; Rosset d. Mattar 7–6(2) 6–3. **USA d. Sweden 4–1, Minneapolis MN USA:** J. Courier d. N. Kulti 4–6 7–6(1) 6–3 7–5; A. Agassi d. S. Edberg 5–7 6–3 7–6(1) 6–3; J. McEnroe/P. Sampras d. Edberg/A. Jarryd 6–1 6–7(2) 4–6 6–3 6–3; Courier lost M. Larsson 6–2 6–7(6) 6–7(5); Agassi d. Kulti 6–7(4) 6–2 6–4.

FINAL – USA d. Switzerland 3–1 (1 not played), Fort Worth TX USA: A. Agassi d. J. Hlasek 6–1 6–2 6–2; J. Courier lost M. Rosset 3-6 7-6 6-3 4-6 4-6; J. McEnroe/P. Sampras d. Hlasek/Rosset 6-7 6-7 7-5 6-1 6-2; Courier d. Hlasek 6-3 3-6 6-3 6-4; Agassi v. Rosset not played.

QUALIFYING ROUND FOR WORLD GROUP 1992

Denmark d. Argentina 3–2, Aarhus DEN: F. Fetterlein lost A. Mancini 6–2 7–5 2–6 1–6 5–7; K. Carlsen d. G. Markus 6–7(4) 6–4 6–3 6–1; Carlsen/M. Christensen d. J. Frana/C. Miniussi 6–4 7–6(5) 6–3; Carlsen d. Mancini 6–4 3–6 6–3 7–6(3); Christensen lost Markus 4–6 6–4 5–7. **Austria d. Canada 3–1 (1 unfinished), Vancouver CAN:** A. Antonitsch d. D. Nestor 6–4 6–4 3–6 6–2; T. Prerovsky lost G. Connell 6–7(4) 6–7(6) 2–6; Antonitsch/G. Mandl d. Connell/G. Michibata 6–2 7–6(1) 4–6 3–6; Antonitsch d. Connell 6–2 6–4 7–6(3); Prerovsky v. D. Nestor 6–4 6–7(6) (unfinished). **Germany d. Belgium 5–0, Essen GER:** M. Stich d. B. Wuyts 6–3 6–4 6–4; B. Becker d. F. De Wulf 6–4 6–4 6–4; Becker/Stich d. De Wulf/E. Masso 7–6(5) 6–2 7–5; M. Zoecke d. Wuyts 6–2 6–2; Stich d. De Wulf 6–4 4–6 6–4. **Cuba d. Yugoslavia walkover** (Yugoslavia disqualified, note Cuba had choice of venue and the tie would have been played in Havana); **Netherlands d. Uruguay 4–1, The Hague NED:** R. Krajicek d. D. Perez 6–2 6–4 7–6(5); P. Haarhuis lost M. Filippini 6–3 6–7(8) 6–1 1–6 1–6; Haarhuis/M. Koevermans d. Filippini/Perez 7–5 6–2 6–4; Krajicek d. Filippini 7–5 7–6(3) 6–3; Haarhuis d. V. Caldarelli 6–4 3–6 6–3. **India d. Great Britain 4–1, New Delhi IND:** L. Paes d. J. Bates 6–2 6–7(3) 7–5 6–1; R. Krishnan d. M. Petchey 6–3 3–6 6–3 6–7(2) 6–1; Krishnan/Paes d. N. Broad/Petchey 6–4 3–6 6–3 6–1; G. Natekar lost C. Wilkinson 3–6 1–6; Paes d. Petchey 6–2 6–4. **Spain d. Israel 3–0 (2 not played), Aviles ESP:** J. Arrese d. G. Bloom 6–1 7–5 6–4; C. Costa d. E. Ran 6–2 7–5 6–0; S. Casal/E. Sanchez d. Bloom/S. Perkiss 4–6 6–2 7–6(5) 3–6 6–2; Costa v Bloom and Arrese v Ran not played. **USSR d. Korea, Rep. 5–0, Moscow RUS:** A. Cherkasov d. H–C. Shin 6–2 6–4 6–0; A. Volkov

d. E–J. Chang 6–2 6–2 6–2; Cherkasov/A. Olhovskiy d. C–W. Kim/J–S. Kim 6–2 6–4 7–5; Volkov d. Shin 6–4 7–5; Cherkasov d. Chang 7–5 6–3.

ZONAL COMPETITION

GROUP I

EURO/AFRICAN ZONE – ZONE A

FIRST ROUND – Kenya d. Romania 3–2, Nairobi KEN: P. Wekesa d. A. Marcu 6–3 7–6(4) 6–3; E. Polo d. D. Pescariu 6–4 6–0 7–5; Polo/Wekesa d. G. Cosac/Marcu 7–6(6) 7–6(5) 6–3; N. Odour lost Pescariu 4–6 3–6; Polo lost Marcu 3–6 6–7(7). **SECOND ROUND – USSR d. Portugal 3–2, Oporto POR:** A. Chesnokov lost J. Cunha–Silva 1–6 4–6 3–6; A. Cherkasov d. B. Mota 6–3 6–4 6–2; Cherkasov/V. Gabrichidze lost Cunha–Silva/N. Marques 6–4 2–6 4–6 6–4 5–7; Cherkasov d. Cunha–Silva 6–4 6–3 6–7(4) 6–3; Chesnokov d. Mota 7–6(4) 6–4 6–1. **Denmark d. Kenya 5–0, Holbaek, nr Copenhagen DEN:** C. Camradt d. P. Wekesa 7–6(1) 6–3 6–3; K. Carlsen d. E. Polo 6–1 6–0 6–1; Carlsen/M. Christensen d. Polo/Wekesa 6–4 6–4 6–4; Carlsen. Wekesa 6–4 6–4; Camradt d. Polo 6–4 6–4.

ZONE B

FIRST ROUND – Hungary d. Poland 3–2, Budapest HUN: L. Markovits lost B. Dabrowski 6–7(2) 7–6(7) 7–6(4) 0–6 12–14; S. Noszaly d. T. Lichon 7–5 6–1 4–6 6–4; A. Lanyi/Markovits d. W. Fibak/T. Iwanski 3–6 7–5 6–2 6–2; Noszaly d. Dabrowski 6–7(6) 6–4 6–4 6–4; Lanyi lost Iwanski 7–5 6–7(4) 11–13. **Finland d. Norway 3–2, Oslo NOR:** A. Rahunen d. C. Ruud 7–6(4) 2–6 6–2 6–3; V. Paloheimo lost B. Pedersen 4–6 6–4 6–7(4) 5–7; Paloheimo/O. Rahnasto lost Pedersen/Ruud 3–6 4–6 4–6; Paloheimo d. Ruud 7–6(3) 1–6 3–6 7–6(2) 6–1; Rahunen d. Pedersen 6–2 6–1 6–1. **SECOND ROUND – Israel d. Hungary 5–0, Ramat Hasharon ISR:** G. Bloom d. V. Nagy 7–6(5) 6–1 6–2; S. Perkiss d. S. Noszaly 7–6(3) 6–2 7–5; Bloom/Perkiss d. L. Markovits/Noszaly 6–4 6–2 6–2; Bloom d. Noszaly 6–3 6–4; E. Ran d. Nagy 6–4 6–3. **Austria d. Finland 4–1, Helsinki FIN:** H. Skoff d. O. Rahnasto 6–4 6–3 6–2; A. Antonitsch lost V. Paloheimo 7–6(3) 6–4 2–6 2–6 1–6; Antonitsch/Skoff d. Paloheimo/Rahnasto 7–6(5) 7–5 6–3; Skoff d. Paloheimo 7–6(6) 5–7 2–6 6–3 11–9; T. Prerovsky d. P. Virtanen 6–1 7–5. **RELEGATION PLAY–OFF – Norway d. Poland 4–1, Oslo NOR:** A. Haaseth d. D. Nowicki 5–7 7–6(1) 7–6(4) 6–3; B. Pedersen d. B. Dabrowski 6–2 7–6(5) 2–6 6–2; Pedersen/A. Rolfsen lost Dabrowski/Nowicki 5–7 2–6 4–6; Haaseth d. Dabrowski 4–6 6–2 6–2 6–4; Pedersen d. R. Sliwinski 6–2 6–4.

AMERICAN ZONE

FIRST ROUND – Cuba d. Paraguay 4–1, Asuncion PAR: M. Tabares d. R. Mena 3–6 6–4 6–4 4–6 11–9; J–A. Pino d. R. Alvarenga 1–6 7–5 6–4 6–4; Pino/Tabares d. C. De Los Rios/Mena 6–3 6–3 6–4; Tabares. Alvarenga 6–1 3–6 6–3; Pino lost Mena 5–7 3–6. **SECOND ROUND – Cuba d. Chile 4–1, Santiago CHI:** J–A. Pino lost F. Rivera 3–6 4–6 6–7(1); M. Tabares d. P. Rebolledo 6–4 6–2 3–6 6–1; Pino/Tabares d. J–P. Queirolo/Rivera 5–7 7–6(1) 6–3 7–5; Tabares d. Rivera 6–3 4–6 6–4 7–5; Pino d. Rebolledo 6–1 3–6 11–9. **Uruguay d. Mexico 3–2, Montevideo URU:** M. Filippini d. O. Fernandez 7–5 6–2 6–2; D. Perez lost L. Lavalle 6–7(1) 6–2 6–7(1) 6–7(4); Filippini/Perez d. Lavalle/J. Lozano 6–1 6–4 1–6 6–3; Filippini d. Lavalle 6–3 7–6(3) 6–2; Perez lost Fernandez 2–6 5–7.

ASIA/OCEANIA ZONE

PRELIMINARY ROUND – Korea, Rep. d. China P.R. 5–0, Seoul KOR: E–J. Chang d. B. Pan 7–6(7) 6–3 7–5; S–H. Ji d. J–P. Xia 6–4 5–7 4–6 6–2 7–5; Chang/C–W. Kim d. Q–H. Meng/Xia 6–2 6–4 6–2; Kim d. J–H. Zhang 6–3 6–0; Ji d. Pan 6–3 6–2. **Philippines d. Japan 3–2, Manila PHI:** R. So lost S. Matsuoka 1–6 4–6 4–6; F. Barrientos d. Y. Yamamoto 3–6 6–1 7–5 6–4; Barrientos/So d. T. Sato/R. Tsujino 6–4 7–6(4) 6–1; Barrientos lost Matsuoka 4–6 6–7(4) 3–6; So d. Yamamoto 6–4 1–6 2–6 6–3 6–4. **FIRST ROUND – Korea, Rep. d. Chinese Taipei 5–0, Seoul KOR:** J–S. Kim d. Y–H. Lien 6–4 6–2 6–4; E–J. Chang d. J–Y. Chiang 6–2 6–2 6–0; Chang/S–H. Ji d. C–F. Chuang/Lien 6–2 6–2 6–4; Chang d. Lien 6–4 6–4; Kim d. Chiang 6–4 6–4. **Indonesia d. Philippines 4–1, Manila PHI:** D. Suhendar lost R. So 5–7 6–3 5–7 0–0(30–0) ret.; B. Wijaya d. J. Lizardo 6–4 6–2 6–1; S. Suharyadi/B. Wiryawan d. S. Palahang/So 6–4 6–4 7–6(1); Wijaya d. So 6–4 3–0 ret.; Suharyadi d. Lizardo 1–6 6–3 6–4. **SECOND ROUND – Korea, Rep. d. New Zealand 3–2, Seoul KOR:** E–J. Chang d. B. Steven 6–3 7–5 5–7 6–7(5) 13–11; H–C. Shin lost K. Evernden 2–6 5–7 4–6; Chang/C–W. Kim d. Evernden/Steven 6–2 7–6(5) 6–3; Chang d. Evernden 3–6 6–4 4–6 6–4 6–3; Kim lost Steven 6–7(6) 3–6. **India d. Indonesia 5–0, Jakarta INA:** L. Paes d. B. Wijaya 7–5 6–2 6–4; R. Krishnan d. D. Suhendar 6–2 6–0 6–2; Krishnan/Paes d. S. Suharyadi/B. Wiryawan 7–5 5–7 6–4 6–2; Krishnan d. Wijaya 6–1 7–6(5); Paes d. Suharyadi 6–2 6–3. **RELEGATION PLAY–OFF – Japan d. China P.R. 3–2, Tokyo JPN:** S. Matsuoka d. B. Pan 6–2 6–1 6–3; Y.

Yamamoto lost J–P. Xia 3–6 6–2 3–6 4–6; Matsuoka/T. Sato lost Pan/Xia 2–6 6–7(7) 4–6; Matsuoka d. Xia 6–1 6–2 6–1; Yamamoto d. Pan 7–6(1) 6–7(4) 2–6 7–6(3) 6–2.

GROUP II
EURO/AFRICAN ZONE
FIRST ROUND – Greece d. Ireland 4–1, Athens GRE: A. Bavelas d. D. Farren 7–6(6) 6–1 5–7 6–2; A. Fikas d. O. Casey 6–3 7–5 5–7 7–6(2); Bavelas/Fikas d. E. Collins/P. Wright 3–6 4–6 6–1 6–4 6–4; Bavelas lost Casey 5–7 2–6; Fikas d. Farren 6–4 6–4; **Bulgaria d. Malta 5–0, Sofia BUL:** I. Keskinov d. G. Asciak 6–2 6–1 6–3; M. Petkov d. C. Gatt 6–0 6–3 7–5; Keskinov/M. Markov d. Asciak/Gatt 3–6 6–2 6–2 3–6 6–4; Keskinov d. Gatt 6–4 7–6(9); Petkov d. Asciak 6–3 6–4; **Luxembourg d. Monaco 4–1, Monte Carlo MON:** A. Paris d. C. Boggetti 6–3 4–6 6–3 6–3; J. Goudenbour d. J. Seguin 6–4 7–5 6–2; Goudenbour/Paris d. Boggetti/Seguin 6–4 6–4 7–6(8); T. Neiens lost Seguin 3–6 1–6; Goudenbour d. Boggetti 7–5 6–2; **Egypt d. Zambia 3–2, Cairo EGY:** K. El Salawy d. D. Sweeney 6–3 6–3 6–4; A. Ghonem d. F. Kangwa 6–3 6–2 7–6(5); M. Eleish/El Salawy lost Kangwa/N. Simunyola 6–4 6–4 1–6 4–6 2–6; El Salawy d. Kangwa 6–4 3–6 6–4 6–1; Ghonem lost Sweeney 3–6 4–6 3–6; **Zimbabwe d. Ghana 4–1, Harare ZIM:** B. Black d. M. Amoah 6–2 6–1 7–5; R. Hassan lost F. Ofori 4–6 3–6 7–6(2) 3–6; M. Birch/Black d. Amoah/Ofori 6–4 6–4 7–6(1); Black d. Ofori 6–2 6–3 6–3; Hassan d. Amoah 6–3 6–4; **Cote d'Ivoire d. Togo 3–2, Lome TOG (1–4 May):** I. L'Onfo lost G. Gbedey 6–7(2) 6–7(1) 4–6; Clement N'Goran d. K. Apeti 6–2 6–4 6–4; Claude N'Goran/Clement N'Goran d. Apeti/Gbedey 6–4 6–2 6–2; Clement N'Goran lost Gbedey 6–3 6–4 2–6 6–7(5) 1–6; L'Onfo d. K. Kunkel 5–7 6–2 6–4 6–7(5) 6–1; **Cyprus d. Turkey walkover (Turkey disqualified, note Turkey had choice of venue); Morocco d. Nigeria 5–0, Lagos NGR:** M. Ridaoui d. S. Ladipo 2–6 6–2 1–6 6–4 6–3; K. Alami d. Y. Suleiman 6–3 6–3 3–6 7–6(6); Alami/Ridaoui d. Ladipo/Suleiman 7–6(4) 6–3 7–6(6); Alami d. Ladipo 6–4 6–3; Ridaoui d. Suleiman 6–7(5) 6–3 6–3.
SECOND ROUND – Greece d. Bulgaria 4–1, Athens GRE: G. Kalovelonis d. M. Petkov 3–6 7–5 6–2 3–6 7–5; A. Bavelas d. O. Stanoichev 6–2 6–1 6–2; Bavelas/C. Efremoglou d. I. Keskinov/M. Markov 3–6 6–7(3) 7–6(4) 6–2 6–4; Bavelas d. Petkov 6–1 6–4; Kalovelonis lost Stanoichev 3–6 3–6; **Luxembourg d. Egypt 3–2, Luxembourg LUX:** S. Brueck d. A. Ghonem 4–6 7–5 6–3 6–3; J. Goudenbour lost T. El Sawy 1–6 6–4 1–6 1–6; Goudenbour/A. Paris d. El Sawy/A. El Shafei 6–2 3–6 7–5; Goudenbour d. Ghonem 6–3 7–6(5) 6–1; Brueck lost El Sawy 3–6 1–3 (15–0) ret. **Zimbabwe d. Cote d'Ivoire 4–1, Abidjan CIV:** B. Black d. E. N'Goran 6–2 6–3 6–2; W. Black d. I. L'Onfo 6–7(6) 6–1 7–6(7) 6–4; M. Birch/B. Black d. L'Onfo/N'Goran 6–4 6–7(5) 6–7(5) 6–3 6–4; B. Black d. L'Onfo 6–4 6–4; R. Hassan lost N'Goran 4–6 6–7(6); **Morocco d. Cyprus 5–0, Nicosia CYP:** M. Ridaoui d. A. Papamichael 6–1 6–2 6–0; Y. El Aynaoui d. Y. Hadjigeorgiou 6–2 6–3 6–0; S. Adbib/A. Chekrouni d. L. Christophides/Hadjigeorgiou 6–3 6–4 6–3; Chekrouni d. Papamichael 6–0 7–6(2); Ridaoui d. Christophides 6–1 6–1.
THIRD ROUND – Luxembourg d. Greece 5–0, Luxembourg LUX: J. Radoux d. A. Fikas 6–2 6–0 7–5; S. Brueck d. A. Bavelas 7–5 7–5 6–2; J. Goudenbour/A. Paris d. Bavelas/C. Efremoglou 6–3 6–1 7–6(3); Radoux d. Bavelas 6–1 7–5; Brueck d. Fikas 7–5 6–4. **Zimbabwe d. Morocco 4–1, Harare ZIM:** W. Black lost Y. El Aynaoui 3–6 6–3 3–6 7–5 4–6; B. Black d. M. Ridaoui 6–3 6–2 6–2; Black/Black d. El Aynaoui/Ridaoui 6–1 6–3 6–1; B. Black d. S. Adbib 6–1 6–3 6–2; W. Black d. Ridaoui 6–0 6–4.
RELEGATION PLAY–OFF – Ireland d. Malta 5–0, Galway IRL: E. Collins d. C. Gatt 6–1 6–2 6–0; O. Casey d. G. Asciak 6–1 6–1 6–2; Casey/P. Wright d. Asciak/Gatt 6–1 7–6(6) 6–4; Casey d. Gatt 6–4 6–3; Collins d. Asciak 6–2 6–3; **Monaco d. Zambia 5–0, Monte Carlo MON:** C. Boggetti d. T. Simunyola 6–4 6–4 6–2; J. Seguin d. D. Sweeney 6–1 6–2 6–1; Seguin/J. Vincileoni d. S. Kangwa/N. Simunyola 6–4 6–1 6–3; Boggetti d. Sweeney 6–3 6–3; Seguin d. T. Simunyola 6–2 6–4; **Ghana d. Togo 3–1 (1 not played), Accra GHA:** F. Ofori d. M. Segbeaya 6–3 6–4 6–4; M. Amoah lost G. Gbedey 6–7(4) 1–6 0–6; Ofori/E. Paddi d. Gbedey/Segbeaya 6–3 6–3 6–3; Ofori d. Gbedey 7–6(4) 7–6(5) 6–2; Amoah v. Segbeaya not played; **Nigeria d. Turkey walkover (Turkey disqualified for failing to play Cyprus).**

AMERICAN ZONE
FIRST ROUND – Peru d. Ecuador 3–2, Guayaquil ECU (31 January–3 February): A. Aramburu lost A. Gomez 4–6 4–6 0–6; J. Yzaga d. L. Morejon 6–2 2–6 6–1 6–0; C. Di Laura/Yzaga d. P. Campana/Gomez 7–6(4) 6–2 1–6 6–4; Yzaga lost Gomez 2–6 2–6 3–6; Aramburu d. Morejon 3–6 6–4 6–2 3–1 ret. **Bahamas d. Eastern Caribbean 4–1, Castries, St. Lucia ECA:** R. Smith d. G. Williams 6–1 5–7 6–1 6–1; J. Farrington lost V. Lewis 3–6 6–1 6–0 6–7(2) 2–6; Farrington/Smith d. J. Maginley/Williams 6–4 3–6 7–6(3) 6–3; Smith d. Lewis 2–6 6–4 6–0 2–6 6–2; Farrington d. Williams 6–3 6–4. **Venezuela d. Dominican Rep. 5–0, Caracas VEN:** M. Ruah d. G. De Leon 0–6 7–5 6–3 6–1; N. Pereira d. R. Moreno 6–2 6–7(2) 6–2 6–1; A. Mora/Pereira d. Moreno/M. Olivares 6–2 6–2 6–2; Pereira d. De Leon 4–6 5–5 ret.; Ruah d. Moreno 6–0 6–0. **Colombia d. Barbados 5–0, Cali COL:** J. Cortes d. C. Smith 6–2 6–1 6–0; A. Jordan d. R. Ashby 7–6(8) 6–3 6–2; Jordan/M. Tobon d. Ashby/B. Frost 6–2 7–5 6–2; Cortes d. Ashby 6–2 7–6(3); Jordan d. Smith 6–2 6–2.
SECOND ROUND – Bahamas d. Peru 3–2, Nassau BAH: R. Smith lost J. Yzaga 6–7(4) 7–6(7) 6–3 3–6 4–6; M. Knowles d. C. Di Laura 6–4 6–4 6–2; Knowles/Smith d. Di Laura/Yzaga 6–3 6–2 6–3; Knowles lost

Yzaga 7–6(3) 3–6 6–7(2) 5–6(30–15) ret.; Smith d. Di Laura 6–3 6–1 6–3. *Venezuela d. Colombia 3–2, Cali COL:* M. Ruah lost J. Cortes 1–6 3–6 6–4 2–6; N. Pereira d. A. Jordan 6–2 4–6 6–2 6–2; A. Mora/Pereira lost Jordan/M. Tobon 1–6 4–6 7–6(2) 3–6; Pereira d. Cortes 6–4 6–4 3–6 6–3; Ruah d. Jordan 3–6 7–6(1) 3–6 7–6(5) 6–4.

FINAL – Bahamas d. Venezuela 5–0, Caracas VEN: R. Smith d. M. Ruah 6–2 6–3 6–1; M. Knowles d. N. Pereira 6–2 6–3 6–4; Knowles/Smith d. Pereira/Ruah 6–4 6–7(5) 7–5 6–3; Smith d. J. Szymanski 6–7(3) 6–0 6–2; Knowles d. Ruah 6–3 4–6 6–4.

RELEGATION PLAY–OFF – Ecuador d. Eastern Caribbean 3–2, Basseterre, St. Kitts ECA: P. Campana d. G. Williams 6–3 6–4 6–0; E. Lingen lost V. Lewis 2–6 6–2 6–7(2) 3–6; Campana/H. Nunez d. Lewis/J. Maginley 6–3 7–5 6–4; Campana d. Lewis 6–1 7–6(4) 6–2; Lingen lost Williams 7–6(7) 3–6 6–8. *Dominican Rep. d. Barbados 5–0, Santo Domingo DOM:* G. De Leon d. L. Eli 6–1 6–2 6–4; R. Moreno d. R. Ashby 5–7 5–7 6–0 6–4 6–1; De Leon/Moreno d. Ashby/B. Frost 6–4 6–3 7–5; De Leon d. Ashby 6–3 6–4; Moreno d. Eli 6–4 6–0.

ASIA/OCEANIA ZONE

FIRST ROUND – Thailand d Singapore 5–0, Bangkok THA: N. Srichaphan d. S. Lim 6–3 6–3 6–1; T. Srichaphan d. F. Ho 6–2 6–0 6–2; W. Samrej/W. Thongkhamchu d. Ho/Lim 6–3 6–0 6–1; N. Srichaphan d. Ho 6–2 6–4; T. Srichaphan d. Lim 6–1 6–0. *Malaysia d. Jordan 4–1, Kuala Lumpur MAS:* R. Ramachandran d. H. Al–Ali 7–5 6–4 3–6 6–1; A. Malik d. E. Abou–Hamdeh 6–0 6–2 6–2; Malik/Ramachandran d. Al–Ali/S. Bushnaq 6–4 6–2 6–3; R. Rahim lost Al–Ali 4–6 2–6; Ramachandran d. Abou–Hamdeh 6–2 4–6 6–4. *Sri Lanka d. Bangladesh 4–1, Colombo SRI:* D. Herath lost H–L. Rahman 5–7 6–4 6–2 4–6 5–7; J. Wijeyesekera d. F–S. Haq 6–3 6–0 6–2; Herath/Wijeyesekera d. Haq/Rahman 6–2 6–1 6–1; Wijeyesekera d. Rahman 6–2 6–2 4–6 6–1; Herath d. Haq 7–6(2) 7–5. *Hong Kong d. Pakistan 3–2, Lahore PAK (1–3 February):* L. Pang lost R. Malik 2–6 3–6 2–6; M. Walker d. M. Khalid 6–3 6–3 7–5; M. Bailey/Walker d. H. Ul–Haq/Malik 6–4 7–6(5) 7–6(5); Walker d. Malik 6–3 4–6 6–2 4–6 6–4; Pang lost Khalid 6–7(6) 4–6.

SECOND ROUND – Thailand d. Malaysia 3–2, Kuala Lumpur MAS: T. Srichaphan lost A. Malik 6–4 6–7(2) 6–7(3) 3–6; N. Srichaphan d. R. Ramanchandran 7–5 6–2 6–0; W. Samrej/W. Thongkhamchu d. Malik/Ramanchandran 6–4 6–7(4) 6–4 6–4; N. Srichaphan lost Malik 4–6 0–6 3–6; T. Srichaphan d. Ramanchandran 6–1 4–6 7–5 6–1. *Hong Kong d. Sri Lanka 5–0, Colombo SRI:* M. Walker d. D. Herath 6–0 6–0 6–0; C. Grant d. J. Wijeyesekera 6–1 6–4 6–2; Grant/Walker d. Herath/Wijeyesekera 6–0 6–2 6–2; Walker d. Wijeyesekera 7–5 5–7 6–3; Grant d. Herath 6–0 6–0.

FINAL – Hong Kong d. Thailand 3–2, Causeway Bay, HKG: C. Grant d. N. Srichaphan 3–6 2–6 6–2 6–1 ret.; M. Walker d. T. Srichaphan 6–4 0–6 6–4 6–3; M. Bailey/Walker d. W. Samrej/W. Thongkhamchu 3–6 4–6 6–2 6–3 6–4; Walker lost Thongkhamchu 3–6 7–6(2) 6–8; Grant lost T. Srichaphan 2–6 4–6.

RELEGATION PLAY–OFF – Jordan d. Singapore 4–1, Amman JOR: E. Abou–Hamdeh d. F. Ho 6–2 6–2 6–4; H. Al–Ali d. S. Lim 6–4 6–3 2–6 4–6 9–7; Abou–Hamdeh/Al–Ali d. Ho/Lim 6–4 6–4 6–4; L. Azoni d. D. Yong 7–5 3–6 6–2; Abou–Hamdeh lost Lim 6–3 4–6 2–6. *Pakistan d. Bangladesh 4–1, Dhaka BAN:* R. Malik d. S. Lal 6–2 6–0 6–1; M. Khalid d. H–L. Rahman 6–1 6–1 6–4; Khalid/Malik d. F–S. Haq/Rahman 6–3 6–2 6–2; A. Raja lost Rahman 3–6 7–5 2–6; Khalid d. Lal 6–0 6–2.

GROUP III

EURO/AFRICAN ZONE (Tunisia)

Algeria, Cameroon, Congo, Senegal, South Africa and Tunisia.

South Africa d. Cameroon 3–0: C. Van Rensburg d. L. Kemajou 6–3 6–0; W. Ferreira d. A. Mvogo 7–5 6–2; Van Rensburg/D. Visser d. Kemajou/J. Oyebog 7–5 6–0. *Senegal d. Congo 3–0:* T. Ly d. A. Bemba 6–3 6–3; Y. Doumbia d. C. Bemba 6–0 6–0; A. Berthe/Doumbia d. C. Bemba/C. Ossombi 6–2 6–2. *Algeria d. Tunisia 2–1:* A. Hameurlaine d. A. Lahdhili 7–5 6–2; R. Galou d. S. Zekri 6–4 6–1; Galou/Hameurlaine lost S. Ben–Hadjali/Zekri 4–6 5–7. *South Africa d. Algeria 3–0:* C. Van Rensburg d. A. Hameurlaine 7–6(3) 7–5; W. Ferreira d. R. Galou 6–3 6–2; Ferreira/D. Visser d. Galou/S. Tounsi 6–1 6–3. *Senegal d. Tunisia 3–0:* A. Berthe d. A. Lahdhili 6–2 6–4; Y. Doumbia d. S. Zekri 6–2 6–2; Doumbia/T. Ly d. S. Ben–Hadjali/Zekri 6–2 6–3. *Cameroon d. Congo 2–1:* L. Kemajou lost A. Bemba 4–6 3–6; A. Mvogo d. C. Bemba 6–2 6–2; Kemajou/Mvogo d. A. Bemba/C. Bemba 2–6 6–4 6–4. *South Africa d. Senegal 3–0:* C. Van Rensburg d. A. Berthe 6–1 6–1; W. Ferreira d. Y. Doumbia 6–4 3–6 6–2; Ferreira/Van Rensburg d. Berthe/Doumbia 6–1 6–2; *Algeria d. Cameroon 2–0 (1 not played):* A. Hameurlaine d. L. Kemajou 6–1 4–6 6–1; R. Galou d. A. Mvogo 6–0 6–3; Hameurlaine/S. Tounsi v. Kemajou/J. Oyebog not played. *Tunisia d. Congo 3–0:* A. Lahdhili d. A. Bemba 6–2 6–4; S. Zekri d. C. Bemba 6–2 6–2; S. Ben–Hadjali/Zekri d. A. Bemba/C. Ossombi 6–1 6–2. *South Africa d. Tunisia 3–0:* D. Visser d. S. Ben–Hadjali 6–3 6–3; W. Ferreira d. S. Zekri 6–3 6–1; C. Van Rensburg/Visser d. Ben–Hadjali/Zekri 6–1 6–1. *Senegal d. Cameroon 3–0:* A. Berthe d. J. Oyebog 6–1 6–4; Y. Doumbia d. A. Mvogo 6–3 6–4; Doumbia/T. Ly d. L. Kemajou/Oyebog 6–3 6–2. *Algeria d. Congo 3–0:* A. Hameurlaine d. A. Bemba 6–1 6–1; R. Galou d. C. Bemba 6–1 6–4; Hameurlaine/S. Tounsi d. C. Bemba/C. Ossombi 6–3 6–7(6) 6–2. *South Africa d. Congo 3–0:* C. Van Rensburg d. A. Bemba 6–1

THE DAVIS CUP BY NEC **39**

6–1; W. Ferreira d. C. Bemba 6–0 6–2; Ferreira/D. Visser d. C. Bemba/C. Ossombi 6–2 6–1. *Senegal d. Algeria 2–1:* A. Berthe d. S. Tounsi 6–4 6–2; Y. Doumbia d. A. Hameurlaine 6–1 6–2; Berthe/T. Ly lost Hameurlaine/Tounsi 6–7(3) 6–4 4–6. *Cameroon d. Tunisia 2–1:* L. Kemajou d. S. Ben–Hadjali 2–6 6–4 6–4; A. Mvogo d. S. Zekri 6–3 6–3; Kemajou/J. Oyebog lost Ben–Hadjali/Zekri 4–6 4–6.

AMERICAN ZONE (El Salvador)

GROUP A – Bolivia, El Salvador, Jamaica and Puerto Rico.
El Salvador d. Bolivia 3–0: M. Tejada d R. Aguirre 7–6(11) 6–2; M. Merz d. R. Navarro 6–0 6–0; Merz/Tejada d. Aguirre/Navarro 7–6(6) 6–4. *Puerto Rico d. Jamaica 2–1:* J. Rios d. K. Hale 7–6(4) 6–3; J. Rive lost D. Burke 6–3 3–6 4–6; M. Nido/Rive d. Burke/Hale 6–3 7–6(4). *El Salvador d. Jamaica 3–0:* M. Tejada d. K. Hale 7–5 6–4; M. Merz d. D. Burke 6–3 6–4; Merz/Tejada d. Burke/Hale 3–6 6–3 6–4. *Puerto Rico d. Bolivia 3–0:* J. Rios d. R. Aguirre 6–2 7–5; M. Nido d. R. Navarro 6–0 6–1; Rios/J. Rive d. Aguirre/A. Serrate 6–1 6–1. *Jamaica d. Bolivia 3–0:* K. Hale d. R. Aguirre 6–3 7–5; D. Burke d. R. Navarro 6–2 6–3; Burke/Hale d. Aguirre/Navarro 6–4 3–6 6–1. *Puerto Rico d. El Salvador 3–0:* M. Nido d. M. Tejada 6–2 7–6(10); J. Rive d. M. Merz 7–6(5) 6–3; Nido/Rive d. Merz/Tejada 6–3 6–2.

GROUP B – Costa Rica, Guatemala, Haiti, and Trinidad & Tobago.
Costa Rica d. Guatemala 3–0: K. Thome d. L. Valencia 6–3 7–5; R. Avalos d. D. Chavez 6–4 6–2; F. Thome/K. Thome d. Chavez/Valencia 6–3 6–2. *Haiti d. Trinidad & Tobago 3–0:* P. Baker d. J. Hodges 6–0 6–2; B. Madsen d. O. Adams 6–3 7–5; Baker/Madsen d. Hodges/B. Khan 6–3 6–2. *Guatemala d. Trinidad & Tobago 2–1:* F. Samayoa d. J. Hodges 6–3 6–2; D. Chavez d. O. Adams 6–2 6–1; Chavez/Samayoa lost Adams/B.Khan 6–7(6) 7–6(5) 3–6. *Haiti d. Costa Rica 2–1:* P. Baker lost K. Thome 3–6 6–7(0); B. Madsen d. R. Avalos 6–3 6–4; Baker/Madsen d. F. Thome/K. Thome 6–3 7–5. *Costa Rica d. Trinidad & Tobago 3–0:* K. Thome d. B. Khan 6–4 6–0; R. Avalos d. O. Adams 6–4 7–6(6); F. Thome/K. Thome d. Adams/Khan 6–2 6–7(5) 6–1. *Haiti d. Guatemala 3–0:* P. Baker d. F. Samayoa 6–3 4–6 6–2; B. Madsen d. D. Chavez 6–7(5) 6–2 6–2; R. Lamothe/Madsen d. Samayoa/L. Valencia 3–6 6–3 2–1 ret.

ASIA–OCEANIA ZONE (Bahrain)

Bahrain, Iran, Kuwait, Lebanon, Qatar, Saudi Arabia and Syria.
Iran d. Lebanon 3–0: M. Al Khodafi d. R. Kattoura 6–3 6–4; M. Saleh d. K. Khouri 6–4 6–0; K. Javan/Saleh d. Kattoura/Khouri 6–3 6–4; *Kuwait d. Syria 2–1:* A. Al Ashwak d. S. Mourad 6–2 7–5; K. Al Foudari d. D. Dawoodian 6–4 4–6 9–7; Al Ashwak/K. Ashkanani lost S. Al Din/Mourad 3–6 4–6; *Qatar d. Saudi Arabia 2–1:* A. Gallal d. O. Al Anazi 3–6 7–5 6–3; N–G. Al Khulaifi lost B. Al Megayel 6–4 6–7(5) 2–6; Al Khulaifi/Gallal d. Al Anazi/Al Megayel 6–3 6–2; *Iran d. Bahrain 2–1:* K. Javan lost E. Abdul–Aal 4–6 2–6; M. Saleh d. S. Shehab 6–1 6–1; Javan/Saleh d. Abdul–Aal/A. Shehab 6–3 6–2; *Kuwait d. Saudi Arabia 3–0:* A. Al Ashwak d. O. Al Anazi 6–1 6–0; K. Al Foudari d. B. Al Megayel 6–2 6–2; Al Foudari/K. Ashkanani d. Al Anazi/A. Al Karim 6–4 6–2; *Qatar d. Syria 2–1:* A. Gallal d. S. Al Din 6–1 6–0; N–G. Al Khulaifi lost D. Dawoodian 0–6 1–6; Al Khulaifi/Gallal d. Dawoodian/S. Mourad 6–2 3–6 7–5; *Kuwait d. Qatar 2–1:* A. Al Ashwak lost A. Gallal 1–6 6–7(2); K. Al Foudari d. N–G. Al Khulaifi 6–1 6–2; Al Foudari/K. Ashkanani d. Al Khulaifi/Gallal 6–1 7–6(3); *Lebanon d. Bahrain 2–1:* R. Kattoura lost E. Abdul–Aal 6–7(3) 1–6; K. Khouri d. S. Shehab 6–2 6–2; Kattoura/Khouri d. Abdul–Aal/A. Shehab 7–5 6–2; *Syria d. Saudi Arabia 3–0:* S. Mourad d. O. Al Anazi 6–2 7–5; D. Dawoodian d. B. Al Megayel 6–4 6–3; Dawoodian/Mourad d. Al Anazi/Al Megayel 7–5 6–0; *Iran d. Saudi Arabia 3–0:* M. Al Khodafi d. A. Al Karim 6–3 6–0; M. Saleh d. B. Al Megayel 6–2 6–1; K. Javan/Saleh d. O. Al Anazi/Al Megayel 6–3 4–6 6–2; *Lebanon d. Syria 2–1:* R. Kattoura d. S. Mourad 6–3 6–2; K. Khouri lost D. Dawoodian 6–1 2–6 8–10; Kattoura/Khouri d. S. Al Din/Mourad 6–3 6–2; *Bahrain d. Qatar 2–1:* E. Abdul–Aal d. A. Gallal 6–3 6–2; S. Shehab lost N–G. Al Khulaifi 2–6 7–6(7) 3–6; Abdul–Aal/A. Shehab d. Al Khulaifi/Gallal 4–6 7–5 10–8; *Iran d. Qatar 2–1:* M. Al Khodafi lost A. Gallal 2–6 5–7; M. Saleh d. A. Al Mulla 6–2 6–1; K. Javan/Saleh d. N–G. Al Khulaifi/Gallal 6–2 6–2; *Kuwait d. Lebanon 3–0:* A. Al Ashwak d. R. Kattoura 4–6 7–6(1) 8–6; K. Al Foudari d. K. Khouri 6–3 4–6 6–4; Al Foudari/K. Ashkanani d. Kattoura/Khouri 6–4 6–4; *Bahrain d. Syria 2–1:* E. Abdul–Aal d. S. Mourad 6–4 6–4; S. Shehab lost D. Dawoodian 7–6(5) 4–6 0–6; Abdul–Aal/A. Shehab d. Al Din/Mourad 6–3 6–1; *Iran d. Kuwait 3–0:* M. Al Khodafi d. A. Al Ashwak 7–5 6–4; M. Saleh d. K. Al Foudari 6–0 6–7(7) 6–4; K. Javan/Saleh d. Al Foudari/K. Ashkanani 6–4 3–6 6–2; *Lebanon d. Qatar 2–1:* H. Badredine lost A. Gallal 3–6 4–6; K. Khouri d. N–G. Al Khulaifi 7–5 6–2; R. Kattoura/Khouri d. Al Khulaifi/Gallal 6–2 6–3; *Bahrain d. Saudi Arabia 2–1:* E. Abdul–Aal d. O. Al Anazi 6–2 6–1; S. Shehab lost B. Al Megayel 4–6 4–6; Abdul–Aal/A. Shehab d. Al Anazi/Al Megayel 6–2 7–5; *Iran d. Syria 2–1:* M. Al Khodafi lost S. Mourad 4–6 6–7(6); M. Saleh d. D. Dawoodian 6–2 6–7(1) 6–1; K. Javan/Saleh d. S. Al Din/Mourad 6–2 6–2; *Kuwait d. Bahrain 2–1:* A. Al Ashwak d. A. Shehab 6–3 6–2; K. Al Foudari lost E. Abdul–Aal 3–6 6–3 2–6; Al Foudari/K. Ashkanani d. Abdul–Aal/A. Shehab 6–2 6–0; *Lebanon d. Saudi Arabia 3–0:* R. Kattoura d. O. Al Anazi 6–4 6–2; K. Khouri d. B. Al Megayel 6–7(1) 7–5 6–4; H. Badredine/Khouri d. A. Al Karim/Al Megayel 7–6(2) 6–3.

DAVIS CUP BY NEC – PRIZE MONEY

WORLD GROUP COMPETITION: Champion Nation $347,600. Runner-up $173,800. Semi-finalists $130,900. Quarter-finalists $78,100. First-round $28,600. Qualifying-round winners $22,000. Qualifying-round losers $25,400. ***ZONAL COMPETITION:*** Group I: $5,600 per tie. Bonuses: Second- round winners $3,800. First-round winners $2,500. Play-off/Preliminary round winners $1,200. Group II: $3,800 per tie. Bonuses: 3rd round/Finalists $4,400. 2nd round- winners $2,500. First-round winners $1,300. Play-off winners $400.

Qualifying Round for the World Group

Zonal Winners and World Group First Round Losers	Promoted to World Group 1993
ARGENTINA	Denmark
Denmark	3–2
Canada	Austria
Austria	3–1
GERMANY	GERMANY
Belgium	5–0
Yugoslavia	Cuba
Cuba	w/o
NETHERLANDS	NETHERLANDS
Uruguay	4–1
India	India
Great Britain	4–1
SPAIN	SPAIN
Israel	3–0
Korea	CIS
CIS	5–0

World Group 1992 (16 nations)

FIRST ROUND	SECOND ROUND	SEMI-FINALS	FINAL	WINNERS
FRANCE	FRANCE			
Great Britain	5–0	Switzerland		
NETHERLANDS	Switzerland	3–2		
Switzerland	4–1		Switzerland	
GERMANY	Brazil		5–0	
Brazil	3–1	Brazil		
SPAIN	Italy	3–1		
Italy	4–1			USA
Yugoslavia	AUSTRALIA			3–1
AUSTRALIA	5–0	SWEDEN		
Canada	SWEDEN	5–0		
SWEDEN	3–2		USA	
Belgium	CZECHOSLOVAKIA		4–1	
CZECHOSLOVAKIA	5–0	USA		
Argentina	USA	3–2		
USA	5–0			

Capital letters denote seeded nations.

Zonal Competition

ZONE A

FIRST ROUND	SECOND ROUND	WINNERS
CIS	CIS	CIS
Bye		3–2
Bye	Portugal	(Promoted to QR)
Portugal		
Kenya	Kenya	DENMARK
Romania	3–2	5–0
Bye	DENMARK	(Promoted to QR)
DENMARK		

ZONE B

FIRST ROUND	SECOND ROUND	WINNERS
ISRAEL	ISRAEL	ISRAEL
Bye		5–0
Poland	Hungary	(Promoted to QR)
Hungary	3–2	
Finland	Finland	AUSTRIA
Norway	3–2	4–1
Bye	AUSTRIA	(Promoted to QR)
AUSTRIA		

EURO/AFRICAN GROUP II 1992 (16 nations)

FIRST ROUND	SECOND ROUND	THIRD ROUND	WINNERS
IRELAND	Greece	Greece	LUXEMBOURG
Greece	4–1	4–1	5–0
Malta	Bulgaria		(Promoted to
Bulgaria	5–0	LUXEMBOURG	Zone I in 1993)
LUXEMBOURG	LUXEMBOURG	3–2	
MONACO	4–1		
Zambia	Egypt		
Egypt	3–2		
Zimbabwe	Zimbabwe	Zimbabwe	Zimbabwe
Ghana	4–1	4–1	4–1
Togo	CÔTE D'IVOIRE		(Promoted to
CÔTE D'IVOIRE	3–2		Zone I in 1993)
Cyprus	Cyprus	MOROCCO	
Turkey	w/o	5–0	
Nigeria	MOROCCO		
MOROCCO	5–0		

AMERICAN ZONE GROUP I 1992 (5 Nations)

FIRST ROUND	SECOND ROUND	WINNERS
CHILE	CHILE	Cuba
Bye	Cuba	4–1
Paraguay	4–1	(Promoted to QR)
Cuba		
Uruguay	Uruguay	Uruguay
Bye		3–2
Bye	MEXICO	(Promoted to QR)
MEXICO		

ASIA/OCEANIA ZONE GROUP I 1992 (8 nations)

PRELIMINARY ROUND	FIRST ROUND	SECOND ROUND	WINNERS
	NZ	NEW ZEALAND	
	Bye	Korea	Korea
	Ch.Tapei	5–0	3–2
Korea	Korea		(Promoted to QR)
China	5–0		
Japan	Philippines	Indonesia	INDIA
Philippines	3–2	4–1	5–0
	Indonesia		(Promoted to QR)
	Bye	INDIA	
	INDIA		

AMERICAN ZONE GROUP II 1992 (8 nations)

FIRST ROUND	SECOND ROUND	FINAL	WINNERS
PERU	PERU		
Ecuador	3–2	Bahamas	Bahamas
Eastern Caribbean	Bahamas	3–2	5–0
Bahamas	4–1		(Promoted to
D. Republic	Venezuela		American Zone
Venezuela	5–0	Venezuela	Group I in 1993)
Barbados	COLOMBIA		
COLOMBIA			

ASIA/OCEANIA ZONE GROUP II 1992 (8 nations)

FIRST ROUND	SECOND ROUND	FINAL	WINNERS
THAILAND	THAILAND		HONG KONG
Singapore	5–0	THAILAND	3–2
Malaysia	Malaysia	3–2	(Promoted
Jordan	4–1		to Asia/Oceania
Bangladesh	Sri Lanka		Zone Group I
Sri Lanka	4–1	HONG KONG	in 1993)
Pakistan	HONG KONG	5–0	
HONG KONG	3–2		

Capital letters denote seeded nations.

A first-day win by Andre Agassi (above, T. Hindley) over Jakob Hlasek and the doubles victory by John McEnroe (below, M. Cole) and Pete Sampras on day two were the cornerstones of the US Davis Cup success.

Federation Cup finalists: (above) Germany - L to R: Steffi Graf, Klaus Hofsass(capt.), Anke Huber, Sabine Hack, (absent Barbara Rittner); (below) Spain - L to R: Virginia Ruano, Noelia Perez, Conchita Martinez, Arantxa Sanchez-Vicario.   *(M. Phillips)*

THE FEDERATION CUP BY NEC

Ian Barnes

When Steffi Graf leapt into the arms of the German team captain Klaus Hofsass on a sunny Sunday afternoon in Frankfurt, more than 6,000 spectators roared their approval. Jumping-for-joy Steffi had just hit the winning shot in a 6–4 6–2 win over Arantxa Sanchez-Vicario which won the Federation Cup by NEC for Germany for the first time since 1987. The crowd packed into the picturesque Centre Court of the Waldstadion erupted in a celebration that drowned the noise of planes about to touch down at the nearby international airport.

Spain, who had won the Cup so dramatically with victory over the United States in Nottingham twelve months before, had not surrendered easily and earned the right to a final place with wins against Belgium, Canada, Argentina and Australia.

But Steffi and her young team-mate, Anke Huber, did all that Hofsass had demanded during the week and were fully entitled to enjoy their success. Seventeen-year-old Huber, with a forehand almost as lethal as the one that had earned Miss Graf a fourth Wimbledon championship only two weeks before, had demonstrated immense courage and determination in defeating Conchita Martinez 6–3, 6–7 6–1 – after gaining only one point in the tie-break – just as she had in all her previous matches in the competition.

Victory for Steffi had been assumed a formality by the home supporters and she lived up to their expectations by winning all her matches in straight sets. But Huber, with the responsibility of starting each tie, had given the German fans many anxious moments in both the second round, when she squeezed past Nicole Muns Jagerman of the Netherlands 7–5 3–6 6–1, and the semi-final against the American, Gigi Fernandez, who was finally ground down 7–5 6–3 only after one of the noisiest – in terms of grunting – but most compelling contests of the week.

Getting her hands on the trophy, alongside Steffi, Barbara Rittner and Sabine Hack, made the perfect happy ending to a dismal few weeks of injury worries for the likeable Huber. The fact that Sanchez-Vicario and Martinez won the 'dead' doubles against Rittner and Huber, with Graf sitting in the team captain's chair, could not dim the German celebrations. 'Super, super, super', was Steffi's reply to questions about how she felt at winning the Cup on home soil, about the state of her game and about what she thought of her team and their fans.

For the Spaniards, who were probably the second most popular team in Frankfurt, the disappointment of handing on the trophy was eased by the knowledge that they had played sparkling, entertaining tennis in every match. Sanchez-Vicario had dropped only 14 games in four matches before the final and Martinez had been defeated only by Helen Kelesi of Canada.

As usual at the Federation Cup by NEC, there had been plenty of excitement and no lack of surprise in the earlier rounds. Poland reached the quarter-finals on the back of hard-fought victories over Israel and Sweden while Australia marched past fifth-seeded Bulgaria, Austria and Czechoslovakia, the third seeds, on the way to the semi-finals, where they lost to Spain.

First round interest had centred on the return of South Africa to the main draw of the Federation Cup after an absence of 15 years. Mariaan De Swardt, who had put up such an impressive performance against Steffi Graf at Wimbledon, and Amanda Coetzer both started their singles matches against Canada in promising style and each took the first set. Neither could then explain how they managed to surrender by the identical score, 2–6 6–2 6–2, to Rene Simpson Alter and Patricia Hy respectively.

Elna Reinach and Mariaan De Swardt won the doubles rubber in straight sets but were disappointed that they then had to win two matches in order to qualify for a place in the main draw of the 1993 competition.

Only the 16 first-round winners were assured of places in Frankfurt in 1993 with the 16 losing nations having to play off for four more places with four teams to complete the 24-strong draw from regional qualifying competitions. This was subsequently amended, with the field extended to 32 teams by increasing the number of regional qualifiers, but that decision made no difference to the drama in what were seen by many players as sudden-death encounters in the play-off matches.

The South Africans made certain of their return to Frankfurt with a 2–1 victory over Belgium and a 3–0 defeat of Mexico but there were some notable casualties in the battle for the other three direct places.

New Zealand suffered a 3–0 setback at the hands of Paraguay, who then lost by the same margin to Switzerland, who had ended Israel's hopes. Indonesia also found themselves among the casualties, only 12 months after their quarter-final showing in Nottingham.

Great Britain disappointed their supporters by losing to Finland after defeating Chile while Italy found themselves on the sidelines after a 3–0 defeat by Hungary, who subsequently lost to Bulgaria.

Italy were, however, reprieved later in the year when, following the break-up of the Commonwealth of Independent States, the Federation Cup Committee decided that Italy, rather than Ukraine, Georgia, Russia, or Belarus, should have direct entry into the main draw.

MAIN DRAW

FIRST ROUND – Germany d. New Zealand 3–0 (A. Huber d. H. Guy 6–1 6–0; S. Graf d. C. Toleafoa 6–2 6–1; S. Hack/B. Rittner d. J. Richardson/A. Trail 5–7 6–3 6–2); **Netherlands d. Paraguay 2–1** (N. Muns Jagerman lost to L. Schaerer 6–1 4–6 2–6; M. Bollegraf d. R. De Los Rios 6–2 6–2; M. Bollegraf/N. Muns Jagerman d. L. Schaerer/R. De Los Rios 6–1 7–5); **Poland d. Israel 3–0** (M. Mroz d. Y. Segal 4–6 6–0 6–2; K. Nowak d. A. Smashnova 6–2 6–7 (9–7) 6–1; M. Mroz/K. Teodorowicz d. L. Zaltz/A. Smashnova 6–3 6–2); **Sweden d. Switzerland 2–1** (C. Dahlman d. E. Zardo 6–2 6–3; C. Lindqvist lost to M. Maleeva 0–6 2–6; M. Lindstrom/M. Strandlund d. M. Maleeva/M. Strebel 6–4 5–7 6–4); **France d. China PR 2–1** (M. Pierce d. Chen Li 6–2 6–2; N. Tauziat lost to Li Fang 1–6 7–6 (7–5) 3–6; N. Tauziat/I. Demongeot d. Li Fang/Tang Min 6–3 7–6 (7–4)); **CIS d. Finland 2–1** (E. Makarova d. N. Dahlman 7–6 (7–2) 6–4; E. Maniokova lost to P. Thoren 7–5 4–6 5–7; E. Makarova/E. Maniokova d. N. Dahlman/P. Thoren 6–3 6–2); **Denmark d. Chile 2–1** (K. Ptaszek d. P. Sepulveda 6–1 6–0; S Albinus lost to P Cabezas 3–6 6–0 0–6; K Ptasek/K. Nielsen d. P. Cabezas/M. Miranda 6–3 6–2); **USA d. Great Britain 3–0** (G. Fernandez d. M. Javer 6–4 6–1; L. McNeil d. J. Durie 7–5 6–3; D. Graham/P. Shriver d. J. Durie/C. Wood 6–4 7–6 (8–6)). **Australia d. Bulgaria 2–1** (R. McQuillan lost to M. Maleeva 6–7 (4–7) 2–6; N. Provis d. K. Maleeva 3–6 6–4 6–0; N. Provis/R. Stubbs d. M. Maleeva/K. Maleeva 6–2 6–1); **Austria d. Romania 2–1** (P. Ritter lost to R. Dragomir 4–6 1–6; J. Weisner d. I. Spirlea 6–0 6–3; J. Weisner/P. Ritter d. I. Spirlea/R. Dragomir 7–5 6–3); **Korea d. Italy 2–1** (Il–Soon Kim d. L. Ferrando 4–6 6–3 6–4; Sung–Hee Park lost to S. Cecchini 4–6 0–6; Jeong–Myung Lee/Il–Soon Kim d. S. Cecchini/L. Ferrando 2–6 7–6 (9–7) 6–3); **Czechoslovakia d. Hungary 3–0** (R. Zrubakova d A. Foldenyi 5–7 6–2 6–1; J. Novotna d. A. Temesvari 6–2 6–1; J. Novotna/A. Strnadova d. A. Temesvari/V. Csurgo 1–6 7–5 7–5); **Japan d. Indonesia 2–1** (M. Endo d. R. Tedjakusuma 6–2 7–6 (8–6); K. Date d. Y. Basuki 7–6 (7–2) 5–7 6–3; M. Endo/M. Kidowaki lost to Y. Basuki/S. Wibowo 1–6 1–6); **Argentina d. Mexico 3–0** (F. Labat d. L. Novelo 6–2 6–1; M. Paz d. A. Gavaldon 6–3 5–7 6–2; M. Paz/P. Tarabini d. L. Novelo/A. Gavaldon 4–6 6–4 6–1); **Canada d. South Africa 2–1** (R. Simpson Alter d. M. De Swardt 2–6 6–2 6–2; P. Hy d. A. Coetzer 2–6 6–2 6–2; J. Hetherington/H. Kelesi lost to E. Reinach/M. De Swardt 4–6 3–6); **Spain d. Belgium 2–1** (C. Martinez d. D. Monami 6–1 6–4; A. Sanchez–Vicario d. S. Appelmans 6–1, 6–2; A. Sanchez–Vicario/N. Perez lost to S. Wasserman/D. Monami 5–7 4–6).

SECOND ROUND – Germany d. Netherlands 2–1 (A. Huber d. N. Muns Jagerman 7–5 3–6 6–1; S. Graf d. B. Schultz 6–3 7–6 (8–6); B. Rittner/S. Hack lost to M. Oremans/Muns Jagerman 6–2 5–7 4–6); **Poland d. Sweden 2–1** (M. Mroz lost to C. Dahlman 2–6 1–6; K. Nowak d. C. Lindqvist 7–6 (7–4) 6–7 (4–7) 6–3; M. Mroz/K. Teodorowicz d. M. Strandlund/M. Lindstrom 6–3 6–2). **France d. CIS 3–0** (M. Pierce d. E. Makarova 6–1 6–2; N. Tauziat d. E. Manyukova 6–1 6–3; N. Tauziat/I.

Demongeot d. E. Makarova/E. Pogorelova 6–3 6–3); **USA d. Denmark 3–0** (G. Fernandez d. K. Ptaszek 4–6 6–3 6–0; L. McNeil d. S. Albinus 7–5, 6–0; P. Shriver/D Graham d. K Ptaszek/H Kjar Neilsen); **Australia d. Austria 2–1** (R. McQuillan d. P. Ritter 4–6 6–2 6–0; N. Provis lost to J. Weisner 7–5 3–6 4–6; N. Provis/R. Stubbs d. P. Ritter/J. Weisner 6–2 6–0). **Czechoslovakia d. Korea 3–0** (H. Sukova d. Yeon-Sook Kim 6–1 7–6 (7–3); J. Novotna d Sung-Hee Park 4–6 6–2 6–3; J. Novotna/A. Strnadova d. Il-Soon Kim/Jeong-Myung Lee 6–3 6–3); **Argentina d. Japan 2–1** (F. Labat d. M. Endo 6–1 6–1; M. Paz lost to K. Date 6–4 1–6 3–6; F. Labat/P. Tarabini d. K. Date/M. Kidowaki 7–5 6–3); **Spain d. Canada 2–1** (C. Martinez lost to H. Kelesi 6–7 (4–7) 2–6; A. Sanchez-Vicario d. P. Hy 6–4 6–2; A. Sanchez-Vicario/C Martinez d. J. Hetherington/P. Hy 6–4 6–0).

QUARTER-FINALS – Germany d. Poland 3–0. (A. Huber d. M. Mroz 6–0 6–3; S. Graf d. K. Nowak 6–0 6–0; A. Huber/S. Graf d. M. Mroz/ K. Teodorowicz 6–4 7–5); **USA d. France 2–1** (G. Fernandez d. M. Pierce 6–1 6–4; L. McNeil lost to N. Tauziat 4–6 5–7; G. Fernandez/P. Shriver d. N. Tauziat/ I. Demongeot 6–4, 6–2); **Australia d. Czechoslovakia 2–1** (R. McQuillan lost to H. Sukova 6–7 (8–6) 6–4 1–6; N. Provis d. J. Novotna 7–5 6–0; N. Provis/R. Stubbs d. J. Novotna/A. Strnadova 6–3 6–3). **Spain d. Argentina 2–1** (C. Martinez d. F. Labat 6–0 6–1; A. Sanchez-Vicario d. M. Paz 6–2 6–1; N. Perez/V. Ruano lost to M. Paz/P. Tarabini 4–6 6–7 (9–7)).

SEMI-FINALS – Germany d. USA 2–1 (A. Huber d. G. Fernandez 7–5 6–3; S. Graf d. L. McNeil 6–0 6–3; B. Rittner/S. Hack lost to P. Shriver/D. Graham 2–6 2–6); **Spain d. Australia 3–0** (C. Martinez d. R. McQuillan 6–1 6–4; A. Sanchez-Vicario d. N. Provis 6–2 6–0; A. Sanchez-Vicario/V. Ruano d. J. Byrne/R. Stubbs 6–3 6–3).

FINAL – Germany d. Spain 2–1 (A. Huber d. C. Martinez 6–3 6–7 (1–7) 6–1; S. Graf d. A. Sanchez-Vicario 6–4 6–2; A. Huber/B. Rittner lost to A. Sanchez-Vicario/C. Martinez 6–1 6–2).

1993 QUALIFYING DRAW

FIRST ROUND – Paraguay d. New Zealand 3–0 (L. Schaerer d. H. Guy 3–6 6–2 6–3; R. De Los Rios d. J. Richardson 6–3 6–2; R. De Los Rios/V. Valdovinos d. C. Teleafoa/A. Trail 6–1 6–1); **Switzerland d. Israel 3–0** (C. Fauche d. Y. Segal 6–1 6–0; M. Maleeva Fragnière d. A. Smashnova 6–1 6–0; C. Fauche/E. Zardo d. A. Smashnova/L. Zaltz 6–3 6–1); **Finland d. China PR 2–1** (N. Dahlman d. Chen Li 7–5 7–6 (7–5); P. Thoren lost to Li Fang 7–5 3–6 5–7; N. Dahlman/A. Aallonen d. Li Fang/Tang Min 2–6 6–2 6–1); **Great Britain d. Chile 3–0** (S. Gomer d. B. Castro 6–2 6–0; J. Durie d. P. Cabezas 6–7 (5–7) 6–0 6–1; S. Gomer/C. Wood d. P. Sepulveda/M. Miranda 6–3 6–1); **Bulgaria d. Romania 2–1** (M. Maleeva d. R. Dragomir 6–0 6–1; K. Maleeva d I. Spirlea 6–1 6–0; E. Pampoulova/M. Maleeva lost to R. Dragomir/I. Spirlea 6–7 (5–7) 2–6); **Hungary d. Italy 3–0** (A. Foldenyi d. R. Reggi Concato 6–3 4–6 6–4; A. Temesvari d. A. Cecchini 6–1 1–0 ret.; A. Temesvari/V. Csurgo d. L. Garrone/L. Ferrando 6–3 6–0); **Mexico d. Indonesia 2–1** (L. Novelo d. R. Tedjakusuma 6–3 7–6 (7–4); A. Gavaldon d. Y. Basuki 6–4 0–6 8–6; L. Novelo/A. Gavaldon lost to S. Wibowo/Y. Basuki 5–7 6–3 2–6); **South Africa d. Belgium 2–1** (E. Reinach d. D. Monami 6–3 6–1; A. Coetzer lost to S. Appelmans 3–6 3–6; E. Reinach/M. De Swardt d. S. Appelmans/S. Wasserman 6–0 6–4).

SECOND ROUND – Switzerland d. Paraguay 3–0 (C. Fauche d. L. Schaerer 3–6 6–2 6–1; M. Maleeva Fragnière d. R. De Los Rios 6–2 6–2; M. Strebel/E. Zardo d. R. De Los Rios/V. Valdovinos 6–2 6–2); **Finland d. Great Britain 2–1** (N. Dahlman d. S. Gomer 6–4 6–0; P. Thoren d. J. Durie 6–3 7–5; A. Aallonen/N Dahlman lost to S. Gomer/C. Wood 6–1 6–4); **Bulgaria d. Hungary 2–1** (E. Pampoulova lost to A. Foldenyi 4–6 2–6; K. Maleeva d. A. Temesvari 6–3 6–4; K. Maleeva/E. Pampoulova d. K. Gyorke/V. Csurgo 7–6 (8–6) 4–6 6–1); **South Africa d. Mexico 3–0** (M. DeSwardt d. L. Novelo 6–1 7–6 7–2); A. Coetzer d. A. Gavaldon 6–2 6–1; E. Reinach/M. De Swardt 6–0 6–0).

Switzerland, Finland, Bulgaria and South Africa qualify for 1993 Main Draw.

NEC WORLD YOUTH CUP

Jackie Nesbitt

The two top-seeded nations in both boys' and girls' events at the 1992 NEC World Youth Cup Finals duly took the titles, but the competition was notable for some of the tightest and most exciting ties of recent years.

Played on clay courts at the prestigious Andres Gimeno Tennis Club in Castelldefels, Spain, the event enjoyed the support of Andres Gimeno and the many club members. Just recovered from the Olympic Games, the Real Federacion Espanola de Tenis spared no efforts to organise a first class competition, under the eye of tournament director, Alberto Riba, and the support of RFET President, Agustin Pujol and the ITF's Vice President, Pablo Llorens.

Now in its 8th year, the World Youth Cup, sponsored for five years by NEC, is established as one of the most important competitions open to 16+ Under juniors during the year. The claim that it attracts the best 16 year old's in the world is justified by a glance at the now famous role of past participants, including Jim Courier, Michael Chang, Goran Ivanisevic, Jennifer Capriati and Anke Huber. It was pleasing then that Belgium fielded their two top juniors, the current world best junior doubles pairing of Nancy Feber and Laurence Courtois. Together with Stephanie Deville they formed a formidable team, and as top seeds, swept aside all opposition to reach the final.

Opening round matches saw just one upset, the departure of the 5/8th seeded CIS at the hands of South Africa. Making their return to ITF international junior team competition, South Africa were level after the two singles matches, when to the delight of their captain, Jean Seymour, Nannie De Villiers and Liezel Horn closed out a tense deciding doubles 6–4 7–6, against Anna Linkova and Tatiana Panova.

A further upset looked possible in the quarter-finals when they went into the doubles once more level at 1–1, but this time De Villiers and Horn found Czechoslovakia's Alena Havrlikova and Zuzana Nemsakova too strong, losing out 6–2 6–4.

In her first match, Belgium's Nancy Feber found the going tough against Canada's Sonya Jeyaseelan, but eventually came through 6–3 3–6 8–6, to put the top seeds through. USA dealt fairly comfortably with the challenge from Japan, winning 3–0, and the 2nd seeds, Germany, were expected to proceed against Argentina. Highly fancied Heike Rusch found Laura Montalvo in inspired form for Argentina, however, and was totally overwhelmed 6–1 6–0. Andrea Glass levelled for the Germans by outlasting Luciana Reynares 7–6 6–2, only for Montalvo and Reynares to produce some fierce doubles play to defeat Glass and Catrin Muller 6–3 3–6 6–0 in the deciding match.

With Belgium handling the challenge from Czechoslovakia in the semi-finals, USA were expected to deal with Argentina in a similar manner. Nicole London brought Laura Montalvo down to earth, a stream of winners helping her to a 6–1 3–6 6–0 victory. Finalist at the recent US Open Junior Championships, Julie Steven, looked to be set for victory after taking the first set against Reynares. The Argentine is nothing if not a fighter, and she not only levelled the match with a three set win, but also paired with Montalvo to overwhelm London and Steven, 6–3 6–1, in the deciding doubles.

The final, played before both a large crowd and television, saw the Junior Wimbledon runner-up, Laurence Courtois, in wonderful form. She kept up her record of not having dropped a set in singles with a 6–1 6–3 victory over Montalvo, and would have been a strong No. 1 in most other nations teams. Reynares unsettled Nancy Feber in the opening set of the top singles match with a bizarre display of underarm and pat serves, having apparently lost confidence in her serve overnight. Once she settled, however, Feber produced fine raking ground strokes to win 1–6 6–4 6–1, and claim the title for Belgium. The doubles provided no consolation for Argentina when Montalvo and Mariana Diaz Oliva lost their way, and a commanding position in the match, to lose out 6–1 5–7 4–6 to Courtois and Stephanie Deville.

The boys' competition was notable for the efforts made by all teams, and for the quality of the tennis produced. Australia had prepared their team well for the event and their opening round 3–0 defeat of 5/8th seeded Italy gave justification to the selectors' decision to send them to Spain one week early.

Top-seeded France looked far from convincing against Argentina, needing the deciding doubles to clinch the tie. Sweden disappointed the home crowd by defeating the defending champions, Spain, in the doubles, with Magnus Norman for Sweden looking very impressive when winning his top singles against Sergio Duran, and partnering Kalle Flygt to victory over Duran and Jacobo Diaz.

South Africa versus Canada was the tie of the opening round, with Jeff Coetzee getting South Africa off to a good start following a 6–1 3–6 6–1 win over Yannick Violette. Conrad Hurter had a hard hitting battle against Robert Kokavec, losing out 7–6 6–4 to see matters level, and then had to watch from the sidelines as his compatriots Coetzee and Paul Trumpelmann lost a three set thriller to Kokavec and Violette, 7–5 2–6 6–4.

The biggest upset of the day occurred when Germany faced USA, the 2nd seeds. Alexander Nickel got the Germans off to a good start with a surprising win over John Roddick, 6–3 6–4. Despite dropping the opening set, Rene Nicklisch then outlasted USA's Paul Goldstein 3–6 7–5 7–5 to consign USA to the consolation place play-offs.

The quarter-finals without doubt saw the finest tie of the Competition. France versus Australia produced the most marvellous high quality tennis. Starting off the proceedings, Maxime Boye just edged out Australia's Ben Ellwood 7–6 4–6 7–5, in a match where both players took the opportunity to play at the net whenever possible. Allen Belobrajdic attempted to level the tie in the top singles, but despite all his heroics, Nicolas Escude was just equal to the task and pipped him at the post 7–6 5–7 10–8. The match, however, was played in tremendous spirit and would have been worthy of any final.

For Israel it was a story of lost chances. The scoreline of 3–0 to Brazil does not reflect the fact that Israel, at a set and 4–1 in the opening singles, should have closed out. Instead Danny Erez lost out 6–4 4–6 4–6 to Gustavo Kuerten. The spirit in the Brazilian team was another outstanding memory from the event. Vocal cheering by captain, Luiz Carlos Enck, as well as the girls' team, not only lifted Kuerten, but also spurred on Antonio Wuttke who came back from a set down to post a 4–6 6–1 6–2 victory over Lior Mor to move Brazil into the semi-finals.

The amount of noise coming from Brazil's deciding doubles in the semi-finals against Germany seemed to indicate that they were on the verge of winning. At 2–5 down in the second set, however, the German pairing of Nickel and Nicklisch slowly started to peg back the Brazilians and eventually wore down their resistance for a 6–7 7–5 6–2 win to reach the final.

Whilst Maxime Boye was too strong for Kalle Flygt of Sweden in the other semi-final, Escude was unable to reproduce his previous day's form and lost to the unbeaten Magnus Norman in straight sets. Norman and Flygt then forged a 4–1 first set lead in the doubles only to see it disappear to lose 7–5 6–4.

Another large crowd for the boys' final was treated to a close encounter with Maxime Boye maintaining his good record with a 7–5 0–6 6–3 win over Alexander Nickel. Escude looked good in the opening set, but fell away to Rene Nicklisch 6–2 3–6 6–3, to leave France and Germany at 1–1 going into the doubles. The French team of Boye and Escude struggled early on in the doubles, but eventually used their more powerful serves to overcome Nickel and Nicklisch 6–7 6–0 6–3, and claim the title for France for the first time.

NEC WORLD YOUTH CUP 1992

Boys' and Girls' 16 & Under International Team Championships
64 nations competed, 54 taking part in the boys' event and 54 in the girls' event. Final stages took place in Castelldefels, Spain, 29 September–3 October.

FINAL POSITIONS – BOYS: Champion nation – France; runners-up – Germany; 3rd – Sweden; 4th – Brazil; 5th – Australia; 6th – Israel; 7th – Indonesia; 8th – Canada; 9th – Argentina; 10th – USA; 11th – Japan; 12th – South Africa; 13th – Spain; 14th – Chinese Taipei; 15th – Italy; 16th – Ecuador. **GIRLS:** Champion nation – Belgium; runners–up – Argentina; 3rd – USA; 4th – Czechoslovakia; 5th – Germany; 6th – Canada; 7th – Japan; 8th – South Africa; 9th – CIS; 10th – Spain; 11th – Indonesia; 12th – Korea, Rep of; 13th – Netherlands; 14th – China, PR; 15th – Colombia; 16th – Brazil.

BOYS' CHAMPIONSHIP – Semi-finals: France d. Sweden 2–1 (N.Escude lost to M.Norman 3–6 2–6; M.Boye d. K.Flygt 6–1 6–1; M.Boye/N.Escude d. K.Flygt/M.Norman 7–5 6–4). **Germany d. Brazil 2–1** (R.Nicklisch d. A.Wuttke 6–2 6–4; A.Nickel lost to G.Kuerten 3–6 2–6; A.Nickel/R.Nicklisch d. G.Kuerten/F.Prestes 6–7 7–5 6–2). **3rd place play-off: Sweden d. Brazil 2–1** (M.Norman d. A.Wuttke 7–6 6–7 6–4; A.Stenman lost to G.Kuerten 5–7 4–6; K.Flygt/M.Norman d. G.Kuerten/F.Prestes 3–6 6–3 6–2). **Final: France d. Germany 2–1** (N.Escude lost to R.Nicklisch 6–2 3–6 3–6; M.Boye d. A.Nickel 7–5 0–6 6–3; M.Boye/N.Escude d. A.Nickel/R.Nicklisch 6–7 6–0 6–3).

GIRLS' CHAMPIONSHIP – Semi-finals: Belgium d. Czechoslovakia 2–1 (N.Feber d. Z.Nemsakova 6–2 1–6 7–5; L.Courtois d. A.Havrlikova 7–6 6–4; L.Courtois/S.Deville lost to A.Havrlikova/Z.Nemsakova 5–7 4–6). **Argentina d. USA 2–1** (L.Reynares d. J.Steven 4–6 6–3 6–2; L.Montalvo lost to N.London 1–6 6–3 0–6; L.Montalvo/L.Reynares d. N.London/J.Steven 6–3 6–1). **3rd place play-off: USA d. Czechoslovakia 2–1** (N.London d. Z.Nemsakova 6–0 6–3; K.Miller lost to A.Havrlikova 4–6 6–7; N.London/J.Steven d. A.Havrlikova/Z.Nemsakova 6–4 6–3). **Final: Belgium d. Argentina 3–0** (N.Feber d L.Reynares 1–6 6–4 6–1; L.Courtois d. L.Montalvo 6–1 6–3; L.Courtois/S.Deville d. M.Diaz Oliva/L.Montalvo 1–6 7–5 6–4).

Winners for the first time of the NEC World Youth Cup, the Belgian girls overcame Argentina 3–0 in the final. Left to Right: Stephanie Deville, Nancy Feber, Steve Martens(Capt.), Laurence Courtois.

NTT WORLD JUNIOR TENNIS

Jackie Nesbitt

The second NTT World Junior Tennis Competition, the ITF Team Championships for boys and girls of 14 & Under, was successfully staged at the Yamanakako Tennis Club near Mount Fuji, Japan. A total of 21 nations were represented by the 16 boys' and 16 girls' teams, who had qualified from five regional qualifying zones. An unexpectedly large entry, 61 nations, made competition to qualifying for the finals very tough, but also meant that the best 14 & Under players in the world were to compete for the titles.

The boys' event saw a few upsets in the opening round with the Republic of Korea, seeded 5/8, going down to Chinese Taipei in the deciding doubles. Korea had actually beaten Chinese Taipei by 2–1 in the final of the Asian/Australasian qualifying zone but Wei-Ju Chen managed to revenge his defeat by Dong-Hyun Kim in the top singles match, and then paired with Po-Tsang Huang to defeat Kim and Hee-Bong Park, 7–5 6–4, in the doubles.

Sweden, also seeded 5/8, had avoided Hungary in their regional qualifying zone, but drew them in the first round of the finals and proceeded to lose both opening singles. The tie, however, was notable for one of the best matches of the week, when the clash of the two top singles players, Szilard Szirtesi and Bjorn Rehnqvist, lasted for almost two and a half hours on the artificial grass courts, before Szilard posted a tie-winning 7–6 3–6 6–3 victory.

The biggest upset of the opening round, however, was the defeat of Argentina, seeded 3/4, at the hands of Japan. Level at 1–1 after the singles matches, the tie came down to the deciding doubles and the 6–2 6–4 result in favour of Yasuhiro Horiuchi and Michishisa Onoda over Gaston Gaudio and Mariano Puerta, does not really reflect what a tense affair it was.

A few surprises on the opening day then, but this was to be bettered on the second day when the three top seeded nations all fell. Chinese Taipei continued their giant killing ways with victory over top seeded Germany. A good start for Germany when Jan-Ralph Brandt posted a 6–0 6–1 win over Jen-Tso Lee. Wei-Ju Chen, however, popped up again with a comprehensive 6–2 6–2 victory over Thomas Haas to level matters, and then partnered by Huang defeated Brandt and Haas, 6–2 6–7 6–1, in the doubles to clinch the tie.

Defending champions, Spain, had lost the services of their number one player just prior to the event due to injury, but still managed to field a strong team and their opponents Hungary did well to defeat them in the deciding doubles.

The other two quarter-final match-ups saw Japan overpowered by USA 3–0, and Austria, seeded 5/8, taking both singles in their 2–1 win over Canada, seeded 3/4. In the semi-finals USA faced Chinese Taipei and Austria faced Hungary. Attempting to level up at 1–1, Wei-Ju Chen was unable to cope with the big serving US No.1 Geoff Abrams, by far the tallest person on view. Despite taking the first set after a nervy tie-break, Chen eventually went down 6–7 6–3 6–4.

On the adjoining court Austria and Hungary were battling for the other place in the final. At times it seemed like a battle of the loudest grunt, but in a nonetheless entertaining match, the Austrian boys' took both singles, with Hungary taking some consolation with victory in the doubles.

Austrian No. 2, Clemens Trimmel, looked to be heading for defeat at a set and a break down to Keith Brill of the United States in the boys' final, but got his act together to close out the match 4–6 6–2 6–2. USA were probably hopeful that the ferocious serving of their No.1, Geoff Abrams, would level them, but Markus Hipfl produced a tremendous display, mastering Abrams' serve to record a 6–4 6–0 win and clinch the title for his country.

The girls' event was far kinder to the seeding committee than the boys' had been with all seeded nations except ironically, Chinese Taipei, seeded 5/8, successfully negotiating the opening round. Taipei with Tzu-Ting Weng, highly placed in the Junior World Rankings, were expected to do well but were no match for Hungary losing all three matches quite comprehensively. The only opening round tie to go to the deciding doubles was the match between Brazil and South Africa. Brazil's Miriam D'Agostini had a hard fought 7–5 6–4 win over Surina de Beer only for Jessica Steck to level up with a 6–2 6–1 defeat of Marcia Komlos. With all the singles players pairing up for the deciding doubles it was to be Brazil who ran out 6–2 6–4 winners.

The closest quarter-finals came in the matches involving the two 3/4 seeded nations, USA and Australia. The United States faced Japan, Saori Obata getting the host nation off to a great start with a well deserved 7–5 6–3 victory over Amanda Basica. The impressive Meilen Tu, however, had no problems levelling matters against Nami Urabe, to dampen spirits. Neither top player played the deciding doubles, where Obata and Yasuko Nishimata threatened to push the USA, before falling away 6–4 6–2 to Basica and Amanda Augustus.

Australia's tie against Hungary saw every match go to three sets. Hungary's Reka Vidats got the better of Renee Reid in the gruelling opening match, 6–2 3–6 6–4, and Petra Mandula took the first set against Annabel Ellwood. Competing in her second NTT event, Ellwood was made of sterner stuff, and came storming back to take the next two sets, 6–0 6–3. She and Reid paired for the deciding doubles and gave captain, Janine Thompson, a fright by dropping the first set 5–7, but then composed themselves to close out 6–2 6–4.

It was to be second time unlucky for Ellwood in the final. Having lost to Czechoslovakia the previous year, she and her team mates were to fair no better against USA. Meilen Tu was too strong for Ellwood winning 6–4 6–4, and despite a tremendous effort by Renee Reid, she also lost her singles to Amanda Basica 6–3 6–7 4–6. As she had done all week, Amanda Augustus played doubles and she and Basica finished off a great tournament with a 6–2 7–5 victory over Siobhan Drake-Brockman and Reid in doubles.

The play-off for 3rd/4th was very tight between Czechoslovakia and Germany, with the 1991 defending champions beating the German team 4–6 6–0 7–5 in the deciding doubles.

The event, sponsored by Nippon Telegraph and Telephone Corporation, and organised by the Japan Tennis Association and The Yomiuri Shimbun to a very high standard can be regarded as the first step in team competition for future Davis Cup and Federation Cup players.

NTT WORLD JUNIOR TENNIS 1992
ITF Team Championships for 14 & Under
61 nations competed, 61 taking part in the boys' event and 49 in the girls' event. Final stages took place in Yamanakako, Japan, 25–29 August.

FINAL POSITIONS – BOYS: Champion nation – Austria; runners-up – USA; 3rd – Hungary; 4th – Chinese Taipei; 5th – Germany; 6th – Spain; 7th – Canada; 8th – Japan; 9th – Sweden; 10th – Argentina; 11th – Czechoslovakia; 12th – Ecuador; 13th – Korea, Rep, of; 14th – Australia; 15th – South Africa; 16th – Brazil. **Girls:** Champion nation – USA; runners-up – Australia; 3rd – Czechoslovakia; 4th – Germany; 5th – Brazil; 6th – Hungary; 7th – Japan; 8th – CIS; 9th – Peru; 10th – Italy; 11th – Chinese Taipei; 12th – South Africa; 13th – Sweden; 14th – Argentina; 15th – China, P.R.; 16th – Mexico.

BOYS' CHAMPIONSHIP – Semi-finals: USA d. Chinese Taipei 3–0 (G.Abrams d. W-J.Chen 6–7 6–3 6–4; K.Brill d. J-T.Lee 6–0 6–3; G.Abrams/B.Bryan d. W-J.Chen/P-T.Huang 6–4 6–2). **Austria d. Hungary 2–1** (M.Hipfl d. S.Szirtesi 6–3 7–5; C.Trimmel d. P. Madarassy 6–2 7–5; M/Hipfl/L.Langer lost to P.Madarassy/S.Szirtesi 3–6 3–6). **3rd place play-off: Hungary d. Chinese Taipei 2–1** (S.Szirtesi d. W-J.Chen 6–3 2–6; P.Madarassy d. P-T.Huang 6–2 6–2; M.Jancso/S.Szirtesi lost to W-J.Chen/P-T.Huang 6–1 0–6 4–6). **Final: Austria d. USA 2–1** (M.Hipfl d. G.Abrams 6–4 6–0; C.Trimmel d. K.Brill 4–6 6–2 6–2; M.Hipfl/C.Trimmel lost to G.Abrams/B.Bryan 1–6 3–6).

GIRLS' CHAMPIONSHIP – Semi-finals: Australia d. Czechoslovakia 3–0 (A.Ellwood d. H.Nagyova 6–3 3–6 6–4; R.Reid d. J.Ondrouchova 7–5 6–2; S.Drake-Brockman/R.Reid d. S.Kleinova/J.Ondrouchova 6–4 6–4). **USA d. Germany 3–0** (M.Tu d. A.Barna 6–1 7–5; A.Augustus d. E.Belbl 6–2 6–4; A.Augustus/A.Basica d. E.Belbl/C.Christian 7–6 6–4). **3rd place play-off: Czechoslovakia d. Germany 2–1** (S.Kleinova lost to A.Barna 2–6 5–7; J.Ondrouchova d. C.Christian 4–6 6–3 6–0; S.Kleinova/J.Ondrouchova d. A.Barna/E.Belbl 4–6 6–0 7–5). **Final: USA d. Australia 3–0** (M.Tu d. A.Ellwood 6–4 6–4; A.Basica d. R.Reid 3–6 7–6 6–4; A.Augustus/A.Basica d. S.Drake-Brockman/R.Reid 6–2 7–5).

GRAND SLAM CHAMPIONSHIPS

AUSTRALIAN OPEN CHAMPIONSHIPS
FRENCH OPEN CHAMPIONSHIPS
WIMBLEDON CHAMPIONSHIPS
US OPEN CHAMPIONSHIPS

By his own high standards 1992 was an average year in the Grand Slams for the 21-year-old American Pete Sampras who missed Melbourne through injury, was a quarter-finalist in Paris, a semi-finalist at Wimbledon and the losing finalist in New York. (M. Cole)

The 21-year-old Floridian, Jim Courier, started the year in impressive style with a first Australian Open victory, the prelude to his arrival as world No.1 two weeks later. (T. Hindley)

AUSTRALIAN OPEN CHAMPIONSHIPS

Alan Trengove

As at Roland Garros in 1991, Jim Courier confounded the pundits at Flinders Park. Seeded second, he was not given much chance of becoming the first native born American since Brian Teacher in 1980 to win the Australian crown.

Favoured ahead of him were, among others, Stefan Edberg, who had trounced him in the 1991 US Open final; defending champion Boris Becker; the reigning Wimbledon champion Michael Stich; and the 1989/90 champion, Ivan Lendl.

Courier, one of the most underestimated No.2 seeds in history, didn't mind his underdog status though he was peeved when the Australian press suggested the final would result in another easy victory for Edberg. Jim won convincingly 6–3 3–6 6–4 6–2. He not only upstaged an uncertain Edberg but also Becker who, after the 1991 final, had gone for a dramatic run through a nearby Park. Courier, in his moment of jubilation, also ran out of the stadium and took a dip in the muddy River Yarra some 200 yards away, thus setting a Grand Slam tradition that must remain unique to Melbourne; the Thames, the Seine and the Hudson are not nearly so conveniently located to the other Grand Slam tournament sites.

The women's event contained fewer surprises. Monica Seles conceded only one set, to Leila Meskhi, en route to her second successive Australian crown. Never short of ideas on how to create a sensation, Monica celebrated by turning up at her post-match press conference in a vivid floral gown and a matching soft-brimmed twenties' hats looking rather like Eliza Doolittle at a royal garden party.

Most people could not be blamed for being in the dark about Courier's form. Despite his seeding he made only three Centre Court appearances before the final. In any case there was too much else going on for anyone to notice Jim. The fans were besotted by John McEnroe's wins over Boris Becker and Emilio Sanchez then saddened by the pathos of his loss to the young South African, Wayne Ferreira. They were absorbed, too, by the tortured striving for his old form by Pat Cash, and stunned by Michael Stich's loss to Richard Krajicek.

Besides developing a reputation for producing flamboyant behaviour, Flinders Park seems increasingly to be associated with accidents and illness. Edberg, who won two championships at Kooyong, has had little luck here. In successive years he defaulted in the quarter-finals with a back injury; retired in the final with a stomach injury; and lost to Lendl in a semi-final after holding two match points. This time the Swede hurt his arm while preparing to use an exhibition event at Kooyong as a warm-up tournament and went into the Open with hardly any match practice over the previous two months.

Others to suffer misfortune were Pete Sampras, forced to pull out for the second year running (with a shoulder strain), Richard Krajicek (tendinitis in the shoulder), Aaron Krickstein (heat exhaustion), Steffi Graf (rubella), and Manuela Maleeva Fragnière (a sore big toe).

However, most of the upsets had nothing to do with physical mishaps. Ninth seed Petr Korda and 12th seed Derrick Rostagno departed on the first days, ousted by Jeff Tarango and Lars Wahlgren respectively. Seventh seed Guy Forget, who had won a poignant five-set match over Davis Cup team-mate Henri Leconte, inexplicably lost in the second round to the dogged Christian Bergstrom; eighth seed Karel Novacek went down to Ferreira (who later put out Compaq Grand Slam Cup champion David Wheaton, as well as McEnroe); 10th seed Goran Ivanisevic lost to Krickstein 6–1 in the third set; and 11th seed Magnus Gustafsson fell to Marc Rosset.

The greatest sensation was Becker's third-round 6–4 6–3 7–5 defeat by McEnroe. This and McEnroe's marathon win over Emilio Sanchez in the following round will remain the tournament's most vivid memories. McEnroe's subjection of Becker, who had beaten him in their last six matches, was one of the highlights of his amazing career because, as he said, it showed that at 32 and without any major success over the last eight years he still had the ability on the day to beat a top player.

A solid win over the tireless Andrei Cherkasov in the second round had boosted his confidence, and the night-time schedule also assisted him. He nullified Becker's power with clever tactics and perfect timing, invariably choosing the right shot at the right time and executing it with the masterly touch of his early years. His use of angles and changes of pace were inspired. Nor did he ever lose control, determined as he was to keep his infamous temper in check. For much of the match Becker gave one of his loud, anguished soliloquys, but neither this nor his usual courage was of avail. 'He didn't give me much time to breathe', he said.

The Sanchez match was entirely different. On the same day and on the same court on which he had been disqualified two years earlier, McEnroe won the first two sets 7–5 7–6. However, when the Spaniard took the next two 6–4 6–2 it seemed Mac was destined to lose. The fifth set was nip-and-tuck, until McEnroe, leading 5–4, had Sanchez 0–40 down on service. Sanchez, in his moments of truth, usually displays the mental strength of a matador; and sure enough, he saved those three match points and won the game. Next he broke McEnroe's serve and served for the match. He went to 40–15, then served a double-fault, and on the next point he mis-hit a forehand out of court. The matador had blinked! He had one more match point – and netted a volley. McEnroe levelled at 6–all; then, leading 7–6, he had Sanchez in trouble a second time. But it took three more match points before he could wrap up victory. After being on court for 4 hours 41 minutes he was so drained that he asked to be given a saline glucose drip.

Two clear days elapsed. McEnroe did not play again until the evening of the third day. It should have been long enough for him to recover physically, but his reservoir of nervous energy was still depleted; against Ferreira, whom he had never played before, he was flat. This time the night-time conditions, with the roof closed because of the threat of rain, worked against him. The court was slower – and so was Mac. He never quite worked out Ferreira's unsettling, disjointed game, losing 6–4 6–4 6–4.

What Ferreira was doing in the top half of the draw, Krajicek was more than equalling in the other half. He put out Michael Chang, seeded 14th, in the third round after winning the first two sets and losing the next two. He was not just a strapping young fellow with a huge serve; he had good hands and could volley. Against Stich in the quarters, Krajicek came back from two sets to one down to win 6–4 in the fifth, out-serving the German with 23 aces, no mean feat. But the effort took its toll. His shoulder was so sore he had to retire from the men's doubles and give Courier a default in the singles, a big blow to the tournament as well as himself.

Meanwhile, Courier quietly did whatever he needed to do to fill his allotted place in the final. He beat Rodolphe Gilbert, Thomas Enqvist, Thomas Muster, Marc Rosset and Amos Mansdorf, then went for a jog in lieu of his semi-final.

Edberg had another of his see-saw encounters with Lendl, but was generally happy with his form. He wasn't convincing in the first set against Ferreira and saved two set points, whereupon the South African's game collapsed.

Perhaps that shaky first set prompted some nagging doubts in Edberg's mind. He knew he would have to serve well against Courier or the American's brutal ground shots would do him a lot of damage. When Edberg serves well, he invariably volleys beautifully. He did neither in the final; most of his seven double-faults came at critical points, such as the two at 4–5 and deuce that cost him the third set.

The Swede looked as though he was about to find his rhythm when he won the second set. Indeed, he broke Courier's opening serve in the third. But he immediately lost his own serve and Courier, the more positive of the two, struck out for victory like the resolute competitor he is, often running around his backhand and smiting his forehand harder and harder as the match wore on. After the thrashing he had received at Flushing Meadow, the manner of this victory said something about Courier's character.

The women's event suffered greatly by the withdrawal of Steffi Graf. In her absence no-one was able to prevent a Seles cake-walk. Leila Meskhi's speed and willingness to attack the net gave Seles a scare in the fourth round, but thereafter no real challenge emerged, although a spirited Anke Huber pushed the champion to 7–5 6–3.

The best match was the quarter-final between Gabriela Sabatini and Jennifer Capriati. Following Capriati's defeat of Sabatini and her brave showing against Seles at the US Open, she was given a chance of upstaging Seles by becoming the youngest winner of the Australian title. But she was a far more tense and unhappy girl than the youngster who had made such a big impression on the tennis world almost two years earlier. She had brought her schoolbooks to Melbourne and was tutored at her hotel, so it could not have been the 'fun' trip that her first travels to Paris and London had been.

The Capriati–Sabatini match was played at a cracking pace and swayed to and fro. The Argentine produced the greater range of shots and made good use of her net-attacking ability. However Capriati led 4–2 in the first set and fought from 1–3 down in the second set to force a tie-break. This she played badly, dropping the first six points, and Sabatini clinched a 6–4 7–6 victory.

At this stage Sabatini seemed to be a threat for the title. She had won the lead-up tournament at Sydney in fine style and should have been buoyed by the Capriati match. Alas for her many fans, her semi-final against seventh seed Mary Joe Fernandez whom she had easily beaten in Sydney, was an anti-climax. She served badly, hit the ball short, and rarely ventured to the net. Fernandez had been encouraged by her new coach, Harold Solomon, to be more aggressive, and it was she who hit most of the winning volleys. She won 6–1 6–4.

Seles dealt just as decisively with Arantxa Sanchez-Vicario in their semi-final, and so we were left with a final that no-one had predicted. This was Mary Joe's second Australian final; she had been runner-up to Graf in 1990. The American puts more sting in her shots now and she promised to reproduce the bold play that had enabled her to beat Sabatini. If she broke that promise it was only because the tenacious young lady from Novi Sad was never a party to the contract. Seles hit the ball from corner to corner so hard and so deep that Fernandez had few opportunities to advance to the net. Whenever she did, she was invariably passed or forced into error. Perhaps she could have taken more chances, but the result would have been much the same. The 6–2 6–3 win gave Seles her second successive Australian crown.

Australia has virtually given up hope of producing a homegrown winner of the two singles titles in the foreseeable future. There was some consolation, though, in the victories of Mark Woodforde and Todd Woodbridge in the men's doubles, and of Woodforde and Nicole Provis in the mixed doubles. Possibly significant, too, were the triumphs of local players Grant Doyle and Joanne Limmer in the junior singles.

MEN'S SINGLES

Holder: B. Becker (GER)

Final: 6-3 3-6 6-4 6-2

FIRST ROUND

1 S. EDBERG (SWE) (1)
2 J. Bates (GBR) (Q)
3 C. Mezzadri (SUI)
4 J. Morgan (AUS) (WC)
5 J. Palmer (USA) (Q)
6 J. Siemerink (NED)
7 J. Fitzgerald (AUS) (WC)
8 M. Koevermans (NED)
9 M. Gontz (ESP)
10 G. Bloom (ISR)
11 A. Chesnokov (CIS)
12 F. Fontang (FRA)
13 P. McEnroe (USA)
14 M. Cierro (ITA)
15 J. Tarango (USA)
16 P. KORDA (TCH) (9)
17 D. ROSTAGNO (USA) (12)
18 C. Limberger (AUS) (Q)
19 B. Gilbert (USA)
20 L. Wahlgren (SWE) (Q)
21 S. Youl (AUS) (Q)
22 G. Raoux (FRA)
23 T. Hogstedt (SWE)
24 O. Camporese (ITA)
25 J. Frana (ARG)
26 C. Pioline (FRA)
27 M. Zoecke (GER)
28 G. Connell (CAN)
29 R. Rasheed (AUS) (WC)
30 D. Marcelino (BRA)
31 J. Fromberg (AUS)
32 I. LENDL (TCH) (5)
33 B. BECKER (GER) (3)
34 J. Gunnarsson (SWE)
35 B. Shelton (USA)
36 G. Pozzi (ITA)
37 J. McEnroe (USA)
38 B. Dyke (US) (Q)
39 P. Kuhnen (GER)
40 A. Cherkasov (CIS)
41 T. Champion (FRA)
42 M. Schapers (NED)
43 J. Eltingh (NED)
44 K. Braasch (GER)
45 H. Skoff (AUT)
46 P. Cash (AUS) (WC)
47 P. Arraya (PER)
48 G. SANCHEZ (ESP) (13)
49 D. WHEATON (USA) (15)
50 J. Cask (AUS) (WC)
51 N. Kulti (SWE)
52 T. Witsken (USA)
53 B. Black (ZIM)
54 C. Arias (USA)
55 J. Arias (USA)
56 L. Koslowski (GER)
57 F. Clavet (ESP)
58 M. Strelba (TCH)
59 M. Woodforde (AUS)
60 J. Yzaga (PER)
61 W. Ferreira (RSA)
62 L. Lavalle (MEX) (Q)
63 D. Pate (USA) (Q)
64 K. NOVACEK (TCH) (8)

SECOND ROUND

EDBERG (1) 6-4 6-2 6-4
Mezzadri 4-2 4-6 6-3 6-4 6-2
Siemerink 6-4 4-6 6-3 4-6 6-2
Fitzgerald 7-6 6-4 7-6
Bloom 6-7 6-2 6-0 6-1
Chesnokov 6-3 7-6 6-1
McEnroe 6-3 6-4
ROSTAGNO (12) 4-6 4-6 6-3 6-3 6-4
Wahlgren 2-6 6-3 1-6 6-3 6-4
Youl 1-6 6-2 6-1 3-6 6-2
Camporese 6-2 6-2 6-2
Pioline 3-6 6-2 6-2 2-6 6-1
Zoecke 7-6 6-1 6-1
Rasheed 7-6 3-6 6-3
LENDL (5) 6-4 2-6 4-6 6-2 6-4
BECKER (3) 6-4 6-2
Pozzi 6-1 6-2
McEnroe 4-6 7-6 2-6 6-2 6-2
Cherkasov 6-2 6-0 6-1
Schapers 6-7 7-5 6-0 6-1
Eltingh 4-6 6-1 6-2 6-4
Cash 2-6 5-7 6-3 6-4 7-5
SANCHEZ (13) 6-1 7-5 7-6
WHEATON (15) 6-4 6-0 6-0
Kulti 6-0 6-1 6-7 6-3
Cane 6-4 6-1
Koslowski 6-1 7-6 6-0
Clavet 6-2 7-2 6-7 5
Woodforde 6-4 7-6 6-1
Ferreira 6-2 6-4 1-6 6-3
NOVACEK (8) 2-6 7-5 6-4 6-1

THIRD ROUND

EDBERG (1) 6-1 6-2 6-1
Fitzgerald 7-5 6-1 7-6
Chesnokov 4-6 6-3 6-4 6-4
McEnroe 6-1 4-6 6-4 6-3
Wahlgren 6-1 7-5 7-6
Camporese 6-3 6-4 7-6
Zoecke 3-6 6-2 7-6 7-6
LENDL (5) 6-3 6-2 6-3
BECKER (3) 7-5 7-6 6-2
McEnroe 7-5 3-6 6-4 6-3
Schapers 1-6-4 5-7 6-1 6-3
SANCHEZ (13) 7-6 6-2 6-7 3-6 6-1
WHEATON (15) 6-3 6-4 2-6 8-6
Koslowski 6-2 1/6 7/6 6/2
Woodforde 6-7 6-4 6-1 3-6 7-5
Ferreira 3-6 6-3 7-6 7-6

FOURTH ROUND

EDBERG (1) 7-5 6-1 6-4
Chesnokov 6-4 1-6 1-6 6-1 6-3
Camporese 6-4 6-2 7-6
LENDL (5) 6-4 6-4 7-6
McEnroe 6-4 6-3 7-5
SANCHEZ (13) 6-3 6-4 7-6
WHEATON (15) 6-4 6-3 6-3
Ferreira 4-6 6-3 6-2 6-2

QUARTER-FINALS

EDBERG (1) 6-1 7-5 6-2
LENDL (5) 7-6 6-1 6-3
McEnroe 7-5 7-6 4-6 2-6 8-6
Ferreira 6-7 6-4 6-2 6-2

SEMI-FINALS

EDBERG (1) 4-6 7-5 6-1 6-7 6-1
Ferreira 6-4 6-4 6-4

FINAL

EDBERG (1) 7-6 6-1 6-2

J. COURIER (USA) (2)

Semifinal

COURIER (2)
w/o

Quarterfinals

Krajicek
5-7 7-6 6-7 6-4 6-4

COURIER (2)
6-3 6-2 6-2

Round 4

Krajicek
7-5 7-6 6-3

STICH (4)
3-6 6-4 7-6 6-4

Mansdorf
6-2 4-6 1-6 7-6 4-1 Ret

COURIER (2)
6-3 6-1 6-3

Round 3

Bergstrom
6-2 6-3 4-6 6-2

Krajicek
6-4 6-1 5-7 1-6 6-3

CHANG (14)
6-3 6-6 4-6 6-4

Masur
6-3 6-4

STICH (4)
6-0 2-6 7-5 6-2

Mansdorf
6-1 6-4 6-3

Krickstein
6-4 5-7 6-7 6-1 8-6

COURIER (2)
6-1 6-4 6-2

Round 2

Bergstrom
7-6 2-6 6-3 6-4

Garnett
4-6 1-6 7-5 6-2 6-2

Krajicek
6-2 7-6 6-1

CHANG (14)
6-3 6-6 4-6 4-6

Washington
6-2 6-4 6-3

Masur
7-6 6-0 6-4

Jaite
3-6 6-0 1-0 Ret

STICH (4)
6-4 6-1 1-6 6-4

Mansdorf
6-1 7-5 6-0

Reneberg
6-3 3-6 6-7 6-4 10-8

Volkov
6-4 6-4 6-2

Krickstein
6-4 5-7 6-7 6-1 8-6

Rosset
6-3 7-5 4-4 3-6 6-3

Steeb
6-4 6-2 7-5

Muster
6-4 6-4 7-6

COURIER (2)
2-6 6-3 6-1 6-4

Round 1

FORGET (7)
2-6 6-4 6-7 6-4 6-3
Bergstrom
7-6 7-6 6-3
Stolle
3-6 6-2 7-5 4-6 6-2
Garnett
6-4 6-2 6-4
Grabb
3-6 6-0 7-6 6-2
Krajicek
6-3 6-3 6-3
Caratti
6-7 6-3 6-3 6-0
CHANG (14)
6-2 6-3 6-0
PRPIC (16)
6-3 6-4 7-6
Washington
6-4 6-2 6-1
Masur
4-6 6-4 4-6 6-2 6-2
Pescosolido
6-4 6-4 7-5
Delaitre
6-7 6-4 6-3 6-2
Jaite
3-6 7-5 6-1 3-6 8-6
Svensson
6-0 7-5 6-3
STICH (4)
7-5 6-1 4-6 6-3
Mansdorf
6-3 6-3 6-4
Boetsch
6-3 6-3 6-4
Poliakov
6-3 3-6 4-6 6-3 6-3
Reneberg
6-2 6-2 7-5
Baur
6-3 6-4 6-7 6-1
Volkov
6-3 6-2 6-1
Krickstein
6-3 6-7 6-2 6-3
IVANISEVIC (10)
7-6 6-3 6-4
GUSTAFSSON (11)
6-4 6-3 6-3
Rosset
6-1 6-2 6-1
Rahunen
4-6 3-6 6-4 6-3 6-4
Steeb
7-4 6-1 7-5
Haarhuis
6-0 2-6 2-6 6-4 6-2
Enqvist
7-5 7-6
COURIER (2)
6-4 7-6 6-3

65 **G. FORGET** (FRA) (7)
66 H. Leconte (FRA) (WC)
67 L. Jonsson (SWE)
68 C. Bergstrom (SWE)
69 J. Oncins (BRA)
70 S. Stolle (AUS) (WC)
71 R. Garnett (USA) (Q)
72 G. Doyle (AUS) (WC)
73 P. Rafter (AUS) (Q)
74 J. Grabb (USA)
75 R. Krajicek (NED)
76 C. Saceanu (GER)
77 C. Caratti (ITA)
78 C. Adams (USA)
79 R. Roese (BRA)
80 **M. CHANG** (USA) (14)
81 **G. PRPIC** (CRO) 16
82 G. Lavendecker (USA) (Q)
83 M. Washington (USA)
84 G. Stafford (RSA) (Q)
85 W. Masur (AUS)
86 M. Vajda (TCH)
87 S. Pescosolido (ITA)
88 D. Nestor (CAN) (Q)
89 O. Delaitre (FRA)
90 C. Miniussi (ARG)
91 M. Jaite (ARG)
92 C. Van Rensburg (RSA)
93 J. Svensson (SWE)
94 S. Matsuoka (JPN)
95 J. Sanchez (ESP)
96 **M. STICH** (GER) (4)
97 P. Lundgren (SWE) (LL)
98 A. Mansdorf (ISR)
99 A. Gargasi (ITA)
100 A. Boetsch (FRA)
101 C. Pistolesi (ITA)
102 D. Poliakov (CIS)
103 A. Reneberg (CIS)
104 B. Wuyts (BEL)
105 P. Baur (GER)
106 N. Kroon (SWE) (Q)
107 A. Volkov (CIS)
108 T. Woodbridge (AUS)
109 A. Jarryd (SWE)
110 T. Krickstein (USA)
111 J. Stoltenberg (AUS)
112 **G. IVANISEVIC** (CRO) (10)
113 **M. GUSTAFSSON** (SWE) (11)
114 G. Muller (RSA)
115 M. de la Pena (ARG)
116 M. Rosset (SUI)
117 A. Gomez (ECU)
118 A. Rahunen (FIN) (Q)
119 R. Furlan (ITA)
120 C. Steeb (GER)
121 J. Fleurian (FRA)
122 T. Muster (AUT)
123 J. Hlasek (SUI)
124 P. Haarhuis (NED)
125 M. Larsson (SWE)
126 T. Enqvist (SWE) (Q)
127 R. Gilbert (FRA)
128 **J. COURIER** (USA) (2)

Capital letters denote seeded players. Number following player's name gives seeding order (Q) – Qualifier, (WC) – Wild Card, (LL) – Lucky Loser.

WOMEN' SINGLES

Holder: M. Seles (YUG)

6–2 6–3

FIRST ROUND	SECOND ROUND	THIRD ROUND	FOURTH ROUND	QUARTER-FINALS	SEMI-FINALS	FINAL

First round / draw:

1 M. SELES (YUG) (1)
2 A. Kijimuta (JPN)
3 M. Paz (ARG)
4 K. Date (JPN)
5 S. Gomer (GBR)
6 L. Field (AUS) (WC)
7 Y. Basuki (INA)
8 P. Tarabini (ARG)
9 M. Kidowaki (JPN)
10 A. Minter (AUS)
11 M. Kochta (GER)
12 H. Ludloff (USA)
13 P. O'Reilly (USA) (Q)
14 N. Arendt (USA) (Q)
15 A. Gavaldon (MEX) (Q)
16 L. MESKHI (CIS) (13)
17 A. HUBER (GER) (12)
18 M. Zivec-Skuj (GER)
19 M. Bollegraf (NED)
20 M. Jaggard (AUS) (WC)
21 R. Fairbank-Nideffer (USA)
22 C. Rubin (USA)
23 D. Szabova (TCH)
24 J. Emmons (USA) (Q)
25 R. Bobkova (TCH)
26 R. Stubbs (AUS) (WC)
27 F. Li (CHN) (Q)
28 F. Hiraki (JPN)
29 R. Alter (CAN)
30 B. Paulus (AUT)
31 P. Zrubakova (TCH)
32 A. NOVOTNA (TCH) (6)
33 A. SANCHEZ VICARIO (ESP) (4)
34 N. Provis (AUS)
35 S. Testud (FRA)
36 L. McNeil (USA)
37 L. Gildemeister (PER)
38 M. Werdel (USA)
39 A. Strnadova (TCH)
40 I. Demongeot (FRA)
41 K. Po (USA)
42 S. Smith (GBR)
43 E. Zardo (SUI)
44 J. Limmer (AUS) (WC)
45 J. Durie (GBR)
46 F. Labat (ARG)
47 S. Savchenko-Neiland (LAT)
48 M. APPELMANS (BEL) (16)
49 M. MALEEVA-FRAGNIERE (SUI) (9)
50 G. Helgeson (USA)
51 G. Fernandez (USA)
52 H. Habsudova (TCH)
53 C. Lindqvist (SWE)
54 M. Daniels (USA)
55 T. Whitlinger (USA)
56 J. Faull (AUS) (LL)
57 D. Faber (USA)
58 N. Dahlman (FIN) (Q)
59 N. Herreman (FRA)
60 R. White (USA)
61 E. Sviglerova (TCH)
62 S. Rehe (USA)
63 S. Stafford (USA)
64 C. MARTINEZ (ESP) (8)

Second round:

- SELES (1) 6-2 6-0
- Date 6-2 6-4
- Field 6-3 6-2
- Basuki 6-3 7-5
- Kidowaki 6-2 6-4
- Kochta 6-3 6-4
- Arendt 6-3 6-4
- MESKHI (13) 6-2 6-2
- HUBER (12) 2-6 6-3 6-1
- Jaggard 2-6 6-4 9-7
- Fairbank-Nideffer 6-4 6-1
- Emmons 6-4 6-2
- Stubbs 6-0 6-1
- Li 6-2 6-4
- Alter 6-4 6-0
- NOVOTNA (6) 7-6 6-3
- SANCHEZ VICARIO (4) 6-2 6-1
- Testud 6-2 3-6 6-4
- Gildemeister 6-4 6-7 6-1
- Strnadova 6-3 6-4
- Po 6-4 2-6 6-1
- Limmer 6-3 6-2
- Durie 7-5 6-1
- Savchenko-Neiland
- MALEEVA-FRAGNIERE (9) 4-6 6-3 6-1
- Habsudova 6-4 6-4
- Lindqvist 6-2 6-3
- Whitlinger 6-1 5-7 6-4
- Dahlman 2-6 6-3 7-5
- White 6-0 6-1
- Rehe 6-2 6-4
- MARTINEZ (8) 6-3 6-1

Third round:

- SELES (1) 6-2 7-5
- Basuki 6-7 6-3 6-4
- Kochta 6-3 6-1
- MESKHI (13) 6-1 6-7
- HUBER (12) 6-0 6-1
- Fairbank-Nideffer 6-4 6-2
- Li 7-5 6-2
- NOVOTNA (6) 6-3 6-2
- SANCHEZ VICARIO (4) 6-1 6-1
- Strnadova 4-6 4-6 9-7
- Po 3-6 6-4 7-5
- Savchenko-Neiland 6-4 4-6 6-1
- MALEEVA-FRAGNIERE (9) 6-3 6-3
- Whitlinger 6-3 7-6
- White 6-2 6-4
- MARTINEZ (8) 6-1 6-2

Fourth round:

- SELES (1) 6-1 6-1
- MESKHI (13) 6-1 7-6
- HUBER (12) 6-0 7-5
- NOVOTNA (6) 6-3 6-1
- SANCHEZ VICARIO (4) 1-6 6-0 6-3
- Savchenko-Neiland 6-2 6-6-1
- MALEEVA-FRAGNIERE (9) 6-2 6-1
- MARTINEZ (8) 7-5 6-0

Quarter-finals:

- SELES (1) 6-4 4-6 6-2
- HUBER (12) 5-7 7-6 6-4
- SANCHEZ VICARIO (4) 6-1 7-6
- MALEEVA-FRAGNIERE (9) 6-4 2-6 6-2

Semi-finals:

- SELES (1) 7-5 6-3
- SANCHEZ VICARIO (4) w/o

Final:

- SELES (1) 6-2 6-2

M. SELES (YUG) (1)

Women's Singles — bottom half of draw (entrants 65–128)

First-round entrants

65	J. CAPRIATI (USA) (5)
66	N. Medvedeva (CIS)
67	Y. Kamio (JPN) (Q)
68	N. Van Lottum (FRA)
69	M. Maruska (AUT)
70	I. Gorrochategui (ARG)
71	L. Cueto (GER)
72	K. Adams (USA)
73	L. Stacey (AUS) (WC)
74	P. Shriver (USA)
75	P. Thoren (CIS)
76	N. Zvereva (CIS)
77	C. Kohde-Kilsch (GER)
78	C. Porwik (GER)
79	S. Frankl (GER)
80	Z. GARRISON (USA) (11)
81	K. MALEEVA (BUL) (10)
82	D. Graham (USA)
83	D. Kamstra (NED)
84	N. Housset (FRA) (Q)
85	S. Meier (GER)
86	K. Sharpe (AUS) (WC)
87	M. Babel (GER)
88	A. Foldenyi (HUN)
89	P. Ritter (AUT)
90	M. Drake (CAN) (LL)
91	B. Mulej (SLO)
92	J. Byrne (AUS) (WC)
93	P. Hy (CAN)
94	M. Maleeva (BUL)
95	J. Halard (FRA)
96	G. SABATINI (ARG) (3)
97	M. FERNANDEZ (USA) (7)
98	B. Schultz (NED)
99	B. Rittner (GER)
100	H. Kelesi (CAN)
101	L. Harvey-Wild (USA)
102	R. McQuillan (AUS)
103	R. Sloane-Lundy (USA)
104	P. Fendick (USA)
105	S. Niox-Chateau (FRA)
106	T. Cioffi (USA)
107	C. Wood (GBR)
108	C. Fulco-Villela (ARG)
109	B. Dechaume (FRA)
110	C. Tessi (ARG)
111	H. WIESNER (AUT) (14)
112	H. SUKOVA (TCH) (15)
113	V. Martinek (GER)
114	K. Goodridge (AUS)
115	N. Muns-Jagerman (NED)
116	E. Maniokova (CIS)
117	D. Monami (BEL)
118	N. Pratt (AUS) (WC)
119	M. Miyagi (JPN)
120	M. Endo (JPN)
121	R. Rajchrtova (TCH)
122	S. Hack (GER)
123	C. Tanvier (FRA)
124	A. Frazier (USA)
125	C. Cunningham (USA)
126	K. Oeljeklaus (GER)
127	A. Devries (BEL) (LL)

First round

- CAPRIATI (5) 6-3 6-4
- Van Lottum 6-4 6-2
- Gorrochategui 4-6 6-4 6-3
- Adams 4-1 Ret
- Shriver 6-0 6-1
- Zvereva 6-4 6-4
- Kohde-Kilsch 6-1 1-6 7-5
- GARRISON (11) 6-2 6-2
- MALEEVA (10) 6-4 6-4
- Housset 4-6 6-4 6-4
- Sharpe 6-2 7-5
- Foldenyi 6-2 6-4
- Ritter 6-3 6-0
- Byrne 6-1 6-0
- Hy 4-6 6-3
- SABATINI (3) 6-2 6-0
- FERNANDEZ (7) 6-4 6-4
- Rittner 6-1 3-6 6-4
- Harvey-Wild 6-1 6-4
- McQuillan 6-1 6-4
- Fendick 6-1 6-3
- Cioffi 6-4 6-2
- Dechaume 6-4 6-1
- WIESNER (14) 6-4 6-3
- SUKOVA (15) 6-3 6-2
- Muns-Jagerman 6-4 7-6
- Monami 4-6 7-5 6-1
- Pratt 6-3 6-3
- Rajchrtova 7-6 2-6 7-5
- Hack 6-4 7-5
- Frazier 6-3 7-5
- Devries 6-1 7-5

Second round

- CAPRIATI (5) 6-0 6-0
- Adams 6-1 7-5
- Shriver 6-4 7-6
- GARRISON (11) 6-2 6-3
- MALEEVA (10) 6-2 6-1
- Sharpe 6-2 6-3
- Byrne 6-4 6-2
- SABATINI (3) 6-1 6-1
- FERNANDEZ (7) 6-4 6-4
- McQuillan 6-2 4-6 6-0
- Fendick 6-1 6-3
- Dechaume 6-2 7-6
- SUKOVA (15) 7-5 6-3
- Monami 6-4 7-6
- Hack 7-5 3-6 6-2
- Frazier 6-1 7-6

Third round

- CAPRIATI (5) 6-4 6-0
- GARRISON (11) 6-4 7-6
- MALEEVA (10) 6-0 6-4
- SABATINI (3) 6-1 6-0
- FERNANDEZ (7) 6-1 2-6 6-1
- Fendick 5-7 6-2 6-3
- Monami 2-6 6-4 6-4
- Frazier 6-1 3-6 6-2

Fourth round

- CAPRIATI (5) 6-4 6-4
- SABATINI (3) 6-1 7-5
- FERNANDEZ (7) 6-4 6-1
- Frazier 6-3 6-4

Quarter-finals

- SABATINI (3) 6-4 7-6
- FERNANDEZ (7) 6-4 7-6

Semi-final

- FERNANDEZ (7) 6-1 6-4

Capital letters denote seeded players. Number following player's name gives seeding order (Q) – Qualifier, (WC) – Wild Card, (LL) – Lucky Loser.

MEN'S DOUBLES

Holders: S. Davis (USA)/D. Pate (USA)

WOODBRIDGE (AUS)/**WOODFORDE** (AUS) (4)

6-4 6-3 6-4

FIRST ROUND	SECOND ROUND	THIRD ROUND	QUARTER-FINALS	SEMI-FINALS	FINAL
1 FITZGERALD/JARRYD (1)	FITZGERALD/JARRYD (1)	FITZGERALD/JARRYD (1)			
2 Dwel/Lundgren	6-4 6-2	6-2 3-6 6-3			
3 Elingh/Kempers	Elingh/Kempers				
4 Clavet/Gorriz	6-3 6-3				
5 Palmer/Stark	Palmer/Stark	Palmer/Stark	Palmer/Stark		
6 Becker/Smid	6-3 6-1	6-4 5-7 6-4	7-6 6-4		
8 **GRABB/RENEBERG** (15)	**GRABB/RENEBERG** (15)				
9 Gar/Perez	6-4 6-2				
10 Nelson/Stoltenberg	Nelson/Stoltenberg	Krajicek/Siemerink		Krajicek/Siemerink	
11 **GALBRAITH/IVANISEVIC** (12)	7-5 6-1	6-4 6-2		6-7 6-2 7-5 7-6	
12 Krajicek/Siemerink	Krajicek/Siemerink		Krajicek/Siemerink		
13 Broad/Muller	6-7 7-6 6-3		3-6 7-6 6-3		
14 Albano/Cannon	Albano/Cannon				WOODBRIDGE/WOODFORDE (4)
15 Annacone/Pugh	6-3 6-3				4-6 3-1 Ret
16 **JENSEN/WARDER** (6)	**JENSEN/WARDER** (6)	**JENSEN/WARDER** (6)			
17 **WOODBRIDGE/WOODFORDE** (4)	7-6 7-5	9-7 3-5			
18 Arthurs/Rasheed (WC)	**WOODBRIDGE/WOODFORDE** (4)				
19 Kratzmann/Van Rensburg	6-1 6-1	**WOODBRIDGE/WOODFORDE** (4)	**WOODBRIDGE/WOODFORDE** (4)		
20 Patridge/Corazza	Kratzmann/Van Rensburg	6-3 6-4	6-3 4-6 6-3		
21 Aciolly/Menezes	6-2 6-1				
22 Bathman/Bergh	Bathman/Bergh	Bathman/Bergh			
23 Miniussi/Rosset	6-4 6-7 6-3	7-5 7-5			WOODBRIDGE/WOODFORDE (4)
24 **HAARHUIS/KOEVERMANS** (13)	Miniussi/Rosset				6-1 6-4 6-4
25 **FRANA/LAVALLE** (9)	1-6 6-2 9-7				
26 Morgan/Stolle (WC)	Morgan/Stolle	Eagle/Doyle			
27 De La Pena/Pozzi	6-1 1-1 Ret	6-4 1-6 6-3			
28 Eagle/Doyle	Eagle/Doyle		Borwick/Youl		
29 Anderson/Fromberg (WC)	5-7 7-6 6-4		3-6 6-3 8-6		
30 Borwick/Youl (AUS)	Borwick/Youl	Borwick/Youl			
31 Bates/Edberg	6-4 6-2	6-2 6-2			
32 **CASAL/SÁNCHEZ** (7)	**CASAL/SÁNCHEZ** (7)				
33 **NIJSSEN/SUK** (8)	6-2 6-1				
34 Middleton/Scherman	**NIJSSEN/SUK** (8)	**NIJSSEN/SUK** (8)			
35 Layendecker/Talbot	6-3 6-7 7-5	7-5 3-6 6-2	NIJSSEN/SUK (8)		
36 Gomez/Sanchez	Gomez/Sanchez		7-6 6-3		
37 Garrow/Pearce	6-3 3-6 6-2				
38 Aldrich/Visser	Aldrich/Visser	Aldrich/Visser			
39 Beckman/Salumaa	6-2 6-1	6-3 7-6			
40 **FERREIRA/NORVAL** (10)	**FERREIRA/NORVAL** (10)		JONES/LEACH (11)	JONES/LEACH (11)	
41 **JONES/LEACH** (11)	6-4 6-2		7-5 6-1	6-0 2-6 7-6 7-5	
42 Kruger/Van Emburgh	**JONES/LEACH** (11)	**JONES/LEACH** (11)			
43 Flegl/Pimek	6-6 6-2	6-4 6-2			
44 Rafter/Tramacchi (WC)	Rafter/Tramacchi				
45 Adams/Black	3-6 6-3 6-4				
46 Devries/Macpherson	Adams/Black				JONES/LEACH (11)
47 Ferreira/Reneberg	6-4 5-7 6-3				4-6 4-6 7-6 6-4 6-3
48 **CONNELL/MICHIBATA** (3)	**CONNELL/MICHIBATA** (3)	**CONNELL/MICHIBATA** (3)			
49 **GALBRAITH/WITSKEN** (5)	6-3 6-4	6-2 4-6 6-1			
50 Schapers/Vacek	Schapers/Vacek				
51 Bloom/Wekesa	6-0 7-5		Bloom/Wekesa		
52 Bloom/Wekesa	Bloom/Wekesa	Bloom/Wekesa	7-6 6-2		
53 Smith/Thorne	6-3 6-1	6-4 3-6 6-1			
54 Novacek/Prpic	Novacek/Prpic				
55 Sobel/Zivojinovic	6-3 7-6	Novacek/Prpic			
56 Kuhnen/Oosting	Kuhnen/Oosting	6-3 6-3			DAVIS/PATE (2)
57 **RIGLEWSKI/STICH** (14)	7-6 7-6				6-3 6-4 6-7 6-3
58 **HLASEK/McENROE** (16)	**HLASEK/McENROE** (16)	Keil/Montana			
59 Garnett/Svantesson	6-4 6-1	4-6 6-3 6-1	Keil/Montana	DAVIS/PATE (2)	
60 Keil/Montana	Keil/Montana		4-6 6-3 6-1	6-3 6-4 6-7 6-3	
61 Oncins/Roese	6-4 6-1				
62 Korda/Masur	Korda/Masur	DAVIS/PATE (2)	DAVIS/PATE (2)		
63 Olhovskiy/Poliakov	6-1 6-2	6-1 6-3	6-4 6-7 6-3		
64 **DAVIS/PATE** (2)	**DAVIS/PATE** (2)				

Capital letters denote seeded pairings. Number following player's name gives seeding order (Q) – Qualifier, (WC) – Wild Card, (LL) – Lucky Loser.

WOMEN'S DOUBLES

Holders: P. Fendick (USA)/M.J. Fernandez (USA)

Winner: SANCHEZ (ESP)/SUKOVA (TCH) (4) — 6-4 7-6

FIRST ROUND

1 NOVOTNA/SAVCHENKO (1)
2 Halard/Huber
3 Kijimuta/Nishiya
4 Helgeson/Whitlinger
5 Morton/Wood
6 Fuchs/Miyagi
7 Cunningham/Gildemeister
8 FAIRBANK/GREGORY (13)
9 MESKHI/PAZ (9)
10 K. Maleeva/Medvedeva
11 Hodder/Schneider
12 Testud/Van Lottum
13 Basuki/Dürie
14 Barclay/Taylor (WC)
15 Graham/Po
16 M.J. FERNANDEZ/GARRISON (5)
17 FENDICK/FERNANDEZ (3)
18 Limmer/Woodcock (WC)
19 Henricksson/Ludloff
20 Babel/Rittner
21 Harvey-Wild/Pfaff
22 Gorrochategui/Herreman
23 Frazier/Hiraki
24 KOHDE-KILSCH/WIESNER (11)
25 REHE/SCHULTZ (16)
26 Novelo/Radford
27 Dechaume/Labat
28 Byrne/Stacey (WC)
29 Kidowaki/Lindqvist
30 Hirose/Kamio
31 Tarabini/Temesvari
32 McNeil/Provis (7)
33 Hetherington/Rinaldi (6)
34 Rehmova/Zrubakova
35 Dhélivás/Fleming
36 Date/Jaggard
37 Field/Minter
38 Arendt/Kelesi
39 Faber/Thoren
40 McQUILLAN/PORWIK (15)
41 DANIELS/WHITE (12)
42 Gooden/Kuhlman
43 Benjamin/Scott
44 Maruska/Ritter
45 Fukuoka/Muns-Jagerman
46 Berger/Smith
47 Faull/Richardson
48 SANCHEZ VICARIO/SUKOVA (4)
49 ADAMS/BOLLEGRAF (8)
50 Svigilerova/Szabova
51 O'Reilly/O'Reilly
52 Borneo/Guse
53 M. Maleeva/Maleeva-Fragniere
54 Glitz/Somerville
55 STRNADOVA/TANVIER (14)
56 Dahlman/Frankl
57 APPELMANS/DEMONGEOT (10)
58 Hack/Meier
59 Alter/Hy
60 Godridge/Pratt
61 Stafford/Werdel
62 Bobkova/Habsudova
63 Devries/Maniokova
64 SHRIVER/ZVEREVA (2)

SECOND ROUND

NOVOTNA/SAVCHENKO (1) 7-6 3-6 7-5
Helgeson/Whitlinger
Morton/Wood 6-3 6-3
FAIRBANK/GREGORY (13)
MESKHI/PAZ (9) 6-7 7-5 6-4
Testud/Van Lottum
Basuki/Dürie 6-0 6-1
FERNANDEZ/GARRISON (5) 6-4 6-4
FENDICK/FERNANDEZ (3) 6-4 6-4
Babel/Rittner 6-3 7-5
Harvey-Wild/Pfaff
KOHDE-KILSCH/WIESNER (11) 6-3 6-3
REHE/SCHULTZ (16) 6-4 3-6 6-1
Byrne/Stacey (WC) 7-5 6-3
Hirose/Kamio
McNEIL/PROVIS (7) 6-1 6-1
HETHERINGTON/RINALDI (6)
Date/Jaggard 7-6 7-6 6-1
Arendt/Kelesi
McQUILLAN/PORWIK (15) 4-6 6-1 6-3
DANIELS/WHITE (12) 6-4 7-6
Benjamin/Scott 6-4 2-6 6-4
Fukuoka/Muns-Jagerman 6-3 6-3
SANCHEZ/SUKOVA (4) 6-2 4-6 6-1
ADAMS/BOLLEGRAF (8) 6-2 4-6 6-2
Borneo/Guse 6-2 6-4
Maleeva/Maleeva-Fragniere
STRNADOVA/TANVIER (14) 3-6 6-3 6-2
APPELMANS/DEMONGEOT (10) 6-0 6-2
Godridge/Pratt 3-6 6-1 6-1
Stafford/Werdel
SHRIVER/ZVEREVA (2) 6-2 6-2

THIRD ROUND

NOVOTNA/SAVCHENKO (1) 6-2 6-3
Morton/Wood 6-3 6-3
MESKHI/PAZ (9) 6-4 7-6
FERNANDEZ/GARRISON (5) 6-2 7-6
FENDICK/FERNANDEZ (3) 6-0 6-3
KOHDE-KILSCH/WIESNER (11) 5-7 6-2 6-1
REHE/SCHULTZ (16) 6-4 6-2
McNEIL/PROVIS (7) 6-2 6-4
Date/Jaggard
McQUILLAN/PORWIK (15) 6-2 6-4
DANIELS/WHITE (12) 6-4 6-2
SANCHEZ/SUKOVA (4) 6-1 6-1
ADAMS/BOLLEGRAF (8) 6-2 6-2
Maleeva/Maleeva-Fragniere 7-5 7-5
APPELMANS/DEMONGEOT (10) 7-5 6-4
SHRIVER/ZVEREVA (2) 7-5 6-4

QUARTER-FINALS

NOVOTNA/SAVCHENKO (1) 6-4 6-3
FERNANDEZ/GARRISON (5) 6-2 7-6
FENDICK/FERNANDEZ (3) 7-6 6-4
REHE/SCHULTZ (16) 7-5 6-3
Date/Jaggard 6-4 6-7 7-5
SANCHEZ/SUKOVA (4) 6-4 6-4
ADAMS/BOLLEGRAF (8) 4-5 Ret
SHRIVER/ZVEREVA (2) 5-7 6-0 6-0

SEMI-FINALS

FERNANDEZ/GARRISON (5) 2-6 6-2 8-6
REHE/SCHULTZ (16) 7-6 6-0
SANCHEZ/SUKOVA (4) 6-2 6-4
SHRIVER/ZVEREVA (2) 7-5 7-5

FINAL

FERNANDEZ/GARRISON (9) 6-2 6-1
SANCHEZ/SUKOVA (4) 6-3 6-3

Capital letters denote seeded pairings. Number following player's name gives seeding order (Q) – Qualifier, (WC) – Wild Card, (LL) – Lucky Loser.

MIXED DOUBLES

Holders: J. Bates (GBR)/J. Durie (GBR)

FIRST ROUND	SECOND ROUND	THIRD ROUND	QUARTER-FINALS	SEMI-FINALS	FINAL
1 WOODBRIDGE/SANCHEZ VICARIO (1)	WOODBRIDGE/SANCHEZ (1) 6-0 6-2	WOODBRIDGE/SANCHEZ (1) 6-1 4-6 6-4	WOODBRIDGE/SANCHEZ (1) 6-2 6-3	WOODBRIDGE/SANCHEZ (1) 6-3 7-6	WOODFORDE (AUS)/PROVIS (AUS) (3) 6-3 4-6 11-9
2 Connell/Alter					
3 Devries/Fendick	Suk/Schultz 6-1 7-6				
4 Suk/Schultz					
5 Ivanisevic/Rehe	Ivanisevic/Rehe 5-7 6-2 6-1	Ivanisevic/Rehe 3-6 6-3 8-6			
6 Aldrich/Gregory					
7 Bergh/Appelmans	NIJSSEN/BOLLEGRAF (7) 7-5 3-6 6-4				
8 NIJSSEN/BOLLEGRAF (7)					
9 LAVALLE/PAZ (6)	LAVALLE/PAZ (6) 4-6 7-6 6-2	Macpherson/McQuillan 6-2 4-6 6-3	Macpherson/McQuillan 6-7 6-2 6-2		
10 Galbraith/Helgeson					
11 Youl/Minter	Macpherson/McQuillan 6-2 7-5				
12 Macpherson/McQuillan					
13 Kinnear/Fairbank-Nideffer	Kinnear/Fairbank-Nideffer 7-6 6-3	PUGH/ZVEREVA (4) 7-6 7-5			
14 Leach/Stafford					
15 Visser/Stubbs	PUGH/ZVEREVA (4) 5-7 6-4 9-7				
16 PUGH/ZVEREVA (4)					
17 WOODFORDE/PROVIS (3)	WOODFORDE/PROVIS (3) 6-4 7-6	WOODFORDE/PROVIS (3) 6-3 6-3	WOODFORDE/PROVIS (3) 6-4 7-6	WOODFORDE/PROVIS (3) 6-2 6-1	
18 Amacone/McNeil					
19 Van Emburgh/Adams	Van Emburgh/Adams 6-4 4-6 6-4				
20 Warder/Wood					
21 Frana/Gildemeister	Kratzmann/Shriver 7-6 6-2	Kratzmann/Shriver 6-7 6-3 6-2			
22 Kratzmann/Shriver					
23 Norval/Daniels	SALUMAA/SAVCHENKO-NEILAND (8) 6-4 6-2				
24 SALUMAA/SAVCHENKO-NEILAND (8)					
25 DAVIS/WHITE (5)	DAVIS/WHITE (5) 6-4 6-3	DAVIS/WHITE (5) 6-2 6-7 6-3	DAVIS/WHITE (5) 6-3 7-6		
26 Vacek/Tanvier					
27 Jensen/Cunningham	Jensen/Cunningham 7-5 6-2				
28 Beckman/Demongeot					
29 Morgan/Godridge (WC)	Bates/Durie 7-6 6-3	Bates/Durie 7-6 6-4			
30 Bates/Durie					
31 Broad/Faull	Broad/Faull 6-4 5-7 6-4				
32 MICHIBATA/HETHERINGTON (2)					

Capital letters denote seeded pairings. Number following player's name gives seeding order (Q) – Qualifier, (WC) – Wild Card, (LL) – Lucky Loser.

JUNIOR EVENTS

BOYS' SINGLES – Final: Grant Doyle(AUS)(1) d. Brian Dunn(USA)(2) 6–2 6–0
GIRLS' SINGLES – Final: Joanne Limmer(AUS)(2) d. Lindsay Davenport(USA)(6) 7–5 6–2
BOY'S DOUBLES – Final: Grant Doyle(AUS)/ Bradley Sceney(AUS)(1) d Alexander
Carrington(USA)/Jason Thompson(USA) 6–4 6–4
GIRLS' DOUBLES – Final: Lindsay Davenport(USA)/Julie London(USA) (2) d. Maija
Avotins(AUS)/Joanne Limmer(AUS)(1) 6–2 7–5
SENIOR INVITATIONAL MEN'S OVER 35 DOUBLES – Final: Mark Edmondson(AUS)/Kim Warwick
d. Peter McNamara(AUS)/Paul McNamee(AUS) 6–3 7–5
SENIOR INVITATIONAL MEN'S OVER 45 DOUBLES – Final: Ken Rosewall(AUS)/Fred Stolle(AUS)
d. John Newcombe(AUS) Tony Roche(AUS) 4–6 7–5 ret.
SENIOR INVITATIONAL MIXED DOUBLES – Final: Allan Stone(AUS)/Wendy Turnbull(AUS) d. Bob
Carmichael(AUS)/Judy Dalton(AUS) 6–4 6–1

AUSTRALIAN OPEN CHAMPIONSHIPS PRIZE MONEY – AUS $5,459,200

MEN'S AND WOMEN'S SINGLES – Winner $360,000. Runner-up $180,000. Semi-finalists
$90,000. Quarter-finalists $46,800. Fourth-round losers $22,200. Third-round losers
$14,500. Second-round losers $8.800. First-round losers $ 5,400.
Total: MEN and WOMEN $1,968,000 each.
MEN'S AND WOMEN'S DOUBLES (per team) – Winners $147,500. Runners-up $73,750.
Semi-finalists $37,900. Quarter-finalists $19,500. Third-round losers $10,500. Second-round
losers $5,700. First-round losers $3,300.
Total MEN and WOMEN $655,850 each
MIXED DOUBLES (per team) – Winners $62,600. Runners-up $31,300. Semi-finalists
$15,600. Quarter-finalists $7,200. Second-round losers $3,600. First-round losers $1,800.
Total $211,500

(Plus prize money for senior events and per diem allowances)

In the finest French Open final anyone could remember, Monica Seles fought like a tigress to retain her title against the athletic challenge of Steffi Graf.   *(M. Cole)*

FRENCH OPEN CHAMPIONSHIPS

David Irvine

It is rare, especially these days that rankings, critics and results speak out in accord. Yet the 1992 French Open, despite some absorbing distractions en route, ended as most observers and the seedings suggested they would, with the 21-year-old American Jim Courier still firmly entrenched as the men's champion and the precocious Yugoslav teenager, Monica Seles, as the women's. So, for once, it was *deja vu* at Roland Garros.

In every practical sense their joint successes offered an emphatic and timely confirmation of their champion status. For Courier it was his third Grand Slam title in five attempts – matching even fellow American John McEnroe's best run – and for 18-year-old Seles, her sixth in eight. There may be more to come.

If there was some mild surprise, it was that Courier succeeded more easily than he had done at the Australian Open, dropping only one set in Paris compared to the two he had let slip in Melbourne, whereas Seles (thanks to Steffi Graf's glorious last ditch challenge) had to dig much deeper than she had done Down Under to maintain her recent supremacy.

Yet Seles won despite the disappointment of missing four match points at 5–3 in the third and having twice to hold her serve to stay in the match. That was a measure of her character. The 6–3 3–6 10–8 score says it all. In statistical terms it was the longest final (2 hours 43 minutes) for 37 years; longer by 45 minutes than the men's. And viewed as a piece of sporting theatre, arguably it ranked alongside the best of the Chris Evert v Martina Navratilova series in the mid-eighties.

Though a poorish second to the men's competition for most of the fortnight, the climax to the women's singles was by any standard a treat to savour. A one-sided first set in which Graf was outclassed gave no hint whatever of the recovery to come. Then, playing her best tennis since her 1988 Grand Slam year, the German courageously fought her way back into contention. She took more chances, hit more winners and, for the most part, looked the more complete player of the two – until, that is, she was put under intolerable pressure. Then her forehand, so often her greatest strength, became her crucial weakness. In the mind game she ultimately had to settle for second best; moreover, she knew it.

'Even when it's close, even when she's tired, she's always going for it', Graf acknowledged. 'That's definitely the big quality she has. She's tough.' Tough yes, but relieved nonetheless. As Seles said, 'It was so close, both of us deserved to win.'

A full house made it clear that, given a choice, they would have preferred Graf to have taken the trophy. 'I have played a lot of tournaments in a lot of places but I've never ever known a crowd like this', she told them. Courting popularity, though, is not Seles' aim. Winning is – and, once again, she had proved herself a winner.

Courier, apart from one set conceded to Goran Ivanisevic when it rained (in his view play should have been suspended), suffered no serious traumas. He either despatched his main challengers with an almost disdainful air or saw them melt away in the opposite half of the draw before they could reach and threaten him.

No-one had seriously considered that the sole survivor from a lower half that included Stefan Edberg, Michael Stich, Michael Chang and Ivan Lendl would be the Czech matchstick man, Petr Korda. Yet the 24-year-old left-hander from Prague happily took advantage of the more fancied candidates' misfortunes to reach his first Grand Slam final without ever facing a single seed.

Inevitably the triple gear-change then required was beyond him. Korda drowned in his own errors. Having watched others crushed by Courier's power, Korda tried to confuse the champion with a mixture of chips, drop shots and changes of pace. It was a high-risk strategy that collapsed alarmingly as his nerve went and his touch deserted him.

Courier said he had not known what to expect. 'He can be very dangerous. I just didn't know whether he would come out swinging or react tightly.' In fact he did neither – if anything his multifarious game plan, which could have been devised by that master of disguise, Miloslav Mecir, was an attempt at gentle assassination.

'But I had to try something different', protested Korda, 'because he was playing like a machine.' It worked up to 3–4. But then he lost serve to love with four appalling errors. Thereafter he won only five more games, Courier taking the last 12 at the cost of just 22 points.

Not since Tony Trabert in 1955 and 1956 had an American successfully defended the French title. Indeed, no American had won the title post-Trabert until the 17-year-old Michael Chang's unexpected win in 1989. Courier, however, did so worthily. In fact since the days of Bjorn Borg in the seventies, no-one had triumphed with such minimum fuss or maximum efficiency.

During the two weeks of the Championships, a competition constantly plagued by rain, more than 30 men's matches stretched to anything between three-and-a-half and five hours' play. It was an indication of Courier's application and concentration that his matches lasted, on average, two hours and seven minutes.

Early interest focused, inevitably, on two veterans – Jimmy Connors and John McEnroe – who had hinted at 'farewell' appearances. Never one to depart without a flourish, Connors, in his 40th year, won two sets off the Wimbledon champion, Michael Stich, before he succumbed 7–5 3–6 6–7 6–1 6–2. 'I made my first excursion into a dark hole today,' said Connors. 'It was scary. It was not a beautiful sight.'

Nor was McEnroe, at 33 still eager to prove something in Paris where he has never won the title. All he proved was a lasting inability to control himself. He had yet another verbal punch-up with courtside photographers before losing in four sets to the 21-year-old Swede, Nicklas Kulti, and was fined a total of $4,200.

Jakob Hlasek(16) and Brad Gilbert(15) were the first seeds to fall, being followed out rather ignominiously by Guy Forget(6) in round two – the Frenchman losing to the Belgian Bart Wuyts – though even that result was overshadowed by the premature dismissal of former champion Lendl(10) 8–6 in the final set by Jaime Oncins of Brazil.

By the end of week one this thinning-out process had further accounted for Edberg(2), Stich(4) and Chang(5), beaten respectively by the unseeded Andrei Cherkasov, Henri Leconte and Kulti who all won again to advance with Korda to the quarter-finals in the lower half. In the upper section Courier was bracketed with Ivanisevic and the rival American pair Pete Sampras(3) and Andre Agassi(11). Though Agassi had looked impressive ending Sampras' charge, the assumption that a semi-final against Courier would be as close as their 1991 final which Courier had won in five torrid sets, proved well wide of the mark. Agassi was savaged 6–3 6–2 6–2.

Though level at 4–4 in previous meetings Courier, significantly, had taken their three most recent encounters and it was easy to see why as the 22-year-old from Dade City pumped out the points with his awesomely powerful groundstrokes. Often he hit winners from the baseline that Agassi, quick as he was, simply could not reach.

Agassi had claimed rather tactlessly prior to the match that he was a more natural talent than Courier, but, as the champion said – and proved – there is a lot more to talent than fancy shot-making. Guts and a will to win are equally important.

Not that the Parisians cared too much. All interest on semi-finals day focused on the left-handed extrovert Leconte, hero of France's Davis Cup triumph the previous December in Lyon, who had made his way impressively and unexpectedly through the draw with dashing victories – in particular over Stich and Kulti.

Unfortunately those five successes had taken their toll on the wild card. The younger, fitter Korda wisely kept his emotions in check, offering a packed and partisan audience nothing to feed off, and a weary Leconte was finally put to rest 6–2 7–6 6–3.

Korda thus became the fifth Czech to reach the final, following in the steps of Roderick Menzel, Jaroslav Drobny, Jan Kodes and Lendl. His hope for the final, he said, was 'to enjoy myself, play the best tennis I can and make the people happy.' It was a laudable ambition but needed Courier's co-operation. That was not forthcoming.

Seles opened her defence impressively, sailing through the first three rounds at a cost of six games. Then came the news that the United Nations had decided to apply sporting sanctions on Yugoslavia – prompting fears that she might have to be disqualified. Even when that threat had passed ('She is competing here as an individual,' said officials), she almost came a cropper against the tiny Japanese, Akiko Kijimuta, ranked 150th in the world.

Seles was within six points of losing in steady drizzle but had the umpire's support in playing out a match Kijimuta felt should have been suspended to win 6–1 3–6 6–4. From 1–4 and deuce in the last set, the No.1 seed lost only a further five points.

Other seeds were not so fortunate. Anke Huber(9), on whom the Germans placed high hopes, fell in round two to the veteran British player Jo Durie. The beaten Australian finalist, Mary Joe Fernandez (6), went out in round three, by which time both the Maleeva sisters had fallen – and by the time the quarter-finalists emerged two non-seeds, Natalia Zvereva from Minsk and Manon Bollegraf of Holland, were poised for glory.

Neither achieved it, although the Dutch player took a set off Arantxa Sanchez-Vicario, and to no-one's surprise but general delight, the top four seeds emerged as semi-finalists: Graf (2) versus Sanchez (4), who had twice beaten her in Paris, and Seles (1) against Gabriela Sabatini (3), the victor on their most recent clash in Rome three weeks earlier.

Another Sanchez humiliation for Graf seemed likely when the lively Spaniard grabbed the first set in 27 minutes without one game going the German's way but Graf scrambled her way back to win 0–6 6–2 6–2. 'I was a bit unlucky,' ventured Sanchez. Unlucky? The truth was she made a hash of it.

Seles v Sabatini was of an altogether higher class. Not the serving, of course, but the accuracy of their groundstrokes, the subtlety of their drop shots and the tactical variations each in turn employed in trying to establish the upper hand – these were the qualities to savour. In the end it was probably Seles' mental strength and greater consistency that saw her home 6–3 4–6 6–4.

It was not an occasion that reflected too much credit on the women's game. Of the 51 service games played 26 produced breaks. Had a Martina Navratilova at her peak been involved, one suspects she would have had a field day. Still, it did at least set up the final everyone had wanted and that was a corker.

In the men's doubles Jacob Hlasek and Marc Rosset scored a notable first for Switzerland while, in the women's, Gigi Fernandez and Zvereva – who were on opposite sides of the net in the 1991 final – joined forces to win; Sanchez, who made the semi-finals of all three events, found some consolation in the mixed, where she teamed up successfully with Todd Woodbridge.

MEN'S SINGLES

Holder: J. Courier (USA)

Final result: 7-5 6-2 6-1

Column headers: FIRST ROUND · SECOND ROUND · THIRD ROUND · FOURTH ROUND · QUARTER-FINALS · SEMI-FINALS · FINAL

FIRST ROUND

1 J. COURIER (USA) (1)
2 N. Kroon (SWE) (Q)
3 C. Motta (BRA) (Q)
4 T. Muster (AUT)
5 G. Bloom (ISR)
6 J. Siemerink (NED)
7 A. Mancini (ARG)
8 A. Corretja (ESP) (Q)
9 A. Boetsch (FRA)
10 T. Woodbridge (AUS)
11 D. Rostagno (USA)
12 K. Novacek (TCH)
13 K. Curren (USA)
14 G. Perez-Roldan (ARG)
15 A. Medvedev (CEI) (Q)
16 J. HLASEK (SUI) (16)
17 C. COSTA (ESP) (9)
18 K. Braasch (GER)
19 G. Schaller (AUT) (Q)
20 J. Yzaga (PER)
21 A. Thoms (GER)
22 W. Ferreira (RSA)
23 M. Zoecke (GER)
24 R. Fromberg (AUS)
25 D. Wheaton (USA)
26 A. Chesnokov (CEI)
27 A. Berasategui (ESP) (Q)
28 M. Larsson (SWE)
29 M. Limberger (AUS) (Q)
30 T. Champion (FRA)
31 S. Youl (AUS)
32 G. IVANISEVIC (CRO) (8)
33 P. SAMPRAS (USA) (3)
34 P. Roset (SUI)
35 B. Black (ZIM)
36 L. Prades (FRA) (WC)
37 H. de la Pena (ARG)
38 T. Guardiola (FRA) (WC)
39 R. Gilbert (FRA)
40 G. Raoux (FRA) (WC)
41 B. Shelton (USA)
42 P. McEnroe (USA)
43 G. Connell (CAN)
44 C. Steeb (GER)
45 J. Stoltenberg (AUS)
46 M. Naewie (GER)
47 M. Vajda (TCH) (Q)
48 A. VOLKOV (CEI) (14)
49 A. AGASSI (USA) (11)
50 J. Frana (ARG)
51 G. Pozzi (ITA)
52 G. Delaitre (FRA)
53 G. Prpic (CRO)
54 R. Reneberg (USA)
55 E. Masso (BEL)
56 C. Pistolesi (ITA)
57 H. Skoff (AUT)
58 E. Sanchez (ESP)
59 J. Etringh (NED)
60 W. Masur (AUS)
61 B. Wuyts (BEL)
62 R. Jarryd (SWE)
63 L. Mattar (BRA)
64 G. FORGET (FRA) (6)

SECOND ROUND

COURIER (1) 7-6 6-4 6-2
Muster 6-4 6-4 5-7 6-2
Bloom 5-7 6-4 6-4 4-6 6-2
Mancini 6-3 6-2 5-7 7-6
Woodbridge 4-6 5-7 6-4 6-4 6-2
Rostagno 3-6 7-5 6-3 6-7 6-3
Curren
Medvedev 6-2 6-4 6-7 6-3
COSTA (9) 6-1 6-3 6-4
Schaller 1-6 7-6 5-7 7-5 8-7
Ferreira 7-5 6-2 7-6
Fromberg 6-4 7-5
Wheaton
Larsson 3-6 3-6 6-4 6-0 6-2
Limberger 6-3 6-2
IVANISEVIC (8) 6-7 6-3 6-2 6-1
SAMPRAS 7-6 4-6 6-4 3-6 6-3
Prades 6-3 6-3 6-3
Guardiola 6-1 1-6 6-4 7-5
Gilbert 6-1 6-3 7-6
McEnroe 4-6 6-3 6-4 7-6
Steeb 6-4 6-2 6-2
Naewie 7-6 6-3
VOLKOV (14) 4-6 7-6 6-1 1-6 7-5
AGASSI (11) 6-1 6-3 6-4
Pozzi 6-1 6-3 6-4
Prpic
Pistolesi 6-7 6-2 2-6 6-2
E. Sanchez 6-4 6-2 6-2
Masur 6-3 6-3 6-1
B. Wuyts 7-5 6-2
FORGET 5-7 6-3 6-7 6-4

THIRD ROUND

COURIER (1) 6-1 6-4 6-4
Mancini 6-3 6-2 5-7 7-6
Woodbridge 4-6 7-6 6-3 6-3
Medvedev 6-4 4-6 6-1 6-3
COSTA (9) 7-6 6-3 6-2
Ferreira 6-3 7-5 6-4
Larsson 7-6 6-4 6-1
IVANISEVIC (8) 6-2 6-2 6-4
SAMPRAS 7-6 6-4 7-6
Gilbert 6-1 7-6 6-1
Steeb 6-2 6-4 3-6 6-3
VOLKOV (14) 6-4 4-6 4-6 6-2 6-2
AGASSI (11) 6-0 6-2 6-1
Prpic 6-2 6-4 6-3
E. Sanchez 3-4-5 7-6 3-6-4 13-11
Wuyts 6-3 6-3 6-3

FOURTH ROUND

COURIER (1) 6-4 6-2 6-0
Medvedev 7-6 6-2 6-1
COSTA (9) 2-6 6-2 6-2 6-2
IVANISEVIC (8) 6-7 6-3 6-1 3-6 9-7
SAMPRAS 6-3 6-2 6-3
Steeb 6-2 6-4 6-4
AGASSI (11) 2-6 6-4 6-1 7-6
E. Sanchez 6-0 6-4 7-6

QUARTER-FINALS

COURIER (1) 6-1 6-4 6-2
IVANISEVIC (8) 6-3 4-6 6-1 6-1
SAMPRAS (3) 6-4 6-3 6-2
AGASSI (11) 6-1 6-3 7-5

SEMI-FINALS

COURIER (1) 6-2 6-1 2-6 7-5
AGASSI (11) 7-6 6-2 6-1

FINAL

COURIER (1) 6-3 6-2

Winner: J. Courier — 7-5 6-2 6-1

COURIER (USA) (1)

No.	Player	Round 1	Round 2	Round 3	Round 4	Round 5
65	**M. CHANG** (USA) (5)	CHANG (5) 6-4 6-3 6-3				
66	P. Haarhuis (NED)					
67	O. Camporese (ITA)	Gorriz	CHANG (5) 6-3 2-6 6-3 6-0			
68	G. Gorriz (ESP)					
69	M. Zillner (GER) (Q)	Zillner		Kulti 7-6 2-6 6-3 8-6		
70	A. Mansdorf (ISR)		Kulti 4-6 6-1 2-6 7-6 6-2			
71	J. McEnroe (USA)	Kulti 1-6 5-7 7-6 6-0 6-3			Kulti 6-0 3-6 7-5 6-4	
72	N. Kulti (SWE)					
73	D. Perez (URU) (Q)	Perez 6-2 7-5 6-7 7-5				
74	F. Pescosolido (ITA)		Perez 6-4 6-1 6-1			
75	D. Nargiso (ITA)	3-6 6-4 6-3 7-5		Perez 6-4 6-3 6-7 5-8 8-6		
76	F. Davin (ARG)	Nargiso 6-4 3-6 6-3 0-6 6-1				
77	M. Gustafsson (SWE)	Gustafsson	KRAJICEK (12) 6-3 6-4 6-1			
78	F. Clavet (ESP)					
79	J. Sanchez (ESP)	KRAJICEK (12) 7-6 6-7 6-3 7-6		KRAJICEK (12) 4-6 6-3 6-7 7-5 8-6		
80	**R. KRAJICEK** (NED) (12)					
81	**A. KRICKSTEIN** (USA) (13)	KRICKSTEIN (13)	KRICKSTEIN (13) 4-6 5-7 6-4 7-6 6-3			
82	M. Koevermans (NED)				Filippini 6-2 1-0 ab.	
83	M. Washington (USA)	Washington 3-6 6-3 6-1 6-3				
84	B. Reneberg (GER)			Filippini 6-4 3-6 6-3		
85	M. Woodforde (AUS)	Filippini 3-6 4-6 6-2	Filippini 6-4 3-6 6-3			
86	M. Filippini (URU)					Leconte 6-7 3-6 6-3 6-3 6-3
87	G. Lopez (ESP)	Filippini 6-3 7-6 6-1				
88	T. Carbonell (ESP)	Lopez 0-6 6-3 6-4 6-0	Leconte 6-3 6-4 6-3			
89	J. Grabb (USA)					
90	A. Fleurian (FRA) (WC)	Grabb 2-6 2-7 6-6 6-3		Leconte 6-3 6-2 6-4		
91	M. Cierro (ITA) (Q)	Leconte 6-1 7-5 6-0			Leconte 7-6 6-4 6-4	
92	H. Leconte (FRA) (WC)					
93	E. Roux (FRA) (WC)	Roux 4-6 3-6 6-4 6-4 6-3	Leconte 7-6 6-4 6-4			
94	M. Jaite (ARG)					
95	J. Connors (USA)	STICH (4) 7-5 3-6 6-7 6-1 6-2	STICH (4) 6-1 6-4 6-4			
96	**M. STICH** (GER) (4)					**KORDA** (7) 6-2 7-6 6-3
97	**P. KORDA** (TCH) (7)	KORDA (7) 6-4 6-2 6-2				
98	C. Bergstrom (SWE)		KORDA (7) 1-6 4-6 6-4 6-4 6-4			
99	C. Orsanic (ARG) (Q)	Matsuoka		KORDA (7) 6-4 6-2 3-6 6-1		
100	S. Matsuoka (JPN)					
101	B. Sloman (FRA) (WC)	Schapers 0-1 6-4 6-4			KORDA (7) 6-4 6-3 6-3	
102	C. Pridham (CAN)	Prinosil 6-4 6-3 6-7 6-7 6-3				
103	M. Schapers (NED)	Schapers 6-1 6-4 6-4	Schapers 7-4 5-7 6-2 3-6 6-3			
104	R. Furlan (ITA)					
105	R. Agenor (HAI)	Tarango 5-7 6-3 6-4 3-6 6-3	Prinosil 7-6 1-6 4-6 7-6 6-2	KORDA (7) 6-4 6-3 6-3		
106	J. Tarango (USA)					
107	J. Svensson (SWE)	Prinosil 6-2 6-1 3-6 6-3				
108	D. Prinosil (GER) (Q)		Oncins 6-3 6-2 6-2			
109	J. Oncins (BRA)	Oncins		Oncins 6-3 6-2 6-2		
110	B. Karbacher (GER) (Q)				Cherkasov 6-3 6-2 3-7 6	
111	S. Bruguera (ESP)	LENDL (10) 6-3 2-6 3-6 6-2 8-6				
112	**I. LENDL** (TCH) (10)		Pioline 7-5 6-3 7-5			
113	**B. GILBERT** (USA) (15)	Pioline 2-6 5-7 7-5 6-2 6-1				
114	C. Pioline (FRA)			Pioline 6-2 7-6 2-6 6-2		
115	F. Fontang (FRA)	Daufresne	Pioline 6-2 7-6 2-6 6-2			
116	X. Daufresne (BEL) (Q)					
117	C. Minussi (ARG)	Gomez 6-5 2-3 6-3				
118	A. Gomez (ECU)		Jonsson 3-6 7-6 6-4 6-4			
119	F. Santoro (FRA)	Jonsson 2-6 3-6 6-2 7-6		Cherkasov 6-3 6-3 7-6		
120	L. Jonsson (SWE)					
121	J. Arrese (ESP)	Cherkasov 6-1 6-3 5-7 6-7 6-3	Cherkasov 5-7 7-6 6-1 6-2			
122	A. Cherkasov (CEI)					
123	J. Azar (ARG)	Azar 4-6 7-6 6-3 7-5				
124	H. Holm (SWE) (Q)		EDBERG (2) 4-6 7-6 7-5 4-6 6-4			
125	L. Koslowski (GER)	Markus				
126	G. Markus (ARG)					
127	O. Soules (FRA) (WC)	EDBERG (2) 7-5 6-1 6-7 7-5				
128	**S. EDBERG** (SWE) (2)					

Capital letters denote seeded players. Number following player's name gives seeding order (Q) – Qualifier, (WC) – Wild Card, (LL) – Lucky Loser.

WOMEN'S SINGLES

Holder: M. Seles (YUG)

FIRST ROUND	SECOND ROUND	THIRD ROUND	FOURTH ROUND	QUARTER-FINALS	SEMI-FINALS	FINAL
1 **M. SELES** (YUG) (1)	**SELES** (1) 6-1 6-0	**SELES** (1) 6-2 6-2	**SELES** (1) 6-0 6-1	**SELES** (1) 6-1 3-6 6-4	**SELES** (1) 6-2 6-2	**SELES** (1) 6-3 4-6 6-4
2 C. Mothes (FRA)						
3 S. Rottier (NED)	Kschwendt 6-4 6-3	McNeil 6-2 6-3				
4 K. Kschwendt (GER) (Q)						
5 C. Kuhlman (USA)	McNeil 6-2 6-2					
6 L. McNeil (USA)						
7 L. Harvey-Wild (USA)	Harvey-Wild 6-4 6-2	Kijimuta 7-6 3-6 8-6	Kijimuta 6-7 6-4 6-4			
8 R. Stubbs (AUS)						
9 E. Reinach (RSA)	Kijimuta 7-6 4-6 9-7					
10 A. Kijimuta (JPN)						
11 A. Fusai (FRA) (WC)	Tessi 6-1 6-0	Durie 6-1 7-5				
12 C. Tessi (ARG)						
13 J. Durie (GBR)	Durie					
14 N. Dahlman (FIN)						
15 N. Zrubakova (TCH)	**HUBER** (9) 6-2 6-1	**PIERCE** (13) 6-2 6-3	**PIERCE** (13) 7-6 6-4	**CAPRIATI** (5) 6-4 6-3		
16 **A. HUBER** (GER) (9)						
17 **M. PIERCE** (FRA) (13)	**PIERCE** (13) 6-1 6-1					
18 R. Reichtova (TCH)						
19 L. Savchenko-Neiland (LAT)	Savchenko-Neiland 6-4 6-0	Strnadova 6-4 6-3				
20 F. Collet (FRA) (WC)						
21 M. Werdel (USA)	Strnadova 0-6 6-2 6-4					
22 A. Strnadova (TCH)						
23 M. Kidowaki (JPN)	Kidowaki	Habsudova 7-5 6-1	**CAPRIATI** (5) 4-6 6-4 6-3			
24 A. Keller (USA)						
25 M. Habsudova (TCH)	Habsudova 6-1 6-2					
26 C. Porwik (GER)						
27 K. Adams (USA)	van Lottum 4-6 6-4 6-3	**CAPRIATI** (5) 6-4 6-4				
28 R. van Lottum (FRA)						
29 S. Testud (FRA)	Testud 6-3 6-1					
30 N. Muns-Jagerman (NED)						
31 B. Ritter (AUT) (Q)	**CAPRIATI** (5) 6-2 6-2					
32 **J. CAPRIATI** (USA) (5)						
33 **G. SABATINI** (ARG) (3)	**SABATINI** (3) 6-0 6-0	**SABATINI** (3) 6-0 6-1	**SABATINI** (3) 6-1 6-3	**SABATINI** (3) 6-3 6-1	**SABATINI** (3) 3-6 6-3 6-2	
34 S. Farina (ITA)						
35 M. Javer (GBR)	Cecchini	Halard 6-1 6-2				
36 S. Cecchini (ITA)						
37 B. Fulco-Villella (ARG)	Halard 6-2 6-4					
38 J. Halard (FRA)						
39 R. Fairbank-Nideffer (USA)	Fairbank-Nideffer 3-6 6-4 6-2	Hy 7-6 6-0	Hy 6-0 7-5			
40 K. Po (USA)						
41 I. Spirlea (ROM) (Q)	Hy 6-2 4-6 2-1 ab.					
42 P. Hy (CAN)						
43 C. Lindqvist (SWE)	Gomer 7-5 6-4	Brioukhovets 4-6 6-4 6-1				
44 S. Gomer (GBR)						
45 E. Brioukhovets (UKR)	Brioukhovets 6-1 6-2					
46 K. Boogert (NED) (Q)						
47 P. Paradis-Mangon (FRA)	**MALEEVA** (11) 6-1 6-4	**MESKHI** (15) 6-1 6-1	**MESKHI** (15) 1-6 7-6 6-4	**MARTINEZ** (7) 6-4 7-5		
48 **A. MALEEVA** (BUL) (11)						
49 **L. MESKHI** (GEO) (15)	**MESKHI** (15) 6-1 6-3					
50 L. Garrone (ITA)						
51 F. Bonsignori (ITA)	Bonsignori 6-3 6-4	Ferrando 6-4 6-4				
52 N. Herreman (FRA)						
53 N. Niox-Chateau (FRA)	Bowes 7-5					
54 B. Bowes (USA)						
55 L. Ferrando (ITA)	Ferrando 6-1 6-3	Grossman 6-4 6-4	**MARTINEZ** (7) 6-2 6-2			
56 R. Reggi-Concato (ITA)						
57 P. Fendick (USA)	Grossman 6-3 6-3					
58 A. Grossman (USA)						
59 K. Nowak (POL)	Probst 7-5 6-0	**MARTINEZ** (7) 6-2 6-0				
60 W. Probst (GER)						
61 E. Sviglerova (TCH)	Martinek 6-2 6-1					
62 K. Martinek (GER)						
63 L. Gildemeister (PER)	**MARTINEZ** (7) 6-2 7-6					
64 **C. MARTINEZ** (ESP) (7)						

6-2 3-6 10-8

M. SELES (YUG) (1)

Women's Singles — bottom half of draw

First round (players)

65 **M. MALEEVA-FRAGNIE** (SUI) (8)
66 H. Cioffi (USA)
67 D. Szabová (TCH) (LL)
68 B. Rittner (GER)
69 M. Bollegraf (NED)
70 E. Maniokova (ICIS)
71 J. Reynares (ARG) (Q)
72 P. Thoren (FIN)
73 S. Wasserman (BEL) (Q)
74 R. Hiraki (JPN)
75 C. Cunningham (USA)
76 D. Faber (USA)
77 S. Amiach (FRA) (WC)
78 G. Helgeson (USA)
79 I. Gorrochategui (ARG)
80 **N. TAUZIAT** (FRA) (12)
81 **K. DATE** (JPN) (14)
82 N. Sawamatsu (JPN)
83 S. Olivier (FRA) (WC)
84 S. Meier (GER)
85 K. Piccolini (ITA)
86 J. Byrne (AUS)
87 I. Demongeot (FRA)
88 M. Endo (JPN)
89 A. Frankl (GER)
90 C. Suire (FRA) (WC)
91 F. Labat (ARG)
92 J. Wiesner (AUT)
93 E. Zardo (SUI)
94 K. Li (CHN)
95 K. Oellekilaus (GER)
96 **A. SANCHEZ-VICARIO** (ESP) (4)
97 **M. FERNANDEZ** (USA) (6)
98 P. Langrova (TCH) (LL)
99 S. Stafford (USA) (Q)
100 K. Rinaldi (USA)
101 P. Tarabini (ARG)
102 S. Hack (GER)
103 M. de Swardt (RSA)
104 A. Zugasti (FRA) (WC)
105 M. Maleeva (BUL)
106 N. Provis (AUS)
107 J. Allen (USA)
108 D. Monami (BEL)
109 N. Zvereva (CIS)
110 C. Kohde-Kilsch (GER)
111 F. Whitlinger (USA)
112 **S. APPELMANS** (BEL) (16)
113 **J. NOVOTNA** (TCH) (10)
114 D. Graham (USA)
115 N. Medvedeva (UKR)
116 M. Babel (GER)
117 C. Rubin (USA)
118 B. Schultz (NED)
119 M. Paz (ARG)
120 A. Frazier (USA)
121 S. Dopfer (AUT) (Q)
122 N. Guerre (FRA) (WC)
123 A. Coetzer (RSA)
124 A. Dechaume (FRA)
125 N. Housset (FRA) (WC)
126 S. Wang (TPE)
127 R. Simpson-Alter (CAN)
128 **S. GRAF** (GER) (2)

Second round

MALEEVA-FRAGNIE (8) 6-4 7-6
Rittner 6-3 6-3
Bollegraf 6-2 6-3
Thoren 6-4 4-6 8-6
Wasserman 7-5 6-3
Faber 6-2 0-6 6-3
Helgeson 6-4 5-7 6-4
TAUZIAT (12) 7-5 6-4
DATE (14) 6-2 6-7 6-3
Meier 6-3 6-3
Piccolini 3-6 7-6 6-2
Endo 6-1 6-2
Frankl 6-4 6-3
Wiesner 6-2 6-3
Zardo 6-0 6-2
SANCHEZ-VICARIO (4) 6-0 6-2
FERNANDEZ (6) 6-3 6-1
Stafford 6-3 2-6 6-3
Hack 6-3 6-0
de Swardt 6-2 6-4
Maleeva 6-2 6-4
Allen 5-7 6-4 6-3
Zvereva 6-2 6-3
APPELMANS (16) 6-4 6-3
NOVOTNA (10) 6-3 6-2
Medvedeva 6-4 6-4
Schultz 6-2 5-7 6-4
Frazier 6-2 3-6 6-4
Dopfer 7-6 1-6 6-3
Coetzer 6-4 3-6 6-3
Housset 4-6 6-4 9-7
GRAF (2) 6-3 6-1

Third round

MALEEVA-FRAGNIERE (8) 5-7 6-1 6-2
Bollegraf 6-2 4-6 7-5
Wasserman 7-5 6-4
TAUZIAT (12) 3-6 6-1 6-3
DATE (14) 4-6 6-4 6-3
Endo 7-6 6-0
Wiesner 6-3 6-2
SANCHEZ-VICARIO (4) 6-3 6-1
FERNANDEZ (6) 6-1 6-4
Hack 0-6 6-4 6-4
Maleeva 4-6 7-6 6-1
Zvereva 6-1 7-6
NOVOTNA (10) 6-4 6-1
Schultz 6-1 3-6 6-2
Coetzer 7-6 4-6 6-3
GRAF (2) 6-2 6-1

Fourth round

Bollegraf 7-5 6-2
TAUZIAT (12) 6-4 6-2
DATE (14) 6-3 6-2
SANCHEZ-VICARIO (4) 6-1 6-2
Hack 7-6 6-2
Zvereva 6-4 6-4
NOVOTNA (10) 6-3 6-4
GRAF (2) 6-1 6-4

Round of 16

Bollegraf 6-4 1-6 6-2
SANCHEZ-VICARIO (4) 6-3 6-2
Zvereva 6-3 6-3
GRAF (2) 6-1 6-4

Quarter-finals

SANCHEZ-VICARIO (4) 6-2 6-3
GRAF (2) 6-1 6-4

Semi-final

GRAF (2) 6-3 6-7 6-3

Final

GRAF (2) 0-6 6-2 6-2

MEN'S DOUBLES

Holders: J. Fitzgerald (AUS)/A. Jarryd (SWE)

Winner: HLASEK (SUI)/ROSSET (SUI) — 7-6 6-7 7-5

FIRST ROUND

1 FITZGERALD/JARRYD (1)
2 Schapers/Vacek
3 Guerici/Van Rensburg
4 Albano/Motta
5 Bates/Broad
6 Goellner/Pozzi
7 Gomez/Sanchez
8 GALBRAITH/P. McENROE (15)
9 DEVRIES/MACPHERSON (10)
10 Boetsch/Fleurian (WC)
11 Agassi/J. McEnroe (WC)
12 Nelson/Stoltenberg
13 Costing/Siemerink
14 Briggs/Kronemann
15 Poline/Raoux (WC)
16 FLACH/WITSKEN (7)
17 JONES/LEACH (4)
18 Aldrich/Visser
19 Adams/Olhovskiy
20 Camporese/Ivanisevic
21 Nargiso/Riglewski
22 Dyke/Lundgren
23 Haarhuis/Koevermans
24 KINNEAR/SALUMAA (14)
25 JENSEN/WARDER (11)
26 Bathman/Bergh
27 Borwick/Youl
28 Forget/Leconte
29 Jonsson/Rahnasto
30 Garnett/Svantesson
31 Mratz/Oncins
32 NIJSSEN/SUK (5)
33 DAVIS/PATE (6)
34 Hlasek/Rosset
35 Keil/Randall
36 Beckman/Brown
37 Limberger/Zdrazila
38 Damm/Riki
39 Davids/Pimek
40 FRANA/LAVALLE (12)
41 KORDA/SANCHEZ (13)
42 Korda/Pugh
43 Cannon/Van Emburgh
44 Fleig/Prinosil
45 Carbonell/Roig
46 Montana/Thorne
47 Chamberlin/Santoro (WC)
48 CONNELL/MICHIBATA (3)
49 FERREIRA/NORVAL (8)
50 Bloom/Wekesa
51 Shelton/Stolle
52 Kruger/Layendecker
53 Black/Cahill
54 Delaitre/Gilbert (WC)
55 Minussi/Perez
56 GRABB/RENEBERG (9)
57 KRATZMANN/MASUR (16)
58 Eltingh/Kempers
59 Pic/Wheaton
60 Aciolv/Menezes
61 Palmer/Wheaton
62 Pearce/Talbot
63 Glavel/Lozano
64 WOODBRIDGE/WOODFORDE (2)

SECOND ROUND

- FITZGERALD/JARRYD (1) — 6-3 6-3
- Albano/Motta — 6-4
- Bates/Broad — 6-4 3-6 6-3
- GALBRAITH/P. McENROE (15) — 6-4 6-3
- DEVRIES/MACPHERSON (10) — 4-6 6-4 6-3
- Agassi/J. McEnroe — 6-3 6-2
- Briggs/Kronemann
- FLACH/WITSKEN (7) — 6-4 6-4
- Aldrich/Visser — 7-6 7-5
- Adams/Olhovskiy
- Dyke/Lundgren — 7-6 6-2
- KINNEAR/SALUMAA (14) — 6-7 6-3 8-6
- JENSEN/WARDER (11) — 6-4 6-2
- Forget/Leconte — 7-6 6-3
- Garnett/Svantesson — 6-3 6-4
- NIJSSEN/SUK (5) — 4-6 6-3 6-4
- Hlasek/Rosset
- Keil/Randall — 6-4 6-3
- Limberger/Zdrazila — 1-6 6-4 6-3
- FRANA/LAVALLE (12) — 6-3 6-1
- Korda/Pugh
- Fleig/Prinosil — 1-6 7-6 9-7
- Carbonell/Roig
- CONNELL/MICHIBATA (3) — 3-6 6-3 6-4
- FERREIRA/NORVAL (8) — 7-6 7-6
- Kruger/Layendecker
- Delaitre/Gilbert — 6-4 7-5
- GRABB/RENEBERG (9)
- KRATZMANN/MASUR (16) — 6-4 1-6 6-4
- Eltingh/Kempers — 6-4 7-5
- Palmer/Wheaton — 6-3 3-6 10-8
- WOODBRIDGE/WOODFORDE (2) — 6-3 6-2

THIRD ROUND

- Albano/Motta — 7-6 5-7 7-5
- GALBRAITH/P. McENROE (15) — 7-5 7-5
- Agassi/J. McEnroe — 6-4 7-5
- Briggs/Kronemann — 7-6 7-6
- Adams/Olhovskiy — 6-4 4-6 6-4
- Dyke/Lundgren — 6-4 6-7 6-3
- JENSEN/WARDER (11) — 7-6 6-4
- Garnett/Svantesson — 7-6 6-1
- Hlasek/Rosset — 6-2 7-5
- Frana/Lavalle — 6-4 6-3
- Korda/Pugh — 6-2 6-4
- Carbonell/Roig — 7-5 6-3
- FERREIRA/NORVAL (8) — 7-6 6-4
- GRABB/RENEBERG (9) — 6-1 7-6
- KRATZMANN/MASUR (16) — 6-7 6-4 6-4
- WOODBRIDGE/WOODFORDE (2) — 6-2 6-7 6-4

QUARTER-FINALS

- Albano/Motta — 6-4 7-6
- Agassi/J. McEnroe — 6-2 6-1
- Adams/Olhovskiy — 6-7 6-3 7-5
- JENSEN/WARDER (11) — 7-6 6-2
- Hlasek/Rosset — 6-3 6-7 6-4
- Korda/Pugh — 4-6 6-4 6-1
- GRABB/RENEBERG (9) — 6-3 3-6 6-4
- KRATZMANN/MASUR (16) — 6-4 4-6 6-3

SEMI-FINALS

- Albano/Motta — 6-4 7-6
- Adams/Olhovskiy — 6-2 6-3
- Hlasek/Rosset — 6-0 6-4
- KRATZMANN/MASUR (16) — 6-0 6-3

FINAL

- Adams/Olhovskiy — 6-3 6-7 6-3
- Hlasek/Rosset — 6-7 6-4 9-7

HLASEK (SUI)/ROSSET (SUI) — 7-6 6-7 7-5

Capital letters denote seeded pairings. Number following player's name gives seeding order (Q) – Qualifier, (WC) – Wild Card, (LL) – Lucky Loser.

WOMEN'S DOUBLES

Holders: G. Fernandez (USA)/J. Novotna (TCH)

Winner: G. FERNANDEZ (USA)/ZVEREVA (CIS) (2) — 6-3 6-2

FIRST ROUND

1. NOVOTNA/SAVCHENKO-NEILAND (1)
2. Nohejlova/Reichtova
3. Faull/Richardson
4. Segura/Souto
5. Date/Kidowaki
6. Muns-Jageman/Schultz
7. Harvey-Wild/Stubbs
8. MESKHI/PAZ (10)
9. PIERCE/TARABINI (14)
10. Benjamin/Santrock
11. Fulco-Villella/Simpson-Alter
12. Kiene/Oremans
13. Langova/Zrubakova
14. Lindstrom
15. Etchemendy/Sabas (WC)
16. COLLINS/REINACH (7)
17. MARTINEZ/SANCHEZ-VICARIO (4)
18. Cecchini/Gildemeister
19. Broukhovets/Medvedeva
20. Bobkova/Ruano
21. Habsudova/Smoller
22. May/Po
23. Farina/Fernando
24. APPELMANS/PORWIK (12)
25. KOHDE-KILSCH/WIESNER (16)
26. Driehuis/Van Lottum
27. Housset/Niox-Chateau (WC)
28. Glitz/Kuhlman
29. Fuchs/Strandlund
30. Kschwendt/Labat
31. Caverzasio/Herreman
32. McNEIL/PROVIS (6)
33. HETHERINGTON/RINALDI (8)
34. Hodder/Pospisilova
35. Gatono/Golarsa
36. Field/Sharpe
37. Novelo/Radford
38. Graf/Huber
39. Amiach/Fusai (WC)
40. FENDICK/STRNADOVA (9)
41. DEMONGEOT/TAUZIAT (13)
42. Guse/Pleming
43. Cunningham/Whitinger
44. Godridge/Woolcock
45. Maleeva/Maleeva-Fragniere
46. Phil/Suire
47. Morton/Wood
48. M.J. FERNANDEZ/GARRISON (3)
49. ADAMS/BOLLEGRAF (5)
50. Paradis-Mangon/Testud
51. Burgin/de Swardt
52. Keller/Sawamatsu
53. Dechaume/Halard
54. Bowes/Emmons
55. Babel/Probst
56. MALEEVA/RITTNER (15)
57. FAIRBANK-NIDEFFER/REGGI-CONC (11)
58. Collet/Guerree (WC)
59. Coetzer/Gorrochategui
60. Graham/Helgeson
61. Frazier/Pirila
62. Jaggard-Lai/Vis
63. Stafford/Wendel
64. G. FERNANDEZ/ZVEREVA (2)

SECOND ROUND

- NOVOTNA/SAVCHENKO (1) — 6-1 6-1
- Segura/Souto — 1-6 6-3 6-4
- Muns-Jageman/Schultz — 6-1 7-5
- Harvey-Wild/Stubbs — 6-1 6-2
- PIERCE/TARABINI (14) — 6-4 6-1
- Kiene/Oremans — 6-2 6-1
- Langova/Zrubakova — 6-4 7-6
- Collins/Reinach — 6-2 6-0
- MARTINEZ/SANCHEZ (4) — 6-2 6-1
- Broukhovets/Medvedeva — 6-2 6-2
- May/Po — 6-4 6-2
- APPELMANS/PORWIK (12) — 6-1 6-2
- Driehuis/Van Lottum — 6-0 2-1 ab
- Glitz/Kuhlman — 6-4 6-4
- Kschwendt/Labat — 6-7 6-1 13-11
- McNEIL/PROVIS (6) — 6-1 6-1
- HETHERINGTON/RINALDI (8) — 6-1 4-6 6-1
- Field/Sharpe — 6-2 5-7 6-2
- Graf/Huber — 6-1 6-3
- FENDICK/STRNADOVA (9) — 7-5 6-3
- DEMONGEOT/TAUZIAT (13) — 6-4 6-3
- Godridge/Woolcock — 6-4 7-6
- Pfaff/Suire
- Morton/Wood — 7-5 3-6 8-2
- ADAMS/BOLLEGRAF (5) — 6-4 6-3
- Burgin/de Swardt
- Dechaume/Halard — 6-0 6-2
- MALEEVA/RITTNER (15) — 6-1 6-3
- FAIRBANK/REGGI (11) — 6-1 6-3
- Coetzer/Gorrochategui — 1-6 6-0 8-6
- Jaggard-Lai/Vis
- G. FERNANDEZ/ZVEREVA (2) — 6-3 6-4

THIRD ROUND

- NOVOTNA/SAVCHENKO (1) — 6-2 6-0
- Harvey-Wild/Stubbs — 4-6 7-6 6-4
- PIERCE/TARABINI (14) — 7-6 6-3
- Collins/Reinach — 6-4 4-6 6-4
- MARTINEZ/SANCHEZ (4) — 6-1 6-1
- APPELMANS/PORWIK (12) — 6-4 6-2
- Driehuis/Van Lottum — 6-2 6-3
- McNEIL/PROVIS (6) — 6-2 6-3
- HETHERINGTON/RINALDI (8) — 7-6 6-2
- Graf/Huber — 6-1 6-4
- DEMONGEOT/TAUZIAT (13) — 6-7 7-6 6-2
- Morton/Wood — 7-5 6-2
- ADAMS/BOLLEGRAF (5) — 4-6 6-4 6-3
- MALEEVA/RITTNER (15) — 6-1 6-4
- FAIRBANK/REGGI (11) — wo
- G. FERNANDEZ/ZVEREVA (2) — 6-3 6-2

QUARTER-FINALS

- NOVOTNA/SAVCHENKO (1) — 6-4 7-6
- PIERCE/TARABINI (14) — 3-6 6-3 6-1
- MARTINEZ/SANCHEZ (4) — 6-1 6-3
- McNEIL/PROVIS (6) — 7-6 6-2
- Graf/Huber — 6-3 6-4
- Demongeot/Tauziat — 2-6 7-6 6-2
- ADAMS/BOLLEGRAF (5) — 6-2 6-3
- G. FERNANDEZ/ZVEREVA (2) — 6-1 6-1

SEMI-FINALS

- NOVOTNA/SAVCHENKO (1) — 6-3 6-4
- MARTINEZ/SANCHEZ (4) — 6-3 6-4
- Graf/Huber — 6-4 6-1
- G. FERNANDEZ/ZVEREVA (2) — 6-3 6-4

FINAL

- MARTINEZ/SANCHEZ-VICARIO (4) — 6-3 6-2
- G. FERNANDEZ/ZVEREVA (2) — 6-0 6-1

Winner: G. FERNANDEZ/ZVEREVA (2) — 6-3 6-2

Capital letters denote seeded pairings. Number following player's name gives seeding order (Q) – Qualifier, (WC) – Wild Card, (LL) – Lucky Loser.

MIXED DOUBLES

Holders: C. Suk (TCH)/H. Sukova (TCH)

Winner: SANCHEZ-VICARIO (ESP)/WOODBRIDGE (AUS) (2) 6–2 6–3

FIRST ROUND	SECOND ROUND	THIRD ROUND	QUARTER-FINALS	SEMI-FINALS	FINAL
1 NOVOTNA/FITZGERALD (1)	NOVOTNA/FITZGERALD (1)				
2 bye		McNeil/Shelton			
3 McNeil/Shelton	McNeil/Shelton 2–6 7–6 6–3	7–6 6–3			
4 Vij/Kemers			McNeil/Shelton		
5 Meskhi/Dzelde	Meskhi/Dzelde		6–7 7–6 6–4		
6 Probst/Randall	3–6 7–6 7–5	FENDICK/DEVRIES (10)			
7 bye		6–2 7–5		McNeil/Shelton	
8 FENDICK/DEVRIES (10)	FENDICK/DEVRIES (10)			6–4 6–4	
9 STUBBS/WARDER (14)	STUBBS/WARDER (14)				
10 bye		Stubbs/Warder			
11 Oremans/Ettingh	Oremans/Ettingh 7–5 6–4	7–6 7–5			
12 Tarabini/Albano			HETHERINGTON/MICHIBATA (7)		
13 Labat/Frana	Labat/Frana		7–6 7–6 6–1		
14 Harvey-Wild/Flach	6–2 6–2	HETHERINGTON/MICHIBATA (7)			McNeil/Shelton
15 bye		7–5 6–3			6–3 6–3
16 HETHERINGTON/MICHIBATA (7)	HETHERINGTON/MICHIBATA (7)				
17 SAVCHENKO-NEILAND/SUK (3)	SAVCHENKO/SUK (3)				
18 bye		SAVCHENKO/SUK (3)			
19 Whitinger/Galbraith	Whitinger/Galbraith	6–2 6–2			
20 Housset/Raoux (WC)	6–4 6–2		SAVCHENKO/SUK (3)		
21 Benjamin/Kinnear			6–7 6–2 6–3		
22 Wood/Beckman	Wood/Beckman	Wood/Beckman			
23 bye	6–3 6–2	6–2 6–1		BOLLEGRAF/NIJSSEN (6)	
24 COLLINS/NORVAL (11)	COLLINS/NORVAL (11)			4–6 6–3 6–4	
25 DEMONGEOT/TALBOT (16)	DEMONGEOT/TALBOT (16)				
26 bye		Faull/Salumaa			
27 Faull/Salumaa	Faull/Salumaa 6–3 7–6	6–4 3–6 6–1			
28 Bowes/Pearce			BOLLEGRAF/NIJSSEN (6)		
29 Langrova/Pimek	Langrova/Pimek		6–2 6–4		
30 Field/Oosting	6–4 6–3	BOLLEGRAF/NIJSSEN (6)			
31 bye		6–3 6–2			
32 BOLLEGRAF/NIJSSEN (6)	BOLLEGRAF/NIJSSEN (6)				
33 FERNANDEZ/JONES (5)	FERNANDEZ/JONES (5)				
34 bye		Pierce/Palmer			
35 Schultz/Schapers	Pierce/Palmer	6–4 7–6			
36 Pierce/Palmer (WC)	7–6 3–6 6–3		Pierce/Palmer		
37 Fairbank/Jensen			6–2 6–7 6–4		
38 Fairbank-Nideffer/Aldrich	Fairbank/Aldrich				
39 bye	6–3 7–6	ADAMS/WITSKEN (9)			
40 ADAMS/WITSKEN (9)	ADAMS/WITSKEN (9)	6–4 6–2		PROVIS/WOODFORDE (4)	
41 PAZ/MacPHERSON (12)	PAZ/MacPHERSON (12)			6–3 5–7 6–3	
42 bye		PAZ/MacPHERSON (12)			
43 Strandova/Stoltenberg	Sabatini/Motta	7–6 7–5			
44 Sabatini/Motta (WC)	7–5 6–3		PROVIS/WOODFORDE (4)		
45 Jaggard-Lai/Bergh			6–4 6–4		
46 Suire/Bathman	Suire/Bathman	PROVIS/WOODFORDE (4)			
47 bye	6–3 4–6 7–5	w/o			
48 PROVIS/WOODFORDE (4)	PROVIS/WOODFORDE (4)				SANCHEZ/WOODBRIDGE (2)
49 RINALDI/LEACH (8)	RINALDI/LEACH (8)				6–3 6–3
50 bye		RINALDI/LEACH (8)			
51 Testud/Simian (WC)	Maleeva/Lavalle	4–6 7–5 6–6			
52 Maleeva/Lavalle	6–4 6–4		ZVEREVA/KRATZMANN (13)		
53 Frazier/Kronemann			6–0 6–2		
54 Herreman/Bahrami (WC)	Frazier/Kronemann	ZVEREVA/KRATZMANN (13)			
55 bye	6–2 6–4	7–6 6–3		ZVEREVA/KRATZMANN (13)	
56 ZVEREVA/KRATZMANN (13)	ZVEREVA/KRATZMANN (13)			6–0 6–2	
57 REINACH/VISSER (15)	REINACH/VISSER (15)				
58 bye		Ponwik/Vacek			
59 Stafford/Brown	Porwik/Vacek	6–7 7–6 9–7			
60 Porwik/Vacek	6–2 6–2		SANCHEZ/WOODBRIDGE (2)		
61 Van Lottum/Davids			6–4 6–7 6–3		
62 Medvedeva/Lozano	Medvedeva/Lozano	SANCHEZ/WOODBRIDGE (2)			
63 bye	2–6 6–1 6–4	6–3 6–4			
64 SANCHEZ-VICARIO/WOODBRIDGE (2)	SANCHEZ/WOODBRIDGE (2)				

JUNIOR EVENTS

BOYS' SINGLES – *Final:* Andrei Pavel(ROM) d. Mose Navara(ITA) 6–1 3–6 6–3
GIRLS' SINGLES – *Final:* Rossana de los Rios(PAR) d. Paola Suarez(ARG) 6–4 6–0
BOYS' DOUBLES – *Final:* Enrique Araboa(MEX)/Grant Doyle(AUS) d. Euguéni Kafelnikov(CIS)/Alexandru Radulescu(ROM)
GIRLS' DOUBLES – *Final:* Laurence Courtois(BEL)/Nancy Feber(BEL)(1) d. Lindsay Davenport(USA)/Chanda Rubin(USA)(2) 6–1 5–7 6–4

FRENCH OPEN CHAMPIONSHIPS PRIZE MONEY — 41,425,000FF

MEN – Total: 21,994,000FF plus Per Diem allowances 1,250,000FF
MEN'S SINGLES – Winner 2,680,000FF. Runner-up 1,340,000FF. Semi-finalists 670,000FF. Quarter-finalists 350,000FF. Fourth-round losers 189,000FF. Third-round losers 109,000FF. Second-round losers 67,000FF. First-round losers 40,000FF.
Total: 14,720,000FF
MEN'S DOUBLES (per team) – Winners 1,100,000FF. Runners-up 550,000FF. Semi-finalists 275,000FF. Quarter-finalists 140,000FF. Third-round losers 80,000FF. Second-round losers 40,000FF. First-round losers 27,000FF.
Total: 4,904,000FF
WOMEN – Total: 18,222,000FF plus Per Diem allowance 1,250,000FF
WOMEN'S SINGLES – Winner 2,470,000FF. Runner-up 1,235,000FF. Semi-finalists 617,000FF. Quarter-finalists 310,000FF. Fourth-round losers 162,000FF. Third-round losers 90,000FF. Second-round losers 53,000FF. First-round losers 33,500FF.
Total: 12,755,000FF
WOMEN'S DOUBLES (per team) – Winners 865,000FF. Runners-up 432,000FF. Semi-finalists 216,000FF. Quarter-finalists 110,000FF. Third-round losers 56,000FF. Second-round losers 30,000FF. First-round losers 17,500FF.
Total: 3,657,000FF
MIXED DOUBLES (per team) – Winners 242,000FF. Runners-up 145,000FF. Semi-finalists 87,000FF. Quarter-finalists 53,200FF. Second-round losers 29,000FF. First-round losers 12,700FF.
Total 1,209,000FF
QUALIFYING – MEN(each): 16 x Third-round losers 23,000FF. 32 x Second-round losers 11,500FF. 64 x First-round losers 6,000FF.
Total: 1,120,000FF
QUALIFYING – WOMEN(each): 8 x Third-round losers 23,000FF. 16 x Second-round losers 11,500FF. 32 x First-round losers 6,000FF.

Andre Agassi won his first Grand Slam title at Wimbledon, a victory that also won him the admiration of his girlfriend Wendy. *(M. Cole)*

THE CHAMPIONSHIPS – WIMBLEDON

John Barrett

The 22-year-old American, Andre Agassi, and Germany's defending champion, Steffi Graf, 23, were the victors at the 1992 Championships, where the prize money totalled a record £4,416,820. For Agassi, the booming baseliner, it was an improbable but glorious first Grand Slam triumph; for Graf a fourth success on the fast grass and her 11th Grand Slam title. It was also an imperious reminder of her sterling qualities of athleticism and groundstroke control.

Each, in their own way, had something to prove, and each had a personal mountain to climb. Agassi, competing at Wimbledon for only the third time, had to quell the haunting fear that he was not, after all the great player he was supposed to be. Failure in three Grand Slam finals, two in Paris one in New York, had gnawed away at the self-confidence upon which every champion depends.

For Graf it was also a matter of confidence, a matter of proving that on grass at least, she is still the equal of Monica Seles who had usurped her position as the world's No.1 player and thwarted her in a magnificent French final the previous month.

The 106th Championship for men and the 99th for women opened in a blaze of sunshine that illuminated some fine performances during a hectic first week. There were 25 Americans, 12 Germans, 11 Australians and 10 Frenchmen among the 128 men from 25 different countries challenging for the first prize of 265,000. Of the seven Britons in the draw, six were wild cards. Only the British No.1, Jeremy Bates, had earned inclusion on merit. How fitting it was that Bates should have scored the first big upset of the meeting by defeating the No.7 seed, Michael Chang in straight sets in the first round! How astonishing it was (to everyone except Jeremy and his fiancee Ruth, of course) that he should have maintained the impetus to dismiss both Javier Sanchez and Thierry Champion before falling heroically in five sets to the Frenchman Guy Forget, seeded No.9.

This was an absorbing battle between Forget's swinging left-handed serve and Bates' piercing backhand returns. As long as Bates could maintain the pressure on his own serve, where he was volleying with commendable authority, he was in with a chance. When the wiry Briton built a two sets to one lead and held a match point on his own serve at 5-3 in the fourth, you could feel the tension that came over the Centre Court as 13,000 supporters held their breath. The silence un-nerved Bates. He caught the ball on his first toss and then served a fault. The second, too short, was dealt with summarily by a grateful Forget. Afterwards Bates explained: 'Somebody sneezed, or something...it was so quiet you could hear a pin drop. I'm very, very disappointed. It's not every day you get the chance to reach the quarters at Wimbledon.' he said. Even in defeat, this was the finest performance by an Englishman at Wimbledon since Roger Taylor reached the quarter-finals in 1973.

Before the tournament began, the experts agreed that the men's winner would come from the small group of grass court experts who had proved their worth on the surface. Boris Becker, seeded 4 and three times the champion, seemed to have regained his zest for the game. After a disappointing first half of the year, Stefan Edberg, the No.2 seed and a two-time winner, had timed his effort perfectly, according to his coach Tony Pickard. The holder Michael Stich, seeded 3, had come fresh from grass court success in Rosmalen while America's Pete Sampras, seeded 5, had set his heart on emulating his US Open success of 1990. The Croatian left-hander, Goran Ivanisevic, seeded 8, was full of confidence after fine-tuning his serve with the help of his coach Bob Brett. By general consent, it had become the fiercest delivery ever to appear at Wimbledon.

The fancied five all came safely through to the quarter-finals. The official favourite, Jim Courier, did not. Already the holder of the Australian and French titles, the competitive American had had his supporters, too. But they were as puzzled as the world No.1 himself by the manner of his surprising exit in the third round at the hands of the little-known Russian qualifier, 26-year-old Andrei Olhovskiy, ranked a lowly 193. 'He simply outplayed me...I came up short, I have no excuses', said Courier. Nor, any longer, did he have dreams of a Grand Slam in 1992.

In the next round John McEnroe made short work of Olhovskiy to enter the quarter-finals for the 8th time since that spectacular debut in 1977 when, still eligible for the junior event, he had surged from the qualifying to the semis and taken a set from Connors. McEnroe, the only unseeded interloper this time, went through to that stage again with a skilful display against Forget who could win no sets from his fellow left-hander. The 33-year-old American was looking good on the firmer Wimbledon courts which had been beautifully prepared by Eddie Seaward and his team. It was apparent that the ground staff had not spared the heavy roller and, because the ball was bouncing higher, there were fewer upsets. The top men could swing through the ball with confidence.

This factor became apparent as Agassi began to believe in himself. Augmenting his control of the baseline with some wonderful serving, as well as some judicious forays to the net, Agassi disposed of Chesnokov and Masso, each in four sets, before carving up two good fast court men – Rostagno and Saceanu – without loss. Against Becker in the quarter-finals, Agassi was awesome. On this evidence one could understand how he had won his last five meetings against the German No.1. Agassi's timing on flashing forehand and deadly double-handed backhand was miraculous. Standing in to take serve, the American was firing back Becker's finest deliveries almost before the German had completed his swing. It was the same on Becker's approach shots. In a flurry of whirling arms and legs, Agassi would smite the ball so hard that Becker was left groping at thin air. My lasting memory of this match is of the look of total disbelief on Becker's face as, time after time, the ball flashed beyond his reach.

It was the same in Agassi's winning semi-final against McEnroe. The former champion was made to look slow and ponderous by the severity of Agassi's counter-hitting as he swept the former champion aside 6–4 6–2 6–3. There was no time for tantrums. As John admitted '...he probably returns serve better than anyone ever has.'

The progress of Ivanisevic in the lower half of the draw was equally impressive. In quick succession the 6ft 4inch Croatian thundered his way past Koslowski, Woodforde and Rosset for the loss of only one set. He then received a default when Ivan Lendl, trailing by one set to two, lost his opening serve in the fourth set and announced that his injured back made it impossible for him to continue. It was another Wimbledon cross to bear for a man who has twice been a finalist but never the winner. I wonder if Ivan knew that this was his 13th challenge.

By this stage Ivanisevic had already served 104 aces – four more than Sampras had delivered in winning his US Open title two years earlier. In the quarter-finals he faced Edberg who the previous year had been beaten by Stich without ever losing his serve. This time the Swede would lose it once in the second set and twice in the third, before scoring a rare break against the Croatian to snatch the fourth set. It had become a magnificent, full-blooded scrap which boiled to an exciting climax as Ivanisevic broke for 5–3 with the help of a net cord and then saved a break point in the next game with his 32nd ace of the match. Another ace took him to match point and Edberg's final return fell long. It had lasted almost three hours on another overcast day but the crowd on No.1 Court had remained absorbed by the quality of Ivanisevic's serving and by the total commitment of both men. The most impressive aspect of the match was Ivanisevic's calmness under pressure. This was not the man who had lost moodily to Nick Brown 12 months earlier. 'I have changed a lot' agreed the winner. 'I'm much stronger in my mind now. I feel great on and off the court.'

In his semi-final against Sampras, played on Court No.1 because rain had interrupted the second week's programming, the same resolution was apparent. With two of the world's finest servers in opposition no-one expected to see many rallies. Nor were there many. Only three games went to deuce. Nevertheless, there was a certain fascination in seeing how both men coped with the frustration of being impotent for so much of the time. This calls for a very special mental quality. One foolish shot, one rash decision, can mean the difference between winning and losing. In the end Ivanisevic proved himself the stronger mentally. He was also the stronger server, his 36 aces answered by a mere 13 from the American who looked dejected as he went down in four sets. '...I had absolutely no idea where his serve was going. He's frustrating to play because you get no rhythm.'

The final became a battle of wills, the all-powerful serve of Ivanisevic (his 169 aces in six matches was a Wimbledon record) against Agassi's pace and deadly accuracy from the back of the court. But it was much more than that. Ivanisevic had already shown how effective he could be from the back of the court with drive and lob – especially on his well disguised two-handed backhand. Edberg knew all about that. Similarly, Agassi had become a shrewd volleyer, never attempting to overdo his advances but choosing the key moments to surprise his opponents.

Never was this ability more necessary than in the closing stages of this five-set thriller. Agassi had lost the opening set on a tie break, quite unable to deal with his opponent's lethal deliveries. It seemed likely that he would lose for a third time to the Croatian who had won their two previous meetings, both in 1991, on a hard court in Sydney and on an indoor carpet in Tokyo. Suddenly, in the second game of the second set, the American connected with four blazing returns of serve. At last he had achieved a break of serve. Thirty minutes later it was one set all.

Ivanisevic seemed mentally scarred, almost in a daze. Another lost service game at the start of the third set revealed his waning confidence. It gave Agassi just the chance he wanted. Losing only three point on his own serve, all in the 4th game, the American took a two sets to one lead and now seemed likely to race ahead to victory. But this complex plot had another twist. Suddenly Ivanisevic burst out of his mental straightjacket and tore into his smaller opponent with a frenzy that was astonishing. With the cheers of the crowd ringing in his ears he won the fourth set 6–1 in a bare 18 minutes. Agassi had been powerless against a barrage of heavy winners.   .

Who would crack first in the decider? It was a question Agassi's coach, Nick Bollettieri, was also asking himself in the courtside box. The key moment came when the American was trailing 3–4 and stood at 30–40 on his serve. To his eternal credit Agassi chose to follow his serve to the net and despatched a forehand volley with complete authority. It was the only chance Ivanisevic was given. Two games later, at 5–4 to Agassi, the Croatian delivered his sixth and seventh double faults of the match to signal sudden self-doubt. Two good serves brought him to 30–30 but the next rally ended with a typical pass form Agassi on the forehand. Now, if ever, Ivanisevic needed help from his most potent weapon. Already he had served 37 aces to bring his total for the Championship to a record-breaking 206. But in his hour of need the trusty cannon misfired. The first delivery ended in the bottom of the net; the second, without its usual bite, was returned, fast but waist high, to the centre of the court. The advancing server, still assailed by self-doubt, pushed at his backhand volley and saw it drop tamely into the net.

Agassi dropped to the ground and lay there face down for a moment, tearful with the sudden release of the tension he had so obviously felt during the past 2hrs 50mins. When he rose and advanced to the net with damp eyes Ivanisevic embraced him and sportingly acknowledged his superiority on the day. 'Listen man, you deserve it. You played great all these two weeks. Well done!'

Well done, indeed. Agassi was the seventh American to reach the final since the start of open tennis in 1968. He followed Stan Smith (1972), Arthur Ashe(1975), Jimmy Connors(1974, 1982), and John McEnroe (1981, 1983, 1984) as the fifth transatlantic champion. Agassi, seeded 12, was also the lowest seed ever to become champion. Both Jaroslav Drobny (1954) and Pat Cash (1987) had been seeded No.11. When the enormity of what he had achieved had sunk in Agassi was suitably humble. 'This tournament has offered me and my life so much, it's a shame I didn't respect it a little earlier' he said. 'If my career is over tomorrow, I have had a lot more than I deserved.'

There were 28 nations represented in the women's draw and, by a curious coincidence,

28 of the 128 competitors vying for a first prize of £240,000 were Americans. Was it an ominous sign for everyone else that there were 13 Germans? The German upon whom all eyes were focused was the No.2 seed Miss Graf. After two straightforward wins against Noelle Van Lottum and Marianne Werdel that cost her three games, the champion faced her first crisis. A few hours after Courier had bowed out unexpectedly on the Centre court on the middle Saturday, the hefty South African 21-year-old, Mariaan de Swardt, nearly provided the same fate for Graf. At 5–5 in the final set it was anyone's match but, to her credit, Graf did not flinch. Still pounding away with her forehand, she inched home 5–7 6–0 7–5 to reach the fourth round. There she dropped the opening set to America's Patty Fendick, the conqueror of 11th seeded Jana Novotna. Again, Graf pulled herself together after a jittery start and finished strongly to record a 4–6 6–3 6–2 win that made her a quarter-finalist for the sixth year in a row.

These two close encounters of the edgy kind seemed to calm the champion's nerves. As she moved through to her fifth final since 1987, we saw the best of Graf. Natalia Zvereva, the only unseeded quarter-finalist, who had beaten the 1990 finalist Zina Garrison, seeded 13, could manage only four games against a barrage of forehands and powerful serves while the 1991 finalist Gabriela Sabatini could muster only six. This was more like the Graf of 1988, the year she added an Olympic gold medal to her first Grand Slam.

The world champion, though, had been equally impressive. Monica Seles had lost only 24 games in moving through to the semi-finals for the first time in three visits. But in her quarter-final against Nathalie Tauziat were sown the seeds of her destruction. Towards the end of the match the Frenchwoman complained to the umpire about Seles' grunting. It was putting her off, she said. Noticeably quieter, Seles completed her 6–1 6–3 win but ran into a barrage of questions at her post-match press conference.

It was a can of worms which never should have been opened. There were many other players who grunted, among them Jimmy Connors, John McEnroe, Arantxa Sanchez and her brother Emilio. But the popular press in Britain had been building this story even before Wimbledon had begun, in fact ever since BBC television's coverage of the French Open final had exaggerated the decibel level of the Seles' grunt because of the sensitivity of the host broadcaster's courtside microphones. Now they turned it into a cause celebre.

To her shame, Martina Navratilova allowed herself to be swept along by the rising tide of false indignation. When, during her semi-final against Seles, she complained it clearly affected the No.1 seed. But it made no difference to the outcome. Seles duly won 6–2 6–7 6–4 and although she entered the final with her hopes of a Grand Slam still very much alive, the adverse comment had had its effect. After an agonizing private debate Seles attempted to remain silent. It robbed her of all intensity, ruined her timing and destroyed the very competitiveness which is central to her success.

So well did Graf play that Monica's reduced effectiveness might not have affected the issue. We shall never know. As it was the final was a non-event. It was also a gloomy occasion, interrupted three times by the squally showers which had dogged much of the second week. Graf's 6–2 6–1 will go down as one of the shortest finals on record. It lasted a bare 59 mins of playing time but ended 5hrs and 22mins after it had begun. Seles was too smart to fall into the trap of using the grunting issue as an excuse. 'I did not lose because I wasn't grunting,' she said. 'Steffi played too well today.'

No-one would disagree with that, least of all Steffi herself. 'I would definitely say this was one of my best matches. I knew I had the strokes and there's no doubt the surface suits me better than her. It's a great satisfaction to beat the No.1 player in the world the way I did.'

A memorable meeting ended with an unscheduled treat on the third Monday. The men's doubles final on Court No.1 had been stopped by failing light at 9.21pm the previous evening. At that stage the American No.4 seeds Jim Grabb and Richey Reneberg were 13–13 in the final set against the unseeded John McEnroe and Michael Stich. Already the Americans had failed on two match points on the Stich serve.

While the free seats on No.1 Court were filling up, the mixed doubles final (delayed by schedule congestion) was in progress. The fans enjoyed this expected bonus and applauded Cyril Suk and Larisa Savchenko Neiland as they imposed a 7–6 6–2 beating on the Dutch pair Jacco Eltingh and Miriam Oremans. Few of them realised the importance of this match to Mrs Savchenko Neiland. For her it was compensation for her loss with Jana Novotna in the final of the Ladies' Doubles to Gigi Fernandez and Natalia Zvereva.

By the time the men came to court all 6,500 seats were filled and the standing room was packed to capacity. For 34 thrilling, emotionally charged minutes the battle raged on. McEnroe was the general, nursing Stich through the tense moments with a jaunty, but deadly serious intensity. As the exuberant fans gave vent to their feelings, like schoolboys at an end of term party, the tennis sparkled. Finally McEnroe hoisted a winning lob with a complete miss-hit. It broke the tension and also spelt the end for their unfortunate opponents, beaten in the end 5–7 7–6 3–6 7–6 19–17. It was Wimbledon's longest doubles final, both in terms of games (83) and duration (5hrs 1min). It was also a great piece of Wimbledon theatre. The picture of Stich pushing his partner forward, cup held proudly aloft, to enjoy one more lap of honour will long remain in my memory. Among the delighted young fans, cheering and snapping their cameras, was McEnroe's 6-year-old son Kevin, there at courtside with his mother Tatum. In view of what lay in store in their private lives, this was a poignant moment.

As she had done in 1991, Steffi Graf kept a firm hold on the Wimbledon trophy in 1992. Her decisive victory over Monica Seles, who had displaced her as the world's No.1, was the German's 11th Grand Slam singles crown. (M. Cole)

MEN'S SINGLES

Holder: M. Stich (GER)

FIRST ROUND	SECOND ROUND	THIRD ROUND	FOURTH ROUND	QUARTER-FINALS	SEMI-FINALS	FINAL
1 **J. COURIER** (USA) (1)	**J. COURIER** (1)	**J. COURIER** (1)				
2 M. Zoecke (GER)	B. Black 6-2 7-5 6-1	6-4 6-1 6-4				
3 G. Fontang (FRA)	K. Kinnear		A. Olhovskiy			
4 B. Black (ZIM)		A. Olhovskiy	6-4 4-6 6-4 6-4			
5 C.-U. Steeb (GER)	A. Olhovskiy	6-4 7-6 6-3				
6 K. Kinnear (USA) (Q)	-6 6-4 6-6 3-6 7-5			J. P. McEnroe		
7 A. Olhovskiy (CIS) (Q)	P. Cash			7-5 6-3 7-6		
8 J. Stark (USA) (Q)	6-4 6-4 7-6	J. P. McEnroe				
9 P. Cash (AUS) (WC)	J. P. McEnroe	6-3 6-4 6-7 6-3 6-2	J. P. McEnroe			
10 J. Eltingh (NED)	5-7 6-1 6-3 6-3		6-3 6-4 6-4			
11 L. Mattar (BRA)	T. Mattar					
12 J. P. McEnroe (USA)		**D. WHEATON** (16)			J. P. McEnroe	
13 H. de la Pena (ARG)	**D. WHEATON** (16)	6-3 6-3 6-3			6-2 7-6 6-3	
14 J. Morgan (USA)	6-3 6-3 6-3					
15 F. Clavet (ESP)	**G. FORGET** (9)					
16 **D. WHEATON** (USA) (16)	6-3 3-6 7-5 7-6					
17 **G. FORGET** (FRA) (9)	**G. FORGET** (9)	**G. FORGET** (9)				
18 A. Mronz (GER)		4-6 6-3 3-6 6-3 10-8				
19 A. Jarryd (SWE)	A. Jarryd		**G. FORGET** (9)			
20 C. B. Bailey (GBR) (WC)	6-4 6-3 6-0		7-6 6-3 3-6 6-3			
21 B. Karbacher (GER)	B. Karbacher	H. Leconte				
22 R. Gilbert (FRA)	2-6 7-5 2-5 6-4 6-4	7-5 6-2 7-6				
23 R. Azar (ARG)	H. Leconte			**G. FORGET** (9)		
24 H. Leconte (FRA) (WC)	6-3 6-0 6-3			6-7 6-4 3-6 7-6 6-3		
25 K. Lavalle (MEX)	L. Lavalle					
26 A. N. Castle (GBR) (WC)	6-4 6-0 7-6	T. Champion				
27 R. A. Reneberg (USA)	T. Champion		M. J. Bates			
28 T. Champion (FRA)	5-7 6-4 3-6 7-6 6-3		7-5 6-4 6-7 4-6 6-4			
29 J. Sanchez (ESP)	J. Sanchez	M. J. Bates				
30 R. Raoux (FRA)	6-4 7-5 5-7 3-6 9-7	7-6 6-3 6-4				
31 J. Bates (GBR)	M. J. Bates					
32 **M. CHANG** (USA) (7)	**B. BECKER** (4)					
33 **B. BECKER** (GER) (4)	**B. BECKER** (4)	**B. BECKER** (4)				
34 O. Camporese (ITA)	7-5 6-3 6-3	4-6 6-4 3-6 6-3				
35 M. Damm (TCH)	M. Damm		**B. BECKER**			
36 C. Pridham (CAN)	6-4 6-4		6-4 3-6 7-6 7-6			
37 K. Curren (USA)		B. Shelton				
38 B. Shelton (USA)	B. Shelton	7-6 3-6 6-3				
39 R. Leach (USA) (Q)	3-6 7-6 4-6 7-6 9-7			**B. BECKER** (4)		
40 O. Delaitre (FRA)	O. Delaitre			3-6 6-3 6-4 6-7 6-1		
41 J. S. Connors (USA)	6-1 7-6 3-6 3-6 6-3					
42 L. Herrera (MEX)	L. Herrera	L. E. Herrera				
43 M. Washington (USA)	6-1 1-6 6-3	6-4 6-4 5-7 4-6 6-3				
44 S. Matsuoka (JPN)	S. Matsuoka		W. FERREIRA (14)			
45 C. J. Van Rensburg (RSA)	7-5 6-4 6-1		7-6 6-1 4-6 6-0			
46 J. Tarango (USA)	**W. FERREIRA** (14)					
47 J. B. Fitzgerald (AUS) (Q)	6-2 6-7 7-5	**W. FERREIRA** (14)			**A. AGASSI** (12)	
48 **W. FERREIRA** (RSA) (14)	**A. AGASSI** (12)	6-3 6-3 6-7 6-3			4-6 6-2 6-2 4-6 6-3	
49 **A. AGASSI** (USA) (12)	**A. AGASSI** (12)	**A. AGASSI** (12)				
50 A. Chesnokov (CIS)	5-7 6-1 7-5 7-5	4-6 6-1 6-3 6-3				
51 E. Masso (BEL)	E. Masso		**A. AGASSI** (12)			
52 N. Kroon (SWE) (Q)	6-4 6-2 2-6 6-4		6-3 7-6 7-5			
53 J. Yzaga (PER)	J. Yzaga	D. Rostagno				
54 M. Goriz (ESP)	6-4 6-4 6-2	6-3 6-3 6-1				
55 D. Rostagno (USA)	D. Rostagno			**A. AGASSI** (12)		
56 T. Carbonell (ESP)	2-6 6-1 6-1 6-2			7-6 6-1 7-6		
57 C. Pioline (FRA)	C. Pioline					
58 F. Roig (ESP)	6-3 6-3 7-5	C. Saceanu				
59 C. Saceanu (GER) (Q)	C. Saceanu	6-4 6-4 0-6 7-5 7-5	C. Saceanu			
60 G. Markus (ARG)	6-3 3-6 6-7		7-6 3-6 6-3 1-6 6-3			
61 J. Hlasek (SUI)	J. Hlasek	J. Hlasek				
62 M. Schapers (NED)		4-6 3-6 6-3 7-6 16-14				
63 C. Bergstrom (SWE)	**P. KORDA** (6)					
64 **P. KORDA** (TCH) (6)	7-5 7-6 6-4					

FINAL

A. AGASSI (12)
6-4 6-2 6-3

6-7 6-4 6-4 1-6 6-4

A. AGASSI (USA) (12)

Gentlemen's Singles — Draw (lower half)

Semi-final winner (advancing): G. IVANISEVIC (8) 6-7 7-6 4-6 6-2

Semi-final:
- P. SAMPRAS (5) — 6-3 6-2 6-4
- G. IVANISEVIC (8) — 6-7 7-6 1-3 6-3

Quarter-finals:
- P. SAMPRAS (5) — 6-3 7-5 7-6
- M. STICH (3) — 3-6 6-1 6-4 6-4
- G. IVANISEVIC (8) — 6-7 6-1 4-1-0 Ret
- S. EDBERG (2) — 6-3 6-4 6-7 6-3

Round 4:
- P. SAMPRAS (5) — 6-1 6-0 6-2
- A. Boetsch — 4-6 7-6 3-6 7-6 6-2
- W. Masur — 6-3 6-7 6-4 6-2
- M. STICH (3) — 6-4 6-1 6-3
- G. IVANISEVIC (8) — 7-6 6-4 6-4
- I. LENDL (10) — 6-3 1-6 2-6 3- 7-5
- H. Holm — 6-4 3-6 6-3 7-6
- S. EDBERG (2) — 6-1 6-0 6-2

Round 3:
- P. SAMPRAS (5) — 6-1 6-0 6-2
- S. E. Davis — 6-7 7-6 7-6 6-3
- A. Boetsch — 6-4 6-2 6-2
- R. KRAJICEK (11) — 7-6 6-3 6-1
- B. GILBERT (13) — 6-1 7-5 7-5
- W. Masur — 6-3 6-4 7-6
- M. Larsson — 7-5 6-3 6-7 6-4
- M. STICH (3) — 4-6 7-6 6-3 6-3
- G. IVANISEVIC (8) — 6-4 6-4 6-7 6-3
- M. Rosset — 7-6 6-2 6-3
- S. Stolle — 3-6 6-4 7-6 6-4
- I. LENDL (10) — 7-5 7-6 1-6 7-5
- A. VOLKOV (15) — 6-4 7-5 6-3
- H. Holm — 6-1 6-2 6-2
- G. Stafford — 6-4 7-6 2-6 6-2
- S. EDBERG (2) — 7-6 6-3 7-6

Round 2 (first-round winners):
- P. SAMPRAS (5) — 6-1 6-3 6-3
- T. A. Woodbridge — 6-2 7-5 6-4
- K. Braasch — 6-7 7-6 6-3
- F. Roig — 6-2 6-3 6-4
- S. E. Davis
- A. Boetsch — 6-3 7-5 6-4
- P. Haarhuis — 6-3 7-5 4-6 4-6 7-5
- R. KRAJICEK (11)
- B. GILBERT (13) — 6-2 6-3 6-2
- S. Youl
- W. Masur — 6-2 6-1
- M. Knowles — 6-2 6-1 6-3
- C. Costa — 6-1 4-6 5-7 6-3 6-3
- M. Larsson
- A. Mansdorf — 6-3 7-6 6-4
- M. STICH (3) — 6-3 6-3 6-2
- G. IVANISEVIC (8) — 6-3 6-2 3-6 7-5
- M. Woodforde
- M. Rosset — 6-2 6-4
- R. J. Petchey — 6-3 2-6 7-6
- S. Stolle — 7-5 7-6 Ret
- C. Wilkinson
- A. Thoms — 6-2 2-6 6-2 6-2
- I. LENDL (10)
- A. VOLKOV (15) — 6-4 6-4 6-3
- B. Stankovic — 6-2 6-4 6-3
- N. Kulti
- T. Holm — 6-0 6-0 6-1
- P. McEnroe
- G. Stafford — 6-4 6-1 6-1
- S. Bryan
- S. EDBERG (2) — 6-1 6-3 7-6

First-round entries (65–128):

65	**P. SAMPRAS** (USA) (5)
66	A. Cherkasov (CIS)
67	T. A. Woodbridge (AUS)
68	F. Roese (BRA) (LL)
69	D. Nargiso (ITA) (LL)
70	K. Braasch (GER)
71	C. Mezzadri (SUI)
72	F. Roig (ESP) (Q)
73	S. E. Davis (USA) (Q)
74	C. Minussi (ARG)
75	A. Boetsch (FRA)
76	J. Grabb (USA)
77	J. Stoltenberg (AUS)
78	P. Haarhuis (NED)
79	J.-L. De Jager (RSA) (Q)
80	**R. KRAJICEK** (NED) (11)
81	**B. GILBERT** (USA) (13)
82	J. P. Fleurian (FRA)
83	S. Youl (AUS)
84	R. Fromberg (AUS)
85	W. Masur (AUS)
86	L. Jonsson (SWE)
87	M. Koevermans (NED)
88	M. Knowles (BAH) (Q)
89	C. A. Limberger (AUS) (LL)
90	C. Costa (ESP)
91	J. Frana (ARG)
92	M. Larsson (SWE)
93	A. Naewie (GER)
94	A. Mansdorf (ISR)
95	S. Pescosolido (ITA)
96	**M. STICH** (GER) (3)
97	**G. IVANISEVIC** (CRO) (8)
98	K. Kosowski (GER)
99	M. Woodforde (AUS)
100	J. Siemerink (NED)
101	A. L. Richardson (GBR) (WC)
102	M. Rosset (SUI)
103	R. J. Petchey (GBR) (WC)
104	M. Randall (USA) (Q)
105	S. Stolle (AUS)
106	K. Novacek (TCH)
107	C. Wilkinson (GBR) (WC)
108	K. Pozzi (ITA)
109	A. Thoms (GER)
110	P. Kuhnen (GER)
111	**I. LENDL** (TCH) (10)
112	**A. VOLKOV** (CIS) (15)
113	E. Sanchez (ESP)
114	B. Stankovic (TCH) (Q)
115	A. L. Foster (GBR) (WC)
116	C. Lopez (ESP)
117	N. Kulti (SWE)
118	T. Holm (SWE) (Q)
119	J. Doyle (AUS)
120	P. McEnroe (USA)
121	F. Montana (USA)
122	G. Stafford (RSA) (LL)
123	T. Muster (AUT)
124	G. Muller (RSA)
125	M. Ondruska (RSA) (LL)
126	S. Bryan (USA) (Q)
127	A. Boetsch (FRA)
128	**S. EDBERG** (SWE) (2)

Capital letters denote seeded players. Number following player's name gives seeding order (Q) – Qualifier, (WC) – Wild Card, (LL) – Lucky Loser.

WOMEN'S SINGLES

Holder: S. Graf (GER)

6–2 6–1

FIRST ROUND	SECOND ROUND	THIRD ROUND	FOURTH ROUND	QUARTER-FINALS	SEMI-FINALS	FINAL

FIRST ROUND

1 M. SELES (YUG) (1)
2 J.M. Byrne (AUS)
3 M. Babel (GER)
4 S. Appelmans (BEL)
5 B. A. Bowes (USA)
6 L. Gildemeister (PER)
7 G. Helgeson (USA)
8 F. Li (CHN)
9 L. Savchenko-Neiland (LAT)
10 C. Porwik (GER)
11 S-A. Siddall (GBR) (WC)
12 D. Lake (GBR) (WC)
13 D. Faber (USA)
14 G. Fernandez (USA)
15 C. E. Kuhlman (USA)
16 K. DATE (JPN) (15)
17 N. TAUZIAT (FRA) (14)
18 B. Schultz (NED)
19 C. J. Wood (GBR) (WC)
20 N. Medvedeva (UKR)
21 N. Provis (AUS)
22 W. Probst (GER)
23 K. Zrubakova (TCH)
24 K. Oeljeklaus (GER)
25 L. K. Allen (USA)
26 S. L. Gomer (GBR)
27 A. Frazier (USA)
28 L. Golarsa (ITA)
29 A. Dahlman (FIN)
30 E. Maniokova (CIS)
31 S. L. Bentley (GBR)
32 M. J. FERNANDEZ (USA) (7)
33 M. NAVRATILOVA (USA) (4)
34 M. Maleeva (BUL)
35 K. Po (USA)
36 B. D. Simpson-Alter (CAN)
37 S. Frankl (GER)
38 E. Sviglerova (TCH)
39 B. Rittner (GER)
40 S. Wohlfinger (USA)
41 F. Labat (ARG)
42 Y. Basuki (INA)
43 S. Hack (GER)
44 P. Paradis-Mangon (FRA)
45 C. Tessi (ARG) (Q)
46 L. Ferrando (ITA)
47 L. Harland (RSA)
48 A. HUBER (GER) (10)
49 K. MALEEVA (BUL) (12)
50 C. Hall (GBR) (WC)
51 M. M. Bollegraf (NED)
52 C. Wegink (NED) (Q)
53 A. L. Grunfeld (GBR) (WC)
54 S. Meier (GER)
55 B. Fulco-Villella (ARG)
56 M. Endo (JPN)
57 J-A. Faull (AUS) (LL)
58 H. Sukova (TCH)
59 S. J. Loosemore (GBR) (WC)
60 A. Dechaume (FRA)
61 R. Rajchrtova (TCH)
62 J. Halard (FRA)
63 L. Meskhi (GEO)
64 A. SANCHEZ VICARIO (ESP) (5)

SECOND ROUND

M. SELES (1) 6–2 6–2
S. Appelmans 6–0 6–2
L. Gildemeister 6–0 6–2
G. Helgeson 6–1 6–2
C. Porwik
S-A. Siddall 6–4 6–3
G. Fernandez 6–4 4–6 6–3
K. DATE (15) 7–6 6–2
N. TAUZIAT (14) 6–4 6–4
N. Medvedeva 6–3 6–3
N. Provis
R. Zrubakova 6–0 6–3
L. K. Allen 3–6 6–1 7–5
A. Frazier 6–2 6–1
N. Dahlman 7–6 6–4
M. J. FERNANDEZ (7) 6–1 6–0
M. NAVRATILOVA (4)
K. Po 6–4 6–3
S. Frankl 6–2 6–0
B. Rittner 6–1
Y. Basuki 6–1
S. Hack 6–3 1–6 12–10
C. Tessi 4–6 6–4
A. HUBER (10) 6–4 6–4
K. MALEEVA 6–2 6–2
M. M. Bollegraf 6–1 6–2
A. L. Grunfeld 4–6 6–2 6–4
M. Endo 6–1 6–2
H. Sukova 6–1 7–5
A. Dechaume 3–6 6–1 7–5
J. Halard 6–1 4–6 6–4
A. SANCHEZ VICARIO (5) 6–3 7–6

THIRD ROUND

M. SELES (1) 6–3 6–2
L. Gildemeister 3–6 6–4 7–5
C. Porwik 6–4 6–2
G. Fernandez 6–1 6–3
N. TAUZIAT (14) 7–5 2–6 6–3
N. Provis 6–2 6–4
A. Frazier 7–6 6–1
M. J. FERNANDEZ (7) 7–5 6–2
M. NAVRATILOVA (4) 6–2 3–6 6–0
B. Rittner 6–0 6–0
Y. Basuki 7–5 6–3
A. HUBER (10) 6–2 6–2
K. MALEEVA (12) 6–4 6–1
M. Endo 5–7 6–2 7–5
H. Sukova 7–5 6–2
J. Halard 6–3 2–6 6–3

FOURTH ROUND

M. SELES (1) 6–4 6–1
G. Fernandez 6–2 6–0
N. TAUZIAT (14) 4–6 7–5 6–3
A. Frazier 6–3 6–3
M. NAVRATILOVA (4) 7–5 6–1
Y. Basuki 6–2 6–3
K. MALEEVA (12) 7–5 6–3
J. Halard 4–6 6–1 6–3

QUARTER-FINALS

M. SELES (1) 6–4 6–2
N. TAUZIAT (14) 6–0 6–3
M. NAVRATILOVA (4) 7–5 6–2
K. MALEEVA (12) 6–0 6–3

SEMI-FINALS

M. SELES (1) 6–1 6–3
M. NAVRATILOVA (4) 6–3 7–6

FINAL

M. SELES 6–2 6–7 6–4

S. GRAF (GER) (2)

Entry list (lower half)

65	**J. CAPRIATI** (USA) (6)
66	C. Rubin (USA)
67	E. Brioukhovets (CIS)
68	P. Shriver (USA)
69	E. Reinach (RSA)
70	P. Hy (CAN)
71	J. J. Santrock (USA) (Q)
72	P. Thoren (FIN)
73	A. Strnadova (TCH)
74	L. Field (AUS) (Q)
75	C. Tanvier (FRA)
76	N. Sawamatsu (JPN)
77	K. Novak (POL)
78	S. Humphreys-Davis (GBR) (WC)
79	M. Kidowaki (JPN)
80	**H. WIESNER** (AUT) (16)
81	**M. MALEEVA-FRAGNIERE** (SUI) (9)
82	N. A. M. Muns-Jagerman (NED)
83	A. Devries (BEL) (Q)
84	S. Rinaldi (USA)
85	C. Kohde-Kilsch (GER)
86	R. McQuillan (AUS)
87	M. Oremans (NED) (Q)
88	K. Godridge (AUS)
89	R. Hiraki (JPN) (Q)
90	K. Kschwendt (GER) (Q)
91	S. Niox-Chateau (FRA)
92	T. Whittington (USA) (LL)
93	I. Demongeot (FRA)
94	R. M. White (USA)
95	P. Tauziat (FRA)
96	**G. SABATINI** (ARG) (3)
97	**C. MARTINEZ** (ESP) (8)
98	P. F. Daniels (USA)
99	N. Herreman (FRA)
100	N. Zvereva (CIS)
101	R. P. Stubbs (AUS)
102	N. Baudone (ITA)
103	C. Suire (FRA)
104	L. M. McNeil (USA)
105	K. M. Adams (USA)
106	S. Frankl (ITA)
107	V. Martinek (GER)
108	R. D. Fairbank-Nideffer (RSA)
109	L. M. Harvey-Wild (USA)
110	J. M. Durie (GBR)
111	**Z. GARRISON** (USA) (13)
112	**J. NOVOTNA** (TCH) (11)
113	D. Monami (BEL)
114	P. Tarabini (ARG)
115	C. Lindqvist (SWE)
116	P. Fendick (USA)
117	K. Habsudova (TCH)
118	D. A. Graham (USA)
119	C. E. Cunningham (USA)
120	M. de Swardt (RSA)
121	G. Garrone (ITA)
122	K. Kroupova (TCH)
123	A. A. Keller (USA)
124	A. A. Keller (USA)
125	M. Javer (GBR)
126	M. Werdel (USA)
127	N. Van Lottum (FRA)
128	**S. GRAF** (GER) (2)

First round

- J. CAPRIATI (6) 6-0 7-5
- P. Shriver 1-6 6-3 6-1
- P. Hy 6-4 6-2
- P. Thoren 6-3 7-6
- A. Strnadova 6-2 6-2
- N. Sawamatsu 6-3 7-6
- K. Novak 6-3 6-2
- H. WIESNER (16) 6-2 6-2
- M. MALEEVA-FRAGNIERE (9) 6-2 6-2
- S. Rinaldi 6-2 7-5
- C. Kohde-Kilsch 2-6 6-2 6-4
- K. Godridge 6-3 6-3
- R. Hiraki 6-0 6-3
- T. Whittington 6-1 4-6 7-5
- I. Demongeot 6-2 6-3
- G. SABATINI (3) 6-1 6-1
- C. MARTINEZ (8) 6-1 6-0
- N. Zvereva 6-3 6-2
- R. P. Stubbs 6-2 7-5
- L. M. McNeil 6-1 7-5
- K. M. Adams 6-3 6-2
- R. D. Fairbank-Nideffer 7-6 6-1
- L. M. Harvey-Wild 6-4 6-2
- Z. GARRISON (13) 6-2 6-4
- J. NOVOTNA (11) 6-1 6-2
- C. Lindqvist 6-2 6-4
- P. Fendick 6-2 6-4
- D. A. Graham 6-2 7-6
- M. de Swardt 6-3 6-4
- A. A. Keller 6-3 6-4
- M. Werdel 6-2 4-6 6-0
- S. GRAF (2) 6-1 6-0

Second round

- J. CAPRIATI (6) 6-2 6-4
- P. Hy 6-2 6-7 6-1
- N. Sawamatsu 6-3 7-6
- H. WIESNER (16) 6-0 6-1
- M. MALEEVA-FRAGNIERE (9) 6-2 6-2
- K. Godridge 6-4 7-5
- R. Hiraki 6-1 7-5
- G. SABATINI (3) 6-2 6-3
- N. Zvereva 6-3 5-7 6-4
- L. M. McNeil 6-1 6-3
- R. D. Fairbank-Nideffer 6-3 6-4
- Z. GARRISON (13) 6-4 6-2
- J. NOVOTNA (11) 6-3 6-2
- P. A. Fendick 7-5 7-5
- M. de Swardt 6-2 5-7 7-5
- S. GRAF (2) 6-1 6-1

Third round

- J. CAPRIATI (6) 6-3 6-1
- N. Sawamatsu 6-1 7-5
- M. MALEEVA-FRAGNIERE (9) 4-6 6-3 6-4
- G. SABATINI (3) 6-0 6-4
- N. Zvereva 5-7 6-4 7-5
- Z. GARRISON (13) 6-4 6-2
- P. A. Fendick 6-3 6-3
- S. GRAF (2) 6-1 6-1

Fourth round

- J. CAPRIATI (6) 6-3 4-6 6-4
- G. SABATINI (3) 6-2 6-1
- N. Zvereva 6-2 3-6 6-1
- S. GRAF (2) 4-6 6-3 6-2

Quarter-finals

- G. SABATINI (3) 6-1 3-6 6-3
- S. GRAF (2) 6-3 6-1

Semi-final

- S. GRAF (2) 6-3 6-3

Capital letters denote seeded players. Number following player's name gives seeding order (Q) – Qualifier, (WC) – Wild Card, (LL) – Lucky Loser.

MEN'S DOUBLES

Holders: J. Fitzgerald (AUS)/A. Jarryd (SWE)

Winner: J. McENROE (USA)/STICH (GER) 5-7 7-6 3-6 7-6 19-17

FIRST ROUND	SECOND ROUND	THIRD ROUND	QUARTER-FINALS	SEMI-FINALS	FINAL

FIRST ROUND

1 FITZGERALD/JARRYD (1)
2 Aldrich/Visser
3 Carbonell/Riki
4 J. McEnroe/Stich
5 Flegl/Novacek
6 Pozzi/Rahnasto
7 Bailey/Wilkinson (WC)
8 KINNEAR/SALUMAA (15)
9 FERREIRA/NORVAL (10)
10 Nargiso/Rosset
11 Castle/MacLagan (WC)
12 Haarhuis/Koevermans
13 Holm/Nyborg (Q)
14 Bauer/Joelson (Q)
15 Davids/Pimek
16 FLACH/WITSKEN (8)
17 JONES/LEACH (3)
18 Nelson/Stoltenberg
19 Galbraith/Palmer
20 Annacone/Seguso
21 Bates/Van Rensburg (WC)
22 Adory/Black
23 FORGET/HLASEK (13)
24 DEVRIES/MacPHERSON (11)
25 Dzelde/Vekesa
26 Brown/Richardson (WC)
27 Eltingh/Kronemann
28 Kell/Randall
29 Boetsch/Raoux (Q)
30 Casal/Gilbert
31 DAVIS/PATE (5)
32 CONNELL/MICHIBATA (6)
33 Beckmann/Brown
34 P. McEnroe/Stark
35 Dyke/Lundgren
36 Odizor/Perez
37 Bathman/Bergh
38 Pearce/Tabot
39 JENSEN/WARDER (12)
40 FRANA/LAVALLE (14)
41 Adams/Olhovskiy
42 Ioni/Petchey (WC)
43 Schapers/Vacek
44 De Jager/Ondruska
45 Poliakov/Siemerink
46 GRABB/RENEBERG (4)
47 NIJSSEN/SUK (7)
48 Curren/Muller
49 Eltingh/Kempers
50 Garnett/Svantesson
51 Kruger/Lavendecker
52 Limberger/Oosting
53 Foster/Sapsford (WC)
54 KRATZMANN/MASUR (9)
55 CAMPORESE/IVANISEVIC (16)
56 Eisenman/Knowles (Q)
57 Borwick/Youl
58 Jonsson/Scherman
59 Cannon/Van Emburgh
60 Broad/Shelton
61 Montana/Thorne
62 WOODBRIDGE/WOODFORDE (2)

SECOND ROUND

FITZGERALD/JARRYD (1) 6-3 7-6 6-3
J. McEnroe/Stich 6-2 6-2 6-3
KINNEAR/SALUMAA (15) 6-2 3-6 6-3 7-5
Nargiso/Rosset 6-3 6-7 4-6 6-3 6-4
Haarhuis/Koevermans 4-6 6-4 6-4
Holm/Nyborg 1-6 6-3 6-4 7-6
FLACH/WITSKEN (8) 7-5 3-6 6-7 6-4
JONES/LEACH (3) 6-4 7-6
Galbraith/Palmer 3-6 6-4 7-6 7-6
Bates/Van Rensburg 6-4 3-6 7-5
FORGET/HLASEK (13) 6-3 7-6 6-3
DEVRIES/MacPHERSON (11) 4-6 7-6 3-6 6-0
Brown/Richardson 6-3 6-4 6-3
Boetsch/Raoux 6-2 3-6 6-1 6-3
DAVIS/PATE (5) 6-3 6-7 5-3 Ret
CONNELL/MICHIBATA (6) 7-6 6-1 6-4
P. McEnroe/Stark 6-2 6-3 6-4
Bathman/Bergh 7-5 6-3 6-4
JENSEN/WARDER (12) 6-4 7-6
FRANA/LAVALLE (14) 6-3 7-5 5-7 3-6 6-3
Schapers/Vacek 7-4 7-6 6-3
De Jager/Ondruska 2-6 3-3 6-4 10-8
GRABB/RENEBERG (4) 6-3 6-2 6-1
Curren/Muller 7-5 6-7 7-6 6-3
Eltingh/Kempers 4-6 7-6
Kruger/Lavendecker 6-4 7-6
KRATZMANN/MASUR (9) 6-3 3-6 6-4 6-3
Eisenman/Knowles 7-4 6-7 7-6 6-2
Borwick/Youl 6-1 6-4 7-6
Broad/Shelton 7-6 3-6 6-1 3-6
WOODBRIDGE/WOODFORDE (2) 1-6 6-2 6-2

THIRD ROUND

J. McEnroe/Stich 6-3 7-6 6-3
KINNEAR/SALUMAA (15) 6-2 7-6 7-5
Haarhuis/Koevermans 6-7 6-4 7-6 7-5
FLACH/WITSKEN (8) 6-2 6-4 6-7 7-5
JONES/LEACH (3) 3-6 7-6 7-6 4-6 6-3
FORGET/HLASEK (13) 6-3 3-6 6-4
DEVRIES/MacPHERSON (11) 6-1 7-6 1-6 2
DAVIS/PATE 7-6 6-1 6-2
P. McEnroe/Stark 6-4 7-5 7-6
JENSEN/WARDER (12) 3-6 4-6 6-1 6-4 10-8
FRANA/LAVALLE (14) 7-6 6-7 3-6 6-3 7-5
GRABB/RENEBERG (4) 6-2 4-6 7-5 6-4
Eltingh/Kempers 6-3 4-6 7-6
KRATZMANN/MASUR (9) 6-4 6-4
Borwick/Youl 7-6 6-3 6-3
WOODBRIDGE/WOODFORDE (2) 6-3 7-6 7-6

QUARTER-FINALS

J. McEnroe/Stich 6-3 6-2 6-4
Haarhuis/Koevermans 6-4 6-4 6-2
FORGET/HLASEK (13) 6-3 6-4 6-4
DAVIS/PATE (5) 6-3 6-7 6-3 6-4
P. McEnroe/Stark 6-2 6-4 4-6 6-4
GRABB/RENEBERG (4) 6-1 6-2 6-4
KRATZMANN/MASUR (9) 6-3 6-4 6-4
WOODBRIDGE/WOODFORDE (2) 6-7 6-4 3-6 8-6

SEMI-FINALS

J. McEnroe/Stich 6-3 6-4 6-4
FORGET/HLASEK (13) 4-6 7-6 7-7 6-4
GRABB/RENEBERG (4) 7-6 3-3 6-1 6
WOODBRIDGE/WOODFORDE (2) 6-7 7-5 6-3

FINAL

J. McEnroe/Stich 7-6 6-3 7-6
GRABB/RENEBERG (4) 7-6 4-6 4-6 7-6 6-4

Capital letters denote seeded pairings. Number following player's name gives seeding order. (Q) – Qualifier, (WC) – Wild Card, (LL) – Lucky Loser.

WOMEN'S DOUBLES

Holders: L. Savchenko-Neiland (CIS)/N. Zvereva (CIS)

Winner: G. FERNANDEZ (USA)/ZVEREVA (CIS) (2) 6-4 6-1

FIRST ROUND

1. **NOVOTNA/SAVCHENKO-NEILAND** (1)
2. Benjamin/Santrock
3. Datte/Kidowaki
4. Fuchs/Habsudova
5. Fulco-Villella/Smoller
6. Meskhi/Wiesner
7. Hodder/Sharpe
8. **FENDICK/STRNADOVA** (9)
9. **MAGERS/WHITE** (16)
10. Garrone/Golarsa
11. Stafford/Werdel
12. Basuki/Durie
13. Bakkum/Strandlund
14. Glitz/Kuhlman
15. Frazier/Hiraki
16. **ADAMS/BOLLEGRAF** (6)
17. **NAVRATILOVA/SHRIVER** (4)
18. Jaggard-Lai/Vis
19. Fairbank-Nideffer/Nagelsen
20. Paradis-Mangon/Testud
21. Godridge/Kschwendt
22. Guse/Morton
23. Babel/Probst
24. **HUBER/KOHDE-KILSCH** (14)
25. **McQUILLAN/PORWIK** (12)
26. Faull/Richardson
27. Kijimuta/Sawamatsu
28. Byrne/Tarabini
29. Pospisilova/Van Lottum
30. Bijal/Sidall
31. Burgin/de Swardt
32. **HETHERINGTON/RINALDI** (8)
33. **FERNANDEZ/GARRISON** (5)
34. Arendt/McCarthy
35. Grunfeld/Salmon
36. Fairal/Ferrando
37. Pfaff/Suire
38. Field/Gregory
39. Dechaume/Halard
40. **COLLINS/REINACH** (10)
41. **MALEEVA/RITTNER** (15)
42. Graham/Helgeson
43. Gildemeister/Labat
44. Segura/Souto
45. Langrova/Zrubakova
46. Iida/Lindstrom
47. Borneo/Wood
48. **SANCHEZ VICARIO/SUKOVA** (3)
49. **McNEIL/STUBBS** (7)
50. Harper/MacGregor
51. Brioukhovets/Medvedeva
52. Daniels/Harvey-Wild
53. Jones/Price
54. Javer/Lake
55. Appelmans/Oremans
56. **DEMONGEOT/TAUZIAT** (13)
57. **PROVIS/SMYLIE** (11)
58. Ludloff/Martinez
59. Novelo/Radford
60. Nohakova/Rajchrtova
61. Maleeva/Maleeva-Fragniere
62. Muns-Jageman/Schultz
63. Bowes/Whitlinger
64. **G. FERNANDEZ/ZVEREVA** (2)

SECOND ROUND

- **NOVOTNA/S.-NEILAND** (1) 6-4 6-4
- Fuchs/Habsudova 7-6 6-3
- Meskhi/Wiesner
- **FENDICK/STRNADOVA** (9) 6-3 6-2
- **MAGERS/WHITE** (16) 7-5 6-3
- Basuki/Durie 6-0 6-1
- Bakkum/Strandlund
- **ADAMS/BOLLEGRAF** (6) 6-3 6-4
- **NAVRATILOVA/SHRIVER** (4) 6-1 6-2
- Fairbank-Nideffer/Nagelsen 6-3 6-4
- Guse/Morton
- **HUBER/KOHDE-KILSCH** (14) 6-7 6-3 6-1
- Faull/Richardson 6-4 4-6 6-3
- Kijimuta/Sawamatsu
- Burgin/de Swardt 6-2 6-0
- **FERNANDEZ/GARRISON** (5) 6-2 6-3
- Fanni/Ferrando
- Field/Gregory 6-4 6-1
- **COLLINS/REINACH** (10) 6-4 7-5
- **MALEEVA/RITTNER** (15) 4-6 7-6 6-3
- Gildemeister/Labat
- Iida/Lindstrom
- **SANCHEZ VICARIO/SUKOVA** (3) 6-4 6-3
- **McNEIL/STUBBS** (7) 6-2 1-6 6-2
- Brioukhovets/Medvedeva
- Jones/Price 2-6 6-1 7-5
- **DEMONGEOT/TAUZIAT** (13) 6-2 6-4
- Novelo/Radford 3-6 6-0 6-1
- Muns-Jageman/Schultz
- **G. FERNANDEZ/ZVEREVA** (2) 6-2 6-1

THIRD ROUND

- **NOVOTNA/S.-NEILAND** (1) 6-3 6-1
- **FENDICK/STRNADOVA** (9) 6-4 6-1
- **MAGERS/WHITE** (16) 6-1 6-4
- **ADAMS/BOLLEGRAF** (6) 4-6 6-3 6-0
- **NAVRATILOVA/SHRIVER** (4) 6-4 7-7-5
- **HUBER/KOHDE-KILSCH** (14) 6-3 6-7 6-2
- Faull/Richardson 6-2 6-3
- Burgin/de Swardt 7-5 6-3
- **FERNANDEZ/GARRISON** (5) 6-2 6-3
- **COLLINS/REINACH** (10) 6-3 6-2
- **MALEEVA/RITTNER** (15) 6-0 6-7 7-5
- **SANCHEZ VICARIO/SUKOVA** (3) 7-6 6-1
- **McNEIL/STUBBS** (7) 7-5 6-4
- **DEMONGEOT/TAUZIAT** (13) 6-7 6-2 12-10
- **G. FERNANDEZ/ZVEREVA** (2) 6-3 6-2

QUARTER-FINALS

- **NOVOTNA/S.-NEILAND** (1) 6-2 6-2
- **MAGERS/WHITE** (6) 6-4 3-6 6-3
- **NAVRATILOVA/SHRIVER** (4) 6-1 6-2
- Faull/Richardson 6-4 5-7 6-0
- **G. FERNANDEZ/GARRISON** (5) 6-7 6-4 6-2
- **SANCHEZ VICARIO/SUKOVA** (3) 6-4 6-2
- **McNEIL/STUBBS** (7) 6-4 6-4
- **G. FERNANDEZ/ZVEREVA** (2) 6-2 6-2

SEMI-FINALS

- **NOVOTNA/S.-NEILAND** (1) 6-2 7-6
- **NAVRATILOVA/SHRIVER** (4) 6-3 6-1
- **SANCHEZ VICARIO/SUKOVA** (3) 6-2 6-4
- **G. FERNANDEZ/ZVEREVA** (2) 6-0 6-3

FINAL

- **NOVOTNA/S.-NEILAND** (1) 7-5 6-7 6-3
- **G. FERNANDEZ/ZVEREVA** (2) 6-1 6-7 7-5

Capital letters denote seeded pairings. Number following player's name gives seeding order (Q) – Qualifier, (WC) – Wild Card, (LL) – Lucky Loser.

MIXED DOUBLES

Holders: J. Fitzgerald (AUS)/D. Smylie (AUS)

Winner: SUK (TCH)/SAVCHENKO-NEILAND (CIS) (3) 7-6 (3) 7-6 6-2

Columns: FIRST ROUND — SECOND ROUND — THIRD ROUND — QUARTER-FINALS — SEMI-FINALS — FINAL

First Round

1 WOODBRIDGE/NOVOTNA (1)
2 Talbot/Demongeot
3 Kronemann/Helgeson
4 Kinnear/Fairbank-Nideffer
5 Black/Kuhlman
6 Pugh/Zvereva
7 Lavalle/Novelo
8 FITZGERALD/SMYLIE (9)
9 CONNELL/RINALDI (11)
10 Sabatini/Sure
11 Rahnasto/Habsudova
12 Bates/Durie
13 Briggs/Jaggard-Lai
14 Oosting/Muns-Jagerman
15 Borwick/Vida
16 NIJSSEN/BOLLEGRAF (8)
17 LEACH/GARRISON (4)
18 Aldrich/Gregory
19 Stark/Graham
20 Petchey/Loosemore (WC)
21 Barnett/Radford
22 Flach/Harvey-Wild
23 Schapers/Schultz
24 DEVRIES/FENDICK (14)
25 WARDER/STUBBS (15)
26 Dzelde/Meskhi
27 Novotny/Swardt
28 Flegl/Zrubakova
29 Eltingh/Oremans
30 Bergh/Appelmans
31 Salumaa/Fauli
32 MMBATA/HETHERINGTON (6)
33 WOODFORDE/PROVIS (7)
34 Olhovskiy/Collins
35 Pimek/Langrova
36 Wilkinson/Gomer (WC)
37 Stolterberg/Strnadova
38 Beckmann/Harper
39 Vacek/Porwik
40 MacPHERSON/McQUILLAN (10)
41 WITSKEN/ADAMS (13)
42 Kempers/Vis
43 Broad/Wood
44 Frana/Sabatini (WC)
45 Dyke/MacGregor
46 Youl/Field
47 Guenthardt/Graf (WC)
48 SUK/SAVCHENKO-NEILAND (3)
49 JONES/FERNANDEZ (5)
50 Galbraith/Morton
51 Visser/Reinach
52 Van Emburgh/McCarthy
53 Shelton/McNeil
54 Pleming/Diehuis
55 Adams/Guse
56 KRATZMANN/SHRIVER (12)
57 DAVIS/WHITE (16)
58 Jensen/Capriati
59 Nelson/Magers
60 Rostagno/Probst
61 Anneacone/Burgin (WC)
62 Keil/Van Lottum
63 Brown/Stafford
64 JARRYD/SUKOVA (2)

Second Round

- WOODBRIDGE/NOVOTNA (1) 7-6 7-6
- Kinnear/Fairbank-Nideffer 4-6 7-5 6-3
- FITZGERALD/SMYLIE (9) 6-3 6-1
- CONNELL/RINALDI (11) 6-2 6-0
- Bates/Durie 6-2 6-2
- Briggs/Jaggard-Lai 2-6 6-3 6-4
- NIJSSEN/BOLLEGRAF (8) 6-4 6-2
- LEACH/GARRISON (4) 6-4 6-2
- Stark/Graham 6-2 6-4
- Flach/Harvey-Wild 6-4 6-3
- Schapers/Schultz 4-6 7-6 6-3
- WARDER/STUBBS (15) 7-5 7-6
- Eltingh/Oremans 3-6 7-5 6-4
- Salumaa/Fauli 3-6 7-5 7-5
- WOODFORDE/PROVIS (7) 6-2 6-2
- Pimek/Langrova 3-6 6-3 6-4
- Stolterberg/Strnadova 6-4 6-7 6-4
- Vacek/Porwik 6-3 5-7 6-2
- Kempers/Vis 6-4 7-6
- Frana/Sabatini 7-6 7-5
- Dyke/MacGregor 6-3 6-4
- SUK/SAVCHENKO-NEILAND (3) 6-4 6-4
- JONES/FERNANDEZ (5) 6-1 4-6 6-3
- Visser/Reinach 6-2 6-2
- Shelton/McNeil 6-4 6-2
- KRATZMANN/SHRIVER (12) 7-5 6-3
- Jensen/Capriati 6-3 6-2
- Nelson/Magers 5-7 6-3 6-4
- Keil/Van Lottum 6-2 6-3
- JARRYD/SUKOVA (2) 6-2 6-3

Third Round

- WOODBRIDGE/NOVOTNA (1) 6-3 7-5
- Pugh/Zvereva 6-2 7-6
- Bates/Durie 6-3 7-6
- NIJSSEN/BOLLEGRAF (8) 6-4 6-4
- Stark/Graham 6-4 6-7 8-6
- Schapers/Schultz w/o
- WARDER/STUBBS (15) 6-3 6-4
- Eltingh/Oremans 3-6 6-4 6-4
- WOODFORDE/PROVIS (7) 6-2 6-3
- Stolterberg/Strnadova 6-2 6-4
- Frana/Sabatini 7-6 7-5
- SUK/SAVCHENKO-NEILAND (3) 7-5 6-2
- JONES/FERNANDEZ (5) 3-6 7-5 9-7
- Shelton/McNeil 4-6 7-6 11-9
- Jensen/Capriati 6-2 7-6
- JARRYD/SUKOVA (2) 6-4 6-4

Quarter-Finals

- WOODBRIDGE/NOVOTNA (1) 6-2 7-5
- NIJSSEN/BOLLEGRAF (8) 6-4 7-5
- Stark/Graham 2-6 7-6 6-0
- Eltingh/Oremans 6-3 6-4
- Stolterberg/Strnadova 6-2 6-4
- SUK/SAVCHENKO-NEILAND (3) w/o
- Shelton/McNeil 6-3 7-5
- Jensen/Capriati 6-3 6-3

Semi-Finals

- NIJSSEN/BOLLEGRAF (8) 6-3 0-6 9-7
- Eltingh/Oremans 7-6 6-4
- SUK/SAVCHENKO-NEILAND (3) 4-6 6-4 8-6
- Shelton/McNeil 7-6 6-2

Final

- Eltingh/Oremans 5-7 7-6 6-1
- SUK/SAVCHENKO-NEILAND (3) 7-6 6-4

Capital letters denote seeded pairings. Number following player's name gives seeding order (Q) – Qualifier, (WC) – Wild Card, (LL) – Lucky Loser.

JUNIOR EVENTS

BOYS' SINGLES – Final: David Skoch(TCH)(10) d. Brian Dunn(USA)(4) 6–4 6–3
GIRLS' SINGLES – Final: Chanda Rubin(USA)(2) d. Laurence Courtois(BEL) 6–2 7–5
BOYS' DOUBLES – Final: Steven Baldas/Scott Draper(AUS)(3) d. Mahesh Buhpati/Nitin Kirtane(IND)
6–1 4–6 9–7
GIRLS' DOUBLES – Final: Maija Avotins/Lisa McShea(AUS)(4) d. Pam Nelson/Julie Steven(USA)(7)
2–6 6–4 6–3

OVER–35 INVITATION EVENTS

MEN'S DOUBLES(Round robin in 4 groups of 4 with knock–out sf and f) Final: Peter Fleming/Stan
Smith(USA) d Mark Edmondson/Kim Warwick(AUS) 6–7 7–6 6–4
WOMEN'S DOUBLES(Knock–out for 8 prs.) – Final: Wendy Turnbull(AUS) /Virginia Wade(GBR)(1) d
Rosie Casals(USA)/Miss S.A.Walsh (USA)(2) 3–6 6–3 7–5
OVER–45 INVITATION DOUBLES(Knock–out for 8 prs.)
Final: Marty Riessen/Sherwood Stewart(USA)(1) d. John Newcombe/Tony Roche(AUS)(2) 3–6 6–3 6–3

WIMBLEDON CHAMPIONSHIPS PRIZE MONEY — £4,416,820

MEN'S SINGLES – Winner £265,000. Runner-up £132,500. Semi-finalists £66,250. Quarter-finalists£34,450. Fourth-round losers £18,550. Third-round losers £10,730. Second-round losers £6,490. First-round losers £3,975.
Total: £1,449,960
WOMEN'S SINGLES – Winner £240,000. Runner-up £120,000. Semi-finalist £57,970. Quarter-finalists £29,280. Fourth-round losers £14,840. Third-round losers £8,315. Second-round losers £5,035. First-round losers £3,080.
Total: £1,203,060
MEN'S DOUBLES (per pair) – Winners £108,570. Runners-up £54,280. Semi-finalists £27,860. Quarter-finalists £14,460. Third-round losers £7,710. Second-round losers £4,190. First-round losers £2,450.
Total: £483,530
WOMEN'S DOUBLES (per pair) – Winners £93,920. Runners-up £46,950. Semi-finalists £22,290. Quarter-finalists £11,570. Third-round losers £5,780. Second-round losers £3,130. First-round losers £1,780.
Total: £385,010
MIXED DOUBLES (per pair) – Winners £46.070. Runners-up £23,030. Semi-finalists £11,520. Quarter-finalists £5,300. Third-round losers £2,650. Second-round losers £1,320. First-round losers £600.
Total: £174,860
35 AND OVER MEN'S INVITATION DOUBLES (per pair) – Winners £14,000. Runners-up £10,000. Semi-finalists £7,000. Second place in each group £5,500. Third place in each group £4,500. Fourth place in each group £3,500
Total: £92,000
45 AND OVER MEN'S INVITATION DOUBLES (per pair) – Winners £11,000. Runners-up £9,000. Semi-finalists £6,000. First round losers £3,000.
Total: £4,000
35 AND OVER WOMEN'S INVITATION DOUBLES (per pair) – Winners £10,000. Runners-up £8,000. Semi-finalists £5,000. First-round losers £2,500.
Total: £38,000
QUALIFYING – MEN(each): 16 x Third-round losers £2,650. 32 x Second-round losers £1,325. 64 x First-round losers £660
Total £127,040
QUALIFYING – WOMEN(each): 8 x Third-round losers £2,050. 16 x Second-round losers £1.030. 32 x First-round losers £515.
Total: £49,360

During a second week which saw him three times on the verge of defeat, Sweden's quiet champion, Stefan Edberg, retained his US Open title against Pete Sampras.   *(M. Cole)*

US OPEN CHAMPIONSHIPS
Bud Collins

Usually playing tennis beats working for a living. Monica Seles would probably concur, looking back on her cameos that amounted to another US Open Championship, and a $500,000 payoff. But what about Stefan Edberg, winning his second straight title too? In retrospect, he may consider himself a survivor of hard labour on the green slabs of Flushing Meadow.

Seldom, if ever, has one champ toiled so little and another so much. As her homeland continued to come apart, Yugoslav-born Seles, a Sarasota, Florida resident, was more together than ever. She lost no sets, only 27 games, stayed well out of harm's way in giving a now-you-see-her-now-you-don't performance. In all it lasted just 7 hours and 12 minutes – between Auora Keller (6–1 6–0) and fifth seeded Arantxa Sanchez-Vicario (6–3 6–3). Was Lisa Raymond a moral victor in nudging Seles to a 7–5 set in the second round? Of course Lisa, having aroused moaning Monica to a fury of fierce hitting, did not win a game after that.

Edberg, in contrast, must have felt he spent the fortnight pounding the pavement of the US Tennis Centre like a picket on strike duty. Except Stefan wasn't out of work, but grinding out almost four times as much time in the office as Monica – 25 hours, 42 minutes. Never before had he struck so many balls. He wasn't alone among the men, whose trials, delayed by generally slow play and overabusive use of towels, sometimes seemed interminable.

If the devotees of Seles felt they didn't get enough of Miss Unorthodox herself, Edberg loyalists were delighted to see so much of his sleek, stylish shotmaking, and to revel in his continual rebounding to win the hardest of his six major titles. After three rounds of relatively breezy sailing, Edberg had to navigate one endless sea of troubles. Yet the cool Swede left New York on a winning run of three sets, 4–6 6–4 7–6 (7–5) 6–2 over the 1990 champion, third seeded Pete Sampras, that brought him the prize of a cool half million.

The semi-finals epitomized Edberg's determination to defend his property and become the only Swede to win twice in the New World. That Saturday, he put in 5 hours 26 minutes to defeat fourth seeded Michael Chang, 6–7 (3–7) 7–5 7–6 (7–3) 5–7 6–4.

Sampras needed 20 minutes less than three hours in brushing off Jim Courier in their semi-final, 6–1 3–6 6–2 6–2, but he had to work late, until 9.30 pm. He came off dehydrated and perhaps didn't have enough time to recover in the intervening 15 hours. Sampras remained in the referees' office until 12.30 am for intravenous nourishment and treatment for a virus and diarrhoea. After the final Pete said 'he'd run out of gas' but that 'I had my chances and couldn't finish it off. I pressed.' He smiled wanly, 'I realised it meant more to me than when I won in '90. I didn't understand the importance then. I was so loose. This time I did, and got a little tight.'

Tightness is an affliction that Seles doesn't yet recognise. She overwhelmed the tournament as no one had since Navratilova's victory parade of 1983 (19 games lost in fourteen sets, never more than three in any). Holding the trophy aloft after an untroubled 90–minute baseline wrap-up of Sanchez-Vicario, Seles, at 18 years 9 months, was the most precocious owner of 7 major championships (3 French, 2 Australian, 2 US) in the history of the game. At the conclusion of her Grand Slam of 1953 Maureen Connolly had been an 18 year old with 7, but only days from her 19th birthday.

If the cruise was as smooth for Seles as it was rock-and-rolling for Edberg, and the women's journey as flat as the Dead Sea, there was more to it than her terrorizing two-fistedness from either side. Much of the excitement erupted in the early stages as three of her principal rivals – ex-champ, third seeded Martina Navratilova, sixth seeded, Jennifer Capriati, troublesome tenth seed Jana Novotna – were removed before the round of sixteen. Novotna, a three-set loser to Seles in the 1991 Australian final, was dumped from Seles's sector in the opening round by Ros Fairbank Nideffer, a dangerous volleyer though ranked number 52.

Navratilova, triumphant in 1983, 1984, 1986, 1987, and runner-up to Seles in 1991, crumbled in the second round to Magdelena Maleeva, completing a triple celebration for the Maleevas. Her older sisters, Manuela and Katerina, had defeated Martina (Manuela during the 1990 Open), so was it about time 17-year-old Maggie joined in. A teary-eyed Navratilova, departing her twentieth Open, hadn't exited earlier in sixteen years, since a first round eviction by Janet Newberry in 1976 when she had also been seeded third. Martina let it slip this time by wasting two break points in the fifth game of the third and, immediately, three game points (40–0) to fall behind 4–2. 'I could tell she was very nervous', said Maggie, ranked number 27. 'Why was I nervous? Time's running out for me', said marvellous Martina, five weeks from her 36th birthday.

One round later the Olympic champ, Capriati, of whom too much was expected, headed back to the teen scene at school. Jenny had come within two points of beating Seles in the 1991 semis. However, she lost out to Patricia Hy, 7–5 6–4. The petite, fine-featured Hy, 27 years old and ranked No.36, mixed speeds and spins, ventured in for winning volleys on critical points, and refused to panic when Capriati seemed ready to escape by breaking to 4–4 in the second.

Born in Cambodia and naturalized in Canada, Hy was the first Cambodian to reach a US quarter-final, and the only Canadian, other than Carling Basset in 1984. To get there she pulled off another upset (of 13th seeded, and 1986 finalist, Helena Sukova) before being swept aside by Seles, 6–1 6–2.

Gabriela Sabatini, 1990 champ, seeded 4th but lacklustre since beating Seles in Rome, might have made trouble. But 7th seeded Mary Joe Fernandez, emulating past successes against Gaby, bounced her from Monica's path, 6–2 1–6 6–4, only to be flattened along that route in the semis, 6–3 6–2.

Steffi Graf, the second seeded 1988–89 champion, might have repeated her Wimbledon stomping of Seles, except that Sanchez-Vicario came up tough and more adventuresome in the semis, 7–6 (7–5) 6–3. A shaky tie-breaker, containing 11 unforced errors and a Graf double-fault to 4–4, concluded with Steffi bungling three forehands from 5–4.

Katerina Maleeva, seeded 15th, got dumped by 16-year-old Wimbledon junior champ, Chanda Rubin. But Maggie avenged her 23-year-old sister, 7–5 5–7 6–1, only to give in dutifully to elder sister, Manuela, 25, quitting the uncomfortable quarter-final confrontation in their second set. Manuela, through, was able to take just three games from Sanchez-Vicario. Still, the Maleevas had enhanced the family record as sisterly quarter-finalists. In 1988 Manuela and Katerina were the first sisters to make the last eight.

Abruptly ninth seeded Ivan Lendl, the R2D2 robo-stroker of tennis, became a sentimental favourite – and deserved it on the basis of a late-late showdown with 1989 champion, seventh seeded Boris Becker. During their sour fourth rounder that stretched into a sixth hour and almost until 1 a.m., they battled and bickered continuously. Both were in and out of break point scrapes, until Lendl's forehand pass edged him ahead, 4–3, in a 6–7 (4–7) 6–2 6–7 (4–7) 6–3 6–4, triumph. For three days their 5-hour and 1 minute contest stood as a record, the longest ever in a US Championship.

Was there another Championship within Lendl, now the injury-prone 32-year-old winner of 1985–86–87? Not quite, but at least he was one of four who gave Edberg a hard time.

Lendl's near-miss bid came in the quarters, after Edberg, seeded 2nd, dodged mammoth serving 6-foot-4 inch Richard Krajicek, 6–4 in the fifth, eluding two break points at 15–40 in the penultimate game. Against Edberg, Lendl was two service games from a fifth set victory, and had the points to do it, but he eventually lost the last four points to the escaping Swede. 'This tournament gets too congested playing the quarters on Thursday', was Edberg's legitimate gripe.

Rain closed them down that night at midnight, forcing Ivan and Stefan to return 14 hours later, Friday afternoon, at 1–2, Lendl serving the fifth. It meant matches on the last four days for Edberg, although he appeared gone as Lendl broke through with a low backhand to 4–3, and had three points for 5–3. A lunging volley kept Edberg in the four deuce game, and Lendl missed a backhand. Edberg got to 5–4, quashing a break point with a monster kicker, and was thereafter in tune, winning, 6–3 6–3 3–6 5–7 7–6 (7–3).

The tiny saboteur, Michael Chang, was lurking the next afternoon. Chang's progress to the semis had been sticky too, with five sets against Malivai Washington then five more against Wayne Ferreira. But he had finished both imposingly, 6–1, and was ready to pursue and harass Edberg through the longest of all major matches – 5 hours and 26 minutes.

'I don't know how I got out of that,' said Edberg, who double-faulted 18 times, and rose from 0–3, and 2–4 in the fifth to win the thriller in a roller-coaster set, 6–4. By streaking through the last four games with 17 out of 21 points, Edberg took over the curious set even though he could have lost it. Stefan's abruptly switched-on power finally quelled the pinpoint passing shots of the contentious 20-year-old Californian. Yet Chang had had the points for a golden fifth. Leading 3–0 he missed out on two break points as Edberg bolted from 15–40. Despite two game points, Chang lost his serve to 3–2, broke right back to 4–2 with a passing backhand return. But the Edberg revival began there.

They had exceeded the record 1969 Wimbledon odyssey of Pancho Gonzalez and Charlie Pasarell (5 hours 12 minutes) in time by 14 minutes, but not in games. That pre-tie-breaker contest went to Gonzalez in 112 games, 22–24 1–6 16–14 6–3 11–9 – but there had been no chairs to retreat to on changeovers in the days of 'play shall be continuous.'

In a torrent of thundering groundstrokes No.1 Jim Courier outmuscled eighth seeded Andre Agassi in the quarters, 6–3 6–7 (6–8) 6–1 6–4. But Courier's slugging couldn't stall third seeded Sampras's slickness. In the quarters Sampras quickly dealt with Alexander Volkov. Nevertheless, the Russian lefthander, first round master of Edberg in 1990, had claimed notable scalps again, taking out fifth seeded Wimbledon finalist Goran Ivanisevic in straight sets, plus Brad Gilbert.

Sampras rode a 16-match streak into the final, and, as he said, his chances appeared good. Fluidly, he darted through the first set, breaking to 4–2 with an elegant backhand passer. He held through two break-points to 3–3 in the second, but a slight deterioration set in as he lost the second set on the only break from 40–15. A double fault on his second game point was a sign of worse to come.

Edberg, still ducking nervelessly, got away from 0–40 and four break points as the third began. But he lost his serve to 5–4. It was there that the title may have been decided. Sampras, with two double faults, lost his serve on one of them, the seventh. In the overtime, Edberg's third double fault cut his lead to 5–4, but Sampras promptly reciprocated with his eighth double. In two points Edberg had the tie-breaker, 7–5, and was at long last soaring beyond danger.

A Sampras victory before 20,496 customers (raising another attendance record to 520,868) could have given US men a sort of mass Grand Slam, their first accumulation of the four majors since the original Grand Slammer himself, Don Budge, in 1938. So they settled for three (Courier at the Australian and French, Agassi at Wimbledon), their best achievement since Jimmy Connors's conquest of Australia, Wimbledon and the US in 1974.

Connors was still around to take the cake – presented after he beat Jaime Oncins in the first round on his 40th birthday, to the delight of 20,751 aficionados. Jimmy was soon departing from his 22nd Open, courtesy of Lendl, but the ageing battler extended his tournament matches played–won record to 115–90.

Jim Grabb and Richey Reneberg, who came within two points of winning Wimbledon, beat Kelly Jones and Rick Leach, 3–6 7–6 (7–2) 6–3 6–3 in the first all-American doubles final since 1983 (Peter Fleming–John McEnroe over Fritz Buenning–Van Winitsky).

Gigi Fernandez and Natalia Zvereva's 7–6 (7–4) 6–1, victory over Jana Novotna and Larisa Savchenko Neiland gained the US–Russian coalition their third major of the year, having missed out only on the Australian where they didn't play together.

Mixed doubles, an Australian specialty, was captured by the eighth Championship team from Down Under, Nicole Provis and lefthander Mark Woodforde, 4–6, 6–3, 6–3, over the Czech–Dutch alliance of Helena Sukova and Tom Nijssen. The winners got $23,250 apiece. It did beat working for a living.

MEN'S SINGLES

Holder: S. Edberg (SWE)

FIRST ROUND

1 J. **COURIER** (USA) (1)
2 A. O'Brien (USA) (WC)
3 A. Asano (ARG) (Q)
4 A. Chesnokov (CIS)
5 C. Pioline (FRA)
6 M. Strelba (TCH)
7 B. Black (ZIM)
8 T. Witsken (USA)
9 H. Skoff (AUT)
10 R. Fromberg (AUS)
11 A. Mansdorf (ISR)
12 G. Pozzi (ITA)
13 M. A. Gorriz (ESP)
14 D. Nargiso (ITA)
15 M. Schapers (NED)
16 J. **McENROE** (USA) (16)
17 C. **COSTA** (ESP) (10)
18 C. van Rensburg (RSA)
19 J. Brown (USA) (Q)
20 A. Miron (GER)
21 F. Rivera (CHI) (Q)
22 S. Davis (USA) (Q)
23 G. Raoux (FRA)
24 O. Camporese (ITA)
25 J. Siemerink (NED)
26 L. Herrera (MEX)
27 E. Lopez (ESP)
28 S. Pescosolido (ITA)
29 F. Roig (ESP)
30 A. Antonitsch (AUT)
31 M. Penfors (SWE)
32 A. **AGASSI** (USA) (8)
33 P. **SAMPRAS** (USA) (3)
34 D. DiLucia (USA) (Q)
35 J. Frana (ARG)
36 M. Damm (TCH)
37 B. Shelton (USA)
38 T. Martin (USA) (WC)
39 C. Caratti (ITA) (Q)
40 P. Kuhnen (GER)
41 T. Carbonell (ESP)
42 J. Palmer (USA) (WC)
43 A. Strajder (CAN)
44 D. Wheaton (USA)
45 M. Larsson (SWE)
46 R. Furlan (ITA)
47 J. Grabb (USA)
48 G. **FORGET** (FRA) (13)
49 M. **STICH** (GER) (11)
50 O. Delaitre (FRA)
51 B. Gilbert (USA)
52 S. Bryan (USA) (WC)
53 M. Ho (USA) (Q)
54 F. Meligeni (BRA) (Q)
55 L. Jonsson (SWE)
56 S. Stolle (AUS)
57 C. Miniussi (ARG)
58 B. Wuyts (BEL)
59 A. Volkov (CIS)
60 S. Youl (AUS)
61 L. Lavalle (MEX)
62 A. Mancini (ARG)
63 M. Rosset (SUI)
64 G. **IVANISEVIC** (CRO) (5)

SECOND ROUND

COURIER (1) — 4-6 6-3 6-3 7-6
Pioline — 6-4 6-3 6-3
Witsken — 7-5 2-1 Ret
Fromberg — 7-6 6-4 6-2
Pozzi — 6-3 6-3 6-0
Nargiso — 6-4 6-1 6-3
McENROE (16) — 6-4 6-0 6-2
COSTA (10) — 6-4 5-7 6-3 6-2
Mronz — 6-4 6-4 6-4
Davis — 6-4 6-7 6-2 6-4
Camporese — 6-4 7-6 6-1
Siemerink — 6-4 6-2 6-3
Pescosolido — 6-1 6-4 5-7 6-7 6-3
Roig — 7-5 6-4 4-6 6-2
AGASSI (8) — 6-1 6-3
SAMPRAS (3) — 6-3 7-5 6-2
Damm — 3-6 6-4 6-4 6-4
Shelton — 6-7 6-2 6-4 6-2
Kuhnen — 6-4 6-7 6-2 3-6 7-5
Palmer — 6-3 6-2 6-2
Wheaton — 6-3 6-7 6-3 6-4
Larsson — 6-2 7-5 6-3
FORGET (13) — 6-2 7-5 6-3
STICH (11) — 6-4 6-3 6-4
B. Gilbert — 6-3 6-1 6-4
Ho — 7-6 6-4 6-2
Stolle — 7-6 6-0 6-4
Wuyts — 7-6 6-0 6-4
Volkov — 2-6 7-6 7-6 6-4
Lavalle — 6-4 7-6 6-3
IVANISEVIC (5) — 6-4 6-4 6-4

THIRD ROUND

COURIER (1) — 4-6 6-3 6-1
Pioline — 6-3 5-7 7-5 6-2
Fromberg — 6-3 6-4 7-6
McENROE (16) — 4-6 6-3 6-0 6-2
COSTA (10) — 6-3 6-1 6-2
Camporese — 6-3 4-6 5-7 6-4 7-6
Siemerink — 6-3 6-4 7-6
AGASSI (8) — 6-1 6-3 6-2
SAMPRAS (3) — 7-5 6-1 6-2
Martin — 6-3 6-3 6-6 6-4
Wheaton — 6-4 6-4 6-0
FORGET (13) — 4-6 6-17-6 6-0
B. Gilbert — 5-7 6-3 3-6 6-3 7-6
Ho — 7-6 6-3 6-3
Volkov — 6-1 1-6 1-1 Ret
IVANISEVIC (5) — 7-5 7-6 6-2

FOURTH ROUND

COURIER (1) — 7-6 6-4 3-6 6-3
McENROE (16) — 6-3 6-1 6-4
COSTA (10) — 6-1 6-2 6-3
AGASSI (8) — 6-2 6-3 6-3
SAMPRAS (3) — 7-6 2-6 4-6 7-5 6-4
FORGET (13) — 6-3 7-6 2-6 6-2
B. Gilbert — 6-1 6-7 2-6 6-4 7-6
Volkov — 6-4 6-0 6-3

QUARTER-FINALS

COURIER (1) — 6-2 6-2 7-6
AGASSI (8) — 6-4 6-3 6-2
SAMPRAS (3) — 6-3 1-6 1-6 6-4 6-3
Volkov — 6-2 6-4 5-7 7-6

SEMI-FINALS

COURIER (1) — 6-3 6-7 6-1 6-4
SAMPRAS (3) — 6-4 6-1 6-0

FINAL

SAMPRAS (3) — 6-1 3-6 6-2 6-2

3-6 6-4 7-6 6-2

S. EDBERG (SWE)

EDBERG (2)
6-7 7-5 6-7 6-4

CHANG (4)
7-5 2-6 6-3 6-7 6-1

EDBERG (2)
6-3 6-3 6-5 7-6

First column — players

65	**P. KORDA** (TCH) (6)
66	E. Sanchez (ESP)
67	K. Braasch (GER)
68	C. Pridham (CAN)
69	T. Champion (FRA)
70	C. Pistolesi (ITA)
71	M. Naewie (GER)
72	J. Sanchez (ESP)
73	J. Stark (USA)
74	G. Muller (RSA)
75	W. Masur (AUS)
76	T. Dosedel (TCH) (Q)
77	R. Gilbert (FRA)
78	S. Bruguera (ESP)
79	J. Arrese (ESP)
80	**W. FERREIRA** (RSA) (12)
81	**M. WASHINGTON** (USA) (14)
82	F. Montana (USA)
83	M. Goellner (GER)
84	J. Jarryd (SWE)
85	J. Eltingh (NED)
86	H. Holm (SWE)
87	R. Reneberg (USA)
88	R. Leconte (FRA)
89	A. Mancisidor (ESP) (Q)
90	J. Tarango (USA)
91	A. Cherkasov (CIS)
92	A. Boetsch (FRA)
93	P. McEnroe (USA)
94	R. Matuszewski (USA) (WC)
95	C. Ferreira (RSA) (Q)
96	**M. CHANG** (USA) (4)
97	**B. BECKER** (GER) (7)
98	K. Curren (USA)
99	R. Weiss (USA) (WC)
100	F. Davin (ARG)
101	J. Bergstrom (SWE)
102	F. Santoro (FRA)
103	C. Steeb (GER)
104	C. Ruud (NOR) (Q)
105	B. Dunn (USA) (WC)
106	M. Zoecke (GER)
107	D. Rostagno (USA)
108	C. Adams (USA) (WC)
109	J. Oncins (BRA)
110	J. Connors (USA)
111	J. Yzaga (PER)
112	**I. LENDL** (USA) (9)
113	**R. KRAJICEK** (NED) (15)
114	F. Clavet (ESP)
115	F. Markus (ARG)
116	D. J. Bosse (USA) (Q)
117	J. Woodbridge (AUS)
118	A. Correja (ESP)
119	M. Woodforde (AUS)
120	T. Nelson (USA) (Q)
121	P. Haarhuis (NED)
122	S. Matsuoka (JPN)
123	J. Svensson (SWE)
124	N. Kulti (SWE)
125	J. Hlasek (SUI)
126	M. Gustafsson (SWE)
127	M. Mattar (BRA)
128	**S. EDBERG** (SWE) (2)

Second round

- E. Sanchez 6-2 4-2 6 6-1 7-6
- Pridham 6-7 6-4 6-4
- Champion 6-4 6-3 6-2
- J. Sanchez 6-4 6-4 5-7 7-6
- Stark 7-5 6-1 6-2
- Masur 7-6 6-2 6-4
- Bruguera 4-6 6-4 6-3
- FERREIRA (12) 3-6 7-5 6-3
- WASHINGTON (14) 6-3 7-6 6-3
- Goellner 3-6 6-3 6-4 6-0
- Holm 6-1 6-4 6-7 6-4
- Leconte 6-4 3-6 6-1 6-2
- Tarango 2-6 6-3 2-6 7-5 6-3
- Boetsch 6-4 6-1 7-6
- P. McEnroe 1-6 6-4 6-2 6-4
- CHANG (4) 6-3 6-4
- BECKER (7) 6-2 5-7 7-3 6-4
- Weiss 6-1 Ret
- Santoro 6-4 4-7 6
- Steeb 6-2 7-6 6-2
- Dunn 6-2 6-3
- Adams 6-2 2-6 6-0 0-5 0 Ret
- Connors 6-1 6-2 6-3
- LENDL (9) 3-6 6-3 6-2 6-0
- KRAJICEK (15) 4-2 6-7 6-6 6-1
- Markus 6-7 6-4 6-3 6-2
- Woodbridge 6-2 6-2
- Woodforde 7-6 6-4 7-6
- Haarhuis 7-5 6-2 6-4
- Svensson 2-6 7-5 6-1 3-6 7-5
- Hlasek 7-5 6-3 6-3
- EDBERG (2) 7-5 7-5 6-2

Third round

- E. Sanchez 7-6 6-2 6-4
- J. Sanchez 7-5 4-1 Ret
- Masur 3-6 4-7 6-4 6-6 6-3
- W. FERREIRA (12) 6-7 6-2 3-6 6-1 6-2
- WASHINGTON (14) 6-3 6-3 6-2
- Leconte 6-1 5-7 6-2 6-2
- Boetsch 4-6 4-6 3-7-6
- CHANG (4) 6-3 6-3 6-4
- BECKER (7) 4-6 2 6-1 1-0 Ret
- Steeb 2-6 7-6 5-6 6-2
- Adams 6-2 6-3 7-6
- LENDL (9) 3-6 3-6 2-6 6-0
- KRAJICEK (15) 4-2 6-7 6-6 6-3 6-1
- Woodforde 6-3 6-2 7-6
- Svensson 6-0 7-5 6-3
- EDBERG (2) 7-5 6-2 6-1

Fourth round

- W. FERREIRA (12) 6-4 6-4 6-2
- WASHINGTON (14) 6-4 6-7 6-4 6-3
- CHANG (4) 6-3 6-3 6-1
- BECKER (7) 6-1 4-6 7-6 6-3
- LENDL (9) 2-6 6-4 6-3 6-4
- KRAJICEK (15) 6-1 6-3 6-2
- EDBERG (2) 6-4 6-7 6-3 6-4

Quarter-finals / later rounds

- W. FERREIRA (12) 6-2 6-4 2-6 6-4
- CHANG (4) 6-2 2-6 3-6 6 6-3 6-1
- LENDL (9) 6-7 6-2 6-7 6-3 6-4
- EDBERG (2) 6-4 6-7 6-3 6-6

Capital letters denote seeded players. Number following player's name gives seeding order (Q) – Qualifier, (WC) – Wild Card, (LL) – Lucky Loser.

WOMEN'S SINGLES

Holder: M. Seles (YUG)

FIRST ROUND	SECOND ROUND	THIRD ROUND	FOURTH ROUND	QUARTER-FINALS	SEMI-FINALS	FINAL

6–3 6–3

1 M. **SELES** (YUG) (1) — **SELES** (1) 6–1 6–0 — **SELES** (1) 7–5 6–0 — **SELES** (1) 6–4 6–0 — **SELES** (1) 6–1 6–2 — **SELES** (1) 6–1 6–2 — **SELES** (1) 6–3 6–2

2 A. Keller (USA)

3 P. Ritter (AUT) — Raymond 6–3 6–4

4 L. Raymond (USA) (WC)

5 C. Porwik (GER) — Porwik 6–3 6–4 — Porwik 7–5 7–5

6 C. Benjamin (USA) (Q)

7 V. Ruano-Pascual (ESP) — Gildemeister 7–5 6–2

8 L. Gildemeister (PER)

9 N. Baudone (ITA) — Baudone 6–4 4–6 7–5 — G. Fernandez 6–3 3–6 6–2 — G. Fernandez 6–4 6–1

10 N. Reinstadler (AUT) (Q)

11 G. Fuschi (SUI) — G. Fernandez 6–0 6–2

12 G. Fernandez (USA)

13 S. Hack (GER) — Hack 6–4 6–3 — Hack 7–5 6–4

14 S. McCarthy (USA) (WC)

15 R. Fairbank-Nideffer (USA) — Fairbank-Nideffer 6–3 6–0

16 **J. NOVOTNA** (TCH) (10)

17 **H. SUKOVA** (TCH) (13) — **SUKOVA** (13) 6–0 6–4 — **SUKOVA** (13) 6–2 7–5 — **SUKOVA** (13) 6–2 6–3

18 C. Lindqvist (SWE)

19 K. Date (JPN) — Date 6–1 6–0

20 M. Babel (GER)

21 L. McNeil (USA) — McNeil 6–7 7–6 6–2 — McNeil 6–1 7–5

22 S. Rottier (NED)

23 L. Demongeot (FRA) — Zardo 6–3 6–4

24 E. Zardo (SUI)

25 P. Hy (CAN) — Hy 6–1 6–1 — Hy 6–2 6–2 — Hy 6–1 7–6

26 E. Sviglerova (TCH)

27 J. Wiesner (AUT) — Wiesner 6–3 7–6

28 A. Temesvari-Trunkos (HUN)

29 S. Testud (FRA) — Testud 6–3 6–4 — **CAPRIATI** (6) 6–2 6–3 — **CAPRIATI** (6) 7–6 6–2

30 A. Fusai (FRA) (Q)

31 N. Muns-Jagerman (NED) — **CAPRIATI** (6) 6–1 6–1

32 **J. CAPRIATI** (USA) (6)

33 **G. SABATINI** (ARG) (4) — **SABATINI** (4) 6–1 6–2 — **SABATINI** (4) 6–0 6–4 — **SABATINI** (4) 6–4 5–7 6–4

34 L. Harvey-Wild (USA)

35 J. Halard (FRA) — Halard 6–1 6–3

36 F. Bonsignori (ITA)

37 F. Li (CHN) — Li 7–5 6–0 — Zvereva 6–1 6–2

38 K. Habsudova (TCH)

39 D. Graham (USA) — Zvereva 6–3 6–2

40 N. Zvereva (CIS)

41 T. Whitlinger (USA) — Milvidskaia 6–4 6–1 — Kuhlman 7–5 6–7 6–2 — Appelmans 6–2 6–1

42 E. Maniokova (CIS)

43 E. Kuhlman (USA) (WC) — Kuhlman 6–3 6–1

44 J. Durie (GBR)

45 K. Wood (GBR) (Q) — Wood 6–1 0–6 6–3 — Appelmans 6–3 6–2

46 S. Appelmans (BEL)

47 **A. HUBER** (GER) (11) — Appelmans 6–3 6–4

48 M. Pierce (FRA) (17)

49 **M. PIERCE** (FRA) (17) — **PIERCE** (16) 6–4 6–2 — **PIERCE** (16) 7–5 6–4 — **PIERCE** (16) 6–2 6–1

50 M. Vento (VEN) (WC)

51 L. Ferrando (ITA) — Ferrando 5–7 6–1 6–0

52 P. Thoren (FIN)

53 M. Javer (GBR) — Rehe 6–4 6–4 — White 7–5 5–7 6–0

54 S. Rehe (USA)

55 S. Frankl (GER) — White 6–0 6–3

56 R. White (USA)

57 B. Schultz (NED) — Schultz 6–3 4–6 6–4 — Schultz 6–2 6–0 — **M. J. FERNANDEZ** (7) 3–6 6–3 6–1 — **M. J. FERNANDEZ** (7) 6–4 6–2 — **M. J. FERNANDEZ** (7) 6–0 6–4 — **M. J. FERNANDEZ** (7) 6–2 1–6 6–4

58 M. Werdel (USA)

59 P. Paradis-Mangon (FRA) — Paradis-Mangon 6–1 7–5

60 K. Novacki (POL)

61 N. Medvedeva (UKR) — Medvedeva 6–4 4–1

62 A. Frazier (USA)

63 D. Faber (USA) — **M. J. FERNANDEZ** (7) 3–6 6–0 6–4

64 **M. J. FERNANDEZ** (USA) (7)

M. SELES (YUG) (1)

Entries (bottom half of draw)

65 C. MARTINEZ (ESP) (8)
66 A. Grossman (USA)
67 N. van Lottum (FRA)
68 B. Paulus (AUT)
69 B. Godridge (AUS)
70 K. Rinaldi (USA)
71 M. L. Daniels (USA) (WC)
72 C. Cunningham (USA)
73 A. Strnadova (TCH)
74 B. Rittner (GER)
75 R. Zrubakova (TCH)
76 G. Helgeson (USA)
77 S. Gomer (GBR)
78 L. Allen (USA)
79 E. Reinach (RSA)
80 M. MALEEVA-FRAGNIERE (SUI) (9)
81 K. MALEEVA (BUL) (15)
82 J. Byrne (AUS)
83 T. Whittington (USA)
84 D. Monami (BEL)
85 J. Emmons (USA) (WC)
86 C. Rubin (USA)
87 N. Provis (AUS)
88 K. Nagatsuka (JPN) (LL)
89 N. Arendt (USA) (Q)
90 S. T. Wang (CHN)
91 K. Po (USA)
92 J. Steven (USA) (WC)
93 M. Maleeva (BUL)
94 K. Kroupova (TCH)
95 S. Stafford (USA) (Q)
96 A. NAVRATILOVA (USA) (3)
97 A. SANCHEZ-VICARIO (ESP) (5)
98 L. Savchenko-Neiland (LAT)
99 L. Davenport (USA) (WC)
100 Y. Basuki (IND)
101 P. Fendick (USA)
102 N. Sawamatsu (JPN)
103 A. Dechaume (FRA)
104 L. Meskhi (USA)
105 G. Mothes (FRA)
106 R. McQuillan (AUT)
107 K. Sloane-Lundy (USA)
108 N. London (USA) (Q)
109 F. Perfetti (ITA)
110 S. Meier (GER)
111 K. Kessel (USA)
112 Z. GARRISON (USA) (14)
113 N. TAUZIAT (FRA) (12)
114 N. Ercegovic (CRO)
115 M. Paz (ARG)
116 A. Coetzer (RSA)
117 I. Majoli (CRO)
118 M. de Swardt (RSA)
119 F. Labat (ARG)
120 L. Golarsa (ITA)
121 S. Cecchini (ITA)
122 B. Simpson-Alter (CAN)
123 B. Fulco-Villela (ARG)
124 N. Dahlman (FIN)
125 P. Shriver (USA)
126 N. Perez (ESP)
127 H. Cioffi (USA)
128 S. GRAF (GER) (2)

First round

Grossman 6-3 2-6 6-4
van Lottum 7-5
Rinaldi 6-2 6-3
Cunningham 6-4 2-6 7-5
Strnadova 6-2 6-1
Helgeson 7-5 7-6
Allen 6-4 7-6
MALEEVA-FRAGNIERE (9) 7-5 7-5
K. MALEEVA (15) 7-5 6-2
Monami 6-2 2-6 6-3
Rubin 6-1 7-5
Provis 6-4 6-2
Arendt 6-4 6-2
Po 6-2 6-3
Mag. Maleeva 6-2 6-1
NAVRATILOVA (3) 4-6 6-1 7-5
SANCHEZ-VICARIO (5) 6-7 6-2 6-2
Davenport 6-4 6-4
Sawamatsu 6-1 6-3
Meskhi 4-6 6-0 7-6
McQuillan 6-2 6-0
London 6-3 6-4
Meier 4-6 6-0 6-3
GARRISON (14) 4-6 6-0 6-3
TAUZIAT (12) 6-3 6-2
Coetzer 6-2 4-6 6-4
Labat 6-4 6-4
Simpson-Alter 6-4 6-2
Dahlman 6-3 6-4
Shriver 6-2 6-4
GRAF (2) 6-0 6-2

Second round

van Lottum 7-6 6-4
Cunningham 7-6 6-2
Strnadova 6-3 7-6
MALEEVA-FRAGNIERE (9) 6-7 6-3 6-2
K. MALEEVA (15) 6-3 6-4
Rubin 7-6 6-3
Po 7-6 7-6
Mag. Maleeva 6-4 0-6 6-3
SANCHEZ-VICARIO (5) 6-2 6-1
Sawamatsu 3-6 6-4 6-4
McQuillan 6-1 7-6
GARRISON (14) 6-2 2-6 6-4
Coetzer 6-0 6-0
Labat 6-3 6-3
Dahlman 6-4 6-4
GRAF (2) 7-5 6-3

Third round

Cunningham 2-6 4-6 6-0
MALEEVA-FRAGNIERE (9) 6-7 6-3 6-2
Rubin 6-4 3-6 6-4
Mag. Maleeva 6-2 6-3
SANCHEZ-VICARIO (5) 6-1 6-3
GARRISON (14) 6-3 6-1
Labat 6-3 4-6 6-4
GRAF (2) 6-4 6-2

Quarter-finals

MALEEVA-FRAGNIERE (9) 6-2 5-3 Ret.
Mag. Maleeva 7-5 5-7 6-1
SANCHEZ-VICARIO (5) 6-0 6-1
GRAF (2) 6-2 6-2

Semi-finals

MALEEVA-FRAGNIERE (9) 6-3 7-5
SANCHEZ-VICARIO (5) 7-6 6-3

Final

SANCHEZ-VICARIO (5) 6-2 6-1

Capital letters denote seeded players. Number following player's name gives seeding order (Q) – Qualifier, (WC) – Wild Card, (LL) – Lucky Loser.

MEN'S DOUBLES

Holders: J. Fitzgerald (AUS)/A. Jarryd (SWE)

Winner: GRABB (USA)/RENEBERG (USA) (2) — 3-6 7-6 6-3 6-3

FIRST ROUND

1 **WOODBRIDGE/WOODFORDE (1)**
2 Antonitsch/Oosting
3 Henriksson/Odizor
4 Holm/Pedersen
5 Carbonell/Miniussi
6 Apell/Steeb
7 W. Ferreira/Norval
8 **ADAMS/OLHOVSKIY (16)**
9 **JENSEN/WARDER (10)**
10 Ho/Melville
11 Eltingh/Haarhuis
12 Kratzmann/Rasheed
13 Frana/Lavalle
14 Albano/Motta
15 Kuhnen/Muller
16 **NIJSSEN/SUK (7)**
17 **JONES/LEACH (4)**
18 Brown/Lundgren
19 DiLucia/MacPhie (WC)
20 Davids/Pimek
21 P. McEnroe/Stark
22 Palmer/Wheaton
23 Pearce/Talbot
24 **FLACH/WITSKEN (14)**
25 **KRATZMANN/MASUR (11)**
26 Eisenman/Scherman
27 Brandi/Thorne
28 Bathman/Bergh
29 Garnett/Svantesson
30 Evernden/Lavendecker
31 Black/Nelson
32 **HLASEK/ROSSET (5)**
33 **J. McENROE/STICH (6)**
34 Cocotos/O'Brien (WC)
35 Cannon/Van Emburgh
36 Nargiso/Sanchez
37 Limberger/Zdrazila
38 Kinnear/Salumaa
39 Damm/Stolle
40 **DAVIS/PATE (12)**
41 **CASSAL/E. SANCHEZ (13)**
42 Schapers/Vacek
43 Pozzi/Rinaesto
44 Clavet/Roig
45 Korda/Pugh
46 Montana/Shelton
47 Briggs/Kronemann
48 **FITZGERALD/JARRYD (3)**
49 **DEVRIES/MacPHERSON (8)**
50 Beckman/Dyke
51 Borwick/Youl
52 Middleton/Siemerink
53 Camporese/Ivanisevic
54 Smith/Vekse
55 Gilbert/Spadea (WC)
56 **GALBRAITH/VISSER (9)**
57 **CONNELL/MICHIBATA (15)**
58 Acioly/De Jager
59 Broad/Kruger
60 Ahnonool/Lucena (WC)
61 Brandi/Dralde
62 Deppe/Haygarth
63 Mattar/Oncins
64 **GRABB/RENEBERG (2)**

SECOND ROUND

WOODBRIDGE/WOODFORDE (1) 6-3 6-4
Holm/Pedersen 6-3 6-4
Apell/Steeb 3-2 Ret.
W. Ferreira/Norval 7-6 7-5
Ho/Martin 2-0
Eltingh/Haarhuis 7-3 6-4
Frana/Lavalle 6-7 6-3 7-5
NIJSSEN/SUK (7) 7-5 6-2
JONES/LEACH (4) 6-7 7-6 7-6
Davids/Pimek 6-3
P. McEnroe/Stark 6-2
FLACH/WITSKEN (14) 6-2 6-4
M. KRATZMANN/MASUR (11) 6-4 6-2
Bathman/Bergh 6-4 1-6 6-4
Evernden/Lavendecker 6-3 6-3
HLASEK/ROSSET (5) 6-4 6-4
J. McENROE/STICH (6) 6-3 6-4
Cannon/Van Emburgh 7-5 6-4
Limberger/Zdrazila 7-6 7-6
DAVIS/PATE (12) 7-6 6-3
CASSAL/E. SANCHEZ (13) 7-5 7-6
Pozzi/Rinaesto 6-2 6-4
Montana/Shelton 7-6 6-3
FITZGERALD/JARRYD (3) 3-6 6-3
DEVRIES/MacPHERSON (8) 6-4 6-7 7-6
Borwick/Youl 6-4 6-7 7-6
Camporese/Ivanisevic 6-3
GALBRAITH/VISSER (9) 6-1 6-4
CONNELL/MICHIBATA (15) 6-3 6-4
Broad/Kruger
Deppe/Haygarth 6-3 6-4
GRABB/RENEBERG (2) 7-6 6-4

THIRD ROUND

WOODBRIDGE/WOODFORDE (1) 6-4 7-6
W. Ferreira/Norval 6-7 6-4 6-2
Eltingh/Haarhuis 7-5 6-2
NIJSSEN/SUK (7) 6-3 6-4
JONES/LEACH (4) 6-3 6-7 6-3
P. McEnroe/Stark 6-2 7-6
Bathman/Bergh 6-2 3-6 7-6
Evernden/Lavendecker 6-3 1-6 7-6
J. McENROE/STICH (6) 7-5 6-4
DAVIS/PATE (12) 6-4 6-3
CASSAL/E. SANCHEZ (13) 7-5 6-4
FITZGERALD/JARRYD (3) 1-6 6-2 6-4
Borwick/Youl 7-6 6-3
GALBRAITH/VISSER (9) 6-3 6-1
CONNELL/MICHIBATA (15) 6-3 7-6
GRABB/RENEBERG (2) 4-6 7-6 6-4

QUARTER-FINALS

WOODBRIDGE/WOODFORDE (1) 6-1 6-3
Eltingh/Haarhuis 7-6 6-2
JONES/LEACH (4) 6-2 7-6
Evernden/Lavendecker 6-2 6-4
J. McENROE/STICH (6) 6-3 4-6 6-4
CASSAL/E. SANCHEZ (13) 7-5 2-6 6-3
Borwick/Youl 3-6 7-6 6-4
GRABB/RENEBERG (2) 6-4 6-7 6-3

SEMI-FINALS

WOODBRIDGE/WOODFORDE (1) 6-3 3-6 6-3 6-4
JONES/LEACH (4) 6-3 7-6 6-2
J. McENROE/STICH (6) 6-7 6-3 6-7 6-6-4
GRABB/RENEBERG (2) 6-4 7-6 6-3

FINAL

JONES/LEACH (4) 7-6 7-6 6-2
GRABB/RENEBERG (2) 3-6 7-5 7-6 4-6 6-2

WOMEN'S DOUBLES

Holders: P. Shriver (USA)/N. Zvereva (CIS)

Winner: G. FERNANDEZ (USA)/ZVEREVA (CIS) (3) — 7-6 6-1

FIRST ROUND

1 NOVOTNA/SAVCHENKO-NEILAND (1)
2 Field/Gregory
3 Oremans/Vis
4 Benjamin/Santrock
5 Davenport/Rubin (WC)
6 MacGregor/Po
7 Stafford/Werdel
8 DECHAUME/LABAT (15)
9 MARTINEZ/PAZ (9)
10 Frazier/Hiraki
11 Grossman/Lindqvist
12 Burgin/de Swardt
13 Fauli/Richardson
14 Schulkebir/Steven (WC)
15 M.J. FERNANDEZ/GARRISON (5)
16 NAVRATILOVA/SHRIVER (4)
17 Langrova/Zrubakova
18 Basuki/Durie
19 Kijimuta/Sawamatsu
20 Haard/Huber
21 Farina/Ferrando
22 DEMONGEOT/TAUZIAT (13)
23 MESKHI/REINACH (11)
24 Harper/Harvey-Wild
25 Date/Fleming
26 Emmons/Simpson-Alter
27 Morton/Wood
28 Kuhlman/Novelo
29 Nagelsen/Pierce (WC)
30 FENDICK/STRNADOVA (8)
31 McNEIL/STUBBS (6)
32 Byrne/Provis
33 Paradis-Mangon/Testud
34 Jankovska/Melicharova
35 Broukhovets/Medvedeva
36 Cecchini/Tarabini
37 HETHERINGTON/RINALDI (10)
38 MALEEVA/WITTNER (14)
39 Fulco-Villella/Ruano-Pascual
40 Gildemeister/Habsudova
41 Fuchs/Strandlund
42 Cunningham/Daniels
43 Kschwendt/Ritter
44 Cantzler/Maleeva
45 G. FERNANDEZ/ZVEREVA (3)
46 COLLINS/REHE (7)
47 Graham/Schultz
48 Allen/Henriksson
49 Appelmans/Wiesner
50 Ludloff/Suire
51 Segura/Souto
52 McQUILLAN/PORWIK (12)
53 SMYLIE/WHITE (16)
54 Dahlman/Golarsa
55 Helgeson/McCarthy
56 Fairbank-Nideffer/Magers
57 Ceniza/McCalla
58 Sampras/Whitinger
59 Godridge/Fusai
60 Lapi/Munoz-Jagerman
61 SANCHEZ VICARIO/SUKOVA (2)

SECOND ROUND

NOVOTNA/S.-NEILAND (1) — 6-1 6-3
Oremans/Vis — 6-1 3-6 6-4
MacGregor/Po — 6-1 7-5
MARTINEZ/PAZ (9) — 7-5 6-2
Frazier/Hiraki — 7-6 6-1
Burgin/de Swardt — 3-6 6-3 6-2
Fauli/Richardson — 6-4 6-4
M.J. FERNANDEZ/GARRISON (5) — 6-2 6-0
NAVRATILOVA/SHRIVER (4) — 6-2 6-0
Basuki/Durie — 6-1 6-3
Farina/Ferrando — 6-1 6-3
DEMONGEOT/TAUZIAT (13) — 6-4 6-3
MESKHI/REINACH (11) — 6-3 6-2
Emmons/Simpson-Alter — 6-4 6-4
Morton/Wood — 6-3 7-6
FENDICK/STRNADOVA (8) — 6-4 7-6
McNEIL/STUBBS (6) — 6-2 6-3
Paradis-Mangon/Testud — 4-6 6-2 6-3
Broukhovets/Medvedeva — 6-2 6-2
HETHERINGTON/RINALDI (10) — 4-6 6-3
Fulco-Villella/Ruano-Pascual — 7-5 6-1
Gildemeister/Habsudova — 6-2 6-4
Cunningham/Daniels — 6-0 6-3
G. FERNANDEZ/ZVEREVA (3) — 6-4 6-2
COLLINS/REHE (7) — 6-1 6-1
Allen/Henriksson — 7-5 6-4
Appelmans/Wiesner — 6-2 6-0
McQUILLAN/PORWIK (12) — 6-3 6-3
SMYLIE/WHITE (16) — 6-3 6-3
Fairbank-Nideffer/Magers — 3-6 6-2 6-2
Sampras/Whitinger — 6-2 6-2
SANCHEZ VICARIO/SUKOVA (2) — 6-3 6-2

THIRD ROUND

NOVOTNA/S.-NEILAND (1) — 6-2 6-2
MARTINEZ/PAZ (9) — 6-7 6-3 6-2
Burgin/de Swardt — 6-2 6-2
M.J. FERNANDEZ/GARRISON (5) — 6-4 6-4
NAVRATILOVA/SHRIVER (4) — 6-2 7-5
DEMONGEOT/TAUZIAT (13) — 6-3 6-3
MESKHI/REINACH (11) — 3-6 6-1 6-0
FENDICK/STRNADOVA (8) — 6-2 6-1
McNEIL/STUBBS (6) — 6-3 7-6
HETHERINGTON/RINALDI (10) — 6-3 4-6 6-3
Gildemeister/Habsudova — 6-4 6-3
G. FERNANDEZ/ZVEREVA (3) — 6-1 6-1
COLLINS/REHE (7) — 6-2 7-6
McQUILLAN/PORWIK (12) — 6-4 7-6
Fairbank-Nideffer/Magers — 6-4 4-6 7-6
SANCHEZ VICARIO/SUKOVA (2) — 6-2 6-2

QUARTER-FINALS

NOVOTNA/S.-NEILAND (1) — 6-2 6-3
M.J. FERNANDEZ/GARRISON (5) — 6-2 4-6 7-6
NAVRATILOVA/SHRIVER (4) — 6-4 6-0
FENDICK/STRNADOVA (8) — 6-3 6-4
McNEIL/STUBBS (6) — 6-4 7-5
G. FERNANDEZ/ZVEREVA (3) — 6-2 6-2
McQUILLAN/PORWIK (12) — 6-3 6-2
SANCHEZ VICARIO/SUKOVA (2) — 7-6 6-2

SEMI-FINALS

NOVOTNA/S.-NEILAND (1) — 1-6 6-4 7-6
NAVRATILOVA/SHRIVER (4) — 6-2 6-2
G. FERNANDEZ/ZVEREVA (3) — 6-3 6-2
SANCHEZ VICARIO/SUKOVA (2) — 6-1 1-6 6-4

FINAL

NOVOTNA/S.-NEILAND (1) — 6-4 7-5
G. FERNANDEZ/ZVEREVA (3) — 6-1 6-3

Capital letters denote seeded pairings. Number following player's name gives seeding order (Q) – Qualifier, (WC) – Wild Card, (LL) – Lucky Loser.

MIXED DOUBLES

Holders: T. Nijssen (NED)/M. Bollegraf (NED)

FIRST ROUND	SECOND ROUND	QUARTER-FINALS	SEMI-FINALS	FINAL
1 SANCHEZ VICARIO/WOODBRIDGE (1)	SANCHEZ VICARIO/WOODBRIDGE (1) 6-1 6-3	Fendick/DeVries 7-6 6-4	REINACH/GALBRAITH (7) 6-4 6-3	PROVIS/WOODFORDE (6) 6-0 6-3
2 Faull/Salumaa				
3 Fendick/DeVries	Fendick/DeVries 6-2 6-3			
4 Meskhi/Pimek				
5 Dechaume/Ettingh	Coetzer/Adams 6-2 6-3	REINACH/GALBRAITH (7) 6-3 6-4		
6 Coetzer/Adams				
7 Fairbank-Nideffer/Van Emburgh	REINACH/GALBRAITH (7) 6-3 7-6			
8 REINACH/GALBRAITH (7)				
9 SAVCHENKO/SUK (3)	Schultz/Jensen 6-3 7-6	McNeil/Shelton 6-4 5-7 6-3	PROVIS/WOODFORDE (6) 7-6 6-3	
10 Schultz/Jensen				
11 McNeil/Shelton (WC)	McNeil/Shelton 6-4 3-6 6-2			
12 Durie/Warder				
13 Demongeot/Talbot	Demongeot/Talbot 6-3 6-4	PROVIS/WOODFORDE (6) 6-7 6-3 6-2		
14 Miyagi/Olhovskiy				
15 Paz/Lavalle	PROVIS/WOODFORDE (6) 5-7 6-4 6-3			
16 PROVIS/WOODFORDE (6)				
17 SUKOVA/NIJSSEN (5)	SUKOVA/NIJSSEN (5) 6-0 7-5	SUKOVA/NIJSSEN (5) 6-2 6-2	SUKOVA/NIJSSEN (5) 6-4 6-4	SUKOVA/NIJSSEN (5) 6-3 6-3
18 Tarabini/Bathman				
19 Strnadova/Kratzmann	Davenport/Dunn 6-0 7-5			
20 Davenport/Dunn (WC)				
21 Collins/Cannon (WC)	Collins/Cannon 6-2 6-2	GARRISON/LEACH (4) 6-3 6-3		
22 Magers/Kinnear (WC)				
23 White/Visser	GARRISON/LEACH (4) 7-6 6-3			
24 GARRISON/LEACH (4)				
25 McQUILLAN/MacPHERSON (8)	McQUILLAN/MacPHERSON (8) 6-3 7-6	Helgeson/Kronemann 6-7 6-3 6-2	Hetherington/Michibata 6-4 2-6 6-1	
26 Shriver/Pugh				
27 Helgeson/Kronemann (WC)	Helgeson/Kronemann 6-3 1-1 Ret			
28 Smylie/Fitzgerald				
29 Harper/Briggs	Medvedeva/Davids 6-2 6-4	Hetherington/Michibata 6-2 6-3		
30 Medvedeva/Davids				
31 Hetherington/Michibata	Hetherington/Michibata 7-6 7-5			
32 G. FERNANDEZ/JONES (2)				

PROVIS (AUS)/WOODFORDE (AUS) (6) 4-6 6-3 6-3

Capital letters denote seeded pairings. Number following player's name gives seeding order. (Q) – Qualifier, (WC) – Wild Card, (LL) – Lucky Loser.

JUNIOR EVENTS

BOYS' SINGLES – Final: Brian Dunn(USA)(2) d. Grant Doyle(AUS)(1) 7–5 6–2
GIRLS' SINGLES – Final: Lindsay Davenport(USA)(1) d. Julie Steven(USA)(8) 6–2 6–2
BOYS' DOUBLES – Final: Jimmy Jackson(USA)/Eric Taino(USA)(8) d. Marcelo Rios(CHI)/Gabriel Siberstein(CHI) 6–3 3–6 6–1
GIRLS' DOUBLES – Final: Lindsay Davenport(USA)/Nicole London(USA)(1) d. Katrina Schlukbir(USA)/Julie Steven(USA)(6) 7–5 6–7 6–4

SENIOR EVENTS

MEN'S SINGLES MASTERS CHAMPIONSHIPS – Final: Hank Pfister(USA)(1) d. Peter Fleming(USA)6–3 6–4
MEN'S DOUBLES MASTERS CHAMPIONSHIPS – Final: Paul McNamee(AUS)/Tomas Smid(TCH)(3) d. Bob Lutz(USA)/Ilie Nastase(ROM)(4) 6–2 6–3
WOMEN'S DOUBLES MASTERS CHAMPIONSHIPS – Final: Wendy Turnbull(AUS) /Virginia Wade(GBR)(2) d. JoAnne Russell-Longdon(USA)/Sharon Walsh(USA) 6–3 6–4
MIXED DOUBLES MASTERS CHAMPIONSHIP– Final: Marty Riessen(USA)/ Wendy Turnbull(AUS)(1) d. Gene Mayer(USA)/Virginia Wade(GBR)(2) 6–3 7–6

US OPEN CHAMPIONSHIPS PRIZE MONEY – $8,556,600

MEN'S AND WOMEN'S SINGLES – Winner $500,000. Runner-up $250,000. Semi-finalists $125,000. Quarter-finalists $65,000. Fourth-round losers $35,000. Third-round losers $20,250. Second-round losers $12,400. First-round losers $7,400.
Totals: MEN - $1,367,200; WOMEN - $1,367,200.
MEN'S AND WOMEN'S DOUBLES (per pair) – Winners $184,000. Runners-up $92,000. Semi-finalists $46,000. Quarter-finalists $24,000. Third-round losers $13,000. Second-round losers $7,500. First-round losers $4,500.
Totals: MEN $416,000; WOMEN $416,000.
MIXED DOUBLES (per pair) – Winners $46,500. Runners-up $22,000. Semi-finalists $11,000. Quarter-finalists $6,200. Second-round losers $3,500. First-round losers $1,400.
Total: $165,700
QUALIFYING COMPETITIONS – $256,800
MEN(each): 16 x Third-round losers $3,000. 32 x Second-round losers $1,650. 64 x First-round losers $1,100.
Total: $171,200
WOMEN(each): 32 x Third-round losers $3,000. 16 x Second-round losers $1,650. 32 x First-round losers $1,100.
Total $85,600

TOTAL FOR SENIOR EVENTS – $385,900

TOTAL FOR PER DIEM ALLOWANCES AND OTHER FEES – $615,400

Germany's Michael Stich delighted the Munich fans by winning the Compaq Grand Slam Cup in his adopted home town to augment his income by a cool $2 million. (T. Hindley)

COMPAQ GRAND SLAM CUP

John Barrett

For locally based Michael Stich, success in the 1992 Compaq Grand Slam Cup in Munich's Olympiahalle was worth much more than the first prize of $2 million. The manner of his emphatic 6–2 6–3 6–2 win over the diminutive American Michael Chang in a final that lasted a mere 2hrs 6mins established the 24-year-old right-hander in the minds of German tennis fans as a true champion.

Despite his epic victory over Boris Becker in the 1991 Wimbledon final, Stich had still lived in the shadow of his more famous countryman. At the ATP Tour Championship in Frankfurt that year, where they had met again, the contrast between the adulation for Becker and his own luke warm reception had hurt him.

The Hamburg fans had been more generous last May when Stich had beaten Becker again in the German Championships. It was a pity, therefore, that both Becker and world No.1 Jim Courier, who had fought out the ATP Tour Championship final a few weeks earlier, had not taken up their places for the spectacular season-ending jamboree in Munich. With both Germans in top form the prospect of a further meeting would have added spice to the proceedings. As it was we had to be content with a superb exhibition of power and control from Stich who seemed to be inspired by the presence of his new wife, Jessica (they had been married in September) and his coach, New Zealander Mark Lewis, at courtside.

The week had begun well for Stich. Against the top seed Stefan Edberg he served particularly well and fought back magnificently from 1–4 in the final set to impose a 7–6 6–7 8–6 defeat on the 26-year-old Swede. It was a superb encounter, played by two men who simply forced one another to raise their games to higher and higher levels. For two sets there were no breaks and only four of the 24 games – all of them in the first set – went to deuce. Such complete service dominance, aided by a Supreme court that all the players agreed was really too fast, can be boring but such was the skill on display that even the staccato rallies held a fascination of their own. Not surprisingly there was a full house for the occasion and the 11,000 patriotic spectators were noisy in their support of the local man. After all, Stich had been playing for Munich's Iphitos Club in the Bundesleague for three years and had first met his coach there.

As the climax of the final set was reached the cheers reached a crescendo and immediately it was over there were tears in Stich's eyes. He sat there surveying the scene as the exuberant supporters crowded round him. He had waited a long time for a moment like this. 'I am not ashamed to cry. Maybe this was one of the most important matches I have ever played...just to prove to myself that I can still win, to prove to all the people out there who counted me off already'

The confidence Stich gained from that win was apparent in the second round as he dealt with the heavy serves of Richard Krajicek, who had already blasted Emilio Sanchez from the scene 6–3 6–2. The margin of Stich's 7–6 7–5 victory may have been narrow but there was never the feeling that he might lose again to the Dutchman as he had done in Melbourne at the start of the year. By now his own impressive service was beginning to look more rhythmical, though the occasional frown revealed an impatience for perfection.

Now came an altogether sterner test, a best of five sets semi-final against Pete Sampras, the man who had won the first Compaq Grand Slam Cup two years earlier. With two impressive wins – against the Russian left-hander, Alexander Volkov (6–3 6–4) and Henri Leconte (7–6 6–4) behind him – it was apparent that the American was back in the form that had taken him to the US Open final three months earlier.

It was another high-quality battle with both men serving magnificently, volleying with great precision and projecting occasional returns and passes of incredible pace. In a sense, the 21-year-old American was unlucky not to win. At least the first set could have been his for it was Sampras who created three fleeting chances to break his opponent's serve. But Stich saved them all with total conviction and went on to win the set on a tie-break. Neither man conceded a chance to break in the second set and again it was Stich who was the firmer in the tie-break.

With the patriotic crowd again giving vent to their delight it was commendable that Sampras was able to snatch the third set on the first service break of the match in the sixth game. He simply swung early and connected. It was as simple as that. Yet, to maintain nerve and concentration in such a situation was not easy. In the fourth set it was Stich's turn to penetrate the American's defences for the first time and he went ahead 4–2. Serving for the match two games later, the tall German faltered. At 30–30 he attempted an ill-judged drop shot that Sampras reached easily and drove at him to set up his backhand volley winner. Another good return forced an error from Stich as his backhand volley fell long. But, to his credit, Stich did not panic. From 1–1 in the tie-break the German surged to victory 7–2 playing the last few points with complete assurance. At last the name of Michael Stich would appear in another major final. Wimbledon 1991 seemed so far away.

Chang, the only man in the field to have taken part in all three Grand Slam Cups, made equally impressive progress to his second consecutive final. In the first round he thrashed his old challenger from junior days, Andre Agassi, 6–4 6–2. Agassi's late arrival from Fort Worth following the US victory over Switzerland in the Davis Cup final was unavoidable but seemed to have left him jaded. On a day when extravagant errors outnumbered spectacular winners there could have been only one result. This was a disappointing performance from the Wimbledon champion whose inability to sustain his form across a full season leaves a question-mark above his head.

Next Chang accounted for French Open finalist, Petr Korda, who had been fortunate to survive in his opening round against Wally Masur. The Australian had led 6–2 5–3 and had held a match point before going down 2–6 7–5 6–4. However, Masur was not too disappointed that he had missed out on a prize of at least $300,000. He and Sweden's Nicklas Kulti, a 6–1 6–4 victim of John McEnroe, had filled the last two places in the 16-man draw. Thus they each and took home an early Christmas present of $100,000 instead of the $50,000 that would have been their reward as alternates if Courier and Becker had been present. As it was, last year's winner David Wheaton and Amos Mansdorf enjoyed that largesse.

Chang's semi-final opponent was the 21-year-old Croatian left-hander, Goran Ivanisevic, who had been too consistent for Frenchman Guy Forget in the first round but had then been forced to work hard by McEnroe, another whose Davis Cup duty had made him a late arrival in Munich. For one set we were tantalised with the prospect of one last great tournament triumph for the great man. He stood in and deflected the Croatian's hardest left-handed serves beyond the reach of his groping racket; he darted into the net and glided his angled volleys away with effortless ease; he teased with testing lobs. It could not last. Once Ivanisevic had got his mind focused, we were left in no doubt that McEnroe, at 33, can no longer live at the hot pace set by today's younger, stronger gladiators. So it proved. Ivanisevic duly opened his young shoulders to wrap up the match 3–6 6–4 6–2 and we were left wondering if we had witnessed a moment of tennis history, McEnroe's last serious singles match? As always, he kept us guessing. 'I'm going to take a step back now. I am not going to announce my retirement. I feel like it is better to keep my options open.' Enigmatic to the end.

Against Chang's nagging consistency and lightning court coverage, Ivanisevic tried hard to be patient. Certainly, since he began working with his Australian coach, Bob Brett, in February 1991 he is a much more mature match player. But he is also still a creature of moods. After dominating in the early stages with his booming serves and powerful blows from the backcourt which earned him the opening set on a tie-break, the sunny countenance disappeared behind black clouds of frustration. Ivanisevic played two dreadful sets, full of petulance and poor shot selection, that included a warning and a penalty point.

During the remainder of the match the courageous Chang, at 20 the youngest competitor in the field and at 5'3" the shortest, refused to be overawed – either by his opponent's size (6'4") or by his occasional brilliant winners. Nor was he distracted by his changing moods. Like the thorough professional he is, Michael simply went on doing what he does best – returning the ball to the feet of the advancing server and chasing everything in sight to surprise his foe with those improbable passes that seem drawn to the lines like iron filings to a magnet. He was also advancing to the net himself on occasion, though not yet with the confidence of a natural volleyer. Ivanisevic regrouped briefly to win the fourth set but as he delivered the last of his 23 aces in the decider to bring his season's total to an astonishing 1,015, he began to wilt again mentally and a jaunty Chang completed his 6–7 6–2 6–4 3–6 6–3 win in 3 hours and 38 minutes.

So here was Chang in the final once more, hoping to improve on his performance the previous year when David Wheaton had beaten him in straight sets. It was unfortunate for the brave little American that Stich decided to remind us of his days of glory at Wimbledon in 1991. Certainly the German hit his serve and backhand as well as he had done that day. In fact, after getting over a slightly edgy start, he hit everything as well – volley, lob, pass, return.

From 2–2 in the first set Stich ran off four games to clinch the opening set 6–2 in 43 minutes. The second turned on one break of serve in the 8th game and the momentum carried him to 2–0 in the third. The only blemish on an otherwise perfect performance came in the 4th game when he was broken for the only time. It merely delayed the end. With a flourish of cheeky, angled stop volleys and lobs, mixed in with impeccable serving, the German swept majestically through the last four games to complete his win in 126 minutes. If one could single out one aspect of his play that excelled it was his first volley. For consistency, depth and power that one stroke prevented Chang from ever developing his rallies as receiver.

It had been one of those Medusan days when everything Stich touched had turned to gold. There was one glorious moment when, trapped in mid-court, the German had improvised with an angled stop volley of such impudence and audacity that its unlikely success caused both players to laugh. The winner was in no doubt about the significance of the occasion. 'It was important for German tennis that I won today' he said. He might have added '...and absolutely vital for me personally.'

Even in defeat Chang was able to smile at the closing ceremony. After all, he had just added another $1 million to the family exchequer to bring his total Grand Slam Cup earnings to $2,450,000.

So ended the third edition of this innovative but controversial six million dollar event. As usual, it was staged sumptuously by Axel Meyer-Walden who dispensed with Placido Domingo this time but added a laser show to the proceedings. Bill Dennis, the Tournament Director, did a flawlessly efficient job and the Grand Slam Supervisor, Ken Farrar, was merely an interested spectator for most of the time, which is as it should be. But the Compaq Grand Slam Cup is not yet the true climax to the Grand Slam year it should be. Although it now has greater acceptance among the public (a record 63,200 attended the matches), the media and the players, it will not fulfil its potential until it moves to an October date with the women included and the men playing best-of-five set matches from round one.

COMPAQ GRAND SLAM CUP 1992
MUNICH, 8–13 DECEMBER
1st round: Michael Stich d. Stefan Edberg(1) 7–6 6–7 8–6; Richard Krajicek(8) d. Emilio Sanchez 6–3 6–2; Pete Sampras(3) d. Alexander Volkov 6–3 6–4; Henri Leconte d. Wayne Ferreira(5) 3–6 6–3 6–0; John McEnroe d. Niclas Kulti 6–1 6–4; Goran Ivanisevic (4) d. Guy Forget 7–5 6–4; Petr Korda(7) d. Wally Masur 2–6 7–5 6–4; Michael Chang d Andre Agassi (2) 6–4 6–2. ***Quarter-finals:*** Stich d Krajicek(8) 7–6 7–5; Sampras (3) d. Leconte 7–6 6–4; Ivanisevic (4) d. McEnroe 3–6 6–4 6–2; Chang d Korda(7) 6–3 6–4. ***Semi-finals:*** Stich d. Sampras (3) 7–6 7–6 7–6; Chang d Ivanisevic(4) 6–7 6–2 6–4 3–6 6–3. ***Final:*** Stich d Chang 6–2 6–3 6–2. ***Prize Money:*** Winner $2m; Finalist $1m; Semi-finalists $450,000; Quarter-finalists $300,000; First round losers $100,000; Alternates $50,000.

COMPAQ GRAND SLAM CUP PRIZE MONEY

During the three years of its existence the Compaq Grand Slam Cup has offered a total of $18 million in prize money, as well as contributing $6 million to the ITF's development fund. Of the forty players who have benefitted, only Michael Chang has actually taken part every year. The 1991 champion, David Wheaton, has been the most successful financially by virtue of reaching the semi-finals in 1990 and filling the passive role of alternate in 1992.

NAME	1990	1991	1992	TOTAL
1. WHEATON	450,000	2,000,000	50,00	2,500,000
2. SAMPRAS	2,000,000	—	450,000	2,450,000
3. STICH	—	450,000	2,000,000	2,450,000
4. CHANG	450,000	1,000,000	1,000,000	2,450,000
5. GILBERT	1,000,000	—	—	1,000,000
6. IVANISEVIC	300,000	—	450,000	750,000
7. LENDL	300,000	450,000	—	750,000
8. LECONTE	300,000	—	300,000	600,000
9. KRICKSTEIN	300,000	100,000	—	400,000
10. FORGET	—	300,000	100,000	400,000
11. WOOODBRIDGE	—	300,000	—	300,000
12. HLASEK	—	300,000	—	300,000
13. McENROE, P.	—	300,000	—	300,000
14. KRAJICEK	—	—	300,000	300,000
15. McENROE, J.	—	—	300,000	300,000
16. KORDA	—	—	300,000	300,000
17. EDBERG	100,000	—	100,000	200,000
18. CHAMPION	50,000	100,000	—	150,000
19. MUSTER	100,000	—	—	100,000
20. CHERKASOV	100,000	—	—	100,000
21. CURREN	100,000	—	—	100,000
22. SVENSSON	100,000	—	—	100,000
23. NOAH	100,000	—	—	100,000
24. GOMEZ	100,000	—	—	100,000
25. BERGSTROM	100,000	—	—	100,000
26. HAARHUIS	—	100,000	—	100,000
27. PRPIC	—	100,000	—	100,000
28. YZAGA	—	100,000	—	100,000
29. CONNORS	—	100,000	—	100,000
30. CARATTI	—	100,000	—	100,000
31. COURIER	—	100,000	—	100,000
32. SANCHEZ, E.	—	—	100,000	100,000
33. VOLKOV	—	—	100,000	100,000
34. FERREIRA	—	—	100,000	100,000
35. KULTI	—	—	100,000	100,000
36. MASUR	—	—	100,000	100,000
37. AGASSI	—	—	100,000	100,000
38. NOVACEK	50,000	—	—	50,000
39. SANCHEZ, J.	—	50,000	—	50,000
40. MANSDORF	—	—	50,000	50,000

GRAND SLAM DEVELOPMENT FUND

Ian Barnes

Now that the Compaq Grand Slam Cup has become firmly established and enables the four Grand Slam championships to make an annual contribution of $2 million to the Grand Slam Development, huge strides have been made in providing opportunities for players from many more countries to join the international tennis community.

During 1992, the second year in which the $2 million has been added to approximately $1 million from the ITF's own funds, dramatic expansion of our development initiatives was possible.

Demand for help increased considerably, especially in Eastern Europe, but funds were also provided for a comprehensive world wide educational programme for the training of coaches, in assisting the growth of wheelchair tennis and in the administration of veteran tennis, one of the fastest-growing areas of the game.

The impact in furthering competitive tennis opportunities for players from Africa, South and Central America, Asia and the South Pacific and Caribbean area has exceeded all expectations.

Following the appointment of Angus Macaulay as a Development Officer in East Africa since 1990, the last year has seen an expansion of this concept with the appointment of three more Development Officers – Dan O'Connell in the South Pacific, Frank Couraud in the English-speaking Caribbean, and Gustavo Granitto in Central America and the Spanish-speaking Caribbean.

In addition, the ITF has joined with Tennis South Africa in the establishment of a residential training school for coaches and players in Johannesburg, to which all African member nations will be able to send students.

We have also been able to expand the ITF Touring Team idea. Talented juniors from developing tennis nations have been invited to join ITF teams, which travel under the guidance of an ITF coach to eight different regions and we now have four international touring teams of aspiring young players taking the first steps on the professional ladder. As professionals, the players earn prize money to cover their expenses. The ITF employs the travelling coach and pays his expenses.

There has also been a considerable increase in the number of events for players of this level. Financial support for ITF Women's Futures events and ITF Men's Satellite Circuits has grown to such an extent that approximately $800,000 will be allocated in 1993.

The Equipment Distribution Programme continues to flourish with enthusiastic support from major manufacturers, particularly Prince and Wilson Sporting Goods. Shipping the equipment efficiently and economically is made possible through the generosity of Lufthansa.

The following tennis manufacturers and other groups
whose interests lie in the sport are members of the
ITF FOUNDATION

All materials for the ITF equipment distribution **Lufthansa**
programme are carried by our official carrier.

Any commercial tennis organisation is welcome to apply for membership
– details of the **ITF Foundation** and the benefits it brings
to both sport and member can be obtained from:-

**The ITF Foundation
International Tennis Federation
Palliser Road
Barons Court
London W14 9EN.**

THE CHANGING GAME

Richard Evans

By any standard, the ATP Tour World Championship in Frankfurt last year was a success. With Boris Becker winning in front of his own fanatical fans, it could hardly have been otherwise.

However, tournament director Zelko Franulovic and his staff had been receiving disturbing messages during the week, both from the lips of the players and from their own eyes. The message was simple. The court was playing faster than the previous year.

The question was: Why? Why would a court, not merely manufactured by the same company to strict specifications, but taken from the same strip of material, play faster then it had done when laid in the same hall, with the same underlay, a year earlier? The balls were the same as the previous year; the lighting was the same and although the court had been washed with soap – contrary to manufacturers instructions – this had only happened on the first day and, thereafter, only water was used. The mystery occupied the minds and the time of Greenset's Lee Frankel based in France and former South African Davis Cup star Gordon Forbes, the company's advisor who lives in Johannesburg. Faxes flew back and forth for days as every conceivable angle was analysed.

Eventually Franulovic came up with the simplest and, in some ways, the most disturbing solution of all. 'The blame, if you want to put it that way, must be with the players,' said the former French Open finalist. 'It is the only logical explanation. They are hitting the ball harder, they are serving with greater power and accuracy. They are just getting better all the time. They are ahead of the equipment.' If this seemingly inexorable increase in speed, power and athleticism makes a discernible difference on Greenset – a surface described by Ivan Lendl as being the fairest and most neutral in the world – then what is going to become of tennis on Wimbledon's fast grass?

It was this and other related questions that dominated technical tennis discussions wherever experts met during 1992. The topic had been launched with great deliberation by the ATP Tour who named 'The Speed of the Game' as the subject for their first ever seminar. Held in Miami during the Lipton, it was designed to gather and air opinions from experts on a number of pertinent aspects of the professional game.

Nothing was more pertinent than the fusion of two apparently unstoppable forces - more powerful equipment and more powerful players. The recent advent of the so-called 'wide-body' racket merely accentuated a process that had started with the first non-wood rackets which first came into use in the early seventies, metal to start with and then the sophistication of the big-headed graphite Prince. By the time Prince had established a niche in the market place it was too late for the ITF – which had no rules for what constituted a tennis racket before the mid-seventies – to cry Halt!

Club players and women players will not be unhappy about that. The larger playing surface and greater speed of the ball off the racket has made a difficult game more enjoyable for those who just like to play for fun while the women's game at the professional level has become more enjoyable to watch.

But for the male pros the problem was growing – all too literally. When Stefan Edberg first made it into the top ten he was, at just over six feet, one of the taller players amongst the game's elite, 'Now I feel like a midget,' Stefan laughs as he looks round the locker room at the likes of Goran Ivanisevic, Boris Becker, Guy Forget and Richard Krajicek.

When increasingly fit and powerful athletes are handed rackets that now enable the ball to travel 30% faster off the frame than did off wood, the game itself starts to change. One of the most disturbing observations heard at the Forum and from other sources is that coaches no longer need to bother with the finer points of the game – touch, finesse and angles – because the power is available to do the job for you. He who hits hardest wins. That is not the way it was meant to be, certainly not the way Jaroslav Drobny, Manolo Santana and Ilie Nastase played it. It was not the way John McEnroe wanted to play it although he had to learn to adapt. The statistical evidence is there to back up the theory that power is spoiling the game as a spectacle on faster surfaces. In the seventies the average point of grass lasted 3.8 seconds. Now it lasts 2.7 seconds. The average playing time per hour on grass twenty years ago was 7.18 minutes. Now, incredibly, it has dropped to 3.55. This startling change is not all due to shorter rallies. The increasing time taken between points and at the changes of end is also responsible.

Interestingly the trend on hardcourts is the other way. A point lasts longer today (6.5 seconds as opposed to 5.6) and the playing time per hour is almost identical. The reason for this is simple. Old style cement courts tended to be much harder and faster than the treated Decoturf style surfaces used today. These new courts can be slowed down to such an extent that some play as slow as clay. That, alas, is not the case with grass.

Greenset thought they had discovered the perfect mix with their Trophy court which is now used in Stockholm and Antwerp as well as at other stops on the ATP Tour. But if Becker, Ivanisevic and Krajicek can brutalise the court's intended neutrality with ever-increasing power, it will be back to the drawing board for Frankel and Forbes.

Where will it end? The conclusion of the ATP Tour hierarchy after the Forum in March 1992 was that there was no real mandate for change and CEO Mark Miles warned against hasty alterations to the rules and regulations governing the game. Caution is prudent but things have moved on apace and the whole problem needs to be constantly monitored and action taken before men's professional tennis is turned into a serving contest.

Obviously ball manufacturers will be keeping a close eye on the situation as they have it in their power to determine the speed of the game, up to a certain point. Slowing the game down would be a simple matter if it was just a question of making a heavier ball but solutions are not that easy, as Slazenger are well aware. This famous British company, the makers of the official ball at Wimbledon since 1902, did actually produce some slower balls in the seventies. (Yes, it was seen as a problem then!) But the players complained that the slower balls felt heavier and produced 'tennis elbow'. Professional players do not want their arms falling off as a result of being asked to serve with rocks.

Certainly the ITF should take a lead in asking all internationally recognised ball manufacturers to make proposals to solve the game's most pressing problem. Perhaps this is also the moment for the players to conduct some experiments of their own with the ATP Tour ball that is being manufactured under licence.

The ATP Tour organised a second forum in 1992 to discuss automatic line-call systems. It was held during the Italian Open in Rome and four companies were asked to present their ingenious inventions in an effort to solve another contentious issue. An updated version of Cyclops, the electronic eye that Ilie Nastase attempted to talk to when it first appeared on the Centre Court at Wimbledon in the 1970's and is still most commonly used, was one of the four. Others presented in Rome included the Australian TEL system, DSI of Israel that owed much to the development of military technology and a third system from Canada. Later in the year the TEL system was installed at Indianapolis and the US Open but only in a test capacity and was not taken into account by the umpire during actual match play.

The ITF expressed keen interest in all these experiments and said they were monitoring the situation via their member nations. David Cooper, who is in charge of all on-court rules and regulations for the ATP Tour, said that tests would continue through 1993 before any definitive decision was made. Mark Miles felt that the players would come to accept a total electronic line-calling system if it was proved to be absolutely accurate and reliable. There are, however, those in the game, including players who would be loath to programme the game still further at the expense of the human element. 'I need a human being to scream at occasionally,' one leading player said, and it was not a totally frivolous comment.

Huge rackets, power serves obliterating touch and artistry, bleeps and flashing lights in place of the line-person's cry – is this the way we want the game to go? The debate is pivotal to the future success of professional tennis and it will rage on through 1993.

IBM/ATP TOUR

TOUR REVIEW
POINTS EXPLANATION
IBM/ATP TOURNAMENTS
ATP TOUR WORLD CHAMPIONSHIP

The powerful Croatian left-hander Goran Ivanisevic enjoyed his best-ever season by winning four titles on the IBM/ATP Tour, reaching the Wimbledon final and winning a bronze medal at the Olympics, results which lifted him to a year-end ranking of No.4.   (T. Hindley)

Stefan Edberg was engaged in a year-long struggle for the No.1 ranking which he held for 12 weeks altogether but he ended 1992 in second place behind Jim Courier.   (T. Hindley)

IBM/ATP TOUR REVIEW

John Parsons

The United States could look back on 1992 as very much the year in which it regained clear supremacy in men's tennis. In addition to regaining The Davis Cup, the Americans almost doubled the number of titles won by their players on the IBM/ATP Tour. And a year which also marked the farewell from the regular circuit of John McEnroe, the greatest of their modern masters, finished with Jim Courier first and Pete Sampras third in the ATP world rankings.

Although the United States had still won more titles than any other nation in 1991, the total of 13 was their lowest since rankings based on performances in tournaments all round the world, had been introduced in 1973. In 1992, not only did that figure soar to 24 but so too did the quality of the titles they achieved. These included three of the four Grand Slam tournaments, compared with only one in the previous year.

Even so, it was a European, Boris Becker, who provided a fitting climax to the ATP year at the Championships in Frankfurt. After what hitherto had largely been a frustrating year for the former world champion and world number one, Becker produced some of his most compelling form to bring down both Goran Ivanisevic and Jim Courier.

Individually, though, the men's 1992 tour belonged to Courier. However, a decline in the second half of the year, when he failed to add to the five titles he had collected by the end of the French Open, meant that his status as number one remained in doubt almost to the end. Indeed when the ATP Championships began, both Stefan Edberg and Pete Sampras – the latter somewhat tenuously – had a chance to overtake him.

Such tension led to interesting debates. There were those who questioned the quality of a world number one whose form had slumped so badly that he only managed a 23–12 win loss record in the second half of the year after winning 46 of his 52 matches up to the end of June. Others, including fellow American player, Michael Chang, questioned the reliability of a ranking system which meant that Courier, as holder of the Australian and French Open titles and a semi-finalist at the US Open, could still have been left in such suspense for so long.

Chang was far from alone in making the point that, irrespective of the continuing controversy about the Best 14 rule (which most top players abhor but most tournament directors appear to prefer), there ought to be a greater differential between the number of points allocated for regular tour events and the four Grand Slams. With no disrespect to Sampras it would surely have totally discredited the ATP ranking system had everything fallen into place for him during Frankfurt and he had finished as number one in a year when he did not win any of the Grand Slams. As it was, when Agassi, the Wimbledon winner, only finished in ninth position on their list, tour officials should have realised that their system, while influenced originally by the best intentions, still has obvious flaws.

Courier is the tenth player – and only the third American after Jimmy Connors and John McEnroe – who has so far achieved the world number one ranking. He took over at the top from Stefan Edberg on February 10 after finishing runner-up to Chang in San Francisco. Yet such are the vagaries of the ranking system, especially since the introduction of the Best 14 rule, that twice (for three weeks in March and for another three weeks in September), Edberg won the position back. On the first occasion he was not even playing at the time! Overall it meant the number one position changed hands five times during the year, the most in any year since 1984.

In terms of titles won Courier, with five, finished equal with fellow American, Pete Sampras and Becker. In addition to his Grand Slam successes, Courier also won, in chronological order, the Japan Open, Hong Kong and Rome. Sampras, who was also runner-up at the US Open, earned wins between February and September. His victories at Philadelphia, Kitzbuhel, Cincinnati, Indianapolis and Lyon, also encompassed three different surfaces – carpet, clay and hard. The only other player to demonstrate such broad-based success was Wimbledon champion, Andre Agassi. The three tournaments he won were on grass, clay and hard. Four of Becker's five titles were won on indoor carpet courts, the other on hard. Fiercely though he tries to overcome the problem, clay remains an anathema to him and the scale of his semi-final defeat by fellow German, Michael Stich in Hamburg, did nothing to ease the mental pain.

During Courier's golden period in April and May, which culminated in him becoming the first American since Tony Trabert in 1954 to win at Roland Garros for a second consecutive year, the Floridian also registered the longest winning streak of the year. It lasted 25 matches before his defeat in Wimbledon's fourth round by Russia's expert qualifier, Andrei Olhovskiy. He topped the qualifying list by winning his way into the main draws of nine events altogether during the year.

Only four players won ten or more matches in succession. Sampras, who won 16, beat Edberg, Becker and Courier twice along the way before losing to Edberg in the final of the US Open. Michael Chang and Karel Novacek both won 15 consecutive matches while Spain's Carlos Costa won 12 during a superb spell on European clay in March and April.

In general, though, it was another year when the form of too many leading players too often seemed transient. Chang, for instance, although going down to Richard Krajicek in Australia, dominated on the American hard courts at the start of the year. The battling American won all three of his 1992 titles, including Indian Wells and the Lipton before March was out. While Carlos Costa was emerging as a potential new European clay court contender, Courier swept through the Far East and Europe, hinting, though falsely we quickly discovered, that no-one would stop him anywhere on anything.

Midsummer produced the usual varied crop of winners as most top ten competitors wound down after Wimbledon and prepared for the US Open. This group included Sampras, who began his late push to be number one, and Becker. The powerful German, rediscovering the confidence and authority which had helped him beat Courier in a memorable final from two sets down in Brussels in February, provided a timely reminder that he still has much to offer.

If there was one spectacularly consistent feature during 1992, it was surely the way in which Goran Ivanisevic kept adding to his runaway lead as the player hitting the most aces. There were 105 in five matches in Stuttgart, where he simply outgunned Edberg in the final. At Wimbledon there were a staggering 206 in seven matches. But Agassi's returning of the serve on the fast grass temporarily, at least, silenced the debate on power dominance and various rule changes or restrictions to rackets and tennis balls which some were advocating.

Ivanisevic eventually delivered a total of 957 aces in his 72 matches on the ATP Tour, 212 more than Pete Sampras, his nearest rival, who struck 745 in 76 matches. Richard Krajicek's 733 also beat the highest number in 1991, which was 611 by Guy Forget. With his 49 at the Olympics and 60 at the Grand Slam Cup, Ivanisevic's complete tally for the year was 1,066 in 80 matches.

In 1991, the 80 tournaments were won by 46 different players. In 1992, there were 43 different winners at 82 tournaments. Such widespread success is obviously good in one major respect; the more players there are who are capable of striving for the top as tournament winners, the better is must be for the overall health of the tour and the game.

Yet the number of tournaments won by the top ten dropped by almost ten per cent from 36 to 33. While this is not necessarily a warning sign, is a timely reminder of how important it also is to maintain a proper balance between expanding the honours list and maintaining quality. Shock results are admirable for the game – if not always for promoters – when they are genuinely accomplished on properly tested merit but not when there has been an unmistakeable lack of commitment. However genuine the reasons, it was still disappointing that only Edberg among those who finished in the top ten, went through the year without losing his opening match at least once on the ATP

Tour. Courier, to his credit, lost in this way only once, Sampras and Goran Ivanisevic, twice. At least half went out immediately in four or more of their events.

On the credit side, the number of countries represented on the list of tournament winners rose from 17 to 18, with ten Americans contributing to their total of 24, although appropriately enough three of their winning Davis Cup quartet, Courier, Sampras and Agassi took the lions share with 13 between them.

Germany stayed in second place but their total dropped from ten to eight and was matched by Spain, who climbed from the fifth position they had held for the previous two years. Next came Sweden, who had almost closed the gap on the Americans in 1991 with eleven titles but this time, due mainly to Edberg's personal contribution dropping from six to three, they provided the champion for only seven tournaments.

The number of countries with players ranked in the top 100, maintained last year's five-year-high of 24. Although the United States, with 18 this time (compared with 17 in 1991), again emphasised their numerical as well as practical superiority, there was some fascinating movement lower down the table.

France, for instance, climbed to second place with a record nine players in the top 100, two more than in the previous year, sharing the status with Spain. Both overtook Sweden, who slipped to fourth. Next came Australia, with 7, Germany 6 and then came four nations, Argentina, Italy, Netherlands and the newly created CIS (formerly the Soviet Union), all with five. Finland, Canada, Haiti and Ecuador (thanks to the retirement of Andres Gomez) dropped out of the list and were replaced by Uruguay (Marcelo Filippini), New Zealand (Brett Steven), Mexico (Luis Herrera) and Denmark (Kenneth Carlsen.)

Carlsen, who reached his first tour final when he was runner-up to Frenchman, Guillaume Raoux, at the Queensland Open in Brisbane during the first weekend of October, also made by far the most spectacular ranking progress during 1992, soaring from 1,036 to 69, a quite phenomenal improvement. The next best was an improvement of 241 places by Austrian newcomer, Gilbert Schaller, who climbed from 323 to 82, although in terms of where they eventually finished, the two most outstanding achievements were probably registered by Andrei Medvedev as he lifted his ranking from 226 to 24, and by Henrik Holm. The Swede had started the year ranked 129 but by the end had broken into the top 20 to occupy 19th place.

Medvedev, who had first attracted major attention a year earlier when, at 17, he three times qualified for main draws, had a magnificent year. He won three tournaments, all on clay (Genova in June, Bordeaux in September and Stuttgart in July). Commendably, he had qualified for the latter, a Championship Series million dollar event with a high class pre-Olympic Games entry. There, in successive rounds he defeated Alexander Volkov, Emilio Sanchez, Edberg (after losing the first set 6–1), Thomas Muster and then Wayne Ferreira, in the final.

The only other qualifier to win a title during the year was Carsten Arriens, who had started 1992 ranked only 26th among German players but, with a world ranking of 210, won a modest World Series event in Guaruja, Brazil, in November.

Both Arriens, then 23, and Medvedev, still 17, were among the 16 players (one fewer than the previous year), who won tour events for the first time. Medvedev, with the help of a wild card entry, became the youngest tournament winner of the year in Genova. Only Malivai Washington, however, in Memphis in February, won the first tour title of his career in a Championship Series event. All the other title breakthroughs, including those by Medvedev and Arriens, came in World Series tournaments and were registered also by: Jeff Tarango (Wellington), Tomas Carbonell (Maceio), Stefan Pescosolido (Scottsdale), Carlos Costa (Estoril), Gabriel Markus (Nice), Shuzo Matsuoka (Seoul), Jaime Oncins (Brazil), Wayne Ferreira (Queen's), Jacob Eltingh (Manchester), Bernd Karbacher (Cologne), Guillaume Raoux (Brisbane) and Thomas Enqvist (Bolzano).

Others to win tournaments with the help of wild cards were Ivanisevic (Adelaide), Becker (Brussels), Muster (Florence) and Krajicek (Antwerp). The Dutch player's success on the last regular week of the tour also swept him, out of the blue (for he had not even been included in ATP's list of possible candidates at the start of the week), into the last qualifying place for the Championships in Frankfurt when Ivan Lendl and first reserve,

Agassi, withdrew through injury.

Stefan Edberg won more prize money than anyone else on the Tour for the third successive year and lifted himself above John McEnroe into second place in the all-time list with $13.3 million. He was still nearly $6 million behind Ivan Lendl's $19.1 million. Even so Edberg's $2,341,804 for the year was fractionally down on his $2,363,575 in 1991. Against that, however, this was the first year in which more than one player had surpassed the $2 million mark. Boris Becker won $2,293,687 and Jim Courier $2,253,385. Naturally enough when the $2 million Compaq Grand Slam Cup first prize is included, Michael Stich, as the winner in Munich, overtook not only these two men but also Monica Seles. The top prize money winner in women's tennis with earnings of $2,622,352, is nearly a million dollars ahead of her nearest rival.

The number of players who exceeded $1 million in tournament earnings during 1992 remained at seven, the same as in the previous year, although the number of those winning more than $500,000 rose from 17 to 23.

Mark Woodforde and Todd Woodbridge's outstanding year in doubles, during which they won eight of the 19 tournaments in which they played, including the Tour Championships in Johannesburg, enabled both of them to finish among the top 20 prize money winners, with $706,836 and $656,642 respectively. In the final they beat John Fitzgerald and Anders Jarryd, the Australia–Sweden combination, which had won both the title and the doubles points race in 1991.

In a year when all four Grand Slam doubles titles were won by different pairings, Woodforde and Woodbridge, who set the pace by winning the Australian Open, led the doubles points table for most of the year. Their 6–2 7–6 5–7 3–6 6–3 victory in the Johannesburg final maintained their astonishing unbeaten record in 12 finals together in two years. For Woodbridge it was his 15th consecutive victory in a doubles final, only four short of McEnroe's record of 19.

Jim Grabb and Richey Reneberg finished runners-up in the doubles race, with four tournament wins from 17 tournaments and four other finals – including that record Wimbledon classic against McEnroe and Stich. As McEnroe observed later: 'After a match like that on a day like that, there's only one way you can go.'

IBM/ATP TOUR 1992 – POINTS EXPLANATION

The tables below show the ranking points to be won at the four Grand Slam Championships and all tournaments on the IBM/ATP Tour – including Challengers with minimum prize money of $25,000 – as well as at the Satellite circuits organised by member nations of the I.T.F. A player's ranking alone decides whether or not he is accepted into the main draw or the qualifying event at all Tour tournaments.

Identical points are awarded for singles and doubles. No points are awarded until a player has completed a match. Anyone who reaches the second round via a bye and then loses is considered to have lost in the first round and receives one point, but he does receive second round prize money. There are additional 'Bonus Points' awarded for beating players ranked between 1 and 200 in singles, or a team ranked between 2 and 400 in doubles. In addition to the points won in any tournament, a player or doubles team winning a place in the main draw via qualifying also receives half the points awarded to the second round loser in that tournament. Lucky Losers receive no qualifying points.

POINTS ALLOCATION

CATEGORY	PRIZE(US$)	W	F	S	Q	16	32	64	128
Grand Slams	4.0 Million	520	390	260	130	65	33	17	1
	3.5 Million	500	375	250	125	63	32	16	1
	3.0 Million	480	360	240	120	60	30	15	1
	2.5 Million	460	345	230	115	58	29	15	1
	2.0 Million	440	330	220	110	55	28	14	1
Championship	1,875,000	300	225	150	75	38	19	10	1
Series	1,750,000	290	218	145	73	37	19	10	1
	1,625,000	280	210	140	70	35	18	9	1
	1,500,000	270	203	135	68	34	17	9	1
	1,375,000	260	195	130	65	33	17	1	–
	1,250,000	250	188	125	63	32	16	1	–
	1,125,000	240	180	120	60	30	15	1	–
	1,000,000	230	173	115	58	29	15	1	–
	875,000	220	165	110	55	28	14	1	–
	750,000	210	158	105	53	27	14	1	–
	625,000	200	150	100	50	25	13	1	–
World Series	675,000	170	128	85	43	22	11	1	–
	600,000	160	120	80	40	20	10	1	–
	525,000	150	113	75	38	19	10	1	–
	450,000	140	105	70	35	18	9	1	–
	375,000	130	98	65	33	17	9	1	–
	300,000	120	90	60	30	15	8	1	–
	225,000	110	83	55	28	14	7	1	–
	150,000	100	75	50	25	13	1	–	–
Challenger *	100,000+H	80	60	40	20	10	1	–	–
Series	100,000	70	53	35	18	9	1	–	–
	75,000	60	45	30	15	8	1	–	–
	50,000	50	38	25	13	7	1	–	–
	25,000	40	30	20	10	5	1	–	–

* Any Challenger providing hospitality will receive the points of the next highest prize money level. Monies shown are on-site amounts.

BONUS POINTS

Singles		*Doubles*	
		Team	
Ranking	Bonus Points	Ranking	Bonus Points
1	50	2–3	50
2–5	45	4–10	45
6–10	36	11–20	36
11–20	24	21–40	24
21–30	18	41–60	18
31–50	12	61–100	12
51–75	6	101–150	6
76–100	3	151–200	3
101–150	2	201–300	2
151–200	1	301–400	1

GRAND SLAM CHAMPIONSHIPS AND IBM/ATP TOUR 1992

DATE	VENUE	SURFACE	SINGLES FINAL	DOUBLES WINNERS
30 Dec–5 Jan	Adelaide	Hard	G. Ivanisevic d. C. Bergstrom 1–6 7–6 6–4	G. Ivanisevic/M. Rosset
30 Dec–5 Jan	Wellington	Hard	J. Tarango d. A. Volkov 6–1 6–0 6–3	J. Palmer/J. Stark
6–12 Jan	Auckland	Hard	J. Yzaga d. M. Washington 7–6 6–4	W. Ferreira/J. Grabb
6–12 Jan	Sydney NSW	Hard	E. Sanchez d. G. Forget 6–3 6–4	S. Casal/E. Sanchez
13–20 Jan	Australian Open	Hard	J. Courier d. S. Edberg 6–3 3–6 6–4 6–2	T. Woodbridge/M. Woodforde
3–9 Feb	Milan	Carpet	O. Camporese d. G. Ivanisevic 3–6 6–3 6–4	N. Broad/D. MacPherson
3–9 Feb	San Francisco	Hard	M. Chang d. J. Courier 6–3 6–3	J. Grabb/R. Reneberg
10–16 Feb	Brussels	Carpet	B. Becker d. J. Courier 6–7 2–6 7–6 7–6 7–5	B. Becker/J. McEnroe
10–16 Feb	Memphis	Hard	M. Washington d. W. Ferreira 6–3 6–2	T. Woodbridge/M. Woodforde
17–23 Feb	Philadelphia	Carpet	P. Sampras d. A. Mansdorf 6–1 7–6 2–6 7–6	T. Woodbridge/M. Woodforde
17–23 Feb	Stuttgart	Carpet	G. Ivanisevic d. S. Edberg 6–7 6–3 6–4 6–4	T. Nijssen/C. Suk
24 Feb–1 March	Rotterdam	Carpet	B. Becker d. A. Volkov 7–6 4–6 6–2	M. Goellner/D. Prinosil
24 Feb–1 March	Scottsdale	Hard	S. Pescosolido d. B. Gilbert 6–0 1–6 6–4	M. Keil/D. Randall
2–8 March	Indian Wells	Hard	M. Chang d. A. Chesnokov 6–3 6–4 7–5	S. DeVries/D. Macpherson
2–8 March	Copenhagen	Carpet	M. Larsson d. A. Jarryd 6–4 7–6	N. Kulti/M. Larsson
13–22 March	Key Biscayne	Hard	M. Chang d. A. Mancini 7–5 7–5	K. Flach/T. Witsken
16–22 March	Casablanca	Clay	G. Perez–Roldan d. G. Lopez 2–6 7–5 6–3	H. De la Pena/J. Lozano
30 March–5 April	Lisbon	Clay	C. Costa d. S. Bruguera 4–6 6–2 6–2	H–J. Davids/L. Pimek
30 March–5 April	Johannesburg	Hard	A. Krickstein d. A. Volkov 6–4 6–4	P. Aldrich/D. Visser
30 March–5 April	Singapore	Hard	S. Youl d. P. Haarhuis 6–4 6–1	T. Woodbridge/M. Woodforde
6–12 April	Barcelona	Clay	C. Costa d. M. Gustafsson 6–4 7–6 6–4	A. Gomez/J. Sanchez
6–12 April	Tokyo	Hard	J. Courier d. R. Krajicek 6–4 6–4 7–6	K. Jones/R. Leach
13–19 April	Hong Kong	Hard	J. Courier d. M. Chang 7–5 6–3	B. Gilbert/J. Grabb
13–19 April	Nice	Clay	G. Markus d. J. Sanchez 6–4 6–4	P. Galbraith/S. Melville
13–19 April	Tampa	Clay	J. Yzaga d. M. Washington 4–6 6–3 6–1	M. Briggs/T. Kronemann
20–26 April	Monte Carlo	Clay	T. Muster d. A. Krickstein 6–3 6–1 6–3	B. Becker/M. Stich
20–26 April	Seoul	Hard	S. Matsuoka d. T. Woodbridge 6–3 4–6 7–5	K. Curren/G. Muller
27 April–3 May	Atlanta	Clay	A. Agassi d. P. Sampras 7–5 6–4	S. DeVries/D. Macpherson
27 April–3 May	Madrid	Clay	S. Bruguera d. C. Costa 7–6 6–2 6–2	P. Galbraith/P. McEnroe
27 April–3 May	Munich	Clay	M. Larsson d. P. Korda 6–4 4–6 6–1	D. Adams/M. Oosting
4–10 May	Charlotte	Clay	M. Washington d. C. Mezzadri 6–3 6–3	S. DeVries/D. Macpherson
4–11 May	Hamburg	Clay	S. Edberg d. M. Stich 5–7 6–4 6–1	S. Casal/E. Sanchez
11–17 May	Rome	Clay	J. Courier d. C. Costa 7–6 6–0 6–4	J. Hlasek/M. Rosset
18–24 May	Bologna	Clay	J. Oncins d. R. Furlan 6–2 6–4	L. Jensen/L. Warder
18–24 May	Dusseldorf	Clay	E. Sanchez d. P. Korda 3–6 6–2 7–6	S. Casal/E. Sanchez
25 May–7 June	French Open	Clay	J. Courier d. P. Korda 7–5 6–2 6–1	J. Hlasek/M. Rosset
8–14 June	Florence	Clay	T. Muster d. R. Furlan 6–3 1–6 6–1	M. Filippini/L. Mattar
8–14 June	Queen's	Grass	W. Ferreira d. S. Matsuoka 6–3 6–4	J. Fitzgerald/A. Jarryd
8–14 June	Rosmalen	Grass	M. Stich d. J. Stark 6–4 7–5	J. Grabb/R. Reneberg
15–21 June	Manchester	Clay	J. Eltingh d. M. Washington 6–3 6–4	P. Galbraith/D. MacPherson
15–21 June	Genoa	Clay	A. Medvedev d. G. Perez–Roldan 6–3 6–4	S. Cannon/G. Van Emburgh
22 June–5 July	Wimbledon	Grass	A. Agassi d. G. Ivanisevic 6–7 6–4 6–4 1–6 6–4	J.P. McEnroe/M. Stich
6–12 July	Bastad	Clay	M. Gustafsson d. T. Carbonell 5–7 7–5 6–4	T. Carbonell/C. Miniussi
6–12 July	Newport	Grass	B. Shelton d. A. Antonitsch 6–4 6–4	D. Deppe/D. Rikl
6–12 July	Gstaad	Clay	S. Bruguera d. F. Clavet 6–1 6–4	H. Davids/L. Pimek
13–19 July	Stuttgart	Clay	A. Medvedev d. W. Ferreira 6–1 6–4 6–7 2–6 6–1	G. Layendecker/B. Talbot
13–19 July	Washington	Hard	P. Korda d. H. Holm 6–4 6–4	B. Garnett/J. Palmer
19–25 July	Toronto	Hard	A. Agassi d. I. Lendl 3–6 6–2 6–0	P. Galbraith/D. Visser
20–26 July	Hilversum	Clay	K. Novacek d. J. Arrese 6–2 6–3 2–6 7–5	P. Haarhuis/K. Koevermans
20–26 July	Kitzbuhel	Clay	P. Sampras d. A. Mancini 6–3 7–5 6–3	S. Casal/E. Sanchez
27 July–2 Aug	San Marino	Clay	K. Novacek d. F. Clavet 7–5 6–2	K. Kulti/M. Tillstrom
28 July–8 Aug	Olympics, Barcelona	Clay	M. Rosset d. J. Arrese 7–6 6–3 3–6 4–6 8–6	B. Becker/M. Stich
3–9 Aug	Los Angeles	Hard	R. Krajicek d. M. Woodforde 6–4 2–6 6–4	P. Galbraith/J. Pugh
10–16 Aug	Cincinnati	Hard	P. Sampras d. I. Lendl 6–3 3–6 6–3	T. Woodbridge/M. Woodforde
10–16 Aug	Prague	Clay	K. Novacek d. F. Davin 6–1 6–1	K. Novacek/B. Stankovic
17–23 Aug	Indianapolis	Hard	P. Sampras d. J. Courier 6–4 6–4	J. Grabb/R. Reneberg
17–23 Aug	New Haven	Hard	S. Edberg d. M. Washington 7–6 6–1	K. Jones/R. Leach
24–30 Aug	Long Island	Hard	P. Korda d. I. Lendl 6–2 6–2	F. Montana/G. Van Emburgh
24–30 Aug	Schenectady	Hard	W. Ferreira d. J. Morgan 6–2 7–6–2	J. Eltingh/P. Haarhuis
31 Aug–13 Sept	US Open	Hard	S. Edberg d. P. Sampras 3–6 6–4 7–6 6–2	J. Grabb/R. Reneberg
14–20 Sept	Bordeaux	Clay	A. Medvedev d. S. Bruguera 6–3 1–6 6–2	S. Casal/E. Sanchez
14–20 Sept	Cologne	Clay	B. Karbacher d. M. Ondruska 7–6 6–4	H. De la Pena/G. Luza
28 Sept–4 Oct	Basel	Hard	B. Becker d. P. Korda 3–6 6–3 6–2 6–4	T. Nijssen/C. Suk
28 Sept–4 Oct	Brisbane	Hard	G. Raoux d. K. Carlsen 6–4 7–6	S. Devries/D. Macpherson
28 Sept–4 Oct	Palermo	Clay	S. Bruguera d. E. Sanchez 6–1 6–3	J. Donar/L. Jonsson
5–11 Oct	Sydney	Hard	G. Ivanisevic d. S. Edberg 6–4 6–2	J. McEnroe/J. Stark
5–11 Oct	Athens	Clay	J. Arrese d. S. Bruguera 7–5 3–0 ret.	T. Carbonell/F. Roig
5–11 Oct	Toulouse	Hard	G. Forget d. P. Korda 6–3 6–2	B. Pearce/J. Talbot
12–18 Oct	Tokyo	Carpet	I. Lendl d. H. Holm 6–3 6–4	T. Woodbridge/M. Woodforde
12–18 Oct	Bolzano	Carpet	T. Enqvist d. A. Boetsch 6–2 1–6 7–6	A. Jarryd/G. Pedersen
12–18 Oct	Tel Aviv	Hard	J. Tarango d. S. Simian 4–6 6–3 6–4	P. Bauer/J. Cunha–Silva
19–25 Oct	Lyon	Carpet	P. Sampras d. C. Pioline 6–4 6–2	J. Hlasek/M. Rosset
19–25 Oct	Vienna	Carpet	P. Korda d. G. Pozzi 6–3 6–2 5–7 6–1	R. Bathman/A. Jarryd
19–25 Oct	Taipei	Carpet	J. Grabb d. J. Morgan 6–3 6–3	J. Fitzgerald/S. Stolle
26 Oct–1 Nov	Stockholm	Carpet	G. Ivanisevic d. G. Forget 7–6 4–6 7–6 6–2	M. Woodford/T. Woodbridge
26 Oct–1 Nov	Guaruja	Hard	C. Arriens d. A. Corretja 7–6 6–3	C. Allgardh/C. Limberger
2–8 Nov	Paris	Hard	B. Becker d. G. Ivanesevic 6–1 6–2	J. McEnroe/P. McEnroe
2–8 Nov	Buzios	Clay	J. Oncins d. L. Herrera 6–3 6–2	M. Ruah/M. Tabares
9–15 Nov	Moscow	Carpet	M. Rosset d. C. Steeb 6–2 6–2	M. Barnard/J.L. de Jager
9–15 Nov	Sao Paulo	Hard	L. Mattat d. J. Oncins 6–1 6–4	D. Perez/F. Roig
9–15 Nov	Antwerp	Carpet	R. Krajicek d. M. Woodforde 6–2 6–2	J. Fitzgerald/A. Jarryd
16–22 Nov	Johannesburg	Hard		T. Woodbridge/M. Woodforde
23–29 Nov	Frankfurt		B. Becker d. J. Courier 6–4 6–3 7–5	
8–13 Dec	Munich		M. Stich d. M. Chang 6–2 6–3 6–2	

PLAYER NATIONALITIES AND BIRTHDAYS

The following players have competed in the 1992 Grand Slam Tournaments and the ATP Tour:

Name and Nationality	Date of Birth	Name and Nationality	Date of Birth
Adams, Chuck (USA)	23/04/71	Carbonell, Tomas (ESP)	23/08/68
Adams, David (AUS)	05/01/70	Carlsen, Kenneth (DEN)	17/04/73
Agassi, Andre (USA)	29/04/70	Carlsson, Johan (SWE)	29/01/66
Agenor, Ronald (HAI)	13/11/64	Casal, Sergio (ESP)	08/09/62
Aguilera, Juan (ESP)	22/03/62	Casey, Owen (IRL)	22/10/69
Alami, Karim (MAR)	24/05/73	Cash, Pat (AUS)	27/05/65
Albano, Pablo (ARG)	11/04/67	Cask, Jason (AUS)	07/02/71
Allgardh, Christer (SWE)	20/02/67	Castle, Andrew (GBR)	15/11/63
Altur, Jose-Francisco (ESP)	24/03/68	Chamberlin, Paul (USA)	26/03/62
Alvarez, Roberto (ARG)	23/02/71	Champion, Thierry (FRA)	31/08/66
Anderson, Johan (AUS)	29/09/71	Chang, Cheng-Fong (TPE)	20/04/72
Annacone, Paul (USA)	20/03/63	Chang, Eui-Jong (KOR)	01/04/69
Antonitsch, Alex (AUT)	06/02/66	Chang, Michael (USA)	22/02/72
Aparisi, Jose-Luis (ESP)	11/03/69	Cheng, Chin-Jung (TPE)	24/09/72
Apell, Jan (SWE)	04/11/69	Cherkasov, Andrei (URS)	04/07/70
Arbanas, John (AUS)	07/02/70	Chesnokov, Andrei (URS)	02/02/66
Ardinghi, Massimo (ITA)	06/03/71	Cierro, Massimo (ITA)	07/05/64
Arias, Jimmy (USA)	16/08/64	Clavet, Francisco (ESP)	24/10/68
Arraya, Pablo (PER)	21/10/61	Conde, Jose-Antonio (ESP)	13/03/70
Arrese, Jordi (ESP)	29/08/64	Connell, Grant (CAN)	17/11/65
Arriens, Carsten (GER)	11/04/69	Connors, Jimmy (USA)	02/09/52
Azar, Roberto (ARG)	21/03/66	Corrales Gonzalo (ESP)	26/04/75
Baguena, Juan-Carlos (ESP)	07/01/67	Corretja, Alex (ESP)	11/04/74
Bahrami, Mansour (IRN)	26/04/56	Cortes, Sergio (CHI)	11/01/68
Bailey, Chris (GBR)	29/04/68	Costa, Carlos (ESP)	24/04/68
Bale, Lan (RSA)	07/09/69	Courier, Jim (USA)	17/08/70
Baron, Ivan (USA)	12/11/72	Cousin, Fabien (BEL)	21/01/69
Barrientos, Felix (PHI)	20/11/67	Couto, Emanuel (POR)	06/08/73
Bates, Jeremy (GBR)	19/06/62	Crow, Pat (USA)	04/11/64
Baur, Patrick (GER)	03/05/65	Cunha-Silva, Joao (POR)	27/11/67
Bavelas, Tasos (GRE)	27/02/68	Curren, Kevin (USA)	02/03/58
Becerra, Nicolas (ARG)	06/11/69	Daher, Jose (BRA)	20/04/66
Becker, Boris (GER)	22/11/67	Damm, Martin (TCH)	01/08/72
Benhabiles, Tarik (FRA)	05/02/65	Daufresne, Xavier (BEL)	24/12/68
Berasategui, Alberto (ESP)	28/06/73	Davids, Hendrik-Jan (HOL)	30/01/69
Bergstrom, Christian (SWE)	19/07/67	Davin, Franco (ARG)	11/01/70
Bezecny, George (USA)	24/03/63	Davis, Scott (USA)	27/08/62
Bjorkman, Jonas (SWE)	23/03/72	De Jager, John-Laffnie (RSA)	17/03/73
Black, Byron (ZIM)	06/10/69	De La Pena, Horacio (ARG)	01/08/66
Blackman, Martin (USA)	03/05/70	De Miguel, David (ESP)	07/02/65
Bloom, Gilad (ISR)	01/03/67	Delaitre, Olivier (FRA)	01/06/67
Boetsch, Arnaud (FRA)	01/04/69	Devening, Brian (USA)	16/07/67
Borg, Bjorn (SWE)	06/06/56	Di Lucia, David (USA)	15/01/70
Borwick, Neil (AUS)	15/09/67	Doohan, Peter (AUS)	02/05/61
Bosse, Dick (RSA)	01/08/67	Dosedel, Ctislav (TCH)	14/01/70
Braasch, Karsten (GER)	14/07/67	Doumbia, Yahiya (SEN)	25/08/63
Broad, Neil (GBR)	20/11/66	Doyle, Grant (AUS)	09/01/74
Brown, Jimmy (USA)	28/04/65	Dunn, Brian (USA)	05/04/74
Bruguera, Sergi (ESP)	16/01/71	Dyke, Broderick (AUS)	31/12/60
Bruno, Nicola (ITA)	26/01/71	Dzelde, Girts (URS)	16/07/63
Bryan, Steve (USA)	10/08/70	Edberg, Stefan (SWE)	19/01/66
Buchmayer, Thomas (AUT)	14/02/71	El Ayanaoui, Younes (MAR)	12/09/71
Burillo, Jordi (ESP)	07/12/72	Eltingh, Jacco (HOL)	29/08/70
Burtshcer, Thomas (AUT)	15/06/69	Engel, David (SWE)	17/10/67
Camporese, Omar (ITA)	08/05/68	Enqvist, Thomas (SWE)	13/03/74
Cane, Paolo (ITA)	09/04/65	Etchecoin, Juan-Pablo (BRA)	22/03/69
Cannon, Shelby (USA)	19/08/66	Evernden, Kelly (NZL)	21/09/62
Caratti, Cristiano (ITA)	23/04/70	Farrow, Buff (USA)	28/05/67

Name and Nationality	Date of Birth	Name and Nationality	Date of Birth
Fernandez, Oliver (MEX)	07/12/72	Knowle, Julian (AUT)	29/04/74
Ferreira, Ellis (RSA)	19/02/70	Knowles, Mark (BAH)	04/09/71
Ferreira, Wayne (RSA)	15/09/71	Kodes, Jan (TCH)	11/03/72
Fetterlein, Frederik (DEN)	11/07/70	Koenig, Robbie (RSA)	05/07/71
Fikas, Andreas (GRE)	15/03/72	Koevermans, Mark (HOL)	03/02/68
Filippini, Marcelo (URU)	04/08/67	Korda, Petr (TCH)	23/01/68
Finnberg, Axel (GER)	05/04/71	Koslowski, Lars (GER)	22/05/71
Fitzgerald, John (AUS)	28/12/60	Kovalski, Gil (ISR)	08/10/71
Flach, Ken (USA)	24/05/63	Krajicek, Richard (HOL)	06/12/71
Fleurian, Jean (FRA)	11/09/65	Kratsmann, Andrew (AUS)	03/11/71
Fontang, Frederic (FRA)	16/03/70	Kratzmann, Mark (AUS)	17/05/66
Forget, Guy (FRA)	04/01/65	Krickstein, Aaron (USA)	02/08/67
Foster, Andrew (GBR)	16/03/72	Kriek, Johan (USA)	05/04/58
Frana, Javier (ARG)	25/12/66	Krishnan, Ramesh (IND)	05/06/61
Fromberg, Richard (AUS)	28/04/70	Kroon, Niclas (SWE)	05/02/66
Furlan, Renzo (ITA)	17/05/70	Krumrey, Florian (GER)	27/01/70
Gabrichidze, Vladimir (URS)	16/05/68	Kucera, Karol (TCH)	04/03/74
Garat, Juan-Ignacio (ARG)	16/05/73	Kuhnen, Patrick (GER)	11/02/66
Garner, Chris (USA)	07/04/69	Kulti, Nicklas (SWE)	22/04/71
Garnett, Bret (USA)	02/07/67	Lareau, Sebastien (CAN)	27/04/73
Gauthier, Pier (FRA)	20/04/72	Larsson, Magnus (SWE)	25/03/70
Geserer, Michael (GER)	14/12/69	Laurendeau, Martin (CAN)	10/07/64
Gessner, Scott (GER)	23/02/73	Lavalle, Leonardo (MEX)	14/07/67
Gilbert, Brad (USA)	09/08/61	Layendecker, Glenn (USA)	09/05/61
Gilbert, Rodolphe (FRA)	11/12/68	Leach, Rick (USA)	28/12/64
Gisbert, Juan (ESP)	13/04/74	Leconte, Henri (FRA)	04/07/63
Godwin, Neville (RSA)	31/01/75	Lendl, Ivan (TCH)	07/03/60
Goellner, Marc (GER)	22/09/70	Lien, Yu-Hui (TPE)	19/06/70
Gollwitzer, Thomas (GER)	24/07/66	Limberger, Carl (AUS)	24/01/64
Gomez, Andres (ECU)	27/02/60	Lopez, German (ESP)	29/12/71
Gorriz, Marco-Aurelio (ESP)	04/03/64	Lundgren, Peter (SWE)	29/01/65
Grabb, Jim (USA)	14/04/64	Maciel, Francisco (MEX)	07/01/64
Greenhalgh, James (NZL)	19/02/75	MacPhie, Brian (USA)	11/05/72
Guardiola, Thierry (FRA)	07/08/71	Mancini, Alberto (ARG)	20/05/69
Gunnarsson, Jan (SWE)	30/05/62	Mancisidor, Alejo (ESP)	31/07/70
Gustafsson, Magnus (SWE)	03/01/67	Mandl, Gerald (AUT)	12/11/70
Haarhuis, Paul (HOL)	19/02/68	Mansdorf, Amos (ISR)	20/10/65
Herrera, Luis (MEX)	27/08/71	Marcelino, Danilo (BRA)	08/03/66
Hlasek, Jakob (SUI)	12/11/64	Marco, Daniel (ESP)	31/01/66
Ho, Tommy (USA)	17/06/73	Markus, Gabriel (ARG)	31/03/70
Hogstedt, Thomas (SWE)	21/09/63	Marques, Nuno (POR)	09/04/70
Holm, Henrik (SWE)	22/08/68	Marsh, Clinton (RSA)	19/01/72
Ingaramo, Marcelo (ARG)	13/10/62	Martin, Todd (USA)	08/07/70
Ivanisevic, Goran (CRO)	13/09/71	Mas, Jordan (ESP)	31/10/71
Jabali, Roberto (BRA)	26/05/70	Masso, Eduardo (BEL)	11/01/64
Jaite, Martin (ARG)	09/10/64	Masuda, Kentaro (JPN)	26/08/71
Jarryd, Anders (SWE)	13/07/61	Masur, Wally (AUS)	13/05/63
Jensen, Murphy (USA)	30/10/68	Matsuoka, Shuzo (JPN)	06/11/67
Ji, Seung-Ho (KOR)	28/04/68	Mattar, Luiz (BRA)	18/08/63
Jones, Kelly (USA)	31/03/64	Matuszewski, Richard (USA)	07/09/64
Jonsson, Lars (SWE)	27/06/70	Mayotte, Tim (USA)	03/08/60
Joyce, Michael (USA)	01/02/73	McEnroe, John (USA)	16/02/59
Kafelnikov, Yevgeny (CIS)	18/02/74	McEnroe, Patrick (USA)	01/07/66
Kaneko, Hideki (JPN)	06/03/64	Medvedev, Andrei (CIS)	31/08/74
Karbacher, Bernd (GER)	03/04/68	Meligeni, Fernando (ARG)	12/04/71
Keil, Mark (USA)	03/06/67	Mercer, Tom (USA)	10/11/64
Kempers, Tom (NED)	01/06/69	Mezzadri, Claudio (SUI)	10/06/65
Kilderry, Paul (AUS)	11/04/73	Michelotti, Francesco (ITA)	23/10/69
Kim, Bong-Soo (KOR)	30/11/62	Michibata, Glenn (CAN)	13/06/62
Kim, Chi-Wan (KOR)	01/10/66	Middleton, Todd (USA)	02/05/68
Kim, Jae-Sik (KOR)	17/05/67	Miniussi, Christian (ARG)	05/07/67
Kinnear, Kent (USA)	30/01/66	Molina, Javier (ESP)	19/09/69

Name and Nationality	Date of Birth	Name and Nationality	Date of Birth
Montana, Francisco (USA)	05/11/69	Reneberg, Richey (USA)	05/10/65
Morgan, Jamie (AUS)	08/06/71	Rhode, Stephen (GBR)	05/10/68
Mota, Bernado (POR)	14/06/71	Richardson, Andrew (GBR)	14/03/74
Motta, Cassio (BRA)	22/02/60	Riglewski, Udo (GER)	28/07/66
Mronz, Alexander (GER)	07/04/65	Rikl, David (TCH)	27/02/71
Muller, Gary (RSA)	24/12/64	Rios, Juan-Oscar (PUR)	15/12/66
Muskatirovic, Srdjan (YUG)	10/04/72	Rivera, Felipe (CHI)	10/05/71
Muster, Thomas (AUT)	02/10/67	Roese, Fernando (BRA)	24/08/65
Naewie, Markus (GER)	07/01/70	Roig, Francisco (ESP)	01/04/68
Nainkin, David (RSA)	20/09/70	Rosset, Marc (SUI)	07/11/70
Nargiso, Diego (ITA)	15/03/70	Rostagno, Derrick (USA)	25/10/65
Nelson, Todd (USA)	18/03/61	Roubicek, Vaclav (TCH)	13/12/67
Nemechek, Libor (TCH)	26/10/68	Roux, Lionel (FRA)	12/04/73
Nensel, Sascha (GER)	09/05/70	Ruah, Maurice (VEN)	19/02/71
Nestor, Daniel (CAN)	04/09/72	Rusedski, Greg (CAN)	06/09/73
Nijssen, Tom (HOL)	01/10/64	Ruud, Christian (NOR)	24/08/72
Norman, Dick (BEL)	01/03/71	Rybalko, Andrei (UKR)	05/06/72
Norman, Magnus (SWE)	???????	Saceanu, Christian (GER)	08/07/68
Noszaly, Sandor (HUN)	16/03/72	Salumaa, Sven (USA)	21/10/66
Novacek, Karel (TCH)	30/03/65	Sampras, Pete (USA)	12/08/71
Nyborg, Peter (SWE)	12/12/69	Sanchez, Emilio (ESP)	29/05/65
O'Brien, Alex (USA)	07/03/70	Sanchez, Javier (ESP)	01/02/68
Odizor, Nduka (NGR)	09/08/58	Sansoni, Stephane (FRA)	12/08/67
Olhovskiy, Andrei (CIS)	15/04/66	Santoro, Fabrice (FRA)	09/12/72
Oncins, Jaime (BRA)	16/06/70	Sapsford, Danny (GBR)	03/04/69
Ondruska, Marcos (RSA)	18/12/72	Schaller, Gilbert (AUT)	17/03/79
Orsanic, Daniel (ARG)	11/06/68	Schapers, Michiel (HOL)	11/10/59
Paes, Leander (IND)	17/06/73	Schmidt, Richard (USA)	31/01/65
Palmer, Jared (USA)	02/07/71	Schors, Jorg (GER)	05/11/74
Paloheimo, Veli (FIN)	13/12/67	Shelton, Bryan (USA)	12/12/65
Pate, David (USA)	16/04/62	Siemerink, Jan (HOL)	14/04/70
Pavel, Andrei (ROM)	27/01/74	Silberberg, Fabio (BRA)	25/03/69
Pearce, Brad (USA)	21/03/66	Simian, Stephane (FRA)	28/06/67
Pech, Phillipe (FRA)	09/08/66	Sinner, Martin (GER)	07/02/68
Pennisi, Pietro (ITA)	11/04/70	Skoff, Horst (AUT)	22/08/68
Pereira, Nicolas (VEN)	20/09/70	Smith, Roger (BAH)	20/01/64
Perez, Diego (URU)	09/02/62	Sobel, John (USA)	15/02/64
Perez Hubert, Marcos (ESP)	22/11/68	Song, Hyeong-Kuen (KOR)	16/09/74
Perez Roldan, Guillermo (ARG)	20/10/69	Soules, Olivier (FRA)	24/03/67
Perkiss, Shahar (ISR)	14/10/62	Stadling, Mikael (SWE)	10/08/66
Pernfors, Mikael (SWE)	16/07/63	Stafford, Grant (RSA)	27/05/71
Pescariu, Dinu (ROM)	12/04/74	Stankovic, Branislav (TCH)	30/05/65
Pescosolido, Stefano (ITA)	13/06/71	Stark, Jonathan (USA)	03/04/71
Petchey, Mark (GBR)	01/08/70	Steeb, Carl-Uwe (GER)	01/09/67
Pimek, Libor (BEL)	03/08/63	Stenlund, Ulf (SWE)	21/01/67
Pioline, Cedric (FRA)	15/06/69	Steven, Brett (NZL)	27/04/69
Pistolesi, Claudio (ITA)	25/08/67	Stich, Michael (GER)	18/10/68
Poliakov, Dimitri (CIS)	19/01/68	Stolle, Sandon (AUS)	13/07/70
Pozzi, Gian-Luca (ITA)	17/06/65	Stoltenberg, Jason (AUS)	04/04/70
Prades, Laurent (FRA)	19/07/68	Strelba, Martin (TCH)	22/03/67
Prerovsky, Thomas (AUT)	15/02/69	Stringari, Martin (ARG)	09/10/71
Pridham, Chris (CAN)	11/04/65	Suk, Cyril (TCH)	29/01/67
Prinosil, David (GER)	09/03/73	Svensson, Jonas (SWE)	21/10/66
Prpic, Goran (CRO)	04/05/64	Sznajder, Andrew (CAN)	25/05/67
Pugh, Jim (USA)	05/02/64	Tanizawa, Hidehiko (JPN)	05/12/71
Radulescu, Alexandru (ROM)	07/12/74	Tarango, Jeff (USA)	20/11/68
Rafter, Patrick (AUS)	28/12/72	Thoms, Arne (GER)	01/01/71
Rahunen, Aki (FIN)	24/12/71	Thorne, Kenny (USA)	24/01/66
Ran, Eyal (ISR)	21/11/72	Tillstrom, Mikael (SWE)	05/03/72
Randall, Dave (USA)	08/05/67	Tsuchihashi, Toshihisa (JPN)	18/10/66
Raoux, Guillaume (FRA)	14/02/70	Tsujino, Ryuso (JPN)	24/02/69
Rasheed, Roger (AUS)	10/03/68	Ullyett, Kevin (RSA)	23/05/72

Name and Nationality	Date of Birth	Name and Nationality	Date of Birth
Vajda, Marian (TCH)	24/03/65	Wheaton, David (USA)	02/06/69
Valeri, Massimo (ITA)	13/03/70	Wibier, Fernon (NED)	25/02/71
Van Den Daele, Thierry (FRA)	27/05/66	Wijaya, Benny (INA)	28/10/73
Van Rensburg, Christo (RSA)	23/10/62	Wilkinson, Chris (GBR)	05/01/70
Van Scheppingen, Dennis (NED)	05/07/75	Windisch, Alexander (GER)	25/03/68
Vasek, Radomir (TCH)	23/09/72	Witsken, Todd (USA)	04/11/63
Velev, Milen (BUL)	04/09/71	Witt, David (USA)	02/06/73
Vilas, Guillermo (ARG)	17/08/52	Woodbridge, Todd (AUS)	02/04/71
Viloca, Joan-Albert (ESP)	17/01/73	Woodforde, Mark (AUS)	23/09/65
Visconti, Mario (ITA)	23/10/68	Wostenholme, Martin (CAN)	11/10/62
Viver, Raul-Antonio (ECU)	17/03/61	Wuyts, Bart (BEL)	15/09/69
Vizner, Pavel (TCH)	15/07/70	Yamamoto, Yasufumi (JPN)	03/05/71
Volkov, Alexander (CIS)	03/03/67	Youl, Simon (AUS)	01/07/65
Vysand, Andres (CIS)	10/03/66	Yunis, Francisco (ARG)	12/08/64
Wahlgren, Lars (SWE)	24/08/66	Yzaga, Jaime (PER)	23/10/67
Walker, Michael (HKG)	21/04/65	Zdrazila, Tomas (TCH)	24/06/70
Washington, Malivai (USA)	20/06/69	Zillner, Marcus (GER)	19/03/70
Weiss, Robbie (USA)	01/12/66	Zivojinovic, Slobodan (YUG)	23/07/63
Wekesa, Paul (KEN)	02/07/67	Zoecke, Markus (GER)	10/05/68

Undefeated in singles and doubles, Emilio Sanchez led Spain to an impressive victory in the Peugeot World Team Cup in Dusseldorf. (M.Cole)

CHAMPIONSHIP SERIES

DONNAY INDOOR CHAMPIONSHIP ($665,000)
BRUSSELS, 10–16 FEBRUARY
MEN'S SINGLES – 1st round: S. Edberg (1) (WC) d. S. Bruguera 6–4 4–6 6–4; J. Siemerink d. A.
Boetsch (Q) 6–3 7–6; E. Masso (Q) d. T. Champion 6–2 6–1; K. Novacek (7) d. G. Prpic 6–4 7–6; B.
Becker (3) (WC) d. J. Svensson 6–4 6–0; P. McEnroe d. A. Cherkasov 6–4 7–6; C. Steeb d. C.
Bergstrom 7–5 3–6 7–6; A. Jarryd d. P. Korda (6) 3–6 6–4 6–1; G. Forget (5) d. M. Gustafsson 6–2 6–4;
J. McEnroe d. R. Krajicek 3–6 7–5 6–2; G. Ivanisevic d. J. Hlasek 6–3 6–3; I. Lendl (4) d. P. Nyborg (Q)
6–7 7–5 6–2; A. Agassi (8) d. A. Antonitsch (Q) 6–7 7–5 6–3; A. Volkov d. C. Pioline 6–7 6–4 6–3; H.
Leconte (WC) d. O. Delaitre 6–3 6–3; J. Courier (2) d. F. Santoro 6–2 6–1.
2nd round: Edberg (1) (WC) d. Siemerink 7–5 6–2; Novacek (7) d. Masso (Q) 6–4 6–2; Becker (3) (WC)
d. P. McEnroe 7–6 6–1; Steeb d. Jarryd 6–4 6–4; Forget (5) d. J. McEnroe 6–3 6–2; Lendl (4) d.
Ivanisevic 6–7 7–5 6–4; Volkov d. Agassi (8) 7–6 6–3; Courier (2) d. Leconte (WC) 6–4 7–5.
Quarter-finals: Edberg (1) (WC) d. Novacek (7) 6–2 6–1; Becker (3) (WC) d. Steeb 6–3 7–6; Forget (5)
d. Lendl (4) 6–2 7–6; Courier (2) d. Volkov 7–6 7–6.
Semi-finals: Becker (3) (WC) d. Edberg (1) (WC) 4–6 6–4 6–2; Courier (2) d. Forget (5) 7–6 6–4.
Final: Becker (3) (WC) d. Courier (2) 6–7 2–6 7–6 7–6 7–5.
MEN'S DOUBLES – Final: Becker/J. McEnroe d. Forget/Hlasek 6–3 6–2.

FEDERAL EXPRESS INTERNATIONAL ($630,000)
MEMPHIS, 10–16 FEBRUARY
MEN'S SINGLES – 1st round: M. Stich (1) – bye; T. Martin (LL) d. M. Woodforde (Q) 7–6 5–7 6–3; K.
Curren d. P. Doohan (WC) 6–2 6–4; J. Connors (16) (WC) – bye; A. Krickstein (9) – bye; T. Witsken (Q)
d. R. Agenor 2–6 7–6 7–6; T. Woodbridge d. C. Adams (Q) 7–6 7–6; A. Chesnokov (8) – bye; M. Chang
(3) – bye; P. Baur d. R. Furlan 2–6 7–6 6–4; B. Shelton d. P. Kuhnen 6–4 6–7 7–6; M. Washington (13) –
bye; H. Skoff (11) – bye; J. Stoltenberg d. G. Markus 6–3 6–2; M. Schapers d. C. Saceanu 6–3 6–7 6–3;
D. Rostagno (6) – bye; B. Gilbert (5) – bye; N. Kulti d. P. Annacone (WC) 4–6 7–6 6–4; A. Mansdorf d. R.
Gilbert (Q) 6–4 6–2; F. Clavet (12) – bye; P. Haarhuis (14) – bye; C. Van Rensburg d. M. Koevermans 6–2
6–1; S. Stolle (LL) d. J. Kriek (WC) 6–3 6–4; D. Wheaton (4) – bye; W. Ferreira (7) – bye; W. Masur d. S.
Matsuoka 4–6 6–1 7–6; G. Pozzi d. J. Arias 6–2 5–7 6–3; R. Reneberg (10) – bye; C. Caratti (15) – bye;
G. Connell d. L. Jonsson 4–6 6–3 7–5; R. Fromberg (Q) d. K. Braasch (Q) 6–3 7–5; P. Sampras (2) – bye.
2nd round: Stich (1) d. Martin (LL) 6–2 6–2; Connors (16) (WC) d. Curren 6–2 6–2; Krickstein (9) d.
Witsken (Q) 7–6 6–4; Woodbridge d. Chesnokov (8) 6–4 7–6; Chang (3) d. Baur 6–3 6–3; Washington
(13) d. Shelton 6–0 6–3; Stoltenberg d. Skoff (11) 7–5 6–3; Schapers d. Rostagno (6) 6–3 4–6 6–3;
Gilbert (5) d. Kulti 7–6 6–3; Mansdorf d. Clavet (12) 6–4 6–3; Haarhuis (14) d. Van Rensburg 6–4 6–4;
Wheaton (4) d. Stolle 7–6 6–3; Ferreira (7) d. Masur 6–4 6–4; Reneberg (10) d. Pozzi 6–2 7–5; Connell
d. Caratti (15) 7–6 7–6; Sampras (2) d. Fromberg (Q) 6–4 7–5.
3rd round: Connors (16) (WC) d. Stich (1) 5–7 7–6 7–5; Krickstein (9) d. Woodbridge 6–2 6–2;
Washington (13) d. Chang (3) 7–5 7–6; Schapers d. Stoltenberg 6–1 6–2; Mansdorf d. Gilbert (5) 7–6
7–6; Haarhuis (14) d. Wheaton (4) 4–6 7–6 7–5; Ferreira (7) d. Reneberg (10) 6–2 4–6 6–4; Sampras (2)
d. Connell 7–6 6–1.
Quarter-finals: Connors (16) (WC) d. Krickstein (9) 3–6 6–2 6–3; Washington (13) d. Schapers 6–3 7–5;
Mansdorf d. Haarhuis (14) 7–6 6–3; Ferreira (7) d. Sampras (2) 6–4 6–2.
Semi-finals: Washington (13) d. Connors (16) (WC) 6–2 7–5; Ferreira (7) d. Mansdorf 6–2 6–3.
Final: Washington (13) d. Ferreira (7) 6–3 6–2.
MEN'S DOUBLES – Final: Woodbridge/Woodforde (2) d. Curren/G. Muller 7–5 4–6 7–6.

COMCAST METROPHONE US PRO INDOORS ($865,000)
PHILADELPHIA, 17–23 FEBRUARY
MEN'S SINGLES – 1st round: M. Stich (1) – bye; M. Schapers d. T. Mayotte (WC) 6–3 6–4; C. Van
Rensburg d. M. Woodforde 6–4 7–5; A. Mansdorf (16) – bye; A. Chesnokov (9) – bye; J. Tarango d. P.
Annacone (WC) 6–7 6–1 6–3; C. Pridham (Q) d. S. Matsuoka 6–7 6–4 7–5; W. Ferreira (7) – bye; M.
Chang (3) – bye; J. Grabb d. B. Shelton 6–3 7–6; T. Woodbridge d. G. Connell 7–6 6–4; M. Washington

(13) – bye; F. Clavet (11) – bye; W. Masur d. J. Stoltenberg 6–4 6–1; R. Furlan d. G. Pozzi 7–5 6–3; D. Rostagno (5) – bye; B. Gilbert (6) – bye; G. Layendecker (Q) d. S. Simian (Q) 3–6 6–4 6–2; M. Laurendeau (Q) d. G. Markus 6–2 7–5; H. Skoff (12) – bye; P. Haarhuis (14) – bye; C. Caratti d. R. Fromberg (Q) 6–4 7–5; M. Zoecke d. L. Lavalle (Q) 6–1 6–4; D. Wheaton (4) – bye; R. Reneberg (8) – bye; R. Gilbert d. P. Baur 7–5 6–7 6–4; T. Martin (WC) d. C. Saceanu 6–3 3–6 6–3; A. Krickstein (10) – bye; S. Pescosolido (15) – bye; A. Boetsch d. R. Agenor 6–4 7–6; D. DiLucia (WC) d. K. Curren 7–5 3–6 6–4; P. Sampras (2) – bye.
2nd round: Stich (1) d. Schapers 7–6 6–3; Mansdorf (16) d. Van Rensburg 6–4 6–3; Tarango d. Chesnokov (9) 3–6 6–4 6–1; Ferreira (7) d. Pridham (Q) 6–4 6–4; Grabb d. Chang (3) 6–3 3–6 6–2; Woodbridge d. Washington (13) 6–1 5–7 7–6; Clavet (11) d. Masur 6–7 6–3 7–6; Rostagno (5) d. Furlan 5–7 6–3 6–3; Gilbert (6) d. Layendecker (Q) 6–2 6–4; Laurendeau (Q) d. Skoff (12) 6–3 6–4; Haarhuis (14) d. Caratti 7–6 6–4; Wheaton (4) d. Zoecke 6–4 3–6 6–4; Gilbert d. Reneberg (8) 6–4 6–2; Krickstein (10) d. Martin (WC) 3–6 6–4 6–3; Pescosolido (15) d. Boetsch 7–5 6–4; Sampras (2) d. DiLucia (WC) 6–2 6–1.
3rd round: Mansdorf (16) d. Stich (1) 7–6 7–5; Tarango d. Ferreira (7) 6–3 7–5; Grabb d. Woodbridge 7–6 6–4; Clavet (11) d. Rostagno (5) 7–6 7–6; Gilbert (6) d. Laurendeau (Q) 6–4 6–3; Haarhuis (14) d. Wheaton (4) 6–3 7–6; Krickstein (10) d. Gilbert 3–6 7–6 7–5; Sampras (2) d. Pescosolido (15) 7–6 4–6 6–4.
Quarter-finals: Mansdorf (16) d. Tarango 6–3 6–0; Clavet (11) d. Grabb 2–6 7–5 6–3; Gilbert (6) d. Haarhuis (14) 6–3 3–6 6–1; Sampras (2) d. Krickstein (10) 3–6 7–6 7–6.
Semi-finals: Mansdorf (16) d. Clavet (11) 5–7 6–3 6–2; Sampras (2) d. Gilbert (6) 6–4 6–3.
Final: Sampras (2) d. Mansdorf (16) 6–1 7–6 2–6 7–6.
MEN'S DOUBLES – **Final**: Woodbridge/Woodforde (2) d. Grabb/Reneberg (8) 6–4 7–6.

EUROCARD CLASSICS ($865,000)
STUTTGART, 17–23 FEBRUARY
MEN'S SINGLES – **1st round**: J. Courier (1) d. D. Nargiso (Q) 6–3 6–3; R. Krajicek d. J. Arrese 6–3 6–2; O. Delaitre d. S. Bruguera 7–6 3–6 6–1; G. Ivanisevic (7) d. S. Zivojinovic (WC) 6–3 7–6; I. Lendl (4) d. A. Cherkasov 7–6 6–4; A. Volkov d. P. Kuhnen (WC) 7–6 6–4; C. Bergstrom d. C. Steeb 6–4 7–5; G. Forget (5) d. J. Hlasek 7–6 6–2; P. Korda (6) d. A. Thoms (Q) 7–6 7–5; A. Jarryd d. P. McEnroe 6–2 6–0; J. Siemerink d. M. Gustafsson 6–1 6–4; B. Becker (3) d. J. Svensson 4–6 7–5 6–2; K. Novacek (8) d. J. McEnroe (WC) 3–6 7–6 6–2; O. Camporese d. F. Santoro 6–0 7–5; A. Antonitsch (Q) d. G. Prpic 7–6 6–2; S. Edberg (2) d. M. Larsson (Q) 6–2 6–2.
2nd round: Courier (1) d. Krajicek 6–3 3–6 6–3; Ivanisevic (7) d. Delaitre 6–3 7–6; Volkov d. Lendl (4) 7–6 5–7 6–1; Forget (5) d. Bergstrom 7–6 6–0; Korda (6) d. Jarryd 6–3 7–5; Siemerink d. Becker (3) 6–3 6–4; Camporese d. Novacek (8) 6–3 6–1; Edberg (2) d. Antonitsch (Q) 6–1 6–2.
Quarter-finals: Ivanisevic (7) d. Courier (1) 3–6 7–6 7–6; Volkov d. Forget (5) 6–4 6–4; Korda (6) d. Siemerink 6–4 6–4; Edberg (2) d. Camporese 4–6 6–2 7–5.
Semi-finals: Ivanisevic (7) d. Volkov 3–6 6–3 6–4; Edberg (2) d. Korda (6) 6–4 6–4.
Final: Ivanisevic (7) d. Edberg (2) 6–7 6–3 6–4 6–4.
MEN'S DOUBLES – **Final**: T. Nijssen/C. Suk (3) d. J. Fitzgerald/Jarryd (1) 6–3 6–7 6–3.

NEWSWEEK CHAMPIONS CUP ($825,000)
INDIAN WELLS, 2–8 MARCH
MEN'S SINGLES – **1st round**: J. Courier (1) – bye; C. Van Rensburg d. F. Fontang 6–1 7–5; A. Chesnokov d. S. Youl (Q) 6–4 6–3; W. Ferreira (15) d. M. Zoecke 7–5 6–4; A. Agassi (10) d. J. Yzaga 6–3 6–7 6–3; B. Karbacher (Q) d. T. Witsken (Q) 7–6 5–7 6–2; T. Champion d. A. Mancini 6–2 6–3; E. Sanchez (7) – bye; M. Stich (3) – bye; J. Connors d. C. Caratti 6–4 6–4; R. Reneberg d. B. Gilbert 6–4 6–4; D. Rostagno (14) d. C. Adams (Q) 7–6 6–3; S. Bruguera (11) d. M. Woodforde (Q) 7–6 6–1; C. Costa d. A. Krickstein 6–4 6–2; M. Ondruska (Q) d. F. Santoro 6–3 6–7 6–3; P. Korda (6) – bye; G. Ivanisevic (5) – bye; R. Krajicek (WC) d. R. Fromberg (WC) 5–7 6–4 6–3; J. Sanchez d. O. Delaitre 6–3 6–0; M. Chang (12) d. M. Jaite 6–0 6–7 7–6; M. Gustafsson (13) d. A. Mansdorf (WC) 6–2 6–4; C. Steeb d. J. Stark (Q) 6–7 6–3 6–0; A. Cherkasov d. S. Pescosolido 7–6 6–7 7–5; G. Forget (4) – bye; K. Novacek (8) – bye; A. Boetsch d. J. Frana 7–6 6–1; F. Clavet d. B. MacPhie (WC) 6–4 6–3; D. Wheaton (9) d. W. Masur (LL) 7–6 7–6; J. Hlasek (16) d. T. Woodbridge (WC) 7–5 6–4; C. Pioline d. M. Rosset 6–3 7–5; B. Shelton d. H. Skoff 4–6 6–3 6–2; P. Sampras (2) – bye.
2nd round: Courier (1) d. Van Rensburg 3–6 6–0 6–2; Chesnokov d. Ferreira (15) 6–4 6–1; Agassi (10) d. Karbacher (Q) 6–1 1–6 7–5; E. Sanchez (7) d. Champion 7–6 6–4; Stich (3) d. Connors 6–4 6–3; Rostagno (14) d. Reneberg 6–3 6–7 6–3; Bruguera (11) d. Costa 7–6 6–3; Korda (6) d. Ondruska (Q) 4–6 7–5 6–1; Krajicek (WC) d. Ivanisevic (5) 6–0 6–3; Chang (12) d. J. Sanchez 0–6 6–4 6–1; Gustafsson (13) d. Steeb 6–1 7–6; Cherkasov d. Forget (4) 6–4 6–0; Novacek (8) d. Boetsch 6–2 0–6 7–6; Clavet d. Wheaton (9) 6–2 6–3; Hlasek (16) d. Pioline 7–5 6–2; Sampras (2) d. Shelton 6–7 6–0 6–4.
3rd round: Chesnokov d. Courier (1) 6–4 7–5; E. Sanchez (7) d. Agassi (10) 6–3 6–1; Stich (3) d. Rostagno (14) 6–2 6–4; Bruguera (11) d. Korda (6) 7–5 4–6 6–0; Chang (12) d. Krajicek (WC) 6–3 6–7

7–6; Cherkasov d. Gustafsson (13) 6–3 6–3; Clavet d. Novacek (8) 6–2 4–6 6–3; Hlasek (16) d. Sampras (2) 6–4 3–6 7–5.
Quarter-finals: Chesnokov d. E. Sanchez (7) 7–5 7–5; Stich (3) d. Bruguera (11) 6–1 6–2; Chang (12) d. Cherkasov 6–4 6–2; Clavet d. Hlasek (16) 6–1 6–2.
Semi-finals: Chesnokov d. Stich (3) 1–6 7–6 6–3; Chang (12) d. Clavet 6–0 6–1.
Final: Chang (12) d. Chesnokov 6–3 6–4 7–5.
MEN'S DOUBLES – **Final**: S. DeVries/D. MacPherson d. K. Kinnear/S. Salumaa 4–6 6–3 6–3.

LIPTON INTERNATIONAL PLAYERS CHAMPIONSHIPS ($1,625,000)
KEY BISCAYNE, 13–22 MARCH
MEN'S SINGLES – **1st round**: J. Courier (1) – bye; T. Champion d. C. Miniussi 4–6 6–3 6–4; A. Gomez d. M. Ondruska (Q) 6–4 6–3; H. Skoff (32) – bye; F. Clavet (18) – bye; K. Curren d. C. Saceanu 6–4 3–0 ret.; C. Steeb d. C. Costa 7–6 4–6 6–3; A. Chesnokov (15) – bye; S. Bruguera (9) – bye; J. Grabb d. J. Brown (Q) 7–5 6–3; J. Stark (Q) d. D. Marcelino 6–4 6–3; M. Washington (23) – bye; A. Krickstein (26) – bye; D. Nargiso d. C. Arriens (Q) 7–5 7–5; C. Adams d. J. Fleurian 6–3 6–4; P. Korda (7) – bye; P. Sampras (4) – bye; S. Matsuoka d. M. Schapers 6–4 6–2; T. Carbonell d. P. Kuhnen 7–5 6–3; J. Connors (30) – bye; W. Ferreira (19) – bye; W. Masur d. L. Lavalle 4–6 7–6 6–2; G. Pozzi d. J. Tarango 3–6 6–3 6–4; D. Rostagno (14) – bye; D. Wheaton (12) – bye; M. Zoecke d. A. Mronz 6–4 4–6 6–1; F. Fontang d. J. Sobel (Q) 6–2 6–1; G. Prpic (21) – bye; J. Sanchez (27) – bye; M. Rosset d. C. Van Rensburg 7–5 6–3; R. Krishnan (Q) d. M. Jaite 7–6 6–2; M. Chang (6) – bye; G. Ivanisevic (5) – bye; B. Karbacher (Q) d. G. Connell 7–6 7–6; S. Stolle (WC) d. B. Dunn (WC) 7–6 6–4; J. McEnroe (28) – bye; R. Krajicek (22) – bye; G. Bloom d. V. Paloheimo 6–7 7–6 6–4; B. Shelton d. P. Cane 7–6 7–5; A. Agassi (11) – bye; M. Gustafsson (13) – bye; T. Witsken d. F. Roese 6–1 6–3; R. Agenor d. S. Bryan (Q) 6–1 3–6 6–4; A. Mancini (20) – bye; P. Haarhuis (29) – bye; P. McEnroe d. S. Pescosolido 3–6 6–2 6–1; A. Boetsch d. J. Siemerink 6–4 7–5; B. Becker (3) (WC) – bye; E. Sanchez (8) – bye; J. Frana d. G. Muller 6–7 6–3 6–4; J. Stoltenberg d. J. Oncins 4–6 6–3 6–0; A. Cherkasov (25) – bye; A. Mansdorf (24) – bye; C. Pioline d. G. Markus 6–4 6–4; R. Gilbert d. F. Santoro 6–2 4–6 6–3; K. Novacek (10) – bye; B. Gilbert (16) – bye; J. Yzaga d. J. Gunnarsson 6–3 6–2; M. Blackman (Q) d. P. Baur 3–6 7–5 6–0; J. Hlasek (17) – bye; R. Reneberg (31) – bye; R. Weiss (Q) d. D. Randall (Q) 6–4 6–4; G. Stafford (Q) d. C. Caratti 6–3 2–6 6–1; S. Edberg (2) – bye.
2nd round: Courier (1) d. Champion 5–7 6–1 6–2; Gomez d. Skoff (32) 6–3 6–4; Clavet (18) d. Curren 2–6 6–2 6–2; Steeb d. Chesnokov 4–6 6–2 6–3; Bruguera (9) d. Grabb 6–4 6–2; Stark (Q) d. Washington (23) 3–6 7–6 6–1; Nargiso d. Krickstein (26) 7–5 6–3; Korda (7) d. Adams 7–5 4–6 6–2; Sampras (4) d. Matsuoka 4–6 7–6 6–1; Connors (30) d. Carbonell 6–7 6–2 7–6; Masur d. Ferreira (19) 6–3 6–3; Rostagno (14) d. Pozzi 6–4 2–6 7–6; Zoecke d. Wheaton (12) 6–1 6–2; Prpic (21) d. Fontang 6–3 2–0 ret.; Rosset d. J. Sanchez (27) 6–3 3–6 7–6; Chang (6) d. Krishnan (Q) 6–3 6–1; Ivanisevic (5) d. Karbacher (Q) 6–4 6–1; J. McEnroe (28) d. Stolle (WC) 6–3 6–4; Krajicek (22) d. Bloom 6–3 6–3; Shelton d. Agassi (11) 6–4 6–4; Witsken d. Gustafsson (13) 6–3 6–2; Mancini (20) d. Agenor 1–6 6–1 6–4; Haarhuis (29) d. P. McEnroe 6–3 6–3; Becker (3) (WC) d. Boetsch 3–6 7–5 6–3; E. Sanchez (8) d. Frana 6–2 6–3; Cherkasov (25) d. Stoltenberg 6–2 5–7 6–4; Pioline d. Mansdorf (24) 7–5 7–5; Gilbert d. Novacek (10) 6–4 2–6 7–6; Yzaga d. Gilbert (16) 4–6 6–2 6–3; Hlasek (17) d. Blackman (Q) 6–3 6–4; Weiss (Q) d. Reneberg (31) 6–3 1–0 ret.; Edberg (2) d. Stafford (Q) 5–7 6–1 0–1 ret.
3rd round: Courier (1) d. Gomez 6–4 6–7 4–3 ret.; Steeb d. Clavet (18) 6–1 7–6; Stark (Q) d. Bruguera (9) 6–3 6–4; Nargiso d. Korda (7) 6–2 7–6; Sampras (4) d. Connors (30) 6–3 6–2; Masur d. Rostagno (14) 6–7 7–6 6–3; Zoecke d. Prpic (21) 6–1 6–4; Chang (6) d. Rosset 4–6 6–3 7–6; J. McEnroe (28) d. Ivanisevic (5) 5–7 7–5 7–5; Krajicek (22) d. Shelton 6–3 7–5; Mancini (20) d. Witsken 6–4 6–3; Becker (3) (WC) d. Haarhuis (29) 6–4 7–6; Cherkasov (25) d. E. Sanchez (8) 7–6 6–2; Pioline d. Gilbert 6–2 6–0; Hlasek (17) d. Yzaga 6–3 6–3; Weiss (Q) d. Edberg (2) 6–3 3–6 6–4.
4th round: Courier (1) d. Steeb 7–6 6–2; Nargiso d. Stark 7–5 6–4; Sampras (4) d. Masur 7–6 4–6 6–2; Chang (6) d. Zoecke 4–6 6–3 6–1; Krajicek (22) d. J. McEnroe (28) 7–6 6–4; Mancini (20) d. Becker (3) (WC) 4–6 6–1 6–4; Cherkasov (25) d. Pioline 7–6 6–2; Hlasek (17) d. Weiss (Q) 6–2 6–2.
Quarter-finals: Courier (1) d. Nargiso 6–7 6–2 6–0; Chang (6) d. Sampras (4) 6–4 7–6; Mancini (20) d. Krajicek (22) 6–4 6–7 7–5; Hlasek (17) d. Cherkasov (25) 6–7 6–3 6–4.
Semi-finals: Chang (6) d. Courier (1) 6–2 6–4; Mancini (20) d. Hlasek (17) 7–6 7–5.
Final: Chang (6) d. Mancini (20) 7–5 7–5.
MEN'S DOUBLES – **Final**: K. Flach/Witsken (3) d. K. Kinnear/S. Salumaa (14) 6–4 6–3.

SUNTORY JAPAN OPEN ($865,000)
TOKYO, 6–12 APRIL
MEN'S SINGLES – **1st round**: S. Edberg (1) – bye; K. Evernden d. C. Saceanu 7–6 6–3; J. Fitzgerald d. D. Marcelino 6–1 6–1; W. Masur (15) d. D. Pate (Q) 6–4 6–3; A. Krickstein (9) d. H. Holm 6–3 6–2; S. Youl d. M. Kratzmann (Q) 6–1 3–6 7–6; C. Pridham d. L. Lavalle 6–1 5–7 6–4; B. Gilbert (7) – bye; M. Stich (3) – bye; S. Matsuoka d. B. Karbacher (Q) 6–2 3–6 6–3; M. Damm d. D. Poliakov 6–2 7–5; A.

Jarryd (14) d. P. Cash 6–1 2–6 6–1; J. Siemerink (12) d. T. Tsuchihashi (WC) 6–0 6–3; J. Grabb d. C. Adams 6–7 6–4 6–4; A. Thoms d. A. Mronz 6–4 2–6 6–2; R. Krajicek (6) – bye; D. Rostagno (5) – bye; B. Steven (Q) d. R. Tsujino (WC) 6–7 6–4 7–6; T. Woodbridge d. G. Raoux 6–3 4–6 6–4; J. Connors (WC) (11) d. B. Black 7–6 6–3; M. Zoecke (13) d. S. Stolle 6–4 7–6; K. Jones (Q) d. H. Tanizawa 6–4 6–2; S. Bryan d. K. Masuda 6–1 6–2; M. Chang (4) – bye; A. Mansdorf (8) – bye; M. Laurendeau d. P. Kuhnen 4–6 6–2 7–6; M. Schapers d. B. Pearce (Q) 6–4 3–6 6–1; P. Haarhuis (10) d. A. Antonitsch 6–3 6–3; G. Pozzi (16) d. J. Fleurian 4–6 7–6 6–3; G. Connell d. M. Petchey (Q) 6–4 6–2; K. Curren d. G. Muller 7–5 6–4; J. Courier (2) – bye.
2nd round: Edberg (1) d. Evernden 6–3 6–4; Masur (15) d. Fitzgerald 6–4 6–2; Krickstein (9) d. Youl 6–1 7–6; Gilbert (7) d. Pridham 6–3 6–0; Stich (3) d. Matsuoka 7–6 3–6 7–6; Jarryd (14) d. Damm 6–3 6–1; Grabb d. Siemerink (12) 6–7 7–5 6–1; Krajicek (6) d. Thoms 6–3 7–6; Steven (Q) d. Rostagno (5) 6–2 2–1 ret.; Woodbridge d. Connors (WC) (11) 6–0 6–1; Zoecke (13) d. Jones (Q) 4–6 6–3 6–2; Chang (4) d. Bryan 6–3 6–2; Mansdorf (8) d. Laurendeau 6–4 6–1; Haarhuis (10) d. Schapers 3–6 7–5 6–3; Pozzi (16) d. Connell 7–6 6–7 6–3; Courier (2) d. Curren 6–1 6–1.
3rd round: Edberg (1) d. Masur (15) 6–3 6–4; Gilbert (7) d. Krickstein (9) 6–4 3–6 6–2; Stich (3) d. Jarryd (14) 7–5 6–2; Krajicek (6) d. Grabb 6–4 6–3; Woodbridge d. Steven (Q) 4–6 6–3 6–4; Chang (4) d. Zoecke (13) 6–4 6–2; Mansdorf (8) d. Haarhuis (10) 4–6 6–1 7–6; Courier (2) d. Pozzi (16) 6–3 6–3.
Quarter-finals: Edberg (1) d. Gilbert (7) 4–6 6–2 6–3; Krajicek (6) d. Stich (3) 7–6 6–4; Chang (4) d. Woodbridge 6–4 1–6 6–0; Courier (2) d. Mansdorf (8) 7–6 6–4.
Semi-finals: Krajicek (6) d. Edberg (1) 6–3 7–5; Courier (2) d. Chang (4) 6–2 6–3.
Final: Courier (2) d. Krajicek (6) 6–4 6–4 7–6.
MEN'S DOUBLES – Final: Jones/R. Leach (3) d. Fitzgerald/Jarryd (1) 0–6 7–5 6–3.

TROFEO CONDE DE GODO–WINSTON ($660,000)
BARCELONA, 6–12 APRIL
MEN'S SINGLES – 1st round: B. Becker (1) – bye; J. Burillo (Q) d. C. Steeb 6–4 7–6; F. Fontang d. L. Koslowski 6–1 6–4; H. Skoff (16) d. R. Azar 6–3 6–3; F. Davin d. A. Cherkasov (10) 6–3 7–6; N. Kulti (LL) d. J. Aparisi (Q) 6–1 6–2; A. Corretja (Q) d. S. Casal (WC) 6–2 6–7 7–5; M. Gustafsson (8) – bye; E. Sanchez (3) – bye; F. Roig d. A. Berasategui (WC) 6–2 7–6; J. Svensson d. C. Pioline 7–5 3–6 6–3; J. Arrese (13) d. M Gorrizt (Q) 6–4 7–6; M. Jaite d. G. Prpic (11) 6–2 3–6 7–6; T. Carbonell d. G. Markus 6–1 1–0 ret.; A. Gomez d. C. Pistolesi 3–6 6–3 6–4; S. Bruguera (5) – bye; A. Agassi (6) – bye; J. Eltingh d. J. Gunnarsson 3–6 6–4 6–2; C. Costa d. R. Furlan 6–2 7–5; M. Filippini d. O. Camporese (12) 6–2 6–3; J. Sanchez (14) d. R. Agenor 4–6 7–5 6–1; C. Miniussi d. B. Wuyts 6–2 6–1; R. Gilbert d. J. Viloca (WC) 6–2 6–2; K. Novacek (4) – bye; A. Mancini (7) – bye; M. Koevermans d. H. de la Pena 6–7 6–1 6–4; M. Larsson d. M. Valeri (Q) 6–4 6–1; F. Clavet (9) d. E. Masso 6–7 6–2 7–6; T. Muster (15) d. V. Paloheimo 1–6 6–4 6–2; J. Altur (Q) d. G. Lopez 6–3 6–3; T. Champion d. G. Dzelde (Q) 7–5 6–4; I. Lendl (2) – bye.
2nd round: Burillo (Q) d. Becker (1) 1–6 7–6 6–4; Skoff (16) d. Fontang 6–4 6–2; Kulti (LL) d. Davin 6–4 1–6 6–3; Gustafsson (8) d. Corretja (Q) 5–7 7–6 6–1; Roig d. E. Sanchez (3) 6–4 6–4; Svensson d. Arrese (13) 7–6 6–3; Jaite d. Carbonell 7–6 6–2; Bruguera (5) d. Gomez 6–2 6–4; Eltingh d. Agassi (6) 6–4 1–6 6–1; Costa d. Filippini 6–4 6–4; J. Sanchez (14) d. Miniussi 7–6 7–6; Gilbert d. Novacek (4) 2–6 7–5 7–5; Mancini (7) d. Koevermans 6–4 2–6 7–5; Clavet (9) d. Larsson 6–1 4–6 6–2; Muster (15) d. Altur (Q) 6–3 4–6 6–2; Lendl (2) d. Champion 6–3 6–1.
3rd round: Skoff (16) d. Burillo (Q) 6–4 6–3; Gustafsson (8) d. Kulti (LL) 4–6 6–2 6–0; Svensson d. Roig 6–7 6–0 7–6; Bruguera (5) d. Jaite 7–5 6–1; Costa d. Eltingh 7–6 7–6; Gilbert d. J. Sanchez (14) 7–6 6–3; Mancini (7) d. Clavet (9) 7–6 6–0; Lendl (2) d. Muster (15) 6–3 6–4.
Quarter-finals: Gustafsson (8) d. Skoff (16) 6–3 6–2; Bruguera (5) d. Svensson 6–4 6–4; Costa d. Gilbert 7–6 6–3; Mancini (7) d. Lendl (2) 3–6 6–3 6–4.
Semi-finals: Gustafsson (8) d. Bruguera (5) 6–4 7–5; Costa d. Mancini (7) 6–3 6–3;
Final: Costa d. Gustafsson (8) 6–4 7–6 6–4.
MEN'S DOUBLES – Final: Gomez/J. Sanchez d. Lendl/Novacek 6–4 6–4.

VOLVO MONTE CARLO OPEN ($1,020,000)
MONTE CARLO, 20–26 APRIL
MEN'S SINGLES – 1st round: B. Becker (1) – bye; T. Nijssen (Q) d. P. Haarhuis 6–3 6–4; L. Wahlgren (LL) d. J. Carlsson (Q) 6–3 6–1; A. Krickstein (16) d. J. Siemerink 6–3 7–5; K. Novacek (9) d. A. Cherkasov 6–1 6–4; T. Carbonell d. C. Pioline 4–6 6–2 6–2; A. Chesnokov d. J. Frana (Q) 6–4 6–2; M. Gustafsson (8) – bye; M. Stich (3) (WC) – bye; R. Furlan d. M. Koevermans (Q) 6–3 6–4; J. Sanchez d. J. Arrese 7–6 6–2; C. Bergstrom d. J. Hlasek (14) 6–1 6–7 6–3; S. Bruguera (11) d. F. Clavet 6–4 2–6 7–5; G. Prpic d. O. Camporese 4–6 6–4 6–3; M. Larsson d. J. Svensson 6–4 7–6; P. Korda (6) – bye; M. Tillstroem (Q) – bye; F. Santoro d. F. Fontang 7–6 5–2 ret.; T. Champion d. H. Skoff 7–6 6–2; M. Rosset d. R. Krajicek (12) 6–2 6–4; A. Volkov (13) d. G. Dzelde (Q) 5–7 7–5 6–2; T. Muster d. H. Leconte (WC) 3–6 6–4 6–3; F. Roig (Q) d. J. Yzaga 7–6 6–2; G. Forget (4) – bye; A. Mancini (7) – bye; A. Boetsch d. C. Miniussi 6–3 6–2; S. Pescosolido d. C. Caratti (WC) 1–6 7–6 7–5; E. Sanchez (10) d. O. Delaitre 6–1 6–0;

W. Ferreira (15) d. B. Borg (WC) 7–6 6–2; C. Costa d. G. Perez–Roldan 3–1 ret.; C. Steeb d. M. Jaite 6–2 4–6 7–6; P. Sampras (2) – bye.
2nd round: Becker (1) d. Nijssen (Q) 6–2 3–6 6–2; Krickstein (16) d. Wahlgren (LL) 6–1 6–1; Novacek (9) d. Carbonell 4–6 6–2 6–2; Chesnokov d. Gustafsson (8) 7–6 6–4; Stich (3) (WC) d. Furlan 7–5 6–4; J. Sanchez d. Bergstrom 6–3 7–6; Prpic d. Bruguera (11) 4–6 6–4 6–0; Larsson d. Korda (6) 6–3 6–3; Tillstroem (Q) d. Santoro 6–0 6–4; Rosset d. Champion 7–5 6–2; Muster d. Volkov (13) 6–2 4–6 6–1; Forget (4) d. Roig (Q) 6–1 3–6 6–4; Boetsch d. Mancini (7) 7–5 7–6; E. Sanchez (10) d. Pescosolido 3–6 7–6 7–6; Ferreira (15) d. Costa 4–6 6–3 6–4; Steeb d. Sampras (2) 6–3 6–4.
3rd round: Krickstein (16) d. Becker (1) 6–1 6–4; Chesnokov d. Novacek (9) 6–2 7–5; Stich (3) (WC) d. J. Sanchez 6–4 7–6; Prpic d. Larsson 7–5 3–6 6–3; Tillstroem (Q) d. Rosset 6–7 6–4 6–2; Muster d. Forget (4) 7–6 4–6 6–3; Boetsch d. E. Sanchez (10) 4–6 6–1 6–2; Steeb d. Ferreira (15) 6–2 6–1.
Quarter-finals: Krickstein (16) d. Chesnokov 6–1 7–6; Prpic d. Stich (3) (WC) 7–6 4–6 7–5; Muster d. Tillstroem (Q) 6–3 4–6 6–3; Boetsch d. Steeb 1–6 6–2 6–0.
Semi-finals: Krickstein (16) d. Prpic 6–1 6–1; Muster d. Boetsch 7–5 6–4.
Final: Muster d. Krickstein (16) 6–3 6–1 6–3.
MEN'S DOUBLES – **Final**: Becker/Stich d. Korda/Novacek 6–4 6–4.

PANASONIC GERMAN OPEN ($1,000,000)
HAMBURG, 4–11 MAY
MEN'S SINGLES – **1st round**: S. Edberg (1) – bye; J. Arrese d. G. Lopez 6–3 6–3; A. Berasategui (LL) d. A. Thoms (WC) 6–3 7–5; F. Clavet (16) d. M. Zoecke 6–2 3–6 6–2; J. McEnroe d. A. Mancini (10) 6–1 6–2; S. Pescosolido d. G. Prpic 3–6 6–2 6–4; O. Camporese d. A. Mronz (WC) 6–4 6–2; I. Lendl (7) – bye; M. Chang (4) – bye; A. Cherkasov d. M. Naewie (WC) 6–4 6–3; P. Haarhuis d. J. Sanchez 6–3 7–6; T. Muster (14) d. C. Van Rensburg 6–1 6–1; A. Agassi (11) d. M. Jaite 6–2 6–3; C. Costa d. P. Kuhnen (WC) 6–2 6–2; O. Delaitre d. F. Fetterlein (Q) 6–2 6–1; P. Korda (6) – bye; G. Ivanisevic (5) – bye; C. Bergstrom d. J. Siemerink 6–0 6–2; G. Perez–Roldan d. M. Schapers 3–6 7–5 6–2; R. Krajicek (12) d. S. Bruguera 6–3 3–6 6–2; H. Skoff d. A. Volkov (13) 6–2 1–6 7–6; D. Prinosil (Q) d. S. Nensel (Q) 7–5 6–1; C. Steeb d. A. Gomez 7–5 5–7 6–1; M. Stich (3) – bye; K. Novacek (8) – bye; F. Rivera (Q) d. J. Altur (Q) 6–0 7–6; C. Caratti (Q) d. F. Fontang 6–3 6–3; A. Corretja (Q) d. E. Sanchez (9) 3–6 6–2 6–2; W. Ferreira (15) d. C. Miniussi 7–6 6–3; R. Furlan d. C. Pioline 6–2 6–3; T. Champion d. L. Koslowski 6–0 6–1; B. Becker (2) (WC) – bye.
2nd round: Edberg (1) d. Arrese 6–3 6–4; Clavet (16) d. Berasategui (LL) 6–3 6–2; Pescosolido d. J. McEnroe 7–6 1–6 6–4; Camporese d. Lendl (7) 7–6 6–2; Chang (4) d. Cherkasov 6–1 6–2; Haarhuis d. Muster (14) 5–7 6–3 7–6; Costa d. Agassi (11) 3–6 6–1 6–2; Delaitre d. Korda (6) 5–7 7–6 6–1; Ivanisevic (5) d. Bergstrom 7–5 7–6; Krajicek (12) d. Perez–Roldan 6–3 6–4; Skoff d. Prinosil (Q) 6–2 6–7 7–6; Stich (3) d. Steeb 6–3 6–2; Novacek (8) d. Rivera (Q) 6–0 6–1; Caratti (Q) d. Corretja (Q) 7–5 4–6 7–5; Furlan d. Ferreira (15) 6–7 6–3 6–3; Becker (2) (WC) d. Champion 6–3 7–6.
3rd round: Edberg (1) d. Clavet (16) 6–3 6–1; Camporese d. Pescosolido 6–4 6–4; Haarhuis d. Chang (4) 7–6 7–6; Costa d. Delaitre 6–2 6–3; Krajicek (12) d. Ivanisevic (5) 7–5 6–2; Stich (3) d. Skoff 6–3 7–5; Novacek (8) d. Caratti (Q) 6–3 6–2; Becker (2) (WC) d. Furlan 6–4 6–4 6–3.
Quarter-finals: Edberg (1) d. Camporese 2–6 7–6 6–2; Costa d. Haarhuis 4–6 6–4 6–3; Stich (3) d. Krajicek (12) 6–4 3–6 6–3; Becker (2) (WC) d. Novacek (8) 6–1 7–6.
Semi-finals: Edberg (1) d. Costa 7–5 7–6; Stich (3) d. Becker (2) (WC) 6–1 6–1.
Final: Edberg (1) d. Stich (3) 5–7 6–4 6–1.
MEN'S DOUBLES – **Final**: S. Casal/E. Sanchez (5) d. Steeb/Stich 5–7 6–4 6–3.

ITALIAN OPEN ($1,125,000)
ROME, 11–17 MAY
MEN'S SINGLES – **1st round**: J. Courier (1) d. T. Muster 7–6 6–4; F. Clavet d. M. Schapers 6–2 6–2; A. Corretja (Q) d. F. Fontang 6–3 6–4; S. Bruguera (15) d. J. Svensson (Q) 6–1 6–3; I. Lendl (9) d. J. Arrese 6–1 6–4; M. Rosset d. L. Jonsson (Q) 6–3 7–5; P. Haarhuis d. J. Tarango 7–5 6–4; C. Miniussi d. G. Ivanisevic (7) 7–5 6–3; M. Koevermans (Q) d. D. Nargiso (C) 6–0 4–6 6–2; C. Pistolesi (C) d. G. Lopez 6–3 6–2; P. McEnroe (C) d. M. Jaite 7–5 7–5; C. Steeb d. R. Krajicek (14) 6–4 5–7 6–2; E. Sanchez (11) d. C. Bergstrom 6–4 2–6 6–3; J. Hlasek d. C. Van Rensburg 1–6 6–4 7–6; R. Furlan d. T. Champion 7–5 6–1; M. Chang (5) d. A. Markus (Q) 6–3 2–6 6–3; J. Sanchez d. G. Forget (6) 7–5 4–6 6–4; O. Camporese d. M. Zillner (Q) 6–4 4–6 7–5; J. Yzaga d. R. Agenor (L) 7–6 7–6; T. Carbonell (Q) d. K. Novacek (12) 4–6 6–4 6–3; C. Costa d. A. Krickstein (13) 6–4 6–4; W. Ferreira d. N. Kulti (Q) 6–2 6–7 7–6; A. Mansdorf d. A. Boetsch 6–4 6–3; F. Santoro d. M. Stich (4) 5–7 2–1 ret.; P. Korda (8) d. G. Pozzi 6–4 6–3; A. Cherkasov d. A. Gomez 7–6 6–2; G. Perez–Roldan d. C. Caratti (C) 6–2 6–1; A. Mancini (10) d. J. Siemerink 6–3 3–6 6–3; G. Prpic d. A. Volkov (16) 6–2 4–6 7–5; S. Pescosolido d. M. Larsson 6–3 1–2 ret.; H. Skoff d. C. Pioline 6–3; P. Sampras (2) d. P. Cane (C) 6–4 6–4.
2nd round: Courier (1) d. Clavet 6–2 6–2; Bruguera (15) d. Corretja (Q) 7–6 6–4; Rosset d. Lendl (9) 6–4 2–6 7–6; Miniussi d. Haarhuis 6–4 7–5; Pistolesi (C) d. Koevermans (Q) 7–5 4–6 6–4; Steeb d. P. McEnroe (C) 6–2 6–4; E. Sanchez (11) d. Hlasek 6–4 7–6; Chang (5) d. Furlan 6–1 3–6 6–3; J. Sanchez

d. Camporese 3–6 7–5 6–3; Yzaga d. Carbonell (Q) 6–4 6–0; Costa d. Ferreira 6–3 7–5; Santoro d. Mansdorf 6–1 6–0; Korda (8) d. Cherkasov 6–3 5–7 6–4; Mancini (10) d. Perez–Roldan 7–6 7–6; Prpic d. Pescosolido 6–1 7–6; Sampras (2) d. Skoff 6–3 6–4.

3rd round: Courier (1) d. Bruguera (15) 6–3 6–2; Miniussi d. Rosset 6–3 5–7 7–5; Steeb d. Pistolesi (C) 6–1 6–2; Chang (5) d. E. Sanchez (11) 6–1 7–5; Yzaga d. J. Sanchez 3–6 6–3 7–6; Costa d. Santoro 6–2 7–5; Korda (8) d. Mancini (10) 3–6 7–6 6–3; Sampras (2) d. Prpic 6–2 6–7 6–3.

Quarter-finals: Courier (1) d. Miniussi 4–6 6–4 6–1; Steeb d. Chang (5) 6–4 3–6 6–1; Costa d. Yzaga 6–4 6–0; Korda (8) d. Sampras (2) 1–6 7–6 6–3.

Semi-finals: Courier (1) d. Steeb 5–7 6–1 6–2; Costa d. Korda (8) 6–4 6–3.

Final: Courier (1) d. Costa 7–6 6–0 6–4.

MEN'S DOUBLES – Final: Hlasek/Rosset d. Ferreira/M. Kratzmann (8) 6–4 3–6 6–1.

MERCEDES CUP ($865,000)
STUTTGART, 13–19 JULY

MEN'S SINGLES – 1st round: S. Edberg (1) – bye; C. Miniussi d. G. Perez–Roldan 6–3 4–6 6–3; A. Chesnokov d. J. Burillo (Q) 7–6 7–6; J. Sanchez (16) – bye; E. Sanchez (9) – bye; F. Davin d. T. Champion 6–4 6–4; A. Medvedev (Q) d. G. Prpic 3–6 7–5 6–0; A. Volkov (8) – bye; M. Chang (4) – bye; B. Karbacher (Q) d. F. Roig 6–2 6–4; C. Steeb d. F. Fontang 6–4 6–1; F. Clavet (13) – bye; T. Muster (12) – bye; M. Rosset d. F. Santoro 6–1 6–4; A. Olhovskiy (Q) d. H. Leconte (WC) 7–6 7–6; M. Stich (5) – bye; C. Costa (6) – bye; C. Bergstrom d. G. Markus 4–6 6–3 6–4; C. Pioline d. L. Koslowski (WC) 7–6 6–1; A. Mancini (11) – bye; K. Novacek (14) – bye; A. Berasategui (Q) d. A. Jarryd 6–4 6–3; O. Delaitre d. A. Boetsch 6–4 6–4; B. Becker (3) (WC) – bye; W. Ferreira (7) – bye; C. Dosedel (Q) d. J. Arrese 0–6 7–5 7–5; S. Pescosolido d. M. Gustafsson 7–5 7–5; S. Bruguera (10) – bye; A. Cherkasov (15) – bye; R. Furlan d. M. Naewie (WC) 6–2 6–3; M. Larsson d. O. Camporese 5–7 6–4 6–3; G. Ivanisevic (2) – bye.

2nd round: Edberg (1) d. Miniussi 7–5 6–2; J. Sanchez (16) d. Chesnokov 4–6 7–6 7–5; E. Sanchez (9) d. Davin 6–2 6–4; Medvedev (Q) d. Volkov (8) 6–4 6–2; Karbacher (Q) d. Chang (4) 6–4 4–6 6–3; Clavet (13) d. Steeb 6–3 7–6; Muster (12) d. Rosset 6–3 6–2; Stich (5) d. Olhovskiy (Q) 6–4 7–5; Costa (6) d. Bergstrom 6–3 7–6; Mancini (11) d. Pioline 6–4 6–7 7–6; Novacek (14) d. Berasategui (Q) 6–7 7–6 6–2; Delaitre d. Becker (3) (WC) 6–3 6–4; Ferreira (7) d. Dosedel (Q) 6–4 7–5; Bruguera (10) d. Pescosolido 6–3 6–3; Cherkasov (15) d. Furlan 7–6 6–4; Ivanisevic (2) d. Larsson 6–4 6–4.

3rd round: Edberg (1) d. J. Sanchez (16) 2–6 7–6 6–2; Medvedev (Q) d. E. Sanchez (9) 7–6 6–2; Karbacher (Q) d. Clavet (13) 6–7 6–4 6–4; Muster (12) d. Stich (5) 7–6 6–4; Costa (6) d. Mancini (11) 6–3 6–4; Novacek (14) d. Delaitre 4–6 6–3 6–4; Ferreira (7) d. Bruguera (10) 7–5 6–3; Ivanisevic (2) d. Cherkasov (15) 6–3 7–6.

Quarter-finals: Medvedev (Q) d. Edberg (1) 1–6 6–4 6–4; Muster (12) d. Karbacher (Q) 3–6 6–1 6–3; Novacek (14) d. Costa (6) 6–2 7–6; Ferreira (7) d. Ivanisevic (2) 6–3 6–7 6–4;

Semi-finals: Medvedev (Q) d. Muster (12) 6–2 6–2; Ferreira (7) d. Novacek (14) 6–3 6–2.

Final: Medvedev (Q) d. Ferreira (7) 6–1 6–4 6–7 2–6 6–1.

MEN'S DOUBLES – Final: G. Layendecker/B. Talbot d. J. Sanchez/Rosset 4–6 6–3 6–4.

NATIONS BANK CLASSIC ($490,000)
WASHINGTON, D.C., 13–19 JULY

MEN'S SINGLES – 1st round: P. Korda (1) – bye; J. Brown (Q) d. M. Laurendeau 6–4 4–6 6–4; A. Antonitsch d. C. Caratti 6–3 6–3; L. Lavalle (16) d. S. Youl 6–4 7–6; W. Masur (9) d. A. Thoms 4–6 6–2 6–2; D. Randall (Q) d. B. Garnett (Q) 6–4 6–7 6–2; R. Agenor d. K. Braasch 2–6 6–2 6–0; A. Mansdorf (8) – bye; A. Krickstein (4) – bye; G. Raoux d. J. Stark 6–4 6–2; P. Lundgren d. K. Flach (Q) 7–5 6–2; M. Ondruska d. L. Herrera (13) 7–5 6–1; M. Damm d. M. Zoecke (11) 4–6 6–2 6–1; J. Arias (Q) d. C. Pridham 6–4 3–6 6–1; T. Hogstedt d. B. Borg (WC) 6–4 7–6; M. Washington (6) – bye; J. McEnroe (5) – bye; J. Bates d. F. Montana 7–6 6–3; T. Martin d. T. Witsken 6–3 6–3; H. Holm d. R. Reneberg (12) 6–1 6–3; J. Grabb (14) d. B. Macphie (WC) 6–4 3–6 6–4; A. O'Brien (WC) d. C. Adams 4–6 7–6 7–6; J. Palmer (WC) d. S. Stolle 6–2 6–4; I. Lendl (3) – bye; D. Rostagno (7) – bye; P. Kuhnen d. S. Bryan (Q) 6–1 6–3; R. Koenig (Q) d. G. Bloom 7–5 4–6 7–6; G. Pozzi (10) d. D. Rikl 6–2 6–1; J. Stoltenberg (15) d. R. Weiss 6–4 6–7 6–4; G. Muller d. G. Connell 6–3 6–7 7–6; K. Curren d. A. Mronz 6–7 7–6 6–4; A. Agassi (2) (WC) – bye.

2nd round: Korda (1) d. Brown (Q) 4–6 6–2 6–3; Antonitsch d. Lavalle (16) 4–6 6–0 6–2; Masur (9) d. Randall (Q) 6–2 7–5; Mansdorf (8) d. Agenor 6–2 6–0; Raoux d. Krickstein (4) 7–5 2–6 6–3; Ondruska d. Lundgren 3–6 7–6 6–1; Arias (Q) d. Damm 7–6 6–3; Washington (6) d. Hogstedt 7–5 6–0; Bates d. J. McEnroe (5) 6–2 1–6 6–4; Holm d. Martin 7–6 7–5; Grabb (14) d. O'Brien (WC) 6–3 6–2; Lendl (3) d. Palmer (WC) 6–4 6–1; Rostagno (7) d. Kuhnen 6–3 6–7 6–3; Koenig (Q) d. Pozzi (10) 3–6 6–4 6–4; Muller d. Stoltenberg (15) 6–1 7–6; Curren d. Agassi (2) (WC) 7–5 6–4.

3rd round: Korda (1) d. Antonitsch 6–3 7–5; Mansdorf (8) d. Masur (9) 6–3 6–4; Raoux d. Ondruska 6–4 6–2; Washington (6) d. Arias (Q) 3–6 6–2 6–3; Holm d. Bates 7–5 3–0 15–0 ret.; Lendl (3) d. Grabb (14) 6–1 7–6; Rostagno (7) d. Koenig (Q) 7–6 6–4; Muller d. Curren 4–6 6–3 7–6.

Quarter-finals: Korda (1) d. Mansdorf (8) 7–6 6–2; Washington (6) d. Raoux 7–6 7–6; Holm d. Lendl (3) 3–6 6–3 6–3; Rostagno (7) d. Muller 6–1 6–7 7–6.
Semi-finals: Korda (1) d. Washington (6) 7–6 6–0; Holm d. Rostagno (7) 6–4 6–3.
Final: Korda (1) d. Holm 6–4 6–4.
MEN'S DOUBLES – *Final*: Garnett/Palmer d. Flach/Witsken (3) 6–2 6–3.

PLAYER'S LTD. INTERNATIONAL CANADIAN OPEN ($1,025,000)
TORONTO, 19–25 JULY
MEN'S SINGLES – *1st round*: P. Korda (1) – bye; R. Weiss d. S. Lareau (WC) 6–0 6–2; L. Lavalle d. N. Kroon (Q) 7–5 6–4; R. Reneberg (15) d. P. McEnroe 7–6 6–4; W. Masur (10) d. K. Braasch 4–6 6–3 6–4; B. Pearce (Q) d. M. Stadling (Q) 7–6 2–6 6–2; P. Kuhnen d. M. Damm 7–6 6–3; D. Rostagno (7) – bye; I. Lendl (3) – bye; T. Martin d. J. Bates 6–1 6–4; S. Youl d. D. Marcelino 7–5 6–1; J. Tarango (13) d. F. Montana 6–3 6–3; J. Stark d. B. Shelton (12) 7–6 7–5; T. Witsken d. A. Mronz 4–6 6–4 6–0; J. Grabb d. G. Raoux 6–4 7–6; J. McEnroe (5) – bye; M. Washington (6) – bye; G. Connell d. R. Schmidt (Q) 6–3 6–4; K. Curren d. L. Herrera 2–6 6–3 6–4; G. Bloom d. G. Pozzi (11) 6–1 6–3; S. Stolle d. M. Schapers (14) 7–5 6–4; H. Holm d.K. Thorne (Q) 6–4 6–4; A. Thoms d. F. Roese 7–6 6–1; A. Krickstein (4) – bye; A. Mansdorf (8) – bye; C. Adams d. G. Muller 6–2 6–4; C. Pridham d. A. Sznajder (WC) 6–1 7–6; J. Stoltenberg d. D. Wheaton (9) 6–3 6–4; S. Bryan (Q) d. C. Van Rensburg (16) 6–7 6–4 6–4; G. Rusedski (WC) d. M. Laurendeau (WC) 7–6 3–6 7–5; D. Nestor (WC) d. C. Caratti (Q) 6–4 6–4; A. Agassi (2) – bye.
2nd round: Korda (1) d. Weiss 6–4 6–4; Reneberg (15) d. Lavalle 6–2 6–3; Masur (10) d. Pearce 4–6 6–4 6–1; Kuhnen d. Rostagno (7) 7–5 3–6 7–5; Lendl (3) d. Martin 6–3 6–2; Youl d. Tarango (13) 7–6 6–4; Stark d. Witsken 6–4 7–5; J. McEnroe (5) d. Grabb 6–4 7–6; Washington (6) d. Connell 4–6 7–6 6–1; Curren d. Bloom 6–4 6–3; Holm d. Stolle 7–6 6–3; Krickstein (4) d. Thoms 6–4 6–3; Mansdorf (8) d. Adams 6–3 6–4; Pridham d. Stoltenberg 6–7 7–6 6–4; Rusedski (WC) d. Bryan (Q) 6–4 6–4 6–3; Agassi (2) d. Nestor (WC) 6–1 6–3.
3rd round: Korda (1) d. Reneberg (15) 6–4 6–2; Masur (10) d. Kuhnen 4–6 6–3 6–2; Lendl (3) d. Youl 6–1 6–4; J. McEnroe (5) d. Stark 6–0 6–2; Washington (6) d. Curren 6–4 7–6; Krickstein (4) d. Holm 6–4 7–6; Mansdorf (8) d. Pridham 6–2 7–5; Agassi (2) d. Rusedski (WC) 6–4 6–1.
Quarter-finals: Masur (10) d. Korda (1) 7–6 4–6 6–3; Lendl (3) d. J. McEnroe (5) 6–2 6–4; Washington (6) d. Krickstein (4) 7–6 6–1; Agassi (2) d. Mansdorf (8) 6–2 6–4
Semi-finals: Lendl (3) d. Masur (10) 6–1 6–2; Agassi (2) d. Washington (6) 2–6 6–2 6–1.
Final: Agassi (2) d. Lendl (3) 3–6 6–2 6–0.
MEN'S DOUBLES – *Final*: P. Galbraith/D. Visser (8) d. Agassi/J. McEnroe 6–4 6–4.

THRIFTWAY ATP CHAMPIONSHIP ($1,125,000)
CINCINNATI, 10–16 AUGUST
MEN'S SINGLES – *1st round*: J. Courier (1) – bye; R. Schmidt (Q) d. J. Tarango 4–6 6–4 6–3; D. Wheaton d. T. Witsken 6–2 5–7 6–3; A. Cherkasov (16) d. J. Stoltenberg 6–3 6–4; C. Pioline d. G. Connell 6–2 3–6 6–3; T. Martin (Q) d. S. Pescosolido 6–2 6–2; G. Pozzi d. J. Hlasek 6–2 7–6; I. Lendl (8) – bye; M. Chang (4) – bye; S. Stolle d. C. Van Rensburg 6–4 6–2; S. Youl d. D. Nargiso 6–1 7–5; B. Gilbert (13) d. J. Stark 7–6 6–4; J. Carlsson (Q) d. M. Washington (12) 6–4 6–3 7–6; J. Yzaga d. K. Thorne (Q) 6–7 6–3 7–5; O. Delaitre d. P. McEnroe 5–7 7–5 7–5; A. Agassi (6) – bye; P. Korda (5) – bye; D. Rostagno d. K. Ullyett (Q) 3–6 6–1 7–6; D. Nainkin (Q) d. R. Koenig (LL) 5–7 6–1 6–3; R. Krajicek (11) d. A. Olhovskiy (Q) 6–3 6–2; A. Volkov (14) d. W. Masur 6–4 7–5; M. Woodforde d. J. Siemerink 6–2 7–6; F. Montana d. L. Lavalle 6–2 7–6; P. Sampras (3) – bye; G. Forget (7) – bye; T. Woodbridge d. G. Lopez 6–0 6–2; J. Grabb d. M. Rosset 6–3 6–4; T. Champion d. W. Ferreira (9) 6–0 1–0 ret.; A. Mansdorf (15) d. B. Shelton 2–6 6–4 7–6; R. Reneberg d. A. Jarryd 6–4 1–6 6–1; C. Bergstrom d. K. Curren 6–1 6–1; S. Edberg (2) – bye.
2nd round: Courier (1) d. Schmidt (Q) 6–3 6–2; Wheaton d. Cherkasov (16) 6–2 7–6; Pioline d. Martin (Q) 6–2 5–7 6–4; Lendl (8) d. Pozzi 6–3 3–6 6–1; Chang (4) d. Stolle 6–4 6–3; Gilbert (13) d. Youl 7–6 6–4; Yzaga d. Carlsson (Q) 6–4 7–6; Agassi (6) d. Delaitre 6–4 6–0; Korda (5) d. Rostagno 3–6 7–6 6–4; Krajicek (11) d. Nainkin (Q) 6–2 6–7 6–0; Woodforde d. Volkov (14) 6–1 6–3; Sampras (3) d. Montana 7–6 3–6 6–3; Woodbridge d. Forget (7) 7–5 5–7 6–3; Grabb d. Champion 4–6 6–1 6–4; Mansdorf (15) d. Reneberg 6–3 4–6 6–4; Edberg (2) d. Bergstrom 7–6 6–1.
3rd round: Wheaton d. Courier (1) 7–5 7–6; Lendl (8) d. Pioline 6–1 6–2; Chang (4) d. Gilbert (13) 6–2 6–2; Yzaga d. Agassi (6) 6–3 4–6 7–5; Korda (5) d. Krajicek (11) 6–3 ret.; Sampras (3) d. Woodforde 2–6 7–6 6–2; Grabb d. Woodbridge 6–2 7–6; Edberg (2) d. Mansdorf (15) 6–4 6–3.
Quarter-finals: Lendl (8) d. Wheaton 6–1 6–2; Chang (4) d. Yzaga 6–3 6–1; Sampras (3) d. Korda (5) 6–3 6–3; Edberg (2) d. Grabb 6–3 7–6.
Semi-finals: Lendl (8) d. Chang (4) 6–3 6–2; Sampras (3) d. Edberg (2) 6–2 6–3.
Final: Sampras (3) d. Lendl (8) 6–3 3–6 6–3.
MEN'S DOUBLES – *Final*: Woodbridge/Woodforde (2) d. P. McEnroe/Stark 6–3 1–6 6–3.

RCA CHAMPIONSHIPS ($865,000)

INDIANAPOLIS, 17–23 AUGUST

MEN'S SINGLES – 1st round: J. Courier (1) – bye; C. Pioline d. K. Evernden (Q) 6–4 6–2; D. Engel (Q) d. C. Pridham 4–6 6–3 6–4; M. Gustafsson d. K. Kinnear (WC) 6–4 4–6 6–1; J. Sanchez (9) d. L. Lavalle 4–1 ret.; S. Stolle d. G. Lopez 6–4 6–2; B. Steven d. J. Stoltenberg 4–6 6–0 4–2; D. Rostagno (8) – bye; C. Costa (4) – bye; M. Ondruska (Q) d. D. Witt (WC) 1–6 6–3 6–1; M. Pernfors (Q) d. R. Reneberg 3–6 6–4 6–4; T. Martin d. C. Bergstrom (16) 6–0 6–3; O. Delaitre (12) d. A. Jarryd 4–6 6–4 6–2; J. Stark (WC) d. R. Weiss 6–3 6–4; T. Champion d. R. Fromberg 6–7 7–6 6–0; F. Clavet (6) – bye; W. Ferreira (5) – bye; K. Curren d. P Arraya 7–5 1–6 6–3; S. Youl d. G. Raoux 6–2 6–0; J. Connors (11) d. D. Dilucia (WC) 6–1 6–2; D. Wheaton (13) d. R. Gilbert 2–6 6–2 6–4; F. Roig d. C. Limberger 7–5 6–2; M. Zoecke d. N. Kulti 6–3 7–6; B. Becker (3) – bye; E. Sanchez (7) – bye; T. Ho (Q) d. J. Grabb 6–3 6–3; T. Enqvist d. F. Montana 6–3 5–7 6–4; T. Carbonell d. A. Mancini (10) 6–1 6–4; T. Witsken d. S. Pescosolido (15) 7–5 6–3; G. Muller d. J. Fitzgerald 6–1 6–4; S. Sansoni (Q) d. T. Mercer (Q) 3–6 6–1 6–1; P. Sampras (2) – bye.

2nd round: Courier (1) d. Pioline 6–4 6–2; Engel (Q) d. Gustafsson 6–2 4–6 6–1; Stolle d. J. Sanchez (9) 7–6 5–7 6–4; Steven d. Rostagno (8) 6–3 6–3; Ondruska (Q) d. Costa (4) 6–1 6–3; Martin d. Pernfors (Q) 7–5 6–2; Delaitre (12) d. Stark (WC) 6–4 6–4; Clavet (6) d. Champion 6–4 6–1; Ferreira (5) d. Curren 6–3 6–4; Connors (11) d. Youl 7–5 6–4; Wheaton (13) d. Roig 6–3 2–6 7–5; Becker (3) d. Zoecke 6–4 6–3; Ho (Q) d. E. Sanchez (7) 7–6 6–3; Enqvist d. Carbonell 6–4 6–1; Witsken d. Muller 5–3 ret.; Sampras (2) d. Sansoni (Q) 6–0 6–1.

3rd round: Courier (1) d. Engel (Q) 7–6 6–2; Steven d. Stolle 6–0 1–1 ret.; Martin d. Ondruska (Q) 6–2 6–1; Clavet (6) d. Delaitre (12) 6–3 6–4; Connors (11) d. Ferreira (5) 6–3 6–2; Becker (3) d. Wheaton (13) 7–6 6–3; Enqvist d. Ho (Q) 6–3 7–6; Sampras (2) d. Witsken 6–4 7–5.

Quarter-finals: Courier (1) d. Steven 6–2 6–3; Martin d. Clavet (6) 6–1 6–2; Becker (3) d. Connors (11) 6–4 6–3; Sampras (2) d. Enqvist 6–0 7–6.

Semi-finals: Courier (1) d. Martin 7–6 6–4; Sampras (2) d. Becker (3) 6–7 6–2 7–6.

Final: Sampras (2) d. Courier(1) 6–4 6–4.

MEN'S DOUBLES – Final: Grabb/Reneberg (2) d. G. Connell/G. Michibata 7–6 6–2.

VOLVO INTERNATIONAL ($865,00)

NEW HAVEN, CONNECTICUT, 17–23 AUGUST

MEN'S SINGLES – 1st round: S. Edberg (1) – bye; B. Farrow (Q) d. I. Baron (Q) 7–6 6–4; S. Lareau (Q) d. F. Roese 6–0 6–2; P. Haarhuis (16) d. A. Chesnokov 6–2 6–3; A. Volkov (10) d. R. Krishnan (WC) 6–3 6–3; T. Woodbridge d. D. Nargiso 6–3 7–6; J. Arias (WC) d. D. Marcelino 5–7 6–2 6–4; G. Forget (7) – bye; M. Chang (3) – bye; G. Pozzi d. P. Kilderry (Q) 2–6 6–2 6–2; B. Black d. J. Bates 6–1 6–0; A. Cherkasov (14) d. A. Olhovskiy (14) 4–6 6–4 7–6; A. Mansdorf (12) d. M. Woodforde 6–1 1–6 6–4; W. Masur d. J. Tarango 6–3 6–0; S. Matsuoka d. J. Oncins 7–5 2–1; I. Lendl (5) – bye; R. Krajicek (6) – bye; A. O'Brien (WC) d. Y. Kafelnikov (Q) 6–2 6–1; F. Santoro d. C. Van Rensburg 6–3 6–2; S. Gilbert (11) d. M. Jensen (Q) 6–0 6–1; C. Adams d. J. Hlasek (13) 7–6 7–6; J. Yzaga d. J. Siemerink 7–5 6–4; A. Boetsch d. J. Burillo 6–3 6–2; P. Korda (4) – bye; M. Washington (8) – bye; L. Herrera d. G. Bloom 7–5 6–1; T. Guardiola d. B. Dyke (Q) 6–4 3–6 6–3; J. McEnroe (9) (WC) d. J. Apell 6–1 7–5; M. Damm d. O. Camporese (15) 4–6 7–5 6–2; M. Rosset d. L. Mattar 4–6 6–3 6–3; B. Shelton d. P. McEnroe 6–2 7–6; G. Ivanisevic (2) – bye.

2nd round: Edberg (1) d. Farrow (Q) 6–3 6–1; Haarhuis (16) d. Lareau 7–6 6–7 6–3; Volkov (10) d. Woodbridge 6–4 3–6 7–5; Forget (7) d. Arias (WC) 4–6 6–3 7–5; Chang (3) d. Pozzi 6–3 6–3; Cherkasov (14) d. Black 6–1 3–6 6–4; Mansdorf (12) d. Masur 2–6 7–5 7–6; Lendl (5) d. Matsuoka 6–3 6–4; O'Brien (WC) d. Krajicek (6) 7–6 7–6; Santoro d. Gilbert (11) 6–0 7–6; Adams d. Yzaga 7–6 6–4; Korda (4) d. Boetsch – w/o; Washington (8) d. Herrera 6–7 7–5 7–6; J. McEnroe (9) (WC) d. Guardiola 6–7 7–5 7–6; Rosset d. Damm 6–2 6–2; Ivanisevic (2) d. Shelton 6–3 7–5.

3rd round: Edberg (1) d. Haarhuis (16) 6–2 6–4; Forget (7) d. Volkov (10) 7–6 7–6; Chang (3) d. Cherkasov (14) 6–2 6–1; Lendl (5) d. Mansdorf (12) 6–2 6–3; Santoro d. O'Brien (WC) 6–3 6–3; Korda (4) d. Adams 6–4 6–7 6–4; Washington (8) d. J. McEnroe (9) (WC) 7–6 6–3; Ivanisevic (2) d. Rosset 3–6 7–6 6–4.

Quarter-finals: Edberg (1) d. Forget (7) 6–3 6–7 6–4; Lendl (5) d. Chang (3) 6–3 7–6; Santoro d. Korda (4) 7–6 4–6 6–3; Washington (8) d. Ivanisevic (2) 6–4 7–5.

Semi-finals: Edberg (1) d. Lendl (5) 7–6 4–6 6–3; Washington (8) d. Santoro 6–4 6–2.

Final: Edberg (1) d. Washington (8) 7–6 6–1.

MEN'S DOUBLES – Final: K. Jones/R. Leach (2) d. P. McEnroe/J. Palmer (8) 7–6 6–7 6–2.

AUSTRALIAN INDOOR TENNIS CHAMPIONSHIP ($825,000)

SYDNEY, 5 – 11 OCTOBER

MEN'S SINGLES – 1st round: S. Edberg (1) – bye; P. Baur d. P. McEnroe 6–3 3–6 7–6; L. Bale (Q) d. S. Stolle 6–7 6–3 7–6; R. Reneberg (15) – bye; D. Rostagno (10) – bye; B. Black d. J. Anderson (Q) 6–1 6–3; A. Olhovskiy (Q) d. S. Youl 6–4 7–6; J. McEnroe (7) – bye; A. Agassi (3) – bye; J. Grabb d. J.

Fitzgerald (WC) 6–4 6–4; P. Kuhnen d. D. Nargiso 7–6 7–6; T. Woodbridge (13) – bye; H. Holm (12) – bye; D. Pate (Q) d. B. Shelton 7–6 3–6 7–6; R. Fromberg d. C. Pridham 6–3 6–2; W. Ferreira (5) – bye; R. Krajicek (6) – bye; A. Antonitsch d. S. Davis (Q) 7–5 6–1; N. Borwick (WC) d. J. Bates 6–1 6–4; D. Wheaton (11) – bye ; M. Woodforde (14) – bye; T. Martin d. J. Eltingh 6–3 7–6; B. Steven d. J. Stark 6–7 6–3 6–2; I. Lendl (4) – bye; W. Masur (8) – bye; J. Morgan (WC) d. G. Raoux 6–4 3–6 7–6; G. Doyle (WC) d. G. Muller 7–5 6–2; P. Haarhuis (9) – bye; S. Matsuoka (16) – bye; C. Van Rensburg d. K. Carlsen 7–6 6–4; G. Pozzi d. N. Kroon (Q) 6–2 6–2; G. Ivanisevic (2) – bye.
2nd round: Edberg (1) d. Baur 7–6 7–5; Reneberg (15) d. Bale (Q) 6–0 6–3; Black d. Rostagno (10) 7–6 6–7 6–4; J. McEnroe (7) d. Olhovskiy (Q) 1–6 6–2 6–0; Agassi (3) d. Grabb 6–4 6–2; Kuhnen d. Woodbridge (13) 7–6 6–4; Holm (12) d. Pate (Q) 6–3 6–2; Ferreira (5) d. Fromberg 6–3 6–3; Krajicek (6) d. Antonitsch 6–1 6–1; Borwick (WC) d. Wheaton (11) 6–0 3–6 6–4; Woodforde (14) d. Martin 6–7 7–5 6–3; Lendl (4) d. Steven 7–5 7–5; Masur (8) d. Morgan (WC) 6–4 6–3; Haarhuis (9) d. Doyle (WC) 6–1 6–3; Van Rensburg d. Matsuoka (16) 7–5 7–6; Ivanisevic (2) d. Pozzi 6–2 6–4.
3rd round: Edberg (1) d. Reneberg (15) 6–4 6–2; J. McEnroe (7) d. Black 7–6 3–6 6–1; Kuhnen d. Agassi (3) 6–3 6–4; Holm (12) d. Ferreira (5) 7–6 3–6 6–4; Krajicek (6) d. Borwick (WC) 6–3 4–6 6–2; Lendl (4) d. Woodforde (14) 6–2 6–4; Haarhuis (9) d. Masur (8) 5–3 ret.; Ivanisevic (2) d. Van Rensburg 6–4 6–4.
Quarter-finals: Edberg (1) d. J. McEnroe (7) 6–3 6–3; Holm (12) d. Kuhnen 6–3 6–2; Krajicek (6) d. Lendl (4) 7–6 7–5; Ivanisevic (2) d. Haarhuis (9) 7–6 6–3.
Semi-finals: Edberg (1) d. Holm (12) 6–2 3–6 6–3; Ivanisevic (2) d. Krajicek (6) 6–3 1–0 ret.
Final: Ivanisevic (2) d. Edberg (1) 6–4 6–2 6–4.
MEN'S DOUBLES – Final: J. McEnroe/Stark d. Grabb/Reneberg (1) 6–2 6–3.

SEIKO SUPER TENNIS ($825,000)
TOKYO, 8–12 OCTOBER
MEN'S SINGLES – 1st round: S. Edberg (1) – bye; J. Grabb d. K. Carlsen (Q) 5–7 7–6 6–2; P. McEnroe d. C. Van Rensburg 6–3 6–2; D. Wheaton (15) – bye; E. Sanchez (9) – bye; S. Matsuoka d. S. Youl 5–7 6–2 6–2; R. Fromberg d. P. Baur 4–6 6–2 6–2; A. Volkov (8) – bye; B. Becker (3) – bye; G. Prpic d. B. Black 6–4 4–6 6–4; B. Shelton d. P. Kuhnen 7–6 6–2; H. Holm (14) – bye; P. Haarhuis (12) – bye; C. Pridham d. L. Wahlgren (Q) 6–3 6–3; C. Mezzadri d. Y. Yamamoto (WC) 6–3 3–6 6–3; W. Ferreira (6) – bye; I. Lendl (5) – bye; T. Martin d. S. Stolle 7–6 6–4; G. Raoux d. B. Kim (WC) 6–2 6–3; W. Masur (11) – bye; D. Rostagno (13) – bye; H. Kroon (Q) d. A. Antonitsch 6–3 7–5; R. Reneberg d. J. Eltingh 3–6 6–3 6–2; G. Ivanisevic (4) – bye; R. Krajicek (7) – bye; M. Woodforde d. D. Nargiso 6–3 7–6; K. Thorne (Q) d. H. Kaneko (WC) 6–3 6–2; J. Sanchez (10) – bye; T. Woodbridge (16) – bye; J. Stark d. G. Connell (Q) 6–3 6–4; A. Olhovskiy (Q) d. R. Tsujino (WC) 6–2 6–4; M. Chang (2) – bye.
2nd round: Edberg (1) d. Grabb 6–4 6–4; P. McEnroe d. Wheaton (15) 6–1 2–6 6–4; Matsuoka d. E. Sanchez (9) 7–6 4–6 6–3; Volkov (8) d. Fromberg 6–3 6–1; Becker (3) d. Prpic 6–4 7–5; Holm (14) d. Shelton 6–4 2–6 6–4; Pridham d. Haarhuis (12) 6–4 6–4; Ferreira (6) d. Mezzadri 6–4 3–6 6–3; Lendl (5) d. Martin 7–5 2–6 7–5; Masur (11) d. Raoux 5–7 7–6 6–4; Kroon (Q) d. Rostagno (13) 7–6 6–3; Ivanisevic (4) d. Reneberg 6–3 6–4; Krajicek (7) d. Woodforde 6–4 6–2; Thorne (Q) d. J. Sanchez (10) 6–3 6–2; Stark d. Woodbridge (16) 6–3 5–7 7–6; Chang (2) d. Olhovskiy (Q) 6–2 6–3.
3rd round: Edberg (1) d. P. McEnroe 6–2 7–6; Volkov (8) d. Matsuoka 7–5 6–2; Holm (14) d. Becker (3) 6–1 6–2; Ferreira (6) d. Pridham 7–6 4–6 6–4; Lendl (5) d. Masur 6–7 6–4 7–6; Ivanisevic (4) d. Kroon (Q) 6–4 6–2; Thorne (Q) d. Krajicek (7) 6–3 7–6; Chang (2) d. Stark 6–0 6–7 6–0.
Quarter-finals: Volkov (8) d. Edberg (1) 6–3 3–6 7–5; Holm (14) d. Ferreira (6) 7–6 6–2; Lendl (5) d. Ivanisevic (4) 6–3 6–4; Chang (2) d. Thorne (Q) 7–6 6–3.
Semi-finals: Holm (14) d. Volkov (8) 7–5 6–2; Lendl (5) d. Chang (2) 6–3 6–4.
Final: Lendl (5) d. Holm (14) 7–6 6–4.
MEN'S DOUBLES – Final: Woodbridge/Woodforde (3) d. Grabb/Reneberg (1) 7–6 6–4.

STOCKHOLM OPEN ($1,040,000)
STOCKHOLM, 26 OCTOBER–1 NOVEMBER
MEN'S SINGLES – 1st round: J. Courier (1) – bye; D. Rostagno d. M Norman (Q) 6–1 6–2; J. Hlasek d. J. Carlsson (Q) 6–2 6–4; H. Holm (16) – bye; M. Washington (10) – bye; T. Enquist (WC) d. O. Camporese 7–6 2–6 7–6; M. Larsson d. J. Siemerink 3–6 6–4 6–1; G. Forget (8) – bye; P. Sampras (3) – bye; T. Woodbridge d. T. Hogstedt (Q) 7–5 6–2; L. Wahlgren (Q) d. N. Kulti (WC) 7–6 3–6 6–3; T. Muster (13) – bye; M. Stich (12) – bye; J. Tarango d. S. Pescosolido 2–6 6–3 6–1; W. Masur d. A. Cherkasov 6–4 6–2; P. Korda (5) – bye; B. Becker (6) – bye; J. Svensson (WC) d. B. Gilbert 6–4 6–3; A. Mansdorf d. J. Bjorkman (Q) 6–2 6–1; A. Volkov (11) – bye; F. Clavet (14) – bye; M. Gustafsson (WC) d. C. Steeb 6–3 3–6 6–1; D. Wheaton d. M. Woodforde 6–7 7–6 6–4; G. Ivanisevic (4) – bye; W. Ferreira (7) – bye; A. Boetsch d. J. Sanchez 6–2 4–6 6–3; C. Bergstrom d. P. Haarhuis 6–2 6–1; C. Costa (9) – bye; K. Novacek (15) – bye; A. Chesnokov d. U. Stenlund (Q) 7–5 7–5; A. Medvedev d. O. Delaitre 6–3 6–2; S. Edberg (2) – bye.

2nd round: Courier (1) d. Rostagno 6–1 7–6; Holm (16) d. Hlasek 6–2 1–0 ret.; Enquist (WC) d. Washington (10) 6–2 6–1; Forget (8) d. Larsson 7–6 6–4; Sampras (3) d. Woodbridge 6–2 7–6; Muster (13) d. Wahlgren (Q) 6–4 4–6 6–4; Stich (12) d. Tarango 6–3 7–6; Korda (5) d. Masur 6–3 6–1; Becker (6) d. Svensson (WC) 7–6 7–5; Mansdorf d. Volkov (11) 7–6 6–1; Gustafsson (WC) d. Clavet (14) 6–2 6–2; Ivanisevic (4) d. Wheaton 6–4 6–4; Boetsch d. Ferreira (7) 6–1 6–3; Bergstrom d. Costa (9) 3–6 6–4 6–3; Novacek (15) d. Chesnokov 6–1 3–6 6–4; Edberg (2) d. Medvedev 6–1 7–6.
3rd round: Holm (16) d. Courier (1) 6–4 6–3; Forget (8) d. Enquist (WC) 7–6 6–3; Sampras (3) d. Muster (13) 6–2 6–4; Korda (5) d. Stich (12) 6–3 6–4; Becker (6) d. Mansdorf 7–6 7–5; Ivanisevic (4) d. Gustafsson (WC) 7–6 6–3; Boetsch d. Bergstrom 5–7 6–3 6–4; Edberg (2) d. Novacek (15) 6–3 6–4.
Quarter-finals: Forget (8) d. Holm (16) 7–5 6–7 7–6; Sampras (3) d. Korda (5) 7–6 5–7 6–3; Ivanisevic (4) er (6) 7–5 6–4; Edberg (2) d. Boetsch 7–5 7–6.
Semi-finals: Forget (8) d. Sampras (3) 7–6 7–6; Ivanisevic (4) d. Edberg (2) 6–4 7–6.
Final: Ivanisevic (4) d. Forget (8) 7–6 4–6 7–6 6–2.
MEN'S DOUBLES – *Final*: Woodforde/Woodbridge (1) d. S. Devries/D. MacPherson (7) 6–3 6–4.

OPEN DE LA VILLE DE PARIS ($2,165,000)
PARIS, 2 – 8 NOVEMBER
MEN'S SINGLES – *1st round*: J. Courier (1) – bye; A. Chesnokov d. K. Novacek 5–7 6–1 6–4; M. Larsson d. P. Haarhuis 7–6 7–6; M. Stich (16) – bye; B. Becker (9) – bye; J. McEnroe d. H. Holm 6–3 3–6 6–3; B. Gilbert d. G. Raoux 6–1 6–1; A. Agassi (7) – bye; M. Chang (4) – bye; D. Wheaton d. J. Sanchez 7–6 7–6; E. Sanchez d. A. Cherkasov 7–6 6–4; A. Volkov (14) – bye; R. Krajicek (12) – bye; A. Mansdorf d. C. Steeb 6–3 3–6 6–3; C. Pioline d. O. Camporese 7–6 3–6 6–3; G. Ivanisevic (6) – bye; P. Korda (5) – bye; A. Boetsch d. F. Clavet 6–3 6–3; O. Delaitre d. S. Pescosolido 6–2 7–6; G. Forget (11) – bye; C. Costa (13) – bye; D. Rostagno d. N. Kulti 6–4 6–3; A. Medvedev d. F. Santoro 3–6 6–4 6–3; S. Edberg (3) – bye; W. Ferreira (8) – bye; J. Hlasek d. T. Muster 6–3 6–4; J. Grabb d. G. Markus 6–3 6–2; M.V. Washington (10) – bye; S. Bruguera (15) – bye; W. Masur d. M. Rosset 6–3 6–4; H. Leconte d. J. Tarango 4–6 6–1 6–4; P. Sampras (2) – bye.
2nd round: Courier (1) d. Chesnokov 6–3 6–0; Stich d. Larsson 4–6 7–6 6–4; Becker (9) d. McEnroe 6–4 6–4; Gilbert d. Agassi (7) 6–1 6–2; Wheaton d. Chang (4) 6–1 1–6 6–3; Volkov (14) d. Sanchez 6–3 6–4; Krajicek (12) d. Mansdorf 6–4 6–2; Ivanisevic (6) d. Pioline 6–4 7–5; Boetsch d. Koda (5) 7–5 6–4; Forget (11) d. Delaitre 4–6 6–3 7–6; Rostagno d. Costa (13) 6–3 7–5; Edberg (3) d. Medvedev 6–1 1–6 6–1; Hlasek d. Ferreira (8) 6–3 3–6 6–3; Grabb d. Washington (10) 4–6 6–4 6–0; Masur d. Bruguera (15) 6–3 7–5; Leconte d. Sampras (2) 6–3 7–5.
3rd round: Courier (1) d. Stich 7–6 6–1; Becker (9) d. Gilbert 6–2 6–2; Wheaton d. Volkov (14) 7–5 6–4; Ivanisevic (6) d. Krajicek (12) 6–4 6–3; Forget (11) d. Boetsch 6–2 6–4; Edberg (3) d. Rostagno 7–6 7–6; Hlasek d. Grabb 4–6 6–1 6–2; Leconte d. Masur 6–4 7–6.
Quarter-finals: Becker (9) d. Courier (1) 6–1 6–2; Ivanisevic (6) d. Wheaton 6–4 6–3; Forget (11) d. Edberg (3) 6–7 7–6 6–3; Hlasek d. Leconte w/o.
Semi-finals: Becker (9) d. Ivanisevic (6) 6–1 6–2; Forget (11) d. Hlasek 6–3 7–6.
Final: Becker (9) d. Forget (11) 7–6 6–3 3–6 6–3.
MEN'S DOUBLES – *Final:* J. McEnroe/P. McEnroe d. P. Galbraith/D. Visser 6–4 6–2.

WORLD SERIES

WEST END MEN'S OPEN ($157,500)
ADELAIDE, 30 DECEMBER–5 JANUARY
MEN'S SINGLES – Quarter-finals: G. Ivanisevic (1) (WC) d. M. Rosset 6–4 7–6; B. Shelton d. R. Gilbert 7–5 6–4; C. Steeb (6) d. T. Enqvist (Q) 7–6 7–6; C. Bergstrom d. O. Delaitre (7) 6–1 6–3.
Semi-finals: Ivanisevic (1) (WC) d. Shelton 6–4 6–2; Bergstrom d. Steeb (6) 7–6 6–4.
Final: Ivanisevic (1) (WC) d. Bergstrom 1–6 7–6 6–4.
MEN'S DOUBLES – Final: Ivanisevic/Rosset d. M. Kratzmann/J. Stoltenberg 7–6 7–6.

BP NATIONALS ($157,500)
WELLINGTON, 30 DECEMBER–5 JANUARY
MEN'S SINGLES – Quarter-finals: A. Volkov (1) d. L. Nemecek (Q) 6–3 6–4; M. Washington d. D. Nargiso 3–6 3–2 0–15 ret.; L. Koslowski d. K. Evernden (WC) 3–6 6–1 6–2; J. Tarango d. P. Haarhuis (2) 7–6 6–3.
Semi-finals: Volkov (1) d. Washjngton 6–3 7–6; Tarango d. Koslowski 6–4 2–6 6–0.
Final: Tarango d. Volkov (1) 6–1 6–0 6–3.
MEN'S DOUBLES – Final: J. Palmer/J. Stark d. M. Schapers/D. Vacek (2) 6–3 6–3.

NEW SOUTH WALES OPEN ($235,000)
SYDNEY, 6–12 JANUARY
MEN'S SINGLES – Quarter-finals: E. Sanchez (7) d. T. Muster 6–3 6–3; O. Camporese d. C. Bergstrom 6–7 6–4 6–1; G. Forget (3) d. A. Krickstein 6–1 6–4; D. Wheaton (8) d. J. Hlasek 3–6 6–1 7–5.
Semi-finals: E. Sanchez (7) d. Camporese 6–4 7–6; Forget (3) d. Wheaton (8) 6–3 6–2.
Final: E. Sanchez (7) d. Forget (3) 6–3 6–4.
MEN'S DOUBLES – Final: S. Casal/E. Sanchez (3) d. S. Davis/K. Jones (4) 3–6 6–1 6–4.

BENSON & HEDGES OPEN TENNIS ($157,500)
AUCKLAND, 6–12 JANUARY
MEN'S SINGLES – Quarter-finals: G. Connell d. K. Evernden (WC) 6–4 7–6; J. Yzaga d. M. Naewie (Q) 6–3 7–6; M. Zoecke d. A. Volkov (3) 7–6 6–2; M. Washington (7) d. A. Cherkasov (2) 6–4 6–2.
Semi-finals: Yzaga d. Connell 6–4 6–2; Washington (7) d. Zoecke 6–2 6–4.
Final: Yzaga d. Washington (7) 7–6 6–4.
MEN'S DOUBLES – Final: W. Ferreira/J. Grabb (2) d. Connell/G. Michibata (1) 6–4 6–3.

MURATTI TIME INDOOR ($565,000)
MILAN, 3–9 FEBRUARY
MEN'S SINGLES – Quarter-finals: O. Camporese d. J. Sanchez 6–3 6–4; A. Cherkasov d. G. Prpic 6–2 4–6 6–3; S. Pescosolido d. G. Pozzi 6–2 6–2; G. Ivanisevic (8) d. P. McEnroe 6–3 6–4.
Semi-finals: Camporese d. Cherkasov 6–3 4–6 6–3; Ivanisevic (8) d. Pescosolido 6–2 6–2.
Final: Camporese d. Ivanisevic (8) 3–6 6–3 6–4.
MEN'S DOUBLES – Final: N. Broad/D. MacPherson d. S. Casal/E. Sanchez (1) 5–7 7–5 6–4.

VOLVO/SAN FRANCISCO ($260,000)
SAN FRANCISCO, 3–9 FEBRUARY
MEN'S SINGLES – Quarter-finals: J. Courier (1) d. W. Masur 4–6 6–4 6–3; D. Rostagno (3) d. J. Tarango 7–6 6–1; B. Gilbert (4) d. K. Braasch (Q) 4–6 6–1 6–1; M. Chang (2) d. T. Champion (7) 6–3 6–3.
Semi-finals: Courier (1) d. Rostagno 6–4 6–3 6–2; Chang (2) d. Gilbert (4) 6–0 7–5.
Final: Chang (2) d. Courier (1) 6–3 6–3.
MEN'S DOUBLES – Final: J. Grabb/R. Reneberg (2) d. P. Aldrich/D. Visser 6–4 7–5.

CHEVROLET CLASSIC ($130,000)
MACEIO, 3–9 FEBRUARY
MEN'S SINGLES – Quarter-finals: F. Roig d. M. Jaite (1) 6–2 6–2; C. Miniussi (6) d. G. Markus (4) 6–2 6–3; L. Mattar d. F. Meligeni (WC) 3–6 6–3 6–2; T. Carbonell (8) d. F. Davin 6–2 5–7 6–2.

Semi-finals: Miniussi (6) d. Roig 3–6 7–5 6–4; Carbonell (8) d. Mattar 6–4 7–5.
Final: Carbonell (8) d. Miniussi (6) 7–6 5–7 6–2.
MEN'S DOUBLES – Final: Markus/J. Sobel d. R. Acioly/M. Menezes 6–4 1–6 7–5.

ABN/AMRO WORLD TENNIS TOURNAMENT ($475,000)
ROTTERDAM, 24 FEBRUARY–1 MARCH
MEN'S SINGLES – Quarter-finals: A. Volkov (7) d. J. Siemerink 6–2 6–3; P. Haarhuis d. G. Prpic (5) 7–6 6–2; J. McEnroe (6) d. A. Antonitsch (Q) 2–6 6–3 7–5; B. Becker (2) d. P. McEnroe 6–3 7–5.
Semi-finals: Volkov (7) d. Haarhuis 6–2 6–7 6–2; Becker (2) d. J. McEnroe (6) 6–2 7–6.
Final: Becker (2) d. Volkov (7) 7–6 4–6 6–2.
MEN'S DOUBLES – Final: M. Goellner/D. Prinosil d. Haarhuis/M. Koevermans (3) 6–2 6–7 7–6.

PUREX TENNIS CHAMPIONSHIPS ($235,000)
SCOTTSDALE, 24 FEBRUARY–1 MARCH
MEN'S SINGLES – Quarter-finals: B. Gilbert (7) d. E. Sanchez (1) 6–3 7–5; M. Washington (5) d. A. Mancini (4) 6–3 6–4; S. Pescosolido d. C. Caratti 6–2 7–6; A. Chesnokov d. M. Rosset 7–6 6–4.
Semi-finals: Gilbert (7) d. Washington (5) 3–6 6–2; Pescosolido d. Chesnokov 6–7 6–3 6–3.
Final: Pescosolido d. Gilbert (7) 6–0 1–6 6–4.
MEN'S DOUBLES – Final: M. Keil/D. Randall d. K. Kinnear/S. Salumaa 4–6 6–1 6–2.

COPENHAGEN OPEN ($130,000)
COPENHAGEN, 2–8 MARCH
MEN'S SINGLES – Quarter-finals: D. Nargiso d. K. Carlsen (WC) 7–5 7–6; A. Jarryd (4) d. J. Eltingh 6–1 6–2; C. Saceanu d. N. Kulti 7–6 7–6; M. Larsson (8) d. P. Baur 6–4 6–7 6–1.
Semi-finals: Jarryd (4) d. Nargiso 6–2 3–6 7–5; Larsson (8) d. Saceanu 6–7 7–6 6–4.
Final: Larsson (8) d. Jarryd (4) 6–4 7–6.
MEN'S DOUBLES – Final: Kulti/Larsson d. H. Davids/L. Pimek (1) 6–3 6–4.

TROPHEE HASSAN II ($130,000)
CASABLANCA, 16–22 MARCH
MEN'S SINGLES – Quarter-finals: B. Wuyts (8) d. Y. El Aynaoui (WC) 1–6 7–5 6–1; G. Lopez (4) d. M. Filippini 6–3 6–2; A. Berasategui (Q) d. M. Koevermans 6–3 7–5; G. Perez–Roldan (2) d. L. Mattar 6–0 6–3.
Semi-finals: Lopez (4) d. Wuyts (8) 6–0 6–0; Perez–Roldan (2) d. Rasategui (Q) 6–4 6–2.
Final: Perez-Roldan (2) d. Lopez (4) 2–6 7–5 6–3.
MEN'S DOUBLES: H. De la Pena/J. Lozano d. G. Dzelde/T. J. Middleton 2–6 6–4 7–6.

ESTORIL OPEN ($465,000)
LISBON, 30 MARCH–5 APRIL
MEN'S SINGLES – Quarter-finals: A. Arrese (7) d. I. Lendl (1) 6–3 4–6 7–5; S. Bruguera (4) d. J. Cunha–Silva (WC) 6–2 6–1; C. Costa d. H. de la Pena 6–4 6–1; E. Sanchez (2) d. F. Fontang 7–6 7–6.
Semi-finals: Bruguera (4) d. Arrese (7) 6–1 6–1; Costa d. E. Sanchez (2) 4–6 7–6 7–6.
Final: Costa d. Bruguera (4) 4–6 6–2 6–2.
MEN'S DOUBLES – Final: H. J. Davids/L. Pimek d. L. Jensen/L. Warder (1) 3–6 6–3 7–5.

PANASONIC S.A. OPEN ($270,000)
JOHANNESBURG, 30 MARCH–5 APRIL
MEN'S SINGLES – Quarter-finals: A. Volkov (1) d. C. Limberger 6–3 6–0; W. Ferreira (3) d. X. Daufresne 6–3 6–1; A. Krickstein (4) d. G. Muller 6–2 6–2; C. Pridham d. K. Ullyett (WC) 0–6 6–3 7–5.
Semi-finals: Volkov (1) d. Ferreira (3) 6–4 7–6; Krickstein (4) d. Pridham 6–3 6–4.
Final: Krickstein (4) d. Volkov (1) 6–4 6–4.
MEN'S DOUBLES – Final: P. Aldrich/D. Visser d. Ferreira/P. Norval (2) 6–4 6–4.

EPSON SINGAPORE SUPER TENNIS ($240,000)
SINGAPORE, 30 MARCH–5 APRIL
MEN'S SINGLES: Quarter-finals: R. Krishnan (WC) d. M. Woodforde 4–6 6–1 6–1; P. Haarhuis (3) d. K. Carlsen (WC) 6–4 6–3; S. Youl d. J. Grabb 6–3 6–4; A. Mronz d. J. Fitzgerald 1–6 6–4 6–3.
Semi-finals: Haarhuis (3) d. Krishnan (WC) 6–3 6–4; Youl d. Mronz 7–5 7–5.
Final: Youl d. Haarhuis (3) 6–4 6–1.
MEN'S DOUBLES: T. Woodbridge/Woodforde (1) d. G. Connell/G. Michibata (2) 6–7 6–2 6–4.

SALEM OPEN ($270,000)
HONG KONG, 13–19 APRIL
MEN'S SINGLES – Quarter-finals: J. Courier (1) d. G. Muller 6–2 6–1; B. Gilbert (4) d. S. Matsuoka

4–6 7–6 6–1; M. Chang (3) d. J. Siemerink (6) 6–3 6–2; T. Woodbridge d. K. Curren – w/o.
Semi-finals: Courier (1) d. Gilbert (4) 6–4 6–1; Chang (3) d. Woodbridge 6–3 6–7 6–1.
Final: Courier (1) d. Chang (3) 7–5 6–3.
MEN'S DOUBLES – Gilbert/J. Grabb d. B. Black/B. Talbot 6–2 6–1.

PHILIPS OPEN ($235,000)
NICE, 13–19 APRIL
MEN'S SINGLES – *Quarter-finals:* P. Sampras (1) d. H. Leconte (WC) 6–4 1–6 6–3; G. Markus d. T.
Champion 7–5 6–4; F. Santoro d. M. Larsson 6–1 7–6; J. Sanchez (7) d. G. Forget (2) 7–6 6–4.
Semi-finals: Markus d. Sampras (1) 6–1 2–6 7–6; J. Sanchez (7) d. Santoro 6–3 7–6.
Final: Markus d. J. Sanchez (7) 6–4 6–4.
MEN'S DOUBLES – *Final:* P. Galbraith/S. Melville d. P. Aldrich/D. Visser 6–1 3–6 6–4.

USTA. CLAY COURTS OF TAMPA ($235,000)
TAMPA, 13–19 APRIL
MEN'S SINGLES – *Quarter-finals:* C. Mezzadri d. M. Gorriz 7–5 6–1; J. Yzaga (4) d. M. Woodforde 4–6
6–0 7–5; M. Washington (3) (WC) d. M. Filippini 4–6 7–6 6–4; F. Davin d. A. Agassi (2) (WC) 6–4 7–6.
Semi-finals: Yzaga (4) d. Mezzadri 5–7 6–4 7–6; Washington (3) (WC) d. Davin 6–3 4–6 6–2.
Final: Yzaga (4) d. Washington (3) (WC) 4–6 6–3 6–1.
MEN'S DOUBLES – *Final:* M. Briggs/T. Kronemann d. L. Mattar/A. Olhovskiy 7–6 6–7 6–4.

KAL CUP KOREA OPEN ($145,000)
SEOUL, 20–26 APRIL
MEN'S SINGLES – *Quarter-finals:* G. Pozzi (1) d. J. Fitzgerald 6–4 6–4; S. Matsuoka (5) d. G. Raoux
6–3 6–1; T. Woodbridge (3) d. A. Mronz 6–2 6–1; P. Kuhnen d. G. Muller 6–2 6–3.
Semi-finals: Matsuoka (5) d. Pozzi (1) 6–2 6–4; Woodbridge (3) d. Kuhnen 6–4 6–1.
Final: Matsuoka (5) d. Woodbridge (3) 6–3 4–6 7–5.
MEN'S DOUBLES – *Final:* K. Curren/G. Muller (1) d. K. Evernden/B. Pearce 7–6 6–4.

XXI TROFEO GRUPO ZETA VILLA DE MADRID, MARLBORO OPEN ($700,000)
MADRID, 20–26 APRIL
MEN'S SINGLES – *Quarter-finals:* C. Costa (7) d. A. Boetsch 6–4 6–1; F. Clavet (6) (WC) d. A. Mancini
(3) 7–5 6–1; S. Bruguera (5) d. M. Rosset 6–3 7–6; J. Sanchez d. J. Arrese (8) 6–3 6–4.
Semi-finals: Costa (7) d. Clavet (6) (WC) 7–5 6–4; Bruguera (5) d. J. Sanchez 6–4 6–2.
Final: Bruguera (5) d. Costa (7) 7–6 6–2 6–2.
MEN'S DOUBLES – *Final:* P. Galbraith/P. McEnroe (4) d. Clavet/Costa 6–3 6–2.

BMW OPEN ($275,000)
MUNICH, 27 APRIL–3 MAY
MEN'S SINGLES – *Quarter-finals:* M. Larsson d. M. Stich (1) 6–4 6–4; M. Naewie d. A. Medvedev (Q)
4–6 7–6 6–4; B. Karbacher (WC) d. K. Novacek (4) 7–5 4–6 6–1; P. Korda (2) d. N. Kulti 6–3 3–6 6–3.
Semi-finals: Larsson d. Naewie 6–7 6–4 7–6; Korda (2) d. Karbacher (WC) 3–6 7–6 7–5.
Final: Larsson d. Korda (2) 6–4 4–6 6–1.
MEN'S DOUBLES – *Final:* D. Adams/M. Oosting (4) d. C. Limberger/T. Zdrazila 3–6 7–5 6–3.

AT&T CHALLENGE ($235,000)
ATLANTA, 27 APRIL–3 MAY
MEN'S SINGLES – *Quarter-finals:* P. Sampras (1) d. J. Connors (7) 7–6 6–2; T. Witsken d. F. Roig 7–5
6–3; P. Arraya d. A. Volkov (3) 6–4 6–7 6–3; A. Agassi (2) d. J. Eltingh 3–6 6–3 6–4.
Semi-finals: Sampras (1) d. Witsken 6–4 6–2; Agassi (2) d. Arraya 6–4 6–3.
Final: Agassi (2) d. Sampras (1) 7–5 6–4.
MEN'S DOUBLES – *Final:* S. Devries/D. MacPherson (3) d. M. Keil/D. Randall 6–3 6–3.

USAIR US MEN'S CLAY COURT CHAMPIONSHIPS ($225,000)
CHARLOTTE, 4–10 MAY
MEN'S SINGLES – *Quarter-finals:* J. Tarango d. A. Krickstein (1) 5–7 7–6 6–1; M. Washington (4) d.
F. Davin (6) 6–3 7–5; C. Mezzadri d. R. Fromberg 7–6 6–7 6–2; L. Mattar d. M. Woodforde 6–4 6–3.
Semi-finals: Washington (4) d. Tarango 6–4 6–4; Mezzadri d. Mattar 6–3 3–6 7–5.
Final: Washington (4) d. Mezzadri 6–3 6–3.
MEN'S DOUBLES – *Final:* S. Devries/D. MacPherson (2) d. B. Garnett/J. Palmer 6–4 7–6.

MURATTI TIME CLASSIC ($240,000)
BOLOGNA, 18–24 MAY

MEN'S SINGLES – **Quarter-finals:** J. Oncins d. L. Koslowski 7–6 7–5; A. Gomez (WC) d. C. Pistolesi 6–3 4–6 7–6; R. Furlan d. F. Davin 6–2 6–1; B. Wuyts d. C. Dosedel (Q) 6–2 6–1.
Semi-finals: Oncins d. Gomez (WC) 6–2 6–1; Furlan d. Wuyts 6–4 7–6.
Final: Oncins d. Furlan 6–2 6–4.
MEN'S DOUBLES – **Final:** L. Jensen/L. Warder (2) d. J. Frana/J. Sanchez (4) 6–2 6–3.

STELLA ARTOIS CHAMPIONSHIPS ($475,000)
LONDON, 8–14 JUNE
MEN'S SINGLES – **Quarter-finals:** S. Edberg (1) d. P. Cash (WC) 6–7 7–6 6–3; S. Matsuoka d. G. Raoux 6–4 3–6 9–7; W. Ferreira (12) d. J. Stoltenberg 6–4 6–2; B. Gilbert (7) d. P. Sampras (2) 6–3 6–4.
Semi-finals: Matsuoka d. Edberg (1) 1–6 7–6 10–8; Ferreira (12) d. Gilbert (7) 7–6 6–4.
Final: Ferreira (12) d. Matsuoka 3–6 6–4.
MEN'S DOUBLES – **Final:** J. Fitzgerald/A. Jarryd (1) d. G. Ivanisevic/D. Nargiso 6–4 7–6.

CONTINENTAL GRASS COURT CHAMPIONSHIP ($235,000)
ROSMALEN, 8–14 JUNE
MEN'S SINGLES – **Quarter-finals:** M. Stich (1) d. R. Reneberg 6–2 6–3; J. McEnroe (5) d. A. Volkov (7) 6–4 6–3; J. Stark d. H. Holm 7–6 3–6 6–3; M. Schapers (8) d. R. Krajicek (2) 6–4 6–2.
Semi-finals: Stich (1) d. J. McEnroe (5) 6–3 7–6; Stark d. Schapers (8) 6–4 7–6.
Final: Stich (1) d. Stark 6–4 7–5.
MEN'S DOUBLES – **Final:** J. Grabb/Reneberg (2) d. J. McEnroe/Stich 6–4 6–7 6–4.

TORNEO INTERNAZIONALE 'CITTA'DI FIRENZE ($235,000)
FLORENCE, 8–14 JUNE
MEN'S SINGLES – **Quarter finals:** T. Muster (1) d. L. Mattar 6–4 7–6 6–3; M. Gustafsson (3) (WC) d. F. Yunis (LL) 6–1 6–3; R. Furlan d. F. Davin 6–2 6–4; M. Filippini d. F. Santoro (8) 7–6 6–3.
Semi-finals: Muster (1) d. Gustafsson (3) (WC) 6–4 7–5; Furlan d. Filippini 7–6 6–3.
Final: Muster (1) d. Furlan 6–3 1–6 6–1.
MEN'S DOUBLES – **Final:** Filippini/Mattar d. R. Deppe/B. Haygarth 6–4 6–7 7–4.

VII TORNEO INTERNAZIONALE DI GENOVA ($235,000)
GENOVA, 15–21 JUNE
MEN'S SINGLES – **Quarter-finals:** A. Medvedev (WC) d. J. Oncins 1–6 6–2 7–6; M. Filippini d. M. Gustafsson (5) 6–1 6–4; G. Perez–Roldan d. M. Gorriz 7–5 6–1; H. Skoff d. P. Cane (WC) 7–6 5–7 6–4.
Semi-finals: Medvedev (WC) d. Filippini 6–1 7–6; Perez–Roldan d. Skoff 4–6 7–6 4–0 ret.
Final: Medvedev (WC) d. Perez–Roldan 6–3 6–4.
MEN'S DOUBLES – **Final:** S. Cannon/G. Van Emburgh (2) d. P. Haarhuis/M. Koevermans (1) 6–1 6–1.

DIRECT LINE INSURANCE MANCHESTER OPEN ($235,000)
MANCHESTER, 15–20 JUNE
MEN'S SINGLES – **Quarter-finals:** W. Masur d. J. Tarango 6–3 6–4; J. Eltingh d. A. Thoms (Q) 6–2 3–0 ret.; M. Washington (5) d. S. Youl 6–4 7–5; L. Herrera (Q) d. B. Gilbert 3–6 6–3 7–6.
Semi-finals: Eltingh d. Masur 6–2 7–6; Washington (5) d. Herrera (Q) 6–7 6–1 6–1.
Final: Eltingh d. Washington (5) 6–3 6–4.
MEN'S DOUBLES – **Final:** P. Galbraith/D. MacPherson (1) d. J. Bates/L. Warder 4–6 6–3 6–2.

RADO SWISS OPEN ($300,000)
GSTAAD, 6–13 JULY
MEN'S SINGLES – **Quarter-finals:** F. Santoro d. K. Novacek (8) 6–4 5–7 6–4; F. Clavet d. E. Sanchez (5) 7–5 7–5; S. Bruguera (6) d. G. Ivanisevic (3) (WC) 6–3 6–2; G. Markus d. M. Chang (2) 7–6 7–6.
Semi-final: Clavet d. Santoro 6–3 6–2; Bruguera (6) d. Markus 4–6 7–5 7–6.
Final: Bruguera (6) d. Clavet 6–1 6–4.
MEN'S DOUBLES – **Final:** H. Davids/L. Pimek d. P. Korda/C. Suk (2) w/o.

SWEDISH OPEN ($235,000)
BASTAD, 6–12 JULY
MEN'S SINGLES – **Quarter-finals:** T. Carbonell d. A. Boetsch (7) 3–6 6–2 7–6; G. Perez–Roldan (6) d. M. Larsson (3) 3–6 6–0 6–1; J. Arrese (4) d. C. Bergstrom (5) 6–2 7–5; M. Gustafsson (2) d. T. Enqvist (WC) 2–6 6–3 6–3.
Semi-finals: Carbonell d. Perez–Roldan (6) 7–6 3–6 6–3; Gustafsson (2) d. Arrese (4) 7–5 6–3.
Final: Gustafsson (2) d. Carbonell 5–7 7–5 6–4.
MEN'S DOUBLES – **Final:** Carbonell/G. Miniussi (2) d. Bergstrom/Gustafsson 6–4 7–5.

MILLER LITE HALL OF FAME TENNIS CHAMPIONSHIPS ($175,000)
NEWPORT, 6–12 JULY
MEN'S SINGLES – N. Borwick (Q) d. B. Macphie (Q) 6–4 7–6; A. Antonitsch d. C. Van Rensburg (4) 6–3 7–6; B. Shelton (6) d. J. Stark 6–2 7–5; J. Frana d. S. Stolle 6–4 6–4.
Semi-finals: Antonitsch d. Borwick (Q) 6–4 7–6; Shelton (6) d. Frana 6–1 6–4.
Final: Shelton (6) d. Antonitsch 6–4 6–4.
MEN'S DOUBLES – *Final:* D. Deppe/D. Rikl d. P. Annacone/D. Wheaton 6–4 6–4.

PHILIPS HEAD CUP ($355,000)
KITZBUHEL, 20–26 JULY
MEN'S SINGLES – *Quarter-finals:* A. Mancini (7) d. D. Perez (Q) 6–3 6–4; T. Muster (4) d. M. Strelba 7–6 6–4; M. Filippini d. E. Sanchez (6) 3–6 7–6 6–4; P. Sampras (2) d. G. Markus 6–3 7–6.
Semi-finals: Mancini (7) d. Muster (4) 7–6 6–1; Sampras (2) d. Filippini 6–7 6–3 6–0.
Final: Sampras (2) d. Mancini (7) 6–3 7–5 6–3.
MEN'S DOUBLES – *Final:* S. Casal/E. Sanchez (1) d. H. de la Pena/V. Flegl (8) 6–1 6–2.

INTERNATIONAL CHAMPIONSHIPS OF THE NETHERLANDS ($225,000)
HILVERSUM, 20–26 JULY
MEN'S SINGLES – *Quarter-finals:* F. Santoro (7) d. J. Siemerink 6–3 6–1; K. Novacek (3) d. J. Eltingh 6–3 6–1; M. Tillstrom (WC) d. M. Koevermans 2–6 6–3 6–4; J. Arrese (2) d. B. Wuyts 6–7 6–3 6–2.
Semi-finals: Novacek (3) d. Santoro (7) 6–3 6–1; Arrese (2) d. Tillstrom (WC) 6–3 6–3.
Final: Novacek (3) d. Arrese (2) 6–2 6–3 2–6 7–5.
MEN'S DOUBLES – *Final:* P. Haarhuis/Koevermans (2) d. M. Renstrom/Tillstrom 6–7 6–1 6–4.

INTERNAZIONALI DI SAN MARINO – MURATTI TIME ($235,000)
SAN MARINO, 27 JULY–2 AUGUST
MEN'S SINGLES – *Quarter-finals:* K. Novacek (1) d. B. Wuyts 4–6 6–4 6–4; L. Jonsson d. G. Lopez 6–3 6–2; R. Agenor d. F. Montana 7–5 6–4; F. Clavet (2) d. M. Tillstrom 6–0 6–1.
Semi-finals: Novacek (1) d. Jonsson 6–4 6–1; Clavet (2) d. Agenor 7–6 7–5.
Final: Novacek (1) d. Clavet (2) 7–5 6–2.
MEN'S DOUBLES – *Final:* K. Kulti/Tillstrom d. C. Brandi/F. Mordegan 6–2 6–2.

VOLVO TENNIS/LOS ANGELES ($235,000)
LOS ANGELES, 3–9 AUGUST
MEN'S SINGLES – *Quarter-finals:* A. Krickstein (1) d. G. Pozzi (8) 6–1 6–2; M. Woodforde d. J. Connors (6) (WC) 6–4 4–6 6–4; S. Stolle d. R. Reneberg 6–4 6–4; R. Krajicek (2) d. J. Tarango 6–7 6–0 3–1 ret.
Semi-finals: Woodforde d. Krickstein (1) 4–2 30–40 ret.; Krajicek (2) d. Stolle 6–2 6–4.
Final: Krajicek (2) d. Woodforde 6–4 2–6 6–4.
MEN'S DOUBLES – P. Galbraith/J. Pugh (4) d. F. Montana/D. Wheaton 7–6 7–6.

CZECHOSLOVAK OPEN TENNIS CHAMPIONSHIPS ($320,000)
PRAGUE, 10–16 AUGUST
MEN'S SINGLES – *Quarter-finals:* K. Novacek (1) d. D. Perez (Q) 6–3 6–2; D. Rikl d. R. Fromberg 6–0 6–3; G. Perez–Roldan (4) d. V. Gabrichidze 6–3 6–0; F. Davin d. J. Svensson (8) 6–2 2–6 6–3.
Semi-finals: Novacek (1) d. Rikl 6–2 3–6 6–2; Davin d. Perez–Roldan (4) 6–3 6–2.
Final: Novacek (1) d. Davin 6–1 6–1.
MEN'S DOUBLES – Novacek/B. Stankovic d. J. Bjorkman/J. Ireland 7–5 6–1.

WALDBAUM'S HAMLET CUP ($235,000)
COMMACK, LONG ISLAND, 24–30 AUGUST
MEN'S SINGLES – *Quarter-finals:* S. Edberg (1) d. C. Arriens (Q) 6–4 6–0; P. Korda (4) d. S. Pescosolido 7–6 6–2; I. Lendl (3) d. B. Becker (5) w/o; M. Chang (2) d. A. Volkov (7) 6–1 6–3.
Semi-finals: Korda (4) d. Edberg (1) 7–5 7–5; Lendl (3) d. Chang (2) 6–2 6–3.
Final: Korda (4) d. Lendl (3) 6–2 6–2.
MEN'S DOUBLES – *Final:* F. Montana/G. Van Emburgh (2) d. G. Pozzi/O. Rahnasto 6–4 6–2.

CROATIA OPEN ($235,000)
UMAG, 24–30 AUGUST
MEN'S SINGLES – *Quarter-finals:* T. Muster (1) d. G. Perez–Roldan (8) 7–5 6–0; J. Arrese (WC) d. J. Altur 6–4 6–2; F. Davin (5) d. A. Medvedev (4) (WC) w/o; H. Skoff (WC) d. C. Mezzadri 6–4 6–4.
Semi-finals: Muster (1) d. Arrese (WC) 6–4 6–4; Davin (5) d. Skoff (WC) 2–0 ret.
Final: Muster (1) d. Davin (5) 6–1 4–6 6–4.
MEN'S DOUBLES – *Final:* D. Prinosil/R. Vogel d. S. Groen/L. Koslowski (4) 6–3 6–7 7–6.

OTB INTERNATIONAL TENNIS OPEN ($130,000)
SCHENECTADY, 24–30 AUGUST
MEN'S SINGLES – Quarter-finals: A. Chesnokov (8) (WC) d. A. Olhovskiy (WC) 6–1 7–6; W. Ferreira (3) d. R. Fromberg (Q) 6–7 6–3 6–3; E. Sanchez (5) d. F. Clavet (4) 6–1 6–2; J. Morgan (LL) d. P. Haarhuis (7) 6–3 3–6 7–6.
Semi-finals: Ferreira (3) d. Chesnokov (8) (WC) 6–4 6–2; Morgan (LL) d. E. Sanchez (5) 6–4 7–6.
Final: Ferreira (3) d. Morgan (LL) 6–2 6–7 6–2.
MEN'S DOUBLES – Final: J. Eltingh/Haarhuis (3) d. S. Casal/E. Sanchez (1) 6–3 6–4.

GRAND PRIX PASSING SHOT ($300,000)
BORDEAUX, 14–20 SEPTEMBER
MEN'S SINGLES – Quarter-finals: C. Pioline d. I. Lendl (1) 7–5 6–4; S. Bruguera (4) d. G. Lopez 6–4 6–2; R. Gilbert d. G. Forget (3) 6–4 6–4; A. Medvedev d. C. Costa (2) 7–6 7–6.
Semi-finals: Bruguera (4) d. Pioline 6–2 6–4; Medvedev d. Gilbert 6–4 6–3.
Final: Medvedev d. Bruguera (4) 6–3 1–6 6–2.
MEN'S DOUBLES – Final: S. Casal/E. Sanchez (1) d. A. Boetsch/Forget (4) 6–1 6–4.

COLOGNE OPEN ($300,000)
COLOGNE, 14–20 SEPTEMBER
MEN'S SINGLES – Quarter-finals: B. Karbacher (7) d. T. Muster (1) 6–3 6–3; J. Sanchez (3) d. R. Furlan (5) 6–1 6–4; M. Ondruska d. M. Filippini (4) 6–3 6–3; K. Braasch d. J. Gunnarsson 7–5 6–1.
Semi-finals: Karbacher (7) d. J. Sanchez (3) 7–6 6–3; Ondruska d. Braasch 6–4 6–1.
Final: Karbacher (7) d. Ondruska 7–6 6–4.
MEN'S DOUBLES – Final: H. De La Pena/G. Luza d. R. Bathman/L. Pimek (2) 6–7 6–0 6–2.

QUEENSLAND OPEN ($235,000)
BRISBANE, 28 SEPTEMBER–4 OCTOBER
MEN'S SINGLES – Quarter-finals: D. Nargiso d. N. Borwick (Q) 6–4 6–1; G. Raoux d. L. Wahlgren (Q) 6–1 6–2; T. Hogstedt d. J. Stark 7–6 1–6 6–4; K. Carlsen d. J. Grabb (8) 3–6 6–1 6–4.
Semi-finals: Raoux d. Nargiso 6–3 6–4; Carlsen d. Hogstedt 6–4 6–1.
Final: Raoux d. Carlsen 6–4 7–6.
MEN'S DOUBLES – Final: S. Devries/D. MacPherson (2) d. J. McEnroe/J. Stark (4) 6–4 6–4.

SWISS INDOORS BASEL ($700,000)
BASEL, 29 SEPTEMBER–4 OCTOBER
MEN'S SINGLES – Quarter-finals: P. Korda (1) d. C. Pioline 2–6 6–3 6–2; I. Lendl (3) d. A. Chesnokov 6–1 6–2; M. Rosset d. P. Lundgren (Q) 6–4 6–2; B. Becker (2) d. A. Mansdorf (7) 7–6 6–7 6–3.
Semi-finals: Korda (1) d. Lendl (3) 6–4 6–3; Becker (2) d. Rosset 6–2 6–4.
Final: Becker (2) d. Korda (1) 3–6 6–3 6–2 6–4.
MEN'S DOUBLES – Final: T. Nijssen/C. Suk (2) d. K. Novacek/D. Rikl 6–3 6–4.

**CAMPIONATI INTERNAZIONALI DI SICILIA
TROFEO KIM TOP LINE** ($285,000)
PALERMO, 28 SEPTEMBER–4 OCTOBER
MEN'S SINGLES – Quarter-finals: R. Furlan d. G. Perez–Roldan 6–4 6–4; E. Sanchez (3) d. T. Carbonell 6–2 6–3; F. Clavet (4) d. H. Skoff 6–1 6–1; S. Bruguera (2) d. F. Fontang 6–2 6–2.
Semi-finals: E. Sanchez (3) d. Furlan 6–3 6–4; Bruguera (2) d. Clavet (4) 6–1 6–4.
Final: Bruguera (2) d. E. Sanchez (3) 6–1 6–3.
MEN'S DOUBLES – Final: J. Donar/L. Johnsson d. H. De La Pena/V. Flegl (2) 5–7 6–3–6–4.

GRAND PRIX DE TOULOUSE ($275,000)
TOULOUSE, 5–11 OCTOBER
MEN'S SINGLES – Quarter-finals: P. Korda (1) d. J. Svensson 3–6 6–0 6–1; J. Siemerink d. B. Gilbert (3) (WC) 6–4 7–6; A. Boetsch d. C. Bergstrom 6–3 6–2; G. Forget (2) d. A. Medvedev (7) 6–3 7–6.
Semi-finals: Korda (1) d. Siemerink 7–6 6–3; Forget (2) d. Boetsch 6–3 6–4.
Final: Forget (2) d. Korda (1) 6–3 6–2.
MEN'S DOUBLES – Final: B. Pearce/J. Talbot d. Forget/H. Leconte 6–1 3–6 6–3.

SAAB ATHENS INTERNATIONAL ($130,000)
ATHENS, 5–11 OCTOBER
MEN'S SINGLES – Quarter-finals: S. Bruguera (1) d. M. Gustafsson (7) 6–2 ret.; J. Sanchez (4) d. M. Velev (Q) 2–6 6–3 6–2; J. Arrese (3) d. M. Jaite 6–3 6–2; F. Clavet (2) d. M. Goellner 6–2 6–2.
Semi-finals: Bruguera (1) d. J. Sanchez (4) 7–6 6–7 6–4; Arrese (3) d. Clavet (2) 7–5 6–2.

Final: Arrese (3) d. Bruguera (1) 7–5 3–0 ret.
MEN'S DOUBLES – *Final:* T. Carbonell/F. Roig d. M. Filippini/M. Koevermans (3) 6–3 6–4.

MELA D'ORO BOLZANO ($270,000)
BOLZANO, 12–18 OCTOBER
MEN'S SINGLES – *Quarter-finals:* O. Delaitre (4) d. P. Cane (WC) 6–4 6–4; A. Boetsch (5) d. O. Camporese 6–4 6–3; T. Enquist d. A. Medvedev (3) 6–7 6–3 2–0 ret.; A. Cherkasov (2) d. J. Svensson (8) 6–4 6–1.
Semi-finals: Boetsch (5) d. Delaitre (4) 7–6 7–5; Enquist d. Cherkasov (2) 4–6 6–3 7–6.
Final: Enquist d. Boetsch (5) 6–2 1–6 7–6.
MEN'S DOUBLES – *Final:* A. Jarryd/G. Pedersen d. T. Nijssen/C. Suk (1) 6–1 6–7 6–3.

THE RIKLIS ISRAEL TENNIS CENTER CLASSIC ($130,000)
TEL AVIV, 12–17 OCTOBER
MEN'S SINGLES – *Quarter-finals:* T. Muster (1) d. G. Bloom 0–6 6–2 6–4; J. Tarango (5) d. A. Mansdorf (3) 6–1 3–6 7–6; J. Cunha–Silva d. R. Matuszewski 6–4 7–5; S. Simian d. M. Ondruska 2–6 6–2 6–3.
Semi-finals: Tarango (5) d. Muster (1) 6–2 6–4; Simian d. Cunha–Silva 7–6 6–4.
Final: Tarango (5) d. Simian 4–6 6–3 6–4.
MEN'S DOUBLES – *Final:* P. Bauer/Cunha–Silva d. M. Koevermans/T. Svantesson (1) 6–3 6–4.

GRAND PRIX TENNIS DE LYON ($550,000)
LYON, 19–25 OCTOBER
MEN'S SINGLES – *Quarter-finals:* P. Sampras (1) d. M. Zoecke 6–4 6–3; M. Washington (3) d. K. Novacek (5) 6–3 6–1; R. Reneberg d. D. Randall (LL) 6–3 6–2; C. Pioline d. A. Boetsch 6–3 1–6 6–4.
Semi-finals: Sampras (1) d. Washington (3) 6–0 6–2; Pioline d. Reneberg 6–2 6–7 7–5.
Final: Sampras (1) d. Pioline 6–4 6–2.
MEN'S DOUBLES – *Final:* J. Hlasek/M. Rosset (1) d. N. Broad/Kruger 6–1 6–3.

PACIFIC CUP INTERNATIONAL ($270,000)
TAIPEI, 19–25 OCTOBER
MEN'S SINGLES – *Quarter-finals:* P. Kuhnen (8) d. G. Bloom 6–0 7–5; J. Grabb (3) d. B. Steven 5–7 6–3 6–2; A. Olhovskiy d. D. Nargiso (6) 7–6 4–6 6–4; J. Morgan d. K. Carlsen (2) 6–3 6–4.
Semi-finals: Grabb (3) d. Kuhnen (8) 6–3 6–1; Morgan d. Olhovskiy 6–7 7–5 7–5.
Final: Grabb (3) d. Morgan 6–3 6–3.
MEN'S DOUBLES – *Final:* J. Fitzgerald/S. Stolle d. P. Baur/C. Van Rensburg 7–6 7–2.

CA TENNIS TROPHY ($280,000)
VIENNA, 19–25 OCTOBER
MEN'S SINGLES – *Quarter-finals:* P. Korda (1) d. A. Antonitsch 7–6 6–4; J. Siemerink d. B. Gilbert (4) 6–1 1–6 6–3; G. Pozzi d. D. Prinosil 6–4 6–0; A. Chesnokov d. T. Gollwitzer 7–6 6–2.
Semi-finals: Korda (1) d. Siemerink 7–5 6–7 6–3; Pozzi d. Chesnokov 6–2 6–7 6–4.
Final: Korda (1) d. Pozzi 6–3 6–2 5–7 6–1.
MEN'S DOUBLES – *Final:* R. Bathman/A. Jarryd (2) d. K. Kinnear/U. Riglewski (4) 6–3 7–5.

ALMANARA CUP ($130,000)
GUARUJA, 26 OCTOBER–1 NOVEMBER
MEN'S SINGLES – *Quarter-finals:* C. Arriens (Q) d. J. Arrese (1) 6–4 2–6 6–1; F. Roese (Q) d. A. Mancisidor (Q) 6–1 6–2; J. Frana d. L. Koslowski 6–2 6–4; A. Corretja d. M. Jaite (WC) 6–4 6–3.
Semi-finals: Arriens (Q) d. Roese (Q) 7–6 6–3; Corretja d. Frana 6–3 3–6 7–6.
Final: Arriens (Q) d. Corretja 7–6 6–3.
MEN'S DOUBLES – *Final:* C. Allgardh/C. Limberger (4) d. D. Perez/F. Roig 6–4 6–3.

KOLYNOS CUP ($182,000)
BUZIOS, 2–8 NOVEMBER
MEN'S SINGLES – *Quarter-finals:* F. Roig (8) d. F. Roese 3–6 7–5 6–4; J. Oncins (5) d. M. Jaite 6–3 7–6; C. Motta d. M. Filippini 4–6 7–5 6–4; L. Herrera (7) d. A. Mancini (2) 6–3 6–3.
Semi-finals: Oncins (5) d. Roig (8) 6–1 6–3; Herrera (7) d. Motta 7–6 6–4.
Final:: Oncins (5) d. Herrera (7) 6–3 6–2.
MEN'S DOUBLES – *Final::* M. Ruah/M. Tabares d. M. Kell/T. Mercer 7–6 6–7 6–4.

BANESPA OPEN ($235,000)
SAO PAULO, 9–15 NOVEMBER
MEN'S SINGLES – *Quarter-finals:* A. Mancini (1) d. F. Roese 6–3 4–6 6–3; J. Oncins (5) d. M. Jaite

6–4 6–2; L. Mattar (6) d. C. Adams 3–6 7–6 6–2; J. Yzaga (2) d. P. Baur 7–6 7–6.
Semi-finals: Oncins (5) d. Mancini (1) 6–3 6–3; Mattar (6) d. Yzaga (2) 7–6 6–2.
Final:: Mattar (6) d. Oncins (5) 6–1 6–4.
MEN'S DOUBLES – Final:: D. Perez/F. Roig d. C. Allgardh/C. Limberger 6–2 7–6.

ITALTEL KREMLIN CUP, ($314,000)
MOSCOW, 9–15 NOVEMBER
MEN'S SINGLES – Quarter-finals: M. Rosset (8) d. K. Novacek (1) 6–4 6–2; C. Pioline (6) d. A. Cherkasov (4) 6–4 7–6; C. Steeb (5) d. A. Medvedev (3) 6–4 6–7 6–3; J. Hlasek d. G. Bloom 6–1 6–2.
Semi–finals: Rosset (8) d. Pioline (6) 7–6 6–1; Steeb (5) d. Hlasek 7–6 6–4.
Final:: Rosset (8) d. Steeb (5) 6–2 6–2.
MEN'S DOUBLES – Final:: M. Barnard/J.L. de Jager d. D. Adams/A. Olhovskiy 6–4 3–6 7–6.

EUROPEAN COMMUNITY CHAMPIONSHIPS ($1,000,000)
ANTWERP, 9–15 NOVEMBER
MEN'S SINGLES – Quarter-finals: Courier (1) d. Forget (8) 6–7 6–4 6–4; Krajicek (6) d. Korda (3) 3–6 6–1 7–6; Woodforde d. Larsson 6–0 7–6; Chang (2) d. Stich 6–3 6–4.
Semi-finals: Krajicek (6) d. Courier (1) 4–6 6–4 7–5; Woodforde d. Chang (2) 7–6 6–3.
Final: Krajicek (6) d. Woodforde 6–2 6–2.
MEN'S DOUBLES – Final: J. Fitzgerald/A. Jarryd d. P. McEnroe/J. Palmer 6–2 6–2.

STANDARD BANK ATP TOUR WORLD DOUBLES CHAMPIONSHIPS ($2,500,000)
JOHANNESBURG, 25–29 NOVEMBER
MEN'S DOUBLES – 1st round: J. Fitzgerald/A. Jarryd d. T. Nijssen/C. Suk 7–6 6–4; T. Woodbridge/M. Woodforde d. S. DeVries/D. McPherson 6–3 6–3; S. Casal/E. Sanchez d. J. Grabb/R. Reneberg 6–4 3–6 7–6; M. Kratzmann/W. Masur d. K. Jones/R. Leach 7–5 4–6 6–1.
2nd round: Grabb/Reneberg d. Jones/Leach 7–6 7–6; DeVries/Macpherson d. Nijssen/Suk 7–6 3–6 7–6; Fitzgerald/Jarryd d. Woodbridge/Woodforde 7–5 7–6; Casal/Sanchez d. Kratzmann/Masur 6–4 7–6.
3rd round: Fitzgerald/Jarryd d. DeVries/Macpherson 6–2 6–3; Jones/Leach d. Casal/Sanchez 6–3 7–6; Kratzmann/Masur d. Grabb/Reneberg 4–6 7–6 6–4; Woodbridge/Woodforde d. Nijssen/Suk 6–4 3–6 6–1.
Semi-finals: Fitzgerald/Jarryd d. Kratzmann/Masur 7–6 6–3; Woodbridge/Woodforde d. Casal/Sanchez 4–6 6–1 6–4.
Final: Woodbridge/Woodforde d. Fitzgerald/Jarryd 6–2 7–6 5–7 3–6 6–3.

ATP TOUR WORLD CHAMPIONSHIP

Andrew Longmore

After a year spent in slumber, the giant awoke, yawned and decided that the little people were in need of a reminder. On this occasion, the cast of Lilliputians included Jim Courier and Stefan Edberg, who between them had won three of the year's four Grand Slam titles, and Goran Ivanisevic, the Wimbledon finalist. Boris Becker reduced all three to miniature on consecutive days, losing just one set in beating the world numbers one (Courier), two (Edberg) and four (Ivanisevic) and winning his first ATP world championship title in Frankfurt, though he had won the old Masters in New York in 1988.

The sigh of relief from a nation which had begun to question the commitment of their champion was almost as loud as the message Becker himself delivered after his 6–4 6–3 7–5 victory over Courier in the final. 'For this evening at least, I feel like I am number one. I am playing better now than maybe ever in my career.' To cap a perfect day for Germany, it was Becker's 25th birthday and the post-match celebrations included a hearty rendition of 'Happy birthday' and the arrival of a cake. The cake, in fact, provided Becker with almost his toughest test of his week. He bent the knife trying to cut it and nearly ran out of breath blowing out the trick candles, which kept relighting. Only Pete Sampras, who beat Becker in the opening group match, offered more resistance, though Ivanisevic came to within an ace or two of victory in a rollicking semi-final of astonishing power and skill, the best match of the week.

Becker's victory ended the American domination of the ATP finals, which had been won in previous years by Andre Agassi and Sampras, and at last vindicated the huge investment in the tournament by SAT 1. The German satellite television station reported an audience of 9.17 million at match point for Becker against Ivanisevic on Saturday, the largest viewing figure for any programme in the six-year history of the network. The same semi-final enjoyed an average of 5.96 million viewers, making it the highest rated tennis broadcast ever on the station. The economic base of the ATP tour, which rests largely on the Deutschmark, seems safe for a few more years yet, so it was no wonder there were several smiling faces among the hierarchy of the ATP and SAT 1. Just a month earlier, it seemed Becker would not even qualify for an event financed for his benefit.

For Courier, beaten in the final for the second year in succession – last year he lost to Sampras – there was the consolation of becoming the first American since John McEnroe to be world number one at the end of the year. That position was confirmed when his year-long rival, Edberg, was annihilated 6–4 6–0 by Becker in the final group match. On a fast indoor surface against big servers, Courier did well to reach the final because he is not a fan of indoor tennis and, by his own admission, was not playing his best. After a long season, which had reached its apex on the main court at Roland Garros in early June, Courier looked jaded and out of sorts. 'Tired?' he asked after the final. 'I'm every spectrum of tired.' Spontaneity is not Courier's game and with the greenset court favouring the serve-and-volley men, there were few rallies for the hard-hitting baselining American to get his teeth into.

During his opening victory against Richard Krajicek, Courier had expressed his feelings by screaming 'boring' as another ace thundered by. He had a point. Much of the tennis in the Festhalle, though breathtaking in its skill, power and athleticism, was too one-paced and too lacking in variety to be of lasting interest. With Wimbledon champion, Andre Agassi, back in Las Vegas nursing a leg injury, no one in the eight-man field had the speed of eye and hand to give the big servers a taste of their own medicine on the fast Greenset surface. Becker and Ivanisevic, therefore, won 98 per cent of their service games and

Ending the season in superlative form, Boris Becker won the ATP Championship for the first time with decisive victories over Ivanisevic and Courier in the last two rounds. (T. Hindley)

Sampras 90 per cent. Nearly a third of the 36 sets played in the finals were decided by the tie-break, while the statisticians were kept busy counting the number of aces Ivanisevic added to his tally. He began the week with 909 and ended it with 957.

Krajicek, though, had no complaints about the style of play, despite being narrowly outslogged by the American. 'If he finds that boring, he should go and take a cold shower,' he said in reference to Courier's criticism. The big Dutchman, who had begun the year by reaching the semi-finals of the Australian Open and maintained his form well through a long season, had only qualified two days before the start of the $2.5 million event when he won the title in Antwerp, gaining his place in the absence of the injured Ivan Lendl and Agassi. None of his other three opponents in the Rod Laver Group – Ivanisevic, Chang and Courier – could have relished the presence of Krajicek, who ended the year at the head of the IBM/ATP fastest service league with a service timed at 132mph (212km/h) in Indian Wells in March. The Ken Rosewall group of Edberg, Sampras, Becker and Petr Korda was equally competitive.

The opening night featured six sets, four of which ended in tie-breaks. Surprisingly, on the basis of pre-match confidence rather than rankings, Sampras beat Becker 7–6 7–6 with a nonchalance which reduced the home crowd to stunned silence. The American had been responsible for Becker's exit in the qualifying stages last year and the same fate seemed to await the German again, particularly as Edberg had shown himself to be in good working order with a 6–3 7–6 win over the mercurial Czech left-hander Petr Korda in the opening group match.

Once Becker had beaten the hapless Korda the following night and Sampras had ousted the Swede 6–3 3–6 7–5, it became inevitable that the 30th instalment of Becker v Edberg, a rivalry which dates back to junior Wimbledon, would decide the second semi-finalist from the Rosewall Group. It could not have fallen better for the German television companies and their champion did not let them down.

Slowly at first, then with ever increasing assurance, Becker dismantled Edberg's confidence with a stunning display of serving and returning which gave his pre-tournament suggestion that he was playing some of the best tennis of his career a solid ring of truth. Rarely can the Swede have been made to feel so empty, alone and inadequate on a tennis court. His second serve, one of the best in the business, was treated with utter disdain, his volleying became erratic, clumsy even, under the pressure of the onslaught and the home crowd greeted every thundering winner with a rising echo of praise.

Edberg stayed level for the first six games until Becker hit a purple patch, winning ten straight points and taking the first set in 38 minutes. Two double-faults cost Edberg his opening service game and betrayed his fears, which were compounded by three successive aces from Becker. Another double-fault gave Becker a 3–0 lead and the execution was sharp and swift. It was only the third 6–0 score – all in Becker's favour – in the 89 completed sets between the pair since their first professional senior meeting in Cologne in 1984. 'He was just too good for me today. It was as simple as that,' Edberg admitted. So Becker, together with the unbeaten and untroubled Sampras, strode into the semi-final, while Edberg went home to rest weary limbs.

The names of the two other semi-finalists were not decided until the final match in the round robin series. Krajicek, who had just managed to make his power tell against the plucky Chang the previous night, needed to beat Ivanisevic in straight sets. Even for the 6 feet 4 inch 'Crackerjack', that was a tall order and Ivanisevic duly claimed his place opposite Becker, his stablemate under Ion Tiriac's management, in the semi-final. Becker had won comfortably at the Paris Open, but knew this time he would be in a fight. Not even he anticipated quite how tough.

The pair went at it for two hours and 22 minutes, the physiques very different, the power identical. Ivanisevic, tall and lean, the dragster to Becker's Mercedes, whipped down 23 aces with that deceptively simply action. Becker, more muscular, banged down 16 in return. Only nine of the 33 games did not include an ace. There were just five break points. One break apiece settled the first two sets, which were mere skirmishes compared to the full-blooded hand-to-hand drama of the tie-break. Ivanisevic produced two aces and a stunning forehand pass to save three match points at 3–6 in the tie-break, saved another at 6–7. But the best was kept to the last, Becker diving one way then the other, like a soccer goalkeeper, to parry Ivanisevic's passes and take the tie-break 9–7. The hall erupted, the gladiators embraced at the net. 'About seven or eight years ago, I played the same kind of tennis as he does,' Becker said, which was praise indeed for Ivanisevic in defeat.

The all-American affair in the other semi-final was more sedate but no less competitive, Courier's 7–6 7–6 victory over Sampras proving a triumph of courage and tenacity over natural skill. The two used to be good friends, but the pressures of business have dulled the warmth and lent an edge of bitterness to their rivalry. Sampras led the series 6–1 going into the semi-final and was favourite to widen the gap. But he endured one of his meandering days and never found his rhythm, though if he had taken either of two set points at 5–4 in the first set the outcome might just have been different. Courier, fired up by a bad call in the first set tie-break, harried and hustled, ran hard and hit harder when it mattered to earn the dubious privilege of being the potential party pooper on Becker's 25th birthday.

In the event, the American only briefly threatened to spoil the celebrations. He broke Becker for the first time at the start of the third set, but once he failed to hold his own serve seemed to sense that the cause was lost. Becker, who had served with all the authority of old, hit his groundstrokes with a certainty and timing seen only too briefly in the year. He simply outplayed the world number one at every turn, cutting off each avenue until Courier's khaki shorts were drenched with sweat and defeat. This was his sixth loss in as many matches against Becker. 'He just beat me every time we played. Fair and square,' Courier said. None, though, have been on clay, Courier's best surface.

Only after his best victory since the final of the Australian Open in 1991 did Becker reveal the full extent of his mid-summer disillusionment with the game. 'I didn't really care whether I qualified for Frankfurt or not. I was thinking whether or not I should keep playing. It was a question of me being a tennis player or not,' he said. The 6–1 6–1 defeat by Michael Stich in Hamburg set Becker back on the right road. 'Can you imagine how it is to lose like that against the number two in Germany? I decided then that the next time I played, I had to be fit, to be hungry. Then everything just came back together.' Becker earned just over $1 million for becoming ATP world champion, but the lift to his morale could prove priceless.

For 1993, the ATP tour will feature nine super series events in Europe and North America, each worth a minimum of $1.7 million. All, though, will be eclipsed by the Stuttgart Indoor tournament organised by Ion Tiriac in February, which is not one of the elite nine, but will be, with prize money of $2.25 million, the richest tour event outside the Frankfurt finals. There will be 87 events in 34 countries, an increase of six on 1992, with Beijing, Qatar, Dubai, Jakarta and Halle, in Germany, among the new venues. Mark Miles, chief executive of the ATP, was also able to report a 13 per cent increase in attendance for the year and record revenues of $42.6 million. 'Recession?', he might legitimately have asked. 'What recession?'.

ATP TOUR WORLD CHAMPIONSHIPS
ROUND ROBIN SECTION – Rod Laver Group: 1st: G. Ivanisevic (CRO) d. Chang 7–6 6–2, Courier 6–3 6–3, Krajicek 6–4 6–3. 2nd: J. Courier (USA) d. Chang 7–5 6–2, Krajicek 6–7 7–6 7–5. 3rd: R. Krajicek (NED) d. Chang 2–6 6–3 7–6. 4th: M. Chang (USA).

Ken Rosewall Group: 1st: P. Sampras (USA) d. Becker 7–6 7–6, Edberg 6–3 3–6 7–5, Korda 3–6 6–3 6–3. 2nd: B. Becker (GER) d. Korda 6–4 6–2, Edberg 6–4 6–0. 3rd: Edberg (SWE) d. Korda 6–3 7–6, 4th: P. Korda (TCH).

PLAY-OFFS – Semi-finals: Courier d. Sampras 7–6 7–6; Becker d. Ivanisevic 4–6 6–4 7–6. **Final:** Becker d. Courier 6–4 6–3 7–5.

PRIZE MONEY AND (POINTS): Becker $1,090,000 (435); Courier $465,000 (260); Sampras $270,000 (195); Ivanisevic $270,000 (195); Krajicek $130,000 (65), Edberg $130,000 (65), Korda $60,000, Chang $60,000.

KRAFT WORLD TOUR

TOUR REVIEW
POINTS EXPLANATION
KRAFT SERIES TOURNAMENTS
VIRGINIA SLIMS CHAMPIONSHIPS

Appearing in 8 finals in 1992, including the US Open, Arantxa Sanchez-Vicario won the Lipton and Canadian Open titles to consolidate her position among the top four and won $1.38 million in the process. (M. Cole)

Five more tournament wins in 1992 brought Gabriela Sabatini's career tally to 25 but she was thwarted at the semi-finals stage in three of the four Grand Slams and could only reach the quarter-finals at the US Open. *(M. Cole)*

KRAFT WORLD TOUR
Barry Wood

Monica Seles ended 1992 by setting a new record for career earnings in a single year, her $2,622,352 eclipsing Stefan Edberg's $2,363,575 of the previous year. It was not all about money, however. She repeated her 1991 achievement of capturing the Australian, French and US Open titles, with Wimbledon eluding her this time not because of her absence, but because of Steffi Graf.

Seles won 10 tournaments, and was the undisputed world champion. She went through the entire year losing just once before the final (in 1991 she had reached the final of every event she played), with her only early defeat coming in the quarter-finals of the Lipton International to Jennifer Capriati. That ended a winning run of 27 matches dating back to November 1991, and her streak of reaching 21 consecutive finals stretching back to October 1990, leaving Seles one short of breaking the record set by Graf.

Despite her domination, there was one point of the year when, having lost three consecutive finals, Seles could mathematically have lost her number 1 ranking to Graf. That was at the US Open, but Seles retained her title while Graf stumbled at the quarter-final stage against Arantxa Sanchez-Vicario.

The year began disastrously for Graf when she had to withdraw from the Australian Open with a virus and, ironically, German measles. It didn't end too well either, with her first round loss to Lori McNeil at the Virginia Slims Championships, her first opening round defeat since Jo Durie beat her in January 1985. In between, however, she had a solid year, winning eight titles, including Wimbledon for the fourth time. She narrowly lost the French Open title in a magnificent tussle with Seles in what was widely acclaimed to be one of the finest women's matches in many years. In stark contrast to their Wimbledon final four weeks later, which Graf won 6–2 6–1, the result of that match was 6–2 3–6 10–8. The German also came up just short in the Olympic final, which she conceded to a revitalised and slimmed-down Capriati, 3–6 6–3 6–4.

Capriati had suffered a dreadful start to 1992, the result largely of passing through a teenage rebellion phase. Following a reluctance to apply herself seriously to practise, her newly appointed coach Pavel Slozil was dismissed, and it was a remark about her weight by a reporter at the Italian Open that finally made her re-assess the direction she was taking.

The Olympic title was an isolated success however, for although she retained her title in San Diego she lost to Patricia Hy, ranked 36, in the third round of the US Open, and suffered the heaviest defeat of her young career when she managed just one game against Graf in Philadelphia in November.

Navratilova set a new record for career titles by winning her 158th at the Virginia Slims of Chicago in February. It was an interesting location for her to achieve that landmark, for she has won more titles in Chicago (now 12) than at any other place. Her last defeat there was to Evonne Goolagong in 1976, although in 1989 she had to default to Larisa Savchenko in the quarter-finals because of injury. Her 7–6 4–6 7–5 win over Jana Novotna, during which she saved two match points, surpassed Chris Evert's career total, and she won her 161st title at Filderstadt on her 36th birthday in October. That victory marked the first time since the 1981 Australian Open that she had won an event seeded as low as third. Navratilova is the second oldest player to win an event, with the record held by Billie Jean King who won the Birmingham title in 1983 aged 39 years 6 months.

As the year came to a close Navratilova announced that 1993 would be her last, although it is difficult to imagine her walking away when she can still beat the No. 1 player, as she did in Los Angeles.

Gabriela Sabatini, as is her habit, enjoyed her most successful period prior to the French Open, winning five titles. Of her 25 career titles, 19 have occurred in the first six months of the year. In the big events she was runner-up to Sanchez-Vicario at Lipton, a semi-finalist at the Australian and French Opens and at Wimbledon, and a quarter-finalist at Flushing Meadows. A good, but unspectacular, year then for the popular Argentinian.

Sanchez-Vicario set a new record for the number of matches played in one year, her total of 167 exceeding Navratilova's 165 set in 1982. Although she was the victim of two upsets during the year, losing to Kimiko Date at the quarter-final stage of the Pan Pacific and to Julie Halard in the second round of Wimbledon, she enjoyed an excellent year in both singles and doubles. She won the Lipton title (defeating Sabatini) and the Canadian Open (defeating Seles), and was runner-up in five other events. The Canadian win marked the first time since 1989 that Seles had lost in three consecutive finals (Wimbledon, Los Angeles, Montreal).

In doubles Sanchez-Vicario won 10 titles (6 with Helena Sukova, including the Virginia Slims Championships). However, the Sanchez-Vicario/Sukova achievement was surpassed by Gigi Fernandez and Natalia Zvereva, who won the French Open (beat Conchita Martinez and Sanchez-Vicario), Wimbledon and the US Open (beat Novotna and Savchenko Neiland).

Mary Joe Fernandez had another successful year while managing to remain outside the spotlight. She reached the final of the Australian Open and the semi-finals of the US Open. Although she suffered third round defeats at both the French Open and Wimbledon, she failed to reach the semi-finals on only two other occasions. She also won an Olympic gold medal with Gigi Fernandez.

A strong contender for the most impressive 'newcomer' award was Amanda Coetzer, who elevated herself into the top 20. Her rise began when, ranked 61, she defeated third ranked Sabatini in the quarter-finals of the Virginia Slims of Florida, and she followed that with a win over Capriati at the Italian Open.

The year began in Brisbane with the first all-Australian final for nearly nine years as Nicole Provis beat Rachel McQuillan to win her first title. The last all-Aussie final was in Kansas City in 1983, when Elizabeth Smylie defeated Anne Minter.

Another highlight of the year occurred in the final of the Virginia Slims of Oklahoma, where Zina Garrison defeated Lori McNeil 7–5 3–6 7–6 (12–10), with the tiebreak lasting a dramatic twenty minutes. Interestingly, it was only the seventh time in five years that the outcome of a final had been decided by a tiebreak.

Navratilova proved her stamina by playing three matches on the final day of the US Hardcourt Championships in San Antonio. She defeated Natalie Tauziat 6–2 6–1 in the final, played a doubles semi-final with Pam Shriver, and after a break of just ten minutes they returned to a 3–6 6–2 7–6 (7–4) victory over Patty Fendick and Andrea Strnadova which finished at 9.15 p.m.

While talking of Strnadova, she has set a sad record of her own, losing in all five finals she has reached. In 1991 she was defeated at Auckland and Wellington, and in 1992 she was again runner-up in Auckland, and in Pattaya and Kuala Lumpur.

One of the biggest upsets of the year occurred at Eastbourne in June, when Linda Harvey-Wild overcame ten-time champion Navratilova in the second round. It was only Navratilova's second defeat at Eastbourne in 62 matches dating back to 1982. No 'one-win wonder', Harvey-Wild continued to the final, where she lost to McNeil. She proved her worth again in November by reaching the final of the Indianapolis Open, where she lost to Sukova.

Other significant upsets during the year included Maggie Maleeva (ranked 39) over Capriati (6) in Tokyo, Veronika Martinek (83) over Capriati (6) at Hilton Head, Natalia Zvereva (27) over Navratilova (4) also at Hilton Head, Manon Bollegraf (57) over Manuela Maleeva (10) at the French Open, Jo Durie (50) over Anke Huber (9) also at the French Open, and Sabine Hack (42) over Mary Joe Fernandez (7) also in Paris. At the US Open, Maggie Maleeva (27) defeated Navratilova (3), Ann Grossman (45) beat Conchita Martinez (8) and Chanda Rubin (75) beat Katerina Maleeva (15).

Pam Shriver came within two matches of becoming only the third player to win singles titles in three separate decades, but was defeated by eventual champion Brenda Schultz in the Edgbaston semi-finals. The only players to achieve that distinction are Navratilova and King.

In September, Sandra Cecchini won the Clarins Open in Paris to keep alive an impressive record of winning at least one title in each of the last ten years. The only other players to achieve that in the Open era are Navratilova, Evert and Goolagong.

In October, Graf began a streak that gave her twenty straight wins (the longest of any player in 1992) as she retained the titles of Leipzig, the European Indoor Championships and Brighton, and won Philadelphia.

Another significant event occurred in October, when on the 5th Maggie Maleeva entered the top 20, placing all three sisters there at the same time.

Several new names began to make their mark during the year. Shi-Ting Wang, long a promising junior and with 32 wins in 36 matches during 1991, ended 1992 ranked 55 after following-up quarter-final finishes at Pattaya and Taipei by defeating top seed Anke Huber and reaching the semi-finals at Indianapolis.

Another to make giant strides was Iva Majoli, a Croatian now resident at Nick Bollettieri's academy in Florida. In her first major tournament, in Houston, she upset McNeil in the second round before losing to Garrison in the quarter-finals. Her ranking rose from 537 to 185, she beat McNeil again in Oakland, and ended the year ranked 50.

Katerina Kroupova, also from Czechoslovakia, made steady progress throughout the year without making any impact whatsoever in the major events. But she enjoyed considerable success on the satellite circuit with two wins, a runner-up finish and three quarter-finals. Beginning the year at 297, she finished at 61.

Patricia Hy cannot strictly be described as a new name, for she has been playing since 1982. But she enjoyed a splendid year and reached the top 30 for the first time. Her rise began in April at Hilton Head, where she defeated Novotna. But it was on home ground in Montreal that she excelled by beating Katerina Maleeva and then taking a set from Seles, and she followed up at the US Open with wins over Capriati and Sukova.

Six players won titles for the first time. They were Sabine Hack (Sao Paulo), Noelle Van Lottum (unseeded, Wellington), Kimiko Date (Japan Open), Magdalena Maleeva (San Marino), Barbara Rittner (Schenectady) and Shaun Stafford (unseeded, Taipei). Other unseeded winners were Robin White (Auckland, and her first title since 1985), Natalia Medvedeva (beating top seed Katerina Maleeva in the second round at Linz) and Wiltrud Probst (Brussels).

Two players of some quality missed most of 1992 because of injury and illness, Helen Kelesi and Barbara Paulus. Kelesi did return at the Federation Cup after an absence of several months to defeat Martinez, but she later collapsed with bronchitis on court in San Marino, and also had to retire from two further events in November.

Finally, for the record, a Czechoslovakian player made her debut during August at a satellite event in Germany. Her name – Gabriela Navratilova. No relation!

KRAFT WORLD TOUR 1992

DATE	VENUE	SURFACE	SINGLES FINAL	DOUBLES WINNERS
2-8 Dec	Sao Paulo	Clay	S. Hack d. V. Martinek 6-3 7-5	I. Gorrochategui/M. Paz
30 Dec-5 Jan	Brisbane	Clay	N. Provis d. R. McQuillan 6-3 6-2	J. Novotna/L. Savchenko Neiland
6-12 Jan	Sydney	Hard	G. Sabatini d. A. Sanchez-Vicario 6-1 6-1	A. Sanchez-Vicario/H. Sukova
13-20 Jan	**Australian Open**	**Hard**	**M. Seles d. M.J. Fernandez 6-2 6-3**	**A. Sanchez-Vicario/H. Sukova**
27 Jan-2 Feb	Auckland	Hard	R. White d. A. Strnadova 2-6 6-4 6-3	R. Fairbank-Nideffer/R. Reggi-Concato
28 Jan-2 Feb	Tokyo	Carpet	G. Sabatini d. M. Navratilova 6-2 4-6 6-2	A. Sanchez-Vicario/H. Sukova
3-9 Feb	Essen	Carpet	M. Seles d. M. J. Fernandez 6-0 6-3	K. Maleeva/B. Rittner
3-9 Feb	Wellington	Hard	N. van Lottum d. D. Faber 6-4 6-0	B. Borneo/C. Wood
4-9 Feb	Osaka	Carpet	H. Sukova d. L. Gildemeister 6-2 4-6 6-1	R. Stubbs/H. Sukova
10-16 Feb	Chicago	Carpet	N. Navratilova d. J. Novotna 7-6 4-6 7-5	M. Navratilova/P. Shriver
10-16 Feb	Linz	Carpet	N. Medvedeva d. P. Paradis Mangon 6-4 6-2	M. Kiene/M. Oremans
17-23 Feb	Oklahoma City	Carpet	Z. Garrison Jackson d. L. McNeil 7-5 3-6 7-6	L. McNeil/N. Provis
17-23 Feb	Cesena	Carpet	M. Pierce d. C. Tanvier 6-1 6-1	C. Suire/C. Tanvier
24 Feb-1 March	Indian Wells	Hard	M. Seles d. C. Martinez 6-3 6-1	C. Kohde-Kilsch/S. Rehe
2-8 March	Boca Raton	Hard	S. Graf d. C. Martinez 3-6 6-2 6-0	L. Savchenko Neiland/N. Zvereva
13-29 March	Key Biscayne	Hard	A. Sanchez-Vicario d. G. Sabatini 6-1 6-4	A. Sanchez-Vicario/L.Savchenko Neiland
23-29 March	San Antonio	Hard	M. Navratilova d. N. Tauziat 6-2 6-1	M. Navratilova/P. Shriver
26-29 March	Wesley Chapel	Clay		J. Novotna/L. Savchenko Neiland
30 March-5 April	Hilton Head Island	Clay	G. Sabatini d. C. Martinez 6-1 6-4	A. Sanchez-Vicario/N. Zvereva
6-12 April	Amelia Island	Clay	G. Sabatini d. S. Graf 6-2 1-6 6-3	A. Sanchez-Vicario/N. Zvereva
6-12 April	Tokyo	Hard	K. Date d. S. Appelmans 7-5 3-6 6-3	A. Frazier/R. Hiraki
13-19 April	Houston	Clay	M. Seles d. Z. Garrison Jackson 6-1 6-1	P. Fendick/G. Fernandez
13-19 April	Pattaya City	Hard	S. Appelmans d. A. Strnadova 7-5 3-6 7-5	I. Demongeot/N. Medvedeva
20-26 April	Barcelona	Clay	M. Seles d. A. Sanchez-Vicario 3-6 6-2 6-3	C. Martinez/A. Sanchez-Vicario
20-26 April	Kuala Lumpur	Carpet	Y. Basuki d. A. Strnadova 6-3 6-0	I. Demongeot/N. Medvedeva
27 April-3 May	Hamburg	Clay	S. Graf d. A. Sanchez-Vicario 7-6 6-2	S. Graf/R. Stubbs
28 April-3 May	Taranto	Clay	J. Halard d. E. Zardo 6-0 7-5	A. Coetzer/I. Gorrochategui
4-10 May	Rome	Clay	G. Sabatini d. M. Seles 7-5 6-4	M. Seles/H. Sukova
4-10 May	Waregem	Clay	W. Probst d. M. Babel 6-2 6-3	M. Bollegraf/C. Vis
11-17 May	Berlin	Clay	S. Graf d. A. Sanchez-Vicario 4-6 7-5 6-2	J. Novotna/L. Savchenko Neiland
18-24 May	Lucerne	Clay	A. Frazier d. R. Zrubakova 6-4 4-6 7-5	A. Frazier/E. Reinach
18-24 May	Strasbourg	Clay	J. Wiesner d. N. Sawamatsu 6-1 6-3	P. Fendick/A.Strnadova
25 May-7 June	**French Open**	**Clay**	**M. Seles d. S. Graf 6-2 3-6 10-8**	**G. Fernandez/N. Zvereva**
8-14 June	Birmingham	Grass	B. Schultz d. J. Byrne 6-2 6-2	L. McNeil/R. Stubbs

DATE	VENUE	SURFACE	SINGLES FINAL	DOUBLES WINNERS
15–20 June	Eastbourne	Grass	L. McNeil d. L. Harvey-Wild 6–4 6–4	J. Novotna/L. Savchenko Neiland
22 June–5 July	**Wimbledon**	**Grass**	**S. Graf d. M. Seles 6–2 6–1**	**G. Fernandez/N. Zvereva**
6–12 July	Palermo	Clay	M. Pierce d. B. Schultz 6–1 6–7 6–1	H. Cioffi/M. Gaidano
6–12 July	Kitzbuhel	Clay	C. Martinez d. M. Maleeva Fragnière 6–0 3–6 6–2	F. Labat/A. Dechaume
20–26 July	Prague	Clay	R. Zrubakova d. K. Kroupova 6–3 7–5	K. Kschwendt/P. Ritter
20–26 July	San Marino	Clay	Mag. Maleeva d. Fed. Bonsignori 7–6 6–4	A. Dechaume/F. Labat
10–16 Aug	Manhattan Beach	Hard	M. Navratilova d. M. Seles 6–4 6–2	A. Sanchez-Vicario/H. Sukova
17–23 Aug	Montreal	Hard	A. Sanchez-Vicario d. M. Seles 6–3 4–6 6–4	L. McNeil/R. Stubbs
24–30 Aug	San Diego	Hard	J. Capriati d. C. Martinez 6–3 6–2	J. Novotna/L. Savchenko Neiland
24–30 Aug	Schenectady	Hard	B. Rittner d. B. Schultz 7–6 6–3	A. Dechaume/F. Labat
31 Aug–13 Sept	**US Open**	**Hard**	**M. Seles d. A. Sanchez-Vicario 6–3 6–3**	**J. Novotna/L. Savchenko Neiland**
14–14–20 Sept	Paris	Hard	C. Cecchini d. E. Zardo 6–2 6–1	C. Cecchini/P. Tarabini
21–27 Sept	Tokyo	Carpet	M. Seles d. G. Sabatini 6–2 6–0	M.J. Fernandez/R. White
28 Sept–4 Oct	Leipzig	Carpet	S. Graf d. J. Novotna 6–3 1–6 6–4	J. Novotna/L. Savchenko Neiland
28 Sept–4 Oct	Bayonne	Carpet	M. Maleeva Fragnière d. N. Tauziat	L. Farrando/P. Langrova
28 Sept–4 Oct	Taipei	Hard	S. Stafford d. A. Grossman 6–1 6–3	J. Faull/J. Richardson
5–11 Oct	Zurich	Carpet	S. Graf d. M. Navratilova 7–5 7–5	H. Sukova/N. Zvereva
12–18 Oct	Filderstadt	Carpet	M. Navratilova d. G. Sabatini 7–6 6–3	A. Sanchez-Vicario/H. Sukova
20–25 Oct	Brighton	Carpet	S. Graf d. J. Novotna 4–6 6–4 7–6	J. Novotna/L. Savchenko Neiland
26 Oct–1 Nov	San Juan	Hard	M. Pierce d. G. Fernandez 6–1 7–5	A. Coetzer/E. Reinach
2–8 Nov	Oakland	Carpet	M. Seles d. M. Navratilova 6–4 6–3	G. Fernandez/N. Zvereva
9–15 Nov	Philadelphia	Carpet	S. Graf d. A. Sanchez-Vicario 6–3 3–6 6–1	G. Fernandez/N. Zvereva
9–14 Nov	Indianapolis	Carpet	H. Sukova d. L. Harvey-Wild 6–4 6–3	K. Adams/E. Reinach
16–22 Nov	New York	Carpet	M. Seles d. M. Navratilova 7–5 6–3 6–1	A. Sanchez-Vicario/H. Sukova

KRAFT WORLD TOUR 1992 – POINTS EXPLANATION

The Kraft World Tour is the equivalent of the men's IBM/ATP Tour. The 1992 women's tour began on 2nd December 1991 with the tournament in Sao Paolo, Brazil and ended with the $1 million Virginia Slims Championships in New York in November 1992, where the $2 million bonus pool was distributed to the top 42 singles players (8 were ineligible because they had not played the required number of tournaments) and 10 doubles players. Altogether 57 tournaments (including the four Grand Slam Championships) were staged in 20 countries, plus the season-ending Championships for the top 16 players and the top eight pairs on the Kraft General Foods points table. The player who heads that table at the end of the Championships is automatically declared the official World Champion.

Events carrying points on the 1992 Kraft World Tour were:

Grand Slam Championships: The Championships of Australia, France, Great Britain and the United States.

Virginia Slims Championships: The season ending event for 16 singles players and eight doubles pairs played at Madison Square Garden, New York with $1 million in prize money and $2 million in the Virginia Slims Bonus Pool.

Lipton International Players Championships: A ten-day tournament in Key Biscayne, Florida with minimum prize money for women of $800,000 and a 96 main draw.

Light n' Lively Doubles: A doubles-only event in Saddlebrook, Florida for eight teams with prize money of $175,000

OTHER TOURNAMENTS (All of which receive guaranteed WTA player designations).

Tier I: Five tournaments, approved by the Women's International Professional Tennis Council, with prize money of $500,000.

Tier II: Fifteen tournaments approved by the WIPTC with prize money of $350,000.

Tier III: Six tournaments approved by the WIPTC with prize money of $$225,000.

Tier IV: Twelve tournaments approved by the WIPTC with prize money of $150,000. Three additional tournaments in this category do not carry the WTA player designation.

Tier V: Tournaments approved by the WIPTC with prize money of $100,000. The number of tournaments allowed in this category is at the discretion of the WIPTC.

KRAFT TOUR POINTS TABLE (Equal points are awarded for singles and doubles)

Category	Winner	Finalist	Semi-finalist	Quarter-finalist	9-16	17-32	33-64	Round of 128
Grand Slams	820	575	370	190	100	50	25	13
VS Champs(S	820	575	370	190	100	–	–	–
Lipton Int.	470	330	210	110	55	25	13	6
Light 'n Liv.	400	280	180	90	50	24	12	–
Tier I	400	280	180	90	50	24	12	–
Tier II	300	210	135	70	35	18	9	–
Tier III	240	170	110	55	30	14	7	–
Tier IV	190	135	85	45	20	10	5	–
Tier V	110	75	50	25	10	6	3	–

Note: In both singles and doubles, no points are awarded to a player until she has completed a match.

1992 BONUS POOLS ($US - TOTAL $2 million)

Singles Players 1-50 (TOTAL $1,508,000) **1** 500,000; **2** 350,000; **3** 200,000; **4** 100,000; **5** 50,000; **6** 40,000; **7** 35,000; **8** 30,000; **9** 25,000; **10** 20,000; **11** 17,000; **12** 15,000; **13** 12,000; **14** 10,000; **15** 7,000; **16** 6,000; **17** 5,000; **18** 5,000; **19** 4,000; **20** 4,000. Players **21-30** $3,500, Players **31-40** $2,500, Players **41-50** $1,300

Doubles (TOTAL $117,000) **1** 50,000; **2** 25,000; **3** 10,000; **4** 10,000; **5** 5,000; **6** 5,000; **7** 4,000; **8** 4,000; **9** 2,000; **10** 2,000.

Incentive Bonus Pool ($208,500) Special prizes for winners of Tier IV and Tier V events, provided they have completed the required number of tournaments.

Special Incentive Fund ($375,000) Designed to encourage top 20 players to play tournaments above their minimum commitment when a tournament does not have its commitment. Payments are made as follows: Players listed 1 and 2 - $75,000; players listed 3 and 4 - $50,000; players listed 5 to 8 - 25,000; players listed 9 to 10 - $12,000; players listed 11 to 20 - $7,500.

VIRGINIA SLIMS 1992 BONUS POOL DISTRIBUTION

Monica Seles finished first in the 1992 $2 million Virginia Slims Bonus Pool with a prize of $500,000. A total of only $1,775,950 was distributed to the 46 players who were eligible to receive bonuses. The Bonus Pool contains four categories: Singles, Doubles, Special Incentive Fund and Tier IV/V Winners Pool. (All amounts shown in US Dollars)

PLAYER	SINGLES	DOUBLES	SPECIAL INCENTIVE FUND	TIER IV/V WINNERS BONUS POOL	TOTAL
1. SELES Monica	500,000				500,000
2. GRAF Steffi	350,000				350,000
3. SABATINI Gabriela	200,000		50,000		250,000
4. SANCHEZ-VICARIO Arantx	100,000	25,000	25,000		150,000
5. ZVEREVA Natalia	5,000	50,000			55,000
6. NAVRATILOVA Martina	50,000				50,000
7. MARTINEZ Conchita	35,000			8,000	43,000
8. FERNANDEZ Mary Joe	40,000				40,000
9. SHRIVER Pam	3,500	4,000	25,000		32,500
10. McNEIL Lori	30,000	2,000			32,000
11. SUKOVA Helena	7,000	5,000		16,000	28,000
12. NOVOTNA Jana	20,000	5,000			25,000
13. GARRISON JACKSON Zina	12,000	4,000		8,000	24,000
14. FERNANDEZ Gigi	3,500	10,000	7,500		21,000
15. TAUZIAT Nathalie	15,000				15,000
16. FRAZIER Amy	6,000			8,000	14,000
17. SCHULTZ Brenda	4,000			8,000	12,000
18. WIESNER Judith	3,500			8,000	11,500
19. SAVCHENKO NEILAND Larisa	1,300	10,000			11,300
20. MALEEVA Katerina	10,000				10,000
21. PROVIS Nicole	1,300			8,000	9,300
22. APPELMANS Sabine	3,500			5,000	8,500
ZRUBAKOVA Radka	3,500			5,000	8,500
24. RITTNER BarbarA	2,500			5,000	7,500
25. MEDVEDEVA Natalia	1,300			5,000	6,300
VAN LOTTUM Noelle	1,300			5,000	6,300
27. WHITE Robin				5,000	5,000
BASUKI Yayuk				5,000	5,000
STAFFORD Shaun				5,000	5,000
HUBER Anke	5,000				5,000
31. MALEEVA Magdalena	1,750			2,500	3,750
32. COETZER Amanda	4,000				4,000
33. HACK Sabine	1,250			2,500	3,750
34. STRNADOVA Andrea	2,500				2,500
GILDEMEISTER Laura	2,500				2,500
HARVEY-WILD Linda	2,500				2,500
GROSSMAN Ann	2,500				2,500
38. STUBBS Rennae		2,000			2,000
39. MESKHI Leila	1,750				1,750
HY Patricia	1,750				1,750
41. GRAHAM Debbie	1,300				1,300
DECHAUME Alexia	1,300				1,300
PARADIS MANGON Pascale	1,300				1,300
FAIRBANK NIDEFFER Ros	1,300				1,300
LABAT Florencia	1,300				1,300
46. FENDICK Patty	1,250				1,250

$1.775,950

NOTE: Jennifer Capriati, Sandra Cecchini, Kimiko Date, Julie Halard, Manuela Maleeva-Fragniere, Rachel McQuillan, Mary Pierce and Naoko Sawamatsu were ineligible for bonuses because they were at least two tournaments short of their minimum commitment. Fendick, Hack, Hy, Magdalena Maleeva and Meskhi each received 50% of their bonus because they were one tournament short of their minimum commitment.

PLAYER NATIONALITIES AND BIRTHDAYS

The following players have competed in the 1992 Grand Slam Tournaments and Kraft World Tour:

Name and Nationality	Date of Birth	Name and Nationality	Date of Birth
Adams, Katrina (USA)	05/08/68	Dreyer, Kirsten (USA)	27/03/69
Allen, Louise (USA)	07/01/62	Durie, Jo (GBR)	27/07/60
Amiach, Sophie (FRA)	10/11/63	Emmons, Jessica (USA)	13/09/70
Appelmans, Sabine (BEL)	12/04/72	Endo, Mana (JPN)	06/02/71
Arendt, Nicole (USA)	26/08/69	Ercegovic, Nadin (YUG)	02/02/73
Avila, Neus (ESP)	26/07/71	Etchemendy, Pascale (FRA	06/06/66
Babel, Meike (GER)	22/11/74	Faber, Donna (USA)	05/07/71
Bacheva, Lubomira (BUL)	07/03/75	Fairbank Nideffer, Ros (USA)	02/11/60
Baranski, Renata (POL)	24/02/65	Farina, Silvia (ITA)	27/04/72
Bassett Seguso, Carling (CAN)	09/10/67	Fauche, Christelle (SUI)	09/06/73
Basuki, Yayuk (INA)	30/11/70	Faull, Jo-Anne (AUS)	13/01/71
Baudone, Nathalie (ITA)	12/07/72	Feber, Nancy (BEL)	05/02/76
Begerow, Petra (GER)	14/04/75	Fendick, Patty (USA)	31/03/65
Benjamin, Camille (USA)	22/06/66	Fernandez, Gigi (USA)	22/02/64
Bentley, Sarah (GBR)	08/03/73	Fernandez, Mary Joe (USA)	19/08/71
Berger, Ilana (ISR)	31/12/65	Ferrando, Linda (ITA)	12/01/66
Bes, Eva (ESP)	14/01/73	Field, Louise (AUS)	25/02/67
Blumberga, Agnesse (CIS)	09/04/71	Foeldenyi, Anna-Maria (HUN)	22/08/74
Bobkova, Radka (TCH)	12/02/73	Frankl, Silke (GER)	29/05/70
Bollegraf, Manon (HOL)	10/04/64	Frazier, Amy (USA)	19/09/72
Bonsignori, Federica (ITA)	20/11/67	Fulco Villella, Bettina (ARG)	23/10/68
Boogert, Kristie (NED)	16/12/73	Fusai, Alexandra (FRA)	22/11/73
Boschiero, Gabriella (ITA)	13/01/72	Gaidano, Maria Jose (ARG)	25/05/73
Bottini, Estefania (ESP)	03/02/74	Garrison Jackson, Zina (USA)	16/11/63
Bowes, Beverly (USA)	09/09/65	Garrone, Laura (ITA)	15/11/67
Brioukhovets, Elena (CIS)	08/06/71	Gavaldon, Angelica (MEX)	03/10/73
Bueche, Katharina (AUT)	19/06/74	Gildemeister, Laura (PER)	12/01/64
Burgin, Elise (USA)	05/03/62	Giusto, Sabrina (BRA)	31/08/71
Byrne, Jenny (AUS)	25/02/67	Glass, Andrea (GER)	17/07/76
Callens, Els (BEL)	20/08/70	Godridge, Kristin (AUS)	07/02/73
Capriati, Jennifer (USA)	29/03/76	Golarsa, Laura (ITA)	27/11/67
Carlsson, Asa (SWE)	16/06/75	Gomer, Sara (GBR)	13/05/64
Cavina, Cristina (ITA)	02/02/69	Gorrochategui, Ines (ARG)	13/06/73
Cecchini, Sandra (ITA)	27/02/65	Graf, Steffi (GER)	14/06/69
Chabalgoity, Claudia (BRA)	13/03/71	Graham, Debbie (USA)	25/08/70
Cioffi, Halle (USA)	05/08/69	Grossman, Ann (USA)	13/10/70
Coetzer, Amanda (RSA)	22/10/71	Grunfeld, Amanda (GBR)	01/03/67
Collet, Barbara (FRA)	13/02/74	Guerree, Nathalie (FRA)	07/07/68
Collins, Sandy (USA)	13/10/58	Guglielmi, Monica (ITA)	02/09/74
Corsato Owsianka, Luciana (BRA)	21/01/66	Guse, Kerry-Anne (AUS)	04/12/72
Cristea, Catalina (ROM)	02/06/75	Habsudova, Karina (TCH)	02/08/73
Cueto, Isabel (GER)	03/12/68	Hack, Sabine (GER)	07/12/69
Cunningham, Carrie (USA)	28/04/72	Halard, Julie (FRA)	10/09/70
Dahlman, Cecilia (SWE)	24/07/68	Hall, Colette (GBR)	03/07/73
Dahlman, Nanne (FIN)	07/09/70	Harper, Peanut (USA)	15/08/60
Daniels, Mary-Lou (USA)	06/08/61	Harvey-Wild, Linda (USA)	11/02/71
Date, Kimiko (JPN)	28/09/70	Helgeson, Ginger (USA)	14/09/68
Davenport, Lindsay (USA)	08/06/76	Henricksson, Ann (USA)	31/10/59
De Lone, Erika (USA)	14/10/72	Herman, Dierdre (USA)	11/10/71
De Los Rios, Rosana (PAR)	16/09/75	Herreman, Nathalie (FRA)	28/03/66
De Swardt, Mariaan (RSA)	18/03/71	Hetherington, Jill (CAN)	27/10/64
Dechaume, Alexia (FRA)	03/05/70	Hiraki, Rika (JPN)	06/12/71
Demongeot, Isabelle (FRA)	18/09/66	Hofmann, Christiane (GER)	12/12/68
Devries, Ann (BEL)	27/02/70	Holubova, Petra (TCH)	12/10/68
Dobrovits, Nike (AUT)	02/12/73	Hoogendorn, Esmir (HOL)	31/03/69
Dopfer, Sandra (AUT)	25/05/70	Housset Gilbert, Nathalie (FRA)	29/07/68
Drake, Maureen (CAN)	21/03/71	Huber, Anke (GER)	04/12/74

Name and Nationality	Date of Birth	Name and Nationality	Date of Birth
Hummell, Nicole (USA)	01/08/74	Meskhi, Leila (CIS)	05/06/68
Humphreys Davies, Virginia (GBR)	06/01/72	Milvidskaia, Viktoria (CIS)	20/04/67
Hy, Patricia (CAN)	22/08/65	Miyagi, Nana (JPN)	10/04/71
Iida, Ei (JPN)	09/09/67	Miyauchi, Misumi (JPN)	06/09/71
Jackson Nobrega, Michelle (USA)	28/12/73	Monami, Dominique (BEL)	31/05/73
Javer, Monique (GBR)	22/07/67	Morton, Tracey (AUS)	18/12/67
Jens, Julia (GER)	01/01/75	Mothes, Catherine (FRA)	07/06/70
Jensen, Rachel Ann (USA)	19/11/72	Mueller, Andrea (GER)	21/08/65
Jeyaseelan, Sonya (CAN)	24/04/76	Mulej, Barbara (YUG)	29/05/74
Kamio, Yone (JPN)	22/11/71	Muns Jagerman, Nicole (HOL)	23/07/67
Kamstra, Petra (HOL)	18/03/74	Nagano, Hiromi (JPN)	20/07/71
Kelesi, Helen (CAN)	15/11/69	Nagatsuka, Kyoko (JPN)	22/02/74
Keller, Audra (USA)	17/11/71	Nagelsen, Betsy (USA)	23/10/56
Kerek, Angela (GER)	25/01/72	Navarro, Barbara (ESP)	09/04/73
Khoo, Chin Bee (MAL)		Navratilova, Martina (USA)	18/10/56
Kidowaki, Maya (JPN)	17/05/69	Nelson, Pam (USA)	01/07/75
Kiene, Monique (HOL)		Nemsakova, Zuzana (TCH)	14/09/76
Kijimuta, Akiko (JPN)	01/05/68	Niox-Chateau, Sybille (FRA)	19/10/69
Kijimuta, Naoko (JPN)	26/03/72	Novelo, Lupita (MEX)	05/05/67
Kochta, Marketa (GER)	14/07/75	Novotna, Jana (TCH)	02/10/68
Kohde-Kilsch, Claudia (GER)	11/12/63	Nowak, Katarzyna (POL)	13/01/69
Krizan, Tina (SLO)	18/03/74	O'Reilly, Christine (USA)	18/01/68
Kroupova, Katerina (TCH)	20/02/74	O'Reilly, Patty (USA)	18/01/68
Kruger, Joanette (RSA)	03/09/73	Oeljeklaus, Katja (GER)	10/02/71
Kschwendt, Karin (LUX)	14/09/68	Okagawa, Emiko (JPN)	26/12/64
Kucova, Petra (TCH)	26/02/73	Okamoto, Kumiko (JPN)	19/02/65
Kuhlman, Caroline (USA)	25/08/66	Olivier, Angelique (FRA)	12/06/75
Labat, Florencia (ARG)	12/06/71	Oremans, Miriam (HOL)	19/09/72
Lai, Su-Ying (TPE)		Pampoulova Wagner, Elena (BUL)	17/05/72
Lake, Valda (GBR)	11/10/68	Papadaki, Christina (GRE)	24/02/73
Langrova, Petra (TCH)	27/06/70	Paradis Mangon, Pascale (FRA)	24/04/66
Laskova, Leona (TCH)	07/04/70	Parkhomenko, Svetlana (CIS)	08/10/62
Li, Fang (CHN)	01/01/73	Paulus, Barbara (AUT)	01/09/70
Limmer, Joanne (AUS)	29/03/74	Paz, Mercedes (ARG)	27/06/66
Lindqvist, Catarina (SWE)	13/06/63	Perez, Pilar (ESP)	22/09/73
Lindstrom, Maria (SWE)	07/03/63	Perfetti, Flora (ITA)	29/01/69
Lohmann, Sabine (GER)	13/03/73	Pfaff, Eva (GER)	10/02/61
London, Nicole (USA)	03/02/76	Piccolini, Katia (ITA)	15/01/73
Loosemore, Sarah (GBR)	15/06/71	Pierce, Mary (FRA)	15/01/75
Lord, Holyn (USA)	12/10/73	Pizzichini, Gloria (ITA)	24/07/75
Ludloff, Heather (USA)	11/06/61	Po, Kimberly (USA)	20/10/71
MacGregor, Cammy (USA)	11/10/68	Porwik, Claudia (GER)	14/11/68
Magers, Gretchen (USA)	07/02/64	Pospisilova, Jana (TCH)	23/03/70
Majoli, Iva (CRO)	12/08/77	Pratt, Nicole (AUS)	05/03/73
Maleeva, Katerina (BUL)	07/05/69	Prausa, Wendy (USA)	29/09/60
Maleeva, Magdalena (BUL)	01/04/75	Price, Tessa (RSA)	25/03/67
Maleeva Fragnière, Manuela (SUI)	14/02/67	Probst, Wiltrud (GER)	29/05/69
Malkova, Zdenka (TCH)	19/01/75	Provis, Nicole (AUS)	22/09/69
Maniokova, Eugenia (CIS)	17/05/68	Quentrec, Karine (FRA)	21/10/69
Martin, Stacey (USA)	13/11/70	Radford, Kristine (AUS)	03/03/70
Martinek, Veronika (GER)	03/04/72	Rajchrtova, Regina (TCH)	05/02/68
Martinez, Conchita (ESP)	16/04/72	Ramon, Silvia (ESP)	09/08/72
Maruska, Marion (AUT)	15/12/72	Raymond, Lisa (USA)	10/08/73
Matic, Gorana (CRO)	24/10/73	Reece, Stephanie (USA)	24/04/70
May, Alycia (USA)	31/01/71	Reggi Concato, Raffaella (ITA)	27/11/65
McCarthy, Shannan (USA)	19/05/70	Rehe, Stephanie (USA)	05/11/69
McGrath, Meredith (USA)	28/04/71	Reichel, Sandra (AUT)	24/06/71
McNeil, Lori (USA)	18/12/63	Reinach, Elna (RSA)	02/12/68
McQuillan, Rachel (AUS)	02/12/71	Reinstadler, Beate (AUT)	20/05/67
Medvedeva, Natalia (CIS)	15/11/71	Reynares, Ma Luciana (ARG)	09/02/76
Meier, Silke (GER)	13/07/68	Rinaldi, Kathy (USA)	24/03/67
Menga, Vanessa (BRA)	20/10/76	Ritter, Petra (AUT)	24/05/72

Name and Nationality	Date of Birth	Name and Nationality	Date of Birth
Rittner, Barbara (GER)	25/04/73	Sviglerova, Eva (TCH)	13/07/71
Romano, Francesca (ITA)	07/02/71	Szabova, Denisa (TCH)	18/11/68
Rossides, Eleni (HOL)	23/10/67	Takagi, Tamaka (JPN)	30/12/65
Rottier, Stephanie (NED)	12/01/74	Tampieri, Paola (ITA)	26/04/75
Ruano Pascual, Virginia (ESP)	21/09/73	Tanvier, Catherine (FRA)	28/05/65
Rubin, Chanda (USA)	18/02/76	Tarabini, Patricia (ARG)	06/08/68
Sabas, Sylvie (FRA)	19/02/72	Tauziat, Nathalie (FRA)	17/10/67
Sabatini, Gabriela (ARG)	16/05/70	Tella, Luciana (BRA)	31/12/69
Salvi, Cristina (ITA)	15/05/70	Temesvari Trunkos, Andrea (HUN)	26/04/66
Sampras, Stella (USA)	09/03/69	Tessi, Cristina (ARG)	20/07/72
Sanchez-Vicario, Arantxa (ESP)	18/12/71	Testud, Sandrine (FRA)	03/04/72
Sangaram, Benjamas (THA)	11/01/75	Thoms, Heike (GER)	01/11/61
Santrock, Jennifer (USA)	26/02/69	Thoren, Petra (FIN)	08/08/69
Savchenko Neiland, Larisa (CIS)	21/07/66	Toleafoa, Claudine (NZL)	28/02/70
Savoldi, Elena (ITA)	11/11/72	Tschan, Natalie (SUI)	13/10/71
Sawamatsu, Naoko (JPN)	23/03/73	Van De Zande, Daphne (BEL)	21/07/74
Schett, Barbara (AUT)	10/03/76	Van Lottum, Noelle (FRA)	12/07/72
Schultz, Brenda (HOL)	28/12/70	Van Rensburg, Dinky (RSA)	04/03/68
Schwartz, Amy (USA)	02/09/69	Vento, Ma. Alejandra (VEN)	24/05/74
Segura, Ana (ESP)	05/02/69	Vieira, Andrea (BRA)	05/02/71
Seles, Monica (YUG)	02/12/73	Viqueira, Emilie (USA)	21/03/69
Serra Zanetti, Adriana (ITA)	05/03/76	Wang, Shi-Ting (TPE)	19/10/73
Sharpe, Kirrily (AUS)	25/02/73	Wasserman, Sandra (BEL)	10/03/70
Shiflet, Julie (USA)	07/10/72	Watanabe, Jolene (USA)	31/08/68
Shriver, Pam (USA)	04/07/62	Webb, Vanessa (CAN)	24/01/76
Siddall, Shirli-Ann (GBR)	20/06/74	Weerasuriya, Lihini (SRI)	20/02/72
Simpson Alter, Rene (CAN)	14/01/66	Wegink, Claire (NED)	29/09/67
Sloane Lundy, Susan (USA)	05/12/70	Werdel, Marianne (USA)	17/10/67
Smashnova, Anna (ISR)	16/07/76	White, Robin (USA)	10/12/63
Smith, Samantha (GBR)	27/11/71	Whitlinger, Tami (USA)	13/11/68
Smylie, Elizabeth (AUS)	11/04/63	Whitlinger, Teri (USA)	13/11/68
Spadea, Luanne (USA)	28/12/72	Whittington, Tammy (USA)	12/10/65
Spirlea, Irina (ROM)	26/03/74	Wiesner, Judith (AUT)	02/03/66
Sprung, Heidi (AUT)	10/01/69	Wood, Clare (GBR)	08/03/68
Stacey, Louise (AUS)	10/01/72	Wuillot, Caroline (BEL)	02/07/71
Stafford, Shaun (USA)	13/12/68	Yazawa, Kiyoko (JPN)	08/08/72
Steven, Julie (USA)	24/04/76	Yokobori, Miki (JPN)	13/05/75
Strandlund, Maria (SWE)	17/08/69	Zardo, Emanuela (SUI)	24/04/70
Strnadova, Andrea (TCH)	28/05/72	Zivec Skulj, Maja (GER)	25/09/73
Stubbs, Rennae (AUS)	26/03/71	Zrubakova, Radka (TCH)	26/12/70
Sugiyama, Ai (JPN)	05/07/75	Zugasti, Agnes (FRA)	15/05/72
Suire, Catherine (FRA)	15/09/59	Zvereva, Natalia (CIS)	16/04/71
Sukova, Helena (TCH)	23/02/65		

KRAFT WORLD TOUR

Tournaments with prize money of $225,000 and above

NSW OPEN TOURNAMENT OF CHAMPIONS ($225,000)
SYDNEY, 6–12 JANUARY

WOMEN'S SINGLES – 1st round: G. Sabatini (1) – bye; M. Bollegraf d. P. Shriver 7–5 2–6 7–5; S. Hack d. L. Harvey-Wild 6–3 6–4; L. McNeil (12) d. B. Schultz 3–6 6–3 6–4; G. Fernandez (15) d. P. Thoren (Q) 6–2 4–6 6–1; R. McQuillan d. A. Minter 6–1 6–4; A. Kijimuta d. K. Godridge 7–6 6–1; Z. Garrison Jackson (7) – bye; M.J. Fernandez (4) – bye; C. Cunningham d. M. Jaggard (Q) 6–3 6–0; D. Graham d. H. Cioffi (Q) 4–6 6–4 6–3; H. Sukova (10) d. G. Helgeson 7–5 6–1; K. Date d. N. Zvereva (14) 7–5 6–1; N. Provis d. F. Labat 1–6 7–6 6–1; A. Dechaume d. J. Durie 6–4 6–1; L. Meskhi (9) – bye; A. Huber (8) – bye; I. Demongeot d. H. Kelesi 6–3 7–6; T. Whitlinger d. R. Rajchrtova 6–1 1–0 ret.; S. Appelmans (11) d. R. Stubbs 6–4 4–6 6–1; J. Halard (13) d. E. Sviglerova 6–4 5–7 6–4; L. Savchenko Neiland d. M. Werdel 6–3 1–6 7–6; P. Fendick d. S. Rehe (Q) 7–5 6–4; J. Novotna (3) – bye; C. Martinez (5) – bye; E. Zardo d. S. Stafford (Q) 3–6 7–5 6–3; N. Muns Jagerman d. K. Po (Q) 6–3 6–1; A. Frazier d. B. Paulus 6–0 6–2; R. Zrubakova (16) d. C. Wood (Q) 1–6 6–4 6–3; B. Rittner d. J. Byrne (Q) 7–5 7–5; A. Strnadova d. P. Hy 6–1 4–6 6–3; A. Sanchez-Vicario (2) – bye.

2nd round: Sabatini (1) d. Bollegraf 6–0 6–1; Hack d. McNeil (12) 7–6 3–6 6–3; Fernandez (15) d. McQuillan 6–1 7–5; Garrison Jackson (7) d. Kijimuta 6–4 3–6 6–2; Fernandez (4) d. Cunningham 7–5 6–3; Sukova (10) d. Graham 7–5 6–4; Date d. Provis 6–4 6–0; Meskhi (9) d. Dechaume 6–3 6–4; Huber (8) d. Demongeot 7–5 6–1; Whitlinger d. Appelmans (11) 6–1 6–3; Halard (13) d. Savchenko Neiland 7–6 6–1; Novotna (3) d. Fendick 7–6 2–1 ret.; Martinez (5) d. Zardo 2–6 6–4 6–2; Frazier d. Muns Jagerman 6–4 7–6; Rittner d. Zrubakova (16) 6–2 3–6 6–3; Sanchez-Vicario (2) d. Strnadova 7–6 6–3.

3rd round: Sabatini (1) d. Hack 6–1 6–0; Fernandez (15) d. Garrison Jackson (7) 7–6 5–7 6–3; Fernandez (4) d. Sukova (10) 6–4 6–4; Meskhi (9) d. Date 4–6 6–3 6–2; Huber (8) d. Whitlinger 6–3 6–4; Novotna (3) d. Halard (13) 6–2 7–5; Martinez (5) d. Frazier 6–4 6–4; Sanchez-Vicario (2) d. Rittner 7–5 6–0.

Quarter-finals: Sabatini (1) d. Fernandez (15) 6–2 7–6; Fernandez (4) d. Meskhi (9) 6–1 6–2; Huber (8) d. Novotna (3) 6–3 7–5; Sanchez-Vicario (2) d. Martinez (5) 6–4 6–2.

Semi-finals: Sabatini (1) d. Fernandez (4) 6–2 6–3; Sanchez-Vicario (2) d. Huber (8) 4–6 7–5 6–3.

Final: Sabatini (1) d. Sanchez-Vicario (2) 6–1 6–1.

WOMEN'S DOUBLES – Final: Sanchez-Vicario/Sukova (4) d. Fernandez/Garrison Jackson (5) 7–6 6–7 6–2.

TORAY PAN PACIFIC OPEN ($350,000)
TOKYO, 28 JANUARY–2 FEBRUARY

WOMEN'S SINGLES – 1st round: G. Sabatini (1) – bye; M. Endo (Q) d. J. Durie 6–4 6–1; P. Shriver d. C. Cunningham 6–3 6–2; L. McNeil (6) d. K. Habsudova 7–5 6–3; A. Sanchez-Vicario (3) – bye; R. McQuillan d. K. Okamoto (Q) 7–6 6–4; K. Date d. P. Fendick 6–3 6–1; R. Stubbs (Q) d. N. Zvereva (7) 6–4 7–6; H. Sukova (5) d. E. Sviglerova 6–0 6–3; S. Wang d. A. Minter 6–2 7–5; M. Maleeva d. B. Schultz 7–6 6–4; J. Capriati (4) – bye; L. Gildemeister (8) d. P. Harper 6–1 7–5; A. Kijimuta d. R. Hiraki (LL) 0–6 6–0 6–3; Y. Basuki d. M. Yokobori (Q) 0–6 6–0 6–3; M. Navratilova (2) – bye.

2nd round: Sabatini (1) d. Endo (Q) 6–2 7–6; Shriver d. McNeil (6) 6–4 6–1; Sanchez-Vicario (3) d. McQuillan 3–6 6–3 6–2; Date d. Stubbs (Q) 7–5 6–1; Sukova (5) d. Wang 7–5 6–4; Maleeva d. Capriati (4) 6–1 6–2; Gildemeister (8) d. Kijimuta 6–1 6–4; Navratilova (2) d. Basuki 6–0 7–5.

Quarter-finals: Sabatini (1) d. Shriver 6–2 6–7 6–4; Date d. Sanchez-Vicario (3) 6–3 6–4; Maleeva d. Sukova (5) 6–2 6–4; Navratilova (2) d. Gildemeister (8) 6–4 6–3.

Semi-finals: Sabatini (1) d. Date 6–3 6–0; Navratilova (2) d. Maleeva 6–2 6–2.

Final: Sabatini (1) d. Navratilova (2) 6–2 4–6 6–2.

WOMEN'S DOUBLES – Final: Sanchez-Vicario/Sukova (2) d. Navratilova/Shriver (1) 7–5 6–1.

NOKIA GRAND PRIX ($350,000)
ESSEN, 3–9 FEBRUARY

WOMEN'S SINGLES – 1st round: M. Seles (1) – bye; A. Kerek (Q) d. L. Garrone 2–6 6–3 7–6; C. Tanvier d. S. Meier (Q) 6–5 6–3; C. Lindqvist (8) d. C. Suire 5–7 6–3 6–2; K. Maleeva (3) – bye; W. Probst d. S. Frankl 6–4 6–2; M. Oremans (Q) d. M. Kochta 6–3 6–1; M. Pierce (6) d. P Langrova 6–3 6–1; B.

Turning 36 last year, Martina Navratilova was as hungry for titles as ever and her four successes lifted her past Chris Evert's 157 wins to a record 161 tournament titles. (M. Cole)

Rittner d. S. Cecchini (7) 6–2 6–4; P. Paradis Magnon d. V. Milvidskaia (Q) 6–0 5–7 6–3; C. Kohde-Kilsch d. P. Kamstra 6–4 6–3; A. Huber (4) – bye; S. Appelmans (5) d. E. Pfaff 6–4 7–5; K. Nowak (LL) d. P. Ritter 6–7 7–6 6–1; C. Porwik d. N. Herreman 7–5 6–3; M.J. Fernandez (2) – bye.
2nd round: Seles (1) d. Kerek 6–2 6–2; Lindqvist (8) d. Tanvier 6–1 6–4; Maleeva (3) d. Probst 6–3 7–6; Pierce (6) d. Oremans 6–4 6–3; Rittner d. Paradis Magnon 6–3 7–6; Huber (4) d. Kohde-Kilsch 6–1 6–1; Appelmans (5) d. Nowak (LL) 4–6 6–4 6–1; Fernandez (2) d. Porwik 6–3 6–3.
3rd round: Seles (1) d. Lindqvist (8) 6–3 6–2; Pierce (6) d. Maleeva (3) 6–3 7–5; Rittner d. Huber (4) 4–6 3–1 ret; Fernandez (2) d. Appelmans 6–4 6–4.
Semi-finals: Seles (1) d. Pierce (6) 6–0 6–1; Fernandez (2) d. Rittner 7–5 6–4.
Final: Seles (1) d. Fernandez (2) 6–0 6–3.
WOMEN'S DOUBLES – **Final**: Maleeva/Rittner d. Appelmans/Porwik (1) 7–5 6–3.

VIRGINIA SLIMS OF CHICAGO ($350,000)
CHICAGO, 10–16 FEBRUARY
WOMEN'S SINGLES – 1st round: S. Graf (1) – bye; R. Hiraki d. A. Minter 3–6 6–1 6–4; M. Bollegraf d. M. de Swardt 6–1 6–2; R. Fairbank Nideffer d. G. Fernandez (5) 6–4 6–4; J. Novotna (3) – bye; M. Werdel d. A. Keller 6–4 6–1; D. Graham d. L. Weerasuriya 6–2 6–1; A. Frazier (7) d. P. Hy 0–1 ret; L. McNeil (6) d. E. Reinach 6–4 6–2; G. Helgeson d. K. Adams 3–6 6–3 6–4; L. Harvey-Wild d. T Whitlinger 6–1 6–2; Z. Garrison Jackson (4) – bye; P. Shriver (8) d. P. Harper 6–2 6–2; N. Provis d. R. White 6–1 4–6 6–1; H. Cioffi d. S. Jeyaseelan 6–2 6–1; M. Navratilova (2) – bye.
2nd round: Graf (1) d. Hiraki 6–0 6–0; Bollegraf d. Fairbank Nideffer 3–6 7–6 6–3; Novotna (3) d. Werdel 6–2 6–1; Frazier (7) d. Graham 4–6 6–4 6–1; McNeil (6) d. Helgeson 7–5 6–7 6–2; Garrison Jackson (4) d. Harvey-Wild 6–4 7–6; Shriver (8) d. Provis 6–0 6–1; Navratilova (2) d. Cioffi 6–0 6–0.
3rd round: Graf (1) d. Bollegraf 6–2 6–1; Novotna (3) d. Frazier (7) 7–6 6–1; McNeil (6) d. Garrison Jackson (4) 6–1 6–3; Navratilova (2) d. Shriver (8) 7–6 7–6.
Semi-finals: Novotna (3) d. Graf (1) 0–6 6–3 7–5; Navratilova (2) d. McNeil (6) 1–6 6–4 6–4.
Final: Navratilova (2) d. Novotna (3) 7–6 4–6 7–5.
WOMEN'S DOUBLES – **Final**: Navratilova/Shriver (1) d. K. Adams/Garrison Jackson (2) 6–4 7–6.

MATRIX ESSENTIALS EVERT CUP ($350,000)
INDIAN WELLS, 24 FEBRUARY–1 MARCH
WOMEN'S SINGLES – 1st round: M. Seles (1) – bye; E. Reinach d. K. Po 7–5 5–7 6–0; J. Watanabe (Q) d. C. Toleafoa (Q) 6–1 6–3; T. Whitlinger d. G. Magers 6–3 6–1; G. Helgeson d. R. White (16) 6–1 1–6 6–3; P. Nelson (WC) d. K. Godridge 7–6 6–1; K. Dreyer (Q) d. M. de Swardt 6–1 1–6 7–6; G. Fernandez (7) – bye; K. Maleeva (4) – bye; J. Emmons (Q) d. P. Kamstra 6–3 6–0; A. Coetzer d. A. Henricksson 6–4 6–1; D. Graham (13) d. R. Stubbs (Q) 3–6 6–4 6–1; Y. Basuki (11) d. M. Kidowaki 6–4 6–1; A. Dechaume d. N. Hummell (WC) 6–3 6–1; R. Simpson Alter d. R. Hiraki 6–3 6–1; N. Tauziat (5) – bye; J. Wiesner (6) – bye; R. Fairbank Nideffer d. N. van Lottum 6–3 6–3; A. Gavaldon (Q) d. J. Durie 6–2 6–7 7–5; H. Kelesi (14) d. A. Keller 6–0 6–7 6–2; N. Provis (12) d. I. Demongeot 6–3 6–3; L. Harvey-Wild d. Cam. MacGregor (LL) 4–6 6–2 6–2; S. Rehe d. S. Sloane Lundy 6–1 6–1; C. Martinez (3) – bye; A. Frazier (8) – bye; J. Santrock (Q) d. M. L. Daniels 4–6 6–2 7–6; C. Kohde-Kilsch d. H. Ludloff (LL) 4–6 6–3 7–5; P. Shriver (10) d. P. Harper 6–4 6–1; C. Lindqvist (15) d. M. Javer 6–2 2–6 6–3; A. Grossman d. A. Kijimuta 7–6 6–0; K. Rinaldi d. C. Wood (Q) 6–4 0–6 6–1; V. Milvidskaia (LL) – bye.
2nd round: Seles (1) d. Reinach 6–1 6–1; Whitlinger d. Watanabe (Q) 2–6 6–1 7–5; Helgeson d. Nelson (WC) 6–1 6–3; Fernandez (7) d. Dreyer (Q) 6–3 6–0; Maleeva (4) d. Emmons (Q) 6–2 6–0; Coetzer d. Graham (13) 4–6 6–0 6–0; Dechaume d. Basuki (11) 7–5 4–6 6–2; Tauziat (5) d. Simpson Alter 6–1 6–2; Wiesner (6) d. Fairbank Nideffer 6–2 6–2; Kelesi (14) d. Gavaldon (Q) 6–3 6–0; Provis (12) d. Harvey-Wild 6–7 6–3 6–3; Martinez (3) d. Rehe 6–4 7–6; Frazier (8) d. Santrock (Q) 6–4 6–2; Shriver (10) d. Kohde-Kilsch 6–3 5–7 6–3; Grossman d. Lindqvist (15) 6–2 6–4; Rinaldi d. Milvidskaia (LL) 6–4 7–5.
3rd round: Seles (1) d. Whitlinger 6–2 6–3; Fernandez (7) d. Helgeson 6–4 6–3; Maleeva (4) d. Coetzer 6–2 6–2; Tauziat (5) d. Dechaume 7–6 3–6 6–3; Wiesner (6) d. Kelesi (14) 5–7 7–6 6–2; Martinez (3) d. Provis (12) 6–2 6–2; Frazier (8) d. Shriver (10) 6–2 6–2; Grossman d. Rinaldi 6–1 7–5.
Quarter-finals: Seles (1) d. Fernandez (7) 6–0 6–0; Maleeva (4) d. Tauziat (5) 4–6 6–4 7–5; Martinez (3) d. Wiesner (6) 6–3 6–1; Grossman d. Frazier (8) 6–4 5–7 6–4.
Semi-finals: Seles (1) d. Maleeva (4) 6–1 6–0; Martinez (3) d. Grossman 6–3 6–1.
Final: Seles (1) d. Martinez (3) 6–3 6–1.
WOMEN'S DOUBLES – **Final**: Kohde-Kilsch/Rehe (4) d. J. Hetherington/Rinaldi (3) 6–3 6–3.

VIRGINIA SLIMS OF FLORIDA ($550,000)
BOCA RATON, 2–8 MARCH
WOMEN'S SINGLES – 1st round: S. Graf (1) – bye; L. Ferrando d. S. Stafford (Q) 6–3 6–4; P. Thoren d. L. Savchenko Neiland 6–2 6–1; N. Sawamatsu (14) d. Y. Basuki 6–3 6–2; B. Schultz (15) d. M. Babel

(Q) 6–2 6–1; A. Dechaume d. A. Mueller (Q) 6–1 6–2; M. Kidowaki d. L. Harvey-Wild 6–4 6–4; Z. Garrison Jackson (7) – bye; M. J. Fernandez (3) – bye; Cam. MacGregor (Q) d. I. Demongeot 6–2 6–4; D. Faber (Q) d. G. Helgeson 6–1 6–7 7–5; L. Gildemeister (10) d. J. Emmons (Q) 6–2 6–4; R. Zrubakova (12) d. B. Fulco Villella 7–6 6–1; P. Langrova d. A. Kijimuta 6–4 5–7 6–4; H. Kelesi d. K. Piccolini 6–1 6–4; N. Tauziat (5) – bye; L. Meskhi (6) – bye; S. Gomer d. C. Wood (LL) 7–6 6–2; A. Grunfeld (LL) d. S. Farina 6–3 6–4; B. Rittner (16) d. N. Arendt (Q) 6–4 6–4; K. Date (11) d. C. Bassett Seguso (WC) 6–2 6–1; L. Raymond (WC) d. P. Harper 6–3 6–1; E. Sviglerova d. K. Godridge 7–6 6–4; C. Martinez (4) – bye; J. Wiesner (8) – bye; N. Medvedeva d. E. Reinach 7–6 6–1; A. Coetzer d. S. Rottier (Q) 6–2 6–2; N. Baudone (LL) d. M. Werdel 6–4 7–5; C. Rubin d. N. Zvereva (13) 1–6 6–4 6–0; H. Cioffi d. M. Jackson Nobrega (WC) 6–4 7–5; J. Durie d. R. Rajchrtova 6–3 7–6; G. Sabatini (2) – bye;
2nd round: Graf (1) d. Ferrando 6–1 6–2; Sawamatsu (14) d. Thoren 7–6 6–4; Schultz (15) d. Dechaume 6–2 2–6 6–2; Garrison Jackson (7) d. Kidowaki 6–0 6–1; Fernandez (3) d. MacGregor (Q) 6–4 6–1; Gildemeister (10) d. Faber (Q) 7–6 6–4; Zrubakova (12) d. Langrova 6–2 6–0; Tauziat (5) d. Kelesi 3–6 6–1 6–4; Meskhi (6) d. Gomer 6–2 6–0; Rittner (16) d. Grunfeld (LL) 6–1 6–3; Date (11) d. Raymond (WC) 7–5 6–3; Martinez (4) d. Sviglerova 6–3 6–1; Wiesner (8) d. Medvedeva 3–6 6–4 7–6; Coetzer d. Baudone (LL) 6–3 6–4; Rubin d. Cioffi 4–6 6–1 6–4; Sabatini (2) d. Durie 6–2 6–0.
3rd round: Graf (1) d. Sawamatsu (14) 6–0 6–1; Garrison Jackson (7) d. Schultz (15) 7–5 4–6 6–3; Fernandez (3) d. Gildemeister (10) 6–3 7–5; Tauziat (5) d. Zrubakova (12) 6–2 7–6; Rittner (16) d. Meskhi (6) 6–2 6–3; Martinez (4) d. Date (11) 6–1 7–6; Coetzer d. Wiesner (8) 6–3 6–1; Sabatini (2) d. Rubin 6–2 6–2.
Quarter-finals: Graf (1) d. Garrison Jackson (7) 6–0 5–7 7–5; Fernandez (3) d. Tauziat (5) 6–4 6–2; Martinez (4) d. Rittner (16) 6–1 6–0; Coetzer d. Sabatini (2) 4–6 6–1 6–2.
Semi-finals: Graf (1) d. Fernandez (3) 6–0 7–5; Martinez (4) d. Coetzer 4–6 6–3 6–0.
Final: Graf (1) d. Martinez (4) 3–6 6–2 6–0.
WOMEN'S DOUBLES – *Final*: Savchenko Neiland/Zvereva (1) d. L. Harvey-Wild/Martinez 6–2 6–2.

LIPTON INTERNATIONAL PLAYERS CHAMPIONSHIPS ($800,000)
KEY BISCAYNE, 13–22 MARCH
WOMEN'S SINGLES – *1st round*: M. Seles (1) – bye; C. Benjamin (Q) d. M. Babel 6–4 7–5; L. Savchenko Neiland d. M. Kidowaki 6–1 6–0; T. Whitlinger (30) – bye; R. Zrubakova (17) – bye; M. Oremans (WC) d. H. Kelesi 6–3 2–6 6–4; D. Faber d. M. Daniels (WC) 7–5 6–0; J. Wiesner (11) – bye; Z. Garrison Jackson (9) – bye; P. Paradis Magnon d. L. Ferrando 7–5 6–0; S. Rehe (WC) d. S. Gomer 7–5 6–4; M. Sawamatsu (21) – bye; K. Habsudova (28) – bye; K. Rinaldi (WC) d. K. Piccolini 3–6 6–3 6–3; K. Godridge d. N. Hummell (Q) 6–4 6–4; J. Capriati (5) – bye; A. Sanchez-Vicario (4) – bye; L. Davenport d. M. Drake (Q) 2–6 6–3 6–2; G. Helgeson d. J. Durie 7–6 6–0; Y. Basuki (24) – bye; B. Rittner (20) – bye; B. Fulco Villella d. C. Rubin 6–1 6–2; C. Kuhlman (Q) d. E. de Lone 6–1 6–2; L. McNeil (13) – bye; L. Gildemeister (15) – bye; S. Farina d. G. Magers (WC) 4–6 6–2 6–3; F. Labat d. H. Cioffi 6–2 6–3; C. Lindqvist (32) – bye; D. Graham (25) – bye; A. Coetzer d. C. Bassett–Seguso (Q) 6–4 6–4; P. Langrova d. E. Sviglerova 6–1 6–0; L. Meskhi (7) – bye; N. Tauziat (8) – bye; J. Thoren d. E. Maniokova 2–6 6–0 6–1; P. Tarabini d. M. Bollegraf 6–3 6–3; N. Medvedeva (27) – bye; P. Shriver (23) – bye; N. Van Lottum d. R. Hiraki 6–0 7–5; S. Hack d. M. Kochta 6–4 6–2; A. Frazier (14) – bye; M. Pierce (10) – bye; E. Reinach d. K. Quentrec 3–6 6–4 3–1 ret.; A. Keller d. A. Dechaume 6–3 7–6; B. Schultz (22) – bye; R. White (31) – bye; R. Fairbank Nideffer d. I. Demongeot 6–7 7–6 6–3; K. Adams d. M. Paz 6–3 6–3; G. Sabatini (3) – bye; M. Fernandez (6) – bye; N. Herreman (Q) d. A. Kijimuta 6–2 6–4; S. Stafford (WC) d. M. McGrath (WC) 6–1 6–3; N. Zvereva (18) – bye; A. Strnadova (29) – bye; R. Stubbs d. K. Nagatsuka (Q) 7–5 7–5; K. Po d. C. Suire 7–6 3–6 6–2; G. Fernandez (12) – bye; K. Date (16) – bye; L. Harvey-Wild d. C. Porwik 6–3 6–3; C. Cunningham d. R. Rajchrtova 6–0 6–0; M. Werdel (26) – bye; S. Cecchini (19) – bye; N. Reggi Concato d. P. Harper 4–6 6–4 6–2; W. Probst (Q) d. E. Brioukhovets 6–2 6–2; S. Graf (2) – bye.
2nd round: Seles (1) d. Benjamin (Q) 6–1 6–3; Savchenko Neiland d. Whitlinger (30) 6–2 6–3; Zrubakova (17) d. Oremans (WC) 6–1 6–1; Wiesner (11) d. Faber 6–4 6–3; Garrison Jackson (9) d. Paradis Magnon 6–3 6–4; Sawamatsu (21) d. Rehe (WC) 6–2 6–7 6–1; Habsudova (28) d. Rinaldi (WC) 3–6 6–1 6–2; Capriati (5) d. Godridge 6–3 7–5; Sanchez-Vicario (4) d. Davenport 6–4 6–4; Helgeson d. Basuki (24) 7–5 6–4; Rittner (20) d. Fulco Villella 6–1 6–3; McNeil (13) d. Kuhlman (Q) 6–4 4–6 6–2; Farina d. Gildemeister (15) 6–3 6–7 6–4; Labat d. Lindqvist (32) 6–2 6–0; Coetzer d. Graham (25) 6–2 6–4; Meskhi (7) d. Langrova 6–7 6–1 6–2; Tauziat (8) d. Thoren 7–5 7–5; Medvedeva (27) d. Tarabini 6–2 6–0; Shriver (23) d. Van Lottum 6–3 6–3; Frazier (14) d. Hack 6–2 7–5; Pierce (10) d. Reinach 0–6 6–3 6–3; Schultz (22) d. Keller 6–2 7–6; Fairbank Nideffer d. White (31) 6–4 6–1; Sabatini (3) d. Adams 6–2 6–3; M. Fernandez (6) d. Herreman (Q) 7–5 6–2; Zvereva (18) d. Stafford (Q) 3–6 7–5 6–1; Strnadova (29) d. Stubbs 6–4 7–6; Fernandez (12) d. Po 6–4 3–6 6–3; Date (16) d. Harvey-Wild 6–2 3–6 6–3; Cunningham d. Werdel (26) 7–5 6–2; Reggi Concato d. Cecchini (19) 6–0 6–4; Graf (2) d. Probst (Q) 6–3 6–1.
3rd round: Seles (1) d. Savchenko Neiland 6–0 6–4; Zrubakova (17) d. Wiesner (11) 7–6 6–4; Garrison Jackson (9) d. Sawamatsu (21) 6–4 6–0; Capriati (5) d. Habsudova (28) 6–3 6–1; Sanchez-Vicario (4) d. Helgeson 6–2 6–2; Rittner (20) d. McNeil (13) 7–6 4–6 6–3; Labat d. Farina 7–5 6–1; Coetzer d. Meskhi (7) 6–3 4–1 ret.; Tauziat (8) d. Medvedeva (27) 6–4 6–2; Frazier (14) d. Shriver (23) 6–2 6–0; Schultz (22)

d. Pierce (10) 7–6 1–6 4–0 ret.; Sabatini (3) d. Fairbank Nideffer 6–2 6–0; M. Fernandez (6) d. Zvereva (18) 6–4 6–4; G. Fernandez (12) d. Strnadova (29) 6–4 3–6 7–5; Date (16) d. Cunningham 3–6 6–1 6–1; Graf (2) d. Reggi Concato 6–2 6–2.

4th round: Seles (1) d. Zrubakova (17) 6–1 6–2; Capriati (5) d. Garrison Jackson (9) 5–7 6–4 6–3; Sanchez-Vicario (4) d. Rittner (20) 6–1 2–1 ret.; Coetzer d. Labat 6–2 3–6 6–2; Frazier (14) d. Tauziat (8) 6–4 7–6; Sabatini (3) d. Schultz (22) 6–1 6–7 6–0; M. Fernandez (6) d. G. Fernandez (12) 6–2 7–5; Graf (2) d. Date (16) 7–6 5–7 6–4.

Quarter-finals: Capriati (5) d. Seles (1) 6–2 7–6; Sanchez-Vicario (4) d. Coetzer 6–1 6–4; Sabatini (3) d. Frazier (14) 6–0 6–1; Graf (2) d. M. Fernandez (6) 7–6 6–4.

Semi-finals: Sanchez-Vicario (4) d. Capriati (5) 6–2 6–4; Sabatini (3) d. Graf (2) 3–6 7–6 6–1.

Final: Sanchez-Vicario (4) d. Sabatini (3) 6–1 6–4.

WOMEN'S DOUBLES – Final: Sanchez-Vicario/Savchenko Neiland (1) d. Hetherington/Rinaldi (5) 7–5 5–7 6–3.

ACURA U.S. HARDCOURT CHAMPIONSHIPS ($225,000)
SAN ANTONIO, 23–29 MARCH

WOMEN'S SINGLES – 1st round: M. Navratilova (1) – bye; L. Allen (LL) d. A. Strnadova (LL) 6–2 6–2; M. Babel (Q) d. P. Harper 6–3 6–7 6–4; R. Reggi Concato d. J. Halard (5) 7–6 6–0; L. McNeil (4) – bye; N. Baudone (Q) d. M. Kochta 6–7 7–5 6–3; M. Javer d. A. Keller 6–2 6–2; P. Shriver (8) d. S. Rehe (WC) 7–6 3–6 7–5; A. Frazier (6) d. C. Benjamin (Q) 4–6 6–0 6–1; C. Rubin d. J. Watanabe (Q) 7–6 6–1; B. Bowes (LL) d. P. Thoren 4–6 6–4 6–4; K. Habsudova – bye; N. Medvedeva d. B. Rittner (7) 7–6 6–2; E. Maniokova d. J. Emmons (WC) 6–3 6–3; P. Fendick d. C. Porwik 7–5 6–3; N. Tauziat (2) – bye.

2nd round: Navratilova (1) d. Lou. Allen (LL) 6–1 6–1; Reggi Concato d. M. Babel (Q) 6–1 6–0; McNeil (4) d. Baudone (Q) 6–1 6–3; Shriver (8) d. Javer 6–2 6–2; Frazier (6) d. Rubin 7–5 3–6 6–1; Habsudova d. Bowes (LL) 6–4 6–3; Maniokova d. Medvedeva 7–6 6–4; Tauziat (2) d. Fendick 7–6 6–3.

Quarter-finals: Navratilova (1) d. Reggi Concato 6–0 6–1; Shriver (8) d. McNeil 6–7 6–2 7–6; Frazier (6) d. Habsudova 6–4 6–2; Tauziat (2) d. Maniokova 6–1 6–3.

Semi-finals: Navratilova (1) d. Shriver (8) 6–4 6–3; Tauziat (2) d. Frazier (6) 4–6 7–6 6–4.

Final: Navratilova (1) d. Tauziat (2) 6–2 6–1.

WOMEN'S DOUBLES – Final: Navratilova/Shriver (1) d. Fendick/Strnadova () 3–6 6–2 7–6.

FAMILY CIRCLE MAGAZINE CUP ($550,000)
HILTON HEAD ISLAND, 30 MARCH–5 APRIL

WOMEN'S SINGLES – 1st round: G. Sabatini (1) – bye; H. Cioffi d. Fed. Bonsignori 6–0 6–2; T. Whitlinger d. K. Nowak 6–4 7–5; A. Coetzer (14) d. A. Kerek (Q) 6–3 6–2; Mag. Maleeva (11) d. R. Jensen (Q) 6–1 6–1; P. Hy d. L. Ferrando 6–4 6–4; P. Tarabini d. E. Maniokova 6–1 6–3; J. Novotna (6) – bye; J. Capriati (4) – bye; V. Martinek d. D. Szabova (Q) 6–1 6–0; S. Martin (WC) d. H. Kelesi 4–0 ret.; B. Schultz (12) d. R. Fairbank Nideffer 7–6 3–6 6–3; S. Frankl d. G. Fernandez (9) 6–7 6–2 6–1; P. Ritter d. S. Meier (Q) 6–3 7–6; C. Kuhlman (Q) d. F. Labat 2–6 6–2 6–3; Z. Garrison Jackson (8) – bye; L. Meskhi (7) – bye; A. Keller d. C. O'Reilly (Q) 5–7 6–1 6–3; A. Grossman d. M. Paz 6–2 2–6 6–2; D. Graham (16) d. L. Garrone 6–3 6–4; I. Gorrochategui d. P. Fendick (15) 7–5 6–3; A. Temesvari (Q) d. E. Brioukhovets 6–0 6–2; S. Hack d. B. Bowes (LL) 6–3 6–1; A. Sanchez-Vicario (3) – bye; C. Martinez (5) – bye; M. L. Daniels d. G. Helgeson 6–1 6–4; C. Kohde-Kilsch d. B. Fulco Villella 6–4 6–4; S. Cecchini (13) d. K. Adams 6–2 6–0; N. Zvereva (10) d. J. Shiflet (Q) 7–6 6–1; S. Stafford d. S. Collins (WC) 6–2 6–1; D. Faber d. L. Harvey-Wild 6–4 3–6 6–2; M. Navratilova (2) – bye.

2nd round: Sabatini (1) d. Cioffi 6–0 6–0; Coetzer (14) d. Whitlinger 6–3 6–4; Hy d. Maleeva (11) 3–6 6–3 6–2; Novotna d. Tarabini 6–4 2–6 6–4; Martinek d. Capriati (4) 6–4 1–6 6–4; Schultz (12) d. Martin (WC) 6–4 6–2; Ritter d. Frankl 6–3 6–3; Kuhlman (Q) d. Garrison Jackson (8) 4–6 6–2 6–3; Meskhi (7) d. Keller 6–1 6–2; Graham (16) d. Grossman 3–6 6–2 6–3; Gorrochategui d. A. Temesvari (Q) 2–6 6–3 7–5; Sanchez-Vicario (3) d. Hack 6–4 6–2; Martinez (5) d. Daniels 6–0 6–1; Cecchini (13) d. Kohde-Kilsch 6–4 6–1; Zvereva (10) d. Stafford 6–1 6–1; Navratilova (2) d. Faber 6–0 6–2.

3rd round: Sabatini (1) d. Coetzer (14) 7–5 6–4; Hy d. Novotna (6) 6–3 3–6 6–1; Schultz (12) d. Martinek 6–2 6–2; Kuhlman (Q) d. Ritter 6–2 7–5; Meskhi (7) d. Graham (16) 3–6 6–2 7–5; Sanchez-Vicario (3) d. Gorrochategui 6–2 6–1; Martinez (5) d. Cecchini (13) 6–1 6–2; Zvereva (10) d. Navratilova 6–4 6–2.

Quarter-finals: Sabatini (1) d. Hy 6–2 6–3; Schultz (12) d. Kuhlman (Q) 6–3 6–1; Sanchez-Vicario (3) d. Meskhi (7) 6–3 6–3; Martinez (5) d. Zvereva (10) 6–2 6–2.

Semi-finals: Sabatini (1) d. Schultz (12) 6–3 6–2; Martinez (5) d. Sanchez-Vicario (3) 6–4 7–5.

Final: Sabatini (1) d. Martinez (5) 6–1 6–4.

WOMEN'S DOUBLES – Final: Sanchez-Vicario/Zvereva (2) d. Novotna/Savchenko Neiland (1) 6–4 6–2.

BAUSCH & LOMB CHAMPIONSHIPS ($350,000)
AMELIA ISLAND, 6–12 APRIL

WOMEN'S SINGLES – 1st round: S. Graf (1) – bye; S. Meier d. B. Fulco Villella 7–6 6–0; F. Labat d. D.

Szabova 4–6 6–1 6–3; B. Schultz (10) d. M. Paz 6–1 6–2; P. Fendick (12) d. E. Burgin (Q) 6–1 4–6 6–2; P. Tarabini d. Cam. MacGregor (LL) 6–3 6–3; B. Bowes d. D. Faber 6–2 6–0; L. Meskhi (7) – bye; A. Sanchez-Vicario (3) – bye; C. Kohde-Kilsch d. S. Stafford 6–4 7–6; T. Whittington d. R. Rajchrtova 6–3 1–6 7–5; I. Gorrochategui d. S. Martin (Q) 6–1 5–7 6–4; T. Whitlinger (14) d. Z. Malkova (Q) 6–1 6–0; S. Hack d. L. Allen 6–0 6–3; H. Cioffi d. M. Jackson Nobrega 6–2 4–6 7–6; K. Maleeva (6) – bye; Z. Garrison Jackson (8) – bye; S. Frankl d. E. Maniokova 7–6 1–6 7–5; C. Bassett Seguso (Q) L. Davenport (Q) 3–6 6–4 6–2; N. Zvereva (9) d. P. Ritter 6–4 7–6; S. Cecchini (11) d. C. Rubin 6–2 6–1; G. Helgeson d. E. Pampoulova Wagner 6–3 7–6; C. Papadaki (Q) d. V. Martinek 6–4 6–3; C. Martinez (4) – bye; J. Novotna (5) – bye; S. Niox–Chateau d. R. Jensen (Q) 6–0 6–2; P. Hy d. A. Keller 1–6 6–4 6–0; Fed. Bonsignori d. A. Temesvari 6–2 7–5; L. Garrone d. A. Grossman (16) 6–4 6–2; K. Rinaldi (WC) d. J. Santrock (Q) 6–2 6–1; L. Harvey-Wild d. R. Fairbank Nideffer 1–6 6–1 7–6; G. Sabatini (2) – bye.

2nd round: Graf (1) d. Meier 7–5 6–1; Schultz (10) d. Labat 1–6 6–3 7–5; Fendick (12) d. Tarabini 5–7 6–1 6–2; Meskhi (7) d. Bowes 6–2 6–4; Sanchez-Vicario (3) d. Kohde-Kilsch 6–2 6–2; Whittington 6–0 6–2; Hack d. Whitlinger (14) 6–0 6–3; Maleeva (6) d. Cioffi 6–4 6–1; Garrison Jackson (8) d. Frankl 7–5 6–3; Zvereva (9) d. Bassett Seguso (Q) 6–3 6–4; Cecchini (11) d. Helgeson 2–6 7–6 6–2; Martinez (4) d. Papadaki (Q) 6–0 6–3; Novotna (5) d. Niox–Chateau 6–7 6–1 6–1; Hy d. Bonsignori 2–6 6–0 6–4; Rinaldi (WC) d. Garrone 7–5 6–2; Sabatini (2) d. Harvey-Wild 6–3 7–5.

3rd round: Graf (1) d. Schultz (10) 6–2 6–2; Meskhi (7) d. Fendick (12) 6–2 6–2; Sanchez-Vicario (3) d. Gorrochategui 6–0 6–2; Hack d. Maleeva (6) 6–4 6–3; Garrison Jackson (8) d. Zvereva (9) 6–3 6–1; Martinez (4) d. Cecchini (11) 6–2 6–0; Novotna (5) d. Hy 6–1 2–1 ret.; Sabatini (2) d. Rinaldi (WC) 6–0 6–3.

Quarter-finals: Graf (1) d. Meskhi (7) 6–0 6–2; Sanchez-Vicario (3) d. Hack 6–1 6–2; Martinez (4) d. Garrison Jackson (8) 6–3 6–1; Sabatini (2) d. Novotna (5) 6–2 6–1.

Semi-finals: Graf (1) d. Sanchez-Vicario (3) 6–7 6–4 6–3; Sabatini (2) d. Martinez (4) 6–3 6–3.

Final: Sabatini (2) d. Graf (1) 6–2 1–6 6–3.

WOMEN'S DOUBLES – *Final*: Sanchez-Vicario/Zvereva (1) d. Garrison Jackson/Novotna (2) 6–1 6–0.

VIRGINIA SLIMS OF HOUSTON ($350,000)
HOUSTON, 13–19 APRIL

WOMEN'S SINGLES – *1st round*: M. Seles (1) – bye; M. Paz d. K. Adams 6–1 7–5; B. Fulco Villella d. A. Keller 6–3 6–0; Mag. Maleeva (8) d. Cam. MacGregor (Q) 6–3 6–2; G. Fernandez (4) – bye; C. Rubin d. L. Allen (Q) 6–7 6–3 6–3; H. Cioffi d. P. O'Reilly (Q) 6–1 6–2; L. Gildemeister (6) d. Fed. Bonsignori 6–2 6–0; L. McNeil (5) d. G. Magers (WC) 7–5 7–6; I. Majoli (WC) d. L. Davenport (LL) 6–3 6–4; E. Burgin (Q) d. J. Santrock (LL) 6–3 6–4; Z. Garrison Jackson (3) – bye; S. Cecchini (7) d. L. Harvey-Wild 3–6 6–3 6–3; S. Hack d. A. Gavaldon (LL) 6–3 6–3; R. Simpson Alter 7–5 7–5; K. Maleeva (2) – bye.

2nd round: Seles (1) d. Paz 6–0 6–0; Fulco Villella d. Maleeva (8) 6–4 6–3; Fernandez (4) d. Rubin 6–1 6–3; Gildemeister (6) d. Cioffi 6–2 6–1; Majoli (WC) d. McNeil (5) 6–3 6–3; Garrison Jackson (3) d. Burgin (Q) 6–1 6–4; Cecchini (7) d. Hack 7–6 7–6; Maleeva (2) d. Simpson Alter 6–2 7–6.

Quarter-finals: Seles (1) d. Fulco Villella 6–1 6–0; Gildemeister (6) d. Fernandez 6–4 3–6 6–1; Garrison Jackson (3) d. Majoli (WC) 6–3 6–4; Maleeva (2) d. Cecchini (7) 6–2 6–3.

Semi-finals: Seles (1) d. Gildemeister (6) 6–4 6–1; Garrison Jackson (3) d. Maleeva (2) 6–1 6–3.

Final: Seles (1) d. Garrison Jackson (3) 6–1 6–1.

WOMEN'S DOUBLES – *Final*: Fendick/G. Fernandez (1) d. J. Hetherington/K. Rinaldi (4) 7–5 6–4.

OPEN SEAT OF SPAIN ($225,000)
BARCELONA, 20–26 APRIL

WOMEN'S SINGLES – *1st round*: M. Seles (1) – bye; N. Muns Jagerman d. C. Mothes 6–2 3–6 6–1; P. Thoren d. E. Bes 6–3 6–4; M. Pierce (6) d. S. Farina 6–1 6–0; M. Maleeva Fragnière (4) – bye; L. Garrone d. S. Niox–Chateau 7–6 7–5; Fed. Bonsignori d. K. Oeljeklaus 6–1 6–4; W. Probst (Q) d. J. Wiesner (7) 6–1 1–6 6–3; N. Tauziat (5) d. E. Bottini (WC) 3–6 7–6 6–2; A. Dechaume d. V. Ruano (Q) 6–1 6–4; N. Guerree (LL) d. I. Spirlea (Q) 7–5 6–7 6–4; C. Martinez (3) – bye; J. Halard (8) d. N. Herreman 6–4 6–4; I. Gorrochategui d. B. Navarro (Q) 7–6 6–0; R. Zrubakova d. E. Zardo 6–1 6–0; A. Sanchez-Vicario (2) – bye.

2nd round: Seles (1) d. Muns Jagerman 6–3 6–1; Pierce (6) d. Thoren 6–2 6–1; Maleeva Fragnière (4) d. Garrone 6–2 6–4; Probst (Q) d. Bonsignori 6–1 6–3; Tauziat (5) d. Dechaume 6–4 6–4; Martinez (3) d. Guerree (LL) 6–1 6–0; Halard (8) d. Gorrochategui 7–6 2–6 6–3; Sanchez-Vicario (2) d. Zrubakova 6–1 6–4.

Quarter-finals: Seles (1) d. Pierce (6) 7–6 6–4; Maleeva Fragnière (4) d. Probst (Q) 6–3 6–4; Martinez (3) d. Tauziat (5) 7–5 6–1; Sanchez-Vicario (2) d. Halard (8) 6–2 6–3.

Semi-finals: Seles (1) d. Maleeva Fragnière (4) 6–3 6–1; Sanchez-Vicario (2) d. Martinez (3) 6–1 6–2.

Final: Seles (1) d. Sanchez-Vicario (2) 3–6 6–2 6–3.

WOMEN'S DOUBLES – *Final*: Martinez/Sanchez-Vicario d. Tauziat/Wiesner (2) 6–4 6–1.

CITIZEN CUP ($350,000)
HAMBURG, 27 APRIL–3 MAY
WOMEN'S SINGLES – 1st round: S. Graf (1) d. D. Graham 6–0 7–6; Mag. Maleeva d. N. Provis 6–3 4–6 7–6; N. van Lottum d. S. Lohmann (WC) 6–0 6–3; L. Meskhi (8) d. N. Muns Jagerman 6–2 4–6 6–4; M. Maleeva Fragnière (4) d. M. Paz 6–1 2–6 6–0; M. Babel (WC) d. D. Szabova 6–4 6–1; J. Durie d. M. Bollegraf 6–3 6–2; A. Huber (6) d. R. Rajchrtova 7–6 6–3; J. Novotna (5) d. E. Brioukhovets 6–3 6–2; P. Hy d. K. Nowak 6–2 6–3; E. Maniokova d. A. Dechaume 6–2 6–2; A. Sanchez-Vicario (3) d. L. Savchenko Neiland 6–0 6–4; J. Wiesner (7) d. B. Fulco Villella 3–6 6–2 6–1; M. Kochta d. C. Hofmann 6–2 6–4; B. Rittner d. P. Thoren 6–2 6–2; G. Sabatini (2) d. S. Cecchini 6–0 6–0.
2nd round: Graf (1) d. Maleeva 6–2 6–3; Meskhi (8) d. van Lottum 7–5 6–0; Maleeva Fragnière (4) d. Babel (WC) 6–3 6–0; Huber (6) d. Durie 6–3 6–2; Novotna (5) d. Hy 6–2 6–2; Sanchez-Vicario (3) d. Maniokova 6–1 6–1; Wiesner (7) d. Kochta 7–6 6–3; Sabatini (2) d. Rittner 6–1 6–1.
Quarter-finals: Graf (1) d. Meskhi (8) 6–2 6–2; Huber (6) d. Maleeva Fragnière (4) 5–7 6–2 7–5; Sanchez-Vicario (3) d. Novotna (5) 6–1 6–4; Sabatini (2) d. Wiesner (7) 6–1 6–2.
Semi-finals: Graf (1) d. Huber (6) 6–3 6–0; Sanchez-Vicario (3) d. Sabatini (2) 3–6 6–4 6–4.
Final: Graf (1) d. Sanchez-Vicario (3) 7–6 6–2.
WOMEN'S DOUBLES – Final: Graf/R. Stubbs d. Bollegraf/Sanchez-Vicario (2) 4–6 6–3 6–4.

XLIX CAMPIONATI INTERNAZIONALE D'ITALIA PEUGEOT OPEN CUP ($550,000)
ROME, 4–10 MAY
WOMEN'S SINGLES – 1st round: M. Seles (1) – bye; N. Baudone (WC) d. P. Hy 6–2 6–4; C. Cunningham d. S. Testud 6–4 2–6 6–3; L. Ferrando d. L. Gildemeister (11) 6–1 6–2; L. Meskhi (10) d. P. Tampieri (Q) 6–1 6–3; M. Kidowaki d. D. Faber 4–6 6–1 6–3; B. Fulco Villella d. P. Etchemendy (Q) 6–3 6–3; K. Maleeva (6) – bye; J. Capriati (3) – bye; S. Cecchini d. P. O'Reilly (Q) 6–4 6–3; B. Mulej (LL) d. A. Kijimuta 6–3 6–0; A. Coetzer (16) d. S. Farina 6–1 6–4; N. Zvereva (14) d. A. Grossman 6–1 4–6 6–2; L. Golarsa (WC) d. S. Dopfer (Q) 2–6 7–6 7–5; R. Reggi Concato d. F. Labat 6–2 6–2; M. Pierce (8) – bye; A. Huber (5) – bye; D. Graham d. K. Piccolini 7–5 6–2; C. Papadaki (Q) d. C. Cavina (Q) 6–4 2–6 6–3; R. Zrubakova (12) – bye; B. Schultz (12) d. G. Pizzichini (Q) 6–1 5–7 7–6; I. Gorrochategui d. F. Romano (WC) d. 7–6 1–6 6–4; I. Demongeot d. C. Kohde-Kilsch 6–3 6–3; M. J. Fernandez (4) – bye; N. Tauziat (7) – bye; L. Garrone d. H. Sprung (Q) 6–2 6–4; R. McQuillan d. F. Bonsignori 5–7 6–3 6–4; H. Sukova (9) d. R. Rajchrtova 6–3 7–5; F. Perfetti (LL) d. B. Rittner (15) 6–2 6–2; N. Provis d. K. Nowak 6–1 6–1; M. Paz d. A. Segura (LL) 6–0 6–0; G. Sabatini (2) – bye.
2nd round: Seles (1) d. Baudone (WC) 6–0 6–4; Cunningham d. Ferrando 6–4 6–1; Meskhi (10) d. Kidowaki 6–2 6–2; Fulco Villella d. Maleeva (6) 2–6 7–6 7–5; Capriati (3) d. Cecchini 6–4 3–6 7–6; Coetzer (16) d. Mulej (LL) 7–5 6–4; Zvereva (14) d. Golarsa (WC) 6–2 6–2; Reggi Concato d. Pierce (8) 7–6 5–7 6–0; Huber (5) d. Graham 6–4 6–4; Zrubakova (12) d. Papadaki (Q) 6–1 6–4; Gorrochategui d. Schultz (12) 7–5 3–6 6–2; Fernandez (4) d. Demongeot 6–3 6–4; Tauziat (7) d. Garrone 6–2 6–0; McQuillan d. Sukova (9) 7–5 6–4; Provis d. Perfetti (LL) 6–2 7–6; Sabatini (2) d. Paz 6–3 6–1.
3rd round: Seles (1) d. Cunningham 6–0 6–1; Meskhi (10) d. Fulco Villella 6–1 6–2; Coetzer (16) d. Capriati (3) 6–1 3–6 6–4; Zvereva (14) d. Reggi Concato 6–1 6–2; Huber (5) d. Zrubakova (12) 6–1 4–6 6–1; Fernandez (4) d. Gorrochategui 3–6 6–2 6–2; Tauziat (7) d. McQuillan 6–2 6–0; Sabatini (2) d. Provis 6–1 6–2.
Quarter-finals: Seles (1) d. Meskhi (10) 6–1 6–4; Coetzer (16) d. Zvereva (14) 6–2 6–3; Fernandez (4) d. Huber (5) 3–6 7–6 6–3; Sabatini (2) d. Tauziat (7) 6–0 6–1.
Semi-finals: Seles (1) d. Coetzer (16) 6–0 6–4; Sabatini (2) d. Fernandez (4) 6–2 6–3.
Final: Sabatini (2) d. Seles (1) 7–5 6–4.
WOMEN'S DOUBLES – Final: Seles/Sukova d. Maleeva/Rittner (8) 6–1 6–2.

LUFTHANSA CUP ($550,000)
BERLIN, 11–17 MAY
WOMEN'S SINGLES – 1st round: S. Graf (1) – bye; M. Paz d. C. Tessi 6–4 6–0; N. van Lottum d. S. Hack 6–3 6–3; H. Sukova (9) d. V. Martinek 4–6 7–5 6–3; J. Halard (11) d. S. Farina 6–4 3–6 6–1; W. Probst d. Fed. Bonsignori 6–4 7–5; S. Frankl d. R. Stubbs 1–6 6–2 6–3; K. Maleeva (7) – bye; J. Capriati (3) – bye; S. Meier (WC) d. M. Kochta 4–6 6–3 6–3; K. Piccolini d. E. Brioukhovets 2–6 6–1 7–5; B. Rittner (15) d. P. O'Reilly (Q) 6–3 6–2; R. Zrubakova (14) d. K. Boogert (Q) 6–1 6–4; N. Sawamatsu d. C. Kuhlman (Q) 6–4 6–4; R. McQuillan d. P. Begerow (Q) 6–3 6–3; J. Novotna (6) – bye; A. Huber (5) – bye; S. Cecchini d. N. Provis 6–4 3–6 6–3; L. Savchenko Neiland d. C. Kohde-Kilsch 6–2 7–5; L. Gildemeister (12) d. P. Thoren 6–1 6–3; J. Wiesner (13) d. M. Babel 6–3 6–2; R. Simpson Alter d. B. Fulco Villella 4–6 6–1 7–6; L. Bacheva (Q) d. C. Hofmann (WC) 6–1 6–0; M. J. Fernandez (4) – bye; N. Tauziat (8) – bye; D. Faber d. S. Niox–Chateau 6–1 6–1; K. Rinaldi d. J. Faull (Q) 4–6 6–1 6–2; S. Appelmans (10) d. A. Glass (Q) 6–2 6–4; N. Zvereva (16) d. D. Graham 6–1 6–3; K. Kschwendt (Q) d. F. Labat 6–0 6–3; M.

Kidowaki d. A. Kijimuta 6–2 5–7 6–3; A. Sanchez-Vicario (2) – bye.
2nd round: Graf (1) d. Paz 6–2 6–4; Sukova (9) d. van Lottum 6–1 6–4; Halard (11) d. Probst 6–2 6–3; Maleeva (7) d. Frankl 6–0 6–1; Capriati (3) d. Meier (WC) 6–3 2–6 6–1; Rittner (15) d. Piccolini 6–1 6–4; Zrubakova (14) d. Sawamatsu 4–6 7–5 6–4; Novotna (6) d. McQuillan 6–3 0–1 ret.; Cecchini d. Huber (5) 1–6 6–2 6–0; Gildemeister (12) d. Savchenko Neiland 6–0 6–3; Wiesner (13) d. Simpson Alter 6–1 6–2; Fernandez (4) d. Bacheva (Q) 6–2 6–1; Tauziat (8) d. Faber 6–2 6–0; Appelmans (10) d. Rinaldi 7–6 4–6 6–4; Zvereva (16) d. Kschwendt (Q) 6–1 6–4; Sanchez-Vicario (2) d. Kidowaki 6–0 6–3.
3rd round: Graf (1) d. Sukova (9) 6–3 3–6 6–2; Halard (11) d. Maleeva (7) 6–2 6–3; Capriati (3) d. Rittner (15) 7–5 6–3; Zrubakova (14) d. Novotna (6) 6–3 6–4; Cecchini d. Gildemeister (12) 6–1 6–2; Fernandez (4) d. Wiesner (13) 6–4 6–4; Appelmans (10) d. Tauziat (8) 6–3 1–6 7–5; Sanchez-Vicario (2) d. Zvereva (16) 7–6 6–3.
Quarter-finals: Graf (1) d. Halard (11) 6–1 6–2; Capriati (3) d. Zrubakova (14) 6–3 7–5; Fernandez (4) d. Cecchini 6–1 7–6; Sanchez-Vicario (2) d. Appelmans (10) 6–0 6–3.
Semi-finals: Graf (1) d. Capriati (3) 2–6 6–3 6–4; Sanchez-Vicario (2) d. Fernandez (4) 7–5 7–6.
Final: Graf (1) d. Sanchez-Vicario (2) 4–6 7–5 6–2.
WOMEN'S DOUBLES – Final: Novotna/Savchenko Neiland (1) d. G. Fernandez/Zvereva (2) 7–6 4–6 7–5.

PILKINGTON GLASS LADIES CHAMPIONSHIPS ($350,000)
EASTBOURNE, 15–20 JUNE
WOMEN'S SINGLES – 1st round: M. Navratilova (1) d. A. Grunfeld (WC) 6–2 6–2; L. Harvey-Wild d. C. Suire (Q) 6–3 7–6; J. Byrne d. T. Price (Q) 6–2 7–5; L. Savchenko Neiland d. M. Bollegraf (16) 6–3 6–3; J. Hetherington (LL) d. C. Tanvier 6–4 6–2; R. Stubbs d. C. Fauche 6–3 6–0; S. Siddall (WC) d. M. Javer 6–2 6–4; J. Durie d. Z. Garrison Jackson (5) 6–3 7–5; J. Novotna (4) d. Y. Basuki 3–6 6–3 6–4; M. Endo d. T. Whitlinger 6–3 6–4; E. Reinach d. V. Lake (WC) 4–6 6–2 7–5; I. Demongeot d. A. Frazier (9) 6–3 6–3; N. Medvedeva (14) d. T. Krizan (Q) 2–6 6–1 6–3; E. Brioukhovets d. T. Morton 2–6 6–4 6–4; R. Fairbank Nideffer d. M. Werdel 6–3 4–6 6–3; K. Date (8) d. M. Kidowaki 6–4 2–6 6–4; N. Tauziat (6) d. G. Magers (Q) 6–3 6–2; P. Paradis Magnon d. C. Lindqvist 6–4 7–5; H. Ludloff (LL) d. G. Helgeson 7–6 6–3; P. Shriver (15) d. C. Rubin 6–0 6–2; L. McNeil (11) d. A. Blumberga (Q) 6–1 6–2; R. White d. S. Gomer 6–3 6–2; N. Provis d. N. Herreman 6–2 6–1; C. Martinez (3) d. K. Adams 6–1 6–1; H. Sukova (7) d. J. Richardson (Q) 6–1 6–4; S. McCarthy (Q) d. N. van Lottum 6–0 4–6 6–4; K. Rinaldi d. L. Golarsa 7–6 2–6 6–4; P. Fendick d. B. Schultz (13) 4–6 7–6 6–4; P. Hy d. G. Fernandez (10) 6–4 6–2; K. Po d. C. Wood 7–5 6–1; S. Testud d. L. Allen 7–5 6–2; M. J. Fernandez (2) d. C. Kohde-Kilsch 6–3 6–1.
2nd round: Harvey-Wild d. Navratilova (1) 6–3 6–7 6–3; Savchenko Neiland d. Byrne 6–2 6–2; Stubbs d. Hetherington (LL) 3–6 6–1 6–4; Durie d. Siddall (WC) 6–0 6–1; Novotna (4) d. Endo 6–4 6–4; Reinach d. Demongeot 3–6 7–5 6–3; Brioukhovets d. Medvedeva (14) 7–6 1–6 6–4; Fairbank Nideffer d. Date (8) 7–6 6–1; Tauziat (6) d. Paradis Magnon 6–2 4–6 7–5; Shriver (15) d. Ludloff (LL) 6–3 6–1; McNeil (11) d. White 6–4 6–4; Martinez (3) d. Provis 5–7 7–6 6–4; Sukova (7) d. McCarthy (Q) 6–4 6–2; Fendick d. Rinaldi 1–6 6–4 6–0; Hy d. Po 6–2 6–3; Fernandez (2) d. Testud 7–6 6–4.
3rd round: Harvey-Wild d. Savchenko Neiland 3–6 7–6 6–4; Stubbs d. Durie 6–3 6–1; Novotna (4) d. Reinach 6–1 6–2; Fairbank Nideffer d. Brioukhovets 7–5 7–5; Tauziat (6) d. Shriver (15) 6–3 6–4; McNeil (11) d. Martinez (3) 6–0 6–3; Sukova (7) d. Fendick 6–4 6–0; Fernandez (2) d. Hy 6–2 6–3.
Quarter-finals: Harvey-Wild d. Stubbs 6–1 6–1; Fairbank Nideffer d. Novotna (4) 6–1 6–3; McNeil (11) d. Tauziat (6) 7–6 6–7 7–5; Fernandez (2) d. Sukova (7) 6–3 6–4.
Semi-finals: Harvey-Wild d. Fairbank Nideffer 6–1 6–3; McNeil (11) d. Fernandez (2) 7–6 6–0.
Final: McNeil (11) d. Harvey-Wild 6–4 6–4.
WOMEN'S DOUBLES – Final: Novotna/Savchenko Neiland (1) d. M. J. Fernandez/Garrison Jackson (4) 6–0 6–3.

VIRGINIA SLIMS OF LOS ANGELES ($350,000)
LOS ANGELES, 10–16 AUGUST
WOMEN'S SINGLES – 1st round: M. Seles (1) – bye; K. Habsudova d. L. Gildemeister 6–1 6–4; L. McNeil d. M. Javer 7–5 6–2; A. Frazier (7) d. L. Raymond (Q) 7–5 7–6; A. Sanchez-Vicario (3) – bye; R. White d. P. Fendick 6–0 6–7 6–4; J. Durie d. N. Provis 6–2 4–6 6–2; H. Sukova (5) d. A. May (WC) 6–2 6–4; R. Fairbank Nideffer d. J. Halard (8) 6–3 6–2; K. Po (Q) d. C. Lindqvist 6–1 6–2; S. Rottier (Q) d. B. Nagelsen (WC) 5–7 7–5 6–3; M. Maleeva Fragnière (4) – bye; Z. Garrison Jackson (6) d. S. Stafford (Q) 6–2 6–2; P. Shriver d. M. Werdel 6–2 6–1; A. Dechaume d. A. Grossman 6–3 6–2; M. Navratilova (2) – bye.
2nd round: Seles (1) d. Habsudova 6–2 6–2; Frazier (7) d. McNeil 3–6 7–6 6–4; Sanchez-Vicario (3) d. White 1–6 6–4 6–0; Sukova (5) 6–4 1–6 6–3; Po (Q) d. Fairbank Nideffer 6–3 3–0 ret.; Maleeva Fragnière (4) d. Rottier (Q) 6–1 6–4; Garrison Jackson (6) d. Shriver 7–5 6–2; Navratilova (2) d. Dechaume 6–3 6–0.
Quarter-finals: Seles (1) d. Frazier (7) 6–2 6–0; Sanchez-Vicario (3) d. Sukova (5) 2–6 6–3 6–2; Maleeva Fragnière (4) d. Po (Q) 6–1 7–6; Navratilova (2) d. Garrison Jackson (6) 6–3 6–0.

Semi-finals: Seles (1) d. Sanchez-Vicario (3) 6–3 6–2; Navratilova (2) d. Maleeva Fragnière (4) 6–4 7–6.
Final: Navratilova (2) d. Seles (1) 6–4 6–2.
WOMEN'S DOUBLES – Final: Sanchez-Vicario/Sukova (1) d. Garrison Jackson/Shriver (2) 6–4 6–2.

MATINEE LTD – CANADIAN OPEN SINGLES ($550,000)
MONTREAL, 17–23 AUGUST
WOMEN'S SINGLES – 1st round: M. Seles (1) – bye; M. Werdel d. C. Porwik 6–3 6–3; Lou. Allen d.
R. Simpson Alter 3–6 6–3 6–3; N. Sawamatsu (14) d. M. Drake (WC) 6–4 6–3; R. Hiraki (Q) d. G.
Fernandez (15) 6–2 2–6 6–4; P. Hy d. K. Rinaldi 2–6 6–3 6–0; N. van Lottum d. V. Webb (WC) 6–2 6–2;
K. Maleeva (5) – bye; M. Maleeva Fragnière (4) – bye; L. Raymond (Q) d. M. de Swardt 6–4 3–6 6–3; C.
Lindqvist d. E. Burgin (Q) 6–2 4–6 6–0; J. Wiesner (9) d. P. Fendick 2–6 6–2 6–2; B. Schultz (12) d. H.
Cioffi 6–2 1–6 7–6; C. Cunningham d. L. Harvey-Wild 6–2 3–6 6–2; D. Faber d. D. Monami 6–0 6–4; L.
McNeil (8) – bye; H. Sukova (7) – bye; C. Wood (Q) d. T. Whittington 7–5 6–4; M. Oremans (Q) d. R.
Stubbs 5–7 6–2 6–4; N. Provis (16) d. S. Rottier 6–0 7–6; N. Zvereva (11) d. I. Demongeot 6–3 7–6; J.
Santrock d. J. Byrne 6–1 6–1; P. Paradis Magnon d. L. Smylie (Q) 6–2 6–2; M.J. Fernandez (3) – bye; N.
Tauziat (6) – bye; H. Kelesi d. A. Temesvari Trunkos 6–0 6–2; E. Reinach d. S. Jeyaseelan (WC) 6–1 6–0;
L. Gildemeister (13) d. A. Keller 6–2 6–7 6–3; A. Coetzer (10) d. K. Habsudova 6–1 6–2; A. Dechaume
d. S. Stafford (Q) 6–1 6–2; C. Kuhlman d. S. Testud 6–4 7–5; A. Sanchez-Vicario (2) – bye.
2nd round: Seles (1) d. Werdel 6–2 6–4; Sawamatsu (14) d. Allen 6–1 6–0; Hy d. Hiraki (Q) 3–6 6–3
6–2; Maleeva (5) d. van Lottum 6–3 6–3; Maleeva Fragnière (4) d. Raymond (Q) 6–2 6–1; Wiesner (9) d.
Lindqvist 6–4 7–5; Cunningham d. Schultz (12) 6–3 5–7 7–6; McNeil (8) d. Faber 6–2 6–3; Sukova (7) d.
Wood (Q) 6–4 6–0; Oremans (Q) d. Provis (16) 6–3 4–6 6–3; Zvereva (11) d. Santrock (Q) 6–3 6–3; M.J.
Fernandez (3) d. Paradis Magnon 6–1 6–4; Tauziat (6) d. Kelesi 6–2 6–4; Reinach d. Gildemeister (13)
6–2 6–1; Coetzer (10) d. Dechaume 6–4 6–0; Sanchez-Vicario (2) d. Kuhlman 6–1 6–1.
3rd round: Seles (1) d. Sawamatsu (14) 6–1 6–2; Hy d. Maleeva (5) 6–3 6–3; Maleeva Fragnière (4) d.
Wiesner (9) 6–3 7–5; McNeil (8) d. Cunningham 7–5 6–4; Sukova (7) d. Oremans (Q) 6–0 7–5; M.J.
Fernandez (3) d. Zvereva (11) 6–4 7–6; Tauziat (6) d. Reinach 6–4 4–6 6–2; Sanchez-Vicario d. Coetzer
(10) 7–6 6–2.
Quarter-finals: Seles (1) d. Hy 6–1 4–6 6–1; McNeil (8) d. Maleeva Fragnière (4) 7–5 6–2; Sukova (7)
d. M.J. Fernandez (3) 6–3 3–6 6–4; Sanchez-Vicario (2) d. Tauziat (6) 6–2 6–4.
Semi-finals: Seles (1) d. McNeil (8) 6–3 6–4; Sanchez-Vicario (2) d. Sukova (7) 6–2 7–5.
Final: Sanchez-Vicario (2) d. Seles (1) 6–3 4–6 6–4.
WOMEN'S DOUBLES – Final: McNeil/Stubbs (3) d. G. Fernandez/Zvereva (2) 3–6 7–5 7–5.

MAZDA TENNIS CLASSIC ($225,000)
SAN DIEGO, 24–30 AUGUST
WOMEN'S SINGLES – 1st round: G. Sabatini (1) – bye; K. Po d. G. Magers 6–3 6–4; K. Date d. P.
Shriver 6–3 6–3; L. Meskhi d. S. Appelmans (8) 6–4 6–1; C. Martinez (3) – bye; I. Demongeot d. Andrea
Strnadova 7–6 6–1; A. Grossman d. R. White 7–6 6–3; J. Novotna (5) d. C. Lindqvist 6–3 6–3; N. Tauziat
(6) d. A. Gavaldon 6–1 6–3; S. Rehe d. M. Paz 6–7 7–6 6–4; D. Graham d. Y. Basuki 6–0 6–3; A. Huber
(4) – bye; Z. Garrison Jackson (7) d. R. Fairbank Nideffer 6–3 6–2; M. Javer d. K. Rinaldi 6–4 6–3; J.
Wiester d. J. Halard 3–6 7–6 6–3; J. Capriati (2) – bye.
2nd round: Sabatini (1) d. Po 6–0 6–0; Meskhi d. Date 6–2 6–3; Martinez (3) d. Demongeot 6–4 7–5;
Grossman d. Novotna (5) 4–6 6–4 4–2 ret.; Tauziat (6) d. Rehe 7–5 3–6 6–3; Huber (4) d. Graham 6–0
6–2; Garrison Jackson (7) d. Javer 6–1 6–0; Capriati (2) d. Wiesner 6–4 6–1.
Quarter-finals: Meskhi d. Sabatini (1) 6–0 6–3; Martinez (3) d. Grossman 6–2 6–3; Huber (4) d. Tauziat
(6) 6–1 6–1; Capriati (2) d. Garrison Jackson (7) 6–4 6–4.
Semi-finals: Martinez (3) d. Meskhi 3–6 7–6 6–2; Capriati (2) d. Huber (4) 7–6 3–6 6–1.
Final: Capriati (2) d. Martinez (3) 6–3 6–2.
WOMEN'S DOUBLES – Final: Novotna/L. Savchenko Neiland (1) d. Martinez/Paz (2) 6–1 6–4.

NICHIREI INTERNATIONAL LADIES CHAMPIONSHIPS ($350,000)
TOKYO, 22–27 SEPTEMBER
WOMEN'S SINGLES – 1st round: M. Seles (1) – bye; S. Wang d. D. Graham 6–2 3–6 6–2; K. Po d. M.
Kidowaki 6–2 6–1; N. Sawamatsu (8) d. N. Miyagi (WC) 5–7 6–2 6–2; M. J. Fernandez (3) – bye; J.
Byrne d. Y. Basuki 6–1 6–4; K. Nagatsuka (Q) d. M. Javer 6–3 6–3; A. Coetzer (5) d. H. Nagano (LL) 6–4
4–6 6–2; M. Werdel d. A. Frazier (6) 6–1 6–4; R. White d. J. Richardson (Q) 6–3 6–3; A. Grossman d. A.
Sugiyama (WC) 6–3 6–1; K. Maleeva (4) – bye; K. Date (7) d. S. Sloane Lundy 6–0 6–1; S. Stafford (Q)
d. Lou. Field (Q) 3–6 6–3 6–2; R. Hiraki d. D. Faber 6–4 6–1; G. Sabatini (2) – bye.
2nd round: Seles (1) d. Wang 6–0 6–1; Sawamatsu (8) d. Po 7–6 6–4; M.J. Fernandez (3) d. Byrne 6–1
6–1; Nagatsuka (Q) d. Coetzer (5) 5–7 6–3 6–1; Werdel d. White 6–1 6–3; Maleeva (4) d. Grossman 6–3
6–1; Date (7) d. Stafford (Q) 6–1 6–1; Sabatini (2) d. Hiraki 6–3 6–3.

Quarter-finals: Seles (1) d. Sawamatsu (8) 6–1 6–0; M.J. Fernandez (3) d. Nagatsuka (Q) 6–0 6–2; Maleeva (4) d. Werdel 6–4 6–4; Sabatini (2) d. Date (7) 6–4 6–2.
Semi-finals: Seles (1) d. M.J. Fernandez (3) 6–0 3–6 6–4; Sabatini (2) d. Maleeva (4) 6–3 6–3.
Final: Seles (1) d. Sabatini (2) 6–2 6–0.
WOMEN'S DOUBLES – Final: M.J. Fernandez/R. White (1) d. Basuki/Miyagi (3) 6–4 6–4.

VOLKSWAGEN CUP DAMEN GP ($225,000)
LEIPZIG, 28 SEPTEMBER–4 OCTOBER
WOMEN'S SINGLES – 1st round: S. Graf (1) d. Bergerow (WC) 6–1 6–0; L. Savchenko Neiland d. M. Kochta 6–3 7–6; Mag. Maleeva d. M. Paz 6–0 6–4; Z. Garrison Jackson (6) d. J. Durie 6–7 6–1 6–1; A. Huber (3) d. B. Rittner 7–6 6–0; C. Porwik d. P. Holubova 3–6 6–0 6–2; J. Wiesner d. E. Maniokova 6–0 6–0; K. Maleeva (7) d. N. Medvedeva 6–3 6–7 7–5; S. Appelmans (8) d. N. Muns Jagerman 6–4 4–6 6–0; J. Santrock d. L. Harvey-Wild 6–2 6–3; R. Zrubakova d. K. Adams 6–3 6–2; J. Novotna (4) d. A. Strnadova 6–2 6–4; H. Sukova (5) d. M. Babel 6–3 6–1; S. Meier d. P. Thoren 0–6 6–3 6–4; A. Dechaume d. W. Probst 5–7 7–6 6–4; C. Martinez (2) d. I. Demongeot 6–2 6–4.
2nd round: Graf (1) d. Savchenko Neiland 6–3 6–3; Mag. Maleeva d. Garrison Jackson (6) 6–4 6–4; Huber (3) d. Porwik 6–2 6–3; Maleeva (7) d. Wiesner 6–0 6–4; Appelmans (8) d. Santrock 6–2 6–3; Novotna (4) d. Zrubakova 6–1 6–3; Sukova (5) d. Meier 6–3 6–3; Martinez (2) d. Dechaume 6–4 3–6 6–2.
Quarter-finals: Graf (1) d. Mag. Maleeva 6–2 6–2; Maleeva (7) d. Huber (3) 1–6 7–6 6–1; Novotna (4) d. Appelmans (8) 3–6 6–1 6–0; Sukova (5) d. Martinez (2) 3–6 6–2 6–2.
Semi-finals: Graf (1) d. Maleeva (7) 6–1 6–1; Novotna (4) d. Sukova (5) 6–3 6–2.
Final: Graf (1) d. Novotna (4) 6–3 1–6 6–4.
WOMEN'S DOUBLES – Final: Novotna/Savchenko Neiland (1) d. P. Fendick/A. Strnadova (3) 7–5 7–6.

EUROPEAN INDOORS – ZURICH ($350,000)
ZURICH, 5–11 OCTOBER
WOMEN'S SINGLES – 1st round: S. Graf (1) d. K. Habsudova; W. Probst d. N. Tschan (WC) 6–2 6–3; P. Shriver d. L. Golarsa 6–3 6–1; J. Wiesner (8) d. L. Gildemeister 7–5 6–4; J. Novotna (4) d. L. Harvey-Wild 6–4 6–3; N. Zvereva d. N. Ercegovic 6–4 6–1; A. Strnadova d. Lou. Allen 4–6 6–3 6–4; H. Sukova (5) d. P. Hy 6–3 6–3; Z. Garrison Jackson (6) d. N. Baudone 6–3 6–7 6–3; J. Durie d. K. Adams 6–2 4–6 6–4; P. Fendick d. K. Kroupova 6–0 6–3; M. Maleeva Fragnière (3) d. M. Kochta 6–1 3–6 7–5; A. Temesvari Trunkos (WC) d. C. Kohde-Kilsch 4–6 7–5 7–6; B. Rittner d. S. Rehe 5–7 6–1 6–4; M. Navratilova (2) d. E. Zardo 6–0 6–0.
2nd round: Graf (1) d. Probst 6–0 6–2; Wiesner (8) d. Shriver 6–4 4–6 6–4; Novotna (4) d. Zvereva 7–5 6–2; Strnadova d. Sukova (5) 7–6 3–6 6–3; Garrison Jackson (6) d. Durie 3–6 6–3 6–4; Fendick d. Maleeva Fragnière 6–3 6–3; Mag. Maleeva (7) d. Temesvari Trunkos (WC) 6–2 6–2; Navratilova (2) d. Rittner 6–3 6–0.
Quarter-finals: Graf (1) d. Wiesner 7–5 6–4; Novotna (4) d. Strnadova 6–4 6–0; Fendick d. Garrison Jackson (6) 6–0 6–2; Navratilova (2) d. Mag. Maleeva (7) 6–2 6–3.
Semi-finals: Graf (1) d. Novotna (4) 6–2 4–6 7–6; Navratilova (2) d. Fendick 6–3 4–1 ret.
Final: Graf (1) d. Navratilova (2) 2–6 7–5 7–5.
WOMEN'S DOUBLES – Final: Sukova/Zvereva (1) d. Navratilova/Shriver (2) 7–6 6–4.

PORSCHE TENNIS GRAND PRIX ($350,000)
FILDERSTADT, 12–18 OCTOBER
WOMEN'S SINGLES – 1st round: G. Sabatini (1) d. K. Kachwendt (Q) 6–4 6–2; N. Medvedeva d. E. Reinach (Q) 6 6–7 7–5; W. Probst d. C. Porwik (WC) 6–1 6–3; A. Temesvari Trunkos (LL) d. L. McNeil (8) 6–7 6–3 7–5; M.J. Fernandez (4) d. B. Schultz 6–2 3–6 6–3; N. Zvereva d. P. Shriver 6–3 6–2; L. Meskhi d. C. Dahlman (Q) 6–4 6–1; A. Huber (5) d. N. Herrerman (Q) 6–4 6–0; H. Sukova (7) d. K. Habsudova 6–1 6–3; R. Zrubakova d. B. Rittner 6–3 7–6; V. Martinek d. D. van Rensburg 4–6 6–2 6–3; M. Navratilova (3) d. P. Hy 7–6 6–1; N. Tauziat (6) d. L. Gildemeister 6–7 6–2 6–1; J. Wiesner d. M. Babel (WC) 6–2 6–4; S. Appelmans d. S. Rehe 6–2 6–3; A. Sanchez-Vicario (2) d. P. Paradis Magnon 7–5 6–4.
2nd round: Sabatini (1) d. Medvedeva 6–4 6–4; Probst d. Temesvari Trunkos (LL) 7–5 6–7 6–1; M.J. Fernandez (4) d. Zvereva 6–2 0–6 6–2; Huber (5) d. Meskhi 4–6 4–0 ret.; Sukova (7) d. Zrubakova 6–4 6–4; Navratilova (3) d. Martinek 6–4 6–1; Wiesner d. Tauziat (6) 6–3 6–4; Sanchez-Vicario (2) d. Appelmans 7–6 6–2.
Quarter-finals: Sabatini (1) d. Probst 6–4 6–1; M.J. Fernandez (4) d. Huber (5) 5–7 6–3 6–1; Navratilova (3) d. Sukova (7) 6–3 7–6; Sanchez-Vicario (2) d. Wiesner 6–1 6–1.
Semi-finals: Sabatini (1) d. M.J. Fernandez (4) 7–5 6–2; Navratilova (3) d. Sanchez-Vicario (2) 6–1 6–1.
Final: Navratilova (3) d. Sabatini (1) 7–6 6–3.
WOMEN'S DOUBLES – Final: Sanchez-Vicario/Sukova (1) d. Shriver/Svereva (2) 6–4 7–5.

MIDLAND BANK CHAMPIONSHIPS ($350,000)
BRIGHTON, 20–25 OCTOBER
WOMEN'S SINGLES – 1st round: S. Graf (1) d. L. Savchenko Neiland 6–2 6–3; A. Strnadova d. A. Grunfeld (WC) 7–6 6–2; L. Meskhi d. R. Zrubakova 2–6 6–2 6–2; L. McNeil (8) d. L. Gildemeister 4–6 6–1 7–5; A. Huber (4) d. B. Schultz 6–1 3–6 6–4; K. Nowak (LL) d. L. Bacheva (Q) 7–5 6–4; C. Dahlman d. E. Maniokova 6–2 0–6 6–4; P. Paradis Magnon d. K. Maleeva (6) 3–6 6–4 6–1; J. Novotna (5) d. P. Hy 6–0 6–3; N. Zvereva d. W. Probst 7–5 6–3; K. Adams (Q) d. S. Siddall (WC) 7–6 6–1; C. Martinez (3) d. N. van Lottum 6–1 6–1; N. Tauziat (7) d. P. Fendick 6–3 6–7 6–2; Mag. Maleeva d. S. Appelmans 6–4 6–1; E. Reinach (Q) d. P. Thoren 6–1 7–6; M.J. Fernandez (2) d. J. Durie 3–2 ret.
2nd round: Graf (1) d. Strnadova 6–0 6–4; McNeil (8) d. Meskhi 7–6 7–6; Huber (4) d. Nowak (LL) 6–1 6–2; Paradis Magnon d. Dahlman 6–4 6–2; Novotna (5) d. Zvereva 6–2 6–0; Martinez (3) d. Adams (Q) 6–0 6–4; Tauziat (7) d. Mag. Maleeva 6–1 6–4; M.J. Fernandez (2) d. Reinach (Q) 6–3 6–0.
Quarter-finals: Graf (1) d. McNeil (8) 6–0 6–2; Huber (4) d. Paradis Magnon 6–3 6–1; Novotna (5) d. Martinez (3) 6–4 6–2; M.J. Fernandez (2) d. Tauziat (7) 6–4 6–3.
Semi-finals: Graf (1) d. Huber (4) 7–5 6–2; Novotna (5) d. M.J. Fernandez (2) 6–3 6–4.
Final: Graf (1) d. Novotna (5) 4–6 6–4 7–6.
WOMEN'S DOUBLES – Final: Novotna/Savchenko Neiland (1) d. Martinez/Zrubakova 6–4 6–1.

BANK OF WEST CLASSIC ($350,000)
OAKLAND, 2–8 NOVEMBER
WOMEN'S SINGLES – 1st round: M. Seles (1) – bye; S. Rehe d. G. Fernandez 6–2 1–0 ret.; I. Majoli (WC) d K. Habsudova 6–2 6–7 6–1; L. McNeil (5) d. K. Po 6–3 6–3; A. Huber (3) – bye; L. Savchenko Neiland d. H. Kelesi 7–6 3–6 6–2; P. Shriver d. R. Fairbank Nideffer 6–2 6–2; Z. Garrison Jackson (8) d. L. Gildemeister 6–4 4–6 7–6; B. Schultz d. A. Frazier (6) 6–4 2–6 6–3; P. Fendick d. B. Nagelsen (WC) 6–7 6–1 6–1; A. Grossman d. R. White 6–1 6–2; K. Maleeva (4) – bye; L. Meskhi d. C. Cunningham 6–4 6–4; N. Zvereva d. L. Harvey-Wild 6–4 6–0; N. Provis d. M. Javer 6–1 7–5; M. Navratilova (2) – bye.
2nd round: Seles (1) d. Rehe 6–4 6–1; Majoli (WC) d. McNeil 6–3 0–6 6–2; Huber (3) d. Savchenko Neiland 1–6 6–0 6–0; Shriver d. Garrison Jackson (8) 2–6 6–4 7–5; Fendick d. Schultz 6–4 6–4; Maleeva (4) d. Grossman 6–4 4–6 6–3; Zvereva d. Meskhi 4–6 7–6 7–6; Navratilova (2) d. Provis 6–1 2–6 6–1.
Quarter-finals: Seles (1) d. Majoli 6–3 6–1; Huber (3) d. Shriver 6–2 6–4; Maleeva (4) d. Fendick 4–6 6–1 6–1; Navratilova (2) d. Zvereva 6–2 6–2.
Semi-finals: Seles (1) d. Huber (3) 6–2 6–3; Navratilova (2) d. Maleeva (4) 6–1 6–2.
Final: Seles (1) d. Navratilova (2) 6–3 6–4.
WOMEN'S DOUBLES – Final: G. Fernandez/Zvereva (1) d. Fairbank Nideffer/G. Magers 3–6 6–2 6–4.

VIRGINIA SLIMS OF PHILADELPHIA ($350,000)
PHILADELPHIA, 9–15 NOVEMBER
WOMEN'S SINGLES – 1st round: S. Graf (1) – bye; E. Brioukhovets d. J. Hetherington 6–2 6–0; Z. Garrison Jackson d. B. Schultz 7–6 7–6; C. Martinez (5) d. N. Herreman 6–4 6–1; J. Capriati (4) – bye; E. Burgin d. R. White 6–2 6–2; G. Fernandez d. L. Savchenko Neiland 7–5 6–4; L. McNeil (8) d. A. Grossman 6–2 6–1; M. Pierce (6) d. K. Rinaldi 6–0 6–1; N. Zvereva d. R. Fairbank Nideffer 6–2 7–5; A. Coetzer d. S. Stafford 6–1 ret.; A. Sanchez-Vicario (3) – bye; A. Frazier (7) d. C. Kuhlman 6–1 6–3; L. Raymond (WC) d. B. Bowes 6–1 6–3; P. Shriver d. B. Nagelsen (WC) 6–1 6–4; G. Sabatini (2) – bye.
2nd round: Graf (1) d. Brioukhovets 6–0 6–1; Martinez (5) d. Garrison Jackson 4–6 6–3 6–4; Capriati (4) d. Burgin 6–2 6–0; McNeil (8) d. Fernandez 6–2 7–5; Zvereva d. Pierce (6) 7–6 6–2; Sanchez-Vicario (3) d. Coetzer 7–6 7–6; Raymond (WC) d. Frazier (7) 6–4 6–4; Sabatini (2) d. Shriver 7–6 7–5.
Quarter-finals: Graf (1) d. Martinez (5) 6–1 6–1; Capriati (4) d. McNeil (8) 6–2 6–1; Sanchez-Vicario (3) d. Zvereva 6–2 6–1; Sabatini (2) d. Raymond (WC) 6–4 7–6.
Semi-finals: Graf (1) d. Capriati (4) 6–0 6–1; Sanchez-Vicario (3) d. Sabatini (2) 4–6 6–3 6–2.
Final: Graf (1) d. Sanchez-Vicario (3) 6–3 3–6 6–1.
WOMEN'S DOUBLES – Final: G. Fernandez/Zvereva (2) d. Martinez/Pierce 6–1 6–3.

VIRGINIA SLIMS CHAMPIONSHIPS ($3,000,000)
NEW YORK, 16–22 NOVEMBER
WOMEN'S SINGLES – 1st round: M. Seles (1) d. N. Tauziat 6–1 6–2; J. Novotna d. M.J. Fernandez (6) 7–6 6–2; G. Sabatini (3) d. A. Frazier 6–0 6–2; J. Capriati (7) d. H. Sukova 7–6 6–1; A. Sanchez-Vicario (5) d. Z. Garrison Jackson 7–6 6–1; M. Navratilova (4) d. M. Maleeva Fragnière 6–2 6–2; C. Martinez (8) d. K. Maleeva 6–4 6–3; L. McNeil d. S. Graf (2) 7–6 6–4.
Quarter-finals: Seles (1) d. Novtotna 3–6 6–4 6–1; Sabatini (3) d. Capriati (7) 6–1 3–6 6–4; Navratilova (4) d. Sanchez Vicario (5) 6–1 2–6 6–2; McNeil d. Martinez (8) 3–6 6–3 6–2.
Semi-finals: Seles (1) d. Sabatini (3) 7–6 6–1; Navratilova (4) d. McNeil 7–6 6–4.
Final: Seles (1) d. Navratilova (4) 7–5 6–3 6–1.
WOMEN'S DOUBLES – Final: Sanchez-Vicario/Sukova d. Novotna/L. Savchenko Neiland 7–6 6–1

A good year for Mary Joe Fernandez who reached the final of the Australian Open, and then won an Olympic gold medal in the doubles with Gigi Fernandez. *(T. Hindley)*

KRAFT WORLD TOUR

Tournaments with prize money below $225,000

NIVEA CUP ($75,000)
SAO PAULO, 2–8 DECEMBER
WOMEN'S SINGLES – Quarter-finals: I. Gorrochategui (5) d. V. Ruano 6–4 6–2; V. Martinek (3) d. L. Spadea 6–4 6–2; S. Hack (6) d. P. Tarabini 6–2 7–6; D. Faber (7) d. F. Labat (2) 6–3 6–4.
Semi-finals: Martinek (3) d. Gorrochategui (5) 6–2 6–1; Hack (6) d. Faber (7) 6–1 6–1.
Final: Hack (6) d. Martinek (3) 6–3 7–5.
WOMEN'S DOUBLES –Final: Gorrochategui/M. Paz (2) d. R. Baranski/L. Glitz 6–2 6–2.

DANONE WOMEN'S OPEN ($150,000)
BRISBANE, 30 DECEMBER–5 JANUARY
WOMEN'S SINGLES – Quarter-finals: N. Provis (14) d. A. Temesvari (LL) 6–3 6–0; M. Maleeva (10) d. R. Zrubakova (4) 6–4 7–5; D. Graham (13) d. M. Endo 6–2 6–3; R. McQuillan (8) d. C. Kohde-Kilsch 6–3 6–3.
Semi-finals: Provis (14) d. Maleeva (10) 4–6 7–5 6–2; McQuillan (8) d. Graham (13) 7–5 6–4.
Final: Provis (14) d. McQuillan (8) 6–3 6–2.
WOMEN'S DOUBLES –Final: J. Novotna/L. Savchenko Neiland (1) d. M. Bollegraf/Provis (2) 6–4 6–3.

NUTRI–METICS BENDON CLASSIC ($100,000)
AUCKLAND, 27 JANUARY–2 FEBRUARY
WOMEN'S SINGLES – Quarter-finals: A. Strnadova (1) d. A. Dechaume (5) 7–6 6–7 6–2; L. Savchenko Neiland (3) d. B. Fulco Villela (8) 6–2 6–4; R. White d. M. Javer 3–6 6–3 6–1; P. Thoren d. R. Reggi Concato (6) 6–3 6–2.
Semi-finals: Strnadova (1) d. Savchenko Neiland (3) 6–2 3–6 6–2; White d. Thoren 6–4 6–3.
Final: White d. Strnadova (1) 2–6 6–4 6–3.
WOMEN'S DOUBLES –Final: R. Fairbank Nideffer/Reggi Concato (3) d. J. Hetherington/K. Rinaldi (1) 1–6 6–1 7–5.

FERNLEAF BUTTER CLASSIC ($100,000)
WELLINGTON, 3–9 FEBRUARY
WOMEN'S SINGLES – Quarter-finals: N. Van Lottum d. J. Faull 6–4 4–6 7–6; M. Javer d. C. Wood 6–4 7–6; A. Grossman (6) d. C. Toleafoa 7–6 2–6 7–5; D. Faber d. L. Field 6–3 6–2.
Semi-finals: Van Lottum d. Javer 7–6 6–4; Faber d. Grossman (6) 6–4 7–5.
Final: Van Lottum d. Faber 6–4 6–0.
WOMEN'S DOUBLES –Final: B. Borneo/Wood (2) d. Faull/J. Richardson (3) 6–0 7–6.

MIZUNO WORLD LADIES ($150,000)
OSAKA, 4–9 FEBRUARY
WOMEN'S SINGLES – Quarter-finals: K. Habsudova d. K. Okamoto 6–0 6–1; L. Gildemeister (3) d. Y. Kamio 6–1 6–2; K. Date (4) d. R. McQuillan (5) 6–3 6–2; H. Sukova (2) d. N. Sawamatsu (7) 6–1 5–7 6–2.
Semi-finals: Gildemeister (3) d. Habsudova 6–3 6–7 6–1; Sukova (2) d. Date (4) 6–2 6–2.
Final: Sukova (2) d. Gildemeister (3) 6–2 4–6 6–1.
WOMEN'S DOUBLES –Final: R. Stubbs/Sukova (3) d. S. Collins/McQuillan (1) 3–6 6–4 7–5.

INTERNATIONAL AUSTRIAN INDOOR CHAMPIONSHIPS ($100,000)
LINZ, 10–16 FEBRUARY
WOMEN'S SINGLES – Quarter-finals: N. Medvedeva d. C. Porwik 6–7 6–1 6–3; E. Maniokova d. M. Pierce (3) 4–6 6–3 6–3; S. Cecchini (4) d. D. Monami 6–4 2–6 6–3; P. Paradis Mangon d. C. Lindqvist (6) 6–4 6–0.
Semi-finals: Medvedeva d. Maniokova 6–3 6–2; Paradis Mangon d. Cecchini (4) 6–2 7–5.
Final: Medvedeva d. Paradis Mangon 6–4 6–2.
WOMEN'S DOUBLES –Final: M. Kiene/M. Oremans d. C. Porwik/R. Reggi Concato (1) 6–4 6–2.

VIRGINIA SLIMS OF OKLAHOMA ($150,000)
OKLAHOMA CITY, 17–23 FEBRUARY
WOMEN'S SINGLES – Quarter-finals: Z. Garrison Jackson (1) d. A. Grossman 6–2 6–0; A. Frazier (4) d. D. Graham (6) 7–6 6–2; L. McNeil (3) d. N. Provis (5) 4–6 6–4 7–6; M. Bollegraf (7) d. G. Fernandez (2) 6–2 6–2.
Semi-finals: Garrison Jackson (1) d. Frazier (4) 6–4 0–6 6–4; McNeil (3) d. Bollegraf (7) 6–3 7–5.
Final: Garrison Jackson (1) d. McNeil (3) 7–5 3–6 7–6.
WOMEN'S DOUBLES – Final: McNeil/Provis (1) d. K. Adams/Bollegraf 3–6 6–4 7–6.

CESENA LADIES CHAMPIONSHIPS ($100,000)
CESENA, 17–23 FEBRUARY
WOMEN'S SINGLES – Quarter-finals: M. Pierce (1) d. L. Ferrando (8) 6–4 1–6 6–3; K. Nowak d. N. Herreman 6–4 2–6 7–6; C. Tanvier d. P. Langrova (6) 6–4 4–6 6–3; L. Golarsa d. P. Paradis Mangon (7) 2–6 6–2 6–4.
Semi-finals: Pierce (1) d. Nowak 6–1 6–1; Tanvier d. Golarsa 6–2 6–1.
Final: Pierce (1) d. Tanvier 6–1 6–1.
WOMEN'S DOUBLES – Final: C. Suire/Tanvier (3) d. S. Appelmans/R. Reggi Concato default.

LIGHT 'N LIVELY DOUBLES ($175,000)
SADDLEBROOK, 26–29 MARCH
WOMEN'S DOUBLES – Quarter-finals: J. Novotna/L. Savchenko Neiland (1) d. L. Meskhi/M. Paz 6–3 6–1; J. Capriati/G. Fernandez d. K. Adams/M. Bollegraf (3) 6–2 7–5; G. Magers/R. White d. S. Collins/E. Reinach (4) 6–1 6–4; A. Sanchez-Vicario/N. Zvereva (2) d. J. Hetherington/K. Rinaldi 6–3 6–2.
Semi-finals: Novotna/Savchenko Neiland (1) d. Capriati/Fernandez 6–2 7–5; Sanchez-Vicario/Zvereva (2) d. Magers/White 2–6 6–2 6–3.
Final: Novotna/Savchenko Neiland (1) d. Sanchez-Vicario/Zvereva (2) 6–4 6–2.

SUNTORY JAPAN OPEN ($150,000)
TOKYO, 6–12 APRIL
WOMEN'S SINGLES – Quarter-finals: A. Frazier (1) d. N. Medvedeva (5) 6–4 6–1; K. Date (3) d. M. Javer 6–4 6–1; N. Sawamatsu (4) d. R. Reggi Concato 6–3 6–2; S. Appelmans (2) d. M. Werdel (8) 7–5 6–2.
Semi-finals: Date (3) d. Frazier (1) 6–3 6–4; Appelmans (2) d. Sawamatsu (4) 7–6 6–3.
Final: Date (3) d. Appelmans (2) 7–5 3–6 6–3.
WOMEN'S DOUBLES – Final: Frazier/R. Hiraki d. Date/S. Rehe (1) 5–7 7–6 6–0.

VOLVO WOMEN'S OPEN ($100,000)
PATTAYA CITY, 13–19 APRIL
WOMEN'S SINGLES – Quarter-finals: S. Appelmans (1) d. C. Lindqvist (6) 6–2 6–4; N. Medvedeva (3) d. S. Wang (LL) 6–2 6–4; Y. Basuki (4) d. P. Paradis Mangon (7) 6–0 6–1; A. Strnadova (5) d. S. Rottier (Q) 6–0 6–1.
Semi-finals: Appelmans (1) d. Medvedeva (3) 6–4 6–3; Strnadova (5) d. Basuki (4) 4–6 6–2 6–2.
Final: Appelmans (1) d. Strnadova (5) 7–5 3–6 7–5.
WOMEN'S DOUBLES – Final: I. Demongeot/Medvedeva (4) d. Paradis Mangon/S. Testud 6–1 6–1.

WOMEN'S OPEN MALAYSIA ($100,000)
KUALA LUMPUR, 20–26 APRIL
WOMEN'S SINGLES – Quarter-finals: M. Javer (8) d. N. Medvedeva (1) 3–6 6–3 6–1; A. Strnadova (3) d. P. Paradis Mangon (5) 6–4 7–6; C. Lindqvist (4) d. L. Fang 7–6 6–0; Y. Basuki (2) d. S. Rottier 6–4 6–0.
Semi-finals: Strnadova (3) d. Javer (8) 6–3 6–1; Basuki (2) d. Lindqvist (4) 6–4 6–1.
Final: Basuki (2) d. Strnadova (3) 6–3 6–0.
WOMEN'S DOUBLES – Final: I. Demongeot/Medvedeva (1) d. R. Hiraki/P. Langrova (4) 2–6 6–4 6–1.

ILVA TROPHY ($100,000)
TARANTO, 28 APRIL–3 MAY
WOMEN'S SINGLES – Quarter-finals: J. Halard (1) d. C. Mothes 6–1 3–6 6–4; L. Ferrando d. A. Coetzer (3) 6–4 6–2; E. Zardo (5) d. V. Martinek 7–5 7–5; R. Zrubakova (2) d. A. Grossman (7) 6–0 6–2.
Semi-finals: Halard (1) d. Ferrando 6–3 6–4; Zardo (5) d. Zrubakova (2) 7–5 5–7 6–4.
Final: Halard (1) d. Zardo (5) 6–0 7–5.
WOMEN'S DOUBLES –Final:: Coetzer/I. Gorrochategui d. R. McQuillan/Zrubakova (1) 4–6 6–3 7–6.

BELGIAN LADIES OPEN ($100,000)
WAREGEM, 4–10 MAY
WOMEN'S SINGLES – ***Quarter-finals:*** N. Dahlman d. E. Hoogendoorn (LL) 6–7 6–2 6–2; M. Babel d. S. Niox–Chateau 6–4 7–6; N. Muns Jagerman (4) d. K. Godridge 7–5 6–1; W. Probst d. E. Zardo (2) 7–5 6–2.
Semi-finals: Babel d. Dahlman 6–3 3–6 6–3; Probst d. Muns Jagerman (4) 7–6 6–4.
Final: Probst d. Babel 6–2 6–3.
WOMEN'S DOUBLES –***Final::*** M. Bollegraf/C. Vis (1) d. E. Brioukhovets/P. Langrova (2) 6–4 6–3.

LUCERNE LADIES EUROPEAN OPEN ($150,000)
LUCERNE, 18–24 MAY
WOMEN'S SINGLES – ***Quarter-finals:*** E. Zardo d. S. Hack 7–5 7–5; R. Zrubakova (3) d. Mag. Maleeva (5) 3–6 6–1 6–4; C. Fauche (WC) d. A. Coetzer (4) 6–2 3–6 6–2; A. Frazier (2) d. L. Harvey-Wild 6–3 6–0.
Semi-finals: Zrubakova (3) d. Zardo 6–4 6–4; Frazier (2) d. Fauche (WC) 7–6 6–2.
Final: Frazier (2) d. Zrubakova (3) 6–4 4–6 7–5.
WOMEN'S DOUBLES – ***Final:*** Frazier/E. Reinach (2) d. K. Habsudova/M. Werdel (4) 7–5 6–2.

INTERNATIONAUX DE STRASBOURG ($150,000)
STRASBOURG, 18–24 MAY
WOMEN'S SINGLES – ***Quarter-finals:*** M. de Swardt d. D. Graham (8) (WC) 6–3 3–6 6–3; N. Sawamatsu (5) d. S. Testud 6–3 3–6 7–5; B. Fulco Villela d. M. Paz 1–6 7–5 6–1; J. Wiesner (2) F. Labat 4–6 6–4 6–3.
Semi-finals: Sawamatsu (5) d. de Swardt 6–3 6–3; Wiesner (2) d. Fulco Villela 6–1 6–1.
Final: Wiesner (2) d. Sawamatsu (5) 6–1 6–3.
WOMEN'S DOUBLES –***Final:*** P. Fendick/A. Strnadova (2) d. L. McNeil/Paz (1) 6–3 6–4.

THE DOW CLASSIC ($150,000)
BIRMINGHAM, 8–14 JUNE
WOMEN'S SINGLES – ***Quarter-finals:*** P. Shriver (7) d. Z. Garrison Jackson (1) 7–5 6–3; B. Schultz (6) d. L. Savchenko Neiland (9) 7–6 7–6; J. Byrne d. L. McNeil (4) 6–2 6–4; J. Durie (10) d. A. Temesvari 6–3 6–2.
Semi-finals: Schultz (6) d. Shriver (7) 6–4 7–6; Byrne d. Durie (10) 6–3 6–1.
Final: Schultz (6) d. Byrne 6–2 6–2.
WOMEN'S DOUBLES –***Final:*** McNeil/R. Stubbs (2) d. S. Collins/E. Reinach (1) 5–7 6–3 8–6.

TORNEO INTERNAZIONALE FEMMINILE DI PALERMO ($100,000)
PALERMO, 6–12 JULY
WOMEN'S SINGLES – ***Quarter-finals:*** M. Pierce (1) d. P. Langrova 6–1 7–6; S. Farina d. C. Mothes (8) 6–1 6–1; N. Ercegovic (Q) d. H. Cioffi 6–1 6–3; B. Schultz (2) d. N. Baudone 6–2 6–4.
Semi-finals: Pierce (1) d. Farina 6–2 6–2; Schultz (2) d. Ercegovic (Q) 6–4 6–2.
Final: Pierce (1) d Schultz (2) 6–1 6–7 6–1.
WOMEN'S DOUBLES – ***Final:*** Cioffi/M. Gaidano d. Langrova/A. Segura (4) 6–3 4–6 6–3

CITROEN CUP AUSTRIAN LADIES OPEN ($150,000)
KITZBUHEL, 6–12 JULY
WOMEN'S SINGLES – ***Quarter-finals:*** C. Martinez (1) d. A. Dechaume 6–2 6–2; A. Coetzer (4) d. W. Probst 7–5 6–2; F. Labat d. J. Wiesner (3) 6–2 6–1; M. Maleeva Fragnière (2) d. S. Cecchini (6) 6–2 6–3.
Semi-finals: Martinez (1) d. Coetzer (4) 6–1 6–3; Maleeva Fragnière (2) d. Labat 4–6 6–0 6–3.
Final: Martinez (1) d. Maleeva Fragnière (2) 6–0 3–6 6–2.
WOMEN'S DOUBLES –***Final:*** Labat/Dechaume (1) d. Coetzer/Probst (2) 6–3 6–3.

HTC PRAGUE OPEN ($100,000)
PRAGUE, 20–26 JULY
WOMEN'S SINGLES – ***Quarter-finals:*** R. Zrubakova (1) d. E. Sviglerova 6–2 5–7 6–2; M. Kiene (Q) d. S. Meier 6–1 0–6 6–2; V. Martinek (5) d. N. van Lottum 7–6 6–4; K. Kroupova d. K. Kschwendt 5–7 6–0 6–4.
Semi-finals: Zrubakova (1) d. Kiene (Q) 6–2 2–6 6–3; Kroupova d. Martinek (5) 6–2 6–3.
Final: Zrubakova (1) d. Kroupova 6–3 7–5.
WOMEN'S DOUBLES –***Final:*** Kschwendt/P. Ritter (4) d. Sviglerova/van Lottum 6–4 2–6 7–5.

INTERNAZIONALI DI TENNIS SAN MARINO ($100,000)
REPUBLIC OF SAN MARINO, 20–26 JULY
WOMEN'S SINGLES – ***Quarter-finals:*** Mag. Maleeva (1) d. F. Perfetti (WC) 6–3 6–2; A. Dechaume (3) d. P. Tarabini 6–4 6–1; Fed. Bonsignori d. F. Labat (6) 6–2 6–4; M. Paz (7) d. B. Fulco Villela 7–6 6–4.
Semi-finals: Maleeva (1) d. Dechaume (3) 2–6 6–3 6–3; Bonsignori d. Paz (7) 6–2 5–7 6–4.

Neither Spain's Conchita Martinez (above) nor the naturalised American Martina Navratilova (below) could reach a Grand Slam final in 1992 but they both retained their places among the top 10 with year-end rankings of 8 and 5 respectively. (T.Hindley)

Final: Maleeva (1) d. Bonsignori 7–6 6–4.
WOMEN'S DOUBLES –Final: Dechaume/Labat (2) d. S. Cecchini/L. Garrone (3) 7–6 7–5.

OTB INTERNATIONAL TENNIS OPEN ($100,000)
SCHENECTADY, 24–30 AUGUST
WOMEN'S SINGLES – Quarter-finals: H. Werdel d. S. Rottier (Q) 6–4 6–4; B. Rittner (3) d. A. Dechaume 6–2 6–2; B. Schultz d. H. Kelesi 6–2 6–3; F. Labat d. R. Zrubakoya (2) 6–4 4–6 6–2.
Semi-finals: Rittner (3) d. Werdel 6–1 ret.; Schultz (4) d. Labat 6–1 6–4.
Final: Rittner (3) d. Schultz (4) 7–6 6–3.
WOMEN'S DOUBLES –Final: Dechaume/Labat (4) d. G. Helgeson/S. McCarthy 6–3 1–6 6–2.

OPEN CLARINS ($150,000)
PARIS, 14–20 SEPTEMBER
WOMEN'S SINGLES – Quarter-finals: J. Halard (1) d. Fed. Bonsignori 6–3 1–6 6–0; E. Zardo (4) d. S. Meier 6–0 6–1; N. Ercegovic d. V. Martinek (7) 3–6 6–1 6–3; S. Cecchini (6) d. S. Hack (2) 6–3 6–2.
Semi-finals: Zardo (4) d. Halard (1) 3–6 7–6 6–4; Cecchini (6) d. Ercegovic 6–1 7–6.
Final: Cecchini (6) d. Zardo (4) 6–2 6–1.
WOMEN'S DOUBLES –Final: Cecchini/P. Tarabini (3) d. R. McQuillan/N. van Lottum (2) 7–5 6–1.

OPEN WHIRLPOOL VILLE DE BAYONNE ($150,000)
BAYONNE, 28 SEPTEMBER–4 OCTOBER
WOMEN'S SINGLES – Quarter-finals: M. Maleeva Fragnière (1) d. D. Monami 5–7 6–0 6–1; P. Paradis Mangon d. N. Dahlman 6–4 6–0; R. McQuillan d. N. van Lottum 6–3 7–5; N. Tauziat (2) d. S. Rehe (8) 6–4 7–6.
Semi-finals: Maleeva Fragnière (1) d. Paradis Mangon 6–1 6–1; Tauziat (2) d. McQuillan 6–3 6–2.
Final: Maleeva Fragnière (1) d. Tauziat (2) 6–7 6–2 6–3.
WOMEN'S DOUBLES –Final: L. Ferrando/P. Langrova d. C. Kohde-Kilsch/Rehe (1) 1–6 6–3 6–4.

P & G TAIWAIN WOMEN'S OPEN ($100,000)
TAIPEI, 29 SEPTEMBER–4 OCTOBER
WOMEN'S SINGLES – Quarter-finals: A. Coetzer (1) d. D. Graham (6) (WC) 6–3 7–5; S. Stafford d. M. Werdel (7) 6–1 3–6 6–4; M. Miyagi d. L. Field 6–2 7–5; A. Grossman (2) d. S. Wang (8) 3–6 6–4 6–3.
Semi-finals: Stafford d. Coetzer (1) 6–1 6–3; Grossman (2) d. Miyagi 6–2 3–0 ret.
Final: Stafford d. Grossman (2) 6–1 6–3.
WOMEN'S DOUBLES –Final: J. Faull/J. Richardson (3) d. Coetzer/Cam. MacGregor (1) 3–6 6–3 6–2.

PUERTO RICAN OPEN ($150,000)
SAN JUAN, 26 OCTOBER–1 NOVEMBER
WOMEN'S SINGLES – Quarter-finals: M. Pierce (1) d. N. Arendt (Q) 6–0 6–1; Lou. Allan d. G. Helgeson 6–3 4–6 6–3; G. Fernandez (4) d. L. Raymond (Q) 7–5 6–3; D. Graham (8) d. A. Coetzer (2) 6–2 3–6 6–3.
Semi-finals: Pierce (1) d. Allen 6–1 6–4; Fernandez (4) d. Graham (8) 6–1 6–2.
Final: Pierce (1) d. Fernandez (4) 6–1 7–5.
WOMEN'S DOUBLES –Final: Coetzer/E. Reinach (3) d. Fernandez/K. Rinaldi (1) 6–2 4–6 6–2.

INDIANAPOLIS TENNIS CLASSIC ($150,000)
INDIANAPOLIS, 9–14 NOVEMBER
WOMEN'S SINGLES – Quarter-finals: S. Wang d. M. Kochta 7–6 1–6 7–5; H. Sukova (4) d. T. Whittlinger 6–2 6–2; K. Maleeva (3) d. L. Gildemeister (6) 6–0 6–2; L. Harvey-Wild (7) d. I. Majoli 6–3 6–3.
Semi-finals: Sukova (4) d. Wang 6–3 6–3; Harvey-Wild (7) d. Maleeva (3) 6–4 7–5.
Final: Sukova (4) d. Harvey-Wild (7) 6–4 6–3.
WOMEN'S DOUBLES –Final: K. Adams/E. Reinach (1) d. S. Collins/M.L. Daniels (3) 5–7 6–2 6–4.

Crowned as the ITF World Champion for 1991 during the French Open, Monica Seles ended the year on a high note with her third consecutive Virginia Slims title, that earned her a Mazda RX-7 to add to the Jaguar XJ-S she had won in 1991. *(M.Cole)*

VIRGINIA SLIMS CHAMPIONSHIPS
Barry Wood

Monica Seles retained her title at the Virginia Slims Championships, defeating Martina Navratilova in a repeat of the 1991 final. The result surprised nobody, including her chief challenger, Steffi Graf, who conceded just the week before that Seles was the favourite for the title and the undisputed number 1 for the year. What was entirely unexpected, however, was Graf's own first round defeat by Lori McNeil, who has always promised so much but rarely delivered. However, having regained her focus with the help and wisdom of coach John Wilkerson, she is now an increasingly potent force again. She showed an impressive resilience under pressure against Graf, and faith in a game plan that led her to attack at every opportunity, no matter what the short term consequences.

Graf, who had not lost in the first round of any Kraft Tour event since she was defeated 2–6 6–4 7–5 by Jo Durie in January 1985, or before the quarter-finals since she was beaten by the same player at Brighton in October of the same year, offered no excuses. She had led 5–1 in the first set and 4–2 in the second, but lost 7–6 6–4, double-faulting on set point in the tiebreak, and cruelly beaten by a net cord on match point. The previous month at Brighton, a defensive approach had led to McNeil taking just two games from Graf, but she had learned her lesson well. Neither player gave an inch, instead dedicating themselves to an all-out attack.

'I stayed aggressive, that was the key. That's my strength. Even when I was down I was serving well but just missing some volleys. But I had made my mind up what I was going to do, and just kept going,' McNeil explained. Although bitterly disappointed to end the year on such a note, especially after victories in her last four tournaments had suggested she was a prime contender for the title, Graf could draw some consolation from the fact that she had been outplayed, and had not succumbed to defeat as the result of her own shortcomings. 'She played an extremely good match. She made very few mistakes, and there was nothing I could do. I never underestimate her, but I didn't expect her to be that consistent. She really deserved to win,' said Graf.

In other matches on that second night at Madison Square Garden, Jana Novotna defeated Mary Joe Fernandez 7–6 6–2, and as the clock ticked past the midnight hour Conchita Martinez defeated Katerina Maleeva 6–4 6–3.

On the opening night, Seles and Navratilova both enjoyed ludicrously easy victories, with Seles taking a mere 53 minutes to overcome Nathalie Tauziat 6–1 6–2, and Navratilova exactly the same time to despatch Manuela Maleeva Fragnière 6–2 6–2. Tauziat held but failed to win seven break points, rushing too many shots. Maleeva Fragnière lobbed a few times, hit a number of decent passing shots, and uncharacteristically produced some aces, but she lacked the self-belief and aggression needed to trouble an opponent playing some of the best tennis of her career. 'I know I have some shots that did not exist in my repertoire eight years ago. I don't know if I'm slower now, but I know I'm hitting shots that I did not have when I was number 1,' said Navratilova.

Jennifer Capriati took time to settle against Helena Sukova, having anxiously awaited the delivery of the contact lenses she had left at her hotel, but she won 7–6 6–1.

Gabriela Sabatini drew Amy Frazier in the first round. The American appeared to be completely overwhelmed by the occasion and was hardly able to play a ball as she was overwhelmed 6–0 6–2.

In the quarter-finals, Seles, who had lost before the final just once in two years – to Capriati at the Lipton International in March 1992 – faced defeat by Novotna, but she recovered to win 3–6 6–4 6–1. Novotna was able to take advantage of Seles' puzzling reluctance to play at her usual blistering pace with some excellent approaches and crisp volleys.

It was not until the Czech led 3–0 in the second set that Seles began to assert herself, and Novotna could not maintain the intensity of her attack. Her fragile serve hardly helped, as she produced nine double-faults, the last on match point. 'I thought that I had to change my game and go for it. I was just pushing the ball back, and you can't play against Jana like that. You have to go for your shots,' said Seles.

Sabatini defeated Capriati 6–1 3–6 6–4 in arguably the most gripping encounter of the week. Surprisingly, it was her determination to get to the net at every opportunity, and her ability to repeatedly produce stunning touch volleys, that won her the match. There was a brief period during which Capriati wrestled control. After leaving the court at 0–5 to change her contact lenses, she returned to launch an astonishing attack that earned her the second set, but in a desperately close final set Sabatini responded adequately to the challenge.

Capriati knew that she had missed her chance of victory by not maintaining the pressure that had seen her overwhelm her opponent in the second set. 'It's always my intention to be aggressive, but sometimes I just don't do it', she admitted. 'I just feel more comfortable doing my thing, which is being at the baseline. I hit good shots and set myself up well so that I could approach the net, but I didn't'.

McNeil followed up her victory over Graf by defeating Martinez 3–6 6–3 6–2. A single break of serve settled the first two sets, but McNeil's better returns eventually earned her a place in the semi-finals.

Navratilova maintained her winning streak against Sanchez-Vicario, her 6–1 2–6 6–2 victory marking her 12th win in 13 meetings, and then resisted a strong challenge from McNeil, winning 7–6 6–4. The quality of McNeil's returns gave her the edge in the first set and she led 5–3. Navratilova finally became more aggressive then and earned a tiebreak. McNeil served for the set at 5–4 but faltered, and she also surrendered a 2–0 lead in the second set. A fightback from 2–5 was in vain, and Navratilova was through.

Seles reached her third consecutive VS Championships final by defeating Sabatini 7–6 6–1. There was nothing to separate them in the first set, as Sabatini ran the risk of being punished by Seles' passing shots as she looked for opportunities to come in to the net. After losing the tiebreak, however, Sabatini's game fell apart. She double-faulted six times to trail 0–3, as Seles also forced errors with her ferocious pace.

In a magnificent final, Seles was inspired to raise her game to the highest level by Navratilova's own performance, and won 7–5 6–3 6–1. Seles took advantage of Navratilova's serve, once so intimidating but now vulnerable, to hit three winning returns and rescue a break in the ninth game of the first set. Navratilova again took the lead in the second for 2–1, and then hit a diving forehand winner at the net for 3–1 that so impressed Seles that she joined Navratilova in watching a replay on a giant tv screen. It also inspired her to even greater efforts, and changed the course of the match.

'She was getting balls back that I've never seen in my life. When she made that incredible shot something just snapped inside me and I decided I had to really go for it,' said Seles, who hit some superb passes down the line, and a spectacular backhand drop volley for the set.

With the comfort of a two set lead, Seles still refused to let down, and the first point of the third set was played with such ferocity that Navratilova bowed to Seles in amazement. The contest was effectively over. 'Had she played like this ten years ago when I was dominating she would have beaten me. At her best she's as good as anybody I've played in 20 years,' Navratilova praised.

"It's a nice thing for her to say, but I do hope this is not the height of my career yet, because I still have a lot of things to learn. I think I need three to four years more practise to feel comfortable playing a match", Seles responded.

In doubles, the 12-year partnership of Navratilova and Pam Shriver was put into voluntary liquidation, after they were defeated 6–4 7–5 by Sanchez-Vicario and Helena Sukova in the semi-finals. They did not rule out playing the occasional tournament together in the future, however.

The title was won by Sanchez-Vicario and Sukova, who defeated Novotna and Larisa Savchenko Neiland 7–6 6–1.

OTHER OFFICIAL PRO TOURNAMENTS

MEN'S CHALLENGER SERIES
MEN'S SATELLITE CIRCUITS
ITF WOMEN'S FUTURES CIRCUIT

After a brilliant start to the year at the Australian Open where he reached the semi-finals, the 20-year-old South African Wayne Ferreira mowed down the field on the grass of Queen's Club to win his first Tour title.   (A. Evans)

MEN'S CHALLENGER SERIES 1992

FINALS

HEILBRONN (GER) 20–26 JANUARY
Singles: K. Braasch (GER) d. M. Naewie (GER) 6–7 6–2 6–2. *Doubles:* D. Eisenman (USA)/B. Pedersen (NOR) d. S. Groen (NED)/T. Nydahl (SWE) 6–1 6–3.

BANGALORE (IND) 27 JANUARY–2 FEBRUARY
Singles: M. Visconti (ITA) d. E. Rossetti 6–4 6–3. *Doubles:* N. Brown/A. Foster (GBR) d. X. Daufresne (BEL)/C. Kist (BRA) 7–3 3–6 7–5.

JAKARTA (INA) 3–9 FEBRUARY
Singles: C. Pistolesi (ITA) d. S. Youl (AUS) 1–6 6–3 6–2. *Doubles:* M. Koevermans (HOL)/L. Lavalle (MEX) d. J. Eltingh/T. Kempers (HOL) w/o.

RENNES (FRA) 24 FEBRUARY–1 MARCH
Singles: K. Braasch (GER) d. M. Naewie (GER) 6–2 3–6 6–2. *Doubles:* F. Montana/K. Thorne (USA) d. M. Damm (TCH)/S. Stolle (AUS).

INDIAN WELLS (USA) 24 FEBRUARY–1 MARCH
Singles: R. Fromberg (AUS) d. T. Woodbridge (USA) 6–4 6–1. *Doubles:* P. Aldrich (RSA)/D. Visser (RSA) d. M. Briggs/T. Kronemann (USA) 7–6 2–6 7–5.

ZARAGOSA (ESP) 2–8 MARCH
Singles: L. Mattar (BRA) d. T. Carbonell (ESP) 7–5 3–6 6–2. *Doubles:* D. Adams (AUS)/A. Olhovsky (CIS) d. M. Damm (TCH)/M. Jensen (USA) 6–2 1–6 6–4.

TUNIS (TUN) 9–15 MARCH
Singles: M. Filippini (URU) d. J. Altur (ESP) 6–4 6–2. *Doubles:* D. Adams (AUS)/ M. Damm (TCH) d. M. Filippini/D. Perez (URU) 7–6 6–1.

SANTIAGO (CHI) 9–15 MARCH
Singles: M. Ingaramo (ARG) d. S. Cortes (COL) 6–4 6–1. *Doubles:* C. Algardh (SWE)/J. Van Duyn (HOL) d. G. Lobo/M. Stringari (ARG) 4–6 7–6 7–5.

AGADIR (MAR) 23–29 MARCH
Singles: G. Perez Roldan (ARG) d. F. Roig (ESP) 6–2 2–6 6–4. *Doubles:* M. Briggs/T. Kronemann (USA) d. P. Henricsson/O. Jonsson (SWE) 6–1 6–1.

PARIOLI (ITA) 30 MARCH–5 APRIL
Singles: F. Davin (ARG) d. F. Roig (ESP) 6–1 6–4. *Doubles:* S. Cannon/G. Van Emburgh (USA) d. G. Lobo/D. Orsanic (ARG) 7–6 6–4.

JERUSALEM (ISR) 6–11 APRIL
Singles: G. Bloom (ISR) d. V. Gabrichidze (CIS) 6–3 6–1. *Doubles:* S. Guy (NZL)/C. Limberger (AUS) d. B. Joelson/R. Matuszewski (USA) 7–6 6–2.

SAN LUIS POTOSI (MEX) 13–19 APRIL
Singles: L. Lavalle (MEX) d. F. Montana (USA) 6–0 6–7 6–4. *Doubles:* L. Herrera/L. Lavalle (MEX) d. F. Maciel/A. Moreno (MEX) 6–2 6–2.

OPPORTO (POR) 20–26 APRIL
Singles: J. Altur (ESP) d. C. Mezzadri (SUI) 1–6 7–6 7–5. *Doubles:* C. Limberger (AUS)/T. Zdrazila (TCH) d. B. Devening (USA)/B. Pedersen (NOR) 3–6 6–1 6–4.

BIRMINGHAM (USA) 20–26 APRIL
Singles: M. Pernfors (SWE) d. L. Mattar (BRA) 7–6 6–4. *Doubles:* B. Garnett (USA)/T. Svantesson (SWE) d. J. Apell/P. Nyborg (SWE) 6–4 7–6.

NAGOYA (JPN) 20–26 APRIL
Singles: C. Adams (AUS) d. D. Nestor (CAN) 7–6 6–3. *Doubles* J. Bates /M. Petchey (GBR) d. B. Madsen (HAI)/L. Paes (IND) 7–5 3–6 7–6.

TAIPEI (TPE) 27 APRIL–3 MAY
Singles: S. Stolle (AUS) d. J. Bates (GBR) 6–3 5–7 7–5. *Doubles:* B. Dyke (AUS)/P. Lundgren (SWE) d.
N. Borwick /A. Kratzmann (AUS) 7–6 7–5.

ACAPULCO (MEX) 27 APRIL–3 MAY
Singles: L. Lavalle (MEX) d. L. Herrera (MEX) 0–6 6–3 6–3. *Doubles:* R. Deppe /B. Haygarth (RSA) d.
G. Guerrero/R. Saad (ARG) 6–3 4–6 7–6.

KUALA LUMPUR (MAS) 4– 10 MAY
Singles: S. Stolle (AUS) d. J. Bates (GBR) 7–6 6–4. *Doubles:* J. Morgan/S. Stolle (AUS) d. T. Ho
(USA)/P. Rafter (AUS) 6–4 7–6.

LJUBLJANA (SLO) 4–10 MAY
Singles: M. Larsson d. M. Tillstroem (SWE) 6–4 6–4. *Doubles:* M. Larsson/M. Tillstroem d. C.
Brandi/F. Mordegan (ITA) 6–3 6–2.

PRAGUE (TCH) 4–10 MAY
Singles: K. Kucera (TCH) d. F. Krumrey (GER) 2–6 6–4 6–4. *Doubles:* M. Damm/D. Rikl (TCH) d. J.
Carlsson/N. Kroon (SWE) 6–2 6–0.

SAO PAULO (BRA) 4–10 MAY
Singles: L. Herrera (MEX) d. J. Oncins (BRA) 6–2 3–6 6–4. *Doubles:* G. Stafford/K. Ullyett (RSA) d. G.
Martinez (MEX)/T. Mercer (USA) 7–6 6–4.

ITU (BRA) 11–17 MAY
Singles: R. Weiss (USA) d. R. Smith (BAH) 3–6 6–3 6–4. *Doubles:* G. Stafford/K. Ullyett (RSA) d. B.
Madsen (HAI)/T. Nelson (USA) 6–1 6–3.

ANTWERP (BEL) 11–17 MAY
Singles: M. Goellner (GER) d. M. Ardinghi (ITA) 4–6 6–3 7–5. *Doubles:* M. Brown (USA)/R. Rasheed
(AUS) d. K. Goossens (BEL)/M. Pernfors (SWE) 6–2 6–4.

FURTH (GER) 1–7 JUNE
Singles: M. Strelba (TCH) d. R. Viver (ECU) 6–1 6–2. *Doubles:* R. Haas/U. Riglewski (GER) d. B.
Joelson (USA)/B. Madsen (HAI) 6–1 6–3.

TURIN (ITA) 1–7 JUNE
Singles: F. Davin (ARG) d. R. Furlan (ITA) 7–6 3–6 6–1. *Doubles:* B. Black (ZIM)/J. De Jager (RSA) d. T.
Middleton/T. Scherman (USA) 6–4 6–2.

YVETOT (FRA) 8–14 JUNE
Singles: R. Agenor (HAI) d. A. Corretja (ESP) 6–4 2–6 7–5. *Doubles:* M. Renstrom/M. Tillstroem (SWE)
d. J. Oncins (BRA)/T. Zdrazila (TCH) 7–6 5–7 6–2.

COLOGNE (GER) 8–14 JUNE
Singles: K. Carlsen (DEN) d. T. Nydahl (SWE) 6–2 1–3 ret. *Doubles:* M. Goellner/B. Karbacher (GER) d.
B. Devening/M. Jensen (USA) 6–4 6–7 6–1.

HALLE (GER) 15–20 JUNE
Singles: M. Goellner (GER) d. T. Enqvist (SWE) 6–3 2–6 7–6. *Doubles:* K. Braasch/L. Koslowski (GER)
4–6 7–6 6–0.

SALZBURG (AUT) 22–28 JUNE
Singles: J. Arrese (ESP) d. G. Schaller (AUT) 7–6 7–6. *Doubles:* J. Apell/M. Tillstroem (SWE) d. J.
Arrese (ESP)/N. Holm (SWE) 3–6 6–2 6–2.

OPPORTO (POR) 29 JUNE–5 JUL
Singles: J. Arrese (ESP) d. L. Jonsson (SWE) 2–6 6–1 6–0. *Doubles:* D. Eisenman (USA)/B. Pedersen
(NOR) d. J. Arrese/A. Corretja (ESP) 1–6 6–4 6–2.

SALERNO (ITA) 29 JUNE–5 JUL
Singles: G. Markus (ARG) d. E. Alvarez (VEN) 7–5 6–1. *Doubles:* A. Kratzmann/R. Rasheed (AUS) d. G.
Markus/D. Orsanic (ARG) 6–4 6–3.

SEVILLE (ESP) 29 JUNE–5 JUL
Singles: M. Hadad (COL) d. K. Carlsen (DEN) 6–7 6–3 6–3. *Doubles:* C. Allgardh/T. Nydahl (SWE) d. S.
Cortes (COL)/C. Kist (BRA) 6–3 6–2.

NEW ULM (GER) 6–12 JULY
Singles: M. Ondruska (RSA) d. M. Goellner (GER) 7–6 6–1. *Doubles:* G. Luza /D. Orsanic (ARG) d. B.
Derlin/S. Guy (NZL) 6–3 6–2.

BRISTOL (GBR) 6–12 JULY
Singles: P. Baur (GER) d. J. Morgan (AUS) 4–6 7–6 6–1. *Doubles:* D. Kirk (GBR)/B. Larkham (AUS) d.
K. Kinnear (USA)/P. Nyborg (SWE) 3–6 7–6 6–4.

GRAMADO (BRA) 6–12 JULY
Singles: N. Bruno (ITA) d. R. Matuszewski ((USA) 6–2 6–2. *Doubles:* R. Matuszewski/J. Sullivan (USA) d. N. Aerts/F. Roese (BRA) 7–6 6–7 6–3.

TAMPERE (FIN) 13–19 JULY
Singles: K. Carlsen (DEN) d. B. Wuyts (BEL) 4–6 7–6 7–6. *Doubles:* J. Bjorkman/J. Donar (SWE) d. J. Gunnarson (SWE)/M. Mortensen (DEN) 6–4 6–4.

NEWCASTLE (GBR) 13–19 JULY
Singles: G. Rusedski (CAN) d. J. Frana (ARG) 6–3 7–6. *Doubles:* J. Frana/C. Van Rensburg (RSA) d. K. Kinnear (USA)/P. Nyborg (SWE) 7–6 7–6.

CAMPOS DO JORDAO (BRA) 13–19 JULY
Singles: R. Matuszewski (USA) d. D. Marcelino (BRA) 4–6 7–6 7–6. *Doubles:* J. Daher (BRA)/M. Tabares (CUB) d. D. Johnson/T. Mercer (USA) 6–3 6–7 6–3.

APTOS (CA) 20–26 JULY
Singles: A. O'Brien (USA) d. B. Black (ZIM) 6–4 2–6 6–1. *Doubles:* P. Annacone/A. O'Brien (USA) d. M. Nido (PUR)/P. Nyborg (SWE) 6–4 4–6 7–5.

OBERSTAUFEN (GER) 20–26 JULY
Singles: M. Valeri (ITA) d. M. Sinner (GER) 6–3 6–3. *Doubles:* J. Anderson (AUS)/L. Wahlgren (SWE) d. F. De Wulf/T. Van Houdt (BEL) 2–6 7–6 6–4.

BELO HORIZONTE (BRA) 20–26 JULY
Singles: G. Schaller (AUT) d. J. Cunha–Silva (POR) 6–4 6–7 6–0. *Doubles:* N. Aerts/A. Hocevar (BRA) d. J. Cunha–Silva/C. Kist (BRA) 6–1 6–7 6–2.

LINS (BRA) 27 JULY–2 AUGUST
Singles: G. Schaller (AUT) d. M. Hadad (COL) 6–3 6–3. *Doubles:* J. Cunha–Silva (POR)/N. Pereira (VEN) d. C. Motta/F. Roese (BRA) 6–3 6–4.

POZNAN (POL) 27 JULY–2 AUGUST
Singles: C. Dosedel (TCH) d. D. Vacek (TCH) 6–4 3–6 7–6. *Doubles:* T. Ivanski (POL)/D. Norman (BEL) d. S. Cortes (COL)/V. Solves (ESP) 4–6 6–3 6–2.

WINNETKA (USA) 27 JULY–2 AUGUST
Singles: C. Adams (USA) d. S. Bryan ((USA) 6–4 6–4. *Doubles:* A. Kratzmann/R. Rasheed (AUS) d. R. Witsken/T. Witsken (USA) 6–3 3–6 6–3.

VIENNA (AUT) 27 JULY–2 AUGUST
Singles: T. Buchmayer (AUT) d. R. Wawra (AUT) 7–6 6–1. *Doubles:* W. Kowalski (POL)/C. Wedenby (SWE) d. A. Hombrecher (USA)/A. Merinov (CIS) 7–6 4–6 6–3.

PESCARA (ITA) 3–9 AUGUST
Singles: F. Sanchez (ESP) d. M. Cierro (ITA) 6–2 7–5. *Doubles:* M. Cierro/N. Utgren (SWE) d. M. Knowles/R. Smith (BAH) 6–4 6–4.

RIBEIRAO (BRA) 3–9 AUGUST
Singles: G. Silberstein (CHI) d. M. Tabares (CUB) 7–6 7–6. *Doubles:* C. Allgardh (SWE)/M. Ruah (VEN) d. L. Bale/B. Curry (RSA) 2–6 7–5 6–4.

LIEGE (BEL) 3–9 AUGUST
Singles: S. Cortes (COL) d. B. Wuyts (BEL) 6–7 6–3 6–4. *Doubles:* J. Baguena (ESP)/E. Masso (BEL) d. D. Fiala/R. Novotny (TCH) 6–2 6–3.

SEGOVIA (ESP) 10–16 AUGUST
Singles: G. Raoux (FRA) d. J. Renzenbrink (HOL) 7–6 7–6. *Doubles:* D. Van Den Berg/J. Wijnhoud (HOL) d. N. Odizor (NGR)/R. Saad (ARG) 7–6 7–6.

NEW HAVEN (USA) 9–14 AUGUST
Singles: J. Arias (USA) d. B. Steven (NZL) 7–6 6–2. *Doubles:* T. Nelson (USA)/L. Paes (IND) d. J. Bates (GBR)/B. Black (ZIM) 7–5 2–6 7–6.

FORTALEZA (BRA) 10–16 AUGUST
Singles: M. Ruah (VEN) d. J. Cunha–Silva (POR) 6–4 3–6 6–4. *Doubles:* A. Kratzmann/R. Rasheed (AUS) d. C. Allgardh (SWE)/M. Ruah 7–6 6–4.

GRAZ (AUT) 17–23 AUGUST
Singles: G. Perez Roldan (ARG) d. K. Novacek (TCH) 3–6 6–2 7–5. *Doubles:* D. Prinosil (GER)/R. Vogel (TCH) d. R. Novotny/M. Trneny (TCH) 6–3 6–4.

ISTANBUL (TUR) 17–23 AUGUST
Singles: H. Holm (SWE) d. S. Simian (FRA) 7–6 6–2. *Doubles:* B. Le Mercier/S. Simian (FRA) d. R. Saad (ARG)/R. Smith (BAH) 7–6 7–6.

GENEVA (SUI) 17–23 AUGUST
Singles: S. Cortes (COL) d. F. De Wulf (BEL) 6–7 6–2 6–4. *Doubles:* F. De Wulf/T. Van Houdt (BEL) d. A. Mora (VEN)/M. Rebolledo (CHI) 6–3 6–2.

SAO PAULO II (BRA) 17–23 AUGUST
Singles: M. Stringari (ARG) d. N. Pereira (VEN) 6–3 3–6 6–2. *Doubles:* P. Albano (ARG)/C. Motta (BRA) d. J. Cunha–Silva (BRA)/N. Pereira w/o.

MERANO (ITA) 31 AUGUST–6 SEPTEMBER
Singles: L. Koslowski (GER) d. R. Azar (ARG) 6–3 6–4. *Doubles:* S. Groen (HOL)/D. Prinosil (GER) d. L. Barthez (FRA)/A. Beust (FRA) 6–4 6–4.

VENICE (ITA) 7–13 SEPTEMBER
Singles: T. Muster (AUT) d. M. Gorriz (ESP) 6–4 6–1. *Doubles:* J. Donar/O. Jonsson (SWE) d. C. Brandi/F. Mordegan (ITA) 6–3 6–2.

AZORES (POR) 7–13 SEPTEMBER
Singles: H. Holm (SWE) d. K. Carlsen (DEN) 6–4 6–3. *Doubles:* M. Holm/N. Utgren (SWE) d. D. Isaak(USA)/P. Nyborg (SWE) 7–6 7–6.

GUARUJA (BRA) 7–13 SEPTEMBER
Singles: N. Pereira (VEN) d. R. Jabali (BRA) 6–4 6–4. *Doubles:* M. Ruah (VEN)/M. Tabares (CUB) d. D. Marcelino (BRA)/F. Meligeni (MEX) w/o.

CASABLANCA (MAR) 14–20 SEPTEMBER
Singles: G. Schaller (AUT) d. F. Sanchez (ESP) 6–4 6–1. *Doubles:* F. De Wulf/T. Van Houdt (BEL) d. K. Kucera (TCH)/A. Merinov (CIS) 7–5 6–3.

BUCHAREST (ROM) 21–26 SEPTEMBER
Singles: H. De La Pena (ARG) d. M. Ondruska (RSA) 6–3 6–0. *Doubles:* H. De La Pena/M. Ondruska d. J. Fleurian (FRA)/M. Naewie (GER) 6–4 6–2.

BOGOTA (COL) 21–27 SEPTEMBER
Singles: D. Marco (ESP) d. A. Sznajder (CAN) 7–6 3–6 6–4. *Doubles:* N. Pereira (VEN)/M. Tabares (CUB) d. W. Kyriakos (BRA)/F. Meligeni (MEX) 7–6 7–5.

FAIRFIELD (USA) 21–27 SEPTEMBER
Singles: J. Palmer (USA) d. A. O'Brien (USA) 7–6 6–2. *Doubles:* J. Palmer/J. Pugh (USA) d. S. Devries/T. Scherman (USA) 6–4 7–6.

SINGAPORE (SIN) 21–26 SEPTEMBER
Singles: L. Roux (FRA) d. T. Nelson (USA) 6–2 6–0. *Doubles:* M. Blackman (USA)/L. Tieleman (ITA) d. P. Baur (GER)/S. Groen (HOL) 6–4 1–6 7–6.

MONTERREY (MEX) 28 SEPTEMBER–4 OCTOBER
Singles: A. O'Brien (USA) d. J. Palmer (USA) 6–2 6–4. *Doubles:* M. Knowles (BAH/A. O'Brien d. R. Matuszewski/J. Sullivan (USA) 3–6 6–3 7–6.

CALI (COL) 28 SEPTEMBER–4 OCTOBER
Singles: M. Hadad (COL) d. M. Visconti (ITA) 6–1 6–2. *Doubles:* M. Geserer(GER)/F. Silberberg (BRA) d. D. Orsanic (ARG)/M. Tabares (CUB) 6–4 6–4.

DUBLIN (IRL) 5–11 OCTOBER
Singles: M. Damm (TCH) d. A. Thoms (GER) 6–3 6–2. *Doubles:* S. Groen (HOL)/A. Thoms d. D. Geiwald (SWE)/R. Koenig (RSA) 5–7 6–4 6–3.

IXTAPA (MEX) 5–11 OCTOBER
Singles: L. Herrera (MEX) d. A. Sznajder (CAN) 6–1 6–2.
Doubles: Cancelled.

REGGIO CALABRIA (ITA) 5–11 OCTOBER
Singles: R. Azar (ARG) d. A. Berasategui (ESP) 6–4 6–2. *Doubles:* B. Haygarth (RSA)/T. Zdrazila (TCH) d. J. Cunha–Silva (BRA)/D. Poliakov (CIS) 6–4 7–6.

PONTE VEDRA (USA) 12–18 OCTOBER
Singles: L. Herrera (MEX) d. J. Yzaga (PER) 7–5 6–4. *Doubles:* J. Palmer/J. Pugh (USA) d. N. Pereira (VEN)/D. Vacek (TCH) 1–6 6–3 6–2.

BUENOS AIRES (ARG) 12–18 OCTOBER
Singles: J. Gisbert (ESP) d. C. Arriens (GER) 6–1 7–6. *Doubles:* P. Albano (ARG)/J. Frana (USA) d. H. De La Pena/G. Markus (ARG) 2–6 6–3 6–4.

CHERBOURG (FRA) 12–18 OCTOBER
Singles: J. Apell (SWE) d. C. Saceanu (GER) 6–3 6–7 7–6. *Doubles:* K. Kinnear (USA)/C. Saceanu d. J. Winnink (HOL)/T. Zdrazila (TCH) 6–1 6–4.

RECIFE (BRA) 12–18 OCTOBER
Singles: L. Mattar (BRA) d. J. Oncins (BRA) 7–6 5–7 7–5. *Doubles:* S. Lareau/D. Nestor (CAN) d. L. Mattar/J. Oncins 5–7 6–4 7–6.

CARACAS (VEN) 19–25 OCTOBER
Singles:
Doubles: D. Eisenman/T. Mercer (USA) d. B. Joelson/T. Scherman (USA) 3–6 6–3 7–5.

BREST (FRA) 26 OCTOBER–1 NOVEMBER
Singles: M. Ondruska (FRA) d. B. Karbacher (GER) 5–7 6–3 6–0. *Doubles:* M. Barnard/B. Haygarth (RSA) d. G. Dzelde (LAT)/B. Pedersen (NOR) 6–2 7–6.

AACHEN (GER) 2–8 NOVEMBER
Singles: M. Damm (TCH) d. B. Steven (NZL) 6–4 7–6. *Doubles:* G. Stafford/C. Van Rensburg (RSA) d. M. Mortensen (DEN)/C. Saceanu (GER) 6–1 6–3.

MANILA (PHI) 2–8 NOVEMBER
Singles: R. Fromberg (AUS) d. N. Borwick (AUS) 7–6 6–4. *Doubles:* R. Fromberg/S. Guy (NZL) d. M. Ardinghi/M. Visconti (ITA) 6–3 6–4.

MUNICH (GER) 9–15 NOVEMBER
Singles: D. Vacek (TCH) d. J. Svensson (SWE) 3–6 7–6 6–4. *Doubles:* S. Groen (HOL)/A. Thoms (GER) d. M. Ondruska (FRA)/ G. Stafford (RSA) 6–4 7–6.

BRUNEL (BRU) 9–15 NOVEMBER
Singles: L. Gloria (USA) d. D. Nestor (CAN) 6–3 2–6 6–2. *Doubles:* O. Casey (IRL)/D. Johnson (USA) d. F. De Wulf/T. Van Houdt (BEL) 6–2 6–3.

HALIFAX (CAN) 9–15 NOVEMBER
Singles: S. Lareau (CAN) d. D. Kass (USA) 7–5 7–6. *Doubles:* E. Ferreira (RSA)/R. Schmidt (USA) d. M. Renstrom (SWE)/C. Ruud (NOR) 4–6 6–1 6–4.

SAO LUIS (BRA) 16–22 NOVEMBER
Singles: L. Mattar (BRA) d. M. Ruah (VEN) 6–4 6–4. *Doubles:* L. Mattar/J. Oncins (BRA) d. M. Ruah/M. Tabares (CUB) 6–3 7–5.

GUADALAJARA (MEX) 16–22 NOVEMBER
Singles: D. Witt (USA) d. M. Koevermans (HOL) 6–4 6–3. *Doubles:* R. Deppe (RSA)/D. Rikl (TCH) d. M. Goellner/C. Saceanu (GER) 7–6 6–4.

KUALA LUMPUR II (MAS) 16– 22 NOVEMBER
Singles: C. Wilkinson (GBR) d. R. Smith (BAH) 6–3 6–1. *Doubles:* M. Michulka (USA)/M. Petchey (GBR) d. O. Casey (IRL)/D. Johnson (USA) 7–6 6–1.

PEMBROKE PINES (USA) 23– 29 NOVEMBER
Singles: L. Lavalle (MEX) d. D. Orsanic (ARG) 6–4 7–6. *Doubles:* R. Bergh (SWE)/T. Kronemann (USA) d. B. Pearce/T. Witsken (USA) 6–3 6–3.

LAUNCESTON (AUS) 23–29 NOVEMBER
Singles: R. Fromberg (NZL) d. D. Nainkin (RSA) 6–1 6–3. *Doubles:* R. Fromberg/P. Rafter (AUS) d. N. Brown/A. Foster (GBR) 7–5 7–6.

NAPLES (USA) 30 NOVEMBER– 6 DECEMBER
Singles: J. Gisbert (ESP) d. K. Braasch (GER) 7–5 1–6 6–4. *Doubles:* T. Nelson (USA)/T. Svantesson (SWE) d. M. Knowles (BAH)/A. O'Brien (USA) 2–6 6–3 6–4.

PERTH (AUS) 30 NOVEMBER–6 DECEMBER
Singles: K. Kinnear (USA) d. D. Adams (AUS) 6–2 6–4. *Doubles:* L. Bale/D. Nainkin (RSA) d. A. Florent/A. McLean (AUS) 3–6 7–6 7–5.

GUANGZHOU (CHN) 7–13 DECEMBER
Singles: L. Paes (IND) d. R. Matuszewski 6–3 6–3. *Doubles:* K. Kinnear (USA)/C. Saceanu (GER) d. R. Matuszewski/J. Sullivan (USA) 6-7 6-3 6-4.

HONG KONG (HKG) 14–20 DECEMBER
Singles: T. Ho (USA) d. G. Rusedski (CAN) 4–6 6–4 7–6. *Doubles:* D. Johnson (USA)/L. Paes (IND) d. R. Matuszewski/J. Sullivan (USA) 6–2 7–6.

MEN'S SATELLITE CIRCUITS 1992

There were 65 satellite circuits for men in 40 countries during 1992, all offering prize money. These circuits, consisting of three tournaments plus a Masters, are organised and run by member nations of the International Tennis Federation. Below are listed the winners of each circuit, together with points won as well as the Masters winner for each circuit and points won.

CIRCUIT	SINGLES WINNER (+ PTS)	MASTERS WINNER (+PTS)
Argentina I	P. Escribano (ARG) (71)	L. Andreotti (ARG) (66)
Argentina II	D. Varela (ARG) (73)	D. Varela (ARG) (73)
Australia I	G. Doyle (AUS) (59)	G. Doyle (AUS) (59)
Australia II	D. Nainkin (RSA) (55)	L. Bale (RSA) (45)
Australia III	J. Grunewald (GER) (65)	J. Grunewald (GER) (65)
Austria	H. Mair (AUT) (52)	H. Mair (AUT) (52)
Bangladesh/Pakistan	S. Cole (GBR) (61)	K. Gyorgy (HUN) (54)
Belgium	J. Frawley (AUS) (74)	K. Goosens (BEL) (59)
Brazil I	C. Allgardh (SWE) (56)	G. Schaller (AUT) (46)
Brazil II	D. Johnson (USA) (50)	D. Johnson (USA) (50)
Brazil III	N. Aerts (BRA) (59)/	N. Aerts (BRA) (59)
	H. Moretti (ARG) (59)	
Bulgaria	P. Albertsson (SWE) (68)	G. Marx (FRA) (50)
Canada	B. Gyetko (CAN)	
Caribbean I	M. Charpentier (ARG) (49)	V. Frieden (SUI) (44)
Caribbean II	O. Casey (IRL) (80)	S. Cole (GBR) (50)
Central Africa	C. Marsh (RSA) (58)	C. Marsh (RSA) (58)
Central America	J. Cortes (COL) (64)	M. Nastase (ROM) (58)
Chile	M. Rios (CHI) (61)	
Chinese Taipei	B. Wijaya (INA) (62)	O. Casey (IRL) (57)
Colombia	M. Rincon (COL) (64)	P. Campana (ECU) (44)
Czechoslovakia	T. Toth (TCH) (62)	J. Bulant (TCH) (59)
Ecuador	E. Diaz (CHI) (48)/	P. Campana (ECU) (36)
	T. Venero (PER) (48)	
Egypt	C. Porumb (ROM) (53)/	G. Schaller (AUT) (53)
	I. Saric (YUG) (53)/	
	G. Schaller (AUT) (53)	
France I	C. Bailey (GBR) (58)	G. Rusedski (CAN) (56)
France II	A. Lopez-Moron (ESP) (68)	A. Lopez-Moron (ESP) (68)
France III	C. Wedenby (SWE) (83)	C. Wedenby (SWE) (83)
Germany I	K. Kucera (TCH) (61)	K. Kucera (TCH) (61)
Germany II	S. Rhode (GER) (69)	S. Rhode (GER) (69)
Germany III	M. Palme (GER) (56)	M. Palme (GER) (56)
Great Britain I	J. Bates (GBR) (73)	J. Donar (SWE) (40)
Great Britain II	P. Norval (RSA) (53)	P. Norval (RSA) (53)
India	L. Paes (IND) (68)	D. Musa (ITA) (41)
Indonesia	O. Casey (IRL) (63)	O. Casey (IRL) (63)
Israel I	E. Ran (ISR) (66)	J. De Jager (RSA) (49)
Italy I	S. Soulie (FRA) (56)	E. Winogradsky (FRA) (48)
Italy II	L. Thomas (TCH) (46)	D. Sanguinetti (ITA) (41)
Italy III	D. Pescariu (ROM) (65)	D. Musa (ITA) (47)

Korea	E. Chang (KOR) (59)/	E. Chang (KOR) (59)
	H. Shin (KOR) (59)	
Malaysia I	R. Rasheed (AUS) (64)	A. Kratzmann (AUS) (36)
Malaysia II	B. Pan (CHN) (75)	A. Chang (CAN) (48)
Mexico	A. Moreno (MEX) (72)	A. Moreno (MEX) (72)
Morocco	M. Ridaoui (MAR) (52)	G. Parino (ARG) (49)
Netherlands	W. Kowalski (POL) (79)	W. Kowalski (POL) (79)
Peru/Bolivia	C. Tarantino (ARG) (64)	R. Alvarenga (PAR) (44)
Philippines	C. Borroni (ITA) (58)	S. Scaiola (ITA) (50.5)
Portugal I	J-L. Rascon (ESP) (54)	L. Gloria (USA) (38)
Portugal II	A. Voinea (ROM) (63)	G. Castrichella (ITA) (54)
Portugal III	N. Marques (POR) (72)	N. Marques (POR) (72)
Romania	G. Cosac (ROM) (77)	G. Cosac (ROM) (77)
Spain I	J. Burillo (ESP) (65)	J. Burillo (ESP) (65)
Spain II	D. De Miguel (ESP) (62)	G. Puentes (ESP) (53.5)
Spain III	J-L. Rascon (ESP) (67)	D. Vacek (TCH) (64)
Spain IV	J. Gisbert (ESP) (52)	A. Moreno (MEX) (42)
Spain V	J. Mas (ESP) (73)	J. Mas (ESP) (73)
Spain VI	O. Kristianson (SWE) (80)	A. Caltrava (ESP) (44)
Spain VII	J. Molina (ESP) (58)	N. Sabas (FRA) (48)
Switzerland	A. Radulescu (ROM) (55)	
Sweden	S. Touzil (GER) (60)	J. Windahl (SWE) (59)
Tunisia	A. Gaudenzi (ITA) (63)	T. Van Houdt (BEL) (59)
Turkey	F. Rizzo (ITA) (48)	E. Ran (ISR) (41)
USA I	N. Utgren (SWE) (78)	N. Utgren (SWE) (78)
USA II	A. Parker (USA) (62)	A. Parker (USA) (62)
USA III	R. Matuszewski (USA) (78)	A. Sznajder (CAN) (66)
USA IV	D. Sachs (USA) (77)	J. Waite (USA) (50)
USA V	M. Joyce (USA) (83)	M. Palme (GER) (53)

ITF WOMEN'S FUTURES CIRCUIT

Acceptance into Kraft Tour events is based on a player's position on the Virginia Slims Rankings computed regularly by the Women's Tennis Association (WTA). It is therefore essential for all players who wish to compete that they earn computer ranking points.

A series of lower level prize money tournaments exist as an apprenticeship circuit to the Kraft Tour. This level has been in existence for over a decade, funded and co-ordinated by Regional and National Associations responsible for development of the grass roots game in their respective countries. In 1990 this worldwide initiative became known as the ITF FUTURES CIRCUIT and is run under Regulations promulgated by the International Tennis Federation, the governing body of the National Associations. In 1992 this Circuit comprised 184 events offering a total in excess of $2.8 million in prize money. This represents a growth of over a quarter of a million dollars in the total amount of prize money which was on offer in 1991 with several additional events scheduled on the calendar as well as new venues. During 1992, ITF Futures Circuit tournaments were staged in no fewer than 52 countries spanning 5 continents. Eligible for WTA computer credit, ITF Futures Events fall into the following categories:-

$20,000 Development Circuits
A Circuit of three tournaments, each offering $5,000 in prize money, plus a Masters tournament offering $5,000 for the most successful players. Total prize money available is $20,000 over four weeks. Players receive computer points for the Main Draw of the Masters event only and therefore these Circuits, which are suitable for national unranked players, provide essential match-play experience for players under professional conditions to enable them to begin to earn an initial ranking.

$40,000 Satellite Circuits
A Circuit of three tournaments, each of $10,000 in prize money, plus a Masters tournament also of $10,000 for the most successful players, offering a total of $40,000 in prize money. Players receive computer credit for each tournament played if they reach the Main Draw, and these Circuits provide essential match-play experience under more international conditions.

$10,000 Satellite Tournaments
Individual tournaments of $10,000 in prize money. Players receive computer points for the Main Draw only and these events therefore help them achieve their minimum three tournaments required to appear on the ranking list, and improve the position of players ranked below 200 on the computer.

$25,000/$50,000/$75,000 Challenger Tournaments
Individual tournaments of $25,000, $50,000 or $75,000 in prize money. Players receive computer credit for the last three rounds of Qualifying and the Main Draw. These events help those ranked higher than 200 on the computer to improve their ranking towards acceptance into Kraft Tour events.

Note: Further information on the $10,000 Satellite Circuits is available on request from the Director of Women's Tennis at the ITF office.

1992 ITF FUTURES CIRCUIT RESULTS
$20,000 - DEVELOPMENT CIRCUITS MASTERS

MEXICO, MONTERREY – MARCH 10–15
SINGLES: R. Pichardo (CUB) d. B. Rodriguez (CUB) 6–3 2–6 6–3
DOUBLES: L. Becerra (MEX)/V. Procacci (USA) d. R. Pichardo (CUB)/B. Rodriguez (CUB) 6–4 6–4

MEXICO, MEXICO CITY – OCTOBER 8–11
SINGLES: L. Becerra (MEX) d. A. Vallejo (MEX) 6–2 3–6 6–1
DOUBLES: L. Becerra (MEX)/C. Mucino (MEX) d. C. Ojeda (MEX)/F. Hernandez (MEX) 6–3 6–1

EL SALVADOR, SAN SALVADOR – NOVEMBER 17–22
SINGLES: B. Rodriquez (CUB) d. C. Hincapie (COL) 6–4 6–4
DOUBLES: B. Rodriquez (CUB)/Y. Montesino (CUB) d. A. Garcia (COL)/C. Hincapie (COL) 6–2 6–2

EGYPT, CAIRO – DECEMBER 14–20
SINGLES: M. Augsburger (SUI) d. M. Neufort (BEL) 7–6 6–3
DOUBLES: M. Augsburger (SUI)/K. Misic (CRO) d. A. Elshishini (EGY)/M. Elway (EGY) 6–1 6–1

$40,000 – SATELLITE CIRCUITS

AUSTRALIA, MILDURA (CIRCUIT I) – MARCH 4–8
SINGLES: J. Taylor (AUS) d. J. Richardson (NZL) 7–6 6–3
DOUBLES: J. Richardson (NZL)/A. Trail (NZL) d. K. Sharpe (AUS)/K. McDonald (AUS) 7–6 7–6

AUSTRALIA, WODONGA (CIRCUIT II) – MARCH 11–15
SINGLES: K. McDonald (AUS) d. J. Richardson (NZL) 6–0, 7–6
DOUBLES: J. Richardson (NZL)/A. Trail (NZL) d. D. Jones (AUS)/K. Radford (AUS) 6–4 6–4

AUSTRALIA, LYNEHAM (CIRCUIT III) – MARCH 18–23
SINGLES: J. Richardson (NZL) d. K. Radford (AUS) 6–2 6–0
DOUBLES: J. Richardson (NZL)/A. Trail (NZL) d. D. Jones (AUS)/K. Radford (AUS) 6–3 6–3

AUSTRALIA, NEWCASTLE (MASTERS) – MARCH 25–29
SINGLES: J. Taylor (AUS) d. J. Richardson (NZL) 6–3 3–6 6–3
DOUBLES: J. Richardson (NZL)/A. Trail (NZL) d. M. Anderson (RSA)/J. Taylor (AUS) 6–4 6–2

CHINESE TAIPEI, TAIWAN (CIRCUIT I) – AUGUST 10–16
SINGLES: S-H. Park (KOR) d. T. Tanasugarn (THA) 6–3 6–1
DOUBLES: Y-H. Lin (TPE)/T–T. Weng (TPE) d. N. Akahori (JPN)/K. Ishida (JPN) 6–4 6–1

CHINESE TAIPEI, TAIWAN (CIRCUIT II) – AUGUST 18–22
SINGLES: S-H. Park (KOR) d. L. Weerasuriya (SRI) 6–3 1–6 7–6
DOUBLES: S-H. Park (KOR)/H-J. Seo (KOR) d. J-J. Doh (KOR)/M-J. Lee (KOR) 6–2 7–5

CHINESE TAIPEI, TAIWAN (CIRCUIT III) – AUGUST 24–30
SINGLES: S-H. Park (KOR) d. L. Weerasuriya (SRI) 7–5 3–6 6–4
DOUBLES: S-H. Park (KOR)/H-J. Seo (KOR) d. J-J. Doh (KOR)/M-J. Lee (KOR) 6–2 7–6

CHINESE TAIPEI, TAIWAN (MASTERS) – AUGUST 31–SEPTEMBER 6
SINGLES: S-H. Park (KOR) d. L. Weerasuriya (SRI) 6–2 3–6 6–4
DOUBLES: J-J. Doh (KOR)/M-J. Lee (KOR) d. M. Beadman (AUS)/A. Evers (NED) 6–3 6–4

MEXICO, CUERNAVACA (CIRCUIT I) – AUGUST 19–23
SINGLES: C. Lucarelli (FRA) d. L. Becerra (MEX) 6–3 7–5
DOUBLES: I. Petrov (MEX)/C. Chabalgoity (BRA) d. S. Gevers (RSA)/L. Horn (RSA) 7–5 3–6 6–2

MEXICO, QUERETARO (CIRCUIT II) – AUGUST 24–30
SINGLES: C. Chabalgoity (BRA) d. M–V. Francesa (VEN) 6–2 6–3
DOUBLES: V. Webb (CAN)/R. Kolkobic (CAN) d. X. Escobedo (MEX)/L. Becerra (MEX) 6–3 6–2

MEXICO, TOLUCA (CIRCUIT III) – AUGUST 31–SEPTEMBER 6
SINGLES: J. Nejedly (CAN) d. N. Kovarcikova (TCH) 6–4 6–4
DOUBLES: L. Becerra (MEX)/X. Escobedo (MEX) d. R. Kolkobic (CAN)/V. Webb (CAN) 7–6 6–7 7–5

MEXICO, MEXICO (MASTERS) – SEPTEMBER 9–12
SINGLES: N.Kovarcikova (TCH) d. L. Becerra (MEX) 7–5 5–7 7–6
DOUBLES: X. Escobedo (MEX)/L. Becerra (MEX) d. I. Petrov (MEX)/C. Chabalgoity (BRA) 6–3 6–2

JAPAN, IBARAGI (CIRCUIT I) – SEPTEMBER 30–OCTOBER 4
SINGLES: F. Yamazaki (JPN) d. H. Hiroko (JPN) 7–5 1–0 (ret)
DOUBLES: N. Kijimuta (JPN)/Y. Hosoki (JPN) d. A. Delone (USA)/L. Meshes (AUS) 6–3 2–2 (ret)

JAPAN, IBARAGI (CIRCUIT II) – OCTOBER 7–12
SINGLES: M. Mizokuchi (JPN) d. M. Yanagi (JPN) 7–5 1–6 6–1
DOUBLES: Y. Hosoki (JPN)/N. Kijimuta (JPN) d. M. Donoshiro (JPN)/Y. Tanaka (JPN) 6–2 6–4

JAPAN, TOKYO (CIRCUIT III) – OCTOBER 14–18
SINGLES: M. Donoshiro (JPN) d. M. Yanagi (JPN) 7–5 6–4
DOUBLES: H. Mochizuki (JPN)/M. Yanagi (JPN) d. Y. Sasano (JPN)/Y. Wauke (JPN) 6–2 3–6 6–2

JAPAN, KYOTO (MASTERS) – OCTOBER 22–25
SINGLES: M. Yanagi (JPN) d. M. Mizokuchi (JPN) 6–2 6–4
DOUBLES: Y. Hosoki (JPN)/N. Kijimuta (JPN) d. M. Yanagi (JPN)/V. Sureephong (USA) 6–3 6–3

$25,000 CHALLENGERS

USA, MIDLAND, MI – JANUARY 28–FEBRUARY 2
SINGLES: H. Kelesi (CAN) d. C. Wegink (NED) 7–6 7–6
DOUBLES: M. Bollegraf (NED)/M. McGrath (USA) d. H. Kelesi (CAN)/C. Vis (NED) 6–3 6–1

SPAIN, BARCELONA – FEBRUARY 18–23
SINGLES: E. Bes (ESP) d. C. Wegink (NED) 7–6 7–4
DOUBLES: P. Holubova (TCH)/M. Stuskova (TCH) d. G. Coorengel (NED)/A. Van Buuren (NED) 5–7 6–4 6–2

USA, KEY BISCAYNE, FL – FEBRUARY 25–MARCH 1
SINGLES: C. Kuhlman (USA) d. K. Nagatsuka (JPN) 4–6 6–2 7–5
DOUBLES: L. Davenport (USA)/K. Schlukebir (USA) d. T. Morton (AUS)/T. Takagi (JPN) 6–1 6–3

SPAIN, VALENCIA – FEBRUARY 25–MARCH 1
SINGLES: F. Romano (ITA) d. A. Olivier (FRA) 5–7 6–1 6–4
DOUBLES: V. Ruano (ESP)/E. Bottini (ESP) d. P. Holubova (TCH)/M. Stuskova (TCH) 6–1 6–2

FRANCE, MOULINS – MARCH 30–APRIL 5
SINGLES: E. Callens (BEL) d. P. Holubova (TCH) 5–7 6–2 6–3
DOUBLES: S. Schilder (NED)/I. Driehuis (NED) d. P. Kucova (TCH)/E. Martincova (TCH) 6–4 7–5

ITALY, MONCALIERI – MARCH 31–APRIL 5
SINGLES: I. Cueto (GER) d. V. Ruano (ESP) 6–3 6–2
DOUBLES: E. Makarova (CIS)/K. Kroupova (TCH) d. R. Bobkova (TCH)/I. Pospisilova (TCH) 6–4 2–6 6–2

FRANCE, LIMOGES – APRIL 7–12
SINGLES: P. Holubova (TCH) d. B. Reinstadler (AUT) 6–1 7–5
DOUBLES: E. Callens (BEL)/M. Strebel (SUI) d. L. Bacheva (BUL)/S. Podlahova (TCH) 4–6 6–1 6–4

ITALY, CASERTA – APRIL 7–12
SINGLES: K. Kroupova (TCH) d. R. Bobkova (TCH) 6–4 6–2
DOUBLES: R. Bobkova (TCH)/J. Pospisilova (TCH) d. V. Ruano (ESP)/E. Bottini (ESP) 6–3 2–6 2–6

ITALY, BARI – APRIL 21–26
SINGLES: S. Dopfer (AUT) d. A. Blumberga (CIS) 6–2 6–3
DOUBLES: J. Hodder (AUS)/K. Sharpe (AUS) d. K. Kroupova (TCH)/E. Martinkova (TCH) 6–2 6–3

INDONESIA, JAKARTA – APRIL 27–MAY 2
SINGLES: N. Dobrovits (AUT) d. H. Nagano (JPN) 6–2 6–4
DOUBLES: K–A. Guse (AUS)/K. Radford (AUS) d. T. Morton (AUS)/J. Richardson (NZL) 7–6 6–2

ISRAEL, ASHKELON – MAY 25–30
SINGLES: K. Studenikova (TCH) d. A. Gima (ROM) 6–4 6–4
DOUBLES: I. Berger (ISR)/P. Kamstra (NED) d. M. Anderson (RSA)/I. Zaltz (ISR) 6–2 2–6 6–4

ITALY, BRINDISI – JUNE 2–7
SINGLES: F. Perfetti (ITA) d. L. Tella (BRA) 7–5 6–3
DOUBLES: N. Baudone (ITA)/C. Salvi (ITA) d. E. Melicharova (TCH)/I. Jankovska (TCH) 4–6 6–3 6–2

ITALY, MODENA – JUNE 7–14
SINGLES: J. Kruger (RSA) d. A. Fusai (FRA) 6–4 6–3
DOUBLES: E. Pampoulova (BUL)/R. Dragomir (ROM) d. A. Fusai (FRA)/N. Tschan (SUI) 6–3 7–6

ITALY, MILAN – JUNE 16–21
SINGLES: E. Zardo (SUI) d. F. Perfetti (ITA) 6–4 6–4
DOUBLES: M. Yokobori (JPN)/K. Nagatsuka (JPN) d. L. Tella (BRA)/A. Vieira (BRA) 3–6 6–1 6–3

USA, ST. SIMONS ISLAND, GA – JUNE 15–21
SINGLES: I. Majoli (CRO) d. B. Bowes (USA) 7–6 7–6
DOUBLES: A. May (USA)/S. Reece (USA) d. S. Cacic (USA)/M. Jackson–Nobrega (USA) 6–3 7–6

ITALY, REGGIO EMILIA – JUNE 23–28
SINGLES: E. Zardo (SUI) d. R. Dragomir (ROM) 6–1 7–6
DOUBLES: R. Dragomir (ROM)/N. Tschan (SUI) d. B. Colette (FRA)/A. Fusai (FRA) 3–6 6–2 6–1

SWEDEN, RONNEBY – JUNE 30–JULY 5
SINGLES: M. Maruska (AUT) d. A. Carlsson (SWE) 4–6 6–1 6–2
DOUBLES: A. Narbe (SWE)/C. Bernstein (SWE) d. C. Thompson (AUS)/R. Mawdsley (AUS) 7–5 6–3

GERMANY, VAIHINGEN – JULY 1–5
SINGLES: J. Kruger (RSA) d. L. Bacheva (BUL) 6–1 6–0
DOUBLES: P. Rajzlova (TCH)/E. Martincova (TCH) d. E. Pampoulova (BUL)/J. Kruger (RSA) 6–4 6–0

GERMANY, ERLANGEN – JULY 8–12
SINGLES: K. Kschwendt (GER) d. A–M. Foeldenyi (HUN) 6–4 6–2
DOUBLES: L. Chen (CHN)/M. Yokobori (JPN) d. C. Schneider (GER)/A. Woolcock (AUS) 6–4 6–2

SPAIN, VIGO – JULY 13–19
SINGLES: A. Narbe (SWE) d. M. Miyauchi (JPN) 6–3 6–3
DOUBLES: R. Bielsa (ESP)/J. Souto (ESP) d. K. Johnson (USA)/S. Lohmann (GER) 2–6 6–3 7–5

USA, EVANSVILLE – JULY 12–19
SINGLES: I. Majoli (CRO) d. A. Sugiyama (JPN) 6–3 6–1
DOUBLES: D. Jones (AUS)/T. Price (RSA) d. M. Bernard (CAN)/C. Delisle (CAN) 6–2 4–6 6–4

ITALY, SEZZE – JULY 14–19
SINGLES: K. Piccolini (ITA) d. M. Grossi (ITA) 6–3 3–6 6–2
DOUBLES: I. Jankovska (TCH)/E. Melicharova (TCH) d. J. Hodder (AUS)/K. Sharpe (AUS) 7–6 5–7 7–5

SPAIN, BILBAO – JULY 21–25
SINGLES: V. Ruano (ESP) d. C. Wegink (NED) 7–5 6–2
DOUBLES: E. Bes (ESP)/V. Ruano (ESP) d. J. Emmons (USA)/C. Thompson (AUS) 6–2 6–4

GERMANY, DARMSTADT – JULY 22–26
SINGLES: A. Foeldenyi (HUN) d. N. Ardent (USA) 6–2 7–6
DOUBLES: N. Ardent (USA)/T. Krizan (SLO) d. A. Popp (GER)/S. Wachterhauser (GER) 6–2 6–1

GERMANY, RHEDA – JULY 29–AUGUST 2
SINGLES: B. Mulej (SLO) d. E. Marakova (CIS) 7–5 6–3
DOUBLES: C. Blahova (TCH)/Z. Malkova (TCH) d. E. Martincova (TCH)/S. Podlahova (TCH) 7–6 6–4

USA, YORK – AUGUST 10–16
SINGLES: N. Miyagi (JPN) d. N. Ardent (USA) 6–2 6–4
DOUBLES: N. Ardent (USA)/S. McCarthy (USA) d. D. Jones (AUS)/T. Price (RSA) 6–3 6–3

POLAND, SOPOT – AUGUST 12–16
SINGLES: R. Bobkova (TCH) d. M. Strandlund (SWE) 6–4 4–6 6–4
DOUBLES: K. Teodorowicz (POL)/M. Stuskova (TCH) d. J. Emmons (USA)/M. Stradlund (SWE) 6–4 6–2

AUSTRIA, KLAGENFURT – SEPTEMBER 1–6
SINGLES: R. Dragomir (ROM) d. A. Carlsson (SWE) 6–4 6–3
DOUBLES: D. Szabova (TCH)/J. Pospisilova (TCH) d. K. Oeljeklaus (GER)/H. Thoms (GER) w.o.

BULGARIA, SOFIA – SEPTEMBER 16–20
SINGLES: H. Rusch (GER) d. S. Van Der AA (NED) 6–3 4–6 6–1
DOUBLES: K. Kuregian (CIS)/K. Sharpe (AUS) d. G. Angelova (BUL)/I. Bacheva (BUL) 7–6 6–2

ITALY, ACIREALE – SEPTEMBER 22–27
SINGLES: K. Piccolini (ITA) d. L. Lapi (ITA) 6–3 6–2
DOUBLES: C. Wegink (NED)/K. Sharpe (AUS) d. A. Segura (ESP)/J. Souto (ESP) 4–6 6–1 6–1

ITALY, S. MARIA C. VETERE – SEPTEMBER 29–OCTOBER 4
SINGLES: R. de los Rios (PAR) d. M. Grossi (ITA) 6–4 6–0
DOUBLES: I. Spirlea (ROM)/A. Devries (BEL) d. G. Mugnani (ITA)/A. Vanc (ROM) 6–0 6–0

USA, SALISBURY, MD – SEPTEMBER 28–OCTOBER 4
SINGLES: B. Bowes (USA) d. M. Drake (CAN) 6–3 6–2
DOUBLES: B. Bowes (USA)/T. Whittington (USA) d. M. Mroz (POL)/K. Teodorowicz (POL) 5–7 6–2 6–0

USA, LEAWOOD, KS – OCTOBER 4–11
SINGLES: R. Alter–Simpson (CAN) d. C. Kuhlman (USA) 7–6 1–6 6–3
DOUBLES: N. Ardent (USA)/A. Gooden (USA) d. R. Jensen (USA)/S. Reece (USA) 6–3 6–1

MEXICO, SAN LUIS POTOSI – OCTOBER 19–25
SINGLES: A. Gavaldon (MEX) d. M. Drake (CAN) 6–1 6–4
DOUBLES: M. Mroz (POL)/K. Teodorowicz (POL) d. I. Petrov (MEX)/J. Watanabe (USA) 4–6 6–4 6–4

PORTUGAL, FUNCHAL – OCTOBER 26–NOVEMBER 1
SINGLES: S. Pitkowski (FRA) d. A. Oliver (FRA) 6–3 3–6 6–1
DOUBLES: K. Ptasek (DEN)/M. Vallin (SWE) d. E. Callens (BEL)/J. Jehs (GER) 6–1 6–3

JAPAN, SAGA – OCTOBER 28–NOVEMBER 1
SINGLES: J. Richardson (NZL) d. T. Price (RSA) 6–2 7–6
DOUBLES: M. Yanagi (JPN)/A. Hirose (JPN) d. K. Studenicova (TCH)/E. Martincova (TCH) 6–2 6–0

GREAT BRITAIN, MANCHESTER – NOVEMBER 10–14
SINGLES: N. Feber (BEL) d. E. Makarova (CIS) 7–5 4–6 6–2
DOUBLES: E. Likhovtseva (CIS)/E. Makarova (CIS) d. E. Pampoulova-Wagner (BUL)/N. Tschan (SUI) 6–1 4–6 6–0

AUSTRALIA, MT GAMBIER – NOVEMBER 11–15
SINGLES: A. Fusai (FRA) d. S. Cacic (USA) 6–4 6–2
DOUBLES: L. Stacey (AUS)/C. Barclay (AUS) d. E. Martincova (TCH)/J. Hubarova (TCH) 7–6 6–7 7–6

GREAT BRITAIN, NOTTINGHAM – NOVEMBER 17–21
SINGLES: E. Makarova (CIS) d. E. Pampoulova–Wagner (BUL) 3–6 6–2 7–5
DOUBLES E. Callens (BEL)/Pampoulova–Wagner (BUL) d. R. Dragomir (ROM)/I. Spirlea (ROM) 7–6 6–4

AUSTRALIA, PORT PIRIE – NOVEMBER 16–22
SINGLES: T. Price (RSA) d. J. Limmer (AUS) 3–6 6–3 6–1
DOUBLES: T. Price (RSA)/D. Jones (AUS) d. R. Mawdsley (AUS)/J. Limmer (AUS) 6–2 5–7 6–3

ISRAEL, RAMAT HASHARON – NOVEMBER 23–30
SINGLES: K. Studenikova (TCH) d. C. Lucarella (FRA) 6–4 6–2
DOUBLES: C. Bakkum (NED)/I. Driehaus (NED) d. G. Coorengel (NED)/Y. Segal (ISR) 6–2 6–1

AUSTRALIA, NURIOOPTA – NOVEMBER 23–29
SINGLES: A. Fusai (FRA) d. M. Jaggard–Lai (AUS) 7–6 3–6 6–3
DOUBLES: K–A. Guse (AUS)/A. Woolcock (AUS) d. K. Sharpe (AUS)/M. Mroz (POL) 4–6 7–6 6–2

FRANCE, LE HAVRE – NOVEMBER 30–DECEMBER 6
SINGLES: R. Dragomir (ROM) d. S. Pitkowski (FRA) 7–6 7–5
DOUBLES: R. Dragomir (ROM)/I. Spirlea (ROM) d. S. Lohmann (FRG)/A. Kerek (FRG) 6–3 7–6

AUSTRALIA, MILDURA – 30 NOVEMBER 30–DECEMBER 6
SINGLES: T. Price (RSA) d. R. de los Rios (PAR) 6–3 6–3
DOUBLES: C. Barclay (AUS)/L. Stacey (AUS) d. M. Jaggard–Lai (AUS)/L. Smylie (AUS) 6–4 6–4

$50,000 CHALLENGERS

INDONESIA, JAKARTA – FEBRUARY 3–9
SINGLES: I. Spirlea (ROM) d. A. Devries (BEL) 6–3 6–2
DOUBLES: A. Woolcock (AUS)/N. Pratt (AUS) d. R. Dragomir (ROM)/I. Spirlea (ROM) 6–1 6–0

ITALY, SALERNO – APRIL 11–19
SINGLES: K. Kroupova (TCH) d. N. Perez (ESP) 6–2 6–3
DOUBLES: L. Ferrando (ITA)/S. Farina (ITA) d. A. Woolcock (AUS)/K. Sharpe (AUS) 6–1 6–4

PORTUGAL, OPORTO – MAY 4–10
SINGLES: A.M. Foldenyi (HUN) d. M. Zivec–Skulj (GER) 6–2 6–3
DOUBLES: M. Jaggard (AUS)/V. Ruano (ESP) d. J. Fuchs (USA)/M. Strandlund (SWE) 6–3 7–5

INDONESIA, JAKARTA – OCTOBER 26–NOVEMBER 1
SINGLES: J. Santrock (USA) d. A. Devries (BEL) 2–6 6–4 7–6
DOUBLES: M. Jaggard–Lai (AUS)/K. Radford (AUS) d. K. Godridge (AUS)/N. Pratt (AUS) 3–6 6–3 6–2

JAPAN, MACHIDA – NOVEMBER 4–8
SINGLES: Y. Kamio (JPN) d. T Price (RSA) 4–6 7–6 6–2
DOUBLES: J. Richardson (NZL)/M. Jaggard Lai (AUS) d. M. Kidowaki (JPN)/I. Driehuis (NED) 6–3 7–5

FRANCE, VAL D'OISE – NOVEMBER 7–13
SINGLES: N. Tauziat (FRA) d. C. Singer (GER) 6–4 6–3
DOUBLES: I. Demongeot (FRA)/C. Suire (FRA) d. S. Appelmans (BEL)/J. Halard (FRA) 7–5 6–4

AUSTRALIA, MELBOURNE – DECEMBER 15–20
SINGLES: E. Delone (USA) d. E. Smylie (AUS) 7–5 7–5
DOUBLES: J. Hodder (AUS)/A. Woolcock (AUS) d. K. Radford (AUS)/K–A. Guse (AUS) 6–4 3–6 6–2

$75,000 CHALLENGERS

ITALY, SPOLETO – AUGUST 18–23
SINGLES: M. Zivec Skulj (GER) d. S. Wasserman (BEL) 6–0 7–6
DOUBLES: F. Perfetti (ITA)/G. Pizzichini (ITA) d. S. Dopfer (AUT)/M. Zivec Skulj (GER) 1–6 6–2 6–1

ITALY, ARZACHENA – SEPTEMBER 8–13
SINGLES: G. Pizzichini (ITA) d. L. Ferrando (ITA) 6–3 6–4
DOUBLES: L. Garrone (ITA)/L. Golarsa (ITA) d. S. Farina (ITA)/L. Ferrando (ITA) 6–4 4–6 6–4

CZECHOSLOVAKIA, KARLOVY VARY – SEPTEMBER 15–20
SINGLES: J. Wiesner (AUT) d. H. Sukova (TCH) 6–4 7–6
DOUBLES: M. Lindstrom (SWE)/M. Strandlund (SWE) d. K. Kroupova (TCH)/J. Pospisilova (TCH) 6–2 6–1

INTERNATIONAL TEAM COMPETITIONS

EUROPEAN CUPS
WORLD TEAM CUP

In the autumn of her career, the British No.1 Jo Durie led her country to a first success in the European Cup competition. *(T. Hindley)*

OTHER INTERNATIONAL TEAM EVENTS

Henry Wancke and John Oakley

EUROPEAN CUP – MEN

An international team event for European nations was first played in 1936 as the Kings Cup and, in the intervening 56 years, the competition has undergone many changes, not least when it became the men's European Cup in 1985. The format at that time was a round robin affair which was continued but in 1992 the European Tennis Association reintroduced a knock-out draw which was last played in 1974.

The competition now consists of three tiers with the top one being aptly named the 'Champions Division' involving the top eight European nations. Relegation and promotion matches still apply though the second division, known as the Promotion Division, consists of 16 nations playing in two groups of eight. The groups also play off in a knock out draw with the winners of each of these groups being promoted, replacing the losers of the relegation matches between first round losers of the 'Champions Division.'

The final tier is now the 'Qualifiers Division' and again two nations can gain access to the 'Promotion Division', replacing losers of relegation matches contested by first round losers of that division. With the emergence of new European nations following the sudden break up of the former communist block, this seems a natural way for nations to establish themselves in the competition as Croatia, Estonia, Slovenia and Ukraine no doubt found out. Another nation competing for the first time was Israel.

Trieste in Italy provided the stage for the 'Champions Division' and the new format produced a series of exciting matches more in keeping with an international team competition. Sweden, seeded to win, eventually emerged as Champions but to do so had to quickly rethink their strategy when Henrik Holm, their leading player, was forced out of the team with a throat infection. With a world ranking of 19, his contribution to the Swedish challenge was expected to be a major factor in the proceedings but as it turned out, his eventual replacement in the team proved more than adequate. Niklas Kulti, playing in the Compaq Grand Slam Cup, was flown in having become available following his first round loss in Munich though the Swedes were forced to play their first round match against the CIS employing the services of Mikael Tillstrom and Thomas Enqvist. They eventually won through with Tillstrom defeating Dmitry Palyonov 6–2 7–5 and Enqvist finally quelling Aleksei Filippov 5–7 7–6 (7–4) 7–6 (7–5) in a match which could have stopped Sweden's campaign at the first hurdle.

In the semi-final against Great Britain (2–1 victors over Czechoslovakia in the previous round) Kulti was available though Mark Petchey kept him on court longer than he expected before claiming a 6–2.1–6 6–2 victory. Chris Wilkinson levelled the tie in the second singles with a superior display of tennis when he beat the 18-year-old Enqvist 6–3 6–4 but in the deciding doubles Kulti and Tillstrom dominated the Britons with their superior returns to claim a place in the final, 7–6 (7–4) 6–4.

In the other half of the draw, the second seeds, Germany, emerged to contest the championship stage with victories over Austria and Italy, dropping a rubber in both ties. Niki Pilic, the German captain, dropped Bernard Karbacher from his line-up as he had failed to score any wins during the previous matches and brought in Markus Naewie at No 1 with Mark Goellner playing at No. 2. The contest was close as highlighted by the first singles when Kulti and Goellner delivered numerous aces in a match full of doubtful calls and rising temperatures. Kulti claimed that first rubber 6–4 7–6 (7–0) for Sweden but then Naewie defeated Enqvist 6–3 6–4 to bring Germany back into contention, thus forcing him back on court in partnership with Tillstrom for the doubles against Naewie and Goellner to decide the championship.

This rubber fittingly, proved to be the match of the competition as both pairs fought for every point and having taken the first set, the Germans stood poised for the title as they served for it in the third set tie-break. A forehand return winner from Kulti kept the Swede's interests alive which, followed by some excellent serve-and-volley play from Tillstrom, put Sweden 8–7 ahead. Goellner, now serving to keep German hopes alive, then sank a very nervous forehand volley into the net to concede the doubles 4–6 6–3 7–6 (9–7) and hand Sweden the title, giving the young Scandanavians their first European Cup championship since 1985.

Austria beat the Netherlands 2–0 and Czechoslovakia defeated the CIS 2–1 to retain 'Champions Division' status for 1993.(H. W.)

CHAMPIONS DIVISION
TRIESTE, ITALY

FIRST ROUND: – Sweden d. CIS 2–0 (M. Tillstrom (SWE) d. D. Palyonov (CIS) 6–2 7–5, T. Enqvist (SWE) d. A. Filipov (CIS) 5–7 7–6 7–6). (Doubles not played); **Gt. Britain d. Czechoslovakia 2–1** (P. Vizne (TCH) d. M. Petchey(GBR) 7–5 6–2, C. Wilkinson (GBR) d. K.I Kucera (TCH) 6–3 6–1, Petchey/Wilkinson(GBR) d. R.Vasek/Vizner(TCH) 6–3 7–6); **Germany d. Austria 2–1** (M. Naewie (GER) d. J. Knowle (AUT) 6–1 6–1, T.Perovsky (AUT) d. B. Karbacher(GER) 7–6 6–3, Goellner/Naewie(GER) d. Mandle/Perovsky(AUT) 6–4 7–6); **Italy d. Netherlands 3–0** (A. Gaudenzi(ITA) d. M. Van Den Bergh(NED) 7–5 6–3, M. Valeri (ITA) d.J. Wiynhoud (NED) 6–2 6–3, Borroni/Navarra(ITA) d. Vandenberg/Wiynhoud (NED) 3–6 7–6 6–4). **SEMI-FINALS: – Sweden d. Gt.Britain 2–1** (N. Kult (SWE) d. Petchey (GBR) 6–2 1–6 6–2, Wilkinson (GBR) d. Enqvist (SWE) 6–3 6–4, Kulti/Tillstrom (SWE) d. Petchey/Wilkinson 7–6 6–4); **Germany d. Italy 2–1** (Naewie (GER) d. Gaudenzi 6–4 6–3, Valeri(ITA) d. Karbacher(GER) 7–5 6–3, Goellner/Naewie d. Gaudenzi/Valeri 6–4 7–5). **FINAL: – Sweden d. Germany 2–1** (Kulti (SWE) d. Goellner (GER) 6–4 7–6, Naewie (GER) d. Enqvist (SWE) 6–3 6–4, Tillstrom/Kulti (SWE) d. Naewie/Goellner (GER) 4–6 6–3 7–6). **RELEGATION PLAY–OFFS (first round losers): – Austria d. Netherlands 2–0, Czechoslovakia d. CIS 2–1.**

EUROPEAN CUP – WOMEN

Jo Durie, a British stalwart for more than a decade, produced her best form for years as Great Britain beat Holland 2–1 in the final to win the European Women's Team championship for the first time, on a fast, indoor court in Prague. Durie was quite superb, for, having to cope with a severe chest cold, she won each of her five matches, three singles and two doubles with Clare Wood, and lost only one service game all week.

Wood, another long-serving member of the British team, also played her part, helping to beat Italy, the second seeds, 3–0 and Belgium 2–1 in group matches and then easily winning the deciding doubles with Durie in the final.

True this event does not attract the world's best women players but for British tennis, which has been in the doldrums for several years, it was a distinct shot in the arm.

Durie, now 32, is one of life's great patriots and she played with the eagerness of an up-and-coming teenager, particularly in her two hour battle with Nicole Muns Jagerman in the final which she won 7–6 6–4 to keep British hopes alive after Wood had lost the opening singles.

Britain, however, were fortunate on two counts. First, they avoided top seeded Czechoslovakia in their three-strong section. Then, in the decisive group match with Belgium, they won a tight doubles against Ann Devries and Dominique Monami, only after Monami was struck on the right elbow by a forehand volley from Wood and, despite treatment, had to retire midway through the second set with the British girls leading 6–2 2–4, and 0–30 in the seventh game.

Holland came through to the final with similar match scores to Britain, beating Switzerland 3–0 and then, to the consternation of the home gallery, defeating Czechoslovakia 2–1.Both Durie and Muns Jagerman had been highly impressive in the group matches with Durie beating diminutive Italian Gloria Pizzichini, unhappy on the fast court, 6–2 6–2 and against Belgium, winning 6–3 6–4 in her singles against Monami even though she lost her service for the only time in the opening game of the match.

Muns Jagerman, ranked only 114 at the time, fared even better for she crushed Emanuela Zardo, the world number 39, 6–0 6–1 in the match with Switzerland and later, in the crucial clash with Czechoslovakia, defeated Radka Zrubakòva, ranked 29th, 6–2 6–7 7–5.

On the last day Switzerland beat Italy 2–1 in the relegation match to send the losers down to the Second Division before Britain and Holland contested the final with the Dutch girls slight favourites, following their victory over Czechoslovakia.

Holland looked like justifying that status when they won the opening rubber with Monique Kiene serving so well she beat Wood 6–2 6–3 in only 74 minutes. Durie, however, again rose to the occasion in a big-serving duel with Muns Jagerman. There were no breaks in the first set though Durie had a set point at 6–5. The pace was unrelenting and an unruffled Muns Jagerman fought back to reach set point herself at 6–5 in the tie-break with her service to come. Then came an astounding rally which Durie won with a remarkable forehand volley after the ball appeared to have gone past her and this one point virtually decided the match. Durie scrambled home 9–7 in the tie-break and, growing in confidence, took the second set with a solitary break in the ninth game.

So it was all on the final rubber and Wood, never beaten in doubles in four years in this event, maintained her 100 per cent record when she and Durie overwhelmed Kiene and a distinctly nervous Miriam Oremans 6–3 6–2 in 66 minutes to give Britain the title. (J.O.)

FIRST DIVISION
PRAGUE, 26–29 NOVEMBER
Group A – Czechoslovakia d. Switzerland 3–0 (K Kroupova d. N Tschan 6–3 6–2; R Zrubakova d. E Zardo 6–1 7–6; Zrubakova and P Langrova d. Tschan and G Dondit 6–4 6–3); ***Holland d. Switzerland 3–0*** (M Kiene d. N Tschan 6–1 6–4; N Muns Jagerman d. E Zardo 6–0 6–1; Kiene and M Oremans d. Zrubakova and P Langrova 6–3 6–3; ***Group B – Belgium d.Italy 3–0*** (S Wasserman d. K Piccolini 6–3 6–2; D. Monami d. G Pizzichini 7–5 6–4; Wasserman and A Devries d. N Baudone and R Grande 7–6 6–4; ***Britain d. Italy 3–0*** (C Wood d. N Baudone 6–3 1–6 6–1; J Durie d. G Pizzichini 6–2 6–2; Wood and S–S Siddall d. Pizzichini and R Grande 7–5 6–2; ***Britain d. Belgium 2–1*** (C Wood lost to A Devries 6–7 6–2 4–6; J Durie d. D Monami 6–3 6–4; Wood and Durie d. Devries and Monami 6–2 2–4 retired.
FINAL: Britain d. Holland 2–1 (C Wood lost to M Kiene 2–6 3–6; J Durie d. N Muns Jagerman 7–6 6–4; Wood and Durie d. Kiene and M Oremans 6–3 6–2. ***RELEGATION PLAY-OFF: Switzerland d. Italy 2–1*** (N Tschan lost to K Piccolini 1–6 0–6; E Zardo d. N Baudone 6–2 6–4; Zardo and Tschan d. G Pizzichini and R Grande 6–3 7–5. Italy were relegated.

PEUGEOT WORLD TEAM CUP
DUSSELDORF, 18–24 MAY
BLUE GROUP RESULTS: USA d. CIS 2–1 (P. Sampras d. A. Volkov 6–2 7–6; D. Rostagno lost to A. Cherkasov 6–4 0–6 3–6; J. Grabb/P. McEnroe d. Cherkasov/Volkov 7–6 4–6 6–3); ***Czechoslovakia d. Germany 3–0*** (P. Korda d. M. Stich 6–3 6–2; K. Novacek d. C. Steeb 7–6 3–6 6–3; Korda/C. Suk d. Steeb/Stich 7–6 6–2); ***Czechoslovakia d. USA 3–0*** (Korda d. Sampras 6–3 6–1; Novacek d. Rostagno 6–3 6–4; Korda/Suk d. Grabb/McEnroe 5–7 6–3 6–4); ***Germany d. CIS 2–1*** (Stich d. Volkov 6–3 6–1; Steeb lost to Cherkasov 6–7 3–6; Steeb/Stich d. Cherkasov/Volkov 7–6 7–6); ***Germany d. USA 3–0*** (Stich d. Sampras 6–7 6–2 6–4; Steeb d. Rostagno 6–1 6–3; Steeb/Stich d. Grabb/McEnroe 7–6 6–2); ***Czechoslovakia d. CIS 2–1*** (Korda d. Volkov 6–4 6–4; Novacek d. Cherkasov 6–7 6–3 6–4; Korda/Suk lost to Cherkasov/Volkov 6–1 3–6 4–6). ***1st:*** Czechoslovakia 3 wins. ***2nd:*** Germany 2 wins. ***3rd:*** USA 1 win. ***4th:*** CIS 0 wins. ***RED GROUP RESULTS: Spain d. Sweden 3–0*** (E. Sanchez d. S. Edberg 1–6 7–6 6–4; S. Bruguera d. M. Gustafsson 5–7 6–4 6–3; S. Casal/Sanchez d. Edberg/A. Jarryd 6–4 7–6); ***France d. Switzerland 2–1*** (G. Forget d. J. Hlasek 6–3 6–2; H. Leconte d. M. Rosset 4–6 7–6 6–1; O. Delaitre/Forget lost to Hlasek/Rosset 6–2 5–7 6–7); ***Spain d. Switzerland 3–0*** (Sanchez d. Hlasek 3–6 6–1 6–4; Bruguera d. Rosset 7–5 6–2; Casal/Sanchez d. Hlasek/Rosset 6–7 7–5 6–4); ***France d. Sweden 2–1*** (Forget d. Edberg 7–5 6–4; Delaitre lost to Gustafsson 3–6 5–7; Forget/Leconte d. Edberg/Jarryd 6–3 6–4); ***Spain d. France 2–1*** (Sanchez d. Forget 4–6 6–2 7–6; Bruguera d. Leconte 6–4 3–6 7–5; Bruguera/Casal lost to Forget/Leconte 6–4 3–6 3–6); ***Sweden d. Switzerland 2–1*** (Edberg d. Hlasek 6–4 3–6 7–6; Gustafsson d. Rosset 6–3 3–6 7–6; Edberg/Jarryd lost to Hlasek/Rosset 7–5 2–6 6–7). ***1st:*** Spain 3 wins. ***2nd:*** France 2 wins. ***3rd:*** Sweden 1 win. ***4th:*** Switzerland 0 wins. ***FINAL: Spain d. Czechoslovakia 3–0*** (Sanchez d. Korda 3–6 6–2 7–6; Bruguera d. Novacek 6–4 6–2; Casal/Sanchez d. Novacek/Suk 1–6 6–4 6–3).

RANKINGS

WORLD RANKINGS
ATP RANKINGS AND PRIZE MONEY
VIRGINIA SLIMS RANKINGS AND PRIZE MONEY

A landmark year for the 20-year-old Dutchman, Richard Krajicek, began with a voyage to the semi-finals at the Australian Open in Melbourne and ended with membership of the exclusive Top Ten club.
(T. Hindley)

WORLD RANKINGS

John Barrett

1992 WORLD RANKINGS (last year's position in brackets)

MEN
1 Jim Courier (USA)(2)
2 Stefan Edberg (SWE) (1)
3 Andre Agassi (USA) (7)
4 Goran Ivanisevic (CRO) (–)
5 Pete Sampras (USA) (8)
6 Boris Becker (GER) (3)
7 Marc Rosset (SUI) (–)
8 Michael Chang (USA) (–)
9 Petr Korda(TCH) (10)
10= Ivan Lendl (USA) (5)
10= Wayne Ferreira (RSA) (–)

WOMEN
1 Monica Seles (YUG) (1)
2 Steffi Graf (GER) (2).
3 Arantxa Sanchez-Vicario (ESP) (5)
4 Jennifer Capriati (USA) (7)
5 Gabriela Sabatini (ARG) (3)
6 Mary Joe Fernandez (USA) (6)
7 Manuela Maleeva Fragnière (SUI) (10)
8 Martina Navratilova (USA) (4)
9 Conchita Martinez (ESP) (9)
10 Natalia Zvereva (CIS) (–)

Despite a wonderful start to the year by Jim Courier during which he captured the Australian and French Opens, as well three events of lesser importance, the 22-year-old American only narrowly held off the late challenge of his old rival, the quiet Swede Stefan Edberg, for the coveted No.1 world ranking. Their rivalry for leadership on the ATP Tour computer was one of the features of the year, just as it had been twelve months earlier. But a computer which considers only a player's best 14 results does not tell the whole story. Nor is the differential between points awarded for the four Grand Slam Championships and the ATP Tour events great enough. Furthermore, the ATP computer does not include Davis Cup results or the Olympic Games – serious omissions these. Accordingly judgement must be brought to bear on the worth of each particular performance, depending upon the stature of the tournament and the strength of the field. The 26-year-old Edberg had a fine year. Not only did he retain his US Open crown with an amazing performance of physical and mental resilience, but he also finished as a finalist at the Australian Open, besides winning two other titles.

How do you deal with Andre Agassi? Although the American had a mediocre year overall, his dramatic win at Wimbledon (a first Grand Slam success, this, after failure in three previous finals) was the season's outstanding performance. Furthermore Agassi did win two other tournaments (Atlanta and Toronto) and contributed significantly to the winning Davis Cup effort by the United States against Switzerland. Taken together, these performances were enough to put him in third place.

More difficult was to separate the two outstanding 20-year-olds, Goran Ivanisevic of Croatia and America's Pete Sampras. Ivanisevic was a finalist at Wimbledon while Sampras reached that stage at the US Open; both were semi-finalists at the two season-ending play-offs – the ATP Tour Championship and the Compaq Grand Slam Cup. Sampras reached the last four at Wimbledon but it was Ivanisevic who beat him there. The Croatian was a semi-finalist at the Olympic Games while the American lost disappointingly in the third round. It was enough to make the difference. As the Olympics come round only once every four years a greater emphasis must be placed on performances there.

Although Boris Becker failed dismally at the Olympic Games (beaten by the 19-year-old Frenchman Fabrice Santoro in the third round), he did claim five tournament titles and the manner of his spectacular finish to the year at the ATP Tour Championship in Frankfurt was enough to place the 25-year-old German ahead of the Olympic champion Marc Rosset.

But what a performance that young man gave us! Rosset was ranked only 43 on the computer at the time, but you would never have guessed it as he carved his way into history. In the stifling heat of Barcelona, the extraordinary exploits of this tall, thin 22-year-old from Geneva were quite simply heroic. He beat in turn Ferreira, Courier (arguably the world's best clay court player), the Spanish No.1 Emilio Sanchez and an exhausted Ivanisevic to reach the most important final of his life. There Rosset survived heatstroke, cramp and the distractions of a fervently patriotic crowd as he beat the local hero Jordi Arrese in five gruelling sets. It was one of the year's highlights.

Like Becker, Michael Chang was an Olympic failure (he lost to Oncins in the second round) but he did win three early tournaments and then made himself a semi-finalist at the US Open. There he pushed Edberg to the limit in one of the year's best matches. Although Petr Korda was the finalist in Paris and won three titles, he was, like Lendl and Ferreira, too inconsistent to earn a higher ranking.

For the second year in a row Monica Seles, the remarkable 18-year-old left-hander from Yugoslavia, was in a class of her own. Her 10 tournament wins included three of the four Grand Slams. Only at Wimbledon was she brought down – and then it was as much the grunting issue as Steffi Graf's superb play that led to her defeat.

Graf was a clear second. Her dramatic failure to wrest the French title from Seles' grasp provided the best match of the year. Her defeat in the Olympic final at the hands of Jennifer Capriati was much more damaging to her morale. In fact it probably contributed to her dismal performances in the last quarter of the year when she fell to Sanchez-Vicario in the quarters at the US Open and to Lori McNeil in the first round of the Virginia Slims final.

Nobody challenged Sanchez-Vicario for third place. For a start no-one played as much. Her 167 matches in 1992–83 singles and 84 doubles is an Open era record. But she was also wonderfully consistent. Arantxa won two tournaments and was the finalist at the US Open. She also reached the last four at the Australian and French Opens and did the same at the Olympics. She could also point to a win over Graf at the US Open and another over Seles at the Canadian Open.

Jennifer Capriati's gold medal win over Graf in Barcelona, plus her defeat of Seles in the quarter-finals of the Lipton in March, lifted the 16-year-old American to fourth position. These were both very impressive wins and suggest that this troubled teenager may yet reach the heights predicted for her.

It was a disappointing year for Gabriela Sabatini who finishes in fifth place. The best she could manage at the Grand Slams was three semi-final finishes and a passage to the quarters at the US Open. This was not the same joyful extrovert who had won that great Championship so spectacularly in 1990.

The last five places go to those who gave us glimpses of greatness during the year without ever threatening to displace the higher ranked women. It is a sign of the times that 36-year-old Martina Navratilova, for so long the pacesetter in women's tennis, is now among this group. The highlight of her year was to beat Seles in the Los Angeles final in August for her 160th tournament win.

JOHN BARRETT'S WORLD RANKINGS 1977–91

MEN

1977	1978	1979	1980	1981
1 Borg	1 Connors	1 Borg	1 Borg	1 McEnroe
2 Vilas	2 Borg	2 McEnroe	2 McEnroe	2 Borg
3 Connors	3 Gerulaitis	3 Connors	3 Connors	3 Connors
4 Gottfried	4 McEnroe	4 Gerulaitis	4 Lendl	4 Lendl
5 Stockton	5 Ramirez	5 Tanner	5 Mayer G.	5 Clerc
6 Gerulaitis	6 Dibbs	6 Vilas	6 Vilas	6 Mayer G.
7 Orantes	7 Gottfried	7 DuPre	7 Solomon	7 Vilas
8 Dent	8 Barazzutti	8 Dibbs	8 Gerulaitis	8 Gerulaitis
9 Ramirez	9 Vilas	9 Pecci	9 Gottfried	9 Pecci
10 Nastase	10 Solomon	10 Solomon	10 Clerc	10 Tanner

1982
1 Connors
2 Lendl
3 McEnroe
4 Vilas
5 Wilander
6 Gerulaitis
7 Mayer G.
8 Noah
9 Clerc
10 Higueras

1983
1 McEnroe
2 Connors
3 Wilander
4 Lendl
5 Noah
=6 Arias
=6 Higueras
8 Solomon
9 Clerc
10 Teltscher

1984
1 McEnroe
2 Lendl
3 Connors
4 Wilander
5 Gomez
6 Cash
7 Sundstrom
8 Jarryd
9 Nystrom
10 Arias

1985
1 Lendl
2 Wilander
3 Edberg
4 Becker
5 McEnroe
6 Connors
7 Jarryd
8 Leconte
9 Nystrom
=10 Gunthardt
=10 Noah

1986
1 Lendl
2 Becker
3 Edberg
4 Leconte
5 Nystrom
6 Mecir
7 Wilander
8 Noah
9 McEnroe
10 Gomez

1987
1 Lendl
2 Edberg
3 Wilander
4 Cash
5 Mecir
6 Connors
7 Becker
8 Noah
9 Mayotte
10 Gomez

1988
1 Wilander
2 Edberg
3 Lendl
4 Becker
5 Agassi
6 Mayotte
7 Mecir
8 Carlsson K.
9 Cash
=10 Leconte
=10 Svensson

1989
1 Becker
2 Lendl
3 Edberg
4 McEnroe J.
5 Chang
6 Gilbert
7 Krickstein
8 Mecir
9 Mayotte
10 Agassi

1990
1 Edberg
2 Lendl
3 Agassi
4 Sampras
5 Becker
6 Gomez
7 Muster
8 Ivanisovic
9 Sanchez
10 McEnroe J.

1991
1 Edberg
2 Courier
3 Becker
4 Stich
5 Lendl
6 Forget
7 Agassi
8 Sampras
9 Novacek
10 Korda

WOMEN

1977
1 Evert Lloyd
2 Wade
3 King
4 Stove
5 Navratilova
6 Barker
7 Turnbull
8 Casals
9 Jausovec
10 Melville Reid

1978
1 Evert Lloyd
2 Navratilova
3 Goolagong
4 Wade
5 Turnbull
6 Ruzici
7 King
=8 Austin
=8 Shriver
10 Jausovec

1979
1 Navratilova
2 Austin
3 Evert Lloyd
4 Goolagong
5 King
6 Fromholtz
7 Wade
8 Turnbull
9 Melville Reid
10 Ruzici

1980
1 Evert Lloyd
2 Austin
3 Navratilova
4 Goolagong
5 Mandlikova
6 Jaeger
7 Turnbull
8 Ruzici
9 Fromholtz
10 Shriver

1981
1 Evert Lloyd
1 Austin
3 Mandlikova
4 Navratilova
5 Jaeger
6 Turnbull
7 Shriver
8 Ruzici
9 Hanika
10 Jausovec

1982
1 Navratilova
2 Evert Lloyd
3 Jaeger
4 Mandlikova
5 Austin
6 Ruzici
7 Bunge
8 Shriver
9 Potter
=10 Garrison
=10 Turnbull

1983
1 Navratilova
2 Evert Lloyd
3 Jaeger
4 Durie
5 Shriver
6 Mandlikova
7 Turnbull
8 Hanika
9 Temesvari
10 Potter

1984
1 Navratilova
2 Evert Lloyd
3 Mandlikova
4 Shriver
5 Bassett
6 Maleeva Man
7 Garrison
8 Jordan K.
9 Turnbull
10 Kohde-Kilsch

1985
1 Navratilova
2 Evert Lloyd
3 Mandlikova
4 Garrison
5 Kohde-Kilsch
6 Sukova
7 Shriver
8 Graf
9 Maleeva Man
=10 Rinaldi
=10 Sabatini

1986
1 Navratilova
2 Evert
3 Graf
4 Sukova
5 Mandlikova
6 Sabatini
7 Shriver
8 Garrison
9 Maleeva Man
10 Rinaldi

1987
1 Graf
2 Navratilova
3 Evert
4 Mandlikova
5 Sabatini
6 Shriver
7 Sukova
8 Kohde-Kilsch
9 Maleeva Fragnière
10 McNeil

1988
1 Graf
2 Sabatini
3 Navratilova
4 Evert
5 Shriver
6 Sukova
7 Zvereva
8 Garrison
9 Maleeva Frag.
10 Kohde-Kilsch

1989
1 Graf
2 Navratilova
3 Sanchez-Vicario
4 Sabatini
5 Seles
6 Evert
7 Garrison
8 Sukova
9 Maleeva Fragnière
10 Lindqvist

1990
1 Graf
2 Seles
3 Sabatini
4 Navratilova
5 Fernandez
6 Maleeva, K.
7 Garrison
8 Sanchez-Vicario
9 Maleeva Fragnière
10 Capriati

1991
1 Seles
2 Graf
3 Sabatini
4 Navratilova
5 Sanchez-Vic.
6 Fernandez
7 Capriati
8 Novotna
9 Martinez
10 Maleeva Fra.

IBM/ATP TOUR RANKINGS AND PRIZE MONEY 1992

The following tables show the rankings of the top 250 in singles, the top 100 in doubles and the top 150 men on the prize money list. For the purposes of rnakings and prize money, the season is deemed to have ended on 30th November rather than the 31st December. Nevertheless, points earned by players who took part in Challenger and Satellite events which took place between the November date and the end of the year still had them added to subsequent lists.

Besides the four Grand Slam Championships, all official IBM/ATP Tour tournaments, including Championship Series, World Series and Challenger Series events, as well as the Satellite Circuits administered by member nations of the ITF, were eligible for ranking purposes. Rankings for 1992, adjusted every week, were based on a player's best 14 results (including bonus points) during a moving twelve month period. Somewhat controversially, in 1992, as in 1991, points were also given for the season-ending IBM/ATP Tour World Championships – a decision with which some of the players themselves do not agree. (Statistics supplied by IBM/ATP Tour)

		T'MNTS	PTS			T'MNTS	PTS
1	Jim Courier (USA)	19	3599	36	Jakob Hlasek (SUI)	22	855
2	Stefan Edberg (SWE)	20	3236	37	Jordi Arrese (ESP)	26	847
3	Pete Sampras (USA)	19	3074	38	Wally Masur (AUS)	26	846
4	Goran Ivanisevic (CRO)	21	2718	39	Paul Haarhuis (NED)	28	832
5	Boris Becker (GER)	19	2530	40	Mark Woodforde (AUS)	24	812
6	Michael Chang (USA)	21	2277	41	Javier Sanchez (ESP)	33	809
7	Petr Korda (TCH)	27	2174	42	Omar Camporese (ITA)	23	793
8	Ivan Lendl (TCH)	25	1985	43	Fabrice Santoro (FRA)	25	772
9	Andre Agassi (USA)	17	1852	44	David Wheaton (USA)	23	753
10	Richard Krajicek (NED)	24	1816	45	Jeff Tarango (USA)	26	747
11	Guy Forget (FRA)	21	1717	46	Franco Davin (ARG)	22	744
12	Wayne Ferreira (RSA)	25	1679	47	Magnus Gustafsson (SWE)	22	722
13	Malivai Washington (USA)	24	1610	48	Jaime Oncins (BRA)	25	722
14	Carlos Costa (ESP)	22	1539	49	Jaime Yzaga (PER)	23	717
15	Michael Stich (GER)	20	1401	50	Guillermo Perez Rold. (ARG)	23	711
16	Sergi Bruguera (ESP)	22	1323	51	Bernd Karbacher (GER)	25	702
17	Alexander Volkov (CIS)	29	1309	52	Luiz Mattar (BRA)	26	699
18	Thomas Muster (AUT)	26	1228	53	Renzo Furlan (ITA)	32	668
19	Henrik Nedm (SWE)	23	1184	54	Todd Woodbridge (AUS)	23	658
20	John McEnroe (USA)	17	1158	55	Jim Grabb (USA)	25	658
21	Emilio Sanchez (ESP)	25	1123	56	Gabriel Markus (ARG)	25	657
22	Francisco Clavet (ESP)	31	1108	57	Jan Siemerink (NED)	26	656
23	Karel Novacek (TCH)	27	1092	58	Christian Bergstrom (SWE)	23	655
24	Andrei Medvedev (URS)	15	1079	59	Luis Herrera (MEX)	23	648
25	Amos Mansdorf (ISR)	27	1066	60	Marcelo Filippini (URU)	25	641
26	Brad Gilbert (USA)	26	1019	61	Henri Leconte (FRA)	14	635
27	Arnaud Boetsch (FRA)	26	1005	62	Stefano Pescosolido (ITA)	28	628
28	Aaron Krickstein (USA)	17	987	63	Thomas Enqvist (SWE)	18	612
29	Carl-Uwe Steeb (GER)	25	947	64	Shuzo Matsuoka (JPN)	17	572
30	Andrei Chesnokov (CIS)	28	917	65	Tomas Carbonell (ESP)	23	568
31	Alberto Mancini (ARG)	20	898	66	Goran Prpic (CRO)	23	551
32	Andrei Cherkasov (CIS)	29	877	67	Marcos Ondruska (RSA)	24	546
33	Cedric Pioline (FRA)	28	866	68	Gianluca Pozzi (ITA)	28	546
34	Magnus Larsson (SWE)	22	861	69	Kenneth Carlsen (SWE)	20	534
35	Marc Rosset (SUI)	23	856	70	Rodolphe Gilbert (FRA)	28	531

#	Player		
71	Sandon Stolle (AUS)	26	525
72	Francisco Roig (ESP)	27	506
73	Brett Steven (NZL)	21	502
74	Bart Wuyts (BEL)	34	502
75	Derrick Rostagno (USA)	24	492
76	Olivier Delaitre (FRA)	26	491
77	Markus Naewie (GER)	30	488
78	Jacco Eltingh (NED)	26	485
79	Nicklas Kulti (SWE)	23	481
80	Andrei Olhovskiy (URS)	24	464
81	Jonas Svensson (SWE)	27	464
82	Gilbert Schaller (AUT)	24	456
83	Richard Fromberg (AUS)	29	454
84	Jimmy Connors (USA)	17	452
85	Jonathan Stark (USA)	21	444
86	Alex Corretja (ESP)	23	444
87	Todd Martin (USA)	21	439
88	Diego Nargiso (ITA)	24	436
89	Patrik Kuhnen (GER)	27	429
90	Karsten Braasch (GER)	24	426
91	Martin Damm (TCH)	25	426
92	Horst Skoff (AUT)	26	425
93	Jamie Morgan (AUS)	15	424
94	Guillaume Raoux (FRA)	19	424
95	Simon Youl (AUS)	27	422
96	Richey Reneberg (USA)	20	420
97	Roberto Azar (ARG)	34	420
98	Claudio Mezzadri (SUI)	23	415
99	Thierry Champion (FRA)	29	406
100	Leonardo Lavalle (MEX)	22	402
101	Bryan Shelton (USA)	26	399
102	Marcos Aurelio Gorriz (ESP)	28	395
103	Marcus Zoecke (GER)	27	391
104	Michiel Schapers (NED)	29	388
105	Todd Witsken (USA)	25	386
106	Jeremy Bates (GBR)	17	385
107	Stephane Simian (FRA)	20	384
108	Daniel Vacek (TCH)	14	383
109	Alex Antonitsch (AUT)	21	382
110	Marc Goellner (GER)	25	381
111	German Lopez (ESP)	24	379
112	Patrick McEnroe (USA)	23	378
113	Chuck Adams (USA)	25	375
114	Horacio de la Pena (ARG)	27	368
115	Alberto Berasategui (ESP)	25	360
116	Lars Koslowski (GER)	29	360
117	Francisco Montana (USA)	27	359
118	Christian Saceanu (GER)	29	359
119	Lars Jonsson (SWE)	29	356
120	Martin Jaite (ARG)	21	354
121	Joao Cunha-Silva (POR)	28	348
122	Robbie Weiss (USA)	6	347
123	Arne Thoms (GER)	22	346
124	Claudio Pistolesi (ITA)	26	346
125	David Prinosil (GER)	23	343
126	Christian Miniussi (ARG)	24	342
127	Alex O'Brien (USA)	15	339
128	Diego Perez (URU)	13	336
129	Nicolas Pereira (VEN)	21	335
130	Patrick Baur (GER)	27	335
131	Chris Pridham (CAN)	21	332
132	Richard Matuszewski USA)	19	331
133	Ronald Agenor (HAI)	25	331
134	Christo Van Rensburg (RSA)	24	326
135	Andrew Sznajder (CAN)	16	325
136	Sergio Cortes (CHI)	18	325
137	Martin Strelba (TCH)	26	325
138	Gilad Bloom (ISR)	19	323
139	Carsten Arriens (GER)	11	321
140	Mark Koevermans (NED)	25	315
141	Jose Francisco Altur (ESP)	19	314
142	Mikael Tillstrom (SWE)	15	303
143	Byron Black (ZIM)	27	295
144	Gary Muller (RSA)	20	291
145	Javier Frana (ARG)	22	289
146	Martin Stringari (ARG)	21	287
147	Kevin Curren (USA)	19	285
148	Juan Gisbert Jr (ESP)	13	284
149	Jared Palmer (USA)	15	284
150	Anders Jarryd (SWE)	17	283
151	David Rikl (TCH)	23	281
152	Jan Apell (SWE)	18	276
153	Fernando Roese (BRA)	23	272
154	Thierry Guardiola (FRA)	28	267
155	Frederic Fontang (FRA)	34	266
156	Jordi Burillo (ESP)	15	257
157	Mauricio Hadad (COL)	13	253
158	Ctislav Dosedel (TCH)	13	253
159	Cristiano Caratti (ITA)	23	249
160	Greg Rusedski (CAN)	15	240
161	Maurice Ruah (VEN)	16	240
162	Paolo Cane (ITA)	17	237
163	Vladimir Gabrichidze (URS)	19	235
164	Tommy Ho (USA)	19	234
165	Chris Wilkinson (GBR)	24	232
166	Mario Visconti (ITA)	23	231
167	John Fitzgerald (AUS)	13	227
168	Daniel Orsanic (ARG)	16	227
169	Jason Stoltenberg (AUS)	17	222
170	Fernando Meligeni (ARG)	24	222
171	Lars Wahlgren (SWE)	12	217
172	Filip Dewulf (BEL)	14	212
173	Libor Nemecek (TCH)	17	212
174	Pablo Arraya (PER)	18	210
175	Neil Borwick (AUS)	11	206
176	Alexander Mronz (GER)	19	206
177	Christer Allgardh (SWE)	15	205
178	Andres Gomez (ECU)	16	204
179	Federico Sanchez (ESP)	18	204
180	Thomas Hogstedt (SWE)	8	201
181	Kenny Thorne (USA)	12	200
182	Carl Limberger (AUS)	17	200
183	Oliver Fernandez (MEX)	19	200
184	Grant Connell (CAN)	17	194
185	Nicklas Utgren (SWE)	16	193
186	Dirk Dier (GER)	18	193
187	Xavier Daufresne (BEL)	27	193
188	Roger Smith (BAH)	16	192
189	Daniel Marco (ESP)	22	188
190	Joern Renzenbrink (GER)	10	187
191	Grant Stafford (RSA)	16	187
192	Lionel Roux (FRA)	12	186
193	Danilo Marcelino (BRA)	26	185
194	Jimmy Arias (USA)	14	182
195	Steve Bryan (USA)	18	182
196	Sebastien Lareau (CAN)	9	180

197	Cassio Motta (BRA)	10	179	224	Paul Annacone (USA)	12	141
198	Kent Kinnear (USA)	16	178	225	Chris Garner (USA)	16	141
199	Tomas Nydahl (SWE)	14	175	226	Mario Tabares (CUB)	17	140
200	Massimo Valeri (ITA)	16	175	227	Dinu Pescariu (ROM)	11	138
201	Roberto Jabali (BRA)	17	172	228	Bernardo Mota (POR)	12	138
202	Pat Cash (AUS)	5	171	229	Olivier Soules (FRA)	23	138
203	Massimo Ardinghi (ITA)	2	169	230	Pier Gauthier (FRA)	11	137
204	Jimmy Brown (USA)	24	167	231	Martin Sinner (GER)	11	135
205	Kelly Evernden (NZL)	14	163	232	Tomas Zdrazila (TCH)	20	132
206	Nicola Bruno (ITA)	18	163	233	Alejo Mancisidor (ESP)	11	131
207	Lan Bale (RSA)	15	162	234	Marcus Zillner (GER)	23	131
208	Fernon Wibier (NED)	15	162	235	Francisco Yunis (ARG)	11	129
209	Leander Paes (IND)	11	156	236	Mikael Pernfors (SWE)	8	127
210	David Engel (SWE)	16	156	237	Peter Nyborg (SWE)	12	127
211	Martin Laurendeau (CAN)	17	156	238	Felipe Rivera (CHI)	14	127
212	Peter Lundgren (SWE)	11	155	239	Johan Carlsson (SWE)	11	126
213	David Witt (USA)	9	152	240	Daniel Nestor (CAN)	11	125
214	Emilio Alvarez (ESP)	14	152	241	Francesco Michelotti (ITA)	14	124
215	Eduardo Masso (BEL)	23	152	242	Michael Geserer (GER)	17	124
216	Massimo Cierro (ITA)	25	150	243	Chris Bailey (GBR)	13	123
217	Karol Kuchera (TCH)	12	149	244	Florian Krumrey (GER)	14	123
218	Tom Nijssen (NED)	6	148	245	Mark Petchey (GBR)	15	120
219	Niclas Kroon (SWE)	12	148	246	Roger Rasheed (AUS)	18	120
220	Dimitri Poliakov (UKR)	14	147	247	Mario Rincon (COL)	8	117
221	Jean-Philippe Fleurian (FRA)	20	146	248	Jaime Cortes (CHI)	19	117
222	Marcelo Ingaramo (ARG)	13	145	249	Thomas Buchmayer (AUT)	10	116
223	Ramesh Krishnan (IND)	10	143	250	Jens Woehrmann (GER)	14	116

DOUBLES
(As at 30 November 1992)

		PTS			PTS
1	Mark Woodforde (AUS)	3085	51	Sven Salumaa (USA)	950
2	Todd Woodbridge (AUS)	3072	52	Mark Keil (USA)	932
3	Jim Grabb (USA)	2961	53	Diego Nargiso (ITA)	930
4	Richey Reneberg (USA)	2895	54	Stefan Kruger (RSA)	922
5	Kelly Jones (USA)	2404	55	Kevin Curren (USA)	919
6	Rick Leach (USA)	2322	56	Henrik Jan Davids (NED)	918
7	Patrick McEnroe (USA)	2235	57	Neil Broad (GBR)	911
8	Jakob Hlasek (SUI)	2219	58	Gary Muller (RSA)	910
9	John McEnroe (USA)	2203	59	Rikard Bergh (SWE)	887
10	Anders Jarryd (SWE)	2107	60	Ken Flach (USA)	884
11	John Fitzgerald (AUS)	1914	61	Francisco Montana (USA)	878
12	Marc Rosset (SUI)	1853	62	Horacio de la Pena (ARG)	875
13	Patrick Galbraith (USA)	1840	63	Neil Borwick (AUS)	859
14	Mark Kratzmann (AUS)	1730	64	Petr Korda (TCH)	844
15	David Macpherson (AUS)	1709	65	Javier Frana (ARG)	833
16	Michael Stich (GER)	1692	66	Simon Youl (AUS)	823
17	Cyril Suk (TCH)	1685	67	Cassio Motta (BRA)	805
18	Tom Nijssen (NED)	1645	68	Jim Pugh (USA)	799
19	Wally Masur (AUS)	1589	69	Brad Pearce (USA)	789
20	Danie Visser (RSA)	1558	70	Menno Oosting (NED)	785
21	Sergio Casal (ESP)	1534	71	David Rikl (TCH)	784
22	Emilio Sanchez (ESP)	1512	72	Tom Kempers (NED)	781
23	Jonathan Stark (USA)	1482	73	Pieter Aldrich (RSA)	780
24	Steve Devries (USA)	1461	74	Glenn Layendecker (USA)	778
25	Jared Palmer (USA)	1443	75	David Prinosil (GER)	767
26	David Adams (AUS)	1400	76	Tomas Carbonell (ESP)	733
27	Glenn Michibata (CAN)	1375	77	Scott Davis (USA)	730
28	Grant Connell (CAN)	1375	78	Royce Deppe (RSA)	722
29	Guy Forget (FRA)	1367	79	Pablo Albano (ARG)	720
30	Laurie Warder (AUS)	1358	80	Boris Becker (GER)	719
31	Wayne Ferreira (RSA)	1342	81	David Pate (USA)	717
32	Andrei Olhovskiy (URS)	1316	82	Leonardo Lavalle (MEX)	712
33	Luke Jensen (USA)	1312	83	Carl Limberger	706
34	Paul Haarhuis (NED)	1302	84	Udo Riglewski (GER)	700
35	Todd Witsken (USA)	1195	85	Bret Garnett (USA)	698
36	Kent Kinnear (USA)	1164	86	Francisco Roig (ESP)	682
37	Libor Pimek (TCH)	1100	87	Brent Haygarth (RSA)	682
38	Byron Talbot (RSA)	1093	88	Broderick Dyke (AUS)	663
39	Piet Norval (RSA)	1089	89	Johan Donar (SWE)	653
40	Greg Van Emburgh (USA)	1062	90	Byron Black (ZIM)	648
41	Trevor Kronemann (USA)	1048	91	Kenny Thorne (USA)	643
42	Goran Ivanisevic (CRO)	1022	92	Diego Perez (URU)	640
43	Mark Koevermans (NED)	1000	93	Tomas Zdrazila (TCH)	631
44	Jacco Eltingh (HOL)	1000	94	Vojtech Flegl (TCH)	622
45	Dave Randall (USA)	996	95	Martin Damm (TCH)	621
46	Ronnie Bathman (SWE)	983	96	Christer Allgardh (SWE)	609
47	Shelby Cannon (USA)	978	97	Michael Tillstrom (SWE)	601
48	Javier Sanchez (ESP)	978	98	Bent-Ove Pedersen (NOR)	600
49	Mike Briggs (USA)	962	99	David Wheaton (USA)	599
50	Karel Novacek (TCH)	951	100	Marc Goellner (GER)	597

PRIZE MONEY (As at 30 November 1992)

Below is a list of players showing their earnings from the four Grand Slam Championships and any IBM/ATP Tour events in which they competed. A further list follows to show the combined earnings of the 16 men who competed in the Compaq Grand Slam Cup. Finally there is a list of players whose career earnings have passed the $1 million mark. During 1992 levels of prize money insisted on rising, despite the worsening economic worldwide recession. For the first time three men exceeded $2 million in earnings from the Grand Slam Championships and IBM/ATP Tour tournaments. Michael Stich's success at the Compaq Grand Slam Cup ensured that he would head the combined earnings table for the year. However, the German No.2 was hotly pursued by last year's top earner, Stefan Edberg, as well as by Boris Becker and Jim Courier. There were four players whose combined earnings for the year topped $2 million (in 1991 there had been one), plus another six who earned more than $1 million – the same number as the previous year. As in 1991, there were seventeen players who earned between $500,000 and $1 million, plus another 19 who took home $300,000–$500,000. Altogether there were 74 men who earned more than $200,000 last year compared to 60 in 1991. Note: Prize money figures include earnings from tournaments, circuit bonuses and play-offs, plus team events where entry is based purely on merit. They do not include earnings from Davis Cup ties, invitation tournaments, exhibitions or special events, nor do they include income from commercial contracts or endorsements.

1	Stefan Edberg (SWE)	$2,341,804	45	Cedric Pioline (FRA)	291,029
2	Boris Becker (GER)	2,293,687	46	Aaron Krickstein (USA)	286,304
3	Jim Courier (USA)	2,253,385	47	David Wheaton (USA)	285,869
4	Pete Sampras (USA)	1,545,087	48	Andrei Chesnokov (CIS)	282,666
5	Goran Ivanisevic (CRO)	1,408,241	49	Rick Leach (USA)	274,963
6	Petr Korda (TCH)	1,050,353	50	Kelly Jones (USA)	269,993
7	Andre Agassi (USA)	1,027,834	51	Magnus Larsson (SWE)	255,801
8	Ivan Lendl (TCH)	961,566	52	Magnus Gustafsson (SWE)	246,083
9	Michael Chang (USA)	924,467	53	Sergio Casal (ESP)	245,084
10	Michael Stich (GER)	777,411	54	Jan Siemerink (NED)	242,182
11	Richard Krajicek (NED)	763,241	55	Andrei Olhovskiy (CIS)	240,218
12	Guy Forget (FRA)	729,487	56	Tom Nijssen (NED)	238,284
13	Mark Woodforde (AUS)	706,836	57	Olivier Delaitre (FRA)	237,052
14	Emilio Sanchez (ESP)	700,983	58	Derrick Rostagno (USA)	234,047
15	Wayne Ferreira (RSA)	679,610	59	Stefano Pescosolido (ITA)	233,471
16	Todd Woodbridge (AUS)	656,642	60	Cyril Suk (TCH)	230,131
17	John McEnroe (USA)	641,077	61	Jonathan Stark (USA)	228,391
18	Sergi Bruguera (ESP)	603,378	62	Jordi Arrese (ESP)	227,253
19	Jim Grabb (USA)	601,189	63	Diego Nargiso (ITA)	221,425
20	Carlos Costa (ESP)	598,547	64	Goran Prpic (CRO)	220,141
21	Jakob Hlasek (SUI)	558,643	65	Jaime Oncins (BRA)	216,597
22	Karel Novacek (TCH)	537,022	66	Gianluca Pozzi (ITA)	213,260
23	Malivai Washington (USA)	516,453	67	Simon Youl (AUS)	213,012
24	Richey Reneberg (USA)	500,057	68	Tomas Carbonell (ESP)	211,898
25	Marc Rosset (SUI)	491,440	69	Mark Kratzmann (AUS)	210,880
26	Wally Masur (AUS)	480,504	70	Jacco Eltingh (NED)	207,621
27	Thomas Muster (AUT)	456,653	71	Todd Witsken (USA)	203,250
28	Alexander Volkov (CIS)	447,331	72	Jeff Tarango (USA)	202,758
29	Anders Jarryd (SWE)	399,116	73	Jaime Yzaga (PER)	202,670
30	Patrick McEnroe (USA)	389,381	74	Renzo Furlan (ITA)	201,168
31	Francisco Clavet (ESP)	377,338	75	Fabrice Santoro (FRA)	199,390
32	Paul Haarhuis (NED)	371,195	76	Grant Connell (CAN)	196,692
33	Carl-Uwe Steeb (GER)	370,278	77	Michiel Schapers (NED)	192,615
34	Javier Sanchez (ESP)	363,990	78	Nicklas Kulti (SWE)	190,945
35	Amos Mansdorf (ISR)	357,625	79	David Macpherson (AUS)	190,047
36	Henrik Nedm (SWE)	345,399	80	Bryan Shelton (USA)	187,777
37	Arnaud Boetsch (GER)	343,596	81	Gabriel Markus (ARG)	186,668
38	Brad Gilbert (USA)	342,949	82	Sandon Stolle (AUT)	185,321
39	Andrei Medvedev (CIS)	335,840	83	Patrick Galbraith (USA)	183,183
40	Henri Leconte (FRA)	319,544	84	Markus Zoecke (GER)	177,186
41	Andrei Cherkasov (CIS)	319,456	85	Steve Devries (USA)	176,785
42	Omar Camporese (ITA)	317,957	86	Francisco Roig (ESP)	176,598
43	John Fitzgerald (AUS)	312,940	87	Christ. Bergstrom (SWE)	173,966
44	Alberto Mancini (ARG)	295,244	88	Luiz Mattar (BRA)	172,588

89 Christian Miniussi (ARG)	172,111	120 Markus Naewie (GER)	133,608
90 Patrik Kuhnen (GER)	170,381	121 Thomas Enqvist (SWE)	132,859
91 Guillermo Perez Roldan (ARG)	169,678	122 German Lopez (ESP)	130,188
92 Thierry Champion (FRA)	167,552	123 Laurie Warder (AUS)	128,530
93 Jonas Svensson (SWE)	167,068	124 Luke Jensen (USA)	126,970
94 Rodolphe Gilbert (FRA)	166,664	125 David Prinosil (GER)	126,231
95 Marcelo Filippini (URU)	166,610	126 Marco Aurelio Gorriz (ESP)	125,973
96 Leonardo Lavalle (MEX)	165,379	127 Frederic Fontang (FRA)	125,661
97 Todd Martin (USA)	162,062	128 Lars Jonsson (SWE)	123,574
98 Mark Koevermans (NED)	160,066	129 Kent Kinnear (USA)	122,824
99 Bernd Karbacher (AUT)	157,850	130 Jeremy Bates (GBR)	120,998
100 Franco Davin (ARG)	156,723	131 Glenn Michibata (CAN)	120,796
101 Guillaume Raoux (FRA)	153,763	132 Chris Pridham (CAN)	120,473
102 Kevin Curren (USA)	153,595	133 Andres Gomez (ECU)	117,075
103 Horst Skoff (AUT)	152,888	134 Diego Perez (URU)	117,071
104 Gary Muller (RSA)	151,537	135 Lars Koslowski (GER)	116,486
105 Shuzo Matsuoka (JPN)	150,097	136 Jason Stoltenberg (AUS)	115,693
106 Francisco Montana (USA)	148,664	137 Claudio Mezzadri (SUI)	115,413
107 Bart Wuyts (BEL)	146,959	138 Gilad Bloom (ISR)	114,521
108 Danie Visser (RSA)	146,711	139 Alex Antonitsch (AUT)	114,520
109 Javier Frana (ARG)	144,864	140 Carl Limberger (AUT)	112,302
110 Jared Palmer (USA)	144,672	141 Claudio Pistolesi (ITA)	111,568
111 Horacio de la Pena (ARG)	142,136	142 Karsten Braasch (GER)	109,635
112 Martin Damm (TCH)	140,238	143 Christian Saceanu (GER)	109,101
113 Richard Fromberg (AUS)	139,813	144 Marc Goellner (GER)	108,617
114 Jimmy Connors (USA)	139,431	145 Arne Thoms (GER)	108,600
115 Marcos Ondruska (RSA)	137,670	146 Chuck Adams (USA)	108,434
116 David Adams (USA)	136,241	147 Patrick Baur (GER)	107,430
117 Christo Van Rensburg (RSA)	136,212	148 Neil Borwick (AUS)	106,281
118 Byron Black (ZIM)	136,189	149 Ronald Agenor (HAI)	105,333
119 Luis Herrera (MEX)	135,488	150 Byron Talbot (RSA)	105,141

COMBINED EARNINGS

The combined earnings of the 16 men who contested the third Compaq Grand Slam Cup, plus the two alternates, were:

	IBM ATP TOUR	COMPAQ GS CUP	TOTAL
Michael Stich	777,411	2,000,000	2,777,411
Stefan Edberg	2,341,804	100,000	2,441,804
Pete Sampras	1,545,087	450,000	1,995,087
Michael Chang	924,467	1,000,000	1,924,467
Goran Ivanisevic	1,408,241	450,000	1,858,241
Petr Korda	1,050,353	300,000	1,350,353
Andre Agassi	1,027,834	100,000	1,127,834
Richard Krajicek	763,241	300,000	1,063,241
John McEnroe	641,077	300,000	941,077
Guy Forget	729,487	100,000	829,487
Emilio Sanchez	700,983	100,000	800,983
Wayne Ferreira	679,610	100,000	779,610
Henri Leconte	319,544	300,000	619,544
Wally Masur	480,504	100,000	580,504
Alexander Volkov	447,331	100,000	547,331
Amos Mansdorf	357,625	50,000	407,625
David Wheaton	285,869	50,000	335,869
Nicklas Kulti	190,945	100,000	290,945

Apart from **Nicklas Kulti (SWE),** everyone in the above list also appears in the list of Millionaires below. The career earnings of Kulti are: $649,178. In addition, there are three players who have earned prize money from the Compaq Grand Slam Cup in other years who have not yet joined the exclusive list of tennis Millionaires. Their combined career earnings are: **Thierry Champion(FRA)** $877,118; **Christian Bergstrom(SWE)** $858,920; **Cristiano Caratti(ITA)** $506,808.

THE MILLIONAIRES

Below is a list of players who, by the end of November 1992 had won more than one million dollars in career prize money. The list includes earnings at the three Compaq Grand Slam Cup tournaments 1990–92.
* Denotes players who appear in the list for the first time.

1	Ivan Lendl (USA)	19,922,627	23	Yannick Noah (FRA)	3,396,395
2	Stefan Edberg (SWE)	13,539,075	24	Henri Leconte (FRA)	3,263,672
3	John McEnroe (USA)	12,527,622	25	Kevin Curren (USA)	3,051,195
4	Boris Becker (GER)	11,670,442	26	Brian Gottfried (USA)	2,782,514
5	Jimmy Connors (USA)	8,571,435	27	Vitas Gerulaitis (USA)	2,778,748
6	Mats Wilander (SWE)	7,377,193	28	John Fitzgerald (AUS)	2,777,424
7	Pete Sampras (USA)	7,007,225	29	Aaron Krickstein (USA)	2,725,692
8	Andre Agassi (USA)	5,451,203	30	Wojtek Fibak (POL)	2,725,133
9	Michael Chang (USA)	5,127,821	31	Tim Mayotte (USA)	2,663,672
10	Jim Courier (USA)	4,946,459	32	Miloslav Mecir (TCH)	2,632,638
11	Guillermo Vilas (ARG)	4,923,132	33	Petr Korda (TCH)	2,462,222
12	Brad Gilbert (USA)	4,904,698	34	Johan Kriek (USA)	2,378,414
13	Michael Stich (GER)	4,843,003	35	Raul Ramirez (MEX)	2,213,671
14	Anders Jarryd (SWE)	4,388,749	36	Ilie Nastase (ROM)	2,076,761
15	Andres Gomez (ECU)	4,357,500	37	Joakim Nystrom (SWE)	2,074,947
16	Guy Forget (FRA)	4,119,041	38	Thomas Muster (AUT)	2,050,694
17	Emilio Sanchez (ESP)	4,048,131	39	Wally Masur (AUS)	2,017,189
18	Jacob Hlasek (SUI)	3,753,325	40	Eddie Dibbs (USA)	2,016,426
19	David Wheaton (USA)	3,746,820	41	Peter Fleming (USA)	1,986,529
20	Thomas Smid (TCH)	3,699,738	42	Jose-Luis Clerc (ARG)	1,984,481
21	Goran Ivanisevic (CRO)	3,658,258	43	Jonas Svensson (SWE)	1,948,660
22	Bjorn Borg (SWE)	3,644,926	44	Karel Novacek (TCH)	1,946,059

45	Scott Davis (USA)	1,920,820	85	Gene Mayer (USA)	1,381,562
46	Robert Seguso (USA)	1,865,159	86	Alberto Mancini (ARG)	1,372,492
47	Martin Jaite (ARG)	1,845,166	87	Carl-Uwe Steeb (GER)	1,349,138
48	Harold Solomon (USA)	1,802,769	88	Richard Krajicek (NED)	*1,328,323
49	Amos Mansdorf (ISR)	1,790,312	89	Vijay Amritraj (IND)	1,312,887
50	Jim Grabb (USA)	1,787,334	90	Derrick Rostagno (USA)	1,304,470
51	Stan Smith (USA)	1,774,811	91	Todd Witsken (USA)	1,298,807
52	David Pate (USA)	1,774,024	92	Tim Wilkison (USA)	1,284,815
53	Andre Chesnokov (CIS)	1,771,779	93	Jan Gunnarsson (SWE)	1,270,840
54	Jimmy Arias (USA)	1,753,425	94	Tom Okker (NED)	1,257,200
55	Mark Woodforde (AUS)	1,752,535	95	Danie Visser (RSA)	1,237,717
56	Roscoe Tanner (USA)	1,696,108	96	Ramesh Krishnan (IND)	1,235,548
57	Pat Cash (AUS)	1,694,970	97	Paul McNamee (AUS)	1,232,826
58	Ken Flach (USA)	1,680,930	98	John Alexander (AUS)	1,214,079
59	Sergio Casal (ESP)	1,655,850	99	Andrei Cherkasov (CIS)	*1,199,070
60	Eliot Teltscher (USA)	1,653,997	100	Horst Skoff (AUT)	1,186,617
61	Todd Woodbridge (AUS)	1,653,938	101	Jaime Yzaga (PER)	*1,177,671
62	Sergi Bruguera (ESP)	1,650,158	102	Robert Lutz (USA)	1,165,276
63	Jim Pugh (USA)	1,612,838	103	Wayne Ferreira (RSA)	*1,160,935
64	Sherwood Stewart (USA)	1,602,565	104	Darren Cahill (AUS)	1,152,379
65	Ken Rosewall (AUS)	1,600,300	105	Marc Rosset (SUI)	*1,131,709
66	Arthur Ashe (USA)	1,584,909	106	Goran Prpic (CRO)	*1,126,344
67	Rod Laver (AUS)	1,564,213	107	Tim Gullikson (USA)	1,121,430
68	Heinz Guenthardt (SUI)	1,550,007	108	Ronald Agenor (HAI)	1,117,353
69	Rick Leach (USA)	1,537,777	109	Jordi Arrese (ESP)	*1,107,350
70	Christo Van Rensburg (RSA)	1,526,608	110	Eric Jelen (GER)	1,100,059
71	Paul Annacone (USA)	1,526,522	111	Steve Denton (USA)	1,084,214
72	Guillermo Perez-Roldan (ARG)	1,506,108	112	Luiz Mattar (BRA)	1,079,625
73	Mark Edmondson (AUS)	1,450,890	113	Peter Lundgren (SWE)	*1,075,847
74	Slobodan Zivojinovic (YUG)	1,450,384	114	Omar Camporese (ITA)	*1,070,612
75	Balazs Taroczy (HUN)	1,437,443	115	Dick Stockton (USA)	1,063,385
76	Patrick McEnroe (USA)	1,435,806	116	John Newcombe (AUS)	1,062,408
77	Alexander Volkov (CIS)	*1,432,763	117	Thierry Tulasne (FRA)	1,058,412
78	Richey Reneberg (USA)	*1,428,633	118	Alexander Mayer (USA)	1,057,738
79	Bill Scanlon (USA)	1,427,007	119	Grant Connell (CAN)	*1,055,911
80	Brian Teacher (USA)	1,426,244	120	Peter McNamara (AUS)	1,046,145
81	Javier Sanchez (ESP)	1,418,488	121	Michiel Schapers (NED)	*1,041,498
82	Magnus Gustafsson (SWE)	1,417,595	122	Paul Haarhuis (NED)	*1,003,939
83	Jose Higueras (ESP)	1,406,355	123	Mark Kratzmann (AUS)	*1,000,408
84	Manuel Orantes (ESP)	1,398,303			

ATP TOUR BOARD OF DIRECTORS (Chief Executive Officer: Mark Miles)

Tournament representatives:
Franco Bartoni (Europe)
Graham Lovett (International Group)
Charlie Pasarell (North America)

Player Representatives:
Paul Annacone
Tim Mayotte
Steve Meister

ADDRESSES

United States:
200 ATP Tour Boulevard,
Ponte Vedra Beach,
Florida,
32082, U.S.A.
Tel:1-904-285 8000
Fax:1-904-285 5966

Europe:
Monte Carlo Sun
74 Boulevard D'Italie,
98000, Monaco
Tel: 33-93-159 565
Fax: 33-93-159 794

International Group:
Suite 2, Level 32,
NORTHPOINT
100 Miller Street,
North Sydney,
N.S.W. 2060
Australia
Tel: 61-2-956 7888
Fax: 61-2-956 7773

VIRGINIA SLIMS RANKINGS AND PRIZE MONEY 1992

RANKINGS

The following tables show the season-ending rankings in singles and doubles. The rankings, updated weekly, are based on points won on the Kraft World Tour. Where players appear to have equal points the complete figures contain the fractional differences. These are not included here. (Statistics supplied by VIRGINIA SLIMS 'SLIMSTAT' SYSTEM.)

SINGLES

		T'MNTS	PTS			T'MNTS	PTS
1	Monica Seles (YUG)	15	283	44	Manon Bollegraf (NED)	10	25
2	Steffi Graf (GER)	14	252	45	Laura Gildemeister (PER)	19	25
3	Gabriela Sabatini (ARG)	17	192	46	Ros Fairbank Nideffer (USA)	16	25
4	Arantxa Sanchez-Vicar. (ESP)	17	177	47	Nicole Provis (AUS)	18	24
5	Martina Navratilova (USA)	12	171	48	Yayuk Basuki (INA)	15	24
6	Mary Joe Fernandez (USA)	16	120	49	Linda Harvey-Wild (USA)	21	24
7	Jennifer Capriati (USA)	13	98	50	Iva Majoli (CRO)	12	23
8	Conchita Martinez (ESP)	17	96	51	Florencia Labat (ARG)	17	22
9	Manuela Maleeva Frag. (SUI)	13	81	52	Debbie Graham (USA)	19	22
10	Jana Novotna (TCH)	17	78	53	Veronika Martinek (GER)	15	22
11	Anke Huber (GER)	15	66	54	Alexia Dechaume (FRA)	19	22
12	Helena Sukova (TCH)	17	66	55	Shi-Ting Wang (TPE)	13	21
13	Mary Pierce (FRA)	12	65	56	Raffaella Reggi Concato (ITA)	11	21
14	Nathalie Tauziat (FRA)	19	59	57	Robin White (USA)	15	19
15	Lori McNeil (USA)	21	59	58	Mana Endo (JPN)	10	19
16	Katerina Maleeva (BUL)	18	58	59	Larisa Savchenko Neil.(CIS)	18	19
17	Amanda Coetzer (RSA)	15	55	60	Jo Durie (GBR)	16	19
18	Zina Garrison Jackson (USA)	20	55	61	Katerina Kroupova (TCH)	11	18
19	Amy Frazier (USA)	18	54	62	Linda Ferrando (ITA)	15	18
20	Magdalena Maleeva (BUL)	15	53	63	Caterina Lindqvist (SWE)	15	18
21	Kimiko Date (JPN)	14	49	64	Marianne Werdel (USA)	17	18
22	Leila Meskhi (CIS)	15	47	65	Federica Bonsignori (ITA)	16	17
23	Natalia Zvereva (CIS)	19	43	66	Ines Gorrochategui (ARG)	10	17
24	Naoko Sawamatsu (JPN)	12	41	67	Karina Habsudova (TCH)	14	17
25	Judith Wiesner (AUT)	18	41	68	Nanne Dahlman (FIN)	15	17
26	Sabine Appelmans (BEL)	16	39	69	Shaun Stafford (USA)	16	17
27	Julie Halard (FRA)	14	39	70	Kimberly Po (USA)	16	16
28	Sabine Hack (GER)	15	38	71	Andrea Temesvari Trunkos (HUN)	15	16
29	Radka Zrubakova (TCH)	19	36	72	Ginger Helgeson (USA)	15	16
31	Pam Shriver (USA)	18	35	73	Monique Javer (GBR)	17	16
32	Patricia Hy (CAN)	15	34	74	Noelle Van Lottum (FRA)	22	15
33	Gigi Fernandez (USA)	16	34	75	Stephanie Rehe (USA)	14	15
34	Brenda Schultz (NED)	21	33	76	Lisa Raymond (USA)	6	15
35	Sandra Cecchini (ITA)	16	33	77	Susan Sloane-Lundy (USA)	15	16
36	Ann Grossman (USA)	17	32	78	Karin Kschwendt (GER)	11	14
37	Andrea Strnadova (TCH)	18	31	79	Claudia Kohde-Kilsch (GER)	14	14
38	Rachel McQuillan (AUS)	13	30	80	Silke Meier (GER)	15	14
39	Enanuela Zardo (SUI)	14	29	81	Catherine Mothes (FRA)	13	14
40	Wiltrud Probst (GER)	15	26	82	Bettina Fulco (ARG)	19	14
41	Natalia Medvedeva (CIS)	17	26	83	Chanda Rubin (USA)	16	14
42	Pascale Paradis Mangon (FRA)	17	26	84	Jenny Byrne (AUS)	19	14
43	Patty Fendick (USA)	17	26	85	Rennae Stubbs (AUS)	16	14

#	Name			#	Name		
86	Eugenia Maniokova (TCH)	14	14	143	Katrina Adams (USA)	16	8
87	Louise Allen (USA)	17	13	144	Petra Nedubova (TCH)	13	8
88	Meike Babel (GER)	18	13	145	Julie Richardson (NZL)	18	8
89	Carrie Cunningham (USA)	13	13	146	Maya Kidowaki (JPN)	17	8
90	Maja Zivec-Skulj (GER)	14	13	147	Akiko Kijimuta (JPN)	16	8
91	Gloria Pizzichini (ITA)	12	13	148	Claire Wegink (NED)	19	8
92	Stephanie Rottier (NED)	14	13	149	Ann Devries (BEL)	16	7
93	Donna Faber (USA)	21	13	150	Misumi Miyauchi (JPN)	13	7
94	Marianne de Swardt (RSA)	9	13	151	Barbara Mulej (SLO)	11	7
95	Nadin Ercegovic (YUG)	14	12	152	Laura Garrone (ITA)	14	7
96	Halle Cioffi (USA)	17	12	153	Cristina Tessi (ARG)	13	7
97	Patricia Tarabini (ARG)	12	12	154	Denisa Szabova (TCH)	15	7
98	Catherine Tanvier (FRA)	8	12	155	Kristine Radford (AUS)	13	7
99	Christelle Fauche (SUI)	11	12	156	Radka Bobkova (TCH)	16	7
100	Claudia Porwik (GER)	19	12	157	Barbara Rittner (GER)	12	7
101	Dominique Monami (BEL)	16	12	158	Christina Singer (GER)	13	7
102	Caroline Kuhlman (USA)	15	12	159	Lindsay Davenport (USA)	12	7
103	Natalia Baudone (ITA)	12	12	160	Michelle Jaggard Lai (AUS)	17	7
104	Katia Piccolini (ITA)	15	12	161	Louise Field (AUS)	20	7
105	Joanette Kruger (RSA)	14	12	162	Sybile Niox-Chateau (FRA)	16	7
106	Petra Thoren (FIN)	20	12	163	Elsie Birgin (USA)	10	7
107	Rene Simpson Alter (CAN)	10	12	164	Kristie Boogert (NED)	21	6
108	Sandrine Testud (FRA)	19	11	165	Irina Spirlea (ROM)	13	6
109	Mercedes Paz (ARG)	19	11	166	Eva Sviglerova (TCH)	17	6
110	Elna Reinach (RSA)	17	11	167	Sylvia Farina (ITA)	17	6
111	Kathy Rinaldi (USA)	16	11	168	Sara Gomer (GBR)	11	6
112	Beverly Bowes (USA)	14	11	169	Esmir Hoogendoorn (NED)	11	6
113	Kataryna Nowak (POL)	14	11	170	Marzia Grossi (ITA)	13	6
114	Nicole Muns Jagerman (NED)	13	11	171	Ma. Luciana Reynares (ARG)	13	6
115	Silke Frankl (GER)	15	11	172	Katarina Studenikova (TCH)	12	6
116	Nana Miyagi (JPN)	11	11	173	Clare Wood (GBR)	19	6
117	Flora Perfetti (ITA)	14	11	174	Nancy Feber (BEL)	8	6
118	Tessa Price (RSA)	14	10	175	Ruxandra Dragomir (ROM)	12	6
119	Fang Li (CHN)	10	10	176	Eva Bes (ESP)	14	6
120	Laura Golarsa (ITA)	13	10	177	Nicole Pratt (AUS)	17	6
121	Kyoko Nagatsuka (JPN)	17	10	178	Nathalie Herreman (FRA)	23	6
122	Jennifer Santrock (USA)	19	10	179	Beate Reinstadler (AUT)	11	6
123	Virginia Ruano-Pascual (ESP)	16	10	180	Ai Sugiyama (JPN)	16	6
124	Sandra Dopfer (AUT)	13	10	181	Andrea Vieira (BRA)	13	6
125	Rika Hiraki (JPN)	19	10	182	Victoria Milvidskaia (CIS)	12	6
126	Nicole Arendt (USA)	15	10	183	Kumiko Okamoto (JPN)	7	6
127	Anna-Maria Foldenyi (HUN)	16	10	184	Tammy Whittington (USA)	11	6
128	Francesca Romano (ITA)	15	10	185	Sung-Hee Park (KOR)	13	6
129	Helen Kelesi (CAN)	14	10	186	Tami Whitlinger (USA)	12	6
130	Noelia Perez (ESP)	11	9	187	Jo-Anne Faull (AUS)	17	6
131	Cecilia Dahlman (SWE)	14	9	188	Rosana de los Rios (PAR)	17	6
132	Miriam Oremans (NED)	18	9	189	Shannan McCarthy (USA)	10	6
133	Yone Kamio (JPN)	15	9	190	Estefania Bottini (ESP)	15	6
134	Elena Brioukhovets (CIS)	17	9	191	Maureen Drake (CAN)	20	6
135	Petra Langrova (TCH)	15	9	192	Nathalie Guerree (FRA)	11	6
136	Sandra Wasserman (BEL)	15	9	193	Hiromi Nagano (JPN)	14	5
137	Angelica Gavaldon (MEX)	18	9	194	Nathalie Housset Gilb.(FRA)	13	5
138	Isabelle Demongeot (FRA)	18	9	195	Cammy MacGregor (USA)	13	5
139	Heather Ludloff (USA)	13	8	196	Angela Kerek (GER)	11	5
139	Kristin Godridge (AUS)	24	9	197	Amanda Grunfeld (GBR)	11	5
140	Marketa Kochta (GER)	15	8	198	Christen Torrens-Valero (ESP)	16	5
141	Alexandra Fusai (FRA)	24	8	199	Asa Carlsson (SWE)	17	5
142	Monique Kiene (NED)	17	8	200	Heike Rusch (GER)	12	5

DOUBLES

		T'MNTS	PTS			T'MNTS	PTS
1	Helena Sukova (TCH)	14	379	26	Sandy Collins (USA)	20	101
2	Natalia Zvereva (CIS)	20	366	27	Amanda Coetzer (RSA)	12	98
3	Arantxa Sanchez-Vicario (ESP)	19	361	28	Nicole Provis (AUS)	17	98
4	Jana Novotna (TCH)	17	341	29	Mercedes Paz (ARG)	19	92
5	Larisa Savchenko Neiland (CIS)	21	302	30	Claudia Porwick (GER)	17	91
6	Gigi Fernandez (USA)	19	287	31	Ros Fairbank Nideffer (RSA)	17	91
7	Pam Shriver (USA)	14	237	32	Gretchen Magers (USA)	10	89
8	Conchita Martinez (ESP)	11	234	33	Isabelle Demongeot (FRA)	19	89
9	Martina Navratilova (USA)	8	218	34	Katerina Maleeva (BUL)	11	85
10	Zina Garrison Jackson (USA)	18	191	35	Brenda Schultz (NED)	20	82
11	Mary Joe Fernandez (USA)	14	173	36	Ines Gorrochategui (ARG)	10	78
12	Stephanie Rehe (USA)	12	166	37	Raffaella Reggi Concato (ITA)	8	76
13	Rennae Stubbs (AUS)	19	157	38	Sabine Appelmans (BEL)	13	75
14	Lori McNeil (USA)	20	153	39	Alexia Dechaume (FRA)	17	75
15	Kathy Rinaldi (USA)	21	138	40	Jo-Anne Faull (AUS)	18	74
16	Patty Fendick (USA)	19	138	41	Mary Pierce (FRA)	6	74
17	Jill Hetherington (CAN)	20	136	42	Anke Huber (GER)	12	74
18	Katrina Adams (USA)	18	129	43	Barbara Rittner (GER)	15	74
19	Manon Bollegraf (NED)	14	126	44	Patricia Tarabini (ARG)	12	72
20	Rachel McQuillan (AUS)	12	124	45	Marian De Swardt (RSA)	12	71
21	Elna Reinach (RSA)	18	113	46	Petra Langrova (TCH)	15	71
22	Steffi Graf (GER)	5	109	47	Amy Frazier (USA)	16	71
23	Robin White (USA)	13	108	48	Nana Miyagi (JPN)	13	70
24	Andrea Strnadova (TCH)	19	104	49	Julie Richardson (NZL)	20	70
25	Claudia Kohde-Kilsch (GER)	15	103	50	Mary Lou Daniels (USA)	12	69

PRIZE MONEY

The following table shows the prize money (including bonuses) won at all recognised tournaments which adopt the WTA guidelines and where direct entry is based solely on merit. (Figures supplied by VIRGINIA SLIMS 'SLIMSTAT' SYSTEM.)

	PRIZE MONEY			PRIZE MONEY
1	Monica Seles (YUG)	$2,622,352	51 Claudia Porwick (GER)	110,793
2	Steffi Graf (GER)	1,691,139	52 Katrina Adams (USA)	108,542
3	Arantxa Sanchez-Vic. (ESP)	1,376,355	53 Elna Reinach (RSA)	105,735
4	Gabriela Sabatini (ARG)	1,207,565	54 Debbie Graham (USA)	102,127
5	Martina Navratilova (USA)	731,933	55 Alexia Dechaume (FRA)	101,596
6	Natalia Zvereva (CIS)	657,694	56 Sabine Hack (GER)	100,003
7	Mary Joe Fernandez (USA)	605,908	57 Ann Grossman (USA)	99,759
8	Jana Novotna (TCH)	511,184	58 Stephanie Rehe (USA)	99,684
9	Gigi Fernandez (USA)	479,187	59 Jo Durie (GBR)	94,954
10	Helena Sukova (TCH)	473,112	60 Isabelle Demongeot (FRA)	94,827
11	Conchita Martinez (ESP)	445,768	61 Shaun Stafford (USA)	90,016
12	Lori McNeil (USA)	427,166	62 Mercedes Paz (ARG)	89,811
13	Larisa Savchenko Neil. (CIS)	407,402	63 Karina Habsudova (TCH)	88,397
14	Zina Garrison Jacks. (USA)	354,947	64 Pascale Paradis Mag. (FRA)	88,386
15	Jennifer Capriati (USA)	315,501	65 Jill Hetherington (CAN)	88,042
16	Manuela Maleeva Frag. (SUI)	291,350	66 Carrie Cunningham (USA)	88,015
17	Nathalie Tauziat (FRA)	271,305	67 Marianne Werdel (USA)	86,168
18	Katerina Maleeva (BUL)	266,207	68 Kimberly Po (USA)	85,919
19	Pam Shriver (USA)	254,458	69 Wiltrud Probst (GER)	85,029
20	Amy Frazier (USA)	233,513	70 Chanda Rubin (USA)	82,575
21	Brenda Schultz (NED)	211,425	71 Ginger Helgeson (USA)	81,995
22	Anke Huber (GER)	209,616	72 Claudia Kohde-Kilsch (GER)	81,839
23	Nicole Provis (AUS)	207,735	73 Bettina Fulco Villel. (ARG)	80,260
24	Judith Wiesner (AUT)	189,380	74 Linda Ferrando (ITA)	79,681
25	Patty Fendick (USA)	184,675	75 Rika Hiraki (JPN)	79,436
26	Mary Pierce (FRA)	183,436	76 Kristin Godridge (AUS)	76,596
27	Magdalena Maleeva (BUL)	183,403	77 Caroline Kuhlman (USA)	76,041
28	Leila Meskhi (CIS)	170,207	78 Emanuela Zardo (SUI)	73,548
29	Andrea Strnadova (TCH)	166,854	79 Tami Whitlinger (USA)	71,612
30	Amanda Coetzer (RSA)	164,962	80 Sandrine Testud (FRA)	70,633
31	Patricia Hy (CAN)	161,815	81 Caterina Lindqvist (SWE)	69,548
32	Barbara Rittner (GER)	161,136	82 Mariaan de Swardt (RSA)	68,498
33	Sabine Appelmans (BEL)	160,927	83 Louise Allen (USA)	68,117
34	Kimiko Date (JPN)	154,925	84 Miriam Oremans (NED)	67,131
35	Manon Bollegraf (NED)	148,884	85 Clare Wood (GBR)	65,147
36	Radka Zrubakova (TCH)	145,498	86 Petra Thoren (FIN)	64,794
37	Robin White (USA)	140,931	87 Sandy Collins (USA)	64,225
38	Laura Gildemeister (PER)	139,624	88 Elena Brioukhovets (CIS)	64,007
39	Linda Harvey-Wild (USA)	137,870	89 Jenny Byrne (AUS)	63,306
40	Rennae Stubbs (AUS)	132,865	90 Meike Babel (GER)	62,897
41	Ros Fairbank Nideffer (USA)	130,009	91 Donna Faber (USA)	62,284
42	Kathy Rinaldi (USA)	125,376	92 Nanne Dahlman (FIN)	62,119
43	Julie Halard (FRA)	122,178	93 Akiko Kijimuta (JPN)	61,877
44	Rachel McQuillan (AUS)	117,271	94 Jo-Anne Faull (AUS)	59,424
45	Noelle Van Lottum (NED)	115,934	95 Julie Richardson (NZL)	59,072
46	Naoko Sawamatsu (JPN)	115,367	96 Rene Simpson Alter (CAN)	57,966
47	Natalia Medvedeva (CIS)	115,202	97 Silke Meier (GER)	56,652
48	Sandra Cecchini (ITA)	114,221	98 Monique Javer (GBR)	56,590
49	Florencia Labat (ARG)	112,097	99 Nicole Muns Jagerman (NED)	56,053
50	Yayuk Basuki (INA)	111,748	100 Halle Cioffi (USA)	55,919

MILLIONAIRES

Players who have won more than $1 million in prize money.

1	Martina Navratilova (USA)	$18,396,526	23	Kathy Jordan (USA)	1,592,111
2	Steffi Graf (GER)	10,332,673	24	Virginia Wade (GBR)	1,542,278
3	Chris Evert (USA)	8,896,195	25	Ros Fairbank Nidef. (USA)	1,468,692
4	Monica Seles (YUG)	6,971,393	26	Evonne Goolagong (AUS)	1,399,431
5	Gabriela Sabatini (ARG)	6,056,672	27	Andrea Jaeger (USA)	1,379,066
6	Pam Shriver (USA)	4,870,516	28	Barbara Potter (USA)	1,376,580
7	Helena Sukova (TCH)	4,343,033	29	Rosie Casals (USA)	1,364,955
8	Zina Garrison Jackson (USA)	3,574,576	30	Sylvia Hanika (GER)	1,296,560
9	Arantxa Sanchez-Vic. (ESP)	3,436,112	31	Elizabeth Smylie (AUS)	1,265,905
10	Hana Mandlikova (AUS)	3,340,959	32	Nathalie Tauziat (FRA)	1,265,802
11	Wendy Turnbull (AUS)	2,769,024	33	Conchita Martinez (ESP)	1,222,345
12	Jana Novotna (TCH)	2,627,657	34	Virginia Ruzici (ROM)	1,183,728
13	Man. Maleeva-Frag. (SUI)	2,574,032	35	Anne Smith (USA)	1,159,717
14	Natalia Zvereva (CIS)	2,363,829	36	Dianne Balestrat (AUS)	1,145,377
15	Mary Joe Fernandez (USA)	2,253,521	37	Jennifer Capriati (USA)	1,134,715
16	Claudia Kohde-Kilsch (GER)	2,224,887	38	Catarina Lindqvist (SWE)	1,126,665
17	Lori McNeil (USA)	2,073,795	39	Bettina Bunge (USA)	1,126,424
18	Billie Jean King (USA)	1,966,487	40	Jo Durie (GBR)	1,118,102
19	Tracy Austin (USA)	1,925,415	41	Kathy Rinaldi (USA)	1,109,354
20	Gigi Fernandez (USA)	1,871,589	42	Betty Stove (NED)	1,047,356
21	Katerina Maleeva (BUL)	1,653,319	43	Robin White (USA)	1,014,495
22	Larisa Savchenko Neil. (CIS)	1,647,143			

WTA ANNUAL AWARDS

Presented at a Gala Dinner held at the Marriott Marquis Hotel, New York, on 31 August 1992 in aid of the New York Special Olympics.

PLAYER OF THE YEAR	Monica Seles
DOUBLES TEAM OF THE YEAR	Larisa Savchenko Neiland/Natalia Zvereva
MOST IMPROVED PLAYER	Kimiko Date
MOST IMPRESSIVE NEWCOMER	Debbie Graham
COMEBACK PLAYER OF THE YEAR	Jenny Byrne
TED TINLING MEDIA AWARD	Robin Finn
KAREN KRANTZCKE SPORTSMANSHIP	Jill Hetherington
PLAYER SERVICE	Elise Burgin
DAVID GRAY SPECIAL SERVICE	Chris Evert

WTA BOARD OF DIRECTORS
(Voted in, August 1992)

PRESIDENT	Pam Shriver	**ADDRESS**
VICE-PRESIDENT	Manon Bollegraf	133 First Street N.E.
SECRETARY	Elizabeth Smylie	St.Petersburg,
TREASURER	Elise Burgin	Florida, 33701
MEMBERS	Katrina Adams	USA.
	Sandy Collins	Tel: 813-895 5000
	Ros Fairbank-Nideffe	Fax: 813-894 1982
	Zina Garrison Jackson	Telex: 441761
	Martina Navratilova	
	Mercedes Paz	
	Judith Wiesner	
	Natalia Zvereva	
BUSINESS ADVISORS	Marvin Koslow	
	Loretta McCarthy	

SENIOR WTA EXECUTIVE STAFF

EXECUTIVE DIRECTOR AND C.E.O.	Gerard Smith
DIRECTOR OF INTERNATIONAL OPERATIONS	Peachy Kellmeyer
DIRECTOR OF FINANCE AND ADMINISTRATION	Jay Meder
DIRECTOR OF PUBLIC RELATIONS	Ana Leaird
DIRECTOR OF MANAGEMENT INFORMATION SYSTEMS	Gene Beckwith

WOMEN'S TENNIS COUNCIL

ADDRESS: 215 Park Avenue South, Suite 1715, New York, N.Y., 10003, USA.
Tel: 212-228 4400; FAX: 212-228 4800; TELEX: 510-6004566

MANAGING DIRECTOR
Ann Person (Appointed March 1991)

ITF REPRESENTATIVES
J.Howard Frazer, USTA
Brian Tobin, ITF
Deborah Jevans, IT

WTA REPRESENTATIVES
Elise Burgin
Pam Shriver
Gerard Smith

TOURNAMENT REPRESENTATIVES
William Goldstein, U.S.A.
George Hendon, Europe
Sara Fornaciari, U.S.A.
Geoffrey Pollard, Rest of the World

KRAFT GENERAL FOODS REPRESENTATIVES Tom Keim, Edy McGoldrick

VIRGINIA SLIMS REPRESENTATIVE
Ina Broeman

REFERENCE SECTION

BIOGRAPHIES
ALL-TIME GREATS
CHAMPIONSHIP ROLLS

At the end of an unbelievably exciting men's doubles final on the third Monday, Michael Stich lifts his partner John McEnroe to celebrate his first Grand Slam doubles success. For the American left-hander it was a ninth such title and a fifth at Wimbledon. (M. Cole)

With three Grand Slam doubles titles to her name in 1992, in partnership with the American Olympic gold medallist Gigi Fernandez, Natalia Zvereva certainly put her new country of Belarus firmly on the map.   (T. Hindley)

BIOGRAPHIES

Christine Forrest

Abbreviations used in this section:

f	final	LIPC	Lipton International
sf	semi-final		Players Championships
qf	quarter-final	Fed Cup	Federation Cup
r/u	runner-up	W Cup	Wightman Cup
def	defaulted	FC Cup	Family Circle Cup
ret'd	retired	GS Cup	Grand Slam Cup
fs	final set	Champ.	Champion/Championship
rr	round-robin	Int	International
b-p	break-point	Inv	Invitation
s-p	set-point	Jun	Junior
m-p	match-point	Nat	National
t-b	tie-break	Pro	Professional
1r	first round	Tourn	Tournament
2s	second set	CS	Colgate Series
RH	right-handed	TS	Toyota Series
LH	left-handed	HC	Hard Court
2HB	2-handed backhand	VS	Virginia Slims
2HF	2-handed forehand	KGF	Kraft General Foods
D Cup	Davis Cup	WCT	World Championship Tennis
US CC	US Clay Court	WTT	World Team Tennis
	Championships	GP	Grand Prix

TOP TEN

Full biographical and statistical details of the top ten men and top ten women head separate men's and women's sections. Each individual's record contains personal details, followed by his or her 1992 prize money, career prize money, the number of career titles won and year end rankings. A paragraph on style is followed by annual notes of career highlights, beginning with the tournaments won each year. A section giving principal singles results in full for 1992 includes all matches where a player has reached at least the semi-final. There follows a complete career record of every match played at each of the four Grand Slam Championships, at the Olympic Games and in Davis Cup or Federation Cup ties.

NEXT 50

Within the two sections are the full 1992 results, the annual notes and the career highlights of the next 50 ranked singles players of each sex, plus the leading doubles players and juniors. The final ranking for each year is shown in brackets following the year.

Note: John Barrett's annual world rankings, as well as the year-end rankings and prize money published by the ATP Tour and the Women's Tennis Association, together with lists of the men and women whose career earning exceed $1 million, can be found in the Rankings Section (pp 197–214).

We gratefully acknowledge the assistance of the ATP Tour, Virginia Slims and the WTA in supplying statistical information.

JIM COURIER (USA)   Turned pro: 1988

Born: Sanford, Fla., 17 August 1970.
Lives: Dade City, Fla.
Father: Jim. **Mother:** Linda. **Sister:** Audra (older).
Agent: International Management Group
Coaches: José Higueras and Brad Stine (on the road).
Height: 6ft 1in(1.85m). **Weight:** 175lb (79kg).
Rankings: 1987: 348; **1988:** 43; **1989:** 24; **1990:** 25; **1991:** 2; **1992:** 1.
Highest: 1 (1992).

1992 Prize Money: $2,253,385. **Career Earnings:** $4,946,459. **Career Titles:** 9.

Style: An aggressive right-hander who blasts his opponents from the court with heavy topspin on western-grip forehand and two-handed backhand. A fine serve and adequate volley, allied to an intense competitiveness, a willingnes to train harder than most, and an ability to reach seemingly impossible shots, make him a formidable opponent.

CAREER HIGHLIGHTS (year: (*titles*))
1986: A prominent junior who was a product of the Nick Bollettieri Tennis Academy. Plays the drums and guitar. Played on US Jun World Cup team r/u to AUS; won Orange Bowl. **1987:** Won French Open Jun doubles with Stark and won Orange Bowl again. **1988:** Sf US CC and Stockholm (d. Jarryd and Pernfors back-to-back; qf Stratton Mountain and Detroit. R/u US Nat 18s to Chang. **1989: (1)** *Basle.* Upset Agassi *en route* to last 16 French Open and beat Edberg to win his 1st GP title at Basle in autumn. In doubles won Italian Open and qualified for Masters with Sampras. **1990:** sf Indian Wells; qf Milan, Philadelphia, LIPC, Munich, Gstaad and Cincinnati. **1991: (3)** *FRENCH OPEN, Indian Wells, Lipton.* He began an extraordinary year by extending Edberg to 5s in last 16 Australian Open, then in March won both singles and doubles (with J. Sanchez) at Indian Wells, following immediately with the title at LIPC over Wheaton, which took him into top 10 for 1st time. Played first D Cup tie in March v Mexico (away) and lost live singles to Herrera and dead one to Lavalle. Then followed the high spot of his career to date, when he won the French Open, beating Edberg *en route* and overpowering Agassi to win his 1st GS final, replacing him as No. 4 in the world. He made a qf appearance at Wimbledon, losing to eventual champion Stich, then swept to f US Open, ending Connors' romantic run in sf, but was completely outplayed by Edberg at the last hurdle. That performance took him to No. 3 behind Edberg and Backer and by Nov. he had edged Becker aside to take 2nd place, a position confirmed by his progress to f ATP World Champ, where he lost to Sampras. Also reached sf Adelaide, Tokyo Suntory, Montreal, Cincinnati, Indianapolis and Stockholm. **1992: (5)** *AUSTRALIAN OPEN, FRENCH OPEN, Tokyo Suntory, Hong Kong, Italian Open.* He won his 2nd GS title at Australian Open, playing no seed until meeting the No. 1 Edberg in f, and followed with the French Open title, but lost the chance of a GS when he lost to Olhovskiy at Wimbledon and at US Open fell in sf to Sampras. After reaching f San Francisco in Feb., he displaced Edberg from the top of the rankings, becoming the 10th man to hold that position since rankings began, but lost his place 6 weeks later (23 March) when he fell to Chang sf LIPC. Throughout the year the top ranking shifted between the two, Courier regaining it in April after winning in Tokyo, where Edberg fell sf, but dropping again to No. 2 after US Open, before returning on 5 Oct, with Edberg dropping to 3 behind Sampras. He finished the year at the top, after taking r/u spot at ATP World Champ to an inspired Becker. Won Tokyo Suntory, Hong Kong and Italian Open, and was r/u San Francisco, Brussels and Indianapolis.

PRINCIPAL 1992 RESULTS (detailed Grand Slam results below)
won Tokyo Suntory (d. Curren 6–1 6–1, Pozzi 6–3 6–3, Mansdorf 7–6 6–4, Chang 6–2 6–3, Krajicek 6–4 6–4 7–6), **won** Hong Kong (d. Kuhnen 7–6 6–4, Damm 6–2 6–1, Muller 6–2 6–1, B. Gilbert 6–4 6–1, Chang 7–5 6–3, **won** Italian Open (d. Muster 7–6 6–4, Clavet 6–2 6–2, Bruguera 6–3 6–2, Miniussi 4–6 6–4 6–1, Steeb 5–7 6–1 6–2, Costa 7–6 6–0 6–4), **r/u**

San Francisco (d. Woodforde 7–6 5–7 7–5, Stoltenberg 7–5 6–4, Masur 4–6 6–4 6–3, Rostagno 4–6 6–3 6–2, lost Chang 6–3 6–3), **r/u** Brussels (d. Santoro 6–2 6–1, Leconte 6–4 7–5, Volkov 7–6 7–6, Forget 7–6 6–4, lost Becker 6–7 2–6 7–6 7–6 7–5), **r/u** Indianapolis (d. Pioline 6–4 6–2, Engel 7–6 6–2, Steven 6–2 6–2, Martin 7–6 7–6, lost Sampras 6–4 6–4), **sf** LIPC (d. Champion 5–7 6–1 6–2, Gomez 6–4 6–7 4–3 ret'd, Steeb 7–6 6–2, Nargiso 6–7 6–2 6–0, lost Chang 6–2 6–4), **sf** Antwerp (d. Connors 6–3 6–3, J. Sanchez 6–3 6–3, Forget 6–7 6–4 6–4, lost Krajicek 4–6 6–4 7–5).

CAREER GRAND SLAM RECORD
AUSTRALIAN OPEN – Played 3, won 1
1990: 2r [seed 14] d. Arias 6–3 6–3 6–1, lost Svensson 2–6 6–2 6–3 6–2. **1991: 4r** [seed 16] d. Gunnarsson 6–3 6–4 6–2, Bloom 6–2 6–3 6–2, Oncins 6–3 6–1 6–1, lost Edberg [seed 1] 4–6 6–0 6–4 5–7 6–2. **1992: won** [seed 2] d. Gilbert 6–4 7–6 6–3, Enquist 2–6 6–3 6–1 6–4, Muster 6–1 6–4 6–2, Rosset 6–3 6–1 6–3, Mansdorf 6–3 6–2 6–2, Krajicek w–o, Edberg [seed 1] 6–3 3–6 6–4 6–2.

FRENCH OPEN – Played 4, won 2
1989: last 16 d.Paloheimo 6–3 6–4 7–6, Brown 6–0 7–5 6–1, Agassi [seed 5] 7–6 4–6 6–3 6–2, lost Chesnokov 2–6 3–6 7–6 6–2 7–5. **1990: last 16** [seed 13] d.Altur 6–1 4–6 6–3 6–4, d.Srejber 7–6 6–1 2–6 6–2, Anderson 6–0 6–2 6–1, lost Agassi [seed] 6–7 6–1 6–4. **1991: won** [seed 9] d Rostagno 6–3 6–3 6–0, Ferreira 6–2 6–3 6–4, Larsson 6–3 4–6 6–4 6–7–5 6–2, Martin 6–2 6–3 6–3, Edberg [seed 1] 6–4 2–6 6–3 6–4, Stich [seed 12] 6–2 6–7 6–2 6–4, Agassi [seed 4] 3–6 6–4 2–6 6–1 6–4. **1992: won** [seed 1]) d Kroon 7–6 6–4 6–2, Muster 6–1 6–4 6–4, Mancini 6–4 6–2 6–0, Medvedev 6–1 6–4 6–2, Ivanisevic [seed 8] 6–2 6–1 2–6 7–5, Agassi [seed 11] 6–3 6–2 6–2.

WIMBLEDON – Played 4, qf 1
1989: 1r lost Seguso 6–2 3–6 6–4 5–7 9–7. **1990: 3r** [seed 9] d.Kaplan 6–1 6–4 6–4, Stoltenberg 6–2 7–6 6–4, lost Woodforde 7–5 5–7 7–5 6–4. **1991: qf** [seed 4] d.Gilbert 6–4 6–2 7–6, Grabb 6–4 7–6 2–6 4–6 6–4, Boetsch 6–2 6–2 6–0, Novacek 6–3 6–4 6–2, lost Stich 3–7 6–6 6–2. **1992: 3r** [seed 1] d.Zoecke 6–2 6–2 6–3, Black 6–4 6–1 6–4, lost Olhovskiy 6–4 4–6 6–4 6–4.

US OPEN – Played 5, r/u 1, sf 1
1988: 2r d. Skoff 7–5 6–4 6–3, lost Pernfors 6–3 6–4 6–4. **1989: 3r** d. Svensson 3–6 7–6 6–2 7–6, Palmer 6–1 6–3 6–3, lost Lendl 6–1 6–2 6–3. **1990: 2r** [seed 14] d. Masur 6–4 6–0 5–7 6–1, lost Muller 4–6 6–4 7–6 7–6. **1991: r/u** [seed 4] d. Kulti 6–3 6–4 6–4, Arias 6–3 6–2 6–0, Jarryd 6–3 6–2 6–2, E.Sanchez [seed 14] 6–4 6–4 6–3, Sampras [seed 6] 6–2 7–6 7–6, Connors 6–3 6–3 6–2, lost Edberg [seed 2] 6–2 6–4 6–0. **1992: sf** [seed 1] d. O'Brien 4–6 6–1 6–4 7–6, Chesnokov 4–6 6–3 6–3 6–1, Pioline 7–6 6–4 3–6 6–3, J.McEnroe [seed 16] 6–2 6–2 7–6, Agassi [seed 8] 6–3 6–7 6–1 6–4, lost Sampras [seed 3] 6–1 3–6 6–2 6–2.

OLYMPIC GAMES
1992: (Barcelona) last 16 [seed 1] d. Krishnan 6–2 4–6 6–1 6–4, Bloom 6–2 6–0 6–0, lost Rosset 6–4 6–2 6–1.

CAREER DAVIS CUP RECORD
1991: March – *World Group 1r (Away) USA d. Mexico 3–2* R1 lost L.Herrera 6–4 2–6 7–5 6–4. R5 lost L.Lavalle 6–4 6–7 7–5. **September –** *World Group S/F (Home) USA d. Germany 3–2* R2 d. C.Steeb 4–6 6–1 6–3 6–4. R4 lost M.Stich 6–4 7–5 6–4. **1992: September –** *World Group sf (Home) USA d. Sweden 4–1* R1 d. N.Kulti 4–6 7–6 6–3 7–5. R4 lost to M.Larsson 2–6 7–6 7–6. **December –** *World Group Final (Home) USA d. Switzerland 3–1* R2 lost to M.Rosset 6–3 6–7 3–6 6–4 6–4. R4 d. J.Hlasek 6–3 3–6 6–3 6–4. (Last rubber not played.)

GRAND PRIX MASTERS/ATP TOUR CHAMPIONSHIP (from 1990)
1991: r/u In rr lost Lendl 6–2 6–3, d. Novacek 6–7 7–5 6–2, d. Forget 7–6 6–4; In sf d. Agassi 6–3 7–5; In f lost Sampras 3–6 7–6 6–3 6–4. **1992: r/u** In rr d. Krajicek 6–7 7–6 7–5, lost Ivanisevic 6–3 6–3, d. Chang 7–5 6–2; In sf d. Sampras 7–6 7–6; In f lost Becker 6–4 6–3 7–5.

STEFAN EDBERG (SWE)   **Turned pro:** 1983

Born: Vastervik, 19 January 1966. **Lives:** London, England.
Father: Bengt. **Mother:** Barbro. **Brother:** Jan (younger). **Wife:**
Married long-time girlfriend Annette Olsen in Vaxjo 18 April 1992.
Agent: ProServ.
Coach: Tony Pickard since 1983. Originally Percy Rosberg.
Height: 6ft 2in (1.89m). **Weight:** 177lb (81kg).
Rankings: 1982: 523; **1983:** 53; **1984:** 20; **1985:** 5; **1986:** 5; **1987:** 2;
1988: 5; **1989:** 3; **1990:** 1; **1991:** 1; **1992:** 2. **Highest:** 1 (13 Aug. 1990).

1992 Prize money: $2,441,804. **Career Earnings:** $13,539,075. **Career Titles:** 36.

Style: A right-hander who changed from a two-handed backhand to a one–handed stroke
on the advice of his shrewd coach Percy Rosberg who had previously advised Bjorn Borg
to stay with his two-hander. Stefan is arguably the best of the present serve–volleyers,
quick of movement and reaction. He also possesses the finest backhand in the game
which he can hit with top or slice.

CAREER HIGHLIGHTS (year:(*titles*)**)**
1983: Became the first player – male or female – to win Jun Grand Slam (Butch Buchholz
won it in 1958 before the tournaments were Championship events), proving prowess on 3
different surfaces, and played 11 events on men's tour. **1984: (1)** *Milan.* Contributed
crucial triumph in D Cup f as Sweden d. USA with doubles win alongside Jarryd over
McEnroe/Fleming, repeating their success over that duo at US Open, where they were r/u.
1985: (4) *Memphis, San Francisco, Basel, AUSTRALIAN OPEN* Reached top 5 with first
GS men's success, upending Lendl and Wilander on grass in Melbourne. **1986 (3):** *Gstaad,
Basel, Stockholm.* Lost four other finals (two to Becker, one to McEnroe, one to Gilbert)
and reached sf US Open. In doubles with Jarryd won Masters and r/u French Open. **1987:
(7)** *AUSTRALIAN OPEN, Memphis, Rotterdam, Tokyo Outdoor and Indoor, Cincinnati,
Stockholm.* Won second Australian singles title, sf Wimbledon and US Open, won titles in
Memphis, Rotterdam, Tokyo (2), Cincinnati and Stockholm, reached 4 more f and achieved
win–loss singles record of 70–11 going into Masters, where he reached sf. In doubles with
Jarryd won Australian and US Opens, and reached sf Masters. **1988: (3)** *Rotterdam,
WIMBLEDON, Basle.* Won Wimbledon over Becker, sf Australian Open and last 16 French
and US Opens. Won Rotterdam and Basel, reached 4 other f and took Olympic bronze
medal. Played virtually no doubles and was restricted at Masters by tendonitis in left knee,
falling to Lendl in sf. **1989: (2)** *Tokyo Suntory, Masters.* Finished the year in triumph with
his first Masters title, beating Lendl in sf and Backer in f. R/u French Open and Wimbledon,
but fell last 16 US Open to Connors and withdrew qf Australian Open with back injury
which kept him our for 5 weeks. His only other title came at Tokyo Suntory, but he reached
f Scottsdale, Cincinnati, Basle and Paris Open. **1990: (7)** *WIMBLEDON, Indian Wells,
Tokyo Suntory, Los Angeles, Cincinnati, Long Island, Paris Open.* Won a second
Wimbledon title and on 13 Aug took over No. 1 ranking for first time from Lendl, holding off
a strong late challenge from Becker to finish the year in that position. He was forced to
retire during f Australian Open with stomach muscle injury, suffered during sf match,
which kept him out for 4 weeks. He was without his coach, Pickard, who was recovering
from a hip operation, from end Australian Open to beginning French, where, as top seed,
he lost 1r to Bruguera, suffering similarly at the hands of Volkov at the same stage US
Open. Altogether in 1990 won 7 titles and reached 5 other finals, including ATP World
Champ, where he lost to Agassi having beaten him in rr. Fined 15% of total earnings on
ATP tour (excluding GS) for falling 2 tourns short of commitment to the tour. Seeded No. 1
GS Cup but lost Chang 1r. Voted Player of the Year. **1991: (6)** *US OPEN, Stuttgart, Tokyo
Suntory, Queen's, Sydney Indoor, Tokyo Seiko.* Lost his No. 1 ranking to Becker for 3
weeks from 28 Jan after falling to Lendl in sf Australian Open, but regained the top position
18 Feb after the German was forced to retire in sf Brussels. His unexpected loss to Stich

in sf Wimbledon cost him the top ranking again until his first US Open title, which he won by playing the best tennis of his life v Courier in f. This took him back to No. 1, where he finished the year. In addition to US Open he won Stuttgart Eurocard, Tokyo Suntory, Queen's (at his 6th attempt), Sydney Indoor and Tokyo Seiko, as well as reaching 2 more f and 4 sf and leading Sweden to victory in World Team Cup. His 6 titles during the year were equalled in the men's game only by Forget. Missed ATP Champs with knee injury, caused by playing too heavy a schedule. Voted Player of the Year again. **1992: (3)** *US OPEN, Hamburg, New Haven.* Surrendered his No. 1 ranking to Courier after losing to the American in f Australian Open, regained the top position on 23 March, but lost it again 6 April after falling to Krajicek sf Tokyo Suntory. Fell to Cherkasov 3r French Open and Ivanisevic qf Wimbledon, but won US Open over Sampras to return to No. 1 albeit briefly On 5 Oct. he dropped to No. 3 behind Courier and Sampras as more 1991 points came off the computer. He needed to win all his matches at ATP World Champs in order to return to the top for the year-end rankings, but he beat only Korda and failed to qualify for sf. He was r/u Stuttgart and Sydney Indoor and reached 6 other sf.

PRINCIPAL 1992 RESULTS (detailed Grand Slam results below)
won Hamburg (d. Arrese 6–3 6–4, Clavet 6–3 6–1, Camporese 2–6 7–6 6–2, Costa 7–5 7–6, Stich 5–7 6–4 6–1), **won** New Haven (d. Farrow 6–3 6–1, Haarhuis 6–2 6–4, Forget 6–3 6–7 6–4, Lendl 7–6 4–6 6–3, Washington 7–6 6–1), **r/u** Stuttgart (d. Larsson 6–2 6–2, Antonitsch 6–1 6–2, Camporese 4–6 6–2 7–5, Korda 6–4 6–4, lost Ivanisevic 6–7 6–3 6–4 6–4), **r/u**Sydney Indoor (d. Baur 7–6 7–5, Reneberg 6–4 6–2, J. McEnroe 6–3 6–3, Holm 6–2 3–6 6–3, lost Ivanisevic 6–4 6–2 6–4), **sf** Brussels (d. Bruguera 6–4 4–6 6–4, Siemerink 7–5 6–2, Novecek 6–2 6–1, lost Becker 4–6 6–4 6–2), **sf** Tokyo Suntory (d. Evernden 6–3 6–4, Masur 6–3 6–4, B. Gilbert 4–6 6–2 6–3, lost Krajicek 6–3 7–5), **sf** Queen's (d. Curren 7–6 6–2, Masur 6–4 6–7 6–4, Cash 6–7 7–6 6–3, lost Matsuoka 1–6 7–6 10–8), **sf** Cincinnati (d. Bergstrom 7–6 6–1, Mansdorf 6–4 6–3, Grabb 6–3 7–6, lost Sampras 6–2 6–3), **sf** Long Island (d. Zoecke 6–2 7–5, Arias 7–6 6–2, Arriens 6–4 6–0, lost Korda 7–5 7–5) **sf** Stockholm (d. Medvedev 6–1 7–6, Novecek 6–3 6–4, Boetsch 7–5 7–6, lost Ivanisevic 6–4 7–6).

CAREER GRAND SLAM RESULTS
AUSTRALIAN OPEN – Played 9, Won 2, r/u 2, sf 2, qf 2
1983: 2r bye, lost Borowiak 6–3 2–6 7–5 6–4. **1984: qf** [seed 8] d. Davis 6–2 6–7 7–5 6–2, Tim Gullikson 6–1 6–2 7–5, Bourne 6–2 6–2 6–2, lost Wilander [seed 2] 7–5 6–3 1–6 6–4. **1985: won** [seed 5] d.Schultz 6–3 6–4 7–6, Anger 5–7 7–6 6–4 7–5, Masur 6–7 2–6 7–6 6–4 6–2 9 (saving 2 MPs), Schapers 6–0 7–5 6–4, Lendl [seed 1] 6–7 7–5 6–1 4–6 9–7, Wilander [seed 3] 6–4 6–3 6–3. **1986: No Championship. 1987: won** [seed 4] bye, d. Letts 3–6 6–1 6–0 6–2, Frawley 6–4 6–3 6–1, Seguso [seed 13] 6–1 6–0 6–1, Mecir [seed 6] 6–1 6–4 6–4, Masur 6–2 6–4 7–6, Cash [seed 11] 6–3 6–4 3–6 5–7 6–3. **1988: sf** [seed 2] d. Davis 4–6 6–2 6–2 7–5, Mronz 6–4 6–3 6–1, Goldie 6–4 7–5 2–6 6–3, Stoltenberg 6–3 6–3 6–4, Chesnokov 4–6 7–6 6–4 6–4, lost Wilander [seed 3] 6–0 6–7 6–3 3–6 6–1 **1989: qf** [seed 4] d. Smith 6–4 6–3 6–4, Moraing 6–4 7–5 7–5, Kriek 7–5 7–5 7–5, Cash [seed 13] 6–4 6–0 6–2, lost Muster [seed 11] w.o. **1990: r/u** [seed 3] d. Anderson 7–6 6–3 6–4, Kuhnen 6–2 6–2 6–4, Chamberlin 6–3 6–4 6–1, Svensson 6–2 6–2 6–4, Wheaton 7–5 7–6 3–6 6–2, Wilander 6–1 6–1 6–2, lost Lendl [seed 1] 4–6 7–6 5–2 ret. **1991: sf** [seed 1] d. Poliakov 6–1 7–6 6–2, Masso 6–1 6–2 6–3, Cash 7–6 7–5 6–2, Courier 4–6 6–0 6–4 5–7 6–2, Yzaga 6–2 6–3 6–2, lost Lendl [seed 3] 6–4 5–7 3–6 7–6 6–4. **1992: r/u** [seed 1] d. Bates 6–4 6–2 6–4, Mezzadri 6–1 6–2 6–1, Fitzgerald 7–5 6–1 6–4, Chesnokov 6–1 7–5 6–2, Lendl [seed 5] 4–6 7–5 6–1 6–7 6–1, Ferreira 7–6 6–1 6–2, lost Courier [seed 2] 6–3 3–6 6–4 6–2.

FRENCH OPEN – Played 9, r/u 1, qf 2
1984: 2r d. Arraya 6–2 6–1 6–2, lost Jarryd 6–4 3–6 7–6 7–5. **1985: qf** [seed 14] d. Panatta 7–6 6–3 6–3, Hlasek 6–2 6–3 6–4, Frawley 7–6 6–3 6–0, Jarryd [seed 6] 6–3 6–7 6–4 6–2, lost Connors [seed 3] 6–4 6–3 7–6. **1986: 2r** [seed 5] d. Perkiss 6–3 3–6 6–4 6–1, lost Pernfors 6–7 7–5 6–3 2–6 6–4. **1987: 2r** [seed 3] d. Leach 6–2 6–3 6–3, lost Winogradsky 7–6 7–6 7–5. **1988: 4r** [seed 2] d. Novacek 4–6 6–3 6–2 6–2, Boetsch 6–0 6–4 6–3,

Gunnersson 6–4 6–4 7–6, lost Perez-Roldan [seed 15] 7–5 6–3 6–3. **1989: r/u** [seed 3] d. Vajda 6–2 6–0 1–6 6–3, Perreira 6–4 6–4 6–2, Arias 6–4 6–4 6–4, Ivanisevic 7–5 6–3 6–3, Mancini 6–1 6–3 7–6, Becker [seed 2] 6–3 6–4 5–7 3–6 6–2, lost Chang [seed 15] 6–1 3–6 4–6 6–4 6–2 **1990: 1r** [seed 1] lost Bruguera 6–4 6–2 6–1. **1991: qf** [seed 1] d. Wuyts 6–2 6–2 6–3, Skopff 6–4 5–7 7–6 6–3, Chesnokov 6–1 6–4 6–3, Cherkasov 7–6 6–4 6–4, lost Courier [seed 9] 6–4 2–6 6–3 6–4. **1992: 3r** [seed 2] d. Soules 7–5 6–1 6–7 7–5, Markus 4–6 7–6 7–5 4–6 6–4, lost Cherkasov 6–4 6–3 7–6.

WIMBLEDON – Played 10, Won 2, r/u 1, sf 2, qf 1
1983: 2r d. Roger-Vasselin 6–2 7–6 6–1, lost Sundstrom 2–6 7–6 7–6 4–6 8–6. **1984: 2r** d. Drewett 6–4 3–6 7–6 6–2, lost Kriek 4–6 6–7 6–4 6–1–6 1. **1985: 4r** [seed 14] d. Doohan 6–2 6–3 6–4, Wilkison 6–1 7–5 3–6 6–7 9–7, Hooper 6–3 6–4 6–4, lost Curren [seed 8] 7–6 6–3 7–6. **1986: 3r** [seed 5] d. Wilder 6–4 6–3 6–1, Annacone 6–4 7–4–6 7–5 6–0, lost Mecir 6–4 6–4 6–4. **1987: sf** [seed 4] d. Eriksson 6–0 6–0 6–0, Purcell 6–4 6–3 6–4, Anger 7–6 6–2 6–2, Hlasek 6–3 6–7 6–1 6–4, Jarryd 4–6 6–4 6–1 6–3, lost Lendl [seed 2] 3–6 6–4 7–6–6–4. **1988: won** [seed 3] d. Forget 6–4 3–6 6–3 6–4, Reneberg 6–3 7–6 5–7 6–2, K.Flach 6–2 7–5 2–6 7–5, Youl 6–2 6–4 6–4, Kuhnen 6–3 4–6 6–1 7–6, Mecir 4–6 2–6 6–4 6–3 6–4, Becker 4–6 7–6 6–4 6–2 **1989: r/u** [seed 2] d. Pridham 6–3 6–4 6–1, Woodbridge 6–4 6–4 1–6 7–6, S.Davis 6–3 6–4 4–6 6–2, Mansdorf [seed 16] 6–4 6–3 6–2, Mayotte [seed 8] 7–6 7–6 6–3 J.McEnroe [seed 5] 7–5 7–6 7–6, lost Becker [seed 3] 6–0 7–6 6–4. **1990: won** [seed 3] d. Dyke 4–6 6–1 6–3 6–1, Mecir 6–2 6–3 6–2, Mansdorf 6–4 5–7 3–6 6–2 9–7, Chang [seed 13] 6–3 6–2 6–1, Bergstrom 6–3 6–2 6–4, Lendl [seed 1] 6–1 7–6 6–3, Becker [seed2] 6–2 6–2 3–6 3–6 6–4. **1991: sf** [seed 1] d. Rosset 6–4 6–4 6–4, Pate 6–2 6–2 6–3, Van Renbsberg 6–1 6–3 6–2, J.McEnroe [seed 16] 7–6 6–1 6–4, Champion 6–3 6–2 7–5, lost Stich [seed 6] 4–6 7–6 7–6 7–6. **1992: qf** [seed 2] d. Bryan 6–1 6–3 6–0, Muller 7–6 6–3 7–6, Stafford 6–2 6–0 6–2, Holm 6–3 6–4 6–7 6–3, lost Ivanisevic [seed 8] 6–7 7–5 6–1 3–6 6–3.

US OPEN – Played 10, Won 2, sf 2
1983: 1r lost Krickstien 6–3 6–2 3–6 4–6 7–6. **1984: 2r** d. Stefanki 6–4 6–3 6–0, lost J.McEnroe [seed 1] 6–1 6–0 6–2. **1985: 4r** [seed 11] d. Clerc 6–3 6–4 6–3, Flach 7–5 6–3 6–4, Gilbert 4–6 6–4 6–1 6–4, lost Connors [seed 4] 6–4 3–6 6–3 6–4. **1986: sf** [seed 4] d. Bonneau 6–0 6–3 6–0, Curren 7–6 3–6 4–6 6–3 6–2, Krishnan 7–6 3–6 6–4 4–6 6–4, Goldie 6–3 6–2 6–2, Wilkison 6–3 6–3 6–3, lost Lendl [seed 1] 7–6 6–2 6–3. **1987: sf** [seed 2] d. Rostagno 6–3 7–6 6–2, Goldie 6–7 6–4 6–2 6–4, Evernden 6–2 6–1 6–4, Svensson 6–2 7–6 6–3, Krishnan 6–2 6–2 6–2, lost Wilander [seed 3] 6–4 3–6 6–3 6–4. **1988: 4r** [seed 3] d. Pimek 6–2 6–2 6–4, Forget 7–5 6–1 6–3, J.Carlsson 6–0 7–5 6–2, lost Krickstein 5–7 7–6 7–6 4–6 7–5. **1989: 4r** [seed 3] d. Frana 7–6 6–2 7–5, Lundgren 6–2 6–2 6–2, Srejber 6–2 1–6 6–2 6–1, lost Connors [seed 13] 6–2 6–3 6–1. **1990: 1r** [seed 1] lost Volkov 6–3 7–6 6–2. **1991: won** [seed 2] d. Shelton 6–4 2–6 7–6 6–1, Tarango 6–3 7–5 6–0, Grabb 7–6 4–6 6–3 6–4, Chang 7–6 7–5 6–3, J.Sanchez 6–3 6–2 6–3, Lendl [seed 5] 6–3 6–3 6–4, Courier [seed 4] 6–2 6–4 6–0. **1992: won** [seed 2] d.Mattar 7–5 7–5 6–2, Hlasek 7–5 6–2 6–1, Svensson 6–4 6–2 6–2, Krajicek [seed 15] 6–4 6–7 6–3 3–6 6–4, Lendl [seed 9] 6–3 6–3 3–6 5–7 7–6, Chang [seed 4] 6–7 7–5 7–6 5–7 6–4, Sampras [seed 3] 3–6 6–4 7–6 6–2.

OLYMPIC GAMES
1984: (Demonstration Event – Under 21) won Final – d. Maciel 6–1 7–6. **1988: Bronze medal** [seed 1] d. Skoff 7–6 6–2 7–3, Moreno 6–2 7–5 6–0, Hlasek [seed 10] 6–2 6–4 7–6, Cane 6–1 7–5 6–4, lost Mecir [seed 3] 3–6 6–0 1–6 6–4 6–2. **1992:(Barcelona) 1r** [seed 2] lost Chesnokov 6–0 6–4 6–4.

CAREER DAVIS CUP RECORD
1984: February – *World Group qf (Home) Sweden d. Paraguay 4–1* R3 (+A. Jarryd) Lost to F.Gonzales/V.Pecci 6–2 8–6 4–6 6–1. **September** – *World Group sf (Home) Sweden d. Czechoslovakia 5–0* R3 (+A.Jarryd) d. P.Slozil/T.Smid 2–6 5–7 6–1 10–8 6–2. **December** – *World Group Final (Home) Sweden d. USA 4–1* R3 (+A. Jarryd) d. P.Fleming/J.McEnroe 7–5 5–7 6–2 7–5. **1985: March** – *World Group 1r (Away) Sweden d. Chile 4–1* R1 Lost to H.

Gildemeister 6–3 2–6 6–4 7–5. R3 (+J.Gunnarsson) d. R.Acuna/H.Gildemeister 6–1 1–6 6–3 6–3. R5 d. P.Rebolledo 6–4 4–6 6–2. **August** – *World Group qf (Away) Sweden d. India 4–1.* R3 (+A.Jarryd) d. A. and V.Amritraj 21–19 2–6 6–3 6–4. **October** – *World Group sf (Home) Sweden d. Australia 5–0.* R3 (+A.Jarryd) d. M.Edmondson/ J.Fitzgerald 6–4 6–3 6–4. **December** – *World Group Final (Away) Sweden d. Germany 3–2.* R2 Lost to B.Becker 6–3 3–6 7–5 8–6. R5 d. M.Westphal 3–6 7–5 6–4 6–3. **1986: July** – *World Group qf (Home) Sweden d. Italy 5–0.* R4 d. P.Cane 6–3 2–6 6–0. **October** – *World Group sf (Away) Sweden d. Czechoslovakia 4–1.* R2 d. M.Srejber 3–6 6–4 6–3 4–6 7–5. R3 (+A.Jarryd) Lost to M.Mecir/ T.Smid 7–5 6–2 6–4. R5 d. M.Mecir 6–4 9–7. **December** – *World Group Final (Away) Australia d. Sweden 3–2.* R1 Lost to P.Cash 13–11 13–11 6–4. R3 (+A.Jarryd) Lost P.Cash/J.Fitzgerald 6–3 6–4 4–6 6–1. R5 d. P.McNamee 10–8 6–4. **1987: July** – *World Group qf (Away) Sweden d. France 4–1.* R3 (+A.Jarryd) Lost to G.Forget/H.Leconte 6–4 6–2 3–6 15–13. **October** – *World Group sf (Away) Sweden d.Spain 3–2.* R2 d. J.Sanchez 6–4 6–2 6–4. R4 d. E.Sanchez 6–4 8–6 6–4. **1988: February** – *World Group 1r (Home) Sweden d. New Zealand 5–0.* R2 d. K.Evernden 12–10 6–2 9–7. R3 (+A.Jarryd) d. K.Evernden/D.Lewis 6–3 7–5 6–4. R5 d. B.Derlin 6–1 6–2. **April** – *World Group qf (Home) Sweden d. Czechoslovakia 3–2.* R1 d. T.Smid 6–3 6–4 6–3. R3 (+M.Wilander) d. M.Mecir/ T.Smid 8–6 6–4 8–6. R5 d. M.Mecir 4–6 6–1 4–6 6–4 9–7. **July** – *World Group sf (Home) Sweden d. France 4–1.* R2 d. H.Leconte 6–4 6–4 8–10 3–6 6–4. **December** – *World Group Final (Home) Germany d. Sweden 4–1.* R2 Lost to B.Becker 6–3 6–1 6–4. R3 (+A.Jarryd) Lost to B.Becker/E.Jelen 3–6 2–6 7–5 6–2. R4 d. C.Steeb 6–4 8–6. **1989: April** – *World Group qf (Away) Sweden d. Austria 3–2.* R1 d. A.Antonisch 6–3 6–2 6–4. R3 (+A.Jarryd) d. Antonisch/H.Skoff 6–3 6–1 6–3. R4 d. H.Skoff 6–3 6–2 6–1. **July** – *World Group sf (Home) Sweden d. Yugoslavia 4–1.* R3 (+A.Jarryd) Lost to G.Ivanisevic/G.Prpic 4–6 6–4 6–4 6–3. **December** – *World Group Final (Away) Germany d. Sweden 3–2* R2 Lost to B.Becker 6–2 6–2 6–4. R5 d. C.Steeb 6–2 6–4. **1990: September** – *World Group qf (Home) Sweden d. Finland 5–0.* R1 d. A.Rahunen 6–1 6–1 7–6. R3 (+P.Lundgren) d. V.Paloheimo/O.Rahnasto 6–2 6–1 6–2. R4 d. Paloheimo 3–6 6–4 6–0. **1991: February** – *World Group 1r (Away) Yugoslavia d. Sweden 4–1.* R2 Lost to G.Prpic(CRO) 6–4 6–3 6–2. R3 (+P.Lundgren) Lost to Ivanisevic/ Prpic(CRO) 6–4 6–4 6–4. R4 Lost to G.Ivanisevic 6–4 6–2. **1992: January** – *World Group 1r (Away) Sweden d. Canada 3–2.* R2 Lost to D.Nestor 4–6 6–3 1–6 6–3 6–4. R3 (+A.Jarryd) d. G.Connell/G.Michibata 3–6 6–3 6–4 6–4. R4 d. G.Connell 6–2 6–2 7–6. **March** – *World Group qf (Home) Sweden d. Australia 5–0.* R2 d. R.Fromberg 6–3 6–2 6–3. R3 (+A.Jarryd) d. J.Fitzgerald/T.Woodbridge 6–3 6–3 3–6 6–1. R4 d. W.Masur 6–4 7–6. **September** – *World Group sf (Away) U.S.A. d. Sweden 4–1.* R2 Lost o A.Agassi 5–7 6–3 7–6 6–3. R3 (+A.Jarryd) Lost to J.McEnroe/P.Sampras 6–1 6–7 4–6 6–3 6–3.

GRAND PRIX MASTERS/ATP TOUR CHAMPIONSHIP (from 1990)

1985: (16–man knock–out) 1r lost Kreik 6–2 4–6 6–2. **1986: sf** In rr lost Lendl 6–3 6–4, d. Noah 4–6 6–3 7–6, d. Gomez 6–2 6–3; sf lost Becker 6–4 6–4. **1987: sf** In rr d. Cash 6–4 4–6 6–1, d. Mecir 6–3 6–3, d. Wilander 6–2 7–6; sf lost Wilander 6–2 4–6 6–3. **1988: sf** In rr d.Becker 7–6 3–6 6–4, d. Wilander 6–2 6–2, lost Leconte 6–4 6–2; sf lost Lendl 6–3 7–6. **1989: won** In rr d. Agassi 6–4 6–2, d. Gilbert 6–1 6–3, lost Becker 6–1 6–4; sf d. Lendl 7–6 7–5; final d. Becker 4–6 7–6 6–3 6–1. **1990: r/u** In rr d. E.Sanchez 6–7 6–3 6–1, d. Agassi 7–6 4–6 7–6, d. Sampras 7–5 6–4; sf d. Lendl 6–4 6–2; final lost Agassi 5–7 7–6 7–5 6–2. **1992: Equal 3rd** In rr d. Korda 6–3 7–6, lost Sampras 6–3 3–6 7–5, lost Becker 6–4 6–0.

PETE SAMPRAS (USA)   Turned pro: 1971

Born: Washington, DC, 12 August 1971. **Lives:** Bradenton, Fla.
Father: Sam, son of Greek immigrants. **Mother:** Georgia. **Sister:**
Stella (older) won 1988 NCAA doubles title at UCLA (with Cooper).
Brother: Gus (older) who sometimes travels with him.
Agent: ProServ.
Coaches: Tim Gullikson. Coached first by Dr Pete Fischer and after they
split in 1989 Robert Lansdorf coached him on forehand, Larry Easley on
volley and Del Little on footwork. Went to Bollettieri Academy and
worked with Joe Brandi. They parted in Dec. 1990, to be reunited
briefly during 1991, and Sampras started working with Pat Etchenbury for strength.
Height: 6ft (1.82m). **Weight:** 170lb (77kg).

Rankings: 1988: 97; **1989:** 81; **1990:** 5; **1991:** 6; **1992:** 3. **Highest:** 2 (2 October 1992).

1992 Prize Money: $1,995,087. **Career Earnings:** $7,007,225. **Career Titles:** 12.

Style: Right-handed, ever since changing from 2HB to 1HB in 1987 on advice of his then
coach, Dr Pete Fischer. Sampras is one of the finest servers and volleyers on the tour and
has flat, orthodox groundstrokes, hit on the rise with awesome power. He is vulnerable to
shin splints that have affected his career at important moments.

CAREER HIGHLIGHTS (year:(*titles*))
1988: sf Schenectady and upset Mayotte *en route* to qf Detroit. **1989:** Reached qf Adelaide
and upset Wilander *en route* to last 16 US Open. In doubles with Courier won Italian Open,
and took 7th place at Masters. **1990: (3)** *Philadelphia, Manchester, US OPEN.* Upset
Mayotte in 70-game struggle 1r Australian Open on his was to last 16, unseeded, and in
Feb. won his 1st tour title at Philadelphia, which took him into top 20. He followed with
Manchester, but the crescendo of his year came in Sept., when he won his 1st GS title at
US Open and moved into the top 10. At 19 yrs 28 days he was the youngest champion
there (the previous youngest was Oliver Campbell, who won in 1890 aged 19 yrs 6 mths).
Also reached sf Milan, Canadian Open, Los Angeles and Stockholm, but withdrew from
Paris Open suffering from shin splints, which had been troubling him since US Open. He
was able to play ATP World Champ, but did not progress beyond rr. Won inaugural GS Cup
and 1st prize $2m. Voted Most Improved Player of The Year. **1991: (4)** *Los Angeles,
Indianapolis, Lyon, IBM/ATP World Champ.* Suffered a string on injuries to shin, foot and
hamstring, returning to action in Feb. He finished the year in tremendous style by winning
ATP World Champ in Frankfurt, the youngest since J. McEnroe in 1979 to win year-end
Champ, beating Courier in f and losing only to Becker in rr. r/u US Pro Indoor, Manchester,
Cincinnati and Paris Open; sf Orlando and Sydney Indoor. In GS he was disappointing at
French Open and Wimbledon, but reached qf US Open. After Frankfurt sacked Brandi
again and sought new coach on eve of D Cup f v France in Lyon where, in his 1st ever tie,
he was humiliated by an inspired Leconte on opening day and lost decisive 3rd rubber to
Forget. **1992 (5)** *Philadelphia, Kitzbuhel, Cincinnati, Indianapolis, Lyon.* Broke into top 3
after winning Philadelphia and on 5 Oct. took 2nd place ahead of Edberg. In GS his best
showing was r/u US Open, where he upset Courier but lost f to Edberg in 4s; upset Stich
to reach sf Wimbledon and fell qf French Open to Agassi. In July he won his 1st title on
clay at Kitzbuhel, followed with back-to-back titles on HC at Cincinnati and Indianapolis and
added Lyon indoors. Was also r/u Atlanta and reached sf Nice, Stockholm and ATP Champ,
where he won all his rr matches before losing to Courier.

PRINCIPAL 1992 RESULTS (detailed Grand Slam results below)
won Philadelphia (d. DiLucia 6–2 6–1, Pescosolido 7–6 4–6 6–4, Krickstein 3–6 7–6 7–6, B.
Gilbert 6–4 6–3, Mansdorf 5–7 6–3 6–2), **won** Kitzbuhel (d. Lopez 4–6 6–3 7–6, Carbonell
6–4 6–1, Markus 6–3 7–6, Filippini 6–7 6–3 6–0, Mancini 6–3 7–5 6–3, **won** Cincinnati (d.
Montana 7–6 3–6 6–3, Woodforde 2–6 7–6 6–3, Korda 6–3 6–3, Edberg 6–2 6–3, Le·dl 6–3
3–6 6–3), **won** Indianapolis (d. Sansoni 6–0 6–1, Witsken 6–4 7–5, Enqvist 6–0 7–6, Becker

6–7 6–2 7–6, Courier 6–4 6–4), **won** Lyon (d. Tarango 7–6 6–3, Rosset 6–3 3–6 6–3, Zoecke 6–4 6–3, Washington 6–0 6–2, Pioline 6–4 6–2), **r/u** US OPEN, **r/u** Atlanta (d. Filippini 7–6 7–5, Mattar 7–6 6–2, Connors 7–6 6–2, Witsken 6–4 6–2, lost Agassi 7–5 6–4), **sf** Nice (d. Jaite 2–6 7–5 6–3, Gomez 7–6 7–5, Leconte 6–4 1–6 6–3, lost Markus 6–1 2–6 7–6), **sf** Stockholm (d. Woodbridge 6–2 7–6, Muster 6–2 6–4, Korda 7–6 5–7 6–3, lost Forget 7–6 7–6), **sf** ATP Champ (d. Edberg 6–3 3–6 7–5, Korda 3–6 6–3 6–3, Becker 7–6 7–6).

CAREER GRAND SLAM RECORD
AUSTRALIAN OPEN – Played 2
1989: 1r lost Saceanu 6–4 6–4 7–6. **1990: 4r** d. Mayotte[seed 6] 7–6 6–7 4–6 7–5 12–10, Arrese 0–6 6–2 3–6 6–1 6–3, Woodbridge 7–5 6–4 6–2, lost Noah 6–3 6–4 3–6 6–2.

FRENCH OPEN – Played 3, qf 1
1989: 2r d. Lozano 6–3 6–2 6–4, lost Chang (seed15) 6–1 6–1 6–1. **1991: 2r** [seed 6] d. Muster 4–6 4–6 6–4 6–1 6–4, lost Champion 6–3 6–1 6–1. **1992: qf** [seed 3] d. Rosset 7–6 4–6 6–4 3–6 6–3, Prades 7–6 6–4 7–6, R.Gilbert 6–3 6–2 6–3, Steeb 6–4 6–3 6–2, lost Agassi [seed 11] 7–6 6–2 6–1.

WIMBLEDON – Played 4, sf 1
1989: 1r lost Woodbridge 7–5 7–6 5–7 6–3. **1990: 1r** lost Van Rensburg 7–6 7–5 7–6. **1991: 2r** [seed 8] d. Marcellino 6–1 6–2 6–2, lost Rostagno 6–4 3–6 7–6 6–4. **1992: sf** [seed 5] d. Cherkasov 6–1 6–3 6–3, Woodbridge 7–6 7–6 6–7 6–4, S.Davis 6–1 6–0 6–2, Boetsch 6–3 7–5 7–6, Stich [seed 3] 6–3 6–2 6–4, lost Ivanisevic [seed 8] 6–7 7–6 6–4 6–2.

US OPEN – Played 5, won 1, r/u 1, qf 1
1988: 1r lost Yzaga 6–7 6–7 6–4 7–5 6–2. **1989: 4r** d. Moreno 6–3 5–7 6–4 6–1, Wilander seed 5] 5–7 6–3 1–6 6–4, Yzaga 4–6 6–4 6–3 6–2, lost Berger [seed11] 7–5 6–2 6–1. **1990: won** [seed 12] d. Goldie 6–1 7–5 6–1. d.Lundgren 6–1 7–5 6–1. d.Lundgren 6–1 7–5 6–1, Hlasek 6–3 6–4 6–1, Muster [seed 6] 6–7 7–6 6–4 6–3, Lendl 6–4 7–6 3–6 4–6 6–2, J.McEnroe 6–2 6–4 3–6 6–3, Agassi 6–4 6–3 6–2. **1991: qf** [seed 6] d. Van Rensburg 6–0 6–3 6–2, Ferreira 6–1 6–2 2–2 ret, Simian 7–6 6–4 6–3, Wheaton [seed 11] 3–6 6–2 6–2 6–4, lost Courier [seed 4] 6–2 7–6 7–6. **1992: r/u** [seed 3] d. Di Lucia 6–3 7–5 6–2, Damm 7–5 6–1 6–2, Martin 7–6 2–6 4–6 7–5 6–4, Forget [seed 13] 6–3 1–6 1–6 6–4 6–3, Volkov 6–4 6–1 6–0, Courier [seed 1] 6–1 3–6 6–2 6–2, lost Edberg [seed 2] 3–6 6–4 7–6 6–2.

OLYMPIC GAMES RECORD
1992: (Barcelona) last 16 [seed 3] d. Masur 6–1 7–6 6–4, Yzaga 6–3 6–0 3–6 6–1, lost Cherkasov [seed 13] 6–7 1–6 7–5 6–0 6–3.

CAREER DAVIS CUP RECORD
1991: November – *World Group Final (Away) France d. USA 3–1* R2 Lost to H.Leconte 6–4 7–5 6–4. R4 Lost to G.Forget 7–6 3–6 6–3 6–4. **1992: January** – *World Group 1R (Home) USA d. Argentina 5–0.* R1 d. M.Jaite 3–6 6–4 6–2 6–4. R4 d. A.Mancini 6–4 6–1. **March** – *World Group qf (Home) USA d. Czechoslovakia 3–2.* R1 d. K. Novacek 6–3 6–4 6–2. R4 Lost to P.Korda 6–4 6–3 2–6 6–3. *September – World Group sf (Home) USA d. Sweden 4–1.* R3 (+ J.McEnroe) d. Edberg/Jarryd 6–1 6–7 4–6 6–3 6–3. *December – World Group Final (Home) USA d. Switzerland 3–1.* R3 (+J.McEnroe) d. J.Hlasek/M.Rosset 6–7 6–7 7–5 6–1 6–2.

GRAND PRIX MASTERS/ATP TOUR CHAMPIONSHIP (from 1990)
1990: Equal 3rd In rr lost Edberg 7–5 6–4, lost Agassi 6–4 6–2, d. E.Sanchez 6–2 6–4. **1991: won** In rr d. Stich 6–2 7–6, d. Agassi 6–3 1–6 6–3, lost Becker 6–4 6–7 6–1; sf d. Lendl 6–2 6–3; f d. Courier 3–6 7–6 6–3 6–4. **1992: sf** In rr d. Becker 7–6 7–6, d. Edberg 6–3 3–6 7–5, d. Korda 3–6 6–3 6–3; sf lost Courier 7–6 7–6.

GORAN IVANISEVIC (CRO)   Turned pro: 1988

Born: Split, 13 September 1971. **Lives:** Split and Monte Carlo, Monaco. **Father:** Srdjan, a teacher **Mother:** Gorana.
Agent: Ion Tiriac.
Coach: Bob Brett since Feb. 1991; formerly by Balazs Taroczy from Sept. 1989.
Height: 6ft 4in (1.93m). **Weight:** 161lb (73kg).
Rankings: 1987: 954; **1988:** 371; **1989:** 40; **1990:** 9; **1991:** 16; **1992:** 4. **Highest:** 4 (6 July 1992).

1992 Prize Money: $1,858,241. **Career Earnings:** $3,658,258. **Career Titles:** 6.

Style: A tall left-hander with a lethal flat or sliced serve, Goran also has fine groundstrokes (single-handed on the forehand, double-handed on the backhand) and improving volleys, that make him one of the best all-rounders in the men's game.

CAREER HIGHLIGHTS(year: *(titles)*)
1987: Won US Open Jun doubles with Nargiso. **1988:** Joined Yugoslav D Cup squad. R/u French Open Jun doubles with Caratti and was No. 3 in ITF Jun singles rankings. **1989:** qf Australian Open after qualifying and last 16 French Open, unseeded. Upset Leconte *en route* to 1st GP sf at Nice, following with 2nd at Palermo and then 1st f at Florence. **1990: (1)** *Stuttgart Outdoor.* Helped his country to win World Team Cup in May, then upset Becker 1r French Open *en route* to qf, following with sf appearance at Wimbledon, both unseeded. Won his 1st career title at Stuttgart; r/u Umag, Long Island, Bordeaux and Basel; 2r GS Cup and broke into the top 10. R/u French Open doubles with Korda. **1991: (1)** *Manchester.* After a good year in 1990, his game fell apart at the beginning of 1991, and he withdrew from LIPC with compact fracture of left index finger. but then he played through the qualifying to gain a place at Manchester, where he won both singles and doubles, reached f New Haven, plus sf Gstaad, Sydney Indoor and Tokyo Seiko and after a last 16 showing at US Open, he finished the year still in the top 20. In doubles with Camporese he won 3 titles from 4 f. Did not play for Yugoslavia in D Cup and, with Prpic, announced in Tokyo in October that henceforth he wanted to be known as a Croatian. **1992: (4)** *Adelaide, Stuttgart, Sydney Indoor, Stockholm.* His most impressive performance in GS came at Wimbledon, where he upset Edberg on his way to a thrilling f v Agassi, which he lost in 5s. At Olympics, where he won 4 consec 5s matches, he won a bronze medal in both singles and doubles (with Prpic). He began the year by winning both singles and doubles titles at Adelaide, in his 1st tourn playing as a Croatian, and also won Stuttgart (d. Courier and Edberg), Sydney Indoor (d. Edberg) and Stockholm (d. Becker and Edberg), as well as r/u Milan and sf Paris Open. Finished the year by qualifying 1st time for ATP World Champ, where he continued his winning ways against Edberg, beating the Swede for 5th time in 5 meetings during the year and winning all his rr matches, before losing a close sf to Becker. Withdrew from Monte Carlo with arythmia heartbeat and also missed Munich.

PRINCIPAL 1992 RESULTS (detailed Grand Slam results below)
SINGLES: won Adelaide (d. Kulti 6–4 6–3, Pescosolido 6–4 6–3, Rosset 6–4 7–6, Shelton 6–4 6–2, Bergstrom 1–6 7–6 6–4), **won** Stuttgart (d. Zivojinovic 6–3 7–6, Delaitre 6–3 7–6, Courier 3–6 7–6 7–6, Volkov 3–6 6–3 6–4, Edberg 6–7 6–3 6–4 6–4), **won** Sydney Indoor (d. Pozzi 6–2 6–4, Van Rensburg 6–4 6–4, Haarhuis 7–6 6–3, Krajicek 6–3 6–0, Edberg 6–4 6–2 6–4), **won** Stockholm (d. Wheaton 6–4 6–4, Gustafsson 7–6 6–3, Becker 7–5 6–4, Edberg 6–4 7–6, Forget 7–6 4–6 7–6 6–2), **r/u** WIMBLEDON, **r/u** Milan (d. Larsson 7–5 5–7 6–4, Haarhuis 6–4 6–3, P. McEnroe 6–3 6–4, Pescosolido 6–2 6–2, lost Camporese 3–6 6–3 6–4), **sf** OLYMPICS (see below), **sf** ATP World Champ (d. Courier 6–3 6–3, Chang 7–6 6–2, Krajicek 6–4 6–3 in rr, lost Becker 4–6 6–4 7–6), **sf** Paris Open (d. Pioline 6–4 7–5, Krajicek 6–4 7–6, Wheaton 6–4 6–3, lost Becker 6–1 6–2), **sf** ATP World Champ (d. Courier 6–3 6–3, Chang 7–6 6–2, Krajicek 6–4 6–3 in rr, lost Becker 4–6 6–4 7–6). **DOUBLES: won** Adelaide (with Rosset) d Kratzmann/Stoltenberg 7–6 7–6, **r/u** Queen's (with Nargiso) lost

Fitzgerald/Jarryd 6–4 7–6, **sf** Olympic Games –bronze medal (with Prpic) lost W.Ferreira/Norval 7–6 3–6 6–3 2–6 6–2.

CAREER GRAND SLAM RECORD
AUSTRALIAN OPEN – Played 4, qf 1
1989: qf d.Larsson 6–3 6–4 2–6 7–6, Fitzgerald [seed 15] 6–3 4–6 6–3 6–4, Nijssen 6–4 6–4 6–0, Lavalle 3–6 3–6 6–3 6–4 6–1, lost Mecir [seed 9] 7–5 6–0 6–3. **1990: 1r** lost Wheaton 7–5 7–5 6–0. **1991: 3r** [seed 5] d. Bruguera 6–4 0–6 6–1 6–4, Krishnan 6–4 3–6 4–6 6–1 6–2, lost Prpic 6–3 6–4 6–3. **1992: 2r** [seed 10] d. Stoltenberg 7–6 6–3 6–4, lost Krickstein 6–2 7–5 6–1.

FRENCH OPEN – Played 4, qf 2
1989: 4r d. Reneberg 0–6 6–2 6–1 6–3,.Stich 6–2 6–3 6–1, Woodforde 6–3 6–4 6–0, lost Edberg 7–5 6–3 6–3. **1990: qf** d. Becker [seed 2] 5–7 6–4 7–5 6–2, Jarryd 6–3 6–0 6–2, d.Kuhnen 7–6 6–1 7–5, Kroon 6–2 6–4 7–5, lost Muster []seed 7) 6–2 4–6 6–4 6–3. **1991: 2r** [seed 8] d. Fontaing 6–4 1–6 6–3 6–1, lost Haarhuis 6–1 6–4 6–1. **1992: qf** [seed 8] d. Youl 6–7 6–3 6–2 6–1, Limberger 6–2 6–2 6–4, Larsson 6–7 6–3 6–1 3–6 9–7, Costa [seed 9] 6–3 4–6 6–1 6–1, lost Courier [seed 1] 6–2 6–1 2–6 7–5.

WIMBLEDON Played 5, r/u 1, sf 1, qf 1
1988: 1r lost Mansdorf [seed15] 6–3 6–2 1–6 6–1. **1989: 2r** d.Champion 6–3 6–4 3–6 6–3, lost Flach 6–4 6–3 4–6 6–3. **1990: sf** d.Leach 6–4 6–0 6–4, Delaitre 6–2 6–0 4–6 6–7 6–3, Rostagno 6–2 6–2. 6–4, Koevermans 4–6 6–3 6–4 7–6, Curren 4–6 6–4 6–4 6–7 6–3, lost Becker [seed 3] 4–6 7–6 6–0 7–6. **1991: 2r** [seed 10] d. Castle 7–6 7–6 6–2, lost Brown 4–6 6–3 7–6 6–3. **1992: r/u** [seed 8] d. Koslowski 6–2 6–2 6–3, Woodforde 6–4 6–4 6–7 6–3, Rosset 7–6 6–4 6–4, Lendl [seed 10] 6–7 6–1 6–4 1–0 ret., Edberg [seed 2] 6–7 7–5 6–1 3–6 6–3, Sampras [seed 5] 6–7 7–6 6–4 6–2, lost Agassi [seed 12] 6–7 6–4 6–4 1–6 6–4.

US OPEN – Played 4
1989: 2r d.Doumbia 6–2 1–6 6–2 6–0, lost Grabb 6–1 6–4 6–2. **1990: 3r** [seed 15] d. Camporese 1–6 6–4 6–1 7–6, d.Fleurian 6–4 6–2 3–6 6–1, lost Cahill 4–6 4–6 6–2 7–6 6–0. **1991: 4r** [seed 12] d. Holm 6–7 6–3 6–3 7–6, Prpic 6–1 6–3 6–4, Mattar 6–3 6–2 6–2, lost Lendl [seed 5] 7–5 6–7 6–4 6–2. **1992: 3r** [seed 5] d. Rosset 6–4 6–4 6–4, Lavalle 7–5 7–6 6–2, lost Volkov 6–4 6–0 6–3.

OLYMPIC GAMES
1992:(Barcelona) sf (Bronze medal) [seed 4] d. Mota 6–2 6–2 6–7 4–6 6–3, Haarhuis 6–7 6–2 1–6 6–3 6–2, Hlasek [seed 15] 3–6 6–0 4–6 7–6 6–7, Santoro 6–7 6–7 6–4 6–4 8–6, lost Rosset 6–3 7–5 6–2.

CAREER DAVIS CUP RECORD
1988: July – *World Group sf (Away) Germany d. Yugoslavia 5–0.* R3 (+S.Zivojinovic) Lost to B.Becker/E.Jelen 5–7 4–6 6–1 11–9 9–7. **1989: February –** *World Group 1R (Home) Yugoslavia d. Denmark 4–1.* R3 (+S.Zivojinovic) d. M.Christensen/M.Mortensen 6–3 6–2 7–6. R4 Lost to M.Fetterlein 0–6 6–3 11–9. **April –** *World Group qf (Home) Yugoslavia d. Spain 4–1.* R1 d. S.Casal 6–3 2–6 7–5 6–3. R3 (+S.Zivojinovic) d. S.Casal/ E.Sanchez 4–6 6–4 4–6 7–6 13–11. R5 d. J.Sanchez 7–5 6–1. **July –** *World Group sf (Away) Sweden d. Yugoslavia 4–1.* R1 Lost to J.Svensson 6–4 7–6 3–6 6–4. R3 (+G.Prpic) d. S.Edberg/A.Jarryd 4–6 6–4 6–4 6–3. R5 Lost to M.Wilander 6–3 6–3. **1990: February –** *World Group 1r (Away) New Zealand d. Yugoslavia 3–2.* R3 (+S.Zivojinovic) d. K.Evernden/S.Guy 7–5 6–3 6–7 7–5. **September –** *Qualifying Round (Home) Yugoslavia d. Switzerland 3–2.* R1 d. M.Rosset 6–4 4–6 6–7 6–3 6–2. R3 d. J.Hlasek/M.Rosset 3–6 6–3 6–4 6–2. R4 d. C.Mezzadri 6–1 6–4 6–2. **1991: February –** *World Group 1r (Home) Yugoslavia d. Sweden 4–1.* R1 d. J.Svensson 6–2 4–6 6–3 6–4. R3 (+G.Prpic) d. S.Edberg/P.Lundgren 6–4 6–4 6–4. R4 d. S.Edberg 6–4 6–2. **March –** *World Group qf (Away) Yugoslavia d. Czechoslovakia 4–1.* R1 d. P.Korda 6–1 7–6 4–6 6–1. R3 (+S.Zivojinovic) d. P.Korda/M.Srejber 7–6 6–4 6–4. R4 d. K.Novacek 6–3 3–6 7–6 3–6 6–4.

GRAND PRIX MASTERS/ATP TOUR CHAMPIONSHIP (from 1990)
1992 sf In rr d. Chang 7–6 6–2, d. Courier 6–3 6–3, d. Krajicek 6–4 6–3; sf lost Becker 6–4 6–4 7–6.

BORIS BECKER (GER)   **Turned pro:** 1984

Born: Leimen, 22 November 1967. **Lives:** Leimen and Monte Carlo, Monaco.
Father: Karl-Heinz is an architect who built tennis centre near the Becker home in Leimen. **Mother:** Elvira. **Sister:** Sabine.
Agent: Ion Tiriac.
Coaches: Austrian D Cup captain Guenther Bresnik; formerly Boris Breskvar, Gunther Bosch, Bob Brett, Nikki Pilic and Tomas Smid.
Height: 6ft 3in (1.92m). **Weight:** 187lb (85kg).

Rankings: 1983: 563; **1984:** 65; **1985:** 6; **1986:** 2; **1987:** 4; **1988:** 4; **1989:** 2; **1990:** 2; **1991:** 3; **1992:** 5. **Highest:** 1 (28 January 1991).

1992 Prize Money: $2,293,687. **Career Earnings:** $11,670,442. **Career Titles:** 36.

Style: A powerful right-hander with one of the best serves in the game who uses his great physical strength and natural athletic ability to force the pace. His backhand is outstanding and his ability to dive for his volleys make him a difficult man to pass.

CAREER HIGHLIGHTS (year:(*titles*))
Played both tennis and soccer as a boy, giving up soccer for tennis at the age of 12. **1982:** Won 1st of 3 consec German Nat Jun Champs. **1983:** R/u Orange Bowl 16s. **1984:** R/u US Open Jun and sf French Jun, both to Kratzmann and qf Australian Open in 1st big men's showing. **1985: (3)** *Queen's, WIMBLEDON, Cincinnati.* At Wimbledon, aged 17 yrs 7 mths, became youngest men's titlist, the 1st German and the 1st unseeded player to capture the world's most prestigious event. Closed year with D Cup wins over Edberg and Wilander in f as FRG lost 3–2 to SWE. Won inaugural Young Masters and was voted ATP Most Improved Player. **1986: (6)** *Chicago, WIMBLEDON, Toronto, Sydney Indoor, Tokyo Indoor, Paris Indoor.* Won Wimbledon again in even more convincing fashion, dismissing Lendl in f without loss of a set and still younger any other champ. Closed year with streak of 3 straight tourns and 21 matches in a row before losing Masters f to Lendl. Won Young Masters in Jan. and Dec. **1987: (3)** *Indian Wells, Milan, Queen's.* Split with coach Gunther Bosch Jan.; trained by Frank Dick. At end of year Bob Brett became coach. Missed LIPC suffering from a form of typhus which seemed to weaken him and restrict his performance for several weeks, and he was further restricted by tendonitis of left knee for last 5 months of year. Won only 3 titles all year and going for his 3rd consec Wimbledon singles title fell 2r to Doohan. After US Open took time off in Germany with his family, returning refreshed in Oct. and qualified for Masters where he extended Lendl to 3s, but lost his Young masters title. **1988: (7)** *Indian Wells, WCT Dallas, Queen's, Indianapolis, Tokyo Indoor, Stockholm, Masters.* He was again plagued by injury problems, withdrawing from Toronto and the Olympics and playing Masters only 10 days after his foot had been removed from plaster following injury in Stockholm sf. He finished the year by taking his 1st Masters title in a thrilling f v Lendl, as well as leading FRG to victory over SWE in D Cup f in Gothenburg. At Wimbledon he was r/u to Edberg and reached last 16 in French Open. **1989: (5)** *Milan, Philadelphia, WIMBLEDON, US OPEN, Paris Indoor.* The high spot of his year was a convincing third title at Wimbledon, where he beat Lendl in a stirring sf and Edberg in f, followed by his 1st triumph at US Open, where he d. Lendl in f, and r/u spot at Masters to Edberg. He won in Milan and on clay reached f Monte Carlo and sf French Open. He also won 3 other titles and led FRG to victory in World Team Cup, and in D Cup where he won 2 singles and doubles (with Jelen) as FRG d. SWE 3-2 in Stuttgart. Voted ATP Player of the Year. **1990: (5)** *Brussels, Stuttgart Indoor, Indianapolis, Sydney Indoor, Stockholm.* R/u Wimbledon to Edberg, sf US Open, qf Australian Open, but his 1r loss to Ivanisevic at French Open was his 1st at that stage in GS. Strongly challenged Edberg for the No. 1 spot at end of year, especially after a stunning performance at Stockholm, where he d. the Swede in f, a result that took his indoor match record since 1988 to 77-5. However, in Paris Open he had to withdraw v the same player with a pulled left thigh, which was still

undergoing treatment when he began play on 2nd day of ATP World Champ, where he fell to Agassi in sf. Won 5 titles and reached 4 more finals. **1991: (2)** *AUSTRALIAN OPEN, Stockholm.* Reached No. 1 on computer 1st time on 28 Jan., after winning his 1st Australian Open; his 5 hr 22 min match in 3r with Camporese was the longest ever played there and lasted only 1 minute less than the marathon at Wimbledon in 1969 between Gonzales and Pasarell. He was overtaken again by Edberg on 18 Feb., after retiring v Cherkasov at Brussels with a right thigh strain, but returned to the top after his appearance in f Wimbledon, where he lost in ss to countryman Stich. His disappointing 3r loss to Haarhuis at US Open saw him slip again to No. 2 and by year's end he had fallen to 3 behind Courier, having narrowly failed to qualify for sf ATP World Champ at Frankfurt. However, he played his best ever CC season, although he again failed to win his 1st title on that surface, losing f Monte Carlo to Bruguera, who had also beaten him at Barcelona. Withdrew from Italian Open with back trouble, but played French Open, where he reached sf for 3rd time. He outlasted Edberg in 5s Stockholm in Oct. for only his 2nd title of the year; also reached f Indianapolis and sf Brussels and Cincinnati. **1992: (5)** *Brussels, Rotterdam, Basle, Paris Indoor, ATP World Champ.* In Jan. dropped out of top 3 1st time since April 1989 and in losing 3r Australian Open to J. McEnroe, he fell from top 5 for 1st time since 1988, eventually slipping as low as 9 in Nov. But working since Sept. with Guenther Bresnik, he found his best form again and finished the year in tremendous style by taking ATP World Champ, surviving a close sf v Ivanisevic and sweeping Courier aside in f. Missed French Open to avoid aggravating a thigh strain and his best showing in a disappointing year in GS was qf Wimbledon (lost to Agassi). His 5 titles during the year were all indoors. Also reached sf Hamburg and Indianapolis. In doubles he won an Olympic gold medal and won Monte Carlo with Stich, plus Brussels with J. McEnroe.

PRINCIPAL 1992 RESULTS (detailed Grand Slam results below)
SINGLES: won Brussels (d. Svensson 6–4 6–0, P. McEnroe 7–6 6–1, Steeb 6–3 7–6, Edberg 4–6 6–4 6–2, Courier 6–7 2–6 7–6 7–6 7–5), **won** Rotterdam (d. Schapers 6–3 6–1, Jarryd 6–2 6–4, P. McEnroe 6–3 7–5, J. McEnroe 6–2 7–6, Volkov 7–6 4–6 6–2), **won** Basle (d. Larsson 7–5 7–6, Kulti 6–4 7–5, Mansdorf 7–6 6–7 6–3, Rosset 6–2 6–4, Korda 3–6 6–3 6–2 6–4), **won** Paris Open (d. J. McEnroe 6–4 6–4, B. Gilbert 6–2 6–2, Courier 7–6 6–3, Ivanisevic 6–1 6–2, Forget 7–6 6–3 3–6 6–3), **won** ATP Champ (d. Edberg 6–4 6–0, Korda 6–4 6–2, lost Sampras 7–6 7–6 in rr, d. Ivanisevic 4–6 6–4 7–6, Courier 7–6 7–6), **sf** Hamburg (d. Champion 6–3 7–6, Furlan 4–6 6–4 6–3, Novacek 6–1 7–6, lost Stich 6–1 6–1), **sf** Indianapolis (d. Zoecke 6–4 6–4, Wheaton 7–6 6–3, Connors 6–4 6–3, lost Sampras 6–7 6–2 7–6). **DOUBLES:** (with Stich unless stated), **won** Olympic gold medal d. W. Ferreira/Norval 7–6 4–6 7–6 6–3, **won** Brussels [+J. McEnroe] d. Forget/Hlasek 6–3 6–2, **won** Monte Carlo d. Korda/Novacek 6–4 6–4.

CAREER GRAND SLAM RECORD
AUSTRALIAN OPEN – Played 7, won 1, qf 2
1984: qf d. .Meyer 6–3 6–1 6–3. d.Mayotte[seed 7] 6–4 7–6 2–6 6–4. d.Pfister 7–5 6–2 6–2, Forget 7–5 6–4 6–3, lost Testerman[seed 14] 6–4 6–3 6–4. **1985: 2r** [seed 4] lost Schapers 3–6 6–4 7–6 4–6 6–3. **1987: 4r** [seed 2] bye. d.Dyke 6–7 6–1 6–4 6–7 6–2, Zivojinovic 6–3 6–3 3–6 6–3, lost Masur 4–6 7–6 6–4 6–7 6–2. **1989: 4r** [seed 3], d.Guy 6–2 3–6 6–2 6–1, Evernden 7–5 6–1 6–3, Pridham 6–0 6–1 6–2, lost Svensson 7–6 6–4 6–3. **1990: qf** [seed 2] d, Haarhuis 6–1 6–2 6–1, S.Davis 6–3 7–6 4–6 6–2 Delaitre 6–3 6–1 6–4, Mecir[seed 16] 4–6 6–7 6–4 6–1 6–1, lost Wilander[seed 8] 6–4 6–4 6–2. **1991: won** [seed 2] d Bates 6–4 6–2 6–3, Vajda 6–4 6–1 6–3, Camporese 7–6 7–6 0–6 4–6 14– 12, Ferreira 6–4 7–6 6–4, Forget [seed 10] 6–2 7 6 6 3, P. McEnroe 7–6 6–3 4–6 4–6 6–2, Lendl [seed 3] 1–6 6–4 6–4 6–4. **1992: 3r** [seed 3] d. Gunnarsson 6–1 6–4 6–2, Pozzi 7–5 7–5 6–2, lost J.McEnroe 6–4 6–3 7–5.

FRENCH OPEN – Played 7, sf 3, qf 2
1985: 2r d.Gerulaitis 6–3 6–7 6–1 6–1, lost Wilander[seed 4] 6–3 6–2 6–1. **1986: qf** [seed 3] d. Potier 6–0 6–3 6–0, Oresar 6–2 6–0 6–7 6–3, d. Teltscher 6–3 6–3 5–7 6–4, E.Sanchez 6–0 4–6 4–6 6–4 6–2, lost Pernfors 2–6 6–4 6–2 6–0. **1987 sf** [seed 2] d. Perez 6–0 6–1 7–5,

Buckley 6–1 4–6 6–3 6–2, d. Sundstrom 6–1 3–6 6–3 6–1, Arias 5–7 6–3 6–2 6–0, Connors[seed 8] 6–3 6–3 7–5, lost Wilander[seed 4] 6–4 6–1 6–2. **1988: qf** [seed 5] d. Mezzadri 6–4 6–2 7–5 d. Korda 6–4 6–3 6–4, Muster 6–1 4–6 7–5 6–3, lost Leconte[seed 11] 6–7 6–3 6–1 5–7 6–4. **1989: sf** [seed 2] d. Pugh 6–4 6–2 6–3, Winogradsky 7–6 7–5 6–3, Bates 7–5 6–1 6–2, Perez-Roldan[seed16] 3–6 6–4 6–2 4–6 7–5, Berger 6–3 6–4 6–1, lost Edberg [seed 3] 6–3 6–4 5–7 3–6 6–2. **1990: 1r** lost Ivanisevic 5–7 6–4 7–5 6–2. **1991: sf** [seed 2] d Arrese 6–2 7–5 6–2, Woodbridge 5–7 1–6 6–4 6–4 6–4, Masur 6–3 6–3 6–2, Clavet 7–6 6–4 6–3, Chang [seed 10] 6–4 6–4 6–2, lost Agassi [seed 4] 7–5 6–3 3–6 6–1. **1992:** Did not play.

WIMBLEDON – Played 9, won 3, r/u 3, qf 1

1984: 3r d.Willenborg 6–0 6–0 6–4. d.Odizor 6–3 6–4 4–2 ret., lost Scanlon 6–2 2–6 7–6 1–2 ret. **1985: won** d.Pfister 4–6 6–3 6–2 6–4. d.Anger 6–0 6–1 6–3, Nystrom 3–6 7–6 6–1 4–6 9–7, Mayotte 6–3 4–6 6–7 7–6 6–2, Leconte 7–6 3–6 6–3 6–4, Jarryd[seed 5] 2–6 7–6 6–3 6–3, Curren[seed 8] 6–3 6–7 7–6 6–4. **1986: won** [seed 4] d. Bengoechea 6–4 6–2 6–1, Tom Gullikson 6–4 6–3 6–2, McNamee 6–4 6–4 4–6 6–4, Pernfors [seed 13] 6–3 7–6 6–2, Mecir 6–4 6–2 7–6, Leconte [seed 7] 6–2 6–4 6–7 6–3, Lendl[seed 1] 6–4 6–3 7–5. **1987: 2r** [seed 1] 2r d. Novacek 6–4 6–2 6–4, I. Doohan 7–6 4–6 6–2 6–4. **1988: r/u** [seed 6] d. Frawley 6–3 6–1 6–2, Novacek 6–3 6–4 6–4, Giammalva 7–6 6–4 6–4, Annacone 6–3 6–4 6–4, Cash [seed 4] 6–4 6–3 6–4, Lendl [seed 1] 6–4 6–3 6–7 6–4 lost Edberg [seed 3] 4–6 7–6 6–4 6–2. **1989: won** [seed 3] d Shelton 6–1 6–4 7–6, Matuszewski 6–3 7–5 6–4, Gunnarsson 7–5 7–6 6–3, Krickstein [seed 13] 6–4 6–4 7–5, Chamberlin 6–1 6–2 6–0, Lendl [seed 1] 7–6 6–7 2–6 6–4 6–3, Edberg[seed 2] 6–0 7–6 6–4). **1990: r/u** [seed 2] d. Herrera 7–6 7–6 7–5, Masur 6–7 6–2 6–3 6–2, Goldie 6–3 6–4 4–6 7–5, Cash 7–6 6–1 6–4, Gilbert [seed 7] 6–4 6–4 6–1, Ivanisevic 4–6 7–6 6–0 7–6, lost Edberg [seed 3] 6–2 6–2 3–6 3–6 6–4. **1991: r/u** [seed 2] d. Steeb 6–4 6–2 6–4, Lundgren 7–6 7–5 7–5, Olhovskiy 6–1 6–4 3–6 6– 3, Bergstrom 6–4 6–7 6–1 7–6, Forget [seed 7] 6–7 7–6 6–2 7–6, Wheaton 6–4 7–6 7–5, lost Stich 6–4 7–6 6–4. **1992: qf** [seed 4] d. Camporese 7–5 6–3 7–5, Damm 4–6 6–4 6–4 3–6 6–3, Shelton 6–4 3–6 7–6 7–6, Ferreira [seed 14] 3–6 6–3 6–4 6–7 6–1, lost Agassi [seed 12] 4–6 6–2 6–2 4–6 6–3.

US OPEN – Played 8, won 1, sf 2

1985: 4r [seed 8] d. Doohan 6–4 6–1 6–2, Van Boeckel 6–3 6–0 6–2, Evernden 7–6 6–3 7–6, lost Nystrom [seed 10] 6–3 6–4 4–6 6–4. **1986: sf** [seed 3] d. Michibata 6–2 5–7 6–4 6–2, Motta 6–3 6–0 6–2, Casal 7–5 6–4 6–2, Donnelly 6–4 6–3 6–7 6–4, Srejber 6–3 6–2 6–1, lost Mecir [seed 16] 4–6 6–3 6–4 3–6 6–3. **1987: 4r** [seed 4] d. Wilkison 4–6 4–6 7–5 6–4 6–2, Canter 6–4 6–2 7–6, Castle 6–4 5–7 6–2 7–5, lost Gilbert [seed.13] 2–6 6–7 7–6 7–5 6–1. **1988: 2r** [seed 5] d. Nelson 6–2 6–0 7–6, lost Cahill 3 6–3 6–2, lost Cahill 3 6–3 6–2. **1989: Won** [seed 2] d. Pate 6–1 6–3 6–1, Rostagno 1–6 6–7 6–3 7–6 6–3, Mecir 6–4 3–6 6–4 6–3, Pernfors 5–7 6–3 6–2 6–1, Noah 6–3 6–3 6–2, Krickstein [seed 14] 6–4 6–3 6–4, Lendl [seed 1] 7–6 1–6 6–3 7–6. **1990: sf** [seed 2] d. Aguilera 7–5 6–3 6–2, Noah 6–4 6–2 –7–6, Carbonell 6–4 6–2 6–2, Cahill 2–6 6–2 6–3 3–6 6–4, Krickstein [seed 9] 3–6 6–3 6–3 6–3, lost Agassi [seed 4] 6–7 6–3 6–2 6–3. **1991: 3r** [seed 1] d. Jaite 7–6 6–4 6–4, Volkov 6–0 7–6 6–1, lost Haarhuis 6–3 6–4 6–2. **1992: 4r** [seed 7] d. Curren 6–2 5–7 6–3 6–4, Weiss 4–6 6–2 6–1 1–0 ret., Steeb 6–1 4–6 7–6 6–3, lost Lendl [seed 9] 6–7 6–2 6–7 6–3 6–4.

OLYMPIC GAMES

1992: (Barcelona) last 16 [seed 5] (d. Ruud.3–6 7–6 5–7 7–6 6–3, El Ayaouni 6–4 5–7 6–4 6–0, lost Santoro 6–1 3–6 6–1 6–3).

CAREER DAVIS CUP RECORD

1985: March – *World Group 1r (Home) Germany d. Spain 3–2* R2 d.J.Aguilera 6–3 6–4 6–4. R3 (+A.Maurer) d.S.Casal/E.Sanchez 4–6 6–3 1–6 6–3 6–4 **August** – *World Group qf (Home) Germany d. USA 3–2* R1 d.E.Teltscher 6–2 6–2 6–3. R3 (+A.Maurer) Lost to K.Flach/R.Seguso 6–2 6–8 6–1 4–6 7–5. R5 d.A.Krickstein 6–2 6–2 6–1. **October** – *World Group sf (Home) Germany d. Czechoslovakia 5–0* R1 d.M.Mecir 6–3 7–5 6–4. R3 (+A.Maurer) d.I.Lendl/T.Smid.6–1 7–5 6–4. R4 d.L.Pimek 6–1 6–4. **December** – *World Group Final (Home) Sweden d. Germany 3–2*. R2 d.S.Edberg 6–2 3–6 7–5 8–6. R3

(+A.Maurer) Lost to J.Nystrom/M.Wilander 6–4 6–2 6–1. R4 d.M.Wilander 6–3 2–6 6–3 6–3. **1986: March –** *World Group 1r (Away) Mexico d. Germany 3–2.* R2 d. L.Lavalle 6–3 6–2 6–4. R3 (+A.Maurer) Lost to Lavalle/F.Perez-Pascal 3–6 6–1 7–5 3–6 6–4. R4 d. F.Maciel 6–3 6–1 6–1. **October –** *Relegation (Home) Germany d. Ecuador 5–0.* R1 d.R.Viver 6–4 6–4 10–8. R3 (+E.Jelen) d. A.Gomez/R.Viver 6–2 6–4 6–4. R5 d. A.Gomez 7–5 6–2. **1987: March –** *World Group 1r (Away) Spain d. Germany 3–2.* R1 d. E.Sanchez 6–4 7–5 5–7 3–6 6–3. R3 (+E.Jelen) d. S.Casal/E.Sanchez 7–5 4–6 6–4 6–3. R5 Lost to S.Casal 6–2 0–6 6–2 6–3. **July –** *Relegation (Away) Germany d. USA 3–2.* R2 d. J.McEnroe 4–6 15–13 8–10 6–2 6–2. R5 d. T.Mayotte 6–2 6–3 5–7 4–6 6–2. **1988: February –** *World Group 1r (Home) Germany d. Brazil 5–0.* R1 d. C.Motta 6–0 6–2 6–0. R3 (+P.Kuhnen) d. R.Acioly/L.Mattar 8–6 15–13 6–4. **April –** *World Group qf (Home) Germany d. Denmark 5–0.* R2 d. M.Tauson 7–5 6–4 6–3. R3 (+E.Jelen) d. M.Mortensen/M.Tauson 6–3 6–4 6–4. R4 d. M.Christensen 6–3 6–4. **July –** *World Group sf (Home) Germany d. Yugoslavia 5–0.* R1 d. S.Zivojinovic 7–5 6–2 6–4. R3 (+E.Jelen) d. G.Ivanisevic/S.Zivojinovic 5–7 4–6 6–1 11–9 9–7. R4 d. G.Prpic 7–5 6–4. **December –** *World Group Final (Away) Germany d. Sweden 4–1.* R2 d. S.Edberg 6–3 6–1 6–4. R3 (+E.Jelen) d. S.Edberg/A.Jarryd.3–6 2–6 7–5 6–3 6–2. **1989: February –** *World Group 1r (Home) Germany d. Indonesia 5–0.* R1 d. A.Mim 6–0 6–1 6–1. R3 (+E.Jelen) d. S.Suharyadi/D.Wailan 6–2 6–4 6–1. R5 T.Wibowo 6–2 7–5. **April –** *World Group qf (Away) Germany d. Czechoslovakia 3–2.* R1 d. K.Novacek 7–6 6–4 6–4. R3 (+E.Jelen) Lost to P.Korda/M.Srejber 6–3 6–7 3–6 7–6 6–3. R5 d. M.Srejber 6–3 6–4 6–3. **July –** *World Group sf (Home) Germany d. USA 3–2.* R2 d. A.Agassi 6–7 6–7 7–6 6–3 6–4. R3 (+E.Jelen) d. K.Flach/R.Seguso 3–6 7–6 6–4 7–6. **December –** *World Group Final (Home) Germany d. Sweden 3–2.* R2 d. S.Edberg 6–2 6–2 6–4. R3 (+E.Jelen) d. J.Gunnarsson/A.Jarryd.7–6 6–4 3–6 6–7 6–4. R4 d. M.Wilander 6–2 6–0 6–2. **1991: February –** *World Group 1r (Home) Germany d. Italy 3–2.* R1 d. P.Cane 3–6 6–1 6–4 6–4. R3 (+E.Jelen) Lost to O.Camporese/D.Nargiso 4–6 6–4 7–6 4–6 6–3. R4 d. O.Camporese 3–6 4–6 6–3 6–4 6–3. **March –** *World Group qf (Home) Germany d. Argentina 5–0.* R2 d. J.Frana 6–3 6–4 6–4. R4 d. M.Jaite 6–1 7–6. **1992: January –** *World Group 1r (Away) Brazil d. Germany 3–1.* R1 d. L.Mattar 6–4 5–7 1–6 7–6 6–0. R3 (+E.Jelen) Lost to C.Motta/F.Roese 7–5 6–3 6–3. **September –** *Qualification (Home) Germany d. Belgium 5–0.* R2 d. F.de Wulf 6–4 6–4 6–4. R3 d. F.de Wulf/E.Masso 7–6 6–2 7–5.

GRAND PRIX MASTERS/ATP CHAMPIONSHIP (from 1990)

1985:(16–man Knock–out) r/u 1r d. Annacone 3–6 6–3 6–2, qf d. Wilander 6–4 4–6 6–3, sf d. Jarryd.6–3 6–4, final lost Lendl 6–2 7–6 6–3. **1986: r/u** In rr d. Nystrom 6–1 6–3, d. Leconte 0–6 6–1 6–1, d. Wilander 6–3 3–6 6–3; In sf d. Edberg 6–4 6–4; In f lost Lendl 6–4 6–4 6–4. **1987: Equal 3rd.**In rr lost Lendl 6–4 6–7 6–3, lost Gilbert 4–6 6–4 6–4, d. Connors 7–5 2–6 6–3. **1988: won** In rr d. Wilander 7–6 6–7 6–1, d. Leconte 6–0 1–0 ret., lost Edberg 7–6 3–6 6–4; In sf d. Hlasek 7–6 7 6; In f d. Lendl 5–7 7–6 3–6 6–2 7–6. **1989: r/u** In rr, d. Gilbert 2–6 6–3 6–4, d. Agassi 6–1 6–3, d. Edberg 6–1 6–4; In sf d. J. McEnroe 6–4 6–4; In f lost Edberg 4–6 7–6 6–3 6–1. **1990: sf** In rr d. Gomez 4–6 6–3 6–3, d. Muster 7–5 6–4, d. Lendl 1–6 7–6 6–4; sf lost Agassi 6–2 6–4. **1991: Equal 3rd** In rr lost to Agassi 6–3 7–5, d. Stich 7–6 6–3, d. Sampras 6–4 6–7 6–1. **1992: won** In rr lost Sampras 7–6 7–6, d. Korda 6–4 6–2, d. Edberg 6–4 6–0; sf d. Ivanisevic 4–6 6–4 7–6; final d. Courier 6–4 6–3 7–5.

MICHAEL CHANG (USA)   Turned pro: 1988

Born: Hoboken, NJ, 22 February 1972. **Lives:** Henderson, Nev.
Father: Joe. **Mother:** Betty. Parents are research chemists from
Taipei. **Brother** Carl (older).
Agent: Advantage International.
Coaches: His brother, Carl, since July 1991. First introduced to the
game by his father who still guides him, and has been coached by
Brian Gottfried, José Higueras and Phil Dent.
Height: 5ft 8in (1.73m). **Weight:** 145lb (65kg).

Rankings: 1987: 63; **1988:** 30; **1989:** 5; **1990:** 15; **1991:** 15; **1992:** :6. **Highest:** 5 (7 Aug. 1989).

1992 Prize Money: $1,924,467. **Career Earnings:** $5,127,821. **Career Titles:** 8.

Style: A small but athletic right-hander with a 2-handed backhand whose astonishing speed
about the court and indomitable will-to-win enable him to beat larger and stronger men. His
return of serve and passing shots make him the bane of every serve-and-volley player.

CAREER HIGHLIGHTS(year:(*titles*))
1987: At 15 yrs 6 mths was youngest player to compete in men's singles at US Open since
1918, and was the youngest ever to win a match in GS tourn, having been granted a wild
card after winning US 18s at Kalamazoo. At 15 yrs 7 mths was youngest to win a pro tourn
at Las Vegas Challenger and was youngest ever GP semi-finalist at Scottsdale. **1988: (1)**
San Francisco. At 16 yrs 4 mths was the youngest for 60 years to win a match in Wimbledon
main draw, and when he won his 1st title at San Francisco at 16 yrs 7 mths, he was
youngest to win a SS event and second-youngest after Krickstein to win a GP title. Upset
Svensson *en route* to last 16 US Open and reached qf Washington and Cincinnati. **1989: (2)**
French Open, Wembley. The highlight of his career to date came at the French Open
where, at 17 yrs 3 mths, he became the youngest known male winner of a GS tourn and the
1st American since Trabert in 1955 to win that title. In 5s of his 4r match v Lendl, he was so
badly affected with cramp that he had to serve underarm. Won Wembley and r/u Los
Angeles, last 16 Wimbledon and US Open to qualify for 1st Masters, where he failed to win
a match. Was the youngest to play D Cup for USA, making his debut v Paraguay, and the
youngest to break into top 5. **1990: (1)** *Canadian Open.* Out until March with stress fracture
of cup of left hip suffered Dec. 1989. He did not reach the heights of the previous year, but
won 1st HC title at Canadian Open, was r.u Los Angeles and Wembley and reached sf
Washington. His best showing in GS was qf French Open. In winning US D Cup team, in sf
coming back from 2 sets to 1 down v Skoff to take US into f, where he d Cahill in 2nd rubber
in 3–2 win v Australia. Reached sf inaugural Cup, losing to eventual winner Sampras. **1991:**
(1) *Birmingham.* He had slipped so far down the rankings that he was not seeded at US
Open, where he reached last 16. At French Open reached qf, but at Wimbledon Mayotte
inflicted his 1st 1r loss in 12 GS tourns. He had to wait until Nov. before winning is 1st title
of the year at Birmingham, having earlier reached sf Memphis, Tokyo Suntory and Paris
Open – upsetting Edberg – and reached 7 more qf. R/u to Wheaton in Compaq GS Cup,
winning $1 million. **1992: (3)** *Indian Wells, LIPC, San Francisco.* Returned to top 10 1st time
since July 1991 after winning Indian Wells, following with LIPC (d. Sampras and Courier)
and San Francisco (d. Courier again). Was also r/u Hong Kong and appeared in sf Tokyo
Suntory (losing both times to Courier) and reached same stage Cincinnati, Long Island and
Tokyo Seiko (losing all 3 to Lendl). His best showing in GS was sf US Open, where he survived
5s matches v Washington and W. Ferreira, but lost a 3rd over the same length v Edberg.
Qualified for ATP World Champs, but won no match there. Wore spectacles on court 1st time
at Gstaad in July, switching from contact lenses after suffering build-up problems.

PRINCIPAL 1992 RESULTS (detailed Grand Slam results see below)
won Indian Wells (d. Jaite 6–0 6–7 7–6, J. Sanchez 0–6 6–4 6–1, Krajicek 6–3 6–7 7–6,
Cherkasov 6–4 6–2, Clavet 6–0 6–1, Chesnokov 6–3 6–4 7–5), **won** LIPC (d. Krishnan 6–3

6–1, Rosset 4–6 6–3 7–6, Zoecke 4–6 6–3 6–1, Sampras 6–4 7–6, Courier 6–2 6–4, Mancini 7–5 7–5), **won** San Francisco (d. Gunnarsson 6–1 6–1, Schapers 6–4 6–3, Champion 6–3 6–3, B. Gilbert 6–0 7–5, Courier 6–3 6–3), **r/u** Hong Kong (d. Connell 7–5 6–3, Grabb 6–2 6–4, Siemerink 6–3 6–2, Woodbridge 6–3 6–7 6–1, lost Courier 7–5 6–3), **sf** Tokyo Suntory (d. Bryan 6–3 6–2, Zoecke 6–4 6–2, Woodbridge 6–4 1–6 6–0, lost Courier 6–2 6–3), **sf** Cincinnati (d. Stolle 6–4 6–3, B. Gilbert 6–2 6–2, Yzaga 6–3 6–1, lost Lendl 6–3 6–2), **sf** Long Island (d. Pozzi 6–0 4–6 6–1, Connors w.o., Volkov 6–1 6–3, lost Lendl 6–2 6–3), **sf** Tokyo Seiko (d. Olhovskiy 6–2 6–3, Stark 6–0 6–7 6–0, Thorne 7–6 6–3, lost Lendl 6–3 6–4).

CAREER GRAND SLAM RECORD
AUSTRALIAN OPEN – Played 1
1992: 3r [seed 14] d Roese 6–2 6–3 6–0, Caratti 6–3 3–6 6–4 6–4, lost Krajicek 6–4 6–1 5–7 1–6 6–3.

FRENCH OPEN – Played 5, won 1, qf 2
1988: 3r d. Seguso 7–5 6–2 6–3, Svantesson 6–4 6–1 6–3, lost McEnroe [seed 16] 6–0 6–3 6–1. **1989: won** [seed 15] d. Masso 6–7 6–3 6–0 6–3, Sampras 6–1 6–1 6–1, Roig 6–0 0–7 5 6–3, Lendl [seed 1] 4–6 4–6 6–3 6–3 6–3, Agenor 6–4 2–6 6–4 7–6, Chesnokov 6–1 5–7 7–6 7–5, Edberg [seed 3] 6–1 2–6 4–6 6–4 6–2. **1990 qf** [seed 11] d. Motta 6–2 7–6 6–1, Rosset 7–5 4–6 6–4 6–3, Bergstrom 2–6 5–7 6–0 6–2 6–4, E.Sanchez [seed 6] 6–4 6–4 6–2, lost Agassi [seed 3] 6–1 6–2 4–6 6–2. **1991: qf** [seed 10] d. Siemerink 6–2 6–0 6–3, Jonsson, 7–6 4–6 6–4 3–6 6–3, Connors 4–6 7–5 6–2 4–6 0–15 ret., Forget [seed 7] 6–1 6–1 4–6 6–3, lost Becker [seed 2] 6–4 6–4 6–2. **1992: 3r** [seed 5] d. Haarhuis 6–4 6–3 6–3, Gorriz 6–3 2–6 6–3 6–0, lost Kulti 7–5 2–6 6–3 3–6 8–6.

WIMBLEDON – Played 5
1988: 2r d. Layendecker 7–5 1–6 6–4 6–2, lost Leconte [seed 7] 2–6 7–6 6–2 6–3. **1989: 4r** [seed 9] d. Scanlon 6–4 6–3 2–6 6–3, Agenor 4–6 6–2 6–1 7–5, Schapers 4–6 6–3 7–5 7–5, lost Mayotte [seed 8] 6–3 6–1 6–3. **1990: 4r** [seed 13] d. Altur 5–7 6–4 6–3 7–5, Pugh 6–3 6–2 6–2, Kratzmann 3–6 4–6 6–4 6–2 6–2, lost Edberg [seed 3] 6–3 6–2 6–1. **1991: 1r** lost Mayotte 6–7 4–6 6–1 7–6 6–2 **1992: 1r** [seed 7] lost Bates 6–4 6–3 6–3.

US OPEN – Played 6, sf 1
1987: 2r d. McNamara 6–3 6–7 6–4 6–4, lost Odizor 6–1 6–2 6–7 3–6 6–4. **1988: 4r** d. Mattar 6–4 6–3 7–5, Svensson [seed 13] 5–7 6–4 2–6 6–4 6–4, Wilkison 4–6 3–6 6–3 6–4 7–5, lost Agassi [seed 4] 7–5 6–3 6–2. **1989: 4r** [seed 7] d. Wilkison 7–5 6–3 6–2, Hogstedt 6–1 6–3 6–3, Aldrich 6–0 7–6 6–4, lost Mayotte [seed 9] 7–5 6–1 1–6 6–3. **1990: 3r** [seed 11] d. Pernfors 6–0 6–2 6–3, Arias 7–6 6–3 6–2, lost Cherkasov 6–4 6–4 6–3. **1991: 4r** d. Woodforde 6–3 6–0 6–2, Witsken 6–3 6–0 6–2, J.McEnroe [seed 16] 6–4 4–6 7–6 2–6 6–3, lost Edberg [seed 2] 7–6 7–5 6–3. **1992: sf** [seed 4] d. E. Ferreira 6–3 6–4 7–6, P.McEnroe 6–3 6–3 6–4, Boetsch 6–3 6–3 6–1, Washington [seed 14] 6–2 2–6 3–6 6–3 6–1, W.Ferreira [seed 12] 7–5 2–6 6–3 6–7 6–1, lost Edberg [seed 2] 6–7 7–5 7–6 5–7 6–4.

OLYMPIC GAMES
1992: (Barcelona) 2r [seed 6] d. Mancini 6–1 6–4 3–6 6–0, lost Oncins 6–2 3–6 6–3 6–3.

CAREER DAVIS CUP RECORD
1989: *World Group 1r (Home) USA d. Paraguay 5–0.* R1 d. V.Pecci 6–7 6–3 6–4 6–2. R4 d. H.Chapacu 5–7 6–0 6–1. **1990:** *World Group sf (Away) USA d. Austria 3–2.* R1 Lost to T.Muster 4–6 6–2 6–2 6–4. R5 d. H.Skoff 3–6 6–7 6–4 6–4 6–3. **1990:** *World Group Final (Home) USA d. Australia 3–2.* R2 d. D. Cahill 6–2 7–6 6–0. R5 Lost to R.Fromberg 7–5 2–6 6–3.

GRAND PRIX MASTERS/ATP TOUR CHAMPIONSHIP (from 1990)
1989: Equal 4th In rr lost Lendl 6–1 6–3, lost McEnroe 6–2 5–7 6–4, lost Krickstein 6–3 7–6. **1992: Equal 4th** In rr lost Ivanisevic 7–6 6–2, lost Krajicek 2–6 6–3 7–6, lost Courier 7–5 6–2.

PETR KORDA (TCH)   Turned pro: 1987

Born: Prague, 23 January 1968. **Lives:** Prague.
Father: Petr, who coached his son until age 18.
Mother: Jana. **Sister:** Eva. **Wife:** Regina Rajchrtova (married autumn 1992).
Agent: ProServ.
Coach: Vladimir Zednik since Feb. 1991; formerly coached by his father.
Height: 6ft 3in (1.90m). **Weight:** 160lb (72kg).

Rankings: 1985: 794; **1986:** 511; **1987:** 87; **1988:** 188; **1989:** 59; **1990:** 38; **1991:** 9; **1992:** 7. **Highest:** 5 (July 1992)..

1992 Prize Money: $1,350,353. **Career Earnings:** $2,462,622. **Career Titles:** 5.

Style: A talented left-hander with the ability to conjure winners from impossible positions – rather like the great Rod Laver used to. His ambitious attempts to go for early winners inevitably produces a higher proportion of unforced errors than is healthy. A good swinging serve, fine touch on the volley and brilliant use of the racket head on forehand and backhand, make him always an exciting player to watch.

CAREER HIGHLIGHTS (year: *(titles)*)
1984: Won Nat 18s at age 16. **1986:** Won Wimbledon Jun doubles with Carbonell. **1987:** Won Budapest challenger; qf Prague (d. Srejber). **1988:** Broke into top 100 in May and upset E. Sanchez in his 1st tourn on grass at Wimbledon. In doubles won Gstaad and Prague. Out of action with shoulder and ankle injuries following a car accident. **1989:** Reached his 1st GP f at Frankfurt in autumn after sf showing at Vienna. In doubles won Stuttgart and reached 3 other f. **1990:** Reached sf Philadelphia, Munich (d. Chang) and Moscow, and upset Gomez at Toronto World Tennis. In doubles r/u French Open with Ivanisevic and reached 3 more f, winning Monte Carlo with Smid. **1991: (2)** *New Haven, Berlin.* Made tremendous strides as he moved into top 10 in autumn. Won his 1st tour singles title at New Haven, following with Berlin and also winning the doubles at both tourns. R/u Tampa, Washing (d. B. Gilbert), Montreal (d. Agassi and Courier), sf Umag and Vienna, and upset Lendl *en route* to qf Stockholm. **1992: (3)** *Washington, Long Island, Vienna.* Having never before passed 3r GS singles, he was r/u French Open to Courier, who was the 1st seeded player he had encountered in the tourn. Won Washington, Long Island (d. Edberg and Lendl) and Vienna, moving into top 5 in Oct; r/u Munich, Toulouse and Basle; sf Italian Open and Stuttgart. Qualified for ATP WorldChamp, but won no match there.

PRINCIPAL 1992 RESULTS (detailed Grand Slam results below)
SINGLES: won Washington (d. Brown 4–6 6–2 6–3, Antonitsch 6–3 7–5, Mansdorf 7–6 6–2, Washington 7–6 6–0, Holm 6–4 6–4), **won** Long Island (d. Oncins 6–0 6–2, Gustafsson 6–3 6–4, Pescosolido 7–6 6–2, Edberg 7–5 7–5, Lendl 6–2 6–2), **won** Vienna (d. Fontang 6–2 6–1, Skoff 6–4 6–3, Antonitsch 7–6 6–4, Siemerink 7–5 6–7 6–3, Pozzi 6–3 6–2 5–7 6–1, **r/u** FRENCH OPEN, **r/u** Munich (d. Steeb 6–2 6–3, L. Jonsson 6–4 6–3, Kulti 6–3 3–6 6–3, Karbacher 3–6 7–6 7–5, lost Larsson 6–4 4–6 6–1), **r/u** Toulouse (d. Hogstedt 6–4 6–1, Roux 6–7 7–5 6–4, Svensson 3–6 6–0 6–1, Siemerink 7–6 6–3, lost Forget 6–3 6–2), **r/u** Basle (d. Cherkasov 6–2 6–2, Oncins 6–2 3–0 ret'd, Pioline 2–6 6–3 6–2, Lendl 6–4 6–2, lost Becker 3–6 6–3 6–2 6–4), **sf** Italian Open (d. Pozzi 6–4 6–3, Cherkasov 6–3 5–7 6–4, Mancini 3–6 7–6 6–3, Sampras 1–6 7–6 6–3, lost Costa 6–4 6–3), **sf** Stuttgart (d. Thoms 7–6 7–5, Jarryd 6–3 7–5, Siemerink 6–4 6–4, lost Edberg 6–4 6–4). **DOUBLES: r/u** Monte Carlo (with Novacek) lost Becker/Stich 6–4 6–4, **r/u** Gstaad (with Suk) lost Davids/Pimek w.o.

CAREER GRAND SLAM RECORD
AUSTRALIAN OPEN – Played 4
1990: 2r d. Hlasek 7–6 6–0 6–3, lost Leconte 6–2 4–6 6–3 6–4. **1991: 2r** d. Volkov 6–1 1–6

1–6 6–4 7–5, lost Krajicek 4–6 7–6 6–3 6–4. **1992: 1r** [seed 9] lost Tarango 4–6 4–6 6–3 6–3 6–3.

FRENCH OPEN - Played 4, r/u 1
1988: 2r d. Duncan 7–6 6–3 6–3, lost Becker [seed 5] 6–3 6–3 6–4. **1990: 2r** d. Paloheimo 6–4 6–1 2–6 6–3, lost Gustafsson [seed 14] 3–6 7–6 1–6 6–1 9–7. **1991: 2r** d. Fleurian 4–6 6–4 6–2 6–4, lost Agassi [seed 4] 6–1 6–2 6–2. **1992: r/u** [seed 7] d. Bergstrom 6–4 6–2 6–2, Matsuoka 1–6 4–6 6–4 6–4 6–4, Schapers 6–4 6–2 3–6 6–1, Oncins 6–4 6–3 6–3, Cherkasov 6–4 6–7 6–2 6–4, Leconte 6–2 7–6 6–3, lost Courier 7–5 6–2 6–1.

WIMBLEDON - Played 4
1988: 3r d. Narducci 6–3 3–6 6–3 6–2, E.Sanchez 7–6 6–3 3–6 0–6 6–1, lost Youl 6–4 7–6 6–0. **1990: 1r** [seed 14] lost Bloom 6–0 –6–4 4–6 6–2. **1991: 1r** lost Wheaton 7–6 6–7 6–4 6–2. **1992: 2r** [seed 6] d. Bergstrom 7–5 7–6 6–4, lost Hlasek 4–6 3–6 6–3 7–6 16–14.

US OPEN - Played 4
1988: 1r lost Bloom 4–6 6–4 2–1 ret. **1990: 2r** d. Jelen 2–6 6–3 6–0 6–3, lost Agassi [seed 4] 7–5 5–7 6–0 6–4. **1991: 1r** [seed 15] lost Boetsch 6–1 6–3 3–6 6–2. **1992: 1r** [seed 6] lost E. Sanchez 6–2 4–6 2–6 6–1 7–6 .

CAREER DAVIS CUP RECORD
1988: February – *World Group 1r (Home) Czechoslovakia d. Paraguay 5–0.* R1 d. H.Chapacu 6–2 6–1 6–2. R5 d. F.Gonzalez 6–4 6–4. **1989: February –** *World Group 1r (Home) Czechoslovakia d. Russia 4–1.* R3 d. A.Olhovskiy/A.Volkov 6–3 6–4 6–4. **April –** *World Group qf (Home) Germany d. Czechoslovakia 3–2.* R3 d. B.Becker/E.Jelen 6–3 6–7 3–6 7–6 6–3. **1990: February –** *World Group 1r (Home) Czechoslovakia d. Switzerland 5–0.* R3 (+M.Srejber) d. H.Guenthardt/ J.Hlasek 6–4 3–6 7–6 7–6. **March –** *World Group qf (Home) USA d. Czechoslovakia 4–1.* R2 d. B.Gilbert 6–2 6–3 6–3. R3 (+M.Srejber) Lost to R.Leach/J.Pugh 6–4 6–4 6–4. R4 Lost A.Krickstein 6–2 6–3 1–6 6–3. **1991: February –** *World Group 1r (Home) Czechoslovakia d Austria 4–1.* R1 d. H.Skoff 6–3 3–6 6–7 6–1 6–3. R3 (+M.Srejber) d. A.Antonitsch/H.Skoff 6–4 7–6 0–6 6–4. **March –** *World Group qf (Home) Yugoslavia d. Czechoslovakia 4–1.* R1 Lost to G.Ivanisevic 6–1 7–6 4–6 6–1. R3 (+M.Srejber) Lost to G.Ivanisevic/S.Zivojinovic 7–6 6–4 6–4. R5 Lost to S.Zivojinovic 7–6 2–6 8–6. **1992: January –** *World Group 1r (Home) Czechoslovakia d. Belgium 5–0.* R2 d. E.Masso 6–1 7–6 6–3. R3 (+C.Suk) d. E.Masso/T.Van Houdt 6–3 6–3 6–3. R4 d. B.Wuyts 6–4 7–5. **March –** *World Group qf (Away) USA d. Czechoslovakia 3–2.* R2 Lost A.Agassi 6–2 6–4 6–1. R3 (+C.Suk) d. R.Leach/J.McEnroe 6–3 6–4 6–4. R4 d. P.Sampras 6–4 6–3 2–6 6–3.

GRAND PRIX MASTERS/ATP TOUR CHAMPIONSHIP (from 1990)
1992: Equal 4th In rr lost Edberg 6–3 7–6, lost Becker 6–4 6–2, lost Sampras 3–6 6–3 6–3.

IVAN LENDL (USA)
Turned pro: 1978

Born: Ostrava, Czechoslovakia, 7 March 1960. **Lives:** Greenwich, Conn. **Father:** Jiri, a lawyer. **Mother:** Olga, former Czech No.3. **Wife:** Samantha Frankl (married 16 Sept. 1989). **Family:** Daughters Marike Lee (born 4 May 1990) and twins Caroline and Isabelle (born 29 July 1991). Became a US citizen 7 July 1992.
Coach: Tony Roche. Hitting partner, former Wimbledon finalist Chris Lewis (since Feb. 1991).
Agent: International Management Group.

Height: 6ft 2in (1.88m). **Weight:** 175lb (79kg).

Rankings: 1978: 74; **1979:** 20; **1980:** 6; **1981:** 2; **1982:** 3; **1983:** 2; **1984:** 3; **1985:** 1; **1989:** 1; **1987:** 1; **1988:** 2; **1989:** 1; **1990:** 3; **1991:** 5; **1992:** 8. **Highest:** 1 (28 February 1983).

1992 Prize Money: $961,566. **Career Earnings:** $19,922,627. **Career Titles:** 92.

Style: A consistent right-hander whose heavy, flat forehand and powerful serve were two of the game's great shots in the 1980's. With a consistency from the back of the court that few could match, Ivan dominated the game during that period. His thorough professionalism set new standards which others have gratefully followed.

CAREER HIGHLIGHTS (year: *(titles)*)
1977: Won Orange Bowl 18s. **1978:** Won Wimbledon, French and Italian Jun and became 1st ITF World Jun Champ. **1979: r/u** Brussels. **1980: (7)** *Houston, Toronto, Barcelona, Basel, Tokyo, Hong Kong, Taipei.* Won his 1st GP title at Houston and added 6 more, beating World No. 1 Borg in Toronto and Basle. **1981: (10)** *Stuttgart, Las Vegas, Montreal, Madrid, Barcelona, Basel, Vienna, Cologne, Buenos Aires, Masters (Jan. 82).* Took 10 titles, closing season with 7 straight tourn wins and 35 straight matches, a streak which was ended at 44 by Noah at La Quinta on 21st Feb.1982. **1982: (15)** *Frankfurt, Washington, North Conway, Cincinnati, WCT Delray Beach, WCT Genoa, WCT Munich, WCT Strasbourg, WCT Houston, WCT Finals Dallas, WCT Forest Hills, WCT Los Angeles, WCT Naples, WCT Hartford, Masters (Jan. 83).* Won 15 of 23 tourns and 106 of 115 matches, and was r/u US Open. **1983: (7)** *WCT Detroit, Milan, WCT Houston, WCT Hilton Head, Montreal, San Francisco, Tokyo Indoor.* Took 7 titles and r/u US Open and Australian Open, his inability still to win a GS casting doubts on his belief in himself as a true champion. **1984: (3)** *FRENCH OPEN, Wembley, Luxembourg.* Silenced his critics by winning French Open for 1st GS in 5 f, coming from 2 sets to 0 down to oust McEnroe in f. Reached sf Wimbledon and f US Open. **1985: (11)** *Fort Myers, Monte Carlo, WCT Finals Dallas, WCT Forest Hills, Indianapolis, US OPEN, Stuttgart, Sydney Indoor, Tokyo Indoor, Wembley, Masters (Jan. 86).* Won 84 of 91 matches (31 consecutively from US Open to sf Australian Open) and 11 of 18 tourns, capturing 1st US Open in 4th straight f and 3rd Masters to cement his status as No. 1 in the World. **1986: (9)** *Philadelphia, Boca West, Milan, Fort Myers, Italian Open, FRENCH OPEN, Stratton Mountain, US OPEN, Masters.* Won 74 of 80 matches and 9 of 15 tourns to take 2nd consec US Open, 2nd French Open, 2nd consec Masters and 4th in all, being beaten by only Becker, Noah, Edberg and Curren all year. **1987: (8)** *Hamburg, FRENCH OPEN, Washington, Montreal, US OPEN, Sydney, Wembley, Masters.* Underwent arthroscopic knee surgery in March, returning to win Hamburg in May. Still vulnerable on grass, he fell in sf Australian Open and 2nd consec Wimbledon f, both to Cash. However, he won 3rd French Open, 3rd US Open crown, a record 5th Masters, 5 other titles and finished the year undisputed No. 1 for 3rd consec year. **1988: (3)** *Monte Carlo, Italian Open, Toronto.* In an injury-plagued year, a fractured bone in his right foot kept him out for 6 weeks in spring, and he underwent arthroscopic surgery on his right shoulder after US Open, returning for Masters, where he lost thrilling f to Becker. Won no GS, losing sf Australian Open to Cash, qf French Open to Svensson, sf Wimbledon to Becker and f US Open to Wilander. Lost to Fitzgerald in Philadelphia – the 1st time he had been beaten by a player outside the top 50 since losing to F. Gonzalez Aug. 1984 – and then to R.Smith at

Stratton Mountain in July – the 1st time he'd lost to a player ranked as low as 150 since losing 1r Wimbledon to Fancutt in 1981. After US Open he lost the No. 1 ranking to Wilander, having held that position continuously for 156 weeks, just 3 weeks short of Connors's record of 159 weeks. **1989: (10)** *AUSTRALIAN OPEN, Scottsdale, LIPC, Forest Hills, Hamburg, Queen's, Montreal, Bordeaux, Sydney Indoor, Stockholm.* Regained the No. 1 ranking after winning his 1st Australian Open. At Queen's won his 1st GP title on grass but failed again to win Wimbledon, lost 5s sf to Becker, and was r/u to the same player at US Open. Won a total of 10 titles and in autumn he achieved the highest No. 1 average ever in the history of the ATP computer rankings (208.5385). Was the 1st to qualify for Masters, but failed for 1st time in 10 appearances to reach f, falling in sf to an inspired Edberg. **1990: (5)** *AUSTRALIAN OPEN, Milan, Toronto Indoor, Queen's, Tokyo Indoor.* Won Australian Open but missed French Open (1st GS he'd missed since Australian Open 1982) to prepare with coach Roche for Wimbledon. He looked to be on course to achieve his greatest ambition of winning there when he beat Becker for 1st time on grass to retain Queen's, but at Wimbledon he never looked secure and fell to Edberg in sf. On 13 Aug. lost No. 1 ranking to Edberg, having held that position for 80 weeks since 30 Jan 1989, and on 20 Aug. slipped to No. 3 behind Becker for 1st time since 1 April 1985. At US Open, seeded 3 for 1st time since 1983, he fell to Sampras in qf. Won a total of 5 titles, reached 1 other f and 3 sf, including ATP World Champ, and 2r GS Cup (lost Wheaton). Fined 15% of total earnings on ATP tour (excluding GS) for falling 2 tourns short of commitment to ATP. **1991: (3)** *Philadelphia, Memphis, Long Island.* He began the year well as r/u Australian Open, where he d. Edberg but lost to Becker. Underwent surgery to remove calluses from racket hand 10 May, missing Italian Open and French Open when scar tissue in the palm of his hand became infected and failed to heal as rapidly as expected. He was again disappointed at Wimbledon, losing in 3r to Wheaton, and in July he was overtaken in the rankings by Stich, slipping from the top 3 for the 1st time since Aug. 1982. In Aug. he dropped to No. 5 behind Courier and was seeded only 5 at US Open, where he lost to Edberg in sf. Maintained a 12-year record of winning 3 or more titles, r/u Rotterdam and Tokyo Suntory and reached 4 other sf, including ATP World Champ, where he won all rr matches but lost to Sampras. Ended year with disappointing sf loss to Chang in Compaq GS Cup after winning 1st 2 sets. **1992: (1)** *Tokyo Seiko.* At Tokyo Seiko he won his 1st title for 14 months, which was to be his only one of the year, in which he was r/u Toronto, Cincinnati and Long Island, reached sf New Haven and Basle and 6 other qf. When he slipped to No. 7 in Feb., he was at his lowest ranking since Oct. 1980, and at French Open, where he fell 2r to Oncins, he was seeded as low as 10, as he was at Wimbledon. Yet again he failed to complete his list of GS titles, being forced to retire with back trouble in 4s last 16 v Ivanisevic at Wimbledon. Qualified for ATP World Champ, but was forced to pull out after suffering a groin injury at Antwerp. He finished the year with fewer titles and with his lowest year-end ranking since 1979.

PRINCIPAL 1992 RESULTS (detailed Grand Slam results below)
SINGLES: won Tokyo Seiko (d. Martin 7-5 2–6 7–5, Masur 6–7 6–4 7–6, Ivanisevic 6–3 6–4, Chang 6–3 6–4, Holm 7–6 6–4, **r/u** Toronto (d. Martin 6–3 6–2, Youl 6–1 6–4, J. McEnroe 6–2 6–4, Masur 6–1 6–2, lost Agassi 3–6 6–2 6–0), **r/u** Cincinnati (d. Pozzi 6–3 3–6 6–1, Pioline 6–1 6–2, Wheaton 6–1 6–2, Chang 6–3 6–2, lost Sampras 6–3 3–6 6–3),**r/u** Long Island (d. Caratti 6–1 6–1, Delaitre 6–4 6–1, Becker w.o., Chang 6–2 6–3, lost Korda 6–2 6–2), **sf** New Haven (d. Matsuoka 6–3 6–4, Mansdorf 6–2 6–3, Chang 6–3 7–6, lost Edberg 7–6 4–6 6–3), **sf** Basle (d. Siemerink 6–4 6–2, Boetsch 6–3 6–4, Chesnokov 6–1 6–2, lost Korda 6–4 6–3). **DOUBLES: r/u** Barcelona (+ Novacek) lost Gomez/J. Sanchez 6–4 6–4.

CAREER GRAND SLAM RECORD
AUSTRALIAN OPEN – Played 10, Won 2, r/u 2, sf 3, qf 1
1980: 2r [seed 2] d. R.Frawley 6–3 6–3 6–1, lost Dupre 7–5 6–3 3–6 2–6 7–6 **1983: r/u** [seed 1] d. Smith 6–2 6–2 6–3, Fleming 6–7 7–6 6–3 6–4, Cash 7–6 6–3 6–3, Smid[seed 7] 6–2 2–6 6–1 6–2, Mayotte[seed 15] 6–1 7–6 6–3, lost Wilander[seed 3] 6–1 6–4 6–4. **1984: 4r** [seed 1] bye, d. Scanlon 4–6 6–4 6–4 6–1, Benhabiles 2–6 6–2 6–4 6–4, lost Curren[seed 9] 6–1

7–6 6–4. **1985: sf** [seed 1] d. Lavalle 6–4 0–6 6–4 6–2, Testerman 6–3 1–6 6–3 6–2, Steyn 6–3 6–2 6–7 6–2, Lloyd 7–6 6–2 6–1, lost Edberg [seed 5] 6–7 7–5 6–1 4–6 9–7. **1986: No Championship**. **1987: sf** [seed 1] bye, d. Saltz 6–4 3–6 6–1 6–1, Anger 6–4 6–2 6–7 6–2, Goldie 2–6 6–4 7–6 6–3, Jarryd[seed 9] 7–6 6–1 6–3. lost Cash[seed 11] 7–6 5–7 7–6 6–4. **1988: sf** [seed 1] d. Roe 6–3 7–6 6–2, Anger 6–0 6–1 6–1, Woodforde 6–4 6–3 6–1, Masur [seed 16] 7–5 6–4 6–4, Witsken 6–2 6–1 7–6, lost Cash[seed 4] 6–4 2–6 6–2 4–6 6–2. **1989: won** [seed 2] d. Mronz 6–0 6–1 6–3, Steeb 6–2 3–6 6–0 6–3, Kulti 6–2 6–4 6–3, Mansdorf [seed 16] 7–6 6–4 6–2, McEnroe[seed 7] 7–6 6–2 7–6, Muster [seed 11] 6–2 6–4 5–7 7–5, Mecir[seed 9] 6–2 6–2 6–2. **1990: won** [seed 1] d. Pugh 6–3 6–2 6–4, Carbonell 6–4 6–2 6–3, Novacek 6–4 3–6 6–4 6–1, Youl 6–1 6–3 6–1, Cherkasov 6–3 6–2 6–3, Noah[seed 12] 6–4 6–1 6–2, Edberg [seed 3] 4–6 7–6 5–2 ret. **1991: r/u** [seed 3] d. Benhabiles 6–1 6–1 6–3, S.Davis 7–6 6–3 6–2, Gustafsson 4–6 6–2 6–3 6–2, Krickstein [seed 13] 6–2 6–2 6–1, Prpic 6–0 7–6 7–6, Edberg[seed 1] 6–2 6–3 6–2, lost Becker[seed 2] 1–6 6–4 6–0 7–6. **1992: qf** [seed 5] d. Fromberg 6–4 6–2 6–2, Rasheed 6–3 6–2 6–3, Zoecke 6–4 6–4 7–6, Camporese 7–6 6–1 6–3, lost Edberg [seed 1] 4–6 7–6 6–1 6–7 6–1.

FRENCH OPEN – Played 13, Won 3, r/u 2, qf 2
1978: 1r lost Clerc 6–3 6–0 6–3. **1979: 4r** d. Fillol 7–6 6–3 4–6 6–3, Dominguez 3–6 6–2 7–5 6–2, Ashe [seed 9] 5–7 7–6 6–2 6–3, lost Gerulaitis [seed 4] 6–2 6–1 6–3. **1980: 3r** [seed 9] d. S.Mayer 7–6 6–2 6–3, Ebehard 6–3 3–6 6–4 7–6, lost Gottfried 2–6 7–6 1–6 7–5 6–3. **1981: r/u** [seed 3] d. Fitzgerald 7–6 7–6 6–4, Gomez 6–2 3–6 2–6 7–6 6–4, Bengoechea 6–2 6–2 4–6 6–3, McNamara 6–2 4–6 7–6 7–6, McEnroe [seed 3] 6–4 6–4 7–5, Clerc 3–6 6–4 4–6 7–6 6–2, lost Borg [seed 1] 6–1 4–6 6–2 3–6 6–1. **1982: 4r** [seed 2] d. Maynetto 6–0 6–4 6–1, Tulasne 7–6 7–5 7–6, Krishnan 6–2 6–1 6–0, lost Wilander [seed] 4–6 7–5 3–6 6–4 6–2. **1983: qf** [seed 3] d. Rebolledo 6–4 6–1 6–3, Casal 6–2 6–2 6–2, Martinez 6–0 6–2 3–6 6–0, Gottfried [seed 12] 7–6 6–4 6–3, lost Noah[seed 6] 7–6 6–3 5–7–6–0. **1984: won** [seed 2] d. Mitchell 6–3 6–2 6–0, Martinez 6–1 6–0 6–1, McNamee 6–1 7–5 6–4, Jarryd[seed 11] 6–4 6–0 6–4, Gomez [seed 7] 6–3 6–7 6–4 6–3, Wilander[seed 4] 6–3 6–3 7–5, McEnroe [seed 1] 3–6 2–6 6–4 7–5 7–5. **1985: r/u** [seed 2] d. Edwards 6–2 6–3 6–1, Gunnarsson 7–6 6–3 6–2, Potier 6–1 6–2 6–2, Krickstein 6–2 6–2 6–0, Jaite 6–4 6–2 6–4, Connors[seed 3] 6–2 6–3 6–1, lost Wilander[seed 4] 3–6 6–4 6–2 6–2. **1986: won** [seed 1] d. Westphal 6–2 6–3 6–4, Hlasek 6–3 6–3 6–3, Minuissi 6–1 6–1 6–2, Keretic 6–1 6–2 6–4, Gomez[seed 9] 6–7 7–6 6–0 6–0, Kriek[seed 13] 6–2 6–1 6–0, Pernfors 6–3 6–2 6–4. **1987; won** [seed 1] d. Agenor 7–5 7–6 0–6 6–3, Canter 3–6 6–1 6–1 6–2, Tulasne 7–6 6–2 6–2, Nystrom 2–6 6–1 5–7 6–0 6–2, Gomez[seed 10] 5–7 6–4 6–1 6–1, Mecir [seed 5] 6–3 6–3 7–6, Wilander [seed 4] 7–6 6–3 3–6 7–6. **1988: qf** [seed 1] d. Pech 6–0 6–3 6–4, Kroon 6–4 6–0 6–1, Tulasne 6–2 3–6 7–6 6–2, McEnroe[seed 16] 6–7 7–6 6–4 6–4, lost Svensson 7–6 7–5 6–2. **1989: 4r** [seed 1] d. Kuhnen 7–6 6–3 6–1, Rostagno 6–1 6–3 6–1, Cahill 7–6 6–3 6–3, lost Chang [seed 15] 4–6 4–6 6–3 6–3 6–3. **1992: 2r** [seed 10] d. Bruguera 6–4 6–2 6–1, lost Oncins 3–6 3–6 6–3 6–2 8–6.

WIMBLEDON – Played 13, r/u 2, sf 5
1979: 1r lost McNamara 6–3 6–2 6–3. **1980: 3r** [seed 10] d. Riessen 6–3 4–6 6–2 6–4, Sadri 6–3 6–4 6–3, lost Dibley 4–6 6–3 6–4 7–6. **1981: 1r** [seed 4] lost T.C.Fancutt 4–6 6–3 6–4 1–6 6–3. **1983: sf** [seed 3] d. Mitton 7–6 6–1 6–0, Waltke 6–4 6–2 6–3, Hlasek 6–1 6–2 6–7 6–4, Cash 6–4 7–6 6–1, Tanner 7–5 7–6 6–3, lost McEnroe[seed 2] 7–6 6–4 6–4. **1984: sf** [seed 2] d. Stockton 4–6 6–0 6–3 5–7 6–4, Tarr 6–3 6–1 6–3, Gehring 6–4 6–2 7–6, S.Davis 4–6 6–4 6–4 5–7 7–5, Smid 6–1 7–6 6–3, lost Connors [seed 3] 6–7 6–3 7–5 6–1. **1985: 4r** [seed 2] d. Purcell 6–4 7–6 7–6, M.Leach 6–3 1–6 6–2 6–7 6–4, Glickstein 7–6 4–6 6–3 6–2, lost Leconte 3–6 6–4 6–3 6–1. **1986: r/u** [seed 1] d. Lavalle 7–6 6–3 6–4, Freeman 6–3 6–2 6–2, Mansdorf 6–2 –4 6–4, Anger 6–7 7–6 7–4 7–6, Mayotte[seed 10] 6–4 4–6 6–3 6–9–7, Zivojinovic 6–2 6–7 6–3 6–7 6–4, lost Becker[seed 4] 6–4 6–3 7–5. **1987: r/u** [seed 2] d. Saceanu 6–2 3–6 6–3 7–5, Cane 3–6 7–6 6–7 7–5 6–1, Reneberg 6–4 6–7 6–3 7–6, Kriek 6–3 7–6 6–2, Leconte[seed 9] 7–6 6–3 7–6, Edberg[seed 4] 3–6 6–4 7–6 6–4, lost Cash[seed 11] 7–6 6–2 7–5. **1988: sf** [seed 1] d. Felgate 6–4 6–1 6–3, Cahill 5–7 6–2 6–4 6–4, Schapers 6–7 7–6 6–4 6–7 6–1, Woodforde 7–5 6–7 6–7 7–5 10–8, Mayotte [seed 10] 7–6 7–6 6–3, lost Becker[seed 6] 6–6–4 6–3 6–7 6–4. **1989: sf** [seed 1] d. Perreira 7–6 4–6 6–3 6–7 6–1,

Bathman 6–7 6–3 6–2 6–2, Carbonell 7–6 6–3 6–1, Lundgren 1–6 7–6 6–3 6–4, Goldie 7–6 7–6 6–0, lost Becker[seed 3] 7–5 6–7 2–6 6–4 6–3. **1990: sf** [seed 1] d. Minuissi 3–6 6–4 6–3 6–4, Hlasek 6–1 6–3 6–0, Shelton 7–6 6–7 6–4 6–4, Antonitsch 3–6 6–4 6–3 6–4, Pearce 6–4 6–4 5–7 6–4, lost Edberg[seed 3] 6–1 7–6 6–3. **1991: 3r** [seed 3] d. Evernden 6–2 7–5 7–6, Washington 4–6 2–6 6–4 6–4 7–5, lost Wheaton 6–3 3–6 7–6 6–3. **1992: 4r** [seed 10] d. Kuhnen 6–1 7–6 7–6, Thoms 7–5 7–6 1–6 7–5, Stolle 6–3 1–6 2–6 6–3 7–5, Ivanisevic [seed 8] 6–7 6–1 6–4 1–0 ret.

US OPEN – Played 14, Won 3, r/u 5, sf 1, qf 3
1979: 2r d. Van Patten 6–4 6–1 6–0, lost Tanner [seed 5] 6–3 6–2 6–1. **1980: qf** [seed 10] d. T.Mayotte 6–4 6–3 7–6, C.Mayotte 6–4 6–4 6–4, Tulasne 6–2 6–0 6–1, Solomon [seed 7] 6–1 6–0 6–0, lost McEnroe [seed 2] 4–6 6–3 6– 7–5. **1981: 4r** [seed 3] d. H.Simonsson 6–2 6–2 6–2, Borowiak 7–6 6–1 7–6, Vines 6–4 3–6 6–2 6–3, lost Gerulaitis [seed 15] 6–3 6–4 3–6 3–6 6–4. **1982: r/u** [seed 3] d. Krishnan 6–4 7–6 6–1, T.Mayotte 6–4 3–6 4–6 7–6 6–4, Solomon 6–3 6–0 6–1, Wilander [seed 11] 6–2 6–2 6–2, Warwick 6–4 3–6 6–1, McEnroe [seed 1] 6–4 6–4 7–6, lost Connors [seed 2] 6–3 6–2 4–6 6–4. **1983: r/u** [seed 2] d. Segarceanu 6–2 6–0 6–2, Glickstein 6–1 6–1 6–2, Levine 6–2 6–2 6–2, Kriek[seed 12] 6–2 6–4 6–1, Wilander [seed 5] 6–4 6–4 7–6, Arias [seed 9] 6–2 7–6 6–1, lost Connors[seed 3] 6–3 6–7 7–5 6–0. **1984: r/u** [seed 2] d. Teacher 6–4 6–4 7–5, Edwards 3–6 7–6 6–3 6–1, J.Brown 6–1 6–2 6–4, Jarryd[seed 14] 6–2 6–2 6–4, Gomez[seed 5] 6–4 6–4 6–1, Cash[seed 15] 3–6 6–3 6–4 6–7 7–6, lost McEnroe[seed 1]6–3 6–4 6–1. **1985: won** [seed 2] d. Lapidus 6–2 6–1 6–3, Scanlon 6–2 6–0 6–3, De la Pena 6–1 6–1 6–3, Yzaga 4–6 6–3 6–4 6–0, Noah[seed 7] 6–2 6–2 6–4, Connors[seed 4] 6–2 6–3 7–5, McEnroe[seed 1] 7–6 6–3 6–4. **1986: won** [seed 1] d. Layendecker 6–3 6–2 6–0, Seguso 6–3 6–1 6–2, Svensson 6–3 6–3 6–4, Gilbert[seed 15] 7–5 6–1 6–2, Leconte[seed 8] 7–5 6–1 1–6 6–1, Edberg[seed 4] 7–6 6–2 6–3, Mecir[seed 16] 6–4 6–2 6–0. **1987: won** [seed 1] d. Moir 6–0 6–0 6–0, Fleurian 6–4 6–2 6–2, Pugh 6–1 6–1 6–2, Jarryd[seed 16] 6–2 7–6 6–4, McEnroe[seed 8] 6–4 7–6 6–3, Connors[seed 6] 6–4 6–2 6–2, Wilander [seed 3] 6–7 6–0 7–6 6–4. **1988: r/u** [seed 1] d. Mansdorf 6–2 6–7 6–1 5–7 6–0, Berger 6–2 6–4 6–1, S.Davis 6–1 6–4 6–2, Hlasek 6–4 5–7 6–2 6–4, Rostagno 6–2 6–2 6–0, Agassi[seed 4] 4–6 6–2 6–3 6–4, lost Wilander [seed 2] 6–4 4–6 6–3 5–7 6–4. **1989: r/u** [seed 1] d. Perez 6–1 7–6 6–4, Fitzgerald 6–2 6–1 6–1, Courier 6–1 6–2 6–3, Chesnokov[seed 16] 6–3 4–6 1–6 6–4 6–3, Mayotte[seed 9] 6–4 6–0 6–1, Agassi[seed 6] 7–6 6–1 3–6 6–1, lost Becker[seed 2] 7–6 1–6 6–3 7–6. **1990: qf** [seed 3] d. Laurendeau 7–5 6–2 6–2, Stich 6–4 5–7 6–4 6–3, Antonitsch 7–6 6–1 6–2, Bloom 6–0 6–3 6–4, lost Sampras[seed 12] 6–4 7–6 3–6 4–6 6–2. **1991: sf** [seed 5] d. Krajicek 3–6 2–6 6–4 7–6 6–0, Kuhnen 6–3 6–2 6–4, Woodbribge 3–6 6–3 6–4 6–3, Ivanisevic[seed 12] 7–5 6–7 6–4 6–2, Stich [seed 3] 6–3 3–6 4–6 7–6 6–1, lost Edberg [seed 2] 6–3 6–3 6–4. **1992: qf** [seed 9] d. Yzaga 6–7 6–1 7–5 4–6 6–3, Connors 3–6 6–3 6–2 6–0, C. Adams 2–6 6–4 6–3 6–4, Becker [seed 7] 6–7 6–2 6–7 6–3 6–4, lost Edberg [seed 2] 6–3 6–3 3–6 5–7 7–6.

CAREER DAVIS CUP RECORD
1978: September – *European Zone Final (Away) Gt.Britain d. Czechoslovakia 5–0.* R2 Lost C.Mottram 6–4 7–5 7–5. R4 Lost M.Cox 6–2 6–4 6–3. **1979: July** – *European Zone sf (Away) Czechoslovakia d. France 4–1.* R1 d. Y.Noah 6–3 6–3 3–6 9–7. R4 d. G.Moretton 6–1 6–2 6–2. **September** – *European Zone Final (Home) Sweden d. Czechoslovakia 3–2.* R2 Lost to B.Borg 6–4 7–5 6–2. R4 d. K.Johansson 8–10 6–4 6–4 4–6 6–1. **October** – *Inter–Zone sf (Away) Italy d. Czechoslovakia 4–1.* R2 Lost to A.Panatta 6–4 1–6 6–0 6–0. R4 Lost to C.Barazzutti 4–6 6–1 6–2 3–6 7–5. **1980: June** – *European Zone sf (Home) Czechoslovakia d. France 5–0.* R2 d. P.Portes 6–4 8–6 6–4. R4 d. C.Roger–Vasselin 6–4 7–5 6–4. **July** – *European Zone Flinal (Away) Czechoslovakia d. Rumania 4–1.* R1 d. d Haradau 6–4 6–1 6–3. R3 (+J.Kodes) d. D.Haradau/ F.Segarceanu 6–3 6–2 6–4. **September** – *Inter–Zone sf (Away) Czechoslovakia d. Argentina 3–2.* R2 d. G.Vilas 7–5 8–6 9–7. R3 (+T.Smid) d. J.Clerc/G.Vilas 6–2 6–4 6–3. R4 d. J.Clerc 6–1 7–5 6–8 6–2. **December** – *World Group Final (Home Czechoslovakia d. Italy 4–1.* R2 d. C.Barazzutti 4–6 6–1 6–1 6–2. R3 (+T.Smid) d. P.Bertolucci/A.Panatta 3–6 6–3 3–6 6–3 6–4. R5 d. G.Ocleppo 6–3 6–3. **1981: March** – *World Group 1r (Away) Czechoslovakia d. Switzerland 3–2..* R1 d. H.Guenthardt 6–3 7–5

6–0. R3 (+T.Smid) Lost to H.Guenthardt/ M.Guenthardt 6–3 3–6 2–6 6–3 6–4. R5 Lost to R.Stadler 6–6 Ret. **July –** *World Group qf (Away) USA d. Czechoslovakia 4–1* R1 d. J.McEnroe 6–4 14–12 7–5. R3 (+T.Smid) Lost to R.Lutz/S.Smith 9–7 6–3 6–2. R5 Lost to J.Connors 7–5 6–4. **1982: March –** *World Group 1r (Home) Czechoslovakia d. Germany 5–0.* R2 d. R.Gehring 6–1 6–2 6–2. R5 d. U.Pinner 6–1 6–3. **July –** *World Group qf (Away) France d. Czechoslovakia 3–2.* R2 d. T.Tulasne 6–3 4–6 6–3 9–11 6–4. R4 Lost to Y.Noah 6–2 3–6 7–9 6–3 6–4. **1983; March –** *World Group 1r (Away) Paraguay d. Czechoslovakia 3–2.* R1 d. F.Gonzalez 6–3 6–4 10–8. R3 Lost to F.Gonzalez/ V.Pecci 6–4 6–4 6–4. **1984: July –** *World Group qf (Home) Czechoslovakia d. France 3–2.* R1 Lost to H.Leconte 6–3 8–6 6–4. R4 d. G.Forget 11–9 6–4 6–2. **September –** *World Group sf (Away) Sweden d. Czechoslovakia 5–0.* R2 Lost to H.Sundstrom 4–6 3–6 6–3 6–1 6–1. R4 Lost to M.Wilander 6–3 4–6 6–2. **1985: August –** *World Group qf (Away) Czechoslovakia d. Ecuador 5–0.* R1 d. A.Gomez 5–3 Ret. R3 (+T.Smid) d. M.Aguirre/R.Ycaza 7–5 6–4 6–4. **October –** *World Group sf (Away) Germany d. Czechoslovakia 5–0.* R3 (+T.Smid) Lost to B.Becker/ A.Maurer 6–1 7–5 6–4.

GRAND PRIX MASTERS/ATP TOUR CHAMPIONSHIP (from 1990)
Played 12, won 5, r/u 4
1980: r/u In rr lost Connors 7–6 6–1, d. Solomon 6–3 6–1, d. Vilas 7–5 6–4; In sf d. G.Mayer 6–3 6–4; In f lost Borg 6–4 6–2 6–2. **1981: won** In rr d. Gerulaitis 4–6 7–5 6–2, d. Vilas 6–4 6–1, d Clerc w.o.; In sf d. McEnroe 6–4 6–2; In f d. Gerulaitis 6–7 2–6 7–6 6–2 6–4. **1982: won (12–man knock–out)** bye, d. Noah 6–4 7–5, Connors 6–3 6–1, McEnroe 6–4 6–4 6–2. **1983: r/u (12–man knock–out)** bye, d Gomez 6–2 1–0 ret., Connors 6–3 6–4, lost McEnroe 6–3 6–4 6–4. **1984: r/u (12–man knock–out)** bye, d. Nystrom 6–4 7–6, Connors 7–5 6–7 7–5, lost McEnroe 7–5 6–0 6–4. **1985: won (16–man knock–out)** d. Smid 6–1 6–0, Mayotte 6–3 6–3, Gomez 6–4 7–5, Becker 6–2 7–6 6–3. **1986: won** In rr d. Noah 6–4 6–4, d. Gomez 6–3 7–5, d. Edberg 6–3 6–4; In sf d. Wilander 6–4 6–2; In f d. Becker 6–4 6–4 6–4. **1987: won** In rr d. Gilbert 6–2 6–2, d. Connors 4–3 ret., d. Becker 6–4 6–7 6–3; In sf d. Gilbert 6–2 6–4; In f d. Wilander 6–2 6–2 6–3. **1988: r/u** In rr lost Hlasek 4–6 6–3 7–5, d. Agassi 1–6 7–6 6–3, d. Mayotte 6–2 3–6 6–3; In sf d. Edberg 6–3 7–6; In f lost Becker 5–7 7–6 3–6 6–2 7–6. **1989: sf** In rr d. Chang 6–1 6–3, d Krickstein 6–1 6–3, d. McEnroe 6–3 6–3; In sf lost Edberg 7–6 7–5. **1990: sf** In rr lost Becker 1–6 7–6 6–4, d. Muster 6–3 6–3, Gomez 6–4 6–1; In sf lost Edberg 6–4 6–2. **1991: sf** In rr d. Forget 6–2 6–4, Courier 6–2 6–3, Novacek 6–2 6–2; In sf lost Sampras 6–2 6–3.

ANDRE AGASSI (USA)   **Turned pro:**1986 (aged 16)

Born: Las Vegas, 29 April 1970, and lives there. **Father:** Emanuel Agassian, who boxed for Iran in the 1952 Olympics, and became Mike Agassi. **Brother:** Philip who usually travels with him. **Sisters:** Tamee, who plays college tennis, Rita who was married to Pancho Gonzales. **Agent:** International Management Group (Bill Shelton). **Coach:** Nick Bollettieri (from age of 13). Assisted from 1989 by Pat Etchenbery for movement and from 1990 by Gil Reyes for strength. **Height:** 5ft 11in (1.80m). **Weight:** 175lbs (79 kg).

Rankings: 1985: 618; **1986:** 91; **1987:** 5; **1988:** 3; **1989:** 7; **1990:** 4; **1991:** 10; **1992:** 9. **Highest:** 3 (7 November 1988).

1992 Prize Money: $1,127,834. **Career Earnings:** $5,451,203. **Career Titles:** 17.

Style: A go-for-broke right-handed hitter from the back of the court with early-ball forehands and double-handed backhands that are amongst the hardest-hit strokes in tennis. A fine serve and improving volleys, added to his agility and speed about the court, make him a fearsome opponent. Inevitably he hits many unforced errors and these sometimes contribute to unexpected losses.

CAREER HIGHLIGHTS (year:(*titles*))

Andre is a born–again Christian who collects motor cars. As a child, suffered from Osgood Schlatter's disease, which causes a bone in the knee to grow improperly. **1984:** Ranked 4 in US Boys' 14s and won Nat 14s. **1985:** Receiving expert counsel from brother-in-law Pancho Gonzales, he tested the waters of men's circuit. **1986:** Downed Mayotte and S.Davis on way to qf Stratton Mountain **1987: (1)** *Itaparica*. Reached first GP f at Seoul, won his 1st GP title at Itaparica at end of season and d Jarryd *en route* to sf Basel. **1988: (6)** *Memphis, Charleston, Forest Hills, Stuttgart, Stratton Mountain, Livingston.* After reaching 1st GS sf in Paris, he took a month's rest, missing Wimbledon. Made d Cup debut and qualified for Masters, but was restricted by a hand injury. **1989: (1)** *Orlando.* Could not maintain the high standards of 1988, having to wait until Orlando in Oct. for his lst title for 14 months. R/u Italian Open; reached 2nd GS sf at US Open and appeared in 4 other sf to qualify for Masters, but won no matches there. **1990: (4)** *San Francisco, Key Biscayne, Washington, ATP Champs.* Reached 1st Grand Slam f at French Open, where he shocked traditionalists with his lurid outfits, which included luminous cycling shorts under black denim shorts. Did not play Australian Open or Wimbledon, but was also r/u at US Open, where he was fined $3,000 for his conduct in 3r match v Korda (allegedly he spat at the umpire). In autumn was fined 20% of total earnings on ATP tour (excluding GS) for falling 2 tourns short of his commitment to the tour and was fined a further $25,000 at end of year for withdrawing from GS Cup after submitting an entry. Early in year won the Lipton at Key Biscayne (d. Jones, Gunnarsson, Gomez 6–7 6–2 6–3, Courier 4–6 6–3 6–1, Berger 5–7 6–1 6–1, Edberg 6–1 6–4 0–6 6–2) and r/u Indian Wells. His year finished on a high note when first he beat world No.1, Edberg, to win ATP Tour World Champ in Nov. and then played in US d Cup team that d Australia 3–2 in final. He withdrew with pulled stomach muscle in 4th rubber v Cahill. **1991: (2)** *Orlando, Washington.* Reached his 3rd GS final at French Open, but in losing to Courier, he again cast doubts on his ability to win a title at the highest level. Known generally for his garish outfits, he delighted both officials and crowds at Wimbledon with his pristine white attire and his enthusiasm. He reached qf there, but disappointed at US Open, falling in to Krickstein in first round At ATP World Champ he reached sf but again fell to Courier to finish the ATP year with just 2 titles and 2 sf finishes. **1992: (3)** *Atlanta, WIMBLEDON, Toronto* In Jan. dropped out of top 10 for 1st time since May 1988 and reached no sf until winning Atlanta in May for 1st title since July 1991. But everything came right for him at Wimbledon, where he removed Becker in 5s and outlasted Ivanisevic in a pulsating 5-set f to take his 1st GS title and return to top 10. Reached sf French Open and qf

US Open, where he wore Wimbledon colours, and won Toronto in summer. Qualified for ATP Champs but was forced to withdraw with an injury to his left thigh.

PRINCIPAL 1992 RESULTS (detailed Grand Slam results see below)
SINGLES: won WIMBLEDON, **won** Atlanta (d. Pernfors 7–5 6–2, de la Pena 6–3 6–3, Eltingh 3–6 6–3 6–4, Arraya 6–4 6–3, Sampras 7–5 6–4), **won** Toronto (d. Nestor 6–1 6–3, Rusedski 6–4 6–1, Mansdorf 6–2 6–4, Washington 2–6 6–2 6–1, Lendl 3–6 6–2 6–0), **sf** FRENCH OPEN. **DOUBLES:** (with J. McEnroe) **r/u** Toronto (lost Galbraith/Visser 6–4 6–4).

CAREER GRAND SLAM RECORD
AUSTRALIAN OPEN – Has never competed

FRENCH OPEN Played 6, r/u 2, sf 2
1987: 2r d. Arraya 6–2 4–6 6–1 7–5, lost Kuchna 6–4 6–3 6–3 **1988: sf** [seed 9] d. Perez Roldan 6–2 6–2 6–4, lost Wilander 4–6 6–2 7–5 5–7 6–0. **1989: 3r** [seed 5] d. J.Carlsson 6–4 6–4 6–1, Cane 6–2 6–3 6–3 lost Courier 7–6 4–6 6–3 6–2. **1990: r/u** [seed 3] d. Wostenholme, Woodbridge. Boetsch, Courier 6–7 6–1 6–4 6–0 , Chang 6–2 6–1 4–6 6–2, Svensson 6–1 6–4 3–6 6–3. lost Gomez 6–3 2–6 6–4 6–4. **1991: r/u** [seed 4] d. Rosset 3–6 7–5 6–4 6–3, Korda 6–1 6–2 6–2, P. McEnroe 6–2 6–2 6–0, Mancini 6–3 6–3 5–7 6–1, Hlasek 6–3 6–1 6–1, Becker [seed 2] 7–5 6–3 6–1, lost Courier [seed 9] 3–6 6–4 2–6 6–1 6–4. **1992: sf** [seed 11] d. Frana 6–1 6–4 6–4, Pozzi 6–0 6–2 6–1, Prpic 2–6 6–4 6–1 7–6, E.Sanchez 6–1 6–3 7–5, Sampras [seed 3] 7–6 6–2 6–1.

WIMBLEDON – Played 3, won 1, qf 1
1987: 1st lost Leconte [seed 9] 6–2 6–1 6–2. **1988–90:** Did not play. **1991: qf** [seed 5] d. Connell 4–6 1–6 7–5 6–3, Prpic 7–6 3–6 6–4 6 2. Krajicek 7–6 6–3 7–6, Eltingh 6–3 6–3 6 4, lost Wheaton (with injury to thigh) 6–2 0–6 3–6 7–6 6–2. **1992: won** [seed 12] d. Chesnokov 5–7 6–1 7–5 7–5, Masso 4–6 6–1 6–3 6–3, Rostagno 6–3 7–6 7–5, Saceanu 7–6 6–1 7–6, Becker [seed 4] 4–6 6–2 6–2 4–6 6–3, J.McEnroe 6–4 6–2 6–3, Ivanisevic [seed 8] 6–7 6–4 6–4 1–6 6–4.

US OPEN – Played 7, r/u 1, sf 2, qf 1
1986: 1st lost Bates 7–6 6–3 3–6 6–4. **1987: 1st** lost Leconte(11) 6–4 7–6 4–6 6–3. **1988: sf** [seed 4] d. Chang 7–5 6–3 6–2, Connors 6–2 7–6 6–1, lost Lendl 4–6 6–2 6–3 6–4. **1989: sf** [seed 6] d. Weiss, Broad, Johnson 6–1 7–6 6–2, Grabb 6–1 7–5 6–3, Connors 6–1 4–6 0–6 6–3 6–4, lost Lendl 7–6 6–1 3–6 6–1. **1990: r/u** [seed 4] d. Connell, Korda, Davin, Berger 7–5 6–0 6–2, Cherkasov 6–2 6–2 6–3, Becker 6–7 6–3 6–2 6–3, lost Sampras 6–4 6–3 6–2. **1991: 1r** [seed 8] lost Krickstein 7–5 7–6 6–2.**1992: qf** [seed 8] d. Pernfors 6–2 6–4 6–1, Roig 6–1 6–3 6–2, Siemerink 6–2 6–3 6–3, Costa [seed 10] 6–4 6–3 6–2, lost Courier [seed 1] 6–3 6–7 6–1 6–4.

CAREER DAVIS CUP RECORD
1988: April – *Zone 1 sf (Away) USA d. Peru 5–0.* R2 d. J.Yzaga 6–8 7–5 6–1 6–2, R5 Versus P.Arraya – Not played **July** – *Zone 1 Final (Away) USA d. Argentina 4–1.* R2 d. M.Jaite 6–2 6–2 6–1. R4 d. G.Perez-Roldan 2–6 6–2 8–6. **1989: February** – *World Group 1r (Home) USA d. Paraguay 5–0.* R2 d. H.Chapacu 6–2 6–1 6–1 R5 d. F.Gonzalez 6–2 6–4. **April** – *World Group Of (Home) USA d. France 5–0.* R2 d. H.Leconte 6–1 6–2 5–7 6–1 R4 d. Y.Noah 6–3 7–6. **July** – *World Group sf (Away) Germany d. USA 3–2.* R2 Lost to B.Becker 6–7 6–7 7–6 6–3 6–4 R4 Lost to C.Steeb 4–6 6–4 6–4 6–2. **1990: September** – *World Group sf (Away) USA d. Austria 3–2.* R2 d. H.Skoff 7–6 6–0 6–1 R4 Lost to T.Muster 6–2 6–2 7–6. **December** – *World Group Final (Home) USA d. Australia 3–2.* R1 d. R.Fromberg 4–6 6–2 4 6–6–2 6–4 R4 Lost to D. Cahill 6–4 4–6 Ret. **1991: September** – *World Group sf (Home) USA d. Germany 3–2.* R1 d. M.Stich 6–3 6–1 6–4. R5 d. C.Steeb 6–2 6–2 6–3. **November** – *World Group Final (Away) France d. USA 3–1.* R1 d. G.Forget 6–7 6–2 6–1 6–2 R5 Versus H.Leconte – Not played **1992: January** – *World Group 1r (Home) USA d. Argentina 5–0.* R2 d. A.Mancini 6–4 6–4 6–4 R5 d. M.Jaite 7–5 6–3. **March** – *World Group qf (Home) USA d. Czechoslovakia 3–2.* R2 d. P.Korda 6–2 6–4 6–1 R5 d. K.Novacek 7–5 6–0 6–0. **September** – *World Group sf*

(Home) USA d. Sweden 4–1. R2 d. S.Edberg 5–7 6–3 7–6 6–3 R5 d. N.Kulti 6–7 6–2 6–4.
December – *World Group Final (Home) USA d. Switzerland 3–1.* R1 d. J.Hlasek 6–1 6–2 6–2
R5 Versus M.Rosset – Not played.

GRAND PRIX MASTERS/ATP TOUR CHAMPIONSHIP (from 1990)
1990: won rr d. Sampras 6–4 6–2, d. E.Sanchez 6–0 6–3 lost Edberg 7–6 4–6 7–6; sf d.
Becker 6–2 6–4. Final: d. Edberg 5–7 7–6 7–5 6–2. **1991: sf** rr d. Becker 6–3 7–5, lost
Sampras 6–3 1–6 6–3, d. Stich 7–5 6–3; sf lost Courier 6–3 7–5.

RICHARD KRAJICEK (NED)   Turned pro: 1989

Born: Rotterdam, 6 December 1971. **Lives:** Monte Carlo, Monaco.
Father and Mother: Were Czech immigrants.
Agent: Advantage International.
Coach: Rohan Goetzke (Australia).
Height: 6ft 5in.(1.96m). **Weight:** 190lb (86 kg).

Rankings: 1989: 392; **1990:** 129; **1991:** 40; **1992:** 10. **Highest:** 10
(16 November 1992).

1992 Prize Money: $1,063,241. **Career Earnings:** $1,328,32. **Career Titles:** 3.

Style: A tall, wiry physique that is susceptible to injury. He has one of the finest serves in
the game plus an aggressive but erratic forehand and improving backhand that he used to
hit with two hands. He volleys with fine touch.

CAREER HIGHLIGHTS (year: *(titles)*)
He twice won Dutch Nat 12s and 14s. His career suddenly took off after he decided to
change from two-handed to one-handed backhand. **1990:** Won Verona and Casablanca
Challengers. **1991: (1)** *Hong Kong.* Reached last 16 Australian Open, unseeded, then at
Hong Kong in April won his 1st tour title in his 1st f. At New Haven upset Edberg *en route* to
qf (where he retired) and Hlasek and J. McEnroe in reaching sf Toulouse. At US Open held
2 mps v Lendl 1r before losing in 5s, and in doubles reached 2 finals with Siemerink, winning
Hilversum. **1992: (2)** *Los Angeles, Antwerp.* Upset Lendl 1r Sydney NSW Open, then made
a tremendous impact at Australian Open where, unseeded, he surprised Chang and Stich as
he swept to sf, where he was forced to def. v Courier with tendonitis of right shoulder. He
followed by winning Los Angeles and Antwerp (d. Courier), r/u Tokyo Suntory (d. Stich and
Edberg) and sf Sydney Indoor (d. Lendl again). These performances saw him become the
1st Dutchman in top 20 since Tom Okker in 1976 and at end of year he broke into the top 10,
the 20th player aged under 21 to do so. His last late surge at Antwerp gained him 8th place
at his 1st ATP Champ when Agassi and Lendl were forced to withdraw, but he won only 1
match there (v Chang).

PRINCIPAL 1992 RESULTS (detailed Grand Slam results below)
won Los Angeles (d. Youl 6–4 7–5, Black 6–3 6–3, Tarango 6–7 6–0 3–1 ret'd, Stolle 6–2
6–4, Woodforde 6–4 2–6 6–4), **won** Antwerp (d. Masur 6–3 4–6 6–2, Connell 6–4 6–4, Korda
3–6 6–1 7–6, Courier 4–6 6–4 7–5, Woodforde 6–2 6–2), **r/u** Tokyo Suntory (d. Thoms 6–3
7–6, Grabb 6–4 6–3, Stich 7–6 6–4, Edberg 6–3 7–5, lost Courier 6–4 6–4 7–6), **sf**
AUSTRALIAN OPEN, **sf** Sydney Indoor (d. Antonitsch 6–1 6–1, Borwick 6–3 4–6 6–2, Lendl
7–6 7–5, lost Ivanisevic 6–3 6–0).

CAREER GRAND SLAM RECORD
AUSTRALIAN OPEN – Played 2
1991: 4r d. Santoro 2–6 6–1 6–2 6–3, Korda 4–6 7–6 6–3 6–4, Cahill 6–7 6–3 6–3 7–6, lost
Caratti 6–3 6–4 6–7 3–6 6–4. **1992: sf** d. Saceanu 6–3 6–3 6–3, Grabb 6–2 7–6 6–1, Chang
[seed 14] 6–4 6–1 5–7 1–6 6–3, Bergstrom 7–5 7–6 6–3, Stich [seed 4] 5–7 7–6 6–7 6–4 6–4,
lost Courier, def.

FRENCH OPEN – Played 2
1991: 2r d. Altur 6–0 6–4 6–1, lost Stich 6–7 7–6 6–3 6–2. **1992: 3r** [seed 12] d. Clavet 7–6
6–7 6–3 7–6, Gustafsson 6–3 6–4 4–6 6–1, lost Perez 6–4 6–1 6–1.

WIMBLEDON – Played 2
1991: 3r d. Ruah 5–7 6–1 3–6 6–3 6–4, Larsson 6–3 6–4 6–3, lost Agassi [seed 5] 7–6 6–3
7–6. **1992: 3r** [seed 11] d. de Jager 7–5 6–1 6–2, Haarhuis 7–6 6–3 6–1, lost Boetsch 4–6 7–6
3–6 7–6 6–2.

US OPEN – Played 2
1991: 1r lost Lendl [seed 5] 3–6 2–6 6–4 7–6 6–0. **1992: 4r** [seed 15] d. Clavet 7–6 6–7 6–3 6–4, Markus 4–6 2–6 7–6 6–3 6–1, Woodforde 6–1 6–3 6–2, lost Edberg [seed 2] 6–4 6–7 6–3 3–6 6–4.

CAREER DAVIS CUP RECORD
1991: September – *World Group Qualifying (Away) Holland d. Mexico 5–0.* R3 (+J.Siemerink) d. L.Lavalle/J.Lozano 6–2 6–3 6–4. **1992: September –** *World Group Qualifying (Home) Holland d. Uruguay 4–1.* R1 d. D. Perez 6–2 6–4 7–6. R4 d. M.Filippini 7–5 7–6 6–3.

GRAND PRIX MASTERS/ATP TOUR CHAMPIONSHIP (from 1990)
1992: Equal 4th In rr lost Courier 6–7 7–6 7–5, d. Chang 2–6 6–3 7–6, lost Ivanisevic 6–4 6–3.

JORDI ARRESE (ESP)
Born Barcelona, 29 August 1964, and lives there; RH; 5ft 9in; 142lb; final 1992 ATP ranking 37; 1992 prize money $227,253.
Coached by Roberto Vizcaino. **1986:** (97) With a sf showing in his first tournament of the season at Nice, he set the tone for a successful year. **1987:** (128) Qf Palermo. **1988:** (33) Won 2 Challenger titles before reaching 1st SS sf at Hamburg and qf Kitzbuhel. **1989:** (44) Reached 1st GP f at Madrid despite being restricted by a back injury during the last 3 matches, for which he wore a neck brace. Upset Krickstein *en route* to sf Italian Open. **1990:** (39) Won San Remo in Aug., following with Prague the next week; sf Estoril and Athens. **1991:** (23) Won Madrid and Buzios; r/u Genova, Hilversum (d. Muster) and Athens; sf Geneva (d. Cherkasov), Palermo and upset Forget at Barcelona. **1992:** The highlight of his year came in Barcelona, where he won a silver Olympic medal. On the tour he won Athens and 2 Challenger titles; r/u Hilversum and sf Lisbon (d. Lendl), Bastad and Umag. **1992 HIGHLIGHTS – SINGLES: French Open 1r** (lost Cherkasov 6–1 6–3 5–7 6–7 6–3), **US Open 1r** (lost W. Ferreira [seed 12] 3–6 7–5 6–3 6–3), **Olympic silver medal** seed 16 (d. E. Chang 6–4 6–2 6–2, Gustafsson 6–2 4–6 6–1 3–6 9–7, Furlan 6–4 6–3 6–2, Lavalle 6–1 7–6 6–1, Cherkasov [seed 13] 6–4 7–6 3–6 6–3, lost Rosset 7–6 6–3 3–6 4–6 8–6); **won** Athens (d. Altur 7–6 6–2, Skoff 6–2 6–4, Jaite 6–3 6–2, Clavet 7–5 6–2, Bruguera 7–5 3–0 ret'd), **won** Salzburg Challenger (d. Schaller 7–6 7–6), **won** Oporto Challenger (d. Jonsson 2–6 6–1 6–0); **r/u** Hilversum (d. L. Jonsson 6–7 6–1 6–4, Champion 6–7 6–2 6–2, Wuyts 6–7 6–3 6–2, Tillstrom 6–3 6–3, lost Novacek 6–2 6–3 2–6 7–5); **sf** Lisbon (d. Azar 6–2 6–3, Riglewski 7–5 6–2, Lendl 6–3 4–6 7–5, lost Bruguera 6–1 6–1), **sf** Bastad (d. Naewie 7–5 5–7 6–2, Gorriz 6–4 2–6 6–2, Bergstrom 6–2 7–5, lost Gustafsson 7–5 6–3), **sf** Umag (d. Strelba 6–4 6–3, Devening 7–5 7–5, Altur 6–4 6–2, lost Muster 6–4 6–4). **CAREER HIGHLIGHTS – SINGLES: Olympics Silver medal 1992.**

JEREMY BATES (GBR)
Born Solihull, 19 June 1962; lives London; RH; 5ft 11in; 160lb; final 1992 ATP ranking 106; 1992 prize money $120,998.
Coached by Warren Jacques. **1982:** (329) Joined British D Cup squad. **1983:** (256). **1984:** (185). **1985:** (99) Sf Tel Aviv, qf Bristol. **1986:** (187) Qf Bristol. **1987:** (89) Sf Hong Kong and won Wimbledon mixed doubles with Durie. **1988:** (152) Qf Guaruja, Lyon and Rye Brook; r/u Australian Open doubles with Lundgren. **1989:** (96) Reached sf Johannesburg and qf Nancy; upset Gilbert at Tel Aviv. **1990:** (126) Won Durban Challenger and in doubles won Queen's with Curren. **1991:** (162) At Australian Open won a second GS mixed doubles title with Durie. **1992:** Played the tennis of his life to reach last 16 at Wimbledon, unseeded; he upset Chang 1r and held mp v Forget for a place in qf. **1992 HIGHLIGHTS – SINGLES: Australian Open 1r** (lost Edberg [seed 1] 6–4 6–2 6–4), **Wimbledon last 16** [unseeded] (d. Chang [seed 7] 6–4 6–3 6–3, J. Sanchez 7–6 6–3 6–4, Champion 7–5 6–4 6–7 4–6 6–4, lost Forget 6–7 6–4 3–6 7–6 6–3). **1992 HIGHLIGHTS – DOUBLES:** (with Warder) **r/u** Manchester (lost Galbraith/MacPherson 4–6 6–3 6–2).

CHRISTIAN BERGSTROM (SWE)
Born Gothenburg, 19 July 1967; lives Monte Carlo; RH; 5ft 11in; 150lb; final 1992 ATP ranking 58; 1992 prize money $173,966.
Coached by Tim Klein. **1984:** (606) Nat Jun Champ. **1985:** (410) European Jun Champ for 2nd year and No. 2 in ITF Jun rankings. **1986:** (120) Won Tampere Challenger. **1987:** (69) Qf Nancy; won Porto Challenger. **1988:** (71) Working with sports psychologist Lars Ryberg, he reached 1st GP sf at Bastad and upset Leconte *en route* to same stage at Toulouse. **1989:** (106) Qf Milan, Bastad and Toulouse. **1990:** (80) A qualifier at the French Open, he was 2 sets up v Chang before losing 3r; at Wimbledon he upset Forget *en route* to qf, unseeded, and in sf Wembley was 4–0 up fs v Chang but lost 7–2 on t-b. Played GS Cup, lost 1r Lendl (2) 6–4 6–0. **1991:** (44) Scored some useful upsets during the year in which he reached sf Wellington (d. Cherkasov), Munich (d. Muster) and Bastad; qf Rotterdam, Copenhagen, Toulouse and Basel (d. Stich); and in GS upset B. Gilbert *en route* to last 16 Wimbledon, unseeded. **1992:** Reached 1st tour f at Adelaide, where he extended

Ivanisevic to 3s, then upset Forget en route to last 16 Australian Open, unseeded; qf Sydney NSW Open, Bastad and Toulouse (d. Mansdorf). *1992 HIGHLIGHTS – SINGLES: Australian Open last 16* [unseeded] (d. L. Jonsson 7–6 7–6 6–2, Forget [seed 7] 7–6 2–6 6–3 6–4, Garnett 6–2 6–3 4–6 6–2, lost Krajicek 7–5 7–6 6–3), *French Open 1r* (lost Korda 6–4 6–2 6–2), *Wimbledon 1r* (lost Korda [seed 6] 7–5 7–6 6–4), *US Open 1r* (lost Santoro 6–4 6–4 7–6); r/u Adelaide (d. Youl 6–3 6–4, Fitzgerald 6–2 6–2, Delaitre 6–1 6–3, Steeb 7–6 6–4, lost Ivanisevic 1–6 7–6 6–4). *1992 HIGHLIGHTS – DOUBLES:* (with Gustafsson) *r/u* Bastad (lost Carbonell/Miniussi 6–4 7–5).

ARNAUD BOETSCH (FRA)
Born Meulam, 1 April 1969; lives Strasbourg; RH; 6ft; 168lb; final 1992 ATP ranking 27; 1992 prize money $343,596.
Coached by Francis Rawsthorne. *1985:* European Jun Champ and won Orange Bowl. *1988:* (275). *1989:* (212). *1990:* (176) Made his mark on the Challenger circuit, although he won no title. *1991:* (54) A wild-card, he reached last 16 French Open, unseeded, and upset Korda at US Open. Played his 1st tour f at Berlin after qualifying and reached qf Prague. Fourth member of winning French D Cup team v USA in Lyon where their 3–1 victory was first French success since 1932. *1992:* Upset Krajicek en route to last 16 Wimbledon, unseeded; r/u Bolzano; sf Monte Carlo (d. E. Sanchez) and Toulouse (d. Chesnokov) and reached 4 more qf. *1992 HIGHLIGHTS – SINGLES: Australian Open 2r* (d. Nargiso 6–3 6–3 6–4, lost Mansdorf 6–1 6–4 6–3), *French Open 1r* (lost Woodbridge 4–6 5–7 7–6 6–4 6–2), *Wimbledon last 16* [unseeded] (d. Grabb 7–6 7–5 6–4, Roig 6–4 6–2 6–2, Krajicek [seed 11] 4–6 7–6 3–6 7–6 6–2, lost Sampras [seed 5] 6–3 7–5 7–6), *US Open 3r* (d. Cherkasov 6–4 6–1 7–6, Tarango 4–6 6–4 6–3 7–6, lost Chang [seed 4] 6–3 6–3 6–1); *r/u* Bolzano (d. Champion 4–6 6–1 7–6, Jarryd 7–6 7–5, Camporese 6–4 6–3, Delaitre 7–6 7–5, lost Enqvist 6–2 1–6 7–6J; *sf* Monte Carlo (d. Miniussi 6–3 6–2, Mancini 7–5 7–6, E. Sanchez 4–6 6–1 6–2, Steeb 1–6 6–2 6–0, lost Muster 7–5 6–4); *sf* Toulouse (d. Chesnokov 6–3 6–2, Pioline 6–2 6–2, Bergstrom 6–3 6–2, lost Forget 6–3 6–4). *1992 HIGHLIGHTS – DOUBLES:* (with Forget) *r/u* Bordeaux (lost Casal/E. Sanchez 6–1 6–4).

SERGI BRUGUERA (ESP)
Born Barcelona, 16 January 1971, and lives there; RH; 6ft 1in; 160lb; final 1992 ATP ranking 16; 1992 prize money $603,378.
Coached by his father, Luis. *1987:* (333) Nat Jun Champ. *1989:* (26) Upset Gomez and Connors en route to 1st GP sf at Italian Open, following with his 2nd and 3rd at Gstaad and Stuttgart, as well as reaching last 16 French Open. Voted ATP Newcomer of the Year. *1990:* (28) Recorded some big upsets during the year. Removed top seed Edberg in ss 1r French Open; r/u Gstaad (d. Chesnokov) and Geneva; sf Adelaide (took Muster to 3s and Paris Open (d. Gomez). Won 2 doubles titles. *1991:* (11) Enjoyed an extraordinary month in April, when he upset Chesnokov at Estoril en route to his 1st career title, upset the same player and Becker back-to-back in reaching f Barcelona and beat Becker again in f Monte Carlo, these triumphs taking him into top 10 1st time. He also won Athens (d. Muster); r/u Gstaad (d. Gomez and Ivanisevic); sf Italian Open and Lyon. *1992:* Continued his winning ways at Madrid, Gstaad (d. Ivanisevic), and Palermo, was r/u Lisbon, Bordeaux and Athens (where he retired v Arrese with a hand injury) and reached sf Barcelona. Won all his matches as ESP won World Team Cup. *1992 HIGHLIGHTS – SINGLES: French Open 1r* (lost Lendl [seed 10] 6–4 6–2 6–1); *US Open 2r* (d. R. Gilbert 4–6 6–3 6–4 6–3, lost W. Ferreira [seed 12] 6–7 6–2 3–6 6–1 6–2), *Olympics 2r* [seed 11] (d. Castle 6–1 6–2 6–3, lost Koevermans 1–6 6–3 6–3 6–2); *won* Madrid (d. Furlan 6–1 3–6 6–3, Fontang 1–6 6–1 6–4, Rosset 6–3 7–6, J. Sanchez 6–4 6–2, Costa 7–6 6–2 6–2), *won* Gstaad (d. Layendecker 6–3 6–4, Rhode 6–4 6–1, Ivanisevic 6–3 6–2, Markus 4–6 7–5 7–6, Clavet 6–1 6–4), *won* Palermo (d. Burillo 6–2 2–6 6–2, Karbacher 6–3 6–1, Fontang 6–2 6–2, Clavet 6–1 6–4, E. Sanchez 6–1 6–3); *r/u* Lisbon (d. Geserer 6–3 6–1, B. Gilbert 7–6 4–1 ret'd, Cunha–Silva 6–2 6–1, Arrese 6–1 6–1, lost Costa 4–6 6–2 6–2), *r/u* Bordeaux (d. Wuyts 6–3 7–5, Gorriz 6–7 6–2 6–0, Lopez 6–4 6–2, Pioline 6–2 6–4, lost Medvedev 6–3 1–6 6–2), *r/u* Athens (d. Bavelas 6–2 6–1, de la Pena 6–3 6–1, Gustafsson 6–2 ret'd, J. Sanchez 7–5 6–7 6–4, lost

Arrese 7–5 3–0 ret'd); *sf* Barcelona (d. Gomez 7–5 6–2, Jaite 7–5 6–1, Svensson 6–4 6–4, lost Gustafsson 6–4 7–5).

OMAR CAMPORESE (ITA)
Born Bologna, 8 May 1968, and lives there; RH; 6ft 2in; 172lb; final 1992 ATP ranking 42; 1992 prize money $317,957.
1986: (766) Won Italian Jun and r/u European Jun Champs. **1987:** (283) R/u Mediterranean Games. **1988:** (216) Qf Bologna and won Vienna Challenger. **1989:** (49) Won Vienna Challenger again and upset Mecir *en route* to qf Italian Open. **1990:** (45) Reached 1st tour f at San Marino; sf Florence, Genova and Hilversum and upset Berger *en route* to qf Italian Open. In doubles with various partners reached 4 f, winning Milan and Madrid. **1991:** (24) Returning from a 3-month lay-off with a knee injury, he reached sf Wellington in Jan. then extended Becker to 14–12 5s in epic 5hr 22min match in 3r at Australian Open – the longest ever played at the tourn and only 1 minute shorter than the marathon between Gonzales and Pasarell at Wimbledon in 1969. Followed in March with the title at Rotterdam, where he d. Lendl in f, reached sf Bologna, and finished the year by upsetting Hlasek and Courier *en route* to qf Paris Open. Won 3 doubles titles from 4 f with Ivanisevic. **1992:** Reached last 16 Australian Open, unseeded, then beat Ivanisevic to win Milan in Feb. These successes took him into top 20 – becoming the 1st Italian to rank there since Panatta in 1981. Appeared in sf Sydney NSW Open and qf Stuttgart, Hamburg (d. Lendl) and Bolzano. **1992 HIGHLIGHTS – SINGLES: Australian Open last 16** [unseeded] (d. Hogstedt 3–6 6–2 6–2 2–6 6–1, Youl 6–3 6–4 7–6, Wahlgren 6–4 6–2 7–6, lost Lendl [seed 5] 7–6 6–1 6–3); **French Open 1r** (lost Gorriz 3–6 6–4 6–4 6–4); **Wimbledon 1r** (lost Becker [seed 4] 7–5 6–3 7–5); **US Open 3r** (d. Raoux 6–4 7–6 6–1, Davis 6–3 3–6 5–7 6–4 7–6, lost Costa [seed 10] 6–1 6–2 6–3); **Olympics 2r** (d. Rios 6–2 6–2 6–0, lost E. Sanchez [seed 12] 6–4 6–2 6–1); **won** Milan (d. Nijssen 5–7 7–5 7–5, Thoms 7–6 4–6 7–6, J. Sanchez 6–3 6–4, Cherkasov 6–3 4–6 6–3, Ivanisevic 3–6 6–3 6–4); *sf* Sydney NSW Open (d. Tarango 7–5 2–6 7–6, Gustafsson 6–3 7–6, Bergstrom 6–7 6–4 6–1, lost E. Sanchez 6–4 7–6).

ANDREI CHERKASOV (CIS)
Born Ufa, 4 July 1970; lives Moscow; RH; 5ft 10in; 160lb; final 1992 ATP ranking 32; 1992 prize money $319,456.
Coached by Natalia Rogova. **1986:** (870) R/u to Courier at Orange Bowl. **1987:** (409) No. 3 in ITF Jun rankings; r/u to Wheaton at US Open Jun and to Courier at Orange Bowl again. **1988:** (236). **1989:** (82) Broke into top 100 after qf showing at Milan and top 50 after winning 2 Challenger titles. At Sydney reached f, having never before reached GP qf. **1990:** (21) Upset Gomez *en route* to his 1st GS qf at Australian Open, and Chang in reaching same stage at US Open, unseeded both times. Won his 1st tour title at Moscow in Oct.; sf Nice (d. Berger) and Umag. Played in GS Cup but lost Sampras 1r. **1991:** (21) Won Moscow, r/u Brussels (d. Chesnokov) and reached 4 more qf. A wild-card entry at French Open, he reached last 16, upsetting J. McEnroe 1r. **1992:** Upset Edberg *en route* to qf French Open, unseeded, and Sampras on his way to a bronze medal at Olympics. Appeared in sf Milan and Bolzano plus 4 more qf. **1992 HIGHLIGHTS – SINGLES: Australian Open 2r** (d. Kuhnen 6–7 7–5 6–0 6–1, lost J. McEnroe 7–5 3–6 6–4 6–3), **French Open qf** [unseeded] (d. Arrese 6–1 6–3 5–7 6–7 6–3, Azar 5–7 7–6 6–1 6–2, Edberg [seed 2] 6–4 6–3 7–6, Pioline 6–3 6–3 7–6, lost Korda 6–4 6–7 6–2 6–4); **Wimbledon 1r** (lost Sampras [seed 5] 6–1 6–3 6–3); **US Open 1r** (lost Boetsch 6–4 6–1 7–6); **Olympic bronze medal** [seed 13] (d. Smith 6–1 6–0 3–6 6–1, Prpic 6–4 6–7 6–4 6–3, Sampras [seed 3] 6–7 1–6 7–5 6–0 6–3, Oncins 6–1 6–4 6–7 4–6 6–2, lost Arrese [seed 16] 6–4 7–6 3–6 6–3); *sf* Milan (d. Furlan 6–2 6–2, Volkov 7–5 7–5, Prpic 6–4 4–6 6–3, lost Camporese 6–3 4–6 6–3), *sf* Bolzano (d. Zoecke 6–4 7–6, Altur 6–1 7–5, Svensson 6–4 6–1, lost Enqvist 4–6 6–3 7–6).

ANDREI CHESNOKOV (CIS)
Born Moscow, 2 February 1966, and lives there; RH; 2HB; 6ft 2in; 167lb; final 1992 ATP ranking 30; 1992 prize money $282,666.
Coached by Tatiana Naoumko. **1980:** Won Russian Nat Jun Champ. **1982:** Won Russian

Nat Jun Champ again. *1984:* Beat Glickstein and Perkis in D Cup. *1985:* (136) Upset Teltscher at French Open. *1986:* (36) Reached qf French Open, upsetting No. 2 seed Wilander in 3r, and last 16 US Open. *1987:* (52) Reached last 16 US Open and won his 1st GP title in his 1st f at Florence, becoming 1st from his country to win a title since Metreveli won S Orange in 1974. *1988:* (14) Won Orlando, r/u Wellington, Sydney and Toulouse. In GS reached qf both Australian Open and French Open (d. Cash). *1989:* (22) Upset Wilander *en route* to sf French Open after winning Nice and Munich back-to-back in spring. *1990:* (12) Won Monte Carlo (d. E. Sanchez and Muster) and Tel Aviv; r/u Auckland and Italian Open (d. E. Sanchez again); sf Barcelona and New Haven *1991:* (31) Upset Lendl in ss *en route* to the title at Montreal, as well as reaching sf Estoril and Brisbane. *1992:* Upset W. Ferreira and Courier back-to-back *en route* to f Indian Wells and handed the same treatment to Edberg at the Olympics. Also reached sf Scottsdale, Schenectady and Vienna. *1992 HIGHLIGHTS – SINGLES: Australian Open last 16* [unseeded] (d. Fontang 6–3 7–6 6–1, Bloom 4–6 6–3 6–4 6–4, P. McEnroe 6–4 1–6 1–6 6–1 6–3, lost Edberg [seed 1] 6–1 7–5 6–2); *French Open 1r* (lost Wheaton 3–6 3–6 6–4 6–0 6–2); *Wimbledon 1r* (lost Agassi [seed 12] 5–7 6–1 7–5 7–5); *US Open 3r* (d. Albano 6–4 6–4 6–3, lost Courier [seed 1] 4–6 6–3 6–3 6–1); *Olympics 2r* (d. Edberg [seed 2] 6–0 6–4 6–4, lost Furlan 7–6 6–4 6–4); *r/u* Indian Wells (d. Youl 6–4 6–3, W. Ferreira 6–4 6–1, Courier 6–4 7–5, E. Sanchez 7–5 7–5, Stich 1–6 7–6 6–3, lost Chang 6–3 6–4 7–5); *sf* Scottsdale (d. Shelton 4–6 6–4 6–2, Pescariu 7–5 6–0, Rosset 7–6 6–4, lost Pescosolido 6–7 6–3 6–3); *sf* Schenectady (d. Schapers 6–4 7–6, Mattar 6–4 6–3, Olhovskiy 6–1 7–6, lost W. Ferreira 6–4 6–2); *sf* Vienna (d. Pescosolido 6–4 6–7 6–4, Poliakov 4–6 7–6 6–1, Gollwitzer 7–6 6–2, lost Pozzi 6–2 6–7 6–4).

FRANCISCO CLAVET (ESP)
Born Aranjuez, 24 October 1968; lives Madrid; LH; 6ft; 156lb; final 1992 ATP ranking 22; 1992 prize money $377,388.
Elder brother of José. *1987:* (638). *1988:* (290). *1989:* (188) Qf Kitzbuhel. *1990:* (90) Won his 1st tour title at Hilversum as a lucky loser, upsetting Jaite on the way. *1991:* (30) Reached sf Stuttgart Mercedes (d. Muster and Gomez), Kitzbuhel, Schenectady, Athens and Sao Paulo, reaching 3 more qf and last 16 French Open, unseeded. *1992:* Enjoying another consistent year he was r/u Gstaad and San Marino and reached sf Philadelphia, Indian Wells, Madrid, Athens and Palermo. *1992 HIGHLIGHTS – SINGLES: Australian Open 2r* (d. Strelba 6–2 7–6 2–6 7–5, lost Woodforde 6–7 6–4 6–1 3–6 7–5); *French Open 1r* (lost Krajicek [seed 12] 7–6 6–7 6–3 7–6); *Wimbledon 1r* (lost Wheaton [seed 14] 6–3 6–3 6–3); *US Open 1r* (lost Krajicek 7–6 6–7 6–3 6–4); *r/u* Gstaad (d. Costa 6–4 3–6 6–3, Hlasek 6–2 6–4, E. Sanchez 7–5 7–5, Santoro 6–3 6–2, lost Bruguera 6–1 6–4); *r/u* San Marino (d. Masso 6–1 1–6 7–6, Mezzadri 6–0 6–1, Tillstrom 6–0 6–1, Agenor 7–6 7–5, lost Novacek 7–5 6–2); *sf* Philadelphia (d. Masur 6–7 6–3 7–6, Rostagno 7–6 7–6, Grabb 2–6 7–5 6–3, lost Mansdorf 5–7 6–3 6–2); *sf* Indian Wells (d. MacPhie 6–4 6–3, Wheaton 6–2 6–3, Novacek 6–2 4–6 6–3, Hlasek 6–1 6–2, lost Chang 6–0 6–1); *sf* Madrid (d. Oncins 6–3 6–4, J. McEnroe 6–2 6–1, Mancini 7–5 6–1, lost Costa 7–5 6–4); *sf* Athens (d. Corrales 6–1 6–2, Carbonell 6–4 7–6, Goellner 6–2 6–2, lost Arrese 7–5 6–2); *sf* Palermo (d. Pistolesi 6–1 1–6 6–3, Prpic 6–4 6–3, Skoff 6–1 6–1, lost Bruguera 6–1 6–4). *1992 HIGHLIGHTS – DOUBLES:* (with Costa) *r/u* Madrid (lost Galbraith/P. McEnroe 6–3 6–2).

JIMMY CONNORS (USA)
Born East St Louis, Ill., 2 September 1952; lives Belleville, Ill. and Santa Ynez, Cal., LH; 2HB; 5ft 10in; 155lb; final 1992 ATP ranking 84; 1992 prize money $139,431.
Wife Patti; son Brett (born 1979); daughter Aubrie-Leigh (born Dec. 1984). One of the game's greatest players, he was taught by his mother and grandmother, growing up outside St Louis in Bellville, Ill. Moving to California, he received expert tutelage from the two great Panchos – Gonzales and Segura – during his crucial late teenage years. His exceptional record from the mid-70s into the mid-80s is an enormous tribute to his skill and willpower. *1971:* Won NCAA title as UCLA freshman. *1972:* Won first pro title in Jacksonville and made Wimbledon debut, upsetting 7th seed Hewitt *en route* to qf, where he lost to Nastase. *1973:* Won first important title – US Pro – signalling that he was ready

to take over American tennis when he stopped Smith in 1r and Ashe in f. Won Wimbledon doubles with Nastase. *1974:* (1) Rose to No. 1 in world, winning Wimbledon, US and Australian Opens and 99 of 103 matches. *1975:* (1) He slipped to No. 2 in minds of most experts, losing in f Wimbledon, US and Australian Opens, falling to Ashe in most critical match of the year in Wimbledon f. Won US Open doubles with Nastase. *1976:* (1) Won second US Open crown (on clay this time). *1977:* (1) Beaten again in Wimbledon and US Open f by Borg and Vilas, but salvaged year with triumph at Masters. *1978:* (1) Avenged Wimbledon f loss to Borg at US Open. *1979:* (2) Beaten in sf Wimbledon by Borg and sf US Open by McEnroe, he slipped to third in world on most experts' lists. *1980:* (3) Ousted by McEnroe in both Wimbledon and US semis he nevertheless played with renewed inspiration and conviction. *1981:* (3) Lost Wimbledon and US semis to Borg and returned briefly to represent US in D Cup for first time since Dec. 75. *1982:* (2) Despite No. 2 computer ranking behind McEnroe, he was everyone else's choice for No. 1 as he won second Wimbledon and fourth US Open crowns and 7 of 18 tournaments entered; was deservedly awarded ITF World Champion's award. *1983:* (3) Took fifth US Open title after disappointment of 4r loss to Curren at Wimbledon, the first time in 12 years he had failed to reach qf. *1984:* (2) Reached fifth Wimbledon and joined forces with McEnroe to lead US into D Cup f where they lost to Sweden. Won Seiko Tokyo. *1985:* (4) For first time since 1972, did not win a singles title but he appeared in his 12th consecutive US Open sf. *1986:* (8) Again did not win a title but reached 4 f. Missed the Masters and suffered first Wimbledon 1r loss in 15 years, then beaten in 3r at US Open after an early-year suspension had kept him out of French Open. *1987:* (4) After taking a 3-month break Nov–Jan, he played a lighter winter schedule and, with the pressure off him to win, he enjoyed his best season for 4 years, reaching f 3 times, with a win–loss record of 52–16 going into Masters for which he qualified a record 11th time. Played superbly and with tremendous spirit to reach sf Wimbledon, coming back from 1–6 1–6 1–4 to d. Pernfors in last 16; sf US Open, qf French Open, r/u Memphis, Orlando and Queen's and reached sf 5 more times. *1988:* (7) At Washington in July won his 1st title since 1984 and followed with his record 107th career title at Toulouse, also reaching f LIPC and Milan, sf Toronto and Basle and qf US Open. However, he was plagued by injury throughout the year and withdrew from Masters to undergo surgery on a growth between 2 toes on his left foot and a long-standing problem with the ball on his right foot. In Oct. he slipped from top 10 for 2 weeks for 1st time since ATP rankings began in 1973, a record approached by no other man. During that time he was No. 1 for a record total of 263 weeks. *1989:* (14) Returned to action in Feb., reaching qf Memphis. Won Toulouse and Tel Aviv during the year and achieved his best showing in GS at US Open, where he d. Edberg to reach qf, narrowly losing to Agassi. *1990:* (936) Returning after foot surgery in Dec. the previous year, he suffered an injury to his left wrist in his 1st tourn at Milan, and although he returned in autumn, he lost 2 consecutive matches and eventually underwent surgery in Oct. *1991:* (48) As determined as ever, and enjoying his tennis all the more in his 20th pro season, this remarkable man confounded all those who had written him off. He beat Riglewski 1r LIPC for his 1st match victory since Oct 1989, then at French Open, in only his 5th tourn back, he reached 3r but was forced to retire in 5s v Chang, suffering from exhaustion and back problems. When he played Krickstein at Wimbledon, where he reached 3r, he became the 1st man to play 100 matches there, and followed at Long Island with his 1st qf appearance since 1989. The triumph of his year, though, came at the US Open where, ranked 174, he was given a wild-card entry. He delighted the crowds by reaching sf at age 39 (oldest to reach that stage since Rosewall in 1974), recovering from 2 sets and 0–3 down v P. McEnroe 1r and outlasting Krickstein in another 5s contest in 4r, both matches lasting more than 4 hours. He followed with sf appearance at Basel. *1992:* Voted Comeback Player of the Year and still a force in the game, he upset Stich *en route* to sf Memphis and reached qf Atlanta, Los Angeles, Indianapolis. *1992 HIGHLIGHTS – SINGLES: French Open 1r* (lost Stich [seed 4] 7–5 3–6 6–7 6–1 6–2), *Wimbledon 1r* (lost Herrera 6–2 1–6 7–5 6–3), *US Open 2r* (d. Oncins 6–1 6–2 6–3, lost Lendl [seed 9] 2–6 6–4 6–3 6–4); *sf* Memphis (d. Curren 6–2 6–2, Stich 5–6 7–6 7–5, Krickstein 3–6 6–2 6–3, lost Washington 6–2 7–5). *CAREER HIGHLIGHTS – SINGLES: Australian Open – won 1974*

(d. Dent 7–6 6–4 4–6 6–3), *r/u 1975* (lost Newcombe 7–5 3–6 6–4 7–6); **Wimbledon– won 1974** (d. Rosewall 6–1 6–1 6–4), **won 1982** (d. Alexander 7–6 4s, Gitlin 7–5 4s, G. Mayer 6–1 6–2 7–6, Edmondson 6–4 6–3 6–1, McEnroe 3–6 6–3 6–7 7–6 6–4), *r/u 1975* (lost Ashe 6–1 6–1 5–7 6–4), *r/u 1977* (lost Borg 3–6 6–2 6–1 5–7 6–4), *r/u 1978* (lost Borg 6–2 6–2 6–3), *r/u 1984* (d. Lendl 6–7 6–3 7–5 6–1, lost McEnroe 6–1 6–1 6–2), *sf 1979* (lost Borg 6–2 6–3 6–2), **sf 1980** seed 3 (lost McEnroe 6–3 3–6 6–3 6–4), **sf 1981** (d. V. Amritraj 2–6 5–7 6–4 6–3 6–2, lost Borg 0–6 4–6 6–3 6–0 6–4), **sf 1985** (lost Curren 6–2 6–2 6–1), **sf 1987** (lost Cash 6–4 6–4 6–1); **US Open – won 1974** (d. Rosewall 6–1 6–0 6–1), **won 1976** (d. Borg 6–4 3–6 7–6 6–4), **won 1978** (d. McEnroe 6–2 6–2 7–5, Borg 6–4 6–2 6–2), **won 1982** (d. Arias 6–4 4–6 6–4 6–1, Nastase 6–3 6–3 6–4, Harmon 6–1 3–6 6–4, Vilas 6–1 3–6 6–2 6–3, Lendl 6–3 6–2 4–6 6–4), **won 1983** (d. Lendl 6–3 6–7 7–5 6–0), *r/u 1975* (lost Orantes 6–4 6–3 6–3), *r/u 1977* (lost Vilas 2–6 6–3 7–6 6–0), **sf 1979** (lost McEnroe 6–3 6–3 7–5), **sf 1980** seed 3 (lost McEnroe 6–4 5–7 0–6 6–3 7–6), **sf 1981** (lost Borg 6–2 7–5 6–4), **sf 1984** (lost McEnroe 6–4 4–6 7–5 4–6 6–3), **sf 1985** (lost Lendl 6–2 6–3 7–5), **sf 1987** (lost Lendl 6–4 6–2 6–2), **sf 1991**; Masters – won 1978 (d. Borg 6–4 1–6 6–4), **sf 1979** seed 3 (lost Gerulaitis 7–5 6–2), **sf 1980** seed 4 (lost Borg 6–4 6–7 6–3), **sf 1982** (lost Lendl 6–3 6–1), **sf 1983** (lost Lendl 6–3 6–4), **sf 1984** (lost Lendl 7–6 5–7 7–5); **WCT Finals – won 1977** (d. Stockton 6–7 6–1 6–4 6–3), **won 1980** seed 2 (d. Scanlon, Lendl, McEnroe 2–6 7–6 6–1 6–2); **US CC – won 1974** (d. Borg 5–7 6–3 6–4), **won 1976** (d. Fibak 6–2 6–4) **won 1978** (d. Higueras 7–5 6–1), **won 1978** (d. Vilas 6–1 2–6 6–4), *r/u 1972* (lost Hewitt 6–1 7–6), *r/u 1977* (lost Orantes 6–1 6–3); **US Pro Indoor – won 1976** (d. Borg 7–6 6–4 6–0), **won 1978** (d. Tanner 4–6 2–6 3), **won 1979** (d. Ashe 6–3 6–4 6–1), **won 1980** (d. McEnroe 6–3 2–6 6–3 3–6 6–4); **US Indoor – won 1973** (d. Meiler), **won 1974** (d. McMillan), **won 1975** (d. Gerulaitis 6–1 fs), **won 1978** (d. Tim Gullikson 7–6 6–3), **won 1979** (d. Ashe 6–4 5–7 6–3), **won 1983** (d. G. Mayer 7–5 6–0), **won 1984** (d. Leconte 6–3 4–6 7–5); **39 (lost** Clerc **4–6 6–2 4–6 7–5 6–0),** sf 1985 (d. Edberg, lost Lendl 6–2 6–3 6–1). **CAREER HIGHLIGHTS – DOUBLES:** (with Nastase) **Wimbledon – won 1973** (d. Cooper/Fraser 3–6 6–3 6–4 8–9 6–1); **US Open – won 1975** (d. Okker/Riessen); **French Open – r/u 1973** (lost Newcombe/Okker 6–4 fs). **MIXED DOUBLES:** (with Evert) **US Open – r/u 1974** (lost Masters/Teeguarden 6–1 7–6).

CARLOS COSTA (ESP)
Born Barcelona, 22 April 1968, and lives there; RH; 6ft; 162lb; final 1992 ATP ranking 14; 1992 prize money $598,547.
Coached by Robert Vizcaino. **1986:** Nat Jun Champ. **1988:** (243). **1989:** (201) Won Madrid doubles with Carbonell. **1990:** (151) Won Zaragoza Challenger; upset Korda and Cherkasov at Barcelona. **1991:** (55) Reached sf Florence and sf Guaruja Bliss; won Venice and Siracusa Challengers. Reached 2 doubles, winning San Marino with Arrese. **1992:** Really came into his own during the year and broke into the top 20 after upsetting E. Sanchez and Bruguera *en route* to his 1st tour title at Lisbon, and following with Barcelona in April. R/u Madrid and Italian Open; sf Hamburg (d. Agassi). **1992 HIGHLIGHTS – SINGLES: French Open last 16** [seed 9] (d. Braasch 6–1 6–0 3–6 6–3, Schaller 7–6 6–3 6–2, W. Ferreira 2–6 6–2 6–2 6–2, lost Ivanisevic 6–3 4–6 6–1 6–1); **Wimbledon 2r** (d. Limberger 6–1 4–6 5–7 6–3 6–3); **US Open last 16** [seed 10] (d. Van Rensburg 6–4 5–7 6–3 6–2, Mronz 6–3 6–1 6–2, Camporese 6–1 6–2 6–3, lost Agassi [seed 8] 6–4 6–3 6–2); **won** Lisbon (d. Prpic 6–1 7–6, Gomez 6–2 6–4, de la Pena 6–4 6–1, E. Sanchez 4–6 7–6 7–6, Bruguera 4–6 6–2 6–2); **won** Barcelona (d. Furlan 6–2 7–5, Filippini 6–4 6–4, Eltingh 7–6 7–6, R. Gilbert 7–6 6–3, Mancini 6–3 6–3, Gustafsson 6–4 7–6 6–4); *r/u* Madrid (d. Viloca 7–6 7–6, Lopez 6–2 6–0, Boetsch 6–4 6–1, Clavet 7–5 6–4, lost Bruguera 7–6 6–2 6–2); *r/u* Italian Open (d. Krickstein 6–4 6–4, W. Ferreira 6–3 7–5, Mansdorf 6–2 7–5, Yzaga 6–4 6–0, Korda 6–4 6–3, lost Courier 7–6 6–0 6–4); **sf** Hamburg (d. Kuhnen 6–2 6–2, Agassi 3–6 6–1 6–2, Delaitre 6–2 6–3, Haarhuis 4–6 6–4 6–3, lost Edberg 7–5 7–6). **1992 HIGHLIGHTS – DOUBLES:** (with Clavet) *r/u* Madrid (lost Galbraith/P. McEnroe 6–3 6–2).

FRANCO DAVIN (ARG)
Born Buenos Aires, 11 January 1970 and lives there; LH; 5ft 8in; 140lb; final 1992 ATP ranking 46; 1992 prize money $156,723.

Coached by Raul Perez-Roldan. *1985:* (508). *1986:* (111) R/u Buenos Aires. *1987:* (166) Qf Bari and Bologna. *1988:* (94) Qf St Vincent and won Marrakech Challenger. 1989: (73) Won his first tour title at St Vincent as well as reaching f Bologna, sf Athens and Prague. 1990: (35) Won Palermo (d. Aguilera); r/u Estoril (d. Aguilera again) and Athens; sf Bologna. *1991:* (111) Reached qf French Open, unseeded, and appeared at same stage at Madrid, San Marino and Hilversum. *1992:* Won 2 Challenger titles and on the main tour was r/u Prague and Umag; upset Agassi *en route* to sf Tampa and reached 4 other qf. *1992 HIGHLIGHTS – SINGLES: French Open 1r* (lost Nargiso 6–4 3–6 6–3 0–6 6–1); *US Open 1r* (lost Weiss 6–1 ret'd); won Parioli Challenger (d. Roig 6–1 6–4); *won* Turin Challenger (d. Furlan 7–6 3–6 6–1); *r/u* Prague (d. Vajda 6–7 6–2 7–6, Arrese 6–2 6–2, Svensson 6–2 2–6 6–3, Perez-Roldan 6–3 6–2, lost Novacek 6–1 6–1); *r/u* Umag (d. Zillner 6–1 6–2, Corretja 6–4 6–4, Medvedev w.o., Skoff 2–0 ret'd, lost Muster 6–1 4–6 6–4); *sf* Tampa (d. Fromberg 6–4 6–3, Fleurian 4–6 6–3 6–4, Agassi 6–4 7–6, lost Washington 3–6 6–4 2–6).

BRIAN DUNN (USA)
Born Tampa, Fla., 5 April 1974; lives Brandon, Fla.; RH; 2HB; 6ft 6in; 200lb; final 1992 ATP ranking 473; 1992 prize money $22,405.
1991: Won Nat 18s CC. *1992:* In Jun tennis won US Open over Behr; r/u Australian Open to Doyle and Wimbledon to Skoch; won Nat 18s. *1992 HIGHLIGHTS – SINGLES: US Open 2r* (d. Zoecke 6–4 6–2 6–3, lost C. Adams 6–2 6–3 7–6).

TOMAS ENQVIST (SWE)
Born Stockholm, 13 March, 1974, and lives there; RH; 6ft 3in; 185lb; final 1992 ATP ranking 63; 1992 prize money $132,859.
Coached by Martin Bohm. *1990:* R/u French Open Jun to Gaudenzi. *1991:* (229) In Jun singles won Australian Open over Gleeson, Wimbledon over Joyce and was r/u French Open to Medvedev to finish the year at No. 1 in the ITF Jun singles rankings. In Jun doubles won French Open with Martinelle.*1992:* Made his mark in the senior game right from the start of the year at Australian Open, where he was the only player apart from Edberg to take a set off Courier. Reached qf Adelaide, Bastad and Indianapolis and in autumn won his 1st tour title at Bolzano. *1992 HIGHLIGHTS – SINGLES: Australian Open 2r* (d. Larsson 7–5 7–6 7–5, lost Courier [seed 2] 2–6 6–3 6–1 6–4); *won* Bolzano (d. Wuyts 6–4 6–2, Pescosolido 6–4 6–7 7–5, Medvedev 6–7 6–3 2–0 ret'd, Cherkasov 4–6 6–3 7–6, Boetsch 6–2 1–6 7–6).

WAYNE FERREIRA (RSA)
Born Johannesburg, 15 September 1971, and lives there; RH; 6ft; 163lb; final 1992 ATP ranking 12; 1992 prize money $679,610.
1989: (229) Finished the year No. 1 doubles player in ITF Jun Rankings, having won US Open Jun with Stafford and r/u Wimbledon Jun with De Jager. *1990:* (173) Upset Noah 1r Wimbledon. *1991:* (50) In singles reached last 16 Australian Open after qualifying and played qf Sydney Indoor (d. Lendl), Brisbane and Birmingham. In doubles s/f Wimbledon with Norval, winning LIPC with him and Adelaide with Kruger. *1992:* Having never before progressed beyond qf on the main tour, he put in a tremendous performance at Australian Open, where he upset Wheaton and Novacek *en route* to sf, unseeded. Took his 1st tour title at Queen's in June and broke into top 20, progressing to top 10 in Sept. after reaching qf US Open. Won a 2nd title at Schenectady, r/u Memphis and Stuttgart and sf Johannesburg. Played 4 doubles f, winning Olympic silver medal with Norval and taking Auckland with Grabb. *1992 HIGHLIGHTS – SINGLES: Australian Open sf* [unseeded] (d. Lavalle 6–2 6–4 1–6 6–3, Novacek [seed 8] 3–6 6–3 7–6 7–6, Woodforde 4–6 6–3 6–2 6–2, Wheaton [seed 15] 6–7 6–4 6–2 6–2, J. McEnroe 6–4 6–4 6–4, lost Edberg [seed 1] 7–6 6–1 6–2); *French Open 3r* (d. Thoms 7–5 6–2 7–6, Fromberg 6–3 7–5 6–4, lost Costa 2–6 6–2 6–2 6–2); *Wimbledon last 16* [seed 14] (d. Fitzgerald 6–2 6–2 6–7 7–5, Van Rensburg 6–3 6–3 6–7 6–3, Herrera 7–6 6–1 4–6 6–0, lost Becker [seed 4] 3–6 6–3 6–4 6–7 6–1); *US Open qf* [seed 12] (d. Arrese 3–6 7–5 6–3 6–3, Bruguera 6–7 6–2 3–6 6–1 6–2, Masur 6–4 6–4 6–2, E. Sanchez 6–2 6–4 2–6 6–4, lost Chang [seed 4] 7–5 2–6 6–3 6–7 6–1); *Olympics*

2r [seed 9] (d. Van Rensburg 7–5 6–2 2–6 6–4, lost Rosset 6–4 6–0 6–2); *won* Queen's (d. Poliakov 6–2 3–6 6–0, Wilkinson 6–3 6–4, Kuhnen 7–5 6–3, Stoltenberg 6–4 6–2, B. Gilbert 7–6 6–4, Matsuoka 6–3 6–4); *won* Schenectady (d. Carbonell 7–5 6–2, Lavalle 6–4 6–0, Fromberg 6–7 6–3 6–3, Chesnokov 6–4 6–2, Morgan 6–2 6–7 6–2); *r/u* Memphis (d. Masur 6–4 6–4, Reneberg 6–2 4–6 6–4, Sampras 6–4 6–2, Mansdorf 6–2 6–3, lost Washington 6–3 6–2); *r/u* Stuttgart (d. Dosedel 6–4 7–5, Bruguera 7–5 6–3, Ivanisevic 6–3 6–7 6–4, Novecek 6–3 6–2, lost Medvedev 6–1 6–4 6–7 2–6 6–1); *sf* Johannesburg (d. de Jager 6–3 5–7 6–4, Stafford 6–4 2–6 6–3, Daufresne 6–3 6–1, lost Volkov 6–4 7–6). *1992 HIGHLIGHTS – DOUBLES:* (with Norval unless stated) *Olympic silver medal* (lost Becker/Stich 7–6 4–6 7–6 6–3); (with Grabb) *won* Auckland (d. Connell/Michibata 6–4 6–3); *r/u* Johannesburg (lost Aldrich/Visser 6–4 6–4); (with Kratzmann) *r/u* Italian Open (lost Hlasek/Rosset 6–4 3–6 6–1). *CAREER HIGHLIGHTS – SINGLES: Australian Open – sf 1992; US Open – qf 1992. CAREER HIGHLIGHTS – DOUBLES:* (with Norval) *LIPC – won 1991* (d. Flach/Seguso 5–7 7–6 6–2); *Olympics – silver medal 1992* (lost Becker/Stich 7–6 4–6 7–6 6–3).

MARCELO FILIPPINI (URU)
Born Montevideo, 4 August 1967 and lives there; RH; 5ft 10in; 145lb; final 1992 ATP ranking 60; 1992 prize money $166,610.
Coached by Alfredo Aroztegni. *1986:* (415). *1987:* (118) Won Sao Paulo Challenger and reached qf there on GP circuit. *1988:* (53) Won 1st GP singles title at Bastad in July – the 1st time he had passed qf in a GP tourn – r/u Bari, sf St Vincent and Barcelona. *1989:* (43) Won Prague and reached 5 more qf, finishing the year with an upset of Hlasek at Itaparica. *1990:* (49) R/u Itaparica; sf Bastad (upset Wilander), San Remo and San Marino. *1991:* (107) R/u Madrid. 1992: Reached last 16 French Open, unseeded; sf Florence, Genova and Kitzbuhel; qf Casablanca, Tampa, Cologne and Buzios. *1992 HIGHLIGHTS – SINGLES: French Open last 16* [unseeded] (d. Woodforde 6–3 7–6 6–1, Lopez 6–4 6–4 3–6 6–3, Krickstein [seed 13] 6–2 1–0 ret'd, lost Leconte 6–3 6–2 6–4); *won* Tunis Challenger (d. Altur 6–4 6–2); *sf* Florence (d. Haarhuis 7–6 0–6 6–2, Schaller 7–5 6–4, Santoro 7–6 6–3, lost Furlan 6–3 3–6 6–1); *sf* Genova (d. Mezzadri 5–7 7–5 6–3, Haarhuis 7–6 6–2, Gustafsson 6–1 6–4, lost Medvedev 6–1 7–6); *sf* Kitzbuhel (d. Daufresne 6–3 6–4, Skoff 6–3 6–2, Mattar 7–5 3–6 7–6, E. Sanchez 3–6 7–6 6–4, lost Sampras 6–7 6–3 6–0). *1992 HIGHLIGHTS – DOUBLES:* (with Mattar) *won* Florence (d. Deppe/Haygarth 6–4 6–7 6–4); (with Koevermans) *r/u* Athens (lost Carbonell/Roig 6–3 6–4).

JOHN FITZGERALD (AUS)
Born Cummins, 28 December 1960; lives Newport Beach, Cal.; RH; 6ft 1in; 170lb; final 1992 ATP ranking 165 singles, 11 doubles; 1992 prize money $312,940.
Wife Jenny, daughters Elizabeth Jean (born July 1988) and Bridget (born Aug. 1990). *1979:* (301). *1980:* (136) Won $25,000 tourn in Tokyo. *1981:* (60) Last 16 Wimbledon and won Kitzbuhel over Vilas. *1982:* (78) Won Australian Open doubles with Alexander, and in singles won Hawaii and r/u Sydney. *1983:* (35) Last 16 Australian Open, where he won mixed doubles with Sayers, and won Newport and Stowe. Member of winning Australian D Cup team. *1984:* (29) Won Sydney NSW and r/u Melbourne; sf Australian Open doubles with Cash. *1985:* (91) In doubles won Auckland with C. Lewis, Las Vegas with Cash and Sydney Indoor with Jarryd, also reaching f Wimbledon (d. McEnroe/Fleming) and Queens Club, both with Cash. *1986:* (102) Won French Open doubles with Smid. In victorious Australian D Cup squad, winning doubles in f over Edberg/Jarryd with Cash. Married Jenny Harper 18 Nov. *1987:* (73) Underwent shoulder surgery in Feb. Reached 1st f in 3 years at Hong Kong and d. Connors 2r Tokyo Seiko. *1988:* (25) Finally free from his nagging shoulder injury, he enjoyed his best season, winning Sydney. En route to f Philadelphia, he upset Lendl, being the 1st player outside the top 50 to do so since F. Gonzalez in Aug. 1984. Beat Gomez and Edberg back-to-back to reach f Tokyo Seiko and appeared in sf Adelaide, Wembley and Brussels. In doubles r/u French Open and Wimbledon with Jarryd, won 4 titles with different partners and qualified for Masters doubles with Jarryd, losing sf to Casal/E. Sanchez. Missed US Open with calf injury. *1989:* (117) Took a 2-month break

mid Feb. to April, returning to reach sf Seoul. The high spot of his year came at Wimbledon, where he upset Gilbert to reach last 16 singles and won the doubles with Jarryd, with whom he was also r/u Masters. *1990:* (188) Out 4 weeks April–May with torn calf muscle. In singles reached sf Brisbane; in doubles reached 2 f with Jarryd and was r/u Wimbledon mixed with Smylie. Won doubles (with Cash) in Aust. D Cup wins over France, New Zealand and Argentina but lost vital 3rd rubber in f during 2–3 loss to USA. *1991:* (216) In singles reached qf Queen's and won Bristol Challenger. In doubles with Jarryd, he finished the year with three–quarters of a Grand Slam, having won French Open, Wimbledon and a first US Open, plus ATP Doubles Champ and 2 other titles. *1992:* In singles reached qf Singapore and Seoul. Played 6 doubles f, winning Queen's and Antwerp with Jarryd, plus Taipei with Stolle; qualified with Jarryd for World Doubles Final, where they lost a closely–fought f to Woodbridge/Woodforde. *1992 HIGHLIGHTS – SINGLES: Australian Open 3r* (d. Koevermans 7–6 6–4 7–5, Siemerink 7–5 6–1 7–5, lost Edberg [seed 1] 7–5 6–1 6–4), *Wimbledon 1r* (lost W. Ferreira [seed 14] 6–2 6–2 6–7 7–5). *1992 HIGHLIGHTS – DOUBLES:* (with Jarryd unless stated) *won* Queen's (d. Ivanisevic/Nargiso 6–4 7–6), (with Stolle) *won* Taipei (d. Baur/Van Rensburg 7–6 6–2), *won* Antwerp (d. P. McEnroe/Palmer 6–2 6–2); *r/u* Stuttgart (lost Nijssen/Suk 6–3 6–7 6–3), *r/u* Tokyo Suntory (lost Jones/Leach 0–6 7–5 6–3), *r/u* World Doubles Final (lost Woodbridge/Woodforde 6–2 7–6 5–7 3–6 6–3).*CAREER HIGHLIGHTS – DOUBLES:* (with Jarryd unless stated) *Australian Open –* [Alexander] *won 1982* (d. Taygan/Rennert, Andrews/Sadri 6–4 7–6) [Cash] *sf 1984* (lost Nystrom/Wilander 6–4 6–4 2–6 6–3); *French Open –* [Smid] *won 1986* (d. Edberg/Jarryd 6–3 4–6 6–3 6–7 14–12), *won 1991, r/u 1988* (lost Gomez/E. Sanchez 6–3 6–7 6–4 6–3); *Wimbledon – won 1989* (d. R. Leach/Pugh 3–6 7–6 6–4 7–6), *won 1991* [Cash] *r/u 1985* (d. McEnroe/Fleming, lost Gunthardt/Taroczy), *r/u 1988* (lost Flach/Seguso 6–4 2–6 6–4 7–6); *US Open – won 1991; Masters/ATP Doubles Champ – won 1991, r/u 1989* (lost Grabb/P. McEnroe 7–5 7–6 5–7 6–3); *LIPC – won 1988* (d. Flach/Seguso 7–6 6–1 7–5).

GUY FORGET (FRA)

Born Casablanca, Morocco, 4 January 1965; lives Marseilles and Neuchatel, Switzerland; LH; 6ft 3in; 177lb; final 1992 ATP ranking 11 singles, 29 doubles; 1992 prize money $729,487.

Wife Isabelle (married May 1989); son Mathieu (born Oct. 1989). *1982:* (70) Was world's second best Jun, winning Orange Bowl in Dec. and making presence felt on GP tour. *1983:* (188) String of 1r losses as he joined men's tour. *1984:* (36) Confidence restored by reaching 3r Wimbledon and last 16 Australian Open where he beat V. Amritraj (seed 15). Qf Queen's, Bordeaux, Stockholm and Wembley where he beat Jarryd and Becker. *1985:* (61) Despite sf appearances in Gstaad and Toulouse, he suffered a hard year. *1986:* (25) Reached last 16 French Open where he held m–p before bowing to Vilas. Won Toulouse, as his grandfather (1946) and father (1966) had done, and lifted his ranking again. R/u Masters doubles with Noah. *1987:* (54) Last 16 Wimbledon, d. his doubles partner Noah, with whom he was r/u French Open and won 5 titles. *1988:* (48) Sf Nice and Queen's and upset Zivojinovic at Olympics. In doubles won 3 titles with different partners. *1989:* (36) Won Nancy for 1st title since Toulouse 1986. Underwent surgery on his left knee in April, returning to action at Geneva in Sept. and upset J. McEnroe *en route* to f Wembley in Nov. *1990:* (16) Broke into top 20 in his most successful year to date in which he reached last 16 Wimbledon and won Bordeaux, overcoming the trauma of the death of his father before qf and funeral before sf and playing on at the insistence of his mother. Also reached f Nice and sf Hamburg and Long Island. In Feb. formed a successful doubles duo with Hlasek, with whom he won IBM/ATP World Doubles (for which both shaved their heads) and 4 other titles (plus a 6th with Becker). *1991:* (7) Improving even on his previous year's performance, and feeling more relaxed, he broke into the top 10 for the 1st time and in April moved as high as 4. He won Sydney NSW, Brussels (upset Edberg), Cincinnati (d. Becker and Sampras as he took his 1st title in US), Bordeaux (where he also won the doubles with Boetsch), Toulouse, and Paris Open (d. Sampras), taking more titles during the year than any other man. In GS reached qf both Australian Open and Wimbledon but progressed no further and in ATP World Champ he did not pass rr. Won decisive 4th rubber v Sampras 7–6 3–6 6–3 6–4 to clinch 3–1 French victory in D Cup f v USA in Lyon after nervously losing opening rubber to Agassi 6–7 6–2 6–1 6–2. This was first French success since 1932. *1992:* In a less spectacular year in which he slipped out of the top 10, he nonetheless reached qf Wimbledon, won Toulouse and was r/u Sydney NSW Open, Stockholm (d. Sampras) and Paris Open (d. Edberg), as well as reaching sf Brussels (d. Lendl) and 5 more qf. *1992 HIGHLIGHTS – SINGLES: Australian Open 2r* [seed 7] (d. Leconte 2–6 6–4 6–7 6–4 6–3, lost Bergstrom 7–6 2–6 6–3 6–4); *French Open 2r* [seed 6] (d. Mattar 5–7 6–3 3–6 7–6 6–4, lost Wuyts 6–3 6–3 6–3); *Wimbledon qf* [seed 9] (d. Mronz 6–3 3–6 7–5 7–6, Jarryd 4–6 6–3 3–6 6–3 10–8, Leconte 7–6 6–3 3–6 6–3, Bates 6–7 6–4 3–6 7–6 6–3, lost J. McEnroe 6–2 7–6 6–3); *US Open last 16* [seed 13] (d. Grabb 6–2 6–3 7–6, Larsson 4–6 6–1 7–6 6–0, Wheaton 6–3 7–6 2–6 6–2, lost Sampras [seed 3] 6–3 1–6 1–6 6–4 6–3); *Olympics 2r* [seed 7] (d. Caratti 6–3 6–4 6–2, lost Larsson 6–3 6–3 6–1); *won* Toulouse (d. Schapers 6–3 3–6 7–5, Santoro 6–7 6–1 6–4, Medvedev 6–3 7–6, Boetsch 6–3 6–4, Korda 6–3 6–2); *r/u* Sydney NSW Open (d. Reneberg 6–3 3–6 6–3, J. Sanchez 6–2 6–4, Krickstein 6–1 6–4, Wheaton 6–3 6–2, lost E. Sanchez 6–3 6–4), *r/u* Stockholm (d. Larsson 7–6 6–4, Enqvist 7–6 6–3, Holm 7–5 6–7 7–6, Sampras 7–6 7–6, lost Ivanisevic 7–6 4–6 7–6 6–2), *r/u* Paris Open (d. Delaitre 4–6 6–3 7–6, Boetsch 6–2 6–4, Edberg 6–7 7–5 6–3, Hlasek 6–3 7–6, lost Becker 7–6 6–3 3–6 6–3); *sf* Brussels (d. Gustafsson 6–2 6–4, J. McEnroe 6–3 6–2, Lendl 6–2 7–6, lost Courier 7–6 6–4). *1992 HIGHLIGHTS – DOUBLES:* (with Hlasek) *r/u* Brussels (lost Becker/J. McEnroe 6–3 6–2); (with Boetsch) *r/u* Bordeaux (lost Casal/E. Sanchez 6–1 6–4); (with Leconte) *r/u* Toulouse (lost Pearce/Talbot 6–1 3–6 6–3).

RENZO FURLAN (ITA)
Born Conegliano, 17 May 1970; lives Codogne; RH; 5ft 8in; 150lb; final 1992 ATP ranking 53 ; 1992 prize money $201,168.
1988: (374). *1989:* (222) Qf San Marino. *1990:* (77) Won Tampere Challenger; qf San Remo (d. Agenor) San Marino and Geneva. *1991:* (52) Reached his 1st GP sf at San Marino, plus qf Estoril, Nice, Athens and Hilversum. Upset E. Sanchez 1r Madrid and Lendl 2r Hamburg. *1992:* Reached last 16 Olympics, upsetting Chesnokov on the way; r/u Bologna and Florence; sf Palermo. 1*992 HIGHLIGHTS – SINGLES: Australian Open 1r* (lost Steeb 6–4 6–2 6–2); *French Open 1r* (lost Schapers 6–1 6–4 6–4); *US Open 1r* (lost Larsson 6–2 7–5 6–3); *Olympics last 16* [unseeded] (d. Matsuoka 6–4 6–3 3–6 6–4, Chesnokov 7–6 6–4 6–4, lost Arrese [seed 16] 6–4 6–3 6–2); *r/u* Bologna (d. Perez-Roldan 6–7 6–3 6–3, Frana 6–4 6–3, Davin 6–2 6–1, Wuyts 6–4 7–6, lost Oncins 6–2 6–4); *r/u* Florence (d. Cane 6–1 6–4, Arrese 7–6 6–1, Davin 6–2 6–4, Filippini 6–3 3–6 6–1, lost Muster 6–3 1–6 6–1); *sf* Palermo (d. Naewie 6–4 6–4, Costa 7–5 6–4, Perez-Roldan 6–4 6–4, lost E. Sanchez 6–3 2–6 6–4).

BRAD GILBERT (USA)
Born Oakland, Cal., 9 August 1961; lives there and San Rafael, Cal.; RH; 6ft 1in; 175lb; final 1992 ATP ranking 26; 1992 prize money $342,949.
Coached by Tom Shivington; trained by Mark Grabow. Wife Kim, son Zachary (born 1988). *1982:* (54) The brother of 1978 US CC titlist Dana Gilbert he played for Allan Fox's Pepperdine team in California and reached f NCAA, losing to M. Leach. Won Taipei. *1983:* (62). *1984:* (23) Won Columbus and Taipei and reached last 16 Australian Open. *1985:* (18) Moved into top 20 winning Livingston, Cleveland and Tel Aviv and capping best year with 1r victory over McEnroe at Masters. *1986:* (11) Made further strides, downing Connors and Edberg for US Indoor crown, adding GP titles in Livingston, Israel and Vienna, reaching last 16 Wimbledon and US Open, and playing D Cup. *1987:* (13) Qf US Open, won Scottsdale and reached 4 more f to qualify for Masters, where he d. Connors and Becker. *1988:* (21) Out of action Jan–March with ankle injury and again, missing Wimbledon, after X-rays revealed a massive build–up of scar tissue on the tendon of left ankle as well as ligament damage from a sprain suffered in 1982. Won his 1st tourn of year at Tel Aviv, was Olympic bronze medallist, and reached f Paris Open plus 3 sf. *1989:* (6) Won Memphis, then in late summer captured Stratton Mountain, Livingston and Cincinnati back-to-back, becoming the first player to win 3 titles in consecutive weeks since Becker in 1986.

Reached qf or better in 17 of 20 tourns – exceptions being 1r losses at Wimbledon, US Open and Tel Aviv – and qualified for Masters, where he won only one match. *1990:* (10) Won Rotterdam, Orlando and Brisbane; r/u Cincinnati; sf Toronto World Tennis, Tokyo Suntory and Washington; and reached 2nd GS qf at Wimbledon. Won $1m as finalist at GS Cup where he competed as alternate when Agassi withdrew. *1991:* (19) Although he won no title, he recorded some significant upsets, beating Sampras to reach f Sydney Indoor, Edberg *en route* to f Los Angeles and Agassi in reaching the same stage at San Francisco and again at Cincinnati. He also reached sf US Pro Indoor and Lyon. *1992:* Again he won no title and slipped out of the top 20. However, he was r/u Scottsdale and reached sf San Francisco, Philadelphia, Hong Kong and Queen's (d. Sampras), as well as upsetting Stich to reach last 16 US Open and Agassi at Paris Open. *1992 HIGHLIGHTS – SINGLES: Australian Open 1r* (lost Wahlgren 1–6 6–2 6–1 3–6 6–2); *French Open 1r* (lost Pioline 2–6 5–7 7–5 6–2 6–1); *Wimbledon 3r* [seed 13] (d. Fleurian 6–2 6–3 6–2, Youl 6–1 7–5 7–5, lost Masur 6–3 6–7 6–7 6–4 6–2); *US Open last 16* [unseeded] (d. Bryan 6–3 6–1 6–4, Stich [seed 11] 5–7 6–3 3–6 6–3 7–6, Ho 6–1 6–7 2–6 6–4 7–6, lost Volkov 6–2 6–4 5–7 7–6); *r/u* Scottsdale (d. Zoecke 6–7 7–6 7–6, Layendecker 6–2 6–2, E. Sanchez 6–3 7–5, Washington 6–3 3–6 6–2, lost Pescosolido 6–0 1–6 6–4); *sf* San Francisco (d. C. Adams 6–1 7–5, Stark 3–6 6–4 6–3, Braasch 4–6 6–1 6–1, lost Chang 6–0 7–5); *sf* Philadelphia (d. Layendecker 6–2 6–4, Laurendeau 6–4 6–3, Haarhuis 6–3 3–6 6–1, lost Sampras 6–4 6–3); *sf* Hong Kong (d. Borwick 3–6 7–5 6–3, Schapers 7–5 6–3, Matsuoka 4–6 7–6 6–1, lost Courier 6–4 6–1); *sf* Queen's (d. Pridham 7–6 6–4, Wheaton 6–4 5–7 11–9, Sampras 6–3 6–4, lost W. Ferreira 7–6 6–4). *1992 HIGHLIGHTS – DOUBLES:* (with Grabb) *won* Hong Kong (d. Black/Talbot 6–2 6–1).

JIM GRABB (USA)

Born Tucson, Arizona, 14 April 1964, and lives there; RH; 6ft 4in; 180lb; final 1992 ATP ranking 55 singles, 3 doubles; 1992 prize money $601,189.

1984: (313) Sf NCAA Champs. *1985:* (250) Senior year at Stanford; reached sf Livingston. *1986:* (94) Qf San Francisco and Scottsdale. *1987:* (66) Won 1st GP title at Seoul. *1988:* (91) Qf Memphis (d. Edberg) and Philadelphia. In doubles, with 6 different partners, won Stockholm and reached 5 f. *1989:* (35) Sf Stratton Mountain then upset E. Sanchez to make an unexpected appearance in last 16 US Open. In doubles with P. McEnroe won French Open and Masters, r/u LIPC and Washington. *1990:* (72) In singles was r/u Washington (d. Gilbert) and reached sf San Francisco. In doubles with 3 different partners appeared in 5 f, winning Wembley. *1991:* (83) In singles reached qf Montreal (d. B. Gilbert) and Moscow; in doubles won 2 titles with Reneberg. *1992:* Won his 2nd career singles title at Taipei in Oct., 5 years and 6 months after his 1st, and reached qf Philadelphia (d. Chang), Singapore, Cincinnati and Brisbane. Won US Open doubles and r/u Wimbledon with Reneberg, as well as reaching another 8 f, of which he won 5 with 3 different partners. Qualified with Reneberg for World Doubles Final. *1992 HIGHLIGHTS – SINGLES: Australian Open 2r* (d. Rafter 3–6 6–0 7–6 6–2, lost Krajicek 6–2 7–6 6–1), *French Open 2r* (d. Fleurian 2–6 6–2 7–6 6–3, lost Leconte 6–3 6–4 6–3); *Wimbledon 1r* (lost Boetsch 7–6 7–5 6–4); *US Open 1r* (lost Forget [seed 13] 6–2 6–3 7–6); *won* Taipei (d. Salumaa 7–5 6–7 6–4, Wijaya 6–3 6–3, Steven 5–7 6–3 6–2, Kuhnen 6–3 6–1, Morgan 6–3 6–3). *1992 HIGHLIGHTS – DOUBLES:* (with Reneberg unless stated) *r/u* Wimbledon (lost J. McEnroe/Stich 5–7 7–6 3–6 7–6 19–17); *won* US Open (d. Jones/Leach 3–6 7–6 6–3 6–3); (with W. Ferreira) *won* Auckland (d. Connell/Michibata 6–4 6–3), won San Francisco (d. Aldrich/Visser 6–4 7–5); (with B. Gilbert) *won* Hong Kong (d. Black/Talbot 6–2 6–1), *won* Rosmalen (d. J. McEnroe/Stich 6–4 6–7 6–4); *won* Indianapolis (d. Connell/Michibata 7–6 6–2); *r/u* Philadelphia (lost Woodbridge/Woodforde 6–4 7–6), *r/u* Sydney Indoor (lost P. McEnroe/Stark 6–2 6–3), *r/u* Tokyo Seiko (lost Woodbridge/Woodforde 7–6 6–4).

MAGNUS GUSTAFSSON (SWE)

Born Lund, 3 January 1967; lives Lindome; RH; 6ft 1in; 172lb; final 1992 ATP ranking 47; 1992 prize money $246,083.

Coached by Tim Klein. *1986:* (273) Nat 18 Champ. *1987:* (53) Reached 1st GP sf at Stockholm, won Tampere Challenger and broke into top 50. *1988:* (51) Upset Mayotte to reach last 16 French Open; sf Hilversum and Barcelona (d. Jaite and Leconte). *1989:* (34) Reached last 16 Australian Open; played 1st GP f at Gstaad, then in autumn upset Wilander and Agassi *en route* to 1st SS f at Stockholm. *1990:* (31) Took a break in March, suffering from shin splints. Reached sf Brussels, Stuttgart (d. E. Sanchez and took Lendl to 3s) and upset Agassi at Hamburg. Reached last 16 French Open, but was forced to default to Gomez owing to a knee injury. *1991:* (12) Won 1st GP title at Munich, upsetting Lendl on the way, and followed with Bastad and Hilversum to break into the top 10 in July. R/u Hamburg, Kitzbuhel and Prague; sf Sydney NSW and reached 2 doubles f. Withdrew from US Open with chronic inflammation of the right elbow. *1992:* Won Bastad and was r/u Barcelona as well as reaching sf Florence and 2 more qf. *1992 HIGHLIGHTS – SINGLES: Australian Open 2r* [seed 11] (d. Muller 6–4 6–3 6–3, lost Rosset 6–3 7–5 4–6 3–6 6–3), *French Open 2r* (d. J. Sanchez 6–3 6–2 6–1, lost Krajicek [seed 12] 6–3 6–4 4–6 6–1), *US Open 1r* (lost Hlasek 7–5 6–3 6–3), *Olympics 2r* (d. Casey 7–6 6–1 6–4, lost Arrese 6–2 4–6 6–1 3–6 9–7); *won* Bastad (d. Miniussi 6–4 6–4, Oncins 2–6 6–2 6–1, Enqvist 2–6 6–3 6–3, Arrese 7–5 6–3, Carbonell 5–7 7–5 6–4); *r/u* Barcelona (d. Corretja 5–7 7–6 6–1, Kulti 4–6 6–2 6–0, Skoff 6–3 6–2, Bruguera 6–4 7–5, lost Costa 6–4 7–6 6–4); *sf* Florence (d. Gorriz 4–6 6–2 6–4, Koevermans 6–2 6–0, Yunis 6–1 6–3, lost Muster 6–4 7–5). *1992 HIGHLIGHTS – DOUBLES:* (with Bergstrom) *r/u* Bastad (lost Carbonell/Miniussi 6–4 7–5).

PAUL HAARHUIS (NED)
Born Eindhoven, 19 February 1966, and lives there; RH; 6ft 2in; 177lb; final 1992 ATP ranking 39 singles, 34 doubles; 1992 prize money $371,195.
Coached by Henk van Hulst. *1987:* (397) Finished 2nd on Dutch satellite circuit. *1988:* (462). *1989:* (57) After winning Lagos Challenger qualified for French Open, where he upset Zivojinovic 1r, and again as a qualifier upset J. McEnroe at US Open, going on to last 16. Qf Hilversum (d. K. Carlsson) and Itaparica. *1990:* (54) Qf Philadelphia (d. Gilbert and took Gomez to 3s) and Estoril. Reached 4 f in doubles with various partners, winning Moscow. *1991:* (37) He again excelled at US Open, upsetting top seed Becker *en route* to qf, unseeded. Reached sf Rotterdam, won Lagos Challenger and scored some other big upsets – E. Sanchez at Estoril and Ivanisevic at Italian Open and French Open. In doubles reached 5 f, winning 3 with different partners, and was r/u French Open mixed with Vis. *1992:* Scored some useful upsets during the year on his way to f Singapore, sf Rotterdam (d. Lendl) and qf Wellington, Memphis (d. Wheaton), Philadelphia (d. Wheaton again), Hamburg (d. Muster and Chang), Schenectady and Sydney Indoor. Reached 4 doubles f, winning Hilversum with Koevermans and Schenectady with Eltingh. *1992 HIGHLIGHTS – SINGLES: Australian Open 2r* (d. Hlasek 6–0 2–6 2–6 6–4 6–2, lost Muster 6–4 6–4 7–6), *French Open 1r* (lost Chang [seed 5] 6–4 6–3 6–3), *Wimbledon 2r* (d. Stoltenberg 6–3 7–5 4–6 4–6 7–5, lost Krajicek [seed 11] 7–6 6–3 6–1), *US Open 2r* (d. Matsuoka 7–5 6–2 6–4, lost Svensson 6–0 7–5 6–3), *Olympics 1r* (lost Mattar 4–6 6–3 6–2 6–2, lost Ivanisevic [seed 4] 6–7 6–2 1–6 6–3 6–2); *r/u* Singapore (d. Antonitsch 6–4 6–1, Stoltenberg 6–1 6–2, Carlsen 6–4 6–3, Krishnan 6–3 6–4, lost Youl 6–4 6–1); *sf* Rotterdam (d. Goellner 6–2 6–2, Lendl 6–1 7–5, Prpic 7–6 6–2, lost Volkov 6–2 6–7 6–2). *1992 HIGHLIGHTS – DOUBLES:* (with Koevermans unless stated) *won* Hilversum (d. Renstrom/Tillstrom 6–7 6–1 6–4); (with Eltingh) *won* Schenectady (d. Casal/E. Sanchez 6–3 6–4); *r/u* Rotterdam (lost Goellner/Prinosil 6–2 6–7 7–6); *r/u* Genova (lost Cannon Van Emburgh 6–1 6–1). *CAREER HIGHLIGHTS – SINGLES: US Open – qf 1991* [unseeded] (d. Jelen 2–6 6–2 6–1 3–6 6–2, Chesnokov 6–1 4–6 6–2 7–6, Becker [seed 1] 6–3 6–4 6–2, Steeb 6–2 6–3 6–4, lost Connors 4–6 7–6 6–4 6–2).

LUIS HERRERA (MEX)
Born Mexico City, 27 August 1971, and lives there; LH; 5ft 7in; 136lb; final 1992 ATP ranking 59; 1992 prize money $135,488.
Won Nat Jun titles in 12s, 14s and 16s. *1987:* (563). *1988:* (471). *1989:* (535) Nat champ and r/u French Open Jun doubles with Knowles. *1990:* (103) Won Challenger titles in Manaus and Ilheus. *1991:* (136) Upset Antonitsch *en route* to sf Seoul, J. McEnroe in reaching qf Washington and Courier in D Cup. *1992:* Concentrated mainly on the

Challenger circuit for first half of year, winning 3 titles. On the main tour he upset B. Gilbert to reach sf Manchester and finished the year by upsetting Mancini on the way to his 1st GP f at Buzios. *1992 HIGHLIGHTS – SINGLES: Wimbledon 3r* (d. Connors 6–2 1–6 7–5 6–3, Matsuoka 6–4 6–4 5–7 4–6 6–3, lost W. Ferreira [seed 14] 7–6 6–1 4–6 6–0), *US Open 1r* (lost Siemerink 6–4 3–6 6–2 6–3); *won* Sao Paulo Challenger (d. Oncins 6–2 3–6 6–4), won Ixtapa Challenger (d. Sznajder 6–1 6–2), *won* Ponte Vedra Challenger (d. Yzaga 7–5 6–4); *r/u* Buzios (d. Perez 6–3 6–4, Albano 4–6 7–6 6–1, Mancini 6–2 6–3, Motta 7–6 6–4, lost Oncins 6–3 6–2); *sf* Manchester (d. Camporese 6–2 6–2, Naewie 6–0 7–5, B. Gilbert 3–6 6–3 7–6, lost Washington 6–7 6–1 6–1).

JAKOB HLASEK (SUI)
Born Prague, Czechoslovakia, 12 November 1964; lives Zurich; 6ft 2in; 165lb; final 1992 ATP ranking 36 singles, 39 doubles; 1992 prize money $558,643.
Family moved to Zurich in 1968. Speaks 6 languages. *1984:* (88) Joined both Olympic and D Cup squads for Switzerland and played prolific schedule including 22 tournaments. *1985:* (33) R/u Rotterdam, sf Milan, Hong Kong and qf 4 times. Won Toulouse doubles with Acuna. *1986:* (32) Played consistent tennis all season, reaching f Hilversum and 8 qf. *1987:* (23) Reached last 16 Wimbledon with 2nd win over Nystrom, sf Toulouse and Wembley (d. Mecir). *1988:* (8) Out of action 34 months after breaking right wrist and 3 ribs in car accident Jan., when he fell asleep at the wheel. Enjoyed a spectacular 2nd half of year, reaching last 16 US Open, f Gstaad and Basel (d. Connors), before taking 1st GP title at Wembley and following with Johannesburg and r/u finish at Brussels to qualify for 1st Masters, where he reached sf. *1989:* (30) Won Rotterdam and r/u Lyon in singles; in doubles won Milan, Indian Wells, LIPC and Wembley with various partners. Out of action with wrist injury July–Oct. *1990:* (17) In singles won Wembley (d. Chang) and reached sf Rotterdam and Canadian Open. Formed a successful doubles duo with Forget in Feb.; together they won 5 titles, including IBM/ATP World Doubles for which both shaved their heads, and he took another with Stich. *1991:* (20) Upset E. Sanchez *en route* to sf French Open, unseeded, and at Basel won both singles and doubles titles. He was also r/u Moscow, reached sf Milan, Copenhagen and Rosmalen, and played 2 other doubles, f. *1992:* Won his 1st GS title in doubles at French Open with Rosset, unseeded, and won both his singles matches as SWZ upset FRA in qf D Cup. On the tour he reached sf LIPC, Paris Open and Moscow, upset Sampras at Indian Wells and Korda at Wimbledon (16–14 5s), and took 2 more doubles titles with Rosset. *1992 HIGHLIGHTS – SINGLES: Australian Open 1r* (lost Haarhuis 6–0 2–6 2–6 6–4 6–2), *French Open 1r*, seed 16 (lost Medvedev 7–6 6–3 6–4), *Wimbledon 3r* (d. Schapers 6–4 6–3 6–2, Korda [seed 6] 4–6 3–6 6–3 7–6 16–14, lost Saceanu 7–6 3–6 6–3 1–6 6–3), *US Open 2r* (d. Gustafsson 7–5 6–3 6–3, lost Edberg [seed 2] 7–5 6–2 6–1), *Olympics last 16* [seed 15] (d. Maciel 6–3 6–4 4–6 6–2, Sznajder 4–6 6–4 6–3 7–6, lost Ivanisevic 3–6 6–0 4–6 7–6 9–7); *sf* LIPC (d. Blackman 6–3 6–4, Yzaga 6–3 6–3, Weiss 6–2 6–2, Cherkasov 6–7 6–3 6–4, lost Mancini 7–6 7–5), *sf* Paris Open (d. Muster 6–3 6–4, W. Ferreira 6–3 3–6 6–3, Grabb 4–6 6–1 6–2, Leconte w.o., lost Forget 6–3 7–6), *sf* Moscow (d. Tarango 6–3 7–5, Schapers 6–7 7–5 6–3, Bloom 6–1 6–2, lost Steeb 7–6 6–4). *1992 HIGHLIGHTS – DOUBLES:* (with Rosset unless stated) *won* French Open (d. D. Adams/Olhovskiy 7–6 6–7 7–5); *won* Italian Open (d. Kratzmann/W. Ferreira 6–4 3–6 6–1), *won* Lyon (d. Broad/Kruger 6–1 6–3); (with Forget) *r/u* Brussels (lost Becker/J. McEnroe 6–3 6–2). *CAREER HIGHLIGHTS – SINGLES: French Open – sf 1991* [unseeded] (d. Pate 6–4 6–1 7–5, E. Sanchez 6–3 4–6 6–2 7–6, Carbonell 7–6 4–6 6–4 6–3, Miniussi 4–6 6–3 5–7 7–5 6–2, lost Agassi [seed 4] 6–3 6–1 6–1). *CAREER HIGHLIGHTS – DOUBLES: French Open –* (with Rosset)*won 1992; LIPC –* (with Jarryd) *won 1989* (d. Grabb/P. McEnroe 6–3 ret'd); *IBM/ATP World Doubles –* (with Forget) *won 1990* (d. Casal/E. Sanchez 6–4 7–6 5–7 6–4).

HENRIK HOLM (SWE)
Born Taby, 22 August 1968; lives Stockholm; RH; 6ft; 170lb; final 1992 ATP ranking 19; 1992 prize money $345,399.
Father, Christer, played D Cup for Sweden and was ranked No. 2 in his country; brother Nils also plays on tour. *1986:* (799). *1987:* (586). *1988:* (434). *1989:* (228) Won Dublin

Challenger. *1990:* (137) Won Aptos Challenger. *1991:* (129) Qf Guaruja. *1992:* Emerging from the minor circuits after winning 2 more Challenger titles, he scored some big upsets and played his 1st 2 f on the main tour – he upset Lendl *en route* to f Washington and surprised Becker, W. Ferreira and Volkov back-to-back in reaching the same stage at Tokyo Seiko. He had beaten Volkov earlier in the year at Wimbledon, on his way to last 16, unseeded, and upset W. Ferreira in reaching sf Sydney Indoor. These performances swept him through the rankings and into the top 20 in November. *1992 HIGHLIGHTS – SINGLES: French Open 1r* (lost Azar 4–6 7–6 6–3 7–5), *Wimbledon last 16* [unseeded] (d. Doyle 6–3 6–2 2–6 6–4, Kulti 6–1 6–2 6–2, Volkov [seed 15] 6–4 3–6 6–3 7–6, lost Edberg [seed 2] 6–3 6–4 6–7 6–3), *US Open 2r* (d. Eltingh 6–1 6–4 6–7 6–4, lost Leconte 6–1 5–7 6–2 6–2); *won* Istanbul Challenger (d. Simian 7–6 6–2), *won* Azores Challenger (d. Carlsen 6–4 6–3); *r/u* Washington (d. Reneberg 6–1 6–3, Martin 7–6 7–5, Bates 7–5 3–0 15–0 ret'd, Lendl 3–6 6–3 6–3, Rostagno 6–4 6–3, lost Korda 6–4 6–4), *r/u* Tokyo Seiko (d. Shelton 6–4 2–6 6–4, Becker 6–1 6–2, W. Ferreira 7–6 6–2, Volkov 7–5 6–2, lost Lendl 7–6 6–4); *sf* Sydney Indoor (d. Pate 6–3 6–2, W. Ferreira 7–6 3–6 6–4, Kuhnen 6–3 6–2, lost Edberg 6–2 3–6 6–3).

ANDERS JARRYD (SWE)

Born Lidkoping, 13 July 1961; lives London and Bastad; RH; 2HB; 5ft 11in; 155lb; final 1992 ATP ranking 149 singles, 10 doubles; 1992 prize money $399,116.
Girlfriend Lotta Sundgren; son Niklas (born Feb. 1988). *1981:* (100). *1982:* (60) Playing second singles in D Cup v US, he stunned Gottfried in straight sets. Won Linz and Ancona. *1983:* (19) Won French Open doubles with H. Simonsson, d. McEnroe in sf Canadian Open, losing f to Lendl, and was r/u Bastad. *1984:* (6) Won 2 GP tourns, including Australian Indoor at Sydney where he d. Lendl in f and was r/u US Open doubles with Edberg. Played on winning Swedish D Cup team, contributing decisive win in doubles with Edberg over McEnroe/Fleming. *1985:* (8) Sf Wimbledon, won Brussels over Wilander; r/u Toronto, Milan and Stockholm and won Masters doubles with Edberg. *1986:* (19) Won WCT Finals in Dallas over Wilander and Becker, and r/u French Open doubles, but slowed down after knee surgery, returning to win Masters doubles with Edberg again in Dec. *1987:* (15) In singles reached qf Australian Open and Wimbledon, r/u Wembley; in doubles won Australian and US Opens with Edberg and French Open with Seguso and sf Masters with Edberg. *1988:* (32) Underwent knee surgery early in year. Qf Australian Open; sf Cincinnati and Frankfurt. In doubles with Fitzgerald r/u French Open and Wimbledon, won LIPC and qualified for Masters, losing sf to Casal/E. Sanchez. *1989:* (31) In singles reached f Rotterdam and San Francisco. In doubles won Wimbledon and r/u Masters with Fitzgerald, taking 3 other titles with various partners. *1990:* (73) Restricted for much of the year by a shoulder injury and persistent cough. However, he upset J. McEnroe and Skoff to win Vienna for his 1st title for 44 years and won The Hague Challenger. *1991:* (45) A year of rejuvenation. In singles reached f Copenhagen and sf Rotterdam, Queen's and Berlin. In doubles with Fitzgerald finished the year with threequarters of a Grand Slam, having won French Open, Wimbledon and US Open, as well as ATP Doubles Champ. With various partners he played 7 other f, winning 4 to regain his place as one of the world's best .*1992:* Underwent arthroscopic surgery 4th time on left knee in April. R/u Copenhagen in singles and continued his success in doubles, joining with 3 different partners to win 4 titles, including the 50th of his career at Vienna. Qualified with Fitzgerald for World Doubles Final, where they lost a closely fought f to Woodbridge/Woodforde. *1992 HIGHLIGHTS – SINGLES: Australian Open 1r* (lost Krickstein 6–3 6–7 6–2 6–3), *French Open 1r* (lost Wuyts 7–5 6–2 6–2), *Wimbledon 2r* (d. Bailey 6–4 6–3 6–0, lost Forget [seed 9] 4–6 6–3 3–6 6–3 10–8), *US Open 1r* (lost Goellner 3–6 6–3 6–4 6–0); *r/u* Copenhagen (d. Riglewski 6–4 6–1, Apell 7–6 4–6 6–2, Eltingh 6–1 6–2, Nargiso 6–2 3–6 7–5, lost Larsson 6–4 7–6). *1992 HIGHLIGHTS – DOUBLES:* (with Fitzgerald unless stated) *won* Queen's (d. Ivanisevic/Nargiso 6–4 7–6), (with Pedersen) *won* Bolzano (d. Nijssen/Suk 6–1 6–7 6–3), (with Bathman) *won* Vienna (d. Kinnear/Riglewski 6–3 7–5), *won* Antwerp (d. P. McEnroe/Palmer 6–2 6–2); *r/u* Stuttgart (lost Nijssen/Suk 6–3 6–7 6–3), *r/u* Tokyo Suntory (lost Jones/Leach 0–6 7–5 6–3), *r/u* World Doubles Final (lost Woodbridge/Woodforde 7–2 7–6 5–7 3–6 6–3).

BERND KARBACHER (GER)
Born Munich, 3 April 1968, and lives there; RH; 6ft 1in; 160lb; final 1992 ATP ranking 51; 1992 prize money $157,850.
Coached by Mark Lewis, who also coaches Stich. *1990:* (271). *1991:* (269). *1992:* Won his 1st tour title at Cologne (d. Muster), as well as reaching sf Munich (d. Novacek and Krickstein) and upsetting Chang and Clavet *en route* to qf Stuttgart to finish the year in the top 50. *1992 HIGHLIGHTS – SINGLES: French Open 1r* (lost Oncins 6–3 2–6 7–5 4–6 6–4), *Wimbledon 2r* (d. R. Gilbert 2–6 7–5 2–6 6–4 6–4, lost Leconte 7–5 6–2 7–6); *won* Hong Kong Challenger (d. Rusedski 6–2 3–6 6–1), *won* Cologne (d. Damm 6–4 6–4, Olhovskiy 6–7 7–6 6–3, Muster 6–3 6–3, J. Sanchez 7–6 6–3, Ondruska 7–6 6–4); *sf* Munich (d. Koslowski 5–7 6–1 6–3, Krickstein 6–2 6–4, Novacek 7–5 4–6 6–1, lost Korda 3–6 7–6 7–5).

AARON KRICKSTEIN (USA)
Born Ann Arbor, Mich., 2 August 1967; lives Grosse Pointe, Mich.; RH; 2HB; 6ft; 160lb; final 1992 ATP ranking 28; 1992 prize money $286,304.
Attended Nick Bollettieri Tennis Academy. Coached by Tim Gullikson from 1989. *1982:* Won US Nat 16 at Kalamazoo. *1983:* (94) Won US Nat 18 at Kalamazoo and turned pro in autumn, after arriving in last 16 at US Open where he upended Edberg and Gerulaitis in 5s before Noah stopped him. He won his first pro event in Tel Aviv to become youngest ever to capture GP tournament at 16 years, 2 months, 13 days. *1984:* (12) Won US Pro and two other GP titles and reached f Italian Open, including Wilander among his major victims. *1985:* (30) Despite r/u showing in Hong Kong and last 16 French Open, he did not live up to promise of previous two years. *1986:* (26) Made history at US Open with two straight triumphs from two–sets–to–love down against Novacek and Annacone, and added a straight–sets dismissal of Purcell to reach last 16. R/u Tel Aviv and contributed to US D Cup win over Ecuador with win over Viver. *1987:* (61) Reached qf 3 times, but progressed no further. Stress fracture of left tibia kept him out Aug–Sept, and before he could return to action, a rib injury sustained in a motor accident sidelined him until Feb. 1988. *1988:* (15) Qf US Open, upsetting Gomez and Edberg back-to-back, r/u Tel Aviv and Detroit and reached 3 other sf. *1989:* (8) Regained his old form, returning to top 10 in Oct. after sf appearance at US Open. At Sydney in Jan. he won his 1st title since Geneva in Sept. 1984. At Los Angeles in Sept. took his 1st SS title since US Pro in July 1984 and followed with Tokyo Seiko in Oct. (d. Edberg). Qualified for Masters. *1990:* (20) *En route* to f Tokyo Suntory had back-to-back wins v Chang and Lendl (for the 1st time), despite nursing a hamstring injury that forced him to withdraw from Orlando. Also appeared in f Brisbane and sf Sydney, reached qf US Open, and reached 2r GS Cup. *1991:* (34) Switched to a remodelled racket in late summer, which seemed to revive his fortunes. Unseeded at US Open, he upset Agassi *en route* to last 16, where he lost in 5s tb to an inspired Connors. He followed with r/u Brisbane, upsetting Chesnokov, and swept to sf Stockholm with back-to-back upsets of Stich and Hlasek. *1992:* In GS upset Ivanisevic *en route* to qf Australian Open, unseeded, where he retired 5s v Mansdorf. At Johannesburg in April he won his 1st title since 1989, despite playing with a foot injury, and followed with r/u spot at Monte Carlo (d. Becker) and sf Los Angeles, appearing in 5 more qf. At that stage at Toronto he fractured the 5th metatarsal of his left foot – the same injury he'd suffered 8 years earlier to the right foot – and in Aug. underwent surgery to pin it, remaining out of action for the rest of what had turned out to be an injury-plagued year. *1992 HIGHLIGHTS – SINGLES: Australian Open last 16* [unseeded] (d. Jarryd 6–3 6–7 6–2 6–3, Ivanisevic [seed 10] 6–2 7–5 6–1, Volkov 6–4 5–7 6–7 6–1 8–6, lost Mansdorf 6–2 4–6 1–6 7–6 4–1 ret'd), *French Open 3r* [seed 13] (d. Koevermans 3–6 6–3 6–1 6–3, Washington 4–6 5–7 6–4 7–6 6–3, lost Filippini 6–2 1–0 ret'd); *won* Johannesburg (d. Roubicek 6–3 6–1, Lavalle 6–2 6–4, Muller 6–2 6–2, Pridham 6–3 6–4, Volkov 6–4 6–4); *r/u* Monte Carlo (d. Siemerink 6–3 7–5, Wahlgren 6–1 6–1, Becker 6–1 6–4, Chesnokov 6–1 7–6, Prpic 6–1 6–1, lost Muster 6–3 6–1 6–3); *sf* Los Angeles (d. Crow 4–6 6–1 6–2, Witsken 6–3 6–7 6–4, Pozzi 6–1 6–2, lost Woodforde 4–2 30–40 ret'd).

MAGNUS LARSSON (SWE)
Born Olofstrom, 25 March 1970; lives Vaxjo and Monte Carlo; RH; 6ft 3in; 172lb; final 1992 ATP ranking 34; 1992 prize money $160,700.

Coached by Martin Bohm. *1986:* Won European Jun doubles with Kulti. *1988:* (381) R/u French Open Jun to Perreira. *1989:* (145) Won Geneva Challenger. *1990:* (56) Won Florence after qualifying, r/u Bstaad and won Ljubliana Challenger. *1991:* (61) He sprung some big upsets during the year, surprising Becker *en route* to sf Adelaide, Edberg at Monte Carlo, Gomez at US Open and Cherkasov on his way to qf Bastad. He reached the same stage at Prague and Florence and extended Courier to 5s French Open, at one stage being 2 sets to 1 ahead. *1992:* Won both singles and doubles at Copenhagen, following with the singles title at Munich (d. Stich and Korda). He also made an unexpected appearance in last 16 Olympics (d. Forget) and reached 3 qf. *1992 HIGHLIGHTS – SINGLES: Australian Open 1r* (lost Enqvist 7–5 7–6 7–5), *French Open 3r* (d. Berasategui 6–3 6–3 6–2, Wheaton 7–6 6–4 6–1, lost Ivanisevic [seed 8] 6–7 6–3 6–1 3–6 9–7), *Wimbledon 3r* (d. Frana 6–3 7–6 6–4, Costa 7–5 6–3 6–7 6–4, lost Stich [seed 3] 6–4 6–1 6–3), *US Open 2r* (d. Furlan 6–2 7–5 6–3, lost Forget [seed 13] 4–6 6–1 7–6 6–0), *Olympics last 16* (unseeded) (d. Skoff 6–2 6–3 6–3, Forget [seed 7] 6–3 6–3 6–1, lost E. Sanchez [seed 12] 6–4 7–6 6–7 6–4); *won* Copenhagen (d. Wahlgren 6–4 7–6, Engel 6–4 6–4, Baur 6–4 6–7 6–1, Saceanu 6–7 7–6 6–4, Jarryd 6–4 7–6), *won* Munich (d. Leconte 6–7 7–6 6–2, Camporese 6–2 6–1, Stich 6–4 6–4, Naewie 6–7 6–4 7–6, Korda 6–4 4–6 6–1), *won* Ljubliana Challenger (d. Tillstroem 6–4 6–4). *1992 HIGHLIGHTS – DOUBLES:* (with Kulti) *won* Copenhagen (d. Davids/Pimek 6–3 6–4).

JOHN McENROE (USA)
Born Wiesbaden, West Germany, 16 February 1959; lives New York and Malibu, Cal.; LH; 5ft 11in; 165lb; final 1992 ATP ranking 20; 1992 prize money $641,077.
Wife Tatum O'Neal (married Aug. 1986); sons Kevin (born May 1986) and Sean Timothy (born Sept. 1987), daughter Emily Catherine (born May 1991). As youth, coached at Pt. Washington Tennis Academy by Harry Hopman. Later by Tony Palafox. Works with Madonna's former trainer, Bob Parr. *1976:* (264) R/u to Larry Gottfried at US Nat 18 Champs and won Orange Bowl 18s. *1977:* (21) Stunned tennis world by reaching sf Wimbledon as qualifier and taking set off Connors. *1978:* (4) Turned pro in June after winning NCAA title as Stanford freshman. Won Hartford, San Francisco, Stockholm and Wembley in autumn, led US D Cup triumph, and closed year by saving 2 mps to beat Ashe in Masters f. *1979:* (3) Won US Open, WCT Finals, New Orleans, Milan, San José, Queen's Club, South Orange, San Francisco, Stockholm and Wembley and again led US D Cup triumph. *1980:* (2) Lost epic Wimbledon f to Borg after saving 7 mps in 4s, finally falling 8–6 5s. Won second straight US Open with 5s triumph over Borg as well as Richmond, Memphis, Milan, Queen's Club, Brisbane, Sydney, Wembley and WCT Montreal. *1981:* (1) Became first male player since Connors in 1974 to win Wimbledon and US Open in same year, stopping Borg in both f to replace the Swede as the No. 1 player in the world. Led US to D Cup victory. *1982:* (1) Lost to Connors in 5s Wimbledon f, coming within three points of victory at 4–3 in 4s tb. After losing to Lendl in sf US Open and f Masters, he was regarded by many experts as No. 3 behind Connors and Lendl. Led US to D Cup victory for 4th time in 5 years and won US Pro Indoor, San Francisco, Sydney, Tokyo and Wembley. *1983:* (1) Won his second Wimbledon and Masters titles, beating Lendl in sf former and f latter. Also won US Pro Indoor, WCT Dallas, Forest Hills, Sydney and Wembley to become undisputed No. 1. *1984:* (1) Won 13 of 15 tournaments and 79 of 82 matches, losing only to Lendl in f French Open, V. Amritraj at Cincinnati and Sundstrom in D Cup f. For the second time he won Wimbledon and US Open, producing glorious form to rout Connors in Wimbledon f and dismissing Lendl with relative ease 6–3 6–4 6–1 in US Open f. Only his loss to Lendl from 2 sets to 0 ahead in f French Open spoiled a nearly perfect year. *1985:* (2) Won Philadelphia, Houston, Chicago, Milan, Atlanta, Stratton, Montreal and Stockholm, but was soundly beaten by Curren in qf Wimbledon and Lendl in f US Open. When he lost to Gilbert in 1r Masters, he elected to take a 6-month sabbatical from the game. *1986:* (14) Returning to competition in Stratton Mountain in July, he lost to Becker in sf after holding 4 mps, then lost to Seguso in 3r Canadian Open and suffered his first 1r defeat at US Open to Annacone. He rebounded with three straight tourn wins (LA, San Francisco and Scottsdale), but was beaten thereafter by Casal in qf of Paris Indoor and Cash in 1r

Wembley. **1987:** (10) In f World Team Cup v Mecir he walked off the court following two disputed umpiring decisions, later claiming that a back injury had prompted his withdrawal, and avoided threatened suspension when MIPTC accepted that he was indeed injured. However, following US Open, when he accumulated fines exceeding $7,500 for the second time in the year, he was suspended for 2 months from 28 Sept. Continuing to be plagued by injuries, and missing Wimbledon with a leg injury, he began working with physical trainers Dae–Shik Seo and Chuck Debus. Reached f 5 times but won no title. **1988:** (11) Won Tokyo for his 71st title and his 1st since Oct. 1986, following with Detroit, and was r/u Indianapolis. Formed a successful partnership with Woodforde in autumn. Coached by Peter Fleming until end of year. **1989:** (4) Playing with renewed confidence he won WCT Finals for record fifth time (d. Lendl for 1st time in 4 years), Lyon and Indianapolis. Missed French Open with back trouble and prepared enthusiastically for Wimbledon, where he reached sf, but fell 2r US Open to qualifier Haarhuis. However, he won the doubles title there with Woodforde. Played Masters for 1st time since losing to Gilbert 1r in 1985, and reached sf (lost Becker). **1990:** (13) At Australian Open became the 1st player since Willy Alvarez at French Open in 1963 to be disqualified from a GS tourn., following a third code of conduct warning for verbal abuse in 4r match v Pernfors. He was fined $6,000 for extreme verbal abuse, although he claimed that he believed GS events were still run on the basis of four warnings. Out nearly 4 months to June with a shoulder injury and lacking motivation, and fell 1r Wimbledon to Rostagno. His ranking dropped to 21 until, unseeded for the 1st time in 12 years, he reached sf US Open. Returned to top 10 for a while, having also won Basel, to become only the 2nd player after Sherwood Stewart to win titles in 3 decades. Sf Milan, Toronto World Tennis, Queen's and Long Island, Reunited during the year with his former coach, Tony Palafox. **1991:** (28) Won Chicago, beating his brother in f, r/u Basel and reached sf US Pro Indoor and Long Island. He missed French Open to be present at the birth of his daughter in May and his best showing in GS was last 16 Wimbledon. **1992:** He thrilled and disappointed fans during the year. He found some of his old touch to reach qf Australian Open, upsetting Becker on the way, and repeated the performance at Wimbledon, where, unseeded, he reached sf – returning to top 20 for 1st time since Aug 1991. Also at Wimbledon, he and Stich, unseeded, won the doubles f in 5 hr 1 min over Grabb/Reneberg. Yet in between he fell 1r French Open to Kulti. He reached sf Rotterdam and Rosmalen, played 2 more qf and upset Ivanisevic at LIPC. In doubles he also won Brussels with Becker and Paris Open with his brother, Patrick (their 2nd together and 1st since 1984). **1992 HIGHLIGHTS – SINGLES: Australian Open qf** [unseeded] (d. Dyke 6–2 6–0 6–1, Cherkasov 7–5 3–6 6–4 6–3, Becker [seed 3] 6–4 6–3 7–5, E. Sanchez [seed 13] 7–5 7–6 4–6 2–6 8–6, lost W. Ferreira 6–4 6–4), **French Open 1r** (lost Kulti 6–2 7–5 6–7 7–5), **Wimbledon sf** [unseeded] (d. Mattar 5–7 6–1 6–3 6–3, Cash 6–7 6–4 6–7 6–3 6–2, Wheaton [seed 14] 6–3 6–4 6–4, Olhovskiy 7–5 6–3 7–6, Forget 6–2 7–6 6–3, lost Agassi 6–4 6–2 6–3), **US Open last 16** [seed 16] (d. Schapers 6–4 6–0 6–4, Nargiso 4–6 6–3 6–0 6–2, Fromberg 6–3 6–1 6–4, lost Courier [seed 1] 6–2 6–2 7–6); **sf** Rotterdam (d. Koevermans 6–3 6–2, Prinosil 7–6 6–3, Antonitsch 2–6 6–3 7–5, lost Becker 6–2 7–6), **sf** Rosmalen (d. Lundgren 6–2 6–3, Grabb 6–2 7–6, Volkov 6–4 6–3, lost Stich 6–3 7–6). **1992 HIGHLIGHTS – DOUBLES:** (with Stich unless stated) **won** Wimbledon (d. Grabb/Reneberg 5–7 7–6 3–6 7–6 19–17); (with Becker) **won** Brussels (d. Forget/Hlasek 6–3 6–2), (with P. McEnroe) **won** Paris Open (d. Galbraith/Visser 6–4 6–2); **r/u** Rosmalen (lost Grabb/Reneberg 6–4 6–7 6–4) [Agassi] **r/u** Toronto (lost Galbraith/Visser 6–4 6–4).

PATRICK McENROE (USA)
Born Manhasset, NY, 1 July 1966; lives Oyster Bay, NY; RH; 2HB; 6ft; 160lb; final 1992 ATP ranking 110 singles, 7 doubles; 1992 prize money $389,381.
Brother of John. Coached by Carlos Goffi. **1983:** R/u US Nat 18s. **1984:** Won Nat GC 18s. **1987:** (452) Won San Francisco doubles with Grabb. **1988:** (494) Graduated from Stanford and in winning NCAA team. 3 times All-American in singles (1986–8). R/u US Open mixed doubles with Smylie. **1989:** (356) Won French Open and Masters doubles with Grabb. Elected ATP Tour Council. **1990:** (120) In singles reached qf Hong Kong and Singapore

before appearing in his 1st tour sf at Rosmalen. In doubles with Grabb won Wembley and reached 2 more f. *1991:* (36) Played the tennis of his life at Australian Open where, unseeded, he reached sf singles before falling to Becker in 4s, and was r/u doubles with Wheaton. He followed with his 1st singles f at Chicago, where he took his brother to 3s, and broke into top 50, before upsetting Becker at LIPC and E. Sanchez at Wimbledon. He reached 2 more doubles f with Hlasek, winning Basel. *1992:* In singles he had a less spectacular year, in which his best showings were qf Milan (d. Forget) and Rotterdam. In doubles played 7 f, winning Madrid with Galbraith, Sydney Indoor with Stark and Paris Open with his brother, John. *1992 HIGHLIGHTS – SINGLES: Australian Open 3r* (d. Cierro 6–3 6–4 6–4, Tarango 6–1 4–6 6–4 6–3, lost Chesnokov 6–1 1–6 1–6 6–1 6–3), *French Open 2r* (d. Shelton 4–6 6–3 6–4 7–6, lost Steeb 6–2 6–4 3–6 6–3), *Wimbledon 2r* (d. Montana 6–4 6–1 6–1, Stafford 6–4 7–6 2–6 6–2), *US Open 2r* (d. Matuszewski 1–6 7–6 6–2 6–4, lost Chang [seed 4] 6–3 6–3 6–4). *1992 HIGHLIGHTS – DOUBLES:* (with Stark unless stated), (with Galbraith) *won* Madrid (d. Clavet/Costa 6–3 6–2), *won* Sydney Indoor (d. Grabb/Reneberg 6–2 6–3), (with J. McEnroe) *won* Paris Open (d. Galbraith/Visser 6–4 6–2); *r/u* Cincinnati (lost Woodbridge/Woodforde 6–3 1–6 6–3), (with Palmer) *r/u* New Haven (lost Jones/Leach 7–6 6–7 6–2), *r/u* Brisbane (lost Devries/MacPherson 6–4 6–4), *r/u* Antwerp (lost Fitzgerald/Jarryd 6–2 6–2).*CAREER HIGHLIGHTS – SINGLES: Australian Open – sf 1991. CAREER HIGHLIGHTS – DOUBLES:* (with Grabb unless stated) *French Open – won 1989* (d. Bahrami/Winogradsky 6–4 2–6 6–4 7–6); *Masters – won 1989* (d. Jarryd/Fitzgerald 7–5 7–6 5–7 6–3); *Australian Open –* (Wheaton) *r/u 1991*; *LIPC – r/u 1989* (lost Hlasek/Jarryd 6–3 ret'd).

ALBERTO MANCINI (ARG)
Born Misiones, 20 May 1969; lives Buenos Aires; RH; 5ft 11in; 164lb; final 1992 ATP ranking 31; 1992 prize money $294,244.
Coached by Francisco (Pancho) Mastelli. *1987:* (130). *1988:* (49) Emerging from the satellite circuits, he won 1st GP title at Bologna and reached sf Madrid, St Vincent and Buenos Aires. Beat E. Sanchez twice during the year. *1989:* (9) Beat Wilander and Becker back-to-back to win Monte Carlo, then followed with Italian Open, saving mp to beat Agassi in f. These performances plus qf showing at French Open and last 16 at US Open took him into the top 10. *1990:* Suffered a difficult year, dropping out of the top 100 and he could manage no better than 2 qf showings at Italian Open and Madrid, although in doubles he won Nice with Noah. *1991:* (22) Returning to form he reached qf Nice and then, as a qualifier, appeared in f Italian Open, where he was forced to retire v E. Sanchez. He reached last 16 French Open as a wild-card entry and followed with r/u Bastad and Stuttgart Mercedes. *1992:* Upset Becker, Krajicek and Hlasek *en route* to a surprise appearance in f LIPC, which took him into the top 20, and reached same stage Kitzbuhel. Sf Barcelona (d. Lendl) and Sao Paulo and played 3 other qf. *1992 HIGHLIGHTS – SINGLES: French Open 3r* (d. Corretja 6–4 1–6 6–4 6–7 6–3, Bloom 6–3 6–2 5–7 7–6, lost Courier [seed 1] 6–4 6–2 6–0), *US Open 1r* (lost Lavalle 6–4 7–6 6–3), *Olympics 1r* (lost Chang [seed 6] 6–1 6–4 3–6 6–0); *r/u* LIPC (d. Agenor 1–6 6–1 6–4, Witsken 6–4 6–3, Becker 4–6 6–1 6–4, Krajicek 6–4 6–7 7–5, Hlasek 7–6 7–5, lost Chang 7–5 7–5), *r/u* Kitzbuhel (d. Saceanu 6–3 4–6 6–4, Azar 6–0 7–5, Perez 6–3 6–4, Muster 7–6 6–1, lost Sampras 6–3 7–5 6–3); *sf* Barcelona (d. Koevermans 6–4 2–6 7–5, Clavet 7–6 6–0, Lendl 3–6 6–3 6–4, lost Costa 6–4 7–6 6–4), *sf* Sao Paulo (d. Allgardh 7–6 7–6, Arriens 7–5 6–4, Roese 6–3 4–6 6–3, lost Oncins 6–3 6–3).

AMOS MANSDORF (ISR)
Born Tel Aviv, 20 October 1965, and lives there; RH; 5ft 9in; 158lb; final 1992 ATP ranking 25; 1992 prize money $357,625.
Coached by Guenther Bresnik. *1984:* (268) Joined Israeli Olympic team; qf US Open Jun. *1985:* (84) R/u Tel Aviv. *1986:* (37) Won first GP title in Johannesburg. *1987:* (27) Beat Mecir and Novacek as he led his country to major upset of TCH in D Cup, d. Connors and Gilbert to win Tel Aviv, and appeared in top 20 in Nov. *1988:* (26) Won Auckland and Paris Open, sf Tel Aviv; upset Becker at Orlando and took Lendl to 5s 1r US Open. *1989:* (39) R/u

Auckland and Singapore; last 16 Australian Open and Wimbledon. *1990:* (33) Won his 1st title on grass at Rosmalen, r/u Tel Aviv, sf Auckland and Toulouse. Upset Gilbert *en route* to last 16 US Open, and in 3r Wimbledon took eventual champion Edberg to 9–7 5s. *1991:* (62) Experienced a quieter year in which his best showing was r/u Toulouse; qf Rosmalen, Manchester and Los Angeles. *1992:* Reached qf Australian Open, unseeded; r/u Philadelphia (d. Stich); sf Memphis (d. B. Gilbert) and appeared in 5 more qf. *1992 HIGHLIGHTS – SINGLES: Australian Open qf* [unseeded] (d. Lundgren 6–4 3–6 6–3 6–4, Boetsch 6–1 6–5 6–0, Reneberg 6–1 6–4 6–3, Krickstein 6–2 4–6 1–6 7–6 4–1 ret'd, lost Courier [seed 2] 6–3 6–2 6–2), *French Open 1r* (lost Zillner 1–6 5–7 7–6 6–0 6–3), *Wimbledon 2r* (d. Naewie 6–3 7–6 6–4, lost Stich [seed 3] 4–6 7–6 6–3 6–3), *US Open 1r* (lost Pozzi 6–7 6–4 6–2 5–7 6–1); *r/u* Philadelphia (d. Van Rensburg 6–4 6–3, Stich 6–4 7–5, Tarango 6–3 6–0, Clavet 5–7 6–3 6–2, lost Sampras 6–1 7–6 2–6 7–6); *sf* Memphis (d. R. Gilbert 6–4 6–2, Clavet 6–4 6–3, B. Gilbert 7–6 7–6, Haarhuis 7–6 6–3, lost W. Ferreira 6–2 6–3).

GABRIEL MARKUS (ARG)
Born Buenos Aires, 31 March 1970, and lives there; RH; 5ft 11in; 155lb; final 1992 ATP ranking 56; 1992 prize money $186,668.
1989: (207) Won Santos Challenger. *1990:* (205). *1991:* (65) Reached his 1st tour qf at Florence, following with the same stage at Sao Paulo, where he also won the Challenger tourn, and broke into the top 100 after an unexpected appearance in last 16 US Open. *1992:* Unseeded, he upset Sampras to win his 1st GP title at Nice, breaking into top 50. He showed he was a player to watch by upsetting Lendl *en route* to sf Madrid, Chang at Gstaad and extending Edberg to 5s at French Open. *1992 HIGHLIGHTS – SINGLES: French Open 2r* (d. Koslowski 7–6 6–3 6–4, lost Edberg [seed 2] 4–6 7–6 7–5 4–6 6–4), Wimbledon 2r (d. Saceanu 7–5 6–3 2–6 7–5), *US Open 2r* (d. Bosse 6–7 6–4 6–3 6–2, lost Krajicek [seed 15] 4–6 2–6 7–6 6–3 6–1); *won* Nice (d. Arrese 6–4 6–2, R. Gilbert 7–6 7–5, Champion 7–5 6–4, Sampras 6–1 2–6 7–6, J. Sanchez 6–4 6–4), *won* Salerno Challenger (d. Alvarez 7–6 6–1); *sf* Gstaad (d. Mancini 6–4 3–6 6–4, Camporese 6–4 3–6 7–6, Chang 7–6 7–6, lost Bruguera 4–6 7–5 7–6). *1992 HIGHLIGHTS – DOUBLES:* (with Sobel) *won* Maceio (d. Acioly/Menezes 6–4 1–6 7–5).

WALLY MASUR (AUS)
Born Southampton, England, 13 May 1963; lives Sydney; RH; 5ft 11in; 167lb; final 1992 ATP ranking 38; 1992 prize money $480,504.
Wife Sue Steel (married 17 Dec. 1989). **1981:** (287) Won Australian Open Jun. *1982:* (125). *1983:* (66) Qf Australian Open and won Hong Kong. *1984:* (106) R/u Taipei. *1985:* (101) R/u Auckland. *1986:* (87) Sf Livingston and Auckland. *1987:* (35) In Adelaide won first tourn since 1983, then upset Becker *en route* to sf Australian Open. *1988:* (46) Won Newport, r/u Adelaide and reached last 16 Australian Open and Wimbledon (d. McEnroe 2r). *1989:* (42) Sf Singapore, Brisbane and Wembley. *1990:* (53) In singles was r/u Memphis; in doubles won Tokyo Suntory with Kratzmann and Hong Kong with Cash. In D Cup won singles v FRA, NZ and ARG, but was dropped from the team that lost 2–3 in f to USA. *1991:* (57) In singles he reached f Hong Kong (upset Hlasek), sf San Francisco, and upset Lendl 1r Sydney. In doubles he won 3 titles with different partners. *1992:* Made unexpected appearances of last 16 Australian Open and Wimbledon (d. B. Gilbert); sf Manchester (d. Volkov) and Toronto; qf San Francisco. Qualified for World Doubles Final with Kratzmann, losing sf to Fitzgerald/Jarryd. *1992 HIGHLIGHTS – SINGLES: Australian Open last 16* [unseeded] (d. Vajda 4–6 6–4 4–6 6–2 6–2, Pescosolido 7–6 6–0 6–4, Washington 6–3 6–3 6–4, lost Stich 3–6 6–4 7–5 6–4), *French Open 2r* (d. Eltingh 6–3 6–3 6–1, lost E. Sanchez 3–6 5–7 6–3 6–4 13–11), *Wimbledon last 16* [unseeded] (d. L. Jonsson 6–2 6–2 6–1, Knowles 6–3 6–4 7–6, B. Gilbert [seed 13] 6–3 6–7 6–7 6–4 6–2, lost Stich [seed 3] 3–6 6–1 6–4 6–4), *US Open 3r* (d. Dosedel 7–6 6–2 6–4, Stark 3–6 6–4 7–6 4–6 6–3, lost W. Ferreira [seed 12] 6–4 6–4 6–2), *Olympics 1r* (lost Sampras [seed 3] 6–1 7–6 6–4); *sf* Manchester (d. Volkov 6–3 4–6 7–5, Pozzi 6–3 7–5, Tarango 6–3 6–4, lost Eltingh 6–2 7–6), *sf* Toronto (d. Braasch 4–6 6–3 6–4, Pearce 4–6 6–4 6–1, Kuhnen 4–6 6–3 6–2, Korda 7–6 4–6 6–3, lost Lendl 6–1 6–2).

ANDREI MEDVEDEV (CIS)

Born Kiev, 31 August 1974, and lives there; RH; 6ft 3in; 178lb; final 1992 ATP ranking 24; 1992 prize money $335,840.
Coach Youri Cherepov. Turned pro 1991. *1990:* Won Orange Bowl over Fernandez. *1991:* (402) Won French Open Jun over Enqvist. *1992:* His run of success began at French Open, where he played through the qualifying and on to the last 16, upsetting Hlasek on the way. Unable to obtain a visa to play the Wimbledon qualifying, he accepted a wild card for Genova and won his 1st tour title there, breaking into the top 100. He followed with the title in Stuttgart after qualifying and upsetting 5 seeds (including Edberg), to reach the top 50, and took a 3rd title at Bordeaux. *1992 HIGHLIGHTS – SINGLES: French Open last 16* [unseeded] (d. Hlasek [seed 16] 7–6 6–3 6–4, Curren 6–4 4–6 6–1 6–3, Woodbridge 7–6 6–2 6–1, lost Courier [seed 1] 6–1 6–4 6–2); *won* Geneva (d. Ardinghi 6–2 6–1, Montana 6–0 6–2, Oncins 1–6 6–2 7–6, Filippini 6–1 7–6, Perez-Roldan 6–3 6–4), *won* Stuttgart (d. Prpic 3–6 7–5 6–0, Volkov 6–4 6–2, E. Sanchez 7–6 6–2, Edberg 1–6 6–4 6–4, Muster 6–2 6–2, W. Ferreira 6–1 6–4 6–7 2–6 6–1), *won* Bordeaux (d. Borg 6–2 6–2, Cherkasov 5–7 6–2 7–5, Costa 7–6 7–6, R. Gilbert 6–4 6–3, Bruguera 6–3 1–6 6–2).

THOMAS MUSTER (AUT)

Born Leibnitz, 2 October 1967; lives there and Monte Carlo; LH; 5ft 11in; 165lb; final 1992 ATP ranking 18; 1992 prize money $456,653.
Coached by Ronald Leitgeb until end 1990 when he became business manager only. *1985:* (98) Won Banana Bowl, r/u French Open Jun and Rolex. Became a member of Austrian D Cup squad and finished 6 on Austrian satellite circuit. *1986:* (47) Won first GP title in Hilversum. *1987:* (56) Sf Vienna (d. E. Sanchez) and won Young Masters. *1988:* (16) Upset Jaite 1r Italian Open and then in the space of 5 weeks won Boston (playing in his 1st GP f), Bordeaux and Prague, following with Bari later in year. *1989:* (21) Reached 1st GS sf at Australian Open. On 1 April, 2 hours after beating Noah to reach f LIPC, which took him into top 10 for 1st time, he was knocked down by a drunken driver in Miami and suffered 2 torn ligaments and torn cartilage in his left knee, requiring reconstructive surgery. In plaster 14 months and was expected to be out of action for about 10 months, but in May he was already practising in a specially designed wheelchair. In Sept., after only 4 months' rehabilitation, he played doubles at Geneva then reached qf Barcelona in singles, following with sf Vienna. *1990:* (7) At Adelaide in Jan. won 1st tour title since injury 10 months earlier, following with Casablanca in March, Italian Open in May and reaching sf French Open to regain his place in the top 10. R/u Monte Carlo and Munich; sf Vienna; qualified for ATP World Champ but failed to reach sf and fell 1r GS Cup to Leconte. Still in pain and advised by doctors to concentrate on CC tourns in 1990. Suspended 5 weeks from 22 Oct. and fined $15,000 (reduced on appeal from a ten-week suspension from US Open plus $25,000 fine) by ATP for violation of best efforts' and unsportsmanlike conduct' – after accepting guarantee to play at Prague he pulled out after just 1 game, having previously expressed his intention to do so. Voted Comeback Player of the Year. *1991:* (35) Underwent arthroscopic surgery on his left knee in March and won no match in his 1st 6 tourns until Italian Open, where he reached 3r, following with qf Bologna. Having dropped out of top 100 for the 1st time since April 1986, he returned after taking the title at Florence, following with Geneva and beating Skoff in f both times. He also reached sf Genova, Prague and Athens. *1992:* He returned to the top 20 with the titles in Monte Carlo, Florence and Umag, plus sf showings at Stuttgart, Kitzbuhel and Tel Aviv. *1992 HIGHLIGHTS – SINGLES: Australian Open 3r* (d. Fleurian 7–6 6–1 7–5, Haarhuis 6–4 6–4 7–6, lost Courier [seed 2] 6–1 6–4 6–2), *French Open 2r* (d. Motta 6–4 6–4 5–7 6–2, lost Courier [seed 1] 6–1 6–4 6–4), *Wimbledon 1r* (lost Stafford 6–3 6–3 7–6), *Olympics 1r* [seed 10] (lost Leconte 7–6 7–6 6–4); *won* Monte Carlo (d. Leconte 3–6 6–4 6–3, Volkov 6–2 4–6 6–1, Forget 7–6 4–6 6–3, Tillstroem 6–3 4–6 6–3, Boetsch 7–5 6–4, Krickstein 6–3 6–1 6–3), *won* Florence (d. Perez-Roldan 6–1 6–7 6–2, Azar 6–1 6–3, Mattar 6–4 6–7 6–3, Gustafsson 6–4 7–5, Furlan 6–3 1–6 6–1), *won* Umag (d. R. Gilbert 6–4 3–6 6–1, Prinosil 6–1 6–0, Perez-Roldan 7–5 6–0, Arrese 6–4 6–4, Davin 6–1 4–6 6–4), *won* Venice Challenger (d. Gorriz 6–4 6–1); *sf* Stuttgart (d. Rosset 6–3 6–2, Stich 7–6 6–4, Karbacher

3–6 6–1 6–3, lost Medvedev 6–2 6–2), *sf* Kitzbuhel (d. Stankovic 6–2 6–3, Oncins 6–4 6–2, Strelba 7–6 6–4, lost Mancini 7–6 6–1), *sf* Tel Aviv (d. Daufresne 7–5 6–4, Bloom 0–6 6–2 6–4, Tarango 6–2 6–4, Simian 4–6 6–3 6–4).

KAREL NOVACEK (TCH)
Born Prostejov, 30 March 1965; lives Prevov; RH; 6ft 3in; 180lb; final 1992 ATP ranking 23; 1992 prize money $650,350.
Wife Maya (married July 1990). Won Nat 12s, 14s, 18s. *1984:* Joined Olympic team. *1985:* (158) Sf Madrid. *1986:* (33) R/u Vienna and captured his first GP title in Washington. Czech Nat champ. *1987:* (76) Reached qf French Open unseeded (d. Jaite); r/u Palermo. *1988:* (127) Qf Nice, Athens and Bastad. *1989:* (74) After splitting with former coach Petr Hutka, he won his 2nd GP title at Hilversum (d. E. Sanchez). *1990:* (34) Scored some major upsets during the year, beating Krickstein and Muster to win Munich, upsetting Krickstein again to reach last 16 French Open and removing Antonitsch, Becker and Skoff back-to-back to reach f Kitzbuhel, as well as appearing in sf Wellington. *1991:* (8) In his best year to date, he broke into the top 20 in April and top 10 in autumn, taking the last berth at ATP World Champ when Edberg withdrew, although he lost all his rr matches there. Won Auckland, Hamburg (d. Sampras), Kitzbuhel and Prague, as well as reaching f Estoril and sf Nice, Madrid, Gstaad (d. Stich) and Hilversum. *1992:* Although he had been selected to play in the Olympics, he chose to stay with his wife, Maya, who was expecting their 1st child and during that time won Hilversum, San Marino and Prague back-to-back. He completed his triumph with the doubles title as well at Prague. He also reached sf Stuttgart as well as qf Brussels, Munich, Gstaad, Lyon and Taipei, but was plagued by lumbago in late summer. *1992 HIGHLIGHTS – SINGLES: Australian Open 2r* [seed 8] (d. Pate 2–6 7–6 6–4 6–1, lost W. Ferreira 3–6 6–3 7–6 7–6), *French Open 1r* (lost Rostagno 3–6 7–5 6–3 6–7 6–3), *Wimbledon 1r* (lost Stolle 7–5 7–6 ret'd); *won* Hilversum (d. Masso 6–4 6–4, Furlan 6–2 0–6 6–3, Eltingh 6–3 6–1, Santoro 6–3 6–1, Arrese 6–2 6–3 2–6 7–5), *won* San Marino (d. Pistolesi 6–2 6–2, Svensson 6–4 6–4, Wuyts 4–6 6–4 6–4, L. Jonsson 6–4 6–1, Clavet 7–5 6–2), *won* Prague (d. Kucera 6–1 7–6, Strelba 7–5 6–1, Perez 6–3 6–2, Rikl 6–2 3–6 6–2, Davin 6–1 6–1); *sf* Stuttgart (d. Berasategui 6–7 7–6 6–2, Delaitre 4–6 6–3 6–4, Costa 6–2 7–6, lost W. Ferreira 6–3 6–2). *1992 HIGHLIGHTS – DOUBLES:* (with Stankovic) *won* Prague (d. Bjorkman/Ireland 7–5 6–1); (with Lendl) *r/u* Barcelona (lost Gomez/J. Sanchez 6–4 6–4), (with Korda) *r/u* Monte Carlo (lost Becker/Stich 6–4 6–4), (with Rikl) *r/u* Basle (lost Nijssen/Suk 6–3 6–4).

JAIME ONCINS (BRA)
Born Sao Paulo, 16 June 1970, and lives there; RH; 6ft 4in; 165lb; final 1992 ATP ranking 48; 1992 prize money $216, 597.
Coached by Paulo Cleto. *1988:* (314). *1989:* (263) Won Lins Challenger. *1990:* (113) Making his mark again on the Challenger circuit, he reached f in 4 tourns, winning Campos and Sao Paulo. *1991:* (64) Won Sao Paulo Challenger again and at end Oct. he reached his 1st tour f at Buzios, following the next week with his 2nd at Sao Paulo to add to his qf showings at Bologna and Geneva. He had overtaken Mattar as No. 1 in his country by end of year. In doubles he reached 4 f with 3 different partners. *1992:* Won his 2 singles matches v Steeb (4s) and Zoecke (5s) as Brazil upset Germany in D Cup. Won his 1st tour title at Bologna in May, following with Buzios in autumn and was r/u Sao Paulo. Upset Lendl on his way to last 16 French Open and at Olympics he surprised Chang *en route* to qf – unseeded both times. *1992 HIGHLIGHTS – SINGLES: Australian Open 1r* (lost Stolle 3–6 6–2 7–5 4–6 6–2), *French Open last 16* [unseeded] (d. Karbacher 6–3 2–6 7–5 4–6 6–4, Lendl [seed 10] 3–6 3–6 6–3 6–2 8–6, Prinosil 6–3 6–2 8–6, lost Korda 6–4 6–3 6–3), *US Open 1r* (lost Connors 6–1 6–2 6–3), *Olympics qf* [unseeded] (d. Muskatirovic 7–6 6–4 6–1 4–6 6–1, Chang [seed 6] 6–2 3–6 6–3 6–3, Koevermans 7–6 6–0 7–6, lost Cherkasov [seed 13] 6–1 6–4 6–7 4–6 6–2); *won* Bologna (d. Youl 6–4 6–3, Roig 3–6 6–4 6–3, Koslowski 7–6 7–5, Gomez 6–2 6–1, Furlan 6–2 6–4), *won* Buzios (d. Frana 6–3 7–6, Azar 7–6 6–4, Jaite 6–3 7–6, Roig 6–1 6–3, Herrera 6–3 6–2); *r/u* Sao Paulo (d. Azar 6–1 6–4, Frana 6–3 4–6 6–4, Jaite 6–4 6–2, Mancini 6–3 6–3, lost Mattar 6–1 6–4).

GUILLERMO PEREZ-ROLDAN (ARG)

Born Tandil, Buenos Aires, 20 October 1969, and lives there; RH; 5ft 10in; 173lb; final 1992 ATP ranking 50; 1992 prize money $169,678.

Coached by his father, Raul. Won Nat. and S American 14s, 16s, 18s. Brother of Mariana. **1985:** (485). **1986:** (109) Sf St Vincent and Buenos Aires and won French Open Jun singles and doubles. **1987:** (19) When he won Munich aged 17 years, 6 months, 10 days he became the second-youngest at the time (after Krickstein) to win a GP title, following with Athens 7 weeks later and Buenos Aires in Nov. to take him into top 20. Won French Open Jun singles again over Stoltenberg. **1988:** (18) Confirmed his CC ability by winning Munich again, taking Lendl to 5s f Italian Open, upsetting Edberg *en route* to qf French Open and also reaching f Hilversum, Prague and Buenos Aires. **1989:** (32) Won Palermo in autumn, r/u Geneva and sf Bologna. **1990:** (14) Won San Marino; r/u Casablanca, Barcelona and Stuttgart; sf Bordeaux and Palermo and reached last 16 French Open. **1991:** (42) Following a slow start to the year with knee and ankle injuries, he won San Marino; upset Ivanisevic *en route* to f Munich, where he was forced to retire in f v Gustafsson; and appeared in sf Barcelona (d. Agassi) and Prague. **1992:** Another solid if unspectacular year in which he won Casablanca and 2 Challenger titles, was r/u Genova and reached sf Bastad and Prague. **1992 HIGHLIGHTS – SINGLES: French Open 1r** (lost Curren 6–2 6–4 6–7 6–3); **won** Casablanca (d. L. Jonsson 5–7 7–6 6–0, Strelba 6–3 6–1, Mattar 6–0 6–3, Berasategui 6–4 6–2, Lopez 2–6 7–5 6–3), **won** Agadir Challenger (d. Roig 6–2 2–6 6–4), **won** Graz Challenger (d. Novacek 3–6 6–2 7–5); **r/u** Genova (d. Fontang 6–1 6–3, Perez 6–4 7–5, Gorriz 7–5 6–1, Skoff 4–6 7–6 4–0 ret'd, lost Medvedev 6–3 6–4); **sf** Bastad (d. Koslowski 6–2 6–0, Pistolesi 6–4 6–1, Larsson 3–6 6–0 6–1, lost Carbonell 7–6 3–6 6–3), **sf** Prague (d. Arriens 6–1 7–6, Krumrey 2–6 7–6 6–2, Garrichidze 6–3 6–0, lost Davin 6–3 6–2).

CEDRIC PIOLINE (FRA)

Born Neuilly sur Seine, 15 June 1969; lives Paris; RH; 6ft 2in; 175lb; final 1992 ATP ranking 33; 1992 prize money $291,029.

Coached by Henri Dumont. **1987:** R/u Nat Jun Champ. **1988:** (461). **1989:** (202). **1990:** (118) Sf Genova and won Brest Challenger. **1991:** (51) Broke into top 100 after reaching sf Nice. (d. Volkov and Leconte back-to-back), following with same stage Bordeaux; qf Genova, Stuttgart Mercedes and Toulouse. **1992:** Scored some useful upsets during the year as he reached last 16 French Open, unseeded (d. B. Gilbert), his 1st tour f at Lyon (d. Forget), sf Bordeaux (d. Lendl) and Moscow (d. Cherkasov) and qf Basle (d. Steeb). **1992 HIGHLIGHTS – SINGLES: Australian Open 2r** (d. Frana 7–6 1–6 6–1 6–1, lost Zoecke 3–6 6–2 7–6 7–6), **French Open last 16** [unseeded] (d. B. Gilbert 2–6 5–7 7–5 6–2 6–1, Daufresne 7–5 6–3 7–5, L. Jonsson 6–2 6–7 6–2 6–2, lost Cherkasov 6–3 6–3 7–6), **Wimbledon 2r** (d. Pistolesi 6–3 3–6 6–3 7–5, lost Saceanu 4–6 6–4 0–6 7–5 7–5), **US Open 3r** (d. Strelba 7–5 2–1 ret'd, Witsken 6–3 5–7 7–5 6–2, lost Courier [seed 1] 7–6 6–4 3–6 6–3); **r/u** Lyon (d. Carbonell 6–0 7–5, Forget 7–5 6–4, Boetsch 6–3 1–6 6–4, Reneberg 6–2 6–7 7–5, lost Sampras 6–4 6–2); **sf** Bordeaux (d. Agenor 2–6 6–3 7–5, Santoro 6–3 6–2, Lendl 7–5 6–4, lost Bruguera 6–2 6–4); **sf** Moscow (d. Antonitsch 6–2 6–4, Reneberg 4–6 6–0 7–6, Cherkasov 6–4 7–6, lost Rosset 7–6 6–1).

RICHEY RENEBERG (USA)

Born Phoenix, Ariz., 5 October 1965; lives Houston, Texas; RH; 5ft 11in; 170lb; final 1992 ATP ranking 95 singles, 4 doubles; 1992 prize money $500,057.

1985: (794) All American at Southern Methodist Univ. for 1st of 3 straight years. **1986:** (337) R/u NCAA singles to Goldie. **1987:** (79) Qf Indianapolis and was voted ATP Newcomer of the Year. No. 1 Collegiate player in US. **1988:** (103) Qf US CC and Vienna. **1989:** (80) Reached 1st GP sf at Auckland and upset Noah *en route* to the same stage at Washington. **1990:** (23) Shot up the rankings into the top 25 with r/u showing at Wellington (d. Chesnokov), plus sf Rosmalen, Indianapolis (d. Sampras) and Tokyo Seiko, and an upset of J. McEnroe at Philadelphia. **1991:** (27) Sidelined at start of year with rotator cuff tendonitis in his right shoulder, he missed the indoor season, but returned to make a surprise appearance in sf LIPC. He went on to win his 1st career singles title at Tampa, breaking into the top 20 in May, and following with sf Birmingham and a surprise defeat of Cherkasov 1r Wimbledon. In doubles won 2 titles with Grabb and reached 2 more f with different partners. *1992:* In singles reached sf Lyon, qf Rosmalen and Los Angeles. Continued his successful doubles partnership with Grabb, winning US Open and r/u Wimbledon to J. McEnroe and Stich, playing a marathon 36-game 5s. They also won San Francisco, Rosmalen and Indianapolis, played 2 more f and qualified for World Doubles Champ. *1992 HIGHLIGHTS – SINGLES: Australian Open 3r* (d. Wuyts 6–2 6–4 7–5, Poliakov 6–3 3–6 6–7 6–4 10–8, lost Mansdorf 6–1 6–4 6–3), *French Open 1r* (lost Prpic 6–0 7–6 6–4), *Wimbledon 1r* (lost Champion 5–7 6–4 3–6 7–6 6–3), *US Open 1r* (lost Leconte 6–4 3–6 6–1 6–2); *sf* Lyon (d. Raoux 7–6 6–4, Steeb 7–6 6–3, Randall 6–3 6–2, lost Pioline 6–2 6–7 7–5). *1992 HIGHLIGHTS – DOUBLES:* (with Grabb) *r/u* Wimbledon (lost J. McEnroe/Stich 5–7 7–6 3–6 7–6 19–17), *won* US Open (d. Jones/Leach 3–6 7–6 6–3 6–3); *won* San Francisco (d. Aldrich/Visser 6–4 7–5), *won* Rosmalen (d. J. McEnroe/Stich 6–4 6–7 6–4), *won* Indianapolis (d. Connell/Michibata 7–6 6–2); *r/u* Philadelphia (lost Woodbridge/Woodforde 6–4 7–6); *r/u* Sydney Indoor (lost P. McEnroe/Stark 6–2 6–3), *r/u* Tokyo Seiko (lost Woodbridge/Woodforde 7–6 6–4). *CAREER HIGHLIGHTS – DOUBLES:* (with Grabb) *US Open – won 1992; Wimbledon – won 1992*

MARC ROSSET (SUI)
Born Geneva, 7 November 1970, and lives there; RH; 6ft 5in; 184lb; final 1992 ATP ranking 35; 1992 prize money $491,440.
Coached by Stephane Oberer. *1988:* Won Orange Bowl and was No. 4 on ITF Jun Rankings. *1989:* (45) On Challenger circuit reached qf or better in 10 tourns, winning 2. Broke into top 100 after winning Geneva in Sept. *1990:* (22) Broke into the top 25 in autumn, following some big upsets during the year. Won his 1st tour title at Lyon (d. Wilander); r/u Madrid (d. E. Sanchez) and Bologna; sf Nice (d. Noah), Gstaad (d. E. Sanchez) and Geneva. *1991:* (60) Sf New Haven (d. Lendl and Chang back-to-back); qf Brussels, LIPC and Hilversum. *1992:* The highlight of his year came in August when he won an Olympic gold medal, unseeded, upsetting Courier (in ss), E. Sanchez and Ivanisevic. He also won Moscow in Nov., reached last 16 Australian Open, unseeded (d. Gustafsson), sf Basle and qf Adelaide, Scottsdale (d. Agassi) and Madrid (d. E. Sanchez). In partnership with Hlasek won his 1st GS title at French Open, plus Italian Open and Lyon, and took Adelaide with Ivanisevic. Played in D Cup squad as SWZ upset FRA in qf. *1992 HIGHLIGHTS – SINGLES: Australian Open last 16* [unseeded] (d. de la Pena 6–1 6–2 6–1, Gustafsson [seed 11] 6–3 7–5 4–6 3–6 6–3, Steeb 6–4 6–4 6–3, lost Courier [seed 2] 6–3 6–1 6–3), *French Open 1r* (lost Sampras [seed 3] 7–6 4–6 6–4 3–6 6–3), *Wimbledon 3r* (d. Richardson 6–2 6–4 6–4, Petchey 7–6 6–2 6–3, lost Ivanisevic [seed 8] 7–6 6–4 6–4), *US Open 1r* (lost Ivanisevic [seed 5] 6–4 6–4 6–4), *Olympic gold medal* [unseeded] (d. Alami 6–2 4–6 2–1 ret'd, W. Ferreira 6–4 6–0 6–2, Courier [seed 1] 6–4 6–2 6–1, E. Sanchez [seed 12] 6–4 7–6 3–6 7–6, Ivanisevic [seed 4] 6–3 7–5 6–2, Arrese 7–6 6–3 3–6 4–6 8–6); *won* Moscow (d. Bates 6–4 6–4, Kafelnikov 6–7 6–3 7–6, Novacek 6–4 6–2, Pioline 7–6 6–1, Steeb 6–2 6–2); *sf* Basle (d. Volkov 7–6 6–4, Svensson 7–5 2–6 6–4, Lundgren 6–4 6–2, lost Becker 6–2 6–4). *1992 HIGHLIGHTS – DOUBLES:* (with Hlasek unless stated) *won* French Open (d. D. Adams/Olhovskiy 7–6 6–7 7–5); (with Ivanisevic) *won* Adelaide (d. Kratzmann/Stoltenberg 7–6 7–6), *won* Italian Open (d. Kratzmann/W. Ferreira 6–4 3–6 6–1), *won* Lyon (d. Broad/Kruger 6–1 6–3); (with J. Sanchez) *r/u* Stuttgart (lost Layendecker/Talbot 4–6 6–3 6–4). *CAREER HIGHLIGHTS – SINGLES: Olympics – gold medal 1992. CAREER HIGHLIGHTS – DOUBLES:* (with Hlasek) *French Open – won 1992.*

EMILIO SANCHEZ (ESP)
Born Madrid, 29 May 1965; lives Barcelona; RH; 5ft 10in; 164lb; final 1992 ATP ranking 21 singles, 22 doubles; 1992 prize money $700,983.
Coached by Pato (Bill) Alvarez. Brother of Javier and Arantxa. *1983:* (208) R/u Orange Bowl and won Spanish Champs. *1984:* (112) Last 16 French Open. *1985:* (64) Upset Nystrom and Jarryd and reached 7 f doubles with Casal, winning 3 titles. *1986:* (16) Emerged as the most improved slow-court player, winning Nice, Munich and Bastad, r/u Italian Open

reaching 5 sfs and twice stopping Wilander and also claiming Becker and Edberg as his victims. *1987:* (17) In singles won Gstaad, Bordeaux, Kitzbuhel, Madrid and reached last 16 French Open and Wimbledon. In doubles with Casal r/u Wimbledon, won 6 titles and qualified for Masters, reaching sf. In mixed doubles won French Open with Shriver and US Open with Navratilova. *1988:* (17) In doubles won French Open with Gomez and Bologna with his brother Javier, while regular partner Casal was undergoing wrist surgery. With Casal won US Open and 7 other titles, plus Olympic silver medal and r/u Masters to R. Leach and Pugh. In singles won Hilversum, reached 3 more f, upset Noah *en route* to qf French Open and d. Mecir to reach same stage at US Open. *1989:* (19) Missed French Open with knee injury which kept him out for 2 months. Won Kitzbuhel in singles and doubles and was r/u Hilversum and Bordeaux. *1990:* (8) In singles won Wellington and Estoril; sf LIPC (d. Lendl), Barcelona, Monte Carlo (d. Becker), Italian Open, Stuttgart, Hilversum and Kitzbuhel. Qualified for ATP World Champ, but won no match there. In doubles reached 9 f, winning 5 with Casal, including French Open, and 1 with Zivojinovic. Qualified with Casal for IBM/ATP World Doubles Final, where they were r/u to Forget/ Hlasek. *1991:* (14) In singles he won Barcelona, Italian Open and Gstaad; r/u Schenectady and Palermo. In doubles won 4 titles with Casal and 1 with Masur, reaching 2 more f with different partners, and in mixed doubles was r/u US Open with his sister, Arantxa. *1992:* Reached last 16 Australian Open, French Open and US Open (d. Korda), qf Olympics and was unbeaten in 7 matches as Spain won World Team Cup. He also won Sydney NSW Open, was r/u Palermo, appeared in sf Lisbon and Schenectady and played 4 other qf. In doubles with Casal won 4 titles in 6 f and qualified for World Doubles Final, where they lost sf to Woodbridge/Woodforde. *1992 HIGHLIGHTS – SINGLES: Australian Open last 16* [seed 13] (d. Arraya 6–3 6–2 6–7 6–3, Cash 7–6 6–2 6–7 6–3 6–1, Schapers 6–3 6–4 7–6, lost J. McEnroe 7–5 7–6 6–2 2–6 8–6), *French Open last 16* [unseeded] (d. Skoff 6–4 6–2 6–2, Masur 3–6 5–7 6–3 6–4 13–11, Wuyts 6–0 6–4 7–6, lost Agassi [seed 11] 6–1 6–3 7–5), *Wimbledon 1r* (lost Volkov [seed 15] 6–3 6–2 4–6 6–4), *US Open last 16* [unseeded] (d. Korda [seed 6] 6–2 4–6 2–6 6–1 7–6, Pridham 7–6 6–7 6–2 6–4, J. Sanchez 5–7 6–1 6–7 7–6 6–4, lost W. Ferreira [seed 12] 6–2 6–4 2–6 6–4), *Olympics qf* [seed 12] (d. Woodbridge 6–1 7–6 6–2, Camporese 6–4 6–2 6–1, Larsson 6–4 7–6 6–7 6–4, lost Rosset 6–4 7–6 3–6 7–6); *won* Sydney NSW Open (d. Skoff 7–6 ret'd, Fitzgerald 6–4 6–4, Muster 6–3 6–3, Camporese 6–4 7–6, Forget 6–3 6–4); *r/u* Palermo (d. Valeri 6–4 6–1, Champion 5–7 7–6 6–4, Carbonell 6–2 6–3, Furlan 6–3 2–6 6–4, lost Bruguera 6–1 6–3); *sf* Lisbon (d. Vysand 6–3 2–6 6–1, Furlan 6–1 6–3, Fontang 7–6 7–6, lost Costa 4–6 7–6 7–6), *sf* Schenectady (d. Naewie 6–3 7–5, Eltingh 4–6 6–4 6–1, Clavet 6–1 6–2, lost Morgan 6–4 7–6). *1992 HIGHLIGHTS – DOUBLES:* (with Casal) *won* Sydney NSW Open (d. S. Davis/Jones 3–6 6–1 6–4), *won* Hamburg (d. Steeb/Stich 5–7 6–4 6–3), *won* Kitzbuhel (d. de la Pena/Flegl 6–1 6–2), *won* Bordeaux (d. Boetsch/Forget 6–1 6–4); *r/u* Milan (lost Broad/MacPherson 5–7 7–5 6–4), *r/u* Schenectady (lost Eltingh/Haarhuis 6–3 6–4). *CAREER HIGHLIGHTS – DOUBLES:* (with Casal unless stated) *French Open* (with Gomez) *won 1988* (d. Fitzgerald/Jarryd 6–3 6–7 6–4 6–3, *won 1990* (d. Ivanisevic/Kulti 7–5 6–3); *US Open – won 1988* (d. R. Leach/Pugh w.o.); *Wimbledon – r/u 1987* (lost Flach/Seguso 3–6 6–7 7–6 6–1 6–4); *Olympics – silver medal 1988* (lost Flach/Seguso 6–3 6–4 6–7 6–7 9–7); *Masters – r/u 1988* (lost R. Leach/Pugh 6–4 6–3 2–6 6–0); *IBM/ATP World Doubles Final – r/u 1990* (lost Forget/Hlasek 6–4 7–6 5–7 6–4). *MIXED DOUBLES: French Open –* (with Shriver) *won 1987* (d. McNeil/Stewart 6–3 7–6); *US Open –* (with Navratilova) *won 1987* (d. Nagelsen/Annacone 6–4 6–7 7–6).

JAVIER SANCHEZ (ESP)
Born Pamplona, 1 February 1968; lives Barcelona; RH; 5ft 10in; 155lb; final 1992 ATP ranking 41 singles, 48 doubles; 1992 prize money $363,990.
Coached by Pato (Bill) Alvarez. Brother of Emilio and Arantxa. *1986:* No. 1 in ITF Jun world rankings. Won Orange Bowl 18s, US Open Jun singles and doubles (with Carbonell), r/u Wimbledon Jun singles and French Open Jun doubles (with Carbonell). *1987:* (110) R/u Madrid to his brother, Emilio. *1988:* (55) Won 1st GP titles at Buenos Aires in both singles and doubles; sf Itaparica and qf Bologna. *1989:* (51) Won both singles and doubles at

Bologna, r/u Sao Paulo singles and took 3 more doubles titles with various partners. *1990:* (70) Reached sf Madrid and last 16 French Open, unseeded. In doubles with various partners reached 6 f, winning 3. *1991:* (32) R/u Umag and Brasilia; sf Buzios and Madrid, upsetting Bruguera there and *en route* to qf US Open, unseeded. In doubles won 3 titles with different partners. *1992:* Upset Forget *en route* to f Nice; sf Madrid, Cologne and Athens. Played 3 doubles f with different partners, winning Barcelona with Gomez. *1992 HIGHLIGHTS – SINGLES: Australian Open 1r* (lost Stich [seed 4] 7–5 6–1 4–6 6–3), *French Open 1r* (lost Gustafsson 6–3 6–2 6–1), *Wimbledon 2r* (d. Raoux 6–4 7–6 5–7 3–6 9–7, lost Bates 7–6 6–3 6–4), *US Open 3r* (d. Naewie 6–4 6–4 5–7 7–6, Champion 7–5 4–1 ret'd, lost E. Sanchez 5–7 6–1 6–7 7–6 6–4); *r/u* Nice (d. Koevermans 2–6 6–4 6–2, Kulti 6–1 6–2, Forget 7–6 6–4, Santoro 6–3 7–6, lost Markus 6–4 6–4); *sf* Madrid (d. P. McEnroe 6–4 6–0, Markus 2–6 6–3 6–2, Arrese 6–3 6–4, lost Bruguera 6–4 6–2), *sf* Cologne (d. Bloom 4–6 6–2 6–2, Jaite 6–2 3–6 6–3, Furlan 6–1 6–4, lost Karbacher 7–6 6–3), *sf* Athens (d. Buchmayer 6–4 7–5, Fontang 6–1 3–6 6–2, Velev 2–6 6–3 6–2, lost Bruguera 7–5 6–7 6–4). *1992 HIGHLIGHTS – DOUBLES:* (with Gomez) **won** Barcelona (d. Lendl/Novacek 6–4 6–4); (with Frana) *r/u* Bologna (lost Jensen/Warder 6–2 6–3), (with Rosset) *r/u* Stuttgart (lost Layendecker/Talbot 4–6 6–3 6–4).

FABRICE SANTORO (FRA)
Born Tahiti, 7 December 1972; lives Toulon; RH; 5ft 10in; 148lb; final 1992 ATP ranking 43; 1992 prize money $199,390.
Nat champ in 12s, 14s and 16s. *1988:* (571) Won Orange Bowl 16s. *1989:* (235) Won French Open Jun over Palmer and was No. 2 in ITF Jun rankings. Upset Gomez at Stuttgart. *1990:* (62) Won Telford Challenger and then upset Gomez again *en route* to his 1st tour f at Toulouse. Qf Nice (d. Chesnokov) and Bordeaux. Voted Newcomer of the Year. *1991:* (43) Won Barcelona, upsetting Bruguera, and Brest Challenger; qf Adelaide, Sydney, Italian Open, Florence, Indianapolis and Bordeaux; last 16 French Open, unseeded. *1992:* Made his mark at the Olympics, where he upset Becker and extended Ivanisevic to 8–6 fs in qf. Scored other big upsets during the year as he moved to sf Nice (d. Chesnokov), Gstaad (d. Novacek), Hilversum and New Haven (d. Korda). *1992 HIGHLIGHTS – SINGLES: French Open 1r* (lost L. Jonsson 2–6 6–3 6–2 7–6), *US Open 2r* (d. Bergstrom 6–4 6–4 7–6, lost Steeb 2–6 7–6 7–5 6–2), *Olympics qf* [unseeded] (d. Miniussi 6–1 7–6 6–4, Frana 4–6 6–2 6–1 6–1, Becker [seed 5] 6–1 3–6 6–1 6–3, lost Ivanisevic [seed 4] 6–7 6–7 6–4 6–4 8–6); *sf* Nice (d. Chesnokov 6–3 0–6 6–3, Delaitre 7–6 7–5, Larsson 6–1 7–6, lost J. Sanchez 6–3 7–6), *sf* Gstaad (d. Rosset 6–4 4–6 7–5, Korda 1–6 7–5 6–2, Novacek 6–4 5–7 6–4, lost Clavet 6–3 6–2), *sf* Hilversum (d. R. Gilbert 6–3 6–3, Nijssen 6–2 6–3, Siemerink 6–3 6–1, lost Novacek 6–3 6–1), *sf* New Haven (d. Van Rensburg 6–3 6–1, B. Gilbert 6–0 7–6, O'Brien 6–3 6–3, Korda 7–6 4–6 6–3, lost Washington 6–4 6–2).

JAN SIEMERINK (NED)
Born Rijnsburg, 14 April 1970, and lives there; LH; 6ft; 156lb; final 1992 ATP ranking 57; 1992 prize money $242,182.
Coached by Rohan Goetze, trained by Fritz Don. *1988:* Nat 18s Champ. *1989:* (477). *1990:* (135) Appeared in his 1st GP sf at Singapore after qualifying. *1991:* (26) Moved into the top 100 with an unscheduled appearance in last 16 Australian Open, then shot through the rankings with his 1st GP title in his 1st f at Singapore in April and r/u placing at Vienna in Oct. (d. Hlasek and Skoff). In addition, he upset Forget at US Open, reached sf Stuttgart Eurocard and won Telford Challenger. From 3 doubles f he won Hilversum with Krajicek. *1992:* It was a less spectacular year, but he scored some more significant upsets in reaching sf Toulouse (d. Steeb) and Vienna (d. B. Gilbert), plus qf Stuttgart (d. Becker), Rotterdam (d. Edberg), Hong Kong and Hilversum. *1992 HIGHLIGHTS – SINGLES: Australian Open 2r* (d. Palmer 6–4 4–6 6–3 4–6 6–2), *French Open 1r* (lost Bloom 5–7 6–4 6–4 4–6 6–2), *Wimbledon 1r* (lost Woodforde 6–3 6–2 3–6 7–5), *US Open 3r* (d. Herrera 6–4 3–6 6–2 6–3, Pescosolido 6–3 6–4 7–6, lost Agassi [seed 8] 6–2 6–3 6–3), *Olympics 1r*

(lost Lavalle 6–4 6–4 6–2); *sf* Toulouse (d. Steeb 7–6 6–7 7–6, Rosset 4–6 6–4 6–4, B. Gilbert 6–4 7–6, lost Korda 7–6 6–3), *sf* Vienna (d. Karbacher 6–1 6–4, Medvedev 6–3 7–6, B. Gilbert 6–1 1–6 6–3, lost Korda 7–5 6–7 6–3).

CARL-UWE (CHARLIE) STEEB (GER)
Born Aalen, 1 September 1967; lives Stuttgart; LH; 5ft 11in; 165lb; final 1992 ATP ranking 29; 1992 prize money $370,278.
1985: (363). **1986:** (150) Won Hauptfeld and r/u Harren on German satellite circuit; qf Buenos Aires. **1987:** (41) Upset Krickstein, Forget and Leconte to reach first GP sf in Stuttgart; qf Munich and Hilversum. **1988:** (73) Upset Zivojinovic *en route* to last 16 Australian Open and Jarryd to reach qf Olympics; sf Lorraine, qf Milan and Munich. Finished the year in style, beating Wilander in 5s as West Germany d. Sweden in D Cup f. **1989:** (15) Won his 1st GP title at Gstaad (d. Krickstein) and reached f Tokyo Seiko. **1990:** (46) Upset Becker and Wilander back-to-back *en route* to f Sydney in Jan.; reached the same stage at Brussels and sf Brisbane, where he d. Wilander again. Pulled out of Paris Open in Oct. with a foot injury, requiring surgery. **1991:** (39) In singles he won Genova, reached sf Milan (d. Chang and Krickstein) and Vienna, made an unexpected appearance in last 16 US Open and upset Ivanisevic at Monte Carlo. In doubles with Jelen he won 2 titles. **1992:** Scored some major upsets as he reached f Moscow, sf Adelaide and Italian Open (d. Chang); last 16 French Open (d. Volkov) and Olympics (d. Stich), unseeded both times; qf Brussels and Monte Carlo (d. Sampras). **1992 HIGHLIGHTS – SINGLES: Australian Open 3r** (d. Furlan 6–4 6–2 6–2, Rahunen 6–4 6–2 7–5, lost Rosset 6–4 6–4 6–3), **French Open last 16** [unseeded] (d. Connell 6–4 6–2 6–2, P. McEnroe 6–2 6–4 3–6 6–3, Volkov [seed 14] 6–2 6–4 6–4, lost Sampras [seed 3] 6–4 6–3 6–2), **Wimbledon 1r** (lost Kinnear 7–6 6–2 6–7 6–1), **US Open 3r** (d. Ruud 6–2 7–6 6–3, Santoro 2–6 7–6 7–5 6–2, lost Becker [seed 7] 6–1 4–6 7–6 6–3), **Olympics last 16** [unseeded] (d. Pavel 7–5 6–2 6–2, Stich [seed 8] 6–4 6–2 4–6 6–3, lost Lavalle 6–4 3–6 6–3 6–2); **r/u** Moscow (d. Carlsen 6–4 6–3, Kulti 6–2 6–3, Medvedev 6–4 6–7 6–3, Hlasek 7–6 6–4, lost Rosset 6–2 6–2); **sf** Adelaide (d. Furlan 6–1 6–4, Stolle 4–6 6–2 6–3, Enqvist 7–6 7–6, lost Bergstrom 7–6 6–4), **sf** Italian Open (d. Krajicek 6–4 5–7 6–2, P. McEnroe 6–2 6–4, Pistolesi 6–1 6–2, Chang 6–4 3–6 6–1, lost Courier 5–7 6–1 6–2). **1992 HIGHLIGHTS – DOUBLES:** (with Stich) **r/u** Hamburg (lost Casal/E. Sanchez 5–7 6–4 6–3).

JEFF TARANGO (USA)
Born Manhattan Beach, Cal., 20 November 1968, and lives there; LH; 5ft 11in; 160lb; final 1992 ATP ranking 45; 1992 prize money $202,758.
1986: Won USTA Boys 18s. 1987: (377) All-American at Stanford. **1988:** (96) Upset Zivojinovic *en route* to 1st GP f at Livingston. **1989:** (137) Qf Schenectady. **1990:** (131) Qf Kiawah Island, d. Leconte and Bruguera at LIPC and won Furth Challenger. **1991:** (106) R/u Seoul, sf Bologna and qf Memphis. **1992:** Won his 1st tour title at Wellington and followed with his second at Tel Aviv in autumn (d. Mansdorf and Muster), breaking into top 50. During the year he also upset Krickstein *en route* to sf US CC and surprised Korda 1r Australian Open. **1992 HIGHLIGHTS – SINGLES: Australian Open 2r** (d. Korda 4–6 4–6 6–3 6–3 6–3, lost P. McEnroe 6–1 4–6 6–4 6–3), **French Open 2r** (d. Agenor 5–7 6–3 6–4 3–6 6–3, lost Prinosil 7–6 1–6 4–6 7–6 6–2), **Wimbledon 1r** (lost Van Rensburg 7–6 6–4 7–5), **US Open 2r** (d. Mancisidor 2–6 6–3 2–6 7–5 6–3, lost Boetsch 4–6 6–4 6–3 7–6); **won** Wellington (d. L. Jonsson 6–2 6–2, Paloheimo 7–5 6–0, Haarhuis 7–6 6–3, Koslowski 6–4 2–6 6–0, Volkov 6–1 6–0 6–3), **won** Tel Aviv (d. Ran 6–3 6–3, Jaite 7–5 7–5, Mansdorf 6–1 3–6 7–6, Muster 6–2 6–4, Simian 4–6 6–3 6–4); **sf** US CC (d. Arias 6–4 6–4, Gorriz 7–6 6–2, Krickstein 5–7 7–6 6–1, lost Washington 6–4 6–4).

ALEXANDER VOLKOV (CIS)
Born Kaliningrad, 3 March 1967, and lives there; LH; 6ft 2in; 175lb; final 1992 ATP ranking 17; 1992 prize money $447,331.
In separate childhood accidents he broke each wrist. Originally played right–handed, then

with either hand, and from 1985, when he broke right wrist, he has played left–handed. *1986:* (529) R/u Nat Champs. *1987:* (104) Upset Gilbert *en route* to last 16 Wimbledon after qualifying, surprised Jaite at Paris Open and broke into top 100 Nov. *1988:* (79) Qf Sydney and won Munich Challenger. *1989:* (50) Sf Adelaide and Munich, then broke into top 50 after reaching 1st GP f at Milan. *1990:* (24) R/u Rosmalen and Berlin; sf Vienna and Stockholm (d. E. Sanchez). In GS reached last 16 Wimbledon, unseeded, and upset top seed Edberg 1r US Open. *1991:* (25) Won his 1st GP title at Milan, breaking into the top 20, and at Wimbledon made an unexpected appearance in last 16, where he took eventual champion Stich to 5s. Reached sf Bastad, Basel, Toulouse and Moscow. *1992:* Won no title, but settled in the top 20 as he scored some big upsets in reaching f Wellington, Rotterdam and Johannesburg (d. W. Ferreira); sf Stuttgart (d. Lendl and Forget) and Tokyo Seiko (d. Edberg), plus 6 qf, including US Open, unseeded (d. Ivanisevic). *1992 HIGHLIGHTS – SINGLES: Australian Open 3r* (d. Woodbridge 6–3 6–2 6–1, Baur 6–4 6–4 6–2, lost Krickstein 6–4 5–7 6–7 6–1 8–6), *French Open 3r* [seed 14] (d. Vajda 4–6 7–6 6–1 1–6 7–5, Naewie 6–4 4–6 4–6 6–2 6–2, lost Steeb 6–2 6–4 6–4), *Wimbledon 3r* [seed 15] (d. E. Sanchez 6–3 6–2 4–6 6–4, Stankovic 6–4 7–5 6–3, lost Holm 6–4 3–6 6–3 7–6), *US Open qf* [unseeded] (d. Youl 2–6 7–6 7–6 6–4, Wuyts 6–1 1–6 1–1 ret'd, Ivanisevic [seed 5] 6–4 6–0 6–3, B. Gilbert 6–2 6–4 5–7 7–6, lost Sampras [seed 3] 6–4 6–1 6–0); *r/u* Wellington (d. Eltingh 6–4 6–4, Bloom 7–6 6–4, Nemecek 6–3 6–4, Washington 6–3 7–6, lost Tarango 6–1 6–0 6–3), *r/u* Rotterdam (d. Larsson 6–7 6–4 6–3, Grabb 6–3 6–3, Siemerink 6–2 6–3, Haarhuis 6–2 6–7 6–2, lost Becker 7–6 4–6 6–2), *r/u* Johannesburg (d. Marsh 6–2 6–0, Bruno 6–0 2–6 6–3, Limberger 6–3 6–0, W. Ferreira 6–4 7–6, lost Krickstein 6–4 6–4); *sf* Stuttgart (d. Kuhnen 7–6 6–4, Lendl 7–6 5–7 6–1, Forget 6–4 6–4, lost Ivanisevic 3–6 6–3 6–4), *sf* Tokyo Seiko (d. Fromberg 6–3 6–1, Matsuoka 7–5 6–2, Edberg 6–3 3–6 7–5, lost Holm 7–5 6–2).

MALIVAI WASHINGTON (USA)
Born Glen Cove, NY, 20 June 1969; lives Swartz Creek, Mich.; RH; 5ft 11in; 175lb; final 1992 ATP ranking 13; 1992 prize money $516,453.
Coached by his father, William. *1987:* R/u Easter Bowl. *1988:* (329) All-American at Univ. of Michigan. *1989:* (199) Won Seattle Challenger. *1990:* (93) Reached sf Orlando after qualifying and appeared at same stage US CC. Upset Lendl in ss 1r New Haven in Aug. *1991:* (49) Sf Chicago, Orlando (d. B. Gilbert), US CC (d. Wheaton) and Queen's. In GS he extended Forget to 7–5 5s at French Open and handed the same treatment to Lendl at Wimbledon. *1992:* Began the year in style with sf showing at Wellington, progressing to his 1st tour f at Auckland a week later and following with his 1st title at Memphis in Feb. (d. Chang), to move into top 25. He won US CC in May and to these successes added r/u Tampa, Manchester and New Haven (d. Ivanisevic); sf Scottsdale, Washington, Toronto and Lyon, so that by end of year he was poised just outside the top 10. *1992 HIGHLIGHTS – SINGLES: Australian Open 3r* (d. Stafford 6–4 6–2 6–1, Prpic 6–2 6–4 6–3, lost Masur 6–3 6–3 6–4), *French Open 2r* (d. Roig 6–3 7–6 4–6 6–2, lost Krickstein [seed 13] 4–6 5–7 6–4 7–6 6–3), *Wimbledon 1r* (lost Matsuoka 7–5 6–4 6–1), *US Open last 16* [seed 14] (d. Montana 6–3 7–6 6–3, Goellner 6–3 6–3 6–2, Leconte 6–4 6–7 6–4 6–3, lost Chang [seed 4] 6–2 2–6 3–6 6–3 6–1); *won* Memphis (d. Shelton 6–0 6–3, Chang 7–6 7–6, Schapers 6–3 7–5, Connors 6–2 7–5, W. Ferreira 6–3 6–2), *won* US CC (d. de la Pena 6–3 6–1, Garner 6–3 6–0, Davin 6–3 7–5, Tarango 6–4 6–4, Mezzadri 6–3 6–3); *r/u* Auckland (d. Gomez 6–3 6–2, Matsuoka 6–3 6–4, Cherkasov 6–4 6–2, Zoecke 6–2 6–4, lost Yzaga 7–6 6–2), *r/u* Tampa (d. Apell 6–2 6–3, Roese 7–6 4–6 6–1, Filippini 4–6 7–6 6–4, Davin 6–3 4–6 6–2, lost Yzaga 4–6 6–3 6–1), *r/u* Manchester (d. Kuhnen 7–6 6–4, Bates 4–6 6–4 6–3, Youl 6–4 7–5, Herrera 6–1 6–1, lost Eltingh 6–3 6–4), *r/u* New Haven (d. Herrera 6–4 6–3, J. McEnroe 7–6 6–3, Ivanisevic 6–4 7–5, Santoro 6–4 6–2, lost Edberg 7–6 6–1); *sf* Wellington (d. Poliakov 6–4 6–3, Olhovskiy 6–1 6–4, Nargiso 3–6 3–2 ret'd, lost Volkov 6–3 7–6), *sf* Scottsdale (d. Furlan 7–6 6–3, Yzaga 6–4 6–3, Mancini 6–3 6–4, lost B. Gilbert 6–3 3–6 6–2), *sf* Washington (d. Hogstedt 7–5 6–0, Arias 3–6 6–2 6–3, Raoux 7–6 7–6, lost Korda 7–6 6–0), *sf* Toronto (d. Connell 4–6 7–6 6–1, Curren 6–4 7–6, Krickstein 7–6 6–1, lost Agassi 2–6 6–2 6–1), *sf* Lyon (d. P. McEnroe 6–3 6–4, Hlasek 6–3 6–4, Novacek 6–3 6–1, lost Sampras 6–0 6–2).

DAVID WHEATON (USA)

Born Minneapolis, Minn., 2 June 1969; lives Lake Minnetonka, Minn.; RH; 6ft 4in; 185lb; final 1992 ATP ranking 44; 1992 prize money $285, 869.
Coached by Jerry Noyce. Spent time at Nick Bollettieri Tennis Academy. Travels with brother John, a lawyer. *1985–87:* Member of US Jun D Cup squad. *1986:* A freshman at Stanford, was r/u Nat Jun Champs. *1987:* (345) Extended Lendl to 3s at Washington and won US Open Jun singles over Cherkasov and US Nat 18s clay court over Courier. *1988:* (441). Played No. 1 singles and doubles for Stanford's NCAA winning team. *1989:* (66) Upset Agassi *en route* to sf Stratton Mountain and won Brasilia Challenger. *1990:* (27) Reached qf Australian Open and US Open and last 16 Wimbledon (lost Gilbert 13–11 5s), all unseeded, and with Annacone reached f doubles at US Open. Out of action 10 weeks early in year with stress fracture of leg, returning in May to win 1st tour title at US CC and broke into top 50. Reached sf inaugural GS Cup. *1991:* (17) Following 4 1r losses at beginning of the year, he enjoyed his best season yet, upsetting Agassi and Edberg *en route* to f LIPC, Lendl and Agassi *en route* to sf Wimbledon, unseeded. He was also r/u Queen's and sf Indianapolis and in doubles with P. McEnroe he reached f Australian Open. Ended year with first Compaq Grand Slam Cup title, winning $2 million. *1992:* It was a disappointing season after the triumphs of the previous year, and he reached only one sf – at Sydney NSW Open – plus qf Cincinnati (d. Courier) and Paris Open (d. Chang). Out for 2 months, returning in May. *1992 HIGHLIGHTS – SINGLES: Australian Open last 16* [seed 15] (d. Cask 6–4 6–0 6–0, Kulti 6–3 5–7 6–4 2–6 8–6, Koslowski 6–4 6–3 6–3, lost W. Ferreira 6–7 6–4 6–2 6–2), *French Open 2r* (d. Chesnokov 3–6 3–6 6–4 6–0 6–2, lost Larsson 7–6 6–4 6–1), *Wimbledon 3r* [seed 14] (d. Clavet 6–3 6–3 6–3, Martin 6–3 6–3 6–7 6–3, lost J. McEnroe 6–3 6–4 6–4), *US Open 3r* (d. Sznajder 6–3 6–7 6–3 6–4, Palmer 6–4 6–4 6–0, lost Forget [seed 13] 6–3 7–6 2–6 6–2); *sf* Sydney NSW Open (d. Masur 7–5 7–5, Delaitre 6–4 6–3, Hlasek 3–6 6–1 7–5, lost Forget 6–3 6–2). *1992 HIGHLIGHTS – DOUBLES:* (with Annacone) *r/u* Newport (lost Deppe/Rikl 6–4 6–4), (with Montana) *r/u* Los Angeles (lost Galbraith/Pugh 7–6 7–6).

TODD WOODBRIDGE (AUS)

Born Sydney, 2 April 1971; lives Woolooware; RH; 5ft 10in; 158lb; final 1992 ATP ranking 54 singles, 2 doubles; 1992 prize money $656,642.
Coached by Ray Ruffels. *1987:* (420) R/u Australian Open Jun to Stoltenberg with whom he won the doubles there and at Wimbledon. *1988:* (213) Won Tasmania and in Jun doubles with Stoltenberg won Australian Open, French Open and Wimbledon. *1989:* (131) Won Brisbane Challenger, upset Fitzgerald *en route* to sf GP event there and finished the year by winning Hobart Challenger. In Jun doubles won Australian and French Open with J. Anderson and in Jun singles r/u Wimbledon to Kulti. *1990:* (50) Upset Chang *en route* to 1st tour f at New Haven and Gilbert *en route* to sf Sydney Indoor. In doubles with various partners reached 4 f, winning 2, and took US Open mixed with Smylie. *1991:* (77) Upset Svensson *en route* to last 16 Australian Open, unseeded, and at French Open extended Becker to 5s. In doubles won 6 titles, 4 with Woodforde, with whom he qualified for ATP Doubles Champ. *1992:* R/u Seoul (d. Chang), sf Hong Kong, qf Tokyo Suntory and upset Stich at Sydney NSW Open. In doubles with Woodforde won a 1st men's GS title at Australian Open, World Doubles Final and 6 other titles, winning every f they played to finish the year as the top–ranked pairing. In mixed doubles with Sanchez-Vicario won French Open and r/u Australian Open. *1992 HIGHLIGHTS – SINGLES: Australian Open 1r* (lost Volkov 6–3 6–2 6–1), *French Open 3r* (d. Boetsch 4–6 5–7 7–6 6–4 6–2, Rostagno 4–6 7–6 6–3 6–3, lost Medvedev 7–6 6–2 6–1), *Wimbledon 2r* (d. Roese 6–2 7–5 6–4, lost Sampras [seed 5] 7–6 7–6 6–7 6–4), *US Open 2r* (d. Corretja 6–2 6–2 6–2, lost Woodforde 6–3 6–2 7–6), *Olympics 1r* (lost E. Sanchez [seed 12] 6–1 7–6 6–2); *r/u* Seoul (d. Saceanu 6–4 6–1, Chang 2–6 6–4 7–5, Mronz 6–2 6–1, Kuhnen 6–4 6–1, lost Matsuoka 6–3 4–6 7–5); *sf* Hong Kong (d. Zoecke 6–7 7–6 6–2, Baur 6–4 6–0, Curren w.o., lost Chang 6–3 6–7 6–1). *1992 HIGHLIGHTS – DOUBLES:* (with Woodforde) *won* Australian Open (d. Jones/Leach 6–4 6–3 6–4), *won* Memphis (d. Curren/Muller 7–5 4–6 7–6), *won* Philadelphia (d. Grabb/Reneberg 6–4 7–6), *won* Singapore (d. Connell/Michibata 6–7 6–2 6–4), *won*

Cincinnati (d. P. McEnroe/Stark 6–3 1–6 6–3), *won* Tokyo Seiko (d. Grabb/Reneberg 7–6 6–4), *won* Stockholm (d. Devries/MacPherson 6–3 6–4), *won* World Doubles Final (d. Fitzgerald/Jarryd 6–2 7–6 5–7 3–6 6–3). *MIXED DOUBLES:* (with Sanchez-Vicario) *r/u* Australian Open (lost Woodforde/Provis 6–3 4–6 11–9), *won* French Open (d. McNeil/Shelton 6–2 6–3). *CAREER HIGHLIGHTS – DOUBLES:* (with Woodforde) *Australian Open – won 1992; World Doubles Final – won 1992. MIXED DOUBLES:* (with Sanchez-Vicario unless stated) *French Open – won 1992; US Open –* (with Smylie) *won 1990.*

MARK WOODFORDE (AUS)
Born Adelaide, 23 September 1965, and lives there; LH; 6ft 2in; 165lb; final 1992 ATP ranking 40 singles, 1 doubles; 1992 prize money $706,836.
Coached by Barry Phillips–Moore. *1984:* (385). *1985:* (127). *1986:* (181) Won 1st pro title at Auckland, sf Bristol. *1987:* (67) Last 16 US Open (d. Mayotte) after qualifying. *1988:* (42) Enjoyed a remarkable year, with success on all surfaces, in which he extended Lendl to 5 close sets in 46–hour 4r match at Wimbledon, conceding only 10–8 in 5s, upset Edberg and J. McEnroe to reach sf Toronto and beat McEnroe again *en route* to last 16 US Open, unseeded. Formed a useful doubles partnership with J. McEnroe in autumn. *1989:* (75) In singles won Adelaide and r/u Brisbane. In doubles won US Open with J. McEnroe and Monte Carlo with Smid. *1990:* (101) Upset Chesnokov 2r Australian Open, but was forced to retire in 3r v Wheaton when he tore 2 ligaments in his ankle, requiring surgery. Out of action until June, when he progressed to last 16 Wimbledon, unseeded and a wild card, and in Aug. reached sf New Haven. *1991:* (101) Upset E. Sanchez *en route* to last 16 Australian Open (unseeded), Chesnokov in reaching qf Copenhagen and Korda 1r Moscow. Won 4 doubles titles with Woodbridge to qualify for ATP Doubles Champ. *1992:* In singles he was r/u Los Angeles and Antwerp (d. Lendl and Chang) and reached qf Singapore, Tampa and US CC. With Woodbridge won Australian Open doubles, World Doubles Final and 6 other titles, winning every f they played to finish the year as the top–ranked pairing. In mixed doubles with Provis, he won Australian Open and US Open.
1992 HIGHLIGHTS – SINGLES: Australian Open 3r (d. Yzaga 6–4 7–6 6–1, Clavet 6–7 6–4 6–1 3–6 7–5, lost W. Ferreira 4–6 6–3 6–2 6–2), *French Open 1r* (lost Filippini 6–3 7–6 6–1), *Wimbledon 2r* (d. Siemerink 6–3 6–2 3–6 7–5, lost Ivanisevic [seed 8] 6–4 6–4 6–7 6–3), *US Open 3r* (d. Nelson 7–6 6–4 7–6, Woodbridge 6–3 6–2 7–6, lost Krajicek [seed 15] 6–1 6–3 6–2); *r/u* Los Angeles (d. Bates 6–3 6–2, Volkov 6–3 6–4, Connors 6–4 4–6 6–4, Krickstein 4–2 30–40 ret'd, lost Krajicek 6–4 2–6 6–4), *r/u* Antwerp (d. Clavet 7–6 2–6 6–2, Lendl 6–4 6–2 M. Larsson 6–0 7–6, Chang 7–6 6–3, lost Krajicek 6–2 6–2). *1992 HIGHLIGHTS – DOUBLES:* (with Woodbridge) *won* Australian Open (d. Jones/Leach 6–4 6–3 6–4); *won* Memphis (d. Curren/Muller 7–5 4–6 7–6), *won* Philadelphia (d. Grabb/Reneberg 6–4 7–6), *won* Singapore (d. Connell/Michibata 6–7 6–2 6–4), *won* Cincinnati (d. P. McEnroe/Stark 6–3 1–6 6–3), *won* Tokyo Seiko (d. Grabb/Reneberg 7–6 6–4), *won* Stockholm (d. Devries/MacPherson 6–3 6–4), *won* World Doubles Final (d. Fitzgerald/Jarryd 6–2 7–6 5–7 3–6 6–3). *MIXED DOUBLES:* (with Provis) *won* Australian Open (d. Woodbridge/Sanchez-Vicario 6–3 4–6 11–9), *won* US Open (d. Sukova/Nijssen 4–6 6–3 6–3). *CAREER HIGHLIGHTS – DOUBLES:* (with Woodbridge unless stated) *Australian Open – won 1992; US Open –* (with J. McEnroe) *won 1989* (d. Flach/Seguso 6–4 4–6 6–3 6–3); *World Doubles Final – won 1992. MIXED DOUBLES:* (with Provis) *Australian Open – won 1992; US Open – won 1992.*

JAIME YZAGA (PER)
Born Lima, 23 October 1967, and lives there; RH; 5ft 7in; 134lb; final 1992 ATP ranking 49; 1992 prize money $202,670.
Coached by Colon Nunez. Has suffered from recurring shoulder injury since 1982. *1981:* Won S. American 16s. *1983:* Won S. American 18s. *1984:* Joined Peruvian D Cup squad. *1985:* (45) Won French Jun and Wimbledon Jun doubles before bursting into last 16 US Open, after qualifying, where he was the only player to take a set off Lendl. Voted Newcomer of the Year. *1986:* (64) Played D Cup for Peru, scored wins over Hlasek, Pecci and Pate and reached sf Tokyo. *1987:* (70) Won first GP singles title at Schenectady,

following with Sao Paulo. *1988:* (65) Finished the year on a high note by winning Itaparica. Upset Gilbert at US Open and reached qf Italian Open, Florence and Sao Paulo. *1989:* (23) Upset Chang *en route* to f Tourn of Champs and Mecir at LIPC, as well as reaching sf Guaruja, Bordeaux, Orlando (d. E. Sanchez) and Itaparica. *1990:* (87) R/u Sao Paulo and upset Berger at Monte Carlo. *1991:* (53) Won US CC, upsetting Chang; sf Washington; and made an unexpected appearance in qf Australian Open. *1992:* Returned from a 4-month absence with patellar tendonitis to win Auckland in Jan., following with Tampa and beating Washington in both f. Reached sf Sao Paulo, qf Italian Open and Cincinnati (d. Agassi) and upset B. Gilbert at LIPC. *1992 HIGHLIGHTS – SINGLES: Australian Open 1r* (lost Woodforde 6–4 7–6 6–1), *French Open 1r* (lost Schaller 1–6 7–6 5–7 7–5 9–7), *Wimbledon 2r* (d. Gomz 6–4 6–4 6–2, lost Rostagno 6–3 6–3 6–1), *US Open 1r* (lost Lendl [seed 9] 6–7 6–1 7–5 4–6 6–3), *Olympics 2r* (d. Paes 1–6 7–6 6–0 6–0, lost Sampras 6–3 6–0 3–6 6–1); *won* Auckland (d. Fleurian 6–2 1–6 6–2, Clavet 6–4 7–6, Naewie 6–3 7–6, Connell 6–4 6–2, Washington 7–6 6–4), *won* Tampa (d. Mattar 7–6 6–7 6–2, Eltingh 6–4 6–4, Woodforde 4–6 6–0 7–5, Mezzadri 5–7 6–4 7–6, Washington 4–6 6–3 6–1); *sf* Sao Paulo (d. Lopez 6–7 7–6 6–0, Meligeni 7–5 6–4, Baur 7–6 7–6, lost Mattar 7–6 6–2).

MONICA SELES (YUG)

Turned pro: 1989

Born: Novi Sad, 2 December 1973.
Lives: Sarasota, Fla.
Father: Karolj is cartoonist and TV director. **Mother:** Esther.
Brother: Zoltan (older). Both parents travel with her, and her brother helps to train her. Discovered at 1985 Orange Bowl by Nick Bollettieri, who moved her family to USA from Yugoslavia in 1986.
Agent: International Management Group.
Coach: Her father, Karolj.

Height: 5ft 9in (1.77m). **Weight:** 130lb (59kg).

Rankings: 1988: 86; **1989:** 6; **1990:** 2; **1991:** 1; **1992:** 1. **Highest:** 1 (March 1991).

1992 Prize Money: $2,622,352. **Career Earnings:** $6,971,393. **Career Titles:** 30.

Style: A naturally competitive left-hander who hits with two-hands on both forehand and backhand. Her ability to hit a rising ball with perfect timing allows her to project thunderous drives on both wings that have destroyed all opposition. An improving serve that is now the equal of any of the women, plus a greater willingness to volley, allied to an acute tactical awareness, make her arguably the finest match player of all time.

CAREER HIGHLIGHTS (year: *(titles)*)
1983: At age 9, reached last 16 Sport Goofy singles. **1984:** Won Sport Goofy singles. **1985:** Won Sport Goofy singles and doubles. **1988:** Upset Kelesi at VS Florida in 1st pro match, took Sabatini to 1s tb 1r LIPC and upset Magers and McNeil to reach sf New Orleans. **1989:(1)** *Houston.* Upset Savchenko and Manuela Maleeva at VS Washington, but had to default sf owing to injury, then won Houston over Evert and was r/u Dallas and Brighton. Unseeded at French Open, she upset Garrison and.Manuela Maleeva before extending Graf to 3s sf; reached last 16 Wimbledon and US Open and qualified for 1st VS Champs, where she lost qf to Navratilova. **1990: (9)** *Berlin, Los Angeles, Oakland FRENCH OPEN, VS Champs, LIPC, San Antonio, Tampa, Italian Open.* Following her acrimonious split in March with Bollettieri, who she considered was spending too much time coaching Agassi, she was coached only by her father. At 16 years 6 months became the youngest French Open women's champion and second-youngest GS champion (after Lottie Dod, who was 15 years 10 months when she won Wimbledon in 1897). She went into the French Open having won 5 consec tourns without dropping a set, but her unbeaten run of 36 matches was ended by Garrison in qf Wimbledon. She in turn had ended Graf's 66-match unbeaten run at Berlin. Her season finished in triumph when she beat Sabatini in 5s in f VS Champs to finish with 9 titles. She beat Graf twice and Navratilova 3 times and by year's end had displaced Navratilova to finish ranked 2. Won WTA Most Improved Player award. **1991: (10)** *AUSTRALIAN OPEN, FRENCH OPEN, US OPEN, VS Champs, LIPC, Houston, Los Angeles, Tokyo Nicherei, Milan, Philadelphia.* Enjoyed a spectacular year in which she reached f in all 16 tourns she entered, winning Australian Open, French Open, US Open and VS Champs, plus 6 more titles. At 17 years 2 moth she became the youngest to take the Australian Open, being 4 months younger than Margaret Smith in 1960, and in March she ousted Graf from the top ranking to become the youngest (17 years 3 months) to reach that spot (Tracy Austin had been 1 month older). Although Graf overtook her again briefly on and off during the summer, Seles finished the year firmly fixed at the top, was voted WTA Singles Player of the Year and was the youngest to be named Official World Champion. She caused much controversy during the year, notably when she pulled out of Wimbledon 72 hours before the start, failing to give a satisfactory explanation and losing her chance of completing a GS. Various explanations were offered, the first being that she had suffered 'a minor accident' but eventually she claimed she had panicked after being given conflicting advice that the shin splints from which she was suffering might keep her out of the game for 6 months or a year. She was fined $6,000 for withdrawing and $20,000

for subsequently appearing in an exhibition tournament. She also missed Fed Cup, claiming injury, although she played an exhibition tournament at the same time. **1992: (10)** *AUSTRALIAN OPEN, FRENCH OPEN, US OPEN, VS Champs, Essen, Indian Wells, Houston, Barcelona, Tokyo Nicherei, Oakland.* After she had won Australian Open and become the 1st woman since Hilde Sperling in 1937 to win 3 consec French Opens, she seemed on course for a GS. But Graf, who had stretched her to 10–8 fs in Paris, demolished her in Wimbledon f and thereafter she seemed less invincible, although she won her 3rd GS title of the year at US Open and finished the season with ss win over Navratilova in f of VS Champs. She was beaten all year only 5 times – by Capriati at LIPC (the only tourn she entered in which she failed to reach the f), by Sabatini at Italian Open, Graf at Wimbledon, Navratilova at Los Angeles and by Sanchez-Vicario at Montreal. She took a total of 10 titles, including Houston for the loss of only 8 games, and when she won Barcelona at 18 years 4 months, she beat Tracy Austin's record of 18 years 8 months as youngest to achieve 25 singles titles. Controversy was never far away, and in 1992 it was her grunting which was the main subject. She played the Wimbledon final almost silently (refusing to make that an excuse for her defeat) and for the rest of the year made an attempt to control the noise, which players and spectators alike found distasteful and disturbing. She was voted Player of Year for second straight year and set a new record for prize money won in one season, beating Edberg's record $2,363,575 in 1991.

PRINCIPAL 1992 RESULTS (detailed Grand Slams results below)
won Essen (d. Kerek 6–2 6–2, Lindqvist 6–3 6–2, Pierce 6–0 6–1, M. J. Fernandez 6–0 6–3, Sanchez-Vicario 6–3 6–3), **won** Indian Wells (d. E. Reinach 6–1 6–1, Tami Whitlinger 6–2 6–3, G. Fernandez 6–0 6–0, K. Maleeva 6–1 6–0, Martinez 6–3 6–1), **won** VS Houston (d. Paz 6–0 6–0, Fulco Villella 6–1 6–0, Gildemeister 6–4 6–1, Garrison 6–1 6–1), **won** Barcelona (d. Muns Jagerman 6–3 6–1, Pierce 7–6 6–4, Maleeva Fragni0re 6–3 6–1, Sanchez-Vicario 3–6 6–2 6–3), **won** Tokyo Nicherei (d. Wang 6–0 6–1, Sawamatsu 6–1 6–0, M. J. Fernandez 6–0 3–6 6–4, Sabatini 6–2 6–0), **won** Oakland (d. Rehe 6–4 6–1, Majoli 6–3 6–1, Huber 6–2 6–3, Navratilova 6–3 6–4), **won** VS Champs (d. Tauziat 6–1 6–2, Novotna 3–6 4–6 6–1, Sabatini 7–6 6–1, Navratilova 7–6 6–3 6–1), **r/u** Italian Open (d. Baudone 6–0 6–4, Cunningham 6–0 6–1, Meskhi 6–1 6–4, Coetzer 6–0 6–4, lost Sabatini 7–5 6–4), **r/u** VS Los Angeles (d. Habsudova 6–2 6–2, Frazier 6–2 6–0, Sanchez-Vicario 6–3 6–2, lost Navratilova 6–4 6–2), **r/u** Montreal (d. Werdel 6–2 6–4, Sawamatsu 6–1 6–2, Hy 6–1 4–6 6–1, McNeil 6–2 6–4, lost Sanchez-Vicario 6–4 3–6 6–4). **DOUBLES** (+Sukova) **won** Italian Open (d. K. Maleeva/Rittner 6–1 6–2).

CAREER GRAND SLAM RECORD
AUSTRALIAN OPEN
1991: won [seed 2] d.Hack 6–0 6–0, Caverzasio 6–1 6–0, Kschwendt 6–3 6–1, Tanvier 6–2 6–1, Huber 6–3 6–1, Fernandez [seed 3] 6–3 0–6 9–7, Novotna [seed 10] 5–7 6–3 6–1. **1992: won** [seed 1] d.Kijimuta 6–2 6–0, Date 6–2 7–5, Basuki 6–1 6–1, Meskhi [seed 13] 6–4 4–6 6–2, Huber [seed 12] 7–5 6–3, Sanchez-Vicario [seed 4] 6–2 6–2, M. J. Fernandez [seed 7] 6–2 6–3.

FRENCH OPEN
1989: sf d.Reis 6–4 6–1, Martin 6–0 6–2, Garrison [seed 4] 6–3 6–2, Faull 6–3 6–2, M.Maleeva [seed 6] 6–3 7–5, lost Graf [seed 1] 6–3 3–6 6–3. **1990: won** [seed 2] d.Piccolini 6–0 6–0, Kelesi 4–6 6–4 6–4, Meskhi 7–6 7–6, Gildemeister [seed 16] 6–4 6–0, Maleeva Fragniere [seed 6] 3–6 6–1 7–5, Capriati 6–2 6–2, Graf [seed 1] 7–6 6–4. **1991: won** [seed 1] d. Zrubakova 6–3 6–0, de Swardt 6–0 6–2, Quentrec 6–1 6–2, Cecchini 3–6 6–3 6–0, Martinez [seed 7] 6–0 7–5, Sabatini [seed 3] 6–4 6–1, Sanchez-Vicario [seed 5] 6–3 6–4. **1992: won** [seed 1] (d. Mothes 6–1 6–0, Kschwendt 6–2 6–2, McNeil 6–0 6–1, Kijimuta 6–1 3–6 6–4, Capriati [seed 5] 6–2 6–2, Sabatini [seed 3] 6–3 4–6 6–4, Graf [seed 2] 6–2 3–6 10–8),

WIMBLEDON
1989: 4r [seed 11] d.Schultz 7–6 1–6 6–4, Porwik 6–2 6–4, Sviglerova 6–4 6–3, lost Graf

[seed 1] 6–0 6–1. **1990: qf** [seed 3] d.Strandlund 6–2 6–0, Benjamin 6–3 7–5, A.Minter 6–3 6–3, Henricksson 6–1 6–0, lost Garrison [seed 5] 6–3 3–6 6–4. **1992: r/u** [seed 1] d. Byrne 6–2 6–2, Appelmans 6–3 6–2, Gildemeister 6–4 6–1, G. Fernandez 6–4 6–2, Tauziat [seed 14] 6–1 6–3, Navratilova [seed 4] 6–2 6–7 6–4, lost Graf 6–2 6–1.

US OPEN

1989: 4r [seed 12] d.Henricksson 4–6 6–2 6–2, A.Smith 7–5 6–2, Stafford 7–6 6–2, lost Evert [seed 4] 6–0 6–2. **1990: 3r** [seed 3] d. Pampoulova 6–0 6–0, Fairbank Nideffer 6–2 6–2, lost Ferrando 1–6 6–1 7–6. **1991: won** [seed 2] d.Arendt 6–2 6–0, Zardo 7–5 6–1, Gomer 6–1 6–4, Rajchrtova 6–1 6–1, G.Fernandez 6–2 6–2, Capriati [seed 7] 6–3 3–6–7–6, Navratilova [seed 6] 7–6 6–1. **1992: won** [seed 1] d. Keller 6–1 6–0, Raymond 7–5 6–0, Porwik 6–4 6–0, G. Fernandez 6–1 6–2, Hy 6–1 6–2, M. J. Fernandez [seed 7], Sanchez-Vicario [seed 5] 6–3 6–3.

STEFFI GRAF (GER)   **Turned pro:** 1982

Born: Bruhl, 14 June 1969.
Lives: There and Gleneagles Country Club, Delray Beach, Fla.
Father: Peter. **Mother:** Heidi.
Brother: Michael. (younger).
Agent: Advantage International.
Coaches: Her father, Peter. Hitting partner is Heinz Gunthardt;
Pavel Slozil was her hitting partner until Nov. 1991.
Height: 5ft 9in (1.75m). **Weight:** 132lb (59kg).

Rankings: 1982: 214; **1983:** 98; **1984:** 22; **1985:** 6; **1986:** 3; **1987:** 1; **1988:** 1; **1989:** 1;
1990: 1; **1991:** 2. **Highest:** 1 (August 1987).

1992 Prize Money: $1,691,139. **Career Earnings:** $10,332,673. **Career Titles:** 70.

Style: A right-hander with the most powerful single-handed forehand in the game and a natural sliced backhand that she uses to open up the court for forehand winners. She also has one of the best serves in women's tennis with an excessively high toss that gives trouble in the wind. A born athlete and graceful mover who is the fastest woman about a tennis court of modern times. Although she can volley, she is reluctant to leave the familiar territory of the baseline from where she can dominate all players except Seles who outdrives her.

CAREER HIGHLIGHTS (year: *(titles)*)
1982: The youngest at the time to receive a WTA ranking at 13 years 4 months; won European 14s and European circuit Masters. **1983: sf** Freiburg. **1984: (1)** *Olympics.* Won demonstration event in LA and reached last 16 Wimbledon. **1985: sf** US Open and LIPC; last 16 French Open and Wimbledon. **1986: (8)** *German Open, Amelia Island, Hilton Head, US CC, Tokyo Pan Pacific, Zurich, Brighton, Mahwah.* Won 8 of her last 11 tourns and 52 of her last 55 matches. Won her 1st pro tourn by beating Evert Lloyd in Hilton Head f, then beat Navratilova in German Open f and had 3 mps in memorable US Open sf loss to Navratilova. Won 4 straight tourns and 23 consec matches in spring. A virus infection affected her performance in Paris and kept her out of Wimbledon, and a freak accident in Prague (a heavy umbrella stand blew over and broke a toe) prevented her from playing in Fed Cup. **1987: (11)** *FRENCH OPEN, VS Florida, LIPC, FC Cup, Amelia Island, Italian Open, Berlin, VS Los Angeles, Hamburg, Zurich, VS Champs.* After a 2-month break Dec.–Jan., missing Australian Open, she took over No. 2 ranking from Evert Lloyd end Feb. and No. 1 from navratilova 16 Aug. Won her 1st GS title at French Open, becoming, at 17 years 11 months and 23 days, the youngest-ever winner of the women's singles there. Unbeaten from 23 Nov. 1986 (VS Champs) until Wimbledon f, where she fell to Navratilova, losing to her again in f US Open when suffering from flu. She won 75 of 77 matches to take 11 titles, confirming her No. 1 ranking by taking VS Champs and being named Official World Champion by virtue of her position at head of VS points table. She became only the 2nd player after Navratilova to earn more than $1m in prize money in a year. **1988: (11)** *AUSTRALIAN OPEN, FRENCH OPEN, WIMBLEDON, US OPEN, Olympics, LIPC, US HC, Berlin, Hamburg, Mahwah, Brighton.* At the age of 19 she achieved a unique 'Golden Slam', becoming only the 3rd woman, after Connolly and Court, to achieve the traditional GS and topping her exceptional year with a gold medal at the Olympics in Seoul. She won 8 other titles and 71 of 74 matches, losing only to Sabatini – at VS Florida (following a 6-week break) and at Amelia Island – and to Shriver (when suffering from flu) at VS Champs, ending run of 46 winning results. Became the 2nd German woman to win Wimbledon after Cilly Aussem in 1931. In doubles won Wimbledon and LIPC with Sabatini, but was forced to default qf VS Champs. **1989: (14)** *AUSTRALIAN OPEN, WIMBLEDON, US OPEN, LIPC, US HC, VS Washington, VS Florida, Hamburg, San Diego, Mahwah, Zurich, Brighton, FC Cup, VS Champs.* A second consec. GS slipped from her grasp when, feeling unwell after suffering from food poisoning, she lost f French Open to Sanchez-Vicario.

However, she retained her titles at Australian Open, Wimbledon and US Open, won VS Champs and took 10 other singles titles. With a record of 82 wins and 2 defeats, losing just 12 sets all year, she was beaten only by Sanchez-Vicario at French Open and Sabatini at Amelia Island in spring. In doubles was r/u French Open with Sabatini. **1990: (10)** *AUSTRALIAN OPEN, Tokyo Toray, Amelia Island, Hamburg, Canadian Open, San Diego, Leipzig, Brighton, VS New England, Zurich.* Began the year in her usual style by winning Australian Open and recorded a 66-match winning streak (the 2nd-highest in women's tennis), which was broken when she lost to Seles in f Berlin. She lost f French Open (her 13th consec. GS f) to the same player, Garrison upset her in sf Wimbledon and Sabatini beat her in f US Open and sf VS Champs. These were the only players to beat her in a year in which she won 10 titles. She was out of action from Feb. to April after breaking her thumb ski-ing, and was hampered through the year by allegations concerning her father and by sinus problems, which caused her to withdraw from the Fed Cup team and required an operation after Wimbledon. On 13 Aug. went into her 157th consec. week at No. 1 (starting 17 Aug. 1987), overtaking Navratilova's women's record of 156 (14 June 1982–9 June 1985); 3 weeks later she passed Jimmy Connors's all-time record of 159 weeks. **1991: (7)** *WIMBLEDON, San Antonio, Hamburg, Berlin, Leipzig, Zurich, Brighton.* Her loss to Novotna in qf Australian Open was her 1st so early in GS since French Open 1986, and until she beat Seles to take San Antonio in April, she had gone 5 tourns since Nov. 1990 without winning a title. she went on to take Hamburg, Berlin, Leipzig, Zurich and Brighton and was r/u VS Florida and Amelia Island. However, she lost her No. 1 ranking to Seles in March, having held that position for a record 86 consec. weeks, regained it briefly after winning her 3rd Wimbledon in a thrilling f over Sabatini, but lost it again in Aug. In sf French Open Sanchez-Vicario inflicted her worst defeat (6–0 6–2) and 1st love set since 1984, Navratilova beat her in sf US Open and Novotna removed her in qf VS Champs. When she d. Wiesner 2r Leipzig, she notched up her 500th career win, the youngest to reach that landmark, being 6 months younger than Evert, although Evert needed only 545 matches to Graf's 568. Split with Slozil in Nov., preferring to work on her own. **1992: (8)** *WIMBLEDON, VS Florida, Hamburg, Berlin, Leipzig, Zurich, Brighton, Philadelphia.* Misfortune continued to dog her as she was forced to withdraw at the last minute from Australian Open with German measles. Then when she returned, at VS Chicago in Feb., she fell sf to Novotna after winning the 1st set to love, but returned to the winner's circle in March when she won VS Florida. She followed with Hamburg, which took her past Evert's $8,827,034 career prize money to $8,907,534 in second place behind Navratilova. At French Open, with the crowd behind her, she saved 5 m-p v Seles in f before losing 8-10 fs and at Wimbledon she ended the No. 1's chance of a GS by allowing her only 3 games in the final, for her 4th title there. She won an Olympic silver medal, losing to Capriati and finished the year with 8 titles, but ended on a disappointing note when she fell 1r VS Champs to McNeil. Led Germany to Fed Cup victory over Spain in f.

PRINCIPAL 1992 RESULTS - (detailed Grand Slam results below)
won VS Florida (d. Ferrando 6–1 6–2, Sawamatsu 6–0 6–1, Garrison 6–0 5–7 7–5, M. J. Fernandez 6–0 7–5, Martinez 3–6 6–2 6–0), **won** Hamburg (d. Graham 6–0 7–6, Magdalena Maleeva 6–2 6–3, Meskhi 6–2 6–2, Huber 6–3 6–0, Sanchez-Vicario 7–6 6–2), **won** Berlin (d. Paz 6–2 6–4, Sukova 6–3 3–6 6–2, Halard 6–1 6–2, Capriati 2–6 6–3 6–4, Sanchez-Vicario 4–6 7–5 6–2), **won** Leipzig (d. Begerow 6–1 6–0, Savchenko Neiland 6–3 6–3, Magdalena Maleeva 6–2 6–2, K. Maleeva 6–1 6–1, Novotna 6–3 1–6 6–4), **won** Zurich (d. Habsudova w.o., Probst 6–0 6–2, Wiesner 7–5 6–4, Novotna 6–2 4–6 7–6, Navratilova 2–6 7–5 7–5), **won** Brighton (d. Savchenko Neiland 6–2 6–3, Strnadova 6–0 6–4, McNeil 6–0 6–2, Huber 7–5 6–2, Novotna 4–6 6–4 7–6), **won** Philadelphia (d.Brioukhovets 6–0 6–1, Martinez 6–1 6–1, Capriati 6–0 6–1, Sanchez-Vicario 6–3 3–6 6–1), **r/u** Amelia Island (d. Meier 7–5 6–1, Schultz 6–2 6–2, Meskhi 6–0 6–2, Sanchez-Vicario 6–7 6–4 6–3, lost Sabatini 6–2 1–6 6–3),. **sf** VS Chicago (d. Hiraki 6–0 6–0, Bollegraf 6–2 6–1, lost Novotna 0–6 6–3 7–5), **sf** LIPC (d. Probst 6–3 6–1, Reggi Concato 6–2 6–2, Date 7–6 5–7 6–4, M. J. Fernandez 7–6 6–4, lost Sabatini 3–6 7–6 6–1). **DOUBLES:** (with Stubbs) **won** Hamburg (d. Bollegraf/Sanchez-Vicario 4–6 6–3 6–4).

CAREER GRAND SLAM RECORD
AUSTRALIAN OPEN – Played 6, won 3, qf 1
1983: 1r lost Sayers 7–6 6–1. **1984: 3r** d.Collins 6–2 6–4, Antonoplis 2–6 6–1 6–0, lost Turnbull [seed 4] 6–4 6–4. **1988: won** [seed 1] d.Jonsson 6–3 6–1, Thompson 6–0 6–1, Cammy Macgregor 6–1 6–2, Lindqvist [seed 13] 6–0 7–5, Mandlikova [seed 5] 6–2 6–2, Kohde-Kilsch [seed 8] 6–2 6–3, Evert [seed 3] 6–1 7–6. **1989: won** [seed 1] d.Guse 6–2 6–1, Simpson 6–0 6–0, Werdel 6–0 6–1, Provis [seed 16] 6–4 6–0, Kohde-Kilsch [seed 8] 6–2 6–3, Sabatini [seed 3] 6–3 6–0, Sukova [seed 5] 6–4 6–4. **1990: won** [seed 1] d.Cunningham 6–2 7–5, de Lone 6–1 6–2, Meskhi 6–4 6–1, Reggi [seed 13] 6–2 6–3, Fendick 6–3 7–5, Sukova [seed 4] 6–3 3–6 6–4, M.-J. Fernandez [seed 6] 6–4 6–4. **1991: qf** [seed 1] d.Santrock 6–3 6–0, Kidowaki 6–1 6–0, Provis 6–4 6–2, Habsudova 6–0 6–1, lost Novotna [seed 10] 5–7 6–4 8–6.

FRENCH OPEN – Played 10, won 2, r/u 3, sf 1, qf 1
1983: 2r d.Karlsson 6–4 6–1, lost Mould 6–0 7–6. **1984: 3r** d.Longo 6–2 7–6, Solomon 6–2 6–1, lost Kohde-Kilsch 6–2 2–6 6–1. **1985: 4r** [seed 11] d.Okagawa 7–5 3–6 6–3, Kim 6–0 6–4, Bunge 6–1 7–6, lost Evert Lloyd [seed 2] 6–2 6–3. **1986: qf** [seed 3] d.Betzner 6–1 6–0, Rush 6–1 6–1, Mesker 6–2 6–1, Casale 6–1 6–3, lost Mandlikova [seed 5] 2–6 7–6 6–1 (held 1 m-p at 5–2 2nd set). **1987: won** [seed 2] d.Bartos Cserepy 6–1 6–1, Budarova 6–1 6–1, Novotna 6–0 67–1, Kelesi 7–6 6–2, M.Maleeva [seed 6] 6–4 6–1, Sabatini[seed 7] 6–4 4–6 7–5, Navratilova[seed 1] 6–4 4–6 8–6. **1988: won** [seed 1] d.Guerree 6–0 6–4, Reis 6–1 6–0, Sloane 6–0 6–1, Tauziat 6–1 6–3, Fulco 6–0 6–1, Sabatini [seed 4] 6–3 7–6, Zvereva [seed 13] 6–0 6–0. **1989: r/u** [seed 1] d.Benjamin 6–1 6–1, Fulco 6–0 6–1, Jagerman 6–1 6–2, La Fratta 6–2 6–1, Martinez [seed 8] 6–0 6–4, Seles 6–3 3–6 6–3, lost Sanchez 7–6 3–6 7–5. **1990: r/u** [seed 1] d.Paradis 6–0 6–2, Santrock 6–1 6–2, Cecchini 6–2 6–3, Tauziat [seed 15] 6–1 6–4, Martinez [seed 9] 6–1 6–3, Novotna [seed 11] 6–1 6–2, lost Seles [seed 2] 7–6 6–4. **1991: sf** [seed 2] d.Mag.Maleeva 6–3 7–6, Langrova 6–0 6–1, Stafford 6–0 6–1, Appelmans 6–2 6–2, Tauziat [seed 13] 6–3 6–2, lost Sanchez-Vicario [seed 5] 6–0 6–2. **1992: r/u** [seed 2] d.Simpson Alter 6–3 6–1, Housset 6–2 6–1, Coetzer 6–2 6–1, Novotna [seed 10] 6–1 6–4, Zvereva 6–3 6–7 6–3, Sanchez-Vicario [seed 4] 0–6 6–2 6–2, lost Seles [seed 1] 6–2 3–6 10–8.

WIMBLEDON – Played 9, won 4, r/u 1, sf 1
1984: 4r d.Mascarin 6–4 5–7 10–8, Barker 7–6 6–3, Bunge 7–5 6–3, lost Durie [seed 10] 2–6 6–3 9–7. **1985: 4r** [seed 11] d.Spain Short 6–7 6–4 6–2, Temesvari 6–3 7–6, Rehe 6–3 6–2, lost Shriver [seed 5] 3–6 6–2 6–4. **1987: r/u**][seed 2] d.Villagran 6–09 6–2, Scheuer-Larsen 6–0 6–0, Gildemeister, 6–2 6–1, Novotna 6–4 6–3, Sabatini [seed 6] 4–6 6–1 6–1, Shriver [seed 5] 6–0 6–2, lost Navratilova [seed 1] 7–5 6–3. **1988: won** [seed 1] d.Hu Na 6–0 6–0, Quentrec 6–2 6–0, Phelps 6–3 6–1, M–J Fernandez [seed 16] 6–2 6–2, Paradis 6–3 6–1, Shriver [seed 4] 6–1 6–2, Navratilova [seed 2] 5–7 6–2 6–1. **1989: won** [seed 1] d.Salmon 6–1 6–2, Kessaris 6–2 6–1, A.Minter 6–1 6–3, Seles [seed 11] 6–4 6–3, Sanchez [seed 7] 7–5 6–1, Evert [seed 4] 6–2 6–1, Navratilova [seed 2] 6–2 6–7 6–1. **1990: sf** [seed 1] d.Porwik 6–1 6–2, McGrath 6–3 6–0, Kohde-Kilsch 6–0 6–4, Capriati [seed 12] 6–2 6–4, Novotna [seed 13] 7–5 6–2, lost Garrison [seed 5] 6–3 3–6 6–4l. **1991: won** [seed 1] d.Appelmans 6–2 6–2, Louie Harper 6–0 6–1, Basuki 6–2 6–3, Frazier [seed 15] 6–2 6–1, Garrison [seed 8] 6–1 6–3, M. J. Fernandez [seed 6] 6–2 7–5, Sabatini [seed 2] 6–4 3–6 8–6. **1992: won** [seed 2] d. Van Lottum 6–1 6–0, Werdel 6–1 6–1, De Swardt 5–7 6–0 7–5, Fendick 4–6 6–3 6–2, Zvereva 6–3 6–1, Sabatini [seed 3] 6–3 6–3, Seles [seed 1] 6–2 6–1.

US OPEN – Played 9, won 2, r/u 2, sf 3, qf 1
1984: 1r lost Hanika 6–4 6–2. **1985: sf** [seed 11] d.Fendick 4–6 6–1 7–5, A.Minter 6–3 7–6, A.White 6–4 6–2, M.Maleeva 6–4 6–2, Shriver [seed 4] 7–6 6–7 7–6, lost Navratilova [seed 2] 6–2 6–3. **1986: sf** [seed 3] d.Mascarin 6–0 6–1, Temesvari 6–1 6–0, Bowes 6–1 1–0 ret., Reggi 6–1 3–6 6–0, Gadusek 6–3 6–1, lost Navratilova [seed 1] 6–1 6–7 7–6. **1987: r/u** [seed 1] d.Fulco 6–0 6–3, Huber 6–2 6–3, Tarabini 6–2 6–0, Hanika [seed 13] 7–54 6–2, Shriver [seed 5] 6–4 6–3, McNeil [seed 11] 4–6 6–2 6–4, lost Navratilova [seed 2] 7–6 6–1.

282 WORLD OF TENNIS 1993

1988: won [seed 1] d. E.Minter 6–1 6–1, Bollegraf 6–1 6–0, Herreman 6–0 6–1, Fendick 6–4 6–2, K.Maleeva [seed 14] 6–3 6–0, Evert [seed 3] w.o., Sabatini [seed 5] 6–3 3 6–6–1. **1989: won** [seed 1] d.Inoue 6–3 6–2, Herreman 6–2 6–1, Phelps 6–1 6–1, Fairbank 6–4 6–0, Sukova [seed 8] 6–1 6–1, Sabatini [seed 3] 3–6 6–4 6–2, Navratilova [seed 2] 3–6 7–5 6–1. **1990: r/u** [seed 1] d.Drake 6–1 6–1, McQuillan 6–1 6–3, Reinach 6–4 3–6 6–1, Capriati [seed 13] 6–1 6–2, Novotna [seed 12] 6–3 6–1, Sanchez-Vicario [seed 6] 6–1 6–2, lost Sabatini [seed5] 6–2 7–6. **1991: sf** [seed 1] d.Temesvari 6–1 6–2, Mothes 6–0 6–0, Sviglerova 6–4 7–5, Wiesner 7–5 6–4, Martinez [seed 8] 6–1 6–3, lost Navratilova [seed 6] 7–6 6–7 6–4. **1992: qf** [seed 2] d.Cioffi 6–0 6–2, Shriver 7–5 6–3, N. Dahlman 6–4 6–2, Labat 6–2 6–2, lost Sanchez-Vicario [seed 5] 7–6 6–3.

OLYMPIC GAMES
1984: (Los Angeles) won Demonstration event (under 21) d.Goles 1–6 6–3 6–4 in final. **1988: (Seoul) won Gold Medal** [seed 1] bye, d.Meskhi 7–5 6–1, Suire 6–3 6–0, Savchenko, [seed 11] 6–2 4–6 6–3, GarrisonJackson [seed 8] 6–2 6–0, Sabatini [seed 3] 6–3 6–3. **1992: (Barcelona) sf (Silver medal)** [seed 1] d.Novelo 6–1 6–1, Schultz 6–1 6–0, Magdalena Maleeva 6–3 6–4, Appelmans [seed 16] 6–1 6–0, M. J. Fernandez [seed 4] 6–4 6–2, Capriati [seed 3] 3–6 6–3 6–4.

CAREER FEDERATION CUP RECORD
1986: lr d. Ann Devries (BEL) 6–3 6–1. (+ Kohde Kilsch) d. Devries/Wasserman 6–1 7–5. **2r** d. Patricia Medrado (BRZ) 6–0 6–2. (+ Bunge) Medrado/Dias 6–2 6–1. **1987: lr** d. Patricia Hy (HK) 6–7 6–2 6–4. **2r** d. Il-Soon Kim (KOR) 6–1 6–1. (+ Kohde Kilsch) d. Lee/Kim 6–1 6–0. **qf** Gabriela Sabatini (ARG) 6–4 6–4. **sf** Hana Mandlikova (TCH) 6–4 6–1. (+ Kohde-Kilsch) Mandlikova/Sukova 7–5 6–2. **Final** d. Chris Evert (USA) 6–2 6–1. (+ Kohde-Kilsch) d. Evert/Shriver (USA) 1–6 7–5 6–4. **1989: lr** d. Anne Aallonen (FIN) 6–0 6–1. **2r** Akiko Kijimuta (JPN) 6–4 6–1. (+ Kohde-Kilsch) d. Date/Inoue 6–4 5–7 6–2. **qf** d. Helena Sukova (TCH) 6–2 6–1. (+ Kohde-Kilsch) **lost** Novotna/Sukova (CZE) 6–2 6–2. **1991: lr** Angeliki Kanellopoulou (GRE) 6–1 6–2. (+Rittner) d. Kanellopoulou/ Papadaki (GRE) 6–3,6–0. **2r** d. Patricia Hy (CAN) 6–3 3–6 6–2. **1992: lr** d. Claudine Toleafoa (NZL) 6–2 6–1. **2r** d. Brenda Schultz (NED) 6–3 7–6(8–6). **qf** d. d. Katarzyna Nowak (POL) 6–0 6–0. (+Huber) Mroz/Teodorowicz (POL) 6–4 7–5. **sf** d. Lori McNeil (USA) 6–0 6–3. **Final** d. Arantxa Sanchez-Vicario (SPA) 6–4 6–2.

GABRIELA SABATINI (ARG)   **Turned pro:** 1985

Born: Buenos Aires, 16 May 1970
Lives: Buenos Aires and Key Biscayne, Fla.
Father: Osvaldo. **Mother:** Beatriz. **Brother:** Osvaldo Jnr (older)
Agent: ProServ.
Coach: Carlos Kirmayr since Wimbledon 1990; formerly Angel
Gimenez for 5 years. Trained by Omar Carminatti and works with
sports psychologist Jim Loehr.
Height: 5ft 8in (1.73m). **Weight:** 130lb (59kg).

Rankings: 1984: 74; **1985:** 11; **1986:** 10; **1987:** 6; **1988:** 4; **1989:** 3; **1990:** 5; **1991:** 3; **1992:** 3. **Highest:** 3 (February 1989).

1992 Prize Money: $1,207,565. **Career Earnings:** $6,056,672. **Career Titles:** 25.

Style: A right-hander with heavily topped groundstrokes and excellent volleys. The Western-grip forehand lacks penetration, as does the backhand but her fitness, strength and determination win her many matches. Her serve is too slow and short, but the weakness can only be exploited by the best of the women because she counter-attacks so well.

CAREER HIGHLIGHTS (year: *(titles)*)

1985: (1) *Japan Open.* Youngest sf at French Open. Won Japan Open and r/u to Evert Lloyd at Hilton Head. **1986: (1)** *Argentine Open.* Youngest sf to date at Wimbledon, r/u French Open. **1987: (3)** *Brighton, Pan Pacific, Argentine Open.* sf French Open, r/u Italian Open. **1988: (4)** *VS Champs, Boca Raton, Italian Open, Canadian Open.* Achieved first-ever win over Graf, ending No. 1's 30-match winning streak, at VS Florida. Upset her again at Amelia island, and was only player to inflict two defeats on the World Champion during the year. Reached sf French Open and last 16 Wimbledon. **1989: (4)** *LIPC, Amelia Island, Italian Open, Filderstadt.* r/u French Open with Graf. Was one of only two players to beat Graf during the year. **1990: (2)** *US Open, Boca Raton.* Working with new coach Carlos Kimayr and sports psychologist Jim Loehr, she developed a serve-and-volley game with which she beat Graf at US Open to win her 1st GS title in her 8th f. **1991: (5)** *Pan Pacific, Boca Raton, Hilton Head, Amelia Island, Italian Open.* In her first Wimbledon f, she lost 8–6 fs to Graf in a thrilling match after serving for it twice. In other GS she lost sf French Open to Seles, qf Australian Open to Sanchez-Vicario and qf US Open to Capriati. Won WTA Most Improved Player Award. **1992: (5)** *Sydney, Tokyo Pan Pacific, FC Cup, Amelia Island, Italian Open.* At Italian Open she was one of only 4 players to beat Seles all year. Won 5 titles, including Italian Open, where she inflicted 1 of only 5 defeats suffered by Seles all year. R/u LIPC, Tokyo Nicherei and Filderstadt and reached 6 other sf, including Australian Open, French Open, Wimbledon and VS Champs.

PRINCIPAL 1992 RESULTS (detailed Grand Slam results below)

won Sydney (d. Bollegraf 6-0 6–1, Hack 6–1 6–0, G. Fernandez 6–2 7–6, M. J. Fernandez 6–2 6–3, Sanchez-Vicario 6–1 6–1), **won** Tokyo Pan Pacific (d. Endo 6–2 7–5, Shriver 6–2 6–7 6–4, Date 6–3 6–0, Navratilova 6–2 4–6 6–2), **won** FC Cup (d. Cioffi 6–0 6–0, Coetzer 7–5 6–4, Hy 6–2 6–3, Schultz 6–3 6–2, Martinez 6–1 6–4), **won** Amelia Island (d. Harvey-Wild 6–3 7–5, Rinaldi 6–0 6–3, Novotna 6–2 6–1, Martinez 6–3 6–3, Graf 6–2 1–6 6–3), **won** Italian Open (d. Paz 6–3 6–1, Provis 6–1 6–2, Tauziat 6–0 6–1, M. J. Fernandez 6–2 6–3, Seles 7–5 6–4), **r/u** LIPC (d. Adams 6–2 6–3, Fairbank Nideffer 6–2 6–0, Schultz 6–1 6–7 6–0, Frazier 6–0 6–1, Graf 3–6 7–6 6–1, lost Sanchez-Vicario 6–1 6–4), **r/u** Tokyo Nicherei (d. Hiraki 6–3 6–3, Date 6–4 6–2, K. Maleeva 6–3 6–3, lost Seles 6–2 6–0), **r/u** Filderstadt (d. Kschwendt 6–4 6–2, Medvedeva 6–4 6–4, Probst 6–4 6–1, M. J. Fernandez 7–5 6–2, lost Navratilova 7–6 6–3), **sf** Hamburg (d. Cecchini 6–0 6–0, Rittner 6–1 6–1, Wiesner 6–1 6–2, lost Sanchez-Vicario 3–6 6–4 6–4), **sf** Philadelphia (d. Shriver 7–6 7–5, Raymond 6–4 7–6, lost Sanchez-Vicario 4–6 6–3 6–2), **sf** VS Champ (d. Frazier 6–0 6–2, Capriati 6–1 3–6 6–4, lost Seles 7–6 6–1).

CAREER GRAND SLAM RECORD
AUSTRALIAN OPEN – Played 4, sf 2, qf 1
1989: sf [seed 3] d. Dahlman 6–0 6–1, Martinez 3–6 6–1 6–2, Benjamin 6–0 6–0, Reggi [seed 13] 6–0 4–6 6–1, Garrison [seed 6] 6–4 2–6 6–4, lost Graf [seed 1] 6–3 6–0. **1990: 3r** [seed 2] d. Frazier 6–4 7–6, Daniels 7–5 6–1, lost Porwick 2–6 0–1 ret. **1991: qf** [seed 4] d. Harvey-Wild 6–3 6–1, Ekstrand 6–1 6–1, Strnadova 6–1 6–1, McQuillan 6–3 6–1, lost Sanchez-Vicario [seed 6] 6–1 6–3. **1992: sf** [seed 3] d. Halard 6–2 6–0, Hy 6–1 6–1, Byrne 6–1 6–0, K. Maleeva [seed 10] 6–1 7–5, Capriati [seed 5] 6–4 7–6, lost M.J.Fernandez [seed 3] 6–4 7–6.

FRENCH OPEN – Played 8, sf 5
1985: sf [seed 14] d. Drescher 6–2 6–2, Barg 6–0 6–2, A.White 6–1 7–6, Fairbank 6–0 1–6 7–5, M.Maleeva [seed 4] 6–3 1–6 6–1, lost Evert Lloyd [seed 2] 6–4 6–1. **1986: 4r** [seed 9] d. Inoue 6–1 6–1, Huber 6–1 6–3, Madruga Osses 6–3 6–3, lost Evert Lloyd [seed 2] 1–6 6–3 6–3. **1987: sf** [seed 7] d. Van Der Torre 6–0 6–2, Ferrando 6–2 6–4, Benjamin 6–0 2–6 6–2, Schimper 6–4 6–1, Sanchez 6–4 6–0, lost Graf [seed 2] 6–4 4–6 7–5. **1988: sf** [seed 4] d. Laval 6–1 7–5, Schimer 6–3 6–0, Yanagi 6–3 6–0, Schultz 6–4 6–1, Kelesi 4–6 6–1 6–3, lost Graf [seed 1] 6–3 7–6. **1989: 4r** [seed 2] d. Nishiya 6–0 6–0, Dechaume 6–3 6–1, Provis 4–6 7–5 6–3, lost M–J Fernandez [seed 15] 6–4 6–4. **1990: 4r** [seed 4] d. Vieira 6–0 7–6, Sloane 6–0 5–7 6–1, Herreman 6–0 6–1, lost Novotna [seed 11] 6–4 7–5. **1991: sf** [seed 3] d. Werdel 6–1 6–1, Zardo 6–1 6–1, Pierce 6–2 6–1, McQuillan 6–3 6–0, Novotna [seed 6] 5–7 7–6 6–0, lost Seles [seed 1] 6–4 6–1. **1992: sf** [seed 3] d. Farina 6–0 6–0, Cecchini 6–0 6–1, Halard 6–1 6–3, Hy 6–3 6–1, Martinez [seed 7] 3–6 6–3 6–2, lost Seles [seed 1] 6–3 4–6 6–4.

WIMBLEDON – Played 8, r/u 1, sf 3, qf 1
1985: 3r [seed 15] d. A.Brown 3–6 6–3 6–3, Benjamin 6–3 6–4, lost Tanvier 6–7 6–4 6–1. **1986: sf** [seed 10] d. Jolissaint 6–2 1–6 6–4, Suire 6–3 6–3, Gerken 6–2 6–1, Reggi 6–4 1–6 6–3, Lindqvist 6–2 6–3, lost Navratilova [seed 1] 6–2 6–2. **1987: qf** [seed 6] d. Gerken 6–3 6–3, Bartos Cserepy 6–1 6–3, Demongeot 6–3 6–4, Zvereva 6–0 2–6 6–4, lost Graf [seed 2] 4–6 6–1 6–1. **1988: 4r** [seed 5] d. Bassett Seguso 6–2 6–2, Zrubakova 6–4 6–3, Tanvier 6–2 6–3, Garrison [seed 12] 6–1 3–6 6–2. **1989: 2r** [seed 3] d. Balestrat 6–1 6–0, lost Fairbank 6–4 6–3. **1990: sf** [seed 4] d. Burgin 6–3 6–3, Huber 6–2 7–6, Tanvier 6–4 6–2, Tauziat 6–2 7–6, Zvereva [seed 11] 6–2 2–6 8–6, lost Navratilova [seed 2] 6–3 6–4. **1991: r/u** [seed 2] d. Javer 6–4 6–0, Quentrec 6–2 6–2, Strnadova 6–1 6–3, Tauziat [seed 12] 7–6 6–3, Gildemeister 6–2 6–1, Capriati [seed 10] 6–4 6–4, lost Graf [seed 1] 6–4 3–6 8–6. **1992: sf** [seed 3] d. Fauche 6–1 6–1, Demongeot 6–2 6–3, Hiraki 6–0 6–4, Godridge 6–2 6–1, Capriati [seed 6] 6–1 3–6 6–3, lost Graf 6–3 6–3.

US OPEN – Played 9, won 1, r/u 1, sf 1, qf 3
1984: 3r d. P.Smith 6–3 3–6 6–2, Shaefer 6–4 6–1, lost Sukova 6–4 6–4. **1985: 1r** [seed 10] lost Potter 6–4 6–2. **1986: 4r** [seed 11] d. Tauziat 6–3 6–2, Casale 6–0 6–3, K.Maleeva 7–5 6–2, lost Navratilova [seed 1] 6–4 6–2. **1987: qf** [seed 8] d. Bowes 6–3 6–3, Gomer 6–3 6–1, Hakami 6–1 6–3, Bunge [seed 12] 1–6 6–1 6–1, lost Navratilova [seed 2] 7–5 6–3 **1988: r/u** [seed 5] d. Fulco 6–3 6–0, Bowes 6–2 6–0, Richardson, 6–1 6–1, Rehe 7–5 6–4, SavchenkoNeiland [seed 16] 4–6 6–4 6–1, Garrison [seed 11] 6–4 7–5, lost Graf [seed 1] 6–3 3–6 6–1. **1989: sf** [seed 3] d. Porwik 6–1 6–2, Caverzasio 6–3 6–2, Meskhi 6–2 6–0, Martinez [seed 15] 6–1 6–1, Sanchez-Vicario [seed 6] 3–6 6–4 6–1, lost Graf [seed 1] 3–6 6–4 6–2. **1990: won** [seed 5] d. Jordan 6–1 6–1, Demongeot 6–1 6–1, Appelmans 6–2 6–4, Sukova [seed 11] 6–2 6–1, Meskhi 7–6 6–4, M.-J. Fernandez [seed 8] 7–5 5–7 6–3, Graf [seed 1] 6–2 7–6. **1991: qf** [seed 3] d. Provis 7–6 6–3, Paulus 6–3 4–6 5–1 ret., Magers 6–3 6–4, Novotna [seed 9] 6–4 7–6, lost Capriati [seed 7] 6–3 7–6. **1992: qf** [seed 4] d. Harvey-Wild 6–1 6–2, Halard 6–0 6–4, Zvereva 6–4 5–7 6–4, Appelmans 6–1 6–3, lost M.-J. Fernandez [seed 7] 6–2 1–6 6–4.

OLYMPIC RECORD
1988: (Seoul) r/u (silver medal) [seed 3] bye, d. Goles 6–1 6–0, Hanika [seed 12] 1–6 6–4 6–2, Zvereva [seed 6] 6–4 6–3, M. Maleeva [seed 7] 6–1 6–1, lost Graf [seed 1] 6–3 6–3.

CAREER FEDERATION CUP RESULTS
1984: lr (+ Longo) lost A Minter/E Minter (AUS) 6–1,6–2. **1985: 1r** d. Laura Gildemeister
(PER) 6–3 6–3. (+Paz) d. Gildemeister/Vasquez 6–0 7–6(7–5). **2r** d. Belinda Cordwell (NZ)
6–1 6–0. (+ Villagran) lost Cordwell/Richardson (NZ) 6–2 6–2. **qf** d. Zina Garrison (USA) 5–7
6–1 6–1. (+ Villagran) lost Jordan/ Walsh 5–7 6–3 6–4. **1986: 1r** d. Fiorella Bonicelli (URU)
6–1 6–1. (+ Paz) d. Bonicelli/Casaretto 6–1 6–1. **2r** d. Soo-ok Kim (KOR) 7–5 6–2. (+ Paz) d.
Jeong Soon Lee/Jumre Park (KOR) 7–5 6–0. **qf** d. Petra Huber (AUT) 6–2 5–7 6–4. (+ Paz)
d. Huber/Poelzl 6–3 6–1. **sf** lost Hana Mandlikova (TCH) 6–2 6–4. (+ Paz) d.
Marsikova/Holikova 6–7(5–7) 6–2 6–2. **1987: 1r** Eva Krapl (SUI) 6–2 6–1. (+ Paz) d.
Cohen/Krapl 6–2 6–0. **2r** d. Belinda Cordwell (NZL) 6–3 7–5,. (+ Paz) d.
Cordwell/Richardson 4–6 6–3 6–1. **qf** lost Steffi Graf (GER) 6–4 6–4 (+Paz) d. Bunge/Meier
6–7 6–1 6–2.

ARANTXA SANCHEZ-VICARIO (ESP)   Turned pro: 1986

Born: Barcelona, 18 December 1971. **Lives:** Andorra.
Father: Emilio. **Mother:** Marisa, whose maiden name, Vicario, she added to her own, travels with her. **Sister:** Marisa (older).
Brothers: Emilio and Javier (both older) who compete on the men's tour.
Agent : International Management Group
Coach: Mervyn Rose (until Jan.1993); formerly Eduardo Osta.
Height: 5ft 6 in (1.69m). **Weight:** 124lb (56kg).

Rankings: 1986: 124; **1987:** 47; **1988:** 18; **1989:** 5; **1990:** 7; **1991:** 5 **1992:** 4. **Highest:** 3 (May 1990).

1992 Prize Money: $1,376,355. **Career Earnings:** $3,436,112. **Career Titles:** 8.

Style: One of the fastest movers on a tennis court whose attacking, all-round game, cheerful demeanour and ready smile has created an enormous following round the world. A right-hander with a good forehand, accurate double-handed backhand and excellent touch on the volley, Arantxa has enjoyed oustanding success both in singles and doubles.

CAREER HIGHLIGHTS (year: *(titles)*)
1986: Emerging from Satellite circuits, she reached sf Spanish Open and played Fed Cup. **1987:** Qf French Open in 1st GS appearance. **1988: (1)** *Belgian Open.* Upset Evert (suffering from a foot injury) at French Open *en route* to qf again and reached last 16 US Open. Won her 1st pro singles title at Brussels and was r/u Tampa. **1989: (2)** *FRENCH OPEN, Barcelona.* At 17 years 6 months became the youngest woman and the 1st Spaniard to win French Open women's title. Qf Wimbledon and US Open, won Barcelona and was r/u Italian Open and Canadian Open, qualifying for 1st VS Champs, where she reached sf. Voted WTA Most Improved Player for 2nd year running. **1990 (2)** *Barcelona, Newport.* In some disappointing performances she fell to Harvey-Wild 1r VS Chicago, to Paz 2r French Open and to Nagelsen 1r Wimbledon. Won 2 titles, r/u Tokyo Toray, VS Houston, Amelia Island, Leipzig and Hamburg, where she d. Navratilova and took Graf to 3s. She lost 1r VS Champs to K. Maleeva and in GS her best showing was sf US Open, but she won French Open mixed doubles with Lozano. In women's doubles won 1 title with Navratilova and 3 with Paz, with whom she was r/u VS Champs. **1991: (1)** *Washington.* Upset Sabatini *en route* to sf Australian Open and Graf on her way to f French Open, inflicting on the former No. 1 her worst defeat and 1st love set since 1984. In other GS lost qf Wimbledon to M.-J. Fernandez and same round US Open to Navratilova, who also stopped her at that stage VS Champs. Had to wait until late Aug. to win her 1st title of the year at VS Washington, although she had reached qf or better in all 13 tourns until then. R/u Sydney, Berlin, Eastbourne, VS Philadelphia and appeared in 6 more sf. Played in the winning Spanish Fed Cup team, winning all her matches. In doubles won Barcelona with Navratilova and took Sydney and Amelia Island with Sukova, with whom she qualified for VS Champs. In mixed doubles r/u US Open with her brother, Emilio. **1992 (2)** *LIPC, Montreal.* Again she was remarkably consistent if not spectacular. She upset Graf qf US Open on her way to f, where she lost to Seles, whom she had beaten 3 weeks earlier at Montreal - one of only 5 defeats the No.1 suffered all year. Reached sf Australian Open and French Open and won an Olympic bronze medal; took 2 titles and was r/u Sydney, Barcelona, Hamburg, Berlin and Philadelphia, reaching 4 more sf and losing qf VS Champs to Navratilova. She enjoyed a terrific year in doubles, winning Australian Open, VS Champs and 4 more titles with Sukova; r/u French Open, Olympic silver medal and 1 title with Martinez; plus 3 more titles with other partners. In mixed with Woodbridge won French Open and r/u Australian Open.

PRINCIPAL 1992 RESULTS (detailed Grand Slam results below)
SINGLES: won LIPC (d. Davenport 6–4 6–4, Helgeson 6–2 6–2, Rittner 6–1 2–1 ret'd,

Coetzer 6–1 6–4, Capriati 6–2 6–4, Sabatini 6–1 6–4), **won** Montreal (d. Kuhlman 6–1 6–1, Coetzer 7–6 6–2, Tauziat 6–2 6–4, Sukova 6–2 7–5, Seles 6–4 3–6 6–4), **r/u** Sydney (d. Strnadova 7–6 6–3, Rittner 7–5 6–0, Martinez 6–4 6–2, Huber 4–6 7–5 6–3, lost Sabatini 6–1 6–1), **r/u** Barcelona (d. Zrubakova 6–1 6–4, Halard 6–2 6–3, Martinez 6–1 6–2, lost Seles 3–6 6–2 6–3), **r/u** Hamburg (d. Savchenko Neiland 6–0 6–4, Maniokova 6–1 6–1, Novotna 6–1 6–4, Sabatini 3–6 6–4 6–4, lost Graf 7–6 6–2), **r/u** Berlin (d. Kidowaki 6–0 6–3, Zvereva 7–6 6–3, Appelmans 6–0 6–3, M.-J. Fernandez 7–5 7–6, lost Graf 4–6 7–5 6–2), **r/u** Philadelphia (d. Coetzer 7–6 7–6, Zvereva 6–2 6–1, Sabatini 4–6 6–3 6–2, lost Graf 6–3 3–6 6–1), **sf** FC Cup (d. Hack 6–4 6–2, Gorrochategui 6–2 6–1, Meskhi 6–3 6–3, lost Martinez 6–4 7–5, **sf** Amelia Island (d. Kohde-Kilsch 6–2 6–2, Gorrochategui 6–0 6–2, Hack 6–1 6–2, lost Graf 6–7 6–4 6–3), **sf** VS Los Angeles (d. R. White 1–6 6–4 6–0, Sukova 2–6 6–3 6–2, lost Seles 6–3 6–2), **sf** Filderstadt (d. Paradis Mangon 7–5 6–4, Appelmans 7–6 6–2, Wiesner 6–1 6–1, lost Navratilova 6–1 6–1). **DOUBLES:** (+Sukova unless stated) **won Australian Open** (+Sukova) d M.J.Fernandez/Garrison 6–4 7–6), **r/u French Open** [+Martinez] lost G. Fernandez/Zvereva 6–3 6–2). **won** Sydney (d. M.-J. Fernandez/Garrison 7–6 7–5), **won** Tokyo Pan Pacific (d. Navratilova/Shriver 7–5 6–1), **won** LIPC[+Savchenko Neiland] (d. Hetherington/Rinaldi 7–5 5–7 6–3), **won** FC Cup[+Zvereva] (d. Novotna/Savchenko Neiland 6–4 6–2), **won** Amelia Island[+Zvereva] (d. Garrison/Novotna 6–1 6–0), **won** Barcelona[+Martinez] (d. Tauziat/Wiesner 6–4 6–1), **won** VS Los Angeles (lost Garrison/Shriver 6–4 6–2), **won** Filderstadt (d. Shriver/Zvereva 6–4 7–5), **won** VS Champs (d. Novotna/Savchenko Neiland 7–6 6–1), **r/u** Light 'n Lively Doubles[+Zvereva] (lost Novotna/Savchenko Neiland 6–4 6–2), **r/u** Hamburg[+Bollegraf] (lost Graf/Stubbs 4–6 6–3 6–4), **MIXED DOUBLES.** (+Woodbridge): **won French Open** d McNeil/Shelton 6–2 6–3. **r/u Australian Open** lost Woodforde/Provis 6–3 4–6 11–9.

CAREER GRAND SLAM RECORD
AUSTRALIAN OPEN – Played 2, sf 2
1991: sf [seed 6] d Medvedeva 6–0 6–2, Javer 4–6 6–4 6–2, McNeil 6–4 3–6 6–0, Frazier [seed 13] 6–3 6–2, Sabatini [seed 4] 6–1 6–3, lost Novotna 6–2 6–4. **1992: sf** [seed 4] (d.Provis 6–2 6–1, Testud 6–1 6–1, Strnadova 1–6 6–0 6–3, Savchenko Neiland 6–1 7–6, Maleeva Fragnière def., Seles [seed 1] 6–2 6–2.

FRENCH OPEN – Played 6, won 1, r/u 1, sf 1
1987: qf d Burgin 7–5 6–3, Dinu 6–0 6–2, Paulus 6–4 6–2, Karlsson 6–1 6–4, lost Sabatini [seed 7] 6–4 6–0. **1988: qf** d Kuczynska 6–2 6–0, Meier 7–5 6–0, Evert [seed 3] 6–1 7–6, Tanvier 6–2 6–0, lost Provis 7–5 3–6 6–4. **1989: won** [seed 7] d Rajchrtova 6–2 6–1, Demongeot 6–4 6–4, Medvedeva 6–0 3–6 6–2, Coetzer 6–3 6–2, Novotna [seed 11] 6–2 6–2, M.-J. Fernandez [seed 15] 6–2 6–2, Graf [seed 1] 7–6 3–6 7–5. **1990: 2r** [seed 3] d Van Lottum 6–1 6–3, lost Paz 7–5 3–6 6–1, **1991: r/u** [seed 5] d McNeil 6–2 6–2, Godridge 6–1 6–2, Fulco 6–1 6–1, Tami Whitlinger 6–2 6–1, M.-J. Fernandez [seed 4] 6–3 6–2, Graf [seed 2] 6–0 6–2, lost Seles [seed 1] 6–3 6–4. **1992: sf** [seed 4] d Oeljeklaus 6–0 6–2, Zardo 6–3 6–2, Wiesner 6–3 6–1, Date [seed 14 6–1 6–2, Bollegraf 6–2 6–3, lost Graf [seed 2] 0–6 6–2 6–2.

WIMBLEDON – Played 6, qf 2
1987: 1r lost Cordwell 6–1 2–6 6–4. **1988: 1r** lost Okamoto 6–3 6–4. **1989: qf** [seed 7] d Pospisilova 6–2 7–5, Halard 6–4 6–3, Reggi 4–6 6–3 7–5, McNeil [seed 15] 6–3 2–6 6–1, lost Graf [seed 1] 7–5 6–1. **1990: 1r** [seed 6] lost Nagelsen 1–6 7–6 9–7. **1991: qf** [seed 3] d Rittner 6–1 6–2, Coetzer 6–4 6–1, McNeil 6–2 6–4, A.Minter 7–5 3–6 6–1, lost M.-J. Fernandez [seed 6] 6–2 7–5. **1992: 2r** [seed 5] d Meskhi 6–3 7–6, lost Halard 6–3 2–6 6–3).

US OPEN Played 6, r/u 1, sf 1, qf 2
1987: 1r lost Dias 6–4 6–2. **1988: 4r** d Keil 6–3 6–0 Steinmetz 6–2 6–2, Sloane 6–3 6–3, lost Garrison [seed 11] 4–6 7–5 6–2. **1989: qf** [seed 6] d Faull 6–3 6–1, Cammy Macgregor 6–1 6–3, Wasserman 6–1 2–6 6–4, Paulus 6–2 6–2, lost Sabatini [seed 3] 3–6 6–4 6–1. **1990: sf** [seed 6] d Provis 6–0 6–3, Kuhlman 6–1 6–2, Fendick 6–2 6–1, Paulus [seed 16] 6–4 6–3, Garrison [seed 4] 6–2 6–2, lost Graf [seed 1] 6–1 6–2. **1991: qf** [seed 4] d Piccolini 6–0 6–1,

Godridge 6–1 6–1, Herreman 6–2 6–2, Zvereva 6–3 7–6, lost Navratilova [seed 6] 7–6 6–7 6–4. **1992: r/u** [seed 5] d Savchenko Neiland 5–7 6–2 6–2, Davenport 6–2 6–1, Sawamatsu 6–1 6–3, Garrison [seed 14] 6–0 6–1, Graf [seed 2] 7–6 6–3, Maleeva Fragnière [seed 9] 6–2 6–1, lost Seles 6–3 6–3.

OLYMPIC GAMES
1988: (Seoul) 1r lost Goles 6–4 6–2. **1992: (Barcelona) sf (bronze medal)** [seed 2] d Spirlea 6–1 6–3, Endo 6–0 6–1, Rittner 4–6 6–3 6–1, Martinez [seed 5] 6–4 6–4, lost Capriati [seed 3] 6–3 3–6 6–1. **DOUBLES:** (with Martinez) **r/u (silver medal)** d McQuillan/Provis 6–3 6–3, lost G. Fernandez/M.-J. Fernandez 7–5 2–6 6–2.

CAREER FEDERATION CUP RECORD
1986: 1r d. Suzanna Anggarkusuma (INA) 7–6 6–3. (+ Almansa) d. Anggarkusuma/ Basuki 7–5 6–4. **2r** lost Martina Navratilova (USA) 6–3 6–0. **1987: 1r** d. Joni van Ryk de Groot (JAM) 6–3 6–1. (+ Llorca) d. Harris/van Ryck de Groot 7–6 6–2. **2r** lost Elizabeth Smylie (AUS) 6–1 4–6 6–1. (+ Llorca) Smylie/Turnbull 6–1 6–2. **1988: 1r** (+ Martinez) d. Bollegraf/Vis 5–7 6–4 6–4. 2r d. Rahay Yayuk Basuki (INA) 6–1 6–1 (+ Martinez) Basuki/Anggarkusuma 6–0 5–7 6–2. **qf** d. Natalia Zvereva (URS) 7–6(7–3) 6–1. (+ Martinez) lost Savchenko/Zvereva 4–6 6–4 6–4. **1989: 1r** d. Natalia Zvereva (URS) 6–4 6–2. **2r** d. Brenda Schultz (NED) 2–6 6–4 10–8, **qf** d. Natalia Zvereva (URS) 7–5 6–3. (+ Martinez) lost Savchenko/Zvereva 6–4 2–6 6–1. **sf** d. Anne Minter (AUS) 6–1 4–6 6–2. **Final** lost Martina Navratilova (USA) 0–6 6–3 6–4. (+ Martinez) lost Garrison/Shriver (USA) 7–5 6–1. **1990: 1r** d. Helen Kelesi (CAN) 6–3 6–2. **2r** d. Yael Segal (ISR) 6–0 6–0. (+ Martinez) **d.** Berger/Zaltz (ISR) 6–3 6–4. **qf** d. Nathalie Tauziat (FRA) 7–6(11–9) 6–1. **d.** (+ Martinez) Demongeot/Pierce 6–4 6–4. **sf** lost Natalia Zvereva (URS) 6–4 2–0 ret. **1991:** 1r d. Sabine Appelmans (BEL) 7–6(7–5) 6–3 **2r** d. Rachel McQuillan (AUS) 6–1 3–6 6–2. (+ Martinez) d. Smylie/Godridge 6–3 6–4. **qf** d. Yayuk Basuki (INA) 4–6 7–5 6–4. **sf** d. Anke Huber (GER) 6–1 2–6 6–2. (+ Martinez) d. Rittner/Huber 6–1 6–1. **Final** d. Mary Joe Fernandez (USA) 6–3 6–4. (+ Martinez) d. Garrison/Fernandez (USA) 3–6 6–1 6–1. **1992: 1r** d. Sabine Appelmans (BEL) 6–1 6–2. (+ N.Perez) lost Wasserman/Monami 7–5 6–4. **2r** d. Patricia Hy (CAN) 6–4 6–2. (+ Martinez) d. Hetherington/Hy 6–4 6–0. **qf** d. Mercedez Paz (ARG) 6–2 6–1. **sf** d. Nicole Provis (AUS) 6–2 6–0 (+ Ruano) d. Byrne/Stubbs (AUS) 6–3 6–3. **Final** lost Steffi Graf (GER) 6–4 6–2 (+ Martinez) d. Huber/Rittner 6–1 6–2.

MARTINA NAVRATILOVA (USA)   **Turned pro:** 1975

Born: Prague, Czechoslovakia, 18 October 1956. Became US citizen 21 July 1981. **Lives:** Aspen, Col. **Father:** Miroslav Subert. **Step Father:** Miroslav (Mirek) Navratil. **Mother:** Jana. **Sister:** Jana. **Agent:** International Management Group.
Coaches: Craig Kardon (from 1989) and Billie Jean King (1990). Formerly Renee Richards(1981), Nancy Lieberman for training, Randy Crawford (1987), Virginia Wade (1987), Tim Gullikson (1988). **Height:** 5ft 8in (1.73m). **Weight:** 145lb (145kg).

Rankings: 1975: 3; **1976:** 4; **1977:** 3. **1978:** 1; **1979:** 1; **1980:** 3; **1981:** 3; **1982:** 1; **1983:** 1; **1984:** 1; **1985:** 1; **1986:** 1; **1987:** 2; **1988:** 2; **1989:** 2; **1990:** 3; **1991:** 4; **1992:** 5. **Highest:** 1 (July 1979).

1992 Prize Money: $731,933. **Career Earnings:** $18,396,526. **Career Titles:** 161.

Style: An athletic and finely trained left-hander with the most powerful serve in women's tennis. Her speed about the court, varied groundstrokes (flat, sliced or topped both sides) plus match-winning volleys have made her the most prolific tournament winner of all time. She has set new standards of training (mental and physical) and diet that others follow.

CAREER HIGHLIGHTS (year: *(title)*)
1973: (1) *Pilsen.* Reached qf French Open. **1974: (1)** *Orlando.* Won first major tourn in Orlando and r/u to Evert in Italian Open. **1975: (4)** *Washington, Boston, Denver, Charlotte.* Led Czechoslovakia to Fed Cup title and r/u to Evert in VS Champs, French and Italian Opens. Announced defection from Czechoslovakia. **1976: (2)** *Houston, Sydney.* Reached first sf at Wimbledon, won first doubles there with Evert, but made tearful exit from US Open, losing 1r. **1977: (6)** *Washington, Houston, Minnesota, Detroit, Edinburgh, Charlotte.* Won 6 tourns and reached f of 5 other events in 20 appearances. **1978: (11)** *WIMBLEDON, VS Champs, Washington, Houston, Los Angeles, Chicago, Seattle, Detroit, Kansas City, Eastbourne, Phoenix.* Ranked 1 on computer in close race with Evert, whom she beat to win first Wimbledon singles title. Won 80 of 89 matches and 11 of 20 tourns, including 37-match winning streak. **1979: (10)** *WIMBLEDON, Avon Champs, Oakland, Houston, Dallas, Chicago, Richmond, Atlanta, Phoenix, Brighton.* Defended Wimbledon title safely and won 11 of 23 tourns. **1980: (11)** *CS Champs, Kansas City, Chicago, Los Angeles, Oakland, Dallas, Amelia Island, Orlando, Montreal, Richmond, Tokyo.* Won 11 of 24 tourns but no majors. **1981: (9)** *AUSTRALIAN OPEN, Avon Champs, Los Angeles, Cincinnati, Dallas, Chicago, Orlando, US Indoors, Tampa.* US Open sf win over Evert Lloyd, another f Australian Open, and success in 8 of 19 tourns. Became US citizen 21 July. **1982: (15)** *FRENCH OPEN, WIMBLEDON, TS Champs, Eastbourne, Canadian Open, Filderstadt, Washington, Seattle, Chicago, Kansas City, Dallas, Sydney, Hilton Head, Orlando, Brighton.* Won 15 of 18 tourns, 90 of 93 matches, including 41 straight from March until September, with third Wimbledon singles and first French Open. **1983: (16)** *AUSTRALIAN OPEN, WIMBLEDON, US OPEN, VS Champs, Eastbourne, Canadian Open, Tampa, Filderstadt, Tokyo Lions Cup, Hilton Head, Washington, Houston, Chicago, Dallas, Orlando, Los Angeles.* Won 16 of 17 tourns, including first US Open and fourth Wimbledon, and 86 of 87 matches, closing season with streak of 50 straight match victories, her only defeat being by Kathleen Horvath in last 16 of French Open. Her 0.988 winning percentage set an Open Tennis' record for men and women. **1984: (13)** *FRENCH OPEN, WIMBLEDON, US OPEN, VS Champs (March), Amelia Island, Eastbourne, US Indoors, Sydney, Orlando, Newport, Mahwah, Fort Lauderdale, New Orleans.* Set modern pro record of 74 straight matches won. Won bonus of $1m from ITF for achieving a modern GS, culminating with French Open win over Evert Lloyd. She extended her GS streak to six with her fifth Wimbledon and second US Open victories, but her bid for traditional GS, as well as her 74-match winning streak, were stopped by Sukova in sf Australian Open. **1985: (12)** *AUSTRALIAN OPEN,*

WIMBLEDON, VS Champs (March), LIPC, Eastbourne, Sydney, Washington, Houston, Dallas, Orlando, Fort Lauderdale, Brisbane. Won her 6th Wimbledon and 3rd Australian titles, 84 of 89 matches and 12 of 17 tourns. Was challenged for No. 1 ranking by Evert Lloyd, who took over top spot for virtually half the year, but Martina clinched No. 1 with 3s triumph over Chris in Australian f. **1986: (14)** *WIMBLEDON, US OPEN, VS Champs (March), VS Champs (Nov.), Eastbourne, Washington, Filderstadt, US Indoors, Chicago, Dallas, Los Angeles, New Orleans, New England (Jan.), New England (Nov.).* . Won 14 of 17 tourns and 89 of 92 matches, including 5th straight Wimbledon (the first since Lenglen 1919–23 to achieve that feat) and her 3rd US Open. Won two VS Champs and closed season with streak of 53 straight matches. Won 1,000th match in Filderstadt. **1987: (4)** *WIMBLEDON, US OPEN, Filderstadt, Chicago.* Losing Australian Open f to Mandlikova, French Open f to Graf, who also beat her in sf LIPC, she won no singles tournament from Nov. 1986 until triumphing over Graf at Wimbledon. Lost her No. 1 computer ranking which she had held continuously since July 1985. However, she won her 1st triple crown at US Open, her 2 GS singles titles confirming her as No. 1 in some eyes until she fell to Sabatini in qf VS Champs. In doubles, won 3rd GS with Shriver in Paris and their 6th VS Champs together. **1988 (9)** *Dallas, Oakland, Washington, New England, Chicago, Hilton Head, Amelia Island, Eastbourne, Filderstadt.* For the first time in 8 years she won no GS title, falling in sf Australian Open to Evert, last 16 French Open to Zvereva, f Wimbledon to Graf and qf US Open to Garrison. Nor did she find consolation at VS Champs, where she fell in qf to Sukova. In doubles won Australian, French Open and VS Champs with Shriver, but failed in both women's and mixed at Wimbledon. However, she won 9 singles titles and her 1,100th career victory at Amelia Island, remaining firmly in the No. 2 position. **1989: (8)** *Los Angeles, Dallas, New England, Sydney, Pan Pacific, Birmingham, Eastbourne, Canadian Open.* Again won no GS singles title, falling qf Australian Open to Sukova, missing French Open to prepare for Wimbledon, where she was r/u to Graf, and losing f US Open also to Graf, despite having been ahead 6-3 4-2. However, was r/u VS Champs to Graf and lost to no one else from April. Took 7 doubles titles, including Australian Open and VS Champs with Shriver and US Open with Mandlikova after ending her partnership with Shriver in July. Called on Billie Jean King mid-season to help her overcome a crisis of confidence and to 'get the fun back' into her game. **1990: (6)** *WIMBLEDON, Chicago, Washington, Indian Wells, Hilton Head, Eastbourne.* Achieved her primary aim of winning a 9th Wimbledon - without dropping a set - to pass Helen Wills Moody's record, and setting a new record of 99 singles victories there, passing Chris Evert's 97. In her only other GS tourn, at US Open, found motivation hard to maintain and lost in last 16 to Maleeva Fragnière, who beat her again in qf Tokyo Nicherei. Won her 150th title at FC Cup in April; r/u Italian Open, Los Angeles and VS California, losing each time to Seles, while Sanchez-Vicario beat her in sf Hamburg and K. Maleeva at same stage Houston. She was overtaken in the rankings by Seles and finished the year ranked 3 for the first time since 1981. In doubles she won US Open with G. Fernandez and took four other titles with various partners. **1991: (5)** *Chicago, Palm Springs, Birmingham, Eastbourne, Oakland.* Missed Australian Open after undergoing knee surgery and returned to reach f Tokyo Pan Pacific end Jan. However, it was her least successful year since 1976, and she slipped out of the top 3 for the 1st time since 1977. R/u Tokyo Pan Pacific, Milan, Filderstadt and VS Champs. In doubles she reached 3 f, winning Barcelona with Sanchez-Vicario, Filderstadt with Novotna and a seventh VS Champs with Shriver. When she d. Seles at Palm Springs, it was the 1st time since 1987 that she'd beaten a player above her in the rankings and she repeated the performance in winning VS California to equal Evert's record of 157 career titles. In beating Reinach 1r Wimbledon – recovering from 4–6 6–2 3–4 0–30 down – she recorded a record 100th single win there, and during the tourn she also passed Evert's record of 111 singles matches played there. She has already set a new record of 1,310 career match wins when she d. M.-J. Fernandez in Milan. However, she failed to take a 10th Wimbledon title, falling in ss to Capriati in qf, and at US Open she was seeded as low as 6. However, she belied that assessment by beating Graf to reach f, which she lost to Seles, who also beat her in 4s f VS Champs. **1992: (4)** *Chicago, San Antonio, Los Angeles, Filderstadt.* At Chicago she won her 158th singles title, passing Evert's record, and finished the year with 161. She also won the doubles at Chicago with Shriver and did the double again at San Antonio, also with Shriver. In 2r Eastbourne Harvey-Wild inflicted her earliest defeat in a tourn since Avon of California in 1981, and in 2r US Open Magdalena Maleeva inflicted her earliest defeat in GS since 1976, when she lost in 1r US Open to Newberry. Hopes of a 10th Wimbledon singles title were dashed in sf by Seles, a defeat which was avenged in f VS Los Angeles. She finished the year in style at VS Champs, where she was r/u to Seles in singles and reached sf doubles with Shriver. Announced at end of season that 1993 would be her last year of competition.

PRINCIPAL 1992 RESULTS: (detailed Grand Slams results below)
SINGLES: won VS Chicago (d. Cioffi 6–0 6–0, Shriver 6–2 7–6, McNeil 1–6 6–4 6–4, Novotna 7–6 4–6 7–5), **won** San Antonio (d. Louise Allen 6–1 6–1, Reggi Concato 6–0 6–1, Shriver 6–4 6–3, Tauziat 6–2 6–1), **won** VS Los Angeles (d. Dechaume 6–3 6–0, Garrison 6–3 6–0, Maleeva Fragnière 6–4 7–6, Seles 6–4 6–2), **won** Filderstadt (d. Hy 7–6 6–1, Martinek 6–4 6–1, Sukova 6–3 7–6, Sanchez-Vicario 6–1 6–1, Sabatini 7–5 6–2), **r/u** Tokyo Pan Pacific (d. Basuki 6–0 7–5, Gildemeister 6–4 6–3, Magdalena Maleeva 6–2 6–2, lost Sabatini 6–2 4–6 6–2), **r/u** Zurich (d. Zardo 6–0 6–0, Rittner 6–3 6–0, Magdalena Maleeva 6–2 6–3, Fendick 6–3 4–1 ret'd, lost Graf 2–6 7–5 7–5), **r/u** Oakland (d. Provis 6–1 2–6 6–1, Zvereva 6–2 6–2, K. Maleeva 6–1 6–2, lost Seles 6–3 6–4), **r/u** VS Champs (d. Maleeva Fragnière 6–3 6–2, Sanchez-Vicario 6–1 2–6 6–2, McNeil 7–6 6–4, lost Seles 7–5 6–3 6–1).
DOUBLES: (with Shriver) **won** VS Chicago (d. Adams/Garrison 6–4 7–6), **won** San Antonio (d. Fendick/ Strnadova 3–6 6–2 7–6), **r/u** Tokyo Pan Pacific (lost Sanchez-Vicario/Sukova 7–5 6–1), **r/u** Zurich (lost Sukova/Zvereva 7–6 6–4).

GRAND SLAM RECORD
AUSTRALIAN OPEN – Played 10, won 3, r/u 3, sf 3, qf 1
1975: r/u d. Gregory 6–0 6–3, Court [seed 1], Chmyreva 6–4 6–4, lost Goolagong 6–3 6–2. **1980: sf** [seed 1] bye, d. Blount 6–3 6–7 6–1, Nagelsen 6–2 6–2, Stevens [seed 5] 4–6 6–1 7–6, lost Turnbull [seed 4] 6–4 7–5. **1981: won** [seed 3] bye, d. Tobin 6–0 6–1, K.Jordan [seed 14] 7–5 3–6 6–2, Cawley [seed 8] 6–4 6–1, Shriver [seed 6] 6–3 7–5, Lloyd [seed 1] 6–7 6–4 7–5. **1982: r/u** [seed 1] bye, d. Budarova 6–1 6–2, Kohde [seed 15] 6–4 6–4, Smith [seed 10] 6–2 6–1, Shriver [seed 5] 6–3 6–4, lost Lloyd [seed 2] 6–3 2–6 6–3. **1983: won** [seed 1] d. Ludloff 6–0 7–5, Sayers 6–1 6–0, Fairbank [seed 16] 6–2 6–2, Durie [seed 8] 4–6 6–3 6–4, Shriver [seed 3] 6–4 6–2, Jordan [seed 9] 6–2 7–6. **1984: sf** [seed 1] d. Vermaak 6–1 6–1, Piatek 6–2 6–1, Rinaldi [seed 15] 4–6 6–0 6–1, Potter [seed 12] 6–3 6–2, lost Sukova [seed 9] 1–6 6–3 7–5. **1985: won** [seed 2] d. Hansel 6–2 6–1, Provis 6–2 6–1, Hobbs 6–3 6–1, Sukova [seed 8] 6–2 6–2, Mandlikova [seed 3] 6–7 6–1 6–4, Evert Lloyd [seed 1] 6–2 4–6 6–2. **1987: r/u** [seed 1] bye, Golder 6–0 6–2, Benjamin 6–2 6–1, Thompson 6–4 6–1, Garrison [seed 7] 6–0 6–3, Lindqvist [seed 10] 6–3 6–2, lost Mandlikova [seed 2] 7–5 7–6. **1988: sf** [seed 2] d. E.Minter 6–3 6–0, A.M.Fernandez 6–1 6–0, Kijimuta 4–6 6–2 6–2, Hanika [seed 11] 6–4 6–0, Sukova [seed 6] 6–4 7–6, lost Evert [seed 3] 6–2 7–5. **1989: qf** [seed 2] d. Betzner 6–0 6–1, Byrne 6–4 7–6, Novotna 6–2 6–2, Mandlikova [seed 15] 6–4 6–1, lost Sukova [seed 5] 6–2 3–6 9–7.

FRENCH OPEN – Played 11, won 2, r/u 4, qf 3
1973: qf d. Kozelubova 6–4 6–3, Giscafre 7–5 6–4, Gunter [seed 5] 6–3 6–3, lost Goolagong[seed 4] 7–6 6–4. **1974: qf** [seed 5] d. Tenney 6–4 6–3, Burton 7–6 6–2, Fromholtz 6–2 3–6 6–3, lost Masthoff [seed 3] 7–6 6–3. **1975: r/u** [seed 2] d. Araujo 6–4 6–4, Fuchs 7–5 6–3, Teeguarden 6–2 2–6 6–3, Ganz 6–1 6–1, Newberry [seed 5] 6–2 6–3, lost Evert [seed 1] 2–6 6–2 6–1. **1981: qf** [seed 2] bye, d. Kuhn Riedl 6–4 6–0, A.White 6–1 6–1, Allen [seed 15] 6–1 6–2, lost Hanika [seed 6] 6–2 6–4. **1982: won** [seed 2] bye, d. C.Reynolds 6–1 6–1, Bonder 6–1 6–3, Rinaldi [seed 15] 6–0 2–6 6–0, Garrison 6–3 6–2, Mandlikova [seed 5] 6–0 6–2, Jaeger [seed 4] 7–6 6–1. **1983: 4r** [seed 1] d. Piatek 6–1 6–1, Skronska 6–1 6–1, W.White 6–0 6–3, lost Horvath 6–4 0–6 6–3. **1984: won** [seed 1] d. Tauziat 6–1 6–2, Mesker 6–1 6–1, Caleja 6–1 6–3, Kohde-Kilsch [seed 14] 6–0 6–1, Horvath [seed 8] 6–4 6–2, Mandlikova [seed 3] 3–6 6–2 6–2, Lloyd [seed 2] 6–3 6–1. **1985: r/u** [seed

1] d. Teeguarden 6–1 6–0, Wade 6–3 6–0, Tanvier 6–0 6–0, Reggi 6–4 6–1, Cecchini 6–2 6–2, Kohde-Kilsch [seed 7] 6–4 6–4, lost Lloyd [seed 2] 6–3 6–7 7–5. **1986: r/u** [seed 1] d. Cecchini 6–3 6–3, Savchenko 6–2 6–3, Porwick 6–3 6–3, Garrone 6–1 6–2, Rinaldi [seed 7] 7–5 6–4, Sukova [seed 6] 4–6 7–6 6–2, lost Lloyd [seed 2] 2–6 6–3 6–3. **1987: r/u** [seed 1] d. Tanvier 6–3 7–6, Villagran 6–0 2–6 6–2, Huber 6–1 6–1, Hanika [seed 15] 6–0 6–2, Kohde-Kilsch [seed 8] 6–1 6–2, Evert [seed 3] 6–2 6–2, lost Graf [seed 2] 6–4 4–6 8–6. **1988: 4r** [seed 2] d. Medrado 6–0 6–3, Ter Riet 6–0 1–0 ret., Paulus 6–2 6–2, lost Zvereva [seed 13] 6–3 7–6.

WIMBLEDON – Played 20, won 9, r/u 2, sf 4, qf 3

1973: 3r d. Janes 6–1 6–4, DuPont 8–6 6–4, lost Hogan 6–4 6–4. **1974: 1r** lost Jausovec 6–4 3–6 6–3. **1975: qf** [seed 2] d. Turnbull 6–2 8–6, Mappin 6–1 6–2, Stevens 6–4 6–3, Chmyreva 6–1 6–0, lost Court [seed 5] 6–3 6–4. **1976: sf** [seed 4] d. DuPont 3–6 6–1 6–3, Gurdal 6–2 6–1, Antonoplis 6–1 6–4, Durr 2–6 6–3 7–5, Barker [seed 7] 6–3 3–6 7–5, lost Evert [seed 1] 6–3 6–0. **1977: qf** [seed 2] d. Coles 6–3 6–0, Lofdahl–Bentzer 6–0 6–3, Charles 6–2 6–2, Holladay 6–4 6–4, lost Stove [seed 7] 9–8 3–6 6–1. **1978: won** [seed 2] d. Anthony 6–1 6–3, Whytcross 7–5 6–1, Jordan 3–6 6–1 6–4, Austin [seed 9] 6–2 6–3, Kruger [seed 11] 6–2 6–4, Cawley [seeded 3] 2–6 6–4 6–4, Evert [seed 1] 2–6 6–4 7–5. **1979: won** [seed 1] d. Harford 4–6 6–2 6–1, Durie 6–4 6–1, Casals 6–3 6–3, Stevens 7–6 6–7 6–3, Fromholtz [seed 6] 2–6 6–3 6–0, Austin [seed 4] 7–5 6–1, Lloyd [seed 2] 6–4 6–4. **1980: sf** [seed 1] d. Kloss 6–0 6–3, Fox 6–1 6–1, Harford 6–3 3–6 6–3, K. Jordan [seed 10] 6–4 6–2, King [seed 5] 7–6 1–6 10–8, lost Lloyd [seed 3] 4–6 6–4 6–2. **1981: sf** [seed 4] d. Portman 6–4 6–0, Mascarin 6–0 6–1, Walsh 6–1 2–6 6–0, Nagelsen, 6–3 6–1, Ruzici [seed 8] 6–2 6–3, lost Mandlikova [seed 2] 7–5 4–6 6–1. **1982: won** [seed 1] bye, d. Norton 6–3 6–3, A.White 6–1 6–4, Garrison 6–3 6–2, Russell 6–3 6–4, Bunge [seed 11] 6–2 6–2, Lloyd [seed 2] 6–1 3–6 6–2. **1983: won** [seed 1] d. Mould 6–1 6–0, Acker 7–6 6–3, Jausovec 6–2 6–1, Kohde-Kilsch [seed 16] 6–1 6–2, Mundel 6–3 6–1, Vermaak 6–1 6–1, Jaeger [seed 3] 6–0 6–3. **1984: won** [seed 1] d. Louie 6–4 6–0, Holton 6–2 7–5, Buderova 6–2 6–2, Sayers 6–0 ret., M.Maleeva [seed 7] 6–3 6–2, K.Jordan [seed 6] 6–3 6–4, Evert Lloyd [seed 2] 7–5 6–2. **1985: won** [seed 1] d. Bonder 6–0 6–2, A.Minter 6–4 6–1, Bunge 7–6 6–3, Uys 6–2 6–2, Shriver [seed 5] 7–6 6–3, Garrison [seed 8] 6–4 7–6, Lloyd [seed 1] 4–6 6–3 6–2. **1986: won** [seed 1] d. Dingwall 6–3 6–2, Forman 6–0 6–4, Kinney 6–0 6–2, Demongeot 6–3 6–3, Bunge 6–1 6–3, Sabatini [seed 10] 6–2 6–2, Mandlikova [seed 3] 7–6 6–3. **1987: won** [seed 1] d. Porwik 6–1 6–0, Inoue 6–1 6–2, Harper 6–2 6–2, G.Fernandez 6–3 6–1, Balestrat 6–2 6–1, Evert [seed 3] 6–2 5–7 6–4, Graf [seed 2] 7–5 6–3. **1988: r/u** [seed 2] d. Goles 6–1 6–2, Hakami 6–2 6–1, Schimper 6–0 6–4, Savchenko [seed 13] 6–4 6–2, Fairbank 4–6 6–4 7–5, Evert [seed 4] 6–1 4–6 7–5, lost Graf [seed 1] 5–7 6–2 6–1. **1989: r/u** [seed 2] d. Hetherington 6–3 6–2, Radford 3–6 6–3 6–3, Provis 6–0 6–3, Mandlikova [seed 14] 6–3 6–2, Magers 6–1 6–2, Lindqvist 7–6 6–2, lost Graf [seed 1] 6–2 6–7 6–1. **1990: won** [seed 2] d. Amiach 6–1 6–1, Smith 6–2 6–3, Kschwendt 6–1 6–1, Wiesner [seed 14] 6–3 6–3, K.Maleeva [seed 7] 6–1 6–1, Sabatini [seed 4] 6–3 6–4, Garrison [seed 5] 6–4 6–1. **1991: qf** [seed 3] d. Reinach 4–6 6–2–6 4, Grunfeld 6–3 6–1, Garrone 6–2 6–2, Lindqvist 6–1 6–3, lost Capriati [seed 9] 6–4 7–5. **1992: sf** [seed 4] d. Magdalena Maleeva 6–2 6–2, Po 6–2 3–6 6–0, Rittner 7–5 6–1, Basuki 7–5 6–2, K. Maleeva [seed 12] 6–3 7–6, lost Seles [seed 1] 6–2 6–7 6–4.

US OPEN – Played 20, won 4, r/u 4, sf 4, qf 2

1973: 1r lost Burton 5–7 6–1 6–3. **1974: 3r** d. Fox 3–6 7–5 7–6, Stove 6–2 6–2, lost Heldman 4–6 6–4 . **1975: sf** [seed 3] d. Mappin 6–3 6–3, Russell 6–2 3–6 6–2, May 6–3 6–0, Court [seed 5] 6–2 6–4, lost Evert [seed 1] 6–4 6–4. **1976: 1r** [seed 3] lost Newberry 1–6 6–4 6–3. **1977: sf** [seed 2] d. Hamm 6–0 6–1, Meyer 6–4 6–1, Harford 6–0 6–2, Kruger 6–1, Jausovec [seed 10] 6–4 6–1, lost Turnbull [seed 12] 2–6 7–5 6–4. **1978: sf** [seed 1] bye, d. Louvera 6–1 6–1, Pinterova 6–1 6–2, Kiyomura 6–4 6–2, Ruzici [seed 11] 6–3 6–2, lost Shriver [seed 16] 7–6 7–6. **1979: sf** [seed 2] bye, d. Moulton 6–4 6–0, Stoll 6–3 6–1, Stevens [seed 10] 6–2 6–2, Reid [seed 8] 6–4 6–1, lost Austin [seed 3] 7–5 7–5. **1980: 4r** [seed 2] d. Sandin 6–4 4–6 6–2, Allen 6–4 4–6 6–2, Morse 6–4 6–1, lost Mandlikova [seed

9] 7–6 6–4. **1981: r/u** [seed 4] d. Gregory 6–0 6–1, A.White 6–2 6–3, Russell 6–2 6–1, K.Jordan [seed 14] 6–0 6–1, Smith 7–5 6–4, Lloyd [seed 1] 7–5 4–6 6–4, lost Austin [seed 3] 1–6 7–6 7–6. **1982: qf** [seed 1] d. DuPont 6–1 6–1, Davis 7–6 6–1, Yeargin 6–3 6–3, Leand [seed 15] 6–1 6–2. lost Shriver [seed 7] 1–6 7–6 6–2. **1983: won** [seed 1] d. Ramponi–Longo 6–1 6–0, Allen 6–2 6–1, Gompert 6–2 6–2, Vasquez 6–0 6–1, Hanika [seed 7] 6–0 6–3, Shriver [seed 5] 6–2 6–1, Lloyd [seed 2] 6–1 6–3. **1984: won** [seed 1] d. Antonoplis 6–4 6–2, Leand 6–4 6–2, Mundel 6–0 6–0, Potter [se0ed 15] 6–4 6–4, Sukova 6–3 6–3, Turnbull [seed 13] 6–4 6–1, Evert Lloyd [seed 2] 4–6 6–4 6–4. **1985: r/u** [seed 2] d. Paradis 6–2 6–1, Bonder 6–1 6–1, Cecchini 6–0 6–1, Lindqvist [seed 13] 6–4 7–5, Garrison [seed 6] 6–2 6–3, Graf [seed 11] 6–2 6–3, lost Mandlikova [seed 3] 7–6 1–6 7–6. **1986: won** [seed 1] d. Holikova 6–4 6–2, Nagelsen 6–2 7–5, Horvath 6–4 6–2, Sabatini [seed 11] 6–4 6–2, Shriver [seed 5] 6–4 6–2, Graf [seed 3] 6–1 6–7 7–6, Sukova [seed 7] 6–3 6–2. **1987: won** [seed 2] d. Gompert 6–1 6–1, R.White 6–1 6–3, Bonder 6–2 6–1, Lindqvist [seed 14] 6–0 6–4, Sabatini [seed 8] 7–5 6–3, Sukova [seed 6] 6–2 6–2, Graf [seed 1] 7–6 6–1. **1988: qf** [seed 2] d. Lindqvist 6–1 6–3, Hakami 6–2 6–1, A. Minter 6–1 6–3, Reinach 6–4 6–1, lost Garrison [seed 11] 6–4 6–7 7–5. **1989: r/u** [seed 2] d. Ida 6–0 6–2, Halard 6–1 56–0, Goles 6–4 6–0,Rajchrtova 6–2 6–0, M.Maleeva [seed 7] 6–0 6–0, Garrison [seed 5] 7–6 6–2, lost Graf [seed 1] 3–6 7–5 6–1. **1990: 4r** [seed 2] d. Haumuller 6–4 6–0, Wood 6–0 6–4, Cioffi 6–2 6–2, lost Maleeva–Fragniere [seed 9] 7–5 3–6 6–3. **1991: r/u** [seed 6] d. Tarabini 6–2 6–2, Graham 6–1 6–4, Shriver 7–5 6–1, Maleeva Fragnière [seed 10] 7–6 1–6 6–2, Sanchez-Vicario [seed 4] 6–7 7–6 6–2, Graf [seed 1] 7–6 6–7 6–4, lost Seles [seed 2] 7–6 6–1. **1992: 2r** [seed 3] d. Stafford 4–6 6–1 7–5, lost Magdalena Maleeva 6–4 0–6 6–3.

OLYMPIC GAMES – Has not competed

CAREER FEDERATION CUP RECORD
1975: lr d. Geraldine Barniville (IRL) 6–1 6–0. (+ Tomanova) d. Barniville/ Lennon 6–3 6–0. **2r** d. Marijke Schaar(NED 6–2 1–0 ret. **qf** d. Helga Masthoff (GER) 6–3 6–2. (+ Tomanova) d. Ebbinghaus/Masthoff (FRG) 8–6 6–1. **sf** d. Gail Chanfreau (FRA) 6–3 6–2. (+ Tomanova) d. Chanfreau/Darmon 6–4 6–3. **Final** d. Evonne Goolagong (AUS) 6–3 6–4. (+ Tomanova) d. Fromholtz/Gourlay (AUS) 6–3 6–1. **1982: lr** d. Suzanna Anggarkusumah (INO) 6–2 6–1. (+ Evert) d. Anggarkusuma/Ultamingsih (INDO) 6–0 6–0. **2r** d. Heliane Steden (MEX) 7–5 6–0. (+ Leand) d. Hernandez/Steden 6–2,6–0. **qf** d. Patricia Medrado (BRZ) 6–0 6–3. (+ Evert) d. Medrado/Monteiro 6–2 6–0. **sf** d. Hana Mandlikova (TCH) 6–4 0–6 6–1. (+ Evert) d. Mandlikova/Sukova 6–3 6–2. **Final** d. Bettina Bunge (GER) 6–4 6–4. (+ Evert) d. Kohde/Bunge (GER) 3–6 6–1 6–2. **1986: lr** d. Li Xinyi (CHN) 6–1 6–0. (+ Shriver) d. Xiufen Pu/Lilan Duan 6–2 6–0. **2r** d. Arantxa Sanchez (ESP) 6–3 6–0. (+Shriver) d. Almansa/Llorca 6–0 6–1. **qf** d.Rafaella Reggi (ITA) 6–2 6–4. (+Shriver) d. Reggi/Garrone (ITA) 6–3 6–1. **sf** d. Claudia Kohde Kilsch (GER) 6–1 6–4. (+ Shriver) d. Bunge/Porwick 6–2 6–3. **Final** d. Hana Mandlikova (TCH) 7–5 6–1. (+ Shriver) d. Mandlikova/Sukova 6–4 6–2. **1989: lr** d. Angeliki Kanellopoulou (GRE) 6–3 6–1. **2r** d. Tine Scheur Larsen (DEN) 7–5 6–3. (+ Garrison) d. Kjaer NielsonScheur Larsen 6–3 6–1. **qf** d. Barbara Paulus (AUT) 6–4 6–1. (+ Shriver) d. Paulus/Wiesner 6–1 6–2. **sf** d. Helena Sukova (TCH) 4–6 6–1 6–4. **Final** d. Arantxa Sanchez-Vicario (ESP) 0–6 6–3 6–4.

MARY JOE FERNANDEZ (USA)　　　　**Turned pro:** 1986

Born: Dominican Republic, 19 August 1971.
Lives: Miami, Fla.
Father: José, born in Spain. **Mother:** Sylvia comes from Cuba.
Sister: Sylvia (older).
Agent: International Management Group. **Manager:** Ion Tiriac.
Coach: Harold Solomon since Dec. 1991; formerly Dean Goldfeen,
Juan Avendano and Tim Gullikson; trainer Ron Zelhov.
Height: 5ft 10in (1.78m). **Weight:** 140lb (63kg).

Rankings: 1985: 99; **1986:** 27; **1987:** 20; **1988:** 15; **1989:** 12; **1990:** 4; **1991:** 8; **1992:** 7.
Highest: 6 (9 September 1991).

1992 Prize Money: $605,908. **Career Earnings:** $2,253,521. **Career Titles:** 2.

Style: With Chris Evert as her model, she is a right-hander with a 2-handed backhand
whose fierce, flat drives on both wings make her a fearsome opponent. Happiest at the
back of the court swapping deep drives, she can volley and does so more frequently now
in an attempt to broaden her game.

CAREER HIGHLIGHTS (year: *(titles)*)
Jun. Record – 1982: Won Orange Bowl 12s, beating Sabatini in f. **1983:** Won Orange Bowl
14s, beating Sabatini in sf. **1984:** In 16s age group won Orange Bowl 16s, US Nat, US CC
and was ranked No. 1 in US. **1985:** Won Orange Bowl 18s, ranked 2 behind Rehe in US
18s. **Prof. Record – 1986:** Demonstrating her uncanny court sense, excellent anticipation,
extraordinary determination and formidable flat forehand and 2HB, she stopped Kohde-
Kilsch to reach qf French Open; had other good CC wins over Rehe and Sabatini during the
year. **1987:** Reached last 16 Wimbledon, qf Geneva and Filderstadt. **1988:** Last 16
Wimbledon and upset Sabatini *en route* to sf both LIPC and Eastbourne. **1989:** Upset
Sabatini again *en route* to sf French Open; r/u Filderstadt and sf Pan Pacific Open. In
doubles r/u US Open with Shriver, and with various partners reached 4 other f, winning VS
Dallas. Qualified for VS Champs for 1st time, but lost 1r to Navratilova. **1990: (2)** *Tokyo
Indoor, Filderstadt.* Her year began on a high note at Australian Open, where she was r/u to
Graf in singles and r/u with Fendick in doubles. She continued to do well in GS, reaching qf
French Open and sf US Open, having missed Wimbledon. In Sept. won her 1st career title
at Tokyo Nicherei (indoors), following with Filderstadt in Oct. In other tourns she reached
sf VS Florida, Barcelona, VS Los Angeles, VS New England and VS Champs to finish the
year in the top 5, ahead of Sabatini. **1991:** Reached sf Wimbledon and Australian Open,
where she extended Seles to 9-7 fs as she suffered the 1st of 6 defeats during the year at
the hands of the new No. 1. R/u VS Houston, Tokyo Ariake; sf Tokyo Pan Pacific, LIPC,
Italian Open, Eastbourne, VS Washington and Milan; and qualified for VS Champs, where
she lost qf to Seles. Won her 1st GS title when she took Australian Open doubles with
Fendick and from 5 more f with various partners she won LIPC with Garrison, with whom
she qualified for VS Champs. Recruited Ion Tiriac to improve her game and image, feeling
that although she was ranked in the top 5 she was relatively little known. **1992:** Working
with Harold Solomon, with whom she developed a serve-and-volley attack, she began the
year with a flourish at Australian Open, upsetting Sabatini to reach her 2nd f there and also
r/u doubles with Garrison. At the Olympics she won a bronze medal in singles and gold in
doubles with G. Fernandez and then upset Sabatini again to reached sf US Open. She was r/u
Essen and appeared in 8 more singles sf – at Sydney, VS Florida, Italian Open, Berlin,
Eastbourne, Tokyo Nicherei, Filderstadt and Brighton. As well as her major triumphs in doubles,
she won Tokyo with R. White and reached 3 more f. So it was rather an anticlimax when, having
qualified for VS Champs in singles and doubles (with Garrison), she lost 1r in both.

PRINCIPAL 1992 RESULTS (detailed Grand Slam results below)
r/u Essen (d. Porwik 6–3 6–3, Appelmans 6–4 6–4, Rittner 7–5 6–4, lost Seles 6–0 6–3), **sf**

Sydney (d. Cunningham 7–5 6–3, Sukova 6–4 6–4, Meskhi 6–1 6–2, lost Sabatini 6–2 6–3), **sf** VS Florida (d. Cammy MacGregor 6–4 6–1, Gildemeister 6–3 7–5, Tauziat 6–4 6–2, lost Graf 6–0 7–5), **sf** Italian Open (d. Demongeot 6–3 6–4, Gorrochategui 3–6 6–2 6–2, Huber 3–6 7–6 6–3, lost Sabatini 6–2 6–3), **sf** Berlin (d. Bacheva 6–2 6–1, Wiesner 6–4 6–4, Cecchini 6–1 7–6, lost Sanchez-Vicario 7–5 7–6), **sf** Eastbourne (d. Kohde-Kilsch 6–3 6–1, Testud 7–6 6–4, Hy 6–3 6–3, Sukova 6–3 6–4, lost McNeil 7–5 6–0), **sf** Tokyo Nicherei (d. Byrne 6–1 6–1, Nagatsuka 6–0 6–2, lost Seles 6–0 3–6 6–4), **sf** Filderstadt (d. Schultz 6–2 3–6 6–3, Zvereva 6–2 0–6 6–2, Huber 5–7 6–3 6–1, lost Sabatini 7–5 6–2), **sf** Brighton (d. Durie 3–2 ret'd, Reinach 6–3 6–0, Tauziat 6–4 6–3, lost Novotna 6–3 6–4). **DOUBLES:** (+GarrisonJackson unless stated) **r/u** Australian Open (lost Sanchez-Vicario/Sukova 6–4 7–6); **[+G. Fernandez] won** Olympic gold medal (see below); **[+R. White] won** Tokyo Nicherei (d. Basuki /Miyagi 6–4 6–4), **r/u** Sydney (lost Sanchez-Vicario/Sukova 7–6 6–7 6–2), **r/u** Eastbourne (lost Novotna/Savchenko Neiland 6–0 6–3); (+Zvereva) **r/u** Montreal (lost McNeil/Stubbs 3–6 7–5 7–5).

CAREER GRAND SLAM RECORD
AUSTRALIAN OPEN – Played 4, r/u 2, sf 1
1989: 3r [seed 10] d. Phelps 6–1 4–6 6–1, Grossman 6–4 7–6, lost Tanvier 6–2 6–3. **1990: r/u** [seed 6] d. Jaggard 6–1 6–3, Rinaldi 6–4 6–4, Halard 6–0 3–6 6–3, Faber 6–4 6–2, Garrison [seed 3] 1–6 6–2 8–6, Porwick 6–2 6–1, lost Graf [seed 1] 6–3 6–4. **1991: sf** [seed 3] d. Gomer 6–1 6–0, Romano 6–1 6–2, Sawamatsu 6–3 6–3, Appelmans [seed 16] 6–3 6–3, K.Maleeva [seed 5] 6–3 6–2, lost Seles [seed2] 6–3 0–6 9–7. **1992: r/u** [seed 7] d. Javer 6–1 6–0, Rittner 6–4 6–4, McQuillan 6–1 2–6 6–1, Fendick 6–4 6–1, Frazier 6–4 7–6, Sabatini 6–1 6–4, lost Seles 6–2 6–3.

FRENCH OPEN Played 7, sf 1, qf 3
1985: 1r lost Mandlikova [seed 3] 6–1 7–5. **1986: qf** d. Kelesi 7–6 6–3, Temesvari 5–7 6–2 6–3, Hobbs 6–2 6–0, Kohde-Kilsch [seed 4] 7–6 7–5, lost Sukova [seed 6] 6–2 7–4. **1987: 2r** [seed 13] d. Horvath 4–6 6–0 6–2, lost Rehe 7–6 1–6 6–4. **1989: sf** [seed 15] d. Herreman 6–2 6–3, Farley 6–7 6–3 6–1, Dias 6–7 6–1 6–1, Sabatini [seed 2] 6–4 6–4, Kelesi [seed 10] 6–2 7–5, lost Sanchez [seed 7] 6–2 6–2. **1990: qf** [seed 7] d. McDonald 6–4 6–2, Pierce 6–4 6–4, Cueto 7–6 6–2, Grossman 6–3 6–2, lost Capriati 6–2 6–4. **1991: qf** [seed 4] d. Romano 6–3 6–0, Hack 6–4 6–0, Thoren 6–4 6–3, Reinach 6–4 7–6, lost Sanchez-Vicario [seed 5] 6–3 6–2. **1992: 3r** [seed 6] d. Langrova 6–3 6–1, Stafford 6–1 6–4, lost Hack 7–6 6–2.

WIMBLEDON – Played 6, sf 1
1986: 1r lost Evert Lloyd [seed 2] 6–4 6–1. **1987: 4r** d. Bonder 6–0 6–2, Potter 6–0 6–1, Moulton 7–6 6–2, lost Balestrat 7–5 6–2. **1988: 4r** [seed 16] d. Jagerman 6–3 6–2, Meskhi 6–1 7–5, Kuczynska 6–4 6–1, lost Graf [seed 1] 6–2 6–2. **1989: 4r** [seed 12] d. Daniels 6–4 7–5, Louise Allen 6–4 6–1, Tanvier 4–6 6–2 6–4, lost Fairbank 6–4 2–6 6–0. **1991: sf** [seed 6] d. Kamstra 6–2 6–4, Keller 7–6 6–1, Shriver 6–3 7–5, Wiesner [seed 9] 6–0 7–5, Sanchez-Vicario [seed 3] 6–2 7–5, lost Graf [seed 1] 6–2 6–4. **1992: 3r** [seed 7] d. Bentley 6–1 6–0, N. Dahlman 7–5 6–2, lost Frazier 6–3 6–3.

US OPEN – Played 8, sf 2
1985: 2r d. Gomer 6–1 6–4, lost Henricksson 6–1 6–4. **1986: 3r** d. Garrone 3–6 6–1 6–3, Hanika 6–2 6–2, lost Evert Lloyd [seed 2] 6–4 6–2. **1987: 3r** d. Marsikova 6–3 6–0, Savchenko 6–1 6–4, lost M.Maleeva [seed 10] 6–0 0–6 6–3. **1988: 3r** [seed 13] d. Byrne 6–1 6–2, Tauziat 6–4 6–4, lost Reinach 7–5 6–3. **1989: 1r** [seed 10] lost W.White 6–4 6–3. **1990: sf** [seed 8] d. Henricksson 6–1 6–1, Oremans 6–4 6–1, R.White 6–1 6–2, Wiesner [seed 15] 6–3 6–2, Maleeva Fragniere [seed 9] 7–5 3–6 6–3, lost Sabatini [seed 5] 7–5 5 7–6–3. **1991: 3r** [seed 5] d. Savchenko 6–3 6–3, Schultz 7–6 6–3, lost Zrubakova 6–1 6–2. **1992: sf** [seed 7] d. Faber 3–6 6–0 6–4, Medvedeva 3–6 6–3 6–1, Schultz 6–4 6–2, Pierce [seed 16] 6–0 6–4, Sabatini [seed 4] 6–2 1–6 6–4, lost Seles 6–3 6–2).

OLYMPIC RECORD
SINGLES – 1992: (Barcelona) SINGLES: sf Bronze medal [seed 4] d. Chen 6–2 6–3, Hy 6–2 1–6 12–10, Zvereva 7–6 6–1, Maleeva Fragnière [seed 6] 5–7 6–1 6–0 lost Graf [seed 1] 6–4 6–2. **DOUBLES – 1992 (+Gigi Fernandez) won Gold Medal** d. Muns/Schultz (NED) 6–0 6–0, Graf/Huber(GER) 7–6 6–4, De Swart/Reinach(RSA) 6–2 6–4, Meskhi/Zvereva(EUN) 6–4 7–5, Martinez/Sanchez-Vicario(ESP) 7–5 2–6 6–2.

CAREER FEDERATION CUP RECORD
1991: 2r d. Katerina Maleeva (BUL) 6–2 6–1, qf d. Barbara Paulus (AUT) 6–1 6–1, sf d. Jana Novotna (TCH) 6–4 0–6 9–7. Final: lost Arantxa Sanchez-Vicario (ESP) 6–3 6–4.

JENNIFER CAPRIATI (USA) Turned pro: 1990

Born: New York, 29 March 1976. **Lives:** Saddlebrook CC, Fla.
Father: Stefano. **Mother:** Denise. **Brother:** Steven (younger).
Agent: International Management Group.
Coach: Coached by her father, Stefano; formerly coached by
Jimmy Evert, and worked with Tom Gullikson in 1990–91 as part of
the USTA support system, then with Pavel Slozil from Dec. 1991 to
April 1992. **Fitness Trainer:** Laurie Schuett.
Height: 5ft 7in (1.70m) **Weight:** 135lb (61kg).

Rankings: 1990: 8; **1991:** 6; **1992:** 7. **Highest:** 6 (September 1991).

1992 Prize Money: $315,501. **Career Earnings:** $1,134,715. **Career Titles:** 5.

Style: A right-hander with a 2-handed backhand who hits the ball as hard as any woman
except Seles from the back of the court. She has a fluent, powerful serve and fine volleys
and tremendous determination but is a little slow on the turn.

CAREER HIGHLIGHTS (year: *(titles)*)
1988: Won Nat 18s at age 12. **1989:** Won French Open Jun (losing no set), US Open Jun,
plus Wimbledon and US Open Jun doubles with McGrath as well as US 18s HC and CC. At
13 years 6 months was youngest to play W Cup, making a sparkling d*but with a 6-0 6–0
drubbing of Wood, but was still too young to compete on the pro tour until March. **1990:**
(1) *Puerto Rico.* At age 13 she became the 1st female to reach f of her 1st pro tourn at VS
Florida, Boca Raton. She upset Sukova there and at LIPC, where she reached last 16,
stunned Sanchez-Vicario and Zvereva *en route* to 2nd tour f at Family Circle Cup, and in
Oct. beat Garrison at Puerto Rico to win her 1st tour title. Reached sf in 1st GS tourn at
French Open, becoming youngest (at 14 years 66 days) to reach that stage; youngest seed
at Wimbledon, where she reached last 16; youngest to win singles match at US Open
where she reached same stage; and youngest to qualify for VS Champs, where she lost 1r
to Graf. She was a member of the winning US Fed Cup team and won WTA Most
Impressive Newcomer award. **1991: (2)** *San Diego, Toronto.* Caused the upset of the
Championships when she stunned Navratilova in ss to become youngest semi-finalist at
Wimbledon, and at US Open d. Sabatini to reach the same stage and took Seles to 3s t-b.
She had earlier upset the No. 1 as she won San Diego, following with Toronto and r/u VS
Philadelphia. Also reached sf VS Florida and Berlin and qualified for VS Champs, where she
lost qf to Sabatini. In doubles won Italian Open with Seles. Played Fed Cup, winning all her
matches as USA reached f. **1992: (2)** *OLYMPICS, San Diego.* Found it a hard year on the
tour, despite winning the Olympic Gold medal. She struggled to recapture her enjoyment of
the game and early in the year was rumoured to be contemplating retirement. By year's end
she was beginning to feel more positive again. Won San Diego and reached sf Berlin,
Philadelphia and LIPC where, in qf, she became one of a handful of players to beat Seles
during the year. In GS she reached qf Australian Open, French Open and Wimbledon, losing
twice to Sabatini and once to Seles, and in VS Champs lost at the same stage to Sabatini.

PRINCIPAL 1992 RESULTS: (detailed Grand Slam results below)
won San Diego (d. Wiesner 6–4 6–1, Garrison 6–4 6–4, Huber 7–6 3–6 6–1, Martinez 3–6
7–6 6–2), **sf** LIPC (d. Godridge 6–3 7–5, Habsudova 6–3 6–1, Garrison Jackson 5–7 6–4 6–3,
Seles 6–2 7–6, lost Sanchez-Vicario 6–2 6–4), **sf** Berlin (d. Meier 6–3 2–6 6–1, Rittner 7–5
6–3, Zrubakova 6–3 7–5, lost Graf 2–6 6–3 6–4), **sf** Philadelphia (d. Burgin 6–2 6–0, McNeil
6–2 6–1, lost Graf 6–0 6–1).

CAREER GRAND SLAM RECORD
AUSTRALIAN OPEN – Played 1, qf 1
1992: qf [seed 5] d. Medvedeva 6–2 6–0, van Lottum 6–3 6–4, Adams 6–0 6–0, Garrison
Jackson [seed 11] 6–4 6–4, lost Sabatini [seed 3] 6–4 7–6.

FRENCH OPEN Played 3, sf 1, qf 1

1990: sf d. Testud 6–1 6–1, Cammy Macgregor 6–1 6–0, wiesner 6–4 6–4, paz 6–0 6–3, M. J. Fernandez [seed 7] 6–2 6–4, lost Seles [seed 2] 6–2 6–2. **1991: 4r** [seed 10] d. Piccolini 6–2 7–5, Temesvari 6–2 6–1, Kidowaki 6–3 6–0, lost Martinez [seed 7] 6–3 6–3. **1992: qf** [seed 5] d. Reinstadler 6–1 6–7 6–3, Testud 6–4 6–4, Habsudova 4–6 6–4 6–3, Pierce [seed 13] 6–4 6–3, lost Seles [seed 1] 6–2 6–2.

WIMBLEDON – Played 3, sf 1, qf 1

1990: 4r [seed 12] d. Kelesi 6–3 6–1, Halard 6–2 7–6, R.White 7–5 6–7 6–3, lost Graf [seed 1] 6–2 6–4. **1991: sf** [seed 10] d. Stafford 6–0 7–5, Zrubakova 6–2 6–3, Probst 6–3 1–6 6–3, Schultz 3–6 6–1 6–1, Navratilova [seed 4] 6–4 7–5, lost Sabatini [seed 2] 6–4 6–4. **1992: qf** [seed 6] d. Rubin 6–0 7–5, Shriver 6–2 6–4, Hy 6–3 6–1, Sawamatsu 6–3 4–6 6–4, lost Sabatini [seed 3] 6–1 3–6 6–3.

US OPEN – Played 3, sf 1

1990: 4r [seed 13] d. Huber 7–5 7–5, Hy 6–3 6–1, Strandlund 6–1 6–4, lost Graf [seed 1] 6–1 6–2. **1991: sf** [seed 7] d. Pfaff 6–1 6–0, Ritter 6–3 6–0, Hy 6–1 6–4, Durie 6–1 6–2, Sabatini [seed 3] 6–3 7–6, lost Seles [seed 2] 3–6 6–3 7–6. **1992: 3r** [seed 6] d. Muns Jagerman 7–6 6–2, Testud 6–2 6–3, lost Hy 7–5 6–4.

OLYMPIC GAMES

1992 (Barcelona) won Gold medal [seed 3] d. Reinach 6–1 6–0, Tarabini 6–4 6–1, Basuki 6–3 6–4, Huber [seed 7] 6–3 7–6, Sanchez-Vicario[seed 2] 6–3 3–6 6–1, Graf [seed 1] 3–6 6–3 6–4.

CAREER FEDERATION CUP RECORD

1990 lr d. Magdalena Mroz (POL) 6–3 6–1, 2r d. Sandra Wasserman (BEL) 6–0 7–6(13–11). qf d. Regina Rajchrtova (TCH) 6–2 7–6 (7–4), sf d. Barbara Paulus (AUT) 6–3 6–4. f d. Leila Meskhi (URS) 7–6 (7–3) 6–3. **1991** lr d. Manon Bollegraf (NED) 6–2 6–3. 2r d. Magdalena Maleeva (BUL) 7–5 6–2. qf lost Judith Wiesner (AUT) 6–2 0–6 8–6. sf d. Radka Zrubakova (TCH) 6–3 6–1. Final d. Conchita Martinez (ESP) 4–6 7–6(7–3) 6–1.

CONCHITA MARTINEZ (ESP)   Turned pro: 1988

Born: Monzon, 16 April 1972. **Lives:** Barcelona.
Father: Cecilio.
Mother: Conchita.
Brothers: Fernando and Roberto (both older).
Agent: Triosports.
Coach: Francisco Lopez; formerly Eric van Harpen.
Trainer: Miguel Mir.
Height: 5ft 7in (1.70m). **Weight:** 132lb (59kg).

Rankings: 1988: 40; **1989:** 7; **1990:** 11; **1991:** 9; **1992:** 8. **Highest:** 7 (November 1989).

1992 Prize Money: $445,768. **Career Earnings:** $1,222,345. **Career Titles:** 11.

Style: A right-hander with a double-handed backhand who hits with topspin on both wings. She is one of the most improved groundstrokers whose strength is her consistency. Despite an above average volley (which makes her a good doubles player) she rarely chooses to advance to the net in singles.

CAREER HIGHLIGHTS (year: *(titles)*)
SINGLES: 1988: (1) *Sofia.* Upset McNeil *en route* to last 16 French Open after qualifying and won 1st pro title in both singles and doubles (+ Paulus) at Sofia. Won Nat Champs over Sanchez and played Fed Cup. **1989: (3)** *Wellington, Tampa, VS Arizona.* Beat Sabatini en route to VS Arizona title; r/u Geneva and Bayonne; qf French Open and qualified for 1st VS Champs. Voted WTA Most Impressive Newcomer. **1990: (3)** *Clarins, Scottsdale, Indianapolis.* sf LIPC (d. Sabatini again), Tampa and Leipzig; qf French Open again. **1991: (3)** *Barcelona, Kitzbuhel, Clarins.* sf Italian Open (d. Navratilova), Geneva, San Diego and Milan. Played in the successful Spanish Fed Cup team and qualified for VS Champs, where she fell 1r to Graf. In GS reached qf French Open again and same stage US Open. **1992: (1)** *Kitzbuhel.* r/u Indian Wells, VS Florida, FC Cup and San Diego; sf Amelia Island and Barcelona; extended Sabatini to 3s in her 4th French Open qf and reached same stage Olympics. Qualified for VS Champs, where she beat K.Maleeva but lost qf to McNeil.
DOUBLES: with Sanchez-Vicario r/u French Open, r/u Olympic Games (silver medal) and won Barcelona, reaching 4 more f with various partners.

PRINCIPAL 1992 RESULTS (detailed Grand Slam results below)
SINGLES: won Kitzbuhel (d. Thoms 6–1 6–2, Fauche 6–2 6–3, Dechaume 6–2 6–2, Coetzer 6–1 6–3, Maleeva Fragnière 6–0 3–6 6–2), **r/u** Indian Wells (d. Rehe 6–4 7–6, Provis 6–2 6–2, Wiesner 6–3 6–1, Grossman 6–3 6–1, lost Seles 6–3 6–1), **r/u** VS Florida (d. Sviglerova 6–3 6–1, Date 6–1 7–6, Rittner 6–1 6–0, Coetzer 4–6 6–3 6–0, lost Graf 3–6 6–2 6–0), **r/u** FC Cup (d. Daniels 6–0 6–2, Cecchini 6–1 6–2, Zvereva 6–2 6–2, Sanchez-Vicario 6–4 7–5, lost Sabatini 6–1 6–4), **r/u** San Diego (d. Demongeot 6–4 7–5, Grossman 6–1 6–3, Meskhi 3–6 7–6 6–2, lost Capriati 6–3 6–2), **sf** Amelia Island (d. Papadaki 6–0 6–3, Cecchini 6–2 6–0, Garrison 6–3 6–1, lost Sabatini 6–3 6–3), **sf** Barcelona (d. Guerree 6–1 6–0, Tauziat 7–5 6–1, lost Sanchez-Vicario 6–1 6–2). **DOUBLES:** (+ Sanchez-Vicario unless stated) **won** Barcelona (d. Tauziat/ Wiesner 6–4 6–1), [Zrubakova] **r/u** Brighton (lost Novotna/Savchenko Neiland 6–4 6–1), [Harvey-Wild] **r/u** VS Florida (lost Savchenko Neiland/Zvereva 6–2 6–2), **r/u** San Diego[+Paz] (lost Novotna/Savchenko Neiland 6–1 6–4), [Pierce] **r/u** Philadelphia (lost G. Fernandez/Zvereva 6–1 6–3).

CAREER GRAND SLAM RECORD
AUSTRALIAN OPEN – Played 2
1989: 2r d. Sviglerova 6–0 6–0, lost Sabatini [seed 3] 3–6 6–1 6–2. **1992 4r** [seed 8] d. Stafford 6–3 6–1, Rehe 6–1 6–2, R. White 7–5 6–0, lost Maleeva Fragnière [seed 9] 6–4 2–6 6–2.

FRENCH OPEN – Played 5, qf 4
1988: 4r d. Dechaume 6–0 6–2, Scheuer Larsen 6–2 6–0, McNeil [seed 9] 1–6 6–3 6–1, lost Fulco 6–2 6–4. **1989: qf** [seed 8] d. Herr 6–3 6–2, Pospisilova 6–0 6–4, Amiach 6–3 6–3, K.Maleeva [seed 9] 6–0 6–1, lost Graf [seed 1] 6–0 6–4. **1990: qf** [seed 9] d. Thompson 7–5 6–1, Etchemendy 7–6 6–3, Zrubakopva 6–1 6–3, Probst 6–3 6–3, lost Graf [seed 1] 6–1 6–3. **1991: qf** [seed 7] d. Wiesner 6–4 6–3, Rehe 6–1 7–6, Cunningham, 6–1 6–4, Capriati [seed 10] 6–3 6–3, lost Seles [seed 1] 6–0 7–5. **1992: qf** [seed 7] d. Gildemeister 6–2 7–6, Martinek 6–2 6–0, Grossman 6–2 6–2, Meskhi [seed 15] 6–4 7–5, lost Sabatini [seed 3] 3–6 6–3 6–2. **DOUBLES: r/u** (+ Sanchez-Vicario) lost G.Fernandez/Zvereva 6–3 6–2.

WIMBLEDON – Played 1
1992: 2r [seed 8] d. Daniels 6–1 6–0, lost Zvereva 6–3 5–7 6–4.

US OPEN – Played 5, qf 1
1988: 1r lost Evert [seed 3] 6–4 6–1. **1989: 4r** [seed 15] d. Birch 6–3 6–2, Amiach 6–3 6–4, Hanika 7–5 6–1, lost Sabatini [seed 3] 6–1 6–1. **1990: 3r** [seed 10] d. Werdel 2–6 7–5 6–2, Bartos 6–4 4–6 6–4, lost Tauziat 6–2 6–1. **1991: qf** [seed 8] d. Dahlman 6–1 6–1, Basuki 6–3 6–4, Fendick 7–5 6–3, Garrison, [seed 12] 6–4 6–4, lost Graf [seed 1] 6–1 6–3. **1992: 1r** [seed 8] lost Grossman 6–3 2–6 6–4.

OLYMPIC GAMES
1992:(Barcelona) qf [seed 5] d. Wiesner 4–6 6–1 6–2, Cecchini 6–4 6–3, Coetzer 6–4 6–3, lost Sanchez-Vicario [seed 2] 6–4 6–4. **DOUBLES: r/u (silver medal)** (+ Sanchez-Vicario) [seed 1] (d..McQuillan/ Provis 6–3 6–3, lost G. Fernandez/M. J. Fernandez 7–5 2–6 6–2).

CAREER FEDERATION CUP RESULTS
1988: 1r d. Manon Bollegraf (NET) 6–2 6–4. (+ Sanchez-Vicario) d.. Bollegraf/Vis 5–7 6–4- 6–4.**2r** d.. Waya Walalangi (INO) 6–0 6–1. (+ Sanchez-Vicario) Basuki/Kusuma 6–0 5–7 6–2. **qf** lost Larisa Savchenko(URS) 7–6(7–4) 6–2. (+ Sanchez-Vicario) lost Savchenko/Zvereva 4–6 6–4 6–4. **1989: d..** Isabelle Demongeot (FRA) 6–7(3–7) 7–6(7–4) 6–4. **2r** d.. Nicole Jagerman (NED) 6–4 7–5. **qf** d. Larisa Savchenko (URS) 6–1 6–1. (+ Sanchez-Vicario) lost Savchenko/Zvereva 6–4 2–6 6–1. **sf** d. Elizabeth Smylie (AUS) 6–3 6–2. **Final** lost Chris Evert (USA) 6–3 6–2. (+Sanchez-Vicario) lost Garrison/Shriver (USA) 7–5 6–1. **1990: lr** d. Jill Hetherington (CAN) 6–1 6–4. (+ Perez) lost Simpson/Hetherington 7–5 2–6 6–2. **2r** d. Ilana Berger (ISR) 6–3 6–2. (+ Sanchez-Vicario) d. Berger/Zaltz (ISR) 6–3 6–4. **qf** d. Julie Halard (FRA) 6–0 6–3. (+ Sanchez-Vicario) d. Demongeot/Pierce (FRA) 6–4 6–4. **sf** d. Leila Meskhi (URS) 6–3 7–5. (+ Perez) lost Savchenko/Zvereva 6–2 6–3. **1991: lr** d. Dominique Monami (BEL) 6–3,6–1. **2r** d. Nicole Provis (AUS) 6–0 2–6 7–5. (+ Sanchez-Vicario) d. Smylie/Godridge 6–3 6–4. **qf** d. Suzanna Wibowo (INO) 6–2 6–0 **sf** d. Barbara Rittner (GER) 6–4 6–1. (+ Sanchez-Vicario) d. Rittner/Huber (GER) 6–1 6–1. **Final** lost Jennifer Capriati (USA) 4–6 7–6(7–3) 6–1. (+ Sanchez-Vicario) d. Garrison/G.Fernandez 3–6 6–1 6–1. **1992: lr** d. Domique Monami (BEL) 6–1 6–4. **2r** lost Helen Kelesi (CAN) 7–6(7–4) 6–2. (+ Sanchez-Vicario) d. Hetherington/Hy 6–4 6–0. **qf** d. Florencia Labat (ARG) 6–0 6–1. **sf** d. Rachel McQuillan (AUS) 6–1 6–4. **Final** lost Anke Huber (GER) 6–3 6–7 6–1(+ Sanchez-Vicario) d. Huber/Rittner 6–1 6–2.

MANUELA MALEEVA FRAGNIERE (SUI) Turned pro: 1982

Born: Sofia, Bulgaria, 14 February 1967. **Lives:** St Legier. **Husband:** Swiss coach Francois Fragnière. **Father:** George, played basketball for Bulgarian nat team. **Mother:** Yulia Berberian, was 9-times Bulgarian women's champ. **Sisters:** Katerina and Magdalena both play on the tour. Has played for Switzerland since Jan.1990. **Agent:** Advantage Internationa.l **Coach:** Husband, Francois; formerly her mother.
Height: 5ft 10in (1.78m). **Weight:** 163lb (73kg).

Rankings: 1982: 60; **1983:** 31; **1984:** 6; **1985:** 7; **1986:** 8; **1987:** 8; **1988:** 6; **1989:** 9; **1990:** 9; **1991:** 10; **1992:** 9. **Highest:** 3 (4 February 1985).

1992 Prize Money: $291,350. **Career Earnings:** $2,574,032. **Career Titles:** 16.

Style: Like so many modern women she is a right-hander with a 2-handed backhand whose great strength is consistency and accuracy from the baseline. She is also quick about the court but lacks a really big shot. Has a good, reliable serve and can volley when necessary.

CAREER HIGHLIGHTS (year: *(titles)*)
1981: Won Orange Bowl 14s. **1982:** Made inroads in women's events, but concluded her jun career on a sad note when her mother ordered her off the court in tears as she trailed Bassett 3-6 3–4 in Orange Bowl final at Miami Beach. **1983:** Upsets of Mandlikova and Bunge signalled her swift advance. **1984: (5)** *US CC, Tokyo Pan Pacific, Italian Open, Tokyo Lions Cup, Swiss Open.* On the last day of Italian Open she completed qf win over Ruzici and then dismissed Bassett and Evert Lloyd Voted WTA's Most Impressive Newcomer. **1985: (1)** *Tokyo Pan Pacific.* Her only singles title. **1986:** Won no tnts. but reached qf or better in 11 of 22 tourns entered, including US Open qf, and joined sister Katerina and mother Yulia to represent Bulgaria in Fed.Cup at Prague. **1987: (2)** *Mahwah, Charleston.* Upset Evert in FC Cup and at Mahwah won 1st tourn since 1985. Qualified for VS Champs, where she reached sf. **1988: (2)** *Kansas, Arizona.* Reached qf US Open and VS Champs and won Olympic bronze medal. **1989: (2)** *Indian Wells, Geneva.* Reached sf VS Dallas, Brighton and VS Chicago. At VS Champs lost qf to Sanchez-Vicario. In GS reached qf French Open and US Open. **1990:** Reached qf French Open, where she took Seles to 3s, and same stage US Open, upsetting Navratilova on the way. R/u VS Chicago, San Antonio and San Diego and appeared in 5 more sf. Qualified for VS Champs, where she fill in qf to M. J. Fernandez. **1991: (3)** *Linz, Geneva, Bayonne.* Won both singles and doubles in Linz. R/u Barcelona (upset Sanchez-Vicario); sf San Antonio (extended Seles to 3s), Toronto and VS California. Qualified for VS Champs, where she lost to Novotna 1r. **1992: (1)** *Bayonne.* r/u Kitzbuhel; sf Barcelona and Los Angeles; and in GS reached sf US Open and qf Wimbledon. Again failed to progress beyond 1r VS Champs, falling to Navratilova.

PRINCIPAL 1992 RESULTS (detailed Grand Slam results below)
won Bayonne (d Ruano 6–1 6-3, Herreman 6–0 6-4, Monami 6–7 6–0 6-1, Paradis Mangon 6–1 6-1, Tauziat 6–3 6-2), **r/u** Kitzbuhel (d. Dopfer 6–2 6-2, Szabova 6–0 6-0, Cecchini 6–2 6-3, Labat 4–6 6–0 6-3, lost Martinez 6–0 3–6 6-2), **sf** Barcelona (d. Garrone 6–2 6-4, Probst 6–3 6-4, lost Seles 6–3 6-1), **sf** VS Los Angeles (d. Rottier 6–1 6-4, Po 6–1 7–6, lost Navratilova 6–4 7–6).

CAREER GRAND SLAM RECORD
AUSTRALIAN OPEN – Played 5, qf 2
1982: 2r d. Acker 6–3 6-3, lost A.Smith [seed 10] 6–2 6-2. **1985: qf** [seed 7] d. Antonoplis 6–1 6-1, Schropp 6–2 6-3, K.Maleeva [seed 16] 6–2 6-1, lost Lloyd [seed 1] 6–3 6-3. **1987: 4r** [seed 6] bye, d. Kuzumi 6–4 6-1, Bartos Cscrepy 6—3 6–7 7-5, lost Lindqvist [seed 10] 6–3 6-3. **1991: 2r** [seed 8] d. Faull 6–2 6-0, lost Huber 6–4 6-4 **1992: qf** [seed 9] d.

Helgeson 4–6 6–3 6–1, Habsudova 6–3 6–3, Tami Whitlinger 6–2 6–1, Martinez [seed 8] 6–4 2–6 6–2, lost Sanchez-Vicario [seed 4] def.

FRENCH OPEN – Played 11, qf 4
1982: 2r bye, lost Bonder 7–5 6–1. **1983: 3r** d. Phelps 6–3 6–2, Bunge [seed 6] 6–4 6–2, lost Rush 2–6 6–2 6–2. **1984: 4r** [seed 10] d. Gerken 6–2 6–2, Vermaak 6–2 6–1, Jausovec 6–1 6–3, lost Lloyd [seed 2] 3–6 6–3 6–2. **1985: qf** [seed 4] d. Collins 6–3 6–3, Delhees–Jauch 6–1 6–2, Calleja 6–0 6–1, Gadusek [seed 10] 7–5 6–3, lost Sabatini [seed 14] 6–3 1–6 6–1. **1986: 3r** [seed 8] d. Skronska 6–1 6–2, Suire 6–0 6–3, lost Paz 5–7 7–6 7–5. **1987: qf** [seed 6] d. Cecchini 3–6 6–3 6–3, Balestrat 6–2 6–0, Wasserman 5–7 6–3 6–1, Rehe 7–6 6–1, lost Graf [seed 2] 6–4 6–1. **1988: 3r** [seed 5] d. Huber 6–3 6–1, Ferrando 6–0 6–2, lost Kelesi 6–4 6–2. **1989: qf** [seed 6] d. Smylie 6–4 6–4, Wasserman 3–6 7–5 6–3, Savchenko 6–1 6–2, Thompson 7–6 6–2, lost Seles 6–3 7–5. **1990: qf** [seed 6] d. Stafford 6–2 6–3, A.Minter 6–1 6–0, Tarabini 2–6 7–5 6–0, Zvereva [seed 10] 6–4 6–2, lost Seles [seed 2] 3–6 6–1 7–5. **1991: 2r** [seed 9] d. Dahlman 6–2 6–2, lost Rajchrtova 6–4 6–0. **1992: 3r** [seed 8] d. Cioffi 6–4 7–6, Rittner 5–7 6–1 6–2, lost Bollegraf 7–5 6–2.

WIMBLEDON – Played 9, qf 1
1982: 2r d. Nelson 2–6 6–4 6–4, lost Preyer 6–3 6–3. **1983: 2r** d. Barker 6–3 6–2, lost Temesvari [seed 14] 7–5 6–4. **1984: qf** [seed 7] d. Mundel 6–4 6–1, Reva 6–2 6–2, Vermaak 6–4 6–4, Hobbs 6–2 3–6 6–3, lost Navratilova [seed 1] 6–2 6–2. **1985: 4r** [seed 4] d. Washington 6–0 6–1, Holladay 6–7 6–1 6–4, R.White 6–3 6–3, lost Van Nostrand 7–5 6–2. **1986: 4r** [seed 8] d. Gompert 6–2 1–0 ret., Mascarin 6–4 7–6, Smylie 7–6 6–3, lost Bunge 3–6 6–2 6–3. **1987: 2r** [seed 7] d. Kelesi 6–3 6–2, lost Balestrat 6–7 6–1 8–6. **1988: 1r** [seed 7] lost Paradis 6–4 6–3. **1990: 1r** [seed 8] lost Gomer 6–2 6–3. **1992: 3r** [seed 9] d. Muns Jagerman 6–1 6–4, Rinaldi 4–6 6–3 6–4, lost Godridge 7–5 7–6.

US OPEN – Played 11, sf 1, qf 4
1982: 3r d. Jones 6–3 6–1, Steinmetz 5–7 6–3 7–5, lost Mandlikova [seed 5] 6–2 6–3. **1983: 3r** d. Allen 6–4 6–1, Rush 6–3 6–0, lost Lloyd [seed 2] 6–4 6–0. **1984: 1r** [seed 6] lost Delhees-Jauch 6–1 5–7 7–5. **1985: 4r** [seed 8] d. Mascarin 6–1 6–1, Cueto 6–0 7–6, Burgin 6–4 7–5, lost Graf [seed 11] 6–2 6–2. **1986: qf** [seed 9] d. Reynolds 6–2 6–4, Gildemeister 6–3 6–1, Benjamin 7–6 6–3, Kohde-Kilsch [seed 6] 6–2 2–6 7–6, lost Lloyd [seed 2] 6–2 6–2. **1987: 4r** [seed 10] d. K.Jordan 7–5 6–2, Tauziat 6–1 6–3, M–J. Fernandez 6–2 0–6 6–3, lost Evert [seed 3] 7–5 6–4. **1988: qf** [seed 6] d. Dias 6–1 6–4, Santrock 7–6 6–2, Cueto 6–1 1–6 6–3, Potter [seed 12] 6–3 6–2, lost Evert [seed 3] 3–6 6–4 6–2. **1989: qf** [seed 7] d. Werdel 6–4 6–3, Cueto 5–7 6–3 5–3 ret., Tauziat 6–1 6–3, Zvereva [seed 13] 6–2 6–2, lost Navratilova [seed 2] 6–0 6–0. **1990: qf** [seed 9] d. Frazier 6–1 6–3, Graham 6–4 6–0, Van Rensburg.6–1 6–0, Navratilova [seed 2] 7–5 3–6 6–3, lost M–J.Fernandez [seed 8] 6–2 2–6 6–1. **1991: 4r** [seed 10] d. Birch 6–3 6–1, Strnadova 7–5 6–2, Pierce 4–6 6–1 5–1 ret. lost Navratilova [seed 6] 7–6 1–6 6–2. **1992: sf** [seed 9] d. Reinach 7–5 7–5, Allen 6–4 6–2, Strnadova 6–7 6–3 6–2, Cunningham 6–3 7–5, Magdalena Maleeva 6–2 5–3 ret., lost Sanchez-Vicario [seed 5] 6–2 6–1.

OLYMPIC RECORD
1988 (Seoul) Bronze Medal sf [seed 7] bye, d. Paz 6–1 6–2, Lindqvist 6–1 6–0, Reggi 6–3 6–4, lost Sabatini [seed 3] 6–1 6–1. **1992 (Barcelona) qf** [seed 6] d. Vieira 6–2 6–3, Reggi Concato 6–2 6–4, Gavaldon 6–0 6–3, lost M. J. Fernandez [seed 4] 5–7 6–1 6–0.

CAREER FEDERATION CUP RECORD
1983: 1r lost Christiane Jolissaint (SKI) 6–4 4–6 6–4. **1984: 1r** d. Jo Durie (GB) 6–4 4–6 6–4. (+ K.Maleeva) d. Hobbs/Brown 7–6 7–5. **2r** d. Natalia Reva (URS) 6–2 6–0. (+ K.Maleeva) lost Eliseenko/Savchenko 5–7 7–5 6–1. **qf** d. Mima Jausovec (YUG) 3–6 6–3 6–1. with K Maleeva) lost Jausovec/Goles 6–3 6–1. **1985: 1r** d. Larisa Savchenko (URS) 6–7 6–4 6–1. (with K Maleeva) d. Cherneva/ Bykova 6–3 7–5. **2r** d. Sabrina Goles (YUG) 6–1 6–3. (+ K.Maleeva) d. Goles/ Winkler 6–4 7–6(9–7). **qf** d. Annabel Croft (GBR) 6–2 6–2. (with K

Maleeva) lost Durie/Hobbs 4–5 retd. **1986: lr** d. Larisa Savchenko (URS) 6–2 6–1. (with K. Maleeva) lost Savchenko/Parkhomenko 6–1 4–6 6–1. **2r** d. Catherine Tanvier (FRA) 6–0 6–1. **qf** d. Claudia Kohde-Kilsch (GER) 6–4 6–2. (+ K.Maleeva) lost Kohde-Kilsch/Bunge 6–4 6–2. **1987**: **lr** d. Angeliki Kanellopoulou (GRE) 6–0 6–0. **2r** d. Nani Rahayu Basuki (INO) 6–4 6–0. **qf** d. Elizabeth Smylie (AUS) 6–4 6–4. **sf** lost Chris Evert (USA) 6–2 2–6 6–4. **1989:lr** d. Ils-Soon Kim (KOR) 6–1 6–0. (+ K.Maleeva) d. Kim/Lee 7–5 6–0. **2r** d. Mercedez Paz (ARG) 4–6 6–1 6–3. (+ K Maleeva) d. Labat/Paz 6–1 3–6 6–1. **qf** lost Anne Minter (AUS) 6–3 2–6 6–4. (+ K.Maleeva) lost Smylie/Thompson 5–7 6—4 6–0. **1991:** lr d. Mercedez Paz (ARG) 6–0 7–6(7–5). **2r** d. Li Fang (CHN) 6–7(5–7) 7–5 6–2. (+ Caverzasio) lost Yi/Fang 1–3 ret. **qf** lost Jana Novotna (TCH) 6–4 6–4. (+ Caverzasio) d. Novotna/Rajchrtova 6–2 2–l ret. **1992: lr** d. Catarina Lindqvist (SWE) 6–0 6–2. with Strebel) d. Lindstrom/Strandlund 6–4 5–7 6–4. **Play-off: 1r** d. Anna Smashnova (ISR) 6–1 6–0. **2r** d. Rosanna de los Rios (PAR) 6–2 6–2.

JANA NOVOTNA (TCH)   Turned pro: 1987

Born: Brno, 2 October 1968.
Lives: Brno.
Father: Frank. **Mother:** Libuse. **Brother:** Paul (older).
Agent: Advantage International.
Coach: Hana Mandlikova since 1990; formerly Mike Estep.
Height: 5ft 9in (1.75m). **Weight:** 142lb (64kg).

Rankings: 1985: 305; **1986:** 172; **1987:** 49; **1988:** 45; **1989:** 11; **1990:** 13; **1991:** 7; **1992:** 10. **Highest:** 6 (April 1991).

1992 Prize Money: $511,184. **Career Earnings:** $2,627,657. **Career Titles:** 5.

Style: A right-handed natural volleyer with good touch who is equally at home on the singles or doubles court. The high toss on her serve sometimes gives timing problems but she can serve-and-volley with the best. Has a large swing on the sometimes erratic forehand and can hit her backhand with slice or topspin.

CAREER HIGHLIGHTS:(year: *(titles)*)
1986: Won US Open Jun doubles with Zrubakova. **1987:** Reached last 16 Wimbledon and US Open, plus qf VS Kansas. In doubles she developed a formidable partnership with Suire, qualifying for VS Champs and taking a set off Navratilova/Shriver. **1988: (1)** *Adelaide.* Won her 1st title on the main tour at Adelaide, r/u Brisbane and upset Sabatini 1r Filderstadt. In doubles won Olympic silver medal with Sukova and took 5 doubles titles with 3 different partners. In mixed, with Pugh, won Australian and US Opens. **1989: (1)** *Strasbourg.* r/u Hamburg and Zurich and reached 4 more sf, as well as qf French Open, to qualify for VS Champs in both singles (lost Graf 1r) and doubles for 1st time. In doubles won 6 women's titles, including Wimbledon and LIPC with Sukova, plus Australian Open and Wimbledon mixed with Pugh. Won WTA Most Improved Player award. **1990: (1)** *Albuquerque.* She continued her successful doubles partnership with Sukova, with whom she won 8 of her 9 titles across the year. The duo were unbeaten until US Open, where, having won Australian Open, French Open and Wimbledon, they failed in their bid for a GS when they lost f to Navratilova/G. Fernandez. They were also disappointed at VS Champs, where they fell 1r to Medvedeva/Meskhi. In singles she upset Sabatini and K. Maleeva *en route* to her 1st GS sf at French Open and followed with qf Wimbledon and US Open. Extended Navratilova to 3s in sf Eastbourne. Qualified for VS Champs in both singles(lost 1r Sabatini) and doubles. **1991: (2)** *Sydney, Oklahoma.* Showing the benefits of her partnership with new coach, Mandlikova, she made a tremendous start to the year, upsetting Garrison, Graf and Sanchez-Vicario back-to-back in ss to reach her 1st GS singles f at Australian Open, where she took the 1st set off Seles. On Tour, r/u Leipzig; sf Berlin and VS Champs, upsetting Graf on the way; and qf French Open. Was voted WTA doubles team of the year with G. Fernandez, with whom she won French Open and was r/u Australian Open, Wimbledon and VS Champs. She completed a full hand of GS doubles f, being r/u US Open with Savchenko, and appeared in 14 f altogether, winning 3 with Fernandez, 3 with Savchenko and 1 with Navratilova. **1992:** qf Sydney, Amelia Island, Hamburg, Eastbourne; upset Graf *en route* to f VS Chicago and extended her to 3s in f both Leipzig and Brighton and sf Zurich, losing twice only on tb. Qualified again for VS Champs, where she took a set off Seles in qf singles and was r/u doubles with Savchenko Neiland. This new pairing was as successful as her previous partnerships and brought 7 titles, plus r/u Wimbledon and US Open.

PRINCIPAL 1992 RESULTS (detailed Grand Slam results below)
SINGLES: r/u VS Chicago (d. Werdel 6–2 6–1, Frazier 7–6 6–1, Graf 0–6 6–3 7–5, lost Navratilova 7–6 4–6 7–5), **r/u** Leipzig (d. Strnadova 6–2 6–4, Zrubakova 6–1 6–3, Appelmans 3–6 6–1 6–0, Sukova 3–6 6–2 6–2, lost Graf 6–3 1–6 6–4), **r/u** Brighton (d. Hy

6–0 6–3, Zvereva 6–2 6–0, Martinez 6–4 6–2, M. J. Fernandez 6–3 6–4, lost Graf 4–6 6–4
7–6), **sf** Zurich (d. Harvey-Wild 6–4 6–3, Zvereva 7–5 6–2, Strnadova 6–4 6–0, lost Graf 6–2
4–6 7–6). **DOUBLES:** (with Savchenko Neiland unless stated) **won** Brisbane (d. Bollegraf/
Provis 6–4 6–3), **won** Light 'n Lively Doubles (d. Sanchez-Vicario/Zvereva 6–4 6–2), **won**
Berlin (d. G. Fernandez/Zvereva 7–6 4–6 7–5), **won** Eastbourne (d. M. J.
Fernandez/Garrison 6–0 6–3), **won** San Diego (d. Martinez/Paz 6–1 6–4), **won** Leipzig (d.
Fendick/Strnadova 7–5 7–6), **won** Brighton (d. Martinez/Zrubakova 6–4 6–1), **r/u**
WIMBLEDON lost G. Fernandez/Zvereva 6–4 6–1, **r/u US OPEN** lost G.
Fernandez/Zvereva 7–6 6–1, **r/u** FC Cup (lost Sanchez-Vicario/Zvereva 6–4 6–2),
[+Garrison] **r/u** Amelia Island (lost Sanchez-Vicario/Zvereva 6–1 6–0), **r/u** VS Champs (lost
Sanchez-Vicario/Sukova 7–6 6–1).

CAREER GRAND SLAM SINGLES RECORD
AUSTRALIAN OPEN – Played 5, r/u 1
1988: 1r lost Inoue 7–6 6–4. **1989: 3r** d. Ingram 7–5 7–5, Cunningham 6–2 6–2, lost
Navratilova [seed 2] 6–2 6–2. **1990: 3r** [seed 5] d. Martin 6–7 6–0 6–0, Temesvari 6–1 6–1,
lost Fendick 1–6 7–6 6–4. **1991: r/u** [seed 10] d. A.Minter 7–6 6–2, Quentrec 6–2 6–2,
Stafford 6–7 6–1 8–6, Garrison [seed 7] 7–6 6–4, Graf [seed 1] 5–7 6–4 8–6, Sanchez-
Vicario [seed 6] 6–2 6–4, lost Seles [seed 2] 5–7 6–3 6–1. **1992: 4r** [seed 6] d. Zrubakova
7–6 6–3, Alter 6–3 6–2, Li 6–3 6–1, lost Huber [seed 12] 5–7 7–6 6–4.

FRENCH OPEN – Played 6, sf 1. qf 1
1986: 1r lost Drescher 6–2 6–3. **1987:3r** d. Durie 6–3 6–1, Zrubakova 6–3 4–6 6–4, lost Graf
[seed 2] 6–0 6–1. **1988: 1r** lost Tarabini 1–6 6—3 6–2. **1989: qf** [seed 11] d. Halard 6–3 6–2,
Porwik 6–3 7–5, Simpson 6–1 6–0, Hanika 6–1 6–4, lost Sanchez-Vicario [seed 7] 6–2 6–2.
1990: sf [seed 11] d. Demongeot 6–0 6–7 10–8, Schultz 6–3 6–1, Sviglerova 7–5 6–2,
Sabatini [seed 4] 6–4 7–5, K.Maleeva [seed 8] 4–6 6–2 6–4, lost Graf [seed 1] 6–1 6–2.
1991: qf [seed 6] d. Farina 7–5 6–2, Hy 6–2 6–1, Brioukhovets 7–6 6–2, Meskhi [seed 14]
6–0 7–6, lost Sabatini [seed 3] 5–7 7–6 6–0. **1992: 4r** seed 10 (d.. Graham 6–3 6–2,
Medvedeva 6–4 6–1, Schultz 6–3 6–4, lost Graf [seed 2] 6–1 6–4.

WIMBLEDON – Played 7, qf 1
1986: 1r lost Mascarin 3–6 7–6 7–2. **1987: 4r** d. Reis 6–3 3–6 8–6, Hu Na 6–2 6–3, Walsh
Pete 6–2 4–6 6–4, lost Graf [seed 2] 6–4 6–3. **1988: 2r** d. Scheuer-Larsen 6–3 7–5, lost
Sukova [seed 6] 6–2 6–2. **1989: 4r** [seed 10] d. Simpson 6–2 6–1, Burgin 6–4 3–6 6–2,
K.Adams 6–4 6–1, lost Golarsa 7–6 2–6 6–4. **1990: qf** [seed 13] d. Golarsa 3–6 7–6 6–2,
Cunningham 6–2 6–1, Faull 6–2 6–1, Fendick 6–2 6–4, lost Graf [seed 1] 7–5 6–2. **1991: 2r**
[seed 6] d. Pratt 6–3 6–0, lost Schultz 4–6 7–6 6–4. **1992: 3r** [seed 11] d. Monami 6–1 6–2,
Lindqvist 6–3 6–2, lost Fendick 6–3 6–3.

US OPEN – Played 6, qf 1
1987: 4r d. Parkhomenko 6–1 7–6, Turnbull [seed 16] 6–2 6–4, Halard 6–4 6–0, lost Shriver
[seed 5] 6–3 7–6. **1988: 1r** lost Wiesner 6–2 6–3. **1989: 2r** [seed 11] d. McGrath 7–5 6–2,
lost Paulus 3–6 6–3 6–2. **1990: qf** [seed 12] d. Lapi 6–3 6–1, Rinaldi 6–4 6–3, Gildemeister
6–3 6–1, K.Maleeva [seed 7] 6–4 6–2, lost Graf [seed 1] 6–3 6–1. **1991: 4r** [seed 9] d.
Grossman 6–3 4–6 6–1, Louie Harper 6–2 6–3, Monami 6–1 6–2, lost Sabatini [seed 3] 6–4
7–6. **1992: 1r** [seed 10] lost Fairbank Nideffer 6–3 7–6.

OLYMPIC GAMES
1988: (Seoul) 2r d. Demongeot 6–4 6–3, lost Paulus 6–4 6–3. **1992: (Barcelona) 1r** [seed
9] lost Zvereva 6–1 6–0.

CAREER FEDERATION CUP RESULTS
1987: 1r (+ Mandlikova) d. Lindqvist/Lindstrom (SWE) 6–3 6–2. **2r** (+ Rajchrtova) d.
Goles/Sasak (YUG) 6–4 5–7 6–4. **1988: 1r** (+Pospisilova) d. Dias/Tella (BRA) 6–3 6–2. **2r**
(+Pospisilova) d. Cordwell/Richardson (NZL) 7–6 7–6. **qf** (+Pospisilova) d. Kjaer

Nielson/Scheur-Larsen (DEN) 6–3,6–2. **sf** (+Pospisilova) d. Kelesi Simpson (CAN) 7–6 6–2. **Final** (+Pospisilova) lost Savchenko/Zvereva (URS) 7–6 7–5. **1989: 1r** d. Caroline van Reneterghem (BEL) 6–0 6–2. **2r** d. Andrea Naszaly (HUN) 6–3,6–3. **qf** d. Claudia Kohde-Kilsch (GER) 6–3 6–3. (+ Sukova) d. Graf/Kohde-Kilsch 6–2 6–2. **Final** lost Chris Evert (USA) 6–2,6–3. **1990: 1r** d. Sook-La Im (KOR) 6–0 6–1. **2r** d. Rachel McQuillan (AUS) 6–4 6–4. **qf** d. Zina Garrison (USA) 6–3 6–3. (+Rajchrtova) lost Garrison/Fernandez 7–6(10–8) 6–4. **1991: 1r** d. Cecilia Dahlman (SWE) 7–6 (7–5) 6–2. **2r** d. Natalia Zvereva (URS) 6–4 6–1. **qf** d. Manuela Fragnière (SUI) 6–4 6–4. **sf** lost Mary Joe Fernandez (USA) 6–4 0–6 9–7. **1992: 1r** d. Andrea Temesvari (HUN) 6–2 6–1. (+Strnadova) Temesvari/Csurgo (HUN) 1–6 7–5 7–5, **2r** d. Sung-Hee Park (KOR) 4–6 6–2 6–3. (+ Strnadova) d. Kim/Lee 6–3 6–3, **qf** lost Nicole Provis (AUS) 7–5 6–0. (+ Strnadova) lost Provis/Stubs 6–3 6–3.

SABINE APPELMANS (BEL)
Born Aalst, 22 April 1972; lives Erembonegen; LH; 2HB; 5ft 5in; 120lb; final 1992 WTA ranking 26; 1992 prize money $160,927.
1987: (283). **1988:** (215) Enjoyed some success on the European satellite circuits and upset Burgin 1r French Open. **1989:** (149) Reached her 1st primary circuit qf at Taipei. **1990:** (22) R/u Auckland (d. Cordwell) and reached sf Wellington and Singapore, breaking into top 100 and finishing the year in the top 25. **1991:** (18) Won her 1st singles title at Phoenix, following with VS Nashville; r/u Tokyo Suntory; sf Oslo and Puerto Rico; reached last 16 Australian Open and French Open and appeared in 3 doubles f. **1992:** Won Pattaya City and r/u Tokyo Suntory, as well as reaching qf Olympics, Essen, Berlin and Leipzig. In GS upset Huber *en route* to last 16 US Open, unseeded. **1992 HIGHLIGHTS – SINGLES: Australian Open 1r** [seed 16] (lost Savchenko Neiland 7–5 6–2), **French Open 2r** [seed 16] (d. Tami Whitlinger 6–4 6–3, lost Zvereva 6–1 7–6), **Wimbledon 2r** (d. Babel 6–0 6–2, lost Seles [seed 1] 6–3 6–2), **US Open last 16** [unseeded] (d. Huber [seed 11] 6–3 6–4, Wood 6–3 6–2, Kuhlman 6–2 6–1, lost Sabatini [seed 4] 6–1 6–3), **Olympics qf** [seed 16] (d. McQuillan 6–3 6–3, Provis 6–2 6–1, Maniokova 6–1 6–3, lost Graf 6–1 6–0); **won** Pattaya City (d. Li 6–2 6–4, Reggi Concato 4–6 6–1 6–3, Lindqvist 6–2 6–4, Medvedeva 6–4 6–3, Strnadova 7–5 3–6 7–5); **r/u** Tokyo Suntory (d. Van Lottum 6–3 6–4, Kamio 6–1 6–2, Werdel 7–5 6–2, Sawamatsu 7–6 6–3, lost Date 7–5 3–6 6–3). **1992 HIGHLIGHTS – DOUBLES:** (with Porwik) **r/u** Essen (lost K. Maleeva/Rittner 7–5 6–3), (with Reggi Concato) **r/u** Cesena (lost Suire/Tanvier def.).

YAYUK BASUKI (INA)
Born Yogyakarta, 30 November 1970, and lives there; RH; 5ft 44in. 122lb; final 1992 WTA ranking 48; 1992 prize money $111,748.
Coached by Mien Gondowiljoyo. **1986:** Joined her country's Fed Cup team. **1988:** (284). **1989:** (377) Made her mark on the satellite circuits. **1990:** (266) Continued to enjoy success on the satellite circuits. **1991:** (35) At Pattaya City, she became 1st native Indonesian to win a primary circuit title; upset Kohde-Kilsch *en route* to qf Eastbourne and reached the same stage at VS Nashville. **1992:** Upset Huber on her way to last 16 Wimbledon and Pierce in reaching the same stage at Olympics, unseeded both times. Won Kuala Lumpur and appeared in sf Pattaya City. **1992 HIGHLIGHTS – SINGLES: Australian Open 3r** (d. Tarabini 6–3 7–5, Field 6–7 6–3 6–4, lost Seles [seed 1] 6–1 6–1), **Wimbledon last 16** [unseeded] (d. Labat 6–2 6–2, Hack 7–5 6–3, Huber [seed 10] 6–2 6–3, lost Navratilova [seed 4] 7–5 6–2), **US Open 1r** (lost Davenport 6–4 6–4), **Olympics last 16** [unseeded] (d. Paz 6–1 6–4, Pierce [seed 13] 0–6 6–3 10–8, lost Capriati [seed 3] 6–3 6–4); **won** Kuala Lumpur (d. Khoo Chin 6–0 6–0, Porwik 7–6 6–2, Rottier 6–4 6–0, Lindqvist 6–4 6–1, Strnadova 6–3 6–1); **sf** Pattaya City (d. Van Lottum 7–5 2–6 7–5, Javer 6–4 6–3, Paradis Mangon 6–0 6–1, lost Strnadova 4–6 6–2 6–2). **1992 HIGHLIGHTS – DOUBLES:** (with Miyagi) **r/u** Tokyo Nicherei (lost M. J. Fernandez/R. White 6–4 6–4).

MANON BOLLEGRAF (NED)
Born Den Bosch, 10 April 1964; lives Ermelo; RH; 2HB; 5ft 8in; 140lb; final 1992 WTA ranking 44 singles, 19 doubles; 1992; prize money $148,884.
Coached by Auke Dijkstra. **1986:** (148) Qf Singapore. **1987:** (120) Qf Little Rock. **1988:** (117) Qf Brisbane. **1989:** (38) In singles won 1st primary circuit title at Oklahoma, reached sf Brussels and Nashville and upset McNeil 2r French Open. In doubles won 4 women's titles plus French Open mixed with Nijssen. **1990:** (32) In singles r/u VS Oklahoma and reached sf Strasbourg. Appeared in 5 doubles f with various partners, winning Wichita with McGrath and Zurich with Pfaff. **1991:** (49) R/u Colorado and sf Oklahoma in singles, won Leipzig with Demongeot in doubles and took US Open mixed with Nijssen. **1992:** Upset Maleeva Fragnière and Tauziat in reaching qf French Open, unseeded; sf VS Oklahoma and qf Chicago; and in doubles reached 4 f with different partners, winning Waregem with Vis. Missed Olympics and US Open after tearing several ligaments at Frankfurt. **1992 HIGHLIGHTS – SINGLES: Australian Open 1r** (lost Jaggard 2–6 6–4 9–7), **French Open qf** [unseeded] (d. Maniokova 6–2 6–3, Thoren 6–2 4–6 7–5, Maleeva Fragnière [seed 8] 7–5

6–2, Tauziat [seed 12] 6–4 1–6 6–2, lost Sanchez-Vicario 6–2 6–3), *Wimbledon 2r* (d. Wegink 6–1 6–2, lost K. Maleeva [seed 12] 6–4 6–1); *sf* VS Oklahoma (d. Amiach 3–6 7–5 7–5, de Lone 3–6 7–6 6–1, G. Fernandez 6–2 6–2, lost McNeil 6–3 7–5). *1992 HIGHLIGHTS – DOUBLES:* (with Vis) *won* Waregem (d. Brioukhovets/Langrova 6–4 6–3); (with Provis) *r/u* Brisbane (lost Novotna/Savchenko Neiland 6–4 6–3), (with Adams) *r/u* VS Oklahoma (lost McNeil/Provis 3–6 6–4 7–6), (with Sanchez-Vicario) *r/u* Hamburg (lost Graf/Stubbs 4–6 6–3 6–4).

ANNA MARIA (SANDRA) CECCHINI (ITA)
Born Bologna, 27 February 1965; lives Ceriva and Monte Carlo; RH; 5ft 64in; 130lb; final 1992 WTA ranking 35; 1992 prize money $114,221.
Prefers to be known by her nickname, Sandra. *1983:* R/u to Spence at Orange Bowl 18s, ranked second among world juniors and third among Italy's women. *1984:* (49) Won Rio de Janeiro. *1985:* (49) Reached qf French Open and won Barcelona, restoring herself after 8 consecutive 1r losses early in year. *1986:* (76) Produced the upset of the year when she stunned Evert Lloyd in Fed Cup, the first time the American had lost in the international team competition. *1987:* (18) Extended Graf to 3s sf Berlin, won VS Arkansas and reached f Strasbourg. *1988:* (21) Won Strasbourg and Nice and reached f Bastad. *1989:* (26) Won Paris Open in singles and doubles; r/u Estoril, sf Tampa and Bastad in singles and won 2 other doubles titles with Tarabini. *1990:* (20) Won Bastad; sf Berlin (upset Sabatini), Kitzbuhel and Clarins. *1991:* (27) At French Open, unseeded, she upset A. Huber to reach last 16, where she was the only player to take a set off Seles. Won Bol, r/u Palermo, sf Houston and reached 2 doubles f. *1992:* When she won Clarins Open in Paris (where she also took the doubles) she became only the 4th player after Goolagong Cawley, Evert and Navratilova to win a singles title in each of 10 consecutive years. She also reached sf Linz and qf VS Houston, Berlin (d. Huber) and Kitzbuhel. *1992 HIGHLIGHTS – SINGLES: French Open 2r* (d. Javer 6–1 6–1, lost Sabatini [seed 3] 6–0 6–1), *US Open 1r* (lost Simpson Alter 6–4 6–3), *Olympics 2r* (d. Sepulveda 6–2 6–3, lost Martinez [seed 5] 6–4 6–3); *won* Clarins (d. Monami 6–4 6–4, Kruger 6–2 6–4, Hack 6–3 6–2, Ercegovic 6–1 7–6, Zardo 6–2 6–1); *sf* Linz (d. Bobkova 6–4 5–7 6–2, Herreman 1–6 6–2 6–2, Monami 6–4 2–6 6–3, lost Paradis Mangon 6–2 7–5). *1992 HIGHLIGHTS – DOUBLES:* (with Tarabini) *won* Clarins (d. McQuillan/Van Lottum 7–5 6–1); (with Garrone) *r/u* San Marino (lost Dechaume/Labat 7–6 7–5).

AMANDA COETZER (RSA)
Born Hoopstad, 22 October 1971, and lives there; RH; 2HB; 5ft 2in; 115lb; final 1992 WTA ranking 17; 1992 prize money $164,962.
1987: (442). *1988:* (153) Won 4 titles on the satellite circuits. *1989:* (63) Made an unexpected appearance in last 16 French Open and reached sf VS Arizona. *1990:* (75) Qf VS Florida, Geneva and VS Albuquerque. *1991:* (67) Upset K. Maleeva at Berlin and G. Fernandez *en route* to her 1st primary circuit f at Puerto Rico. *1992:* Qf LIPC, Taranto, Berlin, Lucerne, Puerto Rico; scored some big upsets during the year surprising Garrison on her way to last 16 Olympics, unseeded, Wiesner and Sabatini *en route* to sf VS Florida, Capriati and Zvereva in reaching the same stage Italian Open and Tauziat at US Open. She also appeared in sf Kitzbuhel and Taipei, plus 5 more qf. In doubles she played 4 f with different partners, winning Taranto with Gorrochategui and Puerto Rico with Reinach. *1992 HIGHLIGHTS – SINGLES: French Open 3r* (d. Dechaume 6–4 3–6 6–3, Dopfer 7–6 4–6 6–3, lost Graf [seed 2] 6–2 6–1), *US Open 3r* (d. Paz 6–2 4–6 6–4, Tauziat [seed 12] 6–0 6–0, lost Labat 6–3 4–6 6–4), *Olympics last 16* [unseeded](d. Garrison [seed 12] 7–5 6–1, Blumberga 6–2 6–4, lost Martinez [seed 5] 6–4 6–3); *sf* VS Florida (d. Rottier 6–2 6–2, Baudone 6–3 6–4, Wiesner 6–3 6–1, Sabatini 4–6 6–1 6–2, lost Martinez 4–6 6–3 6–0), *sf* Italian Open (d. Farina 6–1 6–4, Mulej 7–5 6–4, Capriati 6–1 3–6 6–4, Zvereva 6–2 6–3, lost Seles 6–0 6–4), *sf* Kitzbuhel (d. Fulco Villella 6–2 6–3, Thoren 6–1 6–0, Probst 7–5 6–2, lost Martinez 6–1 6–3), *sf* Taipei (d. Cristea 6–2 7–6, Cammy MacGregor 6–4 7–6, Graham 6–3 7–5, lost Stafford 6–1 6–3). *1992 HIGHLIGHTS – DOUBLES:* (with Gorrochategui) *won* Taranto (d. McQuillan/Zrubakova 4–6 6–3 7–6), (with Reinach) *won* Puerto Rico (d. G. Fernandez/Rinaldi 6–2 4–6 6–2); (with Probst) *r/u* Kitzbuhel (lost Labat/Dechaume 6–3 6–3), (with Cammy MacGregor) *r/u* Taipei (lost Faull/Richardson 3–6 6–3 6–2).

RAFAELLA REGGI CONCATO (ITA)
Born Faenza, 27 November 1965; lives Monte Carlo; RH; 2HB; 5ft 7in; 127lb; final 1992 WTA ranking 56.
Coached by Ferruccio Bonetti; fitness coach Daniele Gatti. Husband Maurizio Concato (married Sept. 1991). **1981:** one of the most spirited performers in the sport, an unwavering competitor, she won Orange Bowl 16s and was ranked No. 1 in Italian 16s. **1982:** (127) Moved up to No. 3 among Italian women and joined Fed Cup Team. **1983:** (48) No. 1 in Italy. **1984:** (62) Sf Swiss Open and qf Italian Open. **1985:** (42) Won Taranto and r/u Barcelona. **1986:** (26) Won Puerto Rican Open and Lugano with victories over Bunge and M. Maleeva, reached last 16 Wimbledon and US Open both unseeded, and won US Open mixed doubles with Casal. Qualified for VS Champ Nov. **1987:** (17) Beat Sukova *en route* to qf French Open, reached last 16 Wimbledon and won VS San Diego. Qualified for VS Champs again. **1988:** (23) At Olympics upset Kohde-Kilsch and Evert to reach qf; r/u Brussels, sf Oklahoma and Filderstadt. **1989:** (21) In GS reached last 16 Australian Open, upset 1988 finalist Zvereva at French Open and held 2 mps v Sanchez at Wimbledon. R/u Eastbourne and VS Indianapolis, sf Oklahoma and Bayonne to qualify for VS Champs (lost Sukova 1r), and in doubles reached 3f. **1990:** (23) Won Taranto and reached last 16 Australian Open. **1991:** (75) In singles r/u Oslo; in doubles won Linz with Maleeva Fragnière and reached 2 more f with Appelmans. **1992:** Reached qf Auckland, San Antonio (d. Halard) and Tokyo Suntory; in doubles played 3 f with different partners, winning Auckland with Fairbank Nideffer. **1992 HIGHLIGHTS – SINGLES:** *French Open 1r* (lost Ferrando 6–1 6–3), **Olympics 2r** (d. Byrne 6–4 7–6, lost Maleeva Fragnière [seed 6] 6–2 6–4). **1992 HIGHLIGHTS – DOUBLES:** (with Fairbank Nideffer) **won** Auckland (d. Hetherington/Rinaldi 1–6 6–1 7–5); (with Porwik) *r/u* Linz (lost Kiene/Oremans 6–4 6–2), (with Appelmans) *r/u* Cesena (lost Suire Tanvier def.).

KIMIKO DATE (JPN)
Born Kyoto, 28 September 1970; lives Amagasaki City; RH; 5ft 4in; 113lb; final 1992 WTA ranking 21; 1992 prize money $154,925.
Coached by Takeshi Koura. Although she plays right-handed, she writes and eats left-handed. **1988:** (321) Won 2 titles on Japanese satellite circuit. **1989:** (120) Qf Tokyo Suntory and Birmingham; won 3 titles on British satellite circuit in May, and played Fed Cup. **1990:** (78) Upset Fairbank Nideffer at Brisbane and then surprised Shriver at Australian Open to become the 1st Japanese woman since 1973 to reach last 16 there, a performance which took her into the top 100. Appeared in qf Tokyo Suntory again. **1991:** (32) Upset Meskhi and Sabatini as she swept to her 1st primary circuit f at VS Los Angeles. **1992:** Won Tokyo Suntory; sf Tokyo Pan Pacific (d. Sanchez-Vicario) and Osaka; reached last 16 French Open and upset Sukova at Sydney. These performances took her into top 25 and earned her the Most Improved Player of Year award. **1992 HIGHLIGHTS – SINGLES: Australian Open 2r** (d. Paz 6–2 6–4, lost Seles [seed 1] 6–1 6–1), **French Open last 16** [seed 14] (d. Sawamatsu 6–2 6–7 6–3, Meier 4–6 6–4 6–3, Endo 6–3 6–2, lost Sanchez-Vicario [seed 4] 6–1 6–2), **Wimbledon 2r** [seed 14] (d. Kuhlman 7–6 6–2, lost G. Fernandez 6–1 6–3), **US Open 2r** (d. Babel 6–1 6–0, lost Sukova [seed 13] 6–2 7–5), **Olympics 2r** [seed 14] (d. Simpson Alter 7–5 6–1, lost Magdalena Maleeva 6–2 6–4); **won** Tokyo Suntory (d. Langrova 5–7 6–0 6–1, Endo 6–4 6–4, Javer 6–4 6–1, Frazier 6–3 6–4, Appelmans 7–5 3–6 6–3); **sf** Tokyo Pan Pacific (d. Fendick 6–3 6–1, Stubbs 7–5 6–1, Sanchez-Vicario 6–3 6–4, lost Sabatini 6–3 6–1), **sf** Osaka (d. Sugiyama 6–1 5–7 6–3, McQuillan 6–3 6–2, lost Sukova 6–2 6–2). **1992 HIGHLIGHTS – DOUBLES:** (with Rehe) *r/u* Tokyo Suntory (lost Frazier/Hiraki 5–7 7–6 6–0).

LINDSAY DAVENPORT (USA)
Born Palos Verdes, Cal., 8 June 1976, and lives there; RH; 6ft 2in; final 1992 WTA ranking 160; 1992 prize money $36,511.
1992: In Jun tennis won US Open over Steven, r/u Australian Open to Limmer; won Australian Open and US Open doubles with London. Ranked No. 1 in Nat 18s. **1992 HIGHLIGHTS – SINGLES: US Open 2r** (d. Basuki 6–4 6–4, lost Sanchez-Vicario [seed 5] 6–1 6–3).

ALEXIA DECHAUME (FRA)

Born La Rochelle, 3 May 1970; lives Bologne; 5ft 44in; 124lb; RH; 2HB; final 1992 WTA ranking 54; 1992 prize money $101,596.
Coached by Patrick Faviäre. **1986:** (225). **1987:** (127) Qf Athens. **1988:** (127) Qf Taranto and won Bayonne on French satellite circuit, breaking into top 100 in June. In doubles with Derly won Paris Open, French Open Jun and r/u Wimbledon Jun. **1989:** (173). **1990:** (84) Reached her first primary circuit f at Taranto and broke into the top 100 in Sept. **1991:** (72) In singles her best showing was qf Barcelona; in doubles she reached 2 f, winning Taranto with Labat. **1992:** In singles she reached sf San Marino plus 3 more qf and upset Wiesner at Australian Open. In partnership with Labat won Kitzbuhel and San Marino back-to-back in July, followed by Schenectady in Aug. **1992 HIGHLIGHTS – SINGLES: Australian Open 3r** (d. Fulco Villella 6–4 6–1, Wiesner [seed 14] 6–2 6–6, lost Fendick 5–7 7–5 6–4), **French Open 1r** (lost Coetzer 6–4 3–6 6–3), **Wimbledon 2r** (d. Loosemore 6–1 4–6 6–4, lost Sukova 7–5 6–2), **US Open 1r** (lost Meskhi 4–6 6–0 7–6); sf San Marino (d. Kelesi 6–3 ret'd, Fusai 6–1 6–0, Tarabini 6–4 6–1, lost Magdalena Maleeva 2–6 6–3 6–3). **1992 HIGHLIGHTS – DOUBLES:** (with Labat) **won** Kitzbuhel (d. Coetzer/Probst 6–3 6–3), **won** San Marino (d. Cecchini/Garrone 7–6 7–5), **won** Schenectady (d. Helgeson/McCarthy 6–3 1–6 6–2).

ROSSANA DE LOS RIOS (PAR)

Born Asuncion, 16 September 1975; lives Callejon; RH; 5ft 6in; 117lb; final 1992 WTA ranking 188.
1992: Won French Open Jun over Suarez and in the women's game won S. Maria C. Vetere Challenger. Ranked No. 1 in Nat 18s. **1992 HIGHLIGHTS – SINGLES: won** S. Maria C. Vetere Challenger (d. Grossi 6–4 6–0).

JO DURIE (GBR)

Born Bristol, 27 July 1960; lives London; RH; 6ft; 150lb; final 1992 WTA ranking 60; 1992 prize money $94,954.
Coached by Alan Jones. **1978:** Top-ranked British jun. **1979:** (73) Sf Wimbledon Plate. **1980:** (53) Out of action 8 months following back surgery. Sf German Indoor Open. **1981:** (31) Last 16 US Open; won British HC. **1982:** (28) No. 1 in Great Britain, taking over from Wade. **1983:** (6) Best year of career when she reached sf US and French Opens, qf Australian Open, and won Sydney and Mahwah. **1984:** (24). **1985:** (26) Sf Brighton (d. Graf). **1986:** (23) Played 17 tournaments and W and Fed Cups, winning 24 of 44 matches, beating McNeil, Lindqvist and K. Jordan, but best showing was sf Mahwah in summer. **1987:** (73) In W Cup ended 23-match winning streak by US when she d. Garrison, and won Wimbledon mixed doubles with Bates, but otherwise suffered a poor year. **1988:** (61) Qf San Diego and California Open. Missed Fed Cup with shoulder injury. **1989:** (118) Sf Auckland. A back injury forced her to withdraw from Wimbledon. **1990:** (64) An appearance in f VS Newport was her best showing since Brighton 1983. **1991:** (60) Reached sf St Petersburg, qf Los Angeles and upset Sukova on her way to an unexpected appearance in last 16 US Open. In mixed doubles won Australian Open with Bates. Won 6th British Nat. singles since beating V. Wade for first win in 1983. **1992:** Upset Huber at French Open and Tauziat *en route* to sf Birmingham. **1992 HIGHLIGHTS – SINGLES: Australian Open 2r** (d. Labat 7–5 6–1, lost Savchenko Neiland 6–4 4–6 6–1), **French Open 3r** (d. N. Dahlman 7–6 6–2, Huber [seed 9] 6–1 7–5, lost Kijimuta 6–7 6–4 6–4), **Wimbledon 1r** (lost Harvey-Wild 6–4 6–2), **US Open 1r** (lost Wood 6–1 0–6 6–3); **sf** Birmingham (d. Emmons 6–3 6–1, Nagelsen 6–3 6–4, Tauziat 5–7 6–3 6–4, Temesvari Trunkos 6–3 6–2, lost Byren 6–3 6–1). **CAREER HIGHLIGHTS – SINGLES: French Open – sf 1983** (d. Moulton, Shriver, Rinaldi, Austin 6–0 fs, lost Jausovec 6–2 fs); **US Open – sf 1983** (d. Madruga Osses 6–2 6–2, lost Evert Lloyd 6–4 6–4); **Australian Open – qf 1983** (lost Navratilova 4–6 6–3 6–4). **CAREER HIGHLIGHTS – DOUBLES:** (with Hobbs unless stated) **Australian Open – sf 1985** (lost Navratilova/Shriver 7–6 6–2); **French Open – sf 1983** (lost Fairbank/Reynolds 6–3 6–2); **Wimbledon – sf 1983** (lost Navratilova/Shriver 6–3 7–5) [Evert Lloyd] **qf 1985** (d. Bunge/Pfaff, lost Navratilova/Shriver 6–4 6–2). **MIXED DOUBLES:** (with Bates) **Australian Open – won 1991; Wimbledon – won 1987** (d. Cahill/Provis 7–6 6–3).

MANA ENDO (JPN)

Born Horishima, 6 February 1971; lives Isukuba City; RH; 5ft 3in; 119lb; final 1992 WTA ranking 58; 1992 prize money $47,378

Coached by her father, Hiroshi, and Bill Conan. **1989:** (377) Won Matsuyama on the Japanese Satellite circuit. **1990:** (197) Still concentrating on the Satellite circuits, she won Kuroshio. **1991:** (117) On the main tour she upset Savchenko at Canadian Open and on the Satellite circuit she won Chiba. **1992:** Played her 1st primary circuit qf at Brisbane, upsetting Shriver. **1992 HIGHLIGHTS – SINGLES: Australian Open 1r** (lost Rajchrtova 7–6 2–6 7–5), **French Open 3r** (d. Demongeot 6–1 6–2, Piccolini 7–6 6–0, lost Date [seed 14] 6–3 6–2), **Wimbledon 3r** (d. Fulco Villella 6–1 6–2, Grunfeld 5–7 6–2 7–5, lost K. Maleeva [seed 12] 7–5 6–3), **Olympics 2r** (d. Pampoulova Wagner 7–6 7–6, lost Sanchez-Vicario [seed 2] 6–0 6–1).

FANG LI (CHN)

Born Hunan, 1 January 1973, and lives there; RH; 2HB; 5ft 5 in; 138lb; final 1992 WTA ranking 130; 1992 prize money $38,863.

Coached by Jiang Hongwei and Xie Fengsen. **1990:** (350) Won Futures titles at Murcia and Fayetteville. **1991:** (153) Won 9 Futures events. **1992:** Emerging from the Satellite circuits, she reached qf Kuala Lumpur, upsetting Reggi Concato. **1992 HIGHLIGHTS – SINGLES: Australian Open 3r** (d. Hiraki 6–2 6–4, Stubbs 7–5 6–2, lost Novotna [seed 6] 6–3 6–1), **French Open 1r** (lost Zardo 6–1 6–2), **Wimbledon 1r** (lost Helgeson 6–1 6–2), **US Open 2r** (d. Habsudova 7–5 6–0, lost Zvereva 6–1 6–2), **Olympics 1r** (lost Schultz 7–5 6–7 6–4).

PATTY FENDICK (USA)

Born Sacramento, Cal., 31 March 1965, and lives there; RH; 5ft 5in; 117lb; final 1992 WTA ranking 43 singles, 16 doubles; 1992 prize money $184,675.

Scar tissue in her eye from an old injury expands and restricts her vision in brightness, obliging her to wear a baseball cap to play tennis. **1983:** Won Wimbledon Jun doubles with Hy, and Orange Bowl 18s singles and doubles. **1984:** Member US Jun Fed Cup team. All-American for Stanford, playing No. 1 on that team. **1985:** (83). **1986:** (94) Sf Wimbledon doubles with Hetherington and won NCAA singles. **1987:** (78) NCAA Champ for second time. While out of action at end of year with intestinal flu, she worked on the mental aspect of her game with John Whittlinger. **1988:** (22) Won her 1st pro title in Auckland, following with Japan Open, and reached sf on 5 other occasions. Last 16 US Open singles, and r/u in doubles with Hetherington, with whom she won 5 of 6 titles during the year and qualified for VS Champs. **1989:** (31) Out 3 months March–June with shoulder injury, returning to reach last 16 Wimbledon. Won Auckland in both singles and doubles with Hetherington, with whom she was r/u Australian Open and won VS California. **1990:** (42) In singles she upset Novotna and Paulus to reach qf Australian Open and, again unseeded, appeared in last 16 Wimbledon. In doubles was r/u Australian Open with M. J. Fernandez, but was less fortunate at US Open, where both her women's and mixed partners withdrew. With various partners she reached sf other doubles f, winning 2. Played in winning US Fed Cup team. **1991:** (55) Reached sf Colorado and Amelia Island. In doubles she won her 1st GS title, taking Australian Open with M. J. Fernandez and going on to reach 7 more f, winning 4 with 3 different partners. **1992:** Unseeded both times, she reached last 16 Australian Open and then Wimbledon, where she upset Novotna and took a set off Graf. At Zurich she beat Maleeva Fragnière and Garrison back-to-back to reach sf where she had to retire v Navratilova. Qf Oakland. Played 4 doubles f, winning VS Houston with G. Fernandez and Strasbourg with regular partner Strnadova, with whom she qualified for VS Champs, but lost 1r. **1992 HIGHLIGHTS – SINGLES: Australian Open last 16** [unseeded] (d. Niox-Chateau 6–1 6–3, Cioffi 5–7 6–2 6–3, Dechaume 5–7 7–5 6–4, lost M. J. Fernandez [seed 7] 6–4 6–1), **French Open 1r** (lost Grossman 6–3 6–3), **Wimbledon last 16** [unseeded] (d. Habsudova 6–2 6–4, Graham 7–5 7–5, Novotna [seed 11] 6–3 6–3, lost Graf [seed 2] 4–6 6–3 6–2), **US Open 1r** (lost Sawamatsu 6–1 6–3); **sf** Zurich (d. Kroupova 6–0 6–3, Maleeva Fragnière 6–3 6–3, Garrison Jackson 6–0 6–2, lost Navratilova 6–3 4–1 ret'd). **1992 HIGHLIGHTS – DOUBLES:** (with Strnadova unless stated); (with G. Fernandez) **won** VS

Houston (d. Hetherington/Rinaldi 7–5 6–4), *won* Strasbourg (d. McNeil/Paz 6–3 6–4); *r/u* San Antonio (lost Navratilova/Shriver 3–6 6–2 7–6), *r/u* Leipzig (lost Novotna/Savchenko Neiland 7–5 7–6). *CAREER HIGHLIGHTS DOUBLES:* (with M. J. Fernandez unless stated) *Australian Open – won 1991* [Hetherington] *r/u 1989* (lost Navratilova/Shriver 3–6 6–3 6–2), *r/u 1990* (lost Novotna/Sukova 7–6 7–6); *US Open –* [Hetherington] *r/u 1988* (lost G. Fernandez/R. White 6–4 6–1).

GIGI FERNANDEZ (USA)
Born Puerto Rico, 22 February 1964; lives Aspen, Col.; 5ft 7in; 145lb; final 1992 WTA ranking 33 singles, 6 doubles; 1992 prize money $479,187.
Coached by Julie Anthony. *1983:* (84) Narrowly beaten 7–6 fs by Herr in f AIAW. *1984:* (27) Buoyed by praise she received from Navratilova after coming within two points of upsetting Shriver at Wimbledon, she reached f Newport as Lucky Loser' and pushed Navratilova to 2s tb. *1985:* (64) Won LIPC doubles with Navratilova. *1986:* (62) Qualified with R. White for VS Champ doubles in Nov. and in singles won her 1st primary circuit title at Singapore. *1987:* (39) Reached last 16 Wimbledon unseeded, qf VS Florida and San Diego and won 3 doubles titles with McNeil. *1988:* (52) In doubles won US Open and Japan Open with R. White, reaching 7 other f with various partners and qualifying for VS Champs. *1989:* (23) R/u Puerto Rico, sf Eastbourne and Newport in singles; in doubles with various partners reached 8 f, winning 4. *1990:* (36) In singles appeared in last 16 US Open plus sf Puerto Rico and qf Tokyo, San Antonio and Birmingham. In doubles won US Open with Navratilova and with various partners took 4 other titles, reaching 3 more f. Played in winning US Fed Cup team. *1991:* (22) At VS Albuquerque she won her 1st singles title since 1986 and reached sf Eastbourne (d. Novotna); qf US Open, unseeded; upset Sukova 1r Wimbledon and Garrison at VS Houston. Voted WTA Doubles Team of the Year with Novotna: together they won French Open, r/u Australian Open, Wimbledon and VS Champs and reached 5 other f, winning 2. In addition she reached 5 more f with 4 different partners, winning a further 3 to bring a total of 6 titles from 14 f. *1992:* In singles was r/u Puerto Rico, played 4 qf and reached last 16 Wimbledon and US Open, unseeded both times. In Oct. began a 5–month rest period, from which she emerged to play VS Champs doubles with Zvereva, progressing to sf. They enjoyed a successful partnership across the year, winning French Open, Wimbledon and US Open plus 2 other titles. She also took an Olympic gold medal with M. J. Fernandez and won a 7th doubles title with Fendick. Won the Eagle Award for Excellence in Sports. *1992 HIGHLIGHTS – SINGLES: Australian Open 1r* (lost Habsudova 6–4 6–4), *Wimbledon last 16* [unseeded] (d. Faber 6–4 4–6 6–3, Date [seed 15] 6–1 6–3, Porwik 6–2 6–0, lost Seles [seed 1] 6–4 6–2), *US Open last 16* [unseeded] (d. Fauche 6–0 6–2, Baudone 6–3 3–6 6–2, Hack 6–4 6–1, lost Seles [seed 1] 6–1 6–2); *r/u* Puerto Rico (d. Paz 6–2 3–6 6–1, Rinaldi 6–3 6–3, Raymond 7–5 6–3, Graham 6–1 6–2, lost Pierce 6–1 7–5). *1992 HIGHLIGHTS – DOUBLES:* (with Zvereva unless stated) *won* French Open (d. Martinez/Sanchez-Vicario 6–3 6–2), *won* Wimbledon (d. Novotna/Savchenko Neiland 6–4 6–1), *won* US Open (d. Novotna/Savchenko Neiland 7–6 6–1), (with M. J. Fernandez) *Olympic gold medal* (d. Meskhi/Zvereva 6–4 7–5, Martinez/Sanchez-Vicario 7–5 2–6 6–2); (with Fendick) won VS Houston (d. Hetherington/Rinaldi 7–5 6–4), *won* Oakland (d. Fairbank Nideffer/Magers 3–6 6–2 6–4), *won* Philadelphia (d. Martinez/Pierce 6–1 6–3); *r/u* Berlin (lost Novotna/Savchenko Neiland 7–6 4–6 7–5), (with Rinaldi) *r/u* Puerto Rico (lost Coetzer/Reinach 6–2 4–6 6–2. *CAREER HIGHLIGHTS – DOUBLES:* (with Novotna unless stated) *French Open – won 1991,1992; US Open – won 1988 , 1992,* (with Navratilova) *won 1990* (d. Novotna/Sukova 6–2 6–4); *Australian Open – r/u 1991; Wimbledon – r/u 1991, won 1992; VS Champs – r/u 1991; LIPC – r/u 1991; Olympics gold medal – 1992.*

AMY FRAZIER (USA)
Born St Louis, Mo., 19 September 1972; lives Rochester Hills, Mich.; RH; 2HB; 5ft 8in; 130lb; final 1992 WTA ranking 19; 1992 prize money $233,513.
Won 7 Nat Jun titles. *1986:* (331). *1987:* (202) Won Kona on USTA circuit. *1988:* (55) Sf Guaruja; qf LA (d. Shriver and Magers), Kansas and Indianapolis (d. Kelesi). *1989:* (33) Won

1st primary circuit singles title at VS Kansas; sf Albuquerque (d. Maleeva Fragnière) and VS Indianapolis. **1990:** (16) Won VS Oklahoma and was r/u Tokyo Nicherei, where she beat Seles and K. Maleeva back-to-back and extended M. J. Fernandez to 3s. In other tourns reached sf Indian Wells and Sydney, where she upset Novotna and took Zvereva to 3s, and upset Fairbank Nideffer at Wimbledon. **1991:** (28) Reached sf Tokyo Nicherei; qf VS Chicago, Tokyo Suntory, Toronto and VS California; last 16 Australian Open and Wimbledon. **1992:** Taking advantage of Graf's withdrawal from her part of the draw, she reached qf Australian Open and, again unseeded, upset M. J. Fernandez to reach last 16 Wimbledon. Won both singles and doubles titles at Lucerne and also took the doubles at Tokyo Suntory. She reached sf singles there, as well as at VS Oklahoma and San Antonio. Qualified for VS Champs 1st time, but lost 1r to Sabatini. **1992 HIGHLIGHTS – SINGLES: Australian Open qf** [unseeded] (d. Cunningham 6–3 7–5, de Vries 6–1 7–6, Hack 6–1 3–6 6–2, Monami 6–3 6–4, lost M. J. Fernandez [seed 7] 6–4 7–6), **French Open 2r** (d. Paz 6–2 3–6 6–4, lost Schultz 6–1 3–6 6–4), **Wimbledon last 16** [unseeded] (d. Golarsa 6–2 6–1, Allen 7–6 6–1, M. J. Fernandez [seed 7] 6–3 6–3, lost Tauziat [seed 14] 6–0 6–3), **US Open 1r** (lost Medvedeva 6–4 6–1); **won** Lucerne (d. Kroupova 7–6 6–0, Harvey-Wild 6–3 6–0, Fauche 7–6 6–2, Zrubakova 6–4 4–6 7–5); **sf** VS Oklahoma (d. Rinaldi 6–1 6–3, Louise Allen 6–4 6–0, Graham 7–6 6–2, lost Garrison 6–4 0–6 6–4), **sf** San Antonio (d. Benjamin 4–6 6–0 6–1, Rubin 7–5 3–6 6–1, Habsudova 6–4 6–2, lost Tauziat 4–6 7–6 6–4), **sf** Tokyo Suntory (d. Po 6–2 6–4, Rehe 6–1 6–2, Medvedeva 6–4 6–1, lost Date 6–3 6–4). **1992 HIGHLIGHTS – DOUBLES:** (Hiraki) **won** Tokyo Suntory (d. Date/Rehe 5–7 7–6 6–0), (with E. Reinach) **won** Lucerne (d. Habsudova/Werdel 7–5 6–2).

LAURA ARRAYA GILDEMEISTER (PER)
Born Cordoba, Argentina, 12 January 1964; lives Lima and Miami, Fla.; RH; 2HB; 5ft 8in; 125lb; final 1992 WTA ranking 45 1992 prize money $162,462.
Coached by her husband, Heinz Gildemeister (married 1984); son Heinz Andre (born June 1988). Having lived in Argentina until age 7, she moved with her family to Peru and became a citizen of that country. **1982:** (69) Burst into her own, beating Bonder, Nagelsen, Temesvari and Horvath. **1983:** (86) R/u Freiburg, qf Hilton Head. **1984:** (34) R/u Tourn of Champs. **1985:** (63) Sf VS Utah and Japan Open; played Fed Cup. **1986:** (31) Upset Lindqvist, M. Maleeva and Kohde-Kilsch during year. **1987:** (46). **1988:** (8) Did not play all year, taking a 9–month break after the birth of her son in June. **1989:** (19) Returned to action at LIPC in March and at Schenectady won 1st primary circuit title for 7 years, following with Puerto Rico (d. Zvereva and G. Fernandez) in Oct. **1990:** (21) R/u Albuquerque and upset Seles in ss en route to sf VS Florida. **1991:** (24) Upset K. Maleeva to reach qf Wimbledon, unseeded, and appeared in sf both tourns in Tokyo and Westchester. 1992: R/u Osaka and sf VS Houston. **1992 HIGHLIGHTS – SINGLES: Australian Open 2r** (d. Werdel 6–4 6–7 6–1, lost Strnadova 4–6 6–4 9–7), **French Open 1r** (lost Martinez [seed 7] 6–2 7–6), **Wimbledon 3r** (d. Bowes 6–0 6–2, Helgeson 3–6 6–4 7–5, lost Seles [seed 1] 6–4 6–1), **US Open 2r** (d. Ruano Pascual 7–5 6–2); **r/u** Osaka (d. Nagatsuka 7–6 6–1, Kamio 6–1 6–2, Habsudova 6–3 6–7 6–1, lost Sukova 6–2 4–6 6–1); **sf** VS Houston (d. F. Bonsignori 6–2 6–0, Cioffi 6–2 6–1, G. Fernandez 6–4 3–6 6–1, lost Seles 6–4 6–1). **CAREER HIGHLIGHTS – SINGLES: Wimbledon – qf 1991.**

DEBBIE GRAHAM (USA)
Born Walnut Greek, Cal., 25 August 1970; lives Fountain Valley, Cal.; RH; 2HB; final 1992 WTA ranking 52; 1992 prize money $102,127.
Coached by Bob Hochstadter and Frank Brenna. Did not join the tour full time until she had finished her education. **1986:** Won Nat 16s. **1988:** (139). **1989:** (252) All-American in singles and doubles for 1st of 2 years. **1990:** (121) Qf Clarins and won NCAA singles, playing for Stanford Univ. **1991:** (42) Qf Westchester, San Diego (d. Paulus) and Tokyo Nicherei (d. Shriver). **1992:** In her 1st full year on tour after graduating in political science from Stanford, she was voted Most Impressive Newcomer, with sf showings at Brisbane and Puerto Rico and 3 more qf appearances. **1992 HIGHLIGHTS – SINGLES: Australian Open 1r** (lost K. Maleeva [seed 10] 6–4 1–6 6–4), **French Open 1r** (lost Novotna [seed 10]

6–3 6–2), *Wimbledon 2r* (d. Cunningham 6–2 7–6, lost Fendick 7–5 7–5), *US Open 1r* (lost Zvereva 6–3 6–2); *sf* Brisbane (d. Kschwendt 6–4 7–6, Tessi 6–3 6–4, Appelmans 6–2 6–2, Endo 6–2 6–3, lost McQuillan 7–5 6–4), *sf* Puerto Rico (d. De Lone 6–0 6–1, Babel 6–0 6–3, Coetzer 6–2 3–6 6–3, lost G. Fernandez 6–1 6–2)

ANN GROSSMAN (USA)
Born Grove City, Ohio, 13 October 1970, and lives there; RH; 2HB; 5ft 3in; 110lb; final 1992 WTA ranking 36; 1992 prize money $99,759.
Coached by Trevor Nettle. *1986:* Won US Int GC 16s. *1987:* (378) Won Nat 18s. *1988:* (48) Upset Fairbank *en route* to f San Diego. *1989:* (55) Reached qf San Diego and last 16 LIPC and French Open. *1990:* (50) Reached last 16 French Open, unseeded, and upset Magers *en route* to f Strasbourg. *1991:* (89) Upset Zvereva at French Open and reached qf VS Houston. *1992:* She returned to top 50 with sf showings at Wellington and Indian Wells (d. Lindqvist and Frazier), plus 3 more qf, and an upset of Martinez 1r US Open. *1992 HIGHLIGHTS – SINGLES: French Open 3r* (d. Fendick 6–3 6–3, Probst 6–3 6–0, lost Martinez [seed 7] 6–2 6–2), *US Open 2r* (d. Martinez [seed 8] 6–3 2–6 6–4, lost Van Lottum 7–6 6–4); *r/u* Taipei (d. Kamio 6–2 6–2, Rossides 7–6 6–3, Wang 3–6 6–4 6–3, Miyagi 6–2 3–0 ret'd, lost Stafford 6–1 6–3); *sf* Wellington (d. I. Berger 6–0 7–5, Smashnova 6–4 4–6 6–1, Toleafoa 7–6 2–6 7–5, lost Faber 6–4 7–5), *sf* Indian Wells (d. Kijimuta 7–6 6–0, Lindqvist 6–2 6–4, Rinaldi 6–1 7–5, Frazier 6–4 5–7 6–4, lost Martinez 6–3 6–1).

SABINE HACK (GER)
Born Ulm, 7 December 1969; lives Ravemburg; RH; 5ft 7in; 130lb; final 1992 WTA ranking 28; 1992 prize money $100,003.
1985: (187) Enjoyed some success on the satellite circuits. *1986:* (263). *1987:* (234). *1988:* (141) Qf Athens and Paris Open. *1989:* (73) Reached 1st tour f at Bastad and broke into top 100. *1990:* (45) Upset Maleeva Fragnière *en route* to sf Geneva and reached same stage Estoril. *1991:* (90) Qf Auckland, Wellington and San Marino. *1992:* Won her 1st tour singles title at Sao Paulo and upset M. J. Fernandez to reach last 16 French Open, unseeded. She also surprised Maleeva Fragnière at Lucerne and was a member of the winning German Fed Cup team. *1992 HIGHLIGHTS – SINGLES: Australian Open 3r* (d. Tanvier 6–4 7–5, Rajchrtova 7–5 3–6 6–2, lost Frazier 6–1 3–6 6–2), *French Open last 16* [unseeded] (d. Tarabini 6–3 6–0, De Swardt 0–6 6–4 6–4, M. J. Fernandez [seed 6] 7–6 6–2, lost Zvereva 6–3 6–3), *Wimbledon 2r* (d. Paradis Mangon 6–3 1–6 12–10, lost Basuki 7–5 6–3), *US Open 3r* (d. McCarthy 6–4 6–3, Fairbank Nideffer 7–5 6–4, lost G. Fernandez 6–4 6–1); *won* Sao Paulo (d. de los Rios 6–2 7–5, Tella 6–1 6–0, Faber 6–1 6–1, Martinek 6–3 7–5).

JULIE HALARD (FRA)
Born Versailles, 10 September 1970; lives La Baule; RH; 2HB; 5ft 7in; 110lb; final 1992 WTA ranking 27; 1992 prize money $122,178.
1986: (8) Won French Open Jun. *1987:* (62) Turned pro June. R/u Wimbledon Jun to Zvereva and reached f Athens. *1988:* (75) Won French Open Jun over Farley. *1989:* (119) Upset Shriver *en route* to qf Moscow. *1990:* (41) Sf Clarins, qf Sydney and Barcelona, and upset Garrison *en route* to last 16 LIPC. *1991:* (20) Won her 1st primary circuit title at Puerto Rico; r/u VS Albuquerque; sf San Antonio, Clarins and Phoenix; and upset M. J. Fernandez at Berlin. Qualified for her 1st VS Champs, but fell 1r to Seles. 1992: Won Taranto, reached sf Clarins and upset Sanchez-Vicario *en route* to last 16 Wimbledon, unseeded. *1992 HIGHLIGHTS – SINGLES: Australian Open 1r* (lost Sabatini [seed 3] 6–2 6–0), *French Open 3r* (d. Fulco Villella 6–2 6–4, Fairbank Nideffer 6–2 6–2, lost Sabatini [seed 3] 6–1 6–3), *Wimbledon last 16* [unseeded] (d. Rajchrtova 6–3 6–1, Sanchez-Vicario [seed 5] 6–3 2–6 6–3, Sukova 4–6 6–1 6–3, lost K. Maleeva [seed 12] 6–0 6–3), *US Open 2r* (d. Federica Bonsignori 6–1 6–3, lost Sabatini [seed] 4 6–0 6–4), *Olympics 2r* [seed 15] (d. Nowak 6–4 7–6, lost Muns Jagerman 7–6 7–6); *won* Taranto (d. Tessi 6–0 1–6 6–1, Pizzichini 6–4 6–2, Mothes 6–1 3–6 6–4, Ferrando 6–3 6–4, Zardo 6–0 7–5); *sf* Clarins (d. Fulco Villella 6–0 6–2, Frankl 6–1 6–4, Federica Bonsignori 6–3 1–6 6–0, lost Zardo 3–6 7–6 6–4).

LINDA HARVEY-WILD (USA)
Born Arlington Heights, Ill., 11 February 1971; lives Hawthorn Woods, Ill.; RH; 5ft 7in; 135lb; final 1992 WTA ranking 49; 1992 prize money $137,870.
Coached by her stepfather, Steve Wild. At Univ. of S. Cal. *1987:* (338). *1988:* (428). *1989:* (153) Won 2 consec. USTA circuit events. *1990:* (83) Qf VS Chicago (upsetting Sanchez–Vicario) and VS Nashville (d. Provis); broke into top 100 in Aug. *1991:* (41) Reached sf Brisbane and VS Houston, upsetting G. Fernandez there and *en route* to qf VS California, and surprised Zvereva 2r Wimbledon. *1992:* R/u Eastbourne, where she caused the upset of the year by removing Navratilova 2r, causing the former No. 1's earliest exit from a tourn since 1981. Reached the same stage Indianapolis (d. K. Maleeva) and appeared in qf Lucerne. *1992 HIGHLIGHTS – SINGLES: Australian Open 2r* (d. Kelesi 6–1 6–4, lost McQuillan 6–2 4–6 6–0), *French Open 2r* (d. Stubbs 6–1 6–2, lost McNeil 6–2 6–3), *Wimbledon 2r* (d. Durie 6–4 6–2, lost Garrison [seed 13] 6–2 6–4), *US Open 1r* (lost Sabatini [seed 4] 6–1 6–2); *r/u* Eastbourne (d. Suire 6–3 7–6, Navratilova 6–3 6–7 6–3, Savchenko Neiland 3–6 7–6 6–4, Stubbs 6–1 6–1, Fairbank Nideffer 6–1 6–3, lost McNeil 6–4 6–4), *r/u* Indianapolis (d. Daniels 6–0 6–3, Adams 6–4 6–1, Majoli 4–6 6–2 6–4, K. Maleeva 6–4 7–6, lost Sukova 6–4 6–3). *1992 HIGHLIGHTS – DOUBLES:* (Martinez) *r/u* VS Florida (lost Savchenko Neiland/Zvereva 6–2 6–2).

ANKE HUBER (GER)
Born Bruchsal, 4 December 1974; lives Karlsdorf; RH; 2HB; 5ft 8in; 120lb; final 1992 WTA ranking 11; 1992 prize money $209,616.
Coached by Boris Breskvar, who coached both Becker and Graf in the early stages of their development. *1986:* Won Nat 12s. *1987:* Won Nat 14s. *1988:* Won Nat 16s. *1989:* (203) Won European Jun Champs. *1990:* (34) She showed great fighting spirit in extending Sabatini to 2s tb in their 2r encounter at Wimbledon. At end Aug. won her 1st tour title at Schenectady after qualifying and followed with r/u Bayonne, upsetting Garrison and breaking into top 100, then shooting up to top 50 by Oct. Voted WTA most impressive newcomer. *1991:* (14) Upset Maleeva Fragnière and Zvereva *en route* to qf Australian Open, unseeded, reached last 16 Wimbledon and ended Sabatini's winning run as she reached qf Berlin. The high spot of her year, though, came at Filderstadt in autumn, where she upset Garrison, Sukova and Navratilova in fs tb to take the title. It was the 1st time for 8 years that Navratilova had been beaten by an unseeded player. *1992:* Upset Novotna *en route* to qf Australian Open and appeared at same stage Olympics; reached sf Sydney, Hamburg, San Diego, Brighton and Oakland and was a member of winning German Fed Cup team. *1992 HIGHLIGHTS – SINGLES: Australian Open qf* [seed 12] (d. Zivec–Skulj 2–6 6–3 6–1, Jaggard 6–0 6–1, Fairbank Nideffer 6–0 7–5, Novotna [seed 6] 5–7 7–6 6–4, lost Seles [seed 1] 7–5 6–3), *French Open 2r* [seed 9] (d. Zrubakova 6–2 6–2, lost Durie 6–1 7–5), *Wimbledon 3r* [seed 10] (d. Ferrando 6–4 6–4, Tessi 6–2 6–2, lost Basuki 6–2 6–3), *US Open 1r* [seed 11] (lost Appelmans 6–3 6–4), *Olympics qf* [seed 7] (d. Sawamatsu 6–0 4–6 6–2, Paulus 6–4 6–1, Muns Jagerman 7–5 7–6, lost Capriati [seed 3] 6–3 7–6); *sf* Sydney (d. Demongeot 7–5 6–1, Tami Whitlinger 6–3 6–4, Novotna 6–3 7–5, lost Sanchez-Vicario 4–6 7–5 6–3), *sf* Hamburg (d. Rajchrtova 7–6 6–3, Durie 6–3 6–2, Maleeva Fragnière 5–7 6–2 7–5, lost Graf 6–3 6–0), *sf* San Diego (d. Graham 6–0 6–2, Tauziat 6–1 6–1, lost Capriati 7–6 6–3 6–1), *sf* Brighton (d. Schultz 6–1 3–6 6–4, Nowak 6–1 6–2, Paradis Mangon 6–3 6–1, lost Graf 7–5 6–2), *sf* Oakland (d. Savchenko Neiland 1–6 6–0 6–0, Shriver 6–2 6–4, lost Seles 6–2 6–3). *CAREER HIGHLIGHTS – SINGLES: Australian Open – qf 1991* [unseeded] (d. Richardson, Maleeva Fragnière 6–4 6–4, Shriver 6–3 7–5, Zvereva 6–3 6–4, lost Seles 6–3 6–1), *qf 1992.*

PATRICIA HY (CAN)
Born Cambodia, 22 August 1965; lives Vancouver; RH; 5ft 4in; 119lb; final 1992 WTA ranking 32; 1992 prize money $161,815.
Coached by her father, Ly. In 1981, living in Kowloon, Hong Kong, she was ranked No. 1 in that country at age 16. *1983:* (65) R/u Wimbledon Jun singles and won doubles there with Fendick. On the senior tour she reached sf Nashville. *1984:* (214) An All-American at UCLA,

she won Fort Lauderdale on USTA circuit. *1985:* (308). *1986:* (101) Won Taipei and reached sf Singapore. *1987:* (101) Extended Graf to 3s in Fed Cup. *1988:* (205) Won USTA Detroit. *1989:* (222) Won USTA Chicago. *1990:* (103) Qf Singapore. *1991:* (57) Qf VS Indian Wells and upset Fairbank Nideffer at Wimbledon. *1992:* Unseeded both times, she reached last 16 French Open and at US Open upset Capriati and Sukova back-to-back to reach qf. She reached the same stage FC Cup (d. Magdalena Maleeva and Novotna), Montreal (d. Maleeva Fragnière) and extended M. J. Fernandez to 12–10 fs at Olympics. *1992 HIGHLIGHTS – SINGLES: Australian Open 2r* (d. Magdalena Maleeva 6–4 6–3, lost Sabatini [seed 3] 6–1 6–1), *French Open last 16* [unseeded] (d. Spirlea 6–2 4–6 2–1 ret'd, Gomer 7–6 6–0, Brioukhovets 6–0 7–5, lost Sabatini [seed 3] 6–3 6–1), *Wimbledon 3r* (d. Reinach 6–4 6–2, Thoren 6–2 6–7 6–1, lost Capriati [seed 6] 6–3 6–1), *US Open qf* [unseeded] (d. Sviglerova 6–1 6–1, Wiesner 6–2 6–2, Capriati [seed 6] 7–5 6–4, Sukova [seed 132] 6–1 7–6, lost Seles [seed 1] 6–1 6–2), *Olympics 2r* (d. D. Randriantefy 6–2 6–1, lost M. J. Fernandez [seed 4] 6–2 1–6 12–10).

ZINA GARRISON JACKSON (USA)

Born Houston, 16 November 1963, and lives there; RH; 5ft 44in; 128lb; final 1991 WTA ranking 18 singles, 10 doubles; 1992 prize money $354,947.

Husband Willard Jackson Jr (married Sept. 1989). Coached by Willis Thomas until Aug. that year when Angel Lopez took over. During 1990 Sherwood Stewart took on that role. Discovered by John Wilkerson in public parks programme in Houston. *1981:* Won Wimbledon and US Open Jun. *1982:* (16) Qf French Open and last 16 Wimbledon. *1983:* (10) Sf Australian Open, Eastbourne and Detroit. *1984:* (9) Won Zurich; r/u VS Washington and New Orleans. *1985:* (8) Won WTA Champs (d. Mandlikova and Evert Lloyd), sf Wimbledon and r/u US CC. *1986:* (11) Won 48 of 69 matches as she won VS Indianapolis, reached f Tampa and sf Canadian Open. *1987:* (9) Suffering stress fracture to foot, was obliged to pull out of French Open and missed Wimbledon. Won NSW Open and VS California, reached f Canadian Open, 5 sf, and qf Australian Open. In doubles was r/u Australian Open with McNeil and won Australian Open mixed with Stewart. Qualified for VS Champs in singles and doubles. *1988:* (9) Qf Wimbledon, where she won mixed doubles with Stewart, and sf US Open, where she d. Navratilova for 1st time in 22 meetings. At Olympics won bronze medal in singles and gold in doubles with Shriver. Qualified for VS Champs singles, but lost 1r to Sukova. *1989:* (4) Won first singles title for 2 years at VS Cal, following with Newport and Chicago as well as reaching 4 more f. At US Open ended Evert's GS career *en route* to sf, reached qf Australian Open and at VS Champs fell qf to Sabatini. In doubles won 4 titles with K. Adams and in mixed was r/u Australian Open with Stewart. *1990:* (10) The high point of her career came at Wimbledon, where she beat Seles and Graf back-to-back before losing f to Navratilova, becoming the 1st black woman to reach f there since Althea Gibson in 1950. Reached qf Australian Open and US Open; won Birmingham; r/u VS Washington and Puerto Rico; sf VS Chicago, Houston, San Diego, Los Angeles and VS California. In doubles won Washington with Navratilova, San Diego with Fendick and Filderstadt with M. J. Fernandez; in mixed with Leach won Wimbledon and r/u Australian Open. Played in winning US Fed Cup team and qualified for VS Champs, where she lost 1r to Martinez. *1991:* (12) Qualified for VS Champs in both singles (lost 1r to Sanchez-Vicario) and doubles (with M. J. Fernandez). Her best showing in GS was qf Wimbledon; r/u VS Chicago and Brighton; sf Sydney, Eastbourne and Birmingham. In doubles won LIPC with M. J. Fernandez and reached 2 more f. *1992:* At VS Oklahoma in Feb. she won her 1st title for 20 months and was r/u Houston, as well as reaching 7 more qf. In doubles she reached 6 f with various partners, including Australian Open with M. J. Fernandez, but won no title. Qualified for VS Champs in both singles and doubles (with M. J. Fernandez), but fell 1r in both. *1992 HIGHLIGHTS – SINGLES: Australian Open last 16* [seed 11] (d. Frankl 6–2 6–2, Kohde-Kilsch 6–2 6–3, Shriver 6–4 6–2, lost Capriati [seed 5] 6–4 4–6), *Wimbledon last 16* [seed 13] (d. Federica Bonsignori 6–0 6–1, Harvey-Wild 6–2 6–4, Fairbank Nideffer 6–4 6–2, lost Zvereva 6–2 3–6 6–1), *US Open last 16* [seed 14] (d. Kelesi 7–5 6–0, Meier 6–2 2–6 6–4, McQuillan 6–3 6–1, lost Sanchez-Vicario [seed 5] 6–0 6–1), *Olympics 1r* [seed 12] (lost Coetzer 7–5 6–1); *won*

VS Oklahoma (d. Cioffi 6–4 6–1, Hiraki 6–2 6–1, Grossman 6–2 6–0, Frazier 6–4 0–6 6–4, McNeil 7–5 3–6 7–6); *r/u* VS Houston (d. Burgin 6–1 6–4, Majoli 6–3 6–4, K. Maleeva 6–1 6–3, lost Seles 6–1 6–1). *1992 HIGHLIGHTS – DOUBLES:* (with M. J. Fernandez unless stated) *r/u* Australian Open (lost Sanchez-Vicario/Sukova 6–4 7–6); *r/u* Sydney (lost Sanchez-Vicario/Sukova 7–6 6–7 6–2), (with McNeil) *r/u* VS Chicago (lost Navratilova/Shriver 6–4 7–6), (with Novotna) *r/u* Amelia Island (lost Sanchez-Vicario/Zvereva 6–1 6–0), *r/u* Eastbourne (lost Novotna/Savchenko Neiland 6–0 6–3), (with Shriver) *r/u* Los Angeles (lost Sukova/Sanchez-Vicario 6–4 6–2). *CAREER HIGHLIGHTS – SINGLES:* Wimbledon – r/u *1990* (d. S. Smith, Dahlman, Leand, Sukova 6–3 6–3, Seles 3–6 6–3 9–7, Graf 6–3 3–6 6–4, lost Navratilova 6–4 6–1), *sf 1985* (d. Tanvier, Van Nostrand, lost Navratilova 6–4 7–6), *qf 1988* (d. Sabatini 6–1 3–6 6–2, lost Shriver 6–4 6–4), *qf 1991*; *USCC – r/u 1983* (lost Temesvari 6–2 6–2), *r/u 1985* (lost Temesvari 7–6 6–3); *Olympics – bronze medal 1988* (lost Graf 6–2 6–0); *Australian Open – sf 1983* (d. Pfaff, Turnbull 6–2 7–6, lost K. Jordan 7–6 6–1), *qf 1985* (d. Henricksson, lost Mandlikova 2–6 6–3 6–3), *qf 1989* (lost Sabatini 6–4 2–6 6–4), *qf 1990* (d. Kijimuta, Thoren, Demongest 5–7 6–3 6–4, Tanvier 6–2 2–0 ret'd, lost M. J. Fernandez 1–6 6–2 8–6); *US Open – sf 1988* (d. Sanchez 4–6 7–5 6–2, Navratilova 6–4 6–7 7–5, lost Sabatini 6–4 7–5), *sf 1989* (d. G. Fernandez, Fendick 6–3 7–5, Faber, Evert 7–6 6–2, lost Navratilova 7–6 6–2), *qf 1985* (d. Gompert, lost Navratilova 6–2 6–3), *qf 1990* (d. Reinstadler, Gavaldon, Meier, Tauziat 6–1 7–5, lost Sanchez-Vicario 6–2 6–2); *French Open – qf 1982* unseeded (d. Bunge, Herr, Jausovec 7–5 6–1, lost Navratilova 6–3 6–2). *CAREER HIGHLIGHTS – DOUBLES: Olympics –* (with Shriver) *gold medal 1988* (d. Novotna/Suire 4–6 6–2 10–8); *LIPC –* (with M J Fernandez) *won 1991*; *Australian Open –* (with McNeil) *r/u 1987* (lost Navratilova/Shriver 6–1 6–0); *US Open –* (with Rinaldi) *qf 1985* unseeded (d. Bassett/Evert Lloyd, lost Kohde-Kilsch/Sukova 5–7 6–4 6–3). *MIXED DOUBLES:* (with Stewart unless stated) *Australian Open – won 1987* (d. Castle/Hobbs 3–6 7–6 6–3), *r/u 1992*; *Wimbledon – won 1988* (d. Magers/Jones 6–1 7–6) [R. Leach] *won 1990* (d. Smylie/Fitzgerald 7–6 6–2).

FLORENCIA LABAT (ARG)
Born Buenos Aires, 12 June 1971, and lives there; LH; 5ft 7in; 135lb; final 1992 WTA ranking 51; 1992 prize money $112,097.
Coached by Roberto Graets. *1987:* Won S American Jun Champs. *1988:* (389) No. 3 in ITF Jun rankings. *1989:* (70) Won S American Jun Champs again. On the pro tour she reached qf Arcachon and VS Arizona as well as upsetting Lindqvist 1r US Open. *1990:* (118) Qf Strasbourg and Puerto Rico and joined her country's Fed Cup team. *1991:* (56) Reached her 1st sf on the main tour at Sao Paulo, appeared in qf Taranto, Kitzbuhel (d. Kelesi) and Schenectady and upset Tauziat at US Open. In doubles won Taranto with Dechaume and Puerto Rico with Hiraki. *1992:* Upset Wiesner *en route* to sf Kitzbuhel and Medvedeva and Zrubakova on her way to same stage Schenectady, winning the doubles at both those tourns with Dechaume and also taking San Marino. Made an unexpected appearance in last 16 US Open. *1992 HIGHLIGHTS – SINGLES: Australian Open 1r* (lost Durie 7–5 6–1), *French Open 1r* (lost Wiesner 6–2 6–3), *Wimbledon 1r* (lost Basuki 6–2 6–2), *US Open last 16* [unseeded] (d. Golarsa 6–4 6–2, Majoli 6–3 6–3, Coetzer 6–3 4–6 6–4, lost Graf [seed 2] 6–2 6–2), *Olympics 1r* (lost Rittner 6–3 6–3); *sf* Kitzbuhel (d. Dobrovits 6–1 6–4, Brioukhovets 6–3 3–0 ret'd, Wiesner 6–2 6–1, lost Maleeva Fragnière 4–6 6–0 6–3), *sf* Schenectady (d. Medvedeva 4–6 6–3 6–4, Rubin 3–6 6–3 6–2, Zrubakova 6–4 4–6 6–2, lost Schultz 6–1 6–4). *1992 HIGHLIGHTS – DOUBLES:* (with Dechaume) *won* Kitzbuhel (d. Coetzer/Probst 6–3 6–3), *won* San Marino (d. Cecchini/Garrone 7–6 7–5), *won* Schenectady (d. Helgeson/McCarthy 6–3 1–6 6–2).

LORI McNEIL (USA)
Born San Diego, Cal., 18 December 1963; lives Houston, Texas; RH; 5ft 7in; 135lb; final 1992 WTA ranking 15 singles, 14 doubles; 1992 prize money $427,166.
Coached by Willis Thomas. *1983:* Member US Jun Fed Cup team, ranked 8 US Intercollegiate list and 4 on USTA satellite circuit. *1984:* (97) Reached last 16 US Open and led Mandlikova by a set and 4–2 before losing. *1985:* (93). *1986:* (14) Burst out of the pack

and established herself as one of top 15 players in world. Won Tampa – over Garrison in first VS Series final between two black women – and VS Tulsa back-to-back in Sept. Ably coached by John Wilkerson, who was also Garrison's instructor, she reached qf Wimbledon unseeded and qualified first time for VS Champs in Nov., clearly the most improved fast-court player in the world. *1987:* (11) Qf Australian Open and sf US Open, where she spoiled Evert's record of winning at least one GS event each year by beating her in qf. Won no singles title but reached f Oklahoma, New Orleans and New Jersey. In doubles r/u Australian Open with Garrison, won 6 titles and r/u 7 more with 5 different partners. Qualified for VS Champs in singles and doubles. *1988:* (13) Won Oklahoma and Newport in singles, took 5 doubles titles with different partners, and won French Open mixed with Lozano. Qualified for VS Champs in both singles and doubles. *1989:* (37) Upset Evert *en route* to f Pan Pacific Open in Tokyo, where she took Navratilova to 3s tb, then won her first singles title for 13 months at Albuquerque. In doubles with various partners she reached 8 f, winning 5. *1990:* (52) Upset Sabatini and G. Fernandez *en route* to sf San Antonio and reached the same stage at Eastbourne. Qualified for VS Champs doubles with K. Adams, upsetting Savchenko/Zvereva to reach sf. *1991:* (19) At Colorado, she won her 1st title for 18 months, following with Tokyo Suntory in April; r/u Westchester and sf VS California to qualify for VS Champs, where she lost 1r to Navratilova. Reached 5 doubles f with different partners, winning Strasbourg with Rehe and Milan with Collins. *1992:* Concentrating more on her tennis, having been somewhat distracted in recent years, she achieved some good results and scored several significant upsets. Won Eastbourne (d. Martinez and M. J. Fernandez); r/u VS Oklahoma, where she extended Garrison to 3s tb; sf VS Champs (d. Graf 1r), VS Chicago (d. Garrison), Montreal (d. Maleeva Fragnière). In women's doubles won 3 titles from 4 f with various partners and qualified for VS Champs with Stubbs. In mixed r/u French Open with Shelton. *1992 HIGHLIGHTS – SINGLES: Australian Open 1r* (lost Testud 6–2 3–6 6–4), *French Open 3r* (d. Kuhlman 6–2 6–2, Harvey-Wild 6–2 6–3, lost Seles 6–0 6–1), *Wimbledon 3r* (d. Suire 6–1 7–5, Stubbs 6–1 6–3, lost Zvereva 5–7 6–4 7–5), *US Open 3r* (d. Rottier 6–7 7–6 6–2, Zardo 6–1 7–5, lost Sukova [seed 13] 6–2 6–3); *won* Eastbourne (d. Blumberga 6–1 6–2, R. White 6–4 6–4, Martinez 6–0 6–3, Tauziat 7–6 6–7 7–5, M. J. Fernandez 7–6 6–0, Harvey-Wild 6–4 6–4); *r/u* VS Oklahoma (d. Sloane Lundy 6–3 6–2, E. Reinach 6–4 6–2, Provis 4–6 6–4 7–6, Bollegraf 6–3 7–5, lost Garrison 7–5 3–6 7–6); *sf* VS Chicago (d. E. Reinach 6–4 6–2, Helgeson 7–5 6–7 6–2, Garrison 6–1 6–3, lost Navratilova 1–6 6–4 6–4), *sf* Montreal (d. Faber 6–2 6–3, Cunningham 7–5 6–4, Maleeva Fragnière 7–5 6–2, lost Seles 6–3 6–4), *sf* VS Champs (d. Graf 1r 6–4, Martinez 3–6 6–3 6–2, lost Navratilova 7–6 6–4). *1992 HIGHLIGHTS – DOUBLES:* (with Stubbs unless stated), (with Provis) *won* VS Oklahoma (d. Adams/Bollegraf 3–6 6–4 7–6), *won* Birmingham (d. Collins/Reinach 5–7 6–3 8–6), *won* Montreal (d. G. Fernandez/Zvereva 3–6 7–5 7–5); (with Paz) *r/u* Strasbourg (lost Fendick/Strnadova 6–3 6–4). *MIXED DOUBLES:* (with Shelton) *r/u* French Open (lost Sanchez-Vicario/Woodbridge 6–2 6–3)*CAREER HIGHLIGHTS – DOUBLES:* (with Garrison) *Australian Open – r/u 1987* (lost Navratilova/Shriver 6–1 6–0). *MIXED DOUBLES:* (with Lozano) *French Open – won 1988* (d. Schultz/Schapers 7–5 6–2), *r/u 1992.*.

RACHEL McQUILLAN (AUS)
Born Waratah, NSW, 2 December 1971; lives Newcastle, NSW; RH; 2HB; 5ft 7in; 132lb; final 1992 WTA ranking 38; 1992 prize money $117,271.
Coached by Ken Richardson and Terry Rocivert. *1987:* (448) In winning World Youth Cup team. *1988:* (202) Won Australian Open and Wimbledon Jun doubles with Faull; r/u US Open Jun to Cunningham. Ranked No. 2 in ITF Jun doubles and No. 5 in singles. *1989:* (79) Qf Adelaide and Hamburg, then upset Cecchini *en route* to f Athens. R/u US Open Jun to Capriati. *1990:* (39) Upset Wiesner twice to make surprise appearances in f Brisbane and Kitzbuhel. In GS overturned Kelesi *en route* to last 16 Australian Open, unseeded, and in doubles reached 2 f with Faull. *1991:* (36) Unseeded she reached last 16 Australian Open (d. Paulus) and French Open (d. Kelesi). R/u Strasbourg (d. Wiesner), sf Bayonne and won Schenectady doubles with Porwik. 1992: R/u Brisbane, sf Bayonne and qf Osaka were her best performances in singles. In doubles she reached 4 f with different partners, winning

an Olympic bronze medal with Provis. *1992 HIGHLIGHTS – SINGLES: Australian Open 3r* (d. Sloane Lundy 6–4 6–4, Harvey-Wild 6–2 4–6 6–0, lost M. J. Fernandez [seed 7] 6–1 2–6 6–1), *Wimbledon 1r* (lost Kohde-Kilsch 2–6 6–2 6–4), *US Open 3r* (d. Mothes 6–2 6–0, London 6–1 7–6, lost Garrison [seed 14] 6–3 6–1), *Olympics 1r* (lost Appelmans [seed 16] 6–3 6–3); *r/u* Brisbane (d. Guse 6–3 6–1, Thoren 6–3 3–6 6–4, Kohde-Kilsch 6–3 6–3, Graham 7–5 6–3, lost Provis 6–3 6–2); *sf* Bayonne (d. Wasserman 6–3 6–3, Kohde-Kilsch 6–2 7–6, Van Lottum 6–3 7–5, lost Tauziat 6–3 6–2). *1992 HIGHLIGHTS – DOUBLES:* (with Provis) *Olympic bronze medal* (lost Martinez/Sanchez-Vicario 6–1 6–2); (with Collins) *r/u* Osaka (lost Stubbs/Sukova 3–6 6–4 7–5), (with Zrubakova) *r/u* Taranto (lost Coetzer/Gorrochategui 4–6 6–3 7–6), (with Van Lottum) *r/u* Clarins (lost Cecchini/Tarabini 7–5 6–1).

IVA MAJOLI (CRO)
Born Zagreb, 12 August 1977; lives Bradenton, Fla.; RH; 2HB; 5ft 8in; 122lb; final 1992 WTA ranking 50; 1992 prize money $46,050.
Coached by her brother Drago. At 12, she moved to USA to attend Bollettieri Tennis Academy. *1992:* Qf VS Houston (d. McNeil), Oakland (d. McNeil again) and Indianapolis (d. Tauziat) to break into top 50. Won St Simons and Evansville Challengers. *1992 HIGHLIGHTS – SINGLES: US Open 2r* (d. De Swardt 6–4 6–4, lost Labat 6–3 6–3); *won* St Simons Challenger (d. Bowes 7–6 7–6), *won* Evansville Challenger (d. Sugiyama 6–3 6–1).

KATERINA MALEEVA (BUL)
Born Sofia, 7 May 1969, and lives there; RH; 2HB; 5ft 6in; 122lb; final 1992 WTA ranking 16; 1992 prize money $266,207.
Coached by her mother, 9 times Bulgarian champion Yulia Berberian. Sister of Manuela and Magdalena. *1984:* (93) Won US Open Jun and was r/u to Sabatini at both Orange Bowl and French Open Jun while making her mark in women's play as well. *1985:* (28) Won Seabrook Island and Hilversum and stopped some of the big names in the sport like Shriver, Sukova and Garrison. *1986:* (28) Did not pass qf in 20 tournaments but won 26 of 47 matches. Played Fed Cup again with sister and mother. *1987:* (13) Beat Sukova 3r Mahwah, won Japan/Asian Open for first title since 1985, following with Athens and qualifying for VS Champs 1st time. *1988:* (11) Upset Sukova to reach f US HC and again *en route* to qf US Open. After reaching f Hamburg, won 1st primary circuit title at Indianapolis, beating Garrison in f. Qualified for VS Champs again. *1989:* (15) Won Bastad, Bayonne and VS Indianapolis; r/u Sofia. *1990:* (6) Won VS Houston (d. Navratilova and Sanchez-Vicario back-to-back), r/u Tampa (d. Sanchez-Vicario) and Canadian Open (d. Sabatini and took Graf to 3s), and appeared in 5 more sf. In GS reached qf Australian Open, French Open and Wimbledon. Broke into the top 10, overtaking her elder sister in the rankings in June, and qualified for VS Champs, where she lost qf to Graf. *1991:* (11) Finished the season in style by taking the title at Indianapolis, although she then fell 1r VS Champs to Sabatini. She was also r/u Toronto and VS Washington (d. M. J. Fernandez), sf Tokyo Nicherei and reached 5 more qf, including Australian Open. *1992:* Reached no f, but played sf Indian Wells, VS Houston, Tokyo Nicherei, Leipzig, Oakland and Indianapolis and reached qf Wimbledon to qualify for VS Champs, where she lost 1r to Martinez. *1992 HIGHLIGHTS – SINGLES: Australian Open last 16* [seed 10] (d. Graham 6–4 1–6 6–4, Housset 6–2 6–1, Sharpe 6–0 6–4, lost Sabatini [seed 3] 6–1 7–5), *French Open 2r* [seed 11] (d. Paradis Mangon 6–1 6–0, lost Brioukhovets 4–6 6–4 6–1), *Wimbledon qf* [seed 12] (d. Hall 6–2 6–2, Bollegraf 6–4 6–1, Endo 7–5 6–2, Halard 6–0 6–3, lost Navratilova [seed 4] 6–3 7–6), *US Open 3r* [seed 15] (d. Byrne 7–5 6–2, Monami 6–3 6–4, lost Rubin 6–4 3–6 6–4), *Olympics 2r* [seed 8] (d. Savchenko Neiland 7–6 6–2, lost Maniokova 7–6 4–6 6–0); *sf* Indian Wells (d. Emmons 6–2 6–0, Coetzer 6–2 6–2, Tauziat 4–6 6–4 7–5, lost Seles 6–1 6–0), *sf* VS Houston (d. Simpson Alter 6–2 7–6, Cecchini 6–2 6–3, lost Garrison 6–1 6–3), *sf* Tokyo Nicherei (d. Grossman 6–3 6–1, Werdel 6–4 6–4, lost Sabatini 6–3 6–3), *sf* Leipzig (d. Medvedeva 6–3 6–7 7–5, Wiesner 6–0 6–4, Huber 1–6 7–6 6–1, lost Graf 6–1 6–1), *sf* Oakland (d. Grossman 6–4 4–6 6–3, Fendick 4–6 6–1 6–1, lost Navratilova 6–1 6–2), *sf* Indianapolis (d. Cioffi 6–1 6–2, Rubin

6–1 6–2, Gildemeister 6–0 6–2, lost Harvey-Wild 6–4 7–6). *1992 HIGHLIGHTS –
DOUBLES:* (with Rittner) *won* Essen (d. Appelmans/Porwik 7–5 6–3); *r/u* Italian Open
(lost Seles/Sukova 6–1 6–2). *CAREER HIGHLIGHTS – SINGLES: Australian Open – qf
1990* (d. McNeil, McDonald, Jagerman, McQuillan 3–6 6–4 6–1, lost Sukova 6–4 6–3), *qf
1991*; *French Open – qf 1990* (d. Appelmans, Faber, Halard, Provis 3–6 6–3 6–3, lost
Novotna 4–6 6–2 6–4); *Wimbledon – qf 1990* (d. B. Romano, Date, DeVries, Herreman
6–3 6–0, lost Navratilova 6–1 6–1), *qf 1992*; *US Open – qf 1988* (d. Sukova 6–1 6–3, lost
Graf 6–3 6–0).

MAGDALENA MALEEVA (BUL)
*Born Sofia, 1 April 1975, and lives there; RH; 2HB; 5ft 6in; 109lb; final 1992 WTA ranking
20; 1992 prize money $183,403.*
Coached by Jan Kurtz and her mother, Yulia Berberian. Sister of Manuela and Katerina.
1988: Won Orange Bowl 12s. *1989:* (211) R/u Bari on Italian satellite circuit in first pro
tourn. *1990:* (72) In Jun singles won Australian Open (over Stacey), French Open (over
Ignatieva) and US Open (over Van Lottum). On the senior tour reached qf Wellington and
after upsetting Lindqvist at Wimbledon she moved into the top 100. *1991:* (38) Upset
Fairbank– Nideffer on her way to an unexpected appearance in last 16 Australian Open and
in April upset Kelesi *en route* to her 1st tour f at Bol, where she also teamed with Golarsa
to win the doubles. *1992:* Won her 1st tour title at San Marino and, unseeded, upset
Navratilova 2r US Open on her way to qf, where she retired against her sister, Manuela,
with a thigh injury. Upset Capriati and Sukova back-to-back at Tokyo Pan Pacific, where she
reached sf, as she did at Brisbane, and surprised Date *en route* to last 16 Olympics,
unseeded. *1992 HIGHLIGHTS – SINGLES: Australian Open 1r* (lost Hy 6–4 6–3), *French
Open 3r* (d. Provis 6–2 6–3, Allen 4–6 7–6 6–1, lost Zvereva 6–4 6–4), *Wimbledon 1r* (lost
Navratilova [seed 4] 6–2 6–2), *US Open qf* [unseeded] (d. Kroupova 6–2 6–1, Navratilova
[seed 3] 6–4 0–6 6–3, Po 6–2 6–3, Rubin 7–5 5–7 6–1, lost Maleeva Fragnière [seed 9] 6–2
5–3 ret'd), *Olympics last 16* [unseeded] (d. Zardo 7–5 6–1, Date [seed 14] 6–2 6–4, lost
Graf [seed 1] 6–3 6–4); *won* San Marino (d. Dopfer 6–1 6–1, Mothes 6–4 6–0, Perfetti 6–3
6–2, Dechaume 2–6 6–3 6–3, Federica Bonsignori 7–6 6–4); *sf* Brisbane (d. Kochta 6–1 6–2,
Alter 6–4 6–1, Zrubakova 6–4 7–5, lost Provis 4–6 7–5 6–2), *sf* Tokyo Pan Pacific (d. Schultz
7–6 6–4, Capriati 6–1 6–2, Sukova 6–2 6–4, lost Navratilova 6–2 6–2). *CAREER
HIGHLIGHTS – SINGLES: US Open – qf 1992.*

PASCALE PARADIS MANGON (FRA)
*Born Troyes, 24 April 1966; lives Paris; RH; 5ft 9in; 135lb; final 1992 WTA ranking 74; 1992
prize money $88,386.*
Coached by Patrick Faviäre. Husband Xavier Mangon (married April 1991). *1981:* Won
French Open Jun. *1983:* (87) Won French and Wimbledon Jun, reached last 16 US Open in
main draw and won Austrian Open. *1984:* (28) R/u Indianapolis and Pittsburgh; sf Brisbane
and Brighton. *1985:* (46) Beat Hanika and Turnbull to reach last 16 Wimbledon. Played Fed
Cup. *1986:* (129). *1987:* (102). *1988:* (20) Having appeared in no qf since 1984, she did so
at Brisbane, Kansas and VS Florida, going on to sf Eastbourne and the highlight of her year
with qf showing at Wimbledon. Upset Sukova (twice), M. Maleeva, Potter and Reggi
during the year and was voted WTA Comeback Player of the Year. *1989:* (121) Qf Mahwah.
1990: (169) Qf Bayonne and on the French satellite circuit won Limoges. *1991:* (74) Upset
Kohde-Kilsch and Dahlman in reaching sf Oslo and appeared in qf Linz. *1992:* Upset
Wiesner, Lindqvist and Cecchini on her way to f Linz; reached sf Bayonne and 4 more qf.
1992 HIGHLIGHTS – SINGLES: French Open 1r (lost K. Maleeva [seed 11] 6–1 6–0),
Wimbledon 1r (lost Hack 6–3 1–6 12–10), *US Open 2r* (d. Nowak 6–1 7–5, lost Schultz
6–2 6–0); *r/u* Linz (d. Maruska 6–3 6–4, Wiesner 6–3 6–3, Lindqvist 6–4 6–0, Cecchini 6–2
7–5, lost Medvedeva 6–4 6–2); *sf* Bayonne (d. Bacheva 4–6 6–3 6–2, Fusai 6–3 3–6 6–2, N.
Dahlman 6–4 6–0, lost Maleeva Fragnière 6–1 6–1). *1992 HIGHLIGHTS – DOUBLES:* (with
Testud) *r/u* Pattaya City (lost Demongeot/Medvedeva 6–1 6–1).

VERONIKA MARTINEK (GER)

Born Usti Nad Laben, Czechoslovakia, 3 April 1972; lives Nuremberg; RH; 2HB; 5ft 3in; 120lb; final 1992 WTA ranking 53; 1992 prize money $148,522.
Coached by her father, Vladimir, and travels with her mother, Jaroslava. Her family defected to West Germany from Czechoslovakia in 1980. **1987:** (397). **1988:** (115) Sf Taranto. **1989:** (157) Won Cava dei Tirreni on the Italian satellite circuit. **1990:** (111) Qf Strasbourg and Kitzbuhel and broke into the top 100 in autumn. **1991:** (64) Won her 1st main tour title at Sao Paulo. **1992:** R/u Sao Paulo, reached sf Prague and upset Capriati in FC Cup. **1992 HIGHLIGHTS – SINGLES: Australian Open 1r** (lost Sukova [seed 15] 6–3 6–2), **French Open 2r** (d. Sviglerova 6–2 6–1, lost Martinez [seed 7] 6–2 6–0), **Wimbledon 1r** (lost Fairbank Nideffer 7–6 6–1); **r/u** Sao Paulo (d. Avila 6–0 6–4, Santrock 6–4 6–0, Spadea 6–4 6–2, Gorrochategui 6–2 6–1, lost Hack 6–3 7–5); **sf** Prague (d. Bobkova 6–1 6–1, Pospisilova 7–5 6–0, Van Lottum 7–6 6–4, lost Kroupova 6–2 6–3).

NATALIA MEDVEDEVA (CIS)

Born Kiev, 15 November 1971, and lives there; RH; 2HB; 5ft 8in; 142lb; final 1992 WTA ranking 41; 1992 prize money $115,202.
Known as Natasha in CIS. **1987:** (196) ITF Jun Champ in doubles; won French Open and Wimbledon Jun doubles with Zvereva. In autumn won 3 consec. titles on LTA British circuit. **1988:** (305). **1989:** (66) Sf Moscow and extended Sanchez-Vicario to 3s at French Open. **1990:** (56) In singles won her 1st tour title at VS Nashville in Oct. and followed the next week with sf showing at Indianapolis. In doubles won Auckland and Wellington at the beginning of the year with Meskhi, with whom she upset Novotna/Sukova at VS Champs, and also took Puerto Rico with Brioukhovets in Oct. **1991:** (82) Reached sf Nashville in singles and won St Petersburg doubles with Brioukhovets. **1992:** Returned to the top 50 after winning Linz (upset K. Maleeva), and reached sf Pattaya City, plus qf Tokyo Suntory and Kuala Lumpur. **1992 HIGHLIGHTS – SINGLES: Australian Open 1r** (lost Capriati [seed 5] 6–2 6–0), **French Open 2r** (d. Babel 6–4 6–4, lost Novotna [seed 10] 6–4 6–1), **Wimbledon 2r** (d. Wood 6–3 6–3, lost Tauziat [seed 14] 7–5 2–6 6–3), **US Open 2r** (d. Frazier 6–4 6–1, lost M. J. Fernandez [seed 7] 3–6 6–3 6–1); **won** Linz (d. Golarsa 6–1 3–6 6–0, K. Maleeva 7–5 6–4, Porwik 6–7 6–1 6–3, Maniokova 6–3 6–2, Paradis Mangon 6–4 6–2); **sf** Pattaya City (d. Drake 6–1 6–2, Wasserman 6–2 7–5, Wang 6–2 6–4, lost Appelmans 6–4 6–3). **1992 HIGHLIGHTS – DOUBLES:** (with Demongeot) **won** Pattaya City (d. Paradis Mangon/Testud 6–1 6–1), **won** Kuala Lumpur (d. Hiraki/Langrova 2–6 6–4 6–1).

LEILA MESKHI (CIS)

Born Tbilisi, 5 January 1968, and lives there; RH; 2HB; 5ft 44in; 120lb; final 1992 WTA ranking 22; 1992 prize money $170,207.
Coached by Temuraz Kakulia and Olga Morozova. Husband Pavil Nadibaidze (married July 1989). **1986:** (241) No. 1 in ITF Jun doubles world rankings. In singles r/u Wimbledon Jun; in doubles won French Open Jun (with Zvereva), r/u Wimbledon (with Zvereva) and US Open Jun (with Brioukhovets). **1987:** (44) Reached 1st sf at VS Indianapolis, qf Athens and Chicago, and upset Bunge 2r Hamburg. **1988:** (46) R/u Singapore, sf Japan Open and Nashville (d. Potter), and stunned Shriver 2r US Open. **1989:** (30) Won VS Nashville (d. K. Maleeva and Kelesi); r/u VS Oklahoma. Joined her country's Fed Cup team. **1990:** (19) In singles she won Auckland and Moscow, was r/u Wellington and Indianapolis (upset K. Maleeva) and, after surprising Zvereva *en route* to qf US Open, she broke into the top 20. In doubles with Medvedeva won 2 titles and upset Novotna/Sukova at VS Champs. **1991:** (15) After winning Wellington and surprising Navratilova *en route* to f FC Cup, she found herself poised just outside the top 10, but despite also reaching f Bayonne and sf Washington, she was still unable to break in. **1992:** Upset Sabatini *en route* to sf San Diego and reached qf Sydney, FC Cup, Amelia Island, Hamburg and Italian Open. She was the only player to take a set off Seles at Australian Open, where she reached last 16, as she did at French Open. In doubles won an Olympic bronze medal with Zvereva. **1992**

HIGHLIGHTS – SINGLES: Australian Open last 16 [seed 13] (d. Gavaldon 6–2 6–2, Arendt 6–1 6–2, Kochta 6–1 7–6, lost Seles [seed 1] 6–4 4–6 6–2), *French Open last 16* [seed 15] (d. Garrone 6–1 6–3, Federica Bonsignori 6–1 6–1, Ferrando 1–6 7–6 6–4, lost Martinez [seed 7] 6–4 7–5), *Wimbledon 1r* (lost Sanchez-Vicario [seed 5] 6–3 7–6), *US Open 2r* (d. Dechaume 4–6 6–0 7–6, lost Sawamatsu 3–6 6–4 6–4), *Olympics 1r* (lost Pierce [seed 13] 7–6 7–5); *sf* San Diego (d. Appelmans 6–4 6–1, Date 6–2 6–3, Sabatini 6–0 6–3, lost Martinez 3–6 7–6 6–2). *1992 HIGHLIGHTS – DOUBLES:* (with Zvereva) *Olympic bronze medal* (lost G. Fernandez/M. J. Fernandez 7–5 2–6 6–2).*CAREER HIGHLIGHTS – SINGLES: US Open – qf 1990* (d. Kijimuta, Zvereva 6–4 6–0, Piccolini 6–2 4–6 7–6, Ferrando 7–6 6–1, lost Sabatini 7–6 6–4).

LARISA SAVCHENKO NEILAND (CIS)
Born Lvov, Ukraine, 21 July 1966; lives Urmala, Latvia; RH; 5ft 64in; 138lb; final 1992 WTA ranking 59 singles, 5 doubles; 1992 prize money $407,402.
Husband Alex Neland, manager of USSR Nat tennis team (married Dec. 1989). *1983:* Ranked 10 on ITF Jun list after reaching qf Wimbledon Jun and first Wimbledon doubles qf with Parkhomenko. *1984:* (138) Wimbledon doubles qf again. *1985:* (55) Third Wimbledon doubles qf and sf VS Denver in singles. Joined Fed Cup team. *1986:* (35) Showed affinity for grass courts, reaching sf Birmingham, qf Eastbourne, and upsetting Rehe at Wimbledon. Qualified with Parkhomenko for VS Champ doubles March and Nov.*1987:* (24) Won 4 doubles titles with Parkhomenko and ousted Navratilova/Shriver *en route* to sf Wimbledon. *1988:* (16) Upset Mandlikova and Sabatini as she swept to f VS California, upset Zvereva *en route* to sf Pan Pacific Open and Kohde-Kilsch *en route* to qf Eastbourne. Reached the same stage at US Open and Olympics and last 16 Wimbledon. In doubles with Zvereva r/u Wimbledon and VS Champs for which she qualified in both singles and doubles. *1989:* (20) Upset Navratilova *en route* to f VS California but then, frustrated by her poor form in singles, she talked of retiring after US Open. However, there she reached last 16, upsetting Shriver, and followed up with sf Moscow and r/u VS Chicago. In doubles won French Open and r/u Wimbledon and VS Champs with Zvereva, reaching 9 more f and winning 4. *1990:* (87) In singles qf Tokyo Toray and Birmingham. In doubles r/u French Open and won 3 titles with Zvereva, taking another with K. Jordan. Qualified for VS Champs with Zvereva but lost 1r to Adams/McNeil. *1991:* (48) Won her 1st singles at St Petersburg and reached sf Brisbane, upsetting Novotna. In doubles played 8 f with Zvereva, winning Wimbledon plus 5 others and r/u French Open to qualify for VS Champs; reached another 4 f with Novotna, winning 3 and r/u US Open; and won Auckland with Fendick. *1992:* In singles reached sf Auckland and last 16 Australian Open, unseeded. In doubles with Novotna won 7 titles and was r/u Wimbledon and US Open to qualify for VS Champs, where they were r/u to Sanchez-Vicario/Sukova. She won 1 more title each with Zvereva and Sanchez-Vicario and in mixed won Wimbledon with Suk. *1992 HIGHLIGHTS – SINGLES: Australian Open last 16* [unseeded] (d. Appelmans [seed 16] 7–5 6–2, Durie 6–4 4–6 6–1, Po 6–2 2–6 6–1, lost Sanchez-Vicario [seed 4] 6–1 7–6), *French Open 2r* (d. Collet 6–4 6–0, lost Pierce [seed 13] 6–2 6–3), *Wimbledon 1r* (lost Porwik 6–0 6–3), US Open 1r (lost Sanchez-Vicario 5–7 6–2 6–2), *Olympics 1r* (lost K. Maleeva [seed 8] 7–6 6–2); sf Auckland (d. Cueto 6–4 6–3, Tessi 6–3 7–6, Fulco Villella 6–2 6–4, lost Strnadova 6–3 3–6 6–2). *1992 HIGHLIGHTS – DOUBLES:* (with Novotna unless stated) *r/u* Wimbledon (lost G. Fernandez/Zvereva 6–4 6–1), *r/u* US Open (lost G. Fernandez/Zvereva 7–6 6–1); *won* Brisbane (d. Bollegraf/Provis 6–4 6–3), (with Zvereva) *won* VS Florida (d. Harvey-Wild/Martinez 6–2 6–2), (with Sanchez-Vicario) *won* LIPC (d. Hetherington/Rinaldi 7–5 5–7 6–3), *won* Light 'n Lively Doubles (d. Sanchez-Vicario/Zvereva 6–4 6–2), *won* Berlin (d. G. Fernandez/Zvereva 7–6 4–6 7–5), *won* Eastbourne (d. M. J. Fernandez/Garrison Jackson 6–0 6–3), *won* San Diego (d. Martinez/Paz 6–1 6–4), *won* Leipzig (d. Fendick/Strnadova 7–5 7–6), *won* Brighton (d. Martinez/Zrubakova 6–4 6–1); *r/u* FC Cup (lost Sanchez-Vicario/Zvereva 6–4 6–2), *r/u* VS Champs (lost Sanchez-Vicario/Sukova 7–6 6–1). *MIXED DOUBLES:* (with Suk) *won* Wimbledon (d. Eltingh/Oremans 7–6 6–2).

ROSALYN FAIRBANK NIDEFFER (USA)

Born Durban, South Africa, 2 November 1960; lives San Diego, Cal.; RH; 5ft 8in; 140lb; final 1992 WTA ranking 46; 1992 prize money $130,009.
Married her coach, sports psychologist Bob Nideffer (May 1989) and became a US citizen.
1978: Seemingly shy and somewhat portly, she displayed extraordinary court sense and a fine flat forehand in her drive to f Orange Bowl, losing to A. Jaeger. **1979:** Established herself firmly on women's tour, winning 22 of 23 matches on Australian satellite tour and reaching f NSW Open. **1980:** (33) Won Wimbledon Plate. **1981:** (43) Won French Open doubles with Harford. **1982:** (17) Won Indianapolis, sf Detroit and Fort Myers. **1983:** (26) Won Richmond. **1984:** (32) Sf VS LA. **1985:** (38) Beat Rehe in San Diego. **1986:** (30) Sf Canadian Open (d. Sabatini) and Brighton, r/u French Open mixed doubles with Edmondson, and sf Wimbledon and US Open doubles with Burgin. **1987:** (37) Reached last 16 Wimbledon, extending Evert to 7–5 fs. **1988:** (37) Reached qf Wimbledon, upsetting McNeil and Zvereva and extending Navratilova to 7–5 3s; sf San Diego and Newport. **1989:** (22) Unseeded, she reached qf Wimbledon again (upset Sabatini and M. J. Fernandez) and last 16 US Open. Sf Eastbourne and Newport in singles and in doubles reached 6 f, winning San Diego. **1990:** (24) Surprised Novotna *en route* to sf San Antonio and G. Fernandez in reaching the same stage at Birmingham. **1991:** (91) Her best performances came at Westchester where she reached sf singles and won the doubles with Gregory. **1992:** Upset Novotna on her way to sf Eastbourne and again 1r US Open. Reached 2 doubles f, winning Auckland with Reggi Concato. **1992 HIGHLIGHTS – SINGLES: Australian Open 3r** (d. Rubin 6–4 6–1, Emmons 6–4 6–2, lost Huber [seed 12] 6–0 7–5), French Open 2r (d. Po 3–6 6–4 6–2, lost Halard 6–2 6–2), **Wimbledon 3r** (d. Martinek 7–6 6–1, Adams 6–3 6–4, lost Garrison Jackson [seed 13] 6–4 6–2), **US Open 2r** (d. Novotna [seed 10] 6–3 7–6, lost Hack 7–5 6–4); sf Eastbourne (d. Werdel 6–3 4–6 6–3, Date 7–6 6–1, Brioukhovets 7–5 7–5, Novotna 6–1 6–3, lost Harvey-Wild 6–1 6–3). **1992 HIGHLIGHTS – DOUBLES:** (with Reggi Concato) **won** Auckland (d. Hetherington/Rinaldi 1–6 6–1 7–5); (with Magers) **r/u** Oakland (lost G. Fernandez/Zvereva 3–6 6–2 6–4). **CAREER HIGHLIGHTS – DOUBLES:** (with Harford unless stated) **French Open – won 1981** (d. Reynolds/P. Smith 6–1 6–3) (with Reynolds) **won 1983** (d. K. Jordan/A. Smith 5–7 7–5 6–2); **US Open –** (with Reynolds) **r/u 1983** (lost Navratilova/Shriver 6–7 6–1 6–3). **MIXED DOUBLES:** (with Edmondson) **French Open – r/u 1986** (lost Flach/K. Jordan 3–6 7–6 6–3).

MARY PIERCE (FRA)

Born Montreal, Canada, 15 January 1975; lives Villeneuve Loubet; RH; 2HB; 5ft 9in; 137lb; final 1992 WTA ranking 13; 1992 prize money $183,436.
Coached by her father, Jim. **1989:** (236) At 14 years 2 months at Hilton Head she was the youngest to make her pro debut – a record broken the following year by Capriati. **1990:** (106) Sf Athens. Moved to France and represented that country in Fed Cup. **1991:** (26) At Palermo she won both singles and doubles for her 1st career title, which took her into the top 50. Upset Fairbank Nideffer *en route* to last 16 LIPC and appeared in sf Puerto Rico. **1992:** Broke into top 20 after winning Cesena; followed with Palermo and Puerto Rico, plus sf Essen. Reached last 16 French Open and US Open, but was forced to withdraw from LIPC with leg and back strains. **1992 HIGHLIGHTS – SINGLES: French Open last 16** [seed 13] (d. Rajchrtova 6–1 6–1, Savchenko Neiland 6–2 6–3, Strnadova 7–6 6–4, lost Capriati [seed 5] 6–4 6–3), **US Open last 16** [seed 16] (d. Vento 6–2 6–2, L. Ferrando 7–5 6–4, R. White 6–2 6–1, lost M. J. Fernandez [seed 7] 6–0 6–4), **Olympics 2r** [seed 13] (d. Meskhi 7–6 7–5, lost Basuki 0–6 6–3 10–8); **won** Cesena (d. Wasserman 6–2 6–1, Reggi Concato 6–2 6–1, Ferrando 6–4 1–6 6–3, Nowak 6–1 6–1, Tanvier 6–1 6–1), **won** Palermo (d. Bobkova 6–4 6–1, Kroupova 6–3 7–6, Langrova 6–1 7–6, Farina 6–2 6–2, Schultz 6–1 6–7 6–1), **won** Puerto Rico (d. Fauche 6–1 4–6 6–0, Reinach 6–3 7–5, Arendt 6–0 6–1, Allen 6–1 6–4, G. Fernandez 6–1 7–5); **sf** Essen (d. Langrova 6–3 6–1, Oremans 6–4 6–3, K. Maleeva 6–3 7–5, lost Seles 6–0 6–1). **1992 HIGHLIGHTS – DOUBLES:** (with Martinez) **r/u** Philadelphia (lost G. Fernandez/Zvereva 6–1 6–3).

WILTRUD PROBST (GER)
Born Nuremberg, 29 May 1969; lives Neunkirchen; RH; 5ft 6in; 129lb; final 1992 WTA ranking 40; 1992 prize money $85,029.
1986: (135) Sf Taipei. ***1987:*** (98) Qf Wild Dunes and Hamburg. ***1988:*** (80) Qf Tampa. ***1989:*** (91) Sf Strasbourg, qf Auckland (d. Magers) and Bayonne. ***1990:*** (40) Won her 1st tour title at Wellington; r/u Eastbourne Under–21; sf Schenectady and upset Garrison *en route* to last 16 French Open, unseeded. ***1991:*** (128). ***1992:*** Won Waregem and reached qf Barcelona (d. Wiesner), Kitzbuhel and Filderstadt. ***1992 HIGHLIGHTS – SINGLES: French Open 2r*** (d. Nowak 7–5 6–0, lost Grossman 6–3 6–0), ***Wimbledon 1r*** (lost Provis 6–0 6–3); ***won*** Waregem (d. van de Zande 7–6 6–1, Monami 6–2 6–1, Zardo 7–5 6–2, Muns Jagerman 7–6 6–4, Babel 6–3 3–6 6–3). ***1992 HIGHLIGHTS – DOUBLES:*** (Coetzer) ***r/u*** Kitzbuhel (lost Labat/Dechaume 6–3 6–3).

NICOLE PROVIS (AUS)
Born Melbourne, 22 September 1969; lives Sandringham, Vic.; RH; 5ft 9in; 141lb; final 1992 WTA ranking 47 singles, 28 doubles; 1992 prize money $207,735.
Coached by Ken Richardson. ***1986:*** (105) R/u French Open Jun. ***1987:*** (77) R/u Australian Open Jun to Jaggard; won doubles with Devries. On senior tour qf Auckland and r/u Wimbledon mixed doubles with Cahill. ***1988:*** (33) Reached sf Strasbourg and qf North California and Berlin, but the high spot of her year came at the French Open, where, unseeded, she upset Kohde-Kilsch, Hanika and Sanchez, before taking Zvereva to 7–5 3s in sf. ***1989:*** (61) Reached last 16 Australian Open and sf VS Arizona. ***1990:*** (49) Reached last 16 French Open, unseeded, and qf VS Washington and Indianapolis. In doubles won Berlin and Strasbourg with Reinach, with whom she qualified for VS Champs, and was r/u French Open mixed with Visser. ***1991:*** (45) In singles reached sf Schenectady, qf Sydney and upset Gildemeister at Berlin and Martinez at VS Nashville. Reached 4 doubles f, winning Geneva and Birmingham with Smylie, with whom she qualified for VS Champs. ***1992:*** Won her 1st tour singles title at Brisbane and reached qf VS Oklahoma, where she won the doubles with McNeil. She also won an Olympic bronze medal in doubles with McQuillan and in mixed with Woodforde won Australian Open and US Open. ***1992 HIGHLIGHTS – SINGLES: Australian Open 1r*** (lost Sanchez-Vicario [seed 4] 6–2 6–1), ***French Open 1r*** (lost Magdalena Maleeva 6–2 6–3), ***Wimbledon 3r*** (d. Probst 6–0 6–3, Zrubakova 6–2 6–4, lost Tauziat [seed 14] 4–6 7–5 6–3), ***US Open 2r*** (d. Nagatsuka 6–4 6–2, lost Rubin 7–6 6–3), ***Olympics 2r*** (d. Piccolini 6–1 6–0, lost Appelmans [seed 16] 6–2 6–1); ***won*** Brisbane (d. Kamstra 6–1 6–1, Po 7–5 6–2, Frankl 6–3 6–2, Temesvari 6–3 6–0, Magdalena Maleeva 4–6 7–5 6–2, McQuillan 6–3 6–2). ***1992 HIGHLIGHTS – DOUBLES:*** (with McQuillan) ***Olympic bronze medal*** (lost Martinez/Sanchez-Vicario 6–1 6–2); (with McNeil) ***won*** VS Oklahoma (d. Adams/Bollegraf 3–6 6–4 7–6); (with Bollegraf) ***r/u*** Brisbane (lost Novotna/Savchenko Neiland 6–4 6–3). ***MIXED DOUBLES:*** (with Woodforde) ***won*** Australian Open (d. Woodbridge/Sanchez/Vicario 6–3 4–6 11–9), ***won*** US Open (d. Sukova/Nijssen 4–6 6–3 6–3). ***CAREER HIGHLIGHTS – SINGLES: French Open – sf 1988*** (d. Kohde-Kilsch 1–6 6–4 7–5, Hanika 7–6 7–6, Sanchez 7–5 3–6 6–4, lost Zvereva 6–3 6–7 7–5).

BARBARA RITTNER (GER)
Born Krefeld, 25 April 1973; lives Odenthal; RH; 2HB; 5ft 8in; 145lb; final 1992 WTA ranking 32; 1992 prize money $161,136.
Coached by Lutz Steinhofel. ***1989:*** (349). ***1990:*** (107) Enjoyed some success on the satellite circuits. ***1991:*** (43) Won Wimbledon Jun over Makarova and Australian Open Jun doubles with Habsudova. In the senior game she reached her 1st tour f at St Petersburg and appeared in qf Wellington, Puerto Rico and Leipzig. ***1992:*** A member of the winning German Fed Cup team, she won her 1st primary circuit title at Schenectady and upset Tauziat on her way to last 16 Olympics, unseeded. She also surprised Zrubakova at Sydney and Cecchini *en route* to sf Essen. ***1992 HIGHLIGHTS – SINGLES: Australian Open 2r*** (d. Schultz 6–1 3–6 6–4, lost M. J. Fernandez [seed 7] 6–4 6–4), ***French Open 2r***

(d. Szabova 6–3 6–3, lost Maleeva Fragnière [seed 8] 5–7 6–1 6–2), **Wimbledon 3r** (d. Tami Whitlinger 6–4 6–1, Frankl 6–0 6–0, lost Navratilova [seed 4] 7–5 6–1), US Open 1r (lost Strnadova 6–2 6–1), **Olympics last 16** [unseeded] (d. Labat 6–3 6–3, Tauziat [seed 10] 6–3 6–2, lost Sanchez-Vicario [seed 2] 4–6 6–3 6–1); **won** Schenectady (d. Majoli 6–3 6–2, Testud 6–7 6–3 6–3, Dechaume 6–2 6–2, Werdel 6–1 ret'd, Schultz 7–6 6–3); **sf** Essen (d. Cecchini 6–2 6–4, Paradis Mangon 6–3 7–6, Huber 4–6 3–1 ret'd, lost M. J. Fernandez 7–5 6–4). **1992 HIGHLIGHTS – DOUBLES:** (with K. Maleeva) **won** Essen (d. Appelmans/Porwik 7–5 6–3); **r/u** Italian Open (lost Seles/Sukova 6–1 6–2).

CHANDA RUBIN (USA)
Born Lafayette, La, 18 February 1976, and lives there; RH; 2HB; 5ft 6in; 128lb; final 1992 WTA ranking 68; 1992 prize money $82,575.
Coached by Ashley Rhoney. **1988:** Won Nat 12s and Orange Bowl in same age group. **1989:** Won Nat 14s. **1990:** (522). **1991:** (83) She announced her presence on the senior tour by upsetting Bollegraf at LIPC in spring, and at end of year borke into the top 100 after reaching her 1st tour f at Phoenix. **1992:** Surprised K. Maleeva on her way to last 16 US Open, unseeded, and upset Zvereva VS Florida. In the Jun game won Wimbledon over Courtois. **1992 HIGHLIGHTS – SINGLES: Australian Open 1r** (lost Fairbank Nideffer 6–4 6–1), **French Open 1r** (lost Schultz 6–2 5–7 6–4), **Wimbledon 1r** (lost Capriati [seed 6] 6–0 7–5), **US Open last 16** [unseeded] (Emmons 6–1 7–5, Provis 7–6 6–3, K. Maleeva [seed 15] 6–4 3–6 6–3, lost Magdalena Maleeva 7–5 5–7 6–1).

NAOKO SAWAMATSU (JPN)
Born Nishinomiya, 23 March 1973, and lives there; RH; 5ft 6in; 130lb; final 1992 WTA ranking 24; 1992 prize money $115,367.
Coached by Hiroyuki Bamba. Niece of Kazuko Sawamatsu, the 1975 Wimbledon doubles titlist. **1988:** Nat champ. **1989:** (256) Won Nagasaki on satellite circuit. **1990:** (31) Won Moulins Challenger, then, a wild–card entry, she beat 3 seeded players to win Singapore, having reached sf Tokyo Suntory 2 weeks earlier. These results saw her break into the top 100 and then top 50 in April. **1991:** (33) Unseeded, she upset Garrison 1r French Open *en route* to last 16, where she took Tauziat to 12–10 fs; r/u Pattaya City and reached sf Strasbourgb. **1992:** Unseeded at Wimbledon, she upset Wiesner on her way to last 16, where she took a set off Capriati. She was r/u Strasbourg and reached sf Tokyo Suntory. **1992 HIGHLIGHTS – SINGLES: French Open 1r** (lost Date [seed 14] 6–2 6–7 6–3), **Wimbledon last 16** [unseeded] (d. Tanvier 6–2 7–5, Strnadova 6–3 7–6, Wiesner [seed 16] 6–1 7–5, lost Capriati [seed 6] 6–3 4–6 6–4), **US Open 3r** (d. Fendick 6–1 6–3, Meskhi 3–6 6–4 6–4, lost Sanchez-Vicario [seed 5] 6–1 6–3), **Olympics 1r** (lost Huber [seed 7] 6–0 4–6 6–2); **r/u** Strasbourg (d. Emmons 6–2 6–3, Cioffi 6–4 6–4, Testud 6–3 3–6 7–5, de Swardt 6–3 6–3, lost Wiesner 6–1 6–3); **sf** Tokyo Suntory (d. Kijimuta 6–3 5–7 6–2, Demongeot 6–2 6–4, Reggi Concato 6–3 6–2, lost Appelmans 7–6 6–3).

BRENDA SCHULTZ (NED)
Born Haarlem, 28 December 1970; lives Heemstede; RH; 6ft 2in; 170lb; final 1992 WTA ranking 34; 1992 prize money $211,425.
Coached by Lada Travnicek. **1987:** (150) Won Chicago on USTA circuit, qf Paris Open. **1988:** (39) Won Wimbledon Jun over Derly and on the senior tour was a finalist at Oklahoma and Taipei. Upset Cecchini to reach last 16 French Open and also scored upsets during the year over Lindqvist, Hanika, Reggi and Fendick. **1989:** (85) Reached f Brisbane and last 16 Australian Open. **1990:** (43) Reached last 16 Wimbledon, unseeded; sf Brisbane (d. Rinaldi); qf Tokyo Toray and Oklahoma (d. Reggi). **1991:** (30) Produced some excellent results on grass, upsetting Kohde-Kilsch and Tauziat on her way to sf Birmingham and then surprising Novotna *en route* to an unexpected appearance in last 16 Wimbledon, where she extended Capriati to 3s. Then went on in Aug. to win her 1st main tour title at Schenectady. In partnership with Schapers, won longest set (56 games) and longest match in games (77) ever recorded in Wimbledon mixed doubles when they beat

Temesvari/Nijssen 6–3 5–7 29–27). *1992:* Won Birmingham, r/u Palermo and Schenectady and reached sf FC Cup. *1992 HIGHLIGHTS – SINGLES: Australian Open 1r* (lost Rittner 6–1 3–6 6–4), *French Open 3r* (d. Rubin 6–2 5–7 6–4, Frazier 6–1 3–6 6–2, lost Novotna [seed 10] 6–3 6–4), *Wimbledon 1r* (lost Tauziat [seed 14] 6–4 6–0), *US Open 3r* (d. Werdel 6–3 4–6 6–4, Paradis Mangon 6–2 6–0, lost M. J. Fernandez [seed 7] 6–4 6–2), *Olympics 2r* (d. Li 7–5 6–7 6–4, lost Graf [seed 1] 6–1 6–0); *won* Birmingham (d. Radford 7–5 4–6 11–9, Stubbs 6–3 4–6 6–2, Savchenko Neiland 7–6 7–6, Shriver 6–4 7–6, Byrne 6–2 6–2); *r/u* Palermo (d. Zivec Skulj 6–1 3–6 6–3, Pizzichini 6–2 6–3, Baudone 6–2 6–4, Ercegovic 6–4 6–2, lost Pierce 6–1 6–7 6–1), *r/u* Schenectady (d. Paradis Mangon 4–6 6–4 6–3, Tami Whitlinger 6–3 6–2, Kelesi 6–2 6–3, Labat 6–1 6–4, lost Rittner 7–6 6–3); *sf* FC Cup (d. Fairbank Nideffer 7–6 3–6 6–3, S. Martin 6–4 6–2, Martinek 6–2 6–2, Kuhlman 6–3 6–1, lost Sabatini 6–3 6–2).

PAM SHRIVER (USA)
Born Baltimore, Md, 4 July 1962, and lives there; RH; 6ft; 150lb; final 1992 WTA ranking 31 singles, 7 doubles; 1992 prize money $25,458.
Coached by Don Candy. *1978:* (13) At age 16 upset top-seeded Navratilova to become youngest finalist in US Open. *1979:* (33) Troubled by nagging shoulder injury, lost 1r US Open. *1980:* (9) Won La Costa and r/u Sydney (d. Navratilova). *1981:* (7) Won first Wimbledon doubles title with Navratilova, sf Wimbledon and Australian Open singles (d. Austin in both) and won Perth. *1982:* (6) Sf US Open (d. Navratilova). *1983:* (4) Sf US Open and won Brisbane. *1984:* (4) Won VS Chicago and r/u Mahwah. *1985:* (4) Won Sydney, Melbourne and Birmingham. Completed double GS with Navratilova by collecting 8th straight GS title in Paris, but record 109-match winning streak broken in f Wimbledon by Jordan/Smylie. *1986:* (6) Won 5th Wimbledon doubles title in 6 years with Navratilova. Won Birmingham and Newport and reached sf VS Champs in Nov. *1987:* (4) Played no singles from March until June, returning to win Edgbaston, Canadian Open (d. Evert 1st time), VS Newport and New England, beating Evert again. With Navratilova won Australian and French Opens for 3rd GS in doubles, won US Open doubles, VS Champs for the 6th time and won French Open mixed doubles with E. Sanchez. *1988:* (5) In singles won Brisbane, Sydney, Pan Pacific Open and Zurich and reached 4 more f, including VS Champs, where she beat Evert in qf and Graf (suffering from flu) in sf. In doubles won Australian Open, French Open and 7th VS Champs with Navratilova and Olympic gold medal with Garrison. However, a form of mononucleosis restricted her performance at Wimbledon, and she lost 2r US Open to Meskhi. *1989:* (17) Struggling to find motivation, she suffered a lacklustre year in singles with r/u Newport her best showing and failed to reach VS Champs in singles, although she qualified again in doubles with Navratilova. Won 8 doubles titles with various partners, including Australian Open and VS Champs with Navratilova, who ended their partnership before US Open, where Shriver was r/u with M. J. Fernandez. Teamed with Navratilova again in winning US Fed Cup team v Spain. *1990:* (66) Out of action from March having fractured her toe when she kicked a chair in frustration after a bad call v Van Rensburg at Boca Raton. She then withdrew from Wimbledon following arthroscopic surgery for a shoulder injury suffered the previous Dec. Sf VS Chicago. *1991:* (37) Returning after a 9-month absence and aiming to return to top 25 after her ranking had dropped a low as 116, she was unseeded at Australian Open in 1st GS for a year. Reached last 16 LIPC, upsetting Caverzasio and Gildemeister then d. Reggi at San Antonio and Sukova *en route* to qf Eastbourne. In doubles she reached 7 f, winning US Open and Brighton with Zvereva, a 7th VS Champs with Navratilova and Tokyo Nicherei with M. J. Fernandez. *1992:* Reached sf San Antonio and Birmingham (d. Garrison), plus qf Tokyo Pan Pacific, VS Chicago and Oakland (d. Garrison again). Reached 6 doubles f with various partners, winning 2 titles with Navratilova; they qualified together for VS Champs, but fell sf to Sanchez-Vicario/Sukova. *1992 HIGHLIGHTS – SINGLES: Australian Open 3r* (d. Stacey 6–0 6–1, Zvereva 6–4 7–6, lost Garrison [seed 11] 6–4 6–2), *Wimbledon 2r* (d. Brioukhovets 1–6 6–3 6–1, lost Capriati [seed 6] 6–2 6–4), *US Open 2r* (d. Perez 6–2 6–4, lost Graf [seed 2] 7–5 6–3); *sf* San Antonio (d. Rehe 7–6 3–6 7–5, Javer 6–2 6–3, McNeil 6–7 6–2 7–6, lost Navratilova 6–4 6–3), *sf* Birmingham (d. Allen 6–4 6–2, Jaggard Lai 6–4 6–1,

Garrison 7–5 6–3, lost Schultz 6–4 7–6). *1992 HIGHLIGHTS – DOUBLES:* (with Navratilova unless stated) *won* VS Chicago (d. Adams/Garrison 6–4 7–6), *won* San Antonio (d. Fendick/Strnadova 3–6 6–2 7–6); *r/u* Tokyo Pan Pacific (lost Sanchez-Vicario/Sukova 7–5 6–1), (Garrison Jackson) *r/u* VS Los Angeles (lost Sukova/Sanchez-Vicario 6–4 6–2), *r/u* Zurich (lost Sukova/Zvereva 7–6 6–4), (with Zvereva) *r/u* Filderstadt (lost Sanchez-Vicario/Sukova 6–4 7–5). *CAREER HIGHLIGHTS – SINGLES: US Open – r/u 1978* (d. Reid, Hunt, Navratilova 7–6 7–6, lost Evert 7–5 6–4), *sf 1982* (d. Navratilova 1–6 7–6 6–2, lost Mandlikova 6–4 2–6 6–2), *sf 1983* (d. Jaeger 7–6 6–3, lost Navratilova 6–2 6–1); *VS Champs – r/u 1988* (d. Hanika, Evert 7–5 6–4, Graf 6–3 7–6, lost Sabatini 7–5 6–2 6–2), *sf 1984* (d. Mandlikova, lost Navratilova), *sf 1986* (lost Navratilova 6–2 4–6 6–4); *Australian Open – sf 1981* (d. Desfor, Durie, Austin 7–5 7–6, lost Navratilova 6–3 7–5), *sf 1982* (lost Navratilova 6–3 6–4), *sf 1983* (d. Bassett 6–0 6–1, lost Navratilova 6–4 6–3); *Wimbledon – sf 1981*, (d. Ekblom, Little, Coles, Durie, Austin 7–5 6–4, lost Evert Lloyd 6–3 6–1), *sf 1987* (d. Hanika, Sukova 4–6 7–6 10–8, lost Graf 6–0 6–2), *sf 1988* (d. K. Maleeva, Garrison 6–4 6–4, lost Graf 6–1 6–2). *CAREER HIGHLIGHTS – DOUBLES:* (with Navratilova unless stated) *Australian Open – won 1982* (d. Kohde-Kilsch/Pfaff 6–4 6–2), *won 1983* (d. Hobbs/Turnbull 6–4 6–7 6–2), *won 1984* (d. Kohde-Kilsch/Sukova 6–3 6–4), *won 1985* (d. Kohde-Kilsch/Sukova 6–3 6–4), *won 1987* (d. Garrison/McNeil 6–1 6–0), *won 1988* (d. Evert/Turnbull 6–0 7–5), *won 1989* (d. Fendick/Hetherington 3–6 6–3 6–2), *r/u 1981* (lost K. Jordan/A. Smith 6–2 7–5); *French Open – won 1984* (d. Kohde-Kilsch/Mandlikova 5–7 6–3 6–2), *won 1985* (d. Kohde-Kilsch/ Sukova 4–6 6–2 6–2), *won 1987* (d. Graf/Sabatini 6–2 6–1), *won 1988* (d. Kohde-Kilsch/ Sukova 6–2 7–5); *Wimbledon – won 1981* (d. K. Jordan/A. Smith 6–3 7–6), *won 1982* (d. K. Jordan/A. Smith 6–4 6–1), *won 1983* (d. Casals/Turnbull 6–2 6–2), *won 1984* (d. K. Jordan/A. Smith 6–3 6–4), *won 1986* (d. Mandlikova/Turnbull 6–1 6–3), *r/u 1985* lost K. Jordan/Smylie 5–7 6–3 6–4); *US Open – won 1983* (d. Fairbank/Reynolds 6–7 6–1 6–3), *won 1984* (d. Turnbull/Hobbs 6–2 6–4), *won 1986* (d. Mandlikova/Turnbull 6–4 3–6 6–3), *won 1987* (d. K. Jordan/Smylie 5–7 6–4 6–2) [Zvereva] *won 1991* [Stove] *r/u 1980* (lost King/Navratilova 7–6 7–5), *r/u 1985* (lost Kohde-Kilsch/Sukova 6–7 6–2 6–3) (with M. J. Fernandez) *r/u 1989* (lost Mandlikova/Navratilova 5–7 6–4 6–4); *Olympics –* (with Garrison) *gold medal 1988* (d. Novotna/Sukova 4–6 6–2 10–8); *TS Champs – won 1982* (d. P. Smith/Reynolds 6–4 7–5); *VS Champs – won 1984* (d. Durie/Kiyomura 6–3 6–1), *won 1985–6* (d. Kohde-Kilsch/Sukova 6–7 6–4 7–6), *won 1986* (d. Kohde-Kilsch/Sukova 7–6 6–3), *won 1987* (d. Kohde-Kilsch/Sukova 6–1 6–1), *won 1988* (d. Savchenko/Zvereva 6–3 6–4), *won 1989* (d. Savchenko/Zvereva 6–3 6–2), *won 1991. MIXED DOUBLES:* (with E. Sanchez) *French Open – won 1987* (d. McNeil/Stewart 6–3 7–6).

ANDREA STRNADOVA (TCH)

Born Prague, 28 May 1972, and lives there; 5ft 9in; 130lb; RH; 2HB; final 1992 WTA ranking 37; 1992 prize money $166,854.
1988: (374). **1989:** (199) Won Wimbledon Jun singles (d. McGrath 6–2 6–3) and in Jun doubles with Sviglerova won Australian Open and r/u Wimbledon to finish No. 1 in ITF Jun doubles rankings. In the senior game won Darmstadt on the German satellite circuit. **1990:** (144) Won Wimbledon Jun singles over Sharpe and took doubles with Habsudova. Qf Leipzig and won Karlov Vary Challenger in the senior game. **1991:** (34) Upset Savchenko *en route* to 1st tour f at Auckland, and beat the same player to reach the same stage at Wellington the following week. Won WTA Most Impressive Newcomer award. **1992:** R/u Auckland, Pattaya City and Kuala Lumpur and upset Sukova on her way to qf Zurich. Reached 3 doubles f with Fendick, winning Strasbourg and qualifying for VS Champs, where they lost 1r to Sanchez-Vicario/Sukova. **1992 HIGHLIGHTS – SINGLES: Australian Open 3r** (d. Demongeot 6–3 6–4, Gildemeister 4–6 6–4 9–7, lost Sanchez-Vicario [seed 4] 1–6 6–0 6–3), *French Open 3r* (d. Werdel 0–6 6–2 6–4, Kidowaki 6–4 6–3, lost Pierce [seed 13] 7–6 6–4), *Wimbledon 2r* (d. Field 6–2 6–2, lost Sawamatsu 6–3 7–6), *US Open 3r* (d. Rittner 6–2 6–1, Helgeson 6–3 7–6, lost Maleeva Fragnière [seed] 6–7 6–3 6–2); *r/u* Auckland (d. Ercegovic 6–3 6–3, Gomer 6–3 6–3, Dechaume 7–6 6–7 6–2, Savchenko Neiland 6–3 3–6 6–2, lost R. White 2–6 6–4 6–3), *r/u* Pattaya City (d. Hiraki 6–2 6–1, Testud 6–3 6–3, Rottier 6–0 6–1, Basuki 4–6 6–2 6–2, lost Appelmans 7–5 3–6 7–5), *r/u* Kuala

Lumpur (d. Testud 6–3 6–1, Faull 6–0 6–2, Paradis Mangon 6–4 7–6, Javer 6–3 6–1, lost Basuki 6–3 6–0). *1992 HIGHLIGHTS – DOUBLES:* (with Fendick) *won* Strasbourg (d. McNeil/Paz 6–3 6–4); *r/u* San Antonio (lost Navratilova/Shriver 3–6 6–2 7–6), *r/u* Leipzig (lost Novotna/Savchenko Neiland 7–5 7–6).

RENNAE STUBBS (AUS)
Born Sydney, 26 March 1971; lives Kingsford; RH; 5ft 10in; 136lb; final 1992 WTA ranking unavailable.
1988: (352). 1989: (225). *1990:* (232) Won Perth on the Australian Satellite circuit. *1991:* (239). *1992:* Upset Zvereva Tokyo Pan Pacific and reached qf Eastbourne. In doubles won 2 titles with McNeil and 1 each with Sukova and Graf; qualified for VS Champs with McNeil, but fell 1r. *1992 HIGHLIGHTS – SINGLES: Australian Open 2r* (d. Bobkova 6–0 6–1, lost Li 7–5 6–2), *French Open 1r* (lost Harvey Wild 6–4 6–2), *Wimbledon 2r* (d. Baudone 6–2 7–5, lost McNeil 6–1 6–3).

HELENA SUKOVA (TCH)
Born Prague, 23 February 1965, and lives there; RH; 6ft 2in; 150lb; final 1991 WTA ranking 12 singles, 1 doubles; 1992 prize money $473,112.
Coached by Jaramir Jirik. Daughter of 1962 Wimbledon finalist, the late Vera Sukova, and Cyril Suk, former President of Czech Tennis Federation. Brother also named Cyril. *1981:* (74) Beat Anne Smith and Barbara Potter to reach last 16 Australian Open at age 16. *1982:* (24) Qf Swiss Open, r/u US CC and Avon Futures Champs. *1983:* (17) Sf Sydney. *1984:* (7) R/u Australian Open (d. Navratilova) and won Brisbane. *1985:* (9) R/u VS Champ and Eastbourne. Qf Australian Open. Voted WTA Most Improved Player. *1986:* (5) Won Canadian Open and Hilversum and r/u US Open (d. Evert Lloyd first time in 15 career meetings). *1987:* (7) Sf US Open, qf Wimbledon, won Eastbourne (d. Evert and Navratilova back-to-back) and New Jersey in singles and Wimbledon doubles with Kohde-Kilsch. Qualified for VS Champs in singles and doubles. *1988:* (8) In singles qf Australian Open, French Open and Wimbledon; r/u Sydney, Pan Pacific and Berlin. In doubles r/u French Open with Kohde-Kilsch, won Olympic silver medal with Novotna, took 4 titles and reached 7 other f with various partners. Qualified for VS Champs in singles and doubles, reaching sf in both and beating Navratilova in qf singles. *1989:* (8) At Brisbane she won her 1st title for 18 months, following with r/u Australian Open (d. Navratilova qf), qf US Open and 5 sf to qualify for VS Champs, where she reached qf. Tore cartilage in right knee at Eastbourne, which kept her out for 2 months, although she played Wimbledon with knee taped and won doubles there with Novotna. Appeared in 7 other doubles f, winning 4. *1990:* (14) Reached sf Australian Open, where she extended Graf to 3s, and was r/u Indian Wells, Birmingham and Brighton. Out for most of CC season undergoing treatment for Achilles' tendon problems, missing French Open singles and playing doubles there only at the request of her partner Novotna, with whom she won 8 of her 10 titles. They captured Australian Open, French Open and Wimbledon, but missed a GS in doubles when they lost US Open f to G. Fernandez/Navratilova. Qualified for VS Champs in both singles and doubles, losing 1r singles to K. Maleeva and 1r doubles to Medvedeva/Meskhi. *1991:* (17) In singles won Brisbane and reached sf VS Chicago (d. Capriati) and Filderstadt (d. M. J. Fernandez), but failed to pass 3r in GS. Qualified for VS Champs in singles and doubles (with Sanchez-Vicario) but was forced to retire 3s v M. J. Fernandez 1r. In women's doubles won 3 titles from 6 f with 4 different partners, and in mixed doubles won French Open with her brother, Cyril. *1992:* Won Osaka and Indianapolis, reached sf Montreal and Leipzig, and played 4 more qf. She had slipped so far down the singles rankings that she was unseeded at Wimbledon, although by year's end she had recovered some ground, despite her 1r loss to Capriati at VS Champs. With 4 different partners she won 9 doubles titles, including Australian Open, VS Champs and 4 others with Sanchez-Vicario. R/u US Open mixed with Nijssen. *1992 HIGHLIGHTS – SINGLES: Australian Open 3r* [seed 15] (d. Martinek 6–3 6–2, Jagerman Muns 7–5 6–3, lost Monami 2–6 6–4 6–4), *Wimbledon 3r* (d. Faull 3–6 6–1 7–5, Dechaume 7–5 6–2, lost Halard 4–6 6–1 6–3), *US Open last 16* [seed 13] (d. Lindqvist 6–0 6–4, Date 6–2 7–5, McNeil 6–2 6–3, lost Hy 6–1 7–6), *Olympics 2r*

[seed 11] (d. N. Randriantefy 6–0 6–1, lost Gavaldon 4–6 6–4 5–3 ret'd); **won** Osaka (d. Hiraki 7–5 7–6, Sawamatsu 6–1 5–7 6–2, Date 6–2 6–2, Gildemeister 6–2 4–6 6–1), **won** Indianapolis (d. Cunningham 6–1 6–3, Gavaldon 7–6 6–4, Tami Whitlinger 6–2 6–2, Wang 6–3 6–3, Harvey-Wild 6–4 7–5); sf Montreal (d. Wood 6–4 6–0, Oremans 6–0 7–5, M. J. Fernandez 6–3 3–6 6–4, lost Sanchez-Vicario 6–2 7–5), **sf** Leipzig (d. Babel 6–3 6–1, Meier 6–3 6–3, Martinez 3–6 6–2 6–2, lost Novotna 6–3 6–2). *1992 HIGHLIGHTS – DOUBLES:* (with Sanchez-Vicario unless stated) **won** Australian Open (d. M. J. Fernandez/Garrison 6–4 7–6); **won** Sydney (d. M. J. Fernandez/Garrison 7–6 7–5), **won** Tokyo Pan Pacific (d. Navratilova/Shriver 7–5 6–1), (with Stubbs) **won** Osaka (d. Collins/McQuillan 3–6 6–4 7–5), (with Seles) **won** Italian Open (d. K. Maleeva/Rittner 6–1 6–2), **won** VS Los Angeles (d. Garrison/Shriver 6–4 6–2), (with Zvereva) **won** Zurich (d. Navratilova/Shriver 7–6 6–4), **won** Filderstadt (d. Shriver/Zvereva 6–4 7–5), **won** VS Champs (d. Novotna/Savchenko Neiland 7–6 6–1). *MIXED DOUBLES:* (with Nijssen) *r/u* US Open (lost Provis/Woodforde 4–6 6–3 6–3). *CAREER HIGHLIGHTS – SINGLES:* Australian Open – *r/u 1984* (d. Kohde-Kilsch, Shriver, Navratilova 1–6 6–3 7–5, lost Evert Lloyd 6–7 6–1 6–3), *r/u 1989* (d. Richardson, Ludloff, O'Neil, Tanvier 7–5 6–4, Navratilova 6–2 3–6 9–7, Cordwell 7–6 4–6 6–2, lost Graf 6–4 6–4), *sf 1990* (d. Morton, Medvedeva, Loosemore 6–3 4–6 6–3, Date 6–4 6–3, K. Maleeva 6–4 6–3, lost Graf 6–3 3–6 6–4); *US Open – r/u 1986* (d. Drescher, Gomer, Bonder, Garrison 6–4 2–6 6–4, Turnbull 6–4 6–0, Evert Lloyd 6–2 6–4, lost Navratilova 6–3 6–2), *sf 1987* (d. Hobbs, Kohde-Kilsch 6–1 6–3, lost Navratilova 6–2 6–2), *qf 1984* (d. K. Jordan, lost Navratilova), *qf 1989* (d. Langrova, Magers 6–2 6–7 6–2, A. Minter 1–6 6–2 6–1, Savchenko 4–6 6–1 6–2, lost Graf 6–1 6–1); *VS Champs – r/u 1985–86* (lost Navratilova 6–3 7–5 6–4), *sf 1986* (lost Graf 7–6 3–6 6–1); *Wimbledon – qf 1986* (d. Parnell, Betzner, A. Minter, R. White 6–3 6–0, lost Evert Lloyd 7–6 4–6 6–4). *CAREER HIGHLIGHTS – DOUBLES:* (with Kohde-Kilsch unless stated) *Australian Open* – (with Novotna) **won 1990** (d. Fendick/M. J. Fernandez 7–6 7–6) **won 1992**, *r/u 1984* (lost Navratilova/ Shriver 6–3 6–4), *r/u 1985* (lost Navratilova/Shriver 6–3 6–4); *French Open* – (with Novotna) **won 1990** (d. Savchenko/Zvereva 6–4 7–5), *r/u 1989* (lost Navratilova/Shriver 4–6 6–2 6–2), *r/u 1988* (lost Navratilova/Shriver 6–2 7–5); *Wimbledon – won 1987* (d. Nagelsen/ Smylie 7–5 7–5)(with Novotna) **won 1989** (d. Savchenko/Zvereva, 6–1 6–2) (with Novotna) **won 1990** (d. K. Jordan/Smylie 6–2 7–6); *US Open – won 1985* (d. Navratilova/Shriver 6–7 6–2 6–3); *LIPC* – (Novotna) **won 1989** (d. G. Fernandez/McNeil 7–6 6–4) (Novotna) **won 1990** (d. Nagelsen/R. White 6–4 6–3); *VS Champs – r/u 1984–85* (lost Navratilova/Shriver 6–7 6–4 7–6), *r/u 1985–86* (lost Mandlikova/Turnbull 6–4 6–7 6–3), *r/u 1986* (lost Navratilova/ Shriver 7–6 6–3), *r/u 1987* (lost Navratilova/Shriver 6–1 6–1); *Olympics* – (Novotna) *silver medal 1988* (lost Shriver/Garrison 4–6 6–2 10–8). *MIXED DOUBLES:* (with Suk) *French Open – won 1991*.

NATHALIE TAUZIAT (FRA)

Born Bangui, Africa, 17 October 1967; lives St Tropez; RH; 5ft 5in; 120lb; final 1992 WTA ranking 14; 1992 prize money $271,305.

Coached by Regis DeCamaret. *1985:* (112) Reached 3r French Open, upsetting 16th seed Casale, and played Fed Cup. *1986:* (67) Qf Hilversum. *1987:* (25) Last 16 French Open, sf Strasbourg, San Diego and Zurich and d. Rinaldi to reach qf LIPC. *1988:* (27) Last 16 French Open, r/u Nice and upset Zvereva and K. Maleeva *en route* to f Mahwah. In doubles with Demongeot upset Kohde-Kilsch/Sukova to win both Berlin and Zurich and qualified for VS Champs. *1989:* (25) Sf Italian Open (d. Manuela Maleeva) and San Diego. *1990:* (18) In GS reached last 16 French Open, Wimbledon and US Open. Won her 1st primary circuit title at Bayonne; r/u Wichita and reached sf LIPC, Birmingham and Canadian Open (d. Maleeva Fragnière). Qualified for VS Champs, where she lost 1r to M. J. Fernandez. *1991:* (13) Appeared in her 1st GS qf at French Open and last 16 Wimbledon. In other tourns she scored some major upsets in reaching f Zurich (d. Sabatini), sf VS Palm Springs, VS Florida (d. M. J. Fernandez), Barcelona (d. Navratilova), San Diego and Bayonne and was close to beating Capriati at VS Champs, eventually losing their 1r match in 3s tb. Reached 3 doubles f, winning Bayonne with Tarabini. *1992:* R/u San Antonio and Bayonne and reached 9 more qf, including Wimbledon. Qualified for VS Champs, but lost 1r to Seles. *1992 HIGHLIGHTS – SINGLES:*

French Open last 16 [seed 12] (d. Gorrochategui 7–5 6–1, Helgeson 3–6 6–1 6–3, Wasserman 6–4 6–2, lost Bollegraf 6–4 1–6 6–2), *Wimbledon qf* [seed 14] (d. Schultz 6–4 6–0, Medvedeva 7–5 2–6 6–3, Provis 4–6 7–5 6–3, Frazier 6–0 6–3, lost Seles [seed 1] 6–1 6–3), *US Open 2r* [seed 12] (d. Ercegovic 6–3 6–2, Coetzer 6–0 6–0), *Olympics 2r* [seed 10] (d. Zrubakova 6–3 6–2, lost Rittner 6–3 6–2); *r/u* San Antonio (d. Fendick 7–6 6–3, Maniokova 6–1 6–3, Frazier 4–6 7–6 6–4, lost Navratilova 6–2 6–1), *r/u* Bayonne (d. Allen 6–3 6–3, Temesvari Trunkos 6–1 6–1, Rehe 6–4 7–6, McQuillan 6–3 6–2, lost Maleeva Fragnière 6–7 6–2 6–3). *1992 HIGHLIGHTS – DOUBLES:* (with Wiesner) *r/u* Barcelona (lost Martinez/Sanchez-Vicario 6–4 6–1). *CAREER HIGHLIGHTS – SINGLES: French Open – qf 1991.*

SHI-TING WANG (TPE)

Born Tainan, 19 October 1973, and lives there; RH; 2HB; 5ft 7 in; 128lb; final 1992 WTA ranking 55; 1992 prize money $40,021.
Coached by her father Wen–Chih. *1989:* Won French Open Jun doubles with Pratt. *1991:* (185) Won 5 titles on the Challenger circuit, including 4 in Taipei. *1992:* Upset Huber in reaching her 1st tour sf at Indianapolis, appeared in qf Pattaya City and Taipei and upset Basuki at Tokyo Suntory. *1992 HIGHLIGHTS – SINGLES: French Open 1r* (lost Housset 4–6 6–4 9–7), *US Open 1r* (lost Arendt 7–6 6–3); *sf* Indianapolis (d. Teri Whitlinger 6–1 6–1, Huber 6–2 6–3, Kochta 7–6 1–6 7–6, lost Sukova 6–3 6–3).

ROBIN WHITE (USA)

Born San Diego, Cal., 10 December 1963; lives Del Mar, Cal.; RH; 5ft 44in; 125lb; final 1992 WTA ranking 57 singles, 23 doubles; 1992 prize money $140,931.
Formerly coached by John Lloyd. *1984:* (105) R/u Wimbledon Plate. *1985:* (32) Last 16 US Open with win over Gadusek and won VS Hershey. *1986:* (20) Won 24 of 42 matches, upsetting Mandlikova and Sabatini to reach sf Eastbourne, and reaching last 16 Wimbledon. Qualified for VS Champ Nov. doubles with G. Fernandez. *1987:* (56) Qf New Orleans in singles and won 4 doubles titles. *1988:* (38) Upset Fendick to reach f North California Open. In doubles with G. Fernandez won US Open and Japan Open, reaching f on 4 other occasions to qualify for VS Champs. *1989:* (90) Qf San Diego was her best showing in singles, but in doubles she took 3 titles with G. Fernandez and won US Open mixed with Cannon. *1990:* (59) In singles reached sf Auckland and in doubles appeared in 6 f with different partners, winning 2 titles. *1991:* (101) Qf Tokyo Pan Pacific in singles, reached 2 f in women's doubles and r/u Australian Open mixed with Davis. *1992:* At Auckland she achieved her 1st singles title since VS Hershey in Pennsylvania in 1985. *1992 HIGHLIGHTS – SINGLES: Australian Open 3r* (d. Herreman 6–0 6–1, N. Dahlman 6–2 6–4, lost Martinez [seed 8] 7–5 6–0), *Wimbledon 1r* (lost Demongeot 6–2 6–3), *US Open 3r* (d. Frankl 6–0 6–3, Rehe 7–5 5–7 6–0, lost Pierce [seed 16] 6–2 6–1); *won* Auckland (d. Godridge 4–6 6–1 6–1, Martinek 6–2 6–1, Javer 3–6 6–3 6–1, Thoren 6–4 6–3, Strnadova 2–6 6–4 6–3). *1992 HIGHLIGHTS – DOUBLES:* (with M. J. Fernandez) *won* Tokyo Nicherei (d. Basuki/Miyagi 6–4 6–4). *CAREER HIGHLIGHTS – DOUBLES:* (with G.Fernandez) *US Open – won 1988* (d. Fendick/Hetherington 6–4 6–1). *MIXED DOUBLES:* (with Cannon) *US Open – won 1989* (d. McGrath/R. Leach 6–7 7–5 6–4).

JUDITH POLZL WIESNER (AUT)

Born Hallein, 2 March 1966; lives Salzburg; RH; 5ft 7in; 138lb; final 1992 WTA ranking 25; 1992 prize money $189,380.
Husband Heinz (married April 1987). Coached by Karel Safarik. *1985:* (305). *1986:* (142) R/u Kitzbuhel and played Fed Cup. *1987:* (34) Sf Bastad and Athens and d. Bunge *en route* to both qf VS Arizona and 2r Italian Open. *1988:* (36) Upset Zvereva to reach f Strasbourg, Cecchini and Hanika as she won her 1st pro singles title at Aix-en-Provence, Kohde-Kilsch to reach sf Italian Open and McNeil *en route* to last 16 US Open. *1989:* (35) Reached last 16 Australian Open and won Arcachon. In doubles won Strasbourg and reached 2 other f.

1990: (17) The high spot of her year came when she beat Novotna, Maleeva Fragnière and Martinez to make an unexpected appearance in f LIPC; also reached sf Brisbane, Sydney, Barcelona, Hamburg and Kitzbuhel to qualify for VS Champs, where she lost 1r to Maleeva Fragnière. *1991:* (16) R/u Kitzbuhel, upset Novotna twice *en route* to sf Hamburg and Filderstadt, and reached last 16 Wimbledon and US Open. Won the Karen Krantzcke Sportsmanship Award. *1992:* Won Strasbourg and reached 5 other qf, as well as winning Karlovy Vary Challenger over Sukova. *1992 HIGHLIGHTS – SINGLES: Australian Open 2r* [seed 14] (d. Tessi 6–4 6–3, lost Dechaume 6–2 7–6), *French Open 3r* (d. Labat 6–2 6–3, Frankl 6–3 6–2, lost Sanchez-Vicario [seed 4] 6–3 6–1), *Wimbledon 3r* [seed 16] (d. Kidowaki 6–2 6–2, Nowak 6–0 6–1, lost Sawamatsu 6–1 7–5), *US Open 2r* (d. Temesvari Trunkos 6–3 7–6, lost Hy 6–2 6–2), *Olympics 1r* (lost Martinez [seed 5] 4–6 6–1 6–2); *won* Strasbourg (d. Paradis Mangon 2–6 6–0 6–2, Labat 4–6 6–4 6–3, Fulco Villella 6–1 6–1, Sawamatsu 6–1 6–3), *won* Karlovy Vary Challenger (d. Sukova 6–4 7–6). *1992 HIGHLIGHTS – DOUBLES:* (with Tauziat) *r/u* Barcelona (lost Martinez/Sanchez-Vicario 6–4 6–1).

EMANUEL ZARDO (SUI)
Born Bellinzona, 24 April 1970; lives Giubiasco; LH; 2HB; 5ft 44in; 114lb; final 1992 WTA ranking 39; 1992 prize money $73,548.
1986: (294) Won Nat Jun Champ. *1987:* (254) Won 3 titles on satellite circuits and joined Swiss Fed Cup team. *1988:* (296). *1989:* (140) Won Oporto on Portuguese satellite circuit. *1990:* (63) Reached sf Geneva, qf Wellington, Palermo and Estoril, and broke into the top 100 in June. *1991:* (31) Moved into the top 50 when she won her 1st primary circuit title at Taranto, playing her 1st f. In addition she reached sf Palermo, won Caserta Challenger and took a set off Seles 2r US Open. *1992:* Won 2 Challenger titles and on the main tour was r/u Taranto and Clarins as well as reaching sf Lucerne. *1992 HIGHLIGHTS – SINGLES: Australian Open 1r* (lost Limmer 6–3 6–2), *French Open 2r* (d. Li 6–1 6–2, lost Sanchez-Vicario [seed 4] 6–3 6–1), *US Open 2r* (d. Demongeot 6–3 6–4, lost McNeil 6–1 7–5), *Olympics 1r* (lost Magdalena Maleeva 6–2 6–4); *won* Milan Challenger (d. Perfetti 6–4 6–4), *won* Reggio Emilia Challenger (d. Dragomir 6–1 7–6); *r/u* Taranto (d. Bottini 6–2 6–2, Golarsa 6–2 7–5, Martinek 7–5 7–5, Zrubakova 7–5 5–7 6–4, lost Halard 6–0 7–5), *r/u* Clarins (d. Testud 6–3 6–2, Ruano Pascual 6–2 6–2, Meier 6–0 6–1, Halard 3–6 7–6 6–4, lost Cecchini 6–2 6–1); *sf* Lucerne (d. Gorrochategui 6–7 6–3 6–2, Dechaume 6–3 6–3, Hack 7–5 7–5, lost Zrubakova 6–4 6–4).

RADKA ZRUBAKOVA (TCH)
Born Bratislava, 26 December 1970, and lives there; RH; 2HB; 5ft 64in; 138lb; final 1992 WTA ranking 29; 1992 prize money $145,498.
1985: In Jun doubles with Holikova won US Open and r/u French Open. *1986:* (409) Won US Open Jun doubles with Novotna. *1987:* (143) Won Helsinki on satellite circuit. *1988:* (35) Last 16 Australian Open, sf Hamburg, qf Taranto, Berlin (d. Mandlikova) and Filderstadt. *1989:* (32) Won 1st tour singles title at Brussels, reached sf Adelaide and upset Sukova at Filderstadt. *1990:* (57) Sf Bastad, upset Sukova again *en route* to qf Sydney and surprised Wiesner in reaching same stage at VS California. In doubles won Kitzbuhel with Langrova. *1991:* (23) Upset Magers at San Antonio, Kelesi at Hamburg and Meskhi *en route* to qf Berlin, before sweeping to the title at Strasbourg, surprising Gildemeister in the process. She then continued her upsetting ways by disposing of M. J. Fernandez to reach last 16 US Open, unseeded, and reached sf Kitzbuhel and Indianapolis. In doubles with Langrova won Clarins and r/u Linz. *1992:* Won Prague, r/u Lucerne and sf Taranto in singles. In doubles she reached 2 f with different partners. *1992 HIGHLIGHTS – SINGLES: Australian Open 1r* (lost Novotna [seed 6] 7–6 6–3), *French Open 1r* (lost Huber [seed 9] 6–2 6–2), *Wimbledon 2r* (d. Oeljeklaus 6–1 6–1, lost Provis 6–2 6–4), *US Open 1r* (lost Helgeson 7–5 7–6), *Olympics 1r* (lost Tauziat [seed 10] 6–3 6–2); *won* Prague (d. Strandlund 6–0 6–4, Kucova 6–0 6–1, Sviglerova 6–2 5–7 6–2, Kiene 6–2 2–6 6–3, Kroupova 6–3 7–5); *r/u* Lucerne (d. Ferrando 4–6 6–2 5–3 ret'd, Magdalena Maleeva 3–6 6–1 6–4, Zardo 6–4 6–4, lost Frazier 6–4 4–6 7–5); *sf* Taranto (d. Bobkova 6–3 6–0,

Spanish No.1 Arantxa Sanchez-Vicario reached the semi-finals or better at no less than 15 tournaments to consolidate her world ranking of No.4. *(M. Cole)*

Frankl 6–3 6–4, Grossman 6–0 6–2, lost Zardo 7–5 5–7 6–4). *1992 HIGHLIGHTS –*
DOUBLES: (with McQuillan) *r/u* Taranto (lost Coetzer/Gorrochategui 4–6 6–3 7–6), (with
Martinez) *r/u* Brighton (lost Novotna/Savchenko Neiland 6–4 6–1).

NATALIA ZVEREVA (CIS)
Born Minsk, 16 April 1971, and lives there; RH; 2HB; 5ft 8in; 138lb; final 1992 WTA ranking
23 singles, 2 doubles; 1992 prize money $657,694.
Nicknamed Natasha. Coached by her father, Marat Zverev. *1985:* Won Bethesda on USTA
circuit and World Jun Champs. *1986:* (92) In singles won Soviet Nat Champs (d.
Savchenko), won Wimbledon Jun singles, USTA Bethesda, and was r/u to Rinaldi at VS
Arkansas after qualifying, becoming youngest player to reach f of VS Series event, at 15
years 7 months. In doubles won French Open Jun and r/u Wimbledon Jun with Meskhi.
1987: (19) ITF Jun Champ; won Nat Champ, Jun singles at French Open, Wimbledon and
US Open and Jun doubles at French Open and Wimbledon with Medvedeva. Did not
compete in Australian Open Jun. Last 16 Wimbledon, beating McNeil and extending
Sabatini to 3s; won Taranto on Italian satellite and reached f in Arkansas and Chicago in
consecutive weeks. *1988:* (7) Played her best tennis to upset Navratilova last 16 French
Open, but disappointed in her 1st GS f there, being totally outclassed 6–0 6–0 in 32
minutes by Graf. Last 16 Wimbledon, qf Olympics, r/u Eastbourne, New England and
Montreal (d. Navratilova and Shriver back-to-back). In doubles with Savchenko r/u
Wimbledon and won 2 titles. At VS Champs reached qf in singles and r/u in doubles. Voted
WTA Newcomer of the Year. *1989:* (27) Was less successful in singles, winning no title,
although she reached f FC Cup (d. Navratilova) and Moscow plus 3 more sf. However, in
doubles with Savchenko she won French Open, was r/u Wimbledon and VS Champs and
reached 7 other f, winning 4. *1990:* (12) Won 1st senior singles title at Brisbane (upset
Sukova qf), following with Sydney the next week. Sf Washington, FC Cup, Amelia Island
(extending Graf to 3s) and Berlin; qf Wimbledon. In doubles with Savchenko r/u French
Open and won 3 titles; in mixed with Pugh won Australian Open and r/u US Open.
Qualified for VS Champs in singles and doubles, losing 1r singles to Sanchez-Vicario and 1r
doubles to Adams/McNeil. *1991:* (21) In singles r/u Birmingham, sf FC Cup and reached
last 16 Australian Open and US Open. In doubles GS won Wimbledon and r/u French Open
with Savchenko and teamed with Shriver 1st time to win US Open. She also won VS
Florida, Berlin, Eastbourne, Toronto and Los Angeles with Savchenko, Brighton with
Shriver and FC Cup with Kohde-Kilsch, as well as reaching 4 more f with various partners,
qualifying for VS Champs with Savchenko. In mixed doubles, r/u Wimbledon with Pugh.
1992: Unseeded in all the major tourns, she always made her mark. At French Open she
upset Appelmans to reach qf, where she took a set off Graf; she reached the same stage
at Wimbledon, upsetting Martinez and Garrison; at US Open she extended Sabatini to 3s
and at Olympics she upset Novotna on her way to last 16. She also upset Navratilova at FC
Cup, reaching qf there as well as at Italian Open, Oakland and Philadelphia. Yet it was in
doubles where she really excelled, reaching 13 f, from which she won French Open,
Wimbledon, US Open plus 2 others with G. Fernandez, 2 with Sanchez-Vicario, 1 with
Savchenko Neiland and 1 with Sukova. In addition she won an Olympic bronze medal with
Meskhi and qualified for VS Champs with G. Fernandez, losing sf to Novotna/Savchenko
Neiland. *1992 HIGHLIGHTS – SINGLES: Australian Open 2r* (d. Thoren 6–4 6–4, lost
Shriver 6–4 7–6), *French Open qf* [unseeded] (d. Kohde-Kilsch 6–2 6–3, Appelmans [seed
16] 6–1 7–6, Magdalena Maleeva 6–4 6–4, Hack 6–3 6–3, lost Graf [seed 2] 6–3 6–7 6–3),
Wimbledon qf [unseeded] (d. Herreman 6–3 6–2, Martinez [seed 8] 6–3 5–7 6–4, McNeil
5–7 6–4 7–5, Garrison [seed 13] 6–2 3–6 6–1, lost Graf [seed 2] 6–3 6–1), *US Open 3r* (d.
Graham 6–3 6–2, Li 6–1 6–2, lost Sabatini [seed 4] 6–4 5–7 6–4), *Olympics last 16*
[unseeded] (d. Novotna [seed 9] 6–1 6–0, Smith 6–1 6–2, lost M. J. Fernandez [seed 4] 7–6
6–1). *1992 HIGHLIGHTS – DOUBLES:* (with G. Fernandez unless stated) *won* French
Open (d. Martinez/Sanchez-Vicario 6–3 6–2), *won* Wimbledon (d. Novotna/Savchenko
Neiland 6–4 6–1), *won* US Open (d. Novotna/Savchenko Neiland 7–6 6–1), (with Meskhi)
Olympic bronze medal (lost G. Fernandez/M. J. Fernandez 7–5 2–6 6–2); (with

Savchenko Neiland) *won* VS Florida (d. Harvey-Wild/Martinez 6–2 6–2), (with Sanchez-Vicario) *won* FC Cup (d. Novotna/Savchenko Neiland 6–4 6–2), (with Sanchez-Vicario) *won* Amelia Island (d. Garrison/Novotna 6–1 6–0), (with Sukova) *won* Zurich (d. Navratilova/Shriver 7–6 6–4), *won* Oakland (d. Fairbank Nideffer/Magers 3–6 6–2 6–4), *won* Philadelphia (d. Martinez/Pierce 6–1 6–3); (with Sanchez-Vicario) *r/u* Light 'n Lively Doubles (lost Novotna/Savchenko Neiland 6–4 6–2), *r/u* Berlin (lost Novotna/Savchenko Neiland 7–6 4–6 7–5), *r/u* Montreal (lost McNeil/Stubbs 3–6 7–5 7–5), (with Shriver) *r/u* Filderstadt (lost Sanchez-Vicario/Sukova 6–4 7–5).

ALL-TIME GREATS

David Gray and John Barrett

WILMER LAWSON ALLISON (USA)
Born 8/1/04. Died 30/4/77. One of the greatest and most spectacular of American doubles specialists, he also gained some notable singles successes. Possessing a fierce smash, a serve with the kick of a Texas mustang', considerable power on the volley, and a fine backhand drive, he found an ideal doubles partner in John Van Ryn. They won at Wimbledon in *1929–30* and were runners–up in *1935.* They took the US title in *1931* and *1935* and reached the final in *1930/32/34/36.* His singles form was less consistent, but on his day could play brilliantly. He defeated Perry to win the US title in *1935,* and in *1930,* after beating Cochet, he was runner-up to Tilden at Wimbledon. Between *1929–35* he played in 45 D Cup rubbers, winning 18 out of 29 singles and 14 of his 16 doubles.

JOSEPH ASBOTH (Hungary)
Born 18/9/17. A stylish righthander whose victory in the *1947* French singles, when he beat Petra, Tom Brown and Sturgess, was Hungary's most important tennis success before their victory in the Saab King's Cup in 1976; 7 times nat champ; 6 times winner of the Hungarian int title; he played 1st at Wimbledon in *1939* and impressed those who saw him against Austin in 1 r. Lost to Bromwich in the *1948* sfs. From *1938–57* he played 41 D Cup rubbers in 16 ties.

ARTHUR ROBERT ASHE (USA)
Born 10/7/43. Died 6/2/93. A cool, thoughtful, dogged competitor, he was the first black American to win the Wimbledon men's singles title and, in *1968,* playing as an amateur, he became the first US Open champion. Always happier on fast courts, he tried hard to succeed on clay but endured regular disappointments in Paris and never progressed further than the semi–finals *(1971)* in Rome. He was a semi-finalist at Wimbledon *1968–69* before surprising Connors in the *1975* final. He defeated Okker to win the US title in *1968* but in *1972* lost to Nastase after leading by two sets to one and 4–2 in the final. He won Australian singles *1970* and the WCT title *1975.* Refused a visa to South Africa in 1970, he broke through apartheid laws to play in Johannesburg *1973,* losing to Connors in the final and winning the doubles with Okker. After missing most of the 1977 season, he regained his place among the leaders of the circuit in *1978* and reached match-point against McEnroe in the Masters final. Between *1963–78,* he appeared in 18 *D Cup* ties, winning 27 out of 32 singles and one of two doubles. US *D Cup* captain *1980–85,* following his retirement from active play owing to a heart condition that had necessitated triple by–pass surgery.

CILLY AUSSEM (Germany)
Born 4/1/09. Died 22/3/63. Later the Contessa della Corta Brae. The first German to win the women's singles at Wimbledon. Her strokes were not strong but she was a model of steadiness and persistence. Quite small and more of a girl in appearance with round brown eyes and a cherub face', wrote Helen Wills. Her agility on court and the distance that she covers in spite of her shortness are really astonishing.' *1931* – when the Californian did not compete – was her best year. She beat Betty Nuthall in the French f and then defeated Hilde Krahwinkel in Wimbledon's only all–German final. That was a disappointing match, because both women were handicapped by blistered feet. Her victory compensated for an

unlucky failure in *1930.* Then she slipped and sprained an ankle at 4–4 in the fs of her sf against Elizabeth Ryan and had to be carried from the court.

HENRY WILFRED AUSTIN (Great Britain)
Born 20/8/06. Bunny Austin's Wimbledon record was remarkable (and unlucky), but his most important contribution to British tennis was in the D Cup. The possessor of elegant groundstrokes, which compensated for a lack of power in his serving and smashing, he played many of the crucial singles, alongside Perry, in Britain's successful campaigns in the 1930s. A former Cambridge Univ captain, he played in 24 ties between *1929–37,* winning 36 of his 48 rubbers, all singles. He won 8 rubbers out of 12 and 5 out of 8 live' rubbers in his 6 Challenge Rounds. At Wimbledon he failed only once to reach the qf or go further between *1929–39.* R/u to Vines *1932* and Budge *1938,* in sf *1929* and *1936/37,* and r/u to Henkel in *1937* French singles.

WILFRED BADDELEY (Great Britain)
Born 11/1/1872. Died 30/1/1929. Youngest winner – at 19 years, 5 months and 23 days – of Wimbledon singles in *1891* until Becker in 1985. Also won singles in *1892/95,* and doubles (with twin brother Herbert) *1891/94/95/96.*

MARCEL BERNARD (France)
Born 18/6/14. Shrewd and stylish, a canny lefthander with considerable touch, he is one of only two French players to have won in Paris since the days of the Musketeers' (the other is Noah, 1983); demonstrated his promise early, reaching the French singles sf and, with Boussus, the doubles in *1932,* still in sufficient form to be chosen for the French D Cup team in *1956.* In *1946* he won 5 set matches against Petra in the sf and Drobny in the final to take the French title; in sf on 3 other occasions; won the doubles with Borotra *(1936)* and with Petra *(1946)* and the mixed with Lollette Payot *(1935)* and Billie Yorke *(1936).* Between *1935–56* he played 42 D Cup rubbers in 25 ties and he has also served as president of the French Tennis Federation.

PAULINE MAY BETZ (USA)
Born 6/8/19. Now Mrs Addie. An agile, athletic competitor, who might have gained many more titles if the war had not interrupted international competition. She was ranked eighth in the US in *1939* and was the most successful player in wartime competitions there, winning the national title from *1942–44.* She won Wimbledon at a cost of only 20 games in *1946,* defeating Louise Brough 6–2 6–4 in the final. She and Miss Hart were runners–up to Miss Brough and Miss Osborne in the doubles and, if she was disappointed in Paris, where Miss Osborne beat her 1–6 8–6 7–5 in the final, after saving two match–points with drop–shots at 5–6 in the second set, she asserted her supremacy again at Forest Hills by defeating Doris Hart 11–9 6–3 in the final. Soon afterwards she turned professional.

BLANCHE BINGLEY (Great Britain)
Born 3/11/1863. Died 6/8/1946. Became Mrs Hillyard. One of the determined pioneers of women's tennis. She competed in the first women's tournament at Wimbledon in *1884* and lost to Maud Watson, the eventual champion, in sfs. The following year Miss Watson defeated her in f, but she avenged those failures by beating the champion in the challenge round in *1886.* That was the first of her six victories. Further successes followed in *1889/94/97/99* and *1900.* Only Lottie Dod, who retired in 1893, troubled her until Mrs Sterry ended her supremacy in 1901. Like many early players, her game was founded on a powerful forehand and strict command of length. A reluctant volleyer who invariably ran round her backhand, she was so quick and so fit that she was difficult to outmanoeuvre. She wore white gloves to give her a better grip and her follow-through on the forehand was said to have been so complete that her left shoulder was often a mass of bruises from the impact of the racket'. She married Commander G. W. Hillyard, secretary of the All England Club from 1907–24; altogether she competed in the championships 24 times.

PENELOPE DORA HARVEY BOOTHBY (Great Britain)
Born 2/8/1881. Died 22/2/1970. Became Mrs Green. One of the group of players from the county of Middlesex who dominated the early years of women's tennis at Wimbledon. She won one of the most exciting of the pre-1914 f, defeating Miss A. M. Morton 6–4 4–6 8–6 (Few closer or more interesting struggles have ever been witnessed on the famous old court', wrote G. W. Hillyard) in *1909,* and lost the most dismal in the history of the championships to Mrs Lambert Chambers, who beat her 6–0 6–0, in the *1911* challenge round. Mrs Lambert Chambers had beaten her by the same score at the Beckenham tournament two weeks earlier and had allowed her only four games in the challenge round in *1910.* Somewhat fortunately she and Mrs McNair became Wimbledon's first women's doubles champions in 1913. They were down 2–6 2–4 to Mrs Lambert Chambers and Mrs Sterry in the final when Mrs Sterry fell and retired with a torn tendon. She and Mrs McNair were also semi-finalists in *1922.*

BJORN BORG (Sweden)
Born 6/6/56. One of the coolest match players the game has ever known, he matured early, winning his first important title, the *1974* Italian Open, shortly before his 18th birthday and the first of his six French Championships just after it. With fierce topspin on both his forehand and his double-handed backhand, a powerful serve and speedy court coverage plus an indomitable will to win, he was virtually invincible on European clay between *1974–81* adding the French Open in *1975/78/79/80/81* and a second Italian title in *1978* as well as the US Pro Championship on US clay in *1974/75/76.* Never an instinctive volleyer, he confounded those observers who thought his game was unsuited to grass by setting a modern record at Wimbledon where he won five successive titles between *1976–80.* Only William Renshaw, in the days of the Challenge Round, won more (1881–86). He learned to win indoors, taking the WCT title in *1976* and the Masters twice *(1979/80)* and leading Sweden to their first D Cup success, a 3–2 victory over Czechoslovakia in Stockholm in *1975.* But he never solved the problems of the high, fast bounce and positive foothold of US hard courts. Four times he was beaten in the US Open final, twice by Connors *(1976/78)* and twice by McEnroe *(1980/81),* the last three being on asphalt at Flushing Meadow. By the autumn of *1981* this great champion felt burnt out and virtually retired from the mainstream, restricting his play to exhibitions and special events. Although he attempted two comebacks, in *1982/84,* he could no longer make the total commitment that had once made him supreme and turned to other interests. Seven years later he again attempted a return but fell in his first match to Jordi Arrese in Monte Carlo and competed no more in 1991. His legacy to Swedish tennis is immeasurable for he sparked the flame that has burned so brightly ever since through Wilander, Sundstrom, Jarryd, Nystrom and Edberg. His style of errorless, counter-attacking topspin inspired a whole generation of players around the world.–J.B.

JEAN BOROTRA (France)
Born 13/8/1898. A brilliantly agile volleyer and a shrewd player. One of the Four Musketeers' who won the D Cup for France from *1927–32.* Enthusiastic and popular, he continued to play competitive lawn tennis long past his 80th year, regularly appearing for France in International Club matches against Britain. Won Wimbledon singles *1924/26* and doubles (with R. Lacoste) *1925* and (with J. Brugnon) *1932/33.* French singles *1924/31,* and doubles *1924/25/28/29/34/36.* Won Australian singles and doubles *1928.* Had long and spectacular covered court record, winning French singles title 12 times, British 11, and US 4. Played 54 D Cup rubbers *1922–47,* winning 36 in 32 ties.

MAUREEN CONNOLLY BRINKER (USA)
Born 17/9/34. Died 21/6/69. The most determined and concentrated of post-war women's champions she hit her groundstrokes with remorseless accuracy. Won US singles in *1951* at the age of 16 and thereafter lost only 4 matches – 2 to Doris Hart, one to Shirley Fry, and another to Beverley Fleitz – before she broke her leg in a riding accident in 1954 and retired. She was never beaten in singles at Wimbledon, winning *1952/53/54.* US singles *1951/52/ 53.* French singles *1953/54* and (with Mrs H. C. Hopman) doubles *1954.*

Australian singles and doubles (with Julie Sampson) *1953*. Italian singles *1954.* She won all 9 of her W Cup rubbers and in *1953* she was the first woman to bring off the Grand Slam of the 4 major singles titles in the same year.

JOHN EDWARD BROMWICH (Australia)
Born 14/11/18. A gracefully unorthodox player whose career might have been even more successful if it had not been interrupted by World War II. Ambidextrous but using both hands on the forehand, he used a very light, softly strung racket to control the ball with great subtlety. He won the Australian singles in *1939* and regained the title from Quist in *1946.* Those were his only major singles victories, although he was agonisingly close to success in f of *1948* Wimbledon when he lost to Falkenburg after leading 5–2 in the fs and holding three match-points. But it was in doubles, mostly with Quist or Sedgman, that he earned most honours. He won at Wimbledon in *1948* (with Sedgman) */50* (with Quist), took the US title three times, and he and Quist ruled in Australia from *1938–40* and *1946–50.* Won the Wimbledon mixed with Louise Brough, *1947/48,* and played in 53 D Cup rubbers between *1937–50.*

SIR NORMAN EVERARD BROOKES (Australia)
Born 14/11/1877. Died 10/1/1968. The first overseas winner of men's singles at Wimbledon. Left-handed and a notable volleyer, he lost to H. L. Doherty in Challenge Round on first visit to Wimbledon 1905. Won singles and doubles (with A. F. Wilding) *1907* and *1914* and Australian singles in *1911* and doubles in *1924* with J. O. Anderson. With Wilding won the D Cup for Australasia in *1907.* Between *1905–20* he played 39 rubbers and was 6 times a member of a side which won the Challenge Round. Returned to Wimbledon in *1924* at 46 and reached the 4r.

ALTHEA LOUISE BROUGH (USA)
Born 11/3/23. Now Mrs Clapp. An aggressive server and volleyer, she played a major part in establishing American domination of women's tennis immediately after World War II. Won Wimbledon singles *1948/49/50* and again in *1955* after the retirement of Maureen Connolly (who beat her in *1952* and *1954* f), US in *1947,* and Australian, *1950.* She and Margaret Osborne du Pont formed a redoubtable doubles partnership, winning 5 times at Wimbledon and 3 times in Paris, and holding the US title from *1942–50* and *1955–57.* She was mixed doubles champ at Wimbledon *1946/47/48/50* and took all 3 titles in *1948* and *1950.* She played 22 W Cup rubbers between *1946–57* and was never beaten.

JACQUES BRUGNON (France)
Born 11/6/1895. Died 20/3/1978. The doubles specialist of the Four Musketeers', he gained most of his early success with Cochet and then formed a partnership with Borotra, which was still capable of reaching the *1939* French f, when he was 44 and Borotra 40, and coming three times within a point of the title. He and Borotra returned to Wimbledon and reached the 3r in *1948.* Won Wimbledon doubles *1926/28* (Cochet) */32/33* (Borotra). Between *1927–34* won French doubles 3 times with Cochet and twice with Borotra. Also Australian doubles (with Borotra) in *1928.* Reached singles sf at Wimbledon, *1926.* Played 31 D Cup doubles and 6 singles *1921–34.*

JOHN DONALD BUDGE (USA)
Born 13/6/15. The first player to bring off the Grand Slam of the 4 historic singles titles in one year – *1938.* A relentless competitor with a majestic backhand he won all 3 titles at Wimbledon in *1937* and *1938.* Won doubles (with G. Mako) and mixed (with Alice Marble). US singles *1937/38* and doubles (with Mako) *1936/38.* French and Australian singles *1938* and between *1935–38* won 25 out of 29 D Cup rubbers in 11 ties. Turned professional in *1938.*

MARIA ESTHER ANDION BUENO (Brazil)
Born 11/10/39. The most gracefully artistic of post-war women's champions. For nearly a decade her rivalry with Margaret Court provided the principal excitement of the women's

game, but at the end she was plagued by injury. Won Wimbledon singles *1959/60/64,* and doubles (with Althea Gibson) *1958,* (with Darlene Hard) *1960/63,* (with Billie Jean King) */65,* and (with Nancy Gunter) */66.* US singles *1959/63/64/66* and doubles (with Darlene Hard) *1960/62,* (with Nancy Gunter) */66,* and (with Margaret Court) */68.* French doubles (with Darlene Hard) *1960.* Australian doubles (with Christine Truman) *1960.* Italian singles, *1958/61/65.*

MAY SUTTON BUNDY (USA)
Born in Plymouth, England, 25/9/1886. Died 4/10/1975. In *1905* the first overseas player to win a Wimbledon title. The seventh and youngest child of a British naval officer, Captain A. de G. Sutton, she learnt tennis on asphalt courts after her family moved to California in 1893. She was forceful and vigorous with a disconcerting top-spin forehand. F. R. Burrow commented: She took a deep breath before every stroke and then hit the ball with all her force to the accompaniment of a very audible expiration.' After winning the US singles and doubles in *1904* she went, aged 18, to Wimbledon *1905* and defeated the holder, Miss Douglass, in the Challenge Round. Miss Douglass regained the title the following year, but then lost a third battle with the Californian in *1907.* After winning the US Clay Court singles *1912,* Miss Sutton married Thomas Bundy, 3 times a US doubles champ. She played doubles in the *1925* W Cup and in *1929* returned to Wimbledon at 42 to defeat Eileen Bennett, seeded 4, and reach the qf. She was still playing 44 years later. Her daughter Dorothy represented the US 3 times in the W Cup and won the Australian singles 1938, and a nephew, John Doeg, was US champ in 1930.

DOROTHEA LAMBERT CHAMBERS (Great Britain)
Born 3/9/1878. Died 7/1/1960. Nee Douglass. The most successful British woman player before 1914, she won Wimbledon singles 7 times and lost dramatically to Suzanne Lenglen in *1919* Challenge Round after holding 2 match-points. Played in *1926* W Cup – 23 years after first success at Wimbledon. The daughter of an Ealing vicar, she became a coach in *1928.* Won Wimbledon singles *1903/04/06/10/11/13/14.*

HENRI COCHET (France)
Born 14/12/01. Died April 1987. The great instinctive genius of lawn tennis, swift and imaginative, a master of the volley and half-volley, whose play could rise to dizzy heights and sometimes slip to unexpected disaster. Won Wimbledon singles *1927/29* and doubles (with J. Brugnon) *1926/28.* US singles *1928.* French singles *1922/26/28/30/32* and doubles (with Brugnon) *1927/30/32.* With the other Musketeers', he played successfully in 6 Challenge Rounds. Between *1922* and *1933,* when he turned professional, he won 44 D Cup rubbers out of 58 in 26 ties. After the war reinstated as an amateur.

ASHLEY JOHN COOPER (Australia)
Born 15/9/36. A strong and determined competitor who maintained Australia's command of the international game after Hoad and Rosewall turned professional. After being overwhelmed by Hoad in the *1957* f at Wimbledon, he returned to beat Fraser in a stern test of endurance in *1958.* He was US champion in *1958* and won Australia *1957–58.* His doubles victories included Australia *1958,* France *1957–58* and US *1958.* He played singles when Australia successfully defended the D Cup in *1957* and *1958,* winning one rubber in each match. He beat Seixas and lost to Mackay *1957* and beat Mackay and lost to Olmedo *1958.*

CHARLOTTE COOPER (Great Britain)
Born 22/9/1870. Died 10/10/1970. Became Mrs Sterry. One of the first successful women volleyers, she won at Wimbledon *1895/96/98/1901/08.* Overshadowed at first by Mrs Hillyard – her first three victories were gained in years when the older player did not compete – she defeated her at last in *1901,* the year of her marriage, after losing to Mrs Hillyard in four previous matches at the championships. In *1902* she lost in the famous re–played challenge round to Muriel Robb (they stopped at 4–6 13–11 on the first evening, then began again and Miss Robb won 7–5 6–1) and then regained the title in *1908* after

beating Mrs Lambert Chambers in the quarter–finals. She reached the all–comers' final in **1912** and took Mrs McNair to 9–7 in the third set of a qf in **1913.** Her attacking spirit delighted her contemporaries. Her smiling good temper and sportsmanship made her as popular a player as ever went on to the Centre Court', wrote Burrow. She had a constitution like the proverbial ostrich. She never knew what it was to be tired and was never sick or sorry', said Hillyard.

BARON GOTTFRIED VON CRAMM (Germany)
Born 7/7/09. Died in car accident in Egypt 9/11/76. An elegant stylist and Germany's most successful player. Won French singles **1934/36** and doubles (with H. Henkel) **1937,** and German singles **1932/33/34/35/48/49** and doubles **1948/49/53/55.** Like F. S. Stolle, he was losing singles finalist at Wimbledon for 3 successive years – 1935–37. Won Wimbledon mixed (with Hilda Krahwinkel) **1933** and US doubles (with Henkel) **1937.** Won 82 D Cup rubbers out of 102 in 37 ties between **1932–53.**

JOHN HERBERT CRAWFORD (Australia)
Born 22/3/08. Died 10/9/91. Classic stylist, he beat H. E. Vines in **1933** in one of the greatest of all Wimbledon f. Won Wimbledon doubles (with A. K. Quist) **1935.** French singles **1933** and doubles (with Quist) **1935,** Australian singles **1931/33** and doubles (with H. C. Hopman) **1929/30,** (with E. F. Moon) **1932,** and (with V. B. McGrath) **1935.** Won 36 out of 58 D Cup rubbers between **1928–37.**

DWIGHT FILLEY DAVIS (USA)
Born 5/7/1879. Died 28/11/1945. The donor of the D Cup, the trophy at stake in the international team championship. A Harvard undergraduate, he played against the British Isles in the first two matches of that competition, winning a single and partnering Holcombe Ward successfully in the doubles in **1900** and, with Ward again, losing to the Dohertys in the doubles in **1902.** A lefthander, he won the US doubles with Ward from **1899–1901,** retiring undefeated, and also the all-comers' final at Wimbledon in **1901,** only to fall to the Dohertys. He was President of the US LTA in **1923,** US Secretary of War 1925–29 and later Governor–General of the Philippines.

MAX DECUGIS (France)
Born 24/9/1882. Died 6/9/1978. The first great French player. He spent his schooldays in England and won his first tournaments there. Short, quick, and wiry, he was an aggressive competitor, whom Lawrie Doherty described as the most promising young player in the world'. He dominated French tennis from **1903,** when he won in Paris for the first time, to the outbreak of World War I, winning the singles title 8 times in 12 years and the doubles from **1902–14** and again in **1920** when the Champs were resumed. He was still playing well enough to reach the singles final in **1923** when he was 41. By that time the age of the Musketeers' was dawning. Although he competed regularly at Wimbledon, he never progressed beyond the singles sf **(1911/12)** but, with Gobert, he gained France's first title by winning the doubles in **1911.**

CHARLOTTE DOD (Great Britain)
Born 24/9/1871. Died 27/6/1960. The first lawn tennis prodigy. Won the first of 5 Wimbledon titles in **1887** at the age of 15 years and 10 months. When she retired, she became an international golfer and hockey player. Nicknamed the Little Wonder', she won Wimbledon singles **1887/88/91/92/93.**

HUGH LAWRENCE DOHERTY (Great Britain)
Born London, 8/10/1875. Died 21/8/1919. Learnt game with elder brother, Reginald Frank (Reggie'), at Westminster School. Played for Cambridge Univ against Oxford in 1896–98 and developed into one of the most spectacular, aggressive, stylish, and successful of British players. Lawrie' Doherty was celebrated for smashing and volleying, and for speed about the court. With his brother, formed one of the greatest doubles partnerships in the

history of the game. Won all-comers' singles at Wimbledon, *1898,* and singles champ *1902–06.* Doubles champ (with R. F. Doherty) *1897–1901, 1903–05.* First overseas player to win US singles, *1903,* and doubles, *1902/03.* In 5 D Cup challenge rounds, *1902–06,* he was never beaten, winning 7 singles rubbers and 5 doubles.

REGINALD FRANK DOHERTY (Great Britain)
Born London, 14/10/1872. Died 29/12/1910. The senior partner of the great Doherty combination and the most notable stylist of early lawn tennis. Contemporary observers called his backhand, produced with back swing, full follow-through and remarkable touch, a model of perfection'. Was Wimbledon singles champ *1897–1900* and doubles champ *1897–1901* and *1903–05.* Reached the doubles challenge round at Wimbledon for first time with H. A. Nisbet in 1896. Thereafter he and his brother, H. L. Doherty, were beaten only by S. H. Smith and F. L. Riseley at Wimbledon. They lost to this pair in 1902, then beat them in the next three challenge rounds before falling to them again in 1906. The Dohertys won the US doubles in *1902/03.* Won South African singles and doubles *1909.*

JAROSLAV DROBNY (Great Britain)
Born 12/10/21. Exiled himself from Czechoslovakia in 1949, became Egyptian subject in 1950 and a naturalised Briton in 1960. One of the great post-war clay court competitors with tremendous left-hand serve and smash, and delicate touch, he played in some of Wimbledon's most dramatic and emotional matches and eventually won the singles in *1954* at the age of 33. In *1946* he beat Kramer, the favourite; he lost to Schroeder in the *1949* f; in *1950* he let a two-set lead slip against Sedgman; Mottram surprised him in *1951;* he fell to Sedgman again in the *1952* f; and in *1953* he never recovered from beating Patty 8–6 16–18 3–6 8–6 12–10 in Wimbledon's second longest singles. The following year, when his chance seemed to be slipping away, he beat Rosewall, then 19, in f. He won in Paris in *1951/52* (after another series of dramatic failures), Italy *1950/51/53* and Germany *1950.* In *1946/47/48/49* he played in 43 D Cup rubbers, and won 37.

FRANCOISE DURR (France)
Born 25/12/42. Now Mrs Browning. The outstanding French woman player of the 1960s and 1970s. Shrewd and unorthodox, particularly in her serve and on the backhand, she excelled in doubles. She gained her major singles successes in *1967* when she won the French and German titles and reached the US semi-finals, but in doubles won a host of titles with a variety of partners, including five successive French victories – with Gail Sheriff (later Mrs Chanfreau and now Mrs Lovera) *1967* and *1970/71,* and with Ann Jones, *1968/69.* Won US doubles *1972* with Betty Stove, and Italian and South African titles *1969* with Jones. She failed, however, in six Wimbledon doubles finals between *1965–75.* Won Wimbledon mixed doubles with Tony Roche *1976* and the French with Jean-Claude Barclay in *1968/71/73.*

ROY STANLEY EMERSON (Australia)
Born 3/11/36. A remarkable athlete, lean, keen, and trained to the last ounce', who led Australia's international challenge for five years after Laver turned professional in 1962. A Queenslander, he won Wimbledon singles *1964/65* but injury in 1966 spoilt his chance of equalling Perry's record of three successive titles. Won the doubles with Fraser *1959/61,* US singles *1961/64* and doubles *1959/60* (with Fraser) and *1965/66* (with Stolle), Australian singles *1961* and *1963/64/65/66/67* and doubles *1960/66.* On clay courts won the French singles *1963/67,* Italian *1959/61/66* and German *1967* and his most interesting doubles achievement was to take the French title from *1960/61/ 63/64/65* with five different partners, Fraser *1960/62,* Laver *1961,* Santana *1963,* Fletcher *1964,* and Stolle *1965.* He won 36 of his 40 D Cup rubbers and played in 9 successive challenge rounds between *1959–67.*

CHRISTINE MARIE EVERT (USA)
Born Fort Lauderdale, Fl., 21/12/54. Now Mrs Andy Mill (married 30th July 1988). Coached

by father Jimmy in Fort Lauderdale to become the most consistent back–court player of her generation: she won at least one Grand Slam singles title every year from **1974** to **1986** during which period her friendly rivalry with Martina Navratilova dominated the women's game. When she and Jimmy Connors (who were engaged at the time) won the two Wimbledon singles titles in **1974** with their double–handed backhands they legitimised the stroke and set a fashion that became a world trend. Her metronomic consistency, unshakeable concentration and fearless resolve to go for her shots were legendary and earned her more professional titles (157) than any other player, male or female, during the open era plus a fortune in prize money ($8,896,195). She competed for 19 consecutive years at the US Open and reached 9 finals, 8 semi-finals and was twice beaten in the quarter-finals, including her last year **1989** when she won her 101st match at these Championships, a record. As a sixteen-year-old, in **1971**, she reached the first of four consecutive semi-finals on grass at Forest Hills. In **1975/76/77** she won the title there on US clay and repeated that success on hard courts at Flushing Meadow in **1978/80/82**, by which time her first husband, John Lloyd (married 17th April 1979, divorced April 1987) had helped her to become a much better volleyer. In 13 challenges in Paris between 1973 and 1988 she won seven of the nine finals she contested (**1974/75/ 79/80/83/85/86**) and only in her last year failed to reach the semi-final, losing in the third round to Arantxa Sanchez-Vicario. She competed at Wimbledon every year from **1972–89** and only in **1983** (when she was ill and lost to Kathy Jordan) did she fail to reach the semi–finals. She was the champion 3 times (**1974/76/81**), a finalist 7 times (**1973/78/79/ 80/82/84/85**) and a semi–finalist 7 times (**1972/75/77/86/87/88/89**). She competed in the Australian Open six times between **1974–88**, winning the title in **1982** and **1984** and reaching the final in **1974/81/85/88**. Her 18 Grand Slam singles titles place her third behind Margaret Court (26) and Helen Wills Moody (19) on the list of great champions. Her streak of 125 consecutive wins on clay courts August **1973** – May **1979** is an all-time record and her prodigious achievement in reaching the semi-finals or better at 52 of her last 56 Grand Slams is unlikely ever to be equalled. She represented the United States eight times in the *Fed Cup* and won all but two of her 42 singles rubbers and 16 of 18 doubles rubbers in 42 ties between **1977–89**. She was unbeaten in 26 W Cup singles rubbers and won 8 of the 12 doubles rubbers she contested in 13 ties between **1971– 85**.–J.B.

ROBERT FALKENBURG (USA)
Born 29/1/26. Won the US Junior Championship in **1943–44** and came to Europe in **1947** with the reputation of possessing the fastest service in the US. He won at Queen's Club, but lost to Pails in qf at Wimbledon and then won the doubles with Kramer, defeating Mottram and Sidwell in f. The following year he won one of Wimbledon's most dramatic f, defeating Bromwich 7–5 0–6 6–2 3–6 7–5 after saving three match-points as 3–5 in 5s. He was born in New York, learnt most of his tennis in Los Angeles and moved to Brazil, for whom he played in D Cup on a residential qualification.

NEALE ANDREW FRASER (Australia)
Born 3/10/33. A consistently aggressive lefthander, with a plain, direct serve-and-volley game, he was trained by Hopman, winning 18 of 21 D Cup rubbers between **1958** and **1963,** and later captained the Australian team which recaptured the trophy at Cleveland in **1973** and at Melbourne in **1978/83**. Fraser started his Wimbledon career in the qualifying competition and ended by winning the singles in **1960** after a remarkable escape in the qf. Buchholz, who had held 5 match-points against him, retired with cramp. He won the doubles with Emerson **1959/61** and mixed with du Pont in **1962** – the year in which he and his brother, John, a Melbourne doctor, both reached the singles sf. Neither got through to the f. He won the US singles **1959/60** and doubles **1957/59/60,** the French doubles **1958/60/62,** and Australian doubles **1957/58/62.**

SHIRLEY JUNE FRY (USA)
Born 30/6/27. Now Mrs Irvin. A persistent competitor, whose most notable performances were in doubles. She was first ranked in the top ten in the US in 1944, but she did not gain

her two major singles successes until *1956* when she won both Wimbledon and Forest Hills. Until then she had always been thwarted by fellow-Americans. She won the Wimbledon doubles from *1951–53* with Doris Hart, losing only four games in capturing the title in *1953* and beat Helen Fletcher and Jean Quertier 6–0 6–0 in sf and Julie Sampson and Maureen Connolly by the same score in f. They won the US title *1951–54.* Her other successes included the Wimbledon mixed, with Seixas, *1956,* the Australian singles and doubles, with Althea Gibson, *1957,* and the French singles, *1951,* and doubles, with Hart, *1950–53.* She played in six W Cup contests, winning 10 matches and losing twice.

ALTHEA GIBSON (USA)
Born 25/8/27. The first black player to dominate international lawn tennis, relying on fierce serving and considerable strength and reach. Won Wimbledon singles *1957/58* and (doubles (with Angela Buxton) *1957* and (with Maria Bueno) */58.* US singles *1957/58.* French singles and doubles (with Angela Buxton) *1956.* Australian doubles (with Shirley Fry) *1957.* Italian singles *1956.* W Cup *1957/58,* turned professional *1958.*

ANDRE HENRI GOBERT (France)
Born 30/9/1890. Died 6/12/1951. Wallis Myers described him as perhaps the greatest indoor player of all time'. With Decugis, he gained France's first Wimbledon title by defeating the holders, Ritchie and Wilding, in *1911.* Although they were beaten by Dixon and Roper Barrett the following year, the brilliant Gobert's compensation was a place in the all-comers' singles f in which he lost to the experienced A. W. Gore. He won the French covered court title from *1911–13* and again in *1920* and the British covered court event in *1911–12* and again from *1920–22.* He first played in D Cup in *1911* and his career ended when the Musketeers' arrived in *1922.* He also won two Olympic gold medals in *1912.*

RICHARD (PANCHO) GONZALES (USA)
Born 9/5/28. A dramatic and spectacular competitor, who was undoubtedly the best player in the world for most of the 1950s. He turned pro in 1949 after winning the US singles in *1948/49,* taking the US Clay Court title *1948/49,* the US indoor title *1949,* and winning the doubles in Paris and at Wimbledon – in his only amateur appearances there – in *1949* with Parker. Thereafter he played his brilliant, angry tennis away from the main arenas of the game until, at last, open competition was allowed. By then he was 40, but he played one last great match for the Wimbledon crowd. In *1969* he beat Pasarell 22–24 1–6 16–14 6–3 11–9 in 5hr 12min – the longest singles seen at Wimbledon.

EVONNE FAY GOOLAGONG (Australia)
Born 31/7/51. Now Mrs Roger Cawley (married in 1975). One of the most naturally gifted of champions, she was the first of her Aborigine race to excel at the game. Suddenly in *1971* at the age of 19, 3 years before her coach Vic Edwards had forecast she would, she swept through both the French Championships and Wimbledon on a cloud of inspiration to win her first major titles. Although she reached the Wimbledon final again the following year and twice more, in *1975* and *1976,* it was not until *1980* that she won again – four years after the birth of her daughter, Kelly. This was the first win by a mother since Dorothea Lambert Chambers's success in 1914. The nine-year gap between her championships was also the greatest since Bill Tilden's wins in 1921 and 1930. She was always more at home on faster surfaces where her beautifully instinctive volleying paid handsome dividends and she won her native Australian Open on that surface four times – *1974/75/76/78*. She was always a competent player on clay but tended to be rather erratic as her famous walkabouts' led to extravagant errors. Nevertheless, besides the French Open in *1971* she also won the Italian title in *1973*. The other highlights of her singles career were the victories in the South African Championships *(1972)* and the Virginia Slims Champs *(1974/76)*. She was a good doubles player and won once at Wimbledon *(1974)*, four times in Melbourne *(1971/74/75/ 76)* and twice in Johannesburg *(1971/72)*. In seven years of Fed Cup duty for Australia from *1971–82* she won 33 of the 38 rubbers she contested in 24 ties. – J.B.

ARTHUR WENTWORTH GORE (Great Britain)
Born 2/1/1868. Died 1/12/1928. Wimbledon's oldest champ and probably the most persistent and industrious competitor in the history of the Champs. He played there for the first time in 1888 and although the Dohertys, Brookes, and Wilding were among his contemporaries, won the singles 3 times *1901* and *1908/09* and, at the age of 44 years and 6 months, won the right to challenge Wilding for the title in *1912.* That was his seventh appearance in the challenge round in 13 years. He was almost entirely a forehand player, hitting the ball flat with the racket in a dead line with his outstretched arm. His lightness of foot enabled him to protect his backhand which was no more than a safe push. He competed at every Wimbledon between *1888–1927* and captained the first British D Cup team at Boston in 1900, reaching sf US Champs on that trip.

KAREN HANTZE (USA)
Born 11/12/42. Now Mrs Susman. One of the new generation of aggressive Californians who arrived on the international scene at the start of the 1960s, she won the doubles at Wimbledon with the 17-year-old Billie Jean Moffitt in *1961* and then defeated Vera Sukova in the *1962* singles final. Marriage and motherhood restricted her tennis, but she won US doubles (again with Moffitt) *1964.* She played W Cup *1960–62* and *1965,* winning six of her nine matches, and *Fed Cup 1965.*

DARLENE R. HARD (USA)
Born 6/1/36. An energetic volleyer, a shrewd tactician, and one of the best doubles players of her generation, she won the US singles in *1960/61* and the French singles *1960,* but she failed in both her Wimbledon finals, losing to Althea Gibson in *1957* and Maria Bueno *1960.* She won the Wimbledon doubles, with Gibson *1957,* Jeanne Arth *1959,* and twice with Bueno *(1960/63)* and the mixed in *1957* (with Rose), *1959–60* (with Laver). She won the US doubles six times and the French doubles three times. Perhaps her most surprising American success came in *1969,* some years after she had retired from regular competition, when she and Francoise Durr defeated Margaret Court and Virginia Wade 0–6 6–3 6–4 in f.

DORIS HART (USA)
Born 20/6/25. In spite of childhood illness which impeded her movement, she became one of the subtlest and most graceful of post-war competitors. Won Wimbledon singles *1951,* doubles (with Pat Todd) *1947* and (with Shirley Fry) *1951/52/53.* US singles *1954/55* and doubles (with Shirley Fry) *1951/52/53/54.* French singles *1950/52* and doubles (with Pat Todd) *1948* and (with Shirley Fry) *1950/51/53.* Australian singles *1949* and doubles (with Louise Brough) *1950.* Italian singles *1951/53* and South African singles *1952.* Also won many mixed titles, notably with E. V. Seixas at Wimbledon *1953/54/55.* Turned professional *1955.*

ADRIANNE (ANN) SHIRLEY HAYDON (Great Britain)
Born 17/10/38. Now Mrs Jones. A shrewd, persistent lefthander, who reached sf at Wimbledon 7 times in 10 years, she captured the title at last in *1969* after beating Margaret Court in sf and Billie Jean King, to whom she had been r/u in *1967,* in f. She achieved international fame as a table tennis player, but decided to concentrate on lawn tennis after being r/u in three events in the 1957 World Table Tennis Champs. She won the French title in *1961/66,* Rome in *1966* and was twice r/u at Forest Hills *1961/67.* She took the French doubles (with Francoise Durr) in *1968/69* and won the Wimbledon mixed with Stolle in *1969.* Her W Cup record – 15 successful rubbers out of 32 in 12 matches – is another remarkable illustration of her tenacity and consistency.

ROBERT ANTHONY JOHN HEWITT (South Africa)
Born in Sydney, Australia, 12/1/40. He moved to South Africa in the early 1960s and started to represent that country when his residential qualification matured in 1967. A big brooding volcano of a man, he had a deceptively fine touch and became one of the greatest right-

court returners of the serve of modern times. He enjoyed two careers – first with fellow-Australian Fred Stolle and then with South Africa's Frew McMillan. With Stolle he won Wimbledon twice *(1962/64)* the Australian Championship twice *(1963/64)* and the Italian twice *(1963/64)* and with McMillan he added three more Wimbledon crowns *(1967/72/78)*, two German *(1967/70)*, one French *(1972)*, one US *(1977)*, one Masters *(1977)* and one WCT *(1974)* title as well as the Italian in *1967* and four at home in South Africa *(1967/70/72/74)*. He registered four major mixed doubles successes with three different partners, winning in Australia with Jan Lehane in *1961*, in Paris with Billie Jean King in *1970* and twice at Wimbledon with his pupil, Greer Stevens, in *1977/79*. He represented South Africa in D Cup *1967–74* and was a member of the successful team of *1974* that won by default from India. – J.B.

LEWIS ALAN HOAD (Australia)
Born 23/11/34. Capable of generating fierce power with great ease, he was one of the boy wonders' Harry Hopman produced to beat the US in the *1953* D Cup match. The other was Rosewall, 21 days his senior, who was to thwart his attempt on the Grand Slam in *1956* by beating him at Forest Hills, in the last of the 4 great f. That year Hoad had won the Australian and French titles, and had beaten Rosewall at Wimbledon. In *1957* he defeated Ashley Cooper in one of the most devastating Wimbledon f ever and then turned professional, but constant back trouble spoilt his pro career and also ended his attempt to return to the circuit when the game was opened to the pros. He won the Wimbledon doubles in *1953/55/56,* the US doubles in *1956,* the French doubles in *1953,* and the Australian doubles in *1953/56/57.* He won 17 rubbers out of 21 in D Cup play between *1953–56.*

HAZEL HOTCHKISS (USA)
Born 20/12/1886. Died 5/12/1974. Became Mrs G. Wightman. One of the most remarkable and enthusiastic competitors that the game has known. She was the donor of the W Cup and a considerable influence in American tennis for more than 60 years. She gained the first of her four US singles titles *(1909/10/11/19)* in 1909 and won the US indoor doubles for the 10th *(1919/21/24/27/28/29/30/31/33/43)* and last time in 1943. A remarkable volleyer with great speed about the court, she and Helen Wills were never beaten in doubles. They won the Wimbledon doubles in *1924* and the US doubles – a title which she had won on 4 other occasions – in *1924–28.* She captained the first US W Cup team in 1923 and between *1923–31* won 3 doubles rubbers in 5 matches.

HELEN HULL JACOBS (USA)
Born 6/8/08. A tenacious competitor, notable for duels with fellow-Californian, Helen Wills Moody, 5 times a Wimbledon finalist between *1929–39* but won only in *1936.* US singles *1932/33/34/35* and doubles (with Sarah Palfrey Fabyan) *1930/34/35.* Italian singles *1934.*

WILLIAM JOHNSTON (USA)
Born 2/11/1894. Died 1/6/1946. Little Bill', a Californian, small in physique but a brilliant volleyer and the possessor of a formidable top-spin forehand, was Big Bill' Tilden's principal rival at home in the first half of the 1920s. He defeated McLoughlin to win the US singles in *1915,* the first year at Forest Hills, lost to Williams in the *1916* final and then regained the title by beating Tilden in straight sets in *1919.* Tilden gained his revenge the following year and, although Johnston reached the final five times between *1920* and *1925,* Tilden always frustrated him. He beat Hunter in the *1923* Wimbledon final, losing only one set in the tournament. He won the US doubles with Griffin *1915/16* and *1920* and played in eight D Cup challenge rounds, winning 18 of his 21 D Cup rubbers.

BILLIE JEAN MOFFITT KING (USA)
Born 22/11/43. Perhaps the most important single figure in the history of tennis, as player, stateswoman, innovator and entrepreneur (usually with lawyer husband Larry King, whom she married in 1965), she has worked tirelessly to gain recognition and respect for the

women's game. One of the founders of the women's pro tour in *1970*, twice President of the Women's Tennis Association, and the prime mover behind Team Tennis, she has been involved in most aspects of the game. As a player her natural exuberance and bubbling personality suited her attacking serve-and-volley game and made her a fearsome opponent. She will best be remembered for her Battle of the Sexes' against Bobby Riggs at the Houston Astrodome on 20 September, *1973* where the world's largest-ever crowd of 30,492 and some 50 million more around the world on TV, saw her win 6–4 6–3 6–3. In *1979* she achieved her 20th Wimbledon title to pass the record she had jointly shared with fellow-Californian Elizabeth Ryan who, ironically, had died on the eve of that unique achievement. Her unparalleled record comprises 6 singles – *1966/67/68/72/73/75*; 10 women's doubles – *1961/62/65/67/68/70/71/72/73/79*; 4 mixed doubles – *1967/71/73/74*. She first played at Wimbledon in *1961* and won the doubles with Karen Hantze. At her last appearance in *1983* she was competing for the 22nd year (she had not entered in *1981*) and reached the mixed doubles final with Steve Denton when she played her 265th and last match at Wimbledon. It was also her 29th final and, as they lost to John Lloyd and Wendy Turnbull 7–5 in the final set, she was losing at that stage for only the 9th time. She was almost as successful in her own US Championships where she won 13 titles, 4 in singles – *1967/71/72/74*, five in doubles – *1964/67/74/78/80* and four in mixed – *1967/71/73/76* and, in addition she became the only woman to win US National titles on all four surfaces – grass, clay, hard and indoor – a feat she repeated in doubles with Rosie Casals with whom she had most of her major doubles successes. She won the French Open singles and doubles in *1972* and the mixed in *1967/70* and was successful in singles and mixed at the Australian Open in *1968*, the first year of open tennis. Her 39 Grand Slam titles put her second only to Margaret Court who won 62. She was also the singles and doubles champion of Italy *(1970)* and of Germany *(1971)* and won the South African title 3 times *1966/67/69)*. With 21 winning rubbers from 26 played in 9 W Cup matches between *1961–78*, plus 52 wins from 58 rubbers in 6 years of Fed Cup play from *1963–79* she contributed hugely to American dominance in those team competitions. – J.B.

JAN KODES (Czechoslovakia)
Born 1/3/46. A dogged, industrious player with great strength and determination. He won his first major victories on clay, winning the French singles *1970/71* and reaching the Italian final *1970/71/72,* but he won the Wimbledon singles in the boycott year of *1973* and was runner-up in the US Champs *1971/73*. Having served his apprenticeship in European junior team competitions (he was on a winning Galea Cup team), he first represented Czechoslovakia in D Cup in *1966,* took them to the final in *1975* and was a member of their winning team in *1980.*

HILDE KRAHWINKEL (West Germany)
Born 26/3/08. Died 7/3/81. Became Mrs Sperling. A tall German, later Danish by marriage, whose dogged ability to retrieve from the back of the court turned her matches into long tests of endurance. She won the German indoor title in *1929* and then, emerging rapidly as an international player, lost to Cilly Aussem in the only all–German women's f at Wimbledon *1931*. She reached the final again in *1936,* losing 6–2 4–6 7–5 to Helen Jacobs, and altogether she was in qf (or better) 8 times. She won the French singles *1935–37*, defeating Mrs Mathieu in each of the three f, the Italian title *1935* and she was German singles champ *1933/35/37/39*. (There was no competition in 1936.) Her last important victory was in the Scandinavian indoor final in *1950.*

JACK ALBERT KRAMER (USA)
Born 1/8/21. A methodical and powerful exponent of the serve-and-volley game. Played for the US in the last pre-war D Cup challenge round against Australia. Won Wimbledon singles title in *1947* after losing dramatically to the then unknown Jaroslav Drobny in 1946. Won doubles *1946/47*. Won US singles *1946/47* and doubles *1940/41/43/47*. Turned pro *1947* and then controlled pro tennis for 15 years. Still appears occasionally as a television commentator and was executive director of ATP Sept. 1972–April 1975.

RENE LACOSTE (France)
Born 2/7/04. In spite of ill health, he became the best groundstroke player and most astute tactician of pre-war lawn tennis. Won Wimbledon singles *1925/28* and doubles (with J. Borotra) *1925*. Won US singles *1926/27,* French singles *1925/27/29* and French doubles (with Borotra) *1924/25/29.* Played in 51 D Cup rubbers between *1923–28* and won the crucial rubbers of the *1927* challenge round which brought France the trophy for the first time, when he beat Tilden and Johnston in the singles.

ARTHUR D. LARSEN (USA)
Born 6/4/25. A graceful, elegant lefthander with exquisite touch and some notable eccentricities, he was famous for his dressing-room superstitions, his physical twitches and his rituals on court. He was known as Tappy because he would have a lucky number for the day and would always tap the baseline, the umpire's chair – even his own toe – with his racket the required number of times before continuing. He won US singles *1950,* US Clay Courts *1952* and US Indoor *1953.* A motor-cycle accident in which he suffered severe head injuries ended his career in 1957.

RODNEY GEORGE LAVER (Australia)
Born 9/8/38. The first player to achieve the Grand Slam twice and the master of the old professional circuit, with Rosewall as his great rival, in its last days. A lefthander, red-haired like Budge, with a spectacularly aggressive style, he brought off the slam of the four major singles titles, as an amateur, in *1962* and then, as a professional, in *1969.* Disciplined, unassuming, quick and light in movement, he could produce sudden bombardments of shots, heavy with spin, which totally disconcerted his opponents. Born at Rockhampton, Queensland, Rocket' was a perfect nickname for the first tennis millionaire. If he had not turned professional in 1963, he would have won many more of the traditional titles. As it was, he won the singles at Wimbledon *1961/62* and *1968/69,* the doubles with Emerson *1971* and the mixed, with Darlene Hard, *1959/60.* He took the US singles and French singles *1962* and *1969,* also winning the French doubles with Emerson and the mixed with Hard in *1961.* His Australian singles victories came in *1960/62/69,* with doubles *1959/61* (Mark) and *1969* (Emerson). He was Italian singles champion *1962* and *1971,* German champion *1961/62* and a member of the undefeated D Cup team from *1959–62.* He returned to D Cup in *1973,* collecting three more rubbers in Australia's 5–0 victory over the US in the final at Cleveland.

SUZANNE LENGLEN (France)
Born 24/5/1899. Died 4/7/1938. The most exciting, and successful of women players. She survived 2 match-points to win at Wimbledon in *1919* against Mrs Lambert Chambers and thereafter lost only in a controversial match to Molla Mallory (US) in 1921 US Champs until her retirement in 1926. Quarrelled with the Wimbledon referee in 1926 and turned pro. Won Wimbledon singles and doubles (with Elizabeth Ryan) *1919/20/21/22/23/25.* French singles and doubles (with various partners) *1920/21/22/23/25/26.*

KATHLEEN McKANE (Great Britain)
Born 7/5/1896. Died 19/6/92. Became Mrs Godfree. A fine match-player with a quick, aggressive game, she achieved the notable distinction of winning the Wimbledon singles twice – even though she was a contemporary of Suzanne Lenglen and Helen Wills. In Lenglen's absence, she beat the Californian (a feat which no other player achieved in the next 14 years at Wimbledon) in the *1924* final after trailing by a set and 1–4, and in *1926* she regained the title after being within a point of 1–4 in the third set against Lili d'Alvarez. She won the Wimbledon mixed (with Gilbert) in *1924* and in *1926* (with her husband, Leslie Godfree). She was r/u to Miss Wills at Forest Hills in 1925 after beating Elizabeth Ryan and Molla Mallory, and she won the US doubles in *1923* (with Mrs Covell) */27* (with Miss Harvey). She won 7 rubbers out of 17 in 7 W Cup matches between *1923–34.*

CHARLES ROBERT McKINLEY (USA)
Born 5/1/41. Died 11/8/86. An energetic and athletic match-player, who won the

Wimbledon singles title in **1963** without meeting another seeded player in the course of the tournament. He was runner-up to Laver in **1961,** a disappointing competitor in **1962** but in **1963** bounced back to take the title. In the US Championships he never progressed further than the semi-finals, failing three times at that stage, but, with Ralston, he won the doubles in **1961** and **1963–64.** He played in 16 D Cup matches between **1960–65** and won 29 of his 38 rubbers.

MAURICE EVANS McLOUGHLIN (USA)
Born 7/1/1890. Died 10/12/1957. The Californian Comet' was the first notable exponent of the cannonball service. Fiercely effective with volley and smash, he was US champ in **1912–13** and his appearance at Wimbledon was, as a contemporary remarked, a sign of the way the modern game was developing. His spectacular style had considerable appeal. When he met Wilding for the title in **1913,** there was such an indecent crush round the barriers of the Centre Court that, to avoid serious injury, several ladies had to be lifted over by policemen into the security of the arena'. Wilding beat him 8–6 6–3 10–8, but McLoughlin had the consolation of winning 2 rubbers in the American capture of the D Cup from Britain at Wimbledon. In the **1914** challenge round at Forest Hills he beat both Brookes and Wilding, but Australasia took the trophy. He did not play after the war. His aggressive style was said to have burnt him out.

FREW DONALD McMILLAN (South Africa)
Born in Springs, a small Transvaal town, 20/5/42. A gifted and unusual doubles player who invariably wore a peaked white cloth cap and held the racket with two hands on both sides to produce just the right blend of disguise, finesse and power. His partnership with expatriate Australian Bob Hewitt was particularly fruitful and they became one of the three greatest pairs of the post-Second World War years. Together they won their native South African title four times **(1967/70/72/74)** and succeeded at Wimbledon three times **(1967/72/78).** They won once each the French **(1972)**, the US **(1977)**, the Masters **(1977** played in Jan '78), the WCT **(1974)** and the Italian **(1967)** titles and won the German twice **(1967/70).** But it was in mixed doubles that he won his first and last major championships. In **1966** he partnered Annette Van Zyl to the French title and in **1981** he captured the Wimbledon mixed for the second time with Betty Stove, with whom he had been successful in 1978 – the same year they won a second US Open together **(1977/78).** He played D Cup from **1965–76** and was a member of the only team ever to win the famous trophy by default – from India in 1974. – J.B.

ALICE MARBLE (USA)
Born 28/9/13. Died 13/12/90. A brilliant server and volleyer whose career was interrupted by ill health and the war. Won Wimbledon singles **1939** and doubles (with Sarah Palfrey Fabyan) **1938/39.** US singles **1936/38/39/40** and doubles (with Sarah Palfrey Fabyan) **1937/38/39/40.** Turned pro **1941.**

SIMONE MATHIEU (France)
Born 31/1/08. Died 7/1/80. A formidable clay court player, she succeeded Lenglen as the leader of the women's game in France. She was junior champ – as a married woman – at 18, and 3 years later reached the French f, losing 6–3 6–4 to Wills. She was r/u again in **1933/36/37** before she won at last in **1938,** defeating Landry, and then retained her title **1939** against Jedrzejowska. She won the French doubles 6 times and the Wimbledon doubles twice with Ryan **1933/34** and once with Yorke **1937.** Her soundness from the baseline carried her 4 times to the singles sf.

HELEN WILLS MOODY (USA)
Born 6/10/05. Later Mrs A. Roark. Lenglen's successor as ruler of Wimbledon. A relentless baseliner, she won the singles 8 times in 9 attempts, losing only to Kitty McKane in 1924. Between **1927–32** she won all the major singles champs, except Australia, without losing a set. Won Wimbledon singles **1927/28/29/30/32/33/35/38** and doubles (with Hazel

Wightman) **1924** and (with Elizabeth Ryan) **/27/30.** US singles **1923/24/25/27/28/29/31,** and doubles (with Mrs J. B. Jessup) **1922,** (with Hazel Wightman) **/24/28,** and (with Mary K. Browne) **/25.** French singles **1928/29/30/32** and doubles (with Elizabeth Ryan) **1930/ 31/32.**

ANGELA MORTIMER (Great Britain)
Born 21/4/32. Now Mrs Barrett. Britain's first post-war Wimbledon singles champ. Coached by Arthur Roberts at Torquay, she used an armoury of firmly controlled ground-strokes most effectively and considerable determination enabled her to overcome a certain frailty of physique. Her first notable success was the capture of the French title in **1955** – the first British victory in Paris since Peggy Scriven won in 1934 – and in the same year she won the Wimbledon doubles (with Anne Shilcock). She won the Australian title in **1958,** after travelling there to recover from illness, and 6 months later was r/u to Althea Gibson at Wimbledon. She won the title in **1961** by beating Christine Truman in the first all–British f of the modern Wimbledon. She won 5 rubbers out of 16 in 6 W Cup matches and became W Cup captain **1964–70** and *Fed Cup* captain **1967–70.**

ILLIE NASTASE (Rumania)
Born 19/8/46. One of the most gifted shot-makers and fluid movers in the game's history, he never quite fulfilled his enormous potential. His two Grand Slam titles were won on different surfaces – on grass in New York in **1972** and on clay in Paris the following year. He could also play beautifully indoors as his four Masters titles in **1971/72/73/75** testify. Sadly for his many admirers, a childlike and sometimes mischievous streak was his undoing on many occasions, particularly towards the end of his playing days when he fell foul of authority for his behaviour. Throughout his career the showman in him struggled constantly with the athlete so that there was often a lack of steel about his match play. This failing, and an inability to put the ball away with his somewhat lightweight volleys, cost him two chances to win the Wimbledon title – in **1972** when Smith beat him and in **1976** when Borg won the first of his five titles. His lightning reflexes made him an excellent doubles player and he won major titles in Paris **(1970)** and Rome **(1970/72),** at Wimbledon **(1973)** and in New York **(1975).** He also won two mixed titles at Wimbledon with Rosie Casals **(1970/72).** His biggest disappointment was his failure to lead Rumania to victory in the **1972** D Cup final against the Americans on clay in Bucharest where his loss to Smith in the opening rubber proved decisive. – J.B.

JOHN DAVID NEWCOMBE (Australia)
Born 23/5/44. The supreme exponent of the simple, rugged style in modern tennis. Splendidly confident and with great strength of personality, Newcombe relied upon a heavy service, forceful volleying and solid, powerful groundstrokes. His best singles successes were on grass – Wimbledon **1967/70/71,** US Championships **1967/73,** and Australia **1973/75** – but he also won, by doggedness and determination, the German **(1968)** and Italian **(1969)** titles. He and Roche formed the most successful of modern doubles partnerships, winning Wimbledon in **1965, 1968–70,** and **1974.** When Roche was injured in **1966,** Fletcher replaced him at short notice and he and Newcombe won the title. He won the US doubles with Roche **1967,** with Taylor **1971,** and with Davidson **1973,** France twice with Roche **(1967/69)** and once with Okker **(1973)** and Australia four times with Roche **(1965/67/71/76)** and once with Anderson **(1973).** In **1981,** aged 37, he and Stolle (42) took McEnroe/Fleming to 5s tie-break in US Open sf. He first played in the *D Cup* in **1963** and finally against Italy in Rome, **1976,** but perhaps his best performance was in **1973** when he and Laver inflicted a 5–0 defeat upon the United States at Cleveland.

BETTY NUTHALL (Great Britain)
Born 23/6/11. Died 8/11/83. Became Mrs Shoemaker. An aggressive and attractive competitor, with a remarkable record as a junior, she never progressed beyond qf at Wimbledon but gained her most impressive victories abroad. At 16, after beating Molla Mallory, No. 6 seed, at Wimbledon in **1927,** she astonished the tennis world by reaching f at F Hills, where Helen Wills beat her 6–1 6–4. In **1930** she became the first British player

to win that title with 6–4 6–1 victory over Mrs Harper. She won the US doubles *1930/31/33* and mixed *1929/31* and the French doubles *1931* and mixed *1931/32.* Her only British success in a nat singles event was the capture of the HC title in *1927.* She won the HC doubles *1926/28/31/32* and the mixed in *1927.* She played in 8 W Cup matches between *1927–39,* winning 6 rubbers and losing 7.

ALEJANDRO OLMEDO (USA)
Born 24/3/36. The son of a groundsman in Peru, this superb natural athlete rose like a comet in *1958* to win D Cup for America in Brisbane almost single-handed. Selected by the captain, Perry T. Jones, Olmedo had rewarded him with two singles wins and a share with Ham Richardson in the doubles win that had sealed the victory. Success in the Australian Championships confirmed the quality of his play as he beat Neale Fraser in four sets. Six months later The Chief', as he was popularly known, won the *1959* Wimbledon from Rod Laver for the loss of only two sets, with one of the most competent displays of power tennis seen since the war. After taking part in the unsuccessful defence of D Cup where he lost to Fraser but beat Laver again, he reached the final of the US Championships but failed once more against Fraser. Immediately he turned professional. – J.B.

MANUEL ORANTES (Spain)
Born 6/2/49. A consummate artist on European clay whose exquisite touch and gentle, generous manners made him an international favourite. A left-hander who, after leading Spain to two Galea Cup victories in *1968/69,* won his first two important titles in *1972* – the German and Italian Opens. His best year was *1975* for, besides winning a second German title, the Canadian Open and the first of his two US Clay Court crowns (he won the second in *1977),* he was triumphant on the clay at Forest Hills. After recovering miraculously to defeat Vilas in a night-time semi-final, having trailed one set to two and 0–5 in the fourth, he was back on court 15 hours later to thrash Jimmy Connors 6–4 6–3 6–3 in a near-perfect display of the clay-court art. In *1976* he won the Spanish Open and at the year's end won Masters in Houston against Fibak with another brave recovery, coming back from one set to two and 1–4. He played in the losing Spanish team in the D Cup challenge round of *1967* in Brisbane but led his country to victory in the World Team Cup in Dusseldorf 11 years later. – J.B.

MARGARET OSBORNE (USA)
Born 4/4/18. Now Mrs du Pont. One of the finest of American doubles players and a formidably successful competitor in singles. With her splendidly consistent serving and her strength and skill at the net, she did much to set the pattern for the period of American supremacy in women's tennis, which began in 1946. Won Wimbledon singles in *1947* Forest Hills *1948/49/50* and Paris in *1946/49.* She and Louise Brough won the Wimbledon doubles in *1946/48/49/50/54.* They ruled the US doubles from *1942–50* and *1955–57,* and held the French title *1946/47/49.* She won the Wimbledon mixed with Neale Fraser in *1962* – 15 years after her first singles victory.

SARAH PALFREY (USA)
Born 18/9/12. Now Mrs Danzig, formerly Mrs Fabyan, and Mrs Cooke. A fine volleyor with a sweeping backhand and a notable doubles player, she partnered Alice Marble to victory at Wimbledon in *1938/39* and won the US doubles title with a variety of partners – Betty Nuthall, Helen Jacobs (3 times), Alice Marble (4 times) and Margaret Osborne – 9 times between *1930–41.* She won the US singles in *1941/45* and was r/u to Helen Jacobs in *1934/35.* She was the US mixed champion on 4 occasions. She played in 10 W Cup matches and won 14 rubbers out of 21.

ADRIANO PANATTA (Italy)
Born 9/7/50. Without doubt, 1976 was the *annus mirabilis* of Panatta's career. Until then he had always been dashing and stylish, but had never made full use of his talent. In *1976,* however, he lived dangerously and survived brilliantly. In Rome he became the first home

player to win in Italy for 15 years after frustrating Warwick no fewer than 11 times at m-p in the first round. In Paris, against Hutka, he again faced a first-round m-p and again went on to take the championship. Four months later, when Italy won D Cup for the first time, Panatta played a major role in their victory. Paris, Rome and D Cup – this was Panatta's year! He was also the leading player in the Italian teams which reached the **1977/79/80** D Cup finals. He reached the French sf in **1973/75** and was runner–up in Rome **1978** and Hamburg **1972.**

GERALD L. PATTERSON (Australia)
Born 17/12/1895. Died 13/6/1967. Formidably aggressive with a cannonball service modelled on McLoughlin's, he was the dominating player when international competition was resumed in 1919. After being r/u to O'Hara Wood in the **1914** Australian singles, he became Wimbledon's first post-war champ by defeating Brookes in **1919.** He lost his Wimbledon title to Tilden in **1920** but regained it against Lycett in **1922.** R/u doubles in **1922** (O'Hara Wood) and **1928** (Hawkes) and won the mixed with Suzanne Lenglen in **1920.** He won the Australian singles in his fourth final in **1927.** Between **1919–28** he played 46 D Cup rubbers for Australia and Australasia and won 4 out of 12 challenge round rubbers. He was a nephew of Dame Nellie Melba and was the first man to win the Wimbledon singles by playing through when the challenge round was abolished there in 1922.

J. EDWARD PATTY (USA)
Born 11/2/24. An American who lived in Paris and developed his game there, Budge' Patty, with his elegant, effective forehand volley, was one of the great post-war stylists. **1950** – when he won both the Wimbledon and French singles – was the peak of his career, but his rivalry with Drobny captured the public's imagination. The most notable of their long and dramatic matches was in the third round at Wimbledon in 1953. After 44 hours Patty lost 8–6 16–18 3–6 8–6 12–10 after holding 6 m–ps. He had beaten the Czech at Wimbledon in **1947** and 3 years later by 6–1 6–2 3–6 5–7 7–5 in his French f. The last of their meetings was in **1954.** Drobny, on his way to the title, won a 4–set sf. Patty won his last title there in **1957** when he and Mulloy, then aged 43, beat Hoad and Fraser to take the men's doubles. He won the Italian singles **1954,** and the German singles **1953/54** and doubles **1953/54/55.**

FRANK A. PARKER (USA)
Born 31/1/16. Shrewd, persistent, and accurate in spite of a certain lightness of shot, he shared with Trabert the distinction, rare for an American, of winning the French title twice. At his best on slow courts, he was ranked in the first 10 in the US for 17 consecutive years between **1933,** the year of the first of his 5 US Clay Court victories, and **1949** when he turned pro. His victories in Paris were in **1948/49**, and in **1949** he won the doubles in Paris and Wimbledon with Gonzales. He won the US singles in **1944/45** as an Army sergeant and the doubles with Kramer in **1943.** He played in the D Cup challenge round against Britain in **1937** when the US regained the trophy after 10 years and in the **1939** and **1948** challenge rounds. He was beaten only twice in 14 D Cup rubbers.

FREDERICK JOHN PERRY (Great Britain)
Born 18/5/09. A US citizen. The most successful modern British player, an aggressive competitor with boundless self-confidence and a remarkable running forehand. Won Wimbledon singles **1934/35/36** – the first player since A. F. Wilding (1910–13) to take the title 3 years in succession – and mixed (with Dorothy Round) **1935/36.** US singles **1933/34/36.** French singles **1935** and doubles (with G. P. Hughes) **1933.** Australian singles **1934** and doubles (with Hughes) **1934.** Won 45 out of 52 D Cup rubbers, 34 out of 38 singles, between **1931–36.** Turned pro in **1936.**

YVON FRANCOIS MARIE PETRA (France)
Born 8/3/16 in Indo–China. Died 11/9/84. Wimbledon's first post-war men's singles champion. Reached mixed f at Wimbledon **1937** with Simone Mathieu and won French

doubles *1938* with Destremau, defeating Budge and Mako in f. Between 1942, when he was released from a prisoner-of-war camp, and 1945, he consolidated his reputation as France's most aggressive competitor in wartime domestic competitions. At Wimbledon, *1946,* his strength, flair and, notably, the consistency of his heavy serving gained this formidably built player an unexpected title. Drobny beat Kramer, the favourite, in 4r. Petra disposed of Pails, the other expected finalist, in qf and then won 5s matches against Tom Brown and Geoff Brown. That was the peak of his career. Marcel Bernard beat him in the French sf – played in July that year – and his consolation was a doubles victory, partnered by Bernard, over Morea and Segura in f. Patty beat him easily on the second day at Forest Hills and in *1947* he lost to Tom Brown in qf at Wimbledon.

NICOLA PIETRANGELI (Italy)
Born 11/9/33. A master of the European clay court style, he was born in Tunis (of a French father and Russian mother) and between *1954–72* played in 163 D Cup rubbers for Italy, more than anyone in history. Won most rubbers (120), played most singles (109) and won most (78), played most doubles (54) and won most (42), and played in most ties (66). Appeared in the *1960/61* challenge rounds against Australia, but won only one dead' singles. Won French singles *1959/60* and doubles (with Sirola), Italian singles *1957/61,* and German singles *1960.* Reached sf at Wimbledon, *1960,* and doubles final (with Sirola) *1956.*

DR JOSHUA PIM (Ireland)
Born 20/6/1869. Died 13/4/1942. A robust, adventurous competitor, regarded by contemporary critics as one of the great geniuses of early tennis. When Pim was at his best he was virtually unplayable', wrote Wallis Myers. It is scarcely exaggerating to say that he could hit a coin placed anywhere on the court.' He reached sf at Wimbledon *1890,* losing to Hamilton, who became Wimbledon's first Irish champ, then lost in *1891* to Wilfred– Baddeley in the all-comers' f and again in *1892* challenge round. He gained his revenge, however, by beating Baddeley in the 2 following Wimbledon f. Pim won the Irish title for the 3rd and last time in *1895* but then played little first-class tennis until he was controversially picked for the D Cup match against USA at New York in 1902. He was preferred to Lawrie Doherty, lost both his singles badly and the British Isles were beaten 3–2. Although still very good, Pim had no more than a shadow of his former skill, but alas! a great deal more than the shadow of his former weight', wrote Commander Hillyard.

ADRIAN KARL QUIST (Australia)
Born 4/8/13. Died 17/11/91. A shrewd, graceful doubles player, whose victories at Wimbledon were separated by a gap of 15 years. Won with J. H. Crawford in *1935* and, when almost a veteran, with J. E. Bromwich *1950.* Held Australian title from *1936–50,* winning twice with D. P. Turnbull and 8 times with Bromwich. Won US doubles (with Bromwich) *1939,* French doubles (with J. H. Crawford) *1935,* and Australian singles *1936/40/48.* Won 42 out of 55 D Cup rubbers in 28 ties between *1933–48.*

WILLIAM CHARLES RENSHAW (Great Britain)
Born 3/1/1861. Died 12/8/1904. The first great champ. Learnt on asphalt at school at Cheltenham with twin brother, Ernest, a more graceful but less determined competitor. They were the first spectacular players and their skill – particularly in volleying and smashing – brought crowds to Wimbledon and contributed considerably to the development of lawn tennis as a spectator sport. Willie' Renshaw was singles champ at Wimbledon from *1881–86* and in *1889.* He held the doubles, with Ernest, in *1884/85/86/88/89.* Ernest won the singles title in *1888* and was beaten by William in the challenge rounds of 1882 and 1883.

NANCY ANN RICHEY (USA)
Born 23/8/42. Later Mrs Gunter. A Texan, famous for her shorts and peaked cap, she was, like her brother, George Clifford Richey, a tenacious baseliner, impressive on clay. Her determination occasionally brought unexpected success on grass. She reached the *1969*

US final, losing 6–2 6–2 to Margaret Court. She won Australia *1967,* beating Lesley Turner, another clay-court specialist, in the final. At Wimbledon she reached qf seven times in nine years *1964–72* but was semi–finalist only in *1968.* She won Wimbledon doubles with Maria Bueno *1966.* On clay she won French singles *1968,* beating Ann Jones to avenge a defeat in the *1966* final, but the best evidence of her quality was her record in US Clay Courts. She won Indianapolis from *1963–68* and even as late as *1975* led Chris Evert 7–5 5–0 in the semi-finals there, twice reaching m–p before retiring with cramp at 2–4 in the final set. She played W Cup from *1962–68* and *Fed Cup 1964–69.*

ROBERT LARIMORE RIGGS (USA)
Born 25/2/18. A shrewd, confident match–player, with remarkable versatility of shot, he won all 3 titles on his first appearance at Wimbledon in *1939.* He also won Forest Hills in *1939,* but lost to McNeill in the French f. He turned pro in 1941 and later became a notable competitor in veterans' events, but his greatest fame came at the age of 55. Profiting from the Women's Lib controversy, he challenged and beat Margaret Court 6–2 6–1 in a singles match in Ramona, Cal, and then lost to Billie Jean King 6–4 6–3 6–3, before a record television audience of almost 50 million and 30,492 paying spectators at the Houston Astrodome in September 1973.

ANTHONY DALTON ROCHE (Australia)
Born 17/6/45. Strong, rugged and a fine volleyer, he was the lefthander in one of Wimbledon's most successful doubles partnerships. He won the doubles with John Newcombe in *1965,* from *1968–70* (the first hat-trick of titles since the Dohertys 1903–5) and in *1974.* Other doubles victories included US *1967,* French *1967–69,* Australia *1965/67/71/76/77* and Italy *1965/71*; and Wimbledon mixed doubles with Francoise Durr *1976.* He did not achieve as much as expected in singles, partly because of injury. The extraordinary operation on his left elbow, performed without knife or anaesthetic in the Philippines by a faith healer, received worldwide publicity. He never reached an Australian final in spite of numerous attempts, but was runner–up to Laver at Wimbledon in *1968* and lost two US Open finals: *1969* when Laver beat him to complete the Grand Slam and *1970* to Rosewall. His most successful year was *1966* when he won French and Italian titles. Played Davis Cup *1964–78* but did not play singles in a final until he beat Panatta in the opening match *1977.*

KENNETH ROBERT ROSEWALL (Australia)
Born 2/11/34. For a quarter of a century Rosewall's grace and easy, economical style delighted the connoisseurs and the only regret about his long and distinguished career is that, in spite of four finals over a period of 20 years, he never won the Wimbledon singles title. He began as a Hopman prodigy and it was not until the end of *1979* that he retired from Grand Prix tennis. In *1953,* aged 18, he won the Australian and French singles and, with Hoad, the French and Wimbledon doubles. In *1954* he lost to Drobny in the Wimbledon final. Hoad beat him in the *1956* Wimbledon final, but Rosewall avenged that defeat in the US final, frustrating Hoad in the last leg of his attempt on the Grand Slam. Turning professional in *1957,* he took over the leadership of the professional circuit from Gonzales until Laver's arrival in *1963.* Rosewall's skills endured. In *1968* he won the first open tournament at Bournemouth and then recaptured some of his former titles. He regained the French singles and doubles (with Stolle) in *1968.* In *1970* – after 14 years and aged 35 – he won the US title again and reached his fourth final at Forest Hills in *1974.* The gap between his Australian successes was even wider. After his victories in *1953/55,* he won again in *1971/72.* But Wimbledon always eluded him. Newcombe beat him in *1970,* his third final, and Connors overwhelmed him in the *1974* final.

DOROTHY EDITH ROUND (Great Britain)
Born 13/7/09. Died 12/11/82. Became Mrs Little. Determined and efficient, possessing a fine forehand drive and shrewd drop-shot, she was one of the two British women's singles champs at Wimbledon between the wars. She gained her first notable victory there

against Lili d'Alvarez in *1931,* was r/u to Helen Wills Moody in *1933,* then beat Helen Jacobs to win the title in *1934* and regained it against Jadwiga Jedrzejowska in *1937.* She won the Australian singles in *1935* and the Wimbledon mixed in *1934* (with Miki) and *1935/36* (with Perry). She won 4 of her 13 W Cup rubbers between *1931–36.*

ELIZABETH RYAN (USA)
Born 5/2/1892. Died 6/7/1979. Suzanne Lenglen's doubles partner and the winner of 19 Wimbledon titles – 12 doubles and 7 mixed. A determined competitor with a cunningly chopped forehand and a great appetite for match-play, she was regarded by contemporaries as the best player never to win a great singles championship'. With a variety of playing partners, she was victorious in the Wimbledon doubles *1914/19/20/21/22/23/25/26/27/30/33/34* and the mixed *1919/21/23/27/28/30/32.* US doubles in *1926,* the French doubles *1930/ 32/33/34.*

JOHN WILLIAM VAN RYN (USA)
Born 30/6/05. Formed one of the most famous of all doubles partnerships with Wilmer Allison. Pat Hughes described their combination as a perfect blending of styles' . . . Van Ryn dipped the ball over from the right court and his partner stepped in at the psychological moment for the final volley.' George Lott thought that their deep personal friendship and knowledge of each other's movements and reactions played an important part in their success. With Allison, Van Ryn succeeded at Wimbledon in *1929–30* and took the US title in *1931/35.* He won Paris and Wimbledon with Lott in *1931.* In the *1929* D Cup challenge round he and Allison beat Cochet and Borotra and in the *1932* match they defeated Cochet and Brugnon. He was a member of the US team from *1929–36* and won 29 of his 32 rubbers in 24 matches. He lost only two of his 24 D Cup doubles.

MANUEL SANTANA (Spain)
Born 10/5/38. Learnt the game as a ballboy and, after a period in which he was the most admired clay court player in Europe, won US singles *1965,* and Wimbledon singles *1966.* Possessed a remarkable forehand and great delicacy of touch. Won French singles *1961/ 64,* defeating Pietrangeli in both finals, and doubles (with Emerson) *1963,* and South African singles *1967.* The most successful Spanish player in history, he won 91 D Cup rubbers out of 119 between *1958–73.*

RICHARD SAVITT (USA)
Born 4/3/27. His talent was discovered in the classic fashion by a complete stranger who saw him playing in a public park, and after a modest junior career he became a powerful exponent of the serve-and-volley game. Concentrating on tennis after a basketball injury in 1949, he rose rapidly on the US ranking–list, moving up from 16th to 6th after reaching sf at Forest Hills, *1950,* with victories over Seixas and Bromwich. His remarkable year was *1951.* He won both the Australian and Wimbledon titles, defeating McGregor in both finals. This was his first trip to Europe and he never achieved the same kind of success again, although he played some memorable matches, notably sf against Rosewall at Forest Hills, *1956,* and a vain defence of his US indoor title in a three–hour f in *1959.* He was a member of the US D Cup team in 1951, but was not chosen to play in the challenge round against Australia.

FREDERICK RUDOLPH SCHROEDER (USA)
Born 20/7/21. A powerful Californian whose aggressive serve-and-volley game brought him much success on fast surfaces. The US National Junior Champion in *1939,* he won the NC Championships from Stanford in *1942* and the same year won the US Championships, defeating Frank Parker in the final. In *1949* he reached the final again but lost in five sets to Pancho Gonzales. Earlier that same year, on his only visit to Wimbledon he had won the singles in heroic fashion after surviving four five–set matches. In the first round he had beaten his doubles partner, Gardnar Mulloy, 7–5 in the fifth (later they reached the doubles final and lost to Gonzales and Parker). In the quarter–finals he had been m-p down to Frank Sedgman and, despite being foot–faulted on his first serve, had followed in his second

serve to hit a winning volley and finally won 9–7 in the final set. In all he played 291 games. Only two champions played more – Boris Becker (292) in 1985 and Ashley Cooper (322) in 1958. In doubles he won the US Championships with Jack Kramer in *1940/41/47* and the mixed with Louise Brough in *1942*. A distinguished member of the US D Cup team between *1946–51*, he played in six challenge rounds, winning eight of his 11 singles and one of his four doubles. – J.B.

FRANCIS ARTHUR SEDGMAN (Australia)
Born 29/10/27. A superb volleyer who seemed to glide about the court, he was Australia's first post-war Wimbledon singles champ and, with Ken McGregor, he achieved the grand slam of the 4 major doubles titles in *1953.* Won Wimbledon singles *1952* and doubles (with J. E. Bromwich) *1948* and (with McGregor) */51/52.* US singles *1951/52* and doubles (with Bromwich) *1950* and (with McGregor) */51.* French doubles (with McGregor) *1951/52.* Australian singles *1949/50* (with McGregor) doubles *1951/52.* Italian singles and doubles (with McGregor) *1952.* Won 25 D Cup rubbers out of 28 between *1949–52.* Turned pro in *1953.*

FRANCISCO 'PANCHO' SEGURA (Ecuador)
Born 20/6/21. An unorthodox showman who made his reputation in his pro years – he achieved little as an amateur. Won the US Clay Court title in *1944* and the US Indoor in *1946,* but made little mark at Wimbledon, losing to Tom Brown and to Drobny in his two singles appearances. He turned pro in 1947 and immediately became one of the great entertainers of the pro game. With his double-fisted forehand, his deadly lobs, his scuttling speed about the court, and his beaming smile, he was a most popular competitor for 20 years. If he did not win as many titles as he deserved, he was always capable of testing players of the quality of Kramer, Rosewall, and Gonzales.

ELIAS VICTOR SEIXAS (USA)
Born 30/8/23. A doggedly successful American competitor. Won Wimbledon singles *1953* and mixed *1953/54/55/56,* 3 times with Doris Hart and once with Shirley Fry. US singles *1954* and doubles (with M. G. Rose) *1952* and (with M. A. Trabert) */54.* French doubles (with Trabert) *1954/55.* Played in 7 successive D Cup challenge rounds and won 38 out of 55 rubbers in 19 ties between *1951–57.*

MARGARET SMITH (Australia)
Born 16/7/42. Now Mrs Court. In 1970 she became the second woman to achieve the Grand Slam of the major singles championships, having brought off a unique mixed doubles slam with Fletcher in *1963.* A powerful athlete, superbly fit, with a heavy service, great stamina and a formidable reach on the volley, she won a record number of 62 GS titles – and would have won more if she had not been afflicted by occasional and often inexplicable losses of confidence. Her major singles successes were Wimbledon *1963/ 65/70,* US Championships *1962/65/69/70/73,* French Championships *1962/64/69/70/ 73,* and Australia *1960–66, 1969–71* and *1973.* She was also three times the holder of the Italian, German and South African titles. In addition, she won the doubles at Wimbledon twice and the mixed five times, the US doubles five times and the mixed on eight occasions, the French four times in doubles and mixed, and she held eight Australian doubles and two mixed titles. She toured successfully, with the help of her husband, Barry, with two children, but retired in 1977 when she found that she was expecting a third baby.

STANLEY ROGER SMITH (USA)
Born 14/12/46. The very epitome of the All-American boy with his tall straight–backed figure, his fair hair and his clean-cut good looks, he became a national hero in *1972*, as well as the world's No. 1 player, when he won a magnificent Wimbledon final against Nastase and then beat the Rumanian again in the opening rubber of the D Cup final on unfriendly clay in Bucharest to launch the United States towards an improbable victory against the odds. Earlier, in *1969*, he had won the US Nationals and the following year had beaten Laver and Rosewall to capture the first–ever Masters which, that year, was a round–robin

competition. When he won the US Open in *1971* on the grass of Forest Hills he was perfecting the serve-and-volley technique that made him such an awkward opponent. Although his groundstrokes were never his strength, he used them intelligently to secure the few breaks of serve that were necessary as he blanketed the net to secure his own service games. His doubles partnership with Lutz was one of the best American pairings there has ever been. They are the only pair to have won US National titles on all four surfaces – grass, clay, hard and indoor. Four times they won the US Open – *1968/74/78/80* and in *1977* they were successful both in South Africa and the US Pro at Boston. In D Cup they are the only American pair to have won three Challenge Round rubbers and two in the Final Round. Overall his D Cup record is 34 wins and 7 losses in 23 ties. – J.B.

FREDERICK SYDNEY STOLLE (Australia)
Born 8/10/38. Former Sydney bank clerk, regarded primarily as doubles specialist, who by diligence and determination became one of the most successful singles players of the 1960s. Powerful serving and volleying, added to dogged consistency in return of service on the backhand, compensated for his lack of mobility and flexibility. Shared with Von Cramm the unlucky distinction of losing in 3 successive Wimbledon singles f, falling to McKinley *(1963)* and Emerson *(1964/65)*. Was also r/u to Lundquist in *1964* Italian f, but won French singles *1965* and US and German titles *1966*. Established himself first as a doubles player with Hewitt. They won Australia *1963/64,* Wimbledon *1962/64* and Italy *1963/64.* With Emerson, who had dominated him in singles, won French and US doubles *1965* and Australia, Italy and US *1966.* In *1981,* aged 42, he and Newcombe (37) took McEnroe/ Fleming to 5s tie–break in US Open sf. Became contract professional *1967* and reached Wimbledon doubles f with Rosewall *1968*, and won mixed doubles there with Ann Jones in *1969*. Between *1964–66* he won 13 out of his 16 D Cup rubbers. Coached NY Sets to victory in World Team Tennis competition *1976.*

ERIC WILLIAM STURGESS (South Africa)
Born 10/6/20. South Africa's most successful singles competitor and their nat champ on no fewer than 11 occasions, beginning a sequence of victories in *1939/40* and continuing in *1946, 1948–54,* and *1957.* Outside Johannesburg his major achievement was the capture of the German singles *1952;* r/u in Paris *1947/51* and lost to Gonzales in *1948* US f. Twice he was in Wimbledon sf, but in spite of speed, steadiness, and elegance, he lacked the weight of shot to win in the highest class and his second service was vulnerable. He won the French doubles with Fannin *1947* and a number of mixed titles, notably Wimbledon *1949* (with Sheila Summers) Land and *1950* (with Louise Brough), and F Hills *1949* (with Brough).

WILLIAM F. TALBERT (USA)
Born 4/11/18. An expert in the practice, technique and strategy of doubles. The best right-court player of his generation, his most important victories were gained with Mulloy, with whom he won the US doubles *1942/45/46/48*, and a total of 84 out of 90 tournaments in ten years. With a variety of partners, he won US Clay Court doubles *1942/44/45/46* and the US Indoor Doubles *1949/50/51/52/54.* Abroad, with the young Trabert, also from Cincinnati, he won French and Italian doubles *1950*. He was runner-up to Parker in US singles *1944/45* and US Indoor champion *1948/51.* He won nine of his ten D Cup rubbers *1946–53*, from *1953–57* he captained the US D Cup team and later became Tournament Director of the US Open. All this was achieved despite the disability of diabetes.

WILLIAM TATUM TILDEN (USA)
Born 10/2/1893. Died 5/6/1953. For many critics the greatest player and student of match-strategy in the history of the game. Tall, with a long reach and a long stride, great strength and versatility of shot, and a powerful sense of drama, Tilden did not win a major title until he was 27. Then won Wimbledon singles *1920/21/30,* and doubles (with F. T. Hunter) *1927,* and US singles *1920/21/22/23/24/25/29,* and doubles *1918/21/22/23/27.* Was first Italian champ in *1930* and played D Cup from *1920–30* winning 34 rubbers out of 41

and 21 out of 28 in challenge rounds. Between *1920–26* won 13 successive challenge round singles. Turned pro in *1931.*

MARION ANTHONY TRABERT (USA)
Born 16/8/30. Won Wimbledon singles *1955* and US singles *1953/55* without losing a set. Won French singles *1954,* and doubles victories included US in *1954* (with E. V. Seixas), French *1950* (with W. F. Talbert) and *1954/55* (with Seixas) and Italian *1950* (with Talbert). Won 27 out of 35 D Cup rubbers between *1951–55.* Turned pro in *1955.*

CHRISTINE CLARA TRUMAN (Great Britain)
Born 16/1/41. Now Mrs Janes. Britain's most popular post-war player. She possessed a powerful forehand, a disconcerting ability to hit her way out of crises, a remarkable capacity for unorthodox volleying, and a temperament and court manners that made her a model for every schoolgirl in the country. She was always regarded as a potential Wimbledon champ and reached sf at the age of 16 at her first Wimbledon, where she lost to Althea Gibson, the eventual winner. Afterwards came a series of spectacular failures until she reached the *1961* f, only to fall to Angela Mortimer. Her best performances were a victory over Miss Gibson in the *1958* W Cup match, which helped to give Britain the trophy for the first time since the war, and the capture of the French and Italian singles titles in *1959.* Won *1960* Australian doubles with Maria Bueno. She and her sister, Nell, formed an aggressively effective – and sometimes erratic – doubles partnership. She won 10 rubbers out of 25 in 11 W Cup matches.

LESLEY ROSEMARY TURNER (Australia)
Born 16/8/42. Now Mrs Bowrey. Clever, strong and persistent, she gained her principal successes on European clay courts. In *1961* on her first European tour she lost to Maria Bueno in the Italian final and was runner-up again *1962/64* before winning the title *1967/68.* She won the French singles *1963,* defeating Ann Jones, and *1965,* beating Margaret Court, and was runner-up *1962/67.* She reached the Australian final *1964/67.* In doubles, with Margaret Court, she won Wimbledon *1964,* Paris *1964/65* and Australia *1965.* Also took the Australian doubles title, with Judy Tegart, *1964/67* and the US doubles, with Darlene Hard, *1961.* Won Wimbledon mixed doubles with Fred Stolle *1961/64.*

H. ELLSWORTH VINES (USA)
Born 28/9/11. The possessor of a fine forehand and one of the fastest services of all time. Defeated Bunny Austin in *1932* 6–4 6–2 6–0 in one of the shortest Wimbledon f and lost title next year in a classic f against Jack Crawford. Won US singles *1931/32* and Australian doubles *1933.* Played D Cup *1932/33,* winning 13 rubbers out of 16. Turned pro *1934.*

SARAH VIRGINIA WADE (Great Britain)
Born 10/7/45. A spectacular and dramatic competitor, at her 16th attempt she finally achieved her ambition of winning the women's singles at Wimbledon in the Centenary year of *1977*. Until then her career had been an extravagant mixture of bitter disappointments, many of the worst endured at Wimbledon, and dazzling successes. Her first major success was gained at US Open *1968* when she defeated Billie Jean King 6–4 6–2 in the final. She won the Australian title, beating Evonne Goolagong, in *1972* and gained her only major clay–court success in *1971,* when she defeated Helga Masthoff in the Italian final. Her best doubles victories – France *1973*, US *1973/75*, Australia *1975* and Italy *1968* – were won with Margaret Court, but she also succeeded in Rome *1971* with Mrs Masthoff and *1973* with Olga Morozova. She also holds the record for the most appearances of any player of any nation in both *Fed Cup* (100 rubbers in 57 ties) and the W Cup (56 rubbers in 20 ties).

ANTHONY FREDERICK WILDING (New Zealand)
Born 31/10/1883. Killed in action in Belgium 9/5/1915. Coached by his father, a notable cricketer, he won the champ of Canterbury, New Zealand, at the age of 17 and went to

Cambridge Univ for which he played **1904–05.** He became one of the great heroes of Edwardian tennis, winning the singles champ at Wimbledon **1910/11/12/13.** Won doubles (with N. E. Brookes) in **1907/14** and (with M. J. G. Ritchie) **/08/10.** He won 21 of the 30 D Cup rubbers which he played for Australasia between **1905–14.**

SIDNEY BURR BEARDSLEE WOOD (USA)

Born 1/11/11. A nephew of the late Julian Myrick, a former President of the US LTA and the prime mover in 1913 in the development of Forest Hills as the national centre of tennis in the US, he made his first appearance at Wimbledon, aged 15, in **1927,** playing Lacoste on the Centre Court. In **1931,** aged 19 years and 243 days, he became Wimbledon's second youngest champion at the time. He won by default. Frank Shields fell in 4s of his sf against Borotra and damaged an ankle. Shields won, but was not fit enough to play in f. A shrewd strategist and a graceful stroke-maker, Wood was r/u to Allison at Forest Hills in **1935** but lost 6–2 6–2 6–3 in one of the tournament's most disappointing finals.

OBITUARIES

ARTHUR ASHE, the greatest black tennis player the world has ever seen, died suddenly of pneumonia at the age of 49 on 6th February 1993. At the time, he was actively engaged in promoting his Arthur Ashe Foundation for the Defeat of Aids for which he had set a fund raising target of $5 million by the end of 1993. Arthur had contracted the virus from a transfusion of contaminated blood during a second major heart operation in 1983. When a national newspaper threatened to publish the fact in April 1992 he decided to call a press conference. It was a very moving occasion as Arthur described his feelings and explained that he would dedicate the remainder of his life to helping others similarly afflicted. Arthur Ashe will certainly be remembered as a great champion, the winner of 33 of the 65 finals he contested during a distinguished career. Growing up in Richmond, Virginia the son of a policeman, he found it difficult to succeed in a white man's sport. But the force of his quiet but persistent personality, plus a wonderful natural ability, enabled him to win the men's singles at the US Open(1968), the Australian Open(1970) and Wimbledon(1975), successes which echoed the achievements of Althea Gibson a decade earlier. With his forthright, attacking game he became a successful Davis Cup player winning 27 of his 32 singles and one of the two doubles rubbers he contested. As player, and later captain, Arthur set standards of behaviour and sportsmanship that were universally admired. He was revered, too, for his uncompromising determination to break down racial prejudices, a determination that forced the South African authorities to grant him a visa to play there in 1973 after several refusals. In an age of fierce competition in sport and ruthless character assassination in politics Arthur Ashe was one of those rare individuals about whom no-one ever uttered an unkind word. He was, indeed, a true gentleman and will be sadly missed not only by his wife and daughter but by a whole generation of young black sportsmen for whom he was a symbol of success.

BRYAN CUTRESS died in May 1992 at the age of 57 after a short illness. As a sports correspondent for the Exchange Telegraph news agency in London for almost 40 years, Brian had earned the respect of tennis players and administrators alike for his straightforward reporting. Accomplished in shorthand, and a speedy touch typist, he was also the envy of his colleagues in the press room who elected him to the post of Chairman of the British Lawn Tennis Writers Association in 1973 and 1974. Brian loved to relax on the golf course and wrote about the sport with the knowledge of a competent performer. He also wrote widely on tennis, rugby, Soccer badminton, table tennis and equestrianism.

KITTY GODFREE died peacefully at the age of 96 on 19th June 1992, just three days before the start of Wimbledon where she had twice made herself the singles champion. By recovering from a set and 1-4 down in her first final against Helen Wills in 1924, Kathleen McKane, as she then was, inflicted the only defeat that the redoubtable American ever suffered in nine visits to Wimbledon. Two years later Kitty was within a point of being 1–4 down in the final set against Lili d'Alvarez of Spain but recovered again to win for the second time. The same year Kitty and her husband Leslie Godfree won the mixed doubles together. To this day they are the only married couple ever to have carried off that title. As the oldest surviving champion for so many years, Kitty was in great demand for interviews from national newspapers and television networks. They were all treated with same the old world courtesy that endeared this grand old lady of British tennis to her legion of admires around the world. Few of them realised that as a young lady Kitty had won the All England Badminton Championships three years in a row, or that as a girl she had cycled with the family to Berlin where her father had business interests. To the last Kitty retained a remarkable vitality and was a familiar figure on her bicycle in East Sheen as she visited the local shops. As recently as 1988 Kitty was a special guest of the Olympic committee in Seoul to commemorate the gold medal in doubles and the bronze in singles she had won in Antwerp in 1920, the last time before 1988 that tennis had been a full medal sport.

GYORGY HOLE, the popular President of the Hungarian Tennis Association, was killed in a motoring accident in May 1992 at the age of 47. Always a progressive thinker Gyorgy had pioneered professional tennis in Hungary and had acted as Tournament Director for 14 professional tournaments. Gyorgy was a printer by trade who became head of the publishing department at the firm where he had started as a hand composer. With his love of tennis, it was no surprise when in 1984 he founded Hungary's most colourful tennis magazine. In 1987 he joined the advertising and marketing department of the national Sports Ministry as executive deputy manager. As a businessman he represented Fila and Pro-Kennex in Hungary and as a journalist he wrote about the game and became secretary of the International Association of Tennis Journalists.

NICOLAS MACCHIAVELLO died on 11th June 1992 at the age of 52 following a period of illness. He had given a life of dedicated service to Ecuadorian tennis. As the President of COSAT since 1990 Nicolas played a leading role in developing every aspect of the game in South America. For four years(1985-1989) he had been the President of the Ecuadorian Tennis Federation after developing junior tennis in the country as captain of the national team in 1983. His work in helping to establish the popularity of Davis Cup tennis throughout South America earned him wide respect.

DAN MASKELL, the doyen of TV tennis commentators, died peacefully on 10th December after a short illness. Dan was 84 and had enjoyed only one year of retirement following his last broadcast for the BBC from the 1991 Grand Slam Cup in Munich. His broadcasting career had begun more than 40 years earlier when he had joined Freddie Grisewood in the Wimbledon commentary box in 1951. The famous mellifluous tones, familiar to tennis lovers the world over, were an integral part of every British summer as he interpreted the matches at Wimbledon with pertinent but restrained comments. Dan had been born in Fulham in 1908, within a stone's throw of Queen's Club where he began his lifelong association with tennis as a ballboy at the age of 15. So adept was he at hitting with the members that after three years he became a full time member of the coaching staff. In 1931 he joined the All England Club as the first professional coach and was attached to the successful British Davis Cup teams of the period where Fred Perry and Bunny Austin came to rely upon his ability as a sparring partner. That playing skill would earn him 19 British Professional titles during the years ahead. In those upstairs downstairs days the teaching professional was not supposed to mix with the amateurs but such was Dan's personality that he helped to break down those social barriers. The award of honorary membership by the All England Club in 1953, the first time a professional had been so honoured, was a cherished moment in Dan's life. During the war Dan spent a productive time as the R.A.F's first Rehabilitation Officer, for which dedicated work he was awarded the O.B.E. After the war he became the Training Manager for the Lawn Tennis Association and set up a scheme to train new coaches. Privately he was asked to coach the royal children and he spent many hours on court at Buckingham palace and elsewhere with Prince Charles, Princess Anne, Princess Alexandra and Prince Andrew. In a very full life Dan experienced two great personal tragedies. In 1970 he lost his only son, Jay, in a flying accident in the West Indies and eight years later he lost his first wife, Connie, in a swimming accident in Antigua. Only the love and understanding of his daughter Robin and his second wife, Kay, whom he married in 1980, enabled him to recover from these blows to make the last years of his life so fruitful. Fittingly for one who had brought so much pleasure to others, Dan was created a CBE in 1982 for his services to tennis and broadcasting.

GIORGIO DE STEFANI, who served for three terms as President of the ITF (1955-56, 1962-63, 1967-69) died during October 1992 at the age of 88. As well as being President of the Italian Federation for 13 years, Giorgio was also a member of the I.O.C. and President of the International Lawn Tennis Club of Italy. As a player he won titles in Greece, Egypt, India, Argentina, Holland and Switzerland and represented Italy in Davis Cup teams between 1926 and 1939. Later he was appointed captain.

WINNIE WOOLDRIDGE who died on 30th March 1992 after a brave but unavailing fight against a terminal illness, will be remembered with affection by all who knew her. Born in Glasgow in 1947 as Winnie Shaw, this talented shotmaker rose quickly to the top of the British junior game and enjoyed a long and successful career as the Scottish No.1, a position she shared over an extended period with her great friend and rival Joyce Barclay, who became Mrs.Williams. Together they were a formidable doubles team and reached the semi-finals at Wimbledon together in 1972. Winnie became a regular member of British Wightman Cup and Federation Cup teams for which she was selected on 26 occasions and when her active days were over she continued to contribute to the game by helping the next generation as coach and captain of junior teams. After her marriage to Keith Wooldridge in 1972 Winnie became equally keen to excel at golf. After twice helping Surrey to win the county title and twice reaching the semi-finals of the Scottish Championships she was particularly proud to be awarded a Scottish cap in 1983, an honour long overdue, according to contemporaries.

CHAMPIONSHIP ROLLS

AUSTRALIAN CHAMPIONSHIPS
MEN'S SINGLES

	CHAMPION	RUNNER-UP	SCORE			
1905	R. W. Heath	A. H. Curtis	4–6	6–3	6–4	6–4
1906	A. F. Wilding	F. N. Fisher	6–0	6–0	6–4	
1907	H. M. Rice	H. A. Parker	6–3	6–4	6–4	
1908	F. B. Alexander	A. W. Dunlop	3–6	3–6	6–0	6–2	6–3
1909	A. F. Wilding	E. F. Parker	6–1	7–5	6–2	
1910	R. W. Heath	H. M. Rice	6–4	6–3	6–2	
1911	N. E. Brookes	H. M. Rice	6–1	6–2	6–3	
1912	J. C. Parke	A. E. Beamish	3–6	6–2	1–6	6–1	7–5
1913	E. F. Parker	H. A. Parker	2–6	6–1	6–3	6–2
1914	A. O'Hara Wood	G. L. Patterson	6–4	6–3	5–7	6–1
1915	F. G. Lowe	H. M. Rice	4–6	6–1	6–1	6–4
1916–18	*Not held*					
1919	A. R. F. Kingscote	E. O. Pockley	6–4	6–0	6–3	
1920	P. O'Hara Wood	V. Thomas	6–3	4–6	6–8	6–1	6–3
1921	R. H. Gemmell	A. Hedeman	7–5	6–1	6–4	
1922	J. O. Anderson	G. L. Patterson	6–0	3–6	3–6	6–3	6–2
1923	P. O'Hara Wood	C. B. St John	6–1	6–1	6–3	
1924	J. O. Anderson	R. E. Schlesinger	6–3	6–4	3–6	5–7	6–3
1925	J. O. Anderson	G. L. Patterson	11–9	2–6	6–2	6–3
1926	J. B. Hawkes	J. Willard	6–1	6–3	6–1	
1927	G. L. Patterson	J. B. Hawkes	3–6	6–4	3–6	18–16	6–3
1928	J. Borotra	R. O. Cummings	6–4	6–1	4–6	5–7	6–3
1929	J. C. Gregory	R. E. Schlesinger	6–2	6–2	5–7	7–5
1930	E. F. Moon	H. C. Hopman	6–3	6–1	6–3	
1931	J. H. Crawford	H. C. Hopman	6–4	6–2	2–6	6–1
1932	J. H. Crawford	H. C. Hopman	4–6	6–3	3–6	6–3	6–1
1933	J. H. Crawford	K. Gledhill	2–6	7–5	6–3	6–2
1934	F. J. Perry	J. H. Crawford	6–3	7–5	6–1	
1935	J. H. Crawford	F. J. Perry	2–6	6–4	6–4	6–4
1936	A. K. Quist	J. H. Crawford	6–2	6–3	4–6	3–6	9–7
1937	V. B. McGrath	J. E. Bromwich	6–3	1–6	6–0	2–6	6–1
1938	J. D. Budge	J. E. Bromwich	6–4	6–2	6–1	
1939	J. E. Bromwich	A. K. Quist	6–4	6–1	6–3	
1940	A. K. Quist	J. H. Crawford	6–3	6–1	6–2	
1941–45	*Not held*					
1946	J. E. Bromwich	D. Pails	5–7	6–3	7–5	3–6	6–2
1947	D. Pails	J. E. Bromwich	4–6	6–4	3–6	7–5	8–6
1948	A. K. Quist	J. E. Bromwich	6–4	3–6	6–3	2–6	6–3
1949	F. A. Sedgman	J. E. Bromwich	6–3	6–2	6–2	
1950	F. A. Sedgman	K. McGregor	6–3	6–4	4–6	6–1
1951	R. Savitt	K. McGregor	6–3	2–6	6–3	6–1
1952	K. McGregor	F. A. Sedgman	7–5	12–10	2–6	6–2
1953	K. R. Rosewall	M. G. Rose	6–0	6–3	6–4	
1954	M. G. Rose	R. N. Hartwig	6–2	0–6	6–4	6–2
1955	K. R. Rosewall	L. A. Hoad	9–7	6–4	6–4	
1956	L. A. Hoad	K. R. Rosewall	6–4	3–6	6–4	7–5
1957	A. J. Cooper	N. A. Fraser	6–3	9–11	6–4	6–2
1958	A. J. Cooper	M. J. Anderson	7–5	6–3	6–4	
1959	A. Olmedo	N. A. Fraser	6–1	6–2	3–6	6–3
1960	R. G. Laver	N. A. Fraser	5–7	3–6	6–3	8–6	8–6
1961	R. S. Emerson	R. G. Laver	1–6	6–3	7–6	6–4
1962	R. G. Laver	R. S. Emerson	8–6	0–6	6–4	6–4
1963	R. S. Emerson	K. N. Fletcher	6–3	6–3	6–1	

1964	R. S. Emerson	F. S. Stolle	6–3	6–4	6–2		
1965	R. S. Emerson	F. S. Stolle	7–9	2–6	6–4	7–5	6–1
1966	R. S. Emerson	A. R. Ashe	6–4	6–8	6–2	6–3	FIRST
1967	R. S. Emerson	A. R. Ashe	6–4	6–1	6–4		PRIZE
1968	W. W. Bowrey	J. M. Gisbert	7–5	2–6	9–7	6–4	(US $)
1969	R. G. Laver	A. Gimeno	6–3	6–4	7–5		5,000
1970	A. R. Ashe	R. D. Crealy	6–4	9–7	6–2		3,800
1971	K. R. Rosewall	A. R. Ashe	6–1	7–5	6–3		10,000
1972	K. R. Rosewall	M. J. Anderson	7–6	6–3	7–5		2,240
1973	J. D. Newcombe	O. Parun	6–3	6–7	7–5	6–1	8,750
1974	J. S. Connors	P. Dent	7–6	6–4	4–6	6–3	9,750
1975	J. D. Newcombe	J. S. Connors	7–5	3–6	6–4	7–5	12,489
1976	M. Edmondson	J. D. Newcombe	6–7	6–3	7–6	6–1	32,000
1977	(Jan) R. Tanner	G. Vilas	6–3	6–3	6–3		32,000
1977	(Dec) V. Gerulaitis	J. M. Lloyd	6–3	7–6	5–7	3–6 6–2	28,000
1978	(Dec) G. Vilas	J. Marks	6–4	6–4	3–6	6–3	41,000
1979	(Dec) G. Vilas	J. Sadri	7–6	6–3	6–2		50,000
1980	(Dec) B. Teacher	K. Warwick	7–5	7–6	6–3		65,000
1981	(Dec) J. Kriek	S. Denton	6–2	7–6	6–7	6–4	65,000
1982	(Dec) J. Kriek	S. Denton	6–3	6–3	6–2		70,000
1983	(Dec) M. Wilander	I. Lendl	6–1	6–4	6–4		77,500
1984	(Dec) M. Wilander	K. Curren	6–7	6–4	7–6	6–2	100,000
1985	(Dec) S. Edberg	M. Wilander	6–4	6–3	6–3		100,000
1986	*Not held*						
1987	(Jan) S. Edberg	P. Cash	6–3	6–4	3–6	5–7 6–3	103,875
1988	M. Wilander	P. Cash	6–3	6–7	2–6	6–1 8–6	104,997
1989	I. Lendl	M. Mecir	6–2	6–2	6–2		140,000
1990	I. Lendl	S. Edberg	4–6	7–6	5–2 ret'd		200,000
1991	B. Becker	I. Lendl	6–4	5–7	3–6	7–6 6–4	246,400
1992	J. Courier	S. Edberg	6–3	3–6	6–4	6–2	274,909

WOMEN'S SINGLES

	CHAMPION	RUNNER–UP	SCORE		
1922	Mrs M. Molesworth	Miss E. F. Boyd	6–3	10–8	
1923	Mrs M. Molesworth	Miss E. F. Boyd	6–1	7–5	
1924	Miss S. Lance	Miss E. F. Boyd	6–3	3–6	6–4
1925	Miss D. Akhurst	Miss E. F. Boyd	1–6	8–6	6–4
1926	Miss D. Akhurst	Miss E. F. Boyd	6–1	6–3	
1927	Miss E. F. Boyd	Mrs S. Harper	5–7	6–1	6–2
1928	Miss D. Akhurst	Miss E. F. Boyd	7–5	6–2	
1929	Miss D. Akhurst	Miss L. M. Bickerton	6–1	5–7	6–2
1930	Miss D. Akhurst	Mrs S. Harper	10–8	2–6	7–5
1931	Mrs C. Buttsworth	Mrs J. H. Crawford	1–6	6–3	6–4
1932	Mrs C. Buttsworth	Miss K. Le Messurier	9–7	6–4	
1933	Miss J. Hartigan	Mrs C. Buttsworth	6–4	6–3	
1934	Miss J. Hartigan	Mrs M. Molesworth	6–1	6–4	
1935	Miss D. E. Round	Miss N. M. Lyle	1–6	6–1	6–3
1936	Miss J. Hartigan	Miss N. Wynne	6–4	6–4	
1937	Miss N. Wynne	Mrs V. Westacott	6–3	5–7	6–4
1938	Miss D. M. Bundy	Miss D. Stevenson	6–3	6–2	
1939	Mrs V. Westacott	Mrs H. C. Hopman	6–1	6–2	
1940	Mrs N. Bolton	Miss T. Coyne	5–7	6–4	6–0
1941–45	*Not held*				
1946	Mrs N. Bolton	Miss J. Fitch	6–4	6–4	
1947	Mrs N. Bolton	Mrs H. C. Hopman	6–3	6–2	
1948	Mrs N. Bolton	Miss M. Toomey	6–3	6–1	
1949	Miss D. J. Hart	Mrs N. Bolton	6–3	6–4	
1950	Miss A. L. Brough	Miss D. J. Hart	6–4	3–6	6–4
1951	Mrs N. Bolton	Mrs T. D. Long	6–1	7–5	
1952	Mrs T. D. Long	Miss H. Angwin	6–2	6–3	
1953	Miss M. Connolly	Miss J. Sampson	6–3	6–2	
1954	Mrs T. D. Long	Miss J. Staley	6–3	6–4	
1955	Miss B. Penrose	Mrs T. D. Long	6–4	6–3	
1956	Miss M. Carter	Mrs T. D. Long	3–6	6–2	9–7
1957	Miss S. J. Fry	Miss A. Gibson	6–3	6–4	
1958	Miss A. Mortimer	Miss L. Coghlan	6–3	6–4	
1959	Mrs S. J. Reitano	Miss R. Schuurman	6–2	6–3	
1960	Miss M. Smith	Miss J. Lehane	7–5	6–2	
1961	Miss M. Smith	Miss J. Lehane	6–1	6–4	
1962	Miss M. Smith	Miss J. Lehane	6–0	6–2	

1963	Miss M. Smith	Miss J. Lehane	6–2	6–2		
1964	Miss M. Smith	Miss L. R. Turner	6–3	6–2		
1965	Miss M. Smith	Miss M. E. Bueno	5–7	6–4	5–2ret'd	
1966	Miss M. Smith	Miss N. Richey	w.o.			FIRST
1967	Miss N. Richey	Miss L. R. Turner	6–1	6–4		PRIZE
1968	Mrs L. W. King	Mrs B. M. Court	6–1	6–2		(US $)
1969	Mrs B. M. Court	Mrs L. W. King	6–4	6–	1	2,000
1970	Mrs B. M. Court	Miss K. Melville	6–1	6–3		700
1971	Mrs B. M. Court	Miss E. Goolagong	2–6	7–5	7–6	1,800
1972	Miss S. V. Wade	Miss E. Goolagong	6–4	6–4		1,200
1973	Mrs B. M. Court	Miss E. Goolagong	6–4	7–5		5,700
1974	Miss E. Goolagong	Miss C. M. Evert	7–6	4–6	6–0	9,000
1975	Miss E. Goolagong	Miss M. Navratilova	6–3	6–2		8,115
1976	Mrs E. Cawley	Miss R. Tomanova	6–2	6–2		12,000
1977	(Jan) Mrs G. Reid	Miss D. Fromholtz	7–5	6–2		12,000
1977	(Dec) Mrs E. Cawley	Mrs H. Cawley	6–3	6–0		9,000
1978	(Dec) Miss C. O'Neil	Miss B. Nagelsen	6–3	7–6		6,000
1979	(Dec) Miss B. Jordan	Miss S. Walsh	6–3	6–3		10,000
1980	(Dec) Miss H. Mandlikova	Miss W. M. Turnbull	6–0	7–5		32,000
1981	(Dec) Miss M. Navratilova	Mrs C. Evert Lloyd	6–7	6–4	7–5	34,000
1982	(Dec) Mrs C. Evert Lloyd	Miss M. Navratilova	6–3	2–6	6–3	40,000
1983	(Dec) Miss M. Navratilova	Miss K. Jordan	6–2	7–6		5,000
1984	(Dec) Mrs J. M. Lloyd	Miss H. Sukova	6–7	6–1	6–3	100,000
1985	(Dec) Miss M. Navratilova	Mrs J. M. Lloyd	6–2	4–6	6–2	100,000
1986	*Not held*					
1987	(Jan) Miss H. Mandlikova	Miss M. Navratilova	7–5	7–6		115,000
1988	Miss S. Graf	Miss C. Evert	6–1	7–6		115,000
1989	Miss S. Graf	Miss H. Sukova	6–4	6–4		135,000
1990	Miss S. Graf	Miss M. J. Fernandez	6–3	6–4		190,000
1991	Miss M. Seles	Miss J. Novotna	5–7	6–3	6–1	246,400
1992	Miss M. Seles	Miss M. J. Fernandez	6–2	6–3		274,909

MEN'S DOUBLES

	CHAMPIONS	RUNNERS–UP	SCORE				
1905	R. Lycett/T. Tachell	E. T. Barnard/B. Spence	11–9	8–6	1–6	4–6	6–1
1906	R. W. Heath/A. F. Wilding	C. C. Cox/H. A. Parker	6–2	6–4	6–2		
1907	W. A. Gregg/H. A. Parker	H. M. Rice/G. W. Wright	6–2	3–6	6–3	6–2	
1908	F. B. Alexander/A. W. Dunlop	G. G. Sharpe/A. F. Wilding	6–3	6–2	6–1		
1909	J. P. Keane/E. F. Parker	C. Crooks/A. F. Wilding	1–6	6–1	6–1	9–7	
1910	A. Campbell/H. M. Rice	R. W. Heath/J. L. O'Dea	6–3	6–3	6–2		
1911	H. W. Heath/R. Lycett	J. J. Addison/N. E. Brookes	6–2	7–5	6–0		
1912	C. P. Dixon/J. C. Parke	A. E. Beamish/F. G. Lowe	6–0	6–4	6–2		
1913	A. H. Hedemann/E. F. Parker	H. Parker/R. Taylor	8–6	4–6	6–4	6–4	
1914	A. Campbell/G. L. Patterson	R. W. Heath/A. O'Hara Wood	7–5	3–6	6–3	6–3	
1915	H. M. Rice/C. V. Todd	F. G. Lowe/C. St John	8–6	6–4	7–9	6–3	
1916–1918	*Not held*						
1919	P. O'Hara Wood/R. V. Thomas	J. O. Anderson/A. H. Lowe	7–5	6–1	7–9	3–6	6–3
1920	P. O'Hara Wood/R. V. Thomas	H. Rice/R. Taylor	6–1	6–0	7–5		
1921	S. H. Eaton/R. H. Gemmell	E. Stokes/N. Breasly	7–5	6–3	6–3		
1922	J. B. Hawkes/G. L. Patterson	J. O. Anderson/N. Peach	8–10	6–0	6–0	7–5	
1923	P. O'Hara Wood/C. B. St John	H. Rice/J. Bullough	6–4	6–3	3–6	6–0	
1924	J. O. Anderson/N. E. Brookes	P. O'Hara Wood/G. L. Patterson	6–2	6–4	6–3		
1925	P. O'Hara Wood/G. L. Patterson	J. O. Anderson/F. Kalms	6–4	8–6	7–5		
1926	J. B. Hawkes/G. L. Patterson	J. O. Anderson/P. O'Hara Wood	6–1	6–4	6–2		
1927	J. B. Hawkes/G. L. Patterson	I. McInnes/P. O'Hara Wood	8–6	6–2	6–1		
1928	J. Borotra/J. Brugnon	E. F. Moon/J. Willard	6–2	4–6	6–4	6–4	
1929	J. H. Crawford/H. C. Hopman	R. O. Cummings/E. F. Moon	6–1	6–8	4–6	6–1	6–3
1930	J. H. Crawford/H. C. Hopman	J. Fitchett/J. B. Hawkes	8–6	6–1	2–6	6–3	
1931	C. Donohoe/R. Dunlop	J. H. Crawford/H. O. Hopman	8–6	6–2	5–7	7–9	6–4
1932	J. H. Crawford/E. F. Moon	H. C. Hopman/G. L. Patterson	12–10	6–3	4–6	6–4	
1933	K. Gledhill/H. E. Vines	J. H. Crawford/E. F. Moon	6–4	10–8	6–2		
1934	G. P. Hughes/F. J. Perry	A. K. Quist/D. P. Turnbull	6–8	6–3	6–4	3–6	6–3
1935	J. H. Crawford/V. B. McGrath	G. P. Hughes/F. J. Perry	6–4	8–6	6–2		
1936	A. K. Quist/D. P. Turnbull	J. H. Crawford/V. B. McGrath	6–8	6–2	6–1	3–6	6–2
1937	A. K. Quist/D. P. Turnbull	J. E. Bromwich/J. E. Harper	6–2	9–7	1–6	6–8	6–4
1938	J. E. Bromwich/A. K. Quist	H. Henkel/G. Von Cramm	7–5	6–4	6–0		
1939	J. E. Bromwich/A. K. Quist	C. F. Long/D. P. Turnbull	6–4	7–5	6–2		
1940	J. E. Bromwich/A. K. Quist	J. H. Crawford/V. B. McGrath	6–3	7–5	6–1		
1941–1945	*Not held*						
1946	J. E. Bromwich/A. K. Quist	M. Newcombe/L. A. Schwartz	6–4	6–2	6–3		

Year	Champions	Runners-up					
1947	J. E. Bromwich/A. K. Quist	F. A. Sedgman/G. Worthington	6–1	6–3	6–1		
1948	J. E. Bromwich/A. K. Quist	C. Long/F. A. Sedgman	1–6	6–8	9–7	6–3	8–6
1949	J. E. Bromwich/A. K. Quist	G. Brown/O. W. Sidwell	6–8	7–5	6–2	6–3	
1950	J. E. Bromwich/A. K. Quist	J. Drobny/E. W. Sturgess	6–3	5–7	4–6	6–3	8–6
1951	K. McGregor/F. A. Sedgman	J. E. Bromwich/A. K. Quist	11–9	2–6	6–3	4–6	6–3
1952	K. McGregor/F. A. Sedgman	D. Candy/M. G. Rose	6–4	7–5	6–3		
1953	L. A. Hoad/K. R. Rosewall	D. Candy/M. G. Rose	9–11	6–4	10–8	6–4	
1954	R. N. Hartwig/M. G. Rose	N. A. Fraser/C. Wilderspin	6–3	6–4	6–2		
1955	E. V. Seixas/M. A. Trabert	L. A. Hoad/K. R. Rosewall	6–3	6–2	2–6	3–6	6–1
1956	L. A. Hoad/K. R. Rosewall	D. Candy/M. G. Rose	10–8	13–11	6–4		
1957	N. A. Fraser/L. A. Hoad	M. J. Anderson/A. Cooper	6–3	8–6	6–4		
1958	A. Cooper/N. A. Fraser	R. S. Emerson/R. Mark	6–5	6–8	3–6	6–3	7–5
1959	R. G. Laver/R. Mark	D. Candy/R. N. Howe	9–7	6–4	6–2		
1960	R. G. Laver/R. Mark	R. S. Emerson/N. A. Fraser	1–6	6–2	6–4	6–4	
1961	R. G. Laver/R. Mark	R. S. Emerson/M. F. Mulligan	6–3	7–5	3–6	7–9	6–2
1962	R. S. Emerson/N. A. Fraser	R. A. J. Hewitt/F. S. Stolle	4–6	4–6	6–1	6–4	11–9
1963	R. A. J. Hewitt/F. S. Stolle	K. N. Fletcher/J. D. Newcombe	6–2	3–6	6–3	3–6	6–3
1964	R. A. J. Hewitt/F. S. Stolle	R. S. Emerson/K. N. Fletcher	6–4	7–5	3–6	4–6	14–12
1965	J. D. Newcombe/A. D. Roche	R. S. Emerson/F. S. Stolle	3–6	4–6	13–11	6–3	6–4
1966	R. S. Emerson/F. S. Stolle	J. D. Newcombe/A. D. Roche	7–9	6–3	6–8	14–12	12–10
1967	J. D. Newcombe/A. D. Roche	W. W. Bowrey/O. K. Davidson	3–6	6–3	7–5	6–8	8–6
1968	R. D. Crealy/A. J. Stone	T. Addison/R. Keldie	10–8	6–4	6–3		
1969	R. S. Emerson/R. G. Laver	K. R. Rosewall/F. S. Stolle	6–4	6–4	6–4		
1970	R. C. Lutz/S. R. Smith	J. G. Alexander/P. Dent	6–3	8–6	6–3		
1971	J. D. Newcombe/A. D. Roche	T. S. Okker/M. C. Riessen	6–2	7–6			
1972	O. K. Davidson/K. R. Rosewall	R. Case/G. Masters	3–6	7–6	6–3		
1973	M. J. Anderson/J. D. Newcombe	J. G. Alexander/P. Dent	6–3	6–4	7–6		
1974	R. Case/G. Masters	S. Ball/R. Giltinan	6–7	6–3	6–4		
1975	J. G. Alexander/P. Dent	R. Carmichael/A. J. Stone	6–3	7–6			
1976	J. D. Newcombe/A. D. Roche	R. Case/G. Masters	7–6	6–4			
1977	A. R. Ashe/A. D. Roche	C. Pasarell/E. Van Dillen	6–4	6–4			
1977	(Dec) R. O. Ruffels/A. J. Stone	J. G. Alexander/P. Dent	7–6	7–6			
1978	(Dec) Fibak/K. Warwick	P. Kronk/C. Letcher	7–6	7–5			
1979	(Dec) P. McNamara/P. McNamee	P. Kronk/C. Letcher	7–6	6–2			
1980	(Dec) M. R. Edmondson/K. Warwick	P. McNamara/P. McNamee	7–5	6–4			
1981	(Dec) M. R. Edmondson/K. Warwick	H. Pfister/J. Sadri	6–3	6–7	6–3		
1982	(Dec) J. G. Alexander/J. Fitzgerald	A. Andrews/J. Sadri	6–4	7–6			
1983	(Dec) M. R. Edmondson/P. McNamee	S. Denton/S. E. Stewart	6–3	7–6			
1984	(Dec) M. R. Edmondson/S. E. Stewart	J. Nystrom/M. Wilander	6–2	6–2	7–5		
1985	(Dec) P. Annacone/C. Van Rensburg	M. R. Edmondson/K. Warwick	3–6	7–6	6–4	6–4	
1986	*Not held*						
1987	(Jan) S. Edberg/A. Jarryd	P. Doohan/L. Warder	6–4	6–4	7–6		
1988	R. Leach/J. Pugh	M. J. Bates/P. Lundgren	6–3	6–2	6–3		
1989	R. Leach/J. Pugh	D. Cahill/M. Kratzmann	6–4	6–4	6–4		
1990	P. Aldrich/D. Visser	G. Connell/G. Michibata	6–4	4–6	6–1	6–4	
1991	S. Davis/D. Pate	P. McEnroe/D. Wheaton	6–7	7–6	6–3	7–5	
1992	M. Woodbridge/M. Woodforde	K. Jones/R. Leach	6–4	6–3	6–4		

WOMEN'S DOUBLES

Year	CHAMPIONS	RUNNERS-UP	SCORE		
1922	E. F. Boyd/M. Mountain	St George/H. S. Utz	1–6	6–4	7–5
1923	E. F. Boyd/S. Lance	M. Molesworth/H. Turner	6–1	6–4	
1924	D. Akhurst/S. Lance	K. Le Mesurier/P. O'Hara Wood	7–5	6–2	
1925	D. Akhurst/R. Harper	E. F. Boyd/K. Le Mesurier	6–4	6–3	
1926	E. F. Boyd/P. O'Hara Wood	D. Akhurst/M. Cox	6–3	6–8	8–6
1927	L. M. Bickerton/P. O'Hara Wood	E. F. Boyd/R. Harper	6–3	6–3	
1928	D. Akhurst/E. F. Boyd	K. Le Mesurier/D. Weston	6–3	6–1	
1929	D. Akhurst/L. M. Bickerton	R. Harper/P. O'Hara Wood	6–2	3–6	6–2
1930	E. Hood/M. Molesworth	M. Cox/R. Harper	6–3	0–6	7–5
1931	L. M. Bickerton/R. Cozens	A. Lloyd/H. S. Utz	6–0	6–4	
1932	C. Buttsworth/J. H. Crawford	K. Le Mesurier/D. Weston	6–2	6–2	
1933	M. Molesworth/V. Westacott	J. Hartigan/J. Van Ryn	6–3	6–3	
1934	M. Molesworth/V. Westacott	J. Hartigan/U. Valkenborg	6–8	6–4	6–4
1935	E. M. Dearman/N. M. Lyle	L. M. Bickerton/N. Hopman	6–3	6–4	
1936	T. Coyne/N. Wynne	M. Blick/K. Woodward	6–2	6–4	
1937	T. Coyne/N. Wynne	N. Hopman/V. Westacott	6–2	6–2	
1938	T. Coyne/N. Wynne	D. M. Bundy/D. E. Workman	9–7	6–4	
1939	T. Coyne/N. Wynne	M. Hardcastle/V. Westacott	7–5	6–4	
1940	T. Coyne/N. Bolton	J. Hartigan/E. Niemeyer	7–5	6–2	
1941–1945	*Not held*				

1946 M. Bevis/J. Fitch	Not available			
1947 N. Bolton/T. D. Long	M. Bevis/J. Fitch	6–3	6–3	
1948 N. Bolton/T. D. Long	M. Bevis/N. Jones	6–3	6–3	
1949 N. Bolton/T. D. Long	D./M. Toomey	6–0	6–1	
1950 L. Brough/D.J. Hart	N. Bolton/T. D. Long	6–3	2–6	6–3
1951 N. Bolton/T. D. Long	J. Fitch/M. Hawton	6–2	6–1	
1952 N. Bolton/T. D. Long	R. Baker/M. Hawton	6–1	6–1	
1953 M. Connolly/J. Sampson	M. Hawton/B. Penrose	6–3	6–2	
1954 M. Hawton/B. Penrose	H. Redick–Smith/J. Wipplinger	6–3	8–6	
1955 M. Hawton/B. Penrose	N. Hopman/A. Thiele	7–5	6–1	
1956 M. Hawton/T. D. Long	M. Carter/B. Penrose	6–3	5–7	9–7
1957 S. J. Fry/A. Gibson	M. Hawton/F. Muller	6–2	6–1	
1958 M. Hawton/T. D. Long	L. Coghlan/A. Mortimer	7–5	6–8	6–2
1959 S. Reynolds/R. Schuurman	L. Coghlan/M. Reitano	7–5	6–4	
1960 M. E. Bueno/C. Truman	L. Robinson/M. Smith	6–2	5–7	6–2
1961 M. Reitano/M. Smith	M. Hawton/J. Lehane	6–3	3–6	7–5
1962 R. Ebbern/M. Smith	D. R. Hard/M. Reintano	6–4	6–4	
1963 R. Ebbern/M. Smith	J. Lehane/L. R. Turner	6–1	6–3	
1964 J. A. M. Tegart/L. R. Turner	R. Ebbern/M. Smith	6–4	6–4	
1965 M. Smith/L. R. Turner	R. Ebbern/B. J. Moffitt	1–6	6–2	6–3
1966 C. Graebner/N. Richey	M. Smith/L. R. Turner	6–4	7–5	
1967 J. A. M. Tegart/L. R. Turner	L. Robinson/E. Terras	6–0	6–2	
1968 K. Krantzcke/K. Melville	J. A. M. Tegart/L. R. Turner	6–4	3–6	6–2
1969 B. M. Court/J. A. M. Tegart	R. Casals/L. W. King	6–4	6–4	
1970 B. M. Court/D. Dalton	K. Krantzcke/K. Melville	6–3	6–4	
1971 B. M. Court/E. F. Goolagong	J. Emmerson/L. Hunt	6–0	6–0	
1972 H. Gourlay/K. Harris	P. Coleman/K. Krantzcke	6–2	6–3	
1973 B. M. Court/S. V. Wade	K. Harris/K. Melville	6–4	6–4	
1974 E. F. Goolagong/M. Michel	K. Harris/K. Melville	7–5	6–3	
1975 E. F. Goolagong/M. Michel	B. M. Court/O. Morozova	7–6	7–6	
1976 E. F. Cawley/H. Gourlay	W. W. Bowrey/R. Tomanova	8–1(one set)		
1977 D. Fromholtz/H. Gourlay	B. Nagelsen/G. E. Reid	5–7	6–1	7–5
1977 (Dec) E. F. Cawley/H. Cawley div'd with M. Guerrant/G. E. Reid				
1978 (Dec) B. Nagelsen/R. Tomanova	N. Sato/P. Whytcross	7–5	6–2	
1979 (Dec) D. D. Chaloner/D. R. Evers	L. Harrison/M. Mesker	6–2	1–6	6–0
1980 (Dec) B. Nagelsen/M. Navratilova	A. Kiyomura/C. Reynolds	6–4	6–4	
1981 (Dec) K. Jordan/A. E. Smith	M. Navratilova/P. H. Shriver	6–2	7–5	
1982 (Dec) M. Navratilova/P. H. Shriver	C. Kohde/E. Pfaff	6–4	6–2	
1983 (Dec) M. Navratilova/P. H. Shriver	A. E. Hobbs/W. M. Turnbull	6–4	6–7	6–2
1984 (Dec) M. Navratilova/P. H. Shriver	C. Kohde–Kilsch/H. Sukova	6–3	6–4	
1985 (Dec) M. Navratilova/P. H. Shriver	C. Kohde–Kilsch/H. Sukova	6–3	6–4	
1986 *Not held*				
1987 (Jan) M. Navratilova/P. H. Shriver	Z. Garrison/L. McNeil	6–1	6–0	
1988 M. Navratilova/P. H. Shriver	C. Evert/W. M. Turnbull	6–0	7–5	
1989 M. Navratilova/P. H. Shriver	P. Fendick/J. Hetherington	3–6	6–3	6–2
1990 J. Novotna/H. Sukova	P. Fendick/M. J. Fernandez	7–6	7–6	
1991 P. Fendick/M. J. Fernandez	G. Fernandez/J. Novotna	7–6	6–1	
1992 A. Sanchez–Vic/H. Sukova	G. Fernandez/Z. Garrison	6–4	7–6	

MIXED DOUBLES

CHAMPIONS	RUNNERS–UP	SCORE		
1922 J. B. Hawkes/Miss E. F. Boyd	H. S. Utz/Mrs Utz	6–1	6–1	
1923 H. M. Rice/Miss S. Lance	C. St John/Miss M. Molesworth	2–6	6–4	6–4
1924 J. Willard/Miss D. Akhurst	G. M. Hone/Miss E. F. Boyd	6–3	6–4	
1925 J. Willard/Miss D. Akhurst	R. E. Schlesinger/Mrs R. Harper	6–4	6–4	
1926 J. B. Hawkes/Miss E. F. Boyd	J. Willard/Miss D. Akhurst	6–2	6–4	
1927 J. B. Hawkes/Miss E. F. Boyd	J. Willard/Miss Y. Anthony	6–1	6–3	
1928 J. Borotra/Miss D. Akhurst	J. B. Hawkes/Miss E. F. Boyd	w.o		
1929 E. F. Moon/Miss D. Akhurst	J. H. Crawford/Miss M. Cox	6–0	7–5	
1930 H. C. Hopman/Miss N. Hall	J. H. Crawford/Miss M. Cox	11–9	3–6	6–3
1931 J. H. Crawford/Mrs Crawford	A. Willard/Mrs V. Westacott	7–5	6–4	
1932 J. H. Crawford/Mrs Crawford	J. Satoh/Mrs P. O'Hara Wood	6–8	8–6	6–3
1933 J. H. Crawford/Mrs Crawford	H. E. Vines/Mrs J. Van Ryn	3–6	7–5	13–11
1934 E. F. Moon/Miss J. Hartigan	R. Dunlop/Mrs V. Westacott	6–3	6–4	
1935 C. Boussus/Miss L. Bickerton	V. G. Kirby/Mrs Bond	1–6	6–3	6–3
1936 H. C. Hopman/Mrs Hopman	A. A. Kay/Miss M. Blick	6–2	6–0	
1937 H. C. Hopman/Mrs Hopman	D. P. Turnbull/Miss D. Stevenson	3–6	6–3	6–2
1938 J. E. Bromwich/Miss J. Wilson	C. Long/Miss N. Wynne	6–3	6–2	
1939 H. C. Hopman/Mrs Hopman	J. E. Bromwich/Miss J. Wilson	6–8	6–2	6–3
1940 C. Long/Mrs N. Bolton	H. C. Hopman/Mrs Hopman	7–5	2–6	6–4

1941–1945	Not held				
1946	C. Long/Mrs N. Bolton	J. Bromwich/Miss J. Fitch	6–0	6–4	
1947	C. Long/Mrs N. Bolton	J. E. Bromwich/Miss J. Fitch	6–3	6–3	
1948	C. Long/Mrs N. Bolton	O. W. Sidwell/Mrs T. D. Long	7–5	4–6	8–6
1949	F. A. Sedgman/Miss D. J. Hart	J. E. Bromwich/Miss J. Fitch	6–1	5–7	12–10
1950	F. A. Sedgman/Miss D. J. Hart	E. W. Sturgess/Miss J. Fitch	6–3	2–6	6–3
1951	G. A. Worthington/Mrs T. D. Long	J. May/Miss C. Proctor	4–6	6–3	6–2
1952	G. A. Worthington/Mrs T. D. Long	T. Warhurst/Mrs A. R. Thiele	9–7	7–5	
1953	R. N. Hartwig/Miss J. Sampson	H. Richardson/Miss M. Connolly	6–4	6–3	
1954	R. N. Hartwig/Mrs T. D. Long	J. E. Bromwich/Miss B. Penrose	8–6	9–7	
1955	G. A. Worthington/Mrs T. D. Long	L. A. Hoad/Miss J. Staley	6–2	6–1	
1956	N. A. Fraser/Miss B. Penrose	R. S. Emerson/Mrs M. Hawton	6–2	6–4	
1957	M. J. Anderson/Miss F. Muller	W. A. Knight/Miss J. Langley	7–5	3–6	6–1
1958	R. N. Howe/Mrs M. Hawton	A. Newman/Miss A. Mortimer	9–11	6–1	6–2
1959	R. Mark/Miss S. Reynolds	R. G. Laver/Miss R. Schuurman	4–6	13–11	6–1
1960	T. Fancutt/Miss J. Lehane	R. Mark/Mrs M. Reitano	6–2	7–5	
1961	R. A. J. Hewitt/Miss J. Lehane	J. Pearce/Mrs M. Reitano	9–7	6–2	
1962	F. S. Stolle/Miss L. R. Turner	R. Taylor/Miss D. R. Hard	6–3	9–7	
1963	K. N. Fletcher/Miss M. Smith	F. S. Stolle/Miss L. R. Turner	7–5	5–7	6–4
1964	K. N. Fletcher/Miss M. Smith	M. J. Sangster/Miss J. Lehane	6–1	6–2	
1965	J. D. Newcombe/Miss M. Smith div'd with O. K. Davidson/Miss R. Ebbern				
1966	A. D. Roche/Miss J. A. Tegart	W. W. Bowrey/Miss R. Ebbern	6–1	6–3	
1967	O. K. Davidson/Miss L. R. Turner	A. D. Roche/Miss J. A. M. Tegart	9–7	6–4	
1968	R. D. Crealy/Mrs L. W. King	A. J. Stone/Mrs B. M. Court	6–2	9–7	
1969	M. C. Riessen/Mrs B. M. Court div'd with F. S. Stolle/Mrs P. F. Jones				
1970–1986	Not held				
1987	S. E. Stewart/Miss Z. Garrison	A. Castle/Miss A. E. Hobbs	3–6	7–6	6–3
1988	J. Pugh/Miss J. Novotna	Tim Gullikson/M. Navratilova	5–7	6–2	6–4
1989	J. Pugh/Miss J. Novotna	S. Stewart/Miss Z. Garrison	6–3	6–4	
1990	J. Pugh/Miss N. Zvereva	R. Leach/Miss Z. Garrison	4–6	6–2	6–3
1991	J. Bates/Miss J. Durie	S. Davis/Miss R. White	2–6	6–4	6–4
1992	M. Woodforde/Miss N. Provis	T. Woodbridge/Miss A. Sanchez–Vic.	6–3	4–6	11–9

FRENCH CHAMPIONSHIPS

Up to 1924 entry was restricted to members of French clubs. In 1925 entry was open to all amateurs. The Championships became open' in 1968.

MEN'S SINGLES

1891	H. Briggs	1903–04	M. Decugis	1920	A. H. Gobert
1892	J. Schopfer	1905–06	M. Germot	1921	J. Samazeuilh
1893	L. Riboulet	1907–09	M. Decugis	1922	H. Cochet
1894–96	A. Vacherot	1910	M. Germot	1923	P. Blanchy
1897–1900	P. Ayme	1911	A. H. Gobert	1924	J. Borotra
1901	A. Vacherot	1912–14	M. Decugis		
1902	M. Vacherot	1915–19	Not held		

	CHAMPION	RUNNER–UP	SCORE		
1925	R. Lacoste	J. Borotra	7–5	6–1	6–4
1926	H. Cochet	R. Lacoste	6–2	6–4	6–3
1927	R. Lacoste	W. T. Tilden	6–4	4–6	5–7	6–3	11–9
1928	H. Cochet	R. Lacoste	5–7	6–3	6–1	6–3
1929	R. Lacoste	J. Borotra	6–3	2–6	6–0	2–6	8–6
1930	H. Cochet	W. T. Tilden	3–6	8–6	6–3	6–1
1931	J. Borotra	C. Boussus	2–6	6–4	7–5	6–4
1932	H. Cochet	G. de Stefani	6–0	6–4	4–6	6–3
1933	J. H. Crawford	H. Cochet	8–6	6–1	6–3
1934	G. von Cramm	J. H. Crawford	6–4	7–9	3–6	7–5	6–3
1935	F. J. Perry	G. von Cramm	6–3	3–6	6–1	6–3
1936	G. von Cramm	F. J. Perry	6–0	2–6	6–2	2–6	6–0
1937	H. Henkel	H. W. Austin	6–1	6–4	6–3
1938	J. D. Budge	R. Menzel	6–3	6–2	6–4
1939	W. D. McNeill	R. L. Riggs	7–5	6–0	6–3
1940–45	Not held				
1946	M. Bernard	J. Drobny	3–6	2–6	6–1	6–4	6–3
1947	J. Asboth	E. W. Sturgess	8–6	7–5	6–4
1948	F. A. Parker	J. Drobny	6–4	7–5	5–7	8–6
1949	F. A. Parker	J. E. Patty	6–3	1–6	6–1	6–4
1950	J. E. Patty	J. Drobny	6–1	6–2	3–6	5–7	7–5
1951	J. Drobny	E. W. Sturgess	6–3	6–3	6–3
1952	J. Drobny	F. A. Sedgman	6–2	6–0	3–6	6–3

Year	Champion	Runner-up					FIRST PRIZE (in French francs)
1953	K. R. Rosewall	E. V. Seixas	6–3	6–4	1–6	6–2	
1954	M. A. Trabert	A. Larsen	6–4	7–5	6–1		
1955	M. A. Trabert	S. Davidson	2–6	6–1	6–4	6–2	
1956	L. A. Hoad	S. Davidson	6–4	8–6	6–3		
1957	S. Davidson	H. Flam	6–3	6–4	6–4		
1958	M. G. Rose	L. Ayala	6–3	6–4	6–4		
1959	N. Pietrangeli	I. C. Vermaak	3–6	6–3	6–4	6–1	
1960	N. Pietrangeli	L. Ayala	3–6	6–3	6–4	4–6	6–3
1961	M. Santana	N. Pietrangeli	4–6	6–1	3–6	6–0	6–2
1962	R. G. Laver	R. S. Emerson	3–6	2–6	6–3	9–7	6–2
1963	R. S. Emerson	P. Darmon	3–6	6–1	6–4	6–4	
1964	M. Santana	N. Pietrangeli	6–3	6–1	4–6	7–5	
1965	F. S. Stolle	A. D. Roche	3–6	6–0	6–2	6–3	
1966	A. D. Roche	I. Gulyas	6–1	6–4	7–5		
1967	R. S. Emerson	A. D. Roche	6–1	6–4	2–6	6–2	
1968	K. R. Rosewall	R. G. Laver	6–3	6–1	2–6	6–2	15,000
1969	R. G. Laver	K. R. Rosewall	6–4	6–3	6–4		35,000
1970	J. Kodes	Z. Franulovic	6–2	6–4	6–0		56,000
1971	J. Kodes	I. Nastase	8–6	6–2	2–6	7–5	48,000
1972	A. Gimeno	P. Proisy	4–6	6–3	6–1	6–1	48,000
1973	I. Nastase	N. Pilic	6–3	6–3	6–0		70,000
1974	B. Borg	M. Orantes	2–6	6–7	6–0	6–1	6–1	120,000
1975	B. Borg	G. Vilas	6–2	6–3	6–4		120,000
1976	A. Panatta	H. Solomon	6–1	6–4	4–6	7–6	130,000
1977	G. Vilas	B. E. Gottfried	6–0	6–3	6–0		190,000
1978	B. Borg	G. Vilas	6–3	6–1	6–3		210,000
1979	B. Borg	V. Pecci	6–3	6–1	6–7	6–4	208,200
1980	B. Borg	V. Gerulaitis	6–4	6–1	6–2		221,000
1981	B. Borg	I. Lendl	6–1	4–6	6–2	3–6	6–1	250,000
1982	M. Wilander	G. Vilas	1–6	7–6	6–0	6–4	400,000
1983	Y. Noah	M. Wilander	6–2	7–5	7–6		500,000
1984	I. Lendl	J. P. McEnroe	3–6	2–6	6–4	7–5	7–5	1,058,600
1985	M. Wilander	I. Lendl	3–6	6–4	6–2	6–2	1,338,200
1986	I. Lendl	M. Pernfors	6–3	6–2	6–4		1,397,250
1987	I. Lendl	M. Wilander	7–5	6–2	3–6	7–6	1,303,800
1988	M. Wilander	H. Leconte	7–5	6–2	6–1		1,500,240
1989	M. Chang	S. Edberg	6–1	3–6	4–6	6–4	6–2	1,791,390
1990	A. Gomez	A. Agassi	6–3	2–6	6–4	6–4	2,226,100
1991	J. Courier	A. Agassi	3–6	6–4	2–6	6–1	6–4	2,448,000
1992	J. Courier	P. Korda	7–5	6–2	6–1		2,680,000

WOMEN'S SINGLES

1897–99	Mlle F. Masson	1906	Mme F. Fenwick	1915–19	Not held
1900	Mlle Y. Prevost	1907	Mme de Kermel	1920–23	Mlle S. Lenglen
1901	Mme P. Girod	1908	Mme F. Fenwick	1924	Mlle D. Vlasto
1902–03	Mlle F. Masson	1909–12	Mlle J. Matthey		
1904–05	Mlle K. Gillou	1913–14	Mlle M. Broquedis		

Up to 1924 entry was restricted to members of French clubs. In 1925 entry was open to all amateurs.

Year	CHAMPION	RUNNER–UP	SCORE		
1925	Mlle S. Lenglen	Miss K. McKane	6–1	6–2	
1926	Mlle S. Lenglen	Miss M. K. Browne	6–1	6–0	
1927	Mlle K. Bouman	Mrs G. Peacock	6–2	6–4	
1928	Miss H. N. Wills	Miss E. Bennett	6–1	6–2	
1929	Miss H. N. Wills	Mme R. Mathieu	6–3	6–4	
1930	Mrs F. S. Moody	Miss H. H. Jacobs	6–2	6–1	
1931	Frl C. Aussem	Miss B. Nuthall	8–6	6–1	
1932	Mrs F. S. Moody	Mme R. Mathieu	7–5	6–1	
1933	Miss M. C. Scriven	Mme R. Mathieu	6–2	4–6	6–4
1934	Miss M. C. Scriven	Miss H. H. Jacobs	7–5	4–6	6–1
1935	Mrs H. Sperling	Mme R. Mathieu	6–2	6–1	
1936	Mrs H. Sperling	Mme R. Mathieu	6–3	6–4	
1937	Mrs H. Sperling	Mme R. Mathieu	6–2	6–4	
1938	Mme R. Mathieu	Mme N. Landry	6–0	6–3	
1939	Mme R. Mathieu	Miss J. Jedrzejowska	6–3	8–6	
1940–45	Not held				
1946	Miss M. E. Osborne	Miss P. M. Betz	1–6	8–6	7–5
1947	Mrs P. C. Todd	Miss D. J. Hart	6–3	3–6	6–4
1948	Mme N. Landry	Miss S. J. Fry	6–2	0–6	6–0

Year	Champion	Runner-up	Score			First Prize
1949	Mrs W. du Pont	Mme N. Adamson	7–5	6–2		
1950	Miss D. J. Hart	Mrs P. C. Todd	6–4	4–6	6–2	
1951	Miss S. J. Fry	Miss D. J. Hart	6–3	3–6	6–3	
1952	Miss D. J. Hart	Miss S. J. Fry	6–4	6–4		
1953	Miss M. Connolly	Miss D. J. Hart	6–2	6–4		
1954	Miss M. Connolly	Mme G. Bucaille	6–4	6–1		
1955	Miss A. Mortimer	Mrs D. P. Knode	2–6	7–5	10–8	
1956	Miss A. Gibson	Miss A. Mortimer	6–0	12–10		
1957	Miss S. J. Bloomer	Mrs D. P. Knode	6–1	6–3		
1958	Mrs Z. Kormoczy	Miss S. J. Bloomer	6–4	1–6	6–2	
1959	Miss C. C. Truman	Mrs Z. Kormoczy	6–4	7–5		
1960	Miss D. R. Hard	Miss Y. Ramirez	6–3	6–4		
1961	Miss A. S. Haydon	Miss Y. Ramirez	6–2	6–1		
1962	Miss M. Smith	Miss L. R. Turner	6–3	3–6	7–5	
1963	Miss L. R. Turner	Mrs P. F. Jones	2–6	6–3	7–5	
1964	Miss M. Smith	Miss M. E. Bueno	5–7	6–1	6–2	
1965	Miss L. R. Turner	Miss M. Smith	6–3	6–4		FIRST
1966	Mrs P. F. Jones	Miss N. Richey	6–3	6–1		PRIZE
1967	Mlle F. Durr	Miss L. R. Turner	4–6	6–3	6–4	(in French francs)
1968	Miss N. Richey	Mrs P. F. Jones	5–7	6–4	6–1	5,000
1969	Mrs B. M. Court	Mrs P. F. Jones	6–1	4–6	6–3	10,000
1970	Mrs B. M. Court	Miss H. Niessen	6–2	6–4		17,800
1971	Miss E. Goolagong	Miss H. Gourlay	6–3	7–5		13,500
1972	Mrs L. W. King	Miss E. Goolagong	6–3	6–3		13,500
1973	Mrs B. M. Court	Miss C. M. Evert	6–7	7–6	6–4	25,000
1974	Miss C. M. Evert	Mrs O. Morozova	6–1	6–2		40,000
1975	Miss C. M. Evert	Miss M. Navratilova	2–6	6–2	6–1	40,000
1976	Miss S. Barker	Miss R. Tomanova	6–2	0–6	6–2	30,000
1977	Miss M. Jausovec	Miss F. Mihai	6–2	6–7	6–1	35,000
1978	Miss V. Ruzici	Miss M. Jausovec	6–2	6–2		100,000
1979	Mrs C. Evert Lloyd	Miss W. M. Turnbull	6–2	6–0		126,900
1980	Mrs C. Evert Lloyd	Miss V. Ruzici	6–0	6–3		178,500
1981	Miss H. Mandlikova	Miss S. Hanika	6–2	6–4		200,000
1982	Miss M. Navratilova	Miss A. Jaeger	7–6	6–1		300,000
1983	Mrs C. Evert Lloyd	Miss M. Jausovec	6–1	6–2		375,000
1984	Miss M. Navratilova	Mrs C. Evert Lloyd	6–3	6–1		791,600
1985	Mrs C. Evert Lloyd	Miss M. Navratilova	6–3	6–7	7–5	1,262,700
1986	Mrs C. Evert Lloyd	Miss M. Navratilova	2–6	6–3	6–3	1,278,400
1987	Miss S. Graf	Miss M. Navratilova	6–4	4–6	8–6	1,178,840
1988	Miss S. Graf	Miss N. Zvereva	6–0	6–0		1,463,390
1989	Miss A. Sanchez	Miss S. Graf	7–6	3–6	7–5	1,593,175
1990	Miss M. Seles	Miss S. Graf	7–6	6–4		1,762,900
1991	Miss M. Seles	Miss A. Sanchez–Vicario	6–3	6–4		2,237,000
1992	Miss M. Seles	Miss S. Graff	6–2	3–6	10–8	2,470,000

MEN'S DOUBLES

	CHAMPIONS	RUNNERS–UP	SCORE				
1925	J. Borotra/R. Lacoste	J. Brugnon/H. Cochet	7–5	4–6	6–3	2–6	6–3
1926	H. O. Kinsey/V. Richards	J. Brugnon/H. Cochet	6–4	6–1	4–6	6–4	
1927	J. Brugnon/H. Cochet	J. Borotra/R. Lacoste	2–6	6–2	6–0	1–6	6–4
1928	J. Borotra/J. Brugnon	R. de Buzelet/H. Cochet	6–4	3–6	6–2	3–6	6–4
1929	J. Borotra/R. Lacoste	J. Brugnon/H. Cochet	6–3	3–6	6–3	3–6	8–6
1930	J. Brugnon/H. Cochet	H. C. Hopman/J. Willard	6–3	9–7	6–3		
1931	G. M. Lott/J. Van Ryn	N. G. Farquharson/V. G. Kirby	6–4	6–3	6–4		
1932	J. Brugnon/H. Cochet	M. Bernard/C. Boussus	6–4	3–6	7–5	6–3	
1933	G. P. Hughes/F. J. Perry	V. B. McGrath/A. K. Quist	6–2	6–4	2–6	7–5	
1934	J. Borotra/J. Brugnon	J. H. Crawford/V. B. McGrath	11–9	6–3	2–6	4–6	9–7
1935	J. H. Crawford/A. K. Quist	V. B. McGrath/D. P. Turnbull	6–1	6–4	6–2		
1936	M. Bernard/J. Borotra	G. P. Hughes/C. R. D. Tuckey	6–2	3–6	9–7	6–1	
1937	G. Von Cramm/H. Henkel	N. G. Farquharson/V. G. Kirby	6–4	7–5	3–6	6–1	
1938	B. Destremau/Y. Petra	J. D. Budge/G. Mako	3–6	6–3	9–7	6–1	
1939	C. Harris/W. D. McNeil	J. Borotra/J. Brugnon	4–6	6–4	6–0	2–6	10–8
1940–1945	Not held						
1946	M. Bernard/Y. Petra	E. Morea/F. Segura	7–5	6–3	0–6	1–6	10–8
1947	E. Fannin/E. W. Sturgess	T. P. Brown/O. W. Sidwel l	6–4	4–6	6–4	6–3	
1948	L. Bergelin/J. Drobny	H. C. Hopman/F. A. Sedgman	8–6	6–1	12–10		
1949	R. A. Gonzales/F. Parker	E. Fannin/E. W. Sturgess	6–3	8–6	5–7	6–3	
1950	W. F. Talbert/M. A. Trabert	J. Drobny/E. W. Sturgess	6–2	1–6	10–8	6–2	
1951	K. McGregor/F. A. Sedgman	G. Mulloy/R. Savitt	6–2	2–6	9–7	7–5	
1952	K. McGregor/F. A. Sedgman	G. Mulloy/R. Savitt	6–3	6–4	6–4		

1953	L. A. Hoad/K. R. Rosewall	M. G. Rose/C. Wilderspin	6–2	6–1	6–1		
1954	E. V. Seixas/M. A. Trabert	L. A. Hoad/K. R. Rosewall	6–4	6–2	6–1		
1955	E. V. Seixas/M. A. Trabert	N. Pietrangeli/O. Sirola	6–1	4–6	6–2	6–4	
1956	D. W. Candy/R. M. Perry	A. J. Cooper/L. A. Hoad	7–5	6–3	6–3		
1957	M. J. Anderson/A. J. Cooper	D. W. Candy/M. G. Rose	6–3	6–0	6–3		
1958	A. J. Cooper/N. A. Fraser	R. N. Howe/A. Segal	3–6	8–6	6–3	7–5	
1959	N. Pietrangeli/O. Sirola	R. S. Emerson/N. A. Fraser	6–3	6–2	14–12		
1960	R. S. Emerson/N. A. Fraser	J. L. Arilla/A. Gimeno	6–2	8–10	7–5	6–4	
1961	R. S. Emerson/R. G. Laver	R. N. Howe/R. Mark	3–6	6–1	6–1	6–4	
1962	R. S. Emerson/N. A. Fraser	W. P. Bungert/C. Kuhnke	6–3	6–4	7–5		
1963	R. S. Emerson/M. Santana	G. L. Forbes/A. Segal	6–2	6–4	6–4		
1964	R. S. Emerson/K. N. Fletcher	J. D. Newcombe/A. D. Roche	7–5	6–3	3–6	7–5	
1965	R. S. Emerson/F. S. Stolle	K. N. Fletcher/R. A. J. Hewitt	6–8	6–3	8–6	6–2	
1966	C. E. Graebner/R. D. Ralston	I. Nastase/I. Tiriac	6–3	6–3	6–0		
1967	J. D. Newcombe/A. D. Roche	R. S. Emerson/K. N. Fletcher	6–3	9–7	12–10		
1968	K. R. Rosewall/F. S. Stolle	R. S. Emerson/R. G. Laver	6–3	6–4	6–3		
1969	J. D. Newcombe/A. D. Roche	R. S. Emerson/R. G. Laver	4–6	6–1	3–6	6–4	6–4
1970	I. Nastase/I. Tiriac	A. R. Ashe/C. Pasarell	6–2	6–4	6–3		
1971	A. R. Ashe/M. C. Riessen	T. W. Gorman/S. R. Smith	6–8	4–6	6–3	6–4	11–9
1972	R. A. J. Hewitt/F. D. McMillan	P. Cornejo/J. Fillol	6–3	'8–6	3–6	6–1	
1973	J. D. Newcombe/T. S. Okker	J. S. Connors/I. Nastase	6–1	3–6	6–3	5–7	6–4
1974	R. D. Crealy/O. Parun	R. C. Lutz/S. R. Smith	6–3	6–2	3–6	5–7	6–1
1975	B. E. Gottfried/R. Ramirez	J. G. Alexander/P. Dent	6–2	2–6	6–2	6–4	
1976	F. McNair/S. E. Stewart	B. E. Gottfried/R. Ramirez	7–6	6–3	6–1		
1977	B. E. Gottfried/R. Ramirez	W. Fibak/J. Kodes	7–6	4–6	6–3	6–4	
1978	G. Mayer/H. Pfister	J. Higueras/M. Orantes	6–3	6–2	6–2		
1979	A. A./G. Mayer	R. Case/P. Dent	6–4	6–4	6–4		
1980	V. Amaya/H. Pfister	B. E. Gottfried/R. Ramirez	1–6	6–4	6–4	6–3	
1981	H. Gunthardt/B. Taroczy	T. Moor/E. Teltscher	6–2	7–6	6–3		
1982	S. E. Stewart/F. Taygan	H. Gildemeister/B. Prajoux	7–5	6–3	1–1 ret'd		
1983	A. Jarryd/H. Simonsson	M. R. Edmondson/S. E. Stewart	7–6	6–4	6–2		
1984	H. Leconte/Y. Noah	P. Slozil/T. Smid	6–4	2–6	3–6	6–3	6–2
1985	M. R. Edmondson/K. Warwick	S. Glickstein/H. Simonsson	6–3	6–4	6–7	6–3	
1986	J. Fitzgerald/T. Smid	S. Edberg/A. Jarryd	6–3	4–6	6–7	6–7	14–12
1987	A. Jarryd/R. Seguso	G. Forget/Y. Noah	6–7	6–7	6–3	6–4	6–2
1988	A. Gomez/E. Sanchez	J. Fitzgerald/A. Jarryd	6–3	6–7	6–4	6–3	
1989	J. Grabb/P. McEnroe	M. Bahrami/E. Winogradsky	6–4	2–6	6–4	7–6	
1990	S. Casal/E. Sanchez	G. Ivanisevic/P. Korda	7–5	6–3			
1991	J. Fitzgerald/A. Jarryd	R. Leach/J. Pugh	6–0	7–6			
1992	J. Hlasek/M. Rosset	C. Adams/A. Olhovskiy	7–6	6–7	7–5		

WOMEN'S DOUBLES

	CHAMPIONS	RUNNERS–UP	SCORE		
1925	S. Lenglen/D. Vlasto	E. Colyer/K. McKane	6–1	9–11	6–2
1926	S. Lenglen/D. Vlasto	E. Colyer/L. A. Godfree	6–1	6–1	
1927	E. L. Heine/G. Peacock	P. Saunders/P. H. Watson	6–2	6–1	
1928	E. Bennett/P. H. Watson	S. Deve/A. Lafaurie	6–0	6–2	
1929	L. de Alvarez/K. Bouman	E. L. Heine/A. Neave	7–5	6–3	
1930	F. S. Moody/E. Ryan	S. Barbier/S. Mathieu	6–3	6–1	
1931	B. Nuthall/E. F. Whittingstall	C. Aussem/E. Ryan	9–7	6–2	
1932	F. S. Moody/E. Ryan	B. Nuthall/E. F. Whittingstall	6–1	6–3	
1933	S. Mathieu/E. Ryan	S. Henrotin/C. Rosambert	6–1	6–3	
1934	S. Mathieu/E. Ryan	H. H. Jacobs/S. Palfrey	3–6	6–4	6–2
1935	M. C. Scriven/K. Stammers	N. Adamoff/H. Sperling	6–4	6–0	
1936	S. Mathieu/A. M. Yorke	S. Noel/J. Jedrzejowska	2–6	6–4	6–4
1937	S. Mathieu/A. M. Yorke	D. Andrus/S. Henrotin	3–6	6–2	6–2
1938	S. Mathieu/A. M. Yorke	A. Halff/N. Landry	6–3	6–3	
1939	J. Jedrzejowska/S. Mathieu	A. Florian/H. Kovac	7–5	7–5	
1940–1945		*Not held*			
1946	L. Brough/M. Osborne	P. Betz/D. Hart	6–4	0–6	6–1
1947	L. Brough/M. Osborne	D. Hart/P. C. Todd	7–5	6–2	
1948	D. Hart/P. C. Todd	S. Fry/M. A. Prentiss	6–4	6–2	
1949	L. Brough/W. du Pont	J. Gannon/B. Hilton	7–5	6–1	
1950	S. Fry/D. Hart	L. Brough/W. du Pont	1–6	7–5	6–2
1951	S. Fry/D. Hart	B. Bartlett/B. Scofield	10–8	6–3	
1952	S. Fry/D. Hart	H. Redick–Smith/J. Wipplinger	7–5	6–1	
1953	S. Fry/D. Hart	M. Connolly/J. Sampson	6–4	6–3	
1954	M. Connolly/N. Hopman	M. Galtier/S. Schmitt	7–5	4–6	6–0
1955	B. Fleitz/D. R. Hard	S. J. Bloomer/P. Ward	7–5	6–8	13–11

Year	Winner	Runner-up					First Prize (£)
1899	R. F. Doherty	A. W. Gore	1–6	4–6	6–2	6–3	6–3
1900	R. F. Doherty	S. H. Smith	6–8	6–3	6–1	6–2	
1901	A. W. Gore	R. F. Doherty	4–6	7–5	6–4	6–4	
1902	H. L. Doherty	A. W. Gore	6–4	6–3	3–6	6–0	
1903	H. L. Doherty	F. L. Riseley	7–5	6–3	6–0		
1904	H. L. Doherty	F. L. Riseley	6–1	7–5	8–6		
1905	H. L. Doherty	N. E. Brookes	8–6	6–2	6–4		
1906	H. L. Doherty	F. L. Riseley	6–4	4–6	6–2	6–3	
1907*	N. E. Brookes	A. W. Gore	6–4	6–2	6–2		
1908*	A. W. Gore	H. Roper Barrett	6–3	6–2	4–6	3–6	6–4
1909	A. W. Gore	M. J. G. Ritchie	6–8	1–6	6–2	6–2	6–2
1910	A. F. Wilding	A. W. Gore	6–4	7–5	4–6	6–2	
1911	A. F. Wilding	H. Roper Barrett	6–4	4–6	2–6	6–2 ret'd	
1912	A. F. Wilding	A. W. Gore	6–4	6–4	4–6	6–4	
1913	A. F. Wilding	M. E. McLoughlin	8–6	6–3	10–8		
1914	N. E. Brookes	A. F. Wilding	6–4	6–4	7–5		
1915–18	*Not held*						
1919	G. L. Patterson	N. E. Brookes	6–3	7–5	6–2		
1920	W. T. Tilden	G. L. Patterson	2–6	6–2	6–3	6–4	
1921	W. T. Tilden	B. I. C. Norton	4–6	2–6	6–1	6–0	7–5
(Challenge Round abolished)							
1922*	G. L. Patterson	R. Lycett	6–3	6–4	6–2		
1923*	W. M. Johnston	F. T. Hunter	6–0	6–3	6–1		
1924	J. Borotra	R. Lacoste	6–1	3–6	6–1	3–6	6–4
1925	R. Lacoste	J. Borotra	6–3	6–3	4–6	8–6	
1926	J. Borotra	Howard Kinsey	8–6	6–1	6–3		
1927	H. Cochet	J. Borotra	4–6	4–6	6–3	6–4	7–5
1928	R. Lacoste	H. Cochet	6–1	4–6	6–4	6–2	
1929	H. Cochet	J. Borotra	6–4	6–3	6–4		
1930	W. T. Tilden	W. L. Allison	6–3	9–7	6–4		
1931*	S. B. Wood	F. X. Shields	w.o.				
1932	H. E. Vines	H. W. Austin	6–4	6–2	6–0		
1933	J. H. Crawford	H. E. Vines	4–6	11–9	6–2	2–6	6–4
1934	F. J. Perry	J. H. Crawford	6–3	6–0	7–5		
1935	F. J. Perry	G. von Cramm	6–2	6–4	6–4		
1936	F. J. Perry	G. von Cramm	6–1	6–1	6–0		
1937*	J. D. Budge	G. von Cramm	6–3	6–4	6–2		
1938	J. D. Budge	H. W. Austin	6–1	6–0	6–3		
1939*	R. L. Riggs	E. T. Cooke	2–6	8–6	3–6	6–3	6–2
1940–45	*Not held*						
1946*	Y. Petra	G. E. Brown	6–2	6–4	7–9	5–7	6–4
1947	J. A. Kramer	T. Brown	6–1	6–3	6–2		
1948*	R. Falkenburg	J. E. Bromwich	7–5	0–6	6–2	3–6	7–5
1949	F. R. Schroeder	J. Drobny	3–6	6–0	6–3	4–6	6–4
1950*	J. E. Patty	F. A. Sedgman	6–1	8–10	6–2	6–3	
1951	R. Savitt	K. McGregor	6–4	6–4	6–4		
1952	F. A. Sedgman	J. Drobny	4–6	6–2	6–3	6–2	
1953*	E. V. Seixas	K. Nielsen	9–7	6–3	6–4		
1954	J. Drobny	K. R. Rosewall	13–11	4–6	6–2	9–7	
1955	M. A. Trabert	K. Nielsen	6–3	7–5	6–1		
1956*	L. A. Hoad	K. R. Rosewall	6–2	4–6	7–5	6–4	
1957	L. A. Hoad	A. J. Cooper	6–2	6–1	6–2		
1958*	A. J. Cooper	N. A. Fraser	3–6	6–3	6–4	13–11	
1959*	A. Olmedo	R. G. Laver	6–4	6–3	6–4		
1960*	N. A. Fraser	R. G. Laver	6–4	3–6	9–7	7–5	
1961	R. G. Laver	C. R. McKinley	6–3	6–1	6–4		
1962	R. G. Laver	M. F. Mulligan	6–2	6–2	6–1		
1963*	C. R. McKinley	F. S. Stolle	9–7	6–1	6–4		
1964	R. S. Emerson	F. S. Stolle	6–1	12–10	4–6	6–3	
1965	R. S. Emerson	F. S. Stolle	6–2	6–4	6–4		FIRST
1966	M. Santana	R. D. Ralston	6–4	11–9		6–4	PRIZE
1967	J. D. Newcombe	W. P. Bungert	6–3	6–1	6–1		(£)
1968	R. G. Laver	A. D. Roche	6–3	6–4	6–2		2,000
1969	R. G. Laver	J. D. Newcombe	6–4	5–7	6–4	6–4	3,000
1970	J. D. Newcombe	K. R. Rosewall	5–7	6–3	6–2	3–6	6–1	3,000
1971	J. D. Newcombe	S. R. Smith	6–3	5–7	2–6	6–4	6–4	3,750
1972*	S. R. Smith	I. Nastase	4–6	6–3	6–3	4–6	7–5	5,000
1973*	J. Kodes	A. Metreveli	6–1	9–8	6–3		5,000
1974	J. S. Connors	K. R. Rosewall	6–1	6–1	6–4		10,000
1975	A. R. Ashe	J. S. Connors	6–1	6–1	5–7	6–4	10,000
1976	B. Borg	I. Nastase	6–4	6–2	9–7		12,500
1977	B. Borg	J. S. Connors	3–6	6–2	6–1	5–7	6–4	15,000

1978	B. Borg	J. S. Connors	6–2	6–2	6–3			19,000
1979	B. Borg	R. Tanner	6–7	6–1	3–6	6–3	6–4	20,000
1980	B. Borg	J. P. McEnroe	1–6	7–5	6–3	6–7	8–6	20,000
1981	J. P. McEnroe	B. Borg	4–6	7–6	7–6	6–4		21,600
1982	J. S. Connors	J. P. McEnroe	3–6	6–3	6–7	7–6	6–4	41,667
1983	J. P. McEnroe	C. J. Lewis	6–2	6–2	6–2			66,600
1984	J. P. McEnroe	J. S. Connors	6–1	6–1	6–2			100,000
1985	B. Becker	K. Curren	6–3	6–7	7–6	6–4		130,000
1986	B. Becker	I. Lendl	6–4	6–3	7–5			140,000
1987	P. Cash	I. Lendl	7–6	6–2	7–5			155,000
1988	S. Edberg	B. Becker	4–6	7–6	6–4	6–2		165,000
1989	B. Becker	S. Edberg	6–0	7–6	6–4			190,000
1990	S. Edberg	B. Becker	6–2	6–2	3–6	3–6	6–4	230,000
1991	M. Stich	B. Becker	6–4	7–6	6–4			240,000
1992	A. Agassi	G. Ivanisevic 6–7		6–4	6–4	1–6	6–4	265,000

WOMEN'S SINGLES

	CHAMPION	RUNNER–UP	SCORE		
1884	Miss M. Watson	Miss L. Watson	6–8	6–3	6–3
1885	Miss M. Watson	Miss B. Bingley	6–1	7–5	
1886	Miss B. Bingley	Miss M. Watson	6–3	6–3	
1887	Miss C. Dod	Miss B. Bingley	6–2	6–0	
1888	Miss C. Dod	Mrs G. W. Hillyard	6–3	6–3	
1889*	Mrs G. W. Hillyard	Miss H. Rice	4–6	8–6	6–4
1890*	Miss H. Rice	Miss M. Jacks	6–4	6–1	
1891*	Miss C. Dod	Mrs G. W. Hillyard	6–2	6–1	
1892	Miss C. Dod	Mrs G. W. Hillyard	6–1	6–1	
1893	Miss C. Dod	Mrs G. W. Hillyard	6–8	6–1	6–4
1894*	Mrs G. W. Hillyard	Miss L. Austin	6–1	6–1	
1895*	Miss C. Cooper	Miss H. Jackson	7–5	8–6	
1896	Miss C. Cooper	Mrs W. H. Pickering	6–2	6–3	
1897	Mrs G. W. Hillyard	Miss C. Cooper	5–7	7–5	6–2
1898*	Miss C. Cooper	Miss L. Martin	6–4	6–4	
1899	Mrs G. W. Hillyard	Miss C. Cooper	6–2	6–3	
1900	Mrs G. W. Hillyard	Miss C. Cooper	4–6	6–4	6–4
1901	Mrs A. Sterry	Mrs G. W. Hillyard	6–2	6–2	
1902	Miss M. E. Robb	Mrs A. Sterry	7–5	6–1	
1903*	Miss D. K. Douglass	Miss E. W. Thomson	4–6	6–4	6–2
1904	Miss D. K. Douglass	Mrs A. Sterry	6–0	6–3	
1905	Miss M. Sutton	Miss D. K. Douglass	6–3	6–4	
1906	Miss D. K. Douglass	Miss M. Sutton	6–3	9–7	
1907	Miss M. Sutton	Mrs Lambert Chambers	6–1	6–4	
1908*	Mrs A. Sterry	Miss A. M. Morton	6–4	6–4	
1909*	Miss D. P. Boothby	Miss A. M. Morton	6–4	4–6	8–6
1910	Mrs Lambert Chambers	Miss D. P. Boothby	6–2	6–2	
1911	Mrs Lambert Chambers	Miss D. P. Boothby	6–0	6–0	
1912*	Mrs D. R. Larcombe	Mrs A. Sterry	6–3	6–1	
1913*	Mrs Lambert Chambers	Mrs R. J. McNair	6–0	6–4	
1914	Mrs Lambert Chambers	Mrs D. R. Larcombe	7–5	6–4	
1915–18	*Not held*				
1919	Mlle S. Lenglen	Mrs Lambert Chambers 10–8		4–6	9–7
1920	Mlle S. Lenglen	Mrs Lambert Chambers	6–3	6–0	
1921	Mlle S. Lenglen	Miss E. Ryan	6–2	6–0	
	(Challenge Round abolished)				
1922	Mlle S. Lenglen	Mrs F. Mallory	6–2	6–0	
1923	Mlle S. Lenglen	Miss K. McKane	6–2	6–2	
1924	Miss K. McKane	Miss H. N. Wills	4–6	6–4	6–4
1925	Mlle S. Lenglen	Miss J. Fry	6–2	6–0	
1926	Mrs L. A. Godfree	Sta E. de Alvarez	6–2	4–6	6–3
1927	Miss H. N. Wills	Sta E. de Alvarez	6–2	6–4	
1928	Miss H. N. Wills	Sta E. de Alvarez	6–2	6–3	
1929	Miss H. N. Wills	Miss H. H. Jacobs	6–1	6–2	
1930	Mrs F. S. Moody	Miss E. Ryan	6–2	6–2	
1931*	Frl C. Aussem	Frl H. Krahwinkel	6–2	7–5	
1932*	Mrs F. S. Moody	Miss H. H. Jacobs	6–3	6–1	
1933	Mrs F. S. Moody	Miss D. E. Round	6–4	6–8	6–3
1934*	Miss D. E. Round	Miss H. H. Jacobs	6–2	5–7	6–3
1935	Mrs F. S. Moody	Miss H. H. Jacobs	6–3	3–6	7–5
1936*	Miss H. H. Jacobs	Mrs S. Sperling	6–2	4–6	7–5
1937	Miss D. E. Round	Miss J. Jedrzejowska	6–2	2–6	7–5

Year	Champion	Runner-up	Score			Prize
1938*	Mrs F. S. Moody	Miss H. H. Jacobs	6–4	6–0		
1939*	Miss A. Marble	Miss K. E. Stammers	6–2	6–0		
1940–45	Not held					
1946*	Miss P. M. Betz	Miss A. L. Brough	6–2	6–4		
1947*	Miss M. E. Osborne	Miss D. J. Hart	6–2	6–4		
1948	Miss A. L. Brough	Miss D. J. Hart	6–3	8–6		
1949	Miss A. L. Brough	Mrs W. du Pont	10–8	1–6	10–8	
1950	Miss A. L. Brough	Mrs W. du Pont	6–1	3–6	6–1	
1951	Miss D. J. Hart	Miss S. J. Fry	6–1	6–0		
1952	Miss M. Connolly	Miss A. L. Brough	6–4	6–3		
1953	Miss M. Connolly	Miss D. J. Hart	8–6	7–5		
1954	Miss M. Connolly	Miss A. L. Brough	6–2	7–5		
1955*	Miss A. L. Brough	Mrs J. G. Fleitz	7–5	8–6		
1956	Miss S. J. Fry	Miss A. Buxton	6–3	6–1		
1957*	Miss A. Gibson	Miss D. R. Hard	6–3	6–2		
1958	Miss A. Gibson	Miss A. Mortimer	8–6	6–2		
1959*	Miss M. E. Bueno	Miss D. R. Hard	6–4	6–3		
1960	Miss M. E. Bueno	Miss S. Reynolds	8–6	6–0		
1961*	Miss A. Mortimer	Miss C. C. Truman	4–6	6–4	7–5	
1962	Mrs J. R. Susman	Mrs V. Sukova	6–4	6–4		
1963*	Miss M. Smith	Miss B. J. Moffitt	6–3	6–4		
1964	Miss M. E. Bueno	Miss M. Smith	6–4	7–9	6–3	
1965	Miss M. Smith	Miss M. E. Bueno	6–4	7–5		FIRST
1966	Mrs L. W. King	Miss M. E. Bueno	6–3	3–6	6–1	PRIZE
1967	Mrs L. W. King	Mrs P. F. Jones	6–3	6–4		(£)
1968	Mrs L. W. King	Miss J. A. M. Tegart	9–7	7–5		750
1969	Mrs P. F. Jones	Mrs L. W. King	3–6	6–3	6–2	1,50
1970*	Mrs B. M. Court	Mrs L. W. King	14–12	11–9		1,500
1971	Miss E. Goolagong	Mrs B. M. Court	6–4	6–1		1,800
1972	Mrs L. W. King	Miss E. Goolagong	6–3	6–3		2,400
1973	Mrs L. W. King	Miss C. M. Evert	6–0	7–5		3,000
1974	Miss C. M. Evert	Mrs O. Morozova	6–0	6–4		7,000
1975	Mrs L. W. King	Mrs R. A. Cawley	6–0	6–1		7,000
1976*	Miss C. M. Evert	Mrs R. A. Cawley	6–3	4–6	8–6	10,000
1977	Miss S. V. Wade	Miss B. F. Stove	4–6	6–3	6–1	13,500
1978	Miss M. Navratilova	Miss C. M. Evert	2–6	6–4	7–5	17,100
1979	Miss M. Navratilova	Mrs C. Evert Lloyd	6–4	6–4		18,000
1980	Mrs R. A. Cawley	Mrs C. Evert Lloyd	6–1	7–6		18,000
1981	Mrs C. Evert Lloyd	Miss H. Mandlikova	6–2	6–2		19,440
1982	Miss M. Navratilova	Mrs C. Evert Lloyd	6–1	3–6	6–2	37,500
1983	Miss M. Navratilova	Miss A. Jaeger	6–0	6–3		60,000
1984	Miss M. Navratilova	Mrs C. Evert Lloyd	7–6	6–2		90,000
1985	Miss M. Navratilova	Mrs C. Evert Lloyd	4–6	6–3	6–2	117,000
1986	Miss M. Navratilova	Miss H. Mandlikova	7–6	6–3		126,000
1987	Miss M. Navratilova	Miss S. Graf	7–5	6–3		139,500
1988	Miss S. Graf	Miss M. Navratilova	5–7	6–2	6–1	148,500
1989	Miss S. Graf	Miss M. Navratilova	6–2	6–7	6–1	171,000
1990	Miss M. Navratilova	Miss Z. Garrison	6–4	6–1		207,000
1991	Miss S. Graf	Miss G. Sabatini	6–4	3–6	8–6	216,000
1992	Miss S.Graf	Miss M. Seles	6–2	6–1		240,000

MEN'S DOUBLES

	CHAMPIONS	RUNNERS–UP	SCORE				
1884	E./W. Renshaw	E. W. Lewis/E. L. Williams	6–3	6–1	1–6	6–4	
1885	E./W. Renshaw	C. E. Farrer/A. J. Stanley	6–3	6–3	10–8		
(Challenge Round instituted)							
1886	E./W. Renshaw	C. E. Farrer/A. J. Stanley	6–3	6–3	4–6	7–5	
1887*	P. Bowes–Lyon/ W. W. Wilberforce	E. Barret–Smith/J. H. Crispe	7–5	6–3	6–2		
1888	E./W. Renshaw	P. Bowes–Lyon/ W. W. Wilberforce	2–6	1–6	6–3	6–4	6–3
1889	E./W. Renshaw	G. W. Hillyard/E. W. Lewis	6–4	6–4	3–6	0–6	6–1
1890*	J. Pim/F. O. Stoker	G. W. Hillyard/E. W. Lewis	6–0	7–5	6–4		
1891	H./W. Baddeley	J. Pim/F. O. Stoker	6–1	6–3	1–6	6–2	
1892	H. S. Barlow/E. W. Lewis	H./W. Baddeley	4–6	6–2	8–6	6–4	
1893	J. Pim/F. O. Stoker	H. W. Barlow/E. W. Lewis	4–6	6–3	6–1	2–6	6–0
1894*	H./W. Baddeley	H. S. Barlow/C. H. Martin	5–7	7–5	4–6	6–3	8–6
1895	H./W. Baddeley	W. V. Eaves/E. W. Lewis	8–6	5–7	6–4	6–3	
1896	H./W. Baddeley	R. F. Doherty/H. A. Nisbet	1–6	3–6	6–4	6–2	6–1
1897	H. L./R. F. Doherty	H./W. Baddeley	6–4	4–6	8–6	6–4	

Year	Winners	Runners-up					
1898	H. L./R. F. Doherty	C. Hobart/H. A. Nisbet	6–4	6–4	6–2		
1899	H. L./R. F. Doherty	C. Hobart/H. A. Nisbet	7–5	6–0	6–2		
1900	H. L./R. F. Doherty	H. A. Nisbet/H. Roper Barrett	9–7	7–5	4–6	3–6	6–3
1901	H. L./R. F. Doherty	D. F. Davis/H. Ward	4–6	6–2	6–3	9–7	
1902	F. L. Riseley/S. H. Smith	H. L./R. F. Doherty	4–6	8–6	6–3	4–6	11–9
1903	H. L./R. F. Doherty	F. L. Riseley/S. H. Smith	6–4	6–4	6–4		
1904	H. L./R. F. Doherty	F. L. Riseley/S. H. Smith	6–3	6–4	6–3		
1905	H. L./R. F. Doherty	F. L. Riseley/S. H. Smith	6–2	6–4	6–8	6–3	
1906	F. L. Riseley/S. H. Smith	H. L./R. F. Doherty	6–8	6–4	5–7	6–3	6–3
1907*	N. E. Brookes/A. F. Wilding	K. Behr/B. C. Wright	6–4	6–4	6–2		
1908*	M. J. G. Ritchie/A. F. Wilding	A. W. Gore/H. Roper Barrett	6–1	6–2	1–6	1–6	9–7
1909*	A. W. Gore/H. Roper Barrett	S. N. Doust/H. A. Parker	6–2	6–1	6–4		
1910	M. J. G. Ritchie/A. F. Wilding	A. W. Gore/H. Roper Barrett	6–1	6–1	6–2		
1911	M. Decugis/A. H. Gobert	M. J. G. Ritchie/A. F. Wilding	9–7	5–7	6–3	2–6	6–2
1912	C. P. Dixon/H. Roper Barrett	M. Decugis/A. H. Gobert	3–6	6–3	6–4	7–5	
1913	C. P. Dixon/H. Roper Barrett	H. Kleinschroth/F. W. Rahe	6–2	6–4	4–6	6–2	
1914	N. E. Brookes/A. F. Wilding	C. P. Dixon/H. Roper Barrett	6–1	6–1	5–7	8–6	
1915–1918	*Not held*						
1919*	P. O'Hara Wood/R. V. Thomas	R. W. Heath/R. Lycett	6–4	6–2	4–6	6–2	
1920*	C. S. Garland/R. N. Williams	A. R. F. Kingscote/J. C. Parke	4–6	6–4	7–5	6–2	
1921*	R. Lycett/M. Woosnam	A. H./F. G. Lowe	6–3	6–0	7–5		
(Challenge Round abolished)							
1922	J. O. Anderson/R. Lycett	P. O'Hara Wood/G. L. Patterson	3–6	7–9	6–4	6–3	11–9
1923	L. A. Godfree/R. Lycett	E. Flaquer/Count de Gomar	6–3	6–4	3–6	6–3	
1924	F. T. Hunter/V. Richards	W. M. Washburn/R. N. Williams	6–3	3–6	8–10	8–6	6–3
1925	J. Borotra/R. Lacoste	R. Casey/J. Hennessey	6–4	11–9	4–6	1–6	6–3
1926	J. Brugnon/H. Cochet	H. Kinsey/V. Richards	7–5	4–6	6–3	6–2	
1927	F. T. Hunter/W. T. Tilden	J. Brugnon/H. Cochet	1–6	4–6	8–6	6–3	6–4
1928	J. Brugnon/H. Cochet	J. B. Hawkes/G. L. Patterson	13–11	6–4	6–4		
1929	W. L. Allison/J. Van Ryn	I. G. Collins/J. C. Gregory	6–4	5–7	6–3	10–12	6–4
1930	W. L. Allison/J. Van Ryn	J. H. Doeg/G. M. Lott	6–3	6–3	6–2		
1931	G. M. Lott/J. Van Ryn	J. Brugnon/H. Cochet	6–2	10–8	9–11	3–6	6–3
1932	J. Borotra/J. Brugnon	G. P. Hughes/F. J. Perry	6–0	4–6	3–6	7–5	7–5
1933	J. Borotra/J. Brugnon	R. Nunoi/J. Satoh	4–6	6–3	6–3	7–5	
1934	G. M. Lott/L. R. Stoefen	J. Borotra/J. Brugnon	6–2	6–3	6–4		
1935	J. H. Crawford/A. K Quist	W. L. Allison/J. Van Ryn	6–3	5–7	6–2	5–7	7–5
1936	G. P. Hughes/C. R. D. Tuckey	C. E. Hare/F. H. D. Wilde	6–4	3–6	7–9	6–1	5–4
1937	J. D. Budge/G. Mako	G. P. Hughes/C. R. D. Tuckey	6–0	6–4	6–8	6–1	
1938	J. D. Budge/G. Mako	H. Henkel/G. von Metaxa	6–4	3–6	6–3	8–6	
1939	E. T. Cooke/R. L. Riggs	C. E. Hare/F. H. D. Wilde	6–3	3–6	6–3	9–7	
1940–1945	*Not held*						
1946	T. Brown/J. A. Kramer	G. E. Brown/D. Pails	6–4	6–4	6–2		
1947	R. Falkenburg/J. A. Kramer	A. J. Mottram/O. W. Sidwell	8–6	6–3	6–3		
1948	J. E. Bromwich/F. A. Sedgman	T. Brown/G. Mulloy	5–7	7–5	7–5	9–7	
1949	R. A. Gonzales/F. A. Parker	G. Mulloy/F. R. Schroeder	6–4	6–4	6–2		
1950	J. E. Bromwich/A. K. Quist	G. E. Brown/O. W. Sidwell	7–5	3–6	6–3	3–6	6–2
1951	K. McGregor/F. A. Sedgman	J. Drobny/E. W. Sturgess	3–6	6–2	6–3	3–6	6–3
1952	K. McGregor/F. A. Sedgman	E. V. Seixas/E. W. Sturgess	6–3	7–5	6–4		
1953	L. A. Hoad/K. R. Rosewall	R. N. Hartwig/M. G. Rose	6–4	7–5	4–6	7–5	
1954	R. N. Hartwig/M. G. Rose	E. V. Seixas/M. A. Trabert	6–4	6–4	3–6	6–4	
1955	R. N. Hartwig/L. A. Hoad	N. A. Fraser/K. R. Rosewall	7–5	6–4	6–3		
1956	L. A. Hoad/K. R. Rosewall	N. Pietrangeli/O. Sirola	7–5	6–2	6–1		
1957	G. Mulloy/B. Patty	N. A. Fraser/L. A. Hoad	8–10	6–4	6–4	6–4	
1958	S. Davidson/U. Schmidt	A. J. Cooper/N. A. Fraser	6–4	6–4	8–6		
1959	R. Emerson/N. A. Fraser	R. Laver/R. Mark	8–6	6–3	1–6	9–7	
1960	R. H. Osuna/R. D. Ralston	M. G. Davies/R. K. Wilson	7–5	6–3	10–8		
1961	R. Emerson/N. A. Fraser	R. A. J. Hewitt/F. S. Stolle	6–4	6–8	6–4	6–8	8–6
1962	R. A. J. Hewitt/F. S. Stolle	B. Jovanovic/N. Pilic	6–2	5–7	6–2	6–4	
1963	R. H. Osuna/A. Palafox	J. C. Barclay/P. Darmon	4–6	6–2	6–2	6–2	

								FIRST
1964	R. A. J. Hewitt/F. S. Stolle	R. Emerson/K. N. Fletcher	7–5	11–9		6–4		PRIZE
1965	J. D. Newcombe/A. D. Roche	K. N. Fletcher/R. A. J. Hewitt	7–5	6–3	6–4			*(£ per*
1966	K. N. Fletcher/J. D. Newcombe	W. W. Bowrey/O. K. Davidson	6–3	6–4	3–6	6–3		*team)*
1967	R. A. J. Hewitt/F. D. McMillan	R. Emerson/K. N. Fletcher	6–2	6–3	6–4			
1968	J. D. Newcombe/A. D. Roche	K. R. Rosewall/F. S. Stolle	3–6	8–6	5–7	14–12	6–3	800
1969	J. D. Newcombe/A. D. Roche	T. S. Okker/M. C. Riessen	7–5	11–9		6–3		1,000
1970	J. D. Newcombe/A. D. Roche	K. R. Rosewall/F. S. Stolle	10–8		6–3	6–1		1,000
1971	R. Emerson/R. Laver	A. R. Ashe/R. D. Ralston	4–6	9–7	6–8	6–4	6–4	750
1972	R. A. J. Hewitt/F. D. McMillan	S. R. Smith/E. Van Dillen	6–2	6–2	9–7			1,000
1973	J. S. Connors/I. Nastase	J. R. Cooper/N. A. Fraser	3–6	6–3	6–4	8–9	6–1	1,000
1974	J. D. Newcombe/A. D. Roche	R. C. Lutz/S. R. Smith	8–6	6–4	6–4			2,000
1975	V. Gerulaitis/A. Mayer	C. Dowdeswell/A. J. Stone	7–5	8–6	6–4			2,000
1976	B. E. Gottfried/R. Ramirez	R. L. Case/G. Masters	3–6	6–3	8–6	2–6	7–6	3,000

1977 R. L. Case/G. Masters	J. G. Alexander/P. C. Dent	6–3	6–4	3–6	8–9	6–4	6,000
1978 R. A. J. Hewitt/F. D. McMillan	P. Fleming/J. P. McEnroe	6–1	6–4	6–2			7,500
1979 P. Fleming/J. P. McEnroe	B. E. Gottfried/R. Ramirez	4–6	6–4	6–2	6–2		8,000
1980 P. McNamara/P. McNamee	R. C. Lutz/S. R. Smith	7–6	6–3	6–7	6–4		8,400
1981 P. Fleming/J. P. McEnroe	R. C. Lutz/S. R. Smith	6–4	6–4	6–4			9,070
1982 P. McNamara/P. McNamee	P. Fleming/J. P. McEnroe	6–3	6–2				16,666
1983 P. Fleming/J. P. McEnroe	T. E./T. R. Gullikson	6–4	6–3	6–4			26,628
1984 P. Fleming/J. P. McEnroe	P. Cash/P. McNamee	6–2	5–7	6–2	3–6	6–3	40,000
1985 H. P. Gunthardt/B. Taroczy	P. Cash/J. Fitzgerald	6–4	6–3	4–6	6–3		47,500
1986 J. Nystrom/M. Wilander	G. Donnelly/P. Fleming	7–6	6–3	6–3			48,500
1987 K. Flach/R. Seguso	S. Casal/E. Sanchez	3–6	6–7	7–6	6–1	6–4	53,730
1988 K. Flach/R. Seguso	J. Fitzgerald/A. Jarryd	6–4	2–6	6–4	7–6		57,200
1989 J. B. Fitzgerald/A. Jarryd	R. Leach/J. Pugh	3–6	7–6	6–4	7–6		65,870
1990 R. Leach/J. Pugh	P. Aldrich/D. Visser	7–6	7–6	7–6			94,230
1991 J. B. Fitzgerald/A. Jarryd	J. Franai/L. Lavalle	6–3	6–4	6–7	6–1		98,330
1992 J. P. McEnroe/M. Stich	J. Grabb/R. Reneberg	5–7	7–6	3–6	7–6	19–17	108,570

WOMEN'S DOUBLES

CHAMPIONS	RUNNERS–UP	SCORE		
1913 R. J. McNair/D. P. Boothby	A. Sterry/D. Lambert Chambers	4–6	2–4 ret'd	
1914 A. M. Morton/E. Ryan	G. Hannam/D. R. Larcombe	6–1	6–3	
1915–1918 *Not held*				
1919 S. Lenglen/E. Ryan	D. Lambert Chambers/D. R. Larcombe	4–6	7–5	6–3
1920 S. Lenglen/E. Ryan	D. Lambert Chambers/D. R. Larcombe	6–4	6–0	
1921 S. Lenglen/E. Ryan	A. E. Beamish/G. Peacock	6–1	6–2	
1922 S. Lenglen/E. Ryan	K. McKane/A. D. Stocks	6–0	6–4	
1923 S. Lenglen/E. Ryan	J. Austin/E. L. Colyer	6–3	6–1	
1924 H. Wightman/H. N. Wills	B. C. Covell/K. McKane	6–4	6–4	
1925 S. Lenglen/E. Ryan	A. V. Bridge/C. G. McIlquham	6–2	6–2	
1926 M. K. Browne/E. Ryan	L. A. Godfree/E. L. Colyer	6–1	6–1	
1927 H. N. Wills/E. Ryan	E. L. Heine/G. Peacock	6–3	6–2	
1928 P. Saunders/M. Watson	E. Bennett/E. H. Harvey	6–2	6–3	
1929 L. R. C. Michell/M. Watson	B. C. Covell/D. C. Shepherd–Barron	6–4	8–6	
1930 F. S. Moody/E. Ryan	E. Cross/S. Palfrey	6–2	9–7	
1931 D. C. Shepherd–Barron/P. E. Mudford	D. Metaxa/J. Sigart	3–6	6–3	6–4
1932 D. Metaxa/J. Sigart	H. H. Jacobs/E. Ryan	6–4	6–3	
1933 S. Mathieu/E. Ryan	F. James/A. M. Yorke	6–2	9–11	6–4
1934 S. Mathieu/E. Ryan	D. B. Andrus/S. Henrotin	6–3	6–3	
1935 F. James/K. E. Stammers	S. Mathieu/H. Sperling	6–1	6–4	
1936 F. James/K. E. Stammers	S. Fabyan/H. H. Jacobs	6–2	6–1	
1937 S. Mathieu/A. M. Yorke	P. King/E. Pittman	6–3	6–3	
1938 S. Fabyan/A. Marble	S. Mathieu/A. M. Yorke	6–2	6–3	
1939 S. Fabyan/A. Marble	H. H. Jacobs/A. M. Yorke	6–1	6–0	
1940–1945 *Not held*				
1946 A. L. Brough/M. E. Osborne	P. M. Betz/D. J. Hart	6–3	2–6	6–3
1947 D. J. Hart/P. C. Todd	A. L. Brough/M. E. Osborne	3–6	6–4	7–5
1948 A. L. Brough/W. du Pont	D. J. Hart/P. C. Todd	6–3	3–6	6–3
1949 A. L. Brough/W. du Pont	G. Moran/P. C. Todd	8–6	7–5	
1950 A. L. Brough/W. du Pont	S. J. Fry/D. J. Hart	6–4	5–7	6–1
1951 S. J. Fry/D. J. Hart	A. L. Brough/W. du Pont	6–3	13–11	
1952 S. J. Fry/D. J. Hart	A. L. Brough/M. Connolly	8–6	6–3	
1953 S. J. Fry/D. J. Hart	M. Connolly/J. Sampson	6–0	6–0	
1954 A. L. Brough/W. du Pont	S. J. Fry/D. J. Hart	4–6	9–7	6–3
1955 A. Mortimer/J. A. Shilcock	S. J. Bloomer/P. E. Ward	7–5	6–1	
1956 A. Buxton/A. Gibson	F. Muller/D. G. Seeney	6–1	8–6	
1957 A. Gibson/D. R. Hard	K. Hawton/T. D. Long	6–1	6–2	
1958 M. E. Bueno/A. Gibson	W. du Pont/M. Varner	6–3	7–5	
1959 J. Arth/D. R. Hard	J. G. Fleitz/C. C. Truman	2–6	6–2	6–3
1960 M. E. Bueno/D. R. Hard	S. Reynolds/R. Schuurman	6–4	6–0	
1961 K. Hantz/B. J. Moffitt	J. Lehane/J. Smith	6–3	6–4	
1962 B. J. Moffitt/J. R. Susman	L. E. G. Price/R. Schuurman	5–7	6–3	7–5
1963 M. E. Bueno/D. R. Hard	R. A. Ebbern/M. Smith	8–6	9–7	
1964 M. Smith/L. R. Turner	B. J. Moffitt/J. R. Susman	7–5	6–2	FIRST
1965 M. E. Bueno/B. J. Moffitt	F. Durr/J. Lieffrig	6–2	7–5	PRIZE
1966 M. E. Bueno/N. Richey	M. Smith/J. A. M. Tegart	6–3	4–6	6–4	*(£ per*
1967 R. Casals/L. W. King	M. E. Bueno/N. Richey	9–11	6–4	6–2	*team)*
1968 R. Casals/L. W. King	F. Durr/P. F. Jones	3–6	6–4	7–5	500
1969 B. M. Court/J. A. M. Tegart	P. S. A. Hogan/M. Michel	9–7	6–2		600
1970 R. Casals/L. W. King	F. Durr/S. V. Wade	6–2	6–3		600
1971 R. Casals/L. W. King	B. M. Court/E. Goolagong	6–3	6–2		450

1972 L. W. King/B. Stove	D. E. Dalton/F. Durr	6–2	4–6	6–3	600
1973 R. Casals/L. W. King	F. Durr/B. Stove	6–1	4–6	7–5	600
1974 E. Goolagong/M. Michel	H. F. Gourlay/K. M. Krantzcke	2–6	6–4	6–3	1,200
1975 A. Kiyomura/K. Sawamatsu	F. Durr/B. Stove	7–5	1–6	7–5	1,200
1976 C. Evert/M. Navratilova	L. W. King/B. Stove	6–1	3–6	7–5	2,400
1977 H. Gourlay–Cawley/J. C. Russell	M. Navratilova/B. Stove	6–3	6–3		5,200
1978 G. E. Reid/W. Turnbull	M. Jausovec/V. Ruzici	4–6	9–8	6–3	6,500
1979 L. W. King/M. Navratilova	B. Stove/W. M. Turnbull	5–7	6–3	6–2	6,930
1980 K. Jordan/A. E. Smith	R. Casals/W. M. Turnbull	4–6	7–5	6–1	7,276
1981 M. Navratilova/P. H. Shriver	K. Jordan/A. E. Smith	6–3	7–6		7,854
1982 M. Navratilova/P. H. Shriver	K. Jordan/A. E. Smith	6–4	6–1		14,450
1983 M. Navratilova/P. H. Shriver	R. Casals/W. M. Turnbull	6–2	6–2		23,100
1984 M. Navratilova/P. H. Shriver	K. Jordan/A. E. Smith	6–3	6–4		34,700
1985 K. Jordan/E. Smylie	M. Navratilova/P. H. Shriver	5–7	6–3	6–4	41,100
1986 M. Navratilova/P. H. Shriver	H. Mandlikova/W. M. Turnbull	6–1	6–3		42,060
1987 C. Kohde–Kilsch/H. Sukova	B. Nagelsen/E. Smylie	7–5	7–5		46,500
1988 S. Graf/G. Sabatini	L. Savchenko/N. Zvereva	6–3	1–6	12–10	49,500
1989 J. Novotna/H. Sukova	L. Savchenko/N. Zvereva	6–1	6–2		56,970
1990 J. Novotna/H. Sukova	K. Jordan/E. Smylie	6–3	6–4		81,510
1991 L. Savchenko/N. Zvereva	G. Fernandez/J. Novotna	6–4	3–6	6–4	85,060
1992 G. Fernandez/N. Zvereva	J. Novotna/L. Savchenko	6–4	6–1		93,920

MIXED DOUBLES

CHAMPIONS	RUNNERS–U	SCORE			
1913 Hope Crisp/Mrs C. O. Tuckey	J. C. Parke/Mrs D. R. Larcombe	3–6	5–3 ret'd		
1914 J. C. Parke/Mrs D. R. Larcombe	A. F. Wilding/Mlle M. Broquedis	4–6	6–4	6–2	
1915–1918 Not held					
1919 R. Lycett/Miss E. Ryan	A. D. Prebble/Mrs D. Lambert Chambers	6–0	6–0		
1920 G. L. Patterson/Mlle S. Lenglen	R. Lycett/Miss E. Ryan	7–5	6–3		
1921 R. Lycett/Miss E. Ryan	M. Woosnam/Miss P. L. Howkins	6–3	6–1		
1922 P. O'Hara Wood/Mlle S. Lenglen	R. Lycett/Miss E. Ryan	6–4	6–3		
1923 R. Lycett/Miss E. Ryan	L. S. Deane/Mrs D. C. Shepherd–Barron	6–4	7–5		
1924 J. B. Gilbert/Miss K. McKane	L. A. Godfree/Mrs D. C. Shepherd–Barron	6–3	3–6	6–3	
1925 J. Borotra/Mlle S. Lenglen	H. L. de Morpurgo/Miss E. Ryan	6–3	6–3		
1926 L. A./Mrs Godfree	H. Kinsey/Miss M. K. Browne	6–3	6–4		
1927 F. T. Hunter/Miss E. Ryan	L. A./Mrs Godfree	8–6	6–0		
1928 P. D. B. Spence/Miss E. Ryan	J. H. Crawford/Miss D. Akhurst	7–5	6–4		
1929 F. T. Hunter/Miss H. N. Wills	I. G. Collins/Miss J. Fry	6–1	6–4		
1930 J. H. Crawford/Miss E. Ryan	D. Prenn/Frl H. Krahwinkel	6–1	6–3		
1931 G. M. Lott/Miss L. A. Harper	I. G. Collins/Miss J. C. Ridley	6–3	1–6	6–1	
1932 E. Maier/Miss E. Ryan	H. C. Hopman/Mlle J. Sigart	7–5	6–2		
1933 G. von Cramm/Frl H. Krahwinkel	N. G. Farquharson/Miss M. Heeley	7–5	8–6		
1934 R. Miki/Miss D. E. Round	H. W. Austin/Mrs D. C. Shepherd–Barron	3–6	6–4	6–0	
1935 F. J. Perry/Miss D. E. Round	H. C./Mrs Hopman	7–5	4–6	6–2	
1936 F. J. Perry/Miss D. E. Round	J. D. Budge/Mrs S. Fabyan	7–9	7–5	6–4	
1937 J. D. Budge/Miss A. Marble	Y. Petra/Mme S. Mathieu	6–4	6–1		
1938 J. D. Budge/Miss A. Marble	H. Henkel/Mrs S. Fabyan	6–1	6–4		
1939 R. L. Riggs/Miss A. Marble	F. H. D. Wilde/Miss N. B. Brown	9–7	6–1		
1940–1945 Not held					
1946 T. Brown/Miss A. L. Brough	G. E. Brown/Miss D. Bundy	6–4	6–4		
1947 J. E. Bromwich/Miss A. L. Brough	C. F. Long/Mrs N. M. Bolton	1–6	6–4	6–2	
1948 J. E. Bromwich/Miss A. L. Brough	F. A. Sedgman/Miss D. J. Hart	6–2	3–6	6–3	
1949 E. E. Sturgess/Mrs S. P. Summer	J. E. Bromwich/Miss A. L. Brough	9–7	9–11	7–5	
1950 E. W. Sturgess/Miss A. L. Brough	G. E. Brown/Mrs P. C. Todd	11–9	1–6	6–4	
1951 F. A. Sedgman/Miss D. J. Hart	M. G. Rose/Mrs N. M. Bolton	7–5	6–2		
1952 F. A. Sedgman/Miss D. J. Hart	E. Morea/Mrs T. D. Long	4–6	6–3	6–4	
1953 E. V. Seixas/Miss D. J. Hart	E. Morea/Miss S. J. Fry	9–7	7–5		
1954 E. V. Seixas/Miss D. J. Hart	K. R. Rosewall/Mrs W. du Pont	5–7	6–4	6–3	
1955 E. V. Seixas/Miss D. J. Hart	E. Morea/Miss A. L. Brough	8–6	2–6	6–3	
1956 E. V. Seixas/Miss S. J. Fry	G. Mulloy/Miss A. Gibson	2–6	6–2	7–5	
1957 M. G. Rose/Miss D. R. Hard	N. A. Fraser/Miss A. Gibson	6–4	7–5		
1958 R. N. Howe/Miss L. Coghlan	K. Nielsen/Miss A. Gibson	6–3	13–11		
1959 R. Laver/Miss D. R. Hard	N. A. Fraser/Miss M. E. Bueno	6–4	6–3		
1960 R. Laver/Miss D. R. Hard	R. N. Howes/Miss M. E. Bueno	13–11	3–6	8–6	
1961 F. S. Stolle/Miss L. R. Turner	R. N. Howe/Miss E. Buding	11–9	6–2		
1962 N. A. Fraser/Mrs W. du Pont	R. D. Ralston/Miss A. S. Haydon	2–6	6–3	13–11	
1963 K. N. Fletcher/Miss M. Smith	R. A. J. Hewitt/Miss D. R. Hard	11–9	6–4		
1964 F. S. Stolle/Miss L. R. Turner	K. N. Fletcher/Miss M. Smith	6–4	6–4		FIRST
1965 K. N. Fletcher/Miss M. Smith	A. D. Roche/Miss J. A. M. Tegart	12–10	6–3		PRIZE
1966 K. N. Fletcher/Miss M. Smith	R. D. Ralston/Mrs L. W. King	4–6	6–3	6–3	(£ per

1967 O. K. Davidson/Mrs L. W. King	K. N. Fletcher/Miss M. E. Bueno	7–5	6–0		*team)*
1968 K. N. Fletcher/Mrs B. M. Court	A. Metreveli/Miss O. Morozova	6–1	14–12		450
1969 F. S. Stolle/Mrs P. F. Jones	A. D. Roche/Miss J. A. M. Tegart	6–3	6–2		500
1970 I. Nastase/Miss R. Casals	A. Metreveli/Miss O. Morozova	6–3	4–6	9–7	500
1971 O. K. Davidson/Mrs L. W. King	M. C. Rieseen/Mrs B. M. Court	3–6	6–2	15–13	375
1972 I. Nastase/Miss R. Casals	K. Warwick/Miss E. Goolagong	6–4	6–4		500
1973 O. K. Davidson/Mrs L. W. King	Mr. Ramirez/Miss J. Newberry	6–3	6–2		500
1974 O. K. Davidson/Mrs L. W. King	M. J. Farrell/Miss L. J. Charles	6–3	9–7		1,000
1975 M. C. Riessen/Mrs B. M. Court	A. J. Stone/Miss B. Stove	6–4	7–5		1,000
1976 A. D. Roche/Miss F. Durr	R. L. Stockton/Miss R. Casals	6–3	2–6	7–5	2,000
1977 R. A. J. Hewitt/Miss G. R. Stevens	F. D. McMillan/Miss B. Stove	3–6	7–5	6–4	3,000
1978 F. D. McMillan/Miss B. Stove	R. O. Ruffels/Mrs L. W. King	6–2	6–2		4,000
1979 R. A. J. Hewitt/Miss G. R. Stevens	F. D. McMillan/Miss B. Stove	7–5	7–6		4,200
1980 J. R. Austin/Miss T. Austin	M. R. Edmondson/Miss D. L. Fromholtz	4–6	7–6	6–3	4,420
1981 F. D. McMillan/Miss B. Stove	J. R. Austin/Miss T. Austin	4–6	7–6	6–3	4,770
1982 K. Curren/Miss A. E. Smith	J. M. Lloyd/Miss W. M. Turnbull	2–6	6–3	7–6	6,750
1983 J. M. Lloyd/Miss W. M. Turnbull	S. Denton/Mrs L. W. King	6–7	7–6	7–5	12,000
1984 J. M. Lloyd/Miss W. M. Turnbull	S. Denton/Miss K. Jordan	6–3	6–3		18,000
1985 P. McNamee/Miss M. Navratilova	J. Fitzgerald/Mrs E. Smylie	7–5	4–6	6–2	23,400
1986 K. Flach/Miss K. Jordan	H. P. Gunthardt/Miss M. Navratilova	6–3	7–6		25,200
1987 M. J. Bates/Miss J. M. Durie	D. Cahill/Miss N. Provis	7–6	6–3		27,900
1988 S. E. Stewart/Miss Z. Garrison	K. Jones/Mrs G. Magers	6–1	7–6		29,700
1989 J. Pugh/Miss J. Novotna	M. Kratzmann/Miss J. Byrne	6–4	5–7	6–4	34,200
1990 R. Leach/Miss Z. Garrison	J. Fitzgerald/Mrs E. Smylie	7–5	6–2		40,000
1991 J. B. Fitzgerald/Mrs E. Smylie	J. Pugh/Miss N. Zvereva	7–6	6–2		41,720
1992 C. Suk/Mrs L. Savchenko Neil.	J. Eltingh/Miss M. Oremans	7–6	6–2		46,070

US NATIONAL CHAMPIONSHIPS 1881–1969
*Holders did not defend the title.

MEN'S SINGLES

	CHAMPION	RUNNER–UP	SCORE				
1881	R. D. Sears	W. E. Glyn	6–0	6–3	6–2		
1882	R. D. Sears	C. M. Clark	6–1	6–4	6–0		
1883	R. D. Sears	J. Dwight	6–2	6–0	9–7		
(Challenge Round instituted)							
1884	R. D. Sears	H. A. Taylor	6–0	1–6	6–0	6–2	
1885	R. D. Sears	G. M. Brinley	6–3	4–6	6–0	6–3	
1886	R. D. Sears	R. L. Beeckman	4–6	6–1	6–3	6–4	
1887	R. D. Sears	H. W. Slocum	6–1	6–3	6–2		
1888*	H. W. Slocum	H. A. Taylor	6–4	6–1	6–0		
1889	H. W. Slocum	Q. A. Shaw	6–3	6–1	4–6	6–2	
1890	O. S. Campbell	H. W. Slocum	6–2	4–6	6–3	6–1	
1891	O. S. Campbell	C. Hobart	2–6	7–5	7–9	6–1	6–2
1892	O. S. Campbell	F. H. Hovey	7–5	3–6	6–3	7–5	
1893*	R. D. Wrenn	F. H. Hovey	6–4	3–6	6–4	6–4	
1894	R. D. Wrenn	M. F. Goodbody	6–8	6–1	6–4	6–4	
1895	F. H. Hovey	R. D. Wrenn	6–3	6–2	6–4		
1896	R. D. Wrenn	F. H. Hovey	7–5	3–6	6–0	1–6	6–1
1897	R. D. Wrenn	W. V. Eaves	4–6	8–6	6–3	2–6	6–2
1898*	M. D. Whitman	D. F. Davis	3–6	6–2	6–2	6–1	
1899	M. D. Whitman	J. P. Paret	6–1	6–2	3–6	7–5	
1900	M. D. Whitman	W. A. Larned	6–4	1–6	6–2	6–2	
1901*	W. A. Larned	B. C. Wright	6–2	6–8	6–4	6–4	
1902	W. A. Larned	R. F. Doherty	4–6	6–2	6–4	8–6	
1903	H. L. Doherty	W. A. Larned	6–0	6–3	10–8		
1904*	H. Ward	W. J. Clothier	10–8	6–4	9–7		
1905	B. C. Wright	H. Ward	6–2	6–1	11–9		
1906	W. J. Clothier	B. C. Wright	6–3	6–0	6–4		
1907*	W. A. Larned	R. LeRoy	6–2	6–2	6–4		
1908	W. A. Larned	B. C. Wright	6–1	6–2	8–6		
1909	W. A. Larned	W. J. Clothier	6–1	6–2	5–7	1–6	6–1
1910	W. A. Larned	T. C. Bundy	6–1	5–7	6–0	6–8	6–1
1911	W. A. Larned	M. E. McLoughlin	6–4	6–4	6–2		
(Challenge Round abolished)							
1912	M. E. McLoughlin	W. F. Johnson	3–6	2–6	6–2	6–4	6–2
1913	M. E. McLoughlin	R. N. Williams	6–4	5–7	6–3	6–1	
1914	R. N. Williams	M. E. McLoughlin	6–3	8–6	10–8		
1915	W. M. Johnston	M. E. McLoughlin	1–6	6–0	7–5	10–8	

1916	R. N. Williams	W. M. Johnston	4–6	6–4	0–6	6–2	6–4
1917	R. L. Murray	N. W. Niles	5–7	8–6	6–3	6–3	
1918	R. L. Murray	W. T. Tilden	6–3	6–1	7–5		
1919	W. M. Johnston	W. T. Tilden	6–4	6–4	6–3		
1920	W. T. Tilden	W. M. Johnston	6–1	1–6	7–5	5–7	6–3
1921	W. T. Tilden	W. F. Johnson	6–1	6–3	6–1		
1922	W. T. Tilden	W. M. Johnston	4–6	3–6	6–2	6–3	6–4
1923	W. T. Tilden	W. M. Johnston	6–4	6–1	6–4		
1924	W. T. Tilden	W. M. Johnston	6–1	9–7	6–2		
1925	W. T. Tilden	W. M. Johnston	4–6	11–9	6–3	4–6	6–3
1926	R. Lacoste	J. Borotra	6–4	6–0	6–4		
1927	R. Lacoste	W. T. Tilden	11–9	6–3	11–9		
1928	H. Cochet	F. T. Hunter	4–6	6–4	3–6	7–5	6–3
1929	W. T. Tilden	F. T. Hunter	3–6	6–3	4–6	6–2	6–4
1930	J. H. Doeg	F. X. Shields	10–8	1–6	6–4	16–14	
1931	H. E. Vines	G. M. Lott	7–9	6–3	9–7	7–5	
1932	H. E. Vines	H. Cochet	6–4	6–4	6–4		
1933	F. J. Perry	J. H. Crawford	6–3	11–13	4–6	6–0	6–1
1934	F. J. Perry	W. L. Allison	6–4	6–3	1–6	8–6	
1935	W. L. Allison	S. B. Wood	6–2	6–2	6–3		
1936	F. J. Perry	J. D. Budge	2–6	6–2	8–6	1–6	10–8
1937	J. D. Budge	C. Von Cramm	6–1	7–9	6–1	3–6	6–1
1938	J. D. Budge	G. Mako	6–3	6–8	6–2	6–1	
1939	R. L. Riggs	S. W. van Horn	6–4	6–2	6–4		
1940	W. D. McNeill	R. L. Riggs	4–6	6–8	6–3	6–3	7–5
1941	R. L. Riggs	F. Kovacs	5–7	6–1	6–3	6–3	
1942	F. R. Schroeder	F. A. Parker	8–6	7–5	3–6	4–6	6–2
1943	J. R. Hunt	J. A. Kramer	6–3	3–6	10–8		6–0
1944	F. A. Parker	W. F. Talbert	6–4	3–6	6–3	6–3	
1945	F. A. Parker	W. F. Talbert	14–12	6–1	6–2		
1946	J. A. Kramer	T. P. Brown	9–7	6–3	6–0		
1947	J. A. Kramer	F. A. Parker	4–6	2–6	6–1	6–0	6–3
1948	R. A. Gonzales	E. W. Sturgess	6–2	6–3	14–12		
1949	R. A. Gonzales	F. R. Schroeder	16–18	2–6	6–1	6–2	6–4
1950	A. Larsen	H. Flam	6–3	4–6	5–7	6–4	6–3
1951	F. A. Sedgman	E. V. Seixas	6–4	6–1	6–1		
1952	F. A. Sedgman	G. Mulloy	6–1	6–2	6–3		
1953	M. A. Trabert	E. V. Seixas	6–3	6–2	6–3		
1954	E. V. Seixas	R. N. Hartwig	3–6	6–2	6–4	6–4	
1955	M. A. Trabert	K. R. Rosewall	9–7	6–3	6–3		
1956	K. R. Rosewall	L. A. Hoad	4–6	6–2	6–3	6–3	
1957	M. J. Anderson	A. J. Cooper	10–8	7–5	6–4		
1958	A. J. Cooper	M. J. Anderson	6–2	3–6	4–6	10–8	8–6
1959	N. A. Fraser	A. Olmedo	6–3	5–7	6–2	6–4	
1960	N. A. Fraser	R. G. Laver	6–4	6–4	9–7		
1961	R. S. Emerson	R. G. Laver	7–5	6–3	6–2		
1962	R. G. Laver	R. S. Emerson	6–2	6–4	5–7	6–4	
1963	R. H. Osuna	F. Froehling	7–5	6–4	6–2		
1964	R. S. Emerson	F. S. Stolle	6–4	6–2	6–4		
1965	M. Santana	E. C. Drysdale	6–2	7–9	7–5	6–1	
1966	F. S. Stolle	J. D. Newcombe	4–6	12–10	6–3	6–4	
1967	J. D. Newcombe	C. Graebner	6–4	6–4	8–6		
1968	A. R. Ashe	R. C. Lutz	4–6	6–3	8–10	6–0	6–4
1969	S. R. Smith	R. C. Lutz	9–7	6–3	6–1		

* Played as National Patriotic tournament.

WOMEN'S SINGLES

	CHAMPION	RUNNER–UP	SCORE				
1887	Miss E. Hansell	Miss L. Knight	6–1	6–0			
1888	Miss B. L. Townsend	Miss E. Hansell	6–3	6–5			
1889	*Miss B. L. Townsend*	*Miss L. D. Voorhees*	*7–5*	*6–2*			
1890	Miss E. C. Roosevelt	Miss B. L. Townsend	6–2	6–2			
1891	Miss M. E. Cahill	Miss E. C. Roosevelt	6–4	6–1	4–6	6–3	
1892	Miss M. E. Cahill	Miss E. H. Moore	5–7	6–3	6–4	4–6	6–2
1893*	Miss A. Terry	Miss A. L. Schultz	6–1	6–3			
1894	Miss H. Hellwig	Miss A. Terry	7–5	3–6	6–0	3–6	6–3
1895	Miss J. Atkinson	Miss H. Hellwig	6–4	6–2	6–1		
1896	Miss E. H. Moore	Miss J. Atkinson	6–4	4–6	6–2	6–2	
1897	Miss J. Atkinson	Miss E. H. Moore	6–3	6–3	4–6	3–6	6–3
1898	Miss J. Atkinson	Miss M. Jones	6–3	5–7	6–4	2–6	7–5
1899*	Miss M. Jones	Miss M. Banks	6–1	6–1	7–5		

1900*	Miss M. McAteer	Miss E. Parker	6–2	6–2	6–0	
1901	Miss E. H. Moore	Miss M. McAteer	6–4	3–6	7–5	2–6 6–2
1902	Miss M. Jones	Miss E. H. Moore	6–1	1–0 ret'd		
1903	Miss E. H. Moore	Miss M. Jones	7–5	8–6		
1904	Miss M. G. Sutton	Miss E. H. Moore	6–1	6–2		
1905*	Miss E. H. Moore	Miss H. Homans	6–4	5–7	6–1	
1906*	Miss H. Homans	Mrs M. Barge–Wallach	6–4	6–3		
1907*	Miss Evelyn Sears	Miss C. Neely	6–3	6–2		
1908	Mrs M. Barger–Wallach	Miss Evelyn Sears	6–3	1–6	6–3	
1909	Miss H. Hotchkiss	Mrs M. Barger–Wallach	6–0	6–1		
1910	Miss H. Hotchkiss	Miss L. Hammond	6–4	6–2		
1911	Miss H. Hotchkiss	Miss F. Sutton	8–10	6–1	9–7	
1912*	Miss M. K. Browne	Miss Eleanora Sears	6–4	6–2		
1913	Miss M. K. Browne	Miss D. Green	6–2	7–5		
1914	Miss M. K. Browne	Miss M. Wagner	6–2	1–6	6–1	
1915*	Miss M. Bjurstedt	Mrs G. W. Wightman	4–6	6–2	6–0	
1916	Miss M. Bjurstedt	Mrs L. H. Raymond	6–0	6–1		
1917	Miss M. Bjurstedt	Miss M. Vanderhoef	4–6	6–0	6–2	
1918	Miss M. Bjurstedt	Miss E. E. Goss	6–4	6–3		
(Challenge Round abolished)						
1919	Mrs G. W. Wightman	Miss M. Zinderstein	6–1	6–2		
1920	Mrs F. Mallory	Miss M. Zinderstein	6–3	6–1		
1921	Mrs F. Mallory	Miss M. K. Browne	4–6	6–4	6–2	
1922	Mrs F. Mallory	Miss H. N. Wills	6–3	6–1		
1923	Miss H. N. Wills	Mrs F. Mallory	6–2	6–1		
1924	Miss H. N. Wills	Mrs F. Mallory	6–1	6–3		
1925	Miss H. N. Wills	Miss K. McKane	3–6	6–0	6–2	
1926	Mrs F. Mallory	Miss E. Ryan	4–6	6–4	9–7	
1927	Miss H. N. Wills	Miss B. Nuthall	6–1	6–4		
1928	Miss H. N. Wills	Miss H. H. Jacobs	6–2	6–1		
1929	Miss H. N. Wills	Mrs P. H. Watson	6–4	6–2		
1930	Miss B. Nuthall	Mrs L. A. Harper	6–1	6–4		
1931	Mrs F. S. Moody	Mrs F. Whittingstall	6–4	6–1		
1932	Miss H. H. Jacobs	Miss C. A. Babcock	6–2	6–2		
1933	Miss H. H. Jacobs	Mrs F. S. Moody	8–6	3–6	3–0 ret'd	
1934	Miss H. H. Jacobs	Miss S. Palfrey	6–1	6–4		
1935	Miss H. H. Jacobs	Mrs S. P. Fabyan	6–2	6–4		
1936	Miss A. Marble	Miss H. H. Jacobs	4–6	6–3	6–2	
1937	Miss A. Lizana	Miss J. Jedrzejowksa	6–4	6–2		
1938	Miss A. Marble	Miss N. Wynne	6–0	6–3		
1939	Miss A. Marble	Miss H. H. Jacobs	6–0		8–10 6–4	
1940	Miss A. Marble	Miss H. H. Jacobs	6–2	6–3		
1941	Mrs E. T. Cooke	Miss P. M. Betz	7–5	6–2		
1942	Miss P. M. Betz	Miss A. L. Brough	4–6	6–1	6–4	
1943	Miss P. M. Betz	Miss A. L. Brough	6–3	5–7	6–3	
1944	Miss P. M. Betz	Miss M. E. Osborne	6–3	8–6		
1945	Mrs E. T. Cooke	Miss P. M. Betz	3–6	8–6	6–4	
1946	Miss P. M. Betz	Miss P. C. Todd	11–9	6–3		
1947	Miss A. L. Brough	Miss M. E. Osborne	8–6	4–6	6–1	
1948	Mrs W. D. du Pont	Miss A. L. Brough	4–6	6–4	15–13	
1949	Mrs W. D. du Pont	Miss D. J. Hart	6–4	6–1		
1950	Mrs W. D. du Pont	Miss D. J. Hart	6–4	6–3		
1951	Miss M. Connolly	Miss S. J. Fry	6–3	1–6	6–4	
1952	Miss M. Connolly	Miss D. J. Hart	6–3	7–5		
1953	Miss M. Connolly	Miss D. J. Hart	6–2	6–4		
1954	Miss D. J. Hart	Miss A. L. Brough	6–8	6–1	8–6	
1955	Miss D. J. Hart	Miss P. E. Ward	6–4	6–2		
1956	Miss S. J. Fry	Miss A. Gibson	6–3	6–4		
1957	Miss A. Gibson	Miss A. L. Brough	6–3	6–2		
1958	Miss A. Gibson	Miss D. R. Hard	3–6	6–1	6–2	
1959	Miss M. E. Bueno	Miss C. C. Truman	6–1	6–4		
1960	Miss D. R. Hard	Miss M. E. Bueno	6–4	10–12	6–4	
1961	Miss D. R. Hard	Miss A. S. Haydon	6–3	6–4		
1962	Miss M. Smith	Miss D. R. Hard	9–7	6–4		
1963	Miss M. E. Bueno	Miss M. Smith	7–5	6–4		
1964	Miss M. E. Bueno	Mrs C. Graebner	6–1	6–0		
1965	Miss M. Smith	Miss B. J. Moffitt	8–6	7–5		
1966	Miss M. E. Bueno	Miss N. Richey	6–3	6–1		
1967	Mrs L. W. King	Mrs P. F. Jones	11–9	6–4		
1968	Mrs B. M. Court	Miss M. E. Bueno	6–2	6–2		
1969	Mrs B. M. Court	Miss S. V. Wade	4–6	6–3	6–0	

* *Played as National Patriotic tournament.*

MEN'S DOUBLES
Holders did not defend the title.

CHAMPIONS	RUNNERS–UP	SCORE				
1881 C. M. Clark/F. W. Taylor	A. Van Rensselaer/A. E. Newbold	6–5	6–4	6–5		
1882 J. Dwight/R. D. Sears	W. Nightingale/G. M. Smith	6–2	6–4	6–4		
1883 J. Dwight/R. D. Sears	A. Van Rensselaer/A. E. Newbold	6–0	6–2	6–2		
1884 J. Dwight/R. D. Sears	A. Van Rensselaer/A. V. R. Berry	6–4	6–1	8–10	6–4	
1885 J. S. Clark/R. D. Sears	W. P. Knapp/H. W. Slocum	6–3	6–0	6–2		
1886 J. Dwight/R. D. Sears	G. M. Brinley/H. A. Taylor	7–5	5–7	7–5	6–4	
1887 J. Dwight/R. D. Sears	H. W. Slocum/H. A. Taylor	6–4	3–6	2–6	6–3	6–3
1888 O. S. Campbell/V. G. Hall	C. Hobart/E. P. MacMullen	6–4	6–2	6–4		
1889 H. W. Slocum/H. A. Taylor	O. S. Campbell/V. G. Hall	6–1	6–3	6–2		
1890 V. G. Hall/C. Hobart	C. W. Carver/J. A. Ryerson	6–3	4–6	6–2	2–6	6–3
(Challenge Round instituted)						
1891 O. S. Campbell/R. P. Huntington	V. G. Hall/C. Hobart	6–3	6–4	8–6		
1892 O. S. Campbell/R. P. Huntington	V. G. Hall/E. L. Hall	6–4	6–2	4–6	6–3	
1893 C. Hobart/F. H. Hovey	O. S. Campbell/R. P. Huntington	6–3	6–4	4–6	6–2	
1894 C. Hobart/F. H. Hovey	C. B. Neel/S. R. Neel	6–3	8–6	6–1		
1895 M. G. Chace/R. D. Wrenn	C. Hobart/F. H. Hovey	7–5	6–1	8–6		
1896*C. B./S. R. Neel	M. G. Chace/R. D. Wrenn	6–3	1–6	6–1	3–6	6–1
1897 L. E. Ware/G. P. Sheldon	H. S. Mahony/H. A. Nisbet	11–13	6–2	9–7	1–6	6–1
1898 L. E. Ware/G. P. Sheldon	D. F. Davis/H. Ward	1–6	7–5	6–4	4–6	7–5
1899 D. F. Davis/H. Ward	L. E. Ware/G. P. Sheldon	6–4	6–4	6–3		
1900 D. F. Davis/H. Ward	F. B. Alexander/R. D. Little	6–4	9–7	12–10		
1901 D. F. Davis/H. Ward	L. E. Ware/B. C. Wright	6–3	9–7	6–1		
1902 H. L./R. F. Doherty	D. F. Davis/H. Ward	11–9	12–10	6–4		
1903 H. L./R. F. Doherty	L. Collins/L. H. Waldner	7–5	6–3	6–3		
1904*H. Ward/B. C. Wright	K. Collins/R. D. Little	1–6	6–2	3–6	6–4	6–1
1905 H. Ward/B. C. Wright	F. B. Alexander/H. H. Hackett	6–3	6–1	6–2		
1906 H. Ward/B. C. Wright	F. B. Alexander/H. H. Hackett	6–3	3–6	6–3	6–3	
1907*F. B. Alexander/B. C. Wright	W. J. Clothier/W. A. Larned	6–3	6–1	6–4		
1908 F. B. Alexander/H. H. Hackett	R. D. Little/B. C. Wright	6–1	7–5	6–2		
1909 F. B. Alexander/H. H. Hackett	G. J. Janes/M. E. McLoughlin	6–4	6–1	6–0		
1910 F. B. Alexander/H. H. Hackett	T. C. Bundy/T. W. Hendrick	6–1	8–6	6–3		
1911 R. D. Little/G. F. Touchard	F. B. Alexander/H. H. Hackett	7–5	13–15	6–2	6–4	
1912 T. C. Bundy/M. E. McLoughlin	R. D. Little/G. F. Touchard	3–6	6–2	6–1	7–5	
1913 T. C. Bundy/M. E. McLoughlin	C. J. Griffin/J. R. Strachan	6–4	7–5	6–1		
1914 T. C. Bundy/M. E. McLoughlin	G. M. Church/D. Mathey	6–4	6–2	6–4		
1915 C. J. Griffin/W. M. Johnston	T. C. Bundy/M. E. McLoughlin	6–2	3–6	4–6	6–3	6–3
1916 C. J. Griffin/W. M. Johnston	W. Dawson/M. E. McLoughlin	6–4	6–3	5–7	6–3	
1917 F. B. Alexander/H. A. Throckmorton	H. C. Johnson/I. C. Wright	11–9	6–4	6–4		
(Challenge Round abolished)						
1918 V. Richards/W. T. Tilden	F. B. Alexander/B. C. Wright	6–3	6–4	3–6	2–6	6–2
(Challenge Round restored)						
1919 N. E. Brookes/G. L. Patterson	V. Richards/W. T. Tilden	8–6	6–3	4–6	6–2	
(Challenge Round abolished)						
1920 C. J. Griffin/W. M. Johnston	W. E. Davis/R. Roberts	6–2	6–2	6–3		
1921 V. Richards/W. T. Tilden	W. M. Washburn/R. N. Williams	13–11	12–10	6–1		
1922 V. Richards/W. T. Tilden	P. O'Hara Wood/G. L. Patterson	4–6	6–1	6–3	6–4	
1923 B. I. C. Norton/W. T. Tilden	W. M. Washburn/R. N. Williams	3–6	6–2	6–3	5–7	6–2
1924 H. O./R. G. Kinsey	P. O'Hara Wood/G. L. Patterson	7–5	5–7	7–9	6–3	6–4
1925 V. Richards/R. N. Williams	J. B. Hawkes/G. L. Patterson	6–2	8–10	6–4	11–9	
1926 V. Richards/R. N. Williams	A. H. Chapin/W. T. Tilden	6–4	6–8	11–9	6–3	
1927 F. T. Hunter/W. T. Tilden	W. M. Johnston/R. N. Williams	10–8	6–3	6–3		
1928 J. F. Hennessey/G. M. Lott	J. B. Hawkes/G. L. Patterson	6–2	6–1	6–2		
1929 J. H. Doeg/G. M. Lott	R. B. Bell/L. N. White	10–8	16–14	6–1		
1930 J. H. Doeg/G. M. Lott	W. L. Allison/J. Van Ryn	8–6	6–3	4–6	13–15	6–4
1931 W. L. Allison/J. Van Ryn	R. B. Bell/G. S. Mangin	6–4	8–6	6–3		
1932 K. Gledhill/H. E. Vines	W. L. Allison/J. Van Ryn	6–4	6–3	6–2		
1933 G. M. Lott/L. R. Stoefen	F. A. Parker/F. X. Shields	11–13	9–7	9–7	6–3	
1934 G. M. Lott/L. R. Stoefen	W. L. Allison/J. Van Ryn	6–4	9–7	3–6	6–4	
1935 W. L. Allison/J. Van Ryn	J. D. Budge/G. Mako	6–4	6–2	3–6	2–6	6–1
1936 J. D. Budge/G. Mako	W. L. Allison/J. Van Ryn	6–4	6–2	6–4		
1937 G. Von Cramm/H. Henkel	J. D. Budge/G. Mako	6–4	7–5	6–4		
1938 J. D. Budge/G. Mako	J. E. Bromwich/A. K. Quist	6–3	6–2	6–1		
1939 J. E. Bromwich/A. K. Quist	J. H. Crawford/H. C. Hopman	8–6	6–1	6–4		
1940 J. A. Kramer/F. R. Schroeder	G. Mulloy/H. J. Prussoff	6–4	8–6	9–7		
1941 J. A. Kramer/F. R. Schroeder	G. Mulloy/W. Sabin	9–7	6–4	6–2		
1942 G. Mulloy/W. F. Talbert	F. R. Schroeder/S. B. Wood	9–7	7–5	6–1		
1943 J. A. Kramer/F. A. Parker	D. Freeman/W. F. Talbert	6–2	6–4	6–4		

1944 R. Falkenburg/W. D. McNeill	F. Segura/W. F. Talbert	7–5	6–4	3–6	6–1	
1945 G. Mulloy/W. F. Talbert	R. Falkenburg/J. Tuero	12–10	8–10	12–10	6–2	
1946 G. Mulloy/W. F. Talbert	G. Guernsey/W. D. McNeill	3–6	6–4	2–6	6–3	20–18
1947 J. A. Kramer/F. R. Schroeder	W. F. Talbert/O. W. Sidwell	6–4	7–5	6–3		
1948 G. Mulloy/W. F. Talbert	F. A. Parker/F. R. Schroeder	1–6	9–7	6–3	3–6	9–7
1949 J. Bromwich/O. W. Sidwell	F. A. Sedgman/G. Worthington	6–4	6–0	6–1		
1950 J. Bromwich/F. A. Sedgman	G. Mulloy/W. F. Talbert	7–5	8–6	3–6	6–1	
1951 K. McGregor/F. A. Sedgman	D. Candy/M. G. Rose	10–8	6–4	4–6	7–5	
1952 M. G. Rose/E. V. Seixas	K. McGregor/F. A. Sedgman	3–6	10–8	10–8	6–8	8–6
1953 R. N. Hartwig/M. G. Rose	G. Mulloy/W. F. Talbert	6–4	4–6	6–2	6–4	
1954 E. V. Seixas/M. A. Trabert	L. A. Hoad/K. R. Rosewall	3–6	6–4	8–6	6–3	
1955 K. Kamo/A. Miyagi	G. Moss/W. Quillian	6–3	6–3	3–6	1–6	6–4
1956 L. A. Hoad/K. R. Rosewall	H. Richardson/E. V. Seixas	6–2	6–2	3–6	6–4	
1957 A. J. Cooper/N. A. Fraser	G. Mulloy/J. E. Patty	4–6	6–3	9–7	6–3	
1958 A. Olmedo/H. Richardson	S. Giammalva/B. McKay	3–6	6–3	6–4	6–4	
1959 R. S. Emerson/N. A. Fraser	E. Buchholz/A. Olmedo	3–6	6–3	5–7	6–4	7–5
1960 R. S. Emerson/N. A. Fraser	R. G. Laver/R. Mark	9–7	6–2	6–4		
1961 C. McKinley/R. D. Ralston	A. Palafox/R. H. Osuna	6–3	6–4	2–6	13–11	
1962 A. Palafox/R. H. Osuna	C. McKinley/R. D. Ralston	6–4	10–12	1–6	9–7	6–3
1963 C. McKinley/R. D. Ralston	A. Palafox/R. H. Osuna	9–7	4–6	5–7	6–3	11–9
1964 C. McKinley/R. D. Ralston	G. Stilwell/M. Sangster	6–3	6–2	6–4		
1965 R. S. Emerson/F. S. Stolle	F. Froehling/C. Pasarell	6–4	10–12	7–5	6–3	
1966 R. S. Emerson/F. S. Stolle	C. Graebner/R. D. Ralston	6–4	6–4	6–4		
1967 J. D. Newcombe/A. D. Roche	O. K. Davidson/W. W. Bowrey	6–8	9–7	6–3	6–3	
1968 R. C. Lutz/S. R. Smith	R. A. J. Hewitt/R. J. Moore	6–4	6–4	9–7		
1969 R. D. Crealy/A. Stone	W. W. Bowrey/C. Pasarell	9–11	6–3	7–5		

* Played as National Patriotic tournament.

WOMEN'S DOUBLES
*Not recognised as an official championship.

CHAMPIONS	RUNNERS–UP	SCORE				
1887*E. F. Hansell/L. Knight	L. Allderdice/Church	6–0	6–4			
1888*E. C. Roosevelt/G. W. Roosevelt	A. K. Robinson/V. Ward	3–6	6–3	6–4		
1889 M. Ballard/B. L. Townsend	M. Wright/L. Knight	6–0	6–2			
1890 E. C. Roosevelt/G. W. Roosevelt	B. L. Townsend/M. Ballard	6–1	6–2			
1891 M. E. Cahill/Mrs W. F. Morgan	E. C. Roosevelt/G. W. Roosevelt	2–6	8–6	6–4		
1892 M. E. Cahill/A. M. McKinlay	Mrs A. H. Harris/A. R. Williams	6–1	6–3			
1893 H. Butler/A. M. Terry	A. L. Schultz/Stone	6–4	6–3			
1894 J. P. Atkinson/H. R. Hellwig	A. R. Williams/A. C. Wistar	6–4	7–5			
1895 J. P. Atkinson/H. R. Hellwig	E. H. Moore/A. R. Williams	6–2	6–2	12–10		
1896 J. P. Atkinson/E. H. Moore	A. R. Williams/A. C. Wistar	6–4	7–5			
1897 J. P. Atkinson/K. Atkinson	F. Edwards/E. J. Rastall	6–2	6–1	6–1		
1898 J. P. Atkinson/K. Atkinson	C. B. Neely/M. Wimer	6–1	2–6	4–6	6–1	6–2
1899 J. W. Craven/M. McAteer	M. Banks/E. J. Rastall	6–1	6–1	7–5		
1900 H. Champlin/E. Parker	M. McAteer/M. Wimer	9–7	6–2	6–2		
1901 J. P. Atkinson/M. McAteer	M. Jones/E. H. Moore	w.o.				
1902 J. P. Atkinson/M. Jones	M. Banks/N. Closterman	6–2	7–5			
1903 E. H. Moore/C. B. Neely	M. Jones/M. Hall	6–4	6–1	6–1		
1904 M. Hall/M. G. Sutton	E. H. Moore/C. B. Neely	3–6	6–3	6–3		
1905 H. Homans/C. B. Neely	V. Maule/M. F. Oberteuffer	6–0	6–1			
1906 Mrs L. S. Coe/Mrs D. S. Platt	C. Boldt/H. Homans	6–4	6–4			
1907 C. B. Neely/M. Wimer	E. Wildey/N. Wildey	6–1	6–4			
1908 M. Curtis/Evelyn Sears	C. B. Neely/M. Steever	6–3	5–7	9–7		
1909 H. V. Hotchkiss/E. E. Rotch	D. Green/L. Moyes	6–1	6–1			
1910 H. V. Hotchkiss/E. E. Rotch	A. Browning/E. Wildey	6–4	6–4			
1911 H. V. Hotchkiss/Eleanora Sears	D. Green/F. Sutton	6–4	4–6	6–2		
1912 M. K. Browne/D. Green	Mrs M. Barge-Wallach/Mrs F. Schmitz	6–2	5–7	6–0		
1913 M. K. Browne/Mrs R. H. Williams	D. Green/E. Wildey	12–10	2–6	6–3		
1914 M. K. Browne/Mrs R. H. Williams	Mrs E. Raymond/E. Wildey	8–6	6–2			
1915 Eleanora Sears/Mrs G. W. Wightman	Mrs G. L. Chapman/Mrs M. McLean	10–8	6–2			
1916 M. Bjurstedt/E. Sears	Mrs E. Raymond/E. Wildey	4–6	6–2	10–8		
1917 M. Bjurstedt/Eleanora Sears	Mrs R. LeRoy/P. Walsh	6–2	6–4			
1918 E. E. Goss/M. Zinderstein	M. Bjurstedt/Mrs J. Rogge	7–5	8–6			
1919 E. E. Goss/M. Zinderstein	Eleanora Sears/Mrs G. W. Wightman	9–7	9–7			
1920 E. E. Goss/M. Zinderstein	H. Baker/E. Tennant	13–11	4–6	6–3		
1921 M. K. Browne/Mrs R. H. Williams	H. Gilleaudeau/Mrs L. G. Morris	6–3	6–2			
1922 Mrs J. B. Jessup/H. N. Wills	Mrs F. I. Mallory/E. Sigourney	6–4	7–9	6–3		
1923 Mrs B. C. Covell/K. McKane	E. E. Goss/Mrs G. W. Wightman	2–6	6–2	6–1		
1924 Mrs G. W. Wightman/H. N. Wills	E. E. Goss/Mrs J. B. Jessup	6–4	6–3			
1925 M. K. Browne/H. N. Wills	Mrs T. C. Bundy/E. Ryan	6–4	6–3			

1926 E. E. Goss/E. Ryan	M. K. Browne/Mrs A. H. Chapin	3–6	6–4	12–10
1927 Mrs L. A. Godfree/E. H. Harvey	J. Fry/B. Nuthall	6–1	4–6	6–4
1928 Mrs G. W. Wightman/H. N. Wills	E. Cross/Mrs L. A. Harper	6–2	6–2	
1929 Mrs L. R. C. Michell/Mrs P. H. Watson	Mrs B. C. Covell/Mrs D. C. Shepherd–Barron	2–6	6–3	6–4
1930 B. Nuthall/S. Palfrey	E. Cross/Mrs L. A. Harper	3–6	6–3	7–5
1931 B. Nuthall/Mrs E. F. Whittingstall	H. H. Jacobs/D. E. Round	6–2	6–4	
1932 H. H. Jacobs/S. Palfrey	A. Marble/Mrs M. Painter	8–6	6–1	
1933 F. James/B. Nuthall	Mrs F. S. Moody/E. Ryan	w.o.		
1934 H. H. Jacobs/S. Palfrey	Mrs D. B. Andrus/C. A. Babcock	4–6	6–3	6–4
1935 H. H. Jacobs/Mrs M. Fabyan	Mrs D. B. Andrus/C. A. Babcock	6–4	6–2	
1936 C. A. Babcock/Mrs J. Van Ryn	H. H. Jacobs/Mrs M. Fabyan	9–7	2–6	6–4
1937 Mrs M. Fabyan/A. Marble	C. A. Babcock/Mrs J. Van Ryn	7–5	6–4	
1938 Mrs M. Fabyan/A. Marble	J. Jedrzejowska/Mrs R. Mathieu	6–8	6–4	6–3
1939 Mrs M. Fabyan/A. Marble	Mrs S. H. Hammersley/K. E. Stammers	7–5	8–6	
1940 Mrs M. Fabyan/A. Marble	D. M. Bundy/Mrs J. Van Ryn	6–4	6–3	
1941 Mrs E. T. Cooke/M. E. Osborne	D. M. Bundy/D. J. Hart	3–6	6–1	6–4
1942 A. L. Brough/M. E. Osborne	P. M. Betz/D. J. Hart	9–7	6–2	6–1
1943 A. L. Brough/M. E. Osborne	P. M. Betz/D. J. Hart	6–4	6–3	
1944 A. L. Brough/M. E. Osborne	P. M. Betz/D. J. Hart	4–6	6–4	6–3
1945 A. L. Brough/M. E. Osborne	P. M. Betz/D. J. Hart	6–4	6–4	
1946 A. L. Brough/M. E. Osborne	Mrs P. C. Todd/Mrs M. A. Prentiss	6–1	6–3	
1947 A. L. Brough/M. E. Osborne	Mrs P. C. Todd/D. J. Hart	5–7	6–3	7–5
1948 A. L. Brough/Mrs W. D. du Pont	Mrs P. C. Todd/D. J. Hart	6–4	8–10	6–1
1949 A. L. Brough/Mrs W. D. du Pont	S. J. Fry/D. J. Hart	6–4	10–8	
1950 A. L. Brough/Mrs W. D. du Pont	S. J. Fry/D. J. Hart	6–2	6–3	
1951 S. J. Fry/D. J. Hart	N. Chaffee/Mrs P. C. Todd	6–4	6–2	
1952 S. J. Fry/D. J. Hart	A. L. Brough/M. Connolly	10–8	6–4	
1953 S. J. Fry/D. J. Hart	A. L. Brough/Mrs W. D. du Pont	6–2	7–9	9–7
1954 S. J. Fry/D. J. Hart	A. L. Brough/Mrs W. D. du Pont	6–4	6–4	
1955 A. L. Brough/Mrs W. D. du Pont	S. J. Fry/D. J. Hart	6–3	1–6	6–3
1956 A. L. Brough/Mrs W. D. du Pont	Mrs B. R. Pratt/S. J. Fry	6–3	6–0	
1957 A. L. Brough/Mrs W. D. du Pont	A. Gibson/D. R. Hard	6–2	7–5	
1958 J. M. Arth/D. R. Hard	A. Gibson/M. E. Bueno	2–6	6–3	6–4
1959 J. M. Arth/D. R. Hard	S. Moore/M. E. Bueno	6–2	6–3	
1960 M. E. Bueno/D. R. Hard	D. M. Catt/A. A. Haydon	6–1	6–1	
1961 D. R. Hard/L. Turner	E. Buding/Y. Ramirez	6–4	5–7	6–0
1962 M. E. Bueno/D. R. Hard	Mrs R. Susman/B. J. Moffitt	4–6	6–3	6–2
1963 R. Ebbern/M. Smith	M. E. Bueno/D. R. Hard	4–6	10–8	6–3
1964 Mrs R. Susman/B. J. Moffitt	M. Smith/L. Turner	3–6	6–2	6–4
1965 N. Richey/Mrs C. Graebner	Mrs R. Susman/B. J. Moffitt	6–4	6–4	
1966 M. E. Bueno/N. Richey	R. Casals/Mrs L. W. King	6–3	6–4	
1967 R. Casals/Mrs L. W. King	M. A. Eisel/Mrs D. Fales	4–6	6–3	6–4
1968 M. E. Bueno/M. Smith	S. V. Wade/Mrs G. M. Williams	6–3	7–5	
1969 Mrs B. M. Court/S. V. Wade	Mrs P. W. Curtis/V. Ziegenfuss	6–1	6–3	

* Played as National Patriotic tournament.
There is some doubt about the accuracy of this result.
5–set finals abolished.

MIXED DOUBLES
Not recognised as an official championship.

CHAMPIONS	RUNNERS–UP	SCORE			
1887* J. S. Clark/Miss L. Stokes	E. D. Faries/Miss L. Knight	7–5	6–4		
1888* J. S. Clark/Miss M. Wright	P. Johnson/Miss A. Robinson	1–6	6–5	6–4	6–3
1889* A. E. Wright/Miss G. W. Roosevelt	C. T. Lee/Miss B. L. Townsend	6–1	6–3	3–6	6–3
1890* R. Beach/Miss M. E. Cahill	C. T. Lee/Miss B. L. Townsend	6–2	3–6	6–2	
1891* M. R. Wright/Miss M. E. Cahill	C. T. Lee/Miss G. W. Roosevelt	6–4	6–0	6–5	
1892 C. Hobart/Miss M. E. Cahill	R. Beach/Miss E. H. Moore	6–1	6–3		
1893 C. Hobart/Miss E. C. Roosevelt	R. N. Willson/Miss Bankson	6–1	4–6	10–8	6–1
1894 E. P. Fischer/Miss J. P. Atkinson	G. Remak/Mrs McFadden	6–2	6–2	6–1	
1895 E. P. Fischer/Miss J. P. Atkinson	M. Fielding/Miss A. R. Williams	4–6	6–1	6–2	
1896 E. P. Fischer/Miss J. P. Atkinson	M. Fielding/Miss A. R. Williams	6–2	6–3	6–3	
1897 D. L. Magruder/Miss L. Henson	R. A. Griffin/Miss M. Banks	6–4	6–3	7–5	
1898 E. P. Fischer/Miss C. B. Neely	J. A. Hill/Miss H. Chapman	Not known			
1899 A. L. Hoskins/Miss E. J. Rastall	J. P. Gardner/Miss J. W. Craven	6–4	6–0 ret'd		
1900 A. Codman/Miss M. J. Hunnewell	G. Atkinson/Miss T. Shaw	11–9	6–3	6–1	
1901 R. D. Little/Miss M. Jones	C. Stevens/Miss M. McAteer	6–4	6–4	7–5	
1902 W. C. Grant/Miss E. H. Moore	A. L. Hoskins/Miss E. J. Rastall	6–2	6–1		
1903 H. F. Allen/Miss H. Chapman	W. H. Rowland/Miss C. B. Neely	6–4	7–5		
1904 W. C. Grant/Miss E. H. Moore	F. B. Dallas/Miss M. Sutton	6–2	6–1		

Year	Winners	Runners-up	Score		
1905	C. Hobart/Mrs Hobart	E. B. Dewhurst/Miss E. H. Moore	6–2	6–4	
1906	E. B. Dewhurst/Miss S. Coffin	J. B. Johnson/Miss M. Johnson	6–3	7–5	
1907	W. F. Johnson/Miss M. Sayres	H. M. Tilden/Miss N. Wildey	6–1	7–5	
1908	N. W. Niles/Miss E. E. Rotch	R. D. Little/Miss L. Hammond	6–4	4–6	6–4
1909	W. F. Johnson/Miss H. V. Hotchkiss	R. D. Little/Miss L. Hammond	6–2	6–0	
1910	J. R. Carpenter/Miss H. V. Hotchkiss	H. M. Tilden/Miss E. Wildey	6–2	6–2	
1911	W. F. Johnson/Miss H. V. Hotchkiss	H. M. Tilden/Miss E. Wildey	6–4	6–4	
1912	R. N. Williams/Miss M. K. Browne	W. J. Clothier/Miss Evelyn Sears	6–4	2–6	11–9
1913	W. T. Tilden/Miss M. K. Browne	C. S. Rogers/Miss D. Green	7–5	7–5	
1914	W. T. Tilden/Miss M. K. Browne	J. R. Rowland/Miss M. Myers	6–1	6–4	
1915	H. C. Johnson/Mrs G. W. Wightman	I. C. Wright/Miss M. Bjurstedt	6–0	6–1	
1916	W. E. Davis/Miss Evelyn Sears	W. T. Tilden/Miss F. A. Ballin	6–4	7–5	
1917	I. C. Wright/Miss M. Bjurstedt	W. T. Tilden/Miss F. A. Ballin	10–12	6–1	6–3
1918	I. C. Wright/Mrs G. W. Wightman	F. B. Alexander/Miss M. Bjurstedt	6–2	6–4	
1919	V. Richards/Miss M. Zinderstein	W. T. Tilden/Miss F. A. Ballin	2–6	11–9	6–1
1920	W. F. Johnson/Mrs G. W. Wightman	C. Biddle/Mrs F. I. Mallory	6–4	6–3	
1921	W. M. Johnston/Miss M. K. Browne	W. T. Tilden/Miss F. I. Mallory	3–6	6–4	6–3
1922	W. T. Tilden/Mrs F. I. Mallory	H. Kinsey/Miss H. N. Wills	6–4	6–3	
1923	W. T. Tilden/Mrs F. I. Mallory	J. B. Hawkes/Miss K. McKane	6–3	2–6	10–8
1924	V. Richards/Miss H. N. Wills	W. T. Tilden/Mrs F. I. Mallory	6–8	7–5	6–0
1925	J. B. Hawkes/Miss K. McKane	V. Richards/Miss E. H. Harvey	6–2	6–4	
1926	J. Borotra/Mrs E. Ryan	R. Lacoste/Mrs G. W. Wightman	6–4	7–5	
1927	H. Cochet/Miss E. Bennett	R. Lacoste/Mrs G. W. Wightman	2–6	6–0	6–2
1928	G. M. Lott/Miss B. Nuthall	H. W. Austin/Mrs B. C. Covell	6–3	6–3	
1929	G. M. Lott/Miss B. Nuthall	H. W. Austin/Mrs B. C. Lovell	6–3	6–3	
1930	W. L. Allison/Miss E. Cross	F. X. Shields/Miss M. Morrill	6–4	6–4	
1931	G. M. Lott/Miss B. Nuthall	W. L. Allison/Mrs L. A. Harper	6–3	6–3	
1932	F. J. Perry/Miss S. Palfrey	H. E. Vines/Miss H. H. Jacobs	6–3	7–5	
1933	H. E. Vines/Miss E. Ryan	G. M. Lott/Miss S. Palfrey	11–9	6–1	
1934	G. M. Lott/Miss H. H. Jacobs	L. R. Stoefen/Miss E. Ryan	4–6	13–11	6–2
1935	E. Maier/Mrs M. Fabyan	R. Menzel/Miss K. E. Stammers	6–3	3–6	6–4
1936	G. Mako/Miss A. Marble	J. D. Budge/Mrs M. Fabyan	6–3	6–2	
1937	J. D. Budge/Mrs M. Fabyan	Y. Petra/Mme S. Henrotin	6–2	8–10	6–0
1938	J. D. Budge/Miss A. Marble	J. E. Bromwich/Miss T. Coyne	6–1	6–2	
1939	H. C. Hopman/Miss A. Marble	E. T. Cooke/Mrs M. Fabyan	9–7	6–1	
1940	R. L. Riggs/Miss A. Marble	J. A. Kramer/Miss D. M. Bundy	9–7	6–1	
1941	J. A. Kramer/Mrs E. T. Cooke	R. L. Riggs/Miss P. M. Betz	4–6	6–4	6–4
1942	F. R. Schroeder/Miss A. L. Brough	A. D. Russell/Mrs P. C. Todd	3–6	6–1	6–4
1943	W. F. Talbert/Miss M. E. Osborne	F. Segura/Miss P. M. Betz	10–8	6–4	
1944	W. F. Talbert/Miss M. E. Osborne	W. D. McNeill/Miss D. M. Bundy	6–2	6–3	
1945	W. F. Talbert/Miss M. E. Osborne	R. Falkenburg/Miss D. J. Hart	6–4	6–4	
1946	W. F. Talbert/Miss M. E. Osborne	R. Kimbrell/Miss A. L. Brough	6–3	6–4	
1947	J. Bromwich/Miss A. L. Brough	F. Segura/Miss G. Morgan	6–3	6–1	
1948	T. P. Brown/Miss A. L. Brough	W. F. Talbert/Mrs W. D. du Pont	6–4	6–4	
1949	E. W. Sturgess/Miss A. L. Brough	W. F. Talbert/Mrs W. D. du Pont	4–6	6–3	7–5
1950	K. McGregor/Mrs W. D. du Pont	F. A. Sedgman/Miss D. J. Hart	6–4	3–6	6–3
1951	F. A. Sedgman/Miss D. J. Hart	M. G. Rose/Miss S. J. Fry	6–3	6–2	
1952	F. A. Sedgman/Miss D. J. Hart	L. A. Hoad/Mrs T. C. Long	6–3	7–5	
1953	E. V. Seixas/Miss D. J. Hart	R. N. Hartwig/Miss J. A. Sampson	6–2	4–6	6–4
1954	E. V. Seixas/Miss D. J. Hart	K. R. Rosewall/Mrs W. D. du Pont	4–6	6–1	6–1
1955	E. V. Seixas/Miss D. J. Hart	L. A. Hoad/Miss S. J. Fry	9–7	6–1	
1956	K. R. Rosewall/Mrs W. D. du Pont	L. A. Hoad/Miss D. R. Hard	9–7	6–1	
1957	K. Nielsen/Miss A. Gibson	R. N. Howe/Miss D. R. Hard	6–3	9–7	
1958	N. A. Fraser/Mrs W. D. du Pont	A. Olmedo/Miss M. E. Bueno	6–3	3–6	9–7
1959	N. A. Fraser/Mrs W. D. du Pont	R. Mark/Miss J. Hopps	7–5	13–15	6–2
1960	N. A. Fraser/Mrs W. D. du Pont	A. Palafox/Miss M. E. Bueno	6–3	6–2	
1961	R. Mark/Miss M. Smith	R. D. Ralston/Miss D. R. Hard	w.o.		
1962	F. S. Stolle/Miss M. Smith	F. Froehling/Miss L. Turner	7–5	6–2	
1963	K. Fletcher/Miss M. Smith	E. Rubinoff/Miss J. Tegart	3–6	8–6	6–2
1964	J. D. Newcombe/Miss M. Smith	E. Rubinoff/Miss J. Tegart	10–8	4–6	6–3
1965	F. S. Stolle/Miss M. Smith	F. Froehling/Miss J. Tegart	5–2	6–2	
1966	O. K. Davidson/Mrs D. Fales	E. Rubinoff/Miss C. A. Aucamp	6–1	6–3	
1967	O. K. Davidson/Mrs L. W. King	S. R. Smith/Miss R. Casals	6–3	6–2	
1968	P. W. Curtis/Miss M. A. Eisel	R. N. Perry/Miss T. A. Fretz	6–4	7–5	
1969	P. Sullivan/Miss P. S. A. Hogan	T. Addison/Miss K. Pigeon	6–4	2–6	12–10

* Played as National Patriotic tournament.

US OPEN CHAMPIONSHIPS

Played at West Side Club, Forest Hills, New York, on grass courts 1968–74, on Har–Tru courts 1975–77. Played at National Tennis Centre, Flushing Meadow, New York, on cement courts, 1978 on.

MEN'S SINGLES

	CHAMPION	RUNNER–UP	SCORE					PRIZE ($)
1968	A. R. Ashe	T. S. Okker	14–12	5–7	6–3	3–6	6–3	14,000
1969	R. G. Laver	A. D. Roche	7–9	6–3	6–1	6–2		16,000
1970	K. R. Rosewall	A. D. Roche	2–6	6–4	7–6	6–3		20,000
1971	S. R. Smith	J. Kodes	3–6	6–3	6–2	7–6		15,000
1972	I. Nastase	A. R. Ashe	3–6	6–3	6–7	6–4	6–3	25,000
1973	J. D. Newcombe	J. Kodes	6–4	1–6	4–6	6–2	6–3	25,000
1974	J. S. Connors	K. R. Rosewall	6–1	6–0	6–1			22,500
1975	M. Orantes	J. S. Connors	6–4	6–3	6–3			25,000
1976	J. S. Connors	B. Borg	6–4	3–6	7–6	6–4		30,000
1977	G. Vilas	J. S. Connors	2–6	6–3	7–6	6–0		33,000
1978	J. S. Connors	B. Borg	6–4	6–2	6–2			38,000
1979	J. P. McEnroe	V. Gerulaitis	7–5	6–3	6–3			39,000
1980	J. P. McEnroe	B. Borg	7–6	6–1	6–7	5–7	6–4	46,000
1981	J. P. McEnroe	B. Borg	4–6	6–2	6–4	6–3		60,000
1982	J. S. Connors	I. Lendl	6–3	6–2	4–6	6–4		90,000
1983	J. S. Connors	I. Lendl	6–3	6–7	7–5	6–0		120,000
1984	J. P. McEnroe	I. Lendl	6–3	6–4	6–1			160,000
1985	I. Lendl	J. P. McEnroe	7–6	6–3	6–4			187,500
1986	I. Lendl	M. Mecir	6–4	6–2	6–0			210,000
1987	I. Lendl	M. Wilander	6–7	6–0	7–6	6–4		250,000
1988	M. Wilander	I. Lendl	6–4	4–6	6–3	5–7	6–4	275,000
1989	B. Becker	I. Lendl	7–6	1–6	6–3	7–6		300,000
1990	P. Sampras	A. Agassi	6–4	6–3	6–2			350,000
1991	S. Edberg	J. Courier	6–2	6–4	6–0			400,000
1992	S. Edberg	P. Sampras	3–6	6–4	7–6	6–2		500,000

WOMEN'S SINGLES

	CHAMPION	RUNNER–UP	SCORE			PRIZE ($)
1968	Miss S. V. Wade	Mrs L. W. King	6–4	6–2		6,000
1969	Mrs B. M. Court	Miss N. Richey	6–2	6–2		6,000
1970	Mrs B. M. Court	Miss R. Casals	6–2	2–6	6–1	7,500
1971	Mrs L. W. King	Miss R. Casals	6–4	7–6		5,000
1972	Mrs L. W. King	Miss K. Melville	6–3	7–5		10,000
1973	Mrs B. M. Court	Miss E. Goolagong	7–6	5–7	6–2	25,000
1974	Mrs L. W. King	Miss E. Goolagong	3–6	6–3	7–5	22,500
1975	Miss C. M. Evert	Mrs R. A. Cawley	5–7	6–4	6–2	25,000
1976	Miss C. M. Evert	Mrs R. A. Cawley	6–3	6–0		30,000
1977	Miss C. M. Evert	Miss W. Turnbull	7–6	6–2		33,000
1978	Miss C. M. Evert	Miss P. Shriver	7–5	6–4		38,000
1979	Miss T. A. Austin	Miss C. M. Evert	6–4	6–3		39,000
1980	Mrs J. M. Lloyd	Miss H. Mandlikova	5–7	6–1	6–1	46,000
1981	Miss T. A. Austin	Miss M. Navratilova	1–6	7–6	7–6	60,000
1982	Mrs J. M. Lloyd	Miss H. Mandlikova	6–3	6–1		90,000
1983	Miss M. Navratilova	Mrs J. M. Lloyd	6–1	6–3		120,000
1984	Miss M. Navratilova	Mrs J. M. Lloyd	4–6	6–4	6–4	160,000
1985	Miss H. Mandlikova	Miss M. Navratilova	7–6	1–6	7–6	187,500
1986	Miss M. Navratilova	Miss H. Sukova	6–3	6–2		210,000
1987	Miss M. Navratilova	Miss S. Graf	7–6	6–1		250,000
1988	Miss S. Graf	Miss G. Sabatini	6–3	3–6	6–1	275,000
1989	Miss S. Graf	Miss M. Navratilova	3–6	7–5	6–1	300,000
1990	Miss G. Sabatini	Miss S. Graf	6–2	7–6		350,000
1991	Miss M. Seles	Miss M. Navratilova	7–6	6–1		400,000
1992	Miss M. Seles	Miss A. Sanchez–Vic.	6–3	6–3		500,000

MEN'S DOUBLES

	CHAMPIONS	RUNNERS–UP	SCORE				
1968	R. C. Lutz/S. R. Smith	A. R. Ashe/A. Gimeno	11–9		6–1	7–5	
1969	K. R. Rosewall/F. S. Stolle	C. Pasarell/R. D. Ralston	2–6	7–5	13–11	6–3	
1970	P. Barthes/N. Pilic	R. S. Emerson/R. G. Laver	6–3	7–6	4–6	7–6	
1971	J. D. Newcombe/R. Taylor	S. R. Smith/E. van Dillen	6–7	6–3	7–6	4–6	7–6
1972	E. C. Drysdale/R. Taylor	O. K. Davidson/J. D. Newcombe	6–4	7–6	6–3		
1973	O. K. Davidson/J. D. Newcombe	R. G. Laver/K. R. Rosewall	7–5	2–6	7–5	7–5	
1974	R. C. Lutz/S. R. Smith	P. Cornejo/J. Fillol	6–3	6–3			
1975	J. S. Connors/I. Nastase	T. S. Okker/M. C. Riessen	6–4	7–6			

	CHAMPIONS	RUNNERS-UP	SCORE				
1976	T. S. Okker/M. C. Riessen	P. Kronk/C. Letcher	6-4	6-4			
1977	R. A. J. Hewitt/F. D. McMillan	B. E. Gottfried/R. Ramirez	6-4	6-0			
1978	R. C. Lutz/S. R. Smith	M. C. Riessen/S. E. Stewart	1-6	7-5	6-3		
1979	P. Fleming/J. P. McEnroe	R. C. Lutz/S. R. Smith	6-2	6-4			
1980	R. C. Lutz/S. R. Smith	P. Fleming/J. P. McEnroe	7-6	3-6	6-1	3-6	6-3
1981	P. Fleming/J. P. McEnroe	H. Gunthardt/P. McNamara	w.o.				
1982	K. Curren/S. Denton	V. Amaya/H. Pfister	6-2	6-7	5-7	6-2	6-4
1983	P. Fleming/J. P. McEnroe	F. Buehning/V. Winitsky	6-3	6-4	6-2		
1984	J. Fitzgerald/T. Smid	S. Edberg/A. Jarryd	7-6	6-3	6-3		
1985	K. Flach/R. Seguso	H. Leconte/Y. Noah	7-6	6-7	7-6	6-0	
1986	A. Gomez/S. Zivojinovic	J. Nystrom/M. Wilander	4-6	6-3	6-3	4-6	6-3
1987	S. Edberg/A. Jarryd	K. Flach/R. Seguso	7-6	6-2	4-6	5-7	7-6
1988	S. Casal/E. Sanchez	R. Leach/J. Pugh	w.o.				
1989	J. P. McEnroe/M. Woodforde	K. Flach/R. Seguso	6-4	4-6	6-3	6-3	
1990	P. Aldrich/D. Visser	P. Annacone/D. Wheaton	6-2	7-6	6-2		
1991	J. B. Fitzgerald/A. Jarryd	S. Davis/D. Pate	6-3	3-6	6-3	6-3	
1992	J. Grabb/R. Reneberg	K. Jones/R. Leach	3-6	7-6	6-3	6-3	

WOMEN'S DOUBLES

	CHAMPIONS	RUNNERS-UP	SCORE		
1968	M. E. Bueno/Mrs B. M. Court	R. Casals/Mrs L. W. King	4-6	9-7	8-6
1969	F. Durr/D. R. Hard	Mrs B. M. Court/S. V. Wade	0-6	6-4	6-4
1970	Mrs B. M. Court/Mrs D. Dalton	R. Casals/S. V. Wade	6-3	6-4	
1971	R. Casals/Mrs D. Dalton	Mrs J. B. Chanfreau/F. Durr	6-3	6-3	
1972	F. Durr/B. Stove	Mrs B. M. Court/S. V. Wade	6-3	1-6	6-3
1973	Mrs B. M. Court/S. V. Wade	R. Casals/Mrs L. W. King	3-6	6-3	7-5
1974	R. Casals/Mrs L. W. King	F. Durr/B. Stove	7-6	6-7	6-4
1975	Mrs B. M. Court/S. V. Wade	R. Casals/Mrs L. W. King	7-5	2-6	7-5
1976	L. Boshoff/I. Kloss	O. Morozova/S. V. Wade	6-1	6-4	
1977	M. Navratilova/B. Stove	R. Richards/B. Stuart	6-1	7-6	
1978	Mrs L. W. King/M. Navratilova	Mrs G. E. Reid/W. M. Turnbull	7-6	6-4	
1979	B. Stove/W. M. Turnbull	Mrs L. W. King/M. Navratilova	7-5	6-3	
1980	Mrs L. W. King/M. Navratilova	P. H. Shriver/B. Stove	7-6	7-5	
1981	K. Jordan/A. E. Smith	R. Casals/W. M. Turnbull	6-3	6-3	
1982	R. Casals/W. M. Turnbull	B. Potter/S. A. Walsh	6-4	6-4	
1983	M. Navratilova/P. H. Shriver	R. Fairbank/C. Reynolds	6-7	6-1	6-3
1984	M. Navratilova/P. H. Shriver	A. E. Hobbs/W. M. Turnbull	6-2	6-4	
1985	C. Kohde-Kilsch/H. Sukova	M. Navratilova/P. H. Shriver	6-7	6-2	6-3
1986	M. Navratilova/P. H. Shriver	H. Mandlikova/W. M. Turnbull	6-4	3-6	6-3
1987	M. Navratilova/P. H. Shriver	K. Jordan/E. Smylie	5-7	6-4	6-2
1988	G. Fernandez/R. White	J. Hetherington/P. Fendick	6-4	6-1	
1989	H. Mandlikova/M. Navratilova	M. J. Fernandez/P. H. Shriver	5-7	6-4	6-4
1990	G. Fernandez/M. Navratilova	J. Novotna/H. Sukova	6-2	6-4	
1991	P. Shriver/N. Zvereva	J. Novotna/L. Savchenko	6-4	4-6	7-6
1992	J. Novotna/L. Savchenko Neil.	G. Fernandez/N. Zvereva	7-6	6-1	

MIXED DOUBLES

	CHAMPIONS	RUNNERS-UP	SCORE		
1968	*Not held*				
1969	M. C. Riessen/Mrs B. M. Court	R. D. Ralston/Miss F. Durr	7-5	6-3	
1970	M. C. Riessen/Mrs B. M. Court	F. D. McMillan/Mrs D. Dalton	6-4	6-4	
1971	O. K. Davidson/Mrs L. W. King	R. R. Maud/Miss B. Stove	6-3	7-5	
1972	M. C. Riessen/Mrs B. M. Court	I. Nastase/Miss R. Casals	6-3	7-5	
1973	O. K. Davidson/Mrs L. W. King	M. C. Riessen/Miss B. M. Court	6-3	3-6	7-6
1974	G. Masters/Miss P. Teeguarden	J. S. Connors/Miss C. M. Evert	6-1	7-6	
1975	R. L. Stockton/Miss R. Casals	F. S. Stolle/Mrs L. W. King	6-3	7-6	
1976	P. Dent/Mrs L. W. King	F. D. McMillan/Miss B. Stove	3-6	6-2	7-5
1977	F. D. McMillan/Miss B. Stove	V. Gerulaitis/Mrs L. W. King	6-2	3-6	6-3
1978	F. D. McMillan/Miss B. Stove	R. O. Ruffels/Mrs L. W. King	6-3	7-6	
1979	R. A. J. Hewitt/Miss G. Stevens	F. D. McMillan/Miss B. Stove	6-3	7-5	
1980	M. C. Riessen/Miss W. M. Turnbull	F. D. McMillan/Miss B. Stove	7-5	6-2	
1981	K. Curren/Miss A. E. Smith	S. Denton/Miss J. Russell	6-4	7-6	
1982	K. Curren/Miss A. E. Smith	F. Taygan/Miss B. Potter	6-7	7-6	7-6
1983	J. Fitzgerald/Miss E. Sayers	F. Taygan/Miss B. Potter	3-6	6-3	6-4
1984	Tom Gullikson/Miss M. Maleeva	J. Fitzgerald/Miss E. Sayers	2-6	7-5	6-4
1985	H. Gunthardt/Miss M. Navratilova	J. Fitzgerald/Mrs E. Smylie	6-3	6-4	
1986	S. Casal/Miss R. Reggi	P. Fleming/Miss M. Navratilova	6-4	6-4	
1987	E. Sanchez/Miss M. Navratilova	P. Annacone/Miss B. Nagelsen	6-4	6-7	7-6

1988 J. Pugh/Miss J. Novotna	P. McEnroe/Mrs E. Smylie	7–6	6–3	
1989 S. Cannon/Miss R. White	R. Leach/Miss M. McGrath	3–6	6–2	7–5
1990 T. Woodbridge/Mrs E. Smylie	J. Pugh/Miss N. Zvereva	6–4	6–2	
1991 T. Nijssen/Miss M. Bollegraf	E. Sanchez/Miss A. Sanchez–Vicario	6–2	7–6	
1992 M. Woodforde/Miss N. Provis	T. Nijssen/Miss H. Sukova	4–6	6–3	6–3

ITALIAN CHAMPIONSHIPS

Staged in Milan 1930 to 1934. Moved to the Foro Italico in Rome in 1935. Not held 1936 to 1949 because of the Abyssinia War and World War II. In 1961 the tournament was staged in Turin. Men's and women's events were held at different dates in 1979. In 1980–1985 the women's events moved to Perugia, but returned to Rome in 1986.

MEN'S SINGLES

CHAMPION	RUNNER–UP	SCORE			
1930 W. T. Tilden	H. L. de Morpurgo	6–1	6–1	6–2	
1931 G. P. Hughes	H. Cochet	6–4	6–3	6–2	
1932 A. Merlin	G. P. Hughes	6–1	5–7	6–0	8–6
1933 E. Sertorio	A. Martin Legeay	6–3	6–1	6–3	
1934 G. Palmieri	G. de Stefani	6–3	6–0	7–5	
1935 W. Hines	G. Palmieri	6–3	10–8	9–7	
1936–49 Not held					
1950 J. Drobny	W. F. Talbert	6–4	6–3	7–9	6–2
1951 J. Drobny	G. Cucelli	6–3	10–8	6–1	
1952 F. A. Sedgman	J. Drobny	7–5	6–3	1–6	6–4
1953 J. Drobny	L. A. Hoad	6–2	6–1	6–2	
1954 J. E. Patty	E. Morea	11–9	6–4	6–4	
1955 F. Gardini	G. Merlo	6–1	1–6	3–6	5–6 ret'd
1956 L. A. Hoad	S. Davidson	7–5	6–2	6–0	
1957 N. Pietrangeli	G. Merlo	8–6	6–2	6–4	
1958 M. G. Rose	N. Pietrangeli	5–7	8–6	6–4	1–6 6–2
1959 L. Ayala	N. A. Fraser	6–3	1–6	6–3	6–3
1960 B. MacKay	L. Ayala	7–5	7–5	0–6	0–6 6–1
1961 N. Pietrangeli	R. G. Laver	6–8	6–1	6–1	6–2
1962 R. G. Laver	R. S. Emerson	6–1	1–6	3–6	6–3 6–1
1963 M. F. Mulligan	B. Jovanovic	6–2	4–6	6–3	8–6
1964 J. E. Lundquist	F. S. Stolle	1–6	7–5	6–3	6–1
1965 M. F. Mulligan	M. Santana	1–6	6–4	6–3	6–1
1966 A. D. Roche	N. Pietrangeli	11–9	6–1	6–2	
1967 M. F. Mulligan	A. D. Roche	6–3	0–6	6–4	6–1
1968 T. S. Okker	R. A. J. Hewitt	10–8	6–8	6–1	1–6 6–0
1969 J. D. Newcombe	A. D. Roche	6–3	4–6	6–2	5–7 6–3
1970 I. Nastase	J. Kodes	6–3	1–6	6–3	8–6
1971 R. G. Laver	J. Kodes	7–5	6–3	6–3	
1972 M. Orantes	J. Kodes	4–6	6–1	7–5	6–2
1973 I. Nastase	M. Orantes	6–1	6–1	6–1	
1974 B. Borg	I. Nastase	6–3	6–4	6–2	
1975 R. Ramirez	M. Orantes	7–6	7–5	7–5	
1976 A. Panatta	G. Vilas	2–6	7–6	6–2	7–6
1977 V. Gerulaitis	A. Zugarelli	6–2	7–6	3–6	7–6
1978 B. Borg	A. Panatta	1–6	6–3	6–1	4–6 6–3
1979 V. Gerulaitis	E. Dibbs	6–7	7–6	6–7	6–4 6–2
1980 G. Vilas	Y. Noah	6–0	6–4	6–4	
1981 J. L. Clerc	V. Pecci	6–3	6–4	6–0	
1982 A. Gomez	E. Teltscher	6–2	6–3	6–2	
1983 J. Arias	J. Higueras	6–2	6–7	6–1	6–4
1984 A. Gomez	A. Krickstein	2–6	6–1	6–2	6–2
1985 Y. Noah	M. Mecir	6–3	3–6	6–2	7–6
1986 I. Lendl	E. Sanchez	7–5	4–6	6–1	6–1
1987 M. Wilander	M. Jaite	6–3	6–4	6–4	
1988 I. Lendl	G. Perez Roldan	2–6	6–4	6–2	4–6 6–4
1989 A. Mancini	A. Agassi	6–3	4–6	2–6	7–6 6–1
1990 T. Muster	A. Chesnokov	6–1	6–3	6–1	
1991 E. Sanchez	A. Mancini	6–3	6–1	3–0 ret'd	
1992 J. Courier	C. Costa	7–6	6–0	6–4	

WOMEN'S SINGLES

CHAMPION	RUNNER–UP	SCORE		
1930 Miss E. de Alvarez	Miss L. Valerio	3–6	8–6	6–0

1931 Mrs L. Valerio	Mrs D. Andrus	2–6	6–2	6–2	
1932 Miss I. Adamoff	Miss L. Valerio	6–4	7–5		
1933 Miss E. Ryan	Miss I. Adamoff	6–1	6–1		
1934 Miss H. Jacobs	Miss L. Valerio	6–3	6–0		
1935 Miss H. Sperling	Miss L. Valerio	6–4	6–1		
1936–49 Not held					
1950 Mrs A. Bossi	Miss P. J. Curry	6–4	6–4		
1951 Miss D. J. Hart	Miss S. J. Fry	6–3	8–6		
1952 Miss S. Partridge	Miss M. P. Harrison	6–3	7–5		
1953 Miss D. J. Hart	Miss M. Connolly	4–6	9–7	6–3	
1954 Miss M. Connolly	Miss P. E. Ward	6–3	6–0		
1955 Miss P. E. Ward	Miss E. Vollmer	6–4	6–3		
1956 Miss A. Gibson	Mrs S. Kormoczy	6–3	7–5		
1957 Miss S. J. Bloomer	Mrs D. P. Knode	1–6	9–7	6–2	
1958 Miss M. E. Bueno	Miss L. Coghlan	3–6	6–3	6–3	
1959 Miss C. C. Truman	Miss S. Reynolds	6–0	6–1		
1960 Mrs S. Kormoczy	Miss A. S. Haydon	6–4	4–6	6–1	
1961 Miss M. E. Bueno	Miss L. R. Turner	6–4	6–4		
1962 Miss M. Smith	Miss M. E. Bueno	8–6	5–7	6–4	
1963 Miss M. Smith	Miss L. R. Turner	6–3	6–4		
1964 Miss M. Smith	Miss L. R. Turner	6–1	6–1		
1965 Miss M. E. Bueno	Miss N. Richey	6–1	1–6	6–3	
1966 Mrs P. F. Jones	Miss A. Van Zyl	8–6	6–1		
1967 Miss L. R. Turner	Miss M. E. Bueno	6–3	6–3		
1968 Mrs W. W. Bowrey	Mrs B. M. Court	2–6	6–2	6–3	
1969 Miss J. M. Heldman	Miss K. Melville	7–5	6–4		
1970 Mrs L. W. King	Miss J. M. Heldman	6–1	6–3		
1971 Miss S. V. Wade	Mrs H. Masthoff	6–4	6–4		
1972 Miss L. Tuero	Mrs O. Morozova	6–4	6–3		
1973 Miss E. F. Goolagong	Miss C. M. Evert	7–6	6–0		
1974 Miss C. M. Evert	Miss M. Navratilova	6–3	6–3		
1975 Miss C. M. Evert	Miss M. Navratilova	6–1	6–0		
1976 Miss M. Jausovec	Miss L. Hunt	6–1	6–3		
1977 Miss J. Newberry	Miss R. Tomanova	6–3	7–6		
1978 Miss R. Marsikova	Miss V. Ruzici	7–5	7–5		
1979 Miss T. A. Austin	Miss S. Hanika	6–4	1–6	6–3	
1980 Mrs J. M. Lloyd	Miss V. Ruzici	5–7	6–2	6–2	
1981 Mrs J. M. Lloyd	Miss V. Ruzici	6–1	6–2		
1982 Mrs J. M. Lloyd	Miss H. Mandlikova	6–0	6–3		
1983 Miss A. Temesvari	Miss B. Gadusek	6–1	6–0		
1984 Miss M. Maleeva	Mrs J. M. Lloyd	6–3	6–3		
1985 Miss R. Reggi	Miss V. Nelson	6–4	6–4		
1986 Not held					
1987 Miss S. Graf	Miss G. Sabatini	7–5	4–6	6–0	
1988 Miss G. Sabatini	Miss H. Kelesi	6–1	6–7	6–1	
1989 Miss G. Sabatini	Miss A. Sanchez	6–2	5–7	6–4	
1990 Miss M. Seles	Miss M. Navratilova	6–1	6–1		
1991 Miss G. Sabatini	Miss M. Seles	6–3	6–2		
1992 Miss G. Sabatini	Miss M. Seles	7–5	6–4		

MEN'S DOUBLES

CHAMPIONS	RUNNERS–UP	SCORE				
1930 W. F. Coen/W. T. Tilden	H. L. de Morpurgo/P. Gaslini	6–0	6–3	6–3		
1931 A. del Bono/G. P. Hughes	H. Cochet/A. Merlin	3–6	8–6	4–6	6–4	6–3
1932 G. P. Hughes/G. de Stafani	J. Bonte/A. Merlin	6–2	6–2	6–4		
1933 J. Lesuer/A. M. Legeay	G. Palmieri/E. Sertorio	6–2	6–4	6–2		
1934 G. Palmieri/G. L. Rogers	G. P. Hughes/G. de Stefani	3–6	6–4	9–7	0–6	6–2
1935 J. H. Crawford/V. B. McGrath	J. Borotra/J. Brugnon	4–6	4–6	6–4	6–2	6–2
1936–49 Not held						
1950 W. F. Talbert/M. A. Trabert	J. E. Patty/O. W. Sidwell	6–3	6–1	4–6 ret'd		
1951 J. Drobny/R. Savitt	G. Cucelli/M. Del Bello	6–2	7–9	6–1	6–3	
1952 J. Drobny/F. A. Sedgman	G. Cucelli/M. Del Bello	3–6	7–5	3–6	6–3	6–2
1953 L. A. Hoad/K. R. Rosewall	J. Drobny/J. E. Patty	6–2	6–4	6–2		
1954 J. Drobny/E. Morea	M. A. Trabert/E. V. Seixas	6–4	0–6	3–6	6–3	6–4
1955 A. Larsen/E. Morea	N. Pietrangeli/O. Sirola	6–1	6–4	4–6	7–5	
1956 J. Drobny/L. A. Hoad	N. Pietrangeli/O. Sirola	11–9	6–2	6–3		
1957 N. A. Fraser/L. A. Hoad	N. Pietrangeli/O. Sirola	6–1	6–8	6–0	6–2	
1958 A. Jancso/K. Nielsen	L. Ayala/D. Candy	8–10	6–3	6–2	1–6	9–7
1959 R. S. Emerson/N. A. Fraser	N. Pietrangeli/O. Sirola	8–6	6–4	6–4		
1960 N. Pietrangeli/O. Sirola	R. S. Emerson/N. A. Fraser	3–6	7–5	2–6	11–11 ret'd	

1961	R. S. Emerson/N. A. Fraser	N. Pietrangeli/O. Sirola	6–2	6–4	11–9		
1962	N. A. Fraser/R. G. Laver	K. N. Fletcher/J. D. Newcombe	11–9	6–2	6–4		
1963	R. A. J. Hewitt/F. S. Stolle	N. Pietrangeli/O. Sirola	6–3	6–3	6–1		
1964	R. A. J. Hewitt/F. S. Stolle	A. D, Roche/J. D. Newcombe	7–5	6–3	3–6	7–5	
1965	A. D. Roche/J. D. Newcombe	C. Barnes/T. Koch	1–6	6–4	2–6	12–10ret'd	
1966	R. S. Emerson/F. S. Stolle	N. Pietrangeli/E. C. Drysdale	6–4	12–10	6–3		
1967	R. A. J. Hewitt/F. D. McMillan	W. W. Bowrey/O. K. Davidson	6–3	2–6	6–3	9–7	
1968	T. S. Okker/M. C. Riessen	A. Stone/N. Kalogeropoulos	6–3	6–4	6–2		
1969	A. D. Roche/J. D. Newcombe	T. S. Okker/M. C. Riessen	6–4	1–6	ret'd		
1970	I. Nastase/I. Tiriac	W. W. Bowrey/O. K. Davidson	0–6	10–8	6–3	6–8	6–1
1971	A. D. Roche/J. D. Newcombe	A. Gimeno/R. Taylor	6–4	6–4			
1972	I. Nastase/I. Tiriac	L. A. Hoad/F. D. McMillan	3–6	3–6	6–4	6–3	5–3ret'd
1973	J. D. Newcombe/T. S. Okker	R. Case/G. Masters	6–3	6–2	6–4		
1974	B. E. Gottfried/R. Ramirez	J. Gisbert/I. Nastase	6–3	6–2	6–3		
1975	B. E. Gottfried/R. Ramirez	J. S. Connors/I. Nastase	6–4	7–6	2–6	6–1	
1976	B. E. Gottfried/R. Ramirez	G. Masters/J. D. Newcombe	7–6	5–7	6–3	3–6	6–3
1977	B. E. Gottfried/R. Ramirez	F. McNair/S. E. Stewart	7–6	6–7	7–5		
1978	V. Pecci/B. Prajoux	J. Kodes/T. Smid	6–7	7–6	6–1		
1979	P. Fleming/T. Smid	J. L. Clerc/I. Nastase	4–6	6–1	7–5		
1980	M. R. Edmondson/K. Warwick	B. Taroczy/E. Teltscher	7–6	7–6			
1981	H. Gildemeister/A. Gomez	B. Manson/T. Smid	7–5	6–2			
1982	H. Gunthardt/B. Taroczy	W. Fibak/J. Fitzgerald	6–4	4–6	6–3		
1983	F. Gonzalez/V. Pecci	J. Gunnarsson/M. Leach	6–2	6–7	6–4		
1984	K. Flach/R. Seguso	J. G. Alexander/M. Leach	3–6	6–3	6–4		
1985	A. Jarryd/M. Wilander	K. Flach/R. Seguso	4–6	6–3	6–2		
1986	G. Forget/Y. Noah	M. R. Edmondson/S. E. Stewart	7–6	6–2			
1987	G. Forget/Y. Noah	M. Mecir/T. Smid	6–2	6–7	6–3		
1988	J. Lozano/T. Witsken	A. Jarryd/T. Smid	6–3	6–3			
1989	J. Courier/P. Sampras	D. Marcelino/M. Menezes	6–4	6–3			
1990	S. Casal/E. Sanchez	J. Courier/M. Davis	7–6	7–5			
1991	O. Camporese/G. Ivanisevic	L. Jensen/L. Warder	6–2	6–3			
1992	J. Hlasek/M. Rosset	W. Ferreira/M. Kratzmann	6–4	3–6	6–1		

WOMEN'S DOUBLES

	CHAMPIONS	RUNNERS–UP	SCORE		
1930	E. de Alvarez/L. Valerio	C. Anet/M. Neufeld	7–5	5–7	7–5
1931	A. Luzzatti/J. Prouse	Mrs D. Andrus Burke/L. Valerio	6–3	1–6	6–3
1932	C. Rosambert/L. Payot	Mrs D. Andrus Burke/L. Valerio	7–5	6–3	
1933	I. Adamoff/ Mrs D. Andrus Burke	E. Ryan/L. Valerio	6–3	1–6	6–4
1934	H. H. Jacobs/E. Ryan	I. Adamoff/ Mrs D. Andrus Burke	7–5	9–7	
1935	E. M. Dearman/N. Lyle	C. Aussem/E. Ryan	6–2	6–4	
1936–49	Not held				
1950	J. Quertier/J. Walker–Smith	B. E. Hilton/K. L. A. Tuckey	1–6	6–3	6–2
1951	S. J. Fry/D. J. Hart	L. Brough/T. D. Long	6–1	7–5	
1952	N. Hopman/ Mrs T. D. Long	N. Migliori/V. Tonoli	6–2	6–8	6–1
1953	M. Connolly/J. Sampson	S. J. Fry/D. J. Hart	6–8	6–4	6–4
1954	P. E. Ward/E. M. Watson	N. Adamson/G. Bucaille	3–6	6–3	6–4
1955	C. Mercellis/P. E. Ward	M. Muller/B. Penrose	6–4	10–8	
1956	M. Hawton/ Mrs T. D. Long	A. Buxton/D. R. Hard	6–4	6–8	9–7
1957	M. Hawton/ Mrs T. D. Long	Y. Ramirez/R. M. Reyes	6–1	6–1	
1958	S. J. Bloomer/C. Truman	M. Hawton/ Mrs T. D. Long	6–3	6–2	
1959	Y. Ramirez/R. M. Reyes	M. E. Bueno/J. Hopps	4–6	6–4	6–4
1960	M. Hellyer/Y. Ramirez	S. J. Brasher/A. Haydon	6–4	6–4	
1961	J. Lehane/L. R. Turner	M. Reitano/M. Smith	2–6	6–1	6–1
1962	M. E. Bueno/D. R. Hard	S. Lazzarino/L. Pericoli	6–4	6–4	
1963	R. Ebbern/M. Smith	S. Lazzarino/L. Pericoli	6–2	6–3	
1964	L. R. Turner/M. Smith	S. Lazzarino/L. Pericoli	6–1	6–2	
1965	M. Schacht/A. Van Zyl	S. Lazzarino/L. Pericoli	2–6	6–2	12–10
1966	N. Baylon/A. Van Zyl	Mrs P. F. Jones/E. Starkie	6–3	1–6	6–2
1967	R. Casals/L. R. Turner	S. Lazzarino/L. Pericoli	7–5	7–5	
1968	Mrs B. M. Court/S. V. Wade	A. Van Zyl/P. Walkden	6–2	7–5	
1969	F. Durr/ Mrs P. F. Jones	R. Casals/ Mrs L. W. King	6–3	3–6	6–2
1970	R. Casals/L. W. King	F. Durr/S. V. Wade	6–2	3–6	9–7
1971	Mrs H. Masthoff/S. V. Wade	Mrs L. Bowrey/H. Gourlay	5–7	6–2	6–2
1972	L. Hunt/ Mrs O. Morozova	Mrs G. Chanfreau/R. Vido	6–3	6–4	
1973	Mrs O. Morozova/S. V. Wade	M. Navratilova/R. Tomanova	3–6	6–2	7–5
1974	C. M. Evert/ Mrs O. Morozova	H. Masthoff/H. Orth	w.o.		
1975	C. M. Evert/M. Navratilova	S. Barker/G. Coles	6–1	6–2	
1976	L. Boshoff/I. Kloss	M. Simionescu/V. Ruzici	6–1	6–2	

1977 B. Cuypers/M. Kruger	B. Bruning/S. A. Walsh	3–6	7–5	6–2
1978 M. Jausovec/V. Ruzici	F. Mihai/B. Nagelsen	6–2	2–6	7–5
1979 B. Stove/W. M. Turnbull	Mrs E. Crawley/G. E. Reid	6–3	6–4	
1980 H. Mandlikova/R. Tomanova	I. Madruga/I. Villagran	6–4	6–4	
1981 C. Reynolds/P. Smith	Mrs J. M. Lloyd/V. Ruzici	7–5	6–1	
1982 K. Horvath/Y. Vermk	Mrs L. W. King/I. Kloss	2–6	6–4	7–6
1983 V. Ruzici/S. V. Wade	I. Madruga Osses/C. Tanvier	6–3	2–6	6–1
1984 I. Budarova/M. Skuherska	K. Horvath/V. Ruzici	7–6	1–6	6–4
1985 A. M. Cecchini/R. Reggi	P. Murgo/B. Romano	1–6	6–4	6–3
1986 Not held				
1987 M. Navratilova/G. Sabatini	C. Kohde–Kilsch/H. Sukova	6–4	6–1	
1988 J. Novotna/C. Suire	J. Byrne/J. Thompson	6–3	4–6	7–5
1989 E. Smylie/J. Thompson	M. Bollegraf/M. Paz	6–4	6–3	
1990 H. Kelesi/M. Seles	L. Garrone/L. Golarsa	6–3	6–4	
1991 J. Capriati/M. Seles	N. Provis/E. Reinach	7–5	6–2	
1992 M. Seles/H. Sukova	K. Maleeva/B. Rittner	6–1	6–2	

MIXED DOUBLES

CHAMPIONS	RUNNERS–UP	SCORE		
1930 H. L. de Morpurgo/Miss E. de Alvarez	G. P. Hughes/Miss L. Valerio	4–6	6–4	6–2
1931 G. P. Hughes/Miss L. Valerio	A. del Bono/Mrs D. Andrus Burke	6–0	6–1	
1932 J. Bonte/Miss L. Payot	A. del Bono/Mrs D. Andrus Burke	6–1	6–2	
1933 A. M. Legeay/Mrs D. Andrus Burke	E. Gabrowitz/Miss Y. Orlandini	6–4	6–3	
1934 H. M. Culley/Miss E. Ryan	F. Puncec/Miss R. Couquerque	6–1	6–3	
1935 H. C. Hopman/Miss J. Jedrzejowska	G. P. Hughes/Miss E. M. Dearman	6–3	1–6	6–3
1936–49 Not held				
1950 A. K. Quist/Miss G. Moran div'd with G. Cucelli/Miss A. Bossi 6–3		1–1	unf.	
1951 F. Ampon/Miss S. J. Fry	L. Bergelin/Miss D. J. Hart	8–6	3–6	6–4
1952 K. Nielsen/Miss A. McGuire	E. Migone/Mrs M. J. de Riba	4–6	6–3	6–3
1953 E. V. Seixas/Miss D. J. Hart	M. G. Rose/Miss M. Connolly	6–4	6–4	
1954 E. V. Seixas/Miss M. Connolly div'd with M. A. Trabert/Miss B. M. Kimbrell		3–6	11–9	3–3 unf.
1955 E. Morea/Miss P. E. Ward div'd with M. G. Rose/Miss B. Penrose				
1956 L. Ayala/Mrs T. D. Long	G. Fachini/Miss S. J. Bloomer	6–4	6–3	
1957 L. Ayala/Mrs T. D. Long	R. N. Howe/Miss S. J. Bloomer	6–1	6–1	
1958 G. Fachini/Miss S. J. Bloomer	L. Ayala/Mrs T. D. Long	4–6	6–2	9–7
1959 F. Contreras/Miss R. M. Reyes	W. A. Knight/Miss Y. Ramirez	9–7	6–1	
1960 Not held				
1961 R. S. Emerson/Miss M. Smith	R. A. J. Hewitt/Miss J. Lehane	6–1	6–1	
1962 F. S. Stolle/Miss L. R. Turner	S. Davidson/Miss M. Schacht	6–4	6–1	
1963 Not held				
1964 J. D. Newcombe/Miss M. Smith	T. Koch/Miss M. E. Bueno	3–6	7–5	6–2
1965 J. E. Mandarino/Miss M. Coronado	V. Zarazua/Miss E. Subirats	6–1	6–1	
1966 Not held				
1967 W. W. Bowrey/Miss L. R. Turner	F. D. McMillan/Miss F. Durr	6–2	7–5	
1968 M. C. Riessen/Mrs B. M. Court	T. S. Okker/Miss S. V. Wade	8–6	6–3	
Event ceased				

THE DAVIS CUP

The International Men's Team Championship of the World was initiated in 1900 when the British Isles, then comprising Great Britain and Ireland, challenged the United States for the trophy presented by Dwight F. Davis. The competition was enlarged in 1904 when Belgium and France took part. Each tie has comprised two players engaged in reverse singles plus a doubles match with the best of five sets throughout. In 1989 the tie–break was introduced for all sets except the fifth, in all matches.

From 1900 to 1971 the Champion Nation stood out until challenged by the winner of a knock–out competition between the challenging nations and had the choice of venue. The format was changed in 1981, when the competition became sponsored by NEC. The Champion Nation was the winner of the World Group of the 16 strongest nations. Other nations competed in zonal groups, with eight earning the right to play against the eight first round losers in the World Group for places alongside the first round winners of the World Group for places in the following year's competition. A Zonal Group Three, in which nations from each geographic region play one another on a round-robin basis during one week at one venue to decide promotion to Zonal Group Two, was introduced in 1992. Entries passed the 100 mark for the 1993 competition when 101 nations entered.

CHALLENGE ROUNDS (In playing order)
1900 USA d. British Isles 3–0, Boston: M. D. Whitman d. A. W. Gore 6–1 6–3 6–2; D. F. Davis d. E. D. Black 4–6 6–2 6–4 6–4; Davis/H. Ward d. Black/H. Roper Barrett 6–4 6–4 6–4; Davis div'd with Gore 9–7 9–9.

1901 Not held
1902 USA d. British Isles 3–2, Brooklyn, New York: W. A. Larned lost to R. F. Doherty 6–2 6–3 3–6 4–6 4–6; M. D. Whitman d. J. Pim 6–1 6–1 1–6 6–0; Larned d. Pim 6–3 6–2 6–3; Whitman d. R. F. Doherty 6–1 7–5 6–4; D. F. Davis/H. Ward lost to R. F./H. L. Doherty 6–3 8–10 3–6 4–6.
1903 British Isles d. USA 4–1, Boston: H. L. Doherty d. R. D. Wrenn 6–0 6–3 6–4; R. F. Doherty lost to W. A. Larnedret'd; R. F./H. L. Doherty d. R. D./G. L. Wrenn 7–5 9–7 2–6 6–3; H. L. Doherty d. Larned 6–3 6–8 6–0 2–6 7–5; R. F. Doherty d. R. D. Wrenn 6–4 3–6 6–3 6–8 6–4.
1904 British Isles d. Belgium 5–0, Wimbledon: H. L. Doherty d. P. de Borman 6–4 6–1 6–1; F. L. Riseley d. W.Lemaire 6–1 6–4 6–2; R. F./H. L. Doherty d. de Borman/Lemaire 6–0 6–1 6–3; H. L. Doherty w.o. Lemaire; Riseley d. de Borman 4–6 6–2 8–6 7–5.
1905 British Isles d. USA 5–0, Wimbledon: H. L. Doherty d. H. Ward 7–9 4–6 6–1 6–2 6–0; S. H. Smith d. W. A. Larned 6–4 6–4 5–7 6–4; R. F./H. L. Doherty d. Ward/B. Wright 8–10 6–2 6–2 4–6 8–6; Smith d. W. J. Clothier 4–6 6–1 6–4 6–3; H. L. Doherty d. Larned 6–4 2–6 6–8 6–4 6–2.
1906 British Isles d. USA 5–0, Wimbledon: S. H. Smith d. R. D. Little 6–4 6–4 6–1; H. L. Doherty d. H. Ward 6–2 8–6 6–3; R. F./H. L. Doherty d. Little/Ward 3–6 11–9 9–7 6–1; Smith d. Ward 6–1 6–0 6–4; H. L. Doherty d. Little 3–6 6–3 6–8 6–1 6–3.
1907 Australasia d. British Isles 3–2, Wimbledon: N. E. Brookes d. A. W. Gore 7–5 6–1 7–5; A. F. Wilding d. H. Roper Barrett 1–6 6–4 6–3 7–5; Brookes/Wilding lost to Gore/Roper Barrett 6–3 6–4 5–7 2–6 11–13; Wilding lost to Gore 6–3 3–6 5–7 2–6; Brookes d. Roper Barrett 6–2 6–0 6–3.
1908 Australasia d. USA 3–2, Melbourne: N. E. Brookes d. F. B. Alexander 5–7 9–7 6–2 4–6 6–3; A. F. Wilding lost to B. Wright 6–3 5–7 3–6 1–6; Brookes/Wilding d. Alexander/Wright 6–4 6–2 5–7 1–6 6–4; Brookes lost to Wright 6–0 6–3 5–7 2–6 10–12; Wilding d. Alexander 3–6 4–6 6–1.
1909 Australasia d. USA 5–0, Sydney: N. E. Brookes d. M. E. McLoughlin 6–2 6–2 6–4; A. F. Wilding d. M. H. Long 6–2 7–5 6–1; Brookes/Wilding d. Long/McLoughlin 12–10 9–7 6–3; Brookes d. Long 6–4 7–5 8–6; Wilding d. McLoughlin 3–6 8–6 6–2 6–3.
1910 Not held
1911 Australasia d. USA 5–0, Christchurch, NZ: N. E. Brookes d. B. Wright 6–4 2–6 6–3 6–3; R. W. Heath d. W. A. Larned 2–6 6–1 7–5 6–2; Brookes/A. W. Dunlop d. Wright/M. E. McLoughlin 6–4 5–7 7–5 6–4; Brookes d. McLoughlin 6–4 3–6 4–6 6–3 6–4; Heath w.o. Wright.
1912 British Isles d. Australasia 3–2, Melbourne: J. C. Parke d. N. E. Brookes 8–6 6–3 5–7 6–2; C. P. Dixon d. R. W. Heath 5–7 6–4 6–4 6–4; A. E. Beamish/Parke lost Brookes/A. W. Dunlop 4–6 1–6 5–7; Dixon lost to Brookes 2–6 4–6 4–6; Parke d. Heath 6–2 6–4 6–4.
1913 USA d. British Isles 3–2, Wimbledon: M. E. McLoughlin lost to J. C. Parke 10–8 5–7 4–6 6–1 5–7; R. N. Williams d. C. P. Dixon 8–6 3–6 6–2 1–6 7–5; H. Hackett/McLoughlin d. Dixon/H. Roper Barrett 5–7 6–1 2–6 7–5 6–4; McLoughlin d. Dixon 8–6 6–3 6–2; Williams lost to Parke 2–6 7–5 7–5 4–6 2–6.
1914 Australasia d. USA 3–2, Forest Hills, NY: A. F. Wilding d. R. N. Williams 7–5 6–2 6–3; N. E. Brookes lost to M. E. McLoughlin 15–17 3–6 3–6; Brookes/Wilding d. T. C. Bundy/McLoughlin 6–3 8–6 9–7; Brookes d. Williams 6–1 6–2 8–10 6–3; Wilding lost to McLoughlin 2–6 3–6 6–2 2–6.
1915–18Not held
1919 Australasia d. British Isles 4–1, Sydney: G. L. Patterson d. A. H. Lowe 6–4 6–3 2–6 6–3; J. O. Anderson lost to A. R. F. Kingscote 5–7 2–6 4–6; N. E. Brookes/Patterson d. A. E. Beamish/Kingscote 6–0 6–0 6–2; Patterson d. Kingscote 6–4 6–4 8–6; Anderson d. Lowe 6–4 5–7 6–3 4–6 12–10.
1920 USA d. Australasia 5–0, Auckland: W. T. Tilden d. N. E. Brookes 10–8 6–4 1–6 6–4; W. M. Johnston d. G. L. Patterson 6–3 6–1 6–1; Johnston/Tilden d. Brookes/Patterson 4–6 6–4 6–0 6–4; Johnston d. Brookes 5–7 7–5 6–3 6–3; Tilden d. Patterson 5–7 6–2 6–3 6–3.
1921 USA d. Japan 5–0, Forest Hills, NY: W. M. Johnston d. I. Kumagae 6–2 6–4 6–2; W. T. Tilden d. Z. Schimidzu 5–7 4–6 7–5 6–2 6–1; W. Washburn/R. N. Williams d. Kumagae/Shimidzu 6–2 7–5 4–6 7–5; Tilden d. Kumagae; 9–7 6–4 6–1; Johnston d. Shimidzu 6–3 5–7 6–2 6–4.
1922 USA d. Australasia 4–1, Forest Hills, NY: W. T. Tilden d. G. L. Patterson 7–5 10–8 6–0; W. M. Johnston d. J. O. Anderson 6–1 6–2 6–3; V. Richards/Tilden lost to P. O'Hara Wood/Patterson 4–6 0–6 3–6; Johnston d. Patterson 6–2 6–2 6–1; Tilden d. Anderson 6–4 5–7 3–6 6–4 6–2.
1923 USA d. Australia 4–1, Forest Hills, NY: W. M. Johnston lost to J. O. Anderson 6–4 2–6 6–2 5–7 2–6; W. T. Tilden d. J. B. Hawkes 6–4 6–2 6–1; Tilden/R. N. Williams d. Anderson/Hawkes 17–15 11–13 2–6 6–3 6–2; Johnston d. Hawkes 6–0 6–2 6–1; Tilden d. Anderson 6–2 6–3 1–6 7–5.
1924 USA d. Australia 5–0, Philadelphia: W. T. Tilden d. G. L. Patterson 6–4 6–2 6–3; V. Richards d. P. O'Hara Wood 6–3 6–2 6–4; W. M. Johnston/Tilden d. O'Hara Wood/Patterson 5–7 6–3 6–4 6–1; Tilden d. O'Hara Wood 6–2 6–1 6–1; Richards d. Patterson 6–3 7–5 6–4.
1925 USA d. France 5–0, Philadelphia: W. T. Tilden d. J. Borotra 4–6 6–0 2–6 9–7 6–4; W. M. Johnston d. R. Lacoste 6–1 6–1 6–8 6–3; V. Richards/R. N. Williams d. Borotra/Lacoste 6–4 6–4 6–3; Tilden d. Lacoste 3–6 10–12 8–6 7–5 6–2; Johnston d. Borotra 6–1 6–4 6–0.
1926 USA d. France 4–1, Philadelphia: W. M. Johnston d. R. Lacoste 6–0 6–4 0–6 6–0; W. T. Tilden d. J. Borotra 6–2 6–3 6–3; V. Richards/R. N. Williams d. J. Brugnon/H. Cochet 6–4 6–4 6–2; Johnston d. Borotra 8–6 6–4 9–7; Tilden lost to Lacoste 6–4 4–6 6–8 6–8.
1927 France d. USA 3–2, Philadelphia: R. Lacoste d. W. M. Johnston 6–3 6–2 6–2; H. Cochet lost to W. T. Tilden 4–6 6–2 2–6 6–8; J. Borotra/J. Brugnon lost to F. Hunter/Tilden 6–3 3–6 3–6 6–4 0–6; Lacoste d. Tilden 6–4 4–6 6–3 6–3; Cochet d. Johnston 6–4 4–6 6–2 6–4.
1928 France d. USA 4–1, Paris: R. Lacoste lost to W. T. Tilden 6–1 4–6 4–6 6–2 3–6; H. Cochet d. J. Hennessey 5–7 9–7 6–3 6–0; J. Borotra/Cochet d. F. Hunter/Tilden 6–4 6–8 7–5 4–6 6–2; Lacoste d. Hennessey 4–6 6–1 7–5 6–3; Cochet d. Tilden 9–7 8–6 6–4.
1929 France d. USA 3–2, Paris: H. Cochet d. W. T. Tilden 6–3 6–1 6–2; J. Borotra d. G. M. Lott 6–1 3–6 6–4 7–5; Borotra/Cochet lost to W. Allison/J. Van Ryn 1–6 6–8 4–6; Cochet d. Lott 6–1 3–6 6–0 6–3; Borotra lost to Tilden 6–4 1–6 4–6 5–7.

1930 France d. USA 4–1, Paris: J. Borotra lost to W. T. Tilden 6–2 5–7 4–6 5–7; H. Cochet d. G. M. Lott 6–4 6–2 6–2; J. Brugnon/Cochet d. W. Allison/J. Van Ryn 6–3 7–5 1–6 6–2; Borotra d. Lott 5–7 6–3 2–6 6–2 8–6; Cochet d. Tilden 4–6 6–3 6–1 7–5.
1931 France d. Great Britain 3–2, Paris: H. Cochet d. H. W. Austin 3–6 11–9 6–2 6–4; J. Borotra lost to F. J. Perry 6–4 8–10 0–6 6–4 4–6; J. Brugnon/Cochet d. G. P Hughes/C. H. Kingsley 6–1 5–7 6–3 8–6; Cochet d. Perry 6–4 1–6 9–7 6–3; Borotra lost to Austin 5–7 3–6 6–3 5–7.
1932 France d. USA 3–2, Paris: H. Cochet d. W. Allison 5–7 7–5 3–6 7–5 6–2; J. Borotra d. H. E. Vines 6–4 6–2 2–6 6–4; J. Brugnon/Cochet lost to Allison/J. Van Ryn 3–6 13–11 5–7 6–4 4–6; Borotra d. Allison 1–6 3–6 6–4 6–2 7–5; Cochet lost to Vines 6–4 6–0 5–7 6–8 2–6.
1933 Great Britain d. France 3–2, Paris: H. W. Austin d. A. Merlin 6–3 6–4 6–0; F. J. Perry d. H. Cochet 8–10 6–4 8–6 3–6 6–1; G. P. Hughes/H. G. N. Lee lost to J. Borotra/J. Brugnon 3–6 6–8 2–6; Austin lost to Cochet 7–5 4–6 6–4 4–6 4–6; Perry d. Merlin 4–6 8–6 6–2 7–5.
1934 Great Britain d. USA 4–1, Wimbledon: F. J. Perry d. S. B. Wood 6–1 4–6 5–7 6–0 6–3; H. W. Austin d. F. X. Shields 6–4 6–4 6–1; G. P. Hughes/H. G. N. Lee lost to G. M. Lott/L. Stoefen 5–7 0–6 6–4 7–9; Perry d. Shields 6–4 4–6 6–2 15–13; Austin d. Wood 4–6 6–0 6–8 6–3.
1935 Great Britain d. USA 5–0, Wimbledon: F. J. Perry d. J. D. Budge 6–0 6–8 6–3 6–4; H. W. Austin d. W. Allison 6–2 2–6 4–6 6–3 7–5; G. P. Hughes/C. R. D. Tuckey d. Allison/J. Van Ryn 6–2 1–6 6–8 6–3 6–3; Perry d. Allison 4–6 6–4 7–5 6–3; Austin d. Budge 6–2 6–4 6–8 7–5.
1936 Great Britain d. Australia 3–2, Wimbledon: H. W. Austin d. J. H. Crawford 4–6 6–3 6–1 6–1; F. J. Perry d. A. K. Quist 6–1 4–6 7–5 6–2; G. P. Hughes/C. R. D. Tuckey lost to Crawford/Quist 4–6 6–2 5–7 8–10; Austin lost to Quist 4–6 6–3 5–7 2–6; Perry d. Crawford 6–2 6–3 6–3.
1937 USA d. Great Britain 4–1, Wimbledon: F. A. Parker lost to H. W. Austin 3–6 2–6 5–7; J. D. Budge d. C. E. Hare 15–13 6–1 6–2; Budge/G. Mako d. C. R. D. Tuckey/F. H. D. Wilde 6–3 7–5 7–9 12–10; Parker d. Hare 6–2 6–4 6–2; Budge d. Austin 8–6 3–6 6–4 6–3.
1938 USA d. Australia 3–2, Philadelphia: R. L. Riggs d. A. K. Quist 4–6 6–0 8–6 6–1; J. D. Budge d. J. E. Bromwich 6–2 6–3 4–6 7–5; Budge/G. Mako lost to Bromwich/Quist 6–0 3–6 4–6 2–6; Budge d. Quist 8–6 6–1 6–2; Riggs lost to Bromwich 4–6 6–4 0–6 2–6.
1939 Australia d. USA 3–2, Philadelphia: J. E. Bromwich lost to R. L. Riggs 4–6 0–6 5–7; A. K. Quist lost to F. A. Parker 3–6 6–2 4–6 6–1 5–7; Bromwich/Quist d. J. R. Hunt/J. Kramer 5–7 6–2 7–5 6–2; Quist d. Riggs 6–1 6–4 3–6 3–6 6–4; Bromwich d. Parker 6–0 6–3 6–1.
1940–45 Not held
1946 USA d. Australia 5–0, Melbourne: F. R. Schroeder d. J. E. Bromwich 3–6 6–1 6–2 0–6 6–3; J. Kramer d. D. Pails 8–6 6–2 9–7; Kramer/Schroeder d. Bromwich/A. K. Quist 6–2 7–5 6–4; Kramer d. Bromwich 8–6 6–4 6–2 6–4; G Mulloy d. Pails 6–3 6–3 6–4.
1947 USA d. Australia 4–1, Forest Hills, NY: J. Kramer d. D. Pails 6–2 6–1 6–2; F. R. Schroeder d. J. E. Bromwich 6–4 5–7 6–3 6–3; Kramer/Schroeder lost to Bromwich/C. F. Long 4–6 6–2 2–6 4–6; Schroeder d. Pails 6–3 8–6 4–6 9–11 10–8; Kramer d. Bromwich 6–3 6–2 6–2.
1948 USA d. Australia 5–0, Forest Hills, NY: F. A. Parker d. O. W. Sidwell 6–4 6–4 6–4; F. R. Schroeder d. A. K. Quist 6–3 4–6 6–0 6–0; G. Mulloy/W. F. Talbert d. C. F. Long/Sidwell 8–6 9–7 2–6 7–5; Parker d. Quist 6–2 6–2 6–3; Schroeder d. Sidwell 6–2 6–1 6–1.
1949 USA d. Australia 4–1, Forest Hills, NY: F. R. Schroeder d. O. W. Sidwell 6–1 5–7 4–6 6–2 6–3; R. A. Gonzales d. F. A. Sedgman 8–6 6–4 9–7; G. Mulloy/W. F. Talbert lost to J. E. Bromwich/Sidwell 6–3 6–4 8–10 7–9 7–9; Schroeder d. Sedgman 6–4 6–3 6–3; Gonzales d. Sidwell 6–1 6–3 6–3.
1950 Australia d. USA 4–1, Forest Hills, NY: F. A. Sedgman d. T. Brown 6–0 8–6 9–7; K. McGregor d. F. R. Schroeder 13–11 6–3 6–4; J. E. Bromwich/Sedgman d. G. Mulloy/Schroeder 4–6 6–4 6–2 4–6 6–4; Sedgman d. Schroeder 6–2 6–2 6–2; McGregor lost to Brown 11–9 10–8 9–11 1–6 4–6.
1951 Australia d. USA 3–2, Sydney: M. G. Rose lost to E. V. Seixas 3–6 4–6 7–9; F. A. Sedgman d. F. R. Schroeder 6–4 6–3 4–6 6–4; K. McGregor/Sedgman d. Schroeder/M. A. Trabert 6–2 9–7 6–3; Rose lost to Schroeder 4–6 11–13 5–7; Sedgman d. Seixas 6–4 6–2 6–2.
1952 Australia d. USA 4–1, Adelaide: F. A. Sedgman d. E. V. Seixas 6–3 6–4 6–3; K. McGregor d. M. A. Trabert 11–9 6–4 6–1; McGregor/Sedgman d. Seixas/Trabert 6–3 6–4 1–6 6–3; Sedgman d. Trabert 7–5 6–4 10–8; McGregor lost to Seixas 3–6 6–8 8–6 3–6.
1953 USA d. Australia 3–2, Melbourne: L. A. Hoad d. E. V. Seixas 6–4 6–2 6–3; K. R. Rosewall lost to M. A. Trabert 3–6 4–6 4–6; R. Hartwig/Hoad lost to Seixas/Trabert 2–6 4–6 4–6; Hoad d. Trabert 13–11 6–3 2–6 3–6 7–5; Rosewall d. Seixas 6–2 2–6 6–3 6–4.
1954 USA d. Australia 3–2, Sydney: M. A. Trabert d. L. A. Hoad 6–4 2–6 12–10 6–3; E. V. Seixas d. K. R. Rosewall 8–6 6–8 6–4 6–3; Seixas/Trabert d. Hoad/Rosewall 6–2 4–6 6–2 10–8; Trabert lost to Rosewall 7–9 5–7 3–6; Seixas lost to R. Hartwig 6–4 3–6 2–6 3–6.
1955 Australia d. USA 5–0, Forest Hills, NY: K. R. Rosewall d. E. V. Seixas 6–3 10–8 4–6 6–2; L. A. Hoad d. M. A. Trabert 4–6 6–3 6–3 8–6; R. Hartwig/Hoad d. Seixas/Trabert 12–14 6–4 6–3 3–6 7–5; Rosewall d. H. Richardson 6–4 3–6 6–1 6–4; Hoad d. Seixas 7–9 6–1 6–4 6–4.
1956 Australia d. USA 5–0, Adelaide: L. A. Hoad d. H. Flam 6–2 6–3 6–3; K. R. Rosewall d. E. V. Seixas 6–2 7–5 6–3; Hoad/Rosewall d. S. Giammalva/Seixas 1–6 6–1 7–5 6–4; Hoad d. Seixas 6–2 7–5 6–3; Rosewall d. Giammalva 4–6 6–1 8–6 7–5.
1957 Australia d. USA 3–2, Melbourne: A. J. Cooper d. E. V. Seixas 3–6 7–5 6–1 1–6 6–3; M. J. Anderson d. B. MacKay 6–3 7–5 3–6 47–9 6–3; Anderson/M. G. Rose d. MacKay/Seixas 6–4 6–4 8–6; Cooper lost to MacKay 4–6 6–1 6–4 4–6 3–6; Anderson lost to Seixas 3–6 6–4 3–6 6–0 11–13.
1958 USA d. Australia 3–2, Brisbane: A. Olmedo d. M. J. Anderson 8–6 2–6 9–7 8–6; B. MacKay lost to A. J. Cooper 6–4 3–6 2–6 4–6; Olmedo/H. Richardson d. Anderson/N. A. Fraser 10–12 3–6 16–14 6–3 7–5; Olmedo d. Cooper 6–3 4–6 6–4 8–6; MacKay lost to Anderson 5–7 11–13 9–11.
1959 Australia d. USA 3–2, Forest Hills, NY: N. A. Fraser d. A. Olmedo 8–6 6–8 6–4 8–6; R. G. Laver lost to B. MacKay 5–7 4–6 1–6; R. S. Emerson/Fraser d. E. Buchholz/Olmedo 7–5 7–5 6–4; Laver lost to Olmedo 7–9 6–4 8–10 10–12;

Fraser d. MacKay 8–6 3–6 6–2 6–4.

1960 Australia d. Italy 4–1, Sydney: N. A. Fraser d. O. Sirola 4–6 6–3 6–3 6–3; R. G. Laver d. N. Pietrangeli 8–6 6–4 6–3; R. S. Emerson/Fraser d. Pietrangeli/Sirola 10–8 5–7 6–3 6–4; Laver d. Sirola 9–7 6–2 6–3; Fraser lost to Pietrangeli 9–11 3–6 6–1 2–6.

1961 Australia d. Italy 5–0, Melbourne: R. S. Emerson d. N. Pietrangeli 8–6 6–4 6–0; R. G. Laver d. O. Sirola 6–1 6–4 6–3; Emerson/N. A. Fraser d. Pietrangeli/Sirola 6–2 6–3 6–4; Emerson d. Sirola 6–2 6–3 4–6 6–2; Laver d. Pietrangeli 6–3 3–6 4–6 6–3 8–6.

1962 Australia d. Mexico 5–0, Brisbane: N. A. Fraser d. A. Palafox 7–9 6–3 6–4 11–9; R. G. Laver d. R. H. Osuna 6–2 6–1 7–5; R. S. Emerson/Laver d. Osuna/Palafox 7–5 6–2 6–4; Fraser d. Osuna 3–6 11–9 6–1 3–6 6–4; Laver d. Palafox 6–1 4–6 6–4 8–6.

1963 USA d. Australia 3–2, Adelaide: R. D. Ralston d. J. D. Newcombe 6–4 6–1 3–6 4–6 7–5; C. R. McKinley lost to R. S. Emerson 3–6 6–3 5–7 5–7; McKinley/Ralston d. Emerson/N. A. Fraser 6–3 4–6 11–9 11–9; Ralston lost to Emerson 2–6 3–6 6–3 2–6; McKinley d. Newcombe 10–12 6–2 9–7 6–2.

1964 Australia d. USA 3–2, Cleveland, Ohio: F. S. Stolle lost to C. R. McKinley 1–6 7–9 6–4 2–6; R. S. Emerson d. R. D. Ralston 6–3 6–1 6–3; Emerson/Stolle lost to McKinley/Ralston 4–6 6–4 6–4 3–6 4–6; Stolle d. Ralston 7–5 6–3 3–6 9–11 6–4; Emerson d. McKinley 3–6 6–2 6–4 6–4.

1965 Australia d. Spain 4–1, Sydney: F. S. Stolle d. M. Santana 10–12 3–6 6–1 6–4 7–5; R. S. Emerson d. J. Gisbert 6–3 6–2 6–2; J. D. Newcombe/A. D. Roche d. J. L. Arilla/Santana 6–3 4–6 7–5 6–2; Emerson lost to Santana 6–2 3–6 4–6 13–15; Stolle d. Gisbert 6–2 6–4 8–6.

1966 Australia d. India 4–1, Melbourne: F. S. Stolle d. R. Krishnan 6–3 6–2 6–4; R. S. Emerson d. J. Mukerjea 7–5 6–4 6–2; J. D. Newcombe/A. D. Roche lost to Krishnan/Mukerjea 6–4 5–7 4–6 4–6; Emerson d. Krishnan 6–0 6–2 10–8; Stolle d. Mukerjea 7–5 6–8 6–3 5–7 6–3.

1967 Australia d. Spain 4–1, Brisbane: R. S. Emerson d. M. Santana 6–4 6–1 6–1; J. D. Newcombe d. M. Orantes 6–3 6–3 6–2; Newcombe/A. D. Roche d. Orantes/Santana 6–4 6–4 6–4; Newcombe lost to Santana 5–7 4–6 2–6; Emerson d. Orantes 6–1 6–1 2–6 6–4.

1968 USA d. Australia 4–1, Adelaide: C. Graebner d. W. W. Bowrey 8–10 6–4 8–6 3–6 6–1; A. R. Ashe d. R. O. Ruffels 6–8 7–5 6–3 6–3; R. C. Lutz/S. R. Smith d. J. G. Alexander/Ruffels 6–4 6–4 6–2; Graebner d. Ruffels 3–6 8–6 2–6 6–3 6–1; Ashe lost to Bowrey 6–2 3–6 9–11 6–8.

1969 USA d. Rumania 5–0, Cleveland, Ohio: A. R. Ashe d. I. Nastase 6–2 15–13 7–5; S. R. Smith d. I. Tiriac 6–8 6–3 5–7 6–4; R. C. Lutz/Smith d. Nastase/Tiriac 8–6 6–1 11–9; Smith d. Nastase 4–6 4–6 6–4 6–1 11–9; Ashe d. Tiriac 6–3 8–6 3–6 4–0 ret'd.

1970 USA d. West Germany 5–0, Cleveland, Ohio: A. R. Ashe d. W. Bungert 6–2 10–8 6–2; C. Richey d. C. Kuhnke 6–3 6–4 6–2; R. C. Lutz/S. R. Smith d. Bungert/Kuhnke 6–3 7–5 6–4; Richey d. Bungert 6–4 6–4 7–5; Ashe d. Kuhnke 6–8 10–12 9–7 13–11 6–4.

1971 USA d. Rumania 3–2, Charlotte, NC: S. R. Smith d. I. Nastase 7–5 6–3 6–1; F. A. Froehling d. I. Tiriac 3–6 1–6 6–1 6–3 8–6; Smith/E. Van Dillen lost to Nastase/Tiriac 5–7 4–6 8–6; Smith d. Tiriac 8–6 6–3 6–0; Froehling lost to Nastase 3–6 1–6 6–1 4–6.

Challenge Round abolished

FINAL ROUND SCORES

1972 USA d. Rumania 3–2, Bucharest: S. R. Smith d. I. Nastase 11–9 6–2 6–3; T. Gorman lost to I. Tiriac 6–4 6–2 4–6 3–6 2–6; Smith/E. Van Dillen d. Nastase/Tiriac 6–2 6–0 6–3; Smith d. Tiriac 4–6 6–2 6–4 2–6 6–0; Gorman lost to Nastase 1–6 2–6 7–5 8–10.

1973 Australia d. USA 5–0, Cleveland, Ohio (indoors): J. D. Newcombe d. S. R. Smith 6–1 3–6 6–3 3–6 6–4; R. G. Laver d. T. Gorman 8–10 8–6 6–8 6–3 6–1; Laver/Newcombe d. Smith/E. Van Dillen 6–1 6–2 6–4; Newcombe d. Gorman 6–2 6–1 6–3; Laver d. Smith 3–6 4–3 6–2.

1974 South Africa w.o. India

1975 Sweden d. Czechoslovakia 3–2, Stockholm (indoors): O. Bengtson lost to J. Kodes 4–6 6–2 5–7 4–6; B. Borg d. J. Hrebec 6–1 6–3 6–0; Bengtson/Borg d. Kodes/V. Zednik 6–4 6–4 6–4; Borg d. Kodes 6–4 6–2 6–2; Bengtson lost to Hrebec 6–3 4–6 1–6 4–6.

1976 Italy d. Chile 4–1, Santiago: C. Barazzutti d. J. Fillol 7–5 4–6 7–5 6–1; A. Panatta d. P. Cornejo 6–3 6–1 6–3; P. Bertolucci/Panatta d. Cornejo/Fillol 3–6 6–2 9–7 6–3; Panatta d. Fillol 8–6 6–4 3–6 10–8; A. Zugarelli lost to B. Prajoux 4–6 4–6 2–6.

1977 Australia d. Italy 3–1, Sydney: A. D. Roche d. A. Panatta 6–3 6–4 6–4; J. G. Alexander d. C. Barazzutti 6–2 8–6 4–6 6–2; Alexander/P. Dent lost to P. Bertolucci/Panatta 4–6 4–6 5–7; Alexander d. Panatta 6–4 4–6 2–6 8–6 11–9; Roche div'd with Barazzutti 12–12.

1978 USA d. Great Britain 4–1, Palm Springs, California: J. P. McEnroe d. J. M. Lloyd 6–1 6–2 6–2; B. E. Gottfried lost to C. J. Mottram 6–4 6–2 8–10 4–6 3–6; R. C. Lutz/S. R. Smith d. M. Cox/D. A. Lloyd 6–2 6–2 6–3; McEnroe d. Mottram 6–2 6–2 6–1; Gottfried d. J. M. Lloyd 6–1 6–2 6–4.

1979 USA d. Italy 5–0, San Francisco (indoors): V. Gerulaitis d. C. Barazzutti 6–3 3–2 ret'd; J. P. McEnroe d. A. Panatta 6–2 6–3 6–4; R. C. Lutz/S. R. Smith d. P. Bertolucci/Panatta 6–4 12–10 6–2; McEnroe d. A. Zugarelli 6–4 6–3 6–1; Gerulaitis d. Panatta 6–1 6–3 6–3.

1980 Czechoslovakia d. Italy 4–1, Prague (indoors): T. Smid d. A. Panatta 3–6 3–6 6–3 6–4 6–4; I. Lendl d. C. Barazzutti 4–6 6–1 6–1 6–2; Lendl/Smid d. P. Bertolucci/Panatta 3–6 6–3 3–6 6–3 6–4; Smid lost to Barazzutti 6–3 3–6 2–6; Lendl d. G. Ocleppo 6–3 6–3.

1981 USA d. Argentina 3–1, Cincinnati (indoors): J. P. McEnroe d. G. Vilas 6–3 6–2 6–2; R. Tanner lost to J. L. Clerc 5–7 3–6 6–8; P. Fleming/McEnroe d. Clerc/Vilas 6–3 4–6 6–4 4–6 11–9; McEnroe d. Clerc 7–5 5–7 6–3 3–6 6–3; Tanner div'd with Vilas 11–10.

1982 USA d. France 4–1, Grenoble (indoors): J. P. McEnroe d. Y. Noah 12–10 1–6 3–6 6–2 6–3; G. Mayer d. H. Leconte 6–2 6–2 7–9 6–4; P. Fleming/McEnroe d. Leconte/Noah 6–3 6–4 9–7; Mayer lost to Noah 1–6 0–6; McEnroe d. Leconte 6–2 6–3.

1983 Australia d. Sweden 3–2, Melbourne: P. Cash lost to M. Wilander 3–6 6–4 7–9 3–6; J. Fitzgerald d. J. Nystrom 6–4 6–2 4–6 6–4; M. R. Edmondson/P. McNamee d. A. Jarryd/H. Simonsson 6–4 6–4 6–2; Cash d. Nystrom 6–4 6–1

6–1; Fitzgerald lost to Wilander 8–6 0–6 1–6.
1984 Sweden d. USA 4–1, Gothenburg: M. Wilander d. J. S. Connors 6–1 6–3 6–3; H. Sundstrom d. J. P. McEnroe 13–11 6–4 6–3; S. Edberg/A. Jarryd d. P. Fleming/McEnroe 7–5 5–7 6–2 7–5; Wilander lost to McEnroe 3–6 7–6 3–6; Sundstrom d. J. Arias 3–6 8–6 6–3.
1985 Sweden d. West Germany 3–2, Munich: M. Wilander d. M. Westphal 6–3 6–4 10–8; S. Edberg lost to B. Becker 3–6 6–3 5–7 6–8; Wilander/J. Nystrom d. Becker/A. Maurer 6–4 6–2 6–1; Wilander lost to Becker 3–6 6–2 3–6 3–6; Edberg d. Westphal 3–6 7–5 6–4 6–3.
1986 Australia d. Sweden 3–2, Melbourne: P. Cash d. S. Edberg 13–11 13–11 6–4; P. McNamee lost to M. Pernfors 3–6 1–6 3–6; Cash/J. Fitzgerald d. Edberg/A. Jarryd 6–3 6–4 4–6 6–1; Cash d. Pernfors 2–6 4–6 6–3 6–4 6–3; McNamee lost to Edberg 8–10 4–6.
1987 Sweden d. India 5–0, Gothenburg: M. Wilander d. R. Krishnan 6–4 6–1 6–3; A. Jarryd d. V. Amritraj 6–3 6–3 6–1; Wilander/J. Nystrom d. An./V. Amritraj 6–3 6–6 1–6 6–2; Jarryd d. Krishnan 6–4 6–3; Wilander d. V. Amritraj 6–2 6–0.
1988 West Germany d. Sweden 4–1, Gothenburg: C.–U. Steeb d. M. Wilander 8–10 1–6 6–2 6–4 8–6; B. Becker d. S. Edberg 6–3 6–1 6–4; Becker/E. Jelen d. Edberg/A. Jarryd 3–6 2–6 7–5 6–3 6–2; Steeb lost to Edberg 4–6 6–8; P. Kuhnen w.o. K. Carlsson.
1989 West Germany d. Sweden 3–2, Stuttgart: C.–U. Steeb lost to M. Wilander 7–5 6–7 7–6 2–6 3–6; B. Becker d. S. Edberg 6–2 6–2 6–4; Becker/E. Jelen d. A. Jarryd/J. Gunnarsson 7–6 6–4 3–6 6–7 6–4; Becker d. Wilander 6–2 6–0 6–2; Steeb lost to Edberg 2–6 4–6.
1990 USA d. Australia 3–2, St Petersburg: A. Agassi d. R. Fromberg 4–6 6–4 4–6 6–2 6–4; M. Chang d. D. Cahill 6–2 7–6 6–0; R. Leach/J. Pugh d. P. Cash/J. Fitzgerald 6–4 6–2 3–6 7–6; Agassi lost to Cahill 4–6 6–4 ret.; Chang lost to Fromberg 5–7 6–2 3–6.
1991 France d. USA 3–1, Lyon: G. Forget lost to A. Agassi 7–6 2–6 1–6 2–6; H. Leconte d. P. Sampras 6–4 7–5 6–4; Forget/Leconte d. K. Flach/R. Seguso 6–1 6–4 4–6 6–2; Forget d. Sampras 7–6 3–6 6–3 6–4; Leconte v Agassi not played.
1992 USA d. Switzerland 3–1, Fort Worth: A. Agassi d. J. Hlasek 6–1 6–2 6–2; J. Courier lost to M. Rosset 3–6 7–6 6–3 4–6 4–6; J. McEnroe/P. Sampras d. Rosset/Hlasek 6–7 6–7 7–5 6–1 6–2; Courier d. Hlasek 6–3 3–6 6–3 6–4; Agassi v Rossi not played.

QUALIFIERS FOR WORLD GROUP

1992 Denmark	Cuba	Austria	Netherlands
Germany	Spain	India	Russia

FEDERATION CUP
International Women's Team Championship, staged on a knock–out basis at one venue with each tie comprising two singles and one doubles match.

FINAL ROUNDS
1963 USA d. Australia 2–1, Queen's Club, London, 18–21 June: D. R. Hard lost to M. Smith 3–6 0–6; B. J. Moffitt d. L. R. Turner 5–7 6–0 6–3; Hard/Moffitt d. Smith/Turner 3–6 13–11 6–3.
1964 Australia d. USA 2–1, Germantown Cricket Club, Philadelphia, 2–5 September: M. Smith d. B. J. Moffitt 6–2 6–3; L. R. Turner d. N. Richey 7–5 6–1; Smith/Turner lost to Moffitt/Mrs J. R. Susman 6–4 5–7 1–6.
1965 Australia d. USA 2–1, Kooyong Stadium, Melbourne, 12–18 January: L. R. Turner d. Mrs C. Graebner 6–3 2–6 6–3; M. Smith d. B. J. Moffitt 6–4 8–6; Smith/J. M. Tegart lost to Graebner/Moffitt 5–7 6–4 4–6.
1966 West Germany 3–0, Turin, 11–15 May: J. M. Heldman d. H. Niessen 4–6 7–5 6–1; Mrs L. W. King d. E. Buding 6–3 3–6 6–1; Mrs C. Graebner/Mrs King d. Buding/H. Schultse 6–4 6–2.
1967 USA d. Great Britain 2–0, Rot-Weiss Club, Berlin, 7–11 June: R. Casals d. S. V. Wade 9–7 8–6; Mrs L. W. King d. Mrs P. F. Jones 6–3 6–4; Casals/Mrs King div'd with Mrs Jones/Wade 6–8 9–7.
1968 Australia d. Netherlands 3–0, Stade Roland Garros, Paris, 23–26 May: K. A. Melville d. M. Jansen 4–6 7–5 6–3; Mrs B. M. Court d. A. Suurbeck 6–1 6–3; Court/Melville d. Suurbeck/L. Venneboer 6–3 6–8 7–5.
1969 USA d. Australia 2–1, Athens, 19–25 May: N. Richey d. K. A. Melville 6–4 6–3; J. M. Heldman lost to Mrs B. M. Court 1–6 6–8; J. Bartkowicz/Richey d. Court/J. M. Tegart 6–4 6–4.
1970 Australia d. West Germany 3–0, Freiburg, Germany, 19–24 May: K. M. Krantzcke d. Mrs H. Hoesl 6–2 6–3; Mrs D. E. Dalton d. H. Niessen 4–6 6–3 6–3; Dalton/Krantzcke d. Hoesl/Niessen 6–2 7–5.
1971 Australia d. Great Britain 3–0, Perth, Australia, 26–29 December 1970: Mrs B. M. Court d. Mrs P. F. Jones 6–8 6–3 6–2; E. F. Goolagong d. S. V. Wade 6–4 6–1; Court/L. Hunt d. W. M. Shaw/Wade 6–4 6–4.
1972 South Africa d. Great Britain 2–1, Ellis Park, Johannesburg, 19–26 March: Mrs Q. C. Pretorius lost to S. V. Wade 3–6 2–6; B. Kirk d. W. M. Shaw 4–6 7–5 6–0; Kirk/Pretorius d. Wade/Mrs G. M. Williams 6–1 7–5.
1973 Australia d. South Africa 3–0, Bad Homburg, Germany, 30 April–6 May: E. F. Goolagong d. Mrs Q. C. Pretorius 6–0 6–2; P. Coleman d. B. Kirk 10–8 6–0; Goolagong/J. Young d. Kirk/Pretorius 6–1 6–2.
1974 Australia d. USA 2–1, Naples, 13–19 May: E. F. Goolagong d. J. M. Heldman 6–1 7–5; D. L. Fromholtz lost to C. M. Evert 6–2 5–7 3–6; Goolagong/J. Young d. Heldman/S. A. Walsh 7–5 8–6.
1975 Czechoslovakia d. Australia 3–0, Aix–en–Provence, 6–11 May: M. Navratilova* d. E. F. Goolagong 6–3 6–4; R. Tomanova d. H Gourlay 6–4 6–2; Navratilova/Tomanova d. D. L. Fromholtz/Gourlay 6–3 6–1.
1976 USA d. Australia 2–1, Spectrum Stadium, Philadelphia, 22–29 August: R. Casals lost to Mrs G. Reid 6–1 3–6 5–7; Mrs L. W. King d. Mrs E. Cawley 7–6 6–4; Casals/King d. Cawley/Reid 7–5 6–3.
1977 USA d. Australia 2–1, Devonshire Park, Eastbourne, 13–18 June: Mrs L. W. King d. D. L. Fromholtz 6–1 2–6 6–2; C. M. Evert d. Mrs G. Reid 7–5 6–3; Casals/Evert lost to Reid/W. M. Turnbull 3–6 3–6.
1978 USA d. Australia 2–1, Kooyong Stadium, Melbourne, 27 November–3 December: T. A. Austin lost to Mrs G. Reid 3–6 3–6; C. M. Evert d. W. M. Turnbull 3–6 6–1 6–1; Evert/Mrs L. W. King d. Reid/Turnbull 4–6 6–1 6–4.
1979 USA d. Australia 3–0, Madrid, 30 April–6 May: T. A. Austin d. Mrs G. Reid 6–3 6–0; Mrs J. M. Lloyd d. D. L. Fromholtz 2–6 6–3 8–6; R. Casals/Mrs L. W. King d. Reid/W. M. Turnbull 3–6 6–3 8–6.

1980 USA d. Australia 3–0, Rot–Weiss Club, Berlin, 19–25 May: Mrs J. M. Lloyd d. D. L. Fromholtz 4–6 6–1 6–1; T. A. Austin d. W. M. Turnbull 6–2 6–3; R. Casals/K. Jordan d. Fromholtz/S. Leo 2–6 6–4 6–4.
1981 USA d. Great Britain 3–0, Tokyo, 9–15 November: A. Jaeger d. S. V. Wade 6–3 6–1; Mrs J. M. Lloyd d. S. Barker 6–2 6–1; R. Casals/K. Jordan d. J. M. Durie/Wade 6–4 7–5.
1982 USA d. West Germany 3–0, Santa Clara, California, 19–25 July: Mrs J. M. Lloyd d. C. Kohde 2–6 6–1 6–3; M. Navratilova d. B. Bunge 6–4 6–4; Lloyd/Navratilova d. Bunge/Kohde 3–6 6–1 6–2.
1983 Czechoslovakia d. West Germany 2–1, Zurich, 18–24 July: H. Sukova d. C. Kohde 6–4 2–6 6–2; H. Mandlikova d. B. Bunge 6–2 3–0 ret'd; I. Budarova/M. Skuherska lost to E. Pfaff/Kohde 6–3 2–6 1–6.
1984 Czechoslovakia d. Australia 2–1, Sao Paulo, 15–22 July: H. Sukova lost to A. Minter 5–7 5–7; H. Mandlikova d. E. Sayers 6–1 6–0; Mandlikova/Sukova d. W. Turnbull/Sayers 6–2 6–2.
1985 Czechoslovakia d. USA 2–1, Nagoya, 7–13 October: H. Sukova d. E. Burgin 6–3 6–7 6–4; H. Mandlikova d. K. Jordan 7–5 6–1; A. Holikova/R. Marsikova lost to Burgin/Jordan 2–6 3–6.
1986 USA d. Czechoslovakia 3–0, Prague, 21–27 July: Mrs J. M. Lloyd d. H. Sukova 7–5 7–6; M. Navratilova d. H. Mandlikova 7–5 6–1; Navratilova/P. H. Shriver d. Mandlikova/Sukova 6–4 6–2.
1987 West Germany d. USA 2–1, Vancouver, 27 July–2 August: C. Kohde–Kilsch lost to P. H. Shriver 0–6 6–7; S. Graf d. C. M. Evert 6–2 6–1; Kohde–Kilsch/Graf d. Evert/Shriver 1–6 7–5 6–4.
1988 Czechoslovakia d. USSR 2–1, Melbourne, 7–11 December: R. Zrubakova d. L. Savchenko 6–1 7–6; H. Sukova d. Zvereva 6–3 6–4; J. Novotna/J. Pospisilova lost to Savchenko/Zvereva 6–7 5–7.
1989 USA d. Spain 3–0, Tokyo, 1–8 October: C. Evert d. C. Martinez 6–3 6–2; M. Navratilova d. A. Sanchez 0–6 6–3 6–4; Z. Garrison/P. H. Shriver d. Martinez/Sanchez 7–5 6–1.
1990 USA d. USSR 2–1, Atlanta, 22–29 July: J. Capriati d. L. Meskhi 7–6 6–2; Z. Garrison lost to N. Zvereva 6–4 3–6 3–6; Z. Garrison/G. Fernandez d. N. Zvereva/L. Savchenko 6–4 6–3.
1991 Spain d. USA 2–1, Nottingham, 22–28 July: C. Martinez lost to J. Capriati 6–4 6–7 1–6; A. Sanchez d. M. J. Fernandez 6–3 6–4; Martinez/Sanchez d. G. Fernandez/Z. Garrison 3–6 6–1 6–1.
1992 Germany d. Spain 2–1, Frankfurt, 13–19 July: A. Huber d. C. Martinez 6–3 6–7 6–1; S. Graf d. A. Sanchez–Vic. 6–4 6–2; A. Huber/B. Rittner lost to A. Sanchez–Vic./C. Martinez 1–6 2–6
* M. Navratilova became a US citizen in 1981.

WIGHTMAN CUP

Women's team contest between USA and Great Britain, each match comprising five singles and two doubles, with reverse singles played between the two top players.
1923 USA d. Great Britain 7–0, Forest Hills: H. Wills d. K. McKane 6–2 7–5, d. Mrs R. Clayton 6–2 6–3; Mrs F. Mallory d. Clayton 6–1 8–6, d. McKane 6–2 6–3; E. Goss d. Mrs W. G. Beamish 6–2 0–6 7–5; Mrs G. W. Wightman/Goss d. McKane/Mrs B. C. Covell 10–8 5–7 6–4; Mallory/Wills d. Beamish/Clayton 6–3 6–2.
1924 Great Britain d. USA 6–1, Wimbledon: Mrs B. C. Covell d. H. Wills 6–2 6–4, d. Mrs F. Mallory 6–2 5–7 6–3; K. McKane d. Mallory 6–3 6–3, d. Wills 6–2 6–2; Mrs W. G. Beamish d. E. Goss 6–1 8–10 6–3; Covell/Mrs D. C. Shepherd–Barron d. Mrs M. Z. Jessup/Goss 6–2 6–2; McKane/E. Colyer lost to Mrs G. W. Wightman/Wills 6–2 2–6 4–6.
1925 Great Britain d. USA 4–3, Forest Hills: K. McKane d. Mrs F. Mallory 6–4 5–7 6–0, lost to H. Wills 1–6 6–1 7–9; J. Fry lost to Wills 0–6 5–7, lost to Mallory 3–6 0–6; Mrs R. Lambert Chambers d. Goss 7–5 3–6 6–1; Lambert Chambers/E. H. Harvey d. Mallory/Mrs T. C. Bundy 10–8 6–1; McKane/E. Colyer d. Wills/M. K. Browne 6–0 6–3.
1926 USA d. Great Britain 4–3, Wimbledon: E. Ryan d. J. Fry 6–1 6–3, lost to Mrs L. A. Godfree 1–6 7–5 4–6; M. K. Browne lost to Godfree 1–6 5–7, lost to Fry 6–3 0–6 4–6; Mrs M. Z. Jessup d. Mrs D. C. Shepherd–Barron 6–1 5–7 6–4; Jessup/E. Goss d. Mrs R. Lambert Chambers/Shepherd–Barron 6–4 6–2; Browne/Ryan d. Godfree/E. L. Colyer 3–6 6–2 6–4.
1927 USA d. Great Britain 5–2, Forest Hills: H. Wills d. J. Fry 6–2 6–0, d. Mrs L. A. Godfree 6–1 6–1; Mrs F. Mallory d. Godfree 6–4 6–2, d. J. Fry 6–2 11–9; H. H. Jacobs lost to B. Nuthall 3–6 6–2 1–6; E. Goss/Mrs A. H. Chapin lost to G. Sterry/Mrs J. Hill 7–5 5–7 5–7; Wills/Mrs G. W. Wightman d. Godfree/E. H. Harvey 6–4 4–6 6–3.
1928 Great Britain d. USA 4–3, Wimbledon: Mrs P. H. Watson lost to H. Wills 1–6 2–6, d. Mrs F. Mallory 2–6 6–1 6–2; E. Bennett d. Mallor 6–1 6–3, lost to Wills 3–6 2–6; B. Nuthall lost to H. H. Jacobs 3–6 1–6; E. H. Harvey/P. Saunders d. E. Goss/Jacobs 6–4 6–1; Bennett/Watson d. Wills/P. Anderson 6–2 6–1.
1929 Great Britain d. USA 4–3, Forest Hills: H. Wills d. Mrs P. H. Watson 6–1 6–4, d. B. Nuthall 8–6 8–6; H. H. Jacobs d. Nuthall 7–5 8–6, lost to Watson 3–6 2–6; E. Goss d. Mrs L. R. C. Michell 6–3 3–6 6–3; Wills/Goss lost to Watson/Michell 4–6 1–6; Mrs G. W. Wightman/Jacobs lost to Mrs B. C. Covell/Mrs D. C. Shepherd–Barron 2–6 1–6.
1930 Great Britain d. USA 4–3, Wimbledon: J. Fry lost to H. Wills 1–6 1–6, lost to H. H. Jacobs 0–6 3–6; Mrs P. H. Watson d. Jacobs 2–6 6–2 6–4, lost to Wills 5–7 1–6; P. Mudford d. S. Palfrey 6–0 6–2; Fry/E. H. Harvey d. Palfrey/E. Cross 2–6 6–2 6–4; Watson/Mrs L. A. Godfree d. Jacobs/Wills 7–5 1–6 6–4.
1931 USA d. Great Britain 5–2, Forest Hills: Mrs F. S. Moody d. P. Mudford 6–1 6–4, d. B. Nuthall 6–4 6–2; H. H. Jacobs d. Nuthall 8–6 6–4, d. Mudford 6–2; Mrs L. A. Harper d. D. E. Round 6–3 4–6 9–7; S. Palfrey/Mrs G. W. Wightman lost to Mudford/Mrs D. C. Shepherd–Barron 4–6 8–10; Moody/Harper lost to Nuthall/Mrs Fearnley Whittingstall 6–8 7–5 3–6.
1932 USA d. Great Britain 4–3, Wimbledon: H. H. Jacobs d. D. E. Round 6–4 6–3, lost to Mrs Fearnley Whittingstall 4–6 6–2 1–6; Mrs F. S. Moody d. Fearnley Whittingstall 6–2 6–4, d. Round 6–2 6–3; Mrs L. A. Harper lost to Mrs M. R. King 6–3 1–6 1–6; Harper/Jacobs d. Mrs L. R. C. Michell/Round 6–4 6–1; Moody/Palfrey lost to Fearnley Whittingstall/B. Nuthall 3–6 6–1 8–10.
1933 USA d. Great Britain 4–3, Forest Hills: H. H. Jacobs d. D. E. Round 6–4 6–2, d. M. Scriven 5–7 6–2 7–5; S. Palfrey d. Scriven 6–3 6–1, lost to Round 4–6 8–10; C. Babcock lost to B. Nuthall 6–1 1–6 3–6; Jacobs/Palfrey d. Round/M. Heeley 6–4 6–2; A. Marble/Mrs J. Van Ryn lost to Nuthall/F. James 5–7 2–6.
1934 USA d. Great Britain 5–2, Wimbledon: S. Palfrey d. D. E. Round 6–3 3–6 8–6, d. M. Scriven 4–6 6–2 8–6; H. H. Jacobs d. Scriven 6–1 6–1, d. Round 6–4 6–4; C. Babcock lost to B. Nuthall 7–5 3–6 4–6; Babcock/J. Cruickshank lost to

N. Lyle/E. M. Dearman 5–7 5–7; Jacobs/Palfrey d. Mrs L. A. Godfree/Nuthall 5–7 6–3 6–2.

1935 USA d. Great Britain 4–3, Forest Hills: H. H. Jacobs lost to K. Stammers 7–5 1–6 7–9, d. D. E. Round 6–3 6–2; Mrs E. B. Arnold lost to Round 0–6 3–6, d. Stammers 6–2 1–6 6–3; S. Palfrey d. Mrs M. R. King 6–0 6–3; Jacobs/Palfrey d. Stammers/F. James 6–3 6–2; Mrs D. B. Andrus/C. Babcock lost to N. Lyle/E. M. Dearman 6–3 A4–6 1–6.

1936 USA d. Great Britain 4–3, Wimbledon: H. H. Jacobs lost to K. Stammers 10–12 1–6, lost to D. E. Round 3–6 3–6; S. Palfrey lost to Round 3–6 4–6, d. Stammers 6–3 6–4; C. Babcock d. M. Hardwick 6–4 4–6 6–2; Babcock/Mrs J. Van Ryn d. N. Lyle/E. M. Dearman 6–2 1–6 6–3; Jacobs/Palfrey d. Stammers/F. James 1–6 6–3 7–5.

1937 USA d. Great Britain 6–1, Forest Hills: A. Marble d. M. Hardwick 4–6 6–2 6–4, d. K. Stammers 6–3 6–1; H. H. Jacobs d. Stammers 6–1 4–6 6–4, d. Hardwick 2–6 6–4 6–2; S. Palfrey d. M. Lumb 6–3 6–1; Marble/Palfrey d. E.M. Dearman/J. Ingram 6–3 6–2; Mrs J. Van Ryn/D. M. Bundy lost to Stammers/F. James 3–6 8–10.

1938 USA d. Great Britain 5–2, Wimbledon: A. Marble lost to K. Stammers 6–3 5–7 3–6, d. M. Scriven 6–3 3–6 6–0); Mrs F. S. Moody d. Scriven 6–0 7–5, d. Stammers 6–2 3–6 6–3; S. Fabyan d. M. Lumb 5–7 6–2 6–3; Marble/Fabyan d. Lumb/F. James 6–4 6–2; Moody/D. Bundy lost to E. M. Dearman/J. Ingram 2–6 5–7.

1939 USA d. Great Britain 5–2, Forest Hills: A. Marble d. M. Hardwick 6–3 6–4, d. K. Stammers 3–6 6–3 6–4; H. H. Jacobs lost to Stammers 2–6 6–1 3–6, d. Hardwick 6–2 6–2; S. Fabyan lost to V. Scott 3–6 4–6; M. Arnold/D. M. Bundy d. B. Nuthall/N. Brown 3–6 6–1; Marble/Fabyan d. Stammers/Mrs S. H. Hammersley 7–5 6–2.

1940–45 Not held.

1946 USA d. Great Britain 7–0, Wimbledon: P. M. Betz d. Mrs J. Bostock 6–2 6–4, d. Mrs M. Menzies 6–4 6–4; M. Osborne d. Bostock 6–1 6–4, d. Menzies 6–3 6–2; L. Brough d. J. Curry 8–6 6–3; Brough/Osborne d. Bostock/Mrs M. Halford 6–2 6–1; Betz/D. Hart d. Mrs B. Passingham/M. Lincoln 6–1 6–3.

1947 USA d. Great Britain 7–0, Forest Hills: M. Osborne d. Mrs J. Bostock 6–4 2–6 6–2, d. Mrs M. Menzies 7–5 6–2; L. Brough d. Menzies 6–4 6–2, d. Bostock 6–4 6–4; D. Hart d. Mrs B. Hilton 4–6 6–3 7–5; Hart/Mrs P. C. Todd d. J. Gannon/J. Quertier 6–1 6–2; Brough/Osborne d. Bostock/Hilton 6–1 6–4.

1948 USA d. Great Britain 6–1, Wimbledon: Mrs W. du Pont d. Mrs J. Bostock 4–8 6–4, d. Mrs B. Hilton 6–3 6–4; L. Brough d. Hilton 6–1 6–1, d. Bostock 6–2 4–6 7–5; D. Hart d. J. Gannon 6–1 6–4; Brough/du Pont d. Mrs M. Menzies/Hilton 6–2 6–2; Hart/Mrs C. Todd lost to Bostock/Mrs N. W. Blair 3–6 4–6.

1949 USA d. Great Britain 7–0, Merion Cricket Club, Philadelphia: D. Hart d. Mrs J. Walker–Smith 6–3 6–1, d. Mrs B. Hilton 6–1 6–3; Mrs W. du Pont d. Hilton 6–1 6–3, d. Walker–Smith 6–4 7–5; B. Baker d. J. Quertier 6–4 7–5; Hart/S. Fry d. Quertier/Mrs N. W. Blair 6–1 6–2; G. Moran/Mrs P. C. Todd d. Hilton/K. Tuckey 6–4 8–6.

1950 USA d. Great Britain 7–0, Wimbledon: Mrs W. du Pont d. Mrs B. Hilton 6–3 6–4, d. Mrs J. Walker–Smith 6–3 6–2; L. Brough d. Hilton 2–6 6–2 7–5, d. Walker–Smith 6–0 6–0; D. Hart d. J. Curry 6–2 6–4; Hart/Mrs P. C. Todd d. Walker–Smith/J. Quertier 6–2 6–3; Brough/du Pont d. Hilton/K. Tuckey 6–2 6–0.

1951 USA d. Great Britain 6–1, Longwood Cricket Club, Boston: D. Hart d. J. Quertier 6–4 6–4, d. Mrs J. Walker–Smith 6–4 2–6 7–5; S. Fry d. Walker–Smith 6–1 6–4; lost to Quertier 3–6 6–8; M. Connolly d. K. Tuckey 6–1 6–3; Mrs P. C. Todd/N. Chaffee d. Mrs J. Mottram/P. Ward 7–5 6–3; S. Fry/D. Hart d. Quertier/Tuckey 6–3 6–3.

1952 USA d. Great Britain 7–0, Wimbledon: D. Hart d. Mrs J. Rinkel–Quertier 6–3 6–3, d. Mrs J. Walker–Smith–5 6–2; M. Connolly d. Walker–Smith 3–6 6–1 7–5, d. Rinkel–Quertier 9–7 6–2; S. Fry d. S. Partridge 6–0 8–6; Fry/Hart d. H. Fletcher/Rinkel 8–6 6–4; L. Brough/Connolly d. Mrs J. Mottram/P. Ward 6–0 6–3.

1953 USA d. Great Britain 7–0, Westchester Club, Rye, NY: M. Connolly d. A. Mortimer 6–1 6–1, d. H. Fletcher 6–1 6–1; Hart d. Fletcher 6–4 7–5, d. Mortimer 6–1 6–1; S. Fry d. Rinkel–Quertier 6–2 6–4; L. Brough/Connolly d. Mortimer/A. Shilcock 6–2 6–3; Fry/Hart d. Fletcher/Rinkel–Quertier 6–2 6–1.

1954 USA d. Great–Britain 6–0, Wimbledon: M. Connolly d. H. Fletcher 6–1 6–3, d. A. Shilcock 6–2 6–2; Hart d. Shilcock 6–4 6–1, d. Fletcher 6–1 6–2; L. Brough d. A. Buxton 8–6 6–2; L. Brough/Mrs W. du Pont d. Buxton/P. Hird 2–6 6–4 7–5; S. Fry/Hart v. Fletcher/Shilcock not played.

1955 USA d. Great Britain 6–1, Westchester Club, Rye, NY: D. Hart lost to A. Mortimer 4–6 6–1 5–7, d. S. J. Bloomer 7–5 6–3; L. Brough d. Bloomer 6–2 6–4, d. Mortimer 6–0 6–2; Mrs D. Knode d. A. Buxton 6–3 6–3; Brough/Mrs W. du Pont d. Bloomer/P. Ward 6–3 6–3; S. Fry/Hart d. Buxton/Mortimer 3–6 6–2 7–5.

1956 USA d. Great Britain 5–2, Wimbledon: L. Brough d. A. Mortimer 3–6 6–4 7–5, d. A. Buxton 3–6 6–3 6–4; S. Fry d. Buxton 6–2 6–8 7–5, lost to Mortimer 4–6 3–6; Mrs D. Knode lost to S. J. Bloomer 4–6 4–6; B. Baker/Knode d. Bloomer/P. Ward 6–1 6–4; Brough/Fry d. Buxton/Mortimer 6–2 6–2.

1957 USA d. Great Britain 6–1, Sewickley, Pennsylvania: A. Gibson d. S. J. Bloomer 6–4 4–6 6–2, d. C. Truman 6–4 6–2; Mrs D. Knode d. Truman 6–2 11–9, d. Bloomer 5–7 6–1 6–2; D. R. Hard lost to A. Haydon 3–6 6–3 4–6; A. Gibson/Hard d. Bloomer/S. M. Armstrong 6–3 6–4; L. Brough/W. du Pont d. Haydon/A. Shilcock 6–4 6–1.

1958 Great Britain d. USA 4–3, Wimbledon: S. J. Bloomer lost to A. Gibson 3–6 4–6, lost to Mrs D. Knode 4–6 2–6; C. Truman d. Knode 6–4 6–4, d. Gibson 3–6 6–3 6–4; A. Haydon d. M. Arnold 6–3 5–7 6–3; Bloomer/Truman d. K. Fageros/Knode 6–2 6–3; A. Shilcock/P. Ward lost to Gibson/J. Jopps 4–6 6–3 3–6.

1959 Great Britain d. USA 4–3, Sewickley, Pennsylvania: Mrs B. Fleits d. A. Mortimer 6–2 6–1, d. C. Truman 6–4 6–4; D. R. Hard lost to Truman 4–6 6–2 3–6, d. Mortimer 6–3 6–8 6–4; S. Moore lost to A. Haydon 1–6 1–6; J. Arth/Hard d. S. J. Bloomer/Truman 9–7 9–7; J. Hopps/Moore lost to Haydon/Mortimer 2–6 4–6.

1960 Great Britain d. USA 4–3, Wimbledon: A. Haydon d. K. Hantze 2–6 11–9 6–1, lost to D. R. Hard 7–5 2–6 1–6; C. Truman lost to Hard 6–4 3–6 4–6, d. Hantze 7–5 6–3; A. Mortimer d. J. Hopps 6–8 6–4 6–1; Haydon/Mortimer lost to Hard/Hantze 0–6 0–6; S. J. Bloomer/Truman d. Hopps/Mrs D. Knode 6–4 9–7.

1961 USA d. Great Britain 6–1, Saddle & Cycle Club, Chicago: K. Hantze d. C. Truman 7–9 6–1 6–1, d. A. Haydon 6–1 6–4; B. J. Moffitt d. Haydon 6–4 6–4, lost to Truman 3–6 2–6; J. Bricka d. A. Mortimer 10–8 4–6 6–3; Hantze/Moffitt d. Truman/D. M. Catt 7–5 6–2; Mrs W. du Pont/M. Varner w.o. Mortimer/Haydon.

1962 USA d. Great Britain 4–3, Wimbledon: D. R. Hard d. C. Truman 6–2 6–2, d. A. Haydon 6–3 6–8 6–4; Mrs J. R. Susman lost to Haydon 8–10 5–7, d. Truman 6–4 7–5; N. Richey lost to D. M. Catt 1–6 5–7; Mrs W. du Pont/M. Varner d. Catt/E. Starkie 6–2 3–6 6–2; Hard/B. J. Moffitt lost to Haydon/Truman 4–6 3–6.

1963 USA d. Great Britain 6–1, Cleveland Skating Club, Cleveland: D. R. Hard lost to Mrs P. F. Jones 1–6 6–0 6–8, d. C. Truman 6–3 6–0); B. J. Moffitt d. Truman 6–4 19–17, d. Jones 6–4 4–6 6–3; N. Richey d. D. M. Catt 14–12 6–3; Hard/Moffitt d. Truman/Jones 4–6 7–5 6–2; Richey/Mrs D. Fales d. Catt/E. Starkie 6–4 6–8 6–2.

1964 USA d. Great Britain 5–2, Wimbledon: N. Richey d. D. M. Catt 4–6 6–4 7–5, d. Mrs P. F. Jones 7–5 11–9; B. J.

Moffitt d. Jones 4–6 6–2 6–3, d. Catt 6–3 4–6 6–3; C. Caldwell d. E. Starkie 6–4 1–6 6–3; Caldwell/Moffitt lost to Catt/Jones 2–6 6–4 0–6; Richey/Mrs D. Fales lost to A. Mortimer/Starkie 6–2 3–6 4–6.

1965 USA d. Great Britain 5–2, Clarke Stadium, Cleveland: B. J. Moffitt lost to Mrs P. F. Jones 2–6 4–6, d. E. Starkie 6–3 6–2; N. Richey d. Starkie 6–1 6–0, lost to Jones 4–6 6–8; Mrs C. Graebner d. S. V. Wade 3–6 10–8 6–4; Graebner/Richey d. F. E. Truman/Starkie 6–1 6–0; Moffitt/Mrs J. R. Susman d. Jones/Wade 6–3 8–6.

1966 USA d. Great Britain 4–3, Wimbledon: N. Richey lost to Mrs P. F. Jones 6–2 4–6 3–6, d. S. V. Wade 2–6 6–2 7–5; Mrs L. W. King d. Wade 6–3 6–3, d. Jones 5–7 6–2 6–3; M. A. Eisel lost to W. Shaw 2–6 3–6; King/J. Albert lost to Jones/Wade 5–7 2–6; Richey/Eisel d. R. Bentley/E. Starkie 6–1 6–2.

1967 USA d. Great Britain 6–1, Clarke Stadium, Cleveland: Mrs L. W. King d. S. V. Wade 6–3 6–2, d. Mrs P. F. Jones 6–1 6–2; N. Richey d. Jones 6–2 6–2, d. Wade 3–6 8–6 6–2; R. Casals lost to C. Truman 6–3 5–7 1–6; Casals/King d. Jones/Wade 10–8 6–4; M. A. Eisel/Mrs C. Graebner d. W. Shaw/Mrs J. Williams 8–6 12–10.

1968 Great Britain d. USA 4–3, Wimbledon: Mrs C. Janes lost to N. Richey 1–6 6–8, lost to M. A. Eisel 4–6 3–6; S. V. Wade d. Eisel 6–0 6–1, d. Richey 6–4 2–6 6–3; W. Shaw lost to J. Bartkowicz 5–7 6–3 4–6; Shaw/Wade d. Eisel/Richey 5–7 6–4 6–3; Janes/F. E. Truman d. S. De Fina/K. Harter 6–3 2–6 6–3.

1969 USA d. Great Britain 5–2, Clarke Stadium, Cleveland: J. M. Heldman d. S. V. Wade 3–6 6–1 8–6, d. W. Shaw 6–3 6–4; N. Richey d. Shaw 8–6 6–2, lost to Wade 3–6 2–6 4–6; J. Bartkowicz d. Mrs C. Janes 8–6 6–0; Mrs P. Curtis/V. Ziengenfuss lost to Janes/F. E. Truman 1–6 6–3 4–6; Heldman/Bartkowicz d. Shaw/ Wade 6–4 6–2.

1970 USA d. Great Britain 4–3, Wimbledon: Mrs L. W. King d. S. V. Wade 8–6 6–4, d. Mrs P. F. Jones 6–4 6–2; N. Richey lost to Jones 3–6 3–6, lost to Wade 3–6 2–6; J. M. Heldman d. Mrs G. Williams 6–3 6–2; Mrs P. Curtis/Heldman lost to Jones/Williams 3–6 2–6; King/J. Bartkowicz d. W. Shaw/Wade 7–5 6–8 6–2.

1971 USA d. Great Britain 4–3, Clarke Stadium, Cleveland: C. Evert d. W. Shaw 6–0 6–4, d. S. V. Wade 6–1 6–1; J. M. Heldman lost to Wade 5–7 5–7; V. Ziegenfuss d. Shaw 6–4 4–6 6–3; K. Pigeon lost to Mrs G. Williams 5–7 6–3 4–6; Mrs P. Curtis/Ziegenfuss d. Mrs C. Janes/F. E. Truman 6–1 6–4; Mrs C. Graebner/Evert lost to Wade/ Williams 8–10 6–4 1–6.

1972 USA d. Great Britain 5–2, Wimbledon: W. Overton lost to Mrs G. Williams 3–6 6–3 3–6, lost to S. V. Wade 6–8 5–7; C. Evert d. Wade 6–4 6–4, d. Williams 6–2 6–3; P. S. A. Hogan d. C. Molesworth 6–8 6–4 6–2; Evert/Hogan d. W. Shaw/F. E. Truman 7–5 6–4; Overton/V. Ziegenfuss d. Wade/Williams 6–3 6–3.

1973 USA d. Great Britain 5–2, Longwood Cricket Club, Boston: C. Evert d. S. V. Wade 6–4 6–2, d. V. Burton 6–3 6–0; P. S. A. Hogan d. Burton 6–4 6–3, lost to Wade 2–6 2–6; L. Tuero d. G. Coles 7–5 6–2; Evert/M. Redondo lost to Coles/Wade 3–6 4–6; J. Evert/Hogan d. L. Beaven/L. Charles 6–3 4–6 8–6.

1974 Great Britain d. USA 6–1, Deeside Leisure Centre, Queensferry, North Wales (indoors): S. V. Wade d. J. M. Heldman 5–7 9–7 6–4, d. J. Newberry 6–1 6–3; G. Coles d. Newberry 4–6 6–1 6–3, d. Heldman 6–0 6–4; S. Barker d. J. Evert 4–6 6–4 6–1; Barker/Charles d. Newberry/B. Nagelsen 4–6 6–2 6–1; Coles/Wade lost to Heldman/M. Schallau 5–7 4–6.

1975 Great Britain d. USA 5–2, Public Auditorium, Cleveland (indoors): S. V. Wade d. M. Schallau 6–2 6–2; lost to C. Evert 3–6 5–7; G. Coles lost to Evert 4–6 1–6, d. Schallau 6–3 7–6; S. Barker d. J. Newberry 6–4 7–5; Mrs P. F. Jones/Wade d. Newberry/J. Anthony 6–2 6–3; Coles/Barker d. Evert/Schallau 7–5 6–4.

1976 USA d. Great Britain 5–2, Crystal Palace, London (indoors): C. Evert d. S. V. Wade 6–2 3–6 6–2, d. S. Barker 2–6 6–2 6–2; R. Casals lost to Barker 6–1 3–6 2–6, lost to Wade 6–3 7–9 ret'd; T. Holladay d. G. Coles 3–6 6–1 6–4; Casals/Evert d. Barker/Wade 6–0 5–7 6–1; Mrs M. Guerrant/A. Kiyomura d. S. Mappin/L. Charles 6–2 6–2.

1977 USA d. Great Britain 7–0, Oakland, California (indoors): C. Evert d. S. V. Wade 7–5 7–6, d. S. Barker 6–1 6–2; Mrs L. W. King d. Barker 6–1 6–4, d. Wade 6–4 3–6 8–6; R. Casals d. M. Tyler 6–2 3–6 6–4; King/J. Russell d. S. Mappin/L. Charles 6–0 6–1; Casals/Evert d. Barker/Wade 6–2 6–4.

1978 Great Britain d. USA 4–3, Albert Hall, London (indoors): S. Barker lost to C. Evert 2–6 1–6, d. T. Austin 6–3 3–6 6–0; S. V. Wade d. Austin 3–6 7–5 6–3, lost to Evert 0–6 1–6; M. Tyler d. P. H. Shriver 7–6 2–6 3; S. Mappin/A. E. Hobbs lost to Mrs L. W. King/Austin 2–6 6–4 2–6; Barker/Wade d. Evert/Shriver 6–0 5–7 6–4.

1979 USA d. Great Britain 7–0, Palm Beach West, Florida: Mrs J. M. Lloyd d. S. Barker 7–5 6–2, d. S. V. Wade 6–1 6–1; T. Austin d. Wade 6–1 6–4, d. Barker 6–4 6–2; K. Jordan d. A. E. Hobbs 6–4 6–7 6–2; Austin/A. Kiyomura d. J. M. Durie/D. A. Jevans 6–3 6–1; Lloyd/R. Casals d. Barker/Wade 6–0 6–1.

1980 USA d. Great Britain 5–2, Albert Hall, London (indoors): Mrs J. M. Lloyd d. S. Barker 6–1 6–2, d. S. V. Wade 7–5 3–6 7–5; A. Jaeger d. Wade 3–6 6–3 6–2, lost to Barker 7–5 3–6 3–6; K. Jordan lost to A. E. Hobbs 6–4 4–6 1–6; Lloyd/R. Casals d. Hobbs/G. Coles 6–3 6–3; A. E. Smith/Jordan d. Barker/Wade 6–4 7–5.

1981 USA d. Great Britain 7–0, International Amphitheatre, Chicago (indoors): T. Austin d. S. Barker 7–5 6–3, d. S. V. Wade 6–3 6–1; Mrs J. M. Lloyd d. Wade 6–1 6–3, d. Barker 6–3 6–0; A. Jaeger d. A. E. Hobbs 6–0 6–0; Jaeger/P. H. Shriver d. J. M. Durie/Hobbs 6–1 6–3; Lloyd/R. Casals d. G. Coles/Wade 6–3 6–3.

1982 USA d. Great Britain 6–1, Albert Hall, London (indoors): B. Potter d. S. Barker 6–2 6–2, d J. M. Durie 5–7 7–6 6–2; Mrs J. M. Lloyd d. Durie 6–2 6–2, d. Barker 6–4 6–3; A. E. Smith d. S. V. Wade 3–6 7–5 6–3; R. Casals/Smith lost to Durie/A. E. Hobbs 3–6 6–2 3–6; Potter/S. A. Walsh d. Barker/Wade 2–6 6–4 6–4.

1983 USA d. Great Britain 6–1, Williamsburg, Virginia (indoors): M. Navratilova d. S. Barker 6–2 6–0, d. J. M. Durie 6–3 6–3; P. H. Shriver d. Durie 6–3 6–2, d. Barker 6–0 6–1; K. Rinaldi d. S. V. Wade 6–3 6–2; C. Reynolds/P. Smith lost to Barker/Wade 5–7 6–3 1–6; Navratilova/Shriver d. Durie/A. Croft 6–2 6–1.

1984 USA d. Great Britain 5–2, Albert Hall, London (indoors): Mrs J. M. Lloyd d. A. E. Hobbs 6–2 6–2; A. Moulton lost to A. Croft 1–6 7–5 4–6; B. Potter lost to J. M. Durie 3–6 6–7; Lloyd/Moulton d. A. Brown/S. V. Wade 6–2 6–2; Potter d. Hobbs 6–1 6–3; Lloyd d. Durie 7–6 6–1; Potter/S. A. Walsh d. Durie/Hobbs 7–6 4–6 9–7.

1985 USA d. Great Britain 7–0, Williamsburg, Virginia (indoors): Mrs J. M. Lloyd d. J. M. Durie 6–2 6–3; K. Rinaldi d. A. E. Hobbs 7–5 7–5; P. H. Shriver d. A. Croft 6–0 6–0; B. Nagelsen/A. White d. Croft/S. V. Wade 6–4 6–1; Shriver d. Durie 6–4 6–4; Lloyd d. Croft 6–3 6–0; Lloyd/Shriver d. Durie/Hobbs 6–3 6–7 6–2.

1986 USA d. Great Britain 7–0, Albert Hall, London (indoors): K. Rinaldi d. S. Gomer 6–3 7–6; S. Rehe d. A. Croft 6–3 6–1; B. Gadusek d. J. M. Durie 6–2 6–4; Gadusek/Rinaldi d. Croft/Gomer 6–3 5–7 6–3; Gadusek d. Hobbs 2–6 6–4 6–4; Rinaldi d. Durie 6–4 6–2; E. Burgin/A. White d. Durie/Hobbs 7–6 6–3.

1987 USA d. Great Britain 5–2, Williamsburg, Virginia (indoors): Z. Garrison d. A. E. Hobbs 7–5 6–2; L. McNeil d. S. Gomer 6–2 6–1; P. H. Shriver d. J. M. Durie 6–1 7–5; G. Fernandez/R. White d. Gomer/C. Wood 6–4 6–1; Shriver d.

Hobbs 6–4 6–3; Garrison lost to Durie 6–7 3–6; Garrison/McNeil lost to Durie/Hobbs 6–0 4–6 5–7.
1988 USA d. Great Britain 7–0, Albert Hall, London (indoors): Z. Garrison d. J. M. Durie 6–2 6–4; P. Fendick d. M. Javer 6–2 6–1; L. McNeil d. S. Gomer 6–7 6–4 6–4; McNeil/B. Nagelsen d. Gomer/J. Salmon 6–3 6–2; Garrison d. C. Wood 6–3 6–2; McNeil d. Durie 6–1 6–2; G. Fernandez/Garrison d. Durie/Wood 6–1 6–3.
1989 USA d. Great Britain 7–0, Williamsburg, Virginia: L. McNeil d. J. Durie 7–5 6–1; J. Capriati d. C. Wood 6–0 6–0; M. J. Fernandez d. S. Gomer 6–1 6–2; McNeil d. Gomer 6–4 6–2; Fernandez d. Durie 6–1 7–5; B. Nagelsen/ Fernandez d. Gomer/Wood 6–2 7–6; P. Fendick/McNeil d. Durie/A. Hobbs 6–3 6–3.

EUROPEAN CUP

Formerly King's Cup

International Men's Team Championship on Indoor Courts. It was staged on a knock–out basis 1936–38, 1952–74, on a league basis 1976–83 with ties home and away. From 1984 the ties in each division were held concurrently at one venue. The Challenge Round system was used in the two opening years, with 1937 the only Challenge Round.

FINALS

1936 France d. Sweden 4–1, Stockholm: J. Borotra d. K. Schroder 2–6 6–2 6–1 6–3, d. C. Ostberg 6–1 6–3 7–5; B. Destremau d. Schroder 3–6 7–5 6–2 6–4, d. Ostberg 6–2 6–2 6–4; C. Boussus/J. Brugnon lost to Ostberg/ Schroder 2–6 6–3 4–6 6–3 4–6.
1937 France d. Sweden 5–0, Paris: B. Destremau d. K. Schroder 8–6 1–6 2–6 11–9 8–6, d. N. Rohlsson 1–6 1–6 6–3 6–1 6–0; Y. Petra d. Rohlsson 6–1 6–4 6–2, d. Schroder 6–3 3–6 6–3 6–4; H. Bolelli/J. Lesueur d. Schroder/H. Wallen 10–8 6–4 6–4.
1938 Germany d. Denmark 5–0, Hamburg: R. Menzel d. H. Plougmann 6–3 6–2 8–6; H. Henkel d. I. Gerdes 6–4 6–0 6–3, d. Plougmann 6–2 6–1 6–3; R. Redl d. Gerdes 6–3 6–3 6–2; Henkel/Menzel d. Gerdes/Plougmann 6–0 6–4 6–2.
1939–51 Not held
1952 Denmark d. Sweden 3–2, Stockholm: K. Nielsen lost to S. Davidson 3–6 7–9 4–6; T. Ulrich d. T. Johansson 7–5 0–6 6–4 6–2; Nielsen/Ulrich d. Davidson/Johansson 6–2 2–6 4–6 8–6 7–5; Nielsen d. Johansson 6–3 6–4 6–1; Ulrich lost to Davidson 6–4 4–6 1–6 6–1 2–6.
1953 Denmark d. Sweden 3–2, Copenhagen: T. Ulrich d. S. Davidson 14–12 11–9 1–6 11–9; J. Ulrich lost to T. Johansson 0–6 2–6 7–9; J. Ulrich/T. Ulrich d. Davidson/N. Rohlsson 6–4 6–4 4–6 3–6 6–3; J. Ulrich lost to Davidson 3–6 4–6 0–6; T. Ulrich d. Johansson 6–3 2–6 6–4 5–7 6–3.
1954 Denmark d. Italy 3–2, Milan: T. Ulrich d. G. Merlo 7–5 2–6 9–7 9–7; K. Nielsen lost to O. Sirola 5–7 6–8 8–6 6–2 3–6; Nielsen/Ulrich d. N. Pietrangeli/Sirola 2–6 2–6 11–9 6–1 12–10; Nielsen lost to Pietrangeli 5–7 6–3 9–7 3–6 5–7; Ulrich d. Sirola 7–5 10–8 6–4.
1955 Sweden d. Denmark 4–1, Copenhagen: S. Davidson d. J. Ulrich 7–5 12–10 6–1; U. Schmidt lost to K. Nielsen 3–6 2–6 6–4 4–6; Davidson/T. Johansson d. Nielsen/J. Ulrich 11–9 6–3 14–12; Davidson d. Nielsen 8–10 6–2 7–9 12–10 7–5; Schmidt d. J. Ulrich 7–9 3–6 6–0 8–6 6–3.
1956 Sweden d. France 4–1, Paris: S. Davidson lost to P. Darmon 7–9 6–2 5–7 6–8; U. Schmidt d. R. Haillet 6–1 /6–2 6–4; Davidson/Schmidt d. Darmon/P. Remy 8–6 3–6 6–1 6–4; Davidson d. Haillet 6–2 2–6 6–4 6–1; Schmidt d. Darmon 6–1 10–8 6–3.
1957 Sweden d. Denmark 3–2, Copenhagen: J. E. Lundqvist d. K. Nielsen 4–6 6–3 10–8 6–4; U. Schmidt lost to T. Ulrich 4–6 7–9 2–6; Lundqvist/Schmidt d. J. Ulrich/T. Ulrich 6–3 5–7 6–0 6–3; Lundqvist d. T. Ulrich 7–5 6–1 6–2; Schmidt lost to Nielsen 6–4 4–6 2–6 5–7.
1958 Sweden d. Denmark 3–2, Stockholm: B. Folke lost to J. Ulrich 11–13 3–6 4–6; S. Davidson d. K. Nielsen 6–0 6–1 6–4; Davidson/T. Johansson d. Nielsen/J. Ulrich 10–8 1–6 6–3 6–8 6–3; Folke lost to Nielsen 4–6 3–6 3–6; Davidson d. J. Ulrich 6–4 6–3 1–6 6–1.
1959 Denmark won, Stockholm: Denmark d. Italy 2–1, lost to Sweden 2–1, d. France 2–1 (12–11 sets); Sweden lost to France 2–1, d. Denmark 2–1, d. Italy 2–1 (10–10 sets); Italy lost to Denmark 2–1, d. France 2–1, lost to Sweden 2–1 (11–11 sets); France d. Sweden 2–1, lost to Italy 2–1, lost to France 2–1 (10–11 sets). Danish team: K. Nielsen and J. Ulrich.
1960 Denmark d. West Germany 3–0, Paris: J. Leschly d. B. Nitsche 6–4 8–6; J. Ulrich d. P. Scholl 6–2 6–3; Leschly/J. Ulrich d. Nitsche/Scholl 6–8 6–2 6–0.
1961 Sweden d. Denmark 2–1, Cologne: U. Schmidt d. J. Leschly 6–4 6–2; J. E. Lundqvist d. J. Ulrich 6–3 6–1; Lundqvist/Schmidt lost to Leschly/J. Ulrich 5–7 6–4 5–7.
1962 Denmark d. Italy 3–0, Copenhagen: J. Leschly d. G. Merlo 6–3 8–6; J. Ulrich d. N. Pietrangeli 6–4 6–2; Leschly/J. Ulrich d. Pietrangeli/O. Sirola 9–7 7–5.
1963 Yugoslavia d. Denmark 3–0, Belgrade: Yugoslav team: B. Jovanovic and N. Pilic.
1964 Great Britain d. Sweden 3–0, Stockholm: M. J. Sangster d. J. E. Lundquist 13–15 10–8 12–10; R. Taylor d. B. Holmstrom 6–3 9–7; Sangster/R. K. Wilson d. Holmstrom/L. Olander 4–6 12–10 6–4.
1965 Great Britain d. Denmark 2–1, Torquay: R. K. Wilson lost to J. Leschly 1–6 4–6; M. Cox d. C. Hedelund 6–4 6–3; A. R. Mills/Wilson d. Leschly/Hedelund 3–6 6–2 6–4 12–10.
1966 Great Britain d. Italy 3–0, Milan: R. Taylor d. N. Pietrangeli 6–4 6–4; M. J. Sangster d. G. Maioli 7–9 6–4 11–9; Sangster/R. K. Wilson d. D. di Maso/Maioli 6–4 6–1.
1967 Great Britain d. Sweden 2–1, Stockholm: R. Taylor d. O. Bengtson 2–6 6–3 9–7; R. K. Wilson d. M. Carlstein 8–6 6–2; M. Cox/Taylor lost to Bengtson/B. Homstrom 4–6 7–9.
1968 Sweden d. Netherlands 2–1, Bratislava: O. Bengtson lost to T. S. Okker 12–14 4–6; M. Carlstein d. J. Hordjik 6–4 6–3; Bengtson/Carlstein d. N. Fleury/Okker 1–6 4–6 7–5 6–3 6–4.
1969 Czechoslovakia d. Sweden 2–1, Cologne: V. Zednik d. H. Zahr 6–4, 7–5; J. Kukal d. O. Bengtson 6–1 5–7 11–9; Kukal/Zednik lost to Bengtson/H. Nerell 4–6 4–6.
1970 France d. Denmark 2–1, Copenhagen: J. B. Chanfreau d. J. Ulrich 6–3 8–6; G. Goven lost to J. Leschly 1–6 3–6;

Chanfreau/Goven d. Ulrich/Leschly 2–6 6–4 7–5.
1971 Italy d. Spain 2–1, Ancona: A. Panatta lost to M. Orantes 2–6 3–6; N. Pietrangeli d. J. Gisbert 7–9 8–6 6–4; Panatta/Pietrangeli d. Gisbert/Orantes 4–6 8–6 6–3 6–4.
1972 Spain d. Hungary 3–0, Madrid: A. Gimeno d. S. Baranyi 10–8 6–2; J. Gisbert d. B. Taroczy 6–1 7–9 6–3; J. Herrera/A. Munoz d. R. Machan/Taroczy 6–4 3–6 7–5.
1973 Sweden d. Italy 2–1, Hanover: L. Johansson d. A. Zugarelli 6–4 6–3; B. Borg d. A. Panatta 4–6 6–2 8–6; Borg/Johansson lost to P. Bertolucci/Zugarelli 6–3 5–7 4–6.
1974 Italy d. Sweden 3–0, Ancona: A. Panatta d. R. Norberg 6–3 6–4; A. Zugarelli d. T. Svensson 6–3 6–4; P. Bertolucci/A. Panatta d. B. Andersson/Norberg 6–2 6–4.
1975 Not held
1976 Hungary 11 wins, Great Britain 10 wins (played entirely as round robin, each tie home and away). Hungarian team: P. Szoke, B. Taroczy. British team: M. Cox, J. M. Lloyd, C. J. Mottram, R. Taylor.
1977 Sweden d. West Germany 5–1, Berlin: R. Norberg d. U. Marten 6–2 4–6 6–4; K. Johansson d. K. Meiler 6–4 6–4; O. Bengtson/Norberg d. P. Elter/Meiler 6–2 6–2. **Linkoping:** Norberg d. U. Pinner 7–6 6–2; Johansson d. Meiler 6–7 6–2 6–3; Bengtson/Norberg lost to Elter/Marten 6–3 4–6 4–6.
1978 Sweden d. Hungary 3–3 (9–7 sets), Uppsala: T. Svensson d. P. Szoke 6–2 6–4; O. Bengtson lost to B. Taroczy 6–7 6–7; Bengtson/Svensson lost to Szoke/Taroczy 6–7 4–6; **Debrecen:** Svensson d. Szoke 6–2 6–2; Bengtson d. Taroczy 6–4 7–6; Bengtson/Svensson lost to Szoke/Taroczy 3–6 6–3 3–6.
1979 Czechoslovakia d. Hungary 4–2, Pecs: I. Lendl lost to J. Benyik 6–7 7–5 6–7; T. Smid d. B. Taroczy 5–7 6–3 6–4; P. Slozil/T. Smid d. P. Szoke/Taroczy 6–4 6–4; **Chrudin:** Lendl lost to Benyik 6–4 2–6 0–6; Smid d. Szoke 6–3 3–6 6–2; Slozil/Smid d. Benyik/Szoke 6–4 6–2.
1980 Czechoslovakia d. Hungary 5–1, Chrudin: T. Smid d. R. Machan 6–4 6–2; I. Lendl d. B. Taroczy 6–2 6–1; Smid/P. Slozil d. P. Szoke/Machan 6–4 7–5; **Debreden:** Smid d. J. Benyik 6–2 3–6 6–2; Lendl d. Machan 6–0 6–2; Smid/Slozil lost to Machan/Szoke 6–3 3–6 2–6.
1981 West Germany d. USSR 3–3 (9–7 sets), Moscow, 2–1, and Hamburg, 1–2.
1982 West Germany d. Czechoslovakia 2–1, Dortmund: K. Eberhard lost to J. Navratil 4–6 1–6; U. Pinnder d. P. Slozilp 6–4 6–4; C. Zipf/H. D. Beutel d. Navratil/Slozil 6–3 6–4.
1983 West Germany d. Czechoslovakia 2–1, Uppsala: H. J. Schwaier lost to L. Pimek 6–4 2–6 3–6; M. Westphal d. J. Navratil 3–6 6–2 6–3; E. Jelen/W. Popp d. Navratil/Piimek 6–1 1–6 7–6.
1984 Czechoslovakia d. Sweden 2–1, Essen: M. Mecir d. J. Gunnarsson 7–6 6–4; L. Pimek lost to J. Nystrom 3–6 5–7; Pimek/J. Navratil d. Gunnarsson/Nystrom 3–6 6–2 6–4.
1985 Sweden d. Switzerland 3–0, Essen: T. Hogstedt d. R. Stadler 6–3 6–2; J. Gunnarsson d. J. Hlasek 7–5 4–6 6–2; S. Simonsson d. Hlasek/Stadler 6–3 6–4.
1986 Switzerland d. Czechoslovakia 2–1, Queen's Club, London: R. Stadler d. M. Vajda 6–4 7–5; J. Hlasek lost L. Pimek 7–5 3–6 5–7; Hlasek/Stadler d. Pimek/P. Korda 6–2 6–3.
1987 Switzerland d. Great Britain 2–1, Hanover: R. Stadler lost to M. J. Bates 6–7 2–6; J. Hlasek d. A. Castle 6–3 6–7 6–2; Hlasek/Stadler d. Bates/Castle 3–6 7–5 6–0.
1988 Czechoslovakia d. Netherlands 2–0, Zurich: P. Korda d. M. Oosting 6–3 7–6; doubles not played.
1989 Czechoslovakia d. West Germany 2–1, Ostrava: P. Korda lost to C.–U. Steeb 3–6 3–6; M. Srejber d. E. Jelen 7–5 6–3; Srejber/Korda d. P. Kuhnen/Jelen 7–6 7–6.
1990 Germany d. USSR 2–1, Metz: U. Riglewski lost to D. Poliakov 7–5 3–6 2–6; M. Stich d. A. Cherkasov 6–3 7–6; Stich/Riglewski d. A. Olhovskiy/V. Gabrichidze 6–3 7–6.
1991 Czechoslovakia d. Netherlands 2–1, Lengnau: D. Rikl lost to T. Kempers 6–3 5–7 1–6; M. Damm d. F. Wibier 6–4 6–1; Damm/T. Zdrazila d. Kempers/Wibier 6–3 6–3.
1992 Sweden d. Germany 2–1, Trieste: N. Kulti d. M. Goellner 6–4 7–6; T. Enqvist lost to M. Naewie 3–6 4–6; M. Tillstrom/N. Kulti d. M. Naewie/M. Goellner 4–6 6–3 7–6

WORLD TEAM CUP

Eight–nation men's team event, qualification by individual ATP rating. Formerly Nations Cup.

FINALS
Played at Kingston, Jamaica
1975 USA d. Great Britain 2–1: R. Tanner d. R. Taylor 6–3 2–6 6–4; A. R. Ashe lost to C. J. Mottram 5–7 7–5 1–6; Ashe/Tanner d. Mottram/Taylor 6–1 1–6 6–4.
1976–77 Not held
Played at Dusseldorf
1978 Spain d. Australia 2–1: J. Higueras d. J. D. Newcombe 6–2 6–3; M. Orantes d. P. Dent 6–3 6–4; Higueras/Orantes lost to Dent/Newcombe 6–7 4–6.
1979 Australia d. Italy 2–1: J. G. Alexander d. C. Barazzutti 6–2 6–0; P. Dent lost to A. Panatta 3–6 3–6; Alexander/Dent d. P. Bertolucci/Panatta d. 3–7 6–4.
1980 Argentina d. Italy 3–0: G. Vilas d. C. Barazzutti 6–3 6–2; J. L. Clerc d. A. Panatta 7–6 6–3; Clerc/Vilas d. P. A. Bertolucci/Panatta 6–2 6–3.
1981 Czechoslovakia d. Australia 2–1: I. Lendl lost to P. McNamara 3–6 4–6; T. Smid d. P. McNamee 6–4 7–6; Lendl/Smid d. McNamara/McNamee 6–4 6–3.
1982 USA d. Australia 2–1: G. Mayer d. K. Warwick 7–6 6–2; E. Teltscher d. P. McNamara 6–4 7–6; Mayer/S. E. Stewart lost to M. R. Edmondson/McNamara 1–6 1–6.
1983 Spain d. Australia 2–1: J. Higueras d. M. R. Edmondson 6–2 6–4; M. Orantes d. P. Cash 6–3 6–2; A. Gimenez/Higueras lost to Cash/Edmondson 5–7 6–4 1–6.
1984 USA d. Czechoslovakia 2–1: J. P. McEnroe d. I. Lendl 6–3 6–2; J. Arias lost to T. Smid 6–4 6–7 4–6; P. Fleming/McEnroe d. Lendl/Smid 6–1 6–2.
1985 USA d. Czechoslovakia 2–1: J. P. McEnroe lost to I. Lendl 7–6 6–7 3–6; J. S. Connors d. M. Mecir 6–3 3–6 7–5; K. Flach/R. Seguso d. Lendl/T. Smid 6–3 7–6

1986 France d. Sweden 2–1: H. Leconte d. A. Jarryd 6–3 3–6 6–1; T. Tulasne lost to M. Wilander 1–6 4–6; G. Forget/Leconte d. Jarryd/Wilander 6–3 2–6 6–2.
1987 Czechoslovakia d. USA 2–1: M. Mecir d. J. P. McEnroe 7–5 2–6 2–1 disqual.; M. Srejber lost to B. Gilbert 4–6 7–5 4–6; Mecir/T. Smid d. Gilbert/R. Seguso 6–3 6–1.
1988 Sweden d. USA 2–1: S. Edberg d. T. Mayotte 6–4 6–2; K. Carlsson d. A. Krickstein 6–4 6–3; Edberg/A. Jarryd lost to K. Flach/R. Seguso 7–6 3–6 6–7.
1989 West Germany d. Argentina 2–1: B. Becker d. G. Perez Roldan 6–0 2–6 6–2; C.–U. Steeb lost to M. Jaite 4–6 3–6; Becker/E. Jelen d. J. Frana/G. Luna 6–4 7–5.
1990 Yugoslavia d. USA 2–1: G. Prpic d. B. Gilbert 6–4 6–4; G. Ivanisevic d. J. Courier 3–6 7–5 6–1; Prpic/S. Zivojinovic lost to K. Flach/R. Seguso 5–7 6–7.
1991 Sweden d. Yugoslavia 2–1: M. Gustafsson d. G. Prpic 6–2 3–6 6–4; S. Edberg d G. Ivanisevic 6–4 7–5; Edberg/Gustafsson lost to Prpic/S. Zivojinovic 6–3 3–6 4–6.
1992 Sweden d. Czechoslovakia 3–0: E. Sanchez d. P. Korda 3–6 6–2 7–6; S. Brugera d. K. Novacek 6–2 6–4; S. Casal/E. Sanchez d. K. Novacek/C. Suk 1–6 6–4 6–3.

GRAND SLAM CUP

A knockout competition held in Munich in December, for the 16 men who have amassed the most points in the four Grand Slam Championships of Australia, France, Great Britain and the USA. The competition, administered by the Grand Slam Committee (the four Chairmen) and an Administrator, is promoted by an independent German company and offers prize money of $6 million. A further $2 million goes annually to the Grand Slam Development Fund, administered by the ITF.

	WINNER	RUNNER–UP	SCORE			FIRST PRIZE
1990	P. Sampras	B. Gilbert	6–3	6–4	6–2	$2,000,000
1991	D. Wheaton	M. Chang	7–5	6–2	6–4	$2,000,000
1992	M. Stich	M. Chang	6–2	6–3	6–2	$2,000,000

MEN'S GRAND PRIX WINNERS

	SINGLES	BONUS	DOUBLES	BONUS	SPONSOR
1970	C. Richey	*$25,000			Pepsi–Cola
1971	S. R. Smith	*$25,000			Pepsi–Cola
1972	I. Nastase	*$50,000			Commercial Union
1973	I. Nastase	*$55,000			Commercial Union
1974	G. Vilas	*$100,000			Commercial Union
1975	G. Vilas	*$100,000	J. Gisbert	$25,000	Commercial Union
1976	R. Ramirez	*$150,000	R. Ramirez	$40,000	Commercial Union
1977	G. Vilas	*$300,000	R. A. J. Hewitt	$85,000	Colgate
1978	J. S. Connors	*$300,000	W. Fibak	$90,000	Colgate
1979	J. P. McEnroe	*$300,000	S. E. Stewart	$90,000	Colgate
1980	J. P. McEnroe	*$300,000	S. R. Smith	$90,000	Volvo
1981	I. Lendl	*$300,000	H. Gunthardt	$90,000	Volvo
1982	J. S. Connors	*$600,000	S. E. Stewart	$150,000	Volvo
1983	M. Wilander	*$600,000	P. Fleming	$150,000	Volvo
1984	J. P. McEnroe	*$600,000	T. Smid	$150,000	Volvo
1985	I. Lendl	*$800,000	R. Seguso	$165,000	Nabisco
1986	I. Lendl	*$800,000	G. Forget	$165,000	Nabisco
1987	I. Lendl	*$800,000	A. Jarryd	$165,000	Nabisco
1988	M. Wilander	*$800,000	R. Leach	$165,000	Nabisco
1989	I. Lendl	*$800,000	R. Leach	$165,000	Nabisco

* Neither Connors nor second–placed B. Borg had played enough tournaments to qualify for the bonus payment, which was awarded to third–placed E. Dibbs.

MEN'S GRAND PRIX MASTERS WINNERS
SINGLES

	VENUE	WINNER	RUNNER–UP	SCORE					FIRST PRIZE
1970	Tokyo	S. R. Smith	R. G. Laver	Round–Robin					$10,000
1971	Paris	I. Nastase	S. R. Smith	Round–Robin					$15,000
1972	Barcelona	I. Nastase	S. R. Smith	6–3	6–2	3–6	2–6	6–3	$15,000
1973	Boston	I. Nastase	T. S. Okker	6–3	7–5	4–6	6–3		$15,000
1974	Melbourne	G. Vilas	I. Nastase	7–6	6–2	3–6	3–6	6–4	$40,000
1975	Stockholm	I. Nastase	B. Borg	6–2	6–2	6–1			$40,000
1976	Houston	M. Orantes	W. Fibak	5–7	6–2	0–6	7–6	6–1	$40,000
1977*	New York	J. S. Connors	B. Borg	6–4	1–6	6–4			$100,000
1978*	New York	J. P. McEnroe	A. R. Ashe	6–7	6–3	7–5			$100,000

1979*	New York	B. Borg	V. Gerulaitis	6–2	6–2			$100,000
1980*	New York	B. Borg	I. Lendl	6–4	6–2	6–2		$100,000
1981*	New York	I. Lendl	V. Gerulaitis	6–7	2–6	7–6	6–2	6–4 $100,000
1982*	New York	I. Lendl	J. P. McEnroe	6–4	6–4	6–2		$100,000
1983*	New York	J. P. McEnroe	I. Lendl	6–3	6–4	6–4		$100,000
1984*	New York	J. P. McEnroe	I. Lendl	7–5	6–0	6–4		$100,000
1985*	New York	I. Lendl	B. Becker	6–2	7–6	6–3		$100,000
1986	New York	I. Lendl	B. Becker	6–4	6–4	6–4		$200,000
1987	New York	I. Lendl	M. Wilander	6–2	6–2	6–3		$200,000
1988	New York	B. Becker	I. Lendl	5–7	7–6	3–6	6–2	7–6 $150,000
1989	New York	S. Edberg	B. Becker	4–6	7–6	6–3	6–1	$285,000

DOUBLES

	WINNERS	RUNNERS–UP	SCORE				
1970	S. R. Smith/A. R. Ashe	R. G. Laver/J. Kodes	Round–Robin				
1971–74	*Not held*						
1975	J. Gisbert/M. Orantes	J. Fassbender/H. J. Pohmann	Round–Robin				
1976	F. McNair/S. E. Stewart	B. E. Gottfried/R. Ramirez	6–3	5–7	5–7	6–4	6–4
1977*	R. A. J. Hewitt/F. D. McMillan	R. C. Lutz/S. R. Smith	7–5	7–6	6–3		
1978*	P. Fleming/J. P. McEnroe	W. Fibak/T. S. Okker	6–4	6–2	6–4		
1979*	P. Fleming/J. P. McEnroe	W. Fibak/T. S. Okker	6–3	7–6	6–1		
1980*	P. Fleming/J. P. McEnroe	P. McNamara/P. McNamee	6–4	6–3			
1981*	P. Fleming/J. P. McEnroe	K. Curren/S. Denton	6–3	6–3			
1982*	P. Fleming/J. P. McEnroe	S. E. Stewart/F. Taygan	6–2	6–2			
1983*	P. Fleming/J. P. McEnroe	P. Slozil/T. Smid	6–2	6–2			
1984*	P. Fleming/J. P. McEnroe	M. R. Edmondson/S. E. Stewart	6–3	6–1			
1985*	A. Jarryd/S. Edberg	J. Nystrom/M. Wilander	6–1	7–6			
1986+	A. Jarryd/S. Edberg	G. Forget/Y. Noah	6–3	7–6	6–3		
1987+	M. Mecir/T. Smid	K. Flach/R. Seguso	6–4	7–5	7–6	6–3	
1988+	R. Leach/J. Pugh	S. Casal/E. Sanchez	6–4	6–3	2–6	6–0	
1989+	P. McEnroe/J. Grabb	A. Jarryd/J. Fitzgerald	7–5	7–6	5–7	6–3	

* Played in January of the following year.* +Played separately from the singles at the Royal Albert Hall, London.

ATP TOUR CHAMPIONSHIP

SINGLES

	VENUE	WINNER	RUNNER–UP	SCORE				FIRST PRIZE
1990	Frankfurt	A. Agassi	S. Edberg	5–7	7–6	7–5	6–2	$950,000
1991	Frankfurt	P. Sampras	J. Courier	3–6	7–6	6–3	6–4	$1,020,000
1992	Frankfurt	B. Becker	J. Courier	6–4	6–3	7–5		$1,020,000

DOUBLES

	VENUE	WINNERS	RUNNERS–UP	SCORE				FIRST PRIZE
1990	Sanc. Cove, Australia	G. Forget/J. Hlasek	S. Casal/E. Sanchez	6–4	7–6	5–7	6–4	$225,000
1991	Johannesburg	J. Fitzgerald/ A. Jarryd	K. Flach/R. Seguso	6–4	6–4	2–6	6–4	$325,000
1992	Johannesburg	T. Woodbridge/ M. Woodforde	J. Fitzgerald/ A. Jarryd	6–2	7–6	5–7	3–6	6–3 $325,000

WOMEN'S WORLD SERIES

	WINNER	BONUS	TOUR SPONSOR
1971	Mrs L. W. King	$10,000	Pepsi–Cola
1972	Mrs L. W. King	$20,000	Commerical Union
1973	Miss C. M. Evert	$23,000	Commercial Union
1974–76	*Not held*		
1977	Miss C. M. Evert	$100,000	Colgate
1978	Miss C. M. Evert	$100,000	Colgate
1979	Mrs J. M. Lloyd	$115,000	Colgate
1980	Miss H. Mandlikova	$115,000	Colgate
1981	Miss M. Navratilova	$125,000	Toyota
1982	Miss M. Navratilova	$130,000	Toyota
1983	Miss M. Navratilova	$150,000	Virginia Slims

1984	Miss M. Navratilova	$150,000	Virginia Slims
1985	Miss M. Navratilova	$150,000	Virginia Slims
1986	Miss M. Navratilova	$200,000	Virginia Slims
1987	Miss S. Graf	$225,000	Virginia Slims
1988	Miss S. Graf	$400,000	Virginia Slims
1989	Miss S. Graf	$400,000	Virginia Slims
1990	Miss S. Graf	$500,000	Kraft General Foods
1991	Miss M. Seles	$500,000	Kraft General Foods
1992	Miss M. Seles	$500,000	Kraft General Foods

WOMEN'S INTERNATIONAL SERIES CHAMPIONSHIPS

SINGLES

	VENUE	WINNER	RUNNER–UP	SCORE			FIRST PRIZE
1977	Palm Springs	Miss C. M. Evert	Mrs L. W. King	6–2	6–2		$75,000
1978	Palm Springs	Miss C. M. Evert	Miss M. Navratilova	6–3	6–3		$75,000
1979*	Landover, Maryland	Miss M. Navratilova	Miss T. A. Austin	6–2	6–1		$75,000
1980*	Palm Springs	Miss T. A. Austin	Miss A. Jaeger	6–2	6–2		$75,000
1981	East Rutherford, NJ	Miss T. A. Austin	Miss M. Navratilova	2–6	6–4	6–2	$75,000
1982	East Rutherford, NJ	Miss M. Navratilova	Mrs J. M. Lloyd	4–6	6–1	6–2	$75,000
1983*	Madison Square Garden, NY	Miss M. Navratilova	Mrs J. M. Lloyd	6–3	7–5	6–1	**$125,000
1984*	Madison Square Garden, NY	Miss M. Navratilova	Miss H. Sukova	6–3	7–5	6–4	**$125,000
1985*	Madison Square Garden, NY	Miss M. Navratilova	Miss H. Mandlikova	6–2 6–1**	6–0	3–6	$125,000
1986	Madison Square Garden, NY	Miss M. Navratilova	Miss S. Graf	7–6	6–3	6–2	**$125,000
1987	Madison Square Garden, NY	Miss S. Graf	Miss G. Sabatini	4–6 6–4**	6–4	6–0	$125,000
1988	Madison Square Garden, NY	Miss G. Sabatini	Miss P. H. Shriver	7–5	6–2	6–2	**$125,000
1989	Madison Square Garden, NY	Miss S. Graf	Miss M. Navratilova	6–4 6–2**	7–5	2–6	$125,000
1990	Madison Square Garden, NY	Miss M. Seles 6–4	Miss G. Sabatini	6–4 6–2	5–7	3–6	$250,000
1991	Madison Square Garden, NY	Miss M. Seles	Miss M. Navratilova	6–4 6–0**	3–6	7–5	$250,000
1992	Madison Square Garden, NY	Miss M. Seles	Miss M. Navratilova	7–5	6–3	6–1	$250,000

*Played in the following year.   ** Best of five sets.

DOUBLES

	WINNERS	RUNNERS–UP	SCORE		
1977	Miss F. Durr/Miss S. V. Wade	Mrs H. Gourlay Cawley/Miss J. Russell	6–1	4–6	6–4
1978	Mrs L. W. King/Miss M. Navratilova	Mrs G. E. Reid/Miss W. M. Turnbull	6–3	6–4	
1979*	Mrs L. W. King/Miss M. Navratilova	Miss R. Casals/Mrs J. M. Lloyd	6–4	6–3	
1980*	Miss R. Casals/Miss W. M. Turnbull	Miss C. Reynolds/Miss P. Smith	6–3	4–6	7–6
1991	Miss M. Navratilova/Miss P. H. Shriver	Miss R. Casals/Miss W. M. Turnbull	6–3	6–4	
1982	Miss M. Navratilova/Miss P. H. Shriver	Miss C. Reynolds/Miss P. Smith	6–4	7–5	
1983*	Miss M. Navratilova/Miss P. H. Shriver	Miss J. M. Durie/Miss A. Kiyomura	6–3	6–1	
1984*	Miss M. Navratilova/Miss P. H. Shriver	Miss C. Kohde–Kilsch/Miss H. Sukova	6–7	6–4	7–6
1985*	Miss H. Mandlikova/Miss W. M. Turnbull	Miss C. Kohde–Kilsch/Miss H. Sukova	6–4	6–7	6–3
1986	Miss M. Navratilova/Miss P. H. Shriver	Miss C. Kohde–Kilsch/Miss H. Sukova	7–6	6–3	
1987	Miss M. Navratilova/Miss P. H. Shriver	Miss C. Kohde–Kilsch/Miss H. Sukova	6–1	6–1	
1988	Miss M. Navratilova/Miss P. H. Shriver	Miss L. Savchenko/Miss N. Zvereva	6–3	6–4	
1989	Miss M. Navratilova/Miss P. H. Shriver	Miss L. Savchenko/Miss N. Zvereva	6–3	6–2	
1990	Miss K. Jordan/Mrs E. Smylie	Miss M. Paz/Miss A. Sanchez–Vicario	7–6	6–4	
1991	Miss M. Navratilova/Miss P. H. Shriver	Miss G. Fernandez/Miss J. Novotna	4–6	7–5	6–4
1992	Miss A. Sanchez–Vic./Miss H. Sukova	Miss J. Novotna/Mrs L. Savchenko Neil.	7–6	6–1	

* Played in the following year.

WORLD CHAMPIONSHIP TENNIS

	WINNER	RUNNER–UP	SCORE					PRIZE
1971	K. R. Rosewall	R. G. Laver	6–4	1–6	7–6	7–6		$50,000
1972	K. R. Rosewall	R. G. Laver	4–6	6–0	6–3	6–7	7–6	50,000
1973	S. R. Smith	A. R. Ashe	6–3	6–3	4–6	6–4		50,000

1974	J. D. Newcombe	B. Borg	4–6	6–3	6–3	6–2		50,000
1975	A. R. Ashe	B. Borg	3–6	6–4	6–4	6–0		50,000
1976	B. Borg	G. Vilas	1–6	6–1	7–5	6–1		50,000
1977	J. S. Connors	R. D. Stockton	6–7	6–1	6–4	6–3		100,000
1978	V. Gerulaitis	E. Dibbs	6–3	6–2	6–1			100,000
1979	J. P. McEnroe	B. Borg	7–5	4–6	6–2	7–6		100,000
1980	J. S. Connors	J. P. McEnroe	2–6	7–6	6–1	6–2		100,000
1981	J. P. McEnroe	J. Kriek	7–6	6–3	4–6	0–6	6–4	100,000
1982	I. Lendl	J. P. McEnroe	6–2	3–6	6–3	6–3		150,000
1983	J. P. McEnroe	I. Lendl	6–2	4–6	6–3	6–7	7–6	150,000
1984	J. P. McEnroe	J. S. Connors	6–1	6–2	6–3			200,000
1985	I. Lendl	T. Mayotte	7–6	6–4	6–1			200,000
1986	A. Jarryd	B. Becker	6–7	6–1	6–1	6–4		200,000
1987	M. Mecir	J. P. McEnroe	6–0	3–6	6–2	6–2		200,000
1988	B. Becker	S. Edberg	6–4	1–6	7–5	6–2		200,000
1989	J. P. McEnroe	B. Gilbert	6–3	6–3	7–6			200,000

WORLD DOUBLES CHAMPIONSHIPS

	VENUE	WINNERS	RUNNERS–UP	SCORE				PRIZE
1973	Montreal	R. C. Lutz/S. R. Smith	T. S. Okker/M. C. Riessen	6–2	7–6	6–0		$40,000
1974	Montreal	R. A. J. Hewitt/F. D. McMillan	J. D. Newcombe/O. K. Davidson	6–2	6–7	6–1	6–2	40,000
1975	Mexico City	B. R. Gottfried/R. Ramirez	M. Cox/C. Drysdale	7–6	6–7	7–6	7–6	40,000
1976	Kansas City	W. Fibak/K. Meiler	R. C. Lutz/S. R. Smith	6–3 6–4	2–6	3–6	6–3	40,000
1977	Kansas City	V. Amritraj/R. D. Stockton	V. Gerulaitis/A. Panatta	7–6	7–6	4–6	6–3	80,000
1978	Kansas City	W. Fibak/T. S. Okker	R. C. Lutz/S. R. Smith	6–7	6–4	6–0	6–3	80,000
1979	Olympia, London	J. P. McEnroe/P. Fleming	I. Nastase/S. E. Stewart	3–6	6–2	6–3	6–1	80,000
1980	Olympia, London	B. E. Gottfried/R. Ramirez	W. Fibak/T. S. Okker	3–6 6–3	6–4	6–4	3–6	80,000
1981	Olympia, London	P. McNamara/P. McNamee	V. Amaya/H. Pfister	6–3 6–2	2–6	3–6	6–3	80.000
1982	Birmingham	H. Gunthardt/B. Taroczy	K. Curren/S. Denton	6–7	6–3	7–5	6–4	80,000
1983	Royal Albert Hall, London	H. Gunthardt/B. Taroczy	B. E. Gottfried/R. Ramirez	6–3	7–5	7–6		80,000
1984	Royal Albert Hall, London	P. Slozil/T. Smid	A. Jarryd/H. Simonsson	1–6 6–3	6–3	3–6	6–4	80,000
1985	Royal Albert Hall, London	K. Flach/R. Seguso	H. Gunthardt/B. Taroczy	6–3 6–0	3–6	6–3	4–6	80,000

From 1986 this event was incorporated into the Masters Doubles.

GRAND SLAMS

The Grand Slam denotes holding the four championship titles of Australia, France, Wimbledon and the United States in the same year (shown in bold below). The list also includes consecutive wins, not in the same year.

MEN'S SINGLES
J. D. Budge: Wimbledon, US 1937, **Australia, France, Wimbledon, US 1938**
R. G. Laver: **Australia, France, Wimbledon, US 1962**
R. G. Laver: **Australia, France, Wimbledon, US 1969**

WOMEN'S SINGLES
Miss M. Connolly: Wimbledon, US 1952, **Australia, France, Wimbledon, US 1953**
Mrs B. M. Court: US 1969, **Australia, France, Wimbledon, US 1970,** Australia 1971
Miss M. Navratilova: Wimbledon, US, Australia 1983, France, Wimbledon, US 1984
Miss S. Graf: **Australia, France, Wimbledon, US 1988**

MEN'S DOUBLES
F. A. Sedgman: (With J. E. Bromwich) US 1950, **(with K. McGregor) Australia, France, Wimbledon, US 1951**, Australia, France, Wimbledon 1952
K. McGregor: **(With F. A. Sedgman) Australia, France, Wimbledon, US 1951**, Australia, France, Wimbledon 1952

WOMEN'S DOUBLES
Miss A. L. Brough: (with Mrs W. du Pont) France, Wimbledon, US 1949, (with Miss D. J. Hart) Australia 1950

Miss M. E. Bueno: **(With Miss C. C. Truman) Australia 1960, (with Miss D. R. Hard) France, Wimbledon, US 1960**
Miss M. Navratilova/Miss P. H. Shriver: Wimbledon, US, Australia 1983, **France, Wimbledon, US, Australia 1984,**
France 1985; *Wimbledon, US 1986, Australia, France 1987
* *Miss Navratilova also won France 1986 with Miss A. Temesvari.*

MIXED DOUBLES
Miss M. Smith: (With F. S. Stolle) US 1962, **(with K. N. Fletcher) Australia, France, Wimbledon, US 1963**, Australia,
France 1964
K. N. Fletcher: **(With Miss M. Smith) Australia, France, Wimbledon, US 1963**, Australia, France 1964
O. K. Davidson: (With Mrs D. Fales) US 1966, **(with Miss L. R. Turner) Australia 1967, (with Mrs L. W. King) France,
Wimbledon, US 1967**
Mrs L. W. King: (With O. K. Davidson) France, Wimbledon, US 1967, (with R. D. Crealy) Australia 1968

JUNIOR SINGLES
E. H. Buchholz: **Australia, France, Wimbledon, US 1958** (*Note:* the US event was not then conducted as an
international event)
S. Edberg: **France, Wimbledon, US, Australia 1983**

ITF VETERAN CHAMPIONSHIPS

MEN

	VENUE	35 SINGLES	35 DOUBLES	45 SINGLES	45 DOUBLES
1981	Sao Paulo			S. Davidson	S. Davidson/H. Stewart
1982	Poertschach			I. Gulyas	J. Morton/J. Nelson
1983	Bahia			I. Gulyas	K. Fuhrmann/F. Seeman
1984	Cervia			I. Gulyas	K. Fuhrmann/F. Seeman
1985	Melbourne			I. Barclay	A. Duestler/J. Nelson
1986	Poertschach			J. Lemann	J. Lemann/I. Ribeiro
1987	Garmisch–Partenkirchen			G. Rohrich	H. Gradischnig P. Pokorny
1988	Huntington Beach, Cal.	A. Gardiner	L. Levai/R. Machan	K. Diepraam	F./G. Krauss
1989	Vina Del Mar, Chile	A. Fillol	R. Machan/L. Levai	H. Elschenbroich	B. Nitsche/G. Krauss
1990	Umag, Yugoslavia	R. Machan	R. Machan/L. Levai	H. Elschenbroich	D. Johnson/J. Parker
1991	Perth	P. Torre	Y. Tarik/A. Wijono	D. McCormick	B. Burns/J. Weaver
1992	Sicily	F. Rocchi	French/S. Birner	R. Staguhn	Penberthy/De Jel

	VENUE	55 SINGLES	55 DOUBLES	60 SINGLES	60 DOUBLES
1981	Sao Paulo	S. Clark	S. Clark/T. Johansson		
1982	Poertschach	R. McCarthy	A. Hussmuller/L. Legenstein	T. Johansson	T. Johansson/A. Ritzenberg
1983	Bahia	R. McCarthy	A. Hussmuller/L. Legenstein	–	–
1984	Cervia	G. Merlo	J. Morton/H. Stewart	–	–
1985	Melbourne	H. Stewart	J. Morton/H. Stewart	R. Sorlein	T. Johansson/V.Zabrodsky
1986	Poertschach	L. Maine	R. Howe/R. Seymour	M. McCarthy	O. Jirkovsky/J. Karlhofer
1987	Garmisch Partenkirchen	I. Gulyas	I. Gulyas/H. Stewart	R. Howe	L. Legenstein/A. Stolpa
1988	Huntington Beach, Cal.	I. Gulyas	S. Davidson/H. Stewart	R. McCarthy	R. Howe/R. McCarthy
1989	Vina Del Mar, Chile	I. Gulyas	C. DeVoe/J. Powless	R. McCarthy	R. Howe/R. McCarthy
1990	Umag, Yugoslavia	I. Gulyas	K. Sinclair/L. Main	S. Davidson	H. Stewart/S. Davidson
1991	Perth	P. Froelich	G. Davis/H. Ahlers	L. Main	F. Sedgman/C. Wilderspin
1992	Sicily	K. Fuhrmann	Stewart/L. Dodson	W. Mertins	Sinclair/Main

	VENUE	65 SINGLES	65 DOUBLES	70 SINGLES	70 DOUBLES
1982	Poertschach	F. Klein	J. Becker/F. Klein	–	–
1983	Bahia	R. San Martin	F. Barboza/H. Pizani	–	–
1984	Cervia	G. Mulloy	G. Mulloy/F. Klein	–	–
1985	Melbourne	J. Gilchrist	R. Ritzenberg/F. Klein	–	–
1986	Poertschach	T. Johansson	G. Mulloy/V. Hughes	–	–
1987	Garmisch–Partenkirchen	A. Swetka	B. Kempa/W. Kessler	–	–
1988	Huntington	T. Brown	L. Hammel/B. Sherman	F. Klein	G. Hippenstiel/G. Young

	Beach, Cal.			
1989	Vina Del Mar, Chile	A. Vieira	A. Vieira/S. Verrati	A. Ritzenberg	A. Ritzenberg/F.Klein
1990	Umag, Yugoslavia	B. McCarthy	O. Jirkovsky/J. Karlhofer	W. Parsons	A. Swetka/A. Ritzenberg
1991	Perth	B. McCarthy	B. McCarthy/B. Howe	B. Sherman	V. Hughes/M. Miller
1992	Sicily	B. McCarthy	B. McCarthy/B. Howe	B. Sherman	B. Sherman/?Isodori

WOMEN

	VENUE	40 SINGLES	40 DOUBLES	50 SINGLES	50 DOUBLES
1981	Sao Paulo	E. de Molina	N. Reed/M. S. Plante	A. Cury	–
1982	Poertschach Burmester	R. Drisaldi	*C. Hillebrand/N. Reed	E. Slytermann	E. Slytermann/I.
1983	Bahia	H. Masthoff	H. Masthoff/H. Orth	I. de Pla	G. Barboza/J. Borzone
1984	Cervia	H. Masthoff	H. Masthoff/H. Orth	C. Mazzoleni	H. Brabanec/P. Wearne
1985	Melbourne	H. Orth	J. Dalton/H. Orth	I. Michael	A. Fotheringham/A. Pilkinghome
1986	Poertschach	H. Masthoff	H. Masthoff/H. Orth	S. Brasher	S. Brasher/L. Cawthorne
1987	Garmisch–Partenkirchen	M. Pinterova	G. Lovera/M. Pinterova	S. Brasher	S. Brasher/L. Cawthorne
1988	Huntington Beach, Cal.	M. Pinterova	G. Lovera/R. Darmon	D. Matthiessen	J. Crofford/D. Matthiessen
1989	Vina Del Mar, Chile	M. Pinterova	M. Pinterova/H. Orth	I. Michael	N. Reed/B. Allendorf
1990	Umag, Yugoslavia	M. Pinterova	B. Mueller/L. Cash	M. Schultze	K. Schiavinato/J. Blackshaw
1991	Perth	C. Baily	C. Baily/B. Mueller	C. Hillebrand	J. Blackshaw/B. Whitelaw
1992	Sicily	M. Rasmussen	M. Rasmussen/?Charles	C. Hillebrand	C. Hillebrand/?Boothman

*held as 45 event.

	VENUE	60 SINGLES	60 DOUBLES
1988	Huntington Beach, Cal.	V. Glass	D. Cheney/C. Murdock
1989	Vina Del Mar, Chile	B. Pratt	D. Cheney/C. Murdock
1990	Umag, Yugoslavia	L. Owen	L. Stock/D. Young
1991	Perth	B. Pratt	R. Illingworth/A. Williams
1992	Sicily	B. Rae	B. Rae/Hobson

DUBLER CUP

International Men's Team Championship for 45 year age group

FINALS

	VENUE*	WINNERS	RUNNERS–UP	SCORE
1958	Monte Carlo	Italy	West Germany	3–1
1959	Zurich	Switzerland	Italy	4–1
1960	Merano, Italy	Italy	Switzerland	5–0
1961	Bologna	Italy	Austria	4–1
1962	Merano, Italy	Italy	France	3–2
1963	Merano, Italy	Italy	Belgium	4–1
1964	Merano, Italy	Italy	West Germany	5–0
1965	Merano, Italy	Italy	Sweden	3–0
1966	Florence	Sweden	Italy	4–1
1967	Avesta, Sweden	France	Sweden	3–2
1968	Paris	USA	France	5–0
1969	St Louis	USA	Sweden	4–1
1970	Cleveland	USA	Sweden	4–1
1971	La Costa, California	USA	Sweden	3–2
1972	Le Touquet	USA	France	4–1
1973	New York	Australia	USA	3–1
1974	New York	USA	Australia	3–2
1975	New York	Australia	USA	5–0
1976	Alassio, Italy	Italy	Canada	3–2
1977	New York	USA	France	4–1
1978	New York	USA	Australia	4–1
1979	Vienna	Austria	USA	3–2
1980	Cervia, Italy	Sweden	Austria	2–1
1981	Buenos Aires	USA	Great Britain	2–1

1982	Athens	USA	Great Britain	2–1
1983	New York	USA	West Germany	2–1
1984	Bastad	West Germany	USA	3–0
1985	Perth	West Germany	Australia	2–1
1986	Berlin	West Germany	Switzerland	3–0
1987	Poertschach	Italy	Austria	2–1
1988	Huntington Beach, Cal.	USA	West Germany	3–0
1989	Montevideo	USA	West Germany	2–1
1990	Bol, Yugoslavia	Germany	USA	2–1
1991	Sydney	USA	Germany	3–0
1992	Portschach, Austria	Germany	Spain	2–1

* From 1958 to 1979 the early rounds were played zonally

AUSTRIA CUP
International Men's Team Competition for 55 year age group.

	VENUE	WINNERS	RUNNERS–UP	FINAL SCORE
1977	Baden b. Wien	Great Britain	Austria	2–1
1978	Brand (Austria)	USA	Sweden	2–1
1979	Brand (Austria)	USA	Sweden	3–0
1980	Brand (Austria)	USA	Sweden	2–1
1981	Poertschach	USA	Sweden	3–0
1982	Cervia, Italy	Australia	USA	2–1
1983	New York	Australia	USA	2–1
1984	Poertschach	USA	Australia	2–1
1985	Perth	Australia	USA	3–0
1986	Poertschach	Australia	Canada	2–1
1987	Umag	Canada	Australia	3–0
1988	Huntington Beach, Cal.	Canada	West Germany	3–0
1989	Buenos Aires	Canada	USA	2–1
1990	Poertschach	Canada	USA	3–0
1991	Sydney	USA	Australia	3–0
1992	Monte Carlo	Germany	USA	3–0

YOUNG CUP
International Women's Team Competition for 40 year age group.

	VENUE	WINNERS	RUNNERS–UP	FINAL SCORE
1977	Malmo	Argentina	Not available	
1978	Ancona	Italy	Not available	
1979	Cannes	West Germany	USA	3–0
1980	Bad Wiessee, Germany	West Germany	Italy	3–0
1981	Bad Wiessee, Germany	France	Italy	2–1
1982	Brand, Austria	France	Italy	3–0
1983	Cervia, Italy	West Germany	France	2–1
1984	Cervia, Italy	USA	France	3–0
1985	Poertschach, Austria	West Germany	France	3–0
1986	Brand	West Germany	USA	2–1
1987	Venice	France	USA	2–1
1988	Bagnoles de l'Orne, France	Great Britain	West Germany	3–0
1989	Poertschach	France	West Germany	3–0
1990	Keszthely, Hungary	France	USA	3–0
1991	Brisbane	Australia	Germany	2–1
1992	Malahaide, Ireland Great Britain		Australia	2–1

MARIA ESTHER BUENO CUP
International Women's Team Competition for 50 year age group.

	VENUE	WINNERS	RUNNERS–UP	FINAL SCORE
1983	Poertschach	Great Britain	USA	2–1
1984	Le Touquet, France	USA	France	3–0
1985	Bremen	USA	Great Britain	3–0
1986	Brand	USA	Great Britain	2–1
1987	Helsinki	USA	Great Britain	2–1
1988	Bahia	USA	Canada	2–1

1989	Bournemouth	USA	Great Britain	2–1
1990	Barcelona	Australia	Spain	2–1
1991	Perth	USA	France	3–0
1992	Bagnoles de L'orne, France	USA	France	2–1

ITALIA CUP
International Men's Team Competition for 35 year age group.

	VENUE	WINNERS	RUNNERS–UP	FINAL SCORE
1982	Cervia, Italy	Italy	USA	2–1
1983	Cervia, Italy	West Germany	USA	2–1
1984	Brand, Austria	West Germany	France	2–1
1985	Reggio Calabria, Italy	USA	Italy	2–0
1986	Normandy, France	West Germany	USA	3–0
1987	Grado	USA	Austria	2–1
1988	Bol, Yugoslavia	West Germany	USA	3–0
1989	Mainz, W. Germany	West Germany	USA	3–0
1990	Glasgow	Spain	Australia	2–1
1991	Melbourne	Australia	Spain	3–0
1992	Ancona, Italy	Italy	France	2–1

BRITANNIA CUP
International Men's Team Competition for 65 year age group.

	VENUE	WINNERS	RUNNERS–UP	FINAL SCORE
1979	Queen's Club, London	USA	Great Britain	3–0
1980	Frinton–on–Sea	USA	Sweden	3–0
1981	Hurlingham Club, London	USA	Sweden	3–0
1982	New York	USA	Canada	3–0
1983	Poertschach	USA	Australia	3–0
1984	Poertschach	USA	Australia	3–0
1985	Poertschach	USA	Australia	3–0
1986	Bournemouth	USA	Norway	3–0
1987	Bastad	USA	Sweden	2–1
1988	Huntington Beach, Cal.	USA	France	3–0
1989	Umag	USA	France	3–0
1990	Bournemouth	USA	Australia	2–1
1991	Canberra	Austria	Australia	2–1
1992	Seefeld, Austria	Australia	Austria2–1	

THE CRAWFORD CUP
International Men's Team Competition for 75 year age group.

	VENUE	WINNERS	RUNNERS–UP	FINAL SCORE
1983	Brand, Austria	USA	Sweden	3–0
1984	Helsinki, Finland	USA	Great Britain	3–0
1985	Brand, Austria	USA	Australia	3–0
1986	Seefeld, Austria	USA	France	3–0
1987	Poertschach	USA	Great Britain	3–0
1988	Keszthely, Hungary	USA	Great Britain	3–0
1989	Bol	USA	Brazil	3–0
1990	Brand, Austria	USA	Brazil	3–0
1991	Canberra	Germany	USA	2–1
1992	Le Touquet, France USA	Germany	3–0	

ALICE MARBLE CUP
International Women's Team Competition for 60 year age group.

	VENUE	WINNERS	RUNNERS–UP	FINAL SCORE
1988	Poertschach	USA	West Germany	3–0
1989	Brand	USA	West Germany	2–1
1990	Paderborn, Germany	USA	Germany	2–1
1991	Perth	USA	Great Britain	3–0
1992	Keszthely, Hungary	Great Britain	USA	2–1

GOTTFRIED VON CRAMM CUP

International Men's Team Competition for 60 year age group.

VENUE	WINNERS	RUNNERS–UP	FINAL SCORE
1989 Kempten	Australia	New Zealand	3–0
1990 Ontario	USA	Austria	2–1
1991 Adelaide	USA	New Zealand	2–1
1992 BournemouthCanada	USA		2–1

FRED PERRY CUP

International Men's Team Competition for 50 year age group.

VENUE	WINNERS	RUNNERS–UP	FINAL SCORE
1991 Bournemouth	Germany	Great Britain	3–0
1992 Berlin	Germany	USA	3–0

AUSTRALIAN INTERNATIONAL JUNIOR CHAMPIONSHIPS

BOYS' SINGLES

1946 F. Sedgman	1956 R. Mark	1965 G. Goven
1947 D. Candy	1957 R. Laver	1966 K. Coombes
1948 K. McGregor	1958 M. Mulligan	1967 B. Fairlie (NZL)
1949 C. Wilderspin	1959 E. Buchholz (USA)	1968 P. Dent
1950 K. Rosewall	1960 W. Coghlan	1969 A. McDonald
1951 L. Hoad	1961 J. Newcombe	1970 J. Alexander
1952 K. Rosewall	1962 J. Newcombe	1971 C. Letcher
1953 W. Gilmour	1963 J. Newcombe	1972 P. Kronk
1954 W. Knight	1964 A. Roche	1973 P. McNamee
1955 G. Moss		

WINNER	RUNNER–UP	SCORE		
1974 H. Brittain				
1975 B. Drewett (AUS)				
1976 R. Kelly				
1977 (Jan.) B. Drewett (AUS)				
1977 (Dec.) R. Kelly				
1978 P. Serrett (AUS)	C. Johnstone (AUS)	6–4	6–3	
1979 G. Whitecross (AUS)	C. Miller (AUS)	6–4	6–3	
1980 C. Miller (AUS)	W. Masur (AUS)	7–6	6–2	
1981 J. Windahl (SWE)	P. Cash (AUS)	6–4	6–4	
1982 M. Kratzman (AUS)	S. Youl (AUS)	6–3	7–5	
1983 S. Edberg (SWE)	S. Youl (AUS)	6–4	6–4	
1984 M. Kratzman (AUS)	P. Flyn (AUS)	6–4	6–1	
1985 S. Barr (AUS)	S. Furlong (AUS)	7–6	6–7	6–3
1986 *Not held*				
1987 J. Stoltenberg (AUS)	T. Woodbridge (AUS)	6–2	7–6	
1988 J. Anderson (AUS)	A. Florent (AUS)	7–5	7–6	
1989 N. Kulti (SWE)	T. Woodbridge (AUS)	6–2	6–0	
1990 D. Dier (FRG)	L. Paes (IND)	6–4	7–6	
1991 T. Enqvist (SWE)	S. Gleeson (AUS)	7–6	6–7	6–1
1992 G. Doyle (AUS)	B. Dunn (USA)	6–2	6–0	

GIRL'S SINGLES

1946 S. Grant	1956 L. Coghlan	1965 K. Melville
1947 J. Tuckfield	1957 M. Rayson	1966 K. Krantzcke
1948 B. Penrose	1958 J. Lehane	1967 A. Kenny
1949 J. Warnock	1959 J. Lehane	1968 L. Hunt
1950 B. McIntyre	1960 L. Turner	1969 L. Hunt
1951 M. Carter	1961 R. Ebbern	1970 E. Goolagong
1952 M. Carter	1962 R. Ebbern	1971 P. Coleman
1953 J. Staley	1963 R. Ebbern	1972 P. Coleman
1954 E. Orton	1964 K. Dening	1973 C. O'Neill
1955 E. Orton		

	WINNER	RUNNER–UP	SCORE		
1974	J. Walker				
1975	S. Barker (GBR)				
1976	S. Saliba (AUS)				
1977	(Jan.) P. Bailey				
1977	(Dec.) A. Tobin (AUS)				
1978	E. Little (AUS)	S. Leo (AUS)	6–1	6–2	
1979	A. Minter (AUS)	S. Leo (AUS)	6–4	6–3	
1980	A. Minter (AUS)	E. Sayers (AUS)	6–4	6–2	
1981	A. Minter (AUS)	C. Vanier (FRA)	6–4	6–2	
1982	A. Brown (GBR)	P. Paradis (FRA)	6–3	6–4	
1983	A. Brown (GBR)	B. Randall (AUS)	7–6	6–3	
1984	A. Croft (GBR)	H. Dahlstrom (SWE)	6–0	6–1	
1985	J. Byrne (AUS)	L. Field (AUS)	6–1	6–3	
1986	*Not held*	.			
1987	M. Jaggard (AUS)	N. Provis (AUS)	6–2	6–4	
1988	J. Faull (AUS)	E. Derly (FRA)	6–4	6–4	
1989	K. Kessaris (USA)	A. Farley (USA)	6–1	6–2	
1990	M. Maleeva (BUL)	L. Stacey (AUS)	7–5	6–7	6–1
1991	N. Pratt (AUS)	K. Godridge (AUS)	6–4	6–3	
1992	J. Limmer (AUS)	L. Davenport (USA)	7–5	6–2	

BOY'S DOUBLES

	WINNERS	RUNNERS–UP	SCORE		
1983	J. Harty (AUS)/D. Tyson (AUS)	A. Lane (AUS)/D. Cahill (AUS)	3–6	6–4	6–3
1984	M. Kratzman (AUS)/M. Baroch (AUS)	B. Custer (AUS)/D. Macpherson (AUS)	6–2	5–7	7–5
1985	B. Custer (AUS)/D. Macpherson	C. Suk (TCH)/P. Korda (TCH) (AUS)	7–5	6–2	
1986	*Not held*				
1987	J. Stoltenberg (AUS)/T. Woodbridge	S. Barr (AUS)/D. Roe (AUS) (AUS)	6–2	6–4	
1988	J. Stoltenberg (AUS)/T. Woodbridge (AUS)	J. Anderson (AUS)/R. Fromberg (AUS)	6–3	6–2	
1989	J. Anderson (AUS)/T. Woodbridge (AUS)	J. Morgan (AUS)/A. Kratzmann (AUS)	6–4	6–2	
1990	R. Petterson (SWE)/M. Renstroem (SWE)	R. Janecek (CAN)/E. Munoz de Cote (MEX)	4–6	7–6	6–1
1991	G. Doyle (AUS)/J. Eagle (AUS)	J. Holmes (AUS)/P. Kilderry (AUS)	7–6	6–4	
1992	G. Doyle (AUS)/B. Sceney (AUS)	L. Carrington (USA)/J. Thompson (USA)	6–4	6–4	

GIRL'S DOUBLES

	WINNERS	RUNNERS–UP	SCORE		
1983	B. Randall (AUS)/K. Staunton (AUS)	J. Byrne (AUS)/J. Thompson (AUS)	3–6	6–3	6–3
1984	L. Field (AUS)/L. Savchenko (URS)	M. Parun (NZL)/J. Masters (AUS)	7–6	6–2	
1985	J. Byrne (AUS)/J. Thompson (AUS)	A. Scott/S. McCann	6–0	6–3	
1986	*Not held*				
1987	N. Provis (AUS)/A. Devries (BEL)	D. Jones (AUS)/G. Dwyer (AUS)	6–3	6–1	
1988	R. McQuillan (AUS)/J. Faull (AUS)	R. Stubbs (AUS)/K. McDonald (AUS)	6–1	7–5	
1989	A. Strnadova (TCH)/E. Sviglerova	N. Pratt (AUS)/A. Woolcock (AUS) (TCH)	6–2	6–0	
1990	L. Zaltz (ISR)/R. Mayer (ISR)	J. Hodder (AUS)/N. Pratt (AUS)	6–4	6–4	
1991	K. Habsudova (TCH)/B. Rittner (GER)	J. Limmer (AUS)/A. Woolcock (AUS)	6–2	6–0	
1992	L. Davenport (USA)/N. London (USA)	M. Avotins (AUS)/J. Limmer (AUS)	6–2	7–5	

FRENCH INTERNATIONAL JUNIOR CHAMPIONSHIPS

	WINNER	RUNNER–UP	SCORE		
1974	C. Casa (FRA)	U. Marten (FRG)	2–6	6–1	6–4
1975	C. Roger–Vasselin (FRA)	P. Elter (FRG)	6–1	6–2	
1976	H. Gunthardt (SUI)	J. L. Clerc (ARG)	4–6	7–6	6–4
1977	J. P. McEnroe (USA)	R. Kelly (AUS)	6–1	6–1	
1978	I. Lendl (TCH)	P. Hjertquist (SWE)	7–6	6–4	
1979	R. Krishnan (IND)	B. Testerman (USA)	2–6	6–1	6–0

1980	H. Leconte (FRA)	A. Tous (ESP)	7–6	6–3	
1981	M. Wilander (SWE)	J. Brown	7–5	6–1	
1982	T. Benhabiles (FRA)	L. Courteau (FRA)	7–6	6–2	
1983	S. Edberg (SWE)	F. Fevrier (FRA)	6–4	7–6	
1984	K. Carlsson (SWE)	M. Kratzman (AUS)	6–3	6–3	
1985	J. Yzaga (PER)	T. Muster (AUT)	2–6	6–3	6–0
1986	G. Perez Roldan (ARG)	S. Grenier (FRA)	4–6	6–3	6–2
1987	G. Perez Roldan (ARG)	J. Stoltenberg (AUS)	6–3	3–6	6–1
1988	N. Pereira (VEN)	M. Larsson (SWE)	7–6	6–3	
1989	F. Santoro (FRA)	J. Palmer (USA)	6–3	3–6	9–7
1990	A. Gaudenzi (ITA)	T. Enqvist (SWE)	2–6	7–6	6–4
1991	A. Medvedev (URS)	T. Enqvist (SWE)	6–4	7–6	
1992	A. Pavel (ROM)	M. Navarra (ITA)	7–6	6–3	

GIRL'S SINGLES

	WINNER	RUNNER–UP	SCORE		
1974	M. Simionescu (RUM)	S. Barker (GBR)	6–3	6–3	
1975	R. Marsikova (TCH)	L. Mottram (GBR)	6–3	5–7	6–2
1976	M. Tyler (GBR)	M. Zoni (ITA)	6–1	6–3	
1977	A. E. Smith (USA)	H. Strachonova (TCH)	6–3	7–6	
1978	H. Mandlikova (TCH)	M. Rothschild (FRG)	6–1	6–1	
1979	L. Sandin (SWE)	M. L. Piatek (USA)	6–3	6–1	
1980	K. Horvath (USA)	K. Henry (USA)	6–2	6–2	
1981	B. Gadusek (USA)	H. Sukova (TCH)	6–7	6–1	6–4
1982	M. Maleeva (BUL)	P. Barg (USA)	7–5	6–2	
1983	P. Paradis (FRA)	D. Spence (USA)	7–6	6–3	
1984	G. Sabatini (ARG)	K. Maleeva (BUL)	6–3	5–7	6–3
1985	L. Garrone (ITA)	D. Van Rensburg (SAF)	6–1	6–3	
1986	P. Tarabini (ARG)	N. Provis (AUS)	6–3	6–3	
1987	N. Zvereva (URS)	J. Pospisilova(TCH)	6–1	6–0	
1988	J. Halard (FRA)	A. Farley (USA)	6–2	4–6	7–5
1989	J. Capriati (USA)	E. Sviglerova (TCH)	6–4	6–0	
1990	M. Maleeva (BUL)	T. Ignatieva (URS)	6–2	6–3	
1991	A. Smashnova (ISR)	I. Gorrochategui (ARG)	2–6	7–5	6–1
1992	R. De Los Rios (PAR)	P. Suarez (ARG)	6–4	6–0	

BOY'S DOUBLES

	WINNERS	RUNNERS–UP	SCORE		
1983	M. Kratzman (AUS)/S. Youl (AUS)	A. Chesnokov (URS)/A. Olhovskiy (URS)	6–2	6–3	
1985	P. Korda (TCH)/C. Suk (TCH)	V. Godrichidze (URS)/V. Volkov (URS)	4–6	6–0	7–5
1986	F. Davin (ARG)/G. Perez–Roldan (ARG)	T. Carbonell (ESP)/J. Sanchez (ESP)	7–5	5–7	6–3
1987	J. Courier (USA)/J. Stark (USA)	F. Davin (ARG)/G. Perez–Roldan (ARG)	6–7	6–4	6–3
1988	J. Stoltenberg (AUS)/T. Woodbridge (AUS)	C. Coratti (ITA)/G. Ivanisevic (YUG)	7–6	7–5	
1989	J. Anderson (AUS)/T. Woodbridge (AUS)	L. Herrera (MEX)/M. Knowles (BAH)	6–3	4–6	6–2
1990	S. La Reau (CAN)/P. Le Blanc (CAN)	C. Marsh (AUS)/M. Ondruska (RSA)	7–6	6–7	9–7
1991	T. Enqvist (SWE)/M. Martinelle (SWE)	J. Knowle (AUT)/J. Unterberger (AUT)	6–1	6–3	
1992	E. Abaroa (MEX)/G. Doyle (AUS)	Y. Kafelnikov (CIS)/A. Radulescu (ROM)	7–6	6–3	

GIRL'S DOUBLES

	WINNERS	RUNNERS–UP	SCORE		
1983	C. Anderholm (SWE)/H. Olsson (SWE)	K./M. Maleeva (BUL)	6–4	6–1	
1985	M.U Perez Roldan (ARG)/P. Tarabini (ARG)	A. Holikova (TCH)/R. Szrubakova (TCH)	6–3	5–7	6–4
1986	L. Meskhi (URS)/N. Zvereva (URS)	J. Novotna (TCH)/R. Rajchrtova (TCH)	1–6	6–3	6–0
1987	N. Medvedeva (URS)/N. Zvereva (URS)	M. Jaggard (AUS)/N. Provis (AUS)	6–3	6–3	
1988	A. Dechaume (FRA)/E. Derly (FRA)	J. Halard (FRA)/M. Laval (FRA)	6–4	3–6	6–3
1989	N. Pratt (AUS)/S.–T. Wang (TPE)	C. Caverzasio (ITA)/S. Farina (ITA)	7–5	3–6	8–6
1990	R. Dragomir (ROM)/I. Spirlea (ROM)	T. Ignatieva (URS)/I. Soukhova (URS)	6–3	6–1	
1991	E. Bes (ESP)/I. Gorrochategui (ARG)	Z. Malkova (TCH)/E. Martincova (TCH)	6–1	6–3	
1992	L. Courtois (BEL)/N. Feber (BEL)	L. Davenport (USA)/C. Rubin (USA)	6–1 5–7 6–4		

INTERNATIONAL WIMBLEDON JUNIOR CHAMPIONSHIPS

The event originated as an invitation tournament, boys' singles in 1947 and girls' singles in 1948. It became a championship event in 1975.

BOY'S SINGLES

1948 S. Stockenberg (SWE)	1957 J. I. Tattersall (GBR)	1966 V. Korotkov (URS)

1949 S. Stockenberg (SWE)	1958 E. Buchholz (USA)	1967 M. Orantes (ESP)
1950 J. A. T. Horn (GBR)	1959 T. Lejus (URS)	1968 J. G. Alexander (AUS)
1951 J. Kupferburger (RSA)	1960 A. R. Mandelstam (RSA)	1969 B. Bertram (RSA)
1952 R. K. Wilson (GBR)	1961 C. E. Graebner (USA)	1970 B. Bertram (RSA)
1953 W. A. Knight (GBR)	1962 S. Matthews (GBR)	1971 R. Kreiss (USA)
1954 R. Krishnan (IND)	1963 N. Kalogeropoulous (GRE)	1972 B. Borg (SWE)
1955 M. P. Hann (GBR)	1964 I. El Shafei (EGY)	1973 W. Martin (USA)
1956 R. Holmberg (USA)	1965 V. Korotkov (URS)	1974 W. Martin (USA)

	WINNER	RUNNER–UP	SCORE		
1975	C. J. Lewis (NZL)	R. Ycaza (ECU)	6–1	6–4	
1976	H. Gunthardt (SUI)	P. Elter (FRG)	6–4	7–5	
1977	V. Winitsky (USA)	E. Teltscher (USA)	6–1	1–6	8–6
1978	I. Lendl (TCH)	J. Turpin (USA)	6–3	6–4	
1979	R. Krishnan (IND)	D. Siegler (USA)	6–3	6–4	
1980	T. Tulasne (FRA)	H. D. Beutel (FRG)	6–4	3–6	6–4
1981	M. Anger (USA)	P. Cash (AUS)	7–6	7–5	
1982	P. Cash (AUS)	H. Sundstrom (SWE)	6–4	6–7	6–3
1983	S. Edberg (SWE)	J. Frawley (AUS)	6–3	7–6	
1984	M. Kratzman (AUS)	S. Kruger (SAF)	6–4	4–6	6–3
1985	L. Lavalle	E. Velez (MEX)	6–4	6–4	
1986	E. Velez (MEX)	J. Sanchez (ESP)	6–3	7–5	
1987	D. Nargiso (ITA)	J. Stoltenberg (AUS)	7–6	6–4	
1988	N. Pereira (VEN)	G. Raoux (FRA)	7–6	6–2	
1989	N. Kulti (SWE)	T. Woodbridge (AUS)	6–4	6–3	
1990	L. Paes (IND)	M. Ondruska (RSA)	7–6	6–2	
1991	T. Enqvist (SWE)	M. Joyce (USA)	6–4	6–3	
1992	D. Skoch (TCH)	B. Dunn (USA)	6–4	6–3	

GIRL'S SINGLES

1948 O. Miskova (TCH)	1957 M. Arnold (USA)	1966 B. Lindstrom (FIN)
1949 C. Mercelis (BEL)	1958 S. M. Moore (USA)	1967 J. Salome (HOL)
1950 L. Cornell (GBR)	1959 J. Cross (RSA)	1968 K. Pigeon (USA)
1951 L. Cornell (GBR)	1960 K. Hantze (USA)	1969 K. Sawamatsu (JAP)
1952 ten Bosch (HOL)	1961 G. Baksheeva (URS)	1970 S. Walsh (USA)
1953 D. Kilian (RSA)	1962 G. Baksheeva (URS)	1971 M. Kroschina (URS)
1954 V. A. Pitt (GBR)	1963 D. M. Salfati (RSA)	1972 I. Kloss (RSA)
1955 S. M. Armstrong (GBR)	1964 P. Barkowicz (USA)	1973 A. Kiyomura (USA)
1956 A. S. Haydon (GBR)	1965 O. Morozova (URS)	1974 M. Jausovec (YUG)

	WINNER	RUNNER–UP	SCORE		
1975	N. Y. Chmyreva (URS)	R. Marsikova (TCH)	6–4	6–3	
1976	N. Y. Chmyreva (URS)	M. Kruger (SAF)	6–3	2–6	6–1
1977	L. Antonoplis (USA)	Mareen Louie (USA)	6–5	6–1	
1978	T. A. Austin (USA)	H. Mandlikova (TCH)	6–0	3–6	6–4
1979	M. L. Piatek (USA)	A. Moulton (USA)	6–1	6–3	
1980	D. Freeman (AUS)	S. Leo (AUS)	7–6	7–5	
1981	Z. Garrison (USA)	R. Uys (SAF)	6–4	3–6	6–0
1982	C. Tanvier (FRA)	H. Sukova (TCH)	6–2	7–5	
1983	P. Paradis (FRA)	P. Hy (HKG)	6–2	6–1	
1984	A. N. Croft (GBR)	E. Reinach (SAF)	3–6	6–3	6–2
1985	A. Holikova (TCH)	J. Byrne (AUS)	7–5	6–1	
1986	N. Zvereva (URS)	L. Meskhi (URS)	2–6	6–2	9–7
1987	N. Zvereva (URS)	J. Halard (FRA)	6–4	6–4	
1988	B. Schultz (HOL)	E. Derly (FRA)	7–6	6–1	
1989	A. Strnadova (TCH)	M. McGrath (USA)	6–2	6–3	
1990	A. Strnadova (TCH)	K. Sharpe (AUS)	6–2	6–4	
1991	B. Rittner (GER)	E. Makarova (URS)	6–7	6–2	6–3
1992	C. Rubin (USA)	L. Courtois (BEL)	6–2	7–5	

BOY'S DOUBLES

	WINNERS	RUNNERS–UP	SCORE		
1982	P. Cash (AUS)/F. Frawley (AUS)	R. Leach (USA)/J. Ross (USA)	6–3	6–2	
1983	M. Kratzman (AUS)/S. Youl (AUS)	M. Nastase (RUM)/O. Rahnasto (FIN)	6–4	6–4	
1984	R. Brown (USA)/R. Weiss (USA)	M. Kratzman (AUS)/J. Svensson (SWE)	1–6	6–4	11–9
1985	A. Moreno (MEX)/J. Yzaga (PER)	P. Korda (TCH)/C. Suk (TCH)	7–6	6–4	
1986	T. Carbonell (ESP)/P. Korda (TCH)	S. Barr (AUS)/H. Karrasch (CAN)	6–1	6–1	

1987	J. Stoltenberg (AUS)/T. Woodbridge (AUS)	D. Nargiso (ITA)/E. Rossi (ITA)	6–3	7–6	
1988	J. Stoltenberg (AUS)/T. Woodbridge (AUS)	D. Rikl (TCH)/T. Zdrazila (TCH)	6–4	1–6	7–6
1989	J. Palmer (USA)/J. Stark (USA)	J.–L. De Jager (RSA)/W. Ferreira (RSA)	7–6	7–6	
1990	S. Lareau (CAN)/S. LeBlanc (CAN)	C. Marsh (RSA)/M. Ondruska (RSA)	7–6	4–6	6–3
1991	K. Alami (MAR)/G. Rusedski (CAN)	J–L. De Jager (RSA)/A. Medvedev (URS)	1–6	7–6	6–4
1992	S. Baldas (AUS)/S. Draper (AUS)	M. Bhupathi (IND)/N. Kirtane (IND)	6–1	4–6	9–7

GIRL'S DOUBLES

	WINNERS	RUNNERS–UP	SCORE		
1982	B. Herr (USA)/P. Barg (USA)	B. S. Gerken (USA)/G. Rush (USA)	6–1	6–4	
1983	P. Fendick (USA)/P. Hy (HKG)	C. Anderholm (SWE)/H. Olsson (SWE)	6–1	7–5	
1984	C. Kuhlman (USA)/S. Rehe (USA)	V. Milvidskaya (URS)/L. Savchenko (URS)	6–3	5–7	6–4
1985	L. Field (AUS)/J. Thompson (AUS)	E. Reinach (SAF)/J. Richardson (NZL)	6–1	6–2	
1986	M. Jaggard (AUS)/L. O'Neill (AUS)	L. Meskhi (URS)/N. Zvereva (URS)	7–6	6–4	
1987	N. Medvedeva (URS)/N. Zvereva (URS)	I. S. Kim (KOR)/P. M. Modena (HKG)	2–6	7–5	6–0
1988	J. Faull (AUS)/R. McQuillan (AUS)	A. Dechaume (FRA)/E. Derly (FRA)	4–6	6–2	6–3
1989	J. Capriati (USA)/M. McGrath (USA)	A. Strnadova (TCH)/E. Sviglerova (TCH)	6–4	6–2	
1990	K. Habsudova (TCH)/A. Strnadova (TCH)	N. Pratt (AUS)/K. Sharpe (AUS)	6–2	6–4	
1991	C. Barclay (AUS)/L. Zaltz (ISR)	J. Limmer (AUS)/A. Woolcock (AUS)	6–4	6–4	
1992	P. Nelson (USA)/J. Steven (USA)	M. Avotins (AUS)/L. McShea (AUS)	2–6	6–4	6–3

US INTERNATIONAL JUNIOR CHAMPIONSHIPS

BOY'S SINGLES

	WINNER	RUNNER–UP	SCORE		
1974	W. Martin (USA)	F. Taygan (USA)	6–4	6–2	
1975	H. Schonfield (USA)	C. J. Lewis (NZL)	6–4	6–3	
1976	Y. Ycaza (ECU)	J. L. Clerc (ARG)	6–4	5–7	6–0
1977	V. Winitsky (USA)	E. Teltscher (USA)	6–4	6–4	
1978	P. Hjertquist (SWE)	S. Simonsson (SWE)	7–6	1–6	7–6
1979	S. Davis (USA)	J. Gunnarsson (SWE)	6–3	6–1	
1980	M. Falberg (USA)	E. Korita (USA)	6–0	6–2	
1981	T. Hogstedt (SWE)	H. Schwaier (FRG)	7–5	6–3	
1982	P. Cash (AUS)	G. Forget (FRA)	6–3	6–3	
1983	S. Edberg (SWE)	S. Youl (AUS)	6–2	6–4	
1984	M. Kratzman (AUS)	B. Becker (FRG)	6–3	7–6	
1985	T. Trigueiro (USA)	J. Blake (USA)	6–2	6–3	
1986	J. Sanchez (ESP)	F. Davin (ARG)	6–2	6–2	
1987	D. Wheaton (USA)	A. Cherkasov (URS)	7–5	6–0	
1988	N. Pereira (VEN)	N. Kulti (SWE)	6–1	6–2	
1989	J. Stark (USA)	N. Kulti (SWE)	6–4	6–1	
1990	A. Gaudenzi (ITA)	M. Tillstroem (SWE)	6–2	4–6	7–6
1991	L. Paes (IND)	K. Alami (MAR)	6–4	6–4	
1992	B. Dunn (USA)	N. Behr (ISR)	7–5	6–2	

GIRL'S SINGLES

	WINNER	RUNNER–UP	SCORE		
1974	I. Kloss (SAF)	M. Jausovec (YUG)	6–4	6–3	
1975	N. T. Chmyreva (URS)	G. Stevens (SAF)	6–7	6–2	6–2
1976	M. Kruger (SAF)	L. Romanov (RUM)	6–3	7–5	
1977	C. Casabianca (ARG)	L. Antonoplis (USA)	6–3	2–6	6–2
1978	L. Siegel (USA)	I. Madruga (ARG)	6–4	6–4	
1979	A. Moulton (USA)	M. L. Piatek (USA)	7–6	7–6	
1980	S. Mascarin (USA)	K. Keil (USA)	6–3	6–4	
1981	Z. Garrison (USA)	K. Gompert (USA)	6–0	6–3	
1982	B. Herr (USA)	G. Rush (USA)	6–3	6–1	
1983	E. Minter (AUS)	M. Werdel (USA)	6–3	7–5	
1984	K. Maleeva (BUL)	N. Sodupe (USA)	6–1	6–2	
1985	L. Garrone (ITA)	A. Holikova (TCH)	6–2	7–6	
1986	E. Hakami (USA)	S. Stafford (USA)	6–2	6–1	
1987	N. Zvereva (URS)	S. Birch (USA)	6–0	6–4	
1988	C. Cunningham (USA)	R. McQuillan (AUS)	6–3	6–1	
1989	J. Capriati (USA)	R. McQuillan (AUS)	6–2	6–3	
1990	M. Maleeva (BUL)	N. Van Lottum (FRA)	7–5	6–2	
1991	K. Habsudova (TCH)	A. Mall (USA)	6–1	6–3	
1992	L. Davenport (USA)	J. Steven (USA)	6–2	6–2	

BOY'S DOUBLES

	WINNERS	RUNNERS–UP	SCORE		
1982	J. Canter (USA)/M. Kures (USA)	P. Cash (AUS)/J. Frawley (AUS)	7–6	6–3	
1983	M. Kratzman (AUS)/S. Youl (AUS)	P. McEnroe (USA)/B. Pearce (USA)	6–1	7–6	
1984	L. Lavelle (MEX)/M. Nastase (RUM)	J. Icaza (PER)/A. Moreno (MEX)	7–6	1–6	6–1
1985	J. Blake (USA)/D. Yates (USA)	P. Flynn (USA)/D. McPherson (USA)	3–6	6–3	6–4
1986	T. Carbonell (ESP)/J. Sanchez (ESP)	J. Tarnago (USA)/D. Wheaton (USA)	6–4	1–6	6–1
1987	G. Ivanisevic (YUG)/D. Nargiso (ITA)	Z. Ali (IND)/B. Steven (NZL)	3–6	6–4	6–3
1988	J. Stark (USA)/J. Yoncey (USA)	M. Boscatta (ITA)/S. Pescosolido (ITA)	7–6	7–5	
1989	W. Ferreira (RSA)/G. Stafford (RSA)	M. Damm (TCH)/J. Kodes (TCH)	6–3	6–4	
1990	M. Renstroem (SWE)/M. Tillstroem (SWE)	S. LeBlanc (CAN)/G. Rusedski (CAN)	6–7	6–3	6–4
1991	K. Alami (MAR)/J–L. De Jager (RSA)	M. Joyce (USA)/V. Spadea (USA)	6–4	6–7	6–1
1992	J. Jackson (USA)/E. Taino (USA)	M. Rios (CHI)/G. Silberstein (CHI)	6–3	6–7	6–4

GIRL'S DOUBLES

	WINNERS	RUNNERS–UP	SCORE		
1982	P. Barg (USA)/B. Herr (USA)	A. Hulbert (AUS)/B. Randall (AUS)	1–6	7–5	7–6
1983	A. Hulbert (AUS)/B. Randall (AUS)	N. Riva (URS)/L. Savchenko (URS)	6–4	6–2	
1984	G. Sabatini (ARG)/M. Paz (MEX)	S. MacGregor (USA)/S. London (USA)	6–4	3–6	6–2
1985	R. Zrubakova (TCH)/A. Holikova (TCH)	P. Tarabini (ARG)/M. Perez Roldan (ARG)	6–4	2–6	7–5
1986	R. Zrubakova (TCH)/J. Novotna (TCH)	E. Brukhovets (URS)/L. Meskhi (URS)	6–4	6–2	
1987	M. McGrath (USA)/K. Po (USA)	Il–Soon Kim (KOR)/Shi–Ting Wang (TPE)	6–4	7–5	
1988	M. McGrath (USA)/K. Po (USA)	K. Caverzasio (ITA)/L. Lapi (ITA)	6–3	6–1	
1989	J. Capriati (USA)/M. McGrath (USA)	J. Faull (AUS)/R. McQuillan (AUS)	6–0	6–3	
1990	K. Godridge (AUS)/K. Sharpe (AUS)	E. deLone (USA)/L. Raymond (USA)	4–6	7–5	6–2
1991	K. Godridge (AUS)/N. Pratt (AUS)	A. Carlsson (SWE)/C. Cristea (ROM)	7–6	7–5	
1992	L. Davenport (USA)/N. London (USA)	K. Schlukebit (USA)/J. Steven (USA)	7–5	6–7	6–4

WORLD YOUTH CUP
International Team Championship for boys and girls aged 16 and under. Early rounds played zonally.

BOY'S FINALS
1985 Australia d. USA 2–1, Kobe Japan: R. Fromberg lost to F. Montana 2–6 2–6; S. Barr d. J. A. Falbo 6–4 6–4; Barr/J. Stoltenberg d. Montana/Falbo 4–6 6–7 7–5.
1986 Australia d. USA 2–1, Tokyo, Japan: J. Stoltenberg d. J. Courier 6–2 6–4; R. Fromberg lost to M. Chang 4–6 4–6; Stoltenberg/T. Woodbridge d. Courier/Kass 7–6 6–2.
1987 Australia d. Netherlands 3–0, Freiburg, West Germany: T. Woodbridge d. P. Dogger 7–5 3–6 6–2; J. Anderson d. F. Wibier 6–0 6–1; J. Morgan/Woodbridge d. Dogger/Wibier 6–3 6–2.
1988 Czechoslovakia d. USA 2–1, Perth, Australia: J. Kodes d. J. Leach 7–6 6–2; M. Damm d. B. MacPhie 6–2 6–7 6–4; Damm/L. Hovorka lost to W. Bull/Leach 4–6 4–6.
1989 West Germany d. Czechoslovakia 2–1, Asuncion, Paraguay: S. Gessner lost to L. Thomas 5–7 5–7; G. Paul d. P. Gazda 6–4 6–4; Paul/D. Prinosil d. Gazda/Thomas 7–5 6–1.
1990 USSR d. Australia 2–1, Rotterdam, Netherlands: D. Thomashevitch d. T. Vasiliadis 6–3 6–2; A. Medvedev lost to G. Doyle 6–2 4–6 5–7; E. Kafelnikov/Medvedev d. Doyle/B. Sceney 7–6 6–3.
1991 Spain d. Czechoslovakia 2–1, Barcelona, Spain: G. Corrales d. D. Skock 7–5 7–5; A. Costa lost to F. Kascak 4–6 5–7; Corrales /Costa d. Kascak/Skock 6–4 6–2.
1992 France d. Germany 2–1, Barcelona, Spain: M. Boye d. A. Nickel 7–5 0–6 6–3; N. Escude lost to R. Nicklish 2–6, 6–3, 3–6; Boye/Escude d. Nickel/Nicklish 6–7 6–0 6–3.

GIRLS' FINALS
1985 Czechoslovakia d. Australia 3–0, Kobe, Japan: J. Pospisilova d. S. McCann 6–4 6–4; R. Zrubakova d. N. Provis 7–6 7–5; Pospisilova/Zrubakova d. Provis/W. Frazer 7–5 6–4.
1986 Belgium d. Czechoslovakia 2–1, Tokyo, Japan: A. Devries d. R. Zrubakova 6–3 6–4; S. Wasserman d. P. Langrova 6–4 7–5; Devries/C. Neuprez lost to Langrova/Zrubakova 4–6 2–6.
1987 Australia d. USSR 2–1, Freiburg, West Germany: J. Faull lost to N. Medvedeva 6–4 2–6 2–6; R. McQuillan d. E. Brioukhovets 3–6 6–2 6–3; Faull/McQuillan d. Brioukhovets/Medvedeva 6–3 6–1.
1988 Australia d. Argentina 3–0, Perth, Australia: K. A. Guse d. F. Haumuller 7–6 6–4; L. Guse d. C. Tessi 7–6 1–6 6–2; K. A. Guse/K. Sharpe d. I. Gorrachategui/Tessi 6–0 6–2.
1989 West Germany d. Czechoslovakia 2–1, Asuncion, Paraguay: M. Skulj–Zivec d. K. Matouskova 6–0 7–5; A. Huber d. K. Habsudova 6–0 6–3; K. Duell/Skulj–Zivec lost to Habsudova/P. Kucova 3–6 0–6.
1990 Netherlands d. USSR 2–1, Rotterdam, Netherlands: P. Kamstra d. I. Soukhova 6–1 7–6; L. Niemantsverdriet lost to T. Ignatieva 0–6 6–1 4–6; Kamstra/Niemantsverdriet d. Ignatieva/Soukhova 6–3 4–6 6–1.
1991 Germany d. Paraguay 2–1, Barcelona, Spain: H. Rusch lost to L. Schaerer 6–7 3–6; M. Kochta d. R de los Rios 6–3 6–1; H. Freye/Kochta d. de los Rios/Schaerer 5–7 6–3 6–3.
1992 Belgium d. Argentina 3–0, Barcelona, Spain: L. Courtois d. L. Montalvo 6–1 6–3; N. Feber d. L. Reynares 1–6 6–4 6–1; Courtois/S. Deville d. M. Oliva/Montalvo 1–6 7–5 6–4.

NTT WORLD JUNIOR TENNIS EVENT
International Team Championship for boys and girls aged 14 and under.

BOY'S FINALS
1991 Spain d. Italy 2–1, Yamanakako, Japan: A. Martin d. C. Zoppi 6–2 7–6; J–A. Saiz d. P. Tabini 6–2 6–1; Martin/J–M. Vincente lost to A. Ciceroni/Tabini 7–5 4–6 6–8.
1992 Austria d. USA 2–1, Yamanakako, Japan: K. Trimmel d. C. Brill 4–6 6–2 6–2; M. Hipfl d. G. Adams 6–4 6–0; Trimmel/Hipfl lost to Abrams/R. Bryan 6–1 6–2.

GIRLS' FINALS
1991 Czechoslovakia d. Australia 3–0, Yamanakako, Japan: L. Cenkova d. A. Ellwood 7–5 6–2; A. Havrlkova d. A. Venkatesan 6–1 6–2; Cenkova/Havrlkova d. Ellwood/E. Knox 6–2 7–6.
1992 USA d. Australia 3–0, Yamanakako, Japan: M. Tu d. A. Ellwood 6–4 6–4; A. Basica d. R. Reid 6–3 6–7 6–4; Basica/A. Augustus d. Reid/S. Drake–Brockman 6–2 7–5.

ORANGE BOWL
International 18 and Under Championship played in Miami each December.

BOYS' SINGLES

	WINNER	RUNNER–UP	SCORE				
1974	W. Martin (USA)	T. Smid (TCH)	6–7	4–6	6–2	6–1	7–6
1975	F. Luna (ESP)	B. E. Gottfried (USA)	6–4	6–4			
1976	J. P. McEnroe (USA)	E. Teltscher (USA)	7–5	6–1			
1977	I. Lendl (TCH)	Y. Noah (FRA)	4–6	7–6	6–3		
1978	G. Urpi (ESP)	S. van der Merwe (SAF)	6–3	6–1			
1979	R. Viver (ECU)	P. Arraya (PER)	7–6	6–4			
1980	J. Nystrom (SWE)	C. Castqtellan (ARG)	7–5	7–6			
1981	R. Arguello (ARG)	R. Joaquim (BRA)	6–2	6–1			
1982	G. Forget (FRA)	J. Bardou (ESP)	7–5	2–6	6–1		
1983	K. Carlsson (SWE)	E. Sanchez (ESP)	6–2	6–4			
1984	R. Brown (USA)	J. Berger (USA)	6–3	6–3			
1985	C. Pistolesi (ITA)	B. Oresar (YUG)	6–2	6–0			
1986	J. Sanchez (ESP)	A. Parker (USA)	6–3	6–4			
1987	J. Courier (USA)	A. Cherkasov (URS)	6–3	6–2			
1988	M. Rosset (USA)	S. Pescosolido (ITA)	7–6	3–6	6–1		
1989	F. Meligeni (ARG)	G. Lopez (ESP)	7–6	7–6			
1990	A. Medvedev (URS)	O. Fernandez (MEX)	6–4	2–6	6–2		
1991	M. Charpentier (ARG)	K. Alami (MAR)	6–4	6–3			
1992	V. Spadea (USA)	G. Etlis(ARG)	7–6	6–3			

GIRLS' SINGLES

	WINNER	RUNNER–UPSCORE			
1974	L. Epstein (USA)	C. Penn (USA)	6–1	6–2	
1975	L. Epstein (USA)	S. McInerny (USA)	6–2	6–1	
1976	M. Kruger (SAF).	A. .E. Smith (USA)	2–6	6–3	6–4
1977	A. E. Smith (USA)	H. Strachonova (TCH)	7–6	7–5	
1978	A. Jaeger (USA)	R. Fairbank (SAF)	6–1	6–3	
1979	K. Horvath (USA)	P. Murgo (ITA)	7–5	6–0	
1980	S. Mascarin (USA)	R. Sasak (YUG)	6–3	3–6	6–4
1981	P. Barg (USA)	H. Fukarkova (TCH)	6–2	6–3	
1982	C. Bassett (CAN)	M. Maleeva (BUL)	6–4 ret'd		
1983	D. Spence (USA)	A. Cecchini (ITA)	2–6	7–5	6–4
1984	G. Sabatini (ARG)	K. Maleeva (BUL)	6–1	6–3	
1985	M. J. Fernandez (USA)	P. Tarabini (ARG)	7–5	6–1	
1986	P. Tarabini (ARG)	B. Fulco (ARG)	6–2	6–2	
1987	N. Zvereva (URS)	L. Lapi (ITA)	6–2	6–0	
1988	C. Cunningham (USA)	L. Lapi (ITA)	6–0	6–1	
1989	L. Spadea (USA)	S. Albinus (DEN)	6–0	6–3	
1990	P. Perez (ESP)	S. Ramon (ESP)	6–1	7–6	
1991	E. Likhovtseva (URS)	M–J. Gaidono (ARG)	7–6	6–1	
1992	B. Mulej (SLO)	R. De Los Rios (PAR)	7–5	7–5	

GALEA CUP
International Men's Team Competition for players aged 20 and under.
FINAL ROUNDS
Played at Deauville
1950 Italy d. France 4–1: U. Bergamo d. R. L. Haillet 6–2 6–3, d. A. Lemyze 8–10 7–5 7–5; F. Gardini d. Lemyze 6–1 6–2; A. Parri lost to F. Nys 3–6 2–6; Gardini/H. Clerici d. Lemyze/Nys 6–1 6–3.

1951 *France d. West Germany 5–0:* A. Lemyze d. B. Pottinger 8–6 10–8; R. L. Haillet d. F. Feldbausch 6–4 6–4; G. Pilet d. C. Biederlack 1–6 6–2 6–2; P. Darmon d. J. Gulcz 6–4 1–6 6–1; Haillet/Lemyze d. Feldbausch/Pottinger 6–1 6–3 6–1. *Played at Vichy*

1952 *Italy d. France 4–1:* N. Pietrangeli d. X. Perreau–Saussine 6–8 6–2 6–2, d. G. Pilet 7–5 6–1; A. Maggi lost to Pilet 3–6 6–2 3–6, d. Perreau–Saussine 6–4 7–5; Maggi/Pietrangeli d. J. N. Grinda/Pilet 10–8 6–3 6–3.

1953 *France d. Italy 4–1:* G. Pilet d. N. Pietrangeli 5–7 6–1 6–0, d. S. Jacobini 6–2 6–4; J. N. Grinda d. Jacobini 6–0 6–2, d. Pietrangeli 6–4 6–1; P. Darmon/Pilet lost to M. Pirro/Pietrangeli 3–6 5–7 7–9.

1954 *Italy d. Yugoslavia 3–2:* S. Jacobini d. L. Jagec 6–2 7–5, d. L. Backor 6–3 4–6 7–5; M. Pirro lost to Backor 6–3 4–6 4–6, lost to Jagec 0–6 5–7; Jacobsini/Pirro d. Backor/Jagec 10–8 4–6 6–4 6–3.

1955 *Italy d. Spain 5–0:* S. Jacobini d. A. Gimeno 3–6 6–3 6–4; F. Bonetti d. J. Moure 6–1 6–4; G. Morelli d. Moure 6–2 6–4; M. Drisaldi d. M. Santana 6–4 6–4; Drisaldi/Jacobini d. A. Arilla/Gimeno 6–3 6–4 2–6 6–1.

1956 *Spain d. Italy 4–1:* M. Santana d. F. Bonetti 6–3 5–7 7–5, d. G. Bonairi 4–6 6–5 7–5; A. Gimeno d. Bonetti 6–3 6–2, d. Bonairi 5–7 6–2 6–3: A. Arilla/A. Gimeno lost to M. Drisaldi/A. Maggi 6–1 4–6 3–6 3–6.

1957 *Spain d. Italy 4–1:* M. Santana d. G. Morelli 9–7 6–4, d. E. Casini 6–4; A. Gimeno d. F. Bonetti 6–3 6–4; J. L. Arilla lost to Morelli 3–6 6–8; A. Arilla/Gimeno d. Bonetti/A. Maggi 6–4 6–3 6–3.

1958 *Spain d. West Germany 3–2:* M. Santana d. W. Bungert 6–3 7–5 4–6 6–0, lost to D. Eklebe 1–6 5–7 6–1 3–6; A. Arilla d. Eklebe 6–1 9–7 4–6 7–5; J. Gisbert lost to W. Stuck 0–6 2–6 0–6; A. Arilla/Santana d. Eklebe/Stuck 7–6 6–3 6–3.

1959 *West Germany d. USSR 4–1:* W. Stuck d. A. Pontanin 6–3 6–0 6–1, d. T. Lejus 6–4 6–1 6–0; W. Bungert d. Lejus 6–2 6–3 6–2; L. Sanders lost to Pontanin 4–6 3–6 6–1 7–5 2–6; Bungert/Stuck d. Lejus/S. Likachev 6–4 5–7 3–6 7–5 6–4.

1960 *France d. USSR 3–2:* A. Bresson d. S. Likachev 6–3 6–2 6–4, d. T. Lejus 2–6 3–6 6–3 6–0 6–3; C. Duxin lost to Lejus 5–7 4–6 8–10, lost to Likachev 2–6 3–6 1–6; D. Contet/F. Jauffret d. Lejus/Likachev 8–6 6–2 4–6 6–2.

1961 *France d. Spain 3–2:* C. Duxin lost to J. Gisbert 1–6 3–6 2–6, d. T. Casado 6–2 6–1 6–1; F. Jauffret d. Casado 6–3 6–2 6–3, lost to Gisbert 6–1 4–6 3–6 4–3–6; D. Contet/Jauffret d. J. L. Arilla/Gisbert 6–2 6–0 6–2.

1962 *France d. USSR 3–2:* J. C. Barclay d. S. Mdzinarichvili 6–4 6–2 6–4, d. A. Metreveli 6–4 6–2 8–6; F. Jauffret lost Metreveli 6–3 2–6 3–6 4–6, d. Mdzinarichvili 8–6 6–1 0–6 6–2; C. Duxin/Jauffret lost to Mdzinarichvili/Metreveli 8–6 3–6 4–6 5–7.

1963 *Czechoslovakia d. Italy 3–2:* S. Koudelka lost to G. Maioli 3–6 6–4 3–6 5–7; d. G. Di Maso 6–4 6–2 6–2; M. Holececk d. Di Maso 6–4 11–9 6–4, d. Maioli 6–0 6–3 8–6; Holecek/Koudelka lost to Di Maso/Maioli 6–8 4–6 9–7 7–9.

1964 *USSR d. Czechoslovakia 3–2:* A. Metreveli d. J. Kodes 6–3 6–3 4–6 17–15, d. S. Koudelka 6–1 6–4 6–1; A. Ivanov lost to Koudelka 6–4 8–10 6–8 2–6, lost to Kodes 7–5 6–4 8–10 6–8 3–6; Ivanov/Metreveli d. Koudelka/F. Pala 6–4 5–7 9–7 8–6.

1965 *Czechoslovakia d. USSR 3–2:* J. Kodes lost to A. Ivanov 5–7 6–3 6–3 2–6 1–6, d. V. Korotkov 6–2 5–7 7–5 6–1; M. Laudin d. Korotkov 6–2 9–7 6–0, lost to Ivanov 8–10 2–6 2–6; Kodes/J. Stoces d. Ivanov/Korotkov 6–2 6–3 6–1.

1966 *Czechoslovakia d. USSR 4–1:* J. Kodes d. S. Kakoulia 6–3 6–1 6–1; M. Laudin d. V. Korotkov 6–2 3–6 6–1 6–4, lost to Kakoulia 1–6 0–6 7–5 3–6; Kodes/J. Medonos d. A. Egorov/Korotkov 6–4 6–3 6–1.

1967 *France d. Great Britain 3–1:* J. B. Chanfreau d. G. Battrick 6–4 6–3 4–6 7–5, d. D. A. Lloyd 6–2 6–3 6–8 7–5; G. Goven d. D. A. Lloyd 3–6 6–2 6–1; Goven/Chanfreau d. Battrick/Lloyd 8–10 6–3 6–4 6–2.

1968 *Spain d. France 3–2:* M. Orantes d. G. Goven 6–4 6–2 6–3, d. P. Proisy 6–1 10–8 6–3; A. Munoz lost to Proisy 6–4 9–11 6–8 6–3 1–6, d. Goven 6–2 3–6 6–3 4–6 7–5; Munoz/Orantes lost to Goven/P. Dominguez 1–6 6–0 1–6 1–6.

1969 *Spain d. Czechoslovakia 3–2:* A. Munoz d. P. Hutka 1–6 6–3 6–3 6–3; M. Orantes d. J. Hrebec 6–2 6–4 7–5; J. Gisbert lost to Hutka 2–6 6–2 3–6 4–6; A. Muntanola lost to J. Pisecki 3–6 1–6 5–7; Munoz/Orantes d. Hrebec/Hutka 5–7 6–3 6–1 6–4.

1970 *Czechoslovakia d. Spain 3–2:* I. Pisecki lost to A. Munoz 7–5 4–6 4–6 2–6, d. A. Riba 6–1 6–2 6–2; J. Hrebec d. Riba 6–3 6–2 6–0, lost to Munoz 3–6 3–6 8–6 1–6; Hrebec/Pisecki d. Munoz/Riba 6–3 6–2 6–0.

1971 *Sweden d. France 5–0:* K. Johansson d. J. Lovera 6–1 0–6 6–1 6–3, d. E. Deblicker 10–12 6–4 6–3 1–6 7–5; T. Svensson d. Deblicker 6–2 6–2 6–2, d. Lovera 5–7 7–5 8–6; K./J. Johansson d. D. Naegelen/J. F. Caujoulle 6–4 6–4 6–2.

1972 *Great Britain d. Spain 4–1:* C. J. Mottram d. J. Herrera 6–1 4–6 6–0 2–6 7–5; S. Warboys d. J. Higueras 6–2 6–2 1–6 6–3, d. Herrera 6–3 6–2 0–6 2–6 7–5; J. M. Lloyd d. Higueras 6–2 10–8; Mottram/Warboys lost to Higueras/J. Moreno 6–3 3–6 4–6 6–1 5–7.

1973 *Spain d. Great Britain 4–1:* J. Higueras d. J. M. Lloyd 4–6 6–2 6–2 0–6 6–4; J. Moreno d. C. J. Mottram 3–6 3–6 6–3 6–1 6–3, d. Lloyd 6–1 6–1 6–3; Higueras/Moreno lost to S. Warboys/M. J. Farrell 7–9 3–6 2–6.

1974 *Czechoslovakia d. Spain 4–1:* P. Slozil d. S. Cabeza 6–4 6–2 6–1; T. Smid d. J. Soler 0–6 6–4 6–0 11–9, d. J. Garcia 6–3 1–6 6–3; J. Granat lost to A. Gimenez 4–6 2–6; Slozil/Smid d. Gimenez/Soler 6–4 6–2 6–4.

1975 *Czechoslovakia d. Spain 3–2:* T. Smid d. A. Gimenez 6–1 4–6 3–6 6–2 6–2, d. M. Mir 3–6 8–6 6–2 7–5; P. Slozil d. Mir 8–6 3–6 6–3 6–2, lost to A. Gimenez 4–6 8–6 1–6 5–7; Slozil/Smid lost to Gimenez/Mir 8–6 6–4 3–6 2–6 1–6.

1976 *West Germany d. Italy 3–2:* W. Zirngibl lost to F. Merlone 2–6 2–6 7–5 4–6, d. G. Ocleppo 6–1 6–1 6–4; P. Elter lost to Ocleppo 2–6 2–6 6–2 4–6, d. Merlone 6–3 3–6 6–4 6–4; U. Marten/K. Eberhard d. V. Vattuone/G. Marchetti 3–6 6–3 6–4 6–4.

1977 *Argentina d. France 3–2:* F. Dalla Fontana lost to C. Roger–Vasselin 4–6 6–1 4–6 4–6, d. C. Casa 6–3 7–6 6–3; J. L. Clerc lost to Casa 4–6 5–7 6–2 4–6, d. Roger–Vasselin 3–6 6–3 6–0 6–4; Clerc/A. Gattiker d. D. Bedel/Noah 2–6 4–6 7–5 6–1 6–4.

1978 *France d. Czechoslovakia 4–1:* Y. Noah d. D. Kulhaj 6–1 6–4 6–4; P. Portes d. I. Lendl 8–6 4–6 6–2 6–2; G. Morreton lost to Lendl 3–6 13–15; Portes d. M. Lacek 6–2 6–1; Morreton/Noah d. Kulhaj/Lendl 9–7 6–1 5–7 3–6 6–4.

1979 *France d. Czechoslovakia 3–2:* Y. Noah d. M. Lacek 6–3 6–1 6–1, d. D. Pohl 6–3 6–2 6–2; P. Portes lost to I. Lendl 1–6 3–6 5–7; T. Pham lost to Lacek 3–6 1–6; Noah/Portes d. Lacek/Lendl 14–12 5–7 8–7 6–7 5.

1980 *France d. Spain 3–2:* T. Tulasne d. A. Tous 6–4 6–3 6–2, d. J. B. Avendano 6–2 6–2 6–1; J. Potier lost to Avendano 6–8 2–6 2–6, lost to Tous 2–6 3–6; H. Leconte/Potier d. Avendano/Tous 6–0 7–5 3–6 6–1.

1981 *West Germany d. Australia 5–0:* C. Zipf d. G. Whitecross 5–7 7–5 9–11 6–2 6–2, d. C. Miller 8–6 3–6 11–9; H. D. Beutel d. Miller 3–6 8–6 6–2 6–1, d. Whitecross 6–4 6–2; Beutel/Zipf d. P. Doohan/Miller 6–4 7–5 6–2.

1982 *Australia d. Spain 3–2:* P. Cash d. A. Tous 4–6 6–2 8–10 6–4 6–1, lost to S. Casal 0–6 1–6; C. Miller d. Casal 6–4 1–6 9–7 6–3, d. Tous 5–7 1–6; Cash/Miller d. Casal/M. Jaite 6–4 6–1 6–4.

1983 *France d. Spain 5–0:* G. Forget d. J. Bardou 6–2 6–2 5–7 4–6 10–8, d. M. Jaite 7–6 6–3; L. Courteau d. Jaite 6–4

10–8 3–6 6–2, d. Bardou 6–3 4–6 6–4; Courteau/Forget d. Bardou/Jaite 6–2 6–3 6–4.
1984 Czechoslovakia d. Argentina 4–1: M. Mecir d. G. Garetto 6–3 2–6 6–8 6–0 6–2, d. E. Masso 7–5 6–3; M. Vajda d. Masso 6–2 8–6 6–2, lost to Garetto 9–7 6–1; Mecir/K. Novacek d. Masso/Mena 6–4 6–4 6–1.
1985 Italy d. USA 3–2: P. Cane d. L. Jensen 6–2 6–1 8–6, d. R. Reneberg 6–3 6–0 6–4; C. Pistolesi lost to Reneberg 3–6 3–6 3–6, d. B. Pearce 10–8 4–6 4–6 6–1 6–1; Cane/M. Fioroni lost to Jensen/B. Pearce 1–6 6–3 1–6 2–6.
1986 Spain d. Czechoslovakia 3–2: J. Sanchez d. M. Strelba, d. P. Korda 6–2 6–3 6–2; F. Garcia lost to Strelba 4–6 12–14 8–10, d. Korda 1–6 6–4 6–4 10–8; Garcia/Sanchez lost to Korda/ C. Suk 11–13 4–6 3–6.
1987 France d. Czechoslovakia 3–1: O. Delaitre d. P. Korda 6–3 6–0, d. C. Suk 6–1 6–1; S. Grenier lost to P. Korda 7–6 2–6 11–13, d. C. Suk 6–3 6–2.
1988 Australia d. Spain 3–2: J. Stoltenberg d. J. Sanchez 6–3 3–6 6–4, lost to T. Carbonell 4–6 3–6; R. Fromberg lost to Sanchez 2–6 3–6, d. Carbonell 6–2 6–3; Stoltenberg/T. Woodbridge d. Carbonell/Sanchez 6–2 6–3.
1989 France d. Australia 3–2: A. Boetsch d. T. Woodbridge 6–1 6–1, d. J. Anderson 6–0 6–2; F. Fontang lost to Woodbridge 4–6 1–6, lost to Anderson 3–6 2–6; Boetsch/G. Raoux d. J. Morgan/Woodbridge 6–1 6–4.
1990 Spain d. Czechoslovakia 3–2: G. Lopez d. D. Rikl 7–6 6–3; d. C. Dosedel 6–3 6–2; J. Conde lost to Dosedel 6–7 5–7; E. Alvarez lost to D. Vacek 3–6 5–7; Lopez/Alvarez d. T. Zdrazila/Rikl 6–3 6–2.
Event ended.

VASCO VALERIO CUP
International Team Championship for boys aged 18 and under. Played zonally with the final stages in Lesa, Italy.

FINALS
1970 Sweden d. France 4–1: L. Johansson d. F. Caujolle 10–8 6–3; T. Svensson d. E. Naegelen 6–4 6–0; R. Norbeg lost to E. Deblicker 4–6 0–6; M. Stig d. A. Collinot 6–3 6–1; Johansson/Stig d. Deblicker/Naegelen 6–3 6–3.
1971 Italy d. West Germany 4–0: M. Consolini d. U. Pinner 6–2 1–0 ret'd; N. Gasparini d. R. Gehring 6–1 3–6 6–0; C. Borea d. A. Hongsag 3–6 6–4 6–3; C. Barazzutti v L. Jelitto 5–1 abandoned; Barazzutti/Gasparini d. Gehring/Jelitto 6–4 6–4.
1972 Czechoslovakia d. USSR 3–2: I. Hora lost to V. Borisov 6–4 7–9 5–7; P. Slozil d. A. Machavez 6–2 2–6 6–4; Slozil/J. Granat d. A. Bogomolov/Borisov 6–3 7–5; T. Smid lost to K. Pugaev 3–6 8–6 4–6; Granat d. Bogomolov 6–3 6–4.
1973 Czechoslovakia d. USSR 4–1: A. Jankowski lost to V. Borisov 6–4 2–3 ret'd; P. Slozil d. A. Machavez 6–3 5–7 6–4; J. Granat d. K. Pugaev 3–6 6–4 6–3; T. Smid d. V. Katsnelson 6–4 6–4; Jankowski/Slozil d. Borisov/Pugaev 6–8 10–8 6–3.
1974 Spain d. Italy 3–2: L. Fargas d. A. Meneschincheri 6–1 6–1; A. Capitan /M. Mir lost to A. Marchetti/A. Vattuone 6–3 4–6 3–6; M. Mir lost to G. Ocleppo 4–6 2–6; A. Torralbo d. Vattuone 9–11 6–4 6–3; Capitan d. G. Marchetti 8–6 3–6 6–3.
1975 Italy d. USSR 3–2: G. Ocleppo d. S. Baranov 7–5 6–5 ret'd; A. Spiga d. S. Molodoikov 6–4 6–8 6–0; A. Merlone d. V. Gruzman 6–2 0–6 6–3; A. Meneschincheri lost to S. Elerdashvili 9–11 4–6; Ocleppo/Merlone lost to Baranov/Gruzman 5–7 4–6.
1976 West Germany d. France 4–1: P. Elter d. P. Portes 6–3 6–2; W. Popp lost to Y. Noah 3–6 0–6; J. Henn d. J. Kuentz 6–2 6–2; A. Maurer d. G. Geniau 6–4 6–3; Elter/Popp d. G. Moretton/Noah 6–3 3–6 6–3.
1977 Italy d. Rumania 5–0: G. Rinaldini d. E. Pana 6–1 6–1; M. Rivaroli d. L. Mancas 6–2 6–4; N. Canessa d. A. Dirzu 6–3 2–6 6–4; P. Parrini d. F. Segarceanu 6–1 6–0; Canessa/Parrini d. Dirzu/Segarceanu 7–5 6–2.
1978 Sweden d. Italy 3–2: M. Wennberg d. F. Moscino 6–2 6–2; P. Hjertquist/S. Simonsson d. M. Alciati/C. Panatta 6–1 6–3; Hjertquist d. M. Ferrari 6–1 6–3; Simonsson lost to Alciati 4–6 1–6; A. Jarryd lost to Panatta 0–6 1–6.
1979 Sweden d. West Germany 4–1: S. Simonsson d. H. D. Beutel 6–4 6–0; T. Svensson d. C. Zipf 2–6 6–4 6–4; A. Jarryd d. K. Vogel 6–2 7–5; J. Gunnarsson d. A. Schulz 7–5 6–4; Simonsson/Svensson lost to Beutel/Zipf 3–6 6–2 6–8.
1980 Spain d. France 4–1: J. Aguilera d. T. Pham 6–4 1–6 6–3; A. Tous/S. Casal d. J. Potier/J. M. Piacentile 6–2 3–6 6–4; Tous lost to Potier 1–6 6–7; R. Mensua d. P. Kuchna 6–4 6–1; Casal d. Miacentile 6–1 6–1.
1981 Sweden d. Italy 3–2: H. Sundstrom d. S. Ercoli 6–4 6–2; J. Nystrom/M. Tideman lost to L. Botazzi/F. Cancellotti 6–1 3–6 4–6; Nystrom d. Botazzi 6–3 6–2; T. Hogstedt lost to Cancellotti 4–6 1–6; Tideman d. S. Colombo 6–2 7–6.
1982 Italy d. Spain 3–2: S. Ercoli lost to M. Jaite 2–6 6–7; M. Fiorini d. D. de Miguel 6–2 7–5; P. Cane d. E. Sanchez 6–1 3–6 6–4; M. Zampieri lost to J. Bardou 4–6 4–6; Cane/Fioroni d. Bardou/Jaite 4–6 6–3 8–6.
1983 Sweden d. Spain 4–1: J. Svensson d. G. R. Fernando 4–6 6–4 7–5; J./K. Carlsson d. D. de Miguel/J. Bardou 6–2 1–6 6–2; J. Carlsson lost to Bardou 4–6 2–6; K. Carlsson d. E. Sanchez 3–6 6–0 6–1; P. Lundgren d. L. F. Garcia 6–3 6–4.
1984 Italy d. France 3–1: F. Ricci d. G. Tournant 6–4 3–6 6–4; N. Devide d. P. Gardarein 6–3 6–4; I. Cappelloni d. O. Cayla 7–5 7–6; Gardarein/Winogradski d. Devide/Pistolesi 5–7 6–4 6–4.
1985 Italy d. Sweden 3–2: A. Baldoni lost to D. Engel 2–6 1–6; C. Pistolesi/S. Mezzadri d. C. Allgaardh/T. Nydahll 6–4 6–4; Pistolesi d. Allgaardh 6–3 6–4; U. Colombini d. C. Bergstrom 7–6 6–2; O. Camporese lost to U. Stenlund 0–6 3–6.
1986 Italy d. Spain 3–2: E. Rossi lost to J. Sanchez 6–7 4–6; O. Camporese lost to T. Carbonell 3–6 4–6; U. Pigato d. F. Anda 6–1 6–3; A. Baldoni d. F. Roig 7–5 6–4; Camporese/Rossi d. Carbonell/Sanchez 3–6 6–3 6–4.
1987 Czechoslovakia d. West Germany 2–0: D. Rikl d. C. Arriens 6–1 6–1; T. Zdrazila d. S. Nensel 6–1 4–6 6–2.
1988 Sweden d. Israel 3–0: N. Kulti d. R. Weidenfeld 7–6 6–2; L. Jonsson d. B. Merenstein 6–2 6–1; Kulti/M. Larsson d. Merenstein/O. Weinberg 6–3 3–6 6–4.
1989 Sweden d. West Germany 2–0: O. Kristiansson d. A. Kloodt 6–2 6–3; R. PettersAoson d. R. Leissler 6–2 6–1; D. Geivald/Kristiansson d. Kloodt/Leissler 6–7 6–1 6–2.
1990 Sweden d. USSR 2–1: M. Renstroem d. A. Rybalko 6–3 7–6; O. Ogorodov lost to R. Petterson 6–3 6–7 0–6; Renstroem/M. Tillstrom d. Ogordov/Rybalko 6–2 6–1
1991 Spain d. Germany 2–0: A. Berasategui d. S. Gessner 6–4 6–2; A. Corretja d. G. Paul 6–2 3–6 6–0.
1992 Spain d. Italy 2–0: A. Corretja d. M. Navarra 6–3 6–1; J. Gisbert d. M. Bertolini 6–1 7–6 (doubles not played)

JEAN BOROTRA CUP
International Team Championship for boys aged 16 and under; originally the Jean Becker Cup. Finals played in Le Touquet.

FINALS
1972 Spain d. France 4–1: M. Mir d. Ph. Gruthchet 6–3 6–2; F. Riba d. C. Freyss 6–2 1–6 6–4; A. Capitan d. R. Brunet

6–3 7–5; Masana/Mir lost to Frantz/Grutchet 6–4 6–7 3–6; Capitan/Riba d. Brunet/Freyss 7–5 3–6 9–7.
1973 Italy d. West Germany 3–2: M. Attolini lost to K. Eberhardt 1–6 1–6; G. Sileo d. P. Elter 7–5 6–4; M. Spiga d. U. Wellerdieck 6–2 7–5; Attolini/Sileo lost to Eberhardt/Elter 0–6 5–7; Mazzocchi/Spiga d. Liebtľial/WellerAdieck 6–3 6–2.
1974 West Germany d. Italy 4–1: Buchbinder d. G. Rinaldi 6–2 6–2; P. Elter d. Risi 6–0 6–1; A. Maurer d. Gardi 6–7 7–5 6–1; Buchbinder/W. Popp lost to Gardi/Rinaldi 6–2 6–7 8–10; Elter/Maurer d. Risi/M. Rivarolli 6–0 6–3.
1975 Czechoslovakia d. Italy 3–2: M. Lacek d. G. Rinaldini 7–5 6–1; I. Lendl d. A. Ciardi 6–1 6–3; J. Kucera d. P. Parreni 6–4 6–4; Lacek/Kucera lost to Parreni/A. Rivaroli 4–6 4–6; Lendl/A. Vantuch lost to Ciardi/Rinaldini 6–1 4–6 3–6.
1976 Sweden d. Czechoslovakia 3–2: P. Hjertquist lost to I. Lendl 6–0 3–6 4–6; S. Simonsson d. A. Vikopa 6–3 6–0; H. Johansson d. T. Pitra 6–3 6–2; Simonsson/A. Fritzner lost to Lendl/J. Kerezek 6–4 3–6 1–6; Hjertquist/Johansson d. Pitra/J. Vikopal 6–3 6–2.
1977 Italy d. Sweden 3–2: A. Costa d. A. Jarryd 7–5 6–2; A. Giacomini lost to S. Simonsson 1–6 1–6; A. Moscino d. S. Svensson 6–4 6–4; Giacomini/A. Odling lost to Simonsson/Jarryd 3–6 4–6; Costa/Moscino d. Svensson/M. Wennberg 6–2 6–4.
1978 Sweden d. France 3–2: S. Svensson d. T. Tulasne 6–4 6–2; H. Simonsson lost to J. Potier 6–3 2–6 7–9 disqualified; J. Gunnarsson d. T. Pham 6–2 5–7 6–2; M. Wilander lost to J. L. Cotard 2–6 7–5 4–6; Svensson/ Simonsson d. Cotard/J. M. Piacentile 6–3 6–1.
1979 Sweden d. France 4–1: J. Windahll lost to T. Tulasne 2–6 1–6; M. Wilander d. H. Leconte 6–2 1–6 6–3; T. Hogstedt d. P. Kuchna 6–2 6–1; J. Sjogren d. J. M. Piacentile 6–1 6–1; Hogstedt/Wilander d. Leconte/Piacentile 3–6 6–3 6–4.
1980 Sweden d. Czechoslovakia 3–0: M. Wilander d. M. Mecir 3–6 6–1 6–1; A. Mansson d. K. Novacek 6–3 6–3; H. Sundstrom/Wilander d. Mecir/B. Stankovic 6–3 3–0 ret'd.
1981 France d. Sweden 3–2: T. Benhabiles d. S. Edberg 6–4 6–4; F. Hamonet d. J. B. Svensson 6–0 6–2; T. Chamsion lost to P. Svensson 3–6 6–2 0–6; O. Cayla lost to A. Henricsson 6–1 4–6 3–6; Hamonet/G. Forget d. Edberg/P. Svensson 6–4 1–6 6–2.
1982 Sweden d. Spain 4–1: J. Svensson d. J. Maso 6–2 6–2; S. Edberg d. F. Garcia 6–4 6–4; P. Svensson d. J. Oltra 6–2 6–1; J. Carlsson lost to S. Castello 5–7 1–6; Edberg/P. Svensson d. Garcia/Oltra 6–2 6–1.
1983 Sweden d. USSR 3–2: D. Engel d. V. Gabritchidze 7–5 6–1; K. Carlsson d. A. Volkov 6–2 6–4; C. Allgaardh d. A. Tchernetsky 7–5 6–3; C. Bergstrom lost to I. Metreveli 6–0 6–7 3–6; Carlsson/Allgaardh d. Volkov/Metreveli 6–3 6–7 6–3.
1984 Italy d. Sweden 4–1: P. Chinellato lost to T. Nydhal 4–6 6–4 3–6; O. Camporese d. H. Holm 6–4 6–0; A. Baldoni d. A. Rosen 6–4 6–0; S. Sorensen d. N. Utgren 6–2 6–4; Baldoni/E. Rossi d. T. Nydal/P. Henricsson 7–6 1–6 6–3.
1985 Sweden d. France 3–2: P. Henricsson lost to A. Boetsch 3–6 2–6; P. Wennberg d. P. Ventura 6–4 6–0; N. Utgren d. S. Blanquie 6–1 6–2; M. Zeile d. C. Sebastiani 6–1 6–3; Henricsson/Utgren lost to Boetsch/R. Pedros 2–6 6–3 4–6.
1986 Italy d. Netherlands 3–2: F. Mordegan lost to P. Dogger 5–7 6–3 1–6; D. Nargiso lost to J. Eltingh 5–7 2–6; C. Caratti d. J. Siemerink 7–5 6–0; R. Furlan d. R. Heethius 7–5 5–7 7–5; Caratti/Nargiso d. Eltingh/Siemerink 4–6 7–5 6–3.
1987 Austria d. Italy 3–2: T. Buchmayer d. F. Pisilli 6–3 6–1; O. Fuchs lost to S. Pescosolido 4–6 1–6; H. Priller d. M. Ardinghi 6–3 6–4; G. Bohm lost to M. Boscatto 6–2 1–6 6–8; Buchmayer/Priller d. Boscatto/Pescosolido 1–6 6–4 6–4.
1988 Sweden d. Czechoslovakia 3–2: J. Alven d. M. Damm 6–1 6–4; R. Pettersson d. J. Kodes 2–6 7–5 6–3; J. Sunnemark lost to L. Hovorka 6–3 0–6 3–6; M. Renstroem d. P. Gazda 6–1 2–6 6–2; Alven/Pettersson lost to Damm/Horkova 0–6 6–3 6–7.
1989 Czechoslovakia d. West Germany 4–1: P. Gazda d. A. Kriebel 7–5 6–3; R. Hanak d. D. Prinosil 6–0 6–4; L. Thomas d. J. Weinzierl 6–2 6–4; B. Galik d. M. Kohlmann 6–4 6–2; Gazda/Thomas lost to M. Kuckenbecker/ Prinosil 6–4 3–6 4–6.
1990 France d. Spain 3–2: N. Kischkewitz d. J. Gisbert 6–4 6–2; P. Lasserre d. A. Corretja 6–4 6–3; J. Hanquez lost to J. Martinez 7–6 5–7 2–6; O. Tauma d. G. Corrales 3–6 6–4 6–0; Kischkewitz/Tauma lost to Corretja/Gisbert 3–6 2–6.
1991 Spain d. Czechoslovakia 4–1: A. Costa d. F. Kascak 6–4 6–2; G. Corrales d. P. Pala 6–7 6–3; R. Carretero d. D. Skoch 5–7 7–6 7–5; J. Balcells lost to D. Miketa 5–7 6–1 1–6; Corrales/Costa d. Kascak/Pala 6–1 6–4.
1992 France d. Sweden 2–1: N. Escude d. M. Norman 2–6 6–4 6–4; M. Huard lost to A. Stenman 5–7 5–7; Esude/Huard d. Norman/M. Sjoquist 6–2 6–2.

DEL SOL CUP
International Team Championship for boys aged 14 and under. Played in zones with finals in Barcelona.

FINALS
1979 Italy d. France 3–2: M. Fioroni d. M. Cartier 6–0 6–2; G. Possani d. G. Forget 6–7 7–5 6–3; A. Paris lost to T. Benhabiles 0–6 5–7; L. Baglioni lost to F. Hamonet 0–6 0–6; Possani/Paris d. Benhabiles/Hamonet 6–1 6–4.
1980 Sweden d. Italy 4–1: P. Svensson d. R. Salemme 6–4 7–6; S. Edberg d. F. Ricci 7–5 6–3; R. Lofquist d. F. Filippi 6–3 6–4; J. Svensson lost to P. Poggioli 4–6 2–6; Edberg/P. Svensson d. Filippi/A. Vacca 6–4 6–1.
1981 Sweden d. Israel 3–2: T. Johansson lost to A. Naor 2–6 6–7; C. Allgaardh lost to G. Blom 4–6 6–2 4–6; K. Carlsson d. R. Weinberg 6–0 6–0; C. Bergstrom d. M. Osherov 2–6 7–5 7–5; Allgaardh/Carlsson d. Blom/ Osherov 6–2 6–1.
1982 Sweden d. West Germany 4–1: H. Kolm d. U. Kraft 6–1 6–0; K. Carlsson d. O. Sachau 6–0 6–0; P. Ekstrand lost to I. Kroll 0–6 2–6; T. Nydahl d. C. Guhl 6–0 1–6 6–1; Carlsson/Nydahl d. Guhl/Kraft 6–1 6–4.
1983 Sweden d. West Germany 3–2: U. Persson d. H. Stang 6–2 6–2; P. Henricsson d. P. Pfleger 6–4 6–1; U. Eriksson lost to U. Kraft 7–6 3–6 2–6; P. Wennberg lost to L. Orzessek 2–6 3–6; Henricsson/M. Urgren d. Kraft/Orzessek 6–2 6–3.
1984 West Germany d. Spain 4–1: S. Scheider d. F. Alfonso 6–3 4–6 7–5; F. Loddenkemper/A. Thoms d. J. Olivert/S. Bruguera 6–3 6–2; Loddenkemper d. Olivert 7–6 7–6; D. Richter d. A. Martinez 6–1 7–5; A. Thoms lost to Bruguera 3–6 6–2 4–6.
1985 Austria d. Italy 5–0: G. Bohm d. F. Casa 6–4 6–2; T. Buchmayer/O. Fuchs d. S. Pescosolido/F. Pisilli 6–2 6–3; Buchmayer d. Pescosolido 6–3 4–6 6–4; Fuchs d. Pisilli 6–3 7–6; H. Prilled d. M. Ardinghi 6–2 6–4.
1986 Sweden d. Yugoslavia 4–1: J. Alven d. S. Hirszon 6–3 6–4; R. Pettersson lost to B. Trupy 2–6 3–6; M. Ekstrand d. A. Tonejc 3–6 6–4 6–3; J. Henriksson d. S. Ban 6–4 7–6; Alven/Pettersson d. Hirszon/Trupej 6–2 6–4.
1987 West Germany d. Austria 4–1: J. Weinzierl lost to R. Wawra 3–6 2–6; G. Paul d. N. Patzak 6–0 6–1; S.

Petraschek d. J. Knowle 3–6 6–2 6–2; A. Kriebel d. H. Kugler 6–2 6–3; Paul/Petraschek d. Knowle/Wawra 4–6 6–2 6–2.
1988 West Germany d. Spain 3–2: M. Kohlman d. A. Corretja 6–2 6–1; T. Ruhle lost to A. Bragado 0–6 3–6; J. Schors
d. J. Martinez 6–2 6–4; G. Hecht lost to J. Velasco 6–0 5–7 1–6; Kohlman/M. Nacke d. Bragado/Corretja 7–6 7–6.
1989 France d. Sweden 4–1: N. Bertsch d. T.A Johansson 7–5 7–6; A. De Cret d. K. Bergh 6–4 6–2; S. Martinez d. P.
Salasca 6–2 6–3; M. Dallay d. D. Winberg 7–5 6–4; Bertsch/De Cret lost to Johansson/Salasca 6–4 3–6 1–6 7–6 7–6.
1990 France d. Spain 5–0: M. Boye d. A. Pastor 7–6 3–6 6–4; N. Maurier d. J. Diaz 7–6 6–4; J. Van Lottum d. A.
Gandarias 1–6 6–2 6–2; K. Dous d. E. Xapelli 6–4 6–1; Boye/Maurier d. Diaz/Pastor 6–2 6–2.
1991 Spain d. USSR 5–0: J–A. Saiz d. I. Pridankine 7–6 6–1; F. Vincente d. J. Michejev 7–6 6–7 6–4; J. Vincente d. A.
Gonopolskij 6–0 6–4; A. Martin d. A. Stoljarov 6–7 6–3 8–6; Martin/J. Vincente d. Pridankine/Stoljarov 7–6 6–3.
1992 Germany d. France 3–1: T. Haas lost to O. Mutis 4–6 4-6; J.-R. Brandt d. J.-R. Lisnard 7–5 6–1; J.-P. Wenner d.
J. Barras 6–3 7–6; Brandt/Haasd. M.-O. Baron/Mutis 6–4 6–3

ANNIE SOISBAULT CUP
International Team Championship for women aged 20 and under. Played zonally with final stages in
Le Touquet.

FINALS
1965 Netherlands d. France 2–1: M. Jansen lost to J. Venturino 1–6 1–6; B. Stove d. C. Spinoza 6–1 1–6 6–3;
Jansen/Stove d. Spinoza/Venturino 10–8 6–4.
1966 France d. Netherlands 2–1: A. A. Seghers lost to A. Bakker 4–6 7–5 2–6; J. Venturino d. M. Jansen 6–4 6–4;
Seghers/Venturino d. Bakker/Jansen 7–5 6–8 6–4.
1967 Netherlands d. France 2–1: A. Bakker lost to O. de Roubin 3–6 0–1 ret'd; A. Suurbeck d. N. Cazeaux 8–6 6–2;
Bakker/Suurbeck d. Cazeaux/de Roubin 6–0 6–0.
1968 USSR d. Czechoslovakia 3–0: O. Morozova d. M. Holubova 6–2 10–8; R. Islanova d. K. Vaneckova 7–5 6–2;
Morozova/A. Eremeeva d. Holubova/Vaneckova 6–3 6–2.
1969 USSR d. Hungary 3–0: O. Morozova d. J. Szorenyi 6–0 6–1; S. Yansone d. A. Graczol 4–6 6–4 6–2; Yansone/E.
Izopajitis d. Szorenyi/A. Barogh 8–6 6–1.
1970 USSR d. France 3–0: E. Izopajitis d. N. Fuchs 6–3 6–1; M. Kroshina d. A. M. Cassaigne 4–6 6–1 9–7; Izopajitis/K.
Zincevic d. Fuchs/M. C. Brochard 6–4 2–6 6–3.
1971 France d. Czechoslovakia 2–1: N. Fuchs d. M. Kozeluhova 6–2 6–3; F. Guedy lost to R. Tomanova 4–6 1–6; M.
C. Brochard/Fuchs d. Kozeluhova/Tomanova 1–6 7–5 6–3.
1972 USSR d. Great Britain 2–1: M. Kroshina d. G. L. Coles 6–3 6–4; E. Biriukova d. V. Burton 6–2 4–6 6–3;
Biriukova/E. Granatuzova lost to L. J. Charles/Coles 3–6 2–6.
1973 Great Britain d. USSR 2–1: G. L. Coles d. M. Kroshina 7–5 4–6 6–3; S. Barker d. E. Granaturova 6–4 7–5;
Barker/Coles lost to Granaturova/Kroshina 4–6 6–3 3–6.
1974 Czechoslovakia d. Great Britain 2–1: M. Navratilova d. G. L. Coles 6–1 6–2; R. Tomanova lost to S. Barker 3–6
2–6; Navratilova/Tomanova d. Baker/Coles 6–2 6–8 7–5.
1975 Great Britain d. Rumania 2–1: S. Barker d. V. Ruzici 4–6 6–4 6–2; L. J. Mottram lost to M. Simionescu 4–6 9–7
1–6; Barker/Mottram d. Ruzici/Simionescu 6–4 6–0.
1976 Czechoslovakia d. Great Britain 2–1: H. Strachonova lost to M. Tyler 7–5 4–6 4–6; R. Marsikova d. L. J. Mottram
6–2 6–4; Marsikova/K. Skronska d. Mottram/B. L. Thompson 6–3 8–10 6–1.
1977 Czechoslovakia d. Switzerland 3–0: H. Strachonova d. A. M. Ruegg 6–0 6–3; R. Marsikova d. M. Simmen 6–0
4–6 6–0; Marsikova/H. Mandlikova d. Ruegg/Simmen 8–6 6–4.
1978 USSR d. Switzerland 3–0: N. Chmyreva d. A. M. Ruegg 6–4 6–4; Eliseenko d. P. Delhees 7–5 6–4; Chmyreva/
Eliseenko d. Ruegg/M. Simmen 6–1 6–0.
1979 Graet Britain d. Czechoslovakia d. 2–1: D. Jevans lost to I. Buderova 5–7 7–9; J. Durie d. H. Mandikova 6–4 6–0;
Durie/Jevans d. Buderova/Mandlikova 6-4 12–10.
1980 Czechoslovakia d. Australia 2–1: I. Budarova d.S. Leo 6–4 6–4; M. Skuherska lost to D. Evers 0–6 3–6;
Budarova/Skuherska d. Evers/M. Sawyer 6–3 6–3.
1981 Netherlands d. USSR 2–0: M. Van Der Torre d. J. Salnikova 6–1 6–4; N. Shutte d. O. Zaitzeva 6–1 6–4.
1982 USSR d. Great Britain 2–1: O. Zaitseva d. S. Walpole 6–2 6–4; N. Reva d. A. Brown 6–1 6–3; J. Kashevarova/
Zaitseva lost to Brown/J. Salmon 5–7 6–0 2–6.
1983 France d. Czechoslovakia 2–1: P. Paradis d. H. Fukarkova 7–5 1–6 6–2; N. Herreman d. O. Votavova 6–4 6–0;
Paradis/P. Thanh lost to Fukarkova/Votavova 6–4 3–6 4–6.
1984 USA d. Czechoslovakia 3–0: G. Rush d. O. Votavova 6–3 6–1; D. Spence d. A. Holikova 6–2 7–5; Rush/N.
Kuhlman d. Votavova/Holikova 6–3 6–2.
1985 Czechoslovakia d. Argentina 3–0: A. Holikova d. P. Tarabini 3–6 7–5 6–4; O. Votavova d. M. Perez–Roldan 0–6
6–3 6–2; Holikova/J. Novotna d. Tarabini/Perez–Roldan 7–5 7–5.
1986 Czechoslovakia d. West Germany 2–1: R. Zrubakova d. M. Schropp 6–2 6–2; R. Rajchrtova d. A. Betzner 6–1
6–2; Rajchrtova/Zrubakova lost to Betzner/Schropp 6–2 7–6.
1987 Australia d. Czechoslovakia 2–1: N. Provis d. R. Rajchrtova 2–6 6–2 6–1; J. Byrne lost to J. Novotna 5–7 6–3 3–6;
Byrne/Provis d. Novotna/Rajchrtova 6–4 0–6 6–3.
1988 Czechoslovakia d. Spain 2–1: R. Zrubakova d. C. Martinez 6–4 6–3; P. Langrova lost to A. Segura 2–6 1–6;
Langrova/Zrubakova d. Martinez/N. Souto 6–3 2–6 9–7.
1989 Czechoslovakia d. Australia 2–0: J. Pospisilova d. J. Faull 6–4 3–6 6–4; P. Langrova d. R. Stubbs 6–0 6–2.
1990 USSR d. Australia 2–1: N. Medvedeva d. K. Sharpe 6–4 6–3; E. Brioukhovets d. K. MacDonald 6–1 1–6 6–3; N.
Biletskaia/S. Komleva lost to MacDonald/R. Stubbs 1–6.
Event ended

HM QUEEN SOFIA CUP
International Team Championship for girls aged 18 and under. Played zonally with the final stages in
Spain.

FINALS
1972 Rumania d. West Germany 3–2: F. Mihai d. A. Spiedel 6–4 7–5; V. Ruzici/M. Simionescu d. B. Portcheller/B. Kasler 8–6 6–1; Ruzici d. Portcheller 2–6 6–0 6–1; Simionescu lost to Kasler 4–6 3–6; M. Neuweiller lost to K. Pohmann 4–6 3–6.
1973 Great Britain d. Spain 4–1: B. L. Thompson d. G. Nogues 6–4 6–4; L. J. Mottram d. J. Mateo 6–3 12–10; S. Barker d. J. Alvarez 7–5 6–0; Barker/Mottram d. Mateo/C. Chillida 6–2 6–2; J. Potterton lost to Chillida 3–6 0–6.
1974 Czechoslovakia d. France 4–1: L. Plchova d. M. Cozaux 6–4 6–1; Y. Brzakova lost to B. Simon 6–8 6–2 4–6; H. Strachonova d. C. Gimmig 6–3 6–0; R. Marsikova d. F. Thibault 8–4 6–4; Brzakova/A. Kulankova d. Thibault/A. Duguy 9–7 4–6 6–4.
1975 Great Britain d. Czechoslovakia 4–1: M. Tyler d. A. Kulhankova 6–1 3–6 6–3; C. Harrison d. J. Kopekova 6–3 6–3; L. J. Mottram d. H. Strachonova 2–6 11–9 6–3; J. Cottrell lost to K. Skronska 1–6 1–6; A. Cooper/Cottrell d. Skronska/Kulhankova 1–6 6–4 6–4.
1976 Great Britain d. Switzerland 3–1: J. M. Durie d. C. Jolissaint 4–6 6–3 6–4; A. Cooper lost to M. Simmen 6–4 0–6 4–6; C. Harrison d. A. Ruegg 6–4 6–7 6–2; M. Tyler d. P. Delhees 6–2 6–2.
1977 Czechoslovakia d. Sweden 5–0: H. Mandlikova d. M. Wiedel 6–2 6–2; I. Budarova d. H. Brywe 6–1 6–1; Mandlikova/Budarova d. A. C. Mansson/A. Nilsson 6–1 6–3; M. Skuherska d. Nilsson 6–0 6–4; H. Strachonova d. Mansson 6–3 7–5.
1978 Czechoslovakia d. Sweden 5–0: M. Skuherska d. L. Jacobson 6–3 6–2; H. Mandlikova d. H. Brywe 6–1 6–1; I. Budarova/Mandlikova d. Jacobson/L. Sandin 6–3 6–1; I. Petru d. A. Nilsson 6–1 6–2; Budarova d. Sandin 6–3 5–7 7–5.
1979 Czechoslovakia d. Switzerland 3–1: I. Bendlova d. P. Frey 6–1 6–1; M. Skuherska/I. Petru lost to C. Jolissaint/I. Villiger 3–6 4–6; Skuherska d. Villiger 3–6 6–1 6–1; I. Novakova d. Jolissaint 6–7 6–3 6–3; Petru v C. Pasquale 5–7 abandoned.
1980 Switzerland d. USSR 3–2: K. Stampfli d. J. Kashevarova 6–3 6–3; I. Villiger/L. Drescher lost to O. Zaitseva/S. Cherneva 4–6 5–7; Villiger d. Zaitseva 6–2 7–5; C. Pasquale lost to Cherneva 4–6 7–5 7–9; Drescher d. J. Salnikova 7–6 6–4.
1981 Sweden d. Czechoslovakia 3–2: B. Bjort d. P. Dutkova 6–2 6–3; M. Lindstrom/C. Lindqvist d. H. Sukova/M. Pazderova 6–3 6–3; C. Jexell lost to Pazderova 6–3 2–6 0–6; Lindqvist d. N. Piskackova 6–2 6–2; Lindstrom lost to Sukova 6–7 3–6.
1982 Italy d. Czechoslovakia 4–1: R. Reggi d. I. Petru 6–3 6–4; N. Virgintino lost to H. Fukarkova 7–5 2–6 3–6; A. Cecchini d. P. Dutkova 7–6 7–6; F. Bonsignori d. A. Souckova 6–3 6–0; Reggi/Virgintino d. Petru/Fukarkova 7–5 4–6 6–2.
1983 Italy d. Czechoslovakia 4–1: L. Ferrando d. A. Souckova 6–0 6–3; B. Romano/N. Virgintino d. A. Holikova/Souckova 6–3 6–7 6–3; A. M. Cecchini d. O. Votavova 6–7 6–3 6–1; Virgintino d. P. Tesarova 6–3 6–1; S. Dalla Valle lost to Holikova 5–7 3–6.
1984 Sweden d. Czechoslovakia 3–2: H. Dahlstrom d. O. Votavova 6–3 6–3; A. Karlsson d. A. Holikova 6–3 6–0; A. Souckova d. M. Lundquist 7–5 7–5; K. Karlsson d. P. Tesarova 6–1 6–2; Votavova/Holikova d. Lundquist/Olsson 6–4 6–3.
1985 Italy d.weden 4–1: L. Lapi lost to C. Dahlman 0–6 1–6; L. Garrone/L. Golarsa d. A. K. Ollson/M. Lundquist 6–1 6–3; Garrone d. H. Dahlstrom 6–2 6–7 6–2; C. Nozzoli d. Ollson 6–4 6–4; Golarsa d. Lundquist 6–2 6–0.
1986 Czechoslovakia d. Sweden 5–0: R. Rajchrtova d. C. Dahlstrom 6–4 6–0; R. Zbrubakova d. J. Jonerup 6–3 6–3; J. Novotna d. M. Stradlund 6–4 6–2; D. Krajcovicova d. M. Ekstrand 6–3 7–5; Novotna/Rajchrtova d. M. Nilsson/ Stradlund 6–0 6–1.
1987 France d. Czechoslovakia 3–0: A. Dechaume d. R. Zrubakova 6–4 6–3; E. Derly d. P. Langrova 7–5 6–1; Dechaume/S. Niox–Chateau d. Langrova/Zrubakova 6–7 6–4 6–3.
1988 Spain d. USSR 2–1: A. Sanchez d. N. Medvedeva 3–6 6–2 6–3; C. Martinez d. E. Brioukhovets 6–2 6–2; Martinez/Sanchez lost to Brioukhovets/Medvedeva 6–7 0–4 ret'd.
1989 Spain d. Czechoslovakia 3–0: A. Sanchez d. A. Strnadova 6–1 6–3; N. Avila d. J. Dubcova 6–3 6–0; S. Ramon/Sanchez d. K. Balnova/Strnadova 6–4 7–5.
1990 Spain d. France 2–1: P. Perez d. A. Zugasti 6–4 6–0; S. Ramon lost to A. Fusai 6–3 4–6 1–6; Perez/Ramon d. Fusai/Zugasti 7–5 6–2.
1991 Spain d. Sweden 3–0: E. Botini d. A. Carlsson 5–7 6–2 6–4; E. Bes d. M. Vallin 6–2 6–1; Botini/C. Torrens d. Vallin/Carlsson 4–6 7–6 6–2.
1992 Germany d. Spain 2–1: P. Begerow d. E. Bottini 6–2 7–5; K. Freye lost to C. Torrens 2–6 3–6; Freye/S. Wachtershauser d. Bottini/E.Jimenez 2–6 7–5 6–2.

HELVETIE CUP
International Team Championship for girls aged 16 and under. Played zonally with final stages at Leysin, Switzerland.

FINALS
1977 Italy d. Switzerland 3–2: P. Cigognani lost to C. Jolissaint 0–6 3–6; B. Rossi d. I. Villiger 6–3 6–7 8–6; M. Calabria d. K. Stampfli 6–1 6–2; P. Murgo d. C. Pasquale 6–3 6–3; Rossi/Murgo lost to Jolissaint/Villiger 4–6 3–6.
1978 Bulgaria d. West Germany 5–0: M. Condova d. C. Kohde 1–6 6–3 6–1; A. Veltcheva d. Haas 6–3 5–7 6–4; I. Chichkova d. Hammig 6–3 6–0; I. Christova d. Wilmsmeyer 3–6 7–6 6–3; Condova/Veltcheva d. Kohde/Haas 3–6 6–2 6–2.
1979 Sweden d. France 5–0: C. Lindqvist d. I. Vernhes 6–7 6–3 6–0; B. Bjork d. C. Vanier 4–6 6–3 6–3; A. Flodin d. S. Gardette 6–0 6–1; H. Olsson/K. Marivall d. M. Callejo/Vanier 6–3 6–3; Olsson d. Callejo 6–2 6–1.
1980 Sweden d. West Germany 3–2: C. Anderholm d. M. Schropp 6–1 6–2; H. Olsson lost to K. Reuter 5–7 4–6; M. Schultz d. P. Keppeler 6–4 6–4; N. Nielson d. M. Reinhard 6–7 6–3 6–2; Olsson/Schultz lost to Reuter/Reinhard 6–1 4–6 5–7.
1981 Sweden d. Italy 3–2: A. Bjork lost to F. Sollenti 2–6 6–7; H. Olsson/C. Anderholm d. R. Reggi/F. Virgintino 0–6 6–2 6–1; Olsson d. A. M. Cecchini 6–4 7–5; Anderholm d. Reggi 6–3 3–6 6–4; I. Sjogreen lost to Virgintino 0–6 0–6.
1982 USSR d. France 3–2: I. Fishkina d. I. Demongeot 6–1 6–2; L. Savchenko/V. Milvidskaya lost to P. Paradis/N. Phan–Thanh 4–6 7–5 4–6; N. Bykova lost to Paradis 1–6 2–6; Savchenko d. Phan–Thanh 6–2 6–3; Mildvidskaya d. N. Herreman 6–1 6–4.
1983 USSR d. Sweden 3–2: A. Kuzmina d. A. K. Olsson 6–3 1–6 6–3; V. Milvidskaya d. H. Dahlmstrom 3–6 6–2 6–4; I. Fischkina lost to M. Lundquist 4–6 4–6; I. Fateeva lost to E. Helmersson 2–6 3–6; Fishkina/Mildvidskaya d.

Dahlstrom/Lundquist 6–4 7–5.
1984 Czechoslovakia d. West Germany 4–1: R. Wlona lost to M. Gartner 7–6 3–6 4–6; J. Novotna/R. Rajchrotova d. S. Meier/R. Weiser 6–0 7–6; Novotna d. Meier 7–5 6–2; Rajchrotova d. Weiser 6–3 4–6 6–1; P. Sedkackova d. S. Hack 6–4 4–6 6–2.
1985 West Germany d. Sweden 4–1: M. Schurhoff d. M. Ekstrand 6–2 4–6 6–4; M. Gartner/S. Hack lost to M. Strandlund/M. Nilsson 3–6 3–6; Gartner/J. Jonerup 7–6 6–2; Hack d. Strandlund 6–1 6–1; W. Probst d. M. Nilsson 6–1 6–1.
1986 Switzerland d. Czechoslovakia 3–1 (one rubber not played)*:* E. Zardo d. M. Frimmelova 6–4 6–2; M. Strebel d. L. Laskova 7–5 6–1; S. Jaquet v. P. Langrova not played; M. Plocher d. E. Sviglerova 6–4 6–2; Jacquet/Plocher lost to Frimmelova/Langrova 6–0 1–6 5–7.
1987 Netherlands d. Switzerland 3–2: N. Van Dierendonck lost to S. Jacquet 6–7 3–6; B. Sonneveld lost to M. Plocher 6–2 3–6 4–6; Y. Grubben d. G. Villiger 7–5 7–6; E. Haslinghuis d. S. Bregnard 6–1 6–0; Sonneveld/Van Dierendonck d. Jacquet/Plocher 7–5 6–3.
1988 West Germany d. Czechoslovakia 3–2: V. Martinek d. K. Balnova 6–3 6–0; K. Duell lost to A. Strnadova 2–6 3–6; M. Skulj–Zivec d. H. Vildova 7–5 6–1; A. Popp lost to R. Bobkova 4–6 6–1 5–7; C. Hofmann/Martinek d. Balnova/Strnadova 7–5 7–5.
1989 Czechoslovakia d. USSR 3–2: R. Bobkova d. S. Komleva 6–2 6–1; K. Habsudova d. E. Makarova 7–6 6–0; K. Matouskova lost to M. Chirikova 3–6 6–3 5–7; K. Kroupova lost to T. Ignatieva 2–6 2–6; Bobkova/Matouskova d. Chirikova/Komleva 4–6 6–0 8–6.
1990 USSR d. West Germany 3–2: T. Ignatieva d. K. Freye 6–4 4–6 6–3; I. Soukhova d. S. Wachterhauser 7–5 6–2; V. Vitels lost to M. Babel 4–6 0–3 ret.; G. Beleni lost to P. Begerow 3–6 3–6; Ignatieva/Soukhova d. Babel/J. Dobberstein 6–4 6–4.
1991 Czechoslovakia d. Spain 4–1: Z. Malkova d. E. Jiminez 6–4 6–0; E. Martincova lost to M. Cruells 3–6 6–7; E. Hostacova d. A. Ortuno 6–3 7–5; M. Hautova d. A. Montolio 4–6 6–3 6–1; Malkova/Martincova d. Cruells/ Jiminez 6–3 6–1.
1992 Belgium d. Germany 2–1: N. feber d. A. Glass 6–3 6–2; L. Courtois lost to H. Rusch 6–3 6–7 3–6; Courtoios/Feber d. Glass/C. Muller 6–7 6–3 6–0

EUROPA CUP
International Team Championship for girls aged 14 and under.

FINALS
1981 West Germany d. France 3–2, Winterslag, Belgium: I. Cueto d. J. Clerin 6–3 2–6 6–1; R. Wieser lost to E. Folcher 1–6 6–3 1–6; S. Graf d. M. Phan–Thanh 7–5 6–3; S. Luidinant d. E. Grousseau 6–2 6–2; Graf/Wieser lost to Folcher/Grousseau 6–4 2–6 1–6.
1982 Sweden d. West Germany 3–2, Mons, Belgium: C. Dahlman d. S. Meier 7–5 7–5: H. Dahlstrom d. B. Herget 6–0 6–4; E. Helmersson lost to I. Cueto 3–6 7–6 0–6; I. Mattiasson lost to E. Walliser 5–7 2–6; Dahlstrom/Helmersson d. Cueto/Walliser 6–2 6–2.
1983 West Germany d. France 3–2, Lee–on–Solent, Hampshire: N. Vassen d. S. N. Chateau 4–6 6–3 6–2; W. Probst d. M. C. Rolet 7–5 5–7 ret'd; S. Hack lost to C. Bourdais 6–3 2–6 0–6; M. Gartner d. A. Dechaume 6–4 4–6 7–5; Gartner/Vassen lost to Bourdais/Dechaume 3–6 1–6.
1984 France d. Sweden 4–1: S. Dussault lost to R. Narbe 0–6 6–4 3–6; A. Dechaume/E. Derly d. M. Ekstrand/H. Johnsson 6–3 6–3; Dechaume d. Ekstrand 7–5 6–2; Derly d. Salsgard 6–4 3–6 6–1; M. Laval d. Johnsson 6–4 6–4.
1985 USSR d. Italy 3–2: N. Zvereva d. A. Dell'Orso 6–2 4–6 6–4; T. Tchernysova lost to F. Romano 3–6 2–6; E. Brihovec lost to S. Favini w.o.; A. Blumberga d. G. Boscheiro 6–3 4–6 6–4; Zvereva/Tchernysova d. Boscheiro/Dell'Orso 6–4 6–3.
1986 Netherlands d. Italy 3–2: Y. Grubben lost to Boscheiro 5–7 4–6; N. Van Lottum d. Favini 6–2 6–1; E. Markestein d. Migliori 6–4 6–4; E. Haslinghuis lost to Bertelloni 2–6 2–6; Grubben/Van Lottum d. Boscheiro/Migliori 6–2 6–2.
1987 Czechoslovakia d. Austria 3–2: P. Kucova lost to U. Priller 3–6 0–6; R. Bobkova d. D. Bidmon 6–2 6–4; P. Markova lost to N. Dobrovits 4–6 1–6; K. Matouskova d. S. Suchan 1–6 6–0 10–8; Bobkova/Kucova d. Dobrovits/ Priller 6–4 4–6 7–5.
1988 Hungary d. West Germany 3–2: A. Foeldenyi d. A. Huber 6–0 3–6 8–6; B. Bathory lost to K. Denn–Samuel 0–6 3–6; M. Zsoldos d. P. Kemper 6–1 4–6 6–4; K. Kocsis lost to M. Kochta 6–4 1–6 1–6; Foeldenyi/Zsoldos d. Denn–Samuel/Huber 4–6 7–6 6–3.
1989 Czechoslovakia d. Italy 5–0: E. Martiucova d. R. Grande 7–6 6–3; I. Malkova d. G. Pizzichini 6–2 7–5; O. Hostakova d. S. Pifferi 5–7 6–1 7–5; M. Hautova d. A. Serra–Zanetti 6–0 6–2; Malkova/Martiucova d. Grande/Pifferi 6–1 6–4.
1990 Czechoslovakia d. Yugoslavia 3–2: S. Radevicova lost to I. Majoli 2–6 6–4 1–6; Z. Rebekova lost to T. Doric 5–7 4–6; A. Havrlikova d. S. Milas 6–1 6–2; A. Gersi d. D. Karadz 7–6 6–0; Havrlikova/Redevicova d. Doric/Majoli 6–3 7–5.
1991 Germany d. Czechoslovakia 5–0: M. Vladulescu d. A. Havrlikova 6–0 6–3; N. Raidt d. R. Surova 7–6 6–2; S. Schmidle d. K. Bakalarova 6–0 6–4; A. Barna d. R. Pelikanova 6–2 6–4; Barna/T. Karsten d. L. Cenkova/Havrlikova 6–2 6–1.
1992 Czechoslovakia d. France 3–2: L. Varmuzova d. I. Taesch 4–6 6–43 6–4; H. Nagyova lost to A. Castera 3–6 2–6; S. Kleinova lost to E. Curutchet 3–6 6–3 2–6; J. Ondrouchova d. G. Goultefard 6–2 6–2; Kleinova/Ondrouchova d. Castera/Curutchet 3–6 7–5 6–4.

US INTERCOLLEGIATE CHAMPIONSHIPS
MEN'S SINGLES

WINNERS		WINNERS	
1883	*Spring:* J. S. Clark (Harvard)	1888	P. S. Sears (Harvard)
1883	*Autumn:* H. A. Taylor (Harvard)	1889	R. P. Huntington (Yale)
1884	W. P. Knapp (Yale)	1890	F. H. Hovey (Harvard)
1885	W. P. Knapp (Yale)	1891	F. H. Hovey (Harvard)
1886	G. M. Brinley (Trinity, Con.)	1892	W. A. Larned (Cornell)
1887	P. S. Sears (Harvard)	1893	M. G. Chace (Brown)

1894	M. G. Chace (Yale)	1944	F. Segura (Miami)
1895	M. G. Chace (Yale)	1945	F. Segura (Miami)
1896	M. D. Whitman (Harvard)	1946	R. Falkenburg (USC)
1897	S. G. Thompson (Princeton)	1947	G. Larned (Wm & Mary)
1898	L. E. Ware (Harvard)	1948	H. E. Likas (U of San Francisco)
1899	D. F. Davis (Harvard)	1949	J. Tuero (Tulane)
1900	R. D. Little (Princeton)	1950	H. Flam (USC)
1901	F. B. Alexander (Princeton)	1951	M. A. Trabert (U of Cincinnati)
1902	W. J. Clothier (Harvard)	1952	H. Stewart (USC)
1903	E. B. Dewhurst (U of Penn)	1953	H. Richardson (Tulane)
1904	R. LeRoy (Columbia)	1954	H. Richardson (Tulane)
1905	E. B. Dewhurst (U of Penn)	1955	J. Aguero (Tulane)
1906	R. LeRoy (Columbia)	1956	A. Olmedo (USC)
1907	G. P. Gardner (Harvard)	1957	B. McKay (U of Michigan)
1908	N. W. Niles (Harvard)	1958	A. Olmedo (USC)
1909	W. F. Johnson (U of Penn)	1959	W. Reed (San Jose State)
1910	R. A. Holden (Yale)	1960	L. Nagler (UCLA)
1911	E. H. Whitney (Harvard)	1961	A. Fox (UCLA)
1912	G. M. Church (Princeton)	1962	R. H. Osuna (USC)
1913	R. N. Williams (Harvard)	1963	R. D. Ralston (USC)
1914	G. M. Church (Princeton)	1964	R. D. Ralston (USC)
1915	R. N. Williams (Harvard)	1965	A. R. Ashe (UCLA)
1916	G. C. Caner (Harvard)	1966	C. Pasarell (UCLA)
1917–18	Not held	1967	R. C. Lutz (USC)
1919	C. S. Garland (Yale)	1968	S. R. Smith (USC)
1920	L. M. Banks (Yale)	1969	J. Loyo–Mayo (USC)
1921	P. Neer (Stanford)	1970	J. Borowiak (UCLA)
1922	R. N. Williams (Yale)	1971	J. S. Connors (UCLA)
1923	C. H. Fischer (Phil. Osteo.)	1972	R. L. Stockton (Trinity, Texas)
1924	W. Scott (Washington)	1973	A. A. Mayer (Stanford)
1925	E. G. Chandler (California)	1974	J. Whitlinger (Stanford)
1926	E. G. Chandler (California)	1975	W. Martin (UCLA)
1927	W. Allison (Texas)	1976	W. Scanlon (Trinity, Texas)
1928	H. Siligson (Lehigh)	1977	M. Mitchell (Stanford)
1929	B. Bell (Texas)	1978	J. P. McEnroe (Stanford)
1930	C. Sutter (Tulane)	1979	K. Curren (Texas)
1931	K. Gledhill (Stanford)	1980	R. Van't Hof (USC)
1932	C. Sutter (Tulane)	1981	T. Mayotte (Stanford)
1933	J. Tidball (UCLA)	1982	M. Leach (Michigan)
1934	G. Mako (USC)	1983	G. Holmes (Utah)
1935	W. Hess (Rice)	1984	M. Pernfors (Georgia)
1936	E. Sutter (Tulane)	1985	M. Pernfors (Georgia)
1937	E. Sutter (Tulane)	1986	D. Goldie (Stanford)
1938	F. D. Guernsey (Rice)	1987	A. Burrow (U of Miami)
1939	F. D. Guernsey (Rice)	1988	R. Weiss (Pepperdine)
1940	D. McNeill (Kenyon Coll)	1989	D. Leaycraft (LSU)
1941	J. R. Hunt (US Naval Acad)	1990	S. Bryan (Texas)
1942	F. R. Schroeder (Stanford)	1991	J. Palmer (Stanford)
1943	F. Segura (Miami)	1992	A. O'Brien (Stanford)

WOMEN'S SINGLES

WINNERS		WINNERS	
1958	D. R. Hard (Pomona)	1976	B. Hallquist (USC)
1959	D. Floyd (Wm & Mary)	1977	B. Hallquist (USC)
1960	L. Vail (Oakland City)	1978	S. Margolin (USC)
1961	T. A. Fretz (Occidental)	1979	K. Jordan (Stanford)
1962	R. Allison (Alabama)	1980	W. White (Rollins)
1963	R. Allison (Alabama)	1981	A. M. Fernandez (Rollins)
1964	J. Albert (Stanford)	1982	A. Moulton (Stanford)
1965	M. Henreid (UCLA)	1983	B. Herr (USC)
1966	C. Martinez (San Francisco State)	1984	L. Spain (Georgia)
1967	O. Rippy (Odessa Jr)	1985	L. Gates (Stanford)
1968	E. Burrer (Trinity, Texas)	1986	P. Fendick (Stanford)
1969	E. Burrer (Trinity, Texas)	1987	P. Fendick (Stanford)
1970	L. DuPont (N Carolina)	1988	S. Stafford (Florida)
1971	P. Richmond (Arizona State)	1989	S. Birch (Stanford)
1972	J. Metcalf (Redlands)	1990	D. Graham (Stanford)
1973	J. Metcalf (Redlands)	1991	S. Birch (Stanford)
1974	C. Meyer (Marymount)	1992	L. Raymond (Florida)
1975	S. Tolleson (Trinity, Texas)		

THE INTERNATIONAL TENNIS FEDERATION

REGIONAL REPORTS
ITF JUNIOR RESULTS
ITF VETERAN TENNIS
WHEELCHAIR TENNIS
NATIONAL RANKINGS

The year started well for Daniela di Toro of Australia who won both the singles and doubles titles at the Australian Open in Melbourne.

THE INTERNATIONAL TENNIS FEDERATION

ASIAN TENNIS FEDERATION

President: Eiichi Kawatei. **Vice Presidents:** Salvador Andrada, Eddy Katimansah, Abdulla Al-Hudaithi. **Secretary General:** Herman Hu. **Hon Treasurer:** Cho Sung-ok. **Executive members:** Lam Seneviratne, Akbar Baba, Ahmed Al-Sabah.

The year 1992 marked the beginning of a new era for the Asian Tennis Federation. A permanent office was established in Hong Kong with a full time co-ordinator from February 1. It was also accepted as an official Regional Association of the ITF at the Annual General Meeting in the Dominican Republic.

Three new members, Vietnam, Myanmar and the Maldives joined the ATF at our AGM in Tokyo in April, boosting membership to 35. Five more countries are expected to join soon as a result of the disintegration of the USSR.

On the playing side, Only Matsuoka of Japan (64) made the top 100 on the ATP computer. However, Asian women players had a much better year with five players – Date (21), Sawamatsu (24) and Endo (57) of Japan; Basuki (48) of Indonesia and Wang Shi-Ting (54) of Taipei – in the top 100.

Asian juniors also started to mushroom. Of the boys, we had four in the top 20 – Suzuki (8) of Japan, Song (10) of Korea, Suwandi (11) of Indonesia and Kohler (13) of Hong Kong. Among the girls, we also had three Japanese in the top 20 – Kuki (10), Yoshida (11) and Mochizuki (12).

On the tennis side, much was accomplished. India was promoted to the World Group of the Davis Cup by NEC for 1993 after defeating Great Britain in Delhi. The Davis Cup by NEC Zonal Group Three competition was successfully organised in Bahrain and Olympic Qualifying was held in Osaka, Japan. Federation Cup by NEC qualifying was held in Colombo, Sri Lanka; World Youth Cup qualifying was held in Manila, Philippines. The NTT World Junior Tennis qualifying was staged in Kuala Lumpur, Malaysia and the Finals were held at the beautiful Yamanaka-ko Resort outside Tokyo.

Several ITF Officiating programmes were held in different parts of Asia with the support and co-operation of the ATF and produced more than 120 qualified officials with white, bronze and silver badges.

The five annual ATF Championships also had another successful year. The Salem Asian Championships and Asian University Championships were held in Hong Kong; the Asian Nations Team Championships was held again in Malaysia; the Asian Junior Championships, which is an ITF B2 tournament, was held in India and the Asian Veteran Championships were once again held in Pattaya, Thailand.

Other tournaments in Asia included 22 ITF Junior tournaments, nine satellite Circuits, 11 Challengers, five ATP Tour events, four Women's circuits, eight futures tournaments and seven Kraft Tour events. With the support of Reebok, for the first time, we organised a series of 16 and Under tournaments with qualifying tournaments in five countries and an Asia/Pacific Championship in Hong Kong. Three 14 and Under tournaments were also organised with ITF Development Funds in Thailand, Philippines and Malaysia.

EUROPEAN TENNIS ASSOCIATION

The activities of the European Tennis Association in organising the official competitions where the titles of European Champions are at stake (for individuals and teams, professionals, juniors and veterans) reached new levels in 1992 in terms of tournament participation, spectator attendance and media coverage.

The increase in participants was due mainly to the entry of countries such as Croatia, Slovenia, Ukraine, Lithuania, Estonia and Latvia into the ETA family.

The figures show clearly the interest generated by the ETA official championships. Thirty nations entered the Men's and 26 nations the Women's team championships which are open to professional players. The events were won respectively by Sweden and Great Britain. A total of 184 national teams competed in the European Junior Team Championships and the European Junior Winter Cups. The European Junior individual championships staged in Athens (14 and under), and Berlin (16/18 and under) registered 340 players from 35 countries.

The European Veterans' Championships (indoor and outdoor) in Seefeld, Baden-Baden and Portschach, were again extremely successful with the participation of around 1,000 enthusiastic players. The European Veterans Clubs Championships for the 45 and 55 age groups are now traditional events and drew entries from 20 teams.

The title of 'European Championship' was awarded in 1992 to the women's tournaments which are part of the Kraft Tour in Zurich and Lucerne .

The ETA pursued its co-operation with the ITF in organising Schools for Officials and working on the levels of support to be provided by the Grand Slam Development Fund. Many European nations benefitted from this help in 1992.

A Coaches Symposium was held in Crete and the European Referees Conference in Hamburg, Germany.

The ETA Development Committee started its development scheme with Poland. It involved ten clubs in Poland which received equipment. The ETA is also handling entries for European events on the ITF Futures Circuit. Entries for 95 tournaments were processed in Basle during the year.

CONFEDERACION SUDAMERICANA DE TENIS

Once again, during 1992, COSAT remained at the forefront of tennis activity throughout the South American region, organising, as usual, a successful junior circuit, and satellite events for both men and women in each of the ten South American nations.

The World Youth Cup qualifying event for the area was splendidly staged at Caracas, Venezuela and the NTT World Junior Tennis qualifying event was held in Santiago de Chile.

A steady improvement in the relationship with the ITF was also a feature of the year.

Doug MacCurdy held a most useful workshop in Mar del Plata, Argentina, with the participation of 200 coaches. All agreed it was a most worthwhile and well organised event.

A new committee was elected during the year comprising Eugenio Saller (Brazil) as President, Vicente Calderon (Bolivia) as Vice President, Martin Rosenbaum (Argentina) as Secretary, Miguel Carrizosa (Paraguay) and Bartolome Puiggros (Peru). Otto Hauser was named as Honorary International Secretary. Eduardo Moline O'Connor was again the South American member of the ITF Committee of Management.

The new committee has pledged itself to improve the existing adminstration by incorporating new methods and facilities for a fluent and effective organisation.

The Veterans' game continued to flourish and a special committee is continuing to support the growing numbers of followers and tournaments; South American players were among the most successful at the ITF Championships in Palermo.

On a sad note, COSAT suffered a severe blow with the death during the year of President Nicolas Macchiavello, who passed away after a short illness. He was a man whose efforts on behalf of South American tennis were appreciated by everybody. He was especially responsible for the unification of all the COSAT nations and his experience will be greatly missed.

CENTRAL AMERICAN AND CARIBBEAN TENNIS CONFEDERATION

The latest grouping of ITF member nations with mutual geographic needs and aspirations was formed during 1992 as a result of discussions among the English and Spanish speaking nations of the Central America and Caribbean area.

Mr Jesus Topete Enriquez, of Mexico was elected President of the new body which has Rolando Martinez, of Cuba as first vice-president and Mrs Glenda Morean, of Trinidad and Tobago as second vice-president.

The secretary is Mario Emilio Guerrero, of the Dominican Republic, the treasurer Enrique Abaroa, of Mexico and the executive secretary Gaston Villegas, of Mexico.

Presidents of various sub-regions are: Lorenzo Molina (Mexico), Enrique Molins (El Salvador), Jose Baldrich (Puerto Rico) and William McComb (US Virgin Islands)

Ambitious plans were announced for the continuing development of tennis throughout the region. Three men's satellite circuits and a development circuit of four events for young women players have been organised to take place in 1993.

Training courses for coaches are also on the agenda and Ken Farrar, the ITF Administrator of Officiating has been invited to organise a training course for umpires during the year.

Training clinics for young players will be organised on a regular basis with particular emphasis on fitness and competitive opportunities will be provided by international youth circuits. The development of tennis in the area is of prime importance to COTECC's Board of Management and every member nation will be encouraged to play its part in increasing the number of tournaments, clinics, and other programmes in the COTECC area.

WHEELCHAIR TENNIS REVIEW

Since its inception in 1976, wheelchair tennis has been the fastest growing and one of the most challenging and exciting of all wheelchair sports. It has provided opportunities for many disabled people to enjoy competitive tennis, as well as sharing experiences with family and able and disabled friends of all age groups.

Wheelchair tennis follows the same rules as able-bodied tennis except the wheelchair tennis player is allowed two bounces of the ball. An official recognition of the two bounce rule was given when The International Tennis Federation included this rule of wheelchair tennis in its official rules of tennis.

Initially, wheelchair tennis was a sport mainly played in the United States. Brad Parks initiated the sport in 1978. In 1980, the National Foundation of Wheelchair Tennis (NFWT) was founded as the organizing body of the sport in the USA. By giving clinics and exhibitions the NFWT has given a lot of exposure to wheelchair tennis worldwide. In October, 1988, The International Wheelchair Tennis Federation (IWTF) was founded as the organising body for wheelchair tennis at an international level.

Representatives from organisations involved in wheelchair tennis present at this meeting came from Australia, Canada, Great Britain, France, Holland, Israel, Japan and the United States of America. With the efforts of the IWTF and its members, wheelchair tennis extended into an international realm. Many countries around the globe began to develop and organise wheelchair tennis nationally. There are currently 24 member nations and additional nations are expected to join in the near future. Today wheelchair tennis is played in approximately 50 countries.

The official team event of the IWTF is the World Team Cup which is played at a different venue, once a year, both for men and women. Since 1992 wheelchair tennis has been an official Paralympic sport.

The establishment of an office in London for the administration of wheelchair tennis worldwide in February 1991 provided this branch of tennis with the biggest boost in its history.

Nineteen ninety-two was an exciting year for wheelchair tennis. NEC gave their generous support to the sport in the form of a grant over the next three years. This support will enable the IWTF to expand its activities all over the world.

Thanks to the initiative of the ITF, one of the major events was the honouring of the wheelchair tennis champions alongside the ITF world champions. Chantal Vandierendonck and Randy Snow received their awards at the same time as Monica Seles and Stefan Edberg, during the World Champions' dinner during the French Open championships in Paris.

The Paralympics was another thrilling event. Fourteen countries were represented in the 32-strong men's draw with the 16 players in the women's event coming from six nations. The event was played at the Vall D'Hebron site, where the able-bodied players had contested the main Olympic event a few weeks before.

Randy Snow, the 1991 World Champion, took the gold medal in the men's singles and Monique van den Bosch won the women's gold medal. All the participants agreed on one thing: this was the best wheelchair tennis event ever held. The organisation was perfect, with everything being done at the same professional level as the Olympic Games. All the matches had full crews of umpires, linesmen and ball boys.

Until 1991 the World Team Cup had always preceded the US Open in Irvine, California. In 1992, however, the event was organised in Belgium in conjunction with the Belgium

IWTF NEC WHEELCHAIR TENNIS CIRCUIT 1992

DATE	TOURNAMENT	CLASS	SINGLES	DOUBLES
Jan 29-Feb 1	Australian Open	M CS3	L.Giammartini d. M.Connell 6-3 6-4	M.Connell/D.Hall d. K.Shibamoto/S.Bitterauf 6-2 6-0
		W CS3	D.Di Toro d. E.de Lange 6-2 7-6	D.DiToro/S.Twelftree d. E.de Lange/K.Koeman 0-6 6-0 6-3
Feb 4-7	New Zealand Open	M CS1	S.Bitterauf d. John Sorenson 6-3 6-0	K.Shibamoto/S.Bitterauf d. W.Fleming/G.Barnes 7-6 4-6 6-3
May 14-17	USTA Outdoor Atlanta	W CS1	R.Snow d. L.Giammartini 6-3 6-2	L.Giammartini/M.Connell d. S.Douglas/K.Schrameyer 6-2 7-6
		M CS1	M.van den Bosch d. R.Isecke 6-2 6-4	M.van den Bosch/R.Isecke d. N.Olson/P.Rollison 6-3 6-1
May 14-17	Spanish Open	M CS3	J.Mistry d. B.Goldbalt 6-4 6-0	B.Goldblat/E.Kirsch d. S.Hatt/J.Mistry 1-6 6-2 6-4
May 28-31	Japan Open	M CS1	L.Giammartini d. M.Connell 6-3 6-4	K.Schrameyer/D.Hall d. L.Giammartini/M.Connell 6-2 6-1
		W CS3	T.Ohi d. K.Kitamoto 6-2 6-3	T.Ohi/K.Kitamoto d. I.Schrank/M.Fink 6-3 6-0
May 29-Jun 13	Baton Rouge USA	M CS3	S.Welch d. J.Black 7-5 6-4	J.Black/S.Douglas d. W.Leavitt/S.Welch 6-7 6-2 6-1
Jun 18-21	Reno USA	W CS2	B.Parks d. J.Black 6-4 2-6 6-4	J.Black/D.Lachman d. B.Parks/M.Foulks 6-0 4-6 6-3
		M CS2	C.Vandierendonck d. N.Olson 6-0 6-3	N.Olson/L.Seideman d. P.Rollison/C.Vandierendonck 6-2 7-5
Jun 30-Jul 5	Israel Open	M CS2	R.Snow d. R.Troppacher 6-1 7-5	R.Snow/S.Bitterauf d. J.Mistry/S.Hatt 6-3 6-2
		W CS3	R.Isecke winner round robin	
Jul 8-12	French Open	W CS2	L.Giammartini d. C.Turner 6-1 6-2	L.Giammartini/A.Naili 6-3 6-3
		M CS2	M.van den Bosch d. C.Vandierendonck 6-4 6-7 6-4	M.van den Bosch/R.Isecke d. O.Marx/A.Racineux 6-0 6-0
Jul 13-19	Dutch Open	M CS1	L.Giammartini d. A.Naili 6-0 6-3	L.Giammartini/T.Caillier d. C.Turner/S.Bitterauf 6-4 3-6 6-3
		W CS1	C.Vandierendonck d. M.van den Bosch 3-6 7-6 6-3	M.van den Bosch/R.Isecke d. E.de Lange/C.Vandierendonck 2-6 6-2 6-4
Jul 24-26	Cleveland USA	M CS3	B.Parks d. L.Montgomery 7-5 6-0	B.Parks/L.Montgomery d. R.Cooper/R.Martin 6-4 2-6 6-0
		W CS3	L.Seidemann d. D.Miller 6-4 6-3	S.Clark/D.Miller d. B.Gilmore/K.Hixenbaugh 6-3 7-6
Jul 23-26	Belgium Open	M CS2	L.Giammartini d. S.Welch 6-4 6-1	L.Giammartini/T.Caillier d. P.Fusade/A.Naili 6-2 7-5
		W CS3	M.van den Bosch w.o	M.van den Bosch/R.Isecke d. N.Olson/P.Rollison 6-0 6-2
Jul 27-Aug 2	British Open	M CS2	C.Turner d. M.Foulks 4-6 6-4 6-4	C.Turner/S.Bitterauf d. M.Foulks/S.Welch 6-2 6-3
		M CS1	M.van den Bosch d. C.Vandierendonck 6-4 6-3	M.van den Bosch/R.Isecke d. E.de Lange/C.Vandierendonck 6-1 6-1
Jul 30-Aug 2	Japan Cup	W CS1	Y.Ohmori d. K.Takeuchi 6-1 7-5	C.Turner/S.Bitterauf d. M.Connell/K.Schrameyer 3-6 6-4 6-3
Aug 4-9	Austrian Open	M CS3	S.Welch d. K.Schrameyer 6-2 6-3	M.van den Bosch/R.Isecke d. H.Taroni/M.Fink 6-0 6-0
		W CS3	M.van den Bosch d. R.Isecke 6-4 6-3	R.Snow/M.Connell d. M.Foulks/S.Douglas 6-4 6-2
Aug 10-16	Swiss Open	M CS1	M.Connell d. R.Snow 5-7 7-5 6-4	M.van den Bosch/R.Isecke d. E.de Lange/C.Vandierendonck 6-3 3-6 7-6
Aug 19-23	German Open	M CS3	M.van den Bosch d. C.Vandierendonck 6-4 6-3	S.Bitterauf/K.Schrameyer d. R.Snow/S.Douglas 6-4 7-6
		W CS3	R.Snow d. L.Giammartini 1-6 7-5 7-5	O.Marx/A.Racineux d. H.Scheffel/K.Petry 6-1 6-3
		W CS3	R.Isecke w.o	D.Lackman/C.Parmelly d. C.Turner/W.Leavitt 6-3 6-2
Sep 11-13	Dallas USA	M CS3	M.Foulks d. C.Parmelly 6-3 6-4	P.Rollison/J.Stout d. S.Clark/A.Mann 6-2 6-3
		W CS3	P.Rollison winner round robin	B.Parks/R.Slaughter d. D.Lachman/C.Parmelly 6-4 6-7 6-2
Sep 17-20	Bloomington USA	M CS3	C.Parmelly d. B.Parks 6-3 6-4	J.Knutsen/N.Olson d. M.J.Kittock/L.Seidemann 6-1 6-3
		W CS3	N.Olson d. L.Seidemann 6-1 6-0	C.Illingworth/M.Thompson d. D.MacArthur/G.MacIntyre 1-6 6-4 7-6
		W CS3	C.Illingworth winner round robin	P.Rollison/J.Stout d. S.Clark/M.J.Kittock 6-4 6-2
Oct 3-4	Lake Tahoe USA	M SS	P.Rollison winner round robin	B.Parks/R.Slaughter d. J.Black/S.Douglas 6-3 6-2
Oct 3-11	US Open	W SS	S.Welch d. J.Black 6-3 7-6	C.Vandierendonc Bosch/R.Isecke d. E.de Lange/C.Vandierendonck 7-5 6-4

SS=Super Series CS=Championship Series M=Men W=Women
SS=100 points winner CS1=80 points winner CS2=70 points winner CS3=50 points winner

Open. The French men defeated the USA 2–0 to take the trophy for the first time since the Cup's inauguration in 1985. The Dutch girls defeated France 2–1 to maintain their 100 per cent record in the championships.

The budget for development was increased in 1992 and clinics and exhibitions were held in Thailand, Hong Kong, The Philippines, South Africa, Mauritius, Russia, Hungary, Czechoslovakia and Denmark.

Some of these countries have now joined the IWTF. Russia and South Africa both sent a team to participate at the World Team Cup in Belgium.

The NEC Wheelchair Tennis Circuit has been formalised with 21 major tournaments (Super Series and Championship Series) and about 50 Satellites worldwide. Each tournament offers different divisions (which are based upon level of play). All results of the Circuit have counted towards international ranking. All players with points will automatically be given a ranking. The ranking is based on a player's best 5 tournament results during the last 12 months. The system caters for both men and women competitors in the open division although, for the moment, it covers only singles competitions.

REVIEW OF THE JUNIOR GAME 1992

Jackie Nesbitt

USA gain their first ever boys' champion, with Brian Dunn finishing the year 200 points ahead of Czechoslovakia's David Skoch in second place, and 240 points ahead of third placed Grant Doyle of Australia.

The only slight falter in Brian's year came at the French Open where he was beaten in the 2nd round by Bjorn Jacob of Germany. This after getting off to a good start in Australia where he had finished as runner-up in the Open to Grant Doyle. Brian redeemed himself on the grass courts in England and began to look like a candidate for the boys' singles champion with victory at the LTA Tournament, Thames Ditton, and a semi-final placing the following week at Surbiton. The big title continued to elude him, however, when at Wimbledon he was not able to overcome David Skoch, finishing as runner-up again in a major group A event. What better way than to break the pattern than with victory in your home major. Brian's win in the US Open, together with victory in the USTA Boys' Closed Championships gave him an unassailable lead, and we look forward to seeing what he is capable of in the seniors in the next few years.

David Skoch gave himself a very busy schedule in 1992 starting with the Australian circuit, followed by Europe and the United States. He met with mixed results in Australia, managing just one semi-final placing in Victoria. However, things started to pick up in Europe, his points beginning to build up thanks to semi-final and runner-up placings in Florence and Santa Croce, Italy, respectively. Victory over top seeded Dunn in Milan set him on track for his first Group A title, but the equally talented Eugeny Kafelnikov, CIS, making one of his brief appearances in the circuit just held on for a 7–6, 6–4 win. Amends were made, of course, at Wimbledon, a title that David will treasure and a sign of his ability to compete on all surfaces.

Third placed Grant Doyle does have the memory of taking his own Australian Open title, but there always seemed to be a few unexpected defeats at the other major tournaments. A disappointing French Open saw him depart in the first round at the hands of Alexandru Radulescu, and at Wimbledon he ran into David Skoch in the quarter-finals.

Eddie Jacques, an unseeded American with relatively little experience, had a wonderful run at the US Open, and it was he who kept his nerve to oust Doyle in two tie-break sets in the quarters of that tournament. Victories at Surbiton and the Canadian Open kept Grant's hope alive, but really it was probably a disappointing year which had got off to the best possible start.

In the girls' singles Rossana de los Rios of Paraguay deserves her title as World Champion after maintaining her position at the top despite considerable pressure from Romania's Catalina Cristea. Victories at the Italian and French Opens were not sufficient to guarantee the title, three group A wins required to pick up bonus points. Going into the Orange Bowl, Rossana was aware that a good result was needed and it was only a strong performance by Slovenia's Barbara Mulej in the final which denied Rossana the perfect ending. Still, a runner-up position extended Rossana's lead, which in the end put her 165 points ahead of Cristea. A win at the South American Closed and a semi-final placing at Wimbledon also contributed towards her success, and it was only really at the US Open that she failed to impress, losing surprisingly to Canada's Sonia Jeyaseelan in the 2nd round.

Not quite so many major titles for Catalina Cristea who travelled as far as Asia in her bid for the title. 16 events worldwide benefitted from Catalina's participation in 1992 and her consistency in all the majors kept her in the hunt. Victory did come in Venezuela and at the European Closed Championships, and there was also a semi-final placing at the French

Open where it was fitting that she was beaten by de los Rios.

Third placed Lindsay Davenport, USA, was another consistent performer who managed to reach this position despite competing in just six circuit events. It does help, of course, to reach the final of the Australian Open and the semi-final of the French Open, but Lindsay's best memory will be of the US Open where she did not drop a set in claiming her home title.

On to doubles where Mexico gained their third championship title when Enrique Abaroa just pipped Czechoslovakia's Filip Kascak by 20 points. Needing something a little special going into the Orange Bowl, Enrique teamed with Nigerian Sule Ladipo and produced just that with victory that earned him 180 points. A timely win for the French doubles champion who also made the semi-finals at Wimbledon with Alexandru Radulescu.

Kascak will be ruing his first round exit at the Orange Bowl which really did cost him the title. Wins at the Group A events in Venezuela and Japan and the Group 1 event at Surbiton set him on his way, but disappointing results at the other group A events also cost him dear.

Steven Baldas, Australia, will be pleased with his third place after good wins in Salsomaggiore, Alessandria and Thames Ditton. However, the highlight of the season will be his win with compatriot Scott Draper at Wimbledon.

The girls' doubles title looked to be heading to the United States with Lindsay Davenport topping the rankings following victory in Australia and the US Open. In fact, only her defeat in the final of the French by Nancy Feber and Laurence Courtois of Belgium prevented her from picking up sufficient bonus points to ensure the title. The decision to miss the end of year events in the United States cost her when her 1991 points from the Orange Bowl were dropped and she moved from first to fifth position after losing 180 points.

In first place we now find the Belgian pairing of Nancy Feber and Laurence Courtois, equal on points and very worthy joint champions. In a marvellous year this pair have reached at least the semi-finals of all circuit events played, their semi-final placing at Wimbledon being bettered by victory at the Italian and French Opens to name but a few. In addition, these two players formed the backbone of the Belgian girls' team which won the NEC World Youth Cup in September, the ITF Team Championships for boys and girls of 16 & Under. Ironically, however, such was their prowess at singles that it was never necessary for them to play doubles together.

Team competitions continue to attract healthy numbers indicating that this type of format is popular amoung the Federations and the players. The European Tennis Federation face a daunting task each year coordinating their numerous age category team championships. In view of the changes taking place in Europe this task will, if anything, become more difficult as more nations receive recognition and wish to submit teams. Nevertheless organisers are found and the youngest of the team categories, the Copa del Sol and the Europa Cup for boys and girls of 14 & Under, were successfully staged in Italy and Spain respectively.

In the boys competition, the Copa del Sol, 21 nations competed for the title with the added incentive of a top 6 placing putting them through to the NTT World Junior Tennis Final, the ITF Team Championship for players of 14 & Under. Germany and France both looked very impressive on their way to the Final, but it was to be Germany's day with a 3–1 victory.

No consolation for France in the girls' equivalent championship, the Europa Cup, when they failed to convert a 2–1 match lead, narrowly losing the deciding doubles to fall 2–3 to Czechoslovakia.

There was an added incentive for the 16's too, with the five top placed nations in the two competitions gaining a berth in the NEC World Youth Cup Finals, the ITF Championships for players of 16 & Under. Nicholas Escude helped France to victory at last in the Jean Borotra Cup, France, with a 2–1 win over Sweden. In the girls' Helvetie Cup Final, Belgium's Nancy Feber and Laurence Courtois dropped the first set of their deciding doubles against Germany's Andrea Glass and Catrina Muller, but rallied to win the title for their country with a 6–7, 6–3 6–0 victory. An incredible 23 nations played the Borotra Cup but this was bettered by the Helvetie Cup entry which totalled 26 nations.

After their sensational year in 1991 when Spain swept the board in boys team competitions, it was inevitable that they would gather a few prizes in 1992. First up was the ETA Vasco Valerio Cup where Spain, represented by Alex Corretja and Juan Gisbert, confortably dealt with rivals Italy 2–0 in the final. Spain went on to finish the year in style, fielding Alberto Costa and Felix Mantilla, defeating USA 2–0 in the final of the Sunshine Cup. Spanish strength in depth, in their junior boys in particular, will be the envy of many nations.

The girls' 18 & Under competitions saw the Spanish team just fail to emulate the boys' team when they lost to the German team of Petra Begerow, Kirstin Freye and Sandra Wachtershauer in the final of the HM Queen Sofia Cup. Germany did, however, need to keep their nerve in the final having dropped the opening set of the deciding doubles.

Julie Steven and Nicole London representing the United States could only finish in third place in the NEC World Youth Cup Final in September. At the Maureen Connolly-Brinker Continental Players' Cup on home ground they once more teamed up and held off the challenge of Italy to take a team title for their country.

PRINCE JUNIOR WORLD RANKING 1992

Only those players who qualified for a year-end ranking are listed. The minimum requirements for this were having played 6 Prince Junior World Ranking events, 3 of which were outside their own country and 3 of which were Group A status.

BOYS' SINGLES
1 Brian Dunn (USA); 2 David Skoch (TCH); 3 Grant Doyle (AUS); 4 Vincent Spadea (USA); 5 Mose Navarra (ITA); 6 Gabriel Silberstein (CHI); 7 Adriano Ferreira (BRA); 8 Takao Suzuki (JPN); 9 Gaston Etlis (ARG); 10 Noam Behr (ISR); 11 Hyeong-Keun Song (KOR); 12 Sule Ladipo (NGR); 13 J.J. Jackson (USA); 14 Sven Kohler (HKG); 15 Gustavo Diaz (ARG); 16 Herbert Wiltschnig (AUT); 17 Erik Casas (MEX); 18 Gregory Carraz (FRA); 19 Andres Zingman (ARG); 20 Filip Kascak (TCH).

GIRLS' SINGLES
1 Rossana De Los Rios (PAR); 2 Catalina Cristea (ROM); 3 Lindsay Davenport (USA); 4 Julie Steven (USA); 5 Larissa Schaerer (PAR); 6 Ninfa Marra (VEN); 7 Nancy Feber (BEL); 8 Ludmila Richterova (TCH); 9 Hiroko Mochizuki (JPN); 10 Lisa McShea (AUS); 11 Zuzana Nemsakova (TCH); 12 Maria-Fernanda Landa (ARG); 13 Laurence Courtois (BEL); 14 Nicole London (USA); 15 Dally Randriantefy (MAD); 16 Anne Miller (USA); 17 Viviana Valdovinos (PAR); 18 Sirilux Mingmolee (THA); 19 Lenka Cenkova (TCH); 20 Anna Smashnova (ISR).

BOYS' DOUBLES
1 Enrique Abaroa (MEX); 2 Filip Kascak (TCH); 3 Steven Baldas (AUS); 4 Miles MacLagen (GBR); 5 Scott Draper (AUS); 6 Alexandru Radulescu (ROM); 7 Mose Navarra (ITA); 8 Massimo Bertolini (ITA); 9 Andrew Richardson (GBR); 10 Eric Taino (USA); 11 Gabriel Silberstein (CHI); 12 J.J. Jackson (USA); 13 Geronimo De Greef (ARG); 14 Marcelo Rios (CHI); 15 David Miketa (TCH); 16 Andres Zingman (ARG); 17 Gaston Etlis (ARG); 18 Sule Ladipo (NGR); 19 Eric Casas (MEX); 20 Tim Henman (GBR).

GIRLS' DOUBLES
1= Nancy Feber (BEL); 1= Laurence Courtois (BEL); 3 Maija Avotins (AUS); 4 Ludmila Richterova (TCH); 5 Lindsay Davenport (USA); 6 Nicole London (USA); 7 Julie Steven (USA); 8 Lisa McShea (AUS); 9 Zuzana Nemsakova (TCH); 10 Eva Martincova (TCH); 11 Lenka Cenkova (TCH); 12 Catalina Cristea (ROM); 13 Ninfa Marra (VEN); 14 Larissa Schaerer (PAR); 15 Sandy Sureephong (USA); 16 Maria-Fernanda Landa (ARG); 17 Hiroko Mochizuki (JPN); 18 Janet Lee (USA); 19 Dally Randriantefy (MAD); 20 Rossana De Los Rios (PAR).

PRINCE JUNIOR WORLD RANKING 1992 – POINTS EXPLANATION

The Prince Junior World Ranking is a world-wide points-linked circuit of 114 tournaments, 5 continental championships and 4 team competitions in 60 countries, under the management of the International Tennis Federation. There are ten separate points categories covering the three types of events. There is no limit to the number of tournaments in which a player may compete each year. The best six results from tournaments (Groups A and 1-5), continental championships (Groups B1-B3) and team competitions (Group C) count towards a player's ranking. To qualify for a final year-end ranking a player must have competed in at least six events, including at least three Group A tournaments and at least three outside his or her own country.

POINTS TABLE (Tournaments & Regional Championships)

SINGLES

	A	1	2	3	4	5	B1	B2	B3
Winner	250	120	80	60	40	30	180	100	80
Runner-up	180	100	65	50	30	20	120	80	50
Semi-Finalists	120	75	50	30	20	10	80	60	30
Quarter-Finalists *	80	50	30	20	10	5	60	40	15
Losers in last 16**	50	30	15	10	5	–	30	25	5
Losers in last 32***	30	20	–	–	–	–	20	10	–

*   only if 16 or more players in draw (excluding withdrawals)
**   only if 32 or more players in draw (excluding withdrawals)
*** only if 64 or more players in draw (excluding withdrawals)

DOUBLES (Each Player)

	A	1	2	3	4	5	B1	B2	B3
Winners	180	100	65	50	30	20	120	80	50
Runners-up	120	75	50	30	20	10	80	60	30
Semi-Finalists *	80	50	30	20	10	5	60	40	15
Quarter-Finalists **	50	30	15	10	5	–	30	25	5
Losers in last 16 ***	30	20	–	–	–	–	20	10	–

*   only if 8 or more pairs in draw (excluding withdrawals)
**   only if 16 or more pairs in draw (excluding withdrawals)
*** only if 32 or more pairs in draw (excluding withdrawals)

POINTS TABLE (Group C - Team Competition)

	No. 1 Singles Player Win	No. 2 Singles Player Win	Doubles Win Each Player
Final	100	80	80
Semi-Final	80	60	60
Quarter-Final	60	40	40

POINTS TABLE (Group A Super Series Bonus Points)

	Singles	Doubles
Winner of 3 or more Group A events	150	150

PRINCE JUNIOR WORLD RANKING RESULTS 1992

DATE	TOURNAMENT	GROUP	BOYS' SINGLES FINAL	GIRLS' SINGLES FINAL
23–29 Dec	Casablanca Cup, Mexico	2	J. Esqueda (MEX) d. A. Ferreira (BRA) 6-3 3-6 6-3	B. Schett (AUT) d. A. Havrlikova (TCH) 4-6 6-4 6-3
27 Dec–1 Jan	African Closed, Ivory Coast	B3	L. Ilou (CIV) d. S. Adbib (MAR) 6-4 7-6	D. Randriantefy (MAD) d. A. Elshishiny (EGY) 6-2 6-3
28 Dec–2 Jan	Queensland Girls, Australia	3		T. Krizan (SLO) d. A. Marik (AUS) 6-3 7-5
28 Dec–2 Jan	South Australian Boys	3	S. Baldas (AUS) d. B. Sceney (AUS) 3-6 6-2 6-3	
30 Dec–5 Jan	Venezuela	A	G. Silberstein (CHI) d. J.J. Jackson (USA) 6-3 6-2	C. Cristea (ROM) d. L. Olave (URU) 6-4 6-3
31 Dec–5 Jan	Coqui Bowl, Puerto Rico	3	H. Wiltschnig (AUT) d. S. Leiner (AUT) 6-1 6-4	L. Pavlov (YUG) d. B. Ivanovic (YUG) 6-4 6-0
1–6 Jan	Salk Indoor, Sweden	3	R. Dellenborg (SWE) d. F. Bergh (SWE) 7-5 6-3	A. Carlsson (SWE) d. A. Norinda (SWE) 6-1 6-4
2–8 Jan	New South Wales, Australia	1	B. Sceney (AUS) d. C. Mahony (AUS) 7-5 7-5	L. McShea (AUS) d. H. Mochizuki (JPN) 4-6 6-2 6-2
6–10 Jan	Vasteras Indoor, Sweden	4	T. Johansson (SWE) d. V. Liukko (FIN) 6-2 6-4	A. Carlsson (SWE) d. M. Wolff (DEN) 6-4 6-4
6–11 Jan	Coffee Bowl, Costa Rica	3	H. Wiltschnig (AUS) d. A. Ferreira (BRA) 6-3 6-2	B. Ivanovic (YUG) d. L. Pavlov (YUG) 6-2 6-1
6–12 Jan	Pony Malta Cup, Colombia	1	A. Ferreira (BRA) d. G. Diaz (ARG) 7-6 6-2	L. Richterova (TCH) d. L. Cenkova (TCH) 6-1 6-1
13–18 Jan	Victoria, Australia	2	M. Hill (AUS) d. S. Draper (AUS) 6-4 6-2	M. Avotins (AUS) d. N. London (USA) 6-0 6-4
13–19 Jan	Ecuador Cup	2	G. Doyle (AUS) d. B. Dunn (USA) 6-2 6-0	L. Richterova (TCH) d. K. Miskolczi (HUN) 6-0 6-1
20–26 Jan	Australian Open	A	G. Fernandes (BRA) d. P. Kudrnac (TCH) 6-4 6-7 7-5	J. Limmer (AUS) d. L. Davenport (USA) 7-5 6-2
20–26 Jan	Inka Bowl, Peru	2	E. Casas (MEX) d. T. Harel (ISR) 7-5 6-2	N. Marra (VEN) d. L. Andrea (ARG) 6-1 3-6 6-1
27 Jan–2 Feb	Condor De Plata, Bolivia	3	G. Silberstein (CHI) d. R. Briones (CHI) 6-4 6-3	N. Marra (VEN) d. C. Ampuero (BOL) 6-3 6-4
3–9 Feb	Milo Cup, Chile	2	G. Diaz (ARG) d. P. Kudrnac (TCH) 6-1 2-6 6-2	L. Andrea (ARG) d. Y. Yoshida (JPN) 6-4 6-2
10–16 Feb	Argentina Cup	2	J. Greenhalgh (NZL) d. G. Diaz (ARG) 6-2 6-2	N. Marra (VEN) d. C. Ampuero (BOL) 3-6 6-3 6-4
17–23 Feb	Carrasco Bowl	2	H-K. Song (KOR) d. N. Kirtane (IND) 6-4 6-0	M-F. Landa (ARG) d. N. Marra (VEN) 6-4 4-6 7-6
17–23 Feb	Asian Closed, India	B2	J. Novak (TCH) d. D. Prchlik (TCH) 0-6 7-6 6-2	H-A. Shin (KOR) d. J-Y. Choi (KOR) 6-2 6-2
18–23 Feb	Czechoslovakian Indoor	3	A. Ghonim (EGY) d. B. Zanaoui (TUN) 6-3 6-2	K. Kroupova (TCH) d. R. Surova (TCH) 6-4 6-2
24–28 Feb	Qatar	5	H. Wiltschnig (AUT) d. C. Reano (PER) 7-6 6-4	
24 Feb–1 March	Asuncion Bowl, Paraguay	2	M. Khaliq (PAK) d. A. Baruah (IND) 6-1 6-4	Y. Yoshida (JPN) d. M-F. Landa (ARG) 6-4 6-2
24 Feb–1 March	Sri Lanka	3	M. Norman (SWE) d. M. Cicek (SWE) 6-7 6-2 7-6	S. Mingmolee (THA) d. S. Sangakkara (SRI) 6-4 6-3
26 Feb–1 March	Swedish Indoor	1	E. Casas (MEX) d. A. Ferreira (BRA) 6-7 7-6 7-6	A. Carlsson (SWE) d. M. Arkbrant (SWE) 7-5 6-3
2–8 March	Banana Bowl, Brazil	4	B. Saluja (IND) d. V. Ramamurthi (IND) 2-1 ret.	L. Schaerer (PAR) d. M-F. Landa (ARG) 7-5 7-5
2–8 March	Hotel Ceylon, Sri Lanka	3	B. Jacob (GER) d. D. Prchlik (TCH) 6-3 1-6 6-3	M. Kuki (JPN) d. R. Prasithikul (THA) 6-2 6-0
5–8 March	Bavarian Indoor, Germany	B2	A. Ferreira (BRA) d. G. Etlis (ARG) 6-4 6-4	E. Krejcova (TCH) d. M. Gargulakova (TCH) 6-3 6-0
9–15 March	South American Closed, Brazil	2	N. Ploysook (THA) d. S. Chukwan (THA) 7-5 6-2	R. De Los Rios (PAR) d. L. Schaerer (PAR) 4-6 6-3 6-3
9–15 March	Thailand	2	F. Veglio (SUI) d. K. Goossens (BEL) 6-4 6-4	B. Sangaram (THA) d. S-H. Chung (KOR) 6-2 7-6
9–15 March	Happy Cup, Belgium	2	N. Kirtane (IND) d. S. Koehler (HKG) 6-2 6-3	N. Feber (BEL) d. L. Courtois (BEL) 6-1 7-6
16–22 March	Hong Kong	2	A. Richardson (GBR) d. T. Henman (GBR) 6-2 6-1	J. Saret (PHI) d. M. Kuki (JPN) 6-4 6-4
18–22 March	British Indoor	5	N. Ploysook (THA) d. S. Yongchanaskul (THA) 5-7 6-2 6-2	S-A. Siddall (GBR) d. Y. Doyle (IRL) 6-1 7-5
23–29 March	Taipei	2	M. Bhupathi (IND) d. C. Halim (INA) 6-4 6-3	S-P. Lin (TPE) d. S. Chatsuthipan (THA) 7-6 3-6 6-1
31 March–5 Apr	Suntory Japan, Tokyo	2	E. Taino (USA) d. J. Schors (GER) 6-1 6-2	J. Saret (PHI) d. D. Sutedja (INA) 6-4 4-6 7-5
6–12 Apr	Croatia	3	M. Linhart (TCH) d. J. Bozic (YUG) 1-6 6-3 6-1	K. Takuma (CIS) d. A. Linkova (CIS) 2-6 6-1 6-2
8–12 Apr	Tashkent, CIS	3	D. Tomachevitch (CIS) d. P. Joromski (CIS) 6-2 3-6 6-4	C. Habernigg (AUT) d. N. Bonacic (CRO) 6-1 6-2
13–19 Apr	Malaysia	3	W-C. Park (KOR) d. V-M. Reddy (IND) 6-7 6-1 6-1	E. Tatarkova (CIS) d. A. Linkova (CIS) 6-1 6-2
13–19 Apr				H-A. Shin (KOR) d. J-Y. Choi (KOR) 6-2 2-2 ret.
14–18 Apr	Dubitzky Tournament, Israel	4	T. Harel (ISR) d. L. Dahan (ISR) 6-3 6-1	S. Burstain (ISR) d. S. Carvin (AUS) 7-5 4-6 6-4

DATE	TOURNAMENT	GROUP	BOYS' SINGLES FINAL	GIRLS' SINGLES FINAL
15–18 Apr	Pascuas Bowl, Paraguay	4	F. Tazza (BRA) d. A. Brause (URU) 6-2 7-5	V. Valdovinos (PAR) d. S. Passos (BRA) 6-7 6-3 6-1
15–20 Apr	Florence, Italy	2	A. Richardson (GBR) d. S. Adbib (MAR) 6-1 6-4	B. Schmitt (AUT) d. F. Lubiana (ITA) 6-1 4-6 6-4
20–26 Apr	Indonesia	3	D. Alfachrizi (INA) d. A. Raturandang (INA) 6-1 7-6	J-Y. Choi (KOR) d. S. Mingmolee (THA) 2-6 6-3 6-3
20–26 Apr	Sochi, CIS	4	E. Kafelnikov (CIS) d. M. Gawlowski (POL) 6-2 6-1	N. Luarsabashvili (CIS) d. A. Casparian (CIS) 6-1 6-1
21–25 Apr	Jerusalem, Israel	5	R. Dellenborg (SWE) d. A. Tishler (ISR) 6-4 6-3	N. Horovitz (ISR) d. D. Kovalevski (ISR) 6-2 6-3
27 Apr–2 May	Salsomaggiore, Italy	5	M. Navarra (ITA) d. G. Terraneo (ITA) 6-2 6-2	K. Bulat (POL) d. J. Angeli (ITA 7-5 6-3
27 Apr–3 May	Brunei	5	A. Baruah (IND) d. M. Misa (PHI) 7-5 6-2	E. Chiew (MAL) d. C-B. Khoo (MAL) 6-0 6-0
29 Apr–3 May	Gesterner Spring Bowl, Austria	3	J. Unterberger (AUT) d. H. Wiltschnig (AUT) 7-5 6-2	L. Nemeckova (TCH) d. M. Gargulakova (TCH) 6-1 6-2
4–9 May	Alessandra, Italy	2	E. Kafelnikov (CIS) d. M. Rios (CHI) 6-4 6-3	L. Cenkova (TCH) d. K. Schlukebir (USA) 6-3 6-0
4–9 May	Singapore	5	J. Greenhalgh (NZL) d. S. Downs (NZL) 6-2 5-7 6-2	M. Kuki (JPN) d. H-H. Shan (KOR) 2-6 6-2 6-1
11–16 May	Santa Croce Sull'Arno, Italy	1	E. Kafelnikov (CIS) d. D. Skoch (TCH) 7-6 6-0	E. Martincova (TCH) d. S. Sureephong (USA) 6-3 6-2
18–23 May	Italian Championships	A	E. Kafelnikov (CIS) d. D. Skoch (TCH) 7-6 6-4	R. De Los Rios (PAR) d. N. Feber (BEL) 6-1 7-5
25–30 May	Astrid Bowl, Belgium	1	C. Tambue (GER) d. A. Zingman (ARG) 6-2 6-2	L. Schaerer (PAR) d. V. Valdovinos (PAR) 4-6 6-4 6-0
31 May–7 June	French Open	A	A. Pavel (ROM) d. M. Navarra (ITA) 6-1 3-6 6-3	R. De Los Rios (PAR) d. P. Suarez (ARG) 6-4 6-0
8–14 June	Flanders Junior Cup, Belgium	2	G. Etlis (ARG) d. S. Ladipo (NGR) 7-5 6-4	N. Feber (BEL) d. E. Likhovtseva (CIS) 6-3 6-2
8–14 June	Apple Bowl, Spain	A	J-I. Carrasco (ESP) d. A. Bragado (ESP) 6-3 2-6 6-1	S. Sierra (ESP) d. V. Garcia (ESP) 6-1 6-3
3–13 June	Danibius Cup, Hungary	4	J. Noval (TCH) d. R. Szymanik (POL) 6-1 6-1	K. Gyorke (HUN) d. G. Nelikova (TCH)
15–21 June	Thames Ditton, England	2	B. Dunn (USA) d. S. Ladipo (NGR) 6-3 6-2	E. Likhovtseva (CIS) d. K. Cross (GBR) 6-4 6-3
22–27 June	Denmark	4	S. Aspelin (SWE) d. C. N'Goran (CIV) 7-5 6-3	K. Petrikova (TCH) d. D. Gerwin (POL) 6-2 6-1
22–28 June	Surbiton, England	1	G. Doyle (AUS) d. L. Arnold (ARG) 6-2 6-1	E. Likhovtseva (CIS) d. Z. Nemsakova (TCH) 6-4 7-6
29 June–5 July	Wimbledon Championships, UK	A	AD. Skoch (TCH) d. B. Dunn (USA) 6-4 6-3	C. Rubin (USA) d. L. Courtois (BEL) 6-2 7-5
29 June–5 July	Netherlands	4	P. Dezort (TCH) d. M. Linhart (TCH) 6-4 6-3	L. Nemeckova (TCH) d. G. Netikova (TCH) 6-1 7-6
7–12 July	German Open	4	D. Pescariu (ROM) d. R. Wassen (NED) 6-2 6-3	S. Haas (GER) d. I. Heise 3-6 6-2 6-1
8–12 July	Friendship Cup	4	M. Hromec (TCH) d. M. Linhart (TCH) 6-4 3-6 6-4	A. Olsza (POL) d. M. Grzybowska (POL) 6-1 6-2
13–18 July	Jamaica	5	N. Malcolm (JAM) d. F. Sierra (MEX) 5-7 6-4 6-4	S. Hanna (JAM) d. M. Rurika (JPN) 1-6 6-3 6-4
13–19 July	Klosters, Switzerland	2	P. Hajek (GER) d. M. Linhart (TCH) 6-1 6-1	D. Randriantefy (MAD) d. I. Heise (GER) 6-1 6-1
17–19 July	Eur. Boys Team Event, Italy	C	Spain d. Italy 2-0	Germany d. Spain 2-1
17–19 July	Eur. Girls Team Event, France	C		
20–25 July	Winchester, England	5	P. Petrovsky (AUS) d. J. Fox (GBR) 7-6 6-3	M. Wagner (LUX) d. K. Llewellyn (GBR) 6-3 4-6 6-4
20–26 July	European Closed, Germany	B1	C.V.Garsse-Lysens (BEL) d. A. Skrzypczak (POL) 6-2 6-4	C. Cristea (ROM) d. K. Hrdlickova (TCH) 6-4 6-3
20–26 July	Guatemala	5	H. Slifa (DOM) d. F. Sierra (MEX) 6-2 6-2	J. Sotomayor (PUR) d. A. Gomez (GUA) 6-1 7-6
25 July–1 Aug	East of Ireland	5	P. Gottesleben (GER) d. C. Hoop (SUI) 6-3 3-6 6-2	K. Nugent (IRL) d. D. Walsh (IRL) 6-0 6-1
27 July–1 Aug	South Africa	5	N. Godwin (RSA) d. A. Walkin (RSA) 6-3 6-2	E. Gevers (RSA) d. J. Neilson (RSA) 6-1 6-2
27 July–2 Aug	El Salvador	5	H. Slifa (DOM) d. C. Giles (MEX) 6-2 6-4	C. Giraldo (COL) d. T. Schroeder (USA) 6-2 6-3
3–8 Aug	Botswana	5	D. Lebeta (LES) d. N. Sangare (CIV) 6-4 6-3	L. Hitge (RSA) d. G. Swart (RSA) 6-2 6-1
5–9 Aug	Slovakia Cup, Czechoslovakia	3	B. Wober (AUS) d. G. Oresic (CRO) 7-5 6-0	M. Gargulakova (TCH) d. R. Surova (TCH) 6-4 6-3
8–15 Aug	USTA Girls Closed, California	1		M. Vento (VEN) d. J. Steven (USA) 6-2 4-6 6-4
8–16 Aug	USTA Boys Closed, Michigan	1	B. Dunn (UAS) d. V. Spadea (USA) 5-7 7-5 1-6 6-3 7-6	
10–15 Aug	Nigeria	5	L. Alakwem (NGR) d. S. Ikpeba (NGR) 6-7 6-4 6-4	C. Udofa (NGR) d. U. Ogherohwo (NGR) 7-5 4-6 6-3
10–16 Aug	Dominican Republic Tournament	5	H. Slifa (DOM) d. C. Giles (MEX) 6-1 6-2	M. Rurika (JPN) d. J. Sotomayor (PUR) 6-3 6-1
11–15 Aug	Nyirfa Cup, Hungary	5	M. Leysek (TCH) d. D. Dudas (ROM) 7-5 6-2	K. Nagy (HUN) d. A. Friganovic (CRO) 6-3 6-1
11–15 Aug	Zimbabwe	5	N. Sangare (CIV) d. C. Hurter (RSA) 6-1 6-3	L. Hitge (RSA) d. C. Black (ZIM 7-5 6-2

DATE	TOURNAMENT	GROUP	BOYS' SINGLES FINAL	GIRLS' SINGLES FINAL
11–16 Aug	Crystal Cup, Czechoslovakia	2	J. Novak (TCH) d. F. Kascak (TCH) 7-5 6-7 7-5	E. Krejcova (TCH) d. G. Netikova (TCH) 6-4 6-3
11–16 Aug	EA-Generali-Jugend, Austria	5	H. Wiltschnig (AUT) d. W. Schranz (AUT) 6-1 6-3	N. Mura (AUT) d. E. Fauth (AUT) 0-6 6-2 6-2
16–22 Aug	USTA Grass Courts, Philadelphia	4	T. Shimada (USA) d. M. Arnold (USA) 6-3 7-6	J. Steven (USA) d. K. Miller (USA) 6-1 6-2
17–22 Aug	South Pacific Closed, Am Samoa	B3	M. Hitesh (FIJ) d. M. Kailahi (TON)	D. So'onalole (SAM) d. L. Leavai (SAM)
18–23 Aug	Zambia	5	D. Omaboe (GHA) d. G. Adenekan (NGR) 6-1 6-4	L. Hitge (RSA) d. G. Swart (RSA) 6-0 7-5
24–30 Aug	Kenya	5	N. Sangare (CIV) d. C. Hurter (RSA) 6-4 6-4	L. Hitge (RSA) d. C. Black (ZIM) 6-4 6-3
25–29 Aug	USTA Hard Courts, Indianapolis	4	J.J. Jackson (USA) d. W. Boich (USA) 6-2 3-6 6-2	A. Wainwright (GBR) d. J. Pullin (GBR) 6-4 1-6 6-2
31 Aug–6 Sep	Canada	1	G. Doyle (AUS) d. M. Bertolini (ITA) 6-3 6-4	P. Kamstra (NED) d. C. Cristea (ROM) 6-2 6-4
2–7 Sep	Romania	4	A. Rechberger (AUT) d. M. Raicea (ROM) 6-1 6-1	L. Zirnoveanu (ROM) d. D. Vlad (ROM) 6-1 6-2
7–13 Sep	U.S. Open	A	B. Dunn (USA) d. N. Behr (ISR) 7-5 6-2	L. Davenport (USA) d. J. Steven (USA) 6-2 6-4
7–13 Sep	Aphrodite Cup, Cyprus	5	T. Larsen (DEN) d. B. Eissa (EGY) 6-1 6-2	M. Foster (DEN) d. M. Pape (DEN) 6-2 6-2
9–13 Sep	Luxembourg	4	M. Linhart (TCH) d. P. Dezort (TCH) 1-6 6-4 7-5	S. Olsen (DEN) d. A. Monhartova (TCH) 6-4 6-2
15–20 Sep	Pelikane Bowl, Bulgaria	5	R. Kukal (TCH) d. D. Bandurowski (POL) 6-4 6-1	A. Pangderova (BUL) d. T. Nedeva (BUL) 6-1 6-3
21–27 Sep	Northern Territory, Australia	5	M. Nielsen (NZL) d. L. Bosio (AUS) 6-2 6-2	A. Venkatesan (AUS) d. K. Hunt (AUS) 7-5 6-2
24–27 Sep	Saloman Melnick, Chile	4	M. Rios (CHI) d. P. Escalona (CHI) 6-3 6-3	B. Castro (CHI) d. C. Morariu (USA) 6-2 6-2
28 Sep–3 Oct	Brunei	4	S. Clark (NZL) d. A. Misra (IND) 6-0 6-4	N. Vaidyanathan (IND) d. P. Kunsirisawat (THA) 6-0 2-6 6-4
5–11 Oct	Malaysia	5	S. Clark (NZL) d. A. Misra (IND) 6-2 6-0	D. Sutedja (INA) d. T-T. Weng (TPE) 6-2 6-1
5–11 Oct	Copa Gerdau, Brazil	5	G. Fernandes (BRA) d. R. Serpa-Guinazu (ARG) 6-0 6-0	S. Rodrigues (BRA) d. L. Kelbert (BRA) 4-6 6-4 6-3
12–18 Oct	Mercu Buana, Indonesia	3	R. Witz (AUT) d. A. Raturandang (INA) 4-6 7-5 6-4	M.V. Widyadharma (INA) d. C. Fan (TPE) 7-5 7-6
12–18 Oct	Copa Banco Economico, Brazil	5	A. Ferreira (BRA) d. P. Zannoni (BRA)	S. Passos (BRA) d. L. Kelbert (BRA)
20–25 Oct	Japan	A	Suwandi (INA) d. T. Suzuki (JPN) 7-6 6-2	M. Kuki (JPN) d. H. Mochizuki (JPN) 3-6 6-1 6-4
26 Oct–1 Nov	East Asian Championships, HK	2	J. Delgado (GBR) d. J. Baily (GBR) 6-4 6-7 6-1	C. Cristea (ROM) d. Y-J. Choi (KOR) 6-0 6-4
3–7 Nov	China, P.R.	3	J. Baily (GBR) d. W-C. Park (KOR) 7-5 5-7 6-3	J-Y. Choi (KOR) d. D. Sutedja (INA) 6-3 7-6
9–15 Nov	Singha Tournament, Thailand	3	A. Baruah (IND) d. P. Waas (GBR) 6-1 6-4	M-H. Park (KOR) d. A. Ponnappa (IND) 6-4 6-3
16–22 Nov	Tea Bowl, Sri Lanka	5	M. Khaliq (PAK) d. Y. Ishii (JPN) 7-5 6-3	N. Schwarz (AUS) d. Y-A. Kim (KOR) 6-4 6-4
23–29 Nov	Pakistan	3	S. Humphries (USA) d. J. Szymanski (VEN) 7-5 7-5	N. Marra (VEN) d. L. Andrea (ARG) 6-4 7-5
29 Nov–5 Dec	Yucatan Cup, Mexico	2	S. Aspelin (SWE) d. N. Behr (ISR) 6-4 6-2	T. Panova (RUS) d. M-A. Vento (VEN) 6-4 2-6 6-0
7–12 Dec	Eddie Herr Tournament, USA	C		
14–19 Dec	Continental Player' Cup, USA	C		USA d. Italy 2-1
14–20 Dec	Sunshine Cup, USA	C	Spain d. USA 2-0	—
20–27 Dec	Orange Bowl, USA	A	V. Spadea (USA) d. G. Etlis (ARG) 7-6 6-3	B. Mulej (SLO) d. R. De Los Rios (PAR) 7-5 7-5
28 Dec–3 Jan 93	Port Washington, USA	2	G. Trifu (ROM) d. A. Roberman (USA) 6-3 6-0	M. Muric (CRO) d. D. Randriantefy (MAD) 6-3 6-2

EUROPA CUP *(Girls' 14 & Under International Team Championship)*
20 nations competed. Semi-finals and finals played in Vercelli, Italy, 3–5 July.
Quarter-finals: Germany d. Sweden 5–0; France d. Hungary 3–2; CIS d. Netherlands 3–2; Czechoslovakia d. Italy 4–1. ***Semi-finals:*** France d. Germany 3–2; Czechoslovakia d. CIS 5–0.
Final: Czechoslovakia d. France 3–2 (L. Varmuzova d. I. Taesch 4–6 6–4 6–4; H.Nagyova lost to A.Castera 3–6 2–6; S.Kleinova lost to E.Curutchet 3–6 6–3 2–6; J.Ondrouchova d. G.Gouttefarde 6–2 6–2; Kleinova/Ondrouchova d. Castera/Curutchet 3–6 7–5 6–4).

COPA DEL SOL CUP *(Boys' 14 & Under International Team Championship)*
21 nations competed. Semi-finals and final played in Playa De Aro, Spain, 3–5 July.
Quarter-finals: Germany d. Hungary 5–0; Sweden d. Italy 3–2; Spain d. Czechoslovakia 3–2; France d. Austria 4–1. ***Semi-finals:*** Germany d. Sweden 4–1; France d. Spain 3–2.
Final: Germany d. France 3–1 (T.Haas lost to O.Mutis 4–6 4–6; J–R. Brandt d. J–R. Lisnard 7–5 6–1; J–P. Wenner d. J.Barras 6–3 7–6; Brandt/Haas d. M-O.Baron/Mutis 6–4 6–3).

VASCO VALERIO CUP *(Boys' 18 & Under International Team Championship)*
22 nations competed. Final played in Lesa, Italy, 16–18 July.
Quarter-finals: Italy d. Great Britain 3–0; Poland d. Sweden 2–1; Czechoslovakia d. Germany 2–1; Spain d. France 2–1. ***Semi-finals:*** Italy d. Poland 2–0; Spain d. Czechoslovakia 3–0. ***Final:*** Spain d. Italy 2–0 (A.Corretja d. M.Navarra 6–3 6–1; J.Gisbert d. M.Bertolini 6–1 7–6; doubles not played).

HM QUEEN SOFIA CUP *(Girls' 18 & Under International Team Championship)*
17 nations competed. Final played in Mimizan, France, 16–18 July.
Quarter-finals: Spain d. CIS 3–0; Sweden d. Italy 3–0; Croatia d. Great Britain 2–1; Germany d. France 3–0. ***Semi-finals:*** Spain d. Sweden 2–1; Germany d. Croatia 2–1.
Final: Germany d. Spain 2–1 (P.Begerow d. E.Bottini 6–2 7–5; K.Freye lost to C.Torrens 2–6 3–6; Freye/S.Wachtershauser d. Bottini/E.Jimenez 2–6 7–5 6–2).

JEAN BOROTRA CUP *(Boys' 16 & Under International Team Championship)*
23 nations competed. Final played in Le Touquet, France, 2–4 August.
Quarter-finals: France d. Hungary 3–0; Israel d. Spain 2–1; Italy d. Czechoslovakia 2–1; Sweden d. Germany 2–1. ***Semi-finals:*** France d. Israel 3–0; Sweden d. Italy 3–0. ***Final:*** France d. Sweden 2–1 (N.Escude d. M.Norman 2–6 6–4 6–4; M.Huard lost to A.Stenman 5–7 5–7; Escude/Huard d. Norman/M.Sjoquist 6–2 6–2).

HELVETIE CUP *(Girls' 16 & Under International Team Championship)*
26 nations competed. Final played in Leysin, Switzerland, 2–4 August.
Quarter-finals: Belgium d. Netherlands 2–1; Czechoslovakia d. Israel 2–1; CIS d. France 2–1; Germany d. Italy 3–0. ***Semi-finals:*** Belgium d. Czechoslovakia 2–1; Germany d. CIS 3–0. ***Final:*** Belgium d. Germany 2–1 (N.Feber d. A.Glass 6–3 6–2; L.Courtois lost to H.Rusch 6–2 6–7 3–6; Courtois/Feber d. Glass/C.Muller 6–7 6–3 6–0).

SUNSHINE CUP *(Boys' 18 & Under International Team Championship)*
38 nations competed. Event played in Delray Beach, Florida, USA, 14–20 December.
Quarter-finals: Chile d. Sweden 2–0; USA d. Czechoslovakia 2–1; Spain d. Argentina 2–1; Israel d. Great Britain 2–1. ***Semi-finals:*** USA d. Chile 2–1; Spain d. Israel 2–0; ***Final:*** Spain d. USA 2–0 (A.Costa d. V.Spadea 6–3 7–5; F.Mantilla d. J.J.Jackson 6–1 6–3; doubles not played).

MAUREEN CONNOLLY–BRINKER CONTINENTAL PLAYERS' CUP *(Girls' 18 & Under International Team Championship)*
27 nations competed. Event played in Delray Beach, Florida, USA, 14–19 December.
Quarter-finals: Spain d. Czechoslovakia 2–1; Italy d. Belgium 3–0; USA d. Russia 2–1; Netherlands d. Japan 3–0; ***Semi-finals:*** Italy d. Spain 2–1; USA d. Netherlands 2–1. ***Final:*** USA d. Italy 2–1 (J.Steven d. R.Grande 6–4 3–6 6–2; N.London lost to F.Bentivoglio 3–6 3–6; London/Steven d. Grande/Bentivoglio 7–6 6–0).

ITF VETERANS' TENNIS

Veteran Events in 1992 returned to Europe with the exception of the new Maureen Connolly Cup Team Event for ladies in the 55 age category. It was agreed that it would be only fitting that the new event supported by the new Maureen Connolly Brinkier Foundation should be the exception. The event was played in Tyler, Texas, at the Tyler Tennis and Swim Club, Tyler being the rose capital of America. Australia were the winners and reaped the privilege of being the first name on the role of honour, beating the Great Britain team 2–1 in the final.

The new event emphasizes the fact that players' requests for age brackets of 5 years are acted upon whenever possible. With the addition of the men's 75, ladies 35 and 65 age categories, there are now 15 in total, 7 for ladies and 8 for men, with 11 team events.

The second year of the Fred Perry Cup sponsored by Fred Perry (Sportswear) UK Ltd. produced the highest number of entries ever received for a Veteran Team Event. A total of 26 teams took part. This large number of teams and supporters were royally treated by the Rot-Weiss Club in Berlin, who, with their sponsors and supporters, Thau & Berendt (Lancia Cars), the Senate of Berlin, the Landessportbund Berlin, the Berlin Brandenburg Tennis Association and the DTP, made this a very memorable event. Our thanks go to the President of the Rot-Weiss Club, Wolfgang Hoffer and the Club Secretary Eberhard Wensky.

The man himself, Fred Perry, accompanied by his wife, Bobby, was in attendance and, as always, was extremely popular with all competitors. The Fred Perry Veterans' Ranking Programme, in its first publicised year, is progressing, and the final year's ranking lists are eagerly awaited. One of the main problem areas in producing an accurate ranking list is the lack of results owing to the average Veteran player competing in only 3 to 4 events a year, and of course the added problem of changing age categories every 5 years. We shall continue in our endeavours to find the most suitable system for all.

Team Events continue to grow. 171 teams took part in 11 events in 1992, an increase of 23% over the previous year. The Championships were held in Palermo, Italy, with an entry of over 330.

Europe again plays host to all events in 1993, with Spain taking on a mini Australian Challenge, hosting 6 Team Events and the Championships, which will be held at the Real Polo Club in Barcelona. The numbers are growing to such an extent that this may be the last time the Championships are held at one venue.

ITALIA CUP
Men's 35 Age Group
ANCONA, ITALY, 14–20 JUNE
Quarter–finals: Italy d. Great Britain 3–0; Brazil d. Portugal 3–0; France d. Indonesia 3–0; USA d. Netherlands 2–1.
Semi–finals: Italy d. Brazil 2–0; France d. USA 2–1.
Final: Italy d. France 2–1 (F. Rocchi d. P. Torre 4–6 6–4 6–2; F. Fanucci d. J. Vanier 7–6 6–4; Zugarelli/Naso lost to Rothwell/Torre 4–6 4–6).

DUBLER CUP
Men's 45 Age Group
PORTSCHACH, AUSTRIA 7–13 JUNE
Quarter–finals: USA d. Australia 2–1; Germany d. Sweden 3–0; France d. Canada 3–0; Spain d.

Switzerland 2–1.
Semi-finals: Germany d. USA 2–1; Spain d. France 2–1.
Final: Germany d. Spain 2–1 (H-J. Plotz lost to J. Velasco 1–6 4–6; H. Rudzinski d. J. Camina 7–5 6–3; Plotz/Rudzinski d. Velasco/Camina 7–5 6–4).

FRED PERRY CUP
Men's 50 Age Group
BERLIN, GERMANY 12–18 JULY
Quarter-finals: Germany d. Canada 3–0; Switzerland 2. Italy 2–1; USA d. Great Britain 3–0; Austria d. Australia 2–1.
Semi-finals: Germany d. Switzerland 3–0; USA d. Austria 3–0.
Final: Germany d. USA 3–0 (H. Elschenbroich d. S. Wilkinson 6–2 6–1; B. Reinholz d. R. Cadwallader 6–2 6–0; Nitsche/Kraus d. Carter/Saputo 7–5 6–4).

AUSTRIA CUP
Men's 55 Age Group
MONTE CARLO, FRANCE 7–13 JUNE
Quarter-finals: USA d. Italy 3–0; Austria d. France 2–0; Australia d. Great Britain 2–0; Germany d. Argentina 2–0.
Semi-finals: USA d. Austria 3–0; Germany d. Australia 2–0.
Final: Germany d. USA 2–1 (K. Fuhrmann d. K. Van Nostrand 5–7 6–4 6–3; H. Loffler d. R. Duesler 6–4 4–6 6–4; J. Nelson/L. Lindborg lost to D. Hamm/F. Seeman 2–6 0–6).

VON CRAMM CUP
Men's 60 Age Group
BOURNEMOUTH, ENGLAND 24–30 MAY
Quarter-finals: Canada d. Norway 3–0; Germany d. Italy 2–1; New Zealand d. France 2–1; USA d. Australia 3–0.
Semi-finals: Canada d. Germany 2–1; USA d. New Zealand 3–0.
Final: Canada d. USA 2–1 (K. Sinclair d. B. Davis 6–3 6–2; L. Main d. C. Devoe 6–4 6–3; L. Miron/K. Sinclair lost to M. Lewis/R. Pharr 5–7 0–6).

BRITANNIA CUP
Men's 65 Age Group
SEEFELD, AUSTRIA 24–30 MAY
Quarter-finals: Austria d. The Netherlands 3–0; USA d. Italy 3–0; Argentina d. Germany 3–0; Australia d. Canada 3–0.
Semi-finals: Austria d. USA 3–0; Australia d. Argentina 2–1.
Final: Australia d. Austria 2–1 (B. McCarthy d. L. Legenstein 4–6 7–6 6–3; D. Billing lost to O. Jirkovsky 6–7 1–6; B. McCarthy/D. Billing d. L. Legenstein/O. Jirkovsky 7–6 7–6).

CRAWFORD CUP
Men's 70 Age Group
LE TOUQUET, FRANCE, 10–15 MAY
Quarter-finals: Germany d. Sweden 2–1; France d. Italy 2–1; Great Britain d. Australia 3–0; USA d. Norway 3–0.
Semi-finals: Germany d. France 2–1; USA d. Great Britain 3–0.
Final: USA d. Germany 3–0 (T. Brown d. R. Rosskopf 6–1 6–0; J. MacGrath d. H. Gantzer 6–2 6–1; Hammel/Swetka d. Rosskopf/Gantzer 6–3 5–7 6–2).

YOUNG CUP
Women's 40 Age Group
MALAHIDE, IRELAND 31 MAY–6 JUNE
Quarter-finals: USA d. Italy 3–0; Austria d. France 2–0; Australia d. Great Britain 2–0; Germany d. Argentina 2–0.
Semi-finals: Australia d. Italy 2–1; Great Britain d. Finland 3–1.
Final: Great Britain d. Australia 2–1 (L. Charles d. M. Rasmussen 6–3 6–0; J. Englefield lost to C. Dorey 4–6 6–3 3–6; L. Charles/J. Englefield d. E. Craig/C. Campling 6–1 6–4).

MARIA ESTHER BUENO CUP
Women's 50 Age Group
BAGNOLES DE L'ORNE, FRANCE, 10–15 MAY

Quarter–finals: USA d. Austria 3–0; Germany d. Canada 3–0; Australia d. Ireland 3–0; France d. Sweden 2–1.
Semi–finals: USA d. Germany 3–0; France d. Australia 2–1.
Final: USA d. France 2–1 (C. Anderson lost to D. Bouteleux 6–3 4–6 3–6; C. Hillebrand d. R. Darmon 6–2 6–4; Hillebrand/Bowden d. Bouteleux/Darmon 6–0 6–0).

MAUREEN CONNOLLY CUP
Women's 55 Age Group
TYLER, USA, 11–16 OCTOBER
Quarter–finals: USA d. Canada 2–1; Australia d. France 3–0; Great Britain d. Ireland 3–0; Germany d. Finland 3–0.
Semi–finals: Australia d. USA 2–0; Great Britain d. Germany 2–1.
Final: Australia d. Great Britain 2–1 (N. Marsh lost to R. Illingworth 6–3 0–6 3–6; J. Dalton d. R. Lauder 6–0 6–1; Dalton/Grigg d. Lauder/Illingworth 6–3 6–2)

MARBLE CUP
Women's 60 Age Group
KESZTHELY, HUNGARY, 10–15 MAY
Quarter–finals: USA d. Hungary 3–0; Australia d. Argentina 2–1; Germany d. Denmark 3–0; Great Britain d. Canada 2–1.
Semi–finals: USA d. Australia 3–0; Great Britain d. Germany 3–0.
Final: Great Britain d. USA 2–1 (R. Lauder d. H. Lum 6–7 6–2 6–2; R. Illingworth lost to B. Pratt 5–7 4–6; R. Lauder/R. Illingworth d. B. Pratt/L. Owen 6–3 6–0).

ITF VETERAN CHAMPIONSHIPS
PALERMO, SICILY 17–23 MAY
MEN'S OVER 35 SINGLES – Final: F. Rocchi (ITA) d. V. Naso (ITA) 6–4 6–1.
MEN'S OVER 35 DOUBLES – Final: French (GBR)/Birner (CSFR) d. Rocchi/Naso (ITA) 6–4 6–3.
MEN'S OVER 45 SINGLES – Final: R. Staguhn (TER) d. B.M. De Jel (NED) 6–3 6–4.
MEN'S OVER 45 DOUBLES – Final: Penberthy (AUS)/De Jel (NED) d. Romero/Perez Corral (ARG) 6–3 6–3.
MEN'S OVER 50 SINGLES – Final: J. P. Lemann (BRA) d. R. Stemmler (GER) 6–0 6–1.
MEN'S OVER 50 DOUBLES – Final: Schelch/Fuchs (AUT) d. Todd (AUS)/Leius (EST) 3-6 7–6 6–4
MEN'S OVER 55 SINGLES – Final: K. Fuhrmann (GER) d. J. Nelson (USA) 6–1 3–2 ret.
MEN'S OVER 55 DOUBLES – Final: Stewart/Dodson (USA) d. Lindberg/Nelson (USA) 7–5 6–4.
MEN'S OVER 60 SINGLES – Final: W. Mertins (GER) d. I. Gulyas (HUN) w/o
MEN'S OVER 60 DOUBLES – Final: Sinclair/Main (CAN) d. Morton/Devoe (USA) 6–3 7–5.
MEN'S OVER 65 SINGLES – Final: B. McCarthy (AUS) d. B. Howe (AUS) 7–5 7–6.
MEN'S OVER 65 DOUBLES – Final: Howe/McCarthy (AUS) d. Hussmuller (GER)/Lenarth (HUN) 6–0 6–2
MEN'S OVER 70 SINGLES – Final: R. Sherman (USA) d. A. Swetka (USA) 3–6 7–5 6–3.
MEN'S OVER 70 DOUBLES – Final: Isidori (ITA)/Sherman (USA) d. Rae (AUS)/Richman (USA)
MEN'S OVER 75 SINGLES – Final: G. Longo (ITA) d. J. Richman (CAN) 6–2 6–4.
MEN'S OVER 75 DOUBLES – Final: De Graad (RUM)/Hunger (GER) d. Richman/Forda (GBR) 7–5 6–2.
WOMEN'S OVER 35 SINGLES – Final: S. Freeman (GBR) d. O. E. Villani (BRA) 7–6 6–76–4.
WOMEN'S OVER 35 DOUBLES – Final: Figueroa (ARG)/Villani (BRA) d. Estradera/Triquell (SPA) 6–0 6–1
WOMEN'S OVER 40 SINGLES – Final: M. Rasmussen (AUS) d. E. Birukova (RUS) 7–6 6–2.
WOMEN'S OVER 40 DOUBLES – Final: Rasmussen (AUS)/Charles (GBR) d. Campling/Craig (AUS) 6–2 6–2.
WOMEN'S OVER 45 DOUBLES – Final: Brasher (GBR)/Pinterova (HUN) d. McLean (USA)/Smith (USA) 6–3 7–5
WOMEN'S OVER 50 SINGLES – Final: C. Hillebrand (USA) d. L. Nette (AUS) 6–1 6–1.
WOMEN'S OVER 50 DOUBLES - Final: Boothman (GBR)/Hillerbrand (USA) d. Anderson/Bowden (USA) 6–3 6–3.
WOMEN'S OVER 55 SINGLES – Final: N. Reed (USA) d. J. Le Caillon (FRA) 6–1 6–4.
WOMEN'S OVER 55 DOUBLES – Final: Reed/Gunderson (USA) d. Wood(USA)/Michael (GER) w/o.
WOMEN'S OVER 60 SINGLES – Final: B. Rae (AUS) d. C. Mazzoleni (ITA) 2–6 7–6 6–2.
WOMEN'S OVER 60 DOUBLES – Final: Hobson/Rae (AUS) d./Owen/Pratt (USA) 6–3 2–6 6–4.

ITF VETERANS WORLD RANKINGS 1992

MEN

35 AGE GROUP
1 F. Rocchi-Landir (ITA); **2** M. Wolf (USA); **3** S. Birner (TCH); **4** H. Seuss (GER); **5** J. Cano (ARG); **6** A. Pereira (BRA); **7** A. Perugia (ARG); **8**. M. Vines (USA); **9 eq** P. Godfroid (BEL); E. Rudi (ARG).

45 AGE GROUP
1 R. Staguhn (GER); **2** P. Pokorny (AUT); **3** B De Jel (NED); **4** J. Ganzabal (ARG); **5** P. Szoke (HUN); **6** J. Martens (GER); **7** T. Lejus (URS); **8** P. Boratisa (THA); **9** R. Ray (CIS); **10** T. Koch (BRA).

50 AGE GROUP
1 J. Paolo Lemann (BRA); **2 eq** R. Howes (AUS); **3** S Labanauskas (URS); **4 eq** O. Escrinabo (ARG); B. Reinholz (GER); **6 eq** B. Burns (AUS); G. Rohrich (ITA); R. Stemmler (GER); **9 eq** H. Elschenbroich (GER); G. Prell (GER).

55 AGE GROUP
1 K. Fuhrmann (GER); **2** P. Froelich (AUS), **3** J. Nelson (USA); **4 eq** L. Dodson (USA); R. Narcio (MEX); **6** F. Hainka (AUT); **7** K. Van Nostrand (USA); 8eq H. Hamzat (AUT); S. Linzbauer (GER); **10** R. Jones (AUS).

65 AGE GROUP
1 F. Kovaleski (USA); **2** L. Legenstein (AUT); **3** B. McCarthy (AUS); **4** O. Jirkovsky (AUT); **5 eq** B. Howe (AUS); L. Lenart (HUN); **7** A. Funes (ARG); **8** B. Tully (USA); **9** H. Stewart (USA); **10** C. Hassell (GBR).

60 AGE GROUP
1 W. Mertins (GER); **2** I. Gulyas (HUN); **3** J. Morton (USA); **4** C. Devoe (AUS); **5** W. Reed USA); **6** A. Mugicat (ARG); **7** J. O'Brien (AUS); **8** A. Kendall (AUS); **9 eq** A.Hussmuller (GER); S. Verrati (FRA).

70 AGE GROUP
1eq T Brown (USA); B. Kempe (GER); **3** A. Swetka (USA); **4** T. Johannson (SWE); **5** B. Sherman (USA); **6** F. Bushman (USA); **7**. M. Kizlink (GBR); **8** G. Henley (AUS); **9 eq** E. Franz Biller (GER); E. Meidhoff (GER); **11** W. Mayr (GER).

75 AGE GROUP
1 G. Henley (AUS); **2**. F. Klein (USA); **3**. A. Swetka (USA); **4** J. Morrison (USA); **5** W. Parsons (USA); **6 eq** J. Bushman (USA); G. Mulloy (USA); **8 eq** F. Henzler (GER); D. Walker (USA); **10 eq** D. Miller (USA); G. Munch (GER).

WOMEN

35 AGE GROUP
1 C. Benzon (USA); **2** K. O'Sullivan (USA);**3** N. Ornstein (USA); **4** C. Nichols (USA); **5 eq** M. Mottola (USA); S. Torrance (USA); **7** C. Farrell (USA); **8 eq** L. Fendig (USA); V. Stilwell (USA); **10** A. Barnes (USA).

40 AGE GROUP
1 M Geyer (AUS); **2** M. Russo (USA); **3** M. Pinterova (HUN); **4** V. Vrankovich (ARG); **5** M. Rasmussen (AUS); **6** C. Bailey (USA); **7** K. Gallagher (USA); **8** R. Schroder (GER); **9** E. Birukova (CIS); **10** R. Martinicova (TCH).

50 AGE GROUP
1 C. Hillebrand (USA); **2** L. Nette (AUS); **3** R. Darmon (FRA); **4** M. Schultze (ESP); **5** A. M. Piotti (ARG); **6** S. Fuhrmann (GER); **7 eq** C. Anderson (USA); R. Mayer-Zdralek (GER); M. L. Tinelli (ITA); **10** E. Collistro (URU).

55 AGE GROUP
1 N. Reed (USA); **2** C. Wagner (GER); **3** I. Michael (GER); **4** E. Perusch (AUT); **5 eq**. J. Crofford (USA); C Wood (USA);.**7 eq** J. Dalton (AUS); D. Matthiessen (USA); **9** T. Sheppard (USA); **10**. B. Jung (GER).

60 AGE GROUP
1 B. Rae (AUS); **2** C. Mazzolleni (ITA); **3** M. Kyburz (SUI); **4** B. Pratt (USA); **5** L. Burling (USA); **6** I. Pla (ARG); **7** H. Lum (USA); **8** E. Szentirmay (HUN); **9** K. Sorge (GER); **10** J. Borzone (ARG).

NATIONAL ASSOCIATIONS, RANKINGS AND CHAMPIONSHIPS

MEMBERS WITH VOTING RIGHTS (108)

Abbreviations: C. = Cable address; T. = Telephone number; TX. = Telex number; Fax. = Facsimile number. Number following country's name denotes year of foundation.

ALGERIA (1962)

Federation Algerienne de Tennis, Centre des Federations Sportives, Cite Olympique B.P. 88 El Biar, Algers 16030.

T. (213–2) 79 0988/3939; TX. 61379 KFS DZ; *Pres.* Col Ali Tounsi; *Ex. Dir.* Mr Yahia Chettab.

MEN: **1**= Abedelhak Hamerlaine/Redha Galou; **2**= Abedellah Harrad/Moncef Zehar; **3**= Samir Tounsi/Mehdi Benyebka; **5** Mohamed Mahmoudi; **6** Toufik Saada; **7** Kheiredine Bounifa; **8** Hassene Bouzidani; **9** Abdelouahab Gouli; **10** Yassine Amier.

WOMEN: **1** Samira Mahmoudi; **2** Warda Bouchabou; **3** Nabila Bouchabou; **4** Lamia Hamerlaine; **5** Hadda Mahmoudi; **6** Samira Takorabt; **7** Niziha Sahbi; **8** Sihem Belbey; **9** Ratiba Ramdani; **10** Amina Bennacer.

National Closed Championships
MEN'S SINGLES – Semi-finals: A. Hamerlaine d. A. Azzi 7–6 6–2; N. Lasla d. N. Mahdoudi 2–6 6–4 6–4. *Final:* Hamerlaine d. Lasla 6–0 6–4.
WOMEN'S SINGLES – S. Mahmoudi d. L. Hamerlaine 6–1 5–7 7–6; W. Bouchabou d. N. Bouchabou 6–2 6–2. *Final:* Bouchabou d. Mahmoudi w/o.

ARGENTINA (1921)

Asociacion Argentina de Tenis, Avda. San Juan 1315/17, (1148) Capital Federal, Buenos Aires.
C. Argtennis, Buenos Aires; T. (54–1) 26 1569/27 0101/26 4696 (1148); TX. 17336 ARGTEN AR; Fax. (54–1) 3340296; *Pres.* Mr Juan Jose Vasquez; *Sec.* Mr Juan Carlos Zamboni, Mr Francisco A Turno.

MEN: **1** Alberto Mancini; **2** Franco Davin; **3** Guillermo Perez Roldan; **4** Gabriel Markus; **5** Roberto Azar; **6** Horacio De La Pena; **7** Martin Jaite; **8** Christian Miniussi; **9** Javier Frana; **10** Martin Stringari.

WOMEN: **1** Gabriela Sabatini; **2** Florencia Labat; **3** Bettina Fulco Villella; **4** Ines Gorrochategui; **5** Mercedes Paz; **6** Patricia Tarabini; **7** Christina Tessi; **8** Luciana Reynares; **9** Paola Suarez; **10** Maria Jose Gaidano.

AUSTRALIA (1904)

Tennis Australia, Private Bag 6060, Richmond South 3121, Victoria.
T. (61–3) 655 1277; TX. 36893 TENCRT AA; Fax. (61–3) 650 2743; *Pres.* Mr Geoff Pollard; *Admin. Man.* Mr Mike Daws; *Tennis Man.* Mr Barry F McMillan.

AUSTRIA (1902)

Osterreichischer Tennisverband, Haekelstrasse 33, 1235 Vienna, Austria.
C. Austriatennis, Vienna; T. (43–222) 8654506/1235 (43–1) 8654506; TX. 131598 OETEN A; Fax. (43–222) 8654506/85 (43–1) 8654506/85; *Pres.* Dr Rudolf Mader; *Sec.* Mr Peter Nader.

MEN: **1** Thomas Muster; **2** Gilbert Schaller; **3** Alexander Antonitsch; **4** Horst Skoff; **5** Thomas Buchmayer; **6** Harald Mair; **7** Roland Burtscher; **8** Reinhard Wawra; **9** Thomas Prerovsky; **10** Hans Priller.

WOMEN: **1** Judith Weisner; **2** Sandra Dopfer; **3** Petra Ritter; **4** Marion Maruska; **5** Barbara Schett; **6** Nike Dobrovits; **7** Katharina Bueche; **8** Beate Reinstadler; **9** Ulli Priller; **10** Heidi Sprung.

National Closed Championships
MEN'S SINGLES – Semi-finals: R. Burtscher d. H. Mair 6–2 3–6 6–3; M. Bauer d. J. Hager 6–2 7–5. *Final:* Burtscher d. Bauer 6–0 6–7 6–0 3–6 6–1.
WOMEN'S SINGLES – Semi-finals: B. Schett d. B. Arming 7–5 6–2; S. Dopfer d. U. Priller 6–3 6–3. *Final:* Dopfer d. Schett 7–5 6–4.

BAHAMAS (1961)

The Bahamas Lawn Tennis Association, PO Box N-10169, Nassau.
T. (1–809) 325 4444; TX. 20170 BRITBEACH B; Fax (1–809) 322 8000; *Pres.* Mr Mickey Williams; *Sec.* Ms Denise Mortimer.
MEN: **1** Sean Cartwright; **2** Leo Rolle; **3**= Sterling Cooke/Nigel Saul; **5**= Admiral Collie/Byron Butler/Vince Andrews/Nikki Fountain/Michael Isaacs.
WOMEN: **1** Kim Cartwright; **2** Lori Feingold; **3** Dyphany Wilkinson; **4**= Karen Turnquest/Terry Demeritte; **6** Jane Wiberg.
National Closed Championships
MEN'S SINGLES – Semi-finals: L. Rolle d. S. Cooke w/o; S. Cartwright d. N. Saul 6–3 6–1. *Final:* Cartwright d. Rolle 7–6 ret.
WOMEN'S SINGLES – Semi-finals: L. Feingold d. Dyphany Wilkinson 6–7 4–5 ret.; K. Cartwright d. T. Demeritte 6–0 6–0. *Final:* Cartwright d. Feingold 6–1 6–1.

BAHRAIN (1981)

Bahrain Lawn Tennis Federation, PO Box 26985, Bahrain.
C. Tennis, Bahrain; T. (973) 687236; TX. 8738 GPIC BN; *Pres.* Shaikh Ahmed Bin Salman Al Kalifa; *Sec:* Mr Yousif Abdulla Ali.

BANGLADESH (1972)

Bangladesh Tennis Federation, Tennis Complex, Ramna Green, Dhaka 1000.
C. Tennisfed, Dhaka; T. (880–2) 863087 (Attn Tennis Fed); TX. 642420 SHER BJ (Att. Tennis); Fax. (880–2) 832975/832915; *Pres.* Mr Khondaker Asaduzzaman; *Sec.* Mr A Morshed Khan Chowdbury.

BARBADOS (1948)

Barbados Lawn Tennis Association, PO Box 615c, Bridgetown.
T. (1–809) 436 0634/6727; Fax. (1–809) 429 4014/4854; *Pres.* Mr Peter G Symmonds; *Sec.* Ms Donna Symmonds.

BELGIUM (1902)

Federation Royal Belge de Tennis, Passage International Rogier 6, BTE 522, 1210 Brussels.
C. Tennisfeder, Brussels; T. (32–2) 217 2365; TX. 24023 TENFED B; Fax. (32–2) 217 6732; *Pres.* Mr Henri Denis; *Sec.* Mr Walter Goethals, Mr Franz Lemaire.

BENIN (1963)

Federation Beninoise de Lawn Tennis, B P 2709, Cotonou I.
C. Lawn Tenkning; T. (229) 315153/312149; TX. 5342 COTONOU; Fax. (229) 314684. *Pres.* Mr Edgar–Yves Monnou; *Sec.* Mr M F. Adedjouma.

BOLIVIA (1937)

Federacion Boliviana de Tenis, Calle Mexico no. 1638, Casilla Postal No.14752, La Paz.
T. (591–2) 378769/391784; TX. 2621 FEDBOTEN BV; Fax. (591–2) 367625/391784; *Pres.* Vicente Calderon Zeballos.
MEN: **1** Jose Medrano; **2** Ricardo Aguirre; **3** Gabriel Flores; **4** Antonio Serrate; **5** Ramiro Benavides; **6** Daniel Berdecio; **7** Jose Claudio Penaloza; **8** Gonzalo Flores; **9** Javier Mendoza; **10** Christian Sandoval.
WOMEN: **1** Sandra Kellemberger; **2** Paola Cespedes; **3** Cecilia Ampuero; **4** Tatiana Uzin; **5** Gabriela Melendres; **6** Fernanda Quiroga; **7** Paola Villarroel; **8** Regina Guzman; **9** Morela Lopez; **10** Monica Rivera.

BOSNIA/HERZOGOVINA (1950)

Tennis Association of Bosnia and Herzegovina, c/o International Tennis Centre Umag, Savudrijska C BB, 51470 Umag, Croatia.
T. (38) 531 541 704; Fax. (38) 531 541 513. *Pres.* Mr Branislav Kovacevic; *Sec.* Ms. Snjezana Kures.

BRAZIL (1956)

Confederacao Brasileira de Tenis, Av. Paulista Nr. 352 - Sala 64, 6 Andar, Conjunto, Cep - 01 310, Sao Paulo.
C. Cebetenis Rio de Janeiro; T. (55–11) 251 3920; TX. 113 2733 CTEN-BR; Fax. (55—11) 289 9404; *Pres.* Mr Walmor Elias; *Vice Pres.* Mr Eugenio Saller; *Supervisor* Mr Carols Alberto Martelotte.
MEN: **1** Jaime Oncins; **2** Luiz Mattar; **3** Fernando Roese; **4** Fernando Meligeni; **5** Danilo Marcelino; **6**

Cassio Motta; **7** Roberto Jabali; **8** Fabio Silberberg; **9** Jose Daher; **10** Nelson Aerts.
WOMEN: 1 Andrea Veira; **2** Luciana Tella; **3** Luciana Corsato; **4** Stephanie Mayorkis; **5** Claudia Chabalgoity; **6** Sumara Passos; **7** Sabrina Giusto; **8** Christina Roswadowski; **9** Eugenia Maia; **10** Marilia Andrade.

BULGARIA (1930)

Bulgarian Tennis Federation, 18 Vassil Levski Blvd, 1000 Sofia.
C. Besefese Tennis, Sofia; T. (359–2) 803710 or 808651 ext. 488; TX. 22723/22724 BSFS BG; Fax. (359–2) 879670; *Pres.* Mr Roumen Serbezov; *Sec.* Mr Tzvetan Tzvetkov.
MEN: 1 Milen Velev; **2** Mihayl Kanev; **3** Ivan Keskinov; **4** Mark Markov; **5** Orlin Stanoytchev; **6** Milko Petkov; **7** Milen Yanakiev; **8** Todor Bandev; **9** Radoslav Radev; **10** Victor Ivantchev.
WOMEN: 1 Katerina Maleeva; **2** Magdalena Maleeva; **3** Lubomira Batcheva; **4** Elena Pampulova–Wagner; **5** Galina Angelova; **6** Svetlana Kriventcheva; **7** Dora Djilianova; **8** Maya Stankova; **9** Ralitza Pavlova; **10** Albena Ivanova.
National Closed Championships
MEN'S SINGLES – Semi-finals: M. Kanev d. V. Ivantchev 6–3 6–3; R. Radev d. M. Yanakiev 7–5 6–1. **Final:** Kanev d. Radev 2–6 6–4 6–0 6–3.
WOMEN'S SINGLES – Semi-finals: S. Kriventcheva d. D. Djilianova 6–2 6–2; G. Angelova d. P. Stoyanova 6–0 6–1. **Final:** Kriventcheva d. Angelova 6–3 6–4.

CAMEROON (1966)

Federation Camerounaise de Lawn Tennis, BP 1121, Yaounde.
C. Fecatennis-MJS-Yaounde; T. (237) 233860/1310 or 224329; TX. 8568 KN/MNFA 8261 KN; *Pres.* Mr Zacharie Noah; *Sec.* Dr Noaki Mboulet.

CANADA (1890)

Tennis Canada, 3111 Steeles Avenue West, Downsview, Ontario M3J 3H2.
T. (1–416) 665 9777; TX. 02618419 CAN TENNIS TOR; Fax. (1–416) 665 9017; *Pres.* Mr. Robert H Moffat; *Sec.* Ms Shelley Evanochko.

CHILE (1920)

Federacion de Tenis de Chile, Almirante Simpson, No. 36 Providencia, Casilla 1149, Santiago.
T. (56–2) 2227279; TX. 240976 COCH CL; Fax. (56–2) 2229291; *Pres.* Mr Javier Flores Mayorga; *Sec.* Mr Guillermo Toledo Olea.

CHINA, PEOPLE'S REPUBLIC OF (1953)

Tennis Association of the People's Republic of China, 9 Tiyukuan Road, Beijing 100016.
C. Sportschine, Beijing; T. (86–1) 7012233; TX. 22034 ACSF CN/22323 CHOC CN; Fax. (86–1) 7015858; *Pres.* Mr Lu Zhengchao; *Sec.* Ms Zhang Dacheng.

CHINESE TAIPEI (1973)

Chinese Taipei Tennis Association, 9th Floor, No. 285, Sec 4, Chung Shaio East Rd, Taipei, Taiwan, ROC.
C. Sinovision, Taipei; T. (886–2) 7313026/7510051 Ext 518/519; TX. 22949 PACICON; Fax. (886–2) 7711696; *Pres.* Mr M C Chang; *Sec-Gen.* Mr Hu Cheng.
MEN: 1 Yu-Hui Lien; **2** Jinn-Yen Chiang; **3** Cheng-Fong Chang; **4** Chih-Jung Chen; **5** Yi-Ta Chuang; **6** Yuen-Hong Lee; **7** Chang-Lung Wu; **8** Chin-Bing Lin; **9** Min-Chin Wu; **10** Hsiu-Ming Lee.
WOMEN: 1 Su-Ying Lai; **2** Chiu-Mei Ho; **3** Yu-Hsien Liu; **4** Ya-Hui Lin; **5** Lin-Ya Wu; **6** Su-Chun Lai; **7** Su-Mei Wang; **8** Shi-Ting Wang; **9** Hong-Lan Liu; **10** Shu-Ping Lin.
National Closed Championships
MEN'S SINGLES – Semi-finals: Lien Yu-Hui d. Chiang Jinn-Yen 6–3 1–6 6–3; Chen Chih-Jung d. Chang Cheng-Fong 7–5 6–2. **Final:** Chen Chih-Jung d. Lien Yu-Hui 6–3 3–6 6–2.
WOMEN'S SINGLES – Semi-finals: Lin Ya-Hui d. Liu Hong-Lan 6–0 6–1; Lai Su–Ying d. Liu Yu-Hsien 6–2 6–4. **Final:** Lai Su-Ying d. Lin Ya-Hui 6–3 4–5 ret.

COLOMBIA (1932)

Federacion Colombiana de Tenis, Apartado No. 10917, Calle 28 No. 25–18 Bogota.
C. Fedetenis, Bogota, T. (57–1) 288 3323/287 7963/283 0618/282 7294; TX. 41275 ICJD CO; Fax (57–1) 287 7963/287 0936/283 2461; *Pres.* Dr Ricardo Mejia P; *Sec.* Mr Arturo Rojas H.
MEN: 1 Carlos Soto; **2** Jaime Cortes; **3** Alvaro Jordan; **4** Jorge Falla; **5** Beimar Zapata; **6** William Espinosa; **7** Ricardo Hernandez; **8** Angel Martinez **9** Mario Aragon; **10** Martin Arenas.
WOMEN: 1 Catalina Ramirez; **2** Cecilia Hincapie; **3** Giana Gutierrez; **4** Ximena Trusillo; **5** Adriana Garcia;

6 Ximena Rodriguez; **7** Carmina Giraldo; **8** Alexandra Schmitt; **9** Natalia Romo; **10** Andrea Montoya.
National Closed Championships
MEN'S SINGLES – *Semi-finals:* A. Jordan d. W. Espinosa 6–3 6–3; M. Tobon d. J. Cortes 6–4 7–5.
Final: Tobon d. Jordan 6–4 6–4.
WOMEN'S SINGLES – *Semi-finals:* C. Ramirez d. X. Rodriguez 6–7 4–6 6–3; C. Hincapie d. M. Mesa
6–2 6–2. *Final:* Hincapie d. Ramirez 6–4 4–6 7–5.

CONGO (1962)

Federation Congolaise de Lawn Tennis, Stade de la Revolution, BP 2061, Brazzaville.
T. (242) 833328; TX. 5237 KG BANKCGO; Fax. (242) 835317; *Pres.* Mr Germain Ickonga Akindou; *Sec.*
Mr Antoine Ouabonzi.

COSTA RICA (1960)

Federacion Costarricense de Tenis, PO Box 326-1005, Barrio Mexico, San Jose.
T. (506) 55 4793/4824, 22 2530; TX. 2509 CODINCO; Fax. (506) 33 5678; *Pres.* Ms Cecilia Sanchez *Sec.*
Mr Domingo Rivera.

COTE D'IVOIRE (1969)

Federation Ivoirienne de Tennis, 01 BP V 273, Abidjan 01.
T. (225) 44 13 54; TX. 23555 or 23493 IHCHOT CI; Fax (225) 44 71 13/44 00 50; *Pres.* Mr Jean-Claude
Delafosse; *Gen. Sec.* Mr Kouame Kouadjo.

CROATIA (1922)

Croatian Tennis Association, Trg Sportova 11, 41 000 Zagreb.
T. (38) 41 33 93 99; Fax. (38) 41 32 58 64/41 32 71 11. *Pres.* Mr Hrvoje Sarinic; *Sec.* Miss Suzana Knezevic

CUBA (1925)

Federacion Cubana de Tenis de Campo, Calle 13 NR 601 Esq AC, Vedado Habana 4.
C. Olimpicuba, Habana; T. (53–7) 403581; TX. 511332 INDER CU; Fax. (53–7)
407677/625604/625605/409037; *Pres.* Mr Rolando Martinez; *Sec.* Mr M O Rodriguez.

CYPRUS (1951)

Cyprus Tennis Federation, Ionos Str 20, PO Box 3931, Nicosia.
T. (357–2) 366822/450875; TX. 5300 OLYMPIC CY; Fax. (357–2) 464355; *Pres.* Mr Philios
Christodoulou; *Sec.* Mr George Georgiades.
MEN: **1** Alkis Papamichael; **2** Yiannos Hadjigeorgiou; **3** Loucas Christofides; **4** Spyros Charalambous; **5**
Savvas Constantinou; **6** Marinos Bagdadi; **7** Alexis Photiades; **8** Paris Christofides; **9** Jacques
Heuchene; **10** Simon Aynedjian.
WOMEN: **1** Persella Ioannidou; **2** Anna Anastassiou; **3** Nicoletta Pericleous; **4** Ioanna Rossi; **5** Tereza
Apostolidou; **6** Kalia Kyriakidou; **7** Aphroditi Karapataki; **8** Benadette Talianou; **9** Olybia Lophitou; **10**
Rose Anne Howell.
National Closed Championships
MEN'S SINGLES – *Semi-finals:* A. Papamichael d. S. Charalambous 6–1 6–2; Y. Hadjigeorgiou d. S.
Constantinou 7–6 6–4. *Final:* Hadjigeorgiou d. Papamichael 6–4 4–6 6–2.
WOMEN'S SINGLES – *Semi-finals:* P. Ioannidou d. N. Pericleous 6–2 6–2; I. Rossi d. K. Kyriakidou 7–6
7–6. *Final:* Ioannidou d. Rossi 6–3 3–6 6–2.

CZECHOSLOVAKIA (1906)

Ceskoslovenska Tenisova Asociace, Ostrov Stvanice 38, 170 00 Prague 7.
C. Sportsvaz, Prague; T. (42–2) 2311484/2311678; TX. 122650 CSTVC; Fax. (42–2) 2311868; *Pres.* Mr
Jiri Lendl; *Sec.* Mr Michal Polak.
MEN: **1** Petr Korda; **2** Karel Novacek; **3** Martin Strelba; **4** Martin Damm; **5** David Rikl; **6** Daniel Vacek; **7**
Ctislav Dosedel; **8** Libor Nemecek; **9** Jaroslav Bulant; **10** Lukas Thomas.
WOMEN: **1** Jana Novotna; **2** Helena Sukova; **3** Radomira Zrubakova; **4** Andrea Strnadova; **5** Karina
Habsudova; **6** Katerina Kroupova; **7** Petra Langrova; **8** Patra Holubova; **9** Kvetoslava Hrdlickova; **10**
Radka Bobkova.
National Closed Championships
MEN'S SINGLES – *Semi-finals:* R. Vasek d. L. Thomas w/o; J. Kahoun d. J. Pelikan 2–6 6–4 7–6. *Final:*
Vasek d. Kahoun 6–1 2–6 6–2.
WOMEN'S SINGLES – *Final:* H. Sukova d. D. Szabova 6–0 7–5.

DENMARK (1920)

Dansk Tennis Forbund, Idraettens Hus, Broendby Stadion 20, 2605 Broendby.
C. Tennisforbund, Copenhagen; T. (45–42) 455555; TX. 33111 IDRAET DK (Att. Tennis); Fax. (45–43) 435045; *Pres.* Mr Jorn Iversen; Vice *Pres.* Mr John Ahlstrand; *Gen. Sec.* Mr Hans Kristensen.
MEN: 1 Michael Tauson; **2** Frederik Fetterlein; **3** Kenneth Carlsen; **4** Christian Camradt; **5** Thomas Sorensen; **6** Morten Christensen; **7** John Larsen; **8** Nick Bendtsen; **9** Thomas G. Andersen; **10**= Peter Flintso/Carsten Gildum/Allan Larsen/Michael Mortensen.
WOMEN: 1 Karin Ptaszek; **2** Tine Scheuer–Larsen; **3** Sofie Albinus; **4** Merete Balling Stockmann; **5** Lone Vandborg; **6** Henriette Kjaer Nielsen; **7** Susanne Gotil; **8** Lotte Gundtoft; **9** Merete Lindahl; **10**= Anja Kostecki/Pernille Sorensen/Maria Wolff.
National Closed Championships
MEN'S SINGLES – Semi-finals: K. Carlsen d. J. Larsen 6–3 6–3; C. Camradt d. T. Sorensen 7–6 4–6 6–3. *Final:* K. Carlsen d. C. Camradt 6–2 6–1.
WOMEN'S SINGLES – Semi-finals: K. Ptaszek d. S. Olsen 6–3 7–6; A. Kostecki d. H.K. Nielsen 1–6 6–3 6–2. *Final:* Ptaszek d. Kostecki 4–6 7–6 6–4.

DJIBOUTI (1978)

Federation Djiboutienne de Tennis, Rue Pierre-Pascal, BP 728, Djibouti.
C. PO Box 16, Djibouti; T. (253) 351781/350611; TX. 5871 DJ PRESIDEN; *Pres.* Mr Houmed Houssein; *Gen. Sec.* Mr Bourhan Daoud.

DOMINICAN REPUBLIC (1929)

Federacion Dominicana de Tenis, Club Deportivo Naco, Calle Central, Ens. Naco, Santo Domingo.
T. (1–809) 541 3685/3488; TX. 3460418 BONELLY; Fax. (1–809) 688 0647/541 0640; *Pres.* Mr Gonzalo Mejia; *Sec.* Mr J. Ravelo.

ECUADOR (1967)

Federacion Ecuatoriana de Tenis, PO Box 716, Guayaquil.
C. Fetenis, Guayaquil; T. (593–4) 313600/304605/306800; TX. 04 3332 BANMAC ED; Fax. (593–4) 313642; *Pres.* Mr Mario Canessa; *Sec.* Ms Nuria Guzman.
MEN: 1 Andres Gomez; **2** Raul Viver; **3** Pablo Campana; **4** Giorgio Carneade; **5** Luis Morejon; **6** Andres Alarcon; **7** Miguel Olvera; **8** Nicolas Lapentti; **9** Ernesto Lingen; **10** Hugo Nunez.
WOMEN: 1 M. Dolores Campana; **2** Nuria Niemes; **3** Cecilia Piedrahita; **4** M. Angeles Ycaza; **5** Alexandra Guzman; **6** Mercedes Ramos; **7** Laura Suarez; **8** Montserrat Martinez; **9** M. Pilar Gallegos; **10** Monica Martinez.

EGYPT (1920)

Egyptian Lawn Tennis Federation, 13 Kasr el Nil Street, Cairo.
C. Gyplawnten, Cairo; T. (20–2) 5740973; TX. 93697 SAFLM UN (Att. Tennis)/21554 STC UN/93000 OLYMP UN; Fax. (20–2) 753235; *Pres Gen.* Mr Mohamed Tawfik; *Sec.* Prof Dr Hussein I Nasr.

EL SALVADOR (1949)

Federacion Salvadorena de Tenis, Apartado Postal (01) 110, San Salvador.
C. Molino; T. (503) 25 6022; TX. 20542 MOLINO SR; Fax. (503) 263832/256366/783278/264247; *Pres.* Mr Enrique Molins Rubio; *Sec.* Mr Roberto Sanchez Alegria.

ESTONIA (1932)

Estonian Tennis Association, Roheline aas 13, 200010 Tallinn.
T. (7) 0142 451 980; Fax. (7) 0142 451 980. *Pres.* Mr. Tiit Nuudi; *Sec.* Mr. Mati Kuum; *Ass. Dir.* Mr. Tonu Ottoson.
MEN: 1 Rene Busch; **2** Aivo Ojassalu; **3** Andrei Luzgin; **4** Ivan Troost; **5** Alti Vahkal; **6** Alo Ojassalu; **7** Redt Reimal; **8** Pavel Ignatenkov; **9** Mart Polakene; **10** Andrus Pirn.
WOMEN: 1 Helen Holter; **2** Kaja Kond; **3** Ande Tulp; **4** Ilona Poljakova; **5** Piret Ilves; **6** Maaren Olander; **7** Pirje Lont; **8** Marje Redel; **9** Kristina Grunberg; **10** Kaire Poldma.
National Closed Championships
MEN'S SINGLES – Semi-finals: R. Busch d. A. Luzgin 5–7 6–2 7–6 6–4; A. Ojassalu d. I. Troost 6–3 6–2 6–2. *Final:* Busch d. Ojassalu 6–3 7–5 7–5.
WOMEN'S SINGLES – Semi-finals: H. Holter d. I. Poljakova 6–1 6–0; K. Kond d. P. Ilves 6–2 6–2. *Final:* Kond d. Holter 6–2 7–6.

FINLAND (1911)

Suomen Tennisliitto, Radiokatu 20, SF-00240 Helsinki.
C. Tennisliitto, Helsinki; T. (358–0) 158 2301; TX. 121797 SVUL SF; Fax. (358–0) 1582328; *Pres.* Mr Raimo Taivalkoski; *Sec.* Mr Eero Kiuttu.
MEN: **1** Veli Paloheimo; **2** Aki Rahunen; **3** Olli Rahnasto; **4** Pasi Virtanen; **5** Janne Holtari; **6** Kimmo Hurme; **7** Juha Lemponen; **8** Juha Pesola; **9** Pasi Kinnunen; **10** Ville Liukko.
WOMEN: **1** Nanne Dahlman; **2** Petra Thoren; **3** Anne Aallonen; **4** Katriina Saarinen; **5** Linda Jansson; **6** Marja–Liisa Kuurne; **7** Nina Karkkainen; **8** Mari Maattanen; **9** Minna Hatakka; **10** Tina Helen Soderstrom.
National Closed Championships
MEN'S SINGLES – **Semi-finals:** A. Rahunen d. P. Virtanen 3–6 6–4 6–0; K. Hurme d. J. Holtari 6–7 6–4 6–4. **Final:** Rahunen d. Hurme 6–0 6–0.
WOMEN'S SINGLES – **Semi-finals:** N. Dahlman d. T. Soderstrom 6–3 6–0; P. Thoren d. K. Saarinen 6–2 6–3. **Final:** Dahlman d. Thoren 6–3 6–4.

FRANCE (1920)

Federation Francaise de Tennis, Stade Roland Garros, 2 Avenue Gordon Bennett, 75016 Paris, France.
C. Tenisfedet Paris; T. (33–1) 47 43 48 00; TX. TENFED 611871 F; Fax. (33–1) 47 43 04 94; *Pres.* Mr Philippe Chatrier; *Sec.* Mr Jean Claude Collinot.

GEORGIA (1992)

Georgian Tennis Federation, K Marjanishvili St 29, Tbilisi.
T. (8832) 952781/953800; Tx. 212180 DIELO/212286 RING; Fax. (8832) 995892/996498. *Pres.* Mr Guzam Mirianashvili; *Sec.* Mr Zurab Katsharava.

GERMANY, FEDERAL REPUBLIC OF (1902)

Deutscher Tennis Bund e.V., Hallerstrasse 89, 2000 Hamburg 13.
T. (49–40) 41178250/251/252; Fax. (49–40) 4104480/41178255/41178275; *Pres.* Dr Claus Stauder; *Exec. Dir.* Mr Gunter Sanders.
MEN: **1** Boris Becker; **2** Michael Stich; **3** Carl–Uwe Steeb; **4** Markus Zoecke; **5** Bernd Karbacher; **6** Markus Naewie; **7** Patrick Baur; **8** Patrick Kuhnen; **9**= Karsten Braasch/Arne Thoms.
WOMEN: **1** Steffi Graf; **2** Anke Huber; **3** Barbara Rittner; **4** Sabine Hack; **5** Wiltrud Probst; **6**= Silke Frankl/Claudia Borwik/Meike Babel; **9**= Veronika Martinek/Karin Kschwendt.
National Closed Championships
MEN'S SINGLES – **Semi-finals:** D. Buljevic d. Rudiger Haas 7–5 4–6 7–5; A. Windisch d. H–J. Schwaier 6–2 6–2. **Final:** Buljevic d. Windisch 6–3 6–2.
WOMEN'S SINGLES – **Semi-finals:** V. Martinek d. E–M. Schurhoff 6–3 6–2; C. Singer d. R. Kochta 7–6 6–4 6–3. **Final:** Martinek d. Singer 7–5 6–0.

GHANA (1909)

Ghana Tennis Association, c/o National Sports Council, PO Box 1272, Accra.
C. Ghansport; T. (233–021) 663924/25/26/27; TX. 2519 GHANSPORT; Fax. (233–021) 223910; *Pres.* Mr Edmund Annan; *Sec.* Mr Gershon Komla Ayiih.

GREAT BRITAIN (1888)

Lawn Tennis Association, The Queens Club, West Kensington, London, W14 9EG.
C. Lawntenna, London W14; T. (44–71) 385 2366; TX. 8956036 THELTA G; Fax. (44–71) 381 5965; *Pres.* Mr. Ian King; *Chief Exec.* Mr Ian D. Peacock; *Sec.* Mr John C. U. James.
MEN: **1** Jeremy Bates; **2** Andrew Castle; **3** Chris Wilkinson; **4** Mark Petchey; **5** Nick Brown; **6** Chris Bailey; **7** Danny Sapsford; **8** David Ison; **9** Nick Fulwood; **10** Laurence Matthews.
WOMEN: **1** Jo Durie; **2** Monique Javier; **3** Sara Gomer; **4** Sam Smith; **5** Clare Wood; **6** Amanda Grunfeld; **7** Sarah Loosemore; **8** Valda Lake; **9** Belinda Borneo; **10** Julie Salmon.
National Closed Championships
MEN'S SINGLES – **Semi-finals:** J. Bates d. P. Hand 6–2 6–3; A. Castle d. C. Bailey 6–2 6–2. **Final:** Bates d. Castle 7–6 6–3.
WOMEN'S SINGLES – **Semi-finals:** J. Durie d. V. Lake 6–1 6–3; J. Salmon d. A. Grunfeld 6–4 3–6 9–7. **Final:** Durie d. Salmon 6–3 6–3.

GREECE (1938)

Hellenic Tennis Federation, Fokionos Negri 9, 115 57 Athens.

C. Efotennis, Athens; T. (30–1) 6852511/512/513; TX. 222415 EFOA GR; Fax. (30–1) 6829112/8654365; *Pres.* Mr Dimitris Stefanides; *Sec.* Mr Dionyssis Gangas.
MEN: 1 Andrew Fikas; **2** Anastassios Bavela; **3** Konstantinos Efremoglou; **4** George Kalovelonis; **5** Kostis Glavas; **6** John Rigas; **7** John Kabakoglou; **8** Michael Papageorgiou; **9** Stravros Michalopoulos; **10** Theodoros Glavas.
WOMEN: 1 Christina Papadaki; **2** Christina Zachariadou; **3** Mairza Georgitsi; **4** Helen Kagalou; **5** Maria Pavlidou; **6** Evi Panteli; **7** Santra Rentzoula; **8** Lidia Soulti; **9** Elpida Alexandrou; **10** Maria Adamopoulou.

GUATEMALA (1950)

Federacion Nacional de Tenis, Palacio de Los Deportes, Zona 4, Guatemala City.
T. (502–2) 310261; TX. 6077 C0G GU; Fax. (502–2) 310261; *Pres.* Lic Enrique Gonzalez Rodriguez; *Sec.* Mr. David Vargas Bettancourt.

HAITI (1950)

Federation Haitienne de Tennis, PO Box 1442, Port-au-Prince.
C. Joetienne, Port-au-Prince; T. (509–4) 50703/51461/51462; Fax. (509–4) 51451/51461; *Pres.* Mr Frantz Liautaud; *Sec.* Mr Hulzer Adolphe.
MEN: 1 Ronald Agenor; **2** Bertrand Madsen; **3** Patrice Baker; **4** Bertrand Lacombe; **5** Ruben Lamothe; **6** Sylvio Joseph; **7** Edduard Delphin; **8** Cressoir Louis; **9** Clifford Brutus; **10** Patrick Derice.
WOMEN: 1 Valerie Marcel; **2** Daphney Rene; **3** Giovanna Marcel; **4** Isabelle Guichard; **5** Nathalie Rehe; **6** Neyssa Etienne; **7** Lynn Bergmann; **8** Brunellie Siess; **9** Gweneelle Romain.

National Closed Championships
MEN'S SINGLES – Semi-finals: S. Joseph d. P. Derice 0–6 7–5 0–6 6–3 2–1 ret.; C. Louis d. A. Chery 6–4 7–6 6–3. **Final:** Joseph d. Louis 6–7 7–6 7–5 7–5.
WOMEN'S SINGLES – Semi-finals: V. Marcel d. G. Marcel 6–0 6–0; D. Rene d. I. Guichard 6–1 6–3. **Final:** Marcel d. Rene 7–5 6–2.

HONG KONG (1909)

Hong Kong Tennis Association Ltd, Victoria Park Centre Court, Victoria Park, Hing Fat Road, Causeway Bay.
C. Tennis, Hong Kong; T. (852) 890 1132; TX. 41224 JSCEN HX (Att HKTA); Fax. (852) 894 8704; *Pres.* Dr. Philip Kwok; *Sec.* Mr Herman Hu; *Exec Dir.* Dr Edward Hardisty.

HUNGARY (1907)

Magyar Tenisz Szovetseg, Dozsa Gyorgy ut 1-3, H-1143 Budapest.
C. Comsport Tennis, Budapest; T. (36–1) 252 6687; TX. 225105 AISHK H; Fax. (36–1) 157 1304/2510107; *Pres.* Mr Gyorgy Hole; *Sec.* Mr Laszlo Nyiro.
International Category: **1** Sandor Noszaly; **2** Karoly Gyorgy.
MEN: 1 Jozsef Krocsko; **2** Victor Nagy; **3** Levente Bartosi; **4** Rudolf Fedkete; **5** Balazs Rajo; **6** Peter Makray; **7** Zultan Nagy; **8** Krisztian Kereztes; **9** Laszlo Rethelyi; **10** Miklos Hornok.
WOMEN: 1 Annamaria Fuldenyi; **2** Petra Gaspar; **3** Virag Csurgo; **4** Rita Kutikis; **5** Barbara Bathory; **6** Maria Zsolbos; **7** Katalin Kocsis; **8** Agnes Muzamel; **9** Zsofia Csapo; **10** Kata Gyorke.
National Closed Championships
MEN'S SINGLES – Semi-finals: J. Krocsko d. V. Nagy 6–1 7–5; L. Baratosi d. R. Fekete 6–4 3–6 6–1. **Final:** Krocsko d. Baratosi 6–2 6–3 6–0.
WOMEN'S SINGLES – Semi-finals: A. Foldenyi d. A. Muzamel 6–3 6–0; Z. Csapo d. M. Zsoldos 6–3 6–3. **Final:** A. Fuldenyi d. Z. Csapo 6–4 6–3.

INDIA (1920)

All India Tennis Association, B-7/3 Asaf Ali Road, New Delhi 110 001.
C. TAX ASSIST NEW DELHI; T. (91–11) 3264250/3274177/3274178; TX. 3163426 RKCO IN; Fax. (91–11)3276716. *Pres.* Mr Raj Khanna; *Gen. Sec.* Mr R D Desai.

INDONESIA (1935)

Indonesian Tennis Association, Gelora Senayan Tennis Stadium, Jakarta 10270.
C. Tennis Indonesia, Jakarta; T. (62 21) 5700157; TX. 62794 PELTI IA; Fax. (62–21) 5700157; *Pres.* Mr Cosmas Batubara; *Gen Sec.* Mr Eddy Katimansah.
MEN: 1 Benny Wijaya; **2** Abdul Kahar Mim; **3** Bonit Wiryawan; **4** Suharyadi Wiryawan; **5** Tjahjono Wiryawan; **6** Dede Suhendar; **7** Sulistyo Wibowo; **8** Suwandi Wibowo; **9** Aga Soemarno; **10** Teddy Tandjung.
WOMEN: 1 Yayuk Basuki; **2** Romana Tedjakusuma; **3** Irawati Moerid; **4** Tanti Trayono; **5** Joice Riana

Sutedja; **6** Maria Veronica Widyadharma; **7** Mima Chernovita; **8** Waya Walalangi; **9** Tanya Soemarno; **10** Lamsriati Moerid.

IRAN (1937)

Tennis Federation of Islamic Republic of Iran, Shahid Shiroodi Stadium, Shahid Mofatteh St., Tehran.
C. Sportsiran; T. (98–21) 826999/832555; TX. 212691 VARZ IR; *Pres.* Mr Mahmood Golsham Shirazi; *Sec.* Mr Nasser Mirzaei.

IRAQ (1959)

Iraqi Tennis Federation, c/o Iraqi National Olympic Committee, PO Box No 441, Baghdad.
C. Iroq, Baghdad; T. (964–1) 7748261; TX. 213409 IROC IK; Fax: (964–1) 7728424; *Pres.* Mr Suhil N Abdulla; *Sec.* Mr Ghazi Shaye'a Hamil.

IRELAND (1895)

Tennis Ireland, Argyle Square, Donnybrook, Dublin 4.
C. Irishtennis Dublin; T. (353–1) 681841; Fax. (353–1) 683411; *Pres.* Mrs Rhoda McAuliffe; *Hon. Sec.* Mrs Mavis Hogg; *Chief Exec.* Mr John Taylor.
MEN: **1** Owen Casey; **2** Peter Wright; **3** Eoin Collins; **4** Scott Barron; **5** Ken Rowe; **6** Michael Nugent; **7** Peter Minnie; **8** Eoin Beiroe; **9** Michael McMahan; **10** Paul Pounch.
WOMEN: **1** Siobhan Nicholson; **2** Gina Niland; **3** Lesley O'Halloran; **4** Yvonne Doyle; **5** Karen Nugent; **6** Catriona McCarthy; **7** Claire Curran; **8** Jenny O'Brien; **9** Deirdre Walsh; **10** Zara Wolseley.
National Closed Championships
MEN'S SINGLES – *Semi-finals:* E. Collins d. S. Barron 6–3 6–4; P. Wright d. E. Flynn 6–4 6–3. *Final:* Wright d. Collins 4–6 7–6 6–4.
WOMEN'S SINGLES – *Semi-finals:* L. O'Halloran d. S. Nicholson 2–6 6–0 7–5; G. Niland d. Y. Doyle 7–6 6–3. *Final:* O'Halloran d. Niland 6–2 3–6 6–2.

ISRAEL

Israel Tennis Association, PO Box 51112, Tel Aviv 67 137
C.ILTA, Tel Aviv; T. (972–3) 5600864; TX. 341118 BXTVIL; Fax. (972–3) 5660319; *Chmn.* Mr. David Harnik; *Sec.* Mr Chava Mazar.
MEN: **1** Amos Mansdorf; **2** Gilad Bloom; **3** Michael Daniel; **4** Oren Motevassel; **5** Eyal Ran; **6** Raviv Weidenfeld; **7** Shahar Perkis; **8** Ofer Sela; **9** Ohad Weinberg; **10** Naom Behr.
WOMEN: **1** Ilana Berger; **2** Anna Smashnova; **3** Limor Zaltz; **4** Yael Segal; **5** Shiri Brustein; **6** Liat Cohen; **7** Tsipora Obziler; **8** Rona Mayer; **9** Hila Rosen; **10** Yael Beckman.
National Closed Championships
MEN'S SINGLES – *Semi-finals:* E. Ran d. E. Erlich 6–1 6–1; O. Sela d. L. Zimmerman 6–1 4–6 6–4. *Final:* Ran d. Sela 6–3 7–6.
WOMEN'S SINGLES – *Semi-finals:* T. Obziler d. S. Burstein 3–6 6–3 6–3; L. Zaltz d. T. Shapovalova 6–3 1–6 6–4. *Final:* Zaltz d. Obziler 6–3 6–4.

ITALY (1910)

Federazione Italiana Tennis, Viale Tiziano 70, 00196 Rome.
C. Italtennis, Rome; T. (39–6) 323 3799/396 6743; TX. 626343 FIT I; Fax. (39–6) 36858166; *Pres.* Mr Paolo Galgani; *Sec.* Mr Giuliano Annibali.
MEN: **1** Omar Camporese; **2** Renzo Fulan; **3** Stefano Pescosolido; **4** Gianluca Pozzi; **5** Diego Nargiso; **6** Claudio Pistolesi; **7** Cristiano Caratti; **8** Paolo Cane; **9** Mario Visconti; **10** Massimo Cierro.
WOMEN: **1** Sandra Cecchini; **2** Raffaella Reggi–Concato; **3** Linda Ferrando; **4** Federica Bonsignori; **5** Katia Piccolini; **6** Gloria Pizzichini; **7** Natalia Baudone; **8** Floria Perfetti; **9** Laura Golarsa; **10** Francesca Romano.
National Closed Championships
MEN'S SINGLES – *Semi-finals:* M. Valeri d. E. Rossetti 7–6 6–2; M. Cierro d. F. Michelotti 6–3 6–3. *Final:* Cierro d. Valeri 4–6 6–1 4–6 6–2 6–4.
WOMEN'S SINGLES – *Semi-finals:* K. Piccolini d. F. Perfetti 6–3 6–4; G. Pizzichini d. L. Lapi 2–6 7–5 7–6. *Final:* Piccolini d. Pizzichini 6–0 6–2.

JAMAICA

Jamaica Lawn Tennis Association, 2A Piccadilly Road, PO Box 175, Kingston 5.
C. Lawntenna, Kingston; T. New Kingston (1–809) 9295878; TX. c/o 2441 JAMINTEL; Fax. (1–809) 9268509; *Pres.* Mr Ken Spencer; *Hon. Sec.* Mr Carmen Bell.

JAPAN (1921)

Japan Tennis Association, c/o Kishi Memorial Hall, 1-1-1 Jinnan, Shibuya-ku, Tokyo 150.
C. Niplotenis, Tokyo; T. (81–3) 3481 2321; TX. 2428222 JTENIS J; Fax. (81–3) 3467 5192; *Pres.* Mr Tokusaburo Kosaka; *Sec.* Mr Shin-ichi Shimizu.
MEN: 1 Shuzo Matsuoka; **2** Bon–Soo Kim; **3** Yasufumi Yamamoto; **4** Hideki Kaneko; **5** Kentaro Masuda; **6** Ryuso Tsujino; **7** Hidehiko Tanizawa; **8** Shin–Ju Lee; **9** Toshitsugu Mori; **10** Toshihisa Tsuchihashi.
WOMEN: 1 Kimiko Date; **2** Naoko Sawamatsu; **3** Mana Endo; **4** Rika Hiraki; **5** Maya Kidowaki; **6** Akiko Kijimuta; **7** Yone Kamio; **8** Misumi Miyauchi; **9** Kyoko Nagatsuka; **10** Hiromi Nagano.

National Closed Championships
MEN'S SINGLES – Semi-finals: Y. Yamamoto d. G. Motomura 6–2 4–6 6–3 6–1; R. Tsujino d. T. Shimada 6–4 3–6 6–3 6–4. **Final:** Yamamoto d. Tsujino 6–4 3–6 7–6 6–1.
WOMEN'S SINGLES – Semi-finals: K. Date d. E. Okagawa 6–3 6–3; M. Endo d. N. Miyagi 6–3 6–4. **Final:** Date d. Endo 6–2 6–2.

JORDAN (1980)

Jordan Tennis Federation, PO Box 961046, Amman.
C. Tenfed, Amman; T. (962 6) 682796; ; TX. 24000 OLYMP; Fax. (962 6) 687950; *Chmn.* Dr Daoud Hanania; *Sec.* Dr Mohammed Sukhen.
MEN: 1 Hani Al–Ali; **2** Imao Abu–Hamdeh; **3** Faris Azzoni; **4** Laith Azzoni; **5** Saleh Bushnaq; **6** Rafat Al–Qasi; **7** Ahmad Maher; **8** Zaid Hanania.
WOMEN: 1 Rand Nafa; **2** Rana Qawar; **3** Arwa Al–Idwan; **4** Suha Qawar; **5** Mai Hanania; **6** Marina Khoder; **7** Madia Nafa.

National Closed Championships
MEN'S SINGLES – Semi-finals: E. Abu Hamdeh d. F. Azzoni 7–5 6–3; H. Al–Ali d. S. Bushnaq 6–3 6–2. **Final:** Abu–Hamdeh d. Al–Ali 6–4 3–6 6–4.
WOMEN'S SINGLES – Semi-finals: R. Nafa d. R. Qawar 6–4 7–5; S. Qawar d. M. Khader 6–3 6–2. **Final:** Nafa d. Qawar 6–4 6–3.

KENYA (1922)

Kenya Lawn Tennis Association, PO Box 43184, Nairobi.
C. Tennis, Nairobi; T. (254–2) 558905/543049; TX. 22119 MTSTRAV KE; Fax. (254–2) 543047; *Chmn.* Mr W D Katibi; *Sec.* Mr B Aggarwal.

KOREA, REPUBLIC OF (1945)

Korea Tennis Association, Room 108, Olympic Gym. No. 2, 88-2, Oryun-dong, Songpa-gu, Seoul 138-678.
C. Kortennis, Seoul; T. (82–2) 420 4285/4286/3333 ext. 659/660; TLX. 24989 KOCSEL K; Fax. (82–2) 420 4284; *Pres.* Mr Choong-Kun Cho; *Sec.* Mr Yeoung-Moo Huh.

KUWAIT (1967)

Kuwait Tennis Federation, PO Box 1462, Hawalli 32015.
C. Tennis Kuwait; T. (965) 265 8148/265 8149; TX. 23192 COMITE KT (Att. Tennis Ass); Fax. (965) 539 0617. *Pres.* Mr Khalid Al-Bannai; *Sec.* Mr Abdul Ridha Ghareeb.

LATVIA (1928)

Latvian Tennis Union, Oskara Kalpaka Prosp 18, 229070 Jurmala.
T. (7) 0132 65 21 41; Fax. (7) 0132 28 44 12/27 26 13. *Pres.* Mr Gvido Zemribo; *Sec.* Ms Marite Mikelsone.

LEBANON (1945)

Federation Libanaise de Tennis, PO Box 113-5591, Hamra, Beirut.
C. Tennispong, Beyrouth; T. (961–1) 342282; TX. 21665/20680 JOEINT LE (Att. Mr E A Yazbeck); *Pres.* Mr Abdel Karim Matar; *Hon. Sec.* Mr Emile A Yazbeck.
MEN: 1 Raymond Kattoura; **2** Said Karam; **3** Karim Khoury; **4** Edouard Nehme; **5** Omar Sadek; **6** Bishara Abourahal; **7** Toufic Zahlan; **8** Ali Tawbe; **9**=Fadi Haddad/Nicolas Kenaan; **10** Adony Abounaoum.
WOMEN: 1 Maya Hajjar; **2** Nahia Aboukhalil; **3** Susanne El Sayed; **4** Tania Zaytouny; **5** Dia Elzeer; **6** Raymonde Ayoub; **7** Sharifa Abouezzeddine; **8** Nicole Salem; **9** Mouna Sakr; **10** Rima Rabbat.

National Closed Championships
MEN'S SINGLES – Semi-finals: R. Kattoura d. E. Nehme 6–1 6–3 6–1; S. Karam d. O. Sadek 6–3 6–3

6–3. *Final:* Kattoura d. Karam 6–4 7–6 5–7 7–6.
WOMEN'S SINGLES – *Semi-finals:* M. Hajjar d. S. Abuezzeddine 6–0 6–0; T. Zaytouny d. N. Aboukhalil 7–5 6–3. *Final:* Hajjar d. Zaytouny 7–5 6–2.

LIBYA (1947)
Jamahiriya Tennis Federation, Alfatah September Street, PO Box 2729, Tripoli.
C. Tennis Libya; T. (218–21) 39150/46883; TX. 20420 OLYMPIC LIBYA; Fax. (218–21) 609 876; *Pres.* Mr Omran Danna; *Sec.* Mr Mohamed Behelil.

LIECHTENSTEIN (1968)
Liechtensteiner Tennisverband, Bartlegroschstrasse 36, 9490 Vaduz.
T. (41–75) 56659; Fax. (41–75) 56518; *Pres.* Mr Walter Walser; *Sec.* Mr Werner Schaechle.

LITHUANIA
Lithuanian Tennis Union, 6 Zemaites Street, 232675 Vilnius.
T. (7) 0122 66 25 17/61 35 80/35 20 32; Fax. (7) 0122 62 40 92. *Pres.* Mr Alfredas Putramentas; *Sec.* Mr Romas Kachanauskas.

LUXEMBOURG (1946)
Federation Luxembourgeoise de Tennis, Boite Postale 38, L 9201 Diekirch, C. Federation Luxembourgeoise de Tennis Luxembourg; T. (352) 81 75 41; Fax. (352) 81 77 25; *Pres.* Mr Michel Wolter; *Vice Pres Gen Sec.* Jean Goederich.
MEN: 1 Johny Goudenbour; 2 Jacques Radoux; 3 Serge Bruck; 4 Thierry Neiens; 5 Patrick Remakel.
WOMEN: 1 Anne Kremer; 2 Marie–Christine Goy; 3 Rosabel Moyen; 4 Michele Wagner; 5 Stephanie Wolf.

National Closed Championships
MEN'S SINGLES – *Semi-finals:* J. Goudenbour d. A. Mills 6–2 1–6 6–2 6–2; T. Neiens d. P. Remakel 6–3 7–6 6–3. *Final:* Goudenbour d. Neiens 6–1 3–6 4–6 7–6 6–3.
WOMEN'S SINGLES – *Semi-finals:* A. Kremer d. M. Wagner 6–4 6–7 6–2; M–C. Goy d. R. Moyen 6–4 6–3. *Final:* Kremer d. Goy 6–3 6–1.

MALAYSIA (1921)
Lawn Tennis Association of Malaysia, c/o National Tennis Centre, Jalan Duta, 50480 Kuala Lumpur, Malaysia.
C. Tennis Kuala Lumpur; T. (60–3) 2938070/2938050; Fax. (60–3) 2925041; TX. 28061 NTC MA; *Pres.* Mr Abdul Ghafar Baba; *Sec.* Mr Zainal Abidin Ali.

MALTA (1966)
\Malta Lawn Tennis Association, PO Box 50, Sliema Post Office, Sliema.
T. (356) 312945/335728/330363 (Sec); TX. 623 MERGRU MW; Fax. (356) 312945; *Pres.* Dr. L. Farrugia Sacco; *Gen. Sec.* Mr Michael J. Borg Cardona.

MEXICO (1952)
Federacion Mexicana de Tenis, Miguel Angel de Quevedo 953, Mexico City 04330 DF.
C. Mextenis, Mexico City, T. (52–5) 689 9733; TX. 1761056 FMDTME; Fax (52–5) 689 6307/549 1956; *Pres.* Mr Jesus Topete Enriquez; *Sec.* Mr Fernando Palafox Valadez.

MONACO (1927)
Federation Monegasque de Lawn Tennis, 27 Boulevard de Belgique, 98000 Monaco.
C. Federation-Tennis-Monaco; T. (33–93) 25 55 74; (Att. LTA); Fax. (33–93) 30 54 82; *Sec.* Mr Bernard Noat.
MEN: 1 Fabien Cousin; 2 Philippe Ventura; 3 Bernard Balleret; 4 Christophe Boggetti; 5 Jerome Seguin; 6 Christian Collange; 7 Jacques Vincileoni; 8 Jacques Guglielmi; 9 Sebastien Graeff.
WOMEN: 1 Alexis Dechaume; 2 Isabelle Demongeot; 3 Florencia Labat; 4 Nathalie Herreman; 5 Agnes Romano; 6 Emmanuelle Gagliardi; 7 Agnes Barthelmy.

National Closed Championships
MEN'S SINGLES – *Semi-finals:* C. Boggetti d. J. Vincileoni 6–4 6–3; J. Seguin d. S. Graeff 6–0 6–0. *Final:* Seguin d. Boggetti 6–1 6–3 6–7 6–3.
WOMEN'S SINGLES – *Final:* E. Gagliardi d. N. Ballerj 6–4 6–1.

MOROCCO (1957)

Federation Royale Marocaine de Tennis, Parc de la Ligue Arabe, BP 15794, Casablanca.
C. Tenisfede, Maroc; T. (212) 234140/230015; TX. 23745 FRTENNIS;
Fax. (212–2) 262663; *Pres.* Mr Mohamed M'Jid; *Sec.* Mr Bouchaib Sbai.

NETHERLANDS (1899)

Koninklijke Nederlandse Lawn Tennis Bond, PO Box 107, 1200 AC Hilversum.
C. Tennisbond, Hilversum; T. (31–35) 246 941; TX. 43061 KNLTB NL; Fax. (31–35) 240 760; *Pres.* Mr Ruurd de Boer; *Vice Pres.* Mrs H V Mook-Grunberg;
MEN: **1** Richard Krajicek; **2** Paul Haarhuis; **3** Jan Simerink; **4** Jacco Eltingh; **5** Mark Koevermans; **6** Michiel Schapers; **7** Fernon Wibier; **8** Sander Groen; **9** Glen Schaap; **10** Tom Nijssen.
WOMEN: **1** Brenda Schultz; **2** Manon Bollegraf; **3** Stephanie Rottier; **4** Nicole Muns–Jagerman; **5** Monique Kiene; **6** Claire Wegink; **7** Miriam Oremans; **8** Kristie Boogert; **9** Esmir Hoogendoorn; **10** Linda Niemantsverdriet.

National Closed Championships
MEN'S SINGLES – Semi-finals: R. Kok d. H. Troost 4–6 6–4 6–4 6–0; G. Schaap d. C. Feenstra 6–3 6–2 7–5. *Final:* Kok d. Schaap 1–6 7–5 6–4 3–6 6–3.
WOMEN'S SINGLES – Semi-finals: S. Rottier d. S. De Vries 6–2 6–2; M. Koutstaal d. L. Niemantsverdrift 6–4 2–6 7–6. *Final:* Rottier d. Koutstaal 6–4 6–2.

NEW ZEALAND (1886)

New Zealand Tennis Inc, PO Box 11541, Manners Street, Wellington.
C. Tennis, Wellington; T. (64–4) 4731115 Fax. (64–4) 4712152 *Chmn.* Mr Ian D Wells; *Admin. Sec.* Ms Maggi Kerr–Andrew.
MEN: **1** Kelly Evernden; **2** Brett Steven; **3** Steven Guy; **4** Bruce Derlin; **5** James Greenhalgh; **6** Alistair Hunt; **7** Phillip Seeman; **8** Justin McKenzie; **9** Glen Wilson; **10** Michael Zoricich.
WOMEN: **1** Claudine Toleafoa; **2** Julie Richardson; **3** Hana Guy; **4** Ruth Seeman; **5** Amanda Trail; **6** Sally Moorfield; **7** Robyn Hunt; **8** Tracey King; **9** Paiao Short; **10** Katherine Costain.

National Closed Championships
MEN'S SINGLES – Semi-finals: J. Greenhalgh d. S. Guy 3–6 7–6 6–2; S. Downs d. R. Moller 6–2 6–4. *Final:* Greenhalgh d. Downs 6–4 7–6.
WOMEN'S SINGLES – Semi-finals: H. Guy d. G. McManus 2–6 6–4 6–4; K. Costain d. A. Trail 7–6 6–3. *Final:* Guy d. Costain 6–3 6–4.

NIGERIA (1927)

Nigeria Lawn Tennis Association, National Stadium, Surulere, PO Box 145, Lagos.
C. Tennis Natsports, Lagos, T. (234–1) 830649/960165; Fax. (234–1) 830535; TX. 26559/2670 ADEFNL NG; Life Patron. Alhaji Raheem A Adejumo; *Chmn.* Mr. Chuka Momah; *Sec.* Mr Simon Ebhojiaye.
MEN: **1** Kyrian Nwokedi; **2** David Imonitie; **3** Mohammed Abdu; **4** Yakubu Suleman; **5** Gabriel Oty; **6** Ganiyu Adenekan; **7** Paul Areh; **8** Innocent Modika; **9** Tom Ikpa; **10** Moses Agera.
WOMEN: **1** Nosa Imafidon; **2** Adepeju Akomolafe; **3** Margaret Olagundoye; **4** Ngozi Uwakwe; **5** Aminat Balogun; **6** Ayoola Shelle; **7** Veronica Okonkwo; **8** Clara Udofa; **9** Osaro Amadin; **10** Ndali Ijomah.

National Closed Championships
MEN'S SINGLES – Semi-finals: G. Omuta d. K. Nwokedi 6–3 7–5; I. Modika d. M. Agera 6–4 6–2. *Final:* Modika d. Omuta 6–4 6–3.
WOMEN'S SINGLES – Semi-finals: N. Imafidon d. V. Okonkwo 6–0 6–2; C. Udofa d. A. Akomolafe 6–1 6–1. *Final:* Udofa d. Imafidon 7–6 6–2.

NORWAY (1909)

Norges Tennisforbund, Haslevangen 33, PO Box 287, 0511, Oslo 5.
C. Norsktennis, Oslo; T. (47–2) 657550; TX. 78586 NIF N (Att. Tennis); Fax. (47–2) 646409; *Pres.* Mr Jarl H Bibow; *Sec.* Mr Jon-Erik Ross.

PAKISTAN (1947)

Pakistan Tennis Federation, 39–A Jinnah Stadium, Pakistan Sports Complex, Kashmir Highway, Islamabad; C. Paktennis, Wah Cantt; T. (92—51) 212846; TX. 54288 ENMAR PK; Fax. (92–51) 212440/212846; *Pres.* Mr Wasim Sajjad; *Vice Pres.* Mr Saeed Hai; *Sec.* Mr Munir Pirzada.

PARAGUAY (1920)

Asociacion Paraguaya de Tenis, Colon 1054, 1st Floor, Asuncion.

T. (595–21) 497756; TX. 25005 DIESA PY; Fax. (595 21) 503721; *Pres.* Mr Miguel Carrizosa; *Exec. Dir.* Mr Daniel Lugo Llamosas.

PERU (1930)

Federacion Peruana de Tenis, Cercado Campo de Marte, s/n Jesus Maria, Casilla 2243, Lima.
T. (51–14) 249979/552394; TX. 25056 PE FPTENIS; Fax. (51–14) 300602/300614/552394; *Pres.* Mr Bartolome Puiggros Planas; *Sec.* Mr Peter Relton Ruddock.

PHILIPPINES (1946)

Philippine Tennis Association, Rizal Memorial Sports Complex, Vito Cruz Street, Manila.
C. Philta, Manila; T. (63–2) 583535/588248; TX. 23297 ALTIS PH/40255 ALTA PM; Fax. (63–2) 522 0229; *Pres.* Col Salvador H Andrada; *Sec.* Mr Romeo Magat.
MEN: **1** Felix Barrientos; **2** Roland So; **3** Sofronio Palahang; **4** Joseph Lizardo; **5** Manuel Tolentino; **6** Robert Angelo; **7** Danilo Pila; **8** Michael Misa; **9** Alberto Alerre, Jr.; **10** Ronald San Andres.
WOMEN: **1** Jennifer Saret; **2** Francesca La'o; **3** Dorothy Jane Suarez; **4** Eva Olivarez; **5** Carol Roque; **6** Josephine Paguyo; **7** Gladys Imperial; **8** Gisselle Sta. Maria; **9** Maricris Fernandez; **10** Mia Fernandez.
National Closed Championships
MEN'S SINGLES – Semi-finals: R. Angelo d. S. Palahang 6–2 6–4; J. Lizardo d. D. Pila 6–3 6–4. *Final:* Angelo d. Lizardo 5–7 6–0 6–4 6–1.
WOMEN'S SINGLES – Semi-finals: J. Saret d. D.J. Suarez 6–1 6–0; F. La'o d. E. Olivarez 7–5 7–5. *Final:* Saret d. La'o 6–2 7–6.

POLAND (1921)

Polski Zwiazek Tenisowy, ul. Marszalkowska 2, 3rd Floor, 00 - 581 Warsaw.
C. Poltenis, Warsaw; T. (48–22) 21 80 01/29 26 21; TX. 816494 PAISP PL/812466 COS PL; *Pres.* Mr Wojtek Fibak; *Vice Pres.* Mr Ryszard Fijalkowski.
MEN: **1** Wojciech Kowalski; **2** Bartlomiej Dabrowski; **3** Tomasz Iwanski; **4** Lech Bienkowski; **5** Tomasz Lichon; **6** Dariusz Nowicki; **7** Aleksander Mierzwinski; **8** Lech Sidor; **9** Pawel Motylewski; **10** Adam Skrzypczak.
WOMEN: **1** Katarzyna Nowak; **2** Magdalena Mroz; **3** Katarzyna Teodorowicz; **4** Karolina Bulat; **5** Katarzyna Malec; **6** Monika Starosta; **7** Agata Werblinska; **8** Maryla Madura; **9** Anna Moll; **10** Malgorzata Listowska.
National Closed Championships
MEN'S SINGLES – Semi-finals: A. Skrzypczak d. L. Bienkowski **6**–0 5–7 2–6 6–3 6–2; L. Sidor d. M. Kost 6–3 4–6 7–5 6–3. *Final:* Sidor d. Skrzypczak 6–1 4–6 6–4 6–0.
WOMEN'S SINGLES – Semi-finals: K. Malec d. K. Teodorowicz 6–2 6–3; M. Starosta d. S. Rynarzewski 7–5 6–3. *Final:* Starosta d. Malec 6–1 6–3.

PORTUGAL (1925)

Federacao Portugesa de Tenis, Estadio Nacional, Apartado 210, 2796 Linda-a-Velha Codex.
C. TENIS PORTUGAL; T. (351–1) 4151356/4151394; TX. 65257 TENFED P; Fax. (351–1) 419 0888; *Pres.* Mr Manuel Cordeiro dos Santos; *Sec.* Mr Antonio Sequeira.
National Closed Championships
MEN'S SINGLES – Semi-finals: J. Cunha E Silva d. E. Couto 6–2 6–3 6–2; N. Marques d. B. Mota 6–4 3–6 6–3 6–2. *Final:* Marques d. Cunha E Silva 7–6 6–3 6–2.
WOMEN'S SINGLES – I. Couto d. J. Pedroso 4–6 6–3 6–1; S. Prazeres d. I. Drumond 6–4 7–5. *Final:* Prazeres d. Couto 3–6 6–1 6–4.

PUERTO RICO (1959)

Puerto Rico Tennis Association, PO Box 40456, Minillas Sta, Santurce, PR 00940.
T. (1–809) 765 7711; TX 345 4212 PRTA PD; Fax. (1–809) 767 7427; *Pres.* Mr Carlos Garcia Rullan; *Sec.* Mr Jaime Ariza.
National Closed Championships
MEN'S SINGLES – Semi-finals: S. Diaz d. J O. Rios 3–6 7–5 6–4; J. Frontera d. M. Nido 2–6 6–3 7–5. *Final:* Diaz d. Frontera 3–6 6–4 6–2.
WOMEN'S SINGLES – Semi-finals: J. Bauza d. M. Amadeo 6–2 6–4; E. Viqueira d. B. Luna 6–4 6–1. *Final:* Viqueira d. Bauza 6–2 6–1.

QATAR (1984)

Qatar Tennis and Squash Federation, PO Box 4959, Doha.

C. QATSF DOHA; T. (974) 351629/351631/454444; TX. 4749 QATFOT DH; Fax. (974) 351626; *Pres.* Mr Ali Al Fardan; *Sec.* Mr Ali Mohammad Yousef

ROMANIA (1929)

Federatia Romana de Tennis, Str. Vasile Conta 16, 70139 Bucharest.
C. Sportrom, Bucharest; T. (40–0) 120 160; TX. 11180 SPORT R; Fax. (40–0) 120 161; *Pres.* Mr Constantin Iurea; *Sec.* Prof Lucian Vasiliu.

SAN MARINO (1956)

Federazione Sammarinese Tennis, Casella Postale no 2, Dogana, 47031 Republic of San Marino.
T. (39-549) 905303; TX. 284 CONSMAR SO; Fax. (39-549) 908187; *Pres.* Mr Remo Raimondi; *Sec.* Maria Teresa Righi.

SAUDI ARABIA (1956)

Saudi Arabian Tennis Federation, PO Box 4674, Riyadh 11412.
C. Koratawla, Riyadh; T. (966–1) 4820188/4822829; TX. 404130 TENNIS SJ; Fax. (966—1) 4822829; *Pres.* Mr Khalid Bin Abdullah Abdul Aziz; *Vice Pres* Mr Abdul Azziz S. Kridis; *Sec.* Mr Mohammed S Al–Ruwashid.

SENEGAL (1960)

Federation Senegalaise de Tennis, Sporting Club, 28 Avenue Roosevelt, BP 510, Dakar.
T. (221) 210239; TX. 61159 SG CTDSENE; Fax. (221) 22 93 93; *Pres.* Mr Mamadou Bary; *Sec.* Mr Layti N'Diaye.

SINGAPORE (1928)

Singapore Lawn Tennis Association, 4 Normanton Park, # 07-115, Singapore 0511.
T. (65) 274 1774; TX. 35467 NASTAD RS; Fax. (65) 272 2704; *Pres.* Dr Ong Leong Boon; *Hon. Sec.* Maj. S Uthrapathy.
MEN: **1** Tung–Yi Kno; **2** Sherman Lim; **3** Art Hobbs; **4** Chee Yen Chen; **5** Derek Yong; **6** Wei–Pin Choo; **7** Mark Choy; **8** Zainuddin Yakin; **9** Wai Yaw Liu; **10** Hock Chai Ang.
WOMEN: **1** Lela Zainal; **2** Laura Liong; **3** Janice Lai; **4** Jean Ho.
National Closed Championships
MEN'S SINGLES – Semi-finals: T. Kho d. A. Hobbs 6–2 4–6 6–4 6–4; S. Lim d. C. Chen 7–6 7–5 6–7 7–5. *Final:* Kho d. Lim 4–6 6–4 6–3 6–0.
WOMEN'S SINGLES – Semi-finals: L. Liong d. J. Ho 6–1 6–1; L. Zainal d. J. Lai 6–1 6–0. *Final:* Zainal d. Liong 6–4 6–1.

SLOVENIA (1946)

Slovene Tennis Association, Gortanova 21, 61000 Ljubljana.
T. (38) 61 44 11 82/44 39 28; Fax. (38) 61 44 14 48; *Pres.* Mr. Janez Erhart; *Sec.* Mr. Fredi Reicher.
MEN: **1** Iztok Bozic; **2** Marko Por; **3** Blaz Trupez; **4** Zaga Janskovec; **5** Andraz Tome; **6** Damjan Klevisar; **7** Miha Furlan; **8** Bostjan Dobersek; **9** Miha Fric; **10** Matjaz Zorko.
WOMEN: **1** Barbara Mulej; **2** Tina Krizan; **3** Tina Vukasovic; **4** Karin Lusnic; **5** Tadeja Florjancic; **6** Vanja Simonic; **7** Urika Radanovic; **8** Dunja Ribianko; **9** Tjasa Jexernik; **10** Srela Rajh.
National Closed Championships
MEN'S SINGLES – Semi-finals: B. Trupej d. U. Sever 7–5 7–6; M. Por d. Z. Janskovec 6–2 6–2. *Final:* ror d. Trupej 2–6 7–6 6–0.
WOMEN'S SINGLES – Semi-finals: B. Mulej d. K. Lusnik 6–7 6–2 6–1; T. Krizan d. T. Vukasovic 6–4 6–7 7–5. *Final:* Mulej d. Krizan 6–2 6–2.

SOUTH AFRICA (1991)

Tennis South Africa, Box 2211, Johannesburg 2000.
T. (27) 11 407 4893 (*Pres.*)/(27) 11 402 3580 (*Chief Exec.*); Fax. (27) 11 407 4662 (*Pres.*)/(27) 11 402 6940 (*Chief Exec.*); *Pres.* Mr Chris Ngcobo; *Chief Exec.* Mr Ian Laxton; *Gen. Sec.* Mr Moss Mashishi

SPAIN (1901)

Real Federacion Espanola de Tenis, Avda. Diagonal 618 3 D, 08021 Barcelona.
C. FEDETENIS Barcelona; T. (34–3) 2005355/2010844/2005878/2015586; Fax. (34–3) 2021279; *Pres.* Mr Agustin Pujol Niubo; *Sec.* Mr Tomas Garcia Balmaseda.
MEN: **1** Carlos Costa; **2** Sergio Bruguera; **3** Emilio Sanchez; **4** Francisco Clavet; **5** Javier Sanchez; **6** Jordi

Arrese; **7** Francisco Roig; **8** German Lopez; **9** Tomas Carbonell; **10** Marcos Gorriz.
WOMEN: 1 Arantxa Sanchez-Vicario; **2** Conchita Martinez; **3** Virginia Ruano; **4** Noelia Perez; **5** Cristina Torrens; **6** Eva Bes; **7** Estefania Bottini; **8** Silvia Ramon; **9** Nelis Avila; **10** Barbara Navarro.
National Closed Championships
MEN'S SINGLES – Semi-finals: C. Costa d. F. Roig 6–4 6–0; F. Clavet d. J. Sanchez 4–6 7–5 6–2. **Final:** Costa d. Clavet 6–2 6–0.
WOMEN'S SINGLES – Semi-finals: A. Sanchez-Vicario d. E. Bes 6–0 6–3; E. Bottini d. C. Torrens 6–4 6–2. **Final:** Sanchez-Vicario d. Bottini 6–0 6–2.

SRI LANKA (1915)
Sri Lanka Tennis Association, 45 Sir Marcus Fernando Mawatha, Colombo 7.
C. Tennis, Colombo; T. (94–1) 686174; TX. 21537 METALIX CE; Fax. (94–1) 580721; *Pres.* Mr D L Seneviratne; *Sec.* Mr L M Fernando.
MEN: 1 Jayendra Wijeyasekera; **2** Chandragupta Soysa; **3** Rohan De Silva; **4** Isuru Gunesekera; **5** Prashan Nagendra; **6** Sanjaya Weerakoon; **7** Genuan Gunewardhana; **8** Nalaka Marashinghe; **9** Sylverster Francis; **10** Sanjaya Wijemanne.
WOMEN: 1 Kishani Wickramasinghe; **2** Anoushka Boralessa; **3** Upekha Wijeratne; **4** Shalini Periera; **5** Lihini Weerasuriya; **6** Sobhini De Silva; **7** Rukshana Kurukulasuriya; **8** Saranga Sangakkara; **9**= Priyanthi Sebaratnam/Lanee De Silva.
National Closed Championships
MEN'S SINGLES – Semi-finals: J. Wijeyesekera d. S. Wijemanne 6–1 5–7 6–4 6–4; R. De Silva d. G. Gunawardhana 6–3 6–1 6–1. **Final:** Wijeyesekera d. De Silva 2–6 1–6 7–5 6–4 6–4.
WOMEN'S SINGLES – Semi-finals: L. Weerasuriya d. K. Wickramasinghe 6–2 6–2; S. Sangakkara d. S. De Silva 6–2 3–6 6–4. **Final:** Weerasuriya d. Sangakkara 6–0 6–1.

SUDAN (1956)
Sudan Lawn Tennis Association, PO Box 1553, Khartoum.
T. (249–11) 70081; TX. 22345 ARART SD/22558 DIGES SD; *Pres.* Mr Mohamed Ahmed Giha; *Sec.* Dr. Fatih Hasabrasoul.

SWEDEN (1906)
The Swedish Tennis Association, Lidingovagen 75, 115 37 Stockholm or Box 27915, S–11594 Stockholm.
C. Svensktennis; T. (46–8) 6679770; Fax. (46–8) 6646606; *Pres.* Mr Olle Bergstrom; *Gen Sec.* Mr Sten Akerstrom.
MEN: 1 Stefan Edberg; **2** Magnus Larsson; **3** Magnus Gustafsson; **4** Christian Bergstrom; **5** Henrik Holm; **6** Nicklas Kulti; **7** Jonas Svensson; **8** Anders Jarryd; **9** Lars Jonsson; **10** Mikael Tillstrom.
WOMEN: 1 Catarina Lindqvist; **2** Asa Carlsson; **3** Cecilia Dahlman; **4** Annika Narbe; **5** Maria Lindstrom; **6** Maria Ekstrand; **7** Catarina Bernstein; **8** Maria Strandlund; **9** Marie Arkbrant; **10** Marianne Vallin.
National Closed Championships
MEN'S SINGLES – Semi-finals: M. Larsson d. P. Nyborg 7–6 6–4; P. Lundgren d. J. Gunnarsson 2–6 6–4 6–4. **Final:** Larsson d. Lundgren 2–6 6–2 6–3.
WOMEN'S SINGLES – Semi-finals: M. Vallin d. M. Linusson 6–2 6–2; C. Dahlman d. M. Ekstrand 6–2 6–3. **Final:** Dahlman d. Vallin 6–3 6–1.

SWITZERLAND (1896)
Schweizerischer Tennisverband, Talgut Zentrum 5, CH 3063, Ittigen/BE.
C. Suissetennis, Bern; T. (41–31) 9217444; TX. 911391 STVCH; Fax. (41–31) 9212924; *Pres.* Mrs Christine Ungricht; *Sec.* Mr Daniel Gundelfinger.
MEN: 1 Marc Rosset; **2** Jakob Hlasek; **3** Claudio Mezzadri; **4** Thierry Grin; **5** Reto Staubli; **6** Valentin Frieden; **7** Ignace Rotman; **8** Patrick Mohr; **9** Zoltan Kuharszky; **10** Stephane Manai.
WOMEN: 1 Manuela Maleeva; **2** Emanuela Zardo; **3** Christelle Fauche; **4** Michele Strebel; **5** Natalie Tschan; **6** Sandrine Jaquet; **7** Cathy Caverzasio; **8** Csilla Bartos; **9** Martina Hingis; **10** Gabrielle Villiger.
National Closed Championships
MEN'S SINGLES – Semi-finals: S. Manai d. V. Frieden 6–2 6–4; R. Staubli d. T. Grin 3–6 6–3 7–6. **Final:** Staubli d. Manai 6–4 7–5 7–6.
WOMEN'S SINGLES – Semi-finals: E. Zardo d. C. Caverzasio 6–1 6–2; N. Tschan d. C. Fauche 7–5 4–6 6–3. **Final:** Zardo d. Tschan 6–1 4–6 6–3.

SYRIA ARAB REPUBLIC (1953)
Syrian Arab Tennis Federation, PO Box 421, Damascus.

T. (963–11) 225026/34/52; TX. 411578 SPOFED SY; *Pres.* Mr M Fahed Al Dahan; *Sec.* Mr Hassan Kudmani.
MEN: 1 Dawood Dawoodian; 2 Samer Murad; 3 Saher Saad Aldin; 4 Ahmed Al–Now; 5 Hasen Al Holou; 6 Rashed Al–Shehaby; 7 Safik Diab; 8 Bassam Shahin; 9 Ramy Seraj Al–Din; 10 Showket Abo–Al Fadle. **WOMEN:** 1 Merna Badawy; 2 Lina Mshaty; 3 Huda Shehate; 4 Rima Al–Taky; 5 Carla Kerkigian; 6 Farah Diayob; 7 Sera Al–Tawil; 8 Rem Khadaj; 9 Paoula Gebily; 10 Raya Rashad.
National Closed Championships
MEN'S SINGLES – Semi-finals: S. Murad d. S. Saad Aldine 6–1 6–2; D. Dawoodian d. A. Alnow 6–1 6–2. **Final:** Dawoodian d. Murad 7–6 3–6 6–4.
WOMEN'S SINGLES – Semi-finals: L. Mshaty d. H. Shehate 0–6 7–5 6–4; M. Badawy d. R. Al–Taky 7–5 3–6 6–4. **Final:** Badawy d. Mshaty 6–2 6–3.

THAILAND (1927)
The Lawn Tennis Association of Thailand, c/o Sports Authority of Thailand, Hua Mark, Bangkok 10240. C. Thai Tennis, Bangkok; T. (66—2) 3190484/3184318; Fax. (66—2) 3195868/2214841; *Pres.* Mr Somchitr Tongpradab; *Sec.* Mr Prachitr Srichaiyan.

TOGO (1955)
Federation Togolaise de Tenis, BP 3601, Lome.
T. (228) 215965/210920/210607; TX. 5442 GRD TG; Fax. (228) 210607; *Pres.* Mr Kwao Aquereburu; *Sec.* Mr Koffi Galokpo.

TRINIDAD AND TOBAGO (1951)
The Lawn Tennis Association of Trinidad and Tobago, 16 Scott Street, St Augustine, Trinidad. C. Lawntenna, Port of Spain; T. (1–809) 662 5876; Fax. (1–809) 627 5278; *Pres.* Mr Emile P. Elias; *Sec.* Mr Richardson Henry.
National Closed Championships
MEN'S SINGLES – Semi-finals: J. Hodge d. K. Boodoosingh 6–4 6–1 6–0; B. Khan d. Ivor Grazette 6–3 6–3 6–3. **Final:** Hodge d. Khan 6–1 6–2 5–7 6–2.
WOMEN'S SINGLES – Semi-finals: E. Gibson d. J. Ayers 6–3 6–0; M. Ward d. F. Look Hong 6–2 6–3. **Final:** Gibson d. Ward 6–2 6–2.

TUNISIA (1954)
Federation Tunisienne de Tennis, Cite Nationale, Sportive - El Menzah, 1004 Tunis.
T. (216—1) 238 144; TX. 15195 TN; Fax. (216—1) 786 188/238144; *Pres.* Mr Fathi Farah; *Sec.* Mr Mohamed Ali Lazrak.
MEN: 1 Selim Ben Hadj Ali; 2 Adel Lahdhiri; 3 Souheil Zekri; 4 Elies Bramly; 5 Walid Caracci; 6 Bessem Zouaoui; 7 Adel Brahim; 8 Karim Jelassi; 9 Selim Baccar; 10 Amine Nabli. **WOMEN:** 1 Selima Sfar; 2 Issem Essaies; 3 Bessima Mahressi; 4 Aicha Ferjani; 5 Dorra Zdiri; 6 Mouna Bey; 7 Imene Ben Arbi; 8 Rim Belkhodja; 9 Lobna Cherif; 10 Dorra Abbassi.
National Closed Championships
MEN'S SINGLES – Semi-finals: S. Ben Hadj Ali d. S. Zekri 6–4 6–2; E. Bramly d. A. Lahdhiri 6–3 5–7 6–4. **Final:** Ben Hadj Ali d. Bramly 3–6 6–4 6–3.
WOMEN'S SINGLES – Semi-finals: I. Essaies d. I. Ben Arbi 6–2 6–3; A. Ferjani d. R. Belkhodj 3–6 6–2 7–5. **Final:** Essaies d. Ferjani 6–3 6–0.

TURKEY (1923)
Turkiye Tenis Federasyonu, Ulus Is Hani, Ankara.
C. Tennis Sport, Ankara; T. (90–4) 310 3960/7345; TX. 44 531 BTGM TR; Fax. (90–4) 311 2554; *Pres.* Mr Gunesi Olcay; *Sec.* Mr Sadi Toker.
MEN: 1 Alaaddin Karagoz; 2 Yavuz Erkancil; 3 Mustafa Azkara; 4 Berk Albayrak; 5 Baris Ergun; 6 Oguz Azkara; 7 Erol Uyar; 8 Aydin Kuntay; 9 Vakur Erturk; 10 Reha Demirdag. **WOMEN:** 1 Duygu Aksit; 2 Gulberk Gultekin; 3 Stela Penciu; 4 Yasemin Kaya; 5 Esra Bayburt; 6 Seden Ozlu; 7 Damla Tokcan; 8 Sanem Berksoy; 9 Meryem Aykul; 10 Isil Cayirli.
National Closed Championships
MEN'S SINGLES – Semi-finals: M. Azkara d. B. Ergun 6–1 7–5; A. Karagoz d. O. Azkara 6–3 6–1. **Final:** Karagoz d. Azkara 3–6 6–2 7–6.
WOMEN'S SINGLES – Semi-finals: G. Gultekin d. S. Elpeze (Penciu) 6–3 6–3; D. Aksit d. Y. Kaya 7–6 1–6 6–1. **Final:** Gultekin d. Aksit w/o.

UKRAINE (1946)

Ukrainian National Lawn Tennis Federation, Kujbesava Str 42, 252023 Kiev.
T. (7) 044 22 00 347, Fax. (7) 044 22 01 294. *Pres.* Mr German Benyaminov; *Sec.* Mr Igor Khokhlov.

UNITED ARAB EMIRATES (1982)

United Arab Emirates Tennis Association, PO Box 87, Dubai.
T. (971–4) 690393; TX. 46347 FAGEN EM; Fax. (971–4) 521802; *Pres.* Mr Hassan Khansaheb; *Sec.* Mr Nasser Madani.

USA (1881)

United States Tennis Association Inc, 12th Floor, 1212 Avenue of the Americas, New York, NY 10036.
C. Ustennis, New York; T. (1–212) 302 3322; TX. 424499 ULTA UI; Fax. (1–212) 764 1838; *Pres.* Mr Robert Cookson; *First Vice Pres.* Mr J Howard Frazer; *Exec. Dir.* Mr M Marshall Happer III; *Sec.* Mr Harry A Marmion.

USSR (1956)

USSR Tennis Federation, Leningradski Prospekt 36, Dinamo Stadium, Petrovski Park Tennis Club, 125167 Moscow.
C. Sportkomitet, Moscow; T. (7–095) 201 1249; TX. 411287 PRIZ SU; Fax. (7–095) 284 6482 ; *Pres.* Mr Shamil Tarpishev; *Gen. Sec.* Mr Boris Fomenko; *Exec. Dir.* Mr Dmitriy Vikharev.

URUGUAY (1915)

Asociacion Uruguya de Tennis, Galicia 1392, CP 11.200, Montevideo.
C. Urutennis, Montevideo; T. (598–2) 91 50 20; TX. 22333 CADE UY; Fax. (598–2) 92 18 09/96 04 10; *Pres.* Mr Carlos Rymer Estrada; *Sec.* Mr Enrique Dentone.
MEN: 1 Federico Dondo; 2 Gonzalo Rodriguez; 3 Enrique Perez; 4 Philippe Pinet; 5 Joaquin Elola; 6 Pablo Casamayou; 7 Alvaro Peyrano; 8 Andres Artia; 9 Sebastian Ravera; 10 Ricardo Ychazo.
WOMEN: 1 Claudia Brause; 2 Laura Olave; 3 Cecilia Juricich; 4 Elena Juricich; 5 Natalia De Coca; 6 Guadalupe Herraiz; 7 Maria Eugenia Fernandez; 8 Sofia Aishemberg; 9 Claudia Perolini; 10 Gloria Scavarelli.
National Closed Championships
MEN'S SINGLES – *Semi-finals:* G. Rodriguez d. E. Perez 6–4 2–6 6–4; F. Dondo d. P. Pinet 7–6 6–2. *Final:* Dondo d. Rodriguez 6–0 7–5.
WOMEN'S SINGLES – *Semi-finals:* C. Brause d. C. Juricich 6–1 6–0; L. Olave d. E. Juricich 6–4 6–2. *Final:* Brause d. Olave 6–4 6–2.

VENEZUELA (1927)

Federacion Venezolana de Tenis, Apartado 70539, Los Ruices, Caracas 1070-A.
C. Fevetenis, Caracas; T. (58–2) 9792421/9791487; Fax (58–2) 9792694/921263; *Pres.* Mr Fermin Perez; *Sec.* Mr Alfredo Lanciani.
MEN: 1 Nicolas Pereira; 2 Maurice Ruah; 3 Jimy Szyhanski; 4 Victor Perez; 5 Rodrigo Diaz; 6 Carlos Parra; 7 Abraham Levy; 8 Javier Lamas; 9 Boro Colvee; 10 Jesus Esteban.
WOMEN: 1 Ninfa Marra; 2 Maria V. Francesa; 3 Maria A. Vento; 4 Eleonora Vegliante; 5 Helene Kappler; 6 Daniela Agostinone; 7 Monica Toledo; 8 Romina Torrealba; 9 Maria Vegliante; 10 Maryori Sequera.
National Closed Championships
MEN'S SINGLES – *Semi-finals:* J. Szymanski d. A. Levy 7–6 6–3; V. Perez d. C. Parra 6–2 6–3. *Final:* Szymanski d. Perez 6–0 6–3.
WOMEN'S SINGLES – *Semi-finals:* M. Toledo d. L. Nastari 6–2 6–1; R. Torrealba d. M. Vegliante 6–4 6–0. *Final:* Toledo d. Torrealba 6–3 7–5.

YUGOSLAVIA (1922)

Tenis Savez Yugoslavije, Terazije 35, 11000 Belgrade.
C. Tesaj, Belgrade; T. (38–11) 33 33 36; TX. 12595 SFKJ YU; *Pres.* Mr Petar Marinkovic; *Sec.* Mr Zoran Peric.

ZAMBIA (1975)

Zambia Lawn Tennis Association, PO Box 31980, Lusaka.
T. (260–1) 224145 (Pres)/22888 (Sec); TX. 43400 ZA; Fax. (260–1) 221440; *Pres.* Mr Mwansa M Mutanuka; *Sec.* Ms Beatrice Nachilombe

ZIMBABWE (1904)

Tennis Association of Zimbabwe, PO Box No A575, Avondale, Harare.
T. (263–4) 24079 (mornings only); TX. 22386 ZW; Fax. (263–4) 61881; *Pres.* Mr Paul Chingoka; T. (263–4) 68377; *Sec.* Ms Julie le Roux.
MEN: 1 Byron Black; 2 Wayne Black; 3 Rashid Hassan; 4 Gwinyayi Tongoona; 5 Malcolm Birch; 6 Mark Gurr; 7 Anthony Harris; 8 Jeremy Du Toit; 9 Gwinyayi Zengeni; 10 Alan Hounsel.
WOMEN: 1 Julia Muir; 2 Paula Iversen; 3 Cara Black; 4 Sally–Ann McDonald; 5 Nicky Wagstaff; 6 Alison Vaughan; 7 Diana Mills; 8 Ashleigh Dolman; 9 Julie Clark; 10 Tara Harvey.
National Closed Championships
MEN'S SINGLES – Semi-finals: W. Black d. J. Du Toit 6–1 6–2 6–0; G. Tongoona d. A. Harris 6–4 6–2 5–7 6–2. *Final:* Black d. Tongoona 6–0 6–1 6–2.
WOMEN'S SINGLES – Semi-finals: C. Black d. A. Vaughan 7–5 6–2; S.A. McDonald d. P. Iversen 6–4 4–6 7–5. *Final:* Black d. McDonald 2–6 6–2 6–0.

Associate Members without voting rights (68)

AFGHANISTAN Afghan Lawn Tennis Association, Sher Pur 1075, Kabul.
T. (9–2) 31561/2 or 32659; TX. 205; *Pres.* Mr Homayun Parvanta; *Sec.* Mr Nematullah Mangal.

AMERICAN SAMOA (1985) American Samoa Tennis Association, PO Box 4489, Pago Pago, American Samoa 96799.
T. (684) 644 5251; Fax. (684) 644 5005; *Pres.* Mr Perelini Perelini; *Sec.* Dr Jerome Amoa.

ANDORRA (1986) Federacio Andorrana de Tenis, Sant Antoni, 5 Entresol A. Escaldes, Principaute d'Andorre.
T. (33–628) 26728; Fax. (33–628) 23182; *Pres.* Mr Alexandre Escale; *Sec.* Mr Claudi Sala.

ANGOLA (1982) Federacao Angolana de Tenis, PO Box 3677, Luanda.
T. (244–1) 361152/350961; TX. 3121 EMISSORA AN/3052 INTSER AN; Fax. (244–1) 33 02 81/ (244–2) 397189; *Pres.* Mr Luis Lopes; *Sec.* Mr Nelson Assis.

ANTIGUA (1982) The Antigua and Barbuda Tennis Association, PO Box 48 (Pres)/PO Box 530 (Sec), St. John's, Antigua.
T. (809) 461 0597 (Pres)/462 3529; . 462 2955/0818 (Sec); *Pres.* Mr Cedric Nanton; *Sec.* Mr Patrick Labadie.

ARUBA (1954) Aruba Lawn Tennis Bond, Fergusonstraat nr 40–A, P O Box 1151, Oranjestad Aruba, Netherlands Antilles.
T. (297–8) 22485; Fax. (297–8) 34605; *Pres.* Mr Herman Kuiperi; *Sec.* Ms Heleen Bongers.

BELIZE (1910) Belize Tennis Association, PO Box 365 (Pres), Belize City.
T. (501) 2 77070; TX. 266 BRODIE BZE; Fax. (501) 2 75593; *Pres.* Mr Edward Nabil Musa; *Sec.* Mr Clement Usher.

BENIN Federation Beninoise de Lawn Tennis, BP 2709, Cotonou 1.
C. Lawn Tenking; T. (229) 315153/312149; TX. 5342 COTONOU; Fax. (229) 314684; *Pres.* Mr Edgar-Yves Monnou; *Sec.* Mr M F Adedjouma.

BERMUDA Bermuda Lawn Tennis Association, PO Box HM 341, Hamilton HM BX.
C. Ernstaudit, Bermuda, T. (1–809) 295 0319/295 7272; TX. 3680 ERNST BA; Fax. (1–809) 295 5193; *Pres.* Mr Allan Simmons; *Sec.* Mrs Gill Butterfield.

BHUTAN (1976) Bhutan Tennis Federation, PO Box 103, Thimphu.
C. Olympic; *Pres.* Mr T Dorji; *Sec.* Mr L Tsering.

BOTSWANA (1964) Botswana Lawn Tennis Association, PO Box 1174, Gaborone.
T. (267–31) 373193; TX. 2424 BD; Fax. (267–31) 373137/373193; *Pres.* Dr Quill Hermans; *Sec.* Mrs J Swift.

BRITISH VIRGIN ISLANDS (1983) British Virgin Islands Tennis Association, PO Box 665, Road Town, Tortola.

C. Veritatem Tortola; T. (1–809) 49 45471; TX. 7918 PMMBVI VB; Fax. (1–809–49) 49 45477; *Pres.* Dr Ken Adamson; *Sec.* Mr Noel Barton.

BRUNEI DARUSSALAM (1967) Brunei Darussalam Lawn Tennis Association, PO Box 859, Pejabat Pos Gadong, Bandar Seri Bagawan 3108.
T. (673–2) 238205; TX. BERSATU BU 2357; Fax. (673–2) 238205; *Pres.* Mr Mohd Ariffin Ajamain; *Sec.* Mr Tom Butcher.

BURKINA FASO (1970) Federation Burkinabe de Tennis, BP 1377, Ouagadougou 1.
Fax. (226) 306116; TX. 5268 CHAMCOM; *Pres.* Mrs Lucile Traore; *Sec.* Mr Halidou Nignan.

CAPE VERDE (1986) Federacao Cabo-Verdiana de Tenis, Ministerio da Informacao, Cultura e Desportos, Rua 5 de Julho, Praia.
T. (238) 613309; Tlx. 6030; *Pres.* Mr Antero Barros; *Sec.* Mr Antonio Ferreira.

CAYMAN ISLANDS (1973) Tennis Federation of the Cayman Islands, PO Box 1352, Grand Cayman, Cayman Islands, British West Indies.
T. (1–809) 949 2077; TX. 4310 CORPSER CP; Fax. (1–809) 949 8154; *Pres.* Mr C. D. Johnson; *Sec.* Mr Barry Smith.

CENTRAL AFRICAN REPUBLIC (1990) Federation Centrafricaine de Tennis, B P 804, Bangui, Republique Centrafricaine (RCA). T. (236) 61 18 05/61 18 10; TX. 5226 FC; Fax. (236) 61 56 60. *Pres.* Mr I Kamach; *Sec.* Jean Ombi.**BRITISH**

COMORES (1985) Federation Comorienne de Tennis, B P 701, Moroni.
T. (269) 732113/732648; TX. 219 MAE RFIC KO; Fax. (269) 733166; *Pres.* Dr Mtara Maecha; *Sec.* Mr Kamal Abdoulwahab.

COOK ISLANDS (1947) Cook Islands Tennis Association, PO Box 72, Rarotonga.
T. (682) 22327 (Pres)/24567 (Sec); TX. 62026 SSIRARO; Fax. (682) 20979; *Pres.* Mr Brian R Baudinet; *Sec.* Mr Bret Gibson.

DOMINICA (1960) Dominica Lawn Tennis Association, c/o The President, PO Box 199; Canefield Industrial Estate, Canefield, Dominica, West Indies.
C "Durapaints" Dominica; T. (1–809) 448 3000/3011; TX. 8655 DOMLEC DO; Fax. (1–809) 449 2051; *Pres.* Mr Ninian Marie; *Sec.* Mr Thomas Dorsett.

ETHIOPIA (1972) Ethiopian Lawn Tennis Federation; c/o Sport Commission; PO Box 3241, Addis Ababa.
C. Addis Ababa (c/o Sports Commission); T. (251 –1) 156795; TX. 21377 NESCO ET; Fax. (251–1) 513 345; *Pres.* Mr Hailu Ballha; *Sec.* Mr Werekey Ferede.

FIJI (1934) Fiji Lawn Tennis Association, PO Box 2399, Government Buildings, Suva OR PO Box 3644, Lautoka (Sec).
T. (679) 315988/300280; TX. 2276 USP FJ; Fax. (679) 305053; *Pres.* Mr Cliff Benson; *Sec.* Mr Paras Naidu.

GABON (1988) Federation Gabonaise de Tennis, BP 2248, Libreville.
T. (241) 733218; Tlx. 5219 CENATEL GO; *Pres.* Mr A. Paul-Apandina; *Sec.* Mr Jean–Jacques Massima Landji.

GAMBIA (1938) Gambia Tennis Association, PO Box 146 or PO Box 194, Banjul, The Gambia.
C. SSHOKSECURITY; T. (220) 28688/29848; TX. 2274 SSHOFIC/2362 MASS GV (Sec); *Pres.* Mr B.O. Semega-Janneh; *Sec.* Mr Geoffrey M Renner.

GRENADA (1973) Grenada Lawn Tennis Association, PO Box 221, St George's.
T. (1–809–440) 2434; *Pres.* Mr E. Gresham; *Sec.* Mr R. L. Hughes.

GUAM Tennis Association of Guam, PO Box 4379, Agana, Guam 96910.
C. Chelsea, Guam; T. (671) 734 2624; Fax. (671) 477 4826; *Pres.* Mr Davey Hairston; *Sec.* Ms Diane Sanchez.

GUINEE CONAKRY (1980) Federation Guineenne de Tennis, BP 4897.
C. FGT BP 262, Conakry Guinee; T. (224) 441962; TX. 22302 MJ GE; *Pres.* Mme Magass–Mala do Diallo; *Sec.* Mr Baba Bayo.

GUYANA (1933) Guyana Lawn Tennis Association, PO Box 10205, Georgetown.

C. Lawntenna, Georgetown. T.(592–2) 62936/53471 (Pres) 56701/72613 (Sec); TX. 3054 REPBANK; Fax. (592–2) 71612; *Pres.* Mr W A Lee; *Sec.* Dr R S Surujbally.

HONDURAS (1989) Federacion Hondurena de Tenis, P O Box 30001, Toncontin, Tegucigalpa. T. (504) 33 2084 (Pres); Fax. (504) 34 0792. *Pres.* Mr W W Kestenbaum; *Sec.* Ms Lourdes Zelaya.

ICELAND (1987) Icelandic Tennis Association, Ithrotamidstoedinni i Laugardal, 104 Reykjavik. T. (354–1) 83377; TX. 2314 ISI-IS; Fax. (354–1) 678848; *Pres.* Mr Pall Stefansson; *Sec.* Mr Sigurdur Halldorsson.

KOREA, PEOPLE'S DEMOCRATIC REPUBLIC (1945) Tennis Association of the Democratic People's Republic of Korea, Munsin-Dong, Dongdaewon Dist. Pyongyang.
C. Tennis Pyongyang; T. (82) 62386/63998/73198/22386/23998; TX. 5472 kp; *Pres.* Mr Kim Ju Yong; *Sec.* Mr Li Won Gun.

LESOTHO (1920) Lesotho Lawn Tennis Association, PO Box 156, Maseru 100.
C. LIPAPALI; TX. 4330 FOREIN LO; Fax. (266) 310047; *Pres.* Mr P. M. Makotoane; *Sec.* Mr Clement M. Nots'i.

LIBERIA (1987) Liberia Lawn Tennis Association, PO Box 1742, Monrovia.
T. (231) 222877/262932; Fax. (231) 261257; *Pres.* Dr W. Taylor Neal.

MADAGASCAR (1979) Federation Malgache de Tennis, BP 8410, Tsaralalana, Antananarivo.
T. (261) 2 215 19; TX. 223 50 MALAKY MG; Fax. (261) 2 260 01; *Pres.* Mr Serge Ramiandrasoa; *Sec.* Mr Josoa Rakatonindriana.

MALAWI (1966) Lawn Tennis Association of Malawi, PO Box 1417, Blantyre.
T. (265) 670033 (Chm); Tx. 44114; Fax. (265) 670808; *Chm.* Mr Duncan Gumbi; *Sec.* Mrs Ann Carter.

THE MALDIVES (1983) Tennis Association of the Maldives, c/o Maldives Olympic Committee, Male.
T. (960) 322 443; TX. 77039 MINHOM MF; Fax. (960) 324 739/323 972 via NOC; *Chmn.* Mr Ahmed Aslam; *Sec.* Mr Abdul Rasheed.

MALI (1963) Federation Malienne de Tennis, B P 1888, Bamako.
T. (223) 226329 (*Vice Pres.*); TX. 2522/2535 (*Vice Pres.*); *Pres.* Mr Alpha Bocar Nafo; *Sec.* Mr Charles Blonda Traore; *Vice Pres.* Mme Bah Youmahane.

MAURETANIA (1989) Federation Mauritanienne de Tennis, c/o Mr Badra Aly Toure, 22 r. Friant, 75014 Paris, France.
T. (33–1) 45 43 03 98 (*Vice Pres.*); *Pres.* Mr M Ragel; *Sec.* Cheickh Ould Horomtala; *Vice Pres.* Mr Badra Aly Toure.

MAURITIUS (1910) Mauritius Lawn Tennis Association, PO Box 46, Rose Hill.
C. Tennis, Mauritius; T. (230) 464 5311; TX. 4729 SPORTS IW (Att. MLTA); Fax. (230) 6319 442; *Pres.* Mr John Glover; *Sec.* Mr Philippe Chan Tin.

MONGOLIA (1990) Mongolian Tennis Association, Central Post Office, PO Box 109, Ulaanbaatar 13.
T. 20311 (via operator); *Pres.* Mr Ch Ganbold; *Sec.* Mr J Batjargal.

MONTSERRAT (1984) Montserrat Tennis Association, PO Box 209, Plymouth, Montserrat, British West Indies.
T. (1–809–491) 3514; Fax. (1–809) 491 5069; *Pres.* Ms Candia Williams; *Sec.* Mr George Barratt.

MOZAMBIQUE (1979) Federacao Mocambicana de Tenis, Caixa Postal 4351, Maputo.
C. JOFIRES, MAPUTO; T. (258) 27027; TX. 6614 BMS MO; Fax. (258–1) 420349/425078; *Pres.* Mr Pedro Figueiredo; *Sec.* Mr Victorino Nhabangue.

MYANMAR (1949) Myanmar Tennis Federation, Aung San Memorial Stadium, Mingala Taung Nyunt, P O Box 11221, Yangon.
C. Ubsped, Rangoon; T. (95–1) 0171731; *Pres.* Mr Tha Oo; *Sec.* Mr Pe Than Tun.

NAMIBIA (1930) Namibia Tennis Association, PO Box 479, Windhoek 9000.
T. (264–61) 51718; Fax (264–61) 51718; *Pres.* Dr Pietie Loubser; *Sec.* Mr Patrick Gardner.

NEPAL (1968) All Nepal Tennis Association, PO Box 2090, Dasarath Stadium, Kathmandu.

T. (977) 211732/215712; TX. 2390 NSCNP/2614 INSURE NP; *Pres.* Mr Siddheshwar Singh; *Sec.* Mr Sarad Lama.

NETHERLANDS ANTILLES (1941) Nederlandse Antilliaanse Tennis Ass, PO Box 3571, Emmastad, Curacao.
T. (599–9) 73192; Fax. (599) 681423; *Pres.* Mr. Maximo Rufino Paul; *Sec.* Mr Hilberto Thomas.

NIGER (1988) Federation Nigerienne de Tennis, BP 10 788, Niamey, Republique du Niger.
T. (227) 735893; TX. 5460 NI; Fax. (227) 735711; *Pres.* Mr. Ahmed Ousman Diallo; *Sec.* Mr. Boubacar Djibo.

NORTHERN MARIANA ISLANDS Northern Mariana Islands Tennis Association, Caller Box PPP, Saipan, MP 96950.
T. (670–234) 8438; TX. 236503484285 MCI UW; Fax. (670–234) 5545; *Pres.* Mr Michael Mason; *Sec.* Mr Peter Sinclair.

OMAN (1986) Oman Tennis Association, PO Box 5226, Ruwi, Sultanate of Oman.
T. (968) 703461; Fax. (968) 798846; *Pres.* Mr Hamoud Sangoor Hashim; *Sec.* Mr Mohamad Salim Khawwar.

PANAMA, REPUBLIC OF (1964) Federacion Panamena de Tenis, Apartado 6-4965, El Dorado.
T. (507) 27 2728/27 2960; TX. 2534 INDE PG or 3429 OLIMPAN PG; *Pres.* Dr Bey Mario Lombana *Sec.* Dr Juan San Martin.

PAPUA-NEW GUINEA (1963) Papua New Guinea Lawn Tennis Association, PO Box 5656, Boroko, Papua New Guinea.
T. (675) 252 889/255 803; Fax. (675) 252 889/255 803; *Pres.* Mr Robert Ainsi; *Sec.* Mr Chris Langton.

RWANDA (1984) Federation Rwandaise de Tennis, B P 1958, Kigali.
T. (250) 7 4032/5892/6130; Fax. (250) 7 4031/3848/2919; Tx 90922517; *Pres.* Mr Gaspard Musabyimana; *Sec.* Mr Vedaste Nkanika.

ST KITTS AND NEVIS (1962) St. Kitts Lawn Tennis Association, c/o Denise Morris, St. Kitts and Nevis Port Authority, PO Box 186, Basseterre, St. Kitts.
T. (1–809) 465 8121 (Sec)/6459 (Pres); Fax. (1–809) 465 8124 (Sec)/1190 (Pres); *Pres.* Mr Raphael Jenkins; *Sec.* Ms Denise Morris.

ST LUCIA St Lucia Lawn Tennis Association, c/o PO 308, Castries, Saint Lucia, West Indies.
T. (1 809 45) 22434; Fax. (1–809–45) 22 534; *Pres.* Mr Ornan Monplaisir.

ST VINCENT AND GRENADINES (1972) St Vincent and the Grenadines Lawn Tennis Association, PO Box 604, Halifax Street, St Vincent.
Pres. Mr Michael Nanton; *Sec.* Miss Diane DaSilva.

SEYCHELLES (1955) Seychelles Tennis Association, PO Box 602, Victoria, Mahe.
T. (248) 47414; TX. 2305 MINED SZ; Fax. (248) 24497; *Pres.* Mr Placid Andre; *Sec.* Kingsley Pouponneau.

SIERRA LEONE (1965) Sierra Leone Lawn Tennis Association, c/o National Sports Council, PO Box 1181, Freetown.
T. (232–22) 40562/40167/41340; TX. 3590 ENG CON; *Pres.* Mr Henry Moore; *Sec.* Mr E T Ngandi.

SOMALIA Somali Amateur Tennis Association, PO Box 523, (Sec: Box 3894) Mogadishu.
T. (252–1) 28042/20589; TX. 3061 SONOC SM; *Pres.* Mr Mohamed Farah Siad; *Sec.* Mr Sa'ad Omar Gedi.

SURINAM (1936) Surinaamse Tennisbond, PO Box 2087, Paramaribo.
T. (597) 463528; TX. 446 IHBO SN; Fax. (597) 465 381/452 781 *Pres.* Dr J H Kolader; *Sec.* Mr W Antonius.

SWAZILAND (1968) Swaziland Tennis Union, Box 2397; Manzini.
T. (268) 4391/44011; TX. 2052; Fax. (268) 45619; *Pres.* Mr Satch Khumalo;

TANZANIA Tanzania Lawn Tennis Association, PO Box 965, Dar Es Salaam.
T. (255–51) 126010; TX. 41446; *Pres.* Mr Richard Rugimbana; *Sec.* Mr Godfrey Zimba.

TONGA (1959) Tonga Amateur National Tennis Association, c/o Tonga Amateur Sports Association, PO Box 1278, Nuku-Alofa.
T. (676) 21041; TX. 66295 TASNOC TS; Fax. (676) 24127; *Acting Pres.* Fuka Kitekeiaho; *Sec.* Miss Dana Sanft.

UGANDA (1948) Uganda Tennis Association, c/o National Council of Sports, PO Box 9825, Kampala. Telegrams. LUGOGO; T. (256–41) 254 478; TX. 61069 OPM UGA; Fax. (256) 412 44574 *Chm.* Prof. Frederick F Ssempebwa; *Sec.* Mr Gideon M Karyoko.

US VIRGIN ISLANDS (1973) Virgin Island Tennis Association, PO Box 6715 VDS, St Thomas, USVI 00803–6715.
T. (1–809) 774 8547; Fax. (1–809) 776 1558; *Pres.* Mr William F McComb; *Sec.* Joyce Wisby.

VANUATU (1990) Federation de Tennis de Vanuatu, B P 563, Port Vila.
T. (678) 2 2698; Fax. (678) 2 2576; *Pres.* Mr Raymond Vallette; *Sec.* Mr Michel Mainguy.

WESTERN SAMOA (1955) Western Samoa Lawn Tennis Association, PO Box 1843, Apia.
T. (685) 21018/21874; TX. 245 SAMSHIP SX; Fax. (685) 24461; *Pres.* Mr Poao Ah Hoy; *Sec.* Mr Keneti Viliamu.

YEMEN(1902) Yemen Tennis Federation, PO Box 19395, Sanaa.
Fax. (967–1) 249768TX. 2710 YOUTH YE; *Sec.* Mr Mohamed Ahmed Abdulgalil.

ZAIRE (1984) Federation Zairoise de Lawn Tennis, BP 20750 Kin 15, Kinshasa.
T. (243–12) 30546/30080/78053; TX. 21160 SGA KIN ZR; Fax. (243–12) 30546; *Pres.* Mr Kanyama Mishindu; *Sec.* Mr Eleko Botuna Bo'osisa.

The Austrian boys and USA girls (above) were victorious in their respective competitions at the NTT World Junior Tennis Championships for the 14 & Under group held in Yamanakako, Japan. Among the major stars of the week were Austria's Markus Hipfl (below left) and Meilen Tu of the United States (below right) who both won important single's matches leading up to the final.

INDEX